Oklahoma Music Guide II

Biographies, Big Hits & Annual Events

by

Hugh W. Foley, Jr.

NEW FORUMS

NEW FORUMS PRESS INC.

Published in the United States of America
by New Forums Press, Inc.1018 S. Lewis St.
Stillwater, OK 74074
www.newforums.com

Copyright © 2013 by New Forums Press, Inc.

Third Printing

All rights reserved. No part of this publication may be reproduced or transmitted in any form or by any means, electronic or mechanical, including photocopy, or any information storage or retrieval system, without permission in writing from the publisher.

Library of Congress Cataloging-in-Publication Data Pending

This book may be ordered in bulk quantities at discount from New Forums Press, Inc., P.O. Box 876, Stillwater, OK 74076 [Federal I.D. No. 73 1123239]. Printed in the United States of America.

ISBN 10: 1-58107-242-2
ISBN 13: 978-1-581072-42-6

Cover design by Mac Crank.

Contents

1. Preface v

2. Acknowledgements viii

3. Oklahoma Music: From Powwows to Power Pop x

4. Scope and Limitations xxxix

5. Key to Abbreviations xli

6. Alphabetical List of *OMG II* Major Entries xlii

7. Index and People's List of Oklahoma Musicians and Musical Groups 1

8. 2013 People's List of Oklahoma Music & *OMG II* Cross Index 754

9. Photo and Image Credits 772

10. About the Author 775

11. Outro Vamp: Some Lessons Learned from Compiling *OMG II* 777

Hugh W. Foley / *iii*

*To Oklahoma musicians & music fans of all backgrounds -
with respect, admiration, and gratitude*

hf

Preface

Started as a personal project of interest in the late 1980s when I discovered several important jazz musicians came from Muskogee, Oklahoma, the town where I graduated high school, the *Oklahoma Music Guide* is an attempt at creating a reference source for he primary musicians, musical groups, and musical traditions in what is now known as the state of Oklahoma, but also includes many pre-statehood musical traditions of American Indian, African-American, and Anglo-American origins.

The first edition of the *Oklahoma Music Guide*, published in 2003, took a first shot at bringing together two hundred primary entities

1927 Sheet Music

of interest to the history of music in Oklahoma. After getting a tumult of positive and constructive feedback, I realized the *Oklahoma Music Guide* belongs to the people in it and those Oklahoma music fans that enjoy finding out more about the incredibly rich history of music in the state, as well as the cultural environment that produced important music in multiple genres. The investment people feel in the guide is inspiring and makes me feel like a temporary caretaker of the information. My charge has been to get out to the public what I know at this point.

Along with establishing some kind of residency in the state, the primary criterion for an entry in the *Oklahoma Music Guide* requires either national or international recognition for musical accomplishment, or extremely significant contributions to the local music world of Oklahoma. Some who are in the guide were born in the state but moved away at an early age (Ray Wylie Hubbard, Edgar Meyer, Chet Baker, and Nokie Edwards of The Ventures), but they get in via birthright. Some moved to the state at an early age from somewhere else (Charlie Christian, Roger Miller, Steve Ripley), but spent their primary early years in the state when they became exposed to music for the first time or enjoyed their first professional experiences. Others moved to the state later in life (Roy Clark and Miranda Lambert), spent some of their professional career in the state (Scott Joplin, Buck Owens, and Hank Thompson), or claimed to be from the state, but weren't (Eddie Cochran and Cowboy Copas). The second edition of the guide addresses some of these issues. By explaining tangential connections some artists have to the state, interested readers will have some answers to often repeated misconceptions about Oklahoma music (Norah Jones), as well as minimum starting points for learning more about the wide variety of music from the state. Additionally, the guide includes a few musicians or groups who are known primarily for their consistent live appearances or recordings over a long period of time within Oklahoma (DC Minner, Mike Hosty). Longevity does create familiarity in show business, especially in local music scenes, which in turn creates affinity for any number of artists. A few of those are included here to provide some context for the quirky (or comfortably consistent) greatness for which the state is so widely appreciated by many of its residents.

As a result of the Internet era's mountainous availability of constantly updated material, I believe new reference works must take an alternative approach to the long tradition of being an all-inclusive resource that exhausts a subject until the next tome under the same title replaces the previous edition. Also being a teacher at the university level, I am a daily witness to this generation's concept of research when any subject can be Googled to a minimum starting point for the inquisitor, and often on one's cell phone. Therefore, contemporary reference information needs to be crisp and to the point, or risk being glossed over completely by over-stimulated brains attempting to sort out the spaghetti of information highways crisscrossing the conscious planet. Concordantly, modern artists also control their own stories, press, discographies, and bibliographies, making a vast amount of personal and professional information available to anyone via their websites. Tremendous resources exist for gathering musical information from multiple for-profit sites that exercise some editorial control of artist biographies and criticism, such as oklahomarock.com, allmusic.com, rollingstone.com, or pick-your-local-online-newspaper. Additionally, non-profit sites such as wikepedia.org have completely democratized the contributions of music fans (and living artists themselves) to the collected body of knowledge about music and musicians worldwide. Some degree of care must be used when using or referencing Wikipedia, but one can glean important reference materials from that database when cited sources are included, or facts can be corroborated by additional sources. All of which leads to the important question: If all this

1938 sheet music

information already exists online, what purpose can the *Oklahoma Music Guide* serve? I believe the answer is in compilation and contextualization.

No single work, in print or online, attempts to collate all of the nationally or internationally recognized musicians, musical groups, or musical traditions from Oklahoma, and place them in a larger critical and historical context of American popular music or ethnomusicology, which is the goal and stated purpose of the *Oklahoma Music Guide*. Special emphasis will be given to musicians or musical traditions not covered extensively heretofore by online or print sources. However, extremely well-known Oklahoma musicians (Woody Guthrie, Garth Brooks, Reba McEntire, Vince Gill, Flaming Lips) are given ample space to provide a place to document and critically assess their career as significant forces of Oklahoma musical nature. As are rule, however, the guide should be a starting point for further research by interested parties, not necessarily the be-all and end-all resource for encyclopedic factoids on every artist or group. To that end, each entry is organized in the following fashion:

1. Name of musician, group, tribe, entity, or musical tradition
    a. Birthdate (b.) (if known)
    b. Deathdate (d.) (if known)
    c. Date group formed (f.)
2. Critical and contextual statement – Example: *Regarded by critics and musicians as one of the 20th century's most technically complicated and stylistically advanced acoustic guitarists, Michael Hedges combined several unusual guitar techniques, such as personal tunings, fret board tapping, and percussive plucking styles, to achieve a musically dense and harmonically rich texture in his playing and compositions, which he called, "violent acoustic," "heavy mental," and "acoustic thrash."*
3. Primary connection to Oklahoma or what the artist's musical experience is/was in the state.
4. Professional accomplishments relative to their time in the state, detailing significant music and/or critical notice
5. Reference source(s) for entry when not cited in-text

With these principles in mind, the *Oklahoma Music Guide* seeks to provide what is known by the author at this time about the major contributions of the state's native-born, temporary, and current residents to the world of music. Additionally, publication of this guide just needs to happen, to begin trying to grasp the enormity of the subject, and to provide a resource for fans, musicians, and those groups working to preserve and promote the Oklahoma music story.. The ever-evolving "people's list" of contributors to Oklahoma music history is kept at www.oklahomamusicguide.com, where the public may make suggestions for inclusion in that list that is published in the back of this book. Readers are also encouraged to make recommendations for future print editions of the

Acknowledgements

The author wishes to thank the following individuals and/or organizations for their gracious assistance in completing *Oklahoma Music Guide II*:

Jack Anquoe, Jr. for several discussions regarding the Oklahoma pow-wow tradition and Kiowa music; Anthony Arkeketa and Louis Headman for insight into Ponca musical traditions; Larry Austin; Chet Baker's estate; Elvin Bishop; Catherine and Clarence Cagle; Jennifer Chancellor for her continued great coverage of Oklahoma music in the *Tulsa World* which is must reading for any contemporary Oklahoma music fan; Joe Cinocca for years of musical fandom and communication with the author; John Cooper and Brad Piccolo of the Red Dirt Rangers; Pete and Joanna Coser; colleagues in the Department of Fine Arts at Rogers State University for their support and friendship , & not to forget work studies who have helped clip and file multiple articles for this guide: Bogie Borchardt, Andrew Jakober, and Cayla Spears; Marvin Diamond for his friendship, brotherhood, insight, and invitation into the spiritual and musical world of the Native American Church in Oklahoma; Doug Dollar at New Forums Press for publishing this book; Nola and Howard Downs for collecting research materials and just being there; Jack Dunham for sharing his knowledge of the Tulsa Sound; Judy and Nokie Edwards; Kenneth Edwards for help with Stoney Edwards' entry; Billy Estes for Toni Estes; the board of directors, members, visitors, and inductees of the Oklahoma Music Hall of Fame and Museum in Muskogee for continued input and inspiration; Curtis Hamilton-Youngbird and June and Donnie Hamilton for sorting out Young Bird's entry, and the star quilt; Scott Booker at Hellfire Management for The Flaming Lips; Patti Page for a great day, remembering me, and reminding young people show business is made up of two parts - "show (the fun)" and "business (the serious work)".

Hutche Chuppa Indian Baptist Church members for continued fellowship, musical inspiration, continued life guidance, and the familiar comfort of a sincere faith community; Jimmy Karstein; Sean Kelly from 1600 AM - KUSH in Cushing; Barney and Phyllis Kessel; Ruth (Hedges) Ipsen for Michael Hedges; Guy Logsdon for sharing his vast expertise on Western swing and Woody Guthrie; Leigh Lust for help with the Willis Brothers entry; Mary Ann and Jay McShann; The Mccubbin Family; Mary Miller for Roger Miller; Malcolm Mills of Proper Records; DC and Selby Minner; Can't say thanks enough to Randy and Melissa Moore, and family, in Pawnee for welcoming me into their home, and the opportunity to learn about the Native American Church; Cornel Pewewardy for his help and encouagement; Mike Pierce for help with Merle Kilgore, Pake McEntire, and Hinder.

Mekko David Proctor and Sam Proctor of the Tallahassee (Wvkokye) Ceremonial Grounds of the Muscogee (Creek) Nation for their friendship, and sharing of the history, purpose, and significance of Muscogee ceremonial traditions; Mike Rabon for the help with the Five Americans entry; Teresa Gaines Rapp for help with the Steve and Cassie Gaines entry; Charlene and Steve Ripley; Tyson Ritter of the All-American Rejects; Dr. Peter C. Rollins for his leadership, academic guidance, and over-all pop culture mentorship; RSU Radio (KRSC-FM) for all the local music access, as well as taking "the format" further; Cynthia Rucker for her patience; John Russell of Admiral Twin; Chad "Charlie 7" Sevigny; Evans Ray Satepauhoodle for his invaluable friendship, mentoring, and detailed history and significance of Kiowa musical traditions and wider Oklahoma powwow music traditions; Mike Shannon of Daddy O's in Stillwater, OK: Don Tolle for his friendship, courtesy, and sharing his vast knowledge of Western swing; Hugh Tudor-Foley for the jazz books in his garage in Rye Brook, NY which really started this journey; Andrew Vasquez; Nan Warshaw of Bloodshot Records; Claude and Blanche Williams; Jimmy Reeder and Stratford Williams for help with the Wichita and Affiliated Tribe's musical traditions; Gary "Turbo" Webb for help with various metal groups; Rosetta Wills for offering helpful corrections and additions to the Wills Brothers entry; John Wilson for his knowledge of Scott Joplin's time in Indian Territory; the Wisner and Burden families for making me feel at home for so many years; John Wooley for his long and valuable chronicle of articles and books on Oklahoma music and musicians – especially relating to Western swing, Red Dirt Music, and the Tulsa Sound.

No work of this type could be possible without the writers and researchers who both preceded me and have continued on as colleagues and admired documentarians of Oklahoma music. Several *Tulsa World* writers, past and present, have made my job easier and more interesting, to include Thomas Conner, Matt Gleason, Jennifer Chancellor, James D. Watts, Jr., and the aforementioned John Wooley. My *Daily Oklahoman* subscription has been worth it many times over due to reporting by Gene Triplett, George Lang, and Brandy McDonnell. Oklahoma's major independent papers, *Currentland, Urban Tulsa,* and the *Oklahoma Gazette,* all deserve credit for tracking above-and-under the radar OK music.

Thanks also to the Oklahoma History Center (Bob Blackburn, and the now-retired Rodger Harris), and Oklahoma Museum of Popular Culture (Larry O'Dell and Jeff Moore) for providing so much access to their documentation of Oklahoma music. Special mention must also be made of OU professor of history, Dr. William W. Savage, Jr. for lighting a signal fire back in 1983 with his *Singing Cowboys and All That Jazz: A Short History of Popular Music in Oklahoma* (OU Press).

Additionally, many big thanks to the various friends, colleagues, students, and family members who have encouraged and jovially endured the author's passion, if not obsession, with Oklahoma's outragesouly rich music heritage and constantly flowering contemporary status.

Oklahoma Music: From Powwows to Power Pop

Oklahoma music is a gusher. Wildcatters in the form of state agencies, non-profit organizations, tourism promoters, academic entities, private entrepreneurs, publications, and musicians of every genre are tapping in to this rich vein of Oklahoma's most significant cultural resource, its music. The 46th state possesses a broad and historic musical heritage, as well as a bevy of 21st century success stories in the music industry. Performers, composers, educational and commercial institutions, promoters, and songwriters have shaped the entire realm of American and world music. The range of important American Indian music from the state historically and in the modern era is unequalled by any other state in terms of variety, the result of thirty-nine tribes having their governmental home offices in the state. Historically, giant names of American music such as Gene Autry, Woody Guthrie, Bob Wills, Patti Page, Wanda Jackson, Hoyt Axton, Jimmy Webb, J.J. Cale, Leon Russell, and Garth Brooks (the biggest selling solo artist in history) are forever linked with Oklahoma as either the place of their birth and maturation, or the site of their musical breakthroughs. American blues, rock, pop, and R&B history is replete with Oklahoma musicians who wrote, played, produced or sang some of the genre's most significant songs. In 2011, modern rock artists such as the Oklahoma-connected Kings of Leon, All-American Rejects, and Hinder swagger through hard rock founded in 1960s British and 1970s Southern rock. Meanwhile, the Flaming Lips, Starlight Mints, Colourmusic and Other Lives all exhibit the quirky meditative "Okie Pop" of the state's progressive music scenes in Tulsa, Oklahoma City, Stillwater, and Norman. Stillwater is also the wellspring of Red Dirt music, a collision of cynical/contemplative/humorous singer/songwriters with blues, country, rock, bluegrass, or waltz influences, depending on the needs of the audience and genre of gig.

Wichita singing group, Grasslodge, 2008 Wichita and Affiliated Tribes Annual Gathering near Anadarko, OK.

If all that weren't confounding enough, the state's most complex active musical entity is Jacob Fred Jazz Odyssey, the contemporary representation of Oklahoma's primary focal point as a fueling and re-fueling of American jazz with musicians from the 19th century to the modern era. Oklahoma jazz begins with slaves of African descent who came with the five Southeastern tribes in the early 19th century, then develops with the Black Town movement of Indian Territory after the Civil War, and evolves with statehood in key towns of Muskogee, Tulsa, and Oklahoma City. At the turn of the 21st century, Tulsa's Wayman Tisdale was a #1 jazz artist on *Billboard*'s Jazz Album chart, giving Oklahoma a primary presence in every jazz subgenre from the jazz string bands of 1910 (think Claude "Fiddler" Williams) through the contemporary smooth jazz hits by Tisdale. Country music hopefuls have stomped out of Oklahoma toward Nashville or L.A. and returned home giants; Reba McEntire, Vince Gill, Toby Keith, and Carrie Underwood are all native-born Oklahomans who have had significant music careers. Reba McEntire is clearly one of the most important women country music performers in American popular music history with her diverse entertainment portfolio of television, concert tours, #1 hit songs (34), and albums in excess of sixty million (all of which allows for generous philanthropy). With her 2009 release, *Keep on Loving You*, McEntire portrays life in song from a mature woman's point of view, to the delight and approval of her fans, male and female, who relate to the subject matter in her songs. To interpret her lyrics in the authentic rhythm (rubato), dialect (Chockie, OK), and vocal twang of a classic country singer, she uses the strong diaphragm for singing she partly developed by singing the "The Star Spangled Banner"at rodeos as a youth.

A crucial component for country music success is an artist understanding that fans need to be able to identify with the experiences of characters in the songs before they will buy in a relationship with a new artist. Having grown alongside her listeners since the 1980s, and achieved a "no questions asked" power in the country music industry, Reba can select songs and release albums that relate to fans who have developed a bond with her over the years, a move that has proven successful in continued sales, popularity and awards recognition. A common thread among Oklahoma songwriters (or those who perform them) is the understanding that songs are stories, peopled by characters having experiences very much like the listener who is in a similar place in life or location as the singer of the song.

The personas in Toby Keith songs must represent identifiable aspects of contemporary human life or he wouldn't have so many fans, and leave it to a modern Oklahoma country artist to actually be discussed in political terms. While the traditional left sees Keith as the jingoistic good ol' boy with an L.C. lifestyle, one only has to see the enthusiastic response from American military members and their families to understand why Keith is a folk hero to them. In a ballad tradition easily traced to England broadside singers of the 1600s, modern country queen Carrie Underwood's first major hit is story about a young woman on an icy patch of road "In Jesus, Take the Wheel". Underwood sings a story of challenge, adversity, and personal victory by faith in a tenuous situation, thematic elements of both modern country music and its centuries-old British Isles story-singing ancestor. As for continuing the country music tradition from the state of Oklahoma, Carrie Underwood has experienced nebulae-bright success since being named an American Idol in 2005. With a gripping voice that can dig out a honky-tonk blues growl or soar through a ballad, Underwood has more than twelve million albums sold, and fifteen #1 singles (so far). By 2008, Underwood's popularity catapulted her to the top of country music concert ticket sales for a female performer. By 2013, Carrie had won her sixth GRAMMY Award, and is one of popular country music's biggest contemporary stars. Whether considering the legacy of Bob Wills, the songwriting of Roger Miller, or the massive success of Garth Brooks, Reba McEntire, and Carrie Underwood, these well-known accolades by Oklahoma musicians have led to extensive discussion and curiosity about Oklahoma music. The most common question is "What is it about Oklahoma that has produced, and continues to produce so many significant musicians and musical performers?"

Carrie Underwood poses in Checotah, OK, in 2005, shortly after winning the American Idol talent competition.

When compared with other states of similar population size, Oklahoma's overall production of musicians is truly astounding. In order to begin grasping how the state's particular and unique historical evolution took place, one might think in terms of a big band or orchestra leader, with each section of musicians representing intrinsic players and historical eras that shaped a complete socio-cultural environment that encouraged and fostered musical performance. The orchestra or big band needs all of its members to produce a cohesive music. However, not every section is taking a lead all the time.

"Hooray, Oklahoma" sheet music, 1942

Occasionally, a section will play a foundational piece such as the rhythm or chord progression. At other points in the music, a section might not play at all, just waiting for the right accent moment or scripted embellishment. Such is the case with Oklahoma music. While many factors contribute to its development, a primary continuum through Oklahoma's history is its geographic position that has encouraged travel through the state. From its first major civilization in the Spiro Mounds era (circa 850 A.D.) when the people of Spiro used the Arkansas and Mississippi River system to govern their people and lands, people have been moving in and out of the state in large numbers. After Comanche and Kiowa began to range into the state after receiving the horse in the late 1600s, multiple tribes were forced by the U.S. to relocate in Indian Territory on foot, horseback, and by boat. After the Civil War, carpetbaggers and speculators arrived with the railroads when Oklahoma had more track crossing it than any other state in the late 19th century. Horse drawn wagons brought thousands of new people to Oklahoma Territory and Indian Territory after Native people were put on government rolls and allotted land, after which tribal governments were abolished. The remaining un-allotted lands, once promised to tribes forever, were opened up for the now historic land runs of the late 19th and early 20th centuries before Oklahoma became a state. Even Oklahoma's early notoriety as an oil state was linked to transportation as automobiles became a popular mode acquisition for an increasingly mobile American society.

Along with multiple connections to the air and space revolutions of the 20th century (without which John Denver's emergence may not have been possible), Oklahoma also sits right in the middle of historic Route 66, providing a steady stream of traffic in and out of the state during the Depression in the 1930s, and World War II of the 1940s, but also as an exotic and archetypal location for U.S. Route 66 tourists of the 1950s. Oklahoma is the state where the roadside attractions indicated to Eastern travelers that they were in the West where American myths hide out, congregate,

American Indian musical traditions in Oklahoma begin with the music of the Plains people, many of which are present in the modern powwow world. Kiowa singer Evans Ray Satepauhoodle (standing) is being honored here at a 2005 powwow in Tulsa, OK.

Musicians from Floris, OK

and spring out at unexpected locations along the road. Along with being a tourist trail in the 1950s, Route 66 also provided a clear road to L.A. which many jazz, blues, rock and pop musicians followed to their enduring musical moments. Contemporarily, two major interstates cross at Oklahoma City in center of the state. I-35 is a north/south path from Mexico and Texas to Canada, and I-40 is an east/west path from coast to coast. The phrase "I drove through Oklahoma once" is a common response to an Oklahoman who has announced as their home state. Musicians and their managers have thought of Oklahoma as a "travel day" since the 1930s, a place that must be crossed to get to more populous and lucrative markets. This still explains why most concerts by major artists in Oklahoma City and Tulsa often occur on weeknights early in the week when major acts are in between weekends in larger cities. Touring entourages can wrap a big Saturday or Sunday night show in Dallas, be ready at one of Oklahoma's two major arenas on Monday or Tuesday, and then be to Kansas City and/or Denver for a Thursday, Friday, or Saturday show. The same kind of planning occurred with the swinging Territory Bands in the 1920s and the Western Swing groups of the Wills brothers in the 1930s. The Wills brand of Western Swing is also a perfect paradigm for the colliding cultures in the American Southwest and, specifically, Oklahoma in the 1930s. To please their audiences, a Wills band needed to be able to make people dance to forget Depression-era troubles, and that meant being able to play fiddle tunes, blues, pop standards of the day, jazz, and whatever else was necessary (hear Red Dirt in there?). That same cultural cross-fertilization was happening within the geographic boundaries of what became Oklahoma.

1923 Sheet Music

Along with the omnipresent American Indian people who still maintain many of their ancient musical traditions at varying levels through the present era, important early musical influences also came from African-Americans who provided a market and formally educated musical resource for the earliest and most popular developments of jazz in Muskogee, Tulsa, and Oklahoma City. Add the full range of British Isle immigrants who brought old time country and Gospel music from the South. Then, count the Easterners who brought both a sensibility of European art music, and knowledge of the early machinations of American popular music. All of this musical activity collides with the late 19th and early 20th century American popular music world of Scott Joplin's ragtime, and the Tin Pan Alley sheet music and piano boom in parlors across "refined" middle-class

America. Additionally, the first commercially available recordings and playback devices in the early 20th century shaped into the music industry as it is known today, and needed musicians, of which there were many in Oklahoma.

Several factors emerge as patterns that have influenced the development of significant musical artists and trends in Oklahoma: 1) the combination of rural isolation and boredom relieved through family and communal music experiences; 2) the prevalence of Oklahoma's significant institutional religious past in which many people received their first musical experiences; 3) performance opportunities in the two major urban centers of Tulsa and Oklahoma City, as well as further opportunities in towns with military bases such as Lawton, Altus, and Enid; in addition, target marketed shows for historic ethnocentric populations in Muskogee, Oklahoma City and Tulsa (jazz), Anadarko (American Indian), Yukon (polka), Hugo (bluegrass); and, finally, experimentation and cross-fertilization in the college towns of Stillwater (Oklahoma State University) and Norman (University of Oklahoma); 5) the prominence of music education in the state from the earliest formation of public education; 6) most significantly, scores of musicians left Oklahoma and blazed a trail for others to follow to American music centers such as Los Angeles, Nashville, Austin, Kansas City, and New York. Before the children started leaving the state, however, the parents and grandparents had to get there.

Consider the settlement patterns of Oklahoma because they reflect the cultural diversity of the state. Charles N. Gould, an early twentieth century travel writer and geographer, emphasizes the state's multicultural traditions: "Oklahoma is a meeting place of many different peoples. Nowhere else is there such a mingling of types. Practically every state in the Union and every civilized nation on the globe is represented among the state's inhabitants."[1] Many different cultural groups brought music in their "cultural baggage" that resulted in the development of a myriad of vibrant musical subcultures. This vast array of people and their music includes the songs and dance music of the American Indian from the southern Great Plains, the southeastern U.S., the northeastern woodlands, Great Lakes, and Ohio Valley regions; Anglo-Celtic ballads from the upland South, country blues from the Mississippi Delta, black and white spirituals from the lowland South, European immigrant music from Italy, Germany, and Czechoslovakia; polka music from the upper Midwest, and Mexican *mariachi* from the Rio Grande Valley. This musical mixture is further reflected in the *WPA Guide to 1930s Oklahoma*: "…each successive immigrant to the state brought the dust of another locale on his feet and the lilt of another people's song on his lips."[3]

Early 20th century musicians in Muskogee, OK

Hugh W. Foley / xv

This cultural confluence of different genres of American music allowed Oklahomans to experiment, innovate, and improvise – traits necessary in the formulation of various forms of American popular and roots music. Within this Oklahoma cultural mosaic, music knew no color. Black, white, and American Indian musical performers borrowed freely from each other, exchanged repertoires and musical ideas, and adopted new techniques and styles. These cross-cultural experiences favored the development of music in Oklahoma. While the earlier-mentioned Western swing of Bob Wills is an easy example of musical hybridization resulting in the diverse tastes of his fans, a lesser-known microcosm of this musical amalgam exists in traditional Muscogee (Creek) Christian hymns.

First introduced to the Muscogee (Creek) people in Alabama and Georgia by Scottish missionaries prior to the forced removal of the Creeks to Indian Territory in the 1830s, the hymns became a primary musical and spiritual vehicle for the shared experiences of the Creek people along with intermarried whites (mostly Scot), and slaves of African descent who were all part of the historic Muscogee (Creek) Nation after removal to Indian Territory. The hymns have Scottish and African melodies with lyrics in the Muscogee (Creek) language. Some of the hymns carry a double meaning, relating both to the Christian faith's experience of going from this world to heaven, as well as commemorating the human angst of forced removal, and subsequent hardship of going to their new unfamiliar place in Indian Territory. Some Creek Hymns refer specifically to the painful removal period in their lyrical content ("Here Suffering, I Pass"/"Yvmv Estemerketvn"). As a result of the songs' use during the long removal trip, and then for extended church services, the hymns can often go on for as long as necessary, just by changing the primary pronoun in the verses with each refrain of a verse in the Creek language. So, a song can cover blessings, meditations, or prayers for just about everyone in the community, family, church, or tribal town before the tune concludes. The music, however, is that learned from both the highly melismatic Scottish "line singing" style ("And Must This Body Die"/"Elkv-este Toyis"), or the slow spirituals in a blues form from plantation slaves of African descent ("God Our Creator"/"Hesaketvmeset Likes").

As a result of all these factors, Muscogee (Creek) Hymns should have a profound place in the history of American music because they are the first tri-cultural artistic product of American Indians, African-Americans, and Anglo/Euro-Americans in U.S. music history. We might even be able to say they are the first truly "American" music since they merge these three important early cultural groups. Additionally, the hymns are a powerful lesson in music as a spiritual vehicle, cathartic expression, healing tool, and form of shared memory that commemorates a dramatic moment in the community's life. Finally, as hymns transport the listener to the 19th century environment of Southern spirituals, the songs also demonstrate artistically the cross-cultural cooperation necessary (even if it was forced) among people of differing backgrounds to endure the social conditions of pre-Civil War and then pre-statehood Oklahoma. In fact, the very first Baptist church in Oklahoma was formed in 1832 by whites, blacks, and Creeks just north of the Arkansas River near present-day Muskogee.

A few independent compact discs and cassettes of Creek hymns have been released by small Creek churches, and Canyon Records released a nearly out-of-print cassette in 1982. However, the Muscogee (Creek) Nation Communications Department recorded a collection of hymns in June, 2011 for a forthcoming official release as teaching tool to help learn and revitalize the hymn singing among young people and those who live away from the Creek Nation. As of 2013, a monthly Creek hymn singing took place at the Muscogee (Creek) Elderly Nutrition Center in Okmulgee, Oklahoma, on the third Thursday evening of each month. Of course, the tradition is still active today in many of the Baptist and Methodist churches of the contemporary Muscogee (Creek) Nation of Oklahoma. Creek hymns are just one example of an extremely significant element of American music history from the state of Oklahoma, but this is just one element of one tribe's music that resonates with significance. As whole concept, one simply cannot understand the history of Oklahoma without studying the history of American Indians here before and after statehood, but this work tries to stay focused on their music, and not the whole stories of their history which are readily available online on tribally maintained websites.

Oklahoma is the modern home for thirty-nine federally recognized North American Indian tribes, nations, bands, and tribal towns, and one state recognized tribe (Euchee). The diversity of indigenous musical influences runs the gamut from some of the oldest songs known among Native people of North America, to the musical roots and formal foundations of the modern powwow world, as well as a cornucopia of active tribal ceremonial music. After the historic Spiro Period, American Indian history in Oklahoma has a jagged history that begins the Caddo, Wichita, and Apache, followed by Plains Tribes such as the Kiowa and Comanche who arrive once they receive the horse. Also, the Pawnee, Osage, and Quapaw are all present before the creation of Indian Territory, set aside for Native people removed from their homelands by the U.S. government through treaty, warfare, or both. As a result, a vast catalog of American Indian music is associated with Oklahoma music history. Just a cursory listing ranges from the Kiowa Gourd Dance or Black Leggins Songs, Wichita Ghost Dance songs, Seneca Green Corn Songs, and Caddo Turkey Dance songs. Along with Tonkawa Scalp Dance Songs, Ponca War Dance Songs, Cheyenne-Arapaho Sun Dance songs, Cherokee and Muscogee (Creek) "Stomp Dance" songs, and Osage In'lonshka Songs, primary music of the Native American Church derives from the state, as does a tremendous amount of contemporary powwow music.

Native American Indian music is very much alive in the state as private, reverent, tribal experience, a very real connection to the ancient musical traditions contemporary tribal people have inherited. Many recordings exist of traditional American Indian music from Oklahoma. Some of the very first recordings ever made in state history are of American Indian music when a German ethnomusicologist, Erich von Hornbostel, recorded about 40 Pawnee songs in Pawnee, Oklahoma, in 1906.[3] Along with participating in individual tribal music traditions, American Indian musicans also embraced the popular music with which they came into contact. Oklahoma historian Rodger Harris documented formal events using string bands in the Cherokee, Choctaw, Seminole, Chickasaw, and Creek Nations from 1840 to 1860. Big Chief's Indian String Band was a Choctaw string band that recorded for RCA Records in 1929.[6] One of the best-known session guitarists of the 1970s rock era is Jesse Ed Davis, a Kiowa/Creek, who played on recordings by John Lennon, Taj Mahal, Ringo Starr, the Monkees, Neil Diamond, John Lee Hooker, Leon Russell, and Eric Clapton, among many, many others.

Furthering the unique story of the tribes in Oklahoma is the connection between the Southeastern tribes and the slaves of African descent who were removed with the tribes beginning in the 1820s. As the Cherokee, Choctaw, Muscogee (Creek), Seminole, and Chickasaw were forced to migrate to Indian Territory beginning in the 1820s, some tribal members, mostly mixed-bloods who had embraced the Southern agricultural model, brought slaves who endured the same "trail of tears" as the owners they accompanied. Thus, a plantation culture emerged in Oklahoma where the spirituals, work songs, and blues of the African-American developed much as they did in other parts of the rural American South. For example, three African-American spirituals are believed to have been first documented before 1862 via Wallis Willis and "Aunt" Minerva Willis, slaves on a large plantation near Doaksville in the Choctaw Nation. The authenticity and origin of spirituals are seldom credited to individuals, however, the Willis family sang "Swing Low, Sweet Chariot," "Steal Away to Jesus," and "I'm a Rollin'" in the cotton fields of Reverend Alexander Reid, superintendent of a Choctaw boarding school. Reid wrote down the words and music, then, forwarded the transcriptions to the Jubilee Singers at Fisk University in Nashville. Subsequently, the group sang the numbers on a tour of the United States and Europe beginning in 1871.[4] The popularity of "Swing Low, Sweet Chariot" extended to the biggest names in mid-20th century American popular music who made their own recordings of the ubiquitous spiritual, to include Benny Goodman, Fats Waller, Tommy Dorsey, Glenn Miller, Gene Autry, Duke Ellington, Louis Armstrong, Johnny Cash, Stevie Wonder, Johnny Cash, Elvis Presley and Eric Clapton. Not only did some of America's

New Dora Missionary Baptist Church Choir of Tom, Oklahoma, 2013.

earliest black spiritual and gospel traditions emerge in Oklahoma, so did the primary secular form of African-American music of the blues.

Acknowledged as the secular counterpart to African-American Christian music, the blues has influenced jazz, R&B, and rock music, with some of its earliest practitioners and subsequent performers and players hailing from Oklahoma. Emerging from field hollers, work songs, and spirituals of slaves of African descent in Indian Territory and early-statehood Oklahoma, people who could play and sing the blues flourished in the territory and the state. Among the first-known, commercially printed twelve-bar blues songs, "Dallas Blues" was published in Oklahoma City by Hart Wand in March, 1912, three months before W.C. Handy's much more famous "Memphis Blues." As a result of the thriving economic environment of all-black towns and major black business districts in Tulsa (Greenwood), Oklahoma City (Deep Deuce), and Muskogee (South Second) in Oklahoma after the Civil War, viable audiences existed for black entertainers throughout the state. Ragtime pianist Scott Joplin performed his opera, *A Guest of Honor*, in Oklahoma City in 1903, and the great Mississippi blues man, Robert Johnson, is documented as having played in the all black town of Taft.[5] Traveling territory bands such as the Oklahoma City Blue Devils and Mighty Clouds of Joy brought the hot riffing jazz music of the Southwest to black audiences in Oklahoma, a style that may have found its summit in Kansas City, but many of its primary musicians came from Oklahoma, such as Jimmy Rushing, Walter Page, Don Byas, Claude Williams, and Jay McShann. Touring bands often picked up extremely capable musicians in Oklahoma, and hinted that better performance opportunities existed in Kansas City, the reason Jay McShann left his native Muskogee and headed to that cauldron of Midwestern jazz. Not only is McShann credited with introducing the world to the great jazz saxophonist Charlie Parker on record and on stage, McShann is a bridge from the jazz age to R&B era of the 1940s when his hits foreshadowed additional blues successes from the period by Roy Milton, Joe Liggins, Lowell Fulson, and Robert Jeffrey. Even the most ardent of music fans are often not aware the "father of funk guitar," Jimmy Nolen, who made his fame playing "chicken scratch" guitar on some of R&B/funk king James Brown's primary recordings, is a native Oklahoman.

By the 1950s and 1960s, many Tulsa musicians embraced the blues with tremendous success, to include Flash Terry, Leon Russell, J.J. Cale, Junior Markham, and Elvin Bishop. By the 1970s, Oklahomans such as Steve Gaines, who contributed to the resuscitation of Lynyrd Skynyrd in the early part of that decade, and Jesse Ed Davis, who recorded with Taj Mahal, John Lennon, Eric Clapton, and B.B. King, kept the state's blues tradition present in the interna-

"Dallas Blues" (1912)

DC Minner

tional spotlight. While not a national star but widely recognized throughout the state in the 1990s and early 2000s as Oklahoma's pre-eminent bluesman, DC Minner brought Oklahoma blues into the 21st century with his seasoned and soulful guitar work and vocals crafted from decades on the road with his group, Blues on the Move. Along with his bassist wife Selby, Minner's experiences urged him to found the Dusk 'til Dawn Blues Festival at the juke joint and on its grounds where he grew up in the historic all-black town of Rentiesville, Oklahoma. Started in 1990, the festival continues in 2013 as one of the region and country's most authentic festivals, drawing consistent crowds every Labor Day weekend to the tiny but historic community near the Honey Springs Civil War Battlefield.

In the realm of R&B, Tulsa's GAP Band became one of the genre's most successful groups with a stellar string of hits in the 1980s, and its lead vocalist, Charlie Wilson has continued working with many top R&B producers and performers of the current era, such as Snoop Dogg, Master P, Trick, and Dr. Dre. Oklahoma City's Color Me Badd parlayed their smooth harmonies and thumping bass lines and beats into several major hits in the 1990s, but the state has yet to produce a major hip hop artist outside of Oklahoma City's Nitro who released one album, *Hustlin' Pays* on Columbia Records in 2000. Muskogee's Ester Dean ("Drop It Low"), OKC'S Meant2B, and Tulsa's Johnny Polygon all may change this before too long. Given Oklahoma's long history of African-American culture and music, and relatively easy contemporary opportunities for recording, one has to wonder when a major hip-hop or rap artist will surface in Oklahoma. Interestingly, many young American Indians are gravitating toward rap as a music that can express their own alienation in contemporary society, such as Muscogee (Creek) hip hop artist, rapper, and musician, Julian B!, a Muscogee (Creek) rapper who incorporates Creek language and cultural concepts into music. While the major hip hop artist may not have yet emerged from Oklahoma, the state's jazz history is filled with titans.

Oklahomans have made huge impacts on the jazz world in every major stylistic era from its inception through the present day. A partial list of jazz titans from Oklahoma include Charles Brackeen and Marshal Royal (saxophone), Jay McShann (piano), Jimmy Rushing (vocals), Don Cherry, and Howard McGhee (trumpet), Chet Baker (trumpet and vocals),

Jay McShann

xx / Oklahoma Music Guide II

Kay Starr and Lee Wiley (vocals), Oscar Pettiford and Aaron Bell (bass), and Claude "Fiddler" Williams (violin). Giants of jazz guitar, Charlie Christian and Barney Kessel, both had their primary musical experiences in the state before setting out to change the electric guitar's role in jazz from primarily a chorded rhythmic instrument to one capable of taking leads on melodies and solos comparable to any instrument in the genre. By the 21st century, Wayman Tisdale (bass) enjoyed number one jazz albums before his untimely death of cancer in 2009. Jacob Fred Jazz Odyssey is considered one of jazz's most progressive and skillful improvisational groups, and Tulsan Oklahoma Music Hall of Fame Inductee Tommy Crook is one of the world's best living guitarists. Crook moves effortlessly between jazz, country, and pop standards, adding his dizzying melodic and chordal interpretations to established melodies. Active in Tulsa in 2013, Tommy Crook's performances are at the core of jazz's primary musical ethos of improvising and "swinging out" on recognizable tunes.

Tommy Crook

While not a jazz artist per se, but difficult to classify otherwise, Enid's Michael Hedges became the first "new age" artist with his unique percussive guitar style he called "violent acoustic" that inspired the foundation of Windham Hill Records, primarily to release Hedges' early material before becoming THE new age record label of the 1980s and 1990s before selling out to Sony. Rarely classified as jazz, Hedges' original guitar ability and technique incorporated modern jazz elements of unique chord progressions, improvisation, and instrumental prowess.

While multiple primary American musicians surfaced from the American Indian and African-American socio-cultural milieu in Indian Territory, Oklahoma Territory, and then Oklahoma, the oldest Anglo-American musical forms migrated into the state first after the Civil War when uncontrollable volumes of people streamed into the territories looking for new opportunities in business, agriculture, and, eventually, oil. Additional immigrants arrived with five land runs, beginning in 1889 when tribal lands were opened for settlement to non-Indians. This additional layer of music consisted of the fiddle dance tunes, such as the entertainment-oriented reels, jigs, schottisches, and strathspeys of the British Isles that formed the basis for old time country music and bluegrass.[6] Anglo sacred music arrived in the form of lined-out hymns, shape note singing instructors, and denominational singing of every hue. Prominent among Southern gospel composers, Spiro's Albert E. Brumley composed one of the best known gospel songs in American history, "I'll Fly Away," as well as additional popular gospel tunes, "Turn Your Radio On," and "Jesus Hold My Hand." The history of contemporary Christian music is also enlivened by modern Oklahoma artists such as Point of Grace, Sandi Patty, and Christian rockers, Pillar.

Also emerging from the traditions of Anglo-Celtic ballads and fairly simple play-party string band music in Oklahoma is the best known Anglo-American folksinger, period, Woody Guthrie from Okemah, Oklahoma. Internationally recognized and lauded for his 1,400-plus folksongs, some of which are still being sung and recorded for the first time by new artists re-visiting Guthrie's massive archives, relocated to Tulsa in 1912. Guthrie wrote songs about the Oklahoma Dust Bowl years, national economic Depression of the 1930s, children songs, ballads about tragic events, celebrations of notable (sometimes notorious) figures, and wry observations on the ironies of life. Guthrie's work has been the wellspring for several books about his life, consistent performances and recordings of his songs by modern artists, and the inspiration for the annual Woody Guthrie Free Folk Festival each July in Okemah. Guthrie is not the only folksinger from Oklahoma, but his influence is felt in Grammy-nominated singer/songwriter Tom Russell who has childhood connections to Bristow. Members of the Red Dirt Music movement such as Bob Childers, Red Dirt Rangers, Tom Skinner, Stoney LaRue, and Jimmy LaFave all cite Guthrie as having a major impact on their music and songwriting. Guthrie also points to the small-town ethos that has governed much of Oklahomans' sensibilities about themselves and their identity.

Mural in Woody Guthrie Memorial Park in Okemah, OK, 2013.

As of the beginning of the 21st century nearly two thirds of Oklahoma's 3.4 million people live in rural areas, small towns, or smaller cities, outside of the major population centers of Oklahoma City and Tulsa.[7] Moreover, the rural and small town residents of Oklahoma have experienced considerable poverty throughout the state's history. Both the rural nature of the state and the poverty challenges confronted by its residents favored the development of the previously mentioned musical genre of blues, but even more so this environment has created an astounding number of contributors to the field of American country music. Oklahoma's high percentage of tenant farmers and sharecroppers in the past forced many to seek music as an avenue for leaving poverty. Several notable musicians were children of Great Depression parents who endured extremely hard times. Parents of the 1930s era who longed for their children to realize a better life moved to the West coast in search of work. Chet Baker, Bonnie Owens, Nokie Edwards, Bob Bogle, Roy Harris, and Jean Shepard were all born in Oklahoma, but moved West with their parents at an early age. Merle Haggard, so closely associated with the state because of his early 1970s hit, "Okie from Muskogee," was born to parents who had given up on their Oklahoma dreams and moved to California in 1934 where Merle was born in 1937. Those who stayed in Oklahoma encouraged their sons and daughters to practice their musical talents and promoted the budding musicians at any venue available in Oklahoma, which, in turn, led to the realm of broadcasting. A number of Oklahoma-based musicians helped turn country music into a profession, including Otto Gray and the Oklahoma Cowboys, Gene Autry, Bob Wills, and Hank Thompson, who often employed local Oklahoma musicians in their groups, or gave first breaks to promising talent. Bob Wills' "Texas Playboys" were mostly Oklahomans, and future stars Patti Page and Wanda Jackson got their first major breaks on local radio. Many children in rural areas who hoped for careers in music were inspired by broadcasts of Otto Gray over KRFU (Bristow), Johnny Bond on WKY (Oklahoma City), and Gene Autry and Bob Wills on KVOO (Tulsa) during the first half of the twentieth century, all of which motivated countless young musicians, and, in turn, fueled country music like dry hay on a barn fire.

Wanda Jackson and Larry Collins perform at the opening of the Oklahoma Rock History Exhibit as the state history center in 2009.

Virtually every sub-genre of country music can attribute substantial elements of its growth to Oklahomans or musicians commonly associated with Oklahoma, including old time fiddlers (Henry Gilliland), singing cowboys (Gene Autry) and cowboy bands (Otto Gray), Western swing (Spade Cooley, Bob Wills, Bob Dunn), bluegrass (Byron Berline), honky tonk (Willis Brothers), country pop (Roger Miller), progressive or "outlaw country" (Ray Wylie Hubbard), "Bakersfield Sound" (Tommy Collins and Bonnie Owens), "Nashville Sound" or pop country (Reba McEntire, Garth Brooks, Toby Keith, Joe Diffie, The Tractors, Ron-

Gene Autry

nie Dunn, Vince Gill, Blake Shelton, Carrie Underwood, Miranda Lambert, Joe Don Rooney of Rascal Flatts, et.al.), alternative country (Kelly Willis, Jason Boland and the Stragglers, Mike McClure, and Cody Canada), and the Red Dirt movement (Bob Childers, Tom Skinner, John Fullbright, Greg Jacobs, Red Dirt Rangers). Oklahoma's contributions to the country music genre are monumental and historic, validated anecdotally by Country Music Television's 2003 list of the "40 Greatest Men of Country Music," a list that includes ten names, or 25% of that group, that are strongly associated with Oklahoma. Three of the men were born in the state (Garth Brooks, Toby Keith, Vince Gill), and two moved to the state at an early age where they had their primary musical experiences (Gene Autry, Roger Miller). As mentioned earlier, Merle Haggard was born to Okie migrants who left the state during the Great Depression for California, and the other four came to Oklahoma for extended performance opportunities (Bob Wills, Buck Owens, Conway Twitty, and Ronnie Dunn). Of course, many more Oklahoma men have contributed to the genre as studio session musicians (Eldon Shamblin and Don White), producers (Tommy Allsup, Scott Hendricks and Tim Dubois), promoters (Jim Halsey), songwriters (Chick Rains, Merle Kilgore, and Jack Dunham), and performers (Wade Hayes, Stoney Edwards, Alvin Crow, Restless Heart, and Ricochet). Both Roy Clark and Merle Travis moved to the state late in their careers.

Although Patti Page was n ot specifically a country music artist, she was an important example of Oklahoma musicians' abilities to transcend genre boundaries. Her massive crossover hit, "Tennessee Waltz", was a hit on the country, pop, and R&B charts, and is now the state song of Tennessee. Many of Page's songs included polished "Nashville Sound" country music elements that landed them on the *Billboard* country music charts. Many other Oklahoma women who enjoyed country music success, such as Lorrie Collins, Gail Davies, Becky Hobbs, Gus Hardin, Norma Jean, Bonnie Owens, Jody Miller, and Jean Shepard. Recent "move-in" women stars include Miranda Lambert who purchased a farm near Tishomingo in 2007 in order to be closer to her eventual husband, Blake Shelton (they were married in 2011). Additionally, Trisha Yearwood is an Owasso resident after marrying Garth Brooks in 2005. While Lambert is still at the beginning of what is already stellar career, Yearwood can choose her recordings carefully and enjoy her life as an artist-at-will, writer, humanitarian, and family person. While country music may have long been the most noticed music out of the state in the national consciousness, American rock and pop have also felt the

Patti Page, 1950s

tidal waves of musical influence from Oklahoma musicians.

With the arrival of the rock era, marked solidly by the volcanic eruption of Elvis Presley on the national pop music scene in 1956 with his hit, "Heartbreak Hotel," co-written by Oklahoman Mae Boren Axton, the state's musicians have contributed mightily to the genre from its inception as a popular music form to the present. However, Oklahomans had already been rocking prior to Elvis, musically with the country boogie of Bob and Johnnie Lee Wills, or lyrically with Woody Guthrie who uses the phrase "rocking and a-rolling" in his "Talking Dust Bowl Blues", a phrase already well known in R&B and blues environments as a euphemistic term for having an extremely good time. While several Oklahomans toiled in proto-rock obscurity (Hank Harral, Tom James, Dale Davis, Charles Jones, Eddie Cletro, Charlie Aldrich), both Larry and Lorrie Collins (The Collins Kids) and Wanda Jackson are now considered primary instigators of the rockabilly movement. Beginning with Wanda, whose 2009 induction in the Rock and Roll Hall of Fame cemented her status as rock music pioneer, and continuing to the present day with successful rock acts such as the two-time Grammy winners Flaming Lips, Hinder, and All-American Rejects, Oklahoma musicians have played major parts in all of rock's stylistic eras.

Oklahoma Today magazine, May/June, 2009

Several musicians who emerged in teen bands of Tulsa in the 1950s, such as David Gates, Leon Russell, Jack Dunham, and J.J. Cale, proceeded to California where they first worked as session musicians before starting individual singing and songwriting careers. Often valued for their versatility between various styles, or laid back and bluesy approach to their playing, a number of Tulsa musicians impacted rock music including drummers Jim Keltner, Chuck Blackwell, David Teegarden, and Jimmy Karstein, bassists Carl Radle and Gary Gilmore, guitarist/pianist Tommy Tripplehorn, and keyboardist Rocky Frisco. Tulsa also became a center for American rock music in the 1970s when Leon Russell established a studio there where many young rockers gained their first recording experiences. Russell's label, Shelter Records, also provided Tulsa power popper Dwight Twilley with his first album, *Sincerely*, in 1976, continuing the trend of Oklahomans supporting

Leon Russell

each other. Rock musicians also broke out in the western part of the state who made major splashes in rock and pop music, to include guitarists Jesse Ed Davis (Norman), Moon Martin (Altus), and Steve Ripley (Tulsa, OKC, Glencoe), as well as singer/songwriters Barry McGuire and Mike Brewer (Oklahoma City), Hoyt Axton (Duncan) and Jimmy Webb (Elk City).

While a number of highly recognizable figures impacted rock music on the national level, more obscure groups also had subtle influences on the splinter subgenres of punk rock that broke off from the mainstream in the 1970s and 1980s. Chickasha's Debris, and their 1976 album, *Static Disposal* is revered as being a proto-punk sound by no less than alternative rock careerists Sonic Youth. East Coast music writers routinely channel the evolution of punk rock on a basic line from the Velvet Underground, Iggy Pop, and the New York Dolls through the official beginning of what gets called "punk rock" with Ramones, and the U.K. bands who followed them. Eventually, the American music industry championed the term safer term "new wave" to categorized and market the buoyant, cynical, and funny antithesis to bloated stadium rock and cocksure Southern rock, which Debris certainly was. The same writers who know all this still fail to acknowledge (or just don't know) that Debris' only studio album, *Static Disposal*, exhibits all the classic touchstones of punk (spitting venomous and/or socially editorial lyrics, short bursts of reckless rock mayhem, and a do-it-yourself ethic that became a mantra for 1980s hardcore), and pre-dates the release of the Ramones first album.[8] Tulsa punk rockers NOTA, New Mysterians, and Los Reactors all figured into the national punk scene of the 1980s, supported by early gigs at ground zero of the underground music scene in Tulsa, a dive known as the Bleu Grotto. Since the 1980s, a number of successful groups indicate the state's level of rock music production is not waning. Alongside previously mentioned groups Flaming Lips, Hinder, and All-American Rejects, 21st century rock groups

Dennis Coyne of Star Death and White Dwarfs

with Oklahoma ties who have landed major record label deals and are touring nationally and internationally include Shiny Toy Guns (Oklahoma City), Starlight Mints (Norman), Other Lives (Stillwater), The Uglysuit (Oklahoma City), Star Death and White Dwarfs (Oklahoma City), Colourmusic (Stillwater), and Anti-Mortem (Chickasha).

Another factor in the development of musicians in the state focuses on the availability of performance venues. As young Oklahoma musicians honed their musical skills at county fairs, churches, school assemblies, nightclubs, and talent contests and festivals throughout the state, many were eventually given the opportunity to perform on the live music radio shows in the state, such as

KOPR in Oklahoma City and KTUL in Tulsa. Moreover, public dance halls and ballrooms, virtually nonexistent before the 1920s, proliferated in great numbers to accommodate the new wave of dance styles, e.g., the foxtrot and Charleston, sweeping the country at the time. The Ritz and Trianon Ballrooms in Oklahoma City, Casa Loma and and Louvre Ballrooms in Tulsa, and the Bluebird Ballroom in Shawnee provided important outlets for

Cain's Ballroom, Tulsa

amateur musicians to perform the music for these dances and gain valuable experience. The trend of performance opportunities in the 21st century has received a boon from the development of a number of tribal casinos, which regularly feature live music, especially the Muscogee (Creek) and Cherokee casinos in Tulsa, both of which feature live music by mostly local artists every night of the week. Longstanding and still active primary venues of the Cain's Ballroom in Tulsa and the Diamond Ballroom in Oklahoma City provide a stage for national acts from whom younger musicians can learn, as well as provide opportunities for local artists to serve as opening acts or headliners on off nights. One of the absolute best rooms in the region for live singer/song-

Jimmy Webb sings at the Blue Door, 2006

writer performers is the Blue Door in Oklahoma City. Opened in 1993 by Greg Johnson, the facility has featured some of America's best singer/songwriters, regularly features Oklahoma artists, and has a stated ethos of supporting up and coming talent.

Of course, a lot of work still exists for live bands in the college towns of Norman, Stillwater, and Tahlequah, as well as honky-tonks and bars that dot Oklahoma highways with signs touting cold beer and hot music. Along with the stages of nightclubs and music halls across the state, Oklahoma music festivals, such as the International Blue Grass Festival in Guthrie, Rocklahoma in Pryor, the Southwestern Oklahoma State University Jazz Festival in Weatherford, and Norman's Music Festival continue offering important developmental opportunities for young and established musicians in the state. These local experiences help Oklahomans launch their professional careers in music, inspire younger musicians in Oklahoma to seek a music profession, and provide important work for professionals.

Music education has also played a historic role in the development of Oklahoma musicians, and current innovative music programs in the state seek to continue this tradition. Music teachers, such as Zelia N. Page Breaux, Evelyn Sheffield, and Cornelius Pittman at Douglas High School in Oklahoma City, Ashley Alexander Sr. At Edison High School in Tulsa, George Bright at Sapulpa High School, and the Manual Training High School Band in Muskogee, provided sound formal training for many jazz musicians from the state in the first half of the twentieth century. Music has always been an important part of Oklahoma's public schools. Even the smallest high school with an 8-man football team has some semblance of a band for playing the fight song in the stands and some kind of half time show, even if the musicians are clad in jeans and matching t-shirts instead of elaborate and expensive band uniforms. Only in the last few years have stories started to appear in the state's newspapers about public school music programs feeling the budget pinch and considering shutting down those programs, but the fact that closing even a small school's music program makes statewide news indicates a continued reverence for music as an important development opportunity for youth in Oklahoma. One program that fosters musical development in youth is the The Oklahoma Arts Institute, a private, non-profit organization with a vision to cultivate established and emerging artists and educators through art workshops, immersion and awareness. Since 1977, the Oklahoma Arts Institute has recruited nationally renowned artists to teach a fine arts program for talented Oklahoma youth and a series of continuing education workshops for adults. Located at Quartz Mountain Arts and Conference Center in southwestern Oklahoma near Altus, the institute hires nationally known musicians to tutor for the Oklahoma Summer Arts Institute and workshops for educators.

While traditional music education programs abound at the university level in the state, a few schools have taken innovative approaches to developing professional musicians in the areas of Broadway, opera, jazz, and popular music. Oklahoma City University's Wanda Bass School of Music seems to be a pipeline to the Broadway and opera performance world with stars such as Kristin Chenowith, Lara Teeter, Kelli O'Hara, and Leona Mitchell as evidentiary products. While Mitchell studied with Inez Silberg at OCU, the Chenowith, Teeter, and O'Hara were mentored by Florence Birdwell who has a reputation among her peers and students as one of the best music teachers in the region. Tulsa University announced in 2009 the beginning of construction on a $34 million arts center that will house the School of Music and Department of Film Studies, and will also be open to community performance groups. The Jazz Lab and Jazz Studies degree at Northeastern State University in Tahlequah provides a top-notch jazz education with a unique performance space, The Jazz Lab (a.k.a. Joe's Place – named after longtime NSU jazz instructor Joe Davis). Along with jazz studies, the University of Central Oklahoma in Edmond has partnered with the London Academy of Contemporary Music to offer degrees in drums, guitar, and vocal performance, as well as studies in music production, recording, and the music industry itself. The CEO of the school, Scott Booker, is widely-known throughout the music industry as the manager of the Flaming Lips and creator of Hellfire Enterprises, an artist management company. In touting the program on the school's website in 2010, Booker explains, "No one in the U.S. or Oklahoma has a program like ACM@UCO – they all have bits and pieces of it within their schools. ACM@UCO combines teaching music skill, production and music business. This is important for Oklahoma because the Oklahoma Department of Commerce has identified the music industry as one of the areas it wants to focus on for development. ACM@UCO will be at the forefront of this development." Booker's statement also indicates a widespread level of support from Oklahoma governmental and non-profit entities that seek to channel Oklahoma's current and historic music into economic development, tourism, and public enlightenment. The Oklahoma City Council highlighted three of its musical giants in 2006 with streets (one each for Vince Gill and Charlie Christian), and an alley (The Flaming Lips), in the Bricktown entertainment district. The alley's naming began a tenuous relationship between the art rocking freaks and the Oklahoma "establishment" intent on honoring them. Lips leader Wayne Coyne let out a few choice enthusiastic words at the alley coronation that made some city politicos blanch. The flap paled in comparison to the national attention raised by the Oklahoma legislature's hissy fit over a Flaming Lips band member wearing a t-shirt with a hammer and sickle logo at the Senate confirmation of their song "Do You Realize?" as the state's official rock song. Some people get the rock sensibility, and some don't, but the state of Oklahoma has made some solid attempts at reckoning with the outrageous legacy of music in the state.

Jill Simpson (left), director of the Oklahoma Film and Music Office, with singer/songwriter, studio engineer, guitar player and tech wizard, Steve Ripley, Tulsa, OK, circa 2004.

The Oklahoma Film & Music Office's mission is to attract film, television, video, and music industries to Oklahoma for the promotion and growth of these industries within the state, sponsoring statewide forums where musicians and music industry figures could express their concerns and interests about music in the state. Outside of the state, office has sponsored an Oklahoma Music Showcase since 2009 at the South by Southwest music and industry festival in Austin, Texas. The showcase features up and coming Oklahoma artists such as Samantha Crain and the Midnight Shivers (Shawnee), The Uglysuit (Oklahoma City), Colourmusic (Stillwater), and Stardeath and White Dwarfs (Oklahoma City). Also at the state agency level, the Oklahoma Arts Council has a strong role in promoting music as an art form and community enrichment activity, awarding grants each year to arts organizations around the state that would not otherwise be able to have such events. In cooperation with the Oklahoma History Center, the Oklahoma Folklife Council actively promotes the preservation, awareness, and presentation of traditional folklife traditions such as music, handcrafted art, and unique foods, as well as sponsoring scholarly forums on the subject's varied off-shoots. Additionally, the Oklahoma History Center put its vast resources to work in documenting and displaying the rock music history of the state in an exhibit and coffee table book, both titled "Another Hot Oklahoma Night" that opened in May, 2009. The exhibit explored Oklahoma rock and roll artists, radio stations, personalities, venues, and fans that have Oklahoma roots. In conjunction with the exhibit, a statewide committee was formed through the Oklahoma History Center to determine a state rock song for Oklahoma, culminating in the Flaming Lips' "Do You Realize?" as the state rock song after a panel of experts decided on a Top 10 list of nominees, which was subsequently voted on by the public via the Internet. The Top 10 list of nominees is a rock history music lesson in itself:

Top 10 Nominees for the Oklahoma State Rock Song in 2009
1. "Heartbreak Hotel" (co-written by Mae Boren Axton, performed by Elvis Presley)
2. "Let's Have a Party" (performed by Wanda Jackson)
3. "Walk Don't Run" (performed by The Ventures featuring Bob Bogle and Nokie Edwards)
4. "Never Been to Spain" (written by Hoyt Axton)
5. "After Midnight" (written by J.J. Cale, performed by J.J. Cale and Eric Clapton)
6. "Home Sweet Oklahoma (written and performed by Leon Russell)
7. "Oklahoma" (written and performed by The Call)
8. "Do You Realize" (written and performed by The Flaming Lips) (Official State Rock Song)
9. "Move Along" (written and performed by All-American Rejects)
10. "Endless Oklahoma Sky" (written and performed by John Moreland and the Black Gold Band

While "Do You Realize?" does not mention the state specifically, the Flaming Lips' youthful, worldwide, and Internet savvy fan base propelled it to the top with an overwhelming percentage of the vote. The song has a positive message of embracing loved ones while the opportunity is present, instead of lamenting lost chances of expressing one's affection after those loved ones are gone. Also interesting is the list of honorable mentions that did not make the Top 10, but also indicate the wide range of rock music associated with the state:

Honorable Mentions for the Oklahoma State Rock Song Ballot (2009)

1. "Bad Case of Loving You" (written by Moon Martin, performed by Robert Palmer
2. "Been There Before" (written and performed by Hanson)
3. "Don't Stop Believin'" (written by Neal Schon, performed by Journey)
4. "Down on the Farm" (written and performed by Big Al Downing)
5. "Happy Song" (written and performed by the Nixons)
6. "I Know a Little" (written by Steve Gaines, performed by Lynyrd Skynyrd)
7. "Joy to the World" (written by Hoyt Axton, performed by Three Dog Night)
8. "Mother Freedom" (written by David Gates, performed by Bread)
9. "Oklahoma Breakdown" (written by Mike Hosty, performed by Hosty Duo)
10. "Red Dirt Boogie, Brother" (written and performed by Jesse Ed Davis)
11. "Summertime Blues" (written and performed by Eddie Cochran)
12. "Yes" (written and performed by Colourmusic)[9]

While The Flaming Lips' "Do You Realize" came out on top, students of Oklahoma music would benefit from a compilation of all of the above-mentioned songs to teach the tremendous impact of Oklahomans on the history of rock music. The state already has a state song/anthem, the well-known title song from the Rodgers and Hammerstein musical, *Oklahoma!*; a state waltz – "Oklahoma Wind"; and, a state country song – "Faded Love". In this writer's opinion, the song penned by Vince Gill and Jimmy Webb for the state's centennial, "Oklahoma Rising", should be considered the state's 21st century song with its lyrical focus on the real history of Oklahoma, its authentic music that relates to the history of the state, and the performance of the song by Oklahomans, elements not present in the Rodgers and Hammerstein number. Primarily available as a collectible through the Oklahoma Centennial Commission in 2007, the song was included on a two-CD set of Oklahoma artists, *Oklahoma Rising: A Tribute to the Artists and Music of Oklahoma*, the proceeds of which benefitted Habitat for Humanity.

A number of non-profit organizations have formed to honor the wide variety of accomplished Oklahoma musicians. Created in 1988 by the state legislature, the Oklahoma Jazz Hall of Fame was created to "to inspire creativity and improve the quality of life for all Oklahomans through preservation, education and performance of jazz, our uniquely American art form," according to its published mission statement. Additionally, the Oklahoma Jazz Hall of Fame wishes "to promote, preserve, and illuminate the true art forms of jazz, blues and gospel music; also to identify, document and honor the Oklahoma musicians who have made significant contributions locally, regionally, nationally and internationally to its development." Located in the historic Union Depot in downtown Tulsa, The Oklahoma Jazz Hall of Fame hosts concerts, educational programs for youth, and an annual induction, but does not focus exclusively on musicians with Oklahoma ties.

Oklahoma Music Hall of Fame and Museum, Muskogee.

Citizens of Muskogee began discussing an Oklahoma Music Hall of Fame in 1995 that would honor and promote all of Oklahoma's music traditions, educate the public about music history in Oklahoma, and hold a yearly induction into a hall of fame for Oklahomans who have made a major impact in their field. The Oklahoma Music Hall of Fame held its first induction in 1997, starting with Woody Guthrie, Patti Page, Merle Haggard, and Claude "Fiddler" Williams. With official sanctioning from the Oklahoma legislature as the entity to operate an Oklahoma Music Hall of Fame and Museum, the organization acquired the historic Frisco railroad depot in Muskogee to establish the first phase of a state music hall of fame and museum. Open to the public with a display of biographies and photographs of all inductees, artifacts of Oklahoma music, and a children's music experience exhibit completed in 2012, the Oklahoma Music Hall of Fame continues in 2013 with plans for more inductions and museum development in Muskogee.

The most recent hall of fame for musicians in Oklahoma, the Oklahoma Blues Hall of Fame, was started by DC and Selby Minner in Rentiesville, Oklahoma, at their Down Home Blues Club, site of the annual Dusk 'til Dawn Blues Festival. Fearing many worthy Oklahoma blues musicians may have a hard time being honored due to the massive numbers of musicians from other genres who are further up front in the induction lines due to popular and commercial notoriety for the Oklahoma Music Hall of Fame or Oklahoma Jazz Hall of Fame, the Minners began inducting Oklahoma blues musicians in 2004, and have held yearly inductions on Memorial Day Weekend through 2011. The Oklahoma Country Music Hall of Fame and Museum in Del City has long been a host of country music variety shows and annual bluegrass festivals, but is not a state-sanctioned hall of fame. The next and most elaborate plan to tell the story of Oklahoma music's impact on the world is a multi-million dollar museum being planned for Tulsa by the Oklahoma History Center, a museum celebrating and properly contextualizing the history of popular culture as influenced and developed by Oklahomans.

Conceived in 2007, and first proposed in 2009, the history center plans on using the theme "Crossroads of Creativity" to detail Oklahomans' impact on American popular culture imagery, Wild West shows, cinema, radio, television, sequential art (comics), music, stage performance, new media, and the legacy of Route 66. The museum's proposed name is the Oklahoma Museum of Music and Popular Culture, but has usually been referred to as the "O.K. Pop Museum", or just "OK Pop", among those who are focused on the project. While a donation from the George Kaiser Family Foundation of one million dollars, and a piece of land donated by Bank of Oklahoma in Tulsa's Historic Brady District furthered the serious nature of the facility's future, the Oklahoma History Center needed cooperation from the state legislature to pass a forty million dollar bond issue to help fund the project, which has not yet happened as of early 2013.[10]

An artist's rendering of the Oklahoma Museum of Music and Popular Culture being planned for Tulsa, OK.

With all of this focus on Oklahoma's musical heritage, one still has to wonder why Oklahoma appears to be a unique place in the realm of musical production. While some states are R&B or country music heavy, they may be light on rock music, or vice versa. Additionally, no other state can boast the

The Miller Brothers Wild West Show operated out of Oklahoma from roughly 1907 to 1928.

Hugh W. Foley / xxxiii

variety of American Indian musical influence in the state. And while Oklahoma features prominent figures from all of those genres, the state has also made impressive contributions to opera (Leona Mitchell/Barbara McAlister), classical (Louis Ballard), and Broadway (Kristin Chenowith/Sam Harris) genres as well. Music is a distinguishing character of place, giving special meaning to one's home area, and, ultimately provides a sense of pride in place. Psychologists call it a "shared ego," while cultural geographers refer to it as "place consciousness." Place itself embodies meaning dependent on the personal history that one brings to it. Through these people-place interactions, one develops a deep psychological attachment with a specific place, such as Oklahoma. Recognition and appreciation of the contributions and innovations of Oklahomans to American music can help create a sense of local awareness, and, translated correctly can become a source of state and civic pride. The various halls of fame, street-namings, and city limits signs, are just another indication people in the state are becoming more sensitive to the unique aspects of being an Oklahoman, as opposed to previous national stereotypes of the "Okie" or a character out of the musical *Oklahoma!*[11] National recognition occurred for Oklahoma music in a profound way in 2010 and 2011 with Wanda Jackson ('10) and Leon Russell ('11) being inducted into the Rock and Roll Hall of Fame in Cleveland, Ohio. Also in 2011, both Reba McEntire and Jean Shepard were inducted into Nashville's pantheon, the Country Music Hall of Fame. While musicians, music aficionados, ardent fans, journalists, and a few cultural historians have long been aware of the high level of musical quality and influence on the part of the state's musicians, citizens of Oklahoma are now becoming more attuned to the rich musical legacy of the state, and realize it is something that makes the state unique in its cultural contributions to the world.

Oklahoma Rock History Exhibit
Oklahoma History Center, 2009

Musicologists agree that music is one of the most important indicators of the cultural milieu in a particular area defined by some kind of city, state, tribal, or geographic boundaries. With the culture of Oklahoma facing increased homogeneity due to the omnipresence of mainstream popular culture, music remains an enduring characteristic of the state's unique character. Many Oklahoma musicians continue to operate outside of the mainstream by living in the state, yet impact their respective musical genres directly. Outsider country music star Toby Keith remains based in the state (Toby Keith), as does country's biggest star ever, Garth Brooks, and some of the genre's newest bright spots in Blake Shelton and Miranda Lambert. Quirky and iconoclastic rockers, Flaming Lips, have won GRAMMY Awards and toured internationally, yet the group's front man and leader, Wayne Coyne, chooses to stay in his Oklahoma City compound of creativity. Recent folk-rock phenom John Fullbright has emerged from Oklahoma's modern folk and red dirt music scene and become a GRAMMY nominated Americana singer/songwriter. Perhaps, the supreme example of an "underground" scene, or music sub-culture, is the tribally specific and ceremonial music of many American Indians based within the state's borders. While American Indian music is often misunderstood, underappreciated, and generally not heard outside of its tribal context beyond an open-to-all intertribal powwow, the multiple variations of indigenous music still active in Oklahoma are a true testament to the perseverance of the people who have maintained their musical traditions in the face of tremendous cultural odds and genuine federal opposition in the 19th century to "abolish" what the U.S. government considered "heathenish customs" of traditional dances and songs of Native people.[12]

Muscogee (Creek) men influenced by Western Swing and popular music included Willie Ben, Smiley Burnett, Amos Barnett, and Haney Barnett, who performed as the Musical Brownies in and around Okmulgee, and on KHBG Radio in Okmulgee from 1948 through 1968.

The American Indian people of the state represent a wider phenomenon of history in Oklahoma, where its people have often reacted against cultural conformity, perhaps explaining the extreme conservatism in the state, as citizens are unwilling to simply accept "culture from the coasts" just because it is offered up by the powerful national media. Perhaps also, the rebellious attitude of a youthful state encourages this demeanor; certainly, the unique cultural mixture of the people who settled here may be the most prominent reason for explaining this contrarian ethos, as Oklahomans have had extreme opportunities to be confronted by cultural norms not present in their own history, and have had to decide to embrace them or not. In Oklahoma, American Indians were not only first here once, but several times, and are still here, unlike many of the states from which the tribes were removed. Additionally, aside from the slaves of African descent that came with some of the Southeastern tribes removed to Oklahoma, free African-Americans came to Oklahoma with a belief in the fair opportunities offered by the all-black town movement of the late 19th century, Even with their disenfranchisement at statehood, blacks in Oklahoma maintained a sense of ownership in the state that continues to the present day in the form of African-American business districts, historic churches, and established leaders in commerce, education, and politics. Finally, immigrants from the British Isles, the European mainland, and first and second generation Americans, migrated to the state after the Civil War, through the land runs, and after statehood, bringing with them the positive attributes of their European backgrounds, along with the negatives of racism that polarized the state's early history and crystallized the differences between the state's people.[13] That same kaleidoscope of ethnicities, beliefs, and musical traditions ultimately completed Oklahoma's palate from which its identity began to take shape at statehood in 1907, and from which musical artists sprang with multiple influences to create hybridized musical forms or were able to shape shift from the requirements of one musical subgenre to another.

Interestingly, the state's entire history can be experienced through the music that has been produced by its inhabitants and citizens, explained in that way because most Native Americans were not considered citizens until 1924. In Oklahoma music, one can hear the first musical interpretations of life on this continent before the arrival of Europeans in the song and chant of the American Indian; one can hear the evolution of old time gospel singing into contemporary Christian pop and rock; one can learn how slave spirituals became blues, how blues merged with marching band music and ragtime to become jazz, and then how Oklahomans varied their jazz styles to find work in every significant jazz era. Oklahoma music and history students can learn how the state's oil booms provided resources for the development of classical music performers and institutions in Tulsa and Oklahoma City. One can follow the trail of old time fiddle tunes as they meander through cowboy songs, Western swing, and bluegrass. Astute listeners will understand how Woody Guthrie's folk songs express the trials of the Dust Bowl era and the subsequent Okie migrations to California in search of a better life, as well as magnify the experience of multiple occupational experiences, life trials, joyful moments, and tragic occurrences of the 1930s and '40s. Hear how honky-tonk, the Nashville Sound and outlaw country all took major cues from Oklahoma musicians, singers and songwriters. Then, witness how blues and country merged to form early rock and roll and R & B. Subsequently, Oklahoma musicians transitioned with every era in rock, and continue to maintain and expand rock music's vocabulary.

By understanding Oklahoma's music, one can understand the cultural and social milieus that provided musically productive environments, and, therefore, better interpret the state's history from a humanities and artistic point of view. Oklahoma's performers, composers, music institutions, and songs can be significant teachers of the state's rich and diverse cultural heritage. As the scholarship associated with American music continues to increase, so does the need for more in-depth research into regional studies of music. When completed, fuller documentation of music at the state level will become a vital part of American history.[14]

With the plethora of information now available on the Internet about many of the artists featured in this book, the author hopes students, teachers, fans, and scholars will use this text as a springboard to more appreciating, researching, and writing about the great array of Oklahoma's impact on the world of music. By all appearances, the gusher of Oklahoma music is not even close to running dry.

> Hugh Foley
> March, 2013
> Stillwater, Oklahoma

Introductory Essay Notes

1. Charles N. Gould, *Travels Through Oklahoma* (Oklahoma City: Harlow Publishing Company, 1928), 127.
2. Writers' Program of the Works Progress Administration, *The WPA Guide to 1930s Oklahoma* (Lawrence: University Press of Kansas, rev. ed.), 104.
3. Evan Tonsing, Letter to the author, 2002.
4. To learn more about the history of the Fisk Jubilee Signers, see www.fiskjubileesingers.org/about/.
5. Peter Guralnick, *Searching for Robert Johnson* (New York: Obelisk Books, 1989), 34.
6. For a few more details about string bands and pre-statehood music in Oklahoma, as well as some commentary on various ethnic music traditions of Oklahoma, see Max Nichols, "State's musical heritage has great range," *The Oklahoman*, 27 March, 2007, section E, p. 3; also see James Hubert Renner, "Geographic Implications of the Fiddling Tradition in Oklahoma" (Master's thesis, Oklahoma State University, 1974).
7. U. S. Census Bureau. http://quickfacts.census.gov/qfd/states/40000
8. For a concise look at the standard history of punk, see Tim Sommer's "Who Invented Punk," *Big Takeover*, Fall, 2010, Volume 31, No. 1, Issue 66, pages 12 and 14.
9. List of honorable mentions for nominations in the process to select a state rock song for Oklahoma are from the personal notes of the author who was the chair of the committee charged with determining the "Top Ten" nominees on which people voted via the Internet.
10. For a complete review of the Oklahoma History Center's 2011 public announcement about the planned Oklahoma Museum of Music and Popular Culture in Tulsa,

see Wayne Green, "New museum proposed for Tulsa," *Tulsa World,* 6 May, 2011, Section A, p. 1; for more on the Bank of Oklahoma's donation of land in Tulsa for the project and the Oklahoma Music Hall of Fame and Museum's public objection to the idea of including "music" in the museum's plan, see Brandy McDonnell, "Bank of Oklahoma plans pop museum donation," *Daily Oklahoma*, 11 May, 2011, Section A, p. 18.

11. For an accounting of Oklahoma's image in the national mindset per a 2007 poll in which the musical *Oklahoma!* and the Oklahoma City bombing were the top two things mentioned when 20, 951 people were asked for their impressions of the state, see Tony Thornton "We're OK," *Daily Oklahoman*, 7 February, 2007, Section A, pages 1 and 3.

12. For early references to the desire on the part of the U.S. government to wipe out American Indian traditional music, see the *Annual Report of the Commissioner of Indian Affairs to the Secretary of the Interior* (Government Printing Office, 1884).

13. Regarding the separation of the races in Oklahoma after statehood, the first set of state laws that went on the books in Oklahoma included the "separate coach," "waiting room," and "restroom" laws. Oklahoma Senate Bill #1 made it "unlawful for any person to use or occupy or remain in any waiting room, toilet room, or at any water tank in any passenger depot in this State, set apart to a race to which he does not belong". See *General Statutes of Oklahoma 1908: A Compilation of All the Laws of a General Nature Including the Session Laws of 1907* (Kansas City: Pipes-Reed, 1908). The effect of the segregationist laws "helped to internalize a behavior toward blacks that led toward increased antipathy and hatred, according to Jimmie L. Franklin, *Journey Toward Hope: A History of Blacks in Oklahoma (Norman: OU Press, 1994), 46.*

14. Burton W. Peretti has called for more regional studies of jazz. See Burton W. Peretti, "The Jazz Studies Renaissance," American Studies 34 (1993), 139-49.

Colourmusic performs at Dfset in Tulsa, OK in 2007.

Scope and Limitations
Comments on fact-checking and citations for the *OMG II*

In the contemporary popular music landscape, most (if not all) major and minor current artists have their own website with an official biography for use in publicity. As a result, much more information about some major artists is available online than we have room to publish here in the *Oklahoma Music Guide*. As this text has taken shape to its present edition, the sheer volume of information about Oklahoma music could triple the pages of this book. As a result, the author has often included the artist's website as the only reference source at the end of a biographical entry about that artist. Some of those biographies have provided foundational sources for the general timeline of an artist's career. Additionally, the author has drawn on many official biographies authorized or submitted by the artists themselves, press releases from a number of record company and radio promoters, as well as the actual musical releases by the artists. While the paradigm is shifting toward a completely digital entertainment product, the author has used many album and CD liner notes for referencing music being discussed in an artist's entry. The data printed on the album and CD covers provide multiple facts such as recording and release dates, songwriters, producers, session musicians, studios used, lyrics, and, occasionally, notes from the artists to their fans, professional colleagues, or family and friend supporters.

While an artist's website is usually the most important starting point for researching a musical entity, the site might be tilted critically toward a favorable interpretation of the artist's career via a hyperbolic publicist apt to amplify mild success (or not much at all) in vague ways, not uncommon as a promotional tactic in show business. Additionally, any website is maintained ultimately by a human being, and a wide variety of typos and or misquotes can occur between the generator of document and its appearance on a website. Therefore, *OMG* researchers are careful to confirm facts such as birthdates, significant performance periods, music release dates, and accurate chart sales or radio chart information to the best of our ability, often checking multiple authoritative sources to corroborate claims by an artist regarding these kinds of facts. However, occasionally an artist will make a claim that is not widely known, but accepted in their own community (such as a #1 hit in an obscure trade magazine or website chart, a concept often embraced by Nashville songwriters).

Another trend with fact-checking for these kinds of reference works is that some contemporary artists are understandably wary of revealing too much more information than everyone already knows, and are protective of their birthdays due to the potential for identity theft. For the hundreds of artists around before that issue was a concern, and if their birthday was already public knowledge, *OMG* includes those here. During the research for this document, some artists declined to include their birth date, and *OMG* has not pursued it further as a person's general age can be determined from photographs of dated performances, and/or a general context of significant dates in an artist's published biography.

As mentioned in the introductory elements to this text, many websites, printed reference works, and published releases by the artists provide a basic guide and commonly known facts regarding the major releases and career trajectory of many current and historic artists discussed in the *Oklahoma Music Guide*; therefore, complete documentation of an artist's career is not as important in this work as naming that artist as part of the whole Oklahoma music story, explaining their connection to the state, providing an overview of their major successes, and attempting to contextualize them critically or historically in the realm of popular or world music (and not make anybody too mad in the process). Additionally, as the need for this book to exist began to outweigh its shortcomings, the author made a decision to go ahead and release what we have at this time so all interested could begin working with the information for their own purposes.

Any mistakes made in the text are the sole responsibility of the author, who is happy to receive corrections and additions for future editions to make the book better for everyone interested. Please share any corrections or additions with the author by contacting Hugh Foley through www.oklahomamusicguide.com..

Ali Harter performs in Stillwater, OK, 2013.

Key to Abbreviations

ACM (Academy of Country Music)
ACM @ UCO (Academy of Contemporary Music at University of Central Oklahoma)
A & R (artist and repertoire, typically applied to record company talent scouts)
ASCAP (American Society of Composers, Authors, and Publishers)
BBC (British Broadcasting Corporation)
BMI (Broadcast Music Incorporated)
BPA (Bonneville Power Administration)
CCM (Contemporary Christian Music)
CD (compact disc)
CMA (Country Music Association)
CMT (Country Music Television)
DJ (disc jockey)
DVD (Digital Video Disc)
EP (extended play release, usually 3 to 6 tracks)
GRAMMY (National Academy of Recording Arts and Sciences Award)
HBO (Home Box Office)
LP (long play album, usually considered vinyl)
Mp3 (digital audio file)
MTV (Music Television)
NAMMY (Native American Music Award)
NEO A & M (Northeastern Oklahoma A & M at Miami)
NSU (Northeastern State University at Tahlequah)
NPR (National Public Radio)
OETA (Oklahoma Educational Television)
OMHOF (Oklahoma Music Hall of Fame)
OSU (Oklahoma State University)
OU (University of Oklahoma)
PBS (Public Broadcasting System)
PSA (public service announcement)
RSU (Rogers State University)
TNN (The Nashville Network)
TU (Tulsa University)
UCO (University of Central Oklahoma at Edmond)
VFW (Veterans of Foreign Wars)
VH1 (cable music network)
WPA (Work Progress Administration)

Oklahoma Music Guide II

Alphabetical List of Major Entries

David Abeyta
Admiral Twin
The Agony Scene
Walter Ahhaitty
The All-American Rejects
Tommy Allsup
AM
Buddy Anderson
Keith Anderson
Tuck Andress
Apache Tribe of Oklahoma
Aqueduct
Larry Austin
Gene Autry
Hoyt Axton
Mae Boren Axton
Chet Baker
Mark Baker
Louis Ballard
Johny Barbata
Glenn Barber
Bobby Barnett
Bob Beckham
Molly Bee
Michael Been (The Call)
Carl Belew
Aaron Bell
Trent Bell
Byron Berline
Elvin Bishop
Chuck Blackwell
Ralph Blane
Noel Boggs
Bob Bogle
Jason Boland
Johnny Bond
Glen Bonham
Scott Booker
Earl Bostic
Charles Brackeen
Mike Brewer
Garth Brooks
Junior Brown
Buddy Bruce
Albert Brumley, Sr.
Anita Bryant
Gary Busey

Don Byas
Caddo Nation of Oklahoma
Chuck Caldwell
J.J. Cale
The Call
The Cannons
Jerry Cantrell
Hank Card
Henson Cargill
Larry Carlton
Caroline's Spine
Jeff Carson
Rose and Roy Carter
Chainsaw Kittens
Greyson Chance
Kristen Chenoweth
Cherokee
Don Cherry
Cheyenne-Arapaho Tribes
Chickasaw Nation
Bob Childers
Choctaw Nation
Charlie Christian
Roy Clark
Sanford Clark
Al Clauser
Eddie Cletro
Sarah Coburn
Eddie Cochran
Kellie Coffey
The Collins Kids
Tommy Collins
Color Me Badd
Colourmusic
Graham Colton
Comanche Nation
John Convertino
David Cook
Spade Cooley
Cowboy Copas
Samantha Crain
Tommy Crook
Crooked X
Cross Canadian Ragweed
Alvin Crow
Edgar Cruz
Agnes "Sis" Cunningham

Gail Davies
Jesse Ed Davis
Ester Dean
Debris
Delta Rhythm Boys
John Denver
Yvonne DeVaney
Joe Diffie
Ernestine Dillard
Dinning Sisters
Mark Dinning
Big Al Downing
Tim DuBois
Jack Dunham
Bob Dunn
Ronnie Dunn
John Durrill
Nokie Edwards
Stoney Edwards
Stephen Egerton
Shelby Eicher
Katrina Elam
Scott Ellison
Ty England
Ester Drang
Toni Estes
The Evangelicals
Ernie Fields
Shug Fisher
The Five Americans
The Flaming Lips
Flash Terry
For Love Not Lisa
Dallas Frazier
Rocky Frisco
Lowell Fulson
Steve and Cassie Gaines
The GAP Band
Benny Garcia, Jr.
Lyle Gaston
David Gates
Vince Gill
Les Gilliam
Gary Gilmore
Al Good
Bill Grant
George Grantham

Otto Gray
Wardell Gray
Great Divide
Barrick Griffiths
Jack Guthrie
Woody Guthrie
Merle Haggard
David Halley
Jim Halsey
Hanson
Gus Hardin
Steve Hardin
Roy Harris
Sam Harris
Ali Harter
Wade Hayes
Lee Hazelwood
Michael Hedges
Scott Hendricks
John Herron
Hinder
Sam Hinton
Becky Hobbs
Hadley Hockensmith
Doyle Holly
Mike Hosty / Hosty Duo
Ray Wylie Hubbard
Charlie Huff
Billy Hughes
Iowa Tribe of Oklahoma
Wanda Jackson
Jacob Fred Jazz Odyssey
Jana Jae
Brett James
Dennis Jernigan
William Johns
Cecil Johnson
Herman Johnson
Claude Jones
Norah Jones
Stacy Jones
Scott Joplin
Jimmy Karstein
Kaw Nation
Jeff Keith (Tesla)
Toby Keith
Jim Keltner
Wayne Kemp
Barney Kessel
Merle Kilgore
Kings Of Leon
Kiowa Tribe

Leo Kottke
Gail Kubik
Jimmy LaFave
Miranda Lambert
Don Lamond
Rodney Lay
Ed Lewis
Jimmy and Joe Liggins
Merl Lindsey
Ryan Lindsey
Little Texas
Guy Logsdon
Los Reactors
Clarence Love
Jimmy Lunceford
Zac Maloy
Kim Manning
Jimmy "Jr." Markham
Moon Martin
Frankie and Johnny Marvin
Tony Mathews
Reed Mathis
Barbara McAlister
Leon McAuliffe
Cecil McBee
Laura Lee McBride
Mike McClure
Mel McDaniel
Pake McEntire
Reba McEntire
Susie McEntire
Howard McGhee
Barry McGuire
Russ McKinnon
J.D. McPherson
Jay McShann
Tyson Meade
Chris Merritt
Edgar Meyer
Mikaila
Jody Miller
Roger Miller
Roy Milton
D.C. Minner
Leona Mitchell
Lucky Moeller
Ralph Mooney
Marilyn Moore
Andy and Semie Moseley
Mourning September
Sonny Murray
Muscogee (Creek) Nation

Scott Musick (The Call)
Marla Nauni
"Doc" Tate Nevaquaya
Grady Nichols
Nitro
The Nixons
No Justice
Jimmy Nolen
Norma Jean
N.O.T.A.
Gary P. Nunn
Kenny O'Dell
Kelli O'Hara
Oklahoma City Blue Devils
Oklahoma
Jamie Oldaker
Oliver Mangum
Osage Nation
Other Lives
Otoe-Missouria Tribe
Tommy Overstreet
Bonnie Owens
Buck Owens
Patti Page
Andy Parker
Billy Parker
Jeff Parker
Sandi Patty
Pawnee Nation
Tom Paxton
Jim Pepper
Stephen Petree
Oscar Pettiford
Tom Petty
Cornel Pewewardy
John Phillips
Pillar
Bobby Pinson
Mary Kay Place
Point Of Grace
Johnny Polygon
Ponca Tribe of Oklahoma
Chick Rains
Red Dirt Music
Red Dirt Rangers
Dick Reinhart
Restless Heart
Ricochet
Steve Ripley
Sam Rivers
Tony Romanello
Joe Don Rooney

Hugh W. Foley / xliii

Marshal Royal
Mark Rubin
Jimmy Rushing
Tim Rushlow
Leon Russell
Tom Russell
Neal Schon
Lynn Seaton
Ronnie Sessions
Mike Settle
Blake Shelton
Jean Shepard
John Simmons
Cal Smith
Michael Smotherman
Tim Spencer
Terry Stafford
Kay Starr

James Talley
B.J. Thomas
Hank Thompson
Floyd Tillman
Wayman Tisdale
Cheevers Toppah
The Tractors
The Tulsa Sound
Dwight Twilley
Linda Twine
Carrie Underwood
Andrew Vasquez
Jimmy Wakely
Wayne Walker
Billy Wallace
Jimmy Webb
Kevin Welch
Bryan White

Wichita Tribe
Wiley and Gene
Lee Wiley
Claude "Fiddler" Williams
Willis Brothers
Kelly Willis
Charlie Wilson (see GAP Band)
Joe Lee Wilson
Sheb Wooley
Young Bird

For additional musicians with ties to Oklahoma, see the People's List of Oklahoma Music on page 754 of this guide.

Harold Aldridge of Tahlequah, OK, is one of Oklahoma's best performer's of traditional acoustic blues.

xliv / Oklahoma Music Guide II

A

Abeyta, David
(lead guitarist for Reckless Kelly)

A gritty, blues-based guitarist for Texas roots rockers Reckless Kelly, David Abeyta is from Bartlesville, OK, according to Reckless Kelly's lead singer, Willy Braun, who introduces Abeyta as an "Oklahoma boy" when introducing the full band in between songs on their live CD, *Was Here* (Sugar Hill, 2006). Also nodding to Abeyta's Latin American heritage, Braun calls Abeyta by what must be band nicknames, the "Angry Enchilada" and the "Hispanic Titanic." Abeyta acknowledges those roots graciously and with good humor by leading the band in the Freddie Fender Tex-Mex crowd favorite, "Hey Say may/Guacamole" at some live performances, as evidenced by the live DVD packaged within *Was Here* (Sugar Hill, 2006). Exhibiting Abeyta's abilities on electric and slide guitar, the *Was Here* DVD is the best place outside of a concert to hear the genre versatility and guts of Abeyta's twang rock guitar leads and arpeggio fills, as well get a sense of the group's modern Texas honky-tonk appeal. While Abeyta was not an original member of the group who relocated from Bend, Oregon, to Austin in 1997, Abeyta's appears prominently on 2000's *The Day* (Reckless), and continued to be a frontline presence through their additional albums on Sugar Hill Records, *Under the Table and Above the Sun* (2003), *Wicked Twisted Road* (2005) and *Best of the Sugar Hill Years* (2008). The band signed to stalwart alternative country independent, Yep Roc Records in 2008, and promptly holed up in Willie Nelson's Pedernales Studio in Lake Travis, Texas, to record *Bulletproof*, released in the summer of that year. The album features an Abeyta solo on almost every track, using a variety of tones, textures and effects to further diversify the guitarist's presence on the recordings, such as the concluding title track, on which Abeyta marries a solo and guitar sound that would not seem out of a place on a late 1960s Pink Floyd album with the tough, forward rocking backup of Reckless Kelly's brawny rhythm section. Fans liked *Bulletproof*, urging the CD to #22 on *Billboard*'s Country Album chart. The band released *Good Luck & True Love* in 2011, peaking at #20 on the same chart, indicating a fairly consistent fan base.

www.recklesskelly.com

David Abeyta

Admiral Twin
(Formed 1990, Tulsa, OK)

Self-proclaimed influences ranging from The Cars, Elvis Costello, The Police, Led Zeppelin, and The Beatles, with some classical music and even a bit of honky-tonk thrown in, Admiral Twin is known for up-tempo power pop, the occasional contextually ironic number with dark lyrics and vibrant music, and kooky live shows. In earlier days, the group brought in marching bands and magicians for their shows, and recruited legendary

Tulsa TV kiddie show host Uncle Zeb to play harmonica with them on stage. Named after a landmark Tulsa drive-in theater, Admiral Twin originally formed around guitarist and vocalist John Russell (b. May 12, 1968, Tulsa, OK), bassist and vocalist Mark Carr (b. June 23, 1968, Sapulpa, OK), drummer and vocalist Jarrod Gollihare (b. October 27, 1966, San Jose, CA), and guitarist, keyboardist, and vocalist Brad Becker (b. February 17, 1969, West Palm Beach, FL).

Not every group gets their first national touring opportunity with a band that has a number-one hit, but it happened to Admiral Twin when **Hanson** asked them to open for the Tulsa pop group's 1998 national tour in the wake of the previous year's smash single, "MMMBop." Admiral Twin had only just recorded their first independent CD, *Unlucky*, in their home studio in Tulsa, when Hanson asked the group to hit the road with them in the summer of 1998. The choice was no surprise to Tulsa local music fans due to Admiral Twin's exuberant live shows that had already created a loyal and fervent following. Not only did the Hanson tour take the band from playing in Tulsa clubs to playing in front of 20,000 people across the U.S. and Canada, Admiral Twin also played performed for a myriad of music industry executives and critics who came out to see what all the Hanson buzz was about. This landed the *Unlucky* CD in some influential ears and the group signed a deal with Mojo Records on Halloween of 1998. Subsequently, Admiral Twin enjoyed their first national release on Mojo, *Mock Heroic* (2000), which collected all of the group's individual tastes and collective abilities for songs that run the gamut from the high-energy pop celebrated in their live shows, to the occasional twangy tune with melancholy lyrics. *Mock Heroic* was recorded in the historic Church Studio in Tulsa, now operated by **Steve Ripley** of Tractors fame.

Admiral Twin had one song featured in the Warner Brothers film, *The In Crowd* (2000), and another song featured in the Universal television program, *Blind Date*. The group released a four-song Christmas EP in 2001, and a collection of previously recorded material in 2002, *Odds and Ends: Demos and Rarities 1996-2000*. The album is made up of songs that did not make previous records, sometimes against their own wishes, demos of songs that did make it out, or songs that never made any album at all. In June of 2002, the band began recording their third album of original material, and continued playing shows in the Midwest and Tulsa, with old friend Isaac Hanson sitting in with them at one show in Tulsa where Isaac debuted two new Hanson songs. By August 2002, original guitarist and vocalist Brad Becker decided to take a job opportunity in San Francisco at a computer software company, and left the group. Playing as a trio was not unknown to Carr, Russell, and Gollihare, however, as they had already played around Tulsa as a cover band without Becker called the Unlucky Ones in the late 1990s.

In 2002, The Becker-less Admiral Twin soldiered on as a trio, recording some backup vocals for Steve Ripley's solo album, *Ripley*, and the group began work on their next album for New Pop Revival Records in their own studio. One of the album's songs includes local musicians like the Hanson Brothers and Brian Parton, as well as fans, friends, and the barroom public on backing vocals that were recorded at Barkley's Uptown Dive in Tulsa's Brookside district. The group released *Creatures of Bread and Wine* in May, 2003, and their second Christmas CD later that same year. Since then, the group's "Better Than Nothing At All" was featured on a the Spanish *Discovery Channel*'s program "Rides" in 2005, and they released their fifth CD, *Center of the Universe* (The Pop Collective) in 2007. The CD's title continues the band's tradition of commemorating Tulsa landmarks, in this case referring to the spot in downtown Tulsa where one can stand and experience a unique acoustic phenomenon of sound echoes due to the circular planter walls at the location. Intended or not, the title also is a sly counterpoint to Hanson's first major label album, *Middle of Nowhere*. Songs from *Center of the Universe* maintained the group's signature sound of Beatle-esque pop harmonies, subtle psychedelic musical accents, and multiple studio effects to create a pleasing melodic palate with enough happening in the texture of the music to reward multiple listens with new audio revelations each time. Among other critical accolades, the CD garnered the group its fifth "Best Pop Act" award from the *Tulsa World*'s annual *Spot* Awards. In 2009, Admiral Twin recorded several songs for an upcoming independent film soundtrack, a new version of the theme song to the animated TV series *Sealab2021*, and their song, "Good as Gold" was featured in the PBS TV series, *Roadtrip Nation*. The band performed live through 2011, but appears to be on hiatus as no new live appearances have been scheduled since that year

www.admiraltwin.com

The Agony Scene
(formed Tulsa, 2001, disbanded 2008)

With three albums on nationally recognized labels during their seven-year existence, Agony Scene was Oklahoma's biggest contribution to hardcore/metal, sometimes known as "metalcore", in the first decade of the 21st century. When calling it quits in 2008, the group's constantly evolving lineup consisted of vocalist Mike Williams, guitarists Chris Emmons and Brian Hodges, bassist Chris Rye, and drummer Ryan Folden. The group's first, self-titled album on Solid State Records, generally known as a Christian rock label, gave an initial impression The Agony Scene was a Christian rock band, an idea that both the band and many Christian rock fans refuted, although some of the lyrics on the first album could be read both as secular and sacred commentary. The band's second album, *The Darkest Red* (Roadrunner) featured new members Hodges on bass, and Steve Kaye as guitarist. Produced by Rob Caggiano, known for his work with Cradle of Filth, the album displays the group's ability to play crunching modern metal, often linked to the melodic metal traditions of Sweden, with screaming verses and melodic choruses, all surrounded by a powerful rhythm section, the biggest of big rhythm guitars, and stinging lead guitar accents. Original drummer, Brent Masters, and vocalist Williams relay some interesting aspects of Tulsa's music scene and how it shaped the band's early work on the Roadrunner Records website: "Mike and I have been in bands together since I was thirteen, and growing up where we did, it made our mindset different, our sense of humor, a lot of things," explains Masters. "I don't want to bash anyone from bigger cities with more of a music scene, but basically, we don't have 'peers' where we come from. There is really no heavy music scene. We write music for ourselves as opposed to latching onto a bandwagon," added Williams. In 2007, the band released *Get Damned* through Century Media. The final album from The Agony Scene mines similar territory as the *The Darker Red*, but abandons the use of melodic vocal choruses and produced a straight-ahead metal core album that still receive raves on the bands myspace site. Clearly linked to both the hardcore and metal traditions, occasionally verging on thrash metal, The Agony scene always featured aggressive, double-kick pedal drum work, power chorded guitar parts, swirling guitar leads and fills, and screaming, back-of-the-throat vocals from Williams that rake over lyrics filled with the darker tropes of death metal on songs such as "Scars of Your Disease", "My Dark Desire", "Prey", "Dances with Devils", "Forever Abandoned", and "Will to Bleed". As of 2008, Williams reportedly was working on solo material that he said "couldn't be further away from hardcore and metal."

The Agony Scene

www.myspace.com/agonyscene

Ahhaitty, Walter
(b. February 2, 1968 – Anaheim, CA)

A member of the widely-traveled Kiowa singing group, Bad Medicine, Walter Ahhaitty is also well-known in powwow circles as a Southern Plains head singer, a style that features deeper voice tones than the higher-pitched northern singing of the powwow world. Of Kiowa, Comanche, and Cherokee heritage, Ahhaitty's 2006 album, *Oklahoma Style*, released on The Sound of Indian America Records, received a 2007 GRAMMY nomination for Best Native American album, and a nomination for Best Historical Album at the 10th annual Native American Music Awards in 2008. Recorded at the 35th Annual Southern California Indian Center Powwow, the CD is compiled of gourd dance songs common to the Kiowa, a grand entry song that is performed at powwows to bring all dancers into the arena , as well the war dance portion of an intertribal gathering, and an intertribal song that is used for everyone to dance, usually including visitors, at most North American powwows. As is the case with many great singers in the powwow world,

Walter Ahhaitty

Ahhaitty is also a competition powwow dancer as depicted above in his Oklahoma-style Fancy Dance regalia. As of 2010, Ahhaitty worked as the executive director for the Kiowa Tribe of Oklahoma.

www.soundofamerica.com

All-American Rejects
(Formed 1999 in Stillwater, OK)

Formed in 2001 by Stillwater natives Nick Wheeler (b. March 20, 1982) on guitars, and vocalist/bassist Tyson Ritter (b. April 24, 1984), the All-American Rejects have parlayed their catchy, power pop sound filled with tons of teen and twenty-something angst into major, international popular music success. With nods to obvious influences such as The Beach Boys and the Cure, the All-American Rejects play catchy power punk in the vein of the bands such as Blink 182, The Ramones, and MXPX. However, the band is now a touchstone in itself with a sound unique to them courtesy of their harmony vocals, tom tom heavy rhythm section, and pleading lyrics. The group's youthful angst subject matter provides a logical palate for this brand of very commercial music that is connecting with millions of teenagers, and now twenty-somethings, experiencing the same life issues as the Rejects.

Nick started playing guitar at age seven, played percussion in the Stillwater school band program, and made extra money by teaching guitar lessons at Daddy-O's music store in Stillwater. Tyson played violin four years in the school orchestra, which led him to playing the bass with Nick in their first group whose name shall remain out of print here. Nick tried a semester at Oklahoma State University, which did not work out, and the two formed the All-American Rejects in 1999. After playing a local Stillwater music festival, they began playing multi-band shows such as the Garden O' Punk in Stillwater, and Playhouse Punk Party in Tulsa, as well as gigs at bars in Stillwater, Tulsa, and Norman, and a Rescue Dog Benefit Show on the OSU campus.

In the spring of 2001, the duo recorded and released an independent CD called *Same Girl, New Songs* which they sold as "five songs for five bucks." This CD and their growing fan base induced Toledo, Ohio-based Doghouse Records to offer them a contract, through which the Rejects recorded their first "proper" album in New York at Mission Sound and Headgear Studio in December, 2001. Produced by Tim O'Heir, who has also worked with Superdrag and Sebadoh, the self-titled release was delayed throughout 2002 by tremendous interest from major labels offering various types of distribution and recording deals for the young band. While the duo recorded all instruments and vocals on the album, they enlisted fellow Oklahomans Mike Kennerty (guitar) and Chris Gaylor (drums) for the touring version of the Rejects, both of whom became permanent members of the band on follow-up albums and an active touring schedule. Both Ken-

Rejects (l to r) Nick Wheeler, Mike Kennerty, Tyson Ritter, Chris Gaylor

nerty and Gaylor had been playing with the Edmond-based Euclid Crash, a group the Rejects met while playing local gigs in Stillwater and Oklahoma City.

In January of 2003, the single, "Swing, Swing" received critical acclaim through *Rolling Stone*'s "Hot List," was picked by the magazine's editors as a favorite single, and landed in the Top 10 of *Billboard*'s Modern Rock chart, an indicator of national commercial airplay. Coinciding with the airplay, the album was a top independent national seller in early 2003, eventually raising it to #25 on Billboard's Top 200 Albums in the country as of March, 2003, and ultimately selling one million copies, enough to certify it as a platinum album. The group's popularity led to performances on *Late Late with Craig Kilborn* and *The Tonight Show with Jay Leno*. Furthering their connection to teen pop culture, "Swing, Swing" was used as the theme song for EA Sports' new baseball simulation game, *MVP Baseball 2003*. Firmly in the groundswell of commercial success and rabid fan interest, through August, 2003 the group had been featured on the cover of *Alternative Press*, and enjoyed press coverage from such teen magazines as *Seventeen*, *YM* (where Tyson was chosen as one of the 20 hottest guys), *Teen People, Tiger Beat*, and *Bop*, as well as several feature articles in daily newspapers from New York to Seattle. Also as a result of the album's success, the group launched their first tour as a headliner in the spring of 2003, titled the *Too Bad for Hell Tour*. A subsequent DVD, *Live from Oklahoma... The Too Bad for Hell DVD!* sold more than 500,000 copies, enough to certify the release as a gold disc.

The group's second album, *Move Along* (Interscope, 2005), ballooned into increasing international pop notoriety for the Rejects. Producing three hit singles, "It Ends Tonight", "Dirty Little Secret" and "Move Along", all of which enjoyed Top 20 success on *Billboard*'s various popular music charts. "Dirty Little Secret" and "Move Along" both sold more than two million digital downloads each, garnering both singles double platinum status, a lofty popular music milestone also achieved by the album. The video for "Move Along" also picked up an MTV Video Music Award for best group video. The album's musical ethos is a tight pop sound with catchy melodies, the Rejects' harmony-laden choruses, and lyrics largely focused on the temporariness and tempestuousness of youthful relationships, long a staple of rock music made by and for young people. After extensive touring to support *Move Along*, to include trips to Japan, Ireland, Great Britain, the band took a break in 2006 to begin writing their next album, *When the World Comes Down* (Interscope, 2008).

While the Rejects toyed with the American Top 40 with their *Move Along* album, *When the World Comes Down* finally landed the group at #1 on the *Billboard* Top 40 radio chart with "Gives You Hell," as well as enjoying Top 5 status in the UK and Australia. While "Gives You Hell" peaked at #4 on the *Billboard* Hot 100, the song enjoyed at least nine months in the Top 50, as of August, 2009. Along with the album's "Real World" being included on the soundtrack for *Transformers: Revenge of the Fallen*, additional singles were released at press time, to include "The Wind Blows" in the US, and "I Wanna" in the UK and Australia. Again featuring more of their trademark sound, *When the World Comes Down* escalates the band's overall sound with orchestrated strings, choirs, and big, sing-along choruses that continue making the Rejects an audience participation experience at concerts. The group had a touring schedule that took them across the US, to Asia, and Europe through the end of 2009. The Rejects continued a heavy performance schedule throughf 2013, releasing their fourth studio album, *Kids on the Street* (Interscope) in 2012. The album notched attention on Australian, Canadian, Irish, Japanese, UK, and US album charts, with its most significant notice being in the US where it reached #18 on the *Billboard* Top 200 album charts..

www.theall-americanrejects.com

Allsup, Tommy
(b. November 24, 1931)

Born in Owasso, but raised in Claremore, only 16 miles from Tulsa, Tommy Allsup is best known as one of the original Buddy Holly's Crickets, a veteran producer of such groups as **Bob Wills** and the Texas Playboys, Asleep at the Wheel, **Hank Thompson**, and Willie Nelson, Grammy Award winner, and instrumentalist on more than 6,500 recordings. He is also recognized as a guitarist, arranger, and percussionist. As a teenager, he would hitchhike from Claremore to Tulsa, where he listened to the noon broadcasts of Bob Wills and the Texas Playboys over radio station KVOO. He began his musical career in Claremore, where he performed with the Oklahoma Swingbillies in 1949, the same year he graduated from Claremore High School. A year later, he played with Art Davis in Miami, Oklahoma, and then moved to Wichita, Kansas, where he performed at the Cowboy Inn with singer and fiddle player Jimmy Hall.

Tommy returned to Tulsa in the early 1950s, and joined **Johnnie Lee Wills**' band, which performed at Cain's Ballroom and over KVOO. Later in the 1950s, he formed his own band, The Southernaires, which played at the Southern Club in Lawton, Oklahoma. On a recording trip to Norman Petty's studio in Clovis, New Mexico, he met Buddy Holly, who asked him to play lead guitar with The Crickets. From 1958 until the ill-fated plane crash in January of 1959 that killed Holly, the Big Bopper, and Ritchie Valens, Tommy was a member of Holly's band. Tommy flipped a coin with Valens for a seat on the Beechcraft Bonanza that resulted in "the day that rock and roll died," while Tommy rode the bus. Tommy's guitar work is heard on the Holly recordings of "Wishing," "It's So Easy," "Love's Made a Fool of You," "Lonesome Tears," and "Come Back Baby."

After Holly's death in 1959, Allsup moved to California where he became the artist and repertoire director for Liberty Records' country music division. In this capacity, he produced Bob Wills and the Texas Playboys from 1960, when he coordinated Wills' *Bob Wills Sings and Plays* album, until 1973, when the *For the Last Time* album was recorded in Dallas on December 2-3. As organizer of the session, Tommy assembled several of the original Texas Playboys, including Leon McAuliffe, Eldon Shamblin, Smokey Dacus, and Al Stricklin. While at Liberty, Tommy produced such well-known artists as Tex Williams, Willie Nelson, and Billy Mize. In 1962 Tommy recorded his first album, *Twistin' the Country Classics*, for Liberty, which was followed in 1968 with *The Buddy Holly Songbook* recorded in the legendary Norman Petty Clovis, New Mexico, studios and released on the Reprise label.

In 1968 Allsup headed for Nashville to assume management of Metromedia Records. Four years later, he met Ray Benson, manager of Asleep at the Wheel, and produced the group's first album for the United Artists label, and continued that relationship when the band recorded four more albums for Capitol Records.

Tommy spent more than thirty years as one of Nashville's top session men, playing guitar, bass guitar, and percussion, and logging more than 10,000 sessions with such notables as Johnny Cash, The Everly Brothers, Janie Fricke, Billy "Crash" Craddock, John Anderson, Jerry Lee Lewis, **Reba McEntire**, Melba Montgomery, Johnny Paycheck,

Marty Robbins, Kenny Rogers, and Ernest Tubb.

Following Wills' death in 1973, McAuliffe chose several of the ex-Playboys to tour under the name Bob Wills' Original Texas Playboys, which was sanctioned by the Wills family. After the death of Al Stricklin, the McAuliffe-led group dissolved in about 1990, but Tommy and Leon Rausch, former vocalist with Wills, assumed the Playboys mantle, and have continued to perform as the Original Texas Playboys, again blessed by the Wills family. Former Playboys who have off and on played with the reconstituted group include Tommy Perkins (drums), Curly Lewis (fiddle), Jimmy Young (fiddle), Curly Hollingsworth (piano), and Bobby Boatright (fiddle). The group performed a tribute to the Wills Family at the 2001 induction of the **Wills** brothers (Bob, Johnnie Lee, Luke, and Billy Jack) into the Oklahoma Music Hall of Fame. Along with Leon Rausch, Allsup has recorded several tribute albums to the late Bob Wills, including *A 50 Song Tribute to the Music of Bob Wills* (1997) on the Sims label, and *Bob Wills Texas Playboys Band Featuring Leon Rausch and Tommy Allsup*, a live recording released by Southland Records in 2000. Tommy has two Southland studio albums, *True Love Ways* and *Tommy Allsup's Gospel Guitar*. As one of the performers on Asleep at the Wheel's tribute to Bob Wills with "Bob's Breakdown," Allsup was part of a GRAMMY Award for Best Country Instrumental of 1999, featuring Allsup, Floyd Domino, Larry Franklin, Vince Gill & Steve Wariner. Allsup was also inducted into the Oklahoma Music Hall of Fame in 2005. In 2011, Allsup teamed with noted Oklahoma music historian, Dr. Guy Logsdon, to produce a chonicle of Allsup's life, *The Flip of a Coin*.

Tommy Allsup

AM

According to the artist's official bio, "Tulsa-born and New Orleans-raised, indie artist AM brings a heady brew of twanging Americana, twinkling Anglified folk-rock-pop, caressing Philly soul and funky R&B whatchacallit — and, best of all, joyously unheard points in-between." Sure enough, the music is a breezy '60s soul-pop with synthesizers, horns, and understated vocals. AM has lived in the New Orleans area since he was thirteen when his family relocated to Mandevill, LA, so his father could pursue a job opportunity. AM's first CD, *Troubled Times*, enjoyed wide distribution via its songs being picked up by a number of televisions shows (HBO's *Big Love* and MTV's *The Hills*, as well as **Brothers And Sisters, Men In Trees, Kyle XY, Trust Me**), and independent films shown at festivals such as the Sundance Film Festival. All ten songs from *Troubled Times* have been featured in films and television shows with over at least 70 commercial placements of AM's music as of 2013.

Recorded in L.A. where AM is based, *Future Sons and Daughters* (Filter/Fontana/

Universal, 2009) quickly piled up critical accolades in the music press, and AM's song "Mainstay" was featured in the Ashton Kutcher vehicle, *Spread* (2009). AM's primary musical experiences are in New Orleans. According to the artist's website: "AM started playing live in bars at age 15 and played throughout high School. While attending college at Loyola University New Orleans, he started writing songs, inspired equally by his own reflective temperament, by the literature and texts he studied as he earned his philosophy degree, and by the music he absorbed simply by living in New Orleans." Even though he may have matured in New Orleans, a casual and relaxed, even breezy, sound familiar to Oklahomans is in his music, and one can only offer conjecture about the kind of childhood in Oklahoma that's a possible source of a laid back, quirky, and easy-going adult's artistic product. AM's music is meditative and unrushed, a thoroughly modern folk-pop, driven by memorable melodies and subtle accents that recall 1960s pop, blue-eyed soul, and the big reverb sound of some new wave music of the early 1980s such as Echo and the Bunnymen, Chameleons UK, or even, occasionally, Big Country. With a steady touring schedule, multiple placements of his music on television programs, and regular positive critical notice, AM is poised to further steady worldwide recognition and commercial success.

AM

www.amsounds.com

Anderson, Bernard Hartwell "Step-Buddy"
(b. October 14, 1919 – d. May 10, 1997)

A native of Oklahoma City, Anderson was born into a musical family. His older brother played alto sax and was a jazz record fan. Anderson was introduced to various brass instruments, especially the bugle, while a member of the Boy Scouts. He began taking violin lessons at the age of seven. Zelia N. Page Breaux, noted Oklahoma City music teacher, was an inspiration for Anderson. Anderson was a member of the Douglass High School marching and jazz bands under the leadership of Ms. Breaux. One of Anderson's first professional opportunities was with the Ted Armstrong band in Clinton, Oklahoma, in 1934. While a student at Xavier University in New Orleans in the late 1930s, he was a member of the university jazz band.

Bernard Anderson on trumpet (far right) in Jay McShann's orchestra, 1941.

In 1939, Anderson returned to Oklahoma City and joined the Leslie Sheffield band that included **Charlie Christian** and Hank Bridges. The next year, he left Oklahoma for the Kansas City jazz scene where he became trumpeter for the **Jay McShann** band. McShann's band had become nationally known by 1942 because it included several widely known instrumentalists, such as Charlie Parker on alto saxophone. One can hear Anderson's bright riffing and counterpoint to Charlie Parker's sax work on the Jay McShann Orchestra's collection of 1941 to 1943 recordings, *Blues from Kanas City* (Decca, 1992). Anderson also shines on one of McShann's signature tunes, "Hootie Blues", as Anderson complements the blues vocals by Walter Brown. Anderson remained with McShann until the band was decimated by the World War II draft. He then moved from one band to another before joining the Billy Eckstine Orchestra in 1944. Shortly thereafter, Anderson contacted tuberculosis and returned to Oklahoma City for medical assistance and to be among family. After recovery from the disease, he was medically advised to abandon the trumpet and switched to piano for a short time.

By 1992, Buddy, then in his seventies, was frequently seen playing his trumpet on street corners in Westport, the historic district in Kansas City, where young people visited to hear him. The handouts he received helped pay his rent. A 1992 article in the *Kansas City Star* by Art Brisbane retold Buddy's jazz legacy, which spawned an organization, The Musicians Emergency Assistance Fund, overseen by the Kansas City Jazz Ambassadors. The first fundraiser, held in 1992 at Obsessions, a club in Westport, honored Buddy. Anderson remained active by entertaining young crowds in Westport, writing plays and poetry, and jamming at the Mutual Musicians Foundation in downtown Kansas City, where he died in 1997.

Buddy "Step-Buddy" Anderson influenced numerous jazz trumpeters, including Dizzy Gillispie and Fats Navarro. Like many Oklahoma-born jazz artists, Buddy Anderson is another of the obscure but important figures in the evolution of modern jazz styles.

Anderson, Keith
(b. January 12, 1968)

Best known as co-composer of "Beer Run," the 2002 duet featuring George Jones and **Garth Brooks**, Keith Anderson was born in Miami, Oklahoma, a town of about 13,000 residents in extreme northeastern Oklahoma. He began writing songs in junior high, primarily inspired by his brother who taught Keith to play guitar, and who constantly played Willie Nelson's *Greatest Hits* for the younger Anderson. His early musical influences represented a cross-section of the music industry, including **Merle Haggard**, Willie Nelson, Kenny Rogers, The Eagles, **Restless Heart**, John Cougar Mellencamp, and Southern rock such as Lynyrd Skynyrd, whose band members **Steve and Cassie Gaines** were raised in his hometown of Miami. During his high school days, Steve competed in football, baseball, and bodybuilding. He was selected for the all-state team in football, finished second in the Mr. Oklahoma bodybuilding contest, and was drafted by the Kansas City Royals baseball organization. A shoulder injury, however, halted his pursuit of a major league baseball career.

Majoring in construction engineering while playing baseball at Oklahoma State University, Keith graduated in 1990 and landed a job with an engineering company in Dallas, but could not divorce himself from music. After about a year and a half with the engineering company, he left to attend physical therapy school at the University of Texas

Southwestern Medical School, and began performing at the Grapevine Opry where Lee Ann Rimes and Kix Brooks had also had early career experiences. His dedication to music interfered with his studies, however, and he decided to focus on writing and singing country music.

After early co-writing experiences with Nashville veterans such as George Ducas, Jeffrey Steele, Bob Dipiero, Craig Wiseman, Kim Williams, and Victoria Shaw, Keith released his eponymous album in 1998, and since 1999 has been based in Nashville, where he performs at such local venues as the Bluebird Café, Wild Horse Saloon, and The Broken Spoke. Anderson's first hit, "Beer Run," co-written with Kim Williams, came about when Williams' daughter returned from college and reminded the two songwriters of the old college party saying "B-Double-E-Are-You-In." Williams' connection with Brooks got the song to the mega-star who cut it as a duet with George Jones. "Beer Run (B-double E-double Are You In?)" was nominated as Vocal Event of the Year for a 2002 CMA award, and led to Anderson signing his first songwriting contract with EMI Music Publishing in Nashville. Anderson won the Jim Beam competition for "Best Unsigned Talent in Country Music" in November of 2002.

After signing with RCA label groups ARISTA imprint in 2004, Anderson's debut, *Three Chord Country and American Rock & Roll* (ARISTA), garnered two Top 10 hits (accompanied by two No. 1 music videos), the slinky country rocker, "Pickin' Wildflowers," and the love-lost ballad, "Every Time I Hear Your Name," along with singles "XXL" and "Podunk," success that prompted music trades *Billboard* and *Radio & Records* to name him country music's No. 1 new male artist of 2005. Not necessarily connected to music, but certainly to his mass appeal, Anderson was named one of *People* Magazine's "50 Hottest Bachelors," *Men's Fitness* magazine's "Ultimate Country Star," and has shown up in *Country Weekly*'s fan-voted "Hottest Bachelor" feature. Also in 2005, the Oklahoma Music Hall of Fame and Museum gave Keith their annual "Rising Star" award for the most promising musical artist from Oklahoma in a given year.

Keith Anderson

Anderson's 2008 album, the stadium-country-sounding *C'mon*, ascended to #3 on *Billboard's* country album charts, with one Top 10 hit, "I Still Miss You," that trotted out the popular country trope of loneliness and having trouble forgetting the love that got away. Also from *C'mon*, "Somebody Needs a Hug" and "She Could Have Been Mine" were moderately successful singles. Anderson also enjoys positive returns when other artists record songs he wrote or worked on, such as Big and Rich who took Anderson's co-written "Lost in the Moment" to #1 on *Billboard's* country songs chart in 2005, and Gretchen Wilson, who included another Keith Anderson co-write, "The Bed", on her number one country album, *Here for the Party* (Epic). In the fall of 2009, Anderson per-

formed on Great American Country television, the Grand Ole Opry, and has continued touring the US thorugh 2013.
www.keithanderson.com

Andress, Tuck

(b. October 28, 1952)

A fluid and expressive guitarist who blends a variety of musical genres together, Tuck Andress was born in Tulsa and gained his first musical experiences, as well as primary professional opportunities there. Growing up, Andress listened to his parents' favorite recordings of big band jazz. His father played piano and had directed a jazz band in college, while his older sister studied classical piano. Both his father and sister often played in the home during Tuck's early years, and he says it provided "tremendous ear training that would serve me for a lifetime," according to his website. After joining forces with Patti Cathcart in 1978, the duo of Tuck and Patti have been thrilling audiences worldwide with their unique approach to jazz, pop, rhythm and blues, gospel, folk, rock and Brazilian genres.

At age seven Tuck learned piano chords from his sister, and he later took formal lessons until age fourteen. In the meantime, his sister was listening to the popular music of the time, and he soon became interested in the Beatles and Rolling Stones. As a teenager, he and two neighborhood boys formed a "garage" band with Tuck on the piano, a boy down the street on drums, and his next-door neighbor playing electric guitar. During this time Tuck decided to learn the guitar, using a Mel Bay instruction book. The first electric guitar he owned was a Ventures Mosrite with a Vox Pacemaker amp, and his guitar idol was Chuck Berry, and his first guitar instructor was the highly regarded Tulsa guitarist, **Tommy Crook**.

According to Carol Wright in a press release on the duo's website, Tuck "spent days his room, "ruthlessly and systematically" learning everything he could about guitar playing, including working his way through all 400 of the orchestral chords, complex jazz chords in the appendix of the Mel Bay chord book. Tuck progressed through "a great deal of practice and experimentation," he says. The guitarist remembers, "From an early point the guitar and I were inseparable. I would conduct my life with a guitar strapped on and my fingers active." Tuck, too, was influenced by Jimi Hendrix, but the rocker's sonic textures were so explosive, that Hendrix actually drove Tuck deeper into jazz. It was two years before he felt confident enough to figure out Hendrix's songs and style. While in high school, Tuck began to listen to jazz guitarists, such as Wes Montgomery and George Benson, although he continued playing in rock bands. His other major guitar influences were B.B. King, Albert King, and Eric Clapton, as well as several Tulsa blues style guitarists such as Steve Hickerson, Jim Byfield, and Tommy Tripplehorn.

After high school graduation, Tuck entered Stanford University in 1970. After the first quarter at Stanford, he moved to Los Angeles, where he rejoined some of the members of his high school band. He auditioned for studio gigs and eventually received an offer as a staff guitarist on the *Sonny and Cher* television program, but turned down the job to Stanford to study classical music theory.

For the next four years, Andress alternated between Stanford and Tulsa. At Stanford, he played in rock and jazz bands as well as the Stanford University Big Band. Whenever he returned to Tulsa, he played with the **GAP Band**, a period Tuck refers to as his "graduate degree in soul music." Meanwhile he doggedly continued studying recordings of guitarists of every style, developing a knack for playing the guitar as several instruments at once. "I learned how to vary the volume and tone of each part independently of the others," Tuck explains, "not knowing that this would become an essential ingredient of the fingerstyle guitar I would take up when Patti and I got together." Also while at Stanford, he teamed with Mike Stillman, a jazz saxophonist, and the duo began playing at the Stanford Coffee House, and took weekly classical guitar lessons for two years.

After leaving Stanford in 1974, Tuck played in countless soul, pop, and rock bands in the Bay Area, while practicing from eight to fourteen hours a day. He immersed himself by listening to jazz legends such as Kenny Burrell, Jimmy Smith, Miles Davis, John Coltrane, and Charlie Parker. In 1978 Tuck met Patti Cathcart in San Francisco, where she auditioned for vocalist in a band of which he was a member. The two soon left the band, began to perform as a duo in 1981, and were married that year Honing their act on the West Coast, the two declined recording contracts until they perfected their sound.

Tuck & Patti

In 1987, Tuck & Patti signed with Windham Hill Jazz, and released their debut album in 1988, *Tears of Joy*, a ten-track jazz-oriented collection, including three songs co-written by them, "Tears of Joy," "Everything's Gonna Be All Right," and "Love Is the Key." *Love Warriors*, featuring songs by Lennon-McCartney and a Jimi Hendrix medley, followed in 1989. Tuck did a solo album of jazz standards for Windham Hill in 1990 entitled *Reckless Precision*, and the duo issued *Dream*, a mix of tracks featuring Stevie Wonder, J.B. Lenoir, and Horace Silver songs, in 1991.

Tuck & Patti switched to the Epic label in 1995, and recorded *Learning How to Fly*, featuring Jimi Hendrix's "Up From the Skies," as well as several of Patti's original songs. They returned to Windham Hill in 1998 with *Paradise Found*, a collection of songs ranging from Lerner and Loewe to Lennon and McCartney. As a result of that album, the duo received the prestigious Dutch Edison Award for best international jazz album of 1999 presented to them at the North Sea Jazz Festival. Just two years later, Tuck and Patti released *Taking the Long Way Home*, with all ten tracks written by Patti. Their 2001 album, *As Time Goes By*, is a mixture of Gershwin, Lerner, Rodgers & Hart, and Lennon-McCartney songs. In 2002, the duo self-released *Chocolate Moment* (T&P Records), a laid-back and soulful collection of the deft, tasteful guitar work and elegant vocals for which Tuck and Patti have become known around the world. In 2002 and 2003 Tuck & Patti continued touring the globe extensively before releasing their tenth album, *A Gift of Love* (T&P Records/33rd Street Records), in 2004. The album, originally a special market project of pop music's greatest love songs for Asia, was met with such an enthusiastic response from European and American fans, the duo released it worldwide.

With their own studio to produce their music and a record label, T&P Records, to license and market their work, the duo continues to tour the world, and look forward to, at long last, taking occasional time off from touring to teach at their Bay Area home, as well as doing workshops while on tour. A concert DVD, *Tuck and Patti Live in Holland*, including a behind-the-scenes documentary, *As We Travel Round this Circle*, was released in 2005. Their album, *I Remember You* (Universal), enjoyed worldwide success in 2007 and 2008, following their earlier formula of covering classic love songs from the great American songbook tradition, inspired by Ella Fitzgerald and Joe Pass. "They are gorgeous tunes, with grand lyrics," shares Patti. "And they sing unabashedly, unapologetically, about love." The duo's website is an incredibly insightful place to begin learning their music, as well extremely interesting information about Tuck's guitars, guitar style, teaching philosophy, and studio techniques, in addition to several articles about his rightful place as one of contemporary music's most diverse and skilled guitarists. Tuck and Patti are continuously booked around the world for performances, with Japan, Germany, Spain, Italy, and California set for shows in 2013.

www.tuckandpatti.com

Apache Tribe of Oklahoma

(In the region of modern Oklahoma as far as human memory exists)

Alternately known in the history books as the Plains-Apache, Prarie-Apache, Eastern Apache, or because of their alliance with the **Kiowa** people, Kiowa-Apache, the contemporary Apache Tribe of Oklahoma is generally considered one of the original tribes of Oklahoma, along with Caddo and Wichita, and other early known residents, the Pawnee, Osage, and Quapaw, at a minimum. According to Alonzo Chalepah in a 1997 interview when he was the cultural preservation officer for the tribe, the people call themselves, Na-I-Sha, related to the concept of "ones who carry things around," or "ones who take things." Chalepah also indicated the tribe has more ancient names,

Raymond "Ace" Chalepah

such as the Cedar People, indicating their homes in the cedar trees, or Whetstone People, derived from their status as knife sharpeners, the indication as such in Plains sign language with the symbolic sharpening of a knife by drawing one hand over the flat palm of another. The group is linked to the other Apachean speaking peoples of New Mexico and Arizona linguistically; however, the Apache Tribe of Oklahoma has known Plains life-ways for more than the last 500 years, which is when they met Coronado in 1541. At that time, the Spanish explorer noted the Apache as buffalo hunters on the high plains of what are now the Oklahoma and Texas panhandles bordering New Mexico. At some point in the mists of history, the tribe became linked with the Kiowa as an ally, perhaps, once the Kiowa received the horse and began migrating down from the northern Plains following the buffalo herds where they met the Apache. In any case, the Apaches traveled and camped with the Kiowa for generations, and were part of Kiowa ceremonies, exemplified by Apaches noted in the Kiowa sun dance circle prior to that ceremony being halted by the U.S. Government after April 10, 1883, when the Secretary of the Interior gave approval to rules governing what the Indian Commissioner called a "court of Indian offenses." The rules for courts of Indian offenses that the Commissioner's office provided to the Secretary on December 2, 1882, were specifically intended to repress religious practices—the Commissioner termed them "heathenish rites"— and by extinguishing the ceremonies, the government could "destroy the tribal relations as fast as possible." After the ceremonies were outlawed, Chalepah remembered that many Apache songs were kept alive secretly in remote parts of their late 19th century reservation, and then 20th century allotments, in what is now southwestern Oklahoma, until the songs could be re-introduced into contemporary life without fear of governmental retribution. This moment of cultural re-introduction occurred for a variety of tribes in the 1950s, such as the resurgence of the Kiowa Gourd Clan, as Native people witnessed the Civil Rights movement of that era. By extension Native Americans believed their own civil rights, such as the freedom to gather ceremonially as a people, and perform songs and dances representing tribal identity, had been subsumed for too long. While the point may seem extreme to make to some, the conquering and "civilizing" Americans knew that music, dance, and ceremony were, and are, at the core of American Indian identity. An effort to erase tribal music by the Federal government is not only a powerful example of imperialist cultural oppression at its most obvious, the process also exhibits the power of music to symbolize one's own self-concepts about life and belonging to a larger whole, in this case, a tribe.

Contemporarily based in Anadarko with active commercial concerns, to include a convenience store, screen printing business, and gaming concerns, The Apache Tribe of Oklahoma also has many contemporary musical traditions. Specifically, many songs go along with the Apache Blackfeet Society's annual ceremonies, a legacy of the tribe's warrior society, and which are a primary identity marker for the tribe, confirming and teaching the social structure, history, and modern concerns of the tribe. The tribe's musical catalog also includes Native American Church songs (sometimes called peyote songs to distinguish them from Anglicized hymns), and specific Christian hymns in the Apache language that borrow non-Indian melodies form missionaries or church planters, but are sung in the Apache language. Additionally, the tribe's members participate in powwows and hand games. A 1969 recording released on the Asch Mankind Series label, *Music of the Plains Apache* (AHM 4252), features various "Plains Apache" singers, to include Irene Chalepah Poolaw, Raymond "Ace" Chalepah, and John Boone-Emhoolah, among others. The Asch album preserves children's songs such as the "Wolf Song," "Turtle Song," "Turkey Song" and "Puppy Song," and a lullaby that translates out to "Go To Sleep Baby Boy". With the evolution of the Native American Church as part of Apache religious traditions, the album also records four peyote songs: "There Is Good Medicine," "We Are In The Peyote Tipi," "It Is On The Curved Mound," and "It Sure Is A Good Morning." Also included on the collection are two dance songs, "Snake Dance Song" and "Buffalo Dance" song, as well as hand game songs and a hand game performance, derived from the ancient guessing and gambling games played traditionally by many Plains tribes during the winter months. Except for the hand game performance, all the previously mentioned tracks are available via mp3 download from online sources such as amazon.com. **Andrew Vasquez**, an Apache Tribe of Oklahoma member, is recognized and recorded Plains flutist with several award-winning CDs on the Makoché label. Also, Darin Cisco recorded one album of Native American Church songs for the Indian Sounds label (Vol. 1 IS-8071). The tribal holds their annual Blackfeet Warrior Society Ceremonies each summer in June, around Father's Day, and politely requests non-tribal videographers and photographers to refrain from "taking" pictures, but welcomes the public to attend the events in a respectful manner.

Recommended Listening
Music of the Plains Apache Recorded and Edited By John Beatty. Asch Mankind Series, 1969 (AHM 4252).

Recommended Reading
For further understanding of the governmental oppression of American Indian music from the reservation era through the Federal Indian Reorganization Act of 1934, see John W. Troutman, *Indian Blues: American Indians and the Politics of Music, 1879-1934*. Norman: University of Oklahoma Press (2009).

Aqueduct
(formed 2003, Tulsa, OK)

Organized and fronted by former Tulsan, David Terry, Aqueduct is a progressive pop outfit heavy on the quirkiness for which a number of Oklahoma progressive groups are known. Merging samples with atypical rock textures and effects-laden vocals for a thoroughly modern sound, as evidenced by Aqueduct's music being tapped for a Jaguar car advertising campaign, the music falls somewhere between Beck and Modest Mouse, the latter being the inspiration for Terry's relocation to Seattle in 2003 with his independent CD, *Power Ballads*, in tow. Since then, Aqueduct has released three albums, *Pistols at Dawn* (Barsuk, 2004), *I Sold Gold* (Barsuk, 2005), and *Or Give Me Death* (Barsuk, 2007), the last of which provided the band with an opportunity to play 53 shows in 62 days, a Herculean musical effort by any standards. Often included in the same breath and college radio charts as contemporaries Of Montreal, Apples in Stereo, and the Starlight Mints, Aqueduct's music is like a sonic flea market. The tunes are filled with bits and pieces of sound effects and studio generated noises, varying tempos, acoustic and electric guitars, horns, and synthesizer keyboard lines, all underpinning Terry's pleading vocals on wry life takes such as "Lying in the Bed I've Made", "As You Wish", and "You'll Get Yours" from *Or Give Me Death*. The band toured into mid-2010, after which Terry took a break from the road to begin working on the next Aqueduct album, which had yet to surface in early 2013.

Aqueduct

www.aqueductisgoodmusic.com

Austin, Larry
(b. September 12, 1930)

Co-founder and editor of *Source*, an *avant-garde* music journal, and well known for his use of electronic, theater, and improvisation in his many compositions, such as *Improvisations for Orchestra and Jazz Soloists* performed and recorded by the New York Philharmonic in 1961 under the direction of Leonard Bernstein, composer and music educator Larry Don Austin was born in Duncan, Oklahoma, a community of roughly 22,000 residents in the south central section of the state. He moved to Texas with his parents when he was five-years-old, graduated from Vernon, Texas High School and received his bachelor's degree in music education and his master's in music theory from the University of North Texas (1947 to 1952). He completed further graduate work in composition and musicology at Mills College, University of California-Berkeley, Stanford University, and the Massachusetts Institute of Technology. His academic appointments have included professorships at the University of California-Davis, University of South Florida, and the University of North Texas in Denton. His many professional activities include president of the International Computer Music Association, founder of the Consortium to Distribute Computer Music, and member of the Academy of the International Institute of Electroacoustic Music, Bourges, France.

According to EMF Media, since 1964 Austin has composed more than seventy works using electro-acoustic and computer music media. His symphonic works include performances by the Boston, Baltimore, Buffalo, Oakland, and National Symphony Orchestras. His credits include *The Maze* (1967), *Agape* (1970), *Walter* (1971), *Plastic Surgery* (1970), *Phantasmagoria* (1982), *Sinfonia Concertanta: A Mozartean Episode* (1986), *Concertante Cybernetica* (1987). Several of his compositions, such as *Life Pulse Prelude* (1974-84), for 20-member percussion orchestra, are based on Charles Ives's compositional sketches for Ives's unfinished *Universe Symphony*. Austin's complete realization of Ives's transcendental *Universe Symphony* was presented and recorded in 1994 by the Cincinnati Philharmonia, followed by performances of the work by the National Philharmonic of Warsaw, Poland, and the Saarland Rundfunk Sinfonieorchester in Saarbrucken, Germany.

Larry Austin

For his composition *BluesAx* (1995-96), for saxophonist and computer music, and for his influential leadership in electro-acoustic music genres for the more than thirty-five years, Austin received the Magistère (Magisterium) title at the twenty-third International Electro-acoustic Music Competition in 1996, Bourges, France. He was the first American composer to receive the Magistère prize.

In 1997 Austin was Magistère composer-in-residence at the BEAST computer music studios at the University of Birmingham in the U.K., where he completed his octophonic computer music, *Djuro's Tree,* and *Singing! The Music of My Own Time,* commissioned by baritone Thomas Buckner. The following year, he was honored with a composer residency at the Rockefeller Center in Bellagio, Italy, where he completed *Tárogató!,* for tárogató and octophonic computer music. In 2000, as a guest research fellow at the Electroacoustic Music Studios at the University of York in York, U.K., he completed *Ottuplo!,* for real and virtual string quartet. In September, 2000, Austin was awarded a month-long composer residency at the International Institute for Electroacoustic Music, Bourges, France, which commissioned his work, *Williams [re]Mix[ed] (1997-2001)*, for octophonic computer music system. Presented on January 30, 2003, in an Interpretations

Series Merkin Concert Hall concert in New York City with composer James Dashow, the world premiere of his most recent work, *Threnos, for* bass clarinet(s) and octophonic computer music, commissioned by Michael Lowenstern, was performed in memory of the victims of September 11, 2001. Other Austin works on the program included *Tárogató!, Williams [re]Mix[ed] and Ottup*lo!

Retiring from his 38-year academic career in 1996, Austin resides with his wife Edna at their Robson Ranch home in Denton, Texas. Working in and out of his Denton studio, *gaLarry*, Austin continues his active composing career with commissions, tours, performances, writing, recordings, and lecturing, anticipating future extended composer residencies in North America, Japan, and Europe.

www.emfmedia.org/artists/austin.html

Autry, Gene
(b. September 29, 1907 - d. October 2, 1998)

Known forever as "Oklahoma's Yodeling Cowboy," Orvon Gene Autry began singing at age five in his grandfather's Tioga, Texas Baptist church choir and rode his smooth vocal chords, handsome visage, and cowboy authenticity through the 20th century as the first major singing cowboy to succeed on records, radio, the silver screen, and television. Autry enjoyed a second career as a broadcasting entrepreneur and major league baseball owner. Gene Autry's use of western themes in his music had tremendous impact on country's music development in the 1930s as the lyrical emphasis of the genre shifted from the rural south to the developing west, and the musical emphasis shifted from the nasal vocal delivery of old time country to the crooning style of the singing cowboy. Musically, Gene Autry also helped popularize the Hawaiian-style slack-keyed guitar which evolved into the use of the Dobro and pedal-steel guitar in Western swing and honky-tonk music. Additionally, along with other singing cowboys such as Tex Ritter and Roy Rogers, Autry's fashion sense of wearing a white cowboy hat impacted country music singers from non-Western states such as Bill Monroe from Kentucky and Hank Williams from Alabama, and continues to influence contemporary country music fashion so much that new country stars with no rural background are often thought of derisively as "hat acts." The mass marketing of Gene Autry's image and name through the Sears and Roebuck catalogues of the 1930s continues to resonate throughout the entertainment industry as a an example of promotion of, and profiting from, star status.

Gene Autry

Born to tenant farmers Delbert Autry and Elnora Ozment Autry in the tiny Grayson County, Texas town of Tioga, just about twenty five miles south of the Oklahoma border, the family moved just across the Red River to Achille, Oklahoma, in Bryan County, when Gene was a small child. In Achille, Gene learned to ride horses and his mother began teaching him to play guitar. When Gene was about fifteen, the Autry family moved to Ravia, Oklahoma, a tiny town in the south central part of the state near Tishomingo, where Gene hauled baggage and did other odd jobs the Frisco Railroad depot leading the station master teach the skills of telegraph operator.

After he finished high school, Gene earned fifteen dollars a week as a ballad singer, saxophone player and black-faced comedian with the Fields Brothers Marvelous Medicine Show for a few months before taking a job as a relief telegrapher for regular Frisco operators from St. Louis to Southern Oklahoma. When the wires were not too busy, Gene had an opportunity to practice his guitar and sing in the style of his hero, Jimmie Rodgers. While riding the Frisco rails and filling in where needed, Gene linked up with another musically inclined railroad man, his boss and uncle-in-law, Jimmy Long, in Sapulpa, Oklahoma, and the two formed a duo that played at dances and parties around Sapulpa and wrote songs together, most notably "That Silver Haired Daddy of Mine" which would later become the music industry's first gold record in 1931 and launched Autry as an up-and-coming star. Popular legend has it that sometime in 1928 the famous Oklahoma humorist Will Rogers heard Gene singing in the Chelsea, Oklahoma railroad depot and suggested the 21-year-old singing telegraph operator head to New York and try to make it in the big city on radio. Gene thought about it while continuing to play locally for a year and then took advantage of a free Frisco railway pass to New York City where he had only the slightest connections to fellow Oklahomans **Frankie** and **Johnny Marvin.** But having met their parents back in Oklahoma, Autry felt connected enough to contact them.

Two of the most popular entertainers in New York, the Marvin Brothers were recording artists and Broadway and vaudeville stars in 1928, giving them ample opportunity to introduce the fresh-faced kid to some industry connections. After auditioning a few tunes for Victor, the talent scout thought Autry had promise but needed more polish and recommended Autry learn some yodeling songs in the manner of Jimmie Rodgers and continue to practice singing somewhere else than under the big microscope in New York. Autry heeded the advice and returned to Tulsa where he landed a job on KVOO, Tulsa as "Oklahoma's Yodeling Cowboy," and performed at schools, private parties, and schools along with his radio work. After getting a year of experience under his belt, Gene returned to New York and Victor Records where the Marvin Brothers helped him get his first songs cut, "My Dreaming of You" and "My Alabama Home" on October 9, 1929. Unfortunately for Autry, the stock market crashed twenty days later and the recording business felt the shock as much as anyone.

Autry turned to several small labels during the period and continued recording ballads in the manner of his idol, Jimmie Rodgers. Autry's style was becoming practically indistinguishable from Rodgers's, leading to Gene recording some of Rodgers's songs such as "Jimmie the Kid" and "T.B. Blues." Autry's version of "Jimmie the Kid" was such a mirror image of Rodgers's that when RCA reissued some of Rodgers's recordings in the 1970s they mistakenly included Autry's version instead of the Rodgers version. By 1931, Autry was becoming a smooth performer, confident with his guitar playing and starting to diverge from the dominant influence of Rodgers. In October of 1931, Gene and Jimmy Long recorded the song they had written way back in Sapulpa, "That Silver Haired Daddy of Mine." The song hinted at Autry's movement away from the Rodgers "blue yodel" style and closer to the style of singing ballads that would evolve into his western model of warm, sincere songs about the West of many Americans' imagination, a much better place to think about than the bread lines and broken fields of the Depression.

As a result of the success enjoyed by "That Silver Haired Daddy of Mine," Art Satherly, vice-president of the American Record Corporation (later subsumed by Columbia), sent Autry to Chicago to audition for the National Barn Dance on fifty thousand watt WLS, a clear channel AM station heard throughout the Midwest. Hired as "Oklahoma's Singing Cowboy" on the National Barn Dance, Autry's success garnered him his own radio show, "Conqueror Record Time," where he portrayed a cowboy fresh off the range who sang tales and tunes of the cattle trails. Before long, Sears Roebuck began taking advantage of the singing cowboy's popularity by marketing songbooks, Gene Autry Round Up Guitars retailing for $9.98 "less case," and Autry recordings on the Conqueror label which was the American Record Corporation's custom-made label for the Sears catalogue and where many Autry recordings appeared. By 1934 Autry was one of the most well-known and successful recording artists in America, but his star had really just started rising compared to the success he would have in the motion picture industry.

As with all elements of the economy during the Great Depression of the 1930s, the motion picture business had to offer special deals and lower prices to entice people into the only audio-visual medium available to them at the time. Although the concept of singing cowboys in a Western had been tried as early as 1930, Autry's entrance into the field came by way of a guest appearance in the film *In Old Santa Fe* (1934) which starred the most popular celluloid singing cowboy to that date, Ken Maynard, and whom filmgoers felt Autry upstaged in the film. Critics and film business types knew they had star in their midst and, in 1935, Autry was cast in the strange, late night cult classic serial, *The Phantom Empire*, a science fiction Western series which ran before main features. Autry's true breakthrough film was *Tumbling Tumbleweeds* (1935), and named after a song Gene recorded the previous January in a trio with his old friend and relative Jimmy Long and film sidekick Smiley Burnette. Just a few weeks after the release of Autry's first film, Republic Pictures released *Melody Trail* (1935), where Gene featured his horse, Champion, for the first time to audiences' rave approval. Two more films, *Sagebrush Troubadour* and *Singing Cowboy* brought the total films to four in just four months at the end of 1935 and provided audiences with the beginnings of Gene's "Cowboy's Code," some of which included the concepts of never shooting first, never hitting a man smaller than yourself, never going back on your word, and never advocating racially or religiously intolerant ideas.

Autry's films were set on a Western landscape and each was an hour long film which gave him the opportunity to break into a song an average of six times per movie which generated a tremendous amount of cross promotion for his records. Over the next eighteen years Autry would star in ninety-one feature films that defined the "B" Western concept, and in 1940, theater exhibitors of America voted Autry the fourth biggest box office attraction behind Mickey Rooney, Clark Gable, and Spencer Tracy. His major records during the 1930s and early 1940s, "Tumblin' Tumbleweeds" (1935), "Mexicali Rose" (1935), "Back in the Saddle Again" (1939), and "(I've Got Spurs That) Jingle, Jangle, Jingle" (1942), sold in the millions.

While Gene's early records such as "Tumblin' Tumbleweeds" and "The Yellow Rose of Texas" featured the simple instrumentation and vocals of his hero Jimmie Rodgers and other cowboy duos of the early 1930s, in 1937 Gene hired a swing fiddle player from Indiana named Carl Cotner to augment the Autry sound. Cotner played in a popular country swing band and was comfortable with everything from orchestrated arrangements popular with the big bands of the time to gutsier and dance-oriented fiddle tunes. Cotner soon began arranging Autry's recordings and originated the sound for which Autry is so famous and which had such an impact on mainstream country music. By adding smooth strings, subtle steel guitar, occasionally a muted horn section, and featuring the two-beat rhythm famous in cowboy songs to replicate a loping horse, Autry's music was appealing to both rural and urban audiences. In 1939, this crossover success landed Autry the CBS national network radio show, *Melody Ranch*, sponsored by Wrigley's Doublemint Gum, which aired on Sunday afternoons until 1956 and which provided Autry with perhaps the one song most associated with him, "Back in the Saddle Again" (1939), the theme song of *Melody Ranch*. Autry built a working Melody Ranch on sixty acres in Newhall, California to provide the backdrop for numerous films, radio shows, and television programs, starring actors such as John Wayne, The Cisco Kid, Ronald Reagan, Hopalong Cassidy, fellow Oklahoman **Johnny Bond,** and a native Arkansan, **Jimmy Wakely**, whom Autry met in Oklahoma in 1938 when he appeared on Wakely's WKY Oklahoma City radio program; ultimately, Autry signed the Jimmy Wakely Trio to become part of the CBS Radio *Melody Ranch Show* in 1940.

Alongside the films, recordings, and radio shows, Autry had a traveling stage show that would often tout the release of a new film and play in the same theaters as the film. Some of his best-known movies are based on his hit records, including *South of the Border* (1939), *Mexicali Rose* (1939), and *Back in the Saddle* (1941). In the fall of 1941, Gene bought a 1,200 acre ranch west of Berwyn, Oklahoma, about 16 miles west of his high school hometown of Ravia. He intended to make the ranch a showplace and headquarters of his traveling rodeo that sold out such venues as Madison Square Garden in New York City. A Berwyn lawman, Cecil Crosby, suggested to residents they change the town's name to honor their famous new neighbor. The Santa Fe Railroad, postal authorities, and residents all agreed and a celebration took place on November 16th, 1941, the 34th anniversary of Oklahoma's statehood. A crowd of 35,000 people, including Oklahoma governor Frank Phillips, assembled to watch the parade and feast on buffalo meat while a movie camera documented the event to include in newsreels throughout the nation's theaters. Gene recorded an episode of *Melody Ranch* that was aired across the country and then replaced the Berwyn town sign with the new Gene Autry sign. Three weeks later, however, U.S. involvement in World War II threw Autry's career, then at its absolute zenith, into uncertainty.

While Autry had a reported income of $600,000 for 1941, he only made $125 per month as a flight officer with the Air Transport Command from 1943 to 1945 flying large cargo planes in the China-Burma-India theater. For those financial reasons, Autry kept his stock at the ranch outside the Oklahoma town bearing his name, he sold the property in 1944. When the war ended, Autry was assigned to Special Services, where he toured with a USO troupe in the South Pacific before resuming his movie career with features such as *The Last Round-Up* (1947) and *Strawberry Roan* (1948). His recording career also took off again with multi-million selling songs "Here Comes Santa Claus" (1947), "Rudolph the Red Nosed Reindeer" (1948), and "Peter Cottontail" (1949). In 1950 Gene became one of the first major movie stars to move into television. For the next five years, he produced and starred in ninety-one half-hour episodes of *The Gene Autry Show* as well as producing popular TV series such as *Annie Oakley*, *The Range Rider*, *Buffalo Bill, Jr.*, *The Adventures of Champion*, and the first thirty-nine episodes of *Death Valley Days*.

With such a strong foundation in popular electronic media, Autry's forays into broadcast ownership were not surprising. Through his company Golden West Broadcasters, Gene owned award-winning stations such as KMPC radio and KTLA television in Los Angeles as well as other stations around the country. Gene also lived out a boyhood dream of being involved with professional baseball when he bought the American League's California (now Anaheim) Angels in 1961. Active in Major League Baseball, Autry held the title of Vice-President of the American League until his death, unfortunately before his Angels won the World Series in 2002. Gene continued his television success in the 1980s when he and his former movie sidekick Pat Buttram hosted the highly rated 90-minute Nashville Network

Autry film box

program, *Melody Ranch Theatre*, for ninety-three episodes in which they highlighted his old Republic and Columbia movies. At the end of the 1980s, Autry fulfilled another longstanding dream by completing the Autry Museum of Western Heritage which houses a fine collection of Western art, artifacts, and memorabilia such as an 1870s-era steam engine from Nevada, guns owned by Annie Oakley and Wyatt Earp, and costumes of TV's Lone Ranger and Tonto.

In 1990, when the school closed in Gene Autry, Oklahoma, citizens converted it into the Gene Autry, Oklahoma History Museum. The museum celebrates singing cowboys of the "B" western movies, especially Autry, and contains hundreds of collectibles to include photographs, clothing, movie posters, musical instruments, and other items associated with the singing cowboys. The museum also sponsors the Gene Autry, Oklahoma Film and Music Festival each year on Autry's birthday. Autry's birthplace of Tioga, Texas also celebrates the anniversary of his birth when 10,000 people arrive annual to enjoy live entertainment, Gene Autry movies, cowboy games, and chuckwagon breakfasts. In 1996, the most notable contemporary singing cowboys, Riders in the Sky, recorded a tribute album, *Public Cowboy #1: The Music of Gene Autry* (Rounder), including many of the songs for which Autry became famous such as "Back in the Saddle Again," "That Silver Haired Daddy of Mine," and "South of the Border."

Among the hundreds of honors and awards Gene Autry received in his lifetime include induction into the Country Music Hall of Fame, the Nashville Songwriters Hall of Fame, the American Academy of Achievement Award, the Los Angeles Area Governor's Emmy from the Academy of Television Arts and Sciences, the National Cowboy Hall of Fame, the National Association of Broadcasters Hall of Fame, and the Oklahoma Music Hall of Fame. He received the Songwriters' Guild Life Achievement Award, the Hubert Humphrey Humanitarian of the Year Award, a Lifetime Achievement Award by the songwriters' organization ASCAP, and not only the first country musician to get a star on the Hollywood Walk of Fame, but the only person to five stars along the walk. In 2009 the U.S. Postal Service announced a Gene Autry stamp would be issued in 2010.

Autry was a 33rd Degree Mason, and for many years ranked on *Forbes* list of the 400 richest Americans, before he fell to the magazine's "near miss" category in 1995 with an estimated net worth of "only" $320 million. In his biography, Autry credits his music's success to its simplicity and straightforwardness. He also describes the fickleness of the music business by saying, "It occurs to me that music, with the possible exception of riding a bull, is the most uncertain way to make a living I know. In either case, you get bucked off, thrown, stepped on, and trampled, if you get on at all. At best, it is a short bumpy ride." Autry's career of 635 recordings, including more than 300 songs written or co-written by him, and 100 million records sold, was more like one long, glorious ride into the sunset of American popular culture for *the* singing cowboy of the 1930s, '40s, and '50s.

www.autry.com

Recommended Reading

George-Warren, Holly. *Public Cowboy No. 1: The Life and Times of Gene Autry*. New York: Oxford University Press, 2009.

Axton, Hoyt

(b. March 25, 1938 - d. October 26, 1999)

Best known for his compositions "The Pusher," "Joy to the World," "Della and the Dealer," and "Jeremiah the Bullfrog," Hoyt Axton was born in Duncan, a community of about 22,000 residents in south central Oklahoma. Hoyt was the oldest son (younger brother named Johnny) of **Mae Boren Axton**, co-writer of Elvis Presley's "Heartbreak Hotel." His father, John T. Axton, was a teacher and high school coach. Both parents were influential in developing Hoyt's musical talents as his mother required him to take piano lessons and his father taught him the finer points of singing, especially how to use his rich baritone voice. Hoyt earned All-State honors in football at Robert E. Lee High School in Jacksonville, Florida, and received a football scholarship to attend Oklahoma State University. Before completion of a degree, he joined the Navy in the late 1950s, where he continued his athletic endeavors through boxing.

After leaving the Navy in 1961, Hoyt turned to the music business—writing and performing folk music. Following a brief period in Nashville, he headed to California, where he played the coffee house circuit in San Francisco in 1962. He recorded his first album in 1962 on the Horizon label. Entitled *The Balladeer* and recorded live at The Troubadour in Hollywood, the album included songs such as "John Henry," "500 Miles," and "Walkin' to Georgia." During the next decade, Axton performed as a folk music artist and co-wrote, "Greenback Dollar," recorded by the Kingston Trio in 1963. It became a Top 20 hit on the *Billboard* charts, however, Hoyt made a grand sum of $800 from the song due to conflicts with the publisher, also known as getting "ripped off" by the business. Other albums, also on the Horizon label, included *Greenback Dollar* (1963), *Thunder 'n' Lightnin,'* (1963), and *Saturday's Child* (1963). He switched record companies in the mid-1960s, and recorded *Hoyt Axton Explodes* (1964) on Vee Jay, The Beatles' first label in the U.S., and *Mr. Greenback Dollar Man* (1965) on the Surrey label.

During the late 1960s, Hoyt composed several major hits, including "The Pusher" and "Snowblind Friend." Recorded by Steppenwolf, "The Pusher" was featured in the 1969 film, *Easy Rider*, and became an iconic 1960s song referencing the drug culture. During the 1960s, he released *Hoyt Axton Sings Bessie Smith* (1965), reflecting his appreciation for other genres of music, including the blues. A constant joker, smirker, and lyrical miracle worker, two of his early albums in the 1970s were released by Capitol, including *Country Anthem* (1971) and *Joy to the World* (1971). In the 1970s, two of Axton's compositions, "Joy to the World" and "Never Been to Spain," were recorded by Three Dog Night, and his "No No Song" was recorded by former Beatle, Ringo Starr. Axton recorded more than thirty albums, primarily in the 1970s. Among these were *Less Than a Song* (1973), *Life Machine* (1974), *Southbound* (1975), *Fearless* (1976), *Road Songs* (1977), *Snowblind Friend* (1977), *Free Sailin'* (1978), and *A Rusty Old Halo* (1979). The latter produced "Della and the Dealer" and "Rusty Old Halo," both of which made the Top 20 charts as singles. As a testament to Hoyt's heavyweight status in the music industry, guests on *Rusty Old Halo* included Garth Hudson, Stephen Stills, Jeff "Skunk" Baxter (of Steely Dan), Paul Butterfield, and Dr. John. Several of his later albums were released by his own recording label, Jeremiah, named after the bullfrog in "Joy to the World," including *Where Did the Money Go* (1980), *Hoyt Axton Live* (1981), and *Pistol Packin' Mama* (1982).

Hoyt Axton

Hoyt's latter albums were *Spin of the Wheel* (1991), *Jeremiah Was a Bullfrog* (1998), and *Gold* (2001). The title song of the *Jeremiah Was a Bullfrog* album was certainly one of his most requested compositions. Additional noteworthy compositions include "When the Mornin' Comes," "Boney Fingers," Viva Pancho Villa," "Wild Bull Rider," and "Evangelina." His songs were covered by a variety of artists, including Waylon Jennings, Glen Campbell, Tanya Tucker, John Denver, and Commander Cody. In 2008, award-winning songwriter Darrel Scott (Dixie Chicks, Garth Brooks, Faith Hill, et. Al.) included Axton's "The Devil" on his album *Modern Hymns* (Appleseed). Scott's aim was to showcase "songs and songwriters who shook me as kid… and guided the way to my own path as a singer-songwriter…"

Hoyt also appeared in several movies and on television, including *We're No Angels, The Black Stallion*, and *Gremlins*, sang the "Head to the Mountains" jingle used in the Busch beer commercial in the 1980s, and was in the hit TV series, *Bonanza*, in 1965. Of particular distinction was his role in Francis Ford Coppola's *Black Beauty* (1979). A singer, guitarist, pianist, songwriter, and actor, Hoyt died of a heart attack at his Victor, Montana, ranch in 1999, after suffering a major stroke in 1995, which had left him confined to a wheel chair. Survived by his third wife, Deborah Hawkins, Hoyt had five children. He was the nephew of former Governor of Oklahoma and U.S. Senator from Oklahoma, David Boren. While remembered widely for his tune, "Jeremiah Was a Bullfrog" with its "Joy to the World" refrain, Axton is also thought of fondly by Oklahomans for one of the lines from "Never Been to Spain": "Well, I've never been to heaven, but I've been to Oklahoma."

www.hoytsmusic.com

Axton, Mae Boren
(b. September 14, 1914 - d. April 9, 1997)

Known as a guardian angel of struggling songwriters, and co-composer of "Heartbreak Hotel," one of Elvis Presley's major hits, Mae Boren Axton was born in Bardwell, Texas, although she was reared in Oklahoma and attended the University of Oklahoma where she earned a journalism degree. She was the sister of David Boren, one of Oklahoma's most celebrated politicians as he served as state senator, governor, and U.S. Senator from the state, as well as serving as president of the University of Oklahoma through 2010. After college, she worked as a reporter for *Life* magazine. She married John T. Axton, a teacher and coach, and they had two sons, Hoyt and Johnny, both born in Duncan, Oklahoma. **Hoyt Axton** was a well-known singer, songwriter, and actor.

Mae Boren Axton

Mae's family moved to Jacksonville, Florida, where she and her husband continued their teaching careers. Moreover, Mae began writing songs with local songwriters Glen Reeves and Thomas Durden, as well as serving as publicist for country singer Hank Snow. It was while working for Snow that she first heard Elvis Presley in May of 1955. According to elvispresleymusic.com, while reading the *Miami Herald* newspaper one day in 1955, Durden and Mae came across an article about a man who had committed suicide in a local hotel. After tearing the labels out of his clothes and destroying his identification, the suicide victim left a note with the line, "I walk a lonely street." Within less than a half hour, Mae and Durden had scribbled out the lyrics and recorded a demo of "Heartbreak Hotel." Some sources say that Mae played the demo tape for Elvis at a radio convention in Nashville, while others say they took it to Colonel Tom Parker, Presley's manager. Elvis liked the song, but hated the title. Elvis mandated that he be listed as co-composer, and received one-third of the royalties. As Elvis' first single for RCA Victor and his first #1 hit on the *Billboard* charts, the song was the biggest selling hit on the *Billboard* charts in 1956, staying at #1 for eight weeks, and eventually won a GRAMMY Hall of Fame award in 1995. Presley, however, never recorded any other Axton songs, although he did record her son Hoyt's "Never Been to Spain." Mae remembered Elvis in a poem, "Elvis (He Was My Friend)," in her independently published book of poems, *From the Window of My Heart (Poems to Live By)*. About Elvis, she writes, "He was young and he was shy, when he first stood by my side… [he] told me of the things he had dreamed… [and he was] anxious to explore a world that he had never seen" (60).

Mae enjoyed other successes as a songwriter, as notable artists such as Patsy Cline ("Pick Me Up On Your Way Down"), **Wanda Jackson** ("Honey Bop"), and Hank Snow ("What Do I Know Today") recorded her songs. In addition, her songs have been covered by a vast array of artists, including The Animals, **J. J. Cale**, Little Jimmy Dickens, Albert King, **Conway Twitty**, Jerry Lee Lewis, **Roger Miller**, Tanya Tucker, Conway Twitty, Faron Young, and Doc Watson. She also wrote the sleeve notes to the Elvis tribute album, *The King Is Gone*, by Ronnie McDowell. In 1973, Mae published her memoirs, *Country Singers As I Know 'em*. She also started a record label called DPJ Records for which son

Hoyt recorded, and gained her status as a struggling songwriter guardian angel for helping boost the careers of such legends as Dolly Parton and Willie Nelson, as well as relative newcomer **Blake Shelton.** Fellow Oklahoman Garth Brooks donated $1 million to the city of Nashville for the establishment of a children's zoo, named in honor of Mae Boren Axton. Mae died at her home in Hendersonville, Tennessee, on April 9, 1997.

Source
Axton, Mae Boren. *From the Window of My Heart (Poems to Live By).* Ada, OK: Cantrell Publishing, 1989.

B

Baker, Chesney H. "Chet"
(b. December 23, 1929 - d. May 13, 1988)

Known as the West Coast cool jazz trumpeter who most intensely represented the ethos of 1950s California jazz with his intimate, hushed vocal style and the clear, warm, subdued tone of his horn, Chesney Henry Baker also endured the rugged lifestyle of a habitual narcotics user which resulted in an uneven, although certainly celebrated and distinctive, international musical career. His sharp, photogenic features led some fans to think of him as the jazz James Dean, while others preferred Chet as an urbane, musically sophisticated antithesis to the grease and leather image popular among 1950s rock icons. To many jazz fans, Chet's musical significance is unquestioned, but biographers, critics, and jazz historians all agree his drug habit limited his career, led to several mediocre recordings in the mid-1960s, and caused too many grisly run-ins with the law and other drug addicts. Chet's father, Chesney Baker, Sr., was a semi-professional country guitar player, who met Vera Ruth (Moser) Baker at a barn dance where he was playing near Yale, Oklahoma, a small farm town in north central Oklahoma. Chet remembers Vera in his 1997 unfinished memoir, *If I Had Wings*: "[she was] a sweet and gentle woman, a country girl who'd been born in Yale, Oklahoma, just as I had." Born two days before Christmas in the first winter of the Great Depression, Chet and the Bakers lived on a small farm his grandfather had acquired in the Oklahoma Territory land runs of 1889. While in Oklahoma his mother took him around to amateur contests where he sang ballads, but never won any contests, and kept him going to church where he sang in the choir. Chet describes his rural childhood bucolically in his memoir, but one has to imagine bleak conditions for supporting a family

Chet Baker

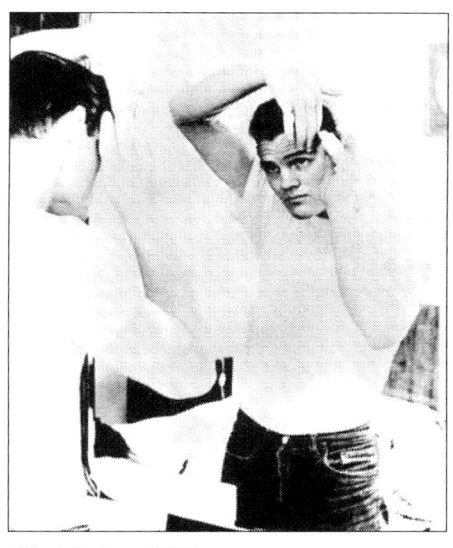

Chet Baker, 1950s

on the dry prairie land smack in the middle of the dust bowl proper. With jobs limited for his parents around Yale, the Bakers moved to Oklahoma City when he was one-year-old to stay with his father's sister, Agnes, who basically raised Chet until he was eight while his mother worked at an ice cream factory and his father as a timekeeper for the WPA. Chet returned to Yale over the summers to visit his grandparents and the farm where he remembers walking dirt roads while picking wild raspberries and eating fresh watermelons out of the fields. If one is looking for reasons for the melancholy elements of Chet Baker's music and life, or even the lonesome, breathy blowings of his trumpet and the near whisper of his singing and scatting, a good place to begin in the imagination is those peaceful ruminations of his rural childhood which were shattered in 1940 when the family moved to Glendale, California, a suburb just north of Los Angeles. Of course, many Oklahomans had to leave the state after being blown out of work by the drought, dust storms, corporate and government led farm takeovers, and the Bakers certainly symbolize that difficult period in state history when the term "Okie" was not one of positive origin.

After living in Glendale for a couple of years, Chet's father, a Jack Teagarden fan, brought home a trombone for thirteen-year-old Chet, but the instrument proved too unwieldy and after a couple of weeks the trombone vanished and a trumpet appeared. Chet started taking lessons at Glendale Jr. High, but given his inclination toward playing by ear he was not successful in band until his high school year when he marched with the high school band, learned all the Sousa marches by ear, and played in the school dance band in the evenings. After one year of high school, his parents moved again to Redondo Beach to stay with some friends from Oklahoma, further indication of the Baker family's travails during the World War II era. Disenchanted with school at Redondo High and distracted by the beach, Chet quit at 16, and joined the U.S. Army.

After basic training at Fort Lewis, Washington in 1946, the Army dubbed Chet a clerk typist who would spend his time filling out forms, and sent him to Berlin, Germany, just after World War II when the city was still in rubble. After arriving in Germany and gaining an audition for the first trumpet player of the 298th Army band, Chet received a transfer from his intended desk chair to playing on freezing tarmacs for high-ranking officials and politicians as they exited planes. At night, he listened closely to the Victory Discs by Dizzy Gillespie and Stan Kenton being played on the Armed Forces Network. Discharged in 1948, Chet returned to Southern California where his parents had finally been able to purchase a home just north of Redondo Beach in Hermosa Beach, and from which he began attending El Camino Junior College on his GI benefits as a music major and English minor. Chet studied theory and harmony at El Camino, but also started developing music contacts in the area. He met Jimmy Rowles, who at the time was pianist for Peggy Lee on Sunset Boulevard in Los Angeles, and Chet immediately befriended Jimmy to the point of showing up at Rowles's house often and asking the pianist to play songs for him. Chet credits Rowles with the inspiration to keep things simple and not get too busy on the trumpet. Many musicians recognized Chet frequently stayed within one octave in his playing, known musically as *mezzo-forte*, which contributes to his perceived subtlety and economic style. Nineteen forty-eight also marked the release of Miles Davis's *Birth of Cool*. The album had an irrevocable impact on Chet's playing as he confirmed in 1978 when he said he "still listens to [*Birth of Cool*] thirty years later." While many critics feel Chet's horn playing is clearly a descendant of Davis's, thus creating one of Baker's critical sobriques, "The West Coast Miles Davis," Baker also has a distinct subtlety of tone and pace instantly recognizable apart from Davis's to those who listen closely. In a 1996 interview, Muskogee-born jazz guitar giant **Barney Kessel** remembered Chet's trumpet playing as "him and nobody else."

During 1948 and 1949, Chet followed the session trail around Los Angeles almost every night and learned from artists such as Dexter Gordon, Shelly Manne, Shorty Rogers, Art Pepper, and others, but also traveled to the suburban spots where he would play with more great players like Russ Freeman, with whom he would play later in the 1950s, and another great Oklahoma-born jazz man, bassist **Oscar Pettiford**. By 1950 Chet dropped out of El Camino because his music teacher told him he would never make it playing by ear all the time, and Chet turned completely toward the valuable sessions cooking all around the Los Angeles metro area. Although he was sitting in occasionally at area clubs clubs, Chet was unable to find consistent work as a musician. Knowing one band where he could make some money, Chet re-enlisted in the U.S. Army to join the Presidio Army band in San Francisco. At Presidio he played for the Army during the day, what he called his "day gig," slept until about 1 a.m., then sat in as a regular at clubs like Bop City which did not open until 2 a.m. On off nights he sat in with Cal Tjader at Fack's, or Dave Brubeck and Paul Desmond at the Blackhawk until 5:30 a.m. and time to get back to the Presidio for reveille. This routine continued for about a year until he tired of the Army part of the musical equation and proceeded to strategize his way out, which he was successful in doing with not a little difficulty by 1952 when a general discharge declared him unadaptable to Army life.

Freed from the confines of wearing the same color clothes every day, Chet went back to Southern California where he found work with Vido Musso and then Stan Getz before learning of an audition to play some West Coast dates with Charlie "Bird" Parker. For many, Parker was *the* architect of bebop who got his first national exposure with a Kansas City based big band led by Muskogee, Oklahoma native **Jay McShann**. After being moved to the front of the audition and playing only two tunes with Bird, "The Song is You" and "Cheryl" in the key of G, Chet got the job and played a series of gigs in California, Washington, and Canada. The twenty-two-year-old Chet and Parker only split when a club manager fired Parker for obliging the club manager to a charity contribution unbeknownst to the manager. Baker went back to L.A. where he played a few nights with Dixieland specialist Freddie "Schnicklefritz" Fisher, and also was recorded for the first time commercially in jam sessions for *Live at the Trade Winds* (1952). By the summer of 1952, Chet met and formed a critically acclaimed quartet with the great jazz baritone saxophonist, Gerry Mulligan, who had arranged the music and written compositions for Miles Davis's *Birth of Cool*. Leaving out the piano, then a standard instrument of almost any jazz combo, the partnership with Chet and Mulligan as the frontline quartet players became known as the archetype for the breezy, laid-back West Coast cool jazz sound. The group proved to be a success commercially and critically, and the band's first recordings as the Gerry Mulligan quartet included Baker's understated, romantic vocals on "My Funny Valentine," recorded for the newly formed Pacific Jazz Records label. While Chet was enjoying his first tastes of national success as a result of the lyrical wispiness of his trumpet and vocals, he also was arrested for the first time on a drug count, a harbinger of the continued peaks and valleys of his career as a musician and his life as an addict. In June of 1953, Gerry Mulligan had time to do himself for a drug charge, and, therefore, Chet's solo career began. He called his old friend Russ Freeman to play piano, and Baker made his first recordings as a bandleader for the Pacific Jazz label. These recordings led to Chet being voted top trumpet player by the readers of *Metronome* and *Downbeat* magazines in 1953 and 1954. When Mulligan returned to the streets and suggested the idea of getting back together, Baker disagreed with him over salary ($300 per week), and when Mulligan balked, Chet walked on to rejoin Charlie Parker briefly, then to gigs around the country with his own groups in the latter half of 1954. That year, Pacific Jazz released *Chet Baker Sings* (1954), enhancing Chet's popularity and cementing his status as a vocalist for the rest of his career, albeit at the expense of estranging some more traditional jazz fans. Eager to exploit his good looks and youth appeal, Hollywood featured Chet in the 1955 film, *Hell's Horizon*. Chet declined the subsequent seven-year contract offered by Columbia Pictures, in favor of playing dates such as the Newport Jazz Festival in July, and touring and recording in Europe from September, 1955 to April, 1956. During these peak years of Chet Baker's early career, he scored the *Metronome* and *Melody Maker* "best trumpet" awards in 1955, and second place in the *Downbeat* poll for that same year. The German publication, *Jazz Echo*, named him the top trumpeter in 1956. The European experience was marred by the untimely heroin overdose of his good friend and pianist, Dick Twardzik, in 1955, which caused Chet to take on the additional challenge of assembling musicians for his group, which he abandoned in April 1956. He returned to the U.S., formed a new quartet and recorded *Chet Baker and Crew* (1956), which leaned more toward the up tempo bop stylings he demonstrated at Newport the year before, as opposed the cool jazz sound for which he was famous. Although still well known and critically lauded through the end of the 1950s, receiving multiple recognitions from *Playboy*'s jazz polls, Chet called the next two years, 1958 and 1959, "difficult" as he both recorded prolifically, if unevenly, and was arrested for drugs repeatedly. Chet left for Europe to stay in 1959, settling in Italy, but Hollywood maintained his rebellious image as a jazz outsider in the 1960 fictionalized film biography of his life, *All the Fine Young Cannibals*, with Robert Wagner starring in the role of Chad Bixby. 1959 was also the year Chet met his third wife, Carol (Jackson) Baker, an English fashion model and show dancer, to whom he was married until his death. In many ways Carol has been responsible for keeping Chet's memory alive through the Chet Baker estate by cooperating with documentary makers, releasing rare recordings, making *The Lost Memoir* available, and maintaining the Chet Baker website.

  Heroin began to seriously interrupt Chet Baker's career in 1960, when he was arrested on a drug charge in Italy and spent nearly eighteen months in jail. Upon release from prison, Chet celebrated with an RCA release *Chet Is Back* (1962), since reissued as *Somewhere Over the Rainbow*. Chet also portrayed himself in the film *The Stolen Hours* (1963), before he endured a series of drug-related deportations in Germany, Switzerland, France, and England. Ironically, Chet remembers the period as "a very good year" in his memoir when he worked with various European musicians and began playing flugelhorn after his trumpet was stolen in Paris, and which can be best heard on *Baby Breeze* (1965).

After another bust in then West Germany, he was deported back to the U.S. in March, 1964, where the Beatles and rock music were anchoring into American music consciousness and jazz's forefront was dominated by the far-reaching, free-jazz master, John Coltrane.

The first fourteen months Chet was back in the states he recorded a number of fine albums: *Lonely Star* (1965), *Stairway to the Stars* (1965), and *On a Misty Night* (1965). Chet also recorded some mediocre albums in 1966 while trying to cash in on the movement in popular instrumental music toward the Tijuana Brass sound of Herb Alpert. The albums were not received well critically but they did help him support his growing family, now with two sons, Dean and Paul. The period is better represented by the album released by Carol Baker known as *Live at Gaetano's* (1966); the recording showcases Chet in a small club in Pueblo, Colorado, with just a few people clapping after some extended jams featuring Chet and his friend Phil Urso, along with some trademark wistful singing by Chet. As Chet slipped steadily into the reclusive world of the addict, a cataclysmic event occurred in Sausalito, California on the same day his daughter, Melissa, was born back in Oklahoma, July 22, 1966. Many accounts exist for what happened that night, but Carol Baker remembers the end result arriving home with a new baby and shortly thereafter receiving a phone call from Chet explaining he had been beaten badly by some thugs who damaged his mouth significantly. One marginal recording exists for 1967, and 1968 is the only year in Chet's professional life when no obvious recording was released. The event forced Chet on welfare for two years when he learned to start playing through the side of his mouth instead of with his embouchure, the point of the upper lip that is pivotal to a brass instrument player's musical dexterity. However, Chet's teeth were bad anyway, and one could argue that the imperfect resonation cavity his jaws formed provided an element of his particular tone. But this injury was also aimed at his lip, and the handicap is immediately apparent on the critically derided *Albert's House* (1969), with Chet barely blowing eleven tunes by Steve Allen, the 1950s and 1960s talk show host and would-be jazz pianist. *Blood, Chet, & Tears* (1970), Baker's final release of the period, was no better with maudlin versions of pop hits such as "Spinning Wheel," "And When I Die," "Something," and "You've Made Me So Very Happy." Chet Baker, who many critics, and certainly his fans, consider *the* jazz trumpeter of the 1950s, was broke, and resorted to working in a gas station as he tried to figure out how to get his life back. Chet began picking up small club dates where he could still play on his legendary name. When Dizzy Gillespie heard Chet was working again, Dizzy helped get Chet a gig in New York at the Half Note in 1973, and Chet began a very slow return to jazz circles, starting with a live reunion at Carnegie Hall with Gerry Mulligan, recorded and released in 1974, followed by several 1970s albums that received better and better reviews such as his "come back" album, *She Is Too Good to You* (1974),

Chet Baker's awards displayed in Drumright, OK 2005.

and three albums in 1977. Out of financial necessity, during this period Chet returned to Italy as he was better known to European jazz fans, and could still get enough gigs to support himself there. He remained in Europe for the rest of his professional life between intermittent trips to Japan, and the U.S., where he would occasionally visit Carol, their children, and his mother who was in a nursing home in Yale. 1977 continued a slow, but important, climb back into the music industry's consciousness and the ears of international jazz fans who remembered Baker's significance. In a 1979 Norwegian television interview, made available by the Chet Baker Foundation, Baker indicated he still felt he was growing "harmonically and lyrically." When asked by the interviewer what kind of music Chet liked at the time, Baker says, "not country and western, not rock, and not pop," but goes on to say at the time he did like Weather Report, "all of Miles [Davis'] old stuff, Dizzy [Gillespie], Keith Jarrett, McCoy Tyner, Wayne Shorter, Michael Brecker, those people…" Commenting on the interviewer's request to discuss the lyrical beauty of his music, Baker explains, "I try to keep it fluid and flowing, from phrase to phrase, a kind of a melodic logic." Finally, with not only a little irony, Baker tells the interviewer he hopes he can last another ten years, but from that point he only last about nine more.

Chet Baker

Although Chet did not regain his critical acclaim of the 1950s in the U.S., his elevated status in Europe, Japan, and among American jazz collectors provided a market in the 1980s for new releases, and reissues, some of which were done without his knowledge and for which he was never paid. A good example of Chet's ability and state of mind in this period is a recording made on Christmas Eve, 1982 when Baker played the Nine of Cups Club in Tulsa, Oklahoma. Baker was in the state visiting his family, borrowed a trumpet (which he never returned) from a local music store, and played the date which emerged as *Out of Nowhere* in 1991 on Fantasy. As of 2003, Chet's discography now totals some 180 individual albums, with another seventy some-odd repackaged box sets available, not even including unreleased material yet to be made available by Carol Baker and the Chet Baker estate. This legacy provided ample substance for Bruce Weber's 1987 documentary on Chet's life, *Let's Get Lost*, which premiered in September, 1988, to vast critical acclaim and garnered an Academy Award nomination. However, Chet never enjoyed the success of the film. On May 13, 1988, at about 3 a.m., he appears to have fallen out of his hotel window in Amsterdam under circumstances never fully explained. While narcotics were certainly involved in the incident, he was fifty-eight-years-old and many critics felt he had not only re-attained his earlier abilities, but was beginning to surpass them with his extensive experience behind the trumpet and microphone as a vocalist. Written a year after Chet's death, J. De Valk's biography/oral history, *Chet Baker: his life and music* (translation by Berkeley Books, 2000), is an excellent overview of Chet's career that uses many interviews and a personal passion for the subject by the author to pursue Chet Baker for a 1987 interview which is fully transcribed in the text. Of particular interest is De Valk's European insight into Chet's career there, especially chapters about his final years through his final moments. The book is well researched and a must read for Baker enthusiasts. Another Baker biographer, James Gavin, did not portray Chet as a flattering character in 2002's *Deep in A Dream: The Long Night of Chet Baker* (Knopf), focusing strongly on Chet's drug abuse, undependability, and selfishness. However, Gavin thought enough of his own project to narrate an audio special for Delta Airlines in 2002 when the airline devoted one of their Delta Radio channels to Baker's life and music on international flights between Europe and the U.S. Also in 2002, six new releases featured Chet Baker's music, to include two sparkling compilations on Blue Note, *Deep in a Dream: The Ultimate Chet Baker*, and *The Definitive Chet Baker*. Like other musicians whose substance abuse problems develop early in their careers, and who subsequently produce a jagged body of work, Chet alternately inspired and disappointed fans, critics, friends and family members who were always willing to give him another chance to match the musical brilliance he brandished from 1954 to 1959 when he was one of the world's best jazz trumpeters. Jazz historians will be discussing his significance for generations to come, but the best confirmation of his self-concept of who he was and where he came from is indicated by the final time he signed into a hotel registry, as Chet Baker of Yale, Oklahoma. As of 2010, the town of his birth continued to acknowledge him. Directly under the name of the weekly newspaper on its front page, *The Yale News* indicates it is "Published in Yale, Oklahoma – Birthplace of Chet Baker and Home of Jim Thorpe."

Chet Baker Foundation: *www.chetbakerjazz.com*

Baker, Mark
(b. February 28, 1953)

Winner of the 1986 Metropolitan Opera National Council Auditions, and performer at New York City's Metropolitan Opera more than 250 times, tenor Mark Baker was born into a "singing family" in Tulsa, but was reared in Florida, and ultimately "found his voice when he moved to Melbourne," Florida.[1] After singing with the Brevard Community College ensemble where he earned an Associate of Arts, and in local community theater productions, he graduated from the University of Indiana with a bachelor's degree in vocal performance and a master's degree in counseling.

Mark made his Met debut as Benvolio during the 1986-87 season, in Gounod's *Roméo et Juliette* in the Outdoor in the Parks season. Later in the same season, he appeared in the "House," as an opera regular in a number of small roles in such operas as Mussorgsky's *Boris Godunov*, Wagner's *Parsifal*, and a repeat of Tibald in *Roméo et Juliette*. Subsequently, he sang at more than 250 Metropolitan Opera performances, averaging ten a year for twenty years. In addition to the Met, he appeared with opera stars Luciano Pavarotti and Placido Domingo, and was a regular performer with such notable U.S. companies as the Lyric Opera of Chicago, Santa Fe Opera, San Francisco Opera, Cincinnati Opera, and Dallas Opera. Overseas, he has performed with the Netherlands Opera; Opera de Lyon, Opera de Nantes, and Bastille in Paris (France); Spoleto Opera and Teatro Bellini in Catania (Italy); Berlin and Bonn Operas (Germany); Santiago Opera (Chile); and Teatro Colon in Buenos Aires (Argentina).

Baker's U.S. credits include Froh in *Das Rheingold*, Grigory/Dimitri in *Boris Godunov*, Narraboth in *Salome*, Vladimir Igorevich in *Prince Igor*, Don Jose in *Carmen*, Siegmund in *Die Walküre*, Florestan in *Fidelio*, and Samson in *Samson et Dalila*. His extensive overseas credits include roles in *Der Fliegende Holländer*, *Salome*, *Wozzeck*, *Peter Grimes*, *Parsifal*, *Die Walküre*, *Katya Kabanova*, *Leonore*, *Jenufa*, and *Samson et Dalila*, and he has appeared on European telecasts of Janácek's *Jenufa* from Glyndebourne and *Wozzeck* from the Berlin State Opera. The "Tulsa tenor" is featured on recordings of Berg's *Wozzeck* (Elektra/WEA, 1997), Wagner's *Das Rheingold* with the Metropolitan Opera Orchestra (Deutsche Grammaphon, 2002), and Anthony Davis's *Amistad*(New World Records, 2008). Additionally, he created roles for two opera premieres, *The Great Gatsby* and *Amistad*.

After retiring from the Met in 2008 to West Melbourne, Florida, as of 2010 he is an adjunct instructor of voice and music literature at Brevard Community College. According to his bio on the Brevard Community College website, his teaching objective is to "help students develop; their vocal technique to become the best singers they can possibly be. This is accomplished best by concentrating on the proper use of breath, support, relaxation, resonance, and diction. It is my hope that students will discover the joy and comfort of *near* effortless singing and they will learn to express themselves in a unique and personal way."[2]

Mark Baker

Sources
1. Maria, Sonnenberg. "World renowned opera singer performs in Melbourne," *metromix.brevard*, 7 November, 2008. http://brevard.metromix.com/events/article/world-renowned-opera-singer/754519/content.
2. Mark Baker faculty biography. *Brevard Community College*. http://www.brevardcc.edu.

Ballard, Louis Wayne (Honganózhe)
(b. July 8, 1931 – d. February 9, 2007)

As a wide-ranging composer who has written many types of music for all instruments and voices, Oklahoma's most successful and prolific classical composer is Louis W. Ballard, a Quapaw-**Cherokee** born at Devil's Promenade in the northeastern corner of Oklahoma near Quapaw. Honganózhe is Ballard's Quapaw name that means "Grand Eagle." His credits include major premiers at Lincoln Center, John F. Kennedy Center, the Smithsonian Institution, Carnegie Hall, the Hollywood Bowl and other major venues around the world. He has received many prestigious awards, such as the National Indian Achievement Award (1972, 1973, 1976), an honorary doctorate from the College of Santa Fe (1973), and the first MacDowell Award for American Chamber Music (1969). He has been awarded grants from the Rockefeller Foundation, Ford Foundation, and National Endowment for the Arts, and, in 1989, he was the first American composer to present an entire program of his music in the Beethoven-House Chamber Music Hall adjoining Beethoven's birthplace. In 1997 he was presented a Lifetime Achievement Award from the First Americans in the Arts, and in 2004 he was inducted into the Oklahoma Music Hall of Fame.

With a mother of pure Quapaw ancestry (Leona Mae (Perry) Ballard) and a father of Cherokee-French-Scot ancestry (Charles Guthrie Ballard), a diverse array of cultural influences surrounded Louis during his youth in northeastern Oklahoma. As a child, he attended the annual Quapaw powwows where he became familiar with Quapaw and inter-tribal American Indian musical traditions. His mother played piano at Spring River Indian Mission, and also wrote fox trots and ballads. Encouraged by his Quapaw grandmother, Newakis Hampton, to play the piano she had in her home, he began taking lessons with his mother at the mission. After attending Bacone College's secondary school, Ballard began his undergraduate education at the University of Oklahoma in 1949 where he sang in the men's glee club, took piano lessons, and studied Latin, harmony, counterpoint, and other rudiments of college music curriculum as well as military science. He also went out for the football team under Bud Wilkinson, but his music suffered and he gave up sports. Financial difficulties caused him to leave OU and he returned home where he attended Northeastern Oklahoma A & M in Miami for his sophomore year. In 1952, Ballard received a loan from the Mayes County Indian Credit Association for his tuition at Tulsa University. He finished his Bachelor of Music Education and Bachelor of Fine Arts at TU and became a music teacher. His first job was in Nelagony, Oklahoma, near Pawhuska, where he taught for two years, and then Ballard taught for two years at Tulsa Webster High School. He left musical teaching due to the low salary and attended Tulsa Technical College to become a mechanical draftsman, after which he designed oil field equipment, huge offshore well platforms, and pressure wells for the National Tank Company. Unsatisfied by the work, Ballard returned to Tulsa University where completed his Masters of Music in composition 1962. During graduate school, Louis gravitated to the music and philosophy of Bela Bartok (1881-1945), the Hungarian composer whose compositions set the stage for 20th century post-modernism by incorporating traditional folk melodies into his formal classical music. Through this exposure, Ballard came to understand the best way of incorporating exotic music into his compositional techniques was to learn as much as possible about the culture, learn as many of the songs as possible, and try to compose music which reflects the quintessence of that culture. Subsequently, Ballard developed his own classical style for which he has become known. Initially, Ballard's compositions sought to generate a greater appreciation for American Indian music, but as his career developed he was determined to shepherd the music into mainstream musical expression. As he writes on his website, Ballard believes, "It is not enough to acknowledge that American

Louis Ballard

Indian music is different from other music. What is needed in America is an awakening and reorienting of our total spiritual and cultural perspective to embrace, understand and learn from the Aboriginal American what motivated his musical and artistic impulses." Ballard's ideas and works at TU brought him to the attention of the Institute of American Indian Arts where he served as director of music and performing arts from 1962 to 1969. While at the school, Ballard developed a new music curriculum in which American Indian tribal music was brought into the classroom and was used to teach the primary elements of music by using tribal songs as examples. As a result, Ballard became the music program director for all the Bureau of Indian Affairs schools throughout the United States from 1969 to 1979. Simultaneously to all of this educational activity, Ballard was writing music at night and on the weekends.

Through a commission from the Harkness Ballet in New York, Ballard wrote music for the ballet *Koshare*, based on the ancient Hopi Creation Story. The ballet premiered in Barcelona, Spain in 1966 and subsequently toured the United States. He continued studying during the summers with the likes of Castelnuovo-Tedesco who taught Andre Previn and Henry Mancini. In 1967 Ballard wrote the ballet *The Four Moons*, inspired by the resilient spirit of the Cherokee, Choctaw, Shawnee, and Osage tribes, and composed in commemoration of Oklahoma's sixtieth anniversary of statehood. Louis's 1968 composition for woodwind quartet, *Ritmo Indio*, impressed German critics as being "ahead of its time," and his *Desert Trilogy* (1969) was nominated for a Pulitzer Prize. In 1969 his instrumental composition, *Mid-Winter of Fire*, was performed at the White House Conference on Children of Youth, and again at the University of Colorado Conference on American Indian Music in 1971. In 1972, he became the first professional musician to be awarded the Indian Achievement Award created by the Indian Council Fire. Nineteen seventy-two was also the year of one Ballard's most popular compositions, *Portrait of Will Rogers [Tribute to a Great American]*, a choral cantata with a libretto by Ballard and quotations by Will Rogers that has been used by many high school, university, and professional choirs. Also in 1972, Murbo Records released Ballard's *Oklahoma Indian Chants for the Classroom*, an album including instructions for singing and dancing to songs from the Quapaw, Shawnee, Kiowa, Creek-Seminole, Cherokee, and Choctaw. In 1974, Ballard composed what many consider one of his most important works for orchestra, *Incident at Wounded Knee* (1974). The piece memorialized the tragedies of the Oglala Sioux in 1890 at Wounded Knee, South Dakota, and resonated with the American Indian Movement's conflict with the U.S. government at Wounded Knee in 1973. Although Ballard hoped the music would remain associated with the events of Wounded Knee, he has also written he hoped it would "rise above all political emotions of this epoch." Although premiered in its entirety during a 1974 performance sponsored by the U.S. State Department in Warsaw, Poland, the state department would not sponsor Ballard on the tour because of the subject matter of *Incident at Wounded Knee*. Apparently, the state department feared the communists would use Ballard to embarrass the U.S. However, Gulf Oil Company paid for Ballard's trip to Poland, and the governor of New Mexico declared Louis Ballard Week because of his achievement. Knowledgeable observers recognized having an American Indian in front of an all-white orchestra said more about democracy than any words could ever express. *Incident at Wounded Knee* received a more recent performance in 1999 at Carnegie Hall as part of the American Composers Orchestra millennium themed concerts, where it received positive comments from listeners such as "most attractive piece in the program," and "Louis Ballard's piece effectively reflected its theme, but also went beyond the theme."

Throughout the 1970s Ballard wrote a number of choral pieces, instrumental pieces, and compositions for orchestra. He also continued his development of educational curriculum materials for classrooms, and served as consultant on the widely distributed film *Discovering American Indian Music*. This film depicts the social and ceremonial functions of American Indian music, and also includes Ballard with a percussion ensemble combining indigenous instruments of various tribes. His use of pine branches brushing across a kettledrum in the ensemble has since appeared in other composers' works. In 1981, Ballard composed *A City of Silver*, a concert fantasy for piano inspired by the composer's visit to Buenos Aires, Argentina, which was featured in 1984 at Carnegie Hall in New York City. Ballard wrote *A City of Fire* in 1983, a concert fantasy for piano inspired by Los Alamos, New Mexico, the birthplace of the atomic era, which was also performed at Carnegie Hall and in Taiwan, China. Ballard continued developing his city theme in 1984 with *City of Light*, inspired by Paris, France, and performed in Austria and in Germany at the Beethoven-House Chamber Music Hall in 1989. His series of fantasies based on American Indian oral history, such as *Fantasy Aborigine No. 5: Naniwaya*, based on the Choctaw creation mound, furthered the explorations of Ballard's primary style of fusing European and American Indian cultural resources. Exhibiting more of the range and diversity of Ballard's compositional skills is *Quetzalcoatl's Coattails* (1992), a solo for classical guitar, inspired by Aztec mythology and written to commemorate the sesquicentennial of the arrival in the Americas by Europeans (1492-1992). Other compositions from the 1990s include art songs for soprano and piano in the Lakota dialect inspired by a Lakota mother's expression of grief, a string quartet composition entitled *The Fire Moon* (1998), and praise songs for American Indian congregational singing that draw their texts from Chippewa, Ojibwa, and Lakota languages. Ballard began the new century with a song called "Thusnelda Louise" (2001) composed for voice and piano and inspired by a 19th century tombstone. In 2002, the composer's *Incident at Wounded Knee* was released with *Cacega Ayuwipi (Decorative Drums)*, and *Music for the Earth and Sky* on Wakan Records. Toward the end of his life, he was preparing some recordings of his orchestral compositions for commercial release; in 2002 Ballard was working on a string quartet, a piano sonata, a concerto, and an opera. Having met Louis Ballard

In October of 2002, The Cherokee Honor Society presented Ballard with the Cherokee Medal of Honor for his outstanding contributions to music. Along with the *Marquis* series of *Who's Who in America, Who's Who in Entertainment,* and *Who's Who in the World*, Louis Ballard's biography has been published in *Baker's Biographical Dictionary of 20th Century Musicians, Grove's Dictionary of American Music, The New Grove Dictionary of Music and Musicians, 2nd Edition,* and *Reference Encyclopedia of the American Indian*. In

Louis Ballard

2004, Ballard was inducted into the Oklahoma Music Hall of Fame. The complete catalogue of Louis Ballard's available instructional materials, compositions for performance, and existing recordings may be viewed on his website. Ballard died February 9, 2007 at his home in Santa Fe, New Mexico, after a lengthy battle with cancer. Having had the opportunity to spend time with Dr. Ballard around his camp at Quapaw powwow, as well as carrying on quite spirited and collegial correspondence with him until the end of his life, this writer feels extremely privileged to have known the man who will most likely be known as the most significant American Indian composer of the 20th century.

Louis Ballard: www.nswmp.com

Barbata, Johny
(b. April 1, 1945)

Drummer on a number of significant pop and rock songs, albums, and world tours in the 1960s, 70s, and 80s, Johny Barbata can be heard on such notable recordings as The Turtles' "Happy Together" (1967), and Crosby, Stills, Nash & Young's massively popular live album, *4 Way Street* (Atlantic, 1971), on which David Crosby says Barbata is "playing his a** off". Barbata moved with his wife, Angie, to Ada, Oklahoma in 1994, where he still made his home as of 2010. Barbata was born in Passaic, New Jersey, and endured parochial school for some of his childhood. Subsequently, he spent his high school years in San Louis Obispo, California, where he started playing in bands when he was sophomore, notably in The Sentinals, where he gained his first musician road experiences via their 1962 West Coast hit, "Latin'ia", included on *Cowabunga! The Surf Box* (Rhino, 1996). This started a career in which Barbata would play on twenty hit singles and more than a hundred albums. He drummed and toured with the Turtles during their peak of seven hit singles over a four years period (1966-70). Subsequently, he joined the supergroup, Crosby, Stills, Nash & Young, during which time Barbata toured and recorded eight albums in four years, including various solo projects and collaborations by the members of C, S, N & Y, such as Neil Young's "Ohio". Barbata's drum work on "Ohio", commemorating the tragic shootings at Kent State University in 1970, is part of the American pop culture aural consciousness of that period in history, forever the beat on documentary programs and films about that moment in time. His militaristic drum roll at the beginning of the song sets up the song's thematic tension in which his drumming is symbolic of the Ohio National Guard, whereas, the song's guitars represent the college students protesting the Vietnam War. He connects the chord and song section changes with unique rhythmic accents that are also evident on his other recordings, and are memorable for their well-timed subtlety.

Johny Barbata

Along with session recordings for over sixty albums for which did not receive credit on the album cover or notes, Barbata also recorded with Eric Clapton, **Leon Russell,** Dave

Mason, and Linda Ronstadt. As work slowed with C, S, N & Y due to their various side projects, Barbata jumped at the opportunity to join Jefferson Airplane in 1972 just as the group morphed into Jefferson Starship, and rocketed to mega-success on the pop hit fuel of "Ride the Tiger" (1974), the double-platinum album, *Red Octopus*, which provided the hit single "Miracles" (1975), and the 1976 *Spitfire* album, shooting "With Your Love" into the top twenty of the pop charts. During his tenure behind the drums for The Turtles, C, S, N & Y, and the Jefferson Airplane/Starship, Barbata played on the biggest hits by each of the three groups.

After an automobile accident that injured his neck in the early 1990s, he and his wife, Angie, a native Oklahoman, moved to her hometown of Ada where they have continued recording music, and playing out with his band, California, which features Angie on vocals. In 2007, Barbata authored an autobiography about his life in music, *Johny Barbata: The Legendary Life of a Rock Star Drummer* (DJ Blues Publishing), and is featured in the 2006 Bob Cianci book, Great Rock Drummers of the Sixties (Hal Leonard).

www.johnybarbata.com

Barber, Glenn
(b. February 2, 1935 – March 28, 2008)

A talented twang-rock, Western swing, and country guitarist, as well as a long favored proto-rocker and rockabilly artist of the mid-1950s, as well as a successful country music artist with 21 chart singles from 1964 to 1980, Martin Glenn Barber was born in Hollis, Oklahoma, a town of roughly 2,500 population located in extreme southwestern Oklahoma near the Texas border. While still living in Oklahoma, Glenn started on the guitar at about age six before the Barber family moved to oil industry town of Pasadena, Texas, just south of Houston, when he was eight-years-old. As he learned to play the banjo, mandolin, steel guitar, dobro, bass, and drums, he began winning numerous talent contests. After starting his own band in high school, made his first recording at age sixteen

Glenn Barber

("Ring Around the Moon") on the Stampede label owned by "Pappy" Dailey. Daily later founded Starday Records, one of the most successful independent labels in Texas, and became Glenn's manager for the next decade. Glenn recorded "Ice Water" for Starday in 1954, easily considered part of the rockabilly boogie tradition emanating from the American Southwest at the time of Elvis Presley's emergence on Sun Records in 1954. Also during this period, Glenn recorded the hilarious rockabilly gem "Atom Bomb", parlaying nuclear paranoia of the 1950s into a talking, joking, jamming novelty number. A funny man with an extroverted personality, Glenn was a popular disc jockey and featured performer on radio station KIKK in Houston from 1962 to 1968, a time in which he and his band, the Western Swingmasters, performed on weekdays and then gigged on the weekends throughout the south Texas region. Barber also was a spokesperson for Pearl beer at the time.

After leaving Houston, Glenn settled in Nashville, where he made his first recordings on the Sims ("How Can I Forget You") and Starday labels ("If Anyone Can Show Cause"/ "Stronger than Dirt," a double-sided hit) in 1964. He remained with Starday until 1966 and then recorded a couple of minor hits, including "Most Beautiful, Most Popular, Most Likely to Succeed" and "You Can't Get Here from There." In addition to recording, Glenn signed a contract with Acuff-Rose Publishing, and wrote songs recorded by Roy Orbison, Don Gibson, and Roy Acuff.

In 1968, Barber signed with Hickory Records and remained on that imprint through 1974, during which time he produced five recordings that made the Top 30, including "Don't Worry 'Bout the Mule Just Load the Wagon" (1968), "Kissed by the Rain, Warmed by the Sun" (1969), "She Cheats on Me" (1970) (also covered by Roy Orbison, Mickey Gilley, and Ferlin Husky), "I'm the Man on Susie's Mind" (1972), and "Unexpected Goodbye" (1972). *Greatest Hits of Hickory Records, Vol. 2*, released in 1993, features two of Glenn's songs, "Unexpected Goodbye" and "She Cheats on Me". He made his debut on the Grand Ole Opry in 1969, and appeared several times thereafter, however, he was never named as a member. One of Glenn's show business gimmicks, or that one thing that will get a performer noticed and remembered, was to have someone in the audience suggest a theme for a song and he would make one up on the spot to the delight of the audience. In 1973, Glenn charted the step-dad favorite, "Daddy Number 2".

After leaving Hickory in 1974, Glenn recorded for several independent labels over the next decade, such as Groovy, Century 21, MMI, Sunbird, Tudor, and Brylen. During this period he produced several low-level entries on the country charts, such as "Yes Ma'am, He Found Me in a Honky Tonk," "Poison Red Berries," "What's the Name of That Song," "Love Songs Just for You," and "Everybody Wants to Disco," clearly a 1970s lament over the rise of that popular dance music form. Barber's choice of songs often showed a wise sense of humor, such as 1976's non-charter, "It Took a Drunk to Drive God's Message Home" and 1977's blip on the top 100 country charts, "(You'd Better Be) One Hell of a Woman".

Although Barber never became a major country music star, he enjoyed the fruits of an artistically successful life. He built a recording studio in the 1970s with the help of his son, enjoyed success as a portrait and mural painter, having sold several of his canvases, and had limited success as screenwriter. After experiencing an early 21st century resurgence of interest in his 1950s rockabilly work, Glenn died March 28, 2008 in Gallatin, Tennessee.

Barnett, Bobby
(b. February 15, 1936)

Known for his country music albums on Oklahoma heritage and heroes, Bobby Glen Barnett was born in Cushing, Oklahoma, an oil field community of approximately 7,000 located about 25 miles southeast of Stillwater. Born to George and Berls Barnett, he had twelve siblings. Following graduation from Cushing High School in 1953, he moved to El Paso, Texas where he worked for the El Paso Natural Gas Company as an engineer. After seven years in El Paso, Bobby decided to enter the country music field. Recording for a local Muskogee, Oklahoma label, Razorback, he cut **Eddie Miller**'s "This Old Heart" in 1960, and it reached #24 on the country charts. Hoping to capitalize on its wider distribution and promotion network, the single was re-released by the Republic label, which also released Barnett's follow up single that failed to chart, "Please Come Home/It Makes No Difference," in 1961.

Bobby Barnett

In 1962, Barnett moved to Reprise Records, only the second country artist on that label. He released two singles, "Crazy Little Lover"/"Last of the Angels" and "Same Old Love"/"Temptation's Calling," neither of which were successful. He then switched to Sims Records in 1963 where he had a #6 hit, "She Looks Good to the Crowd," followed by a Top 50 song, "Worst of Luck" (1964), and a Top 30 number, "Mismatch" (1964). After three years, he returned to the charts with "Down, Down Came My World"/"Moaning the Blues" on the K-Ark label.

Bobby moved to Columbia Records in 1968, based primarily on his friendship with George Richey, then the new A & R director for the label. Bobby's first single release on Columbia was "Love Me, Love," a Top 15 hit, taken from his album, *Lyin', Lovin' & Leavin'*. It was followed with two more low-level chart singles, "Your Sweet Love Lifted Me" and "Drink Canada Dry." Another decade passed before Bobby scored any hits on the country charts. In 1978, Cin Kay Records released Barnett's "Burn Atlanta Down" to little fanfare, followed by one more minor chart single, "Born in Country Music (Raised on Dixieland)" (1981).

Bobby has recorded two albums related to Oklahoma: *Heroes, History and Heritage of Oklahoma, Vol. 1* (1974) and *Vol. 2* (1985), both on the Heritage label. Of particular note on Volume 1 is the appearance on drums by D.J. Fontana, long known for his primary rock and roll drumming with Elvis Presley. In 1997, Bear Family Records (a German company) released *American Heroes and Western Legends* that includes twenty-seven tracks all written or co-written by Barnett, featuring songs about historical Oklahomans, such as Captain David L. Payne, Pretty Boy Floyd, Pawnee Bill, Belle Starr, Bill Pickett, Will Rogers, Sequoyah, Tom Mix, Jim Thorpe, and **Woody Guthrie**.

Beckham, Bob
(b. July 8, 1927)

A child prodigy in the entertainment world and president of Combine Music, where he helped mold the careers of such country notables as Dolly Parton, Kris Kristofferson, Ray Stevens, Jerry Reed, and Tony Joe White, Robert Joseph Beckham has been in the music publishing business for over fifty years, and was born in Stratford, Oklahoma, a community of roughly 1,500 residents located southeast of Oklahoma City.

Beckham began a career in the entertainment field at age eight, when he joined a traveling medicine show. He moved to California and entered the motion picture arena as a child actor, appearing in such movies as *The Starmaker* (1939) and *Junior G-Men* (1940). At age thirteen, he returned to Oklahoma and attended high school, before joining the army at seventeen to fight in World War II. Following discharge as an army paratrooper, he became an electrician for a short period, and then worked in radio with the legendary Arthur Godfrey. He launched a country music career with two Top 40 hits as a singer,

"Just As Much As Ever" and "Crazy Arms". The latter remaining a karaoke favorite to this day.

After a short stint touring with Brenda Lee, Bob settled in 1959 in Nashville, where he joined the Shelby Singleton music-publishing firm. He then moved to Combine Music in 1964, and became its president in 1966. Through his diligence and business acumen, including the use of country songs in commercials, he built Combine into one of the major publishing companies in Nashville. Over a twenty-year period, he shaped the careers of Parton, Stevens, Reed, Kristofferson, and White, as well as others. Beckham produced six Mickey Newbury albums, including *Looks Like Rain* (1969), *Frisco Mabel Joy* (1971), *Heaven Help the Child* (1973), *Live at Montezuma Hall* (1973), *Mickey Newbury Collection* (1998), and *Lulled By the Moonlight* (2000).

Bob Beckham

Combine Music was sold in 1986 to SBK music publishers. After a four-year hiatus from the music publishing business, he was recruited to establish HoriPro Entertainment Group's Nashville office. A division of Taiyo Music, Japan's largest publisher, Beckham has operated HoriPro's Nashville office since 1990, bringing a number of important publishing concerns under its umbrella. Under his leadership, it would acquire an additional four catalogs, namely Merit Music Corp. (1991), Jerry Reed's Vector Music Corp. (1992), Double J Music Group (1999), and the publishing assets of the 1970s and 1980s successful arena rock group, REO Speedwagon (1992). Among artists under the aegis of HoriPro are Kiss, Marilyn Manson, **Reba McEntire**, Usher, George Strait, Elvis Presley, just a tip of a dizzying roster of songs. HoriPro Entertainment Group, Inc.'s catalog includes over 10,000 songs that are heard in every major genre. Diversifying its music business approach, HoriPro also provides record labels, film and television producers, and advertising agencies with quality hit songs that help sell music, enhance film and television projects, and tie in with consumer goods. In addition, HoriPro's catalog is in great demand by new technology services that sell ringtones, download or stream music, and for use as background music in video games.

www.horipro.com

Bee, Molly
(b. August 18, 1939 – d. February 7, 2009)

A childhood star on such television shows as the *Hometown Jamboree*, *Pinky Lee Show*, and *Tennessee Ernie Ford Show*, singer, dancer, and actress Molly Beachboard was born in Oklahoma City, and earned significant recognition as a yodeler. Her early years were spent singing on a farm near Beltbuckle, Tennessee, but her family moved to Tucson, Arizona, where she began her professional career at the age of ten. Her mother encouraged Molly to audition for singing cowboy Rex Allen at one of his concerts, and the blond-haired, blue-eyed youngster responded with her rendition of Hank Williams' "Lovesick Blues." Shortly thereafter, she debuted on Allen's radio show.

At age eleven, Molly's family moved to Hollywood, where she became a regular on the *Hometown Jamboree*, a Los Angeles television show, hosted by Cliffie Stone. She remained with the show throughout her teenage years, while also appearing as a cast member on the NBC *Pinky Lee Show* from 1954 to 1956. At the age of thirteen, Molly signed with Capitol Records and debuted with her single entitled "Tennessee Tango." Released in late 1952, the holiday novelty number, "I Saw Mommy Kissing Santa Claus" was her first hit. It was followed by a duet with Tennessee Ernie Ford, "Don't Start Courtin' in a Hot Rod Ford" in 1953. A year later, she joined the *Tennessee Ernie Ford* daytime television show, and began to develop a large following with her live shows drawing record-breaking crowds.

During the late 1950s, Molly's career began to blossom with such hit singles as "Young Romance," "Don't Look Back," and "5 Points of a Star." During the late 1960s, she joined **Roy Clark**'s *Swingin' Country* nationally televised show, and became a major performer on the Las Vegas showroom circuit.

During the 1960s, Molly also added acting to her career, debuting in the musical *The Boy Friend* in San Francisco. This was followed with *Finian's Rainbow* and *Paint Your Wagon* in which she starred with such notable actors as Alan Young and Buddy Ebsen. She also appeared in several films, including *Summer Love* (1958), *Going Steady* (1958), *Chartreuse Caboose* (1960), *The Young Swingers* (1963), and *Hillbillies in a Haunted House* (1967).

In 1965, Molly signed with MGM Records and cut two albums, *It's Great, It's Molly Bee* (1965) and *Swingin' Country* (1967). A string of singles during the 1960s included "Keep It a Secret"/ "Single Girl Again," "I'm Gonna Change Everything"/ "Together Again," "Losing You"/ "Miserable Me," "How's the World Treating You"/ "It Keeps Right on a Hurtin'," "A World I Can't Live In," "Almost Persuaded," "Heartbreak USA," "I Hate to See Me Go," "You Win Again," and "Fresh Out of Tryin'," the latter was her final MGM release. In 1966, she was nominated for Female Vocalist of the Year by the ACM.

Molly Bee

By the late 1960s, Molly's personal life began to take a turn for the worse as she struggled with drug addiction. After this difficult period in her life, she re-emerged in 1975 with a new album on Cliffie Stone's Granite label, *Good Golly Ms. Molly*, and released four singles on Granite, two of which garnered *Billboard* chart action, "She Kept on Talkin'," and "Right or Left at Oak Street," while the other two, "California Country," and "I Can't Live in the Dark Anymore," did not register with radio or the public. Her last album, *Sounds Fine to Me*, was released on the Accord label in 1982. Capitol

42 / Oklahoma Music Guide II

Nashville released *Christmas on the Range: Singing Cowboy Classics* in 1995, which featured Molly's best-known song, "I Saw Mommy Kissing Santa Claus." She continued performing throughout the 1990s at her restaurant, Molly Bee's, in Oceanside, California, and as a graduate of the Hollywood Professional School, she performed for their reunion in 2000. She died February 7, 2009, at a hospital in Oceanside, following complications and declining health from a stroke.

Been, Michael
(see entry for The Call)

Belew, Carl
(b. April 21, 1931 – d. October 31, 1990)

Best known for his honky tonk songwriting skills, including cathartic weepers such as "Am I That Easy to Forget?", "Lonely Street," "Stop the World (And Let Me Off)," and "What's He Doing in My World," Carl Robert Belew was born on a farm in Punkin' Hollow, near Salina, Oklahoma, a town boasting 1,000 people located in the northeastern part of the state. As a pastime on the farm, he began playing guitar, and left school at age fifteen to become a plumber, but decided on a music career.

In 1955, Marvin Rainwater set up a recording session for Carl with Four Star Records, for which Carl recorded rockabilly stylings popular in the 1950s, such as "I'm Gone", due to Elvis Presley's skyrocketing popularity. After making his way to California, Belew appeared on the Cliffie Stone Show and Town Hall Party in 1956. He then moved to the Louisiana Hayride in 1957. A year later, he co-wrote Johnnie and Jack's Top 10 single, "Stop the World (And Let Me Off)."

In 1958, Andy Williams scored a Top 5 hit on the pop charts with "Lonely Street," which would become Carl's signature song because of subsequent recordings by such artists as Patsy Cline, Rex Allen, Jr., Gene Vincent, and Elvis Presley. It received a BMI Award in 1959. A year later Carl's marriage dissolved, resulting in "Am I That Easy to Forget?" co-written by William A. McCall. It was recorded by Debbie Reynolds as a Top 40 pop hit, and later covered by such artists as Engelbert Humperdinck, Skeeter Davis, Gene Vincent, Don Gibson, Jim Reeves, and **Leon Russell**. Carl also recorded it in 1959 as his first Top 10 hit. Carl also received the BMI One-Million Performance Award for the song.

Carl Belew

In 1960, Carl released his eponymous album on the Decca label, which resulted in a Top 20 single, "Too Much to Lose." His first album with RCA in 1964, *Hello Out There*, produced a Top 10 hit, the title track of the LP, which surprisingly he did not write, as was the case with another one of his Top 20 hits, "Crystal Chandelier" (1965). His follow-up album with RCA in 1965 was *Am I That Easy to Forget?* He then reeled off a series of albums beginning with *Country Songs* (1967) and *Lonely Street* (1967) on the Vocalion label, *Twelve Shades of Belew* (1968) on RCA, and *When My Baby Sings His Song* (1972), a record of duets with Betty Jean Robinson, on Decca. The latter LP yielded another hit single, "All I Need Is You." His last charted single, "Welcome Back to My World," was released in 1974.

Additional songwriting successes included "What's He Doing in My World," a #1 hit for Eddy Arnold in 1965, the Jim Reeves hit in 1968, "That's When I See the Blues (In Your Pretty Brown Eyes)," and "Look at Us," which received the *Music City News* Award for Best Song of the Year in 1992. Other songs he penned included "Here's to the Girls," "Wind Me Up," "Working Like the Devil," "Even the Bad Times Are Good," "Don't Squeeze My Sharmon," and "Help Stamp Out Loneliness."

The list of artists who have recorded Carl's songs is impressive and includes such notables not previously mentioned as Waylon Jennings, Bobby Bare, The Browns, Bobby Darin, Everly Brothers, Emmylou Harris, Clarence "Frogman" Henry, **Wanda Jackson**, Dean Martin, George Jones, Willie Nelson, **Patti Page**, Carl Perkins, Esther Phillips, **B. J. Thomas**, Ernest Tubb, Conway Twitty, Tammy Wynette, and Faron Young.

Carl was inducted into the Nashville Songwriters Hall of Fame in 1976. At his induction ceremony, Carl stated: "I'm just thankful that the Lord has given me some talent, and I feel that I can still go on and write good songs . . . but it's cost me a fortune to learn how to read a contract. I think I could WRITE one now . . . and put a melody to it!" He died of cancer in 1990 at the age of fifty-nine.

Bell, Aaron
(b. April 24, 1922 – d. July 28, 2003)

As well as recording with Billie Holliday, Miles Davis, Count Basie, Coleman Hawkins, Ella Fitzgerald, and Sammy Davis, Jr., Muskogee-born Aaron Bell was Duke Ellington's bassist, and occasional arranger, from 1960 to 1962 on recordings and in concert. Bell came of age in the prime jazz era of Muskogee, a city now recognized for producing more nationally recognized jazz musicians than any town its size in the United States. Bell was surrounded by music via his mother who taught piano, and his father who played trombone. Occasionally, Bell's parents would perform together at their church, Central Baptist. Bell became interested in jazz by hearing a local band in Muskogee, comprised of musicians such as Ellis Ezell and **Jay McShann,** and T. Holder's legendary territory band, as well as traveling groups like The Carolina Cotton Pickers (out of Indiana), Ernie Fields, and the Sunset Royals. Like many other Oklahoma jazz artists (**Don Byas**, **Barney Kessel**, and **Howard McGhee**), Bell was extremely adept at playing different jazz styles in different eras. He played classical and marching pieces in the Manual Training High School Band in Muskogee. He learned the New Orleans style by playing regularly in New Orleans when he attended Xavier University. Bell playerd all popular and military music styles in the US Navy band corps, and after his discharge he played with one of the few remaining post-war hot-blowing territory bands in the Kansas City style (Andy Kirk, 1947). Subsequently, he transitioned easily into the smooth popular jazz of the 1950s (*Three Swinging Bells* (Herald, 1955), and joined in on progressive and modern jazz sessions of the early 1960s (*Duke Ellington & John Coltrane* (Impulse, 1962). A gifted improviser trusted implicitly by Duke Ellington to create appropriate bass lines on his own, Bell's bass work is fluid and understated, holding down the chord changes and rhythm of a tune while adding his own unique voicing to a

Aaron Bell

given piece's melody, a cornerstone of jazz interpretation.

In a 2000 interview with the author, Bell explained his musical background in Muskogee: "First in the family, I studied piano with my mother. All of us, there were nine in my family—seven boys and two girls, at some time or the other studied the piano, but everybody didn't stick with it. I had a sister who was really a great pianist. Both of them could play well, but my oldest sister, Launelia had the best reputation. She played classical music. Later, I tried to get her interested in jazz. We used to play duets together, you know, classical piano duets, and then when I took up the bass we used to play together. I didn't take up bass until my last year of high school. Before that I was playing tuba and trumpet, and the piano." Bell also made his first transcription for the Muskogee (Manual Training) High School Band, foreshadowing his scoring for Ellington, and further illustrating the level of musical direction students received under Manual Training band director, Boston Russell.

After high school Bell went of Xavier University in New Orleans where he was in both the jazz band and concert band. He started playing tuba and piano, before switching to bass and graduating with a B.A. in Music. While in the Navy, Bell played four years in the bands, for which he volunteered to avoid getting drafted by the Army as he had 1-A status, meaning he was fit to serve, and could be called any time. After the service, Bell went back to Muskogee. After hearing Andy Kirk's band was playing in Tulsa, Bell drove over to hear him. After the intermission was over, the bass player was late getting back so Bell asked to sit in, which landed Bell a job with Kirk for a year. After leaving Kirk for a group led by violinist Stuff Smith in Chicago, a job that only last one gig, Bell returned to Muskogee in 1948 and taught music and band at Manual Training where they won a statewide marching award that year. Before too long, opportunities for Bell's skills became too much for him to remain in Muskogee, and he relocated to New York where he played in dance bands and with Cab Calloway. At the same time, he began working on his Master's degree at New York University, culminating in a teaching certification which provided the financial foundation for the rest of his career while he was actively pursued as a session musician and live performer. Due to physical issues later in his life, Bell switched back to his first instrument, piano. He continued an active teaching, lecturing, and performing schedule until his death in 2003.

When asked in 2000, why he thought Muskogee was such as substantial producer of jazz musicians, Bell explained to this author, "I think because the territory was a spontaneous place. We were free to operate, even under the conditions, and experiment any way we wanted to. We weren't chained down by any set ways to play and perform. That way you get musicians who are individuals, and I think that's what makes them stand out, an individual's approach to the music. In a lot of places if you don't play a certain way, you are not accepted. In Oklahoma, if they liked it, you were accepted, it didn't matter is so-and-so did it, or if somebody else did it. You didn't have to match. In other words, a trumped player didn't have to sound like Louis Armstrong to be appreciated."

Recommended Listening
John Coltrane and Duke Ellington (Impulse, 1962)
Three Swinging Bells (Herald, 1955)

Recommended Reading
For more background on Bell's period with Duke Ellington, see Stanley Dance, *The World of Duke Ellington* (Scribner's, 1971).

Bell, Trent

"Music always held my attention better than anything else," studio engineer and longtime **Chainsaw Kittens** guitarist, Trent Bell, told Oklahoma Historical Society interviewers Larry O'Dell and Jeff Moore in a 2009 interview for the Oklahoma History Center's exhibit on rock music from the state of Oklahoma. Bell was a natural interview for that exhibit because he has been at the epicenter of Norman and Oklahoma City's music scene for his entire adult life. Born in Norman, Bell tells O'Dell and Moore he started playing music in middle school when his parents gave him a drum set, and he began forming bands to play at school talent shows. Around the same time, his grandfather gave him a Fender guitar and amp, and Bell began experimenting around before starting guitar lessons at about age fifteen. Instead of wanting to play fast like the majority of rock lead guitar players in the 1980s, Bell was more interested in learning how to put songs together. Consequently, his early bands played mostly originals because they did not feel they had the talent to be a cover band doing other people's songs. The most notable band of Bell's high school career is the Bensons, who opened for alternative music headliners such as The Meat Puppets in Norman. After high school, Bell played in the regionally successful Janis 18 for about a year, then left to join his friends in the Chainsaw Kittens, before the group recorded its first album, *Violent Religion* (Mammoth, 1990) at **Steve Ripley**'s Church Studio in Tulsa.

As a guitarist and co-songwriter, Bell remained with the Chainsaw Kittens for the duration of their recording career, co-composing about half the songs on every album after the debut, through the last release, *The All American* (Four Alarm, 2000). Of the most popular Kittens recordings, Bell's crunchy sweet electric guitars are loud and up front as a melodic hook ("Pop Heiress Dies"/"Dorothy's Last Fling"), leaving no doubt the band is a rock group, but also a pop act via catchy melodies, singer Tyson Meade's unmistakable vocal imprint and lyrics, and a driving, big-drum-kit sound, all seasoned by Oklahoma musical quirks such as sound effects, arrhythmic guitar lines, feedback, and melodic distortion. The Chainsaw Kittens have re-grouped on occasion for special performances of their one-of-a-kind Oklapop, such as at 2008's Norman Music Festival; however, Trent Bell's primary music industry work as of 2010 was being the owner, engineer and producer at Bell Labs, his studio in

Trent Bell

Norman, where he has recorded and produced albums for hundreds of bands and artists, including **The Flaming Lips**, **Watermelon Slim,** and **The Starlight Mints**.

Recommended Listening
Chainsaw Kittens. *Pop Heiress* (Atlantic/Mammoth, 1994)
Chainsaw Kittens. (Mercury/Scratchie, 1996)

Sources
Bell, Trent. 2008 interview with Jeff Moore and Larry O'Dell in Norman, OK for the Oklahoma Historical Society.

www.myspace.com/trentbell

Bennett, Wayne
(b. Dec. 13, 1933 – Nov. 28, 1992)

Born in the south central Oklahoma town of Sulphur, Wayne Bennett played electric lead guitar with many significant blues artists, to include Elmore James, John Lee Hooker, Jimmy Reed, Buddy Guy, and Bobby "Blue" Bland. Merging blues, country, jazz, and pop abilities on his hollow-bodied guitar, Bennett surfaced as a significant guitarist in Chicago with Otis Rush in the 1950s. No doubt as a result of his versatility, Bobby "Blue" Bland hired Bennett for touring and recording, notably on Bland's bigger hits of the period, "I Pity the Fool" (1961) and "Stormy Monday Blues" (1962). Bennett's playing on Bland's version of "Stormy Monday" is considered a defining blues statement via its understated yet powerful compliment to Bland's soulful vocals during the verses and choruses, merging blues licks with chords more often associated with jazz than blues.

Additionally, Bennett's solo in the song fills the bridge with subtle, fluid blues riffs and arpeggiated chords that drip with experience of a thousand-plus bandstands and recording sessions. His ability to play subtle blues compliments, melodic pop with a jazzy flair, and a stinging blues solo lead, made him an in-demand session musician for blues artists such as Junior "Mystery Train" Parker, Fats Domino, and Clarence Gatemouth Brown, as well as jazz artists like Dexter Gordon, Ramsey Lewis, and Cannonball Adderly. According to his *Wikipedia* online biography, Bennett formally studied guitar, harmony, and ear training, and played in various significant theatrical house bands, such as the Apollo (New York City), the Regal Theatre (Chicago), the Howard (Washington D.C.), and the Uptown Theatre (Philadelphia). Bennett recorded one solo album, from which he had one minor hit, the Ruby Andrews classic, "Casanova (Your Playing Days Are Over)" released in 1967 on the Giant label (GT-703). The National Blues Foundation named Bennett Blues Guitarist of the Year in 1981, and he was inducted into the Oklahoma Blues Hall of Fame in Rentiesville, OK, in 2008.

Wayne Bennett

Recommended Listening

While some viewers/listener will want to avoid some "off-color" language Bennett uses to introduce his version of the O'Jay's "She Used To Be My Girl" in a 1979 video performance recorded in Chicago, the video document (available on youtube.com as of 2010) demonstrates the guitarist's considerable skills that rest at the crossroads of jazz and blues, first popularized by **Charlie Christian** with Benny Goodman in the big band era, but carried forward with riveting conviction by Bennett throughout his playing career.

Source

Larkin, Colin. *The Virgin Encyclopedia of the Blues*. (London: Muze UK, 1998).

Berline, Byron

(b. July 6, 1944)

A former three time national fiddle champion, solo artist, film and television music composer, session musician, and actor, Byron Berline has recorded with some of the biggest names in country, pop, and rock music. His staggering list of recording session credits includes the Rolling Stones, The Byrds, The Eagles, Elton John, Bob Dylan, Willie Nelson, and **John Denver**, among several others. Without a doubt, Byron Berline is the best known Anglo fiddler from Oklahoma, although he was born near Caldwell, Kansas, just north of the Oklahoma-Kansas border; however, he was raised on a farm in Oklahoma. His father, Lue, who was an old-time fiddler, encouraging Byron to begin playing the fiddle at age five, and before too long he was accompanying older musicians. After high school graduation, Byron was awarded a football scholarship to the University of Oklahoma, and planned to coach with his physical education degree. While attending the University of Oklahoma, he formed his first band, Cleveland County Ramblers, which performed at campus functions, and also performed on an Oklahoma City television program sponsored by Garrett Household Furniture on which he became acquainted with and performed for **Wiley** (Walker) **and Gene** (Sullivan), who wrote "Live and Let Live" and "When My Blue Moon Turns to Gold Again." In 1963, he was auditioned by the Dillards, who were in concert on campus, and they invited him to play a number. A year later, he joined the Dillards on their *Pickin' and Fiddlin'* album, and won the National Old-Time Fiddling Championship in Missoula, Montana, a feat he would repeat two more times.

Byron Berline

In 1965, Berline performed at the Newport Folk Festival, where he met Bill Monroe, who asked him to join the Blue Grass Boys when he completed his degree. After graduating from OU in 1967, Byron decided to fulfill Monroe's request, and his first performance with the band was on the Grand Ole Opry, as well as recording three songs with Monroe. After six months with the Blue Grass Boys, Byron was drafted into the U.S. Army and assigned to the special services unit. Stationed at Fort Polk, Louisiana, Byron performed with a bluegrass band at the officers' club for two years.

Following his discharge, Berline joined the Dillards for a short time, and then followed Doug Dillard when he teamed up with Gene Clark to form Dillard and Clark (1969-70). During this time, he played sessions for several other artists, including the Flying Burrito Brothers' debut album, *The Gilded Palace of Sin*. Dillard and Clark disbanded in 1970, and Byron again followed Doug Dillard to the Dillard Expedition (1970-71). In 1970, Berline scored the ABC television movie, *Run Simon Run*. During the 1970s, Byron scored several films, including *Stay Hungry* (his first in 1975), *Bound for Glory* (story of **Woody Guthrie**), *White Lightning*, *The Longest Yard*, *Pat Garrett and Billy the Kid* (featured Bob Dylan), and *Stay Hungry* (Arnold Schwarzenegger's first film). When legendary Henry Mancini scored the film, *Sometimes a Great Notion*, he asked Berline to provide the fiddle music. Byron also scored the music for *Northern Exposure*, the 1990s hit television show.

After the break-up of the Dillard Expedition, Byron, bassist Roger Bush, and banjoist Billy Ray Latham formed The Country Gazette in 1971, which later included Oklahoman Alan Munde. The Gazette recorded several albums, including their debut release, *A Traitor in Our Midst* (UA, 1972) and *Don't Give Up Your Day Job* (UA, 1973), and *Bluegrass Special* (1973) on the Ariola label, a European recording company.

Byron left The Gazette in 1975 for a permanent move to Los Angeles to concentrate on songwriting, session work, and scoring films. Later that year, he organized Sundance, a group that included John Hickman, Dan Crary, Jack Skinner, Allen Wald, and Skip Conover, and later **Vince Gill** and Mark Cohen. The band remained together until 1985, releasing one album, *Byron Berline and Sundance*, cut in 1976. The next year, Bryon recorded the album, *Dad's Favorites* (Rounder, 1977), a tribute to his father, Lue. It included such well-known instrumentalists as Doug Dillard, Alan Munde, Vince Gill, Dan Crary, John Hartford, and Byron's wife, Bette on piano. Berline followed up *Dad's Favorites* with *Outrageous* (Flying Fish, 1981).

From 1978 to 1990, Byron led a trio consisting of himself, Crary, and Hickman. The threesome toured Japan and recorded three albums for Sugar Hill. Concurrently, Berline formed the L.A. Fiddle Band (1979-93) comprised of three fiddles, dobro, banjo, guitar, and bass. This group released one album on the Sugar Hill label, *Byron Berline & The L.A. Fiddle Band* (1980). After adding bassist Steven Spurgin, Berline, Crary, and Hickman, changed their name to simply BCH (first initials of their last names) in 1988, and in 1990 when they added mandolinist-guitarist John Moore, the band renamed itself California (1990-96).

In 1995, Byron released the critically acclaimed, two-time Grammy nominated album, *Fiddle & A Song* (Sugar Hill), which included Vince Gill singing the Bill Monroe classic, "My Rose of Old Kentucky," and a reunification of Bill Monroe and Earl Scruggs on "Sally Goodin'" with backup from their sons, James Monroe and Randy Scruggs.

After twenty-six years in California, Byron and his wife, Bette, returned to Oklahoma in 1996 and immediately launched three new projects: the Byron Berline Band with old friend John Hickman on banjo; the Double Stop Fiddle Shop and Music Hall in historic Guthrie, Oklahoma; and the First International Bluegrass Festival, also held in Guthrie the first weekend of October each year since 1997. Recent albums include *Live at the Music Hall* (1997), *One-Eyed Jack* (1999), and *Tribute to Gene Clark and Gram Parsons* by his own label, Double Stop Music. By 2003, the Byron Berline Band consisted of banjoist Hickman, bassist Richard Sharpe, drummer Steve Short, and guitarist Brad Benge who replaced the previous guitarist, Jim Fish. The group plays about thirty to forty shows a year, having performed in California, Nashville, and on the East Coast in 2002 and 2003.

Byron has not only toured the United States, but also Europe, China, Japan, Australia, North Africa, and the South Pacific. As a result, he was named an Oklahoma Ambassador of Good Will since his return to the state. Byron was inducted into the Oklahoma Music Hall of Fame in 1999, and has released a steady stream of albums independently through his Double Stop Fiddle Shop as CDs or downloadable mp3s, notably *My Oklahoma* (2008). According to Berline's website, "[*My Oklahoma*] is based on the concept of recording a collection of styles that would display the diverse personalities of the Byron Berline Band members. We have something for everyone, from old-timey to cowboy to contemporary, all with a bluegrass feel."

www.doublestop.com

Bishop, Elvin
(b. October 21, 1942)

As the lead guitarist in the revolutionary earliest incarnation of The Butterfield Blues Band in 1961, a Top 10 hit to his credit in 1976, and five decades of playing and recording his own saucy mix of rowdy, good-time blues, Elvin Bishop helped usher in the resurgence of American interest in blues masters in the 1960s with his personal style of soulful lead guitar. Known for the sense of humor he expresses through his music, his slide guitar work, and fusing several American roots forms in his music, as of 2003 Bishop remains one of America's great blues guitarists, and continues to embody the sound of one who made a conscious effort to learn from the masters of the genre when he had the opportunity.

Elvin's parents, Elvin Bishop, Sr. and Mylda (Kleege) Bishop, were farmers from Iowa and Nebraska. Elvin's father was in the service and stationed in Glendale, California where Bishop was born. After Elvin Sr.'s service time, the Bishops moved back to Iowa where they continued to farm. In 1952, during an Oklahoma drought, Elvin Sr. brought down a load of hay to Oklahoma and took the opportunity to apply at Douglas Aviation in Tulsa where he was hired. Subsequently, at ten-years-old, Elvin moved with his family to Tulsa where he attended John Ross Grade School, Bell Jr. High, and Will Rogers High School.

As a child, he would hear **Johnnie Lee Wills and His Boys** on the radio in the morning as he ate his cereal. "The country music influence is free in Oklahoma," Elvin remembered in a 2002 interview.

Since Tulsa was still very segregated in the 1950s, Elvin first became exposed to the blues by listening to Lightnin' Hopkins, John Lee Hooker, and Howlin' Wolf on radio stations from Nashville (WLAC), Shreveport, and Mexico. He tried playing guitar for a while but it hurt his fingers so he gave up until he saw all the girls hanging around the guitar players

Elvin Bishop, 2010

from another local band. About that time, in 1959 Elvin Bishop rode a National Merit Scholarship from Will Rogers High to the University of Chicago to be closer to the blues mecca of the South Side of Chicago where blues men like Muddy Waters, Little Walter, and Howlin' Wolf were playing regularly in clubs. "The first thing I did when I got there," Elvin remembers, "was to make friends with the black dudes working in the cafeteria. Within fifteen minutes I was into the blues scene."

Acquaintances included Little Smokey Smothers and who taught Bishop a lot about playing the guitar, as did Sammy Lawhorn, Otis Rush, and Luther Tucker, during hours and hours of lessons in the blues as an art form and as an occupation. Elvin also served an apprenticeship as a sideman with Chicago legends Magic Sam and Junior Wells, and, became an accomplished player. He remembers two of his favorite blues men of the time were artists he had not seen from Oklahoma, **Flash Terry** and **Lowell Fulson**, whose records he collected in Chicago.

In 1960, when Bishop met fellow U of C student Paul Butterfield, a harmonica player and singer who had grown up in Chicago and gotten his start from Smothers as well, the two began frequenting South Side blues clubs where they would jam with Buddy Guy and Otis Rush, or pay two dollars to watch Howlin' Wolf, or Muddy Waters. Soon, they formed a duo and started playing college parties as The Buttercups. Upon the invitation to play a North Side Chicago club, Bishop and Butterfield hired the rhythm section from Howlin' Wolf's group, Sam Lay and Jerome Arnold, and became what was more than likely Chicago's only integrated blues group at the time, The Butterfield Blues Band. The group's popularity among Chicago's white audiences led to gigs at colleges outside of the Chicago area and the music took off.

In 1963, the group added another significant lead guitarist, Michael Bloomfield, as well as organist Mark Naftalin, and the hard-driving, attitude-laden band subsequently popularized the electric Chicago blues sound in America that was already being embraced by British blues enthusiasts John Mayall and the Rolling Stones; however, while the Brits were learning their licks from records, Elvin and company were emerging from the very wellspring of the form. The first recordings made by the group in 1964 became the album *The Paul Butterfield Blues Band* (1965), and were reissued in 1997 as a double CD package with songs not released on the original album. Popular music historians also note the group fueled their sound with the extended jams of the Bishop/Bloomfield twin-guitar attack, such as on 1966's thirteen-plus minute "East West" based on jazz and East Indian raga concepts. These kinds of jams would be the standard by which other late 1960s rock bands, such as the Grateful Dead and the Allman Brothers, based their own multi-lead instrumental techniques.

The group also played a minor part in the shifting tastes of American music listeners. After doing their own set at the 1965 Newport Folk Festival, the group backed Bob Dylan for his controversial electric folk set which sounded the death knell of the acoustic folk resurgence of the late 1950s and early 1960s. Contrary to several published reports, however, Elvin did not play during the set since he was backstage sharing a half pint with Mance Lipscomb and Mississippi John Hurt. Also during this period Bishop adopted the pseudonym of Pigboy Crabshaw to showcase his country material and the band took that name for its 1967 release, *The Resurrection of Pigboy Crabshaw,* which featured a horn section and only Bishop on lead guitar when Bloomfield left to form Electric Flag.

After the group's 1968 album, *In My Own Dream*, Elvin left for good and traveled to New York where he jammed with Jimi Hendrix, whom he called "quiet and humble," and Eric Clapton. Heading to the West coast in 1968, his solid reputation led to releasing three albums on Fillmore Records, a subsidiary of Epic, and two on One Way to include 1975's *Juke Joint Jump*. The latter enjoyed some moderate radio success with "Travelin' Shoes," peaking at #61 on the pop chart, and "Sure Feels Good," registering modestly at #83. Signed by Capricorn Records in 1975 at the urging of Dickey Betts, guitarist for the Allman Brothers who were also on Capricorn, Elvin reevaluated his strategy for commercial success. Lacking the mainstream appeal of his guitar work, Elvin's vocals seemed to be holding back the records, which prompted him to enlist pre-Jefferson Starship singer Mickey Thomas for the vocals to "Fooled Around and Fell in Love," a massive radio hit that landed at #3 on the pop chart and propelled the single's album, *Struttin My Stuff*, to number #68 on the album chart. Bishop's next album, *Hometown Boy Makes* Good (1976), failed to capitalize on his previous hit, even with another vocal by Thomas, however, and prompted critics to wonder if Bishop could ever capture his infectious live spirit on vinyl. Elvin confronted this critique by releasing a 1977 live album, *Raisin' Hell,* which bettered his earlier success on the album charts by reaching #38.

By 1978 Bishop pulled out all the stops and mixed nearly every one of his influences – gospel, R & B, blues, country, funk, and rock – on his final studio album for Capricorn, *Hog Heaven*, the cover art for which shows Elvin pouring beer into a hog's mouth. After a seven-year recording drought, Alligator Records, one of America's most prominent contemporary blues labels, signed Elvin where he has been releasing critically acclaimed recordings and supporting them through touring ever since. His 1991 release, *Don't Let the Bossman Get You Down*, earned a four star review in *Rolling Stone*, and landed him on *Late Night with David Letterman*. In 1992, he toured the U.S. as part of Alligator Records 20th anniversary, and performs on the Grammy-nominated album recorded during that tour. Bishop was also interviewed for the documentary *Pride and Joy: The Story of Alligator Records*.

In 1998, the Oklahoma Jazz Hall of Fame's inducted Bishop in its blues category. In 2000, Bishop joined his former mentor Little Smokey Smothers for three sold out shows in San Francisco which were culled for the album *That's My Partner*, and a best of collection was released as part of Mercury Records' 20th Century Master series.

In a 2003 interview with this author, Bishop said he was writing songs about some "difficult subjects", a reference to his daughter's murder in 2000, and which resulted in *Getting' My Groove Back* (Blind Pig, 2005). The album opens with the aptly stressed out tune, "What the Hell Is Goin' On", and features some blistering leads that are certainly Bishop wailing hard for his daughter, as well as indicting a society in which such an event could happen, singing "Lock your doors up tight. Don't let your children out of your sight." He also gets in some searing catharsis with "Come On Blues", the lyrics of which plead with the blues to make it all better, and includes a *hard* blues guitar workout as tough, ragged, emotion-filled and intense as any ever recorded by Bishop. In the 2005 Blind Pig Records press release for the album, Bishop says of "Come On Blues", "I only did that song once in my life and that's all I'm ever going to do it. I thought about doing it over – maybe the singing could have been better – but it's real. So I just left it." The album is filled with gritty and echo-laden guitar blues born out of Bishop's sorrow, but also some of the up tempo party numbers for which he is well-known. About this dualistic tone of the album, Elvin explains, "Most of my stuff is for entertainment, but that song ["Come On Blues"] and 'What the Hell Is Goin' were written for me, more for therapy than anything." Bishop continued the blues theme, really hitting a powerful stride on his subsequent album, the 2008 GRAMMY-nominated CD, *The Blues Rolls On* (Delta Groove). The collection features a revisit to his 1975 period with a new version of "Struttin' My Stuff", several guest stars (Derek Trucks, George Thorogood, and B.B. King), and a tough, distorted guitar blues boogie on "Oklahoma" where Elvin sings about leaving Oklahoma for San Francisco in the 1960s heyday of Haight-Ashbury. Also re-visiting his youth on the CD, Bishop includes a cover of a Jimmy Reed instrumental "Honest I Do," the first blues song a young Bishop remembers hearing on his transistor radio as a child in Tulsa. "Growing up in Oklahoma," Elvin told this author, "gives you a soulful background for whatever you want to do."

In 2010, Delta Groove released another Bishop album, *Red Dog Speaks,* a reference to Bishop's 1959 Gibson ES -345 guitar, which he plays with reckless abandon on the CD, coaxing bittersweet and celebratory tones out of the cherry-red vintage instrument. *Red Dog Speaks* features story/song-telling ("Red Dog Speaks", "Blues Cruise", and "Clean Livin'"), instrumental jamming ("Barbecue Boogie"), a 1950s-inspired "Doo-Wop Medley", plenty of attitude-laden, peppy blues tunes ("Get Your Hand Out of My Pocket" and "Neighbor Neighbor"), and a slide guitar instrumental "His Eye Is On the Sparrow". Bishop planned a 2010 tour to support the album. He has never really stopped performing throughout the United States at festivals, club dates, and concerts. However, of the musician's road life he says, "The romance of travel has worn off. More than anything, I just like to go out on the weekends and play like hell." Elvin lives with his wife, Cara, in the San Francisco Bay area where he is an avid gardener, canning jars of tomatoes, green beans, fruit, corn, garlic, and a variety of Japanese vegetables. In 2011, Bishop released a live album, *The Raisin' Hell Review*, containing his best known songs and guitar stylings. In 2013, his website indicated a steady touring schedule through fall, 2013.

www.deltagrooveproductions.com

Blackwell, Chuck

(b. August 19, 1940)

Born in Oklahoma City, and then quickly relocating to Tulsa when he was about 1-year-old, Charles E. "Chuck" Blackwell is one of a few top-notch drummers who emerged from the Tulsa environment to national and international recognition among his peers as fame. Focusing more on steady groove keeping instead of a lot of "butterflying around" the drum kit, Blackwell has recorded with Taj Mahal, Leon Russell, Freddie King, Joe Cocker, and Jackie DeShannon, to name a few, and is a primary example of Tulsa's lengthy list of musicians who provided subtle, yet rock solid, backing for numerous significant popular music recordings from the late 1950s to the present. He credits hearing Bill Doggett's 1956 smash R&B/pop hit, "Honky Tonk", for his initial musical and drumming inspiration, and was the first place he ever heard the shuffle rhythm that has become so synonymous with what is called the **Tulsa Sound**, a broad term that has different meanings depending on the era and generation of musicians to which one is referring. Listening to Doggett's "Honky Tonk", one can hear the understated and easy-going shuffle at which Blackwell has always been so adept. At about age 16, Chuck began playing drums with bands in local beer bars and roadhouses, carrying a letter from his father that would permit him play on the bandstand. During this period, he played with other young Tulsa musicians, such as **David Gates**, **Leon Russell** and others discussed in this guide's Tulsa Sound entry, and also toured in a backup group for Jerry Lee Lewis. Once Chuck realized he could improve his scrawny, monthly paper route pay to six, seven, or eight dollars as night a musician, he was convinced he had found his calling.

After graduating Tulsa Central High School, he left for California in 1958, and after a few early professional trials, he again connected with David Gates and Leon Russell in Los Angeles where he started working as a session musician with them backing various artists, such as Jackie DeShannon, and eventually landed a regular gig in the house band of the musically focused ABC television show, *Shindig!* Also in the house band, the Shin-diggers, later the Shindogs, from 1964 to 1966 were a young Glen Campbell, as well as Billy Preston, James Burton, Delaney Bramlett, and **Leon Russell**. As one of L.A.'s recognized session drummers, a series of gigs provided Blackwell with all the work could handle, some of which landed him square in the middle of rock music's elite core of musicians and bands of the late 1960s and 1970s. The connection to Leon Russell proved to be a lengthy one professionally and as comrades, as Russell called on Blackwell over and over for a variety of recordings over the years. Blackwell played with Taj Majal solidly for about four years, contributing drums to Taj Mahal's early albums with fellow Oklahomans **Jesse Ed Davis** (guitar) and **Gary Gilmore** (bass), to include *Taj Mahal* and *The Natch'l Blues* in 1968, and *Giant Step* (1969). He also recorded multiple times with his old buddy Leon Russell on *Leon Russell and the Shelter People* (1971), and Russell's highest charting album, *Carney* (1972), and several other sessions over which Leon had full or semi-control, such and British vocalist Joe Cocker's star-laden *Mad Dogs and Englishmen* album of 1970, co-produced by Russell. Also in the 1970s, Blackwell laid down some tough grooves to accompany American blues man, Freddie King, on three of King's early 1970s albums (*Getting Ready*, 1971; *Texas Cannonball*, 1972; *Woman Across the River*, 1973). Check out King's "Goin Down" for a perfect aural illustration of Blackwell's "groove-ability". Chuck is also present on drums behind Taj Mahal on the Rolling Stones' 1968 *Rock and Roll Circus* film, re-issued in 2004 on DVD.

Around 1970, Blackwell returned his permanent base of operations to Tulsa, where he and his wife formed an architectural design and engineering firm specializing in entry ways to homes, offices, and buildings of all types. As of 2010, he gigged regularly with a local band, Pipe Full of Blues, and continued writing, recording, and playing, occasionally writing lyrics for new material by long-time friend, **Walt Richmond,** known for his own work with Eric Clapton, **J.J. Cale**, and The **Tractors**). Reflecting on his session work resulting in recordings that he considers his personal favorites, Chuck said in a July, 2010 telephone interview, "The early stuff with Taj, 'She Caught the Katy and Left Me a Mule to Ride' and 'Diving Duck Blues'; and the recordings with Leon [Russell]." He added, with not a little weariness, "There are so many stories."

Chuck Blackwell plays percussion with Junior Markham in Tulsa, 2010.

Blane, Ralph

(b. July 26, 1914 – d. November 13, 1995)

Co-composer of "Meet Me in St. Louis," "Have Yourself a Merry Little Christmas," and "The Trolley Song," singer, arranger, and lyricist Ralph Blane was born Ralph Uriah Hunsecker on a farm near Broken Arrow, a suburb of Tulsa, to Tracy Mark and Florence Hazel Wilborn Hunsecker. The Hunseckers also had a second son, Tracy Mark, born in 1921. Ralph's father was a businessman, owning three dry goods stores in Broken Arrow and Coweta. Ralph attended elementary school in Broken Arrow and graduated from Central High School in Tulsa. While at Central, he was active as a singer and dancer, often participating in high school talent shows. At age seventeen, Ralph and his parents attended a Broadway show in New York, and, following that visit, he realized that music would be his calling.

After studying at Northwestern University in Evanston, Illinois, Ralph moved to New York City, where he studied music under Estell Liebling. He made his Broadway stage debut as a vocalist in *New Faces* in 1936, followed in 1937 by another Broadway musical, *Hooray for What?* Responsible for auditions for the latter production was actress Kay Thompson, star of the show, assisted by pianist Hugh Martin, who suggested Blane for a part because of his rich strong voice. In 1941, Blane teamed with Martin to organize a vocal quartet known as The Martins, who performed in New York City nightclubs and made a guest appearance on *The Fred Allen Show* on radio. Sometime while in New York, Ralph began using Blane because his original last name did not fit theater marquees.

In the 1930s, Blane was co-vocal arranger for such Broadway musicals as *Pal Joey*, *DuBarry Was a Lady*, *Cabin in the Sky*, *Too Many Girls*, *Louisiana Purchase*, *Very Warm for May*, and *Stars in Your Eyes*. During the 1940s, the Blane and Martin team contributed songs for the 1941 Broadway hit, *Best Foot Forward* (326 performances), produced and directed by George Abbott and choreographed by Gene Kelly. Blane and Martin helped MGM convert it into the 1943 Vincinte Minnelli movie musical of the same title, starring Lucille Ball. The most celebrated songs from the musical were "Ev'ry Time" and "Buckle Down, Winsocki," a college fight song for the fictitious Winsocki University ("buckle down, Winsocki, buckle down/you can win Winscocki, if you knuckle down"). It was later recorded by such artists as Glenn Miller, Benny Goodman, and Liza Minnelli. Henry Wallace, third party candidate for President in 1948, used the tune for his campaign song, "We Can Win With Wallace," and the National Safety Council in the 1960s and 1970s used the melody for its "Buckle Up for Safety" commercial. While in Hollywood, the Blane-Martin partnership contributed "The Joint is Really Jumpin' (In Carnegie Hall)" for the movie, *Thousands Cheer* in 1943, and reunited in 1954 to score the film *Anthea*, followed by *The Girl Rush* in 1955.

During this era, the Blane-Martin duo wrote musical scores for several other films,

Hugh W. Foley / 55

including *Best Foot Forward* (1943), *Meet Me in St. Louis* (1944) which was their most successful soundtrack, *One Sunday Afternoon* (1948), *My Dream Is Yours* (1949), *My Blue Heaven* (1950), *The French Line* (1954), *The Girl Most Likely* (1957). Star of *Meet Me in St. Louis*, Judy Garland sang several of their best-known compositions, such as "Have Yourself a Merry Little Christmas," "The Boy Next Door," and "The Trolley Song" ("clang, clang, clang went the trolley/ding, ding, ding went the bell"). The latter was nominated for an Academy Award for Best Song in 1945. "Have Yourself a Merry Little Christmas" became a holiday favorite, especially after Perry Como and Tony Bennett's recordings in the late 1960s. It later appeared on seasonal albums by such luminaries as Andy Williams, Barbara Streisand, James Taylor, Peabo Bryson, The Jackson 5, and **Garth Brooks**. "Pass That Piece Pipe," a collaboration of Blane, Martin, and Roger Edens, was written as a duet for Gene Kelly and Fred Astaire in the MGM film, *Ziegfield Follies*, but it never made it into the movie. It did resurface in the 1947 movie *Good News*, starring June Allyson and Peter Lawford, and was nominated for an Oscar as Best Song of the Year in 1948. On October 5, 1947, Blane married Emajo Jo Stage at his brother's home in Broken Arrow, and their marriage resulted in one son, George.

Returning to Broadway in the 1950s, Blane wrote the music and lyrics for the musical, *Three Wishes for Jamie* (1952), starring John Raitt. He and Martin wrote the score for *Sugar Babies*, another Broadway hit in 1979, starring Mickey Rooney, and the team composed several new songs for a stage adaptation of *Meet Me in St. Louis* in 1960, adding more new material for a 1989 revival on Broadway. It was nominated for four Tony Awards, including Best Adapted Score for a Musical.

Additional highlights from the Blane-Martin catalog include "Shady Lady Bird," "Everytime," "The Three B's," "That's How I Love the Blues," "What Do You Think I Am," "Love" (recorded by native Oklahoman **Chet Baker** in 1954), "Just a Little Joint With a Jukebox," "Brazilian Boogie," "Connecticut (Is the Place For Me)," "Venezia," "I Don't Know What I Want," and "You Are For Loving." Blane also collaborated with other composers including Harry Warren ("The Stanley Steamer," Someone Like You," and "My Dream Is Yours") and Harold Arlen ("My Blue Heaven"). He also wrote "Duty, Honor, Country," the musical background for General Douglas MacArthur's famous speech to the Corps of Cadets at the U.S. Military Academy at West Point in 1962. His lone television score was for *Quillow and the Giant*.

During the early 1990s, Blane retired to his native Broken Arrow, where he died November 13, 1995. He is credited with more than 500 songs in the ASCAP directory, and was inducted into the Songwriters Hall of Fame in 1983 by the National Academy of Popular Music. He also received the Richard Rodgers Award, a prestigious honor given by the Richard and Dorothy Rodgers Foundation and ASCAP to recognize the achievements of lyricists and composers historically associated with American music.

In 2001 The Ralph Sharon Quartet recorded *The Ralph Blane Songbook*, a fifteen-track tribute to Blane, on the DRG label. The CD included "Buckle Down, Winsocki," " The Trolley Song," and "Have Yourself a Merry Little Christmas," but also featured some of Blane's lesser known songs, such as "An Occasional Man," "At Last We're Alone," and "I Love a New Yorker." In 2003, Rhino Records released the Original Motion Picture Soundtrack of *Best Foot Forward,* which also included four previously unissued Martin and Songs written for *Abbot and Costello in Hollywood* (1945). In 2011, The Oklahoma Music Hall of Fame inducted Blane for his outstanding accomplishments as a songwriter.

Boggs, Noel

(b. November 14, 1917 – d. August 31, 1974)

Considered one of the finest steel guitarists in the history of the instrument, an inductee into the Steel Guitar Hall of Fame, Oklahoma City-born Noel Boggs made more than 2,000 recordings as a session musician. Boggs' steel guitar helped give Western swing its bounce, twang, and happy feeling, a necessary antidote for the 1930s Depression era Oklahoma environment in which he came of age. Of course, the steel guitar can also dually represent the weepy melancholy of lost love, lost job, or just general feelings of hopelessness, but also the breezy open-range cowboy life from which the steel guitar descends in the first place, as an instrument of working cowboys in Hawaii who brought the instrument back to the mainland. Boggs learned to play the steel guitar during junior high after taking a twelve-lesson course in the fundamentals of music at twenty-five cents per lesson while in junior high school in the early 1930s. While in high school, he worked for three radio stations in Oklahoma City (WKY, KOMA, and KEXR). His first steel guitar was a Rickenbacker. While in Oklahoma City, Noel befriended the legendary jazz guitarist **Charlie Christian**, who worked on Northeast Second Street ("Deep Deuce"). Noel learned many of Christian's guitar solos and techniques, a process that would ultimately enhance Boggs' reputation as a fluid player who could take any melody, improvise on it, and swing out, always keeping the Western sound because of the steel guitar's identifiable twang sound imprint.

In 1936, Noel joined Hank Penny's Radio Cowboys and the band toured the southern and eastern regions of the U.S., as well as recording with the group on Vocalion in 1939. He gained further experience working as a staff musician on radio stations WWL in New Orleans and WAPI and WBRC in Birmingham before returning to Oklahoma City in 1937. Working with **Wiley and Gene** on both their recordings and at radio station WKY for the next four years, Noel launched his own band in 1941 with the encouragement of **Leon McAuliffe**, steel guitarist with **Bob Wills** and the Texas Playboys. After working at the Rainbow Room in Oklahoma City for the next three years with such musicians as **Jimmy Wakely**, Noel joined the Texas Playboys as steel guitarist when McAuliffe left in 1944 to form his own band, the Cimarron Boys. While with the Playboys, he met guitarists Jimmy Wyble and Cameron Hill, with whom he would later created arrangements for three guitars that gave Western swing one of its distinctive sounds. According to a 1978 article by Bea Perry in *Guitar Player*, Boggs, Wyble, and Hill took Charlie Christian solos from Benny Goodman recordings of "Flying Home" or "Good Enough to Keep", and "work them out note-for-note, expanding them into three parts. Each member of the trio made equal contributions to the arrangements, though the actual execution varied; duets of steel plus guitar, or two guitars with a supporting steel… sometimes they traded leads, other times all played at once, in unison or in harmony."

Noel played on some of Wills' Tiffany Transcriptions and Columbia recordings, including "New Spanish Two Step," "Texas Playboy Rag," "Roly Poly," and "Stay a Little Longer." In 1946, he left Wills and reformed a group for an extended engagement at the Hollywood Palladium, but returned to Wills for a brief time before joining another western swing band, the **Spade Cooley** Orchestra in 1947. During this time, he met the famed guitar maker, Leo Fender, while the Cooley band performed at the Santa Monica Ballroom. Fender presented Noel with his first steel guitar, and thereafter Noel became a promoter for Fender's equipment. A friendship between the two ensued and Fender became

Noel Boggs Trio promotional card, circa 1960

godfather of Noel's daughter, Sandy. He remained off and on with Cooley until 1954, recording his trademark classics, "Boggs Boogie" (1947) and "Steelin' Home" (1954).

Noel suffered the first of several heart attacks that curtailed his playing until 1956. After partial recovery from the heart condition, Noel formed his own quintet and toured several western states, and played many of the nightclubs in Las Vegas, Reno, and Lake Tahoe. Along with performances on USO tours, Noel recorded several albums on the Shasta and Repeat labels, including *Magic Steel Guitar* (1960), *Western Swing* (1965), and *Any Time* (1968).

Inducted into the Steel Guitar Hall of Fame in 1981, Noel is recognized as an innovative recording artist who created a unique individual sound via his 'neck-hopping' technique" where he lined up four steel guitars with different tunings to play a wider array of melodic leads and accompaniment. Boggs is often noted for his smooth, complex, and full chord expression, as well as his mellow tone when it was appropriate. During his career, Noel appeared in several films, including *Rhythm Roundup* (1945), *Blazing the Western Trail* (1945), *Lawless Empire* (1946), and *Everybody's Dancin'* (1950). He also worked on radio with a number of the singing cowboys, such as **Gene Autry**, Roy Rogers, Rex Allen, and the Sons of the Pioneers. While his final years were fraught with negative health and family issues, Noel Boggs will always be associated with the heights of the steel guitar in American popular music through his Western swing recordings, certainly in league with **Leon McAuliffe** and **Bob Dunn**. Furthermore, Boggs' "hybrid" style of merging several different popular music traditions into his playing is a repeated hallmark of Oklahoma musicians who have again and again blended the different musical styles of the state's diverse ethnic, geographic, and socio-economic population into something that sounds new and familiar all at the same time. Musicians from Oklahoma have always had to be able to play a variety of musical styles, both to fit the varied stylistic requirements of potential jobs, and to make happy as many people as possible. Noel Boggs made a career out of doing all three. Numerous videos featuring Boggs can be found on www.youtube.com.

Source
Perry, Bea Poling. "Noel Boggs: A Life Devoted To Steel Guitar." *Guitar Player* 12, no. 1 (January, 1978): 24, 112, 116, 120.

Bogle, Bob
(b. January 16, 1934 – June 14, 2009)

As the original and all-time bassist/guitarist for the best and most significant instrumental guitar group of the early 1960s, The Ventures, Bob Bogle is one of Oklahoma's least-known native musicians who has enjoyed popular success on a massive scale. Bob Bogle and another native Oklahoman, lead guitarist **Nokie Edwards**, were half of the original Ventures that redefined and re-popularized the electric guitar combo in the midst of the late 1950s and early 1960s pop music era of homogenized and watered-down rock and roll. With Top 5 hits like "Walk Don't Run" and "Hawaii Five-0," their drum-driven, fast dance music featuring speedy electric guitars inspired countless 1960s surf music groups and garage rock bands from the U.S., the U.K., and Japan. Their heavy influence tumbled into punk rock era of the 1970s, and the alternative country music of the 1980s through the 2000s. Musicians who are on record as being inspired by the group include Jimmy Page, Stanley Clarke, Steve Miller, George Harrison, The Ramones, Jeff "Skunk" Baxter of Steely Dan, and Larry Carlton.

While The Ventures had admirable success on the single charts in the 1960s with fourteen Top 100 singles, The Ventures' thematic LP collections drove their notoriety. They rank sixth among all 1960s artists on the album charts, behind The Beatles, Frank Sinatra, Elvis Presley, Ray Conniff and Ray Charles. According to the band's website, all totaled, Bob Bogle has recorded more than 3,000 songs with The Ventures, had a hand in writing co-writing many of their more than 1,000 original songs, and appeared on over 250 albums with the group, including compilations. Thirty-seven of the albums made the US charts, more than 150 albums have been released in Japan alone, and their 1960s-era *Play Guitar with The Ventures* series was the first and only set of musical instruction records to ever make the album charts. The group had five gold albums, was named *Billboard's* Most Promising Instrumental Group of 1960, sold an unprecedented one million albums per year from 1961 to 1966, and have ultimately sold over one hundred million albums through 2003.

Robert Lenard "Bob" Bogle was born at the rural residence of his family near Wagoner, Oklahoma, a town founded in 1886 where the Arkansas Valley and Kansas Valley Railroad met the developing Missouri, Kansas, and Texas railway that ran north to south through Indian Territory. The thoroughfare was then known as the Texas Road, and is now U.S. Highway 69, still a major transportation artery through northeastern Oklahoma. According to The Ventures' 2003 website in the "Ask a Venture" section, Bob remembers mainly listening to the radio since TV did not yet exist, and "most of the music at that time in that area was Western music," undoubtedly referring to the prominence of **Bob Wills and His Texas Playboys** on Oklahoma radio. He also remembers listening to the Grand Ole Opry "quite a bit" before moving west. when he was six-years-old.

The 1930s Depression-era travails suffered by many of the state's residents led Bogle's father to sell what few animals and basic farm equipment they had on a small leased farm, and move west to California. Not only was that the classic Okie thing to do at the time, but they ran into the classic Okie problem in California, no work. The family migrated up and down the West Coast following the various harvests, and Bob, the second of four boys, worked in the fields doing any kind of farm work available. During school months, they worked in the mornings before school and again in the evenings. After a few years, the

Bob Bogle

family finally settled in Portland where his father found work in a sawmill when Bob was in his early teens.

Bogle's earliest musical experiences came when he was twelve and his brother, Clarence, brought home an acoustic lap steel guitar, allowing Bob to learn chords immediately. Because of its open tuning that allows a player to hold a steel bar in a one position on the instrument's neck and make a perfect chord by striking all the strings, Bob was soon accompanying himself on simple, three-chord songs that make up much of country music's core repertoire. He continued playing the instrument for a couple of years, but left home at age fifteen (and halfway through the 9th grade) to begin working in construction. At eighteen in 1952, Bogle became a journeyman brick mason and a member of the Bricklayers Union in Portland. That year his younger brother, Dennis, bought a regular acoustic guitar, showed Bob a few chords, and eventually gave him the guitar when Dennis left for the Air Force. Bob kept learning chords, accompanying himself, and started figuring out lead guitar lines while getting into "all that Top 40 stuff." That stuff would have been the beginning of the 1950s rock and roll movement about the time Bill Haley hit with "Rock Around the Clock" in 1954. For a precursor to the lickety split guitar work that became a hall mark of Ventures' recordings, check out Haley's solo on that landmark single, commonly acknowledged as the first significant popular rock and roll hit.

In 1959, Bob began working at a construction company in Seattle, Washington. After meeting future Ventures partner Don Wilson (b. February 10, 1937, Tacoma, Washington), who was selling used cars at the time, Wilson expressed interest in getting work in construction and soon the two were working together as mortar removers (or tuckpointers), where they had plenty of time to discuss their mutual interest in guitars. Before long they started practicing together on weekends with guitars and amps purchased from local pawnshops, and began playing as The Versatones at local dances in 1959. With more experience and some acceptance by crowds locally, Bogle and Wilson decided to upgrade their equipment and think about a career in music which couldn't be any worse than a bricklaying career, and might even be a ticket out of that type of work that musicians have been trying to avoid since the time of Orpheus.

Bob's first new guitar was a Fender Stratocaster that came with six lessons, a half-hour a week, for six weeks. Telling the instructor to teach him chords, Bob picked up most of the formal training he would need to play at a rock level that would find national chart success within a year. He began to listen his big three inspirations, Chet Atkins, Duane Eddy, and Les Paul, trying to pick out their songs and key into their primary stylistic aesthetics of playing and tone. While listening to a Chet Atkins album, *Hi-Fi in Focus* (RCA-Victor, 1959), Bob and Don heard "Walk, Don't Run" and decided to record it with a rhythm section they had brought into the group that included bassist **Nokie Edwards** (just out of Buck Owens' band), and drummer Skip Moore (who had played with Edwards in Owens' band). Moore was a local drummer who was given the choice of $25 or ¼ of the song's proceeds, and mistakenly chose the former. Primary drummer Howie Johnson (b. WA, 1938 - d. 1988) was added within a year. While Edwards initially joined the group as a bassist, and soon became the lead guitarist of the band, Bob Bogle played guitar on "Walk, Don't Run," a song that was kept out of the #1 spot in 1960 by Brian Hyland's "Itsy Bittsy Teeny Weeny Yellow Polka Dot Bikini" and Elvis Presley's "It's Now or Never," but forever defined the classic Ventures sound. Bogle also played guitar on the first several Ventures LP releases before switching to bass completely for concerts and recordings when it became obvious Nokie's stratospheric guitar abilities could be showcased to everyone's advantage.

The Ventures are not only widely known for their instrumental prowess, but also for their important innovations in guitar sound and technique, and widely divergent stylistic abilities. Experimenting with such technical innovations like the "fuzzbox" for a guitar that would distort the sound to give a band a unique aural signature, The Ventures are credited with being the first band to record with it on 1962's "2000 Pound Bee." Additionally, not only did their success "formalize" the standard rock combo of lead and rhythm guitars, electric bass, and drums for countless rock bands from the 1960s through the present in the U.S. and U.K., the Ventures appealing guitar sound also inspired thousands of Japanese youngsters to buy guitars and generally create the same sort of general social nuisance that rock and roll had aroused in 1950s U.S. popular culture.

Incidentally, many of the guitars sold by virtue of The Ventures popularity were made by two Oklahoma natives, Semie Moseley (b. Durant, 1935), and his brother, Andy (b. Durant, 1933), who had moved as children with their parents in the Okie migration west during the Great Depression. After a stint building instruments for Rickenbacker in Los Angeles in the early 1950s, Semie started his own line of guitars, Mosrites, which were first picked up by Bakersfield Sound country musicians such as Joe Maphis, and traveling Grand Ole Opry stars always on the lookout for a performance gimmick. Semie's triple-necked guitar with the longest neck strung as a standard guitar, the second-longest neck tuned an octave higher, and the shortest neck an eight-stringed mandolin provided such a versatile and visual instrument. After Nokie Edwards met Moseley in 1962 and enjoyed playing a Mosrite, The Ventures played and marketed the custom guitars by Moseley under an exclusive licensing deal that kept the guitars on their album covers from 1963 to 1968 when the company went bankrupt. At their peak in 1968, Semie and his brother averaged production of 1,000 guitars per month, to include acoustics, standard electrics, double-necks, triple-necks, basses, dobros, and mandolins, but the company's success was largely fueled by The Ventures large following.

The Ventures's fruitful 1960s period was certainly enhanced by recording instrumental collections based on contemporary musical trends in the rapidly changing pop culture world of that decade. According to a 2003 interview posted on his website, Nokie remembers the band members looking at songs bubbling under the various trade charts, listening to those songs, and then picking ones out they though might be hits about the time the album was ready. Recordings of this type included The Animals "House of the Rising Son," The Surfaris "Wipe Out," Henry Mancini's "Pink Panther Theme," and Leiber and Stoller's "Love Potion #9," and Lennon and McCartney's "I Feel Fine," among many others. Not limited by popular music, however, The Ventures also arranged classical music so that it sounded pop, such as "Rap City," based on Brahms' "Hungarian Dance #5," and "Bumble Bee Twist," based on Rimsky-Korsakov's "The Flight of the Bumblebee." Just a sampling of Ventures album titles traces pop culture trends of the period: *Twist with the Ventures* (Dolton, 1962), *The Ventures Surfing* (Dolton, 1963), *The Ventures in Space* (Dolton, 1964), *The Ventures A-Go-Go* (Dolton, 1965), *Wild Things* (Dolton, 1966), *Guitar Freakout* (Dolton, 1967), *Super Psychedelics* (Liberty, 1967), *Underground Fire* (Liberty, 1968), and *Hawaii Five-0* (Liberty, 1969).

After Nokie Edwards left the band in 1968, The Ventures had their last major U.S. hit in 1969, "Hawaii- Five-O," the theme song for the popular television detective drama set in Hawaii that aired on from 1968 to 1980. Not only did the song reach #4 on the U.S. pop charts, the weekly television show kept The Ventures' sound in front of the public and kept them touring the world, especially in Japan where in 1970 and 1971 the Ventures were that country's #1 composers. Five songs during those years reached the top of the Japanese charts when the band's Japanese label would release a Japanese vocal version of the song, known in Japan as "Kayo-kyoku," or a "ballad song," at the same time as The Ventures' original instrumental hit the market and, subsequently, the charts.

After a three-year hiatus (1968-1971) during which Edwards pursued his passion for horses, Gerry McGee played lead guitar for The Ventures while native Oklahoman John Durrill (**The Five Americans**) played keyboards for the band. Nokie returned to play lead guitar in 1972 and The Ventures' 1970s releases again chronicle some of the decade's popular culture musical trends, as well as the group's ability to capitalize on them: *Theme from Shaft* (United Artists, 1971), *Rock 'N' Roll Forever* (1972), *The Jim Croce Songbook* (1974), *Ventures Play the Carpenters* (1974), *TV Themes* (1977), and the *Latin Album* (1978) that surfaced when the disco era and its heavy Latin influences were a prominent part of mainstream pop music. The Ventures continued recording new material with the original lineup through 1983, touring the U.S. and, especially, Japan where they remain hugely popular. Nokie again left in 1984 to pursue his own music and a steady stream of solo engagements, but repeatedly performed and recorded with The Ventures on select occasions through the beginning of the twenty-first century. No less than seventy re-issues of albums have been produced on various labels both in the states and abroad since 1990, and Bogle continued playing with the group through 2007 when he began to slow down due to health issues.

The Ventures legacy remained active in 2010 with a constant demand for the group's performances at festivals, on cruise lines, and their own headlining concerts, sometimes with Nokie Edwards on lead guitar, and sometimes with old friend Gerry McGee taking the spot, albeit with a vital and historic cog, Bob Bogle missing from the band stand. Historically, The Ventures are considered one of rock's all-time greatest bands, finally gaining that recognition by rock's most venerated (and cursed) establishment, the Rock and Roll Hall of Fame, who inducted The Ventures in 2008. Like Nokie Edwards, Bob Bogle did not begin playing music as a child when he lived in Oklahoma. However, one can imagine the state's musical vibe of the 1930s, to include the simultaneous radio presence of Western swing and Grand Ole Opry broadcasts, as well as the musical sensibility (and accent) carried away from the state by his parents, must have planted a little country twang in his ear that has never really left The Ventures, and via their music has found its way across the world. Bob Bogle died in 2009 after a long battle with non-Hodgkin lymphoma, but not before learning The Ventures would be inducted into the Rock and Roll Hall of Fame, a deserving honor for this primary rock guitar group of American popular music.

www.theventures.com

Boland, Jason and the Stragglers
(Formed 1998 in Stillwater, OK)

Playing a rowdy brand of **Red Dirt Music** that leans toward the heavily bowed fiddle, whiney steel guitar, and the bittersweet/cynically insightful lyrical topics of honky-tonk country music, Jason Boland and the Stragglers are one of the most successful country groups playing on the well-worn stages of Oklahoma, Kansas, Arkansas, Louisiana, and

Texas. Led by Oklahoma native and primary songwriter Jason Boland, who began playing professionally with **Cross Canadian Ragweed**'s Cody Canada in Stillwater in 1997, the Stragglers consist of lead singer and rhythm guitarist Boland (b. Harrah), lead guitarist, steel, and dobro player Roger Ray (from Vian), drummer Brad Rice (from Edmond), bassist Grant Tracy (from Vian). The group has added various instrumentalists over the years, most recently, fiddler Noah Jeffries.

Born in Harrah, a farming community of about 4,000 people thirty miles east of Oklahoma City, Jason Boland started playing guitar in the sixth grade after seeing a *Crossroads* with his father, a movie about legendary blues man Robert Johnson who is known to have played in Taft, Oklahoma in the 1930s. Inspired by the film, Boland mentioned to his father he would like to play guitar and the elder Boland pulled an old one down from the attic and showed Jason a few blues licks. Boland was in a few bands, and listened to his older sister's rock records as a teenager that turned him onto Ozzy Osbourne's great guitarist, Randy Rhodes. After moving to Stillwater in 1993 to attend Oklahoma State University, Jason discovered Steve Earle, heard Jimmy Buffett in a new light, and started writing songs. Soon, the **Great Divide**'s Mike McClure pointed Boland in the direction of red dirt music godfathers, Tom Skinner and Bob Childers, as well as toward Cody Canada of Cross Canadian Ragweed. By 1997, Boland met Canada at one of Cross Canadian Ragweed's shows in Stillwater, and the two struck up a musical friendship that evolved into Boland filling the break space between sets in Canada's local solo gigs.

Jason Boland

Enter jazz and fusion drummer Brad Rice, who met Boland the same year at OSU, guitarist and steel player Roger Ray who connected with Boland at "The Farm," a rural meeting place for Stillwater musicians in the 1990s, and, finally, bassist and banjo player Tracy Grant who brought jam-band influences of Phish and the Grateful Dead to the Stragglers' rocking alter ego that surfaces periodically in the midst of all the honk. With a group in place by 1998, the Stragglers headed to Larry Joe Taylor's annual Texas music festival in Meridian where they played campfire jams, by virtue of which they were invited back the next year to play the new artist showcase at the festival. In 1999, the Stragglers released *Pearl Snaps*, an album produced by Texas music legend Lloyd Maines, and a record Jason has said is suited for a "partyin', drinkin', cryin' in your beer type mood." Quickly becoming one of the biggest selling roots country records in Texas for that year, the songs' party mood and sing-along ethos ("Pearl Snaps" and "Drinking Song") is the opposite of the road stories and marginalized-human studies present on *Truckstop Diaries* (2001), an album full of the Stragglers' multiple musical influences, as well as the characters and the experiences of their continued existence on the road.

With songs such as "Truckstop Diaries," a wry observation of the eccentric personalities of travel plazas, and "Falling with Style," a description of the rough and tumble world of rodeo cowboys, Boland carries the bulk of the band's songwriting load. While he wrote or co-wrote eight of the album's songs, he also brought in tunes written or co-written by fellow red dirt luminaries such as Stoney LaRue, Mike McClure, Cody Canada, Bob Childers, and Randy Crouch to fill out the collection. Eagerly anticipated by fans in 2001, *Truckstop Diaries* hit the shelves in late July, and a few days afterwards, Boland and fiddler Dana Hazzard were involved in a one-car accident that broke Jason's hip and shelved him for about three months. The August 1st date earmarked for the album's release party evolved into a benefit concert and auction for Boland's medical expenses, which led to a series of benefits in Texas and Oklahoma that raised almost thirty thousand dollars for the injured singer. Within a few months, and after extensive rehab on the part of Boland, the Stragglers were back on the road in support of *Truckstop Diaries* and have not stopped since. In their short existence, the band has been able to exploit their popularity into opening slots for Merle Haggard, Asleep at the Wheel, Robert Earl Keen, and Willie Nelson, as well as continuing their own schedule of headlining opportunities throughout the five-state area mentioned earlier, along with newly opened markets in Nebraska, New Mexico, Colorado and Alabama. *Truckstop Diaries* was re-released in 2006 on Sustain Records.

In 2002, the group released *Live and Lit at Billy Bob's Texas* as part of a series of live albums recorded in the "The World's Largest Honky Tonk." *Live and Lit*, with lead and rhythm guitarist Travis Linville complementing the band's performance, exemplifies the spirit of the group with many of their best songs from the first two albums, as well as new numbers like the Tex-Mex-influenced, lost love song, "Mexico or Crazy," a Top 20 song by March, 2003 in The Texas Music Chart; one that would make Waylon Jennings proud, "When I'm Stoned"; and "Mary," a desperate song about the lonelier side of life.

The group can also be found on compilations of both red dirt musicians and like-minded Texas artists. "Armor" appears on the spiritually influenced compilation, *Dirt and Spirit*, and "Travelin' Jones" appears on *Texas Road Trip*, an album of "Texas" musicians (even though Boland and Cross Canadian Ragweed, also on the album, are from Oklahoma). Boland also added half of a duet performance with Texas honky-tonker Kevin Fowler on Merle Haggard's "I Think I'll Just Stay Here and Drink," included on an album of drinking songs, *Brewed in Texas* (Compadre).

The powerful Texas magnet and its markets of millions proved too much for the band to keep its Oklahoma home. By late 2002, the band had relocated to Austin, a logical move given the Stragglers' success in the lone star state. Before going south of the Red River, however, The Stragglers backed their old Stillwater friend, Kyle Everett, a young, Oklahoma City-based country singer, on

The Stragglers (l to r) are Grant Tracy, Roger Ray, Brad Rice, with Jason Boland

64 / Oklahoma Music Guide II

Roger Ray

his solo album, *Water for My Horses*. Ultimately, Boland found the Lone Star capitol's distractions too engaging, and moved again to New Braunfels, Texas in 2005 where his old friends Cody Canada (**Cross Canadian Ragweed**) and **Stoney LaRue** also lived. From that base the Stragglers recorded and released *Somewhere in the Middle* (Smith, 2004) with legendary producer, Lloyd Maines, back in the studio after working with Jason on 1999's *Pearl Snaps*. Guests on the honky-tonk party disc include Billy Joe Shaver, Oklahoma red dirt/country fiddler, Randy Crouch, Stoney Larue, and Reckless Kelly's Cody Bronze.

Somewhere in the Middle's songs range from the live favorite "(My Baby Loves Me) When I'm Stoned", and familiar country themes of unrequited love ("If You Want To Hear a Love Song"), to Red Dirt populism rooted in Woody Guthrie's lyrical attitittude ("Somewhere in the Middle"), and the false promise of alcohol's lure ("Mary"). Enjoying the success of *Somewhere in the Middle* landing on the *Billboard* country chart, and a constantly growing fan base in the American Southwest and Midwest, the Stragglers continued touring while Boland kept writing for their next release, *Bourbon Legend* (Sustain, 2006). With a now familiar band sound and Boland's vocal imprint, *Bourbon Legend* continued mining the same themes of previous albums: demise of the rural environment ("Last Country Song"), iconoclastic living ("The Bourbon Legend", "No One Left to Blame", "Lonely By Choice" and "Baby That's Just Me"), alcohol-induced splendor/demise ("Can't Tell If I Drink").

In 2008, Jason and the Stragglers released *Comal County Blue* (Red Distribution), furthering fulfilled expectations by fans for lyrics that range from wise and introspective, to purely celebratory, backed by the confident and experienced country music abilities of the Stragglers. Just as one might think latter albums are starting to show the

Brad Rice

group's weariness of constant touring at an older age, writing, and a consistent recording output, the Stragglers released a 2010 energetic live album, *High in the Rockies: A Live Album* (Thirty Tigers), which shows why the group is so popular among its enthusiastic fan base. Recorded over four consecutive shows in Colorado and Wyoming, *High in the Rockies* debuted at #27 on the Billboard country album chart in April, 2010. The group's spot-on version of "Tulsa Time" from the album, with a guest shot by the songwriter, Danny Flowers, hit #1 on *Billboard*'s "Texas Regional Radio Report" and #1 on the "Texas Music Chart". The group has proven themselves longevity-wise, playing about 200 shows per year. In 2011, the group released their sixth studio album, *Ranch Alto*, on which Boland tips his hat to his **red dirt music** roots by covering Greg Jacobs' "Farmer's Luck" and **Bob Childers**' homage to **Woody Guthrie**, "Woody's Road".

www.thestragglers.com

Bond, Johnny
(b. June 1, 1915 - d. June 22, 1978)

Known for writing the western classic "Cimarron (Roll On)" and the bluegrass standard "I Wonder Where You Are Tonight," as well as being one of the first inductees into the Nashville Songwriter's Hall of Fame in 1970 and an inductee into the Country Music Hall of Fame in 1999, Cyrus Whitfield Bond was born near Enville, Oklahoma, a tiny hamlet located near the Oklahoma-Texas border that closed its post office in 1935, and is no longer included on Oklahoma highway maps.

Johnny was raised in a poor farm family who listened to Jimmie Rodgers recordings. As a young boy, he wanted to become a songwriter and guitarist like Rodgers. Once he had earned enough money, he ordered a 98-cent ukulele from the Montgomery Ward catalogue. Although he played trumpet in the Marietta (Oklahoma) High School band, his first love was the guitar because of the Rodgers' influence. He also listened to the recordings of Milton Brown and the Light Crust Doughboys, one of the first Western swing bands in Fort Worth. Johnny's first professional experience was in 1933 playing in a local string band where he played ukulele, guitar, and banjo.

After graduating from high school in 1934, Bond headed to Oklahoma City, where he auditioned for local radio shows. There he met **Jimmy Wakely**, who was to become a life-long friend. In 1937, the two formed a trio patterning their sound after the popular cowboy singing group, the Sons of the Pioneers, which included as one of its original members Oklahoman **Tim Spencer** from Picher. The third member of the trio alternated between Scotty Harrell and former Light Crust Doughboy, **Dick Reinhart**, a native Oklahoman from Tishomingo. At the outset, the trio called themselves The Singing Cowboy Trio, but later changed their name to The Bell Boys because of sponsorship by the Bell Clothing Company on radio station WKY in Oklahoma City, where they played on a daily show. In addition, the trio cut transcription discs at radio station KVOO in Tulsa. During these first years of his career, Johnny used several pseudonyms, such as Cyrus Whitfield, Johnny Whitfield, and finally Johnny Bond. He also attended the University of Oklahoma for a brief time in 1937.

During this Oklahoma City period, Johnny started writing songs, and in 1938, he completed his first classic, "Cimarron (Roll On)", which was used as a theme song for the *Bell Boys* radio show. **Gene Autry** came through Oklahoma City on tour in the late 1930s and heard the trio. Impressed by their repertoire, which included some of Autry's songs, Autry suggested he could use the trio on his *Melody Ranch* radio show should they ever decide to make a move to California.

In 1939, the group was invited to appear as the Jimmy Wakely Trio in the Hollywood Republic Pictures production of *The Saga of Death Valley*, starring Roy Rogers. This taste of Western movies and Autry's offer set the trio to thinking about a move to Hollywood. Subsequently, in May of 1940, Bond, Wakely, and Reinhart and their families left in Wakely's Dodge automobile for California, where in September, Autry hired them to become regulars on the CBS *Melody Ranch* radio show, where Johnny remained for sixteen years until the show was canceled in 1956. The trio appeared as Jimmy Wakely and His Rough Riders in a second movie, *The Tulsa Kid* (1940), starring "Red" Barry, and a third in the Universal studio film, *Pony Post* (1940), starring Johnny Mack Brown. Johnny continued his work with the original trio members, along with Scotty Harrell, who moved to Hollywood later. They performed at various concerts, ballrooms, and clubs throughout southern California. But by 1941, the Wakely Trio had ceased to exist and Johnny began to look for other opportunities in furthering his career in the Los Angeles area.

While remaining on the *Melody Ranch* show, Bond also appeared in thirty-eight motion pictures through 1947, primarily as a supporting musician to such legendary singing cowboys as Autry, Tex Ritter, and Wakely, who eventually became a star in his own films at Monogram. Some sources indicate that Wakely was the first trio member recorded on Decca in 1940, while others state that Johnny was the first member to record on Okeh, a subsidiary of Columbia Records in 1941. Regardless of this debate, Art Satherly of Okeh did sign Johnny to a contract in 1941, a deal which spanned sixteen years. Satherly knew talent as he had previously signed Gene Autry, Tex Ritter, Leadbelly, and a host of other music legends. Because of his association with Autry, Satherly was familiar with Johnny's work as acoustic guitarist on all of Autry's recordings. The most memorable was the famous Martin guitar introduction to "Back in the Saddle Again," as well as the first song they recorded together, "You Are My Sunshine." Johnny and Gene also co-wrote a number of songs, including "Don't Live a Lie" and "Funny Little Bunny with the Powder Puff Tail".

From left, Johnny Bond, Noel Boggs, Gene Autry, and Jimmy Wakely on 1939 NBC broadcast from Okemah.

Bond's first recording sessions were in August of 1941, and resulted in one notable recording, "Those Gone and Left Me Blues." In April of 1942, Johnny cut three songs, including "Turkey in the Straw", "Mussolini's Letter to Hitler", and "Hitler's Reply to Mussolini", but the company decided not to release them due to a conflict with Carson Robison's then popular recording of "Turkey in the Straw".

As Johnny continued songwriting he began to have some of his songs published, including "I Wonder Where You Are Tonight" and "Cimarron". In July of 1942, he recorded four songs, including "I'm a Pris'ner of War", and "Der Fuhrer's Face", as well as two of his originals, "You Let Me Down" and "Love Gone Cold". On the recordings, he was backed by a band that included **Spade Cooley**, another Oklahoman, on fiddle. In addition to his regular work on the Melody Ranch show, Johnny was the hayseed comedian on *Hollywood Barn Dance* radio show from 1943-47.

Although Johnny's career in the movies ended in 1947, his songwriting and recording flourished in the 1950s. Bond became leader of Tex Ritter's studio band, The Red River Valley Boys, and was involved in playing as a session member on many other West Coast country stars. In terms of recording, Bond scored three Top 5 country hits in 1947, including "So Round, So Firm, So Full Packed" (the Merle Travis big seller), "Divorce Me C.O.D." and "The Daughter of Jole Blon". The next year, he went Top 10 with "Oklahoma Waltz," and in 1949 charted with "Till the End of the World" and "Tennessee Saturday Night". On most of these, he was backed by the Red River Valley Boys. He charted a Top 10 hit in 1950 with "Love Song in 32 Bars", and in 1951, another Top 10 hit, "Sick, Sober and Sorry". Bond made his first guest appearance on the *Grand Ole Opry* in 1948.

By the end of 1957, Bond had written 123 songs. His most significant included "Cimarron", covered by such well-known artists as Sons of the Pioneers, **Bob Wills**, Jimmy Dean, Les Paul and Mary Ford, Harry James, Neal Hefti, and Billy Vaughn. "I Wonder Where You Are Tonight", recorded by such luminaries as Johnny Rodriguez, Porter Waggoner, Bobby Bare, **Roy Clark**, Jerry Lee Lewis, **Norma Jean**, Louvin Brothers, Carl Smith, Hank Snow, and Hank Williams, Jr., became a bluegrass standard as a result of recordings by Flatt & Scruggs, Bill Monroe, and Red Allen & the Kentuckians. Bond's "Tomorrow Never Comes", co-written with Ernest Tubb in 1945, was a hit for Glen Campbell in 1967 as well as being covered by such artists as Elvis Presley, Loretta Lynn, the Statler Brothers, Little Jimmy Dickens, **B. J. Thomas**, and Lynn Anderson. "I'll Step Aside", written in 1947, was covered by three more country legends, **Hank Thompson**, Ernest Tubb, and Marty Robbins. Kitty Wells, Faron Young, Billy Jo Spears, Jim Reeves, Jeannie C. Riley, **Patti Page**, and Ricky Skaggs recorded "Your Old Love Letters". "Glad Rags" was covered by Jimmy Dean, Tennessee Ernie Ford, and Mac Wiseman. Finally, Tex Ritter and Marty Robbins recorded "Conversations with A Gun".

In 1952, Johnny, Tex Ritter, and William Wagnon, Jr., a booking agent, organized a show called *Town Hall Party* in Compton, California, a combination of the *Grand Ole Opry* and *National Barn Dance*. Johnny wrote the script and insisted all songs performed on the show danceable. Filmed by the Armed Forces Network and Screen Gems, the Friday/Saturday night shows aired through 1961.

In 1955 Bond launched the music publishing busines, Red River Songs. Ritter and Wagnon joined him to form Vidor Publications, which signed songs written by **Tommy Collins**, a native Oklahoman, Freddie Hart, Lefty Frizzell, Harlan Howard ("King of Nashville Songwriters"), and Larry and Lorrie Collins (**The Collins Kids**, who often appeared on the *Town Hall Party* shows).

When the rock and roll phenomenon swept the U.S. in the mid-1950s, Johnny adapted his sound to the new genre, and was one of the first to recognize that it had roots in country music. Despite this adjustment, Columbia Records decided not to renew Johnny's contract in 1957. He moved to Gene Autry's Republic Records for a brief period in 1960 during which time he recorded the Charlie Ryan tune, "Hot Rod Lincoln", which became a rock and roll classic made even more popular by Commander Cody and His Lost Planet Airmen in 1977.

Bond signed with the Starday label in 1960, where he remained until 1971. His first single, "Ten Little Bottles", was previously recorded with Columbia in 1951. This new version of the novelty drinking song proved to be the biggest hit of his career. The follow-up single, "Morning After", did not sell as well. Johnny's first album release with Starday was *The Wild, Wicked But Wonderful West* (1961), which he had written between label deals. It was the first of fourteen albums he would record with Starday,. It included "Carry Me Back to the Lone Prairie", "Dusty Skies", and "High Noon," Johnny's own version of the original Tex Ritter recording on which Johnny played guitar. Most of Bond's later albums focused on the tried-and-true honky-tonk theme of drinking songs, such as *Ten Little Bottles* (1965), *Bottled in Bond* (1967), *Bottles Up* (1968), *Ten Nights in a Barroom* (1970), and *Drink Up and Go Home* (1970). These collections appeared to make him a one-theme performer and songwriter, and his contract with Starday ended in 1969. He immediately signed with Capitol and joined Merle Travis in a tribute album to the Delmore Brothers, however, the album sold poorly, and both Johnny and Travis were released by Capitol. He resigned with Starday and recorded five more albums in two years. After one album on the Lion & Lamb label, he recorded two albums with Shasta Records, his old friend Jimmy Wakely's label. The most notable of these was *Johnny Bond Rides Again* (1975) that included "I Wonder Where You Are Tonight", "Hot Rod Lincoln", "Cimarron", and Johnny's version of "Oklahoma Hills", co-written by **Jack** and **Woody Guthrie**. An album entitled *The Singing Cowboy Rides Again*, made in 1976 by Johnny and the **Willis Brothers**, also native Oklahomans, was released in 1992 by CMH. The 18-track release included a host of singing cowboy songs, such as "Riders in the Sky", "The Last Roundup", "Cool Water", and "Take Me Back to Tulsa", Johnny's version of the **Bob Wills** hit.

From 1964 to 1970, Autry revived the *Melody Ranch* weekly series on his own television station, KTTV in Los Angeles, and Johnny reunited with Gene as performer and scriptwriter. In 1965, Johnny was elected to the Board of Directors of the Country Music Association, and also served two terms as president of the Academy of Country Music. He was reunited with Tex Ritter for a *Grand Ole Opry* appearance in 1973. Finally, Johnny toured England and Italy in 1976. Bond was recipient of several awards throughout his career, including the BMI Award for "Your Old Love Letters" (1961), and two more BMI Awards in 1965 ("Ten Little Bottles") and 1971 ("Tomorrow Never Comes"). In 1974, he received the John Edwards Memorial Foundation Art Satherley Annual Award and the ACM Pioneer Award.

During his elder years, Johnny became an author, writing his autobiography, *Reflections*, published in 1976 by the John Edwards Memorial Foundation at U.C.L.A. Bone also wrote a biography of his friend, Tex Ritter, and had begun a book on the history of Western music before his death from a heart attack on June 12, 1978 in Burbank, California. As an early singer-songwriter of country music, in addition to his cowboy and bluegrass songs, he wrote and recorded in several other musical genres, including rockabilly ("The Little Rock Roll"), boogie woogie ("Mean Mama Boogie"), patriotic ("Under the Red, White and Blue"), western swing ("We Might As Well Forget It"), and religious ("Rock My Cradle Once Again").

Bond's music has been continuously released after his death. A 2000 release by King Records, *Country Music Hall of Fame 1999*, features "Ten Little Bottles"; *Country & Western* (Bloodshot, 2001) includes a variety of Bond's cowboy songs such as "Red River Valley" and "Tumbling Tumbleweeds"; and Varese Sarabande's 2002 *Home Recordings*, a twenty track set, included "Oklahoma Waltz", "I Wonder Where You Are Tonight", and "Cherokee Waltz".

www.johnnybond.com

Bonham, Glen

According to the Scena Records online biography, Atoka resident Glen "White Cloud" Bonham is an enrolled member of the Choctaw Nation of Oklahoma who enjoyed a childhood filled with the sounds of his bluegrass-playing family of skilled musicians in southeastern Oklahoma, an area nicknamed "Little Dixie" for its close proximity to the South and legacy of Southern life-ways. A 2003 *No Depression* article by Silas House indicates Bonham's father, of Anglo heritage and 1/16 Choctaw, played fiddle, as did the elder Bonham's brothers, often jamming on the family's front porch. Glen's mother was full-blood Choctaw who had a family gospel group that would travel area churches, sometimes singing hymns in the Choctaw language. Bonham began his professional career in 1971 at age 11 when he sang at Grant's Bluegrass Festival, the oldest bluegrass festival west of the Mississippi. Within a year he was playing with the festival's founders, revered Oklahoma bluegrass artists, **Bill Grant and Delia Bell**. Bonham remained with the group until about 1980, along the way playing with stalwarts of the genre. Bonham was in Bill Monroe's Bluegrass Boys during the 1970s and 1980s, which helps explain Bonham's almost dead-on ability to mirror Monroe's voice. Bonham also played with notable bluegrass figures Ricky Skaggs, The Whites at the Grand Ole Opry, Jimmy Martin, and a still-maturing Vince Gill. Skilled as a guitarist, bassist, and mandolin player, as well as carrying a strong lead and tenor voice, Glen is a welcome accompanist and vocal harmonizer in any bluegrass environment whose "high lonesome" singing abilities achieve splendor and melancholy with equal agility.

After a stint in the Marines, Bonham joined a bluegrass group, Signal Mountain, that was teeming with talent, to include singer **Joe Diffie**, Billy Joe Foster (fiddler for Bill Monroe and Ricky Skaggs), and songwriter Shawn Camp who wrote hits for Garth Brooks and Diamond Rio. Along with performing at major Bluegrass Festivals since 1990, Glen is a prolific songwriter with more than 100 songs to his credit. Glen has also worked as an actor, having been a recurring character for the duration of the television program, *Walker, Texas Ranger*, when he worked with his former martial arts instructor, and native Oklahoman, Chuck Norris. He also appeared in the Jet LiGlen is also an accomplished traditional powwow dancer. He has four albums on Scena Records, the first of which was comprised of bluegrass standards, *Native American Sings American Bluegrass* (2002). Subsequently, Scena released a self-titled collection of bluegrass and country standards with a few of Bonham's compositions. The recording is replete with his perfect lead bluegrass vocal pitch, excellent harmonies, and dynamic picking by the players on country and bluegrass classics, as well as some of his own compositions. Scena followed up with another release, *Cold Cold Winter* (2006), comprised of some of the highlights from the first CD, notably a cover of Merle Haggard's "Silver Wings". In 2007, Glen released a regionally popular gospel CD, *Gospel Favorites Volume 1*, featuring his group, Southern Tradition, and in 2008 was performing with family again in the Bonham Brothers. On listening to his vocals, bluegrass enthusiasts instantly understand why he has been a popular performer since he was child, able to call up the aural ghosts of Bill Monroe while maintaining his own identity as a Choctaw traditional country music singer who merges R&B, rock, blues, and gospel styles, within the bluegrass framework. According to his myspace page, continues performing a wide variety of shows in 2013.

Sources

www.scenarecords.com

www.myspace.com/glenbonham09

House, Silas. "Glen Bonham: Bluegrass Blooded." No Depression (November-December, 2003): 28-29.

Booker, Scott

According to the University of Central Oklahoma website, native Oklahoman and Edmond, OK, resident, Scott Booker began his career in the music industry as a clerk at Sound Warehouse in Midwest City. Subsequently he managed the Rainbow Records chain in Oklahoma City while attending Central State University, now the University of Central Oklahoma. Shortly after graduating from UCO with a degree in education, he met Flaming Lips front man Wayne Coyne in Rainbow Records because Wayne worked down the street at Long John Silver's and shopped for vinyl at Rainbow. By 1990 Booker was the group's manager, grabbing on for a career ride of multiple major label Lips albums on Warner Brothers, international touring to support the records, and the payoff of watching the group garner three GRAMMY Awards. In order to capitalize on his management acumen, Scott and his spouse, Jennifer, created Hellfire Enterprises, Ltd, in 2001 to better organize their management of the Flaming Lips, and other groups such as the **Starlight Mints**, Red Red Meat, Hum, Wheat, **Star Death and White Dwarfs**, British Sea Power, and Oscar nominee, Elliot Smith. In 2003 Scott co-founded World's Fair Label Group – a music industry service company facilitating independent record labels and artist-owned labels for artists to self-release their own music. After selling his ownership in World's Fair, Booker began focusing on launching and growing the Academy of Contemporary Music at the University of Central Oklahoma. The school is the first authorized U.S. version of Britain's renowned Academy of Contemporary Music. Classes and an Associate's degree program in popular music performance, and various business and technical aspects of the music industry, began in fall, 2009. Explaining the curricular emphasis at the school, Booker explains in a UCO press release, "What excites me about the ACM@UCO program is how well-rounded it is. It doesn't just focus on being a great musician – the program also cares about if you can break into the business as well. ACM@UCO provides the skills you need to maneuver through the industry once you start working."

The Flaming Lips' Wayne Coyne (left) with his long-time friend and band manager, Scott Booker.

www.acm-uco.com

www.hellfireltd.com

Bostic, Earl

(b. April 25, 1913 – d. October 28, 1965)

Born in Tulsa, Earl Bostic's gravelly alto saxophone work typified the sultry instrument's front-line position in late 1940s R&B, and 1950s rock & roll. Like almost every other Oklahoma jazz musician of note, Bostic was equally adept at jazz or blues, often adding complicated scales to his R & B recordings that foreshadowed progressive jazz. Partially born out of participating in the early 1940s bebop movement where Charlie Parker had been contributing fast, chromatic scales to bebop, Bostic's musical creativity was obviously a harbinger of later progressive jazz statements by artists such as John Coltrane, who played in one of Bostic's late 1940s combos. Bostic played his first professional gigs at age 18 with Muskogee-based **Terrence Holder** and his Twelve Clouds of Joy, in which the young sax player certainly learned how to blow long and loud in Holder's hot swinging territory group. After he left Oklahoma to study music at Xavier University in New Orleans, and where he played in local bands on riverboats, Bostic relocated to New York City. There he became a featured soloist for Don Redman in 1938, and Lionel Hampton, making his first recordings with Hampton in 1939. As a small combo leader in New York, Bostic hired one of jazz's great saxophonists, John Coltrane as a side man, and made an obvious imprint on Coltrane's evolving style that merged fluid melodic lines with more jagged and disjunct chromatic scales, as did Bostic, who was not known as a soloist until he recorded his biggest hit, "Flamingo", in 1951. "Flamingo" emphasizes Bostic's use of exaggerated vibrato, or holding long notes and manipulating them to the points of fracturing sonically, before descending or ascending through complex scales to the delight of jazz aficionados and high-caliber players. He died in Rochester, New York, in 1952. Of many recommended recordings to experience Earl Bostic's dizzying technical, melodic, and improvisatory skills, interested listeners should certainly pursue "Flamingo", "Up There In Orbit", "Harlem Nocturne", and "Cherokee".

Earl Bostic

Source

Chilton, John. "Earl Bostic," The New Grove Dictionary of Jazz (New York: St. Martin's 1994).

Brackeen, Charles

(b. March 12, 1940)

Regarded as an adventurous *avant-garde* jazz tenor, alto, and soprano saxophonist, pianist, and composer, Charles Brackeen was born in Eufaula, Oklahoma, a community of approximately 2,700 residents, located on Lake Eufaula. While still a teenager, he moved to Los Angeles in 1956, originally studying violin and piano, but settled on reed instruments, and where he met and married jazz pianist Joanne Brackeen.

Charles and Joanne moved in 1966 to New York City, where Charles recorded his first album, *Rhythm X* (Strata-East, 1968), featuring three former members of the Ornette

Coleman Quartet, including fellow Oklahoman and jazz futurist, **Don Cherry,** Charlie Haden, and Ed Blackwell. After playing with Melodic Art-tet regularly on the New York *avant garde* loft scene in the early 1970s, he contributed alto and tenor sax, as well as vocals, on Cherry's *Relativity Suite* album on the JCOA label in 1973. He was featured on tenor sax on Leroy Jenkins' *For Players Only* album, released in 1975 by JCOA, and reappeared on William Parker's *Through Acceptance of the Mystery Peace* in 1979 on the Centering label, and Ronald Shannon Jackson's *Eye on You* in 1980 on the About Time label. His tenor solos with drummer Paul Motian's trio, heard on the *Dance* (1977) and *Le Voyage* (1979) albums, both released on the ECM label, are noteworthy.

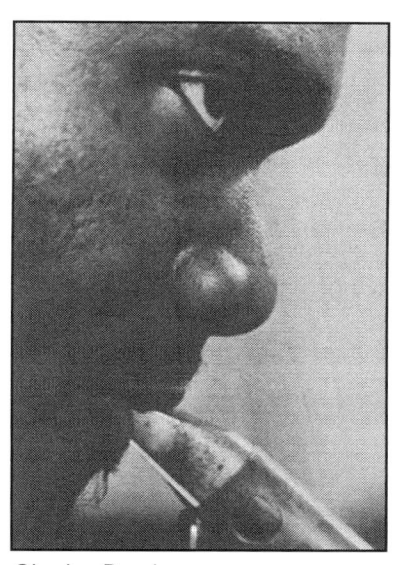

Charles Brackeen

After a period of obscurity, during which time some sources say he worked for a railroad company in Texas, Brackeen resurfaced in Los Angeles in 1987, and was contacted by trumpeter Dennis Gonzalez and Silkheart Records owner Keith Knox to record for their label. With his own quartet, he recorded *Bannar*, a 1987 Silkheart label release, a four-track album all written by Charles. It was followed by two more Silkheart releases, *Worshippers Come Nigh* (1987) and *Attainment* (1987), both of which contained Charles' own compositions.

Brackeen is also included in the Silkheart Records release, *Silkheart Sampler: The Spirit of New Jazz*, released in 1990, and can be heard on DIW's 1999 release, *Live from Soundscape: Hell's Kitchen*, which features him on "Improvisations No. 3 and 4." Finally, Brackeen also appears, along with native Oklahomans **Sam Rivers** and **Sunny Murray**, on *Wildflowers: The New York Loft Jazz Sessions*, a three CD set, released in 2000 on the Knitting Factory label.

Brewer, Michael (of Brewer and Shipley)

(b. April 14, 1944)

As part of the 1970s duo, Brewer and Shipley, singer, guitarist, songwriter Michael Brewer is best known for the 1971 hit, "One Toke Over the Line," which was banned on numerous radio stations because of its drug overtones, yet still reached #10 on *Billboard*'s Hot 100. Born in Oklahoma City, his mother was a music teacher and encouraged young Michael to sing which he did at age four on local radio. His father, a postal worker, was an artist and strongly encouraged the development of Michael's musical talent. Michael was first child in the Brewer family, followed in order of birth by Keith, Charla, and Timothy. During high school, he played drums in a rock and roll band along with **Jesse Ed Davis**, a fellow Oklahoman and guitarist for Eric Clapton. Shortly thereafter, he sold his drums to purchase his first guitar, a Martin D-18. Following graduation from Northeast High School in Oklahoma City in 1962, Brewer hit the road and performed on the coffee house circuit throughout the country. Brewer and Shipley's peak period music is filled with humorous, cynical, and insightful comments on society, especially related to the socio-political environment of the late 1960s and early 1970s, all couched in mostly up tempo folk rock songs that bounce along with tight harmonies, acoustic rhythm guitar, electric guitar leads, piano accompaniment, and a driving rhythm section.

In 1964, Brewer met Tom Shipley at the Blind Owl Coffeehouse in Kent, Ohio, a friendship that would develop into a musical relationship later in the decade. He moved to California in 1965, first to San Francisco and later Los Angeles. It was in L.A. where Michael began working with Tom Mastin, and the duet soon began touring with The Byrds and Buffalo Springfield. After signing a contract with Columbia Records, the record deal was an unsuccessful venture and the duo soon left the label. Brewer then signed on as a songwriter for Good Sam Music Publishing, a subsidiary of A & M Records founded by Herb Alpert in Los Angeles. Shipley moved to Los Angeles and lived in a house around the corner from Brewer, and soon they were collaborating on songs, which led to Shipley joining Brewer as a staff writer for A & M Records. Their 1968 debut album, *Down in L.A.*, featured all original compositions, but garnered no hits. Their second album, *Weeds*, featured an array of talented musicians, including Mike Bloomfield, the tragically ill-fated Chicago blues guitarist par excellence, along with former members of The Electric Flag. Other notable talents who have performed on Brewer and Shipley recordings include **Leon Russell**, the Grateful Dead's Jerry Garcia, Nicky Hopkins (pianist for the Rolling Stones and Beatles), Al Kooper (keyboardist for Bob Dylan and Blood, Sweat, and Tears), and Jim Messina, half of the noted 1970s duo, Loggins & Messina. *Weeds* also featured a cover of fellow Oklahoman Jim Pepper's "Witchi Tai To", based on a song originating within the Native American Church of Pepper's American Indian ancestry, sometimes known as the tipi way, or "red road". *Weeds* still provided no luck for a hit single, but their third album, *Tarkio Road* (1970), provided the group's first chart single via the title track, "Tarkio Road", that made it to #55 on *Billboard*'s Hot 100, but it was the next release that provided the duo with their signpost hit, "One Toke Over the Line", as well as an album full of counterculture and political references via their trademark folk rock sound. "One Toke" was demonized by then U.S. Vice President, Spiro T. Agnew, named Brewer and Shipley as subversives to American youth, at the same time champagne music master, Lawrence Welk, featured the song on his television program, calling it a "gospel song". By the 1990s, the Grateful Dead also featured the song in their set. Brewer and Shipley's fourth album, *Shake off the Demon* (1971), which they co-produced, only charted a minor single with the title track barely cracking *Billboard*'s Hot 100. Their fifth and final album on the Kama Sutra label was *Rural Space* (1973), which included fine renditions of "Blue Highway," "Black Sky," and "Yankee Lady", but was not a commercial success. Following the demise of Kama Sutra Records, the duo signed with Capitol and recorded two albums, *ST-11261* (1974) and *Welcome to Riddle Bridge* (1976), although neither enjoyed the success of their "One Toke" moment. Does that mean we can call Brewer Shipley a "one toke wonder"?

(l to r) Brewer and Shipley

In 1980, Brewer and Shipley parted to explore other possibilities in the music business. Brewer recorded a solo album, *Beauty Lies*, in 1983 with backup contributions from Linda Ronstadt, J. D. Souther, and Dan Fogelberg, who also produced the album. Prompted by Kansas City rock radio station KCFX, Brewer and Shipley presented in 1989 their first live show in seven years. The duo released their first compact disc in 1995, *Shanghai*, on their own label, One Toke Productions, their first release in nearly twenty years. The same year, they joined a national tour, "California Dreamin'," that included Maria Maldaur, New Riders of the Purple Sage, The Mamas and Papas, and a revised version of Canned Heat. In 1997, they recorded the *Heartland* album again on their own label, One Toke Productions. A greatest hits package, *One Toke Over the Line: The Best of Brewer and Shipley*, was released on the Buddha label in 2001.

Brewer's songwriting talents are noteworthy. He has composed such songs as "Hearts Overflowing," "Food on the Table," "Bound to Fall," and "Truly Right," recorded by such luminaries as Stephen Stills, Don McLean, The Nitty Gritty Dirt Band, Jonathan Edwards, The Dillards, and The Seldom Scene. When McLean recorded "Food on the Table," he changed the title to "Love in My Heart," for his 1988 Capitol Records *Love Tracks* album; the song reappeared on the *Very Best of Don McLean* album in 1989, as well as on the 1989 *And I Love You So* collection, released only in the U.K. The Brewer penned-song cracked the Top 10 pop charts in Australia. The duo's peak period music remains popular, as *Weeds* and *Tarkio* were re-issued in 2004 by Collector's Choice as a double-album CD package, and again through Acadia in 2008. Brewer released solo albums in 2004 (*Retro Man*) and 2010 (*It Is What It Is*).

Brewer and Shipley have performed at such well-known venues as Carnegie Hall, The Bottom Line, The Troubadour, The Roxy, and Keil Opera House. As of 2010, Brewer and Shipley were still performing at various venues all over the U.S., including Alaska, and remain superb instrumental and vocal technicians, performing their extremely listenable music in an easy-going manner to audiences appreciative of their humor, wit, and observational insight. Their One Toke Productions is based in Rolla, Missouri.

www.brewerandshipley.com

Brooks, Garth

(b. February 7, 1962)

To begin grasping the enormity of what Garth Brooks has accomplished, one only need mention's his name as the biggest selling solo artist in American popular music, ahead of Elvis Presley who is in second place, and only behind The Beatles in total sales for any artist *ever*. Volumes have already been written about the country singer and performer from Oklahoma who changed the course of American country and pop music in the 1990s. Now with total sales of more than 128 million as of 2010, Garth Brooks is the only solo artist to sell ten million copies of six different albums, and the only artist to take twenty singles to the #1 position on the country charts. Born Troyal Garth Brooks in Tulsa, Oklahoma, the name Troyal is derived from his father and grandfather, and the name Garth came from his great-great grandfather, who was a Civil War general. Colleen Carroll and Troyal

Garth Brooks

Raymond Brooks were previously married; she had three children and he had one. Garth and Kelly were born to Troyal and Colleen with Garth the youngest of the six children. Garth learned his first chords on guitar from his father, who was a guitar and mandolin picker. His father, a former U.S. Marine, was a draftsman for Union Oil. Colleen, born in Kansas City, Missouri, but raised in Arkansas, was a country singer who had a short-lived contract with Cardinal and Camark Records, and performed with Red Foley on the Ozark Jubilee in the 1950s. Garth grew up in a music-filled environment. According to his website, he heard country music standards via his parents' record collection, rock and pop of the period via his siblings, and was also drawn to James Taylor and Dan Fogelberg, artists he covered liberally in his early years of singing at nightclubs and bars in Stillwater where he attended Oklahoma State University. Brooks' vocals mirror one of his biggest stylistic influences, George Strait, but also have a unique imprint that is immediately recognizable as his own, a hallmark of all major artists.

While Garth's first major country release in 1989 provided his initial hits and set the thematic and musical template for the most successful parts of his career, his live shows brought a new level of excitement to country music with stage productions reminiscent of his early arena rock influences, Kiss, but also from witnessing the energy of a 1989 Chris LeDoux show at the Cocky Bull in Victorville, California. That night, Garth and his band opened for LeDoux, and when they saw the show he put on, Brooks knew he wanted to create that kind of environment and energy for his shows. By changing the dynamic of a country concert from a revered observation of a given star standing on stage and delivering their hits, Garth's live concert productions embraced the technical and energetic staging of arena rock shows, as well as the rowdy Cajun party milieu of a Chris LeDoux concert, creating a new aesthetic benchmark for popular country music entertainment.

In 1966, Garth's family moved to Yukon, Oklahoma, where he took part in a number of sports including football, basketball, baseball, and track. He was vice-president of his ninth grade class and received a banjo on his sixteenth birthday. After graduation from Yukon High School in 1980, Garth attended Oklahoma State University on a partial athletic scholarship where he threw the javelin. During his OSU days, he began to perform in public, representing Iba Hall, the athletic dormitory, when he won an annual talent show sponsored by the Residence Halls Association. While at school, one of Garth's roommates was **Ty England**, who became his singing partner and acoustic guitarist once Garth began enjoying success in Nashville. The two had made a pact while in college that if either of them were successful they would call the other, and the first call Garth made when he signed with Capitol was to England. On weekends, Garth performed at local clubs on what's known in the college town of Stillwater as "The Strip" (South Washington Street), most notably "Willie's," owned and operated by Bill Bloodworth since 1974. Sitting at the bar in Willie's on a random July, 2010, afternoon, Bloodworth remembered that Garth would occasionally play with bands, but mostly liked to play by himself. "Kind of like he does now," Bloodworth said, referring to Brooks' wildly popular solo acoustic shows at the Winn Casino in Las Vegas from 2009 through 2014. At Willie's in the mid-1980s, however, Brooks performed a repertoire largely from the pop songs he liked by artists such as James Taylor, Billy Joel, Jimmy Buffet, and Bob Seger with an occasional country song by George Strait. He also worked at Dupree's Sporting Goods on South Washington Street (across the street from Willie's) where he later had his T-shirts printed for concerts. While working at Dupree's, he would have T-shirts printed for his friends saying "Garth Brooks World Tour."

After graduating from OSU in December, 1984 with a B.S. in journalism and an emphasis in advertising, he spent about a year living in Stillwater perfecting his musical act, making some demo tapes for a possible visit to Nashville, and working as a bouncer at Tumbleweed's, a country music nightclub, where he met his future wife, nineteen year old Sandy Mahl, also an OSU student, rodeo barrel rider, and amateur dancer in campus modern dance functions. Local legend in Stillwater has long told that Garth met Sandy in an incident at "The Weed" where she was involved in an altercation in the women's restroom, and as bouncer Garth had to remedy whatever drama was going on in there. Sandy wound up being escorted back to her dormitory by Garth, during which time he asked her for a date.

Willie's Saloon, Stillwater, OK, 2010.

In 1985, Garth made his first attempt at Nashville's music industry. He made the requisite visits to all the major record labels and left demo tapes, but received no encouragement and left Music City, discouraged. He returned to Stillwater and continued to perform at "Willie's," made additional demo tapes, and played shows where possible around Oklahoma. On May 24, 1986, he married Sandy in her hometown of Owasso, Oklahoma. Shortly thereafter, they moved to a house at 227 South Duck Street in Stillwater, across from the YMCA. The house is still a rent house and maintains the local music history by declaring "Garth Brooks and Sandy Lived Here 1987" over the front porch. In May 1987 Garth applied to become a member of ASCAP and was accepted. The next month, he and Sandy and his band (Santa Fe) returned to Nashville, where he and Sandy worked at Cowtown, a boot store in north Nashville, and Santa Fe was disbanded.

Garth found additional work in the advertising sector (his college major) by doing voice-overs on Lone Star Beer commercials. Throughout 1987, he continued to write songs, including "Not Counting You," and was signed by Major Bob Publishing, headed by Bob Doyle, as one of its first two songwriters in 1988. Shortly thereafter, Doyle and publicist Pam Lewis formed Doyle-Lewis Management with Garth as a client. Doyle soon made an appointment with Capitol Records' Jim Foglesong and Lynn Shults for them to listen to Garth in the Nashville office. Shults later attended a Garth performance at the Bluebird Café in Nashville, and made a handshake agreement for a Capitol Nashville (later renamed Liberty Records) contract, which was officially signed on June 18, 1988.

The "Garth Brooks House" in Stillwater, OK.

Garth recorded his first album with producer Allen Reynolds at the end of 1988, and the self-titled album was released in early 1989, supported by an extensive tour by Garth and his newly formed band "Stillwater", named after the town where he attended

Garth Brooks in Willie's Saloon, 1987.

college. The first single "Much Too Young (Too Feel This Damn Old)" climbed to Top 10 by July 1989. The album produced three more hit singles, including "If Tomorrow Never Comes" (Garth's first #1 single), "The Dance" (#1), and "Not Counting You" (#2). All except "The Dance" was either written or co-written by Garth. By learning and being able to sing many different artists' songs, Garth absorbed good songwriting form. While not a country axiom, Garth can get the truth out of four or five chords in a song, often staying within the familiar country, blues, and rock form of a "1-4-5" chord progression, for the amateur strummers out there. His songs are instantly familiar because they often sound like a lot of other classic country songs, but it's his voice, delivery, and lyrical choices that make the songs stand out. But, I digress from the timeline. He also made his Grand Ole Opry debut in June 1989, and in 1990 became the sixty-fifth member of the Opry roster. Throughout the first album, having sold nine million copies by 2010, Garth's sound is not reminiscent of the moribund Nashville pop country of the late 1980s, but more reflective of the dance music, and earthier country band music familiar to Oklahoma and Texas honky-tonk fans. Songs about heartbreak, small towns, cowboys, and falling in love fill the album that swings with fiddle, steel guitar, and electric leads. Also, Garth's recognizable vocal "twang flips" at the end of his words and lines accent lyrics in a unashamed nod to the heritage of country music's nasal singing tradition.

Garth's second album, *No Fences*, released in the fall of 1990, established him as a mega-star as it sold 700,000 copies within the first ten days of its release, and has eventually sold more than sixteen million copies, the biggest selling album in his career. A string of #1 hits were produced from the album, including "Friends in Low Places" (which also was a hit video), "Unanswered Prayers," "Two of a Kind, Workin' on a Full House," and "The Thunder Rolls" (also a hit video). Garth's songwriting abilities on "Unanswered Prayers" and "The Thunder Rolls" were recognized by the Nashville Songwriters Association's Artist of the Year for 1992 as he tied with Alan Jackson for the award. He wrote or co-wrote more than half of the hits on ensuing albums. "Friends in Low Places" is still an incredibly popular sing-along tune, a ubiquitous presence at Oklahoma karaoke bars.

Garth's album successes were matched by his concert appearances. By the end of 1990, he was selling out stadiums, for example, 50,000 at the Dallas State Fair, throughout the country, patterning his show after 1970s rock extravaganzas with cordless microphone so he could move around on stage, bust guitars, douse himself and his band in water, use a flying harness to swing out over the audience while he sang, and feature an explosive laser and pyrotechnics show to dazzle the crowd. It would mark the first time a country artist would incorporate such rock techniques into live concerts. His three 1993 concerts in the 65,000 seat Texas Stadium in Dallas broke the attendance record set by former Beatle Paul McCartney.

By the end of 1990, Garth was nominated for every conceivable country music award possible, including the CMA's Single and Song of the Year ("If Tomorrow Never Comes"), Male Vocalist of the Year, Music Video of the Year (*The Dance*), and the Horizon Award; winning the Horizon and Music Video categories. In addition, the ACM nominations included New Male Vocalist of the Year, Top Song, and Top Single, however, he failed to win any of these three awards. For the first time, Garth performed at Nashville's Fan Fair, and was presented with his first gold album (*Garth Brooks*) by Capitol Records' president Jimmy Bowen.

In 1991 the CMA nominated Garth in five categories, including Entertainer of the Year, Single of the Year ("Friends in Low Places"), Album of the Year (*No Fences*), Male Vocalist of the Year, and Music Video of the Year (*The Thunder Rolls*). He captured three of these awards: Entertainer, Music Video, and Album. "The Thunder Rolls" (song and video) was somewhat controversial because of its domestic violence content, but it paved the way for similarly themed songs like Martina McBride's "Independence Day" and the Dixie Chicks' "Goodbye Earl." His third album, *Ropin' the Wind*, was released in September 1991, and quickly entered the country and pop charts at the #1 position. It was the first country record to debut at the top of the pop charts. The album spawned four #1 singles, including "Shameless" (a rework of the Billy Joel song), "Rodeo," "What She's Doing Now," and "The River," the latter two co-written by Garth, as well as "Papa Loved Mama," which reached #2 on the country charts.

Garth Brooks' tours revolutionized country music's concert production standards.

By the end of 1991, Garth had become an American popular music icon. Even his seasonal album, *Beyond the Season*, went multi-platinum. His hometown of Yukon, Oklahoma, proclaimed a "Garth Brooks Day," and officially dedicated one of the town's water towers with a sign reading "Home of Garth Brooks," with Garth on hand for the ceremonies. Garth was a major winner in the *Billboard* Music Awards in 1991 with top honors in five categories. Moreover, he captured his first Grammy in 1991 for Best Country Performance Male for the *Ropin' the Wind* album. Finally in 1991, Garth swept the ACM Awards with honors as Entertainer of the Year, Male Vocalist of the Year, Album of the Year (*No Fences*), Single of the Year ("Friends in Low Places"), and Song and Video of the Year ("The Dance").

Garth's first major television special, *This is Garth Brooks*, received critical acclaim in 1992, and was the highest rated Friday night program on NBC in two years. Filmed at two sold out concerts in Reunion Arena in Dallas, Trisha Yearwood and Chris LeDoux were the opening acts. According to survey data, the special attracted some sixteen million households with ninety percent of the viewers between eighteen and forty-nine.

In April 1992 Garth appeared on the ACM telecast and captured first place honors in two of his five nominations: Entertainer of the Year and Male Vocalist of the Year. In October 1992 Garth swept the CMA awards show with top honors for Entertainer of the Year and Album of the Year (*Ropin' the Wind*), and was nominated for Male Vocalist of the Year. Garth was also a recipient of the first ASCAP "Voice of Music" award presented in 1992 at the grand opening ceremonies of ASCAP's new Nashville offices. On July 8, 1992, Garth and Sandy's first child, Taylor Mayne Pearl Brooks, was born in Nashville, named after James Taylor and Minnie Pearl, two of Garth's favorite personalities. To conclude 1992, Garth's hometown of Yukon, Oklahoma, designated a stretch of Highway 92 from the Interstate 40 exit to Main Street as "Garth Brooks Boulevard."

Garth's fourth album, *The Chase*, was also released in 1992 and became the second one to enter both the pop and country charts at #1. Although somewhat controversial, the disc generated four more hit singles beginning with "We Shall Be Free," which featured a strong gospel component and peaked at #12. The song was written as a result of Garth's presence in Los Angeles during the 1992 riots with the video featuring such luminaries as Paula Abdul, Burt Bacharach, Harry Belafonte, Michael Bolton, Whoopi Goldbert, Julio Iglesias, Eddie Murphy, Colin Powell, Elizabeth Taylor, and **Reba McEntire**. It was followed by three #1 hits in 1993, including "Somewhere Other Than the Night," "Learning to Live Again," and "That Summer." The eclectic nature of the album was reflected in such diverse numbers as the Patsy Cline classic "Walkin' After Midnight" and a rousing version of the Little Feat rock number "Dixie Chicken." By the end of 1992, the album was certified platinum, and by the end of 1993 had sold in excess of more than six million copies, more than enough attention to get him on the cover of *Rolling Stone* magazine in April, 1993, a publication not known for putting country artists on its cover, but just another indication of Brooks' titan status in American popular music of the period.

In Pieces, Garth's fifth album, was released in 1993 and debuted at #1 on the *Billboard* country charts. It yielded several hits, including "Ain't Goin' Down (Til the Sun Comes Up)," the debut single which rose to #1 on the *Radio & Records* chart, "American Honky-Tonk Bar Association," "Standing Outside the Fire," "One Night a Day," and "Callin' Baton Rouge." Garth performed the National Anthem during pre-game festivities at the 1993 Super Bowl to an estimated viewing audience of more than one billion. His award-winning video, *We Shall Be Free*, premiered during the telecast. Finally in 1993, he was nominated for CMA awards in three categories: Entertainer of the Year, Male Vocalist of the Year, and Album of the Year (*The Chase*), however, he failed to win any of these, but was one of the artists who collaborated on the winning Vocal Event of the Year, "I Don't Need Your Rockin' Chair," teaming with George Jones, **Vince Gill**, and **Joe Diffie**, among others.

In 1994 Brooks was nominated for the CMA Entertainer of the Year and Music Video of the Year ("Standing Outside the Fire"), but failed to win either. By 1995, Garth had earned additional honors both at home and abroad, including five American Music Awards, a Juno Award from Canada, two German-American Country Music Federation Awards, a Dutch Country Award, top award from England's *Country Music Round-Up* publication, and two nominations by the CMA for Entertainer of the Year and Music Video of the Year ("The Red Strokes"). Furthermore, he was named Favorite Country Artist by *Rolling Stone* magazine for the first half of the 1990s, Country Performer of the Year for 1991 through 1993 by *Radio & Records* readers, garnered some eleven *Billboard* awards during this productive era, and received a star in the Hollywood Walk of Fame, under which was buried *The Hits*, a limited edition of eighteen singles spanning his career from 1989 to 1994. In addition to these many laurels, Sandy gave birth to their second daughter, August Anna, in May of 1994.

Released in 1994, *The Hits* was a collec-

Garth Brooks, 1997

tion of Garth's greatest hits and eventually sold more than eight million copies. In late 1995, *Fresh Horses*, Garth's first album of original material in two years, debuted at #1 on *Billboard*'s country list and #2 on the pop charts, achieving first week sales of an estimated 500,000 copies, and sales of more than three million copies within six months of its release. Eight tracks from the album, six of which were co-written by Garth, received national radio airplay, including "She's Every Woman" (#1), "The Fever" (a rework of The Aerosmith number), "The Change," "The Old Stuff," "The Beaches of Cheyenne" (#1 chart buster), "It's Midnight Cinderella," "Rollin'," and "That Ol' Wind." He was again a finalist for Entertainer of the Year by the CMA in 1996, and was also featured on VH1's acclaimed singer/songwriter series, *Storytellers*, in a highly rated show that double ratings of his rock peers of the period. Garth's seventh album, *Sevens*, was released in late 1997, after a management shake-up at Capitol Records and a massive publicity campaign including a concert at New York City's Central Park on August 7, which drew am estimated 250,000, the largest crowd ever to attend a concert there. The concert was also broadcast on HBO. The album quickly catapulted to #1 upon its release and went multi-platinum by the end of the year. Only six of the fourteen tracks were co-written by Garth, but several of them received considerable radio airplay, including "She's Gonna Make It," "Cowboy Cadillac," and "In Another's Eyes." Additional tracks of note were "Longneck Bottle," "You Move Me," and "Two Piña Coladas." The latter also garnered the #1 spot on the country charts, and earned him Entertainer of the Year by the CMA in 1997.

Garth's 1996-98 concert tour was an overwhelming success, but a grueling schedule as he played 350 shows in more than 100 cities totaling 5.3 million tickets sold. One of the major events of the tour was a sold-out show at the Hollywood Bowl with the Hollywood Bowl Orchestra. The concert sold out in twenty-one minutes as "Garthmania" continued to sweep the nation. He captured top honors from the CMA in 1998 for Entertainer of the Year, and was nominated for Album of the Year (*Sevens*) and Vocal Event of the Year, "In Another's Eyes" with Trisha Yearwood.

After these incredible successes in country music, Garth's decided to try something new in the late 1990s, and it centered on a new persona—Chris Gaines, a brooding, leather-clad rock star, complete with a fabricated biography and plans for an accompanying proposed film, *The Lamb*, a thriller about a tortured rock star. The film featured a collection of Gaines' "greatest hits," which was released in 1999 as an album entitled *In the Life of Chris Gaines*, a set of thirteen pop songs ranging from "Lost in You," a smooth ballad, to "Maybe," a self-conscious Beatles tribute, but none of which were written by Brooks. Garth's fans were unforgiving and could not understand the move, akin to Michael Jordan playing baseball at the height of his NBA career, however, Garth defended the attempt as an opportunity to do something new and stretch his own artistic boundaries. It proved to be a commercial disaster, left Garth's fans bewildered, and release of the film was delayed. Moreover, it did not help the sales of Garth's second seasonal album, *Garth Brooks and the Magic of Christmas*, released in late 1999, but he was still a finalist for Entertainer of the Year in 1999 by the CMA. Perhaps most significantly about the Gaines project is his recording of "Main Street", a song co-written by eventual second wife, Trisha Yearwood. Additionally, when looking at the total Garth Brooks oeuvre, the Gaines album also shows Brooks early songwriting and singing influences of Dan Fogelberg and James Taylor, but should ultimately be viewed through the lens of a film's soundtrack, with each song representing a stylized representation of the character's change through a variety of genres.

After the Chris Gaines experiment, Garth kept a low profile through most of 2000 because of several factors, including the dissolution of his marriage with, and in October he announced his retirement from touring to spend more time with his children. He and Jenny Yates (co-writer) did earn a Golden Globe nomination in 2001 for Best Original Song in a Motion Picture for "When You Come Back to Me Again" from the film *Frequency*. Garth returned to the industry in 2001 via *Scarecrow*, his most popular album since *Fresh Horses* and one in which he returned to his country roots. It debuted at #1 on both the *Billboard* pop and country charts, the seventh time one of Garth's albums had accomplished this feat and more times than any other artist. The twelve-tracks featured the George Jones duet "Beer Run," co-written by fellow Oklahoman, **Keith Anderson**; "Pushing Up Daisies," another song co-written by Oklahoman **Kevin Welch**; "Squeeze Me In," a duet with his long-time singing partner and eventual wife, Trisha Yearwood; and "When You Come Back to Me Again," "Why Ain't I Running," "The Storm," and "Rodeo or Mexico," all of which were co-written by Garth. "Thicker Than Blood," another track co-written by Garth, is a family-oriented song that features a tribute to his mother and father, and cracked the Top 10 in the fall of 2002, his forty-seventh Top 20 hit. While the album shows occasional hints of the overproduction and melodrama which is about the only criticism possible of Garth's production and song choices over the years, *Scarecrow* was certified triple platinum in early 2002, making it the best selling album of 2001, and signifying sales of three million. It also garnered the best selling album in Canada in 2002 with an award from the Canadian Country Music Association. So, forget the critics and enjoy it if you like it. In any case, Garth slipped out of public view for a couple of years, even though he continued receiving awards, to reorganize his life through the difficult transition of divorce and reorientation to Oklahoma living when he moved near Owasso to be close to his three daughters (Taylor, August, and Allie).

In March of 2002, Brooks was presented with ASCAP's prestigious Golden Note Award, recognizing his achievements to American music. The ceremony was highlighted by musical tributes to Garth, including vocals by two other Oklahomans, **David Gates** and **Jimmy Webb**. Also in 2002, Garth received the Hitmaker Award from the Nashville Songwriters Hall of Fame, and his *Double Live* album was certified by the R.I.A.A. for shipping more than fifteen million units, making it the best selling live album in American music history. He also accepted in person the People's Choice Award for Favorite Male Musical Performer in 2002. Moreover, he received two CMT Flameworthy Awards in 2002 for Male Video of the Year for "Wrapped Up In You" and Video Collaboration of the Year for "Squeeze Me In," his duet with Trisha Yearwood which also gained him a 2003 GRAMMY nomination for Country Collaboration with Vocals. Finally, Garth's duet with George Jones on Capitol's "Beer Run (B-double E-double Are You In?)" was nominated by the CMA for Vocal Event of the Year in 2002. "Squeeze Me In" was also nominated for a GRAMMY. Seemingly, just for fun, Garth contributed vocals to a song, "Night Birds," on the 2003 album *A Dyin' Breed* (Wondermint) by old friend and songwriting collaborator Royal Wade Kimes. Also in 2003, Garth received the Hitmaker Award from the Songwriters Hall of Fame in New York City, and "If Tomorrow Never Comes" enjoyed new #1 status when it reached the top spot on the UK charts by former Boyzone frontman Ronan Keating.

From the outset of his career, Garth has been active in charitable causes, raising more than $40 million for children's charities, along with other benefit work to raise money for the Oklahoma City bombing victims, helping fund a Nashville zoo in honor of **Mae Boren Axton**, chairing a Read Across America campaign in an effort to improve literacy among children, and assisting with wildfire relief in California. He also accepted promotional invitations to spring training baseball camps of the San Diego Padres (1998 and 1999), New York Mets (2000) and Kansas City Royals (2004) to raise awareness for his Teammates for Kids Foundation.

Not only did Brooks marry his long-time collaborator, Trisha Yearwood, in 2005, he also parted ways with Capitol Records and retained ownership of all of his master recordings. Subsequently, he struck a unique deal with Wal-Mart, now the largest physical music retailer in the United States, ensuring his catalog and new material will be sold exclusively through the mega-chain's stores or website. About the deal with Wal-Mart, Brooks explains it was the most cost effective move to get his music to his fans at the lowest price possible. "If you were going to get this many units at this price, you were going to have to marry somebody," Brooks says in a 2005 radio interview CD issued to promote releases planned with the retailing giant. Once he heard how low the prices could be with Wal-Mart, he says, "Now [they're] talking my language with my people. I love to see [fans] get this much entertainment and, hopefully, not hurt their wallet too bad." The first release through Wal-Mart in 2005 was the five-disc DVD set, comprised of never-before-seen original footage from his four highly rated television specials (*This is Garth Brooks* (1992), *This is Garth Brooks, Too!* (1994), *Live from Central Park* (1997), *Live From Dublin*) and fifteen of his video hits. The second release was another multiple disc boxed set, *The Limited Series* (2005), that included re-issues of *Sevens, Scarecrow,* and *Double Live* (the biggest selling live album in history), but also an excellent collection of unreleased material on *The Lost Sessions* that proved so popular among fans for its back-to-basics Garth sound that it was released as an album in 2006. The songs on the CD were all left over from Garth's Capitol years. When he left the label, he took the masters which were thought of as "vault recordings" by Capitol, or not necessarily releasable demos, and those became the core of that album. About The Lost Sessions, Garth says, "The songs were either in a demo form or little guitar/vocal form, and [we] just built around them." Ten of the eleven songs are all previously recorded material from the vault, and the eleventh one,"Good Ride Cowboy", a tribute to his late friend Chris LeDoux, was the first new recording by Garth since going into "retirement". Including extra tracks on the individual re-release of *The Lost Sessions*, the CD sparkled with on a duet with Trisha Yearwood, "Love Will Always Win", that was a top 25 country single. Selling over a million copies and certified as a platinum video release, *Limited Series* contains a DVD that contains contemporary interview footage with Garth, music videos, live performances, and a huge photo gallery.

Garth's resurgence into the popular mindset continued in 2006 via the *Limited Series'* success and the new song, "Good Ride Cowboy". Also that year, he helped out his alma mater, Oklahoma State University by recording a 30-second TV commercial for the school. His home state further recognized him with the Spirit of Will Rogers Award from the Will Rogers Rotary Club. In 2007, Brooks announced a new box set, *The Ultimate Hits*, featuring two discs with thirty of his hits, three new songs, and a DVD with videos for each of the new tunes. The first single from the collection, "More Than a Memory", debuted at #1 on Billboard's Hot Country Songs chart, the highest-debuting single in the chart's history. In 2007, Brooks performed nine sold-out shows in Kansas City, even though only one was originally planned. Roughly 140,000 tickets sold out in two hours, with the final show simulcast to more than 300 movie theaters across the nation. In 2009, Brooks was inducted into the Oklahoma State University Alumni Hall of Fame alongside OSU football great Barry Sanders, and baseball star Robin Ventura.

To reiterate a few vital statistics indicative of the powerful influence Garth has had on American music, his total sales of more than 126 million make him the all-time biggest selling solo artist in history. He is the only solo artist to have six albums top the ten million-sold benchmark, and has spent more time at #1 on the album sales charts than any other artist. Along with twenty #1 singles on the country charts, Garth has filled up several trophy cases of awards from the Country Music Association (11), People's Choice Awards (12), Academy of Country Music (18, including Entertainer of the Year four times), two GRAMMY awards, American Music Awards (17), World Music Awards (5), and twenty-four *Billboard* Music Awards. The latter achievement is unparalleled in the history of the *Billboard* awards. He was also named as Artist of the Decade (1990s) by the ACM and received the prestigious ACM Jim Reeves Memorial Award in 1994 for promoting international acceptance of country music. As of 2010, he lives with wife, Trisha, near Owasso, OK. Since Garth's career has exceeded all hyperbole, one cannot write an over-exaggerated sentence about Garth Brooks' significance as American country and popular music star. His success is unparalleled in the music industry for a solo performer, and his control of his own artistic destiny is the hope of any musician. And, the fact that he was born, raised, and has his primary musical experiences in Oklahoma should be further inspiration for anyone from this state, or any other, that given the right talent, drive, and circumstances, anyone can take a shot at realizing their dreams. In 2009 Garth accepted an offer to perform series of special concerts in Las Vegas at the Winn Casino, and proceeded to play sold-out solo acoustic shows in the intimate Encore Theatre through 2012, essentially the same thing he was doing at Willie's Saloon in Stillwater in the mid-1980s, albeit with his own hits. Somewhere in the middle of all his activity, Brooks also found time to finish his Master's degree at Oklahoma State University in 2011, and by all counts was happy to just walk across the stage and not have to sing a lick from it. In 2012, Garth Brooks was inducted into the Country Music Hall of Fame

www.garthbrooks.com

Recommended Reading
For insight into Garth's developmental early years in Stillwater, see Matt O'Meilia, Garth Brooks: The Road Out of Santa Fe (Norman: OU Press, 1997). O'Meilia was the drummer in Garth's Stillwater-era band, Santa Fe.

Brown, Junior
(b. June 12, 1952)

A high-octane, miracle working guitarist, famous for his legendary "guit-steel" (half guitar/half lap steel), Junior Brown is a genre defying musician who weaves deftly in and out of Western swing, rock & roll, blues, and honky-tonk. His rich baritone voice fits barroom ballads or up tempo smirkers about the gamut of country music themes: love lost or gained; chasing the blues; oddball characters; working class heroes; partying on a weekend; puttin' it to the "man": and so on. Brown his lived in the Tulsa area since the mid-1980s, most recently near the Mounds/Bixby area, but was born in Cottonwood, Arizona where he began playing melodies on the family piano before he could talk, and a guitar he found in his grandparents attic at age seven. As a child, he played along with contemporary music of the day, such as The Beatles, The Beach Boys, and The Kinks, explaining his penchant for rock. Another set of influences came via his father who introduced Junior to the blues of Lighnin' Hopkins, John Lee Hooker, and other country blues artists. By the early 1970s Junior became enamored with country music, specifically **Merle Haggard**, Ray Price, and Ernest Tubb. As a result, he spent most of that decade maturing musically (and otherwise) in house bands playing six nights a week in little country bars and honky-tonks in the Southwest border area of Arizona. With gigs drying up in the 1980s for country bands, Brown started writing his own songs so he wouldn't just be thought of a cover musician. During this time, he made another change that would cement his unique show business image and sound, the guit-steel.

In the mid-1980s, Junior was tired of awkwardly switching back and forth from guitar to steel. According to a 2004 Telarc Records press release, the idea came to Junior in a dream where the two instruments mysteriously melted into one. He took the idea to guitar maker Michael Stevens, and the result was Junior's now-famous "guit-steel", a double-necked guitar combining a standard guitar with the steel. Also about this time, Junior moved to the Tulsa area so he could play and work with legendary steel guitarist, **Leon McAuliffe**, who was teaching at the **Hank Thompson** School of Country Music at Rogers State College (now Rogers State University) in Claremore, Oklahoma, about twenty-five miles northeast of Tulsa. McAuliffe helped Junior get on board as an instructor of guitar at the school. The opportunity proved fortuitous in a number of ways, as teaching allowed him to meet his future rhythm guitarist, backup vocalist, and eventual wife, Tanya Rae, who was a student in the school's music program. The two were married in 1988, and while they relocated part of their operations to Austin, Texas in the early 1990s, their permanent home base has remained in Oklahoma near Bixby.

Junior Brown

As of 2010, Brown has eight albums of mostly original material that exhibit his multi-faceted guitar skills. While he is routinely thought of as one of the great modern country guitarists, and his collections are certainly filled to the brim with twang, Junior also throws in all kinds of musical references, from Jimi Hendrix and surf-rock to the steel-guitar laden Bakersfield Sound of Merle Haggard, and, of course, the Western swing influences of steel master, Leon McAuliffe. According to his website, *Guitar Player* magazine named Brown in multiple "Best of 1994" named him #1 lap steel player, #2 country artist, his album, *Guit With It* (Curb), the #3 country album of that year. *Guit With It* is the perfect place to start appreciating Junior Brown's artistry. While he had minor country chart hits from the album, "Highway Patrol", a tribute to the trials of being a state trooper, and "My Wife Thinks You're Dead", a funny song about not wanting to see a long gone ex who shows up in town, the industry and/or public at large has not embraced him to the extent that his ardent fans and guitar aficionados have. *Guit With It* also features Tanya Rae's duet with Junior on "So Close Yet So Far Away", obviously about the time the two have spent apart due to his touring schedule, and a song that expresses Junior's affinity for her and for his adopted home state , "The Gal from Oklahoma". Finally, the show-stopping "Guit-Steel Blues" bends, bows, picks, slides, rakes, and races fluidly around the unusual instrument that provides his signature sound of two guitarists playing in the same group as he switches from one neck to the other.

Subsequent albums, *Long Walk Back* (Curb, 1998), *Mixed Bag* (Curb, 2001), and *Down Home Chrome* (Telarc 2004), mined the same outrageous technical guitar skills ("Hill Country Hot Rod Man"), varied musical aesthetic (cover of Henrix's "Foxy Lady"), humorous/melancholy honky-tonk lyrics ("Where Has All The Money Gone"/"It Hurts When I Do That"), a final extended track for guit-steel jamming ("Monkey Wrench Blues" or "Stupid Blues"), and a mostly twang-heavy sound one would expect to hear coming out of a Oklahoma beer joint jukebox. To try and capitalize on his superbly entertaining concerts, Telarc released *Live in the Continental Club* (2005), recorded at the venerable Austin, TX live music spot where Brown gained his first critical notice that led to his early Curb releases. While usual fan favorites are included in the live set, Brown simply amazes and rewards listeners with a "Rock and Roll Medley" where he essentially details the history of stratospheric guitar work. After opening with some Spanish flamenco arpeggios to show some of the modern guitar's ancestry, he plays some blistering blues licks, quotes one of his early influences, John Lee Hooker, then replicates famous guitar riffs from the history of rock, to include nods to the Kinks, Led Zeppelin, Chuck Berry, Cream, and Jimi Hendrix, at a minimum, and improvises solos for each segment that honors the originators, but are all in his own inimitable style that is no one else but Junior Brown. In 2012, Brown releaed his tenth studio album, simply titled *Volume 10*, belying the complexity and texture of his music.

www.juniorbrown.com

Bruce, Buddy

Repeatedly listed as a "Tulsa guitarist" in multiple online references, as well as in local Tulsa publications such as the *Tulsa World, Urban Tulsa*, and Oklahoma Jazz Hall of Fame concert press releases, Buddy Bruce is notable for being the lead guitarist on the 1958 #1 Latin-tinged pop hit by the Champs, "Tequila". Laid down on the third take as a final track to round out a four-song session, the song was based on a repeated riff stage vamp used by the trio to stall for time or transition into another element of their set. Recorded by **Gene Autry**'s Challenge Records in 1957 while Bruce was working as part of the Flores Trio, the primarily instrumental song's only lyrics are "Tequila" being shouted three times. Released initially as a B-side to another song from the same session, the tune shot up the charts to #1 in March of 1958. However, due to the trio's leader and saxophonist, Daniel Flores, already being signed to another label, the song was credited to "Chuck Rio" instead of the Flores Trio. More recording sessions were set up to capitalize on the song by a group whose name had not even been determined yet when it had its first and only hit, but by that point Bruce was out of the picture, eventually winding up back in Tulsa where he played regularly through the rest of the 20th century in Tulsa-area performances, and was a regular session guitarist on numerous local Tulsa recordings. In 2005, Bruce was diagnosed with throat cancer and the Oklahoma Jazz Hall of Fame led efforts to provide assistance to the guitarist. In a press release to promote the benefit concerts for Buddy, long time Tulsa jazz mainstay and founder of the Tulsa Jazz Society, Gayle Williamson, said about Bruce: "He is the consummate musician – especially the consummate guitarist. He has some of the best ears of any musician I've ever worked with, and has a vast knowledge of tunes in his memory bank. He can pick up any tune and improvise on it."

Source
Larkin, Colin. "The Champs," The Virgin Encyclopedia of Fifties Music (London: Muze, 1998).

Brumley, Albert Edward
(b. October 29, 1905 - d. November 15, 1977)

Composer of more than 800 songs and hymns, including such favorites as "I'll Fly Away," "Turn Your Radio On," "Jesus Hold My Hand," and "I'd Rather Be An Old-Time Christian," Albert Edward Brumley was born on a cotton farm near Spiro, Oklahoma, a town of about 2,000 residents in far eastern Oklahoma near the Arkansas border. Albert became interested in music after attending a singing school in around 1921 or 1922 in the Rock Island community near Spiro. Prior to his songwriting career, Albert had learned to play the organ and at age nineteen left his farm near Spiro and attended the Hartford Musical Institute in nearby Hartford, Arkansas, where he sang with the Hartford Quartet, but he was too shy to sing as a soloist, which, in turn ushered him into songwriting. The Hartford Music Company was also a gospel music publishing house that produced the new gospel songs in seven-shape notation systems in the same vein as the James D. Vaughan and Stamps-Baxter publishers (shape-note singing books). Some of Albert's first songs were printed in 1927 in a "convention book" (books designed for all-day singing events) called the *Gates of Glory* published by Hartford. The first song accepted by Hartford was "I Can Hear Them Singing Over There".

Brumley actually composed "I'll Fly Away" in 1929 before he left Oklahoma. According to the Brumley Music website, he recalled that while picking cotton and singing the popular song, "If I Had the Wings of an Angel," he thought about flying away. Brumley was quoted: "actually, I was dreaming of flying away from that cotton field when I wrote 'I'll Fly Away'." Many of his songs were developed along these lines because of his deep spiritual convictions.

Albert Edward Brumley

Albert spent considerable time studying and learning from the veteran songwriters at the Hartford Institute, including Eugene M. Bartlett, original owner of the company and composer of such songs as "Victory in Jesus" and "I Heard My Mother Call My Name in Prayer." After leaving Hartford, Albert traveled the Ozarks of Missouri and Arkansas teaching singing schools. Singing schools were an institution based on an itinerant singer who would move from church to church and teach the local congregations how to use the shape-note method in the published songbooks. Fortuitously, Albert met his future wife, Goldie Edith Schell, at one of these schools, and they were married in 1931 and settled in Powell, Missouri, the home of Goldie's parents. Albert and Goldie raised six children: Bill, Bob, Betty, Al, Tom, and Jackson.

Albert continued to write songs while traveling the singing school circuit, and Goldie encouraged him to publish them. Without a doubt, the biggest song he submitted was "I'll Fly Away," mailed to the Hartford Music Company in 1932. Hartford agreed to publish his song and it appeared in one of their hymnals, *The Wonderful Message*. At the time this song was published, Albert was working in his father-in-law's general store in Powell for a dollar a day. Hartford Music Company invited him to join their staff for $12.50 per month, and he spent the next thirty-four years writing songs for the Hartford and Stamps-Baxter music publishing companies.

In addition to "I'll Fly Away", Albert wrote and published his best known works from 1932 to 1945, including "Jesus Hold My Hand", "I'd Rather Be an Old-Time Christian", "I'll Meet You in the Morning", "Camping in Canaan's Land", "There's a Little Pine Log Cabin", "Turn Your Radio On", "Did You Ever Go Sailing? (River of Memories)", "I've Found a Hiding Place", "Rank Stranger to Me", "By the Side of the Road", "Nobody Answered Me", "God's Gentle People", "The Prettiest Flowers Will Be Blooming", and "If We Never Meet Again."

After his career with Hartford and Stamps-Baxter, Brumley formed the Albert E. Brumley & Sons Music Company, Country Gentlemen Music, and eventually purchased Hartford Music Company in 1948 in order to retain copyright control over his classic gospel numbers. Brumley began to publish his own songbooks, while serving as postmaster, in the late 1930s from his base in Powell, Missouri, including his best known, *Albert E. Brumley's Book of Radio Favorites*, and founded in 1969 the annual Albert E. Brumley Sundown to Sunup Sing, now the Albert E. Brumley Memorial Gospel Sing, reported to be the largest outdoor gospel sing in the nation.

Based on his illustrious career, Brumley's musical significance accounted for man accolades and honors. He was inducted into the Nashville Songwriters Hall of Fame, one of the first inductees (1970), Gospel Music Hall of Fame (1972), and the Oklahoma Music Hall of Fame (1998). The Gospel Music Association named him as one of only five persons in the U.S. whose compositions directly affected twentieth century gospel music, while the Smithsonian Institution in Washington, D.C., described Brumley as "the greatest white gospel songwriter before World War II." Two of his songs have received national and international attention. "Turn Your Radio On" received a Citation of Achievement from BMI in 1972, while "I'll Fly Away" has been recorded more than 500 times, including the Grammy award winning 2000 soundtrack for the film, *O Brother, Where Art Thou?* performed by Gillian Welch and Alison Krauss. Even reggae king Bob Marley could not escape the long reach of Brumley's influence, as Marley borrowed liberally from "I'll Fly Away" for "Rastaman Chant" that appeared on the Wailers' 1973 album *Burnin'* (Island). Contemporary hip hop artist Kanye West also included a very traditional harmonized gospel version of "I'll Fly Away" on his #1 2005 album, *The College Dropout* (Roc-A-Fella).

Brumley's songs have been recorded by a broad spectrum of artists, including Elvis Presley, Ray Charles, The Supremes, Statler Brothers, Bellamy Brothers, Chet Atkins, Larry Gatlin, Blackwood Brothers, Florida Boys, Aretha Franklin, Loretta Lynn, Oak Ridge Boys,

Burl Ives, Roy Rogers, Wynonna, Bill Monroe and the Bluegrass Boys, Chuck Wagon Gang, Red Foley, Stanley Brothers, and even the Boston Pops Orchestra.

Many stories are associated with the use of Brumley's songs, including how "Rank Stranger" was made into a bluegrass standard in the late 1950s by Ralph Stanley, or how Hank Williams "borrowed" the melody and lyric pattern for "I Saw the Light" from Brumley's 1939 "He Set Me Free". Finally, Elvis Presley conveyed that "If We Never Meet Again" was his mother's favorite song, and that it was sung at her funeral.

Although Albert E. Brumley died in 1977, his legacy lives on. His family continues to run the publishing house with Bob, Bill, and Betty still operate the company offices built by their father in the 1940s, as well as promote and direct the gospel festival now in its 42nd year in 2010. Brumley's songbooks can still be purchased through company offices as they were originally published. In 2011, The Five Blind Boys of Alabama included Brumley's "Jesus, Hold My Hand" on their album *Take the High Road* (Seguro). As for his other sons, Tom is a well-known steel guitarist in the country field and manages a show in Branson, Missouri, while Al is a gospel singer with several albums to his credit, and Jackson works as a music publisher and manager. In 2012, the Brumley estate celebrated the 80th anniversary of "I'll Fly Away," and in 2013, Brumley and Sons continued licensing Albert's music, and offering both historic recordings and modern offerings via download on the company's website.

www.brumleymusic.com

Bryant, Anita

(b. March 25, 1940)

Recognized for her million selling single of "Paper Roses", that reached #5 on the pop charts in 1960, Miss America runner-up Anita Bryant was born in her grandparent's house in Barnsdall, Oklahoma, a town of roughly 1,300 residents located northwest of Tulsa. The doctor declared her dead at childbirth, but her Grandpa Berry splashed her with a pan of cold water and she revived. After her sister was born, Anita's parents divorced, and her Grandfather John Berry encouraged her to sing at family gatherings and in church and school activities. Every Saturday night, she listened to the Grand Old Opry on radio. With the encouragement of her Grandpa Berry, she first sang in public at the age of two in a Southern Baptist church in Barnsdall, where her selection was "Jesus Loves Me," a song learned from her grandpa. By the age of eight, Anita made her singing debut on radio, and at nine, had won her first talent contest. With a lovely voice without extreme distinction compared to other Oklahoma women vocalists, Patti Page, Wanda Jackson, and Jean Shepard, and looks that could be marketed as sultry or wholesome, Anita Bryant parlayed her beauty queen status into a ten-year popular music career before transitioning into faith-based music, books, and ministries. Her stance against gay rights in the 1970s caused her career extreme difficulty, from which she never returned to her prominent status as wholesome spokesperson for a number of national products.

After moving to Velma-Alma and then Midwest City, Oklahoma, Anita broke into television at age twelve with her own show on WKY-TV in Oklahoma City, where she sang primarily country songs. Her mother remarried and they moved to Tulsa, where Anita attended Will Rogers High School, and captured the lead as a sophomore in the musical, *South Pacific*. She became known as "Oklahoma's Red Feather Girl," and as a high school junior soon drew the attention of Arthur Godfrey Talent Scout Show, where she competed and won first place. Her first recording was "Sinful to Flirt," released in 1956.

In 1958, Anita won the Miss Tulsa and Miss Oklahoma crown and sang as part of the talent competition in the Miss America contest, in which she was second runner-up. This national attention opened new opportunities for Anita. She became a regular on the Don McNeill Breakfast Club show in Chicago and was given a scholarship to Northwestern University. She left Northwestern to sign with Carlton Records in 1958, and her second single, "Till There Was You," from the musical *The Music Man* (1959), reached #30 on the pop charts. It eventually became a million seller and Anita's first gold record. As a result, *Cash Box* magazine named her Most Promising Female Vocalist. Other singles to follow included "Six Boys and Seven Girls"(1959), "Promise Me a Rose"(1959), and "Do-Re-Mi" (1959).

In 1960, Anita produced three major pop hits on the Carlton label, including "In My Little Corner of the World," which charted at #10 and later revived by Marie Osmond in 1974; "Wonderland By Night," which reached #18 as the vocal version of Bert Kaempfert's #1 instrumental hit; and "Paper Roses," which was her most successful hit at #5 on the charts, garnered her another gold record, and was also later covered by Marie Osmond in 1973. Additional singles on the Carlton label included "One of the Lucky Ones", "A Texan and a Girl from Mexico", and "I Can't Do It By Myself".

In 1962, Anita moved to Columbia Records where she recorded several albums, including *In A Velvet Mood* (1962), *Mine Eyes Have Seen the Glory* (1967), *Christmas with Anita Bryant/Do You Hear What I Hear?* (1967), and *Abide With Me* (1970s). Her singles with Columbia included "The World of Lonely People," "Welcome, Welcome Home," and the popular "Step By Step, Little By Little." She later released a children's album, *Orange Bird*, on the Disney label.

From 1960 to 1967, Anita was vocalist with the Billy Graham Crusades after 1965, a regular performer on Bob Hope's Christmas tours of Vietnam, performed at the White House from 1964 to 1967, sang her signature song "The Battle Hymn of the Republic" at both the Democratic and Republican conventions in 1968, at President Lyndon Johnson's funeral in 1973, and at half time of the Super Bowl in 1976, and. Bryant cut seventy-six ads for the Florida Citrus Commission from 1968 through 1979, and served as television spokesperson for Coca-Cola, Kraft Foods, and Holiday Inns during the 1980s. Toward the end of the 1960s, Anita focused more on religious songs and recorded several albums on the Myrrh and Word labels. In addition, she began a series of books in 1970, including *Mine Eyes Have Seen the Glory* (1970), *Amazing Grace* (1971), *Bless This House* (1972), *Fishers of Men* (1973), *Light My Candle* (1974), *Running a Good Race* (1976), *Raising God's Children* (1977), *The Anita Bryant Story* (1977), *At Any Cost* (1978), and *A New Day* (1992).

In the late 1970s, Anita became an outspoken advocate against gay rights and traveled around the country as a motivational speaker from her base in

Anita Bryant, 1964

Miami, Florida, where she had organized the Anita Bryant Ministries. As a result, she became a target for gay activists who disagreed with her on the subject. For a period in the late 1970s, gay activists made media spectacles out of hitting Anita with a pie in the face at public appearances. Ironically, her stand against homosexuals may have had an opposite effect than she intended, giving gay rights an international media forum. The negative publicity caused her to lose multiple bookings and endorsements; and, in the midst of this professional chaos, Anita divorced her husband in 1980. Subsequently, her career and life spiraled into a psychological low point in the 1980s after her stand against gay rights, a decision she has maintained as the right one in several interviews since then. Through her professed faith in God, she believes she emerged from these "dark years" to renewed optimism, conviction, and professional vigor.

In 1990, she married NASA astronaut test crewman, Charlie Dry, a childhood sweetheart, and they moved from Nashville to Berryville, Arkansas, where they opened a music theater in nearby Eureka Springs, Arkansas, in 1991. She then moved to Branson, Missouri, in 1993, and assumed ownership of the John Davidson Theater in 1995, renaming it the Anita Bryant Theater, which did not pan out as a business decision. In 1998, Anita and Charley purchased the Music Mansion Theater in Pigeon Forge, Tennessee, where she starred in the "Anita, With Love" show. Unfortunately for Bryant, none of these enterprises were successful either, causing Anita and her husband to file for Chapter 11 bankruptcy in 2001. In 2003, Bryant and her husband moved back to Oklahoma, choosing Edmond as their new home. She returned to her hometown of Barnsdall in 2005 where the town named a street near where she was born as Anita Bryant Boulevard. Her latest work includes starting a ministry in the Bricktown area of Oklahoma City, volunteering at a local hospital there, assisting with other charities, writing more inspirational books, and recording children's music. According to her website, "Anita is excited about being back home in Oklahoma and believes her latter days will be greater than in the beginning."

Anita Bryant Ministries: www.anitabmi.org

Busey, Gary

(b. June 29, 1944)

Best known musically for his Oscar-nominated performance as Buddy Holly in the 1978 film about the triumphant and tragic life of the 1950s rocker, *The Buddy Holly Story*, Gary Busey lists himself as an actor, musician, and activist on his myspace.com page. Busey was born in Goose Creek, Texas, but raised in Oklahoma where he graduated from Nathan Hale High School in 1962. After attending Pittsburg State University in Pittsburg, Kansas, he transferred to Oklahoma State University in Stillwater where he played in two successful local bands, The Rubber Band, and Carp. Carp recorded an album for Epic Records in 1966. Busey plays drums and received several songwriting credits on the self-titled release, now considered a collectible and rare LP.

By the early 1970s, Busey was appearing as a character named Teddy Jack Eddy in skits on a local Tulsa television show, *The Uncanny Film Festival and Camp Meeting* hosted by *Mazeppa Pompozoidi*. The actor who portrayed Mazeppa in the show, Gailard Sartain, also played the Big Bopper alongside Busey in *The Buddy Holly Story*. On seeing the way-out-there-and-double-kooky show on Tulsa TV, Leon Russell became a fan of the show and Busey's character. According to tulsatvmemories.com, when Russell discovered the character of Teddy Jack Eddy was actually a drummer, Busey landed on Russell's tour schedule. Eventually, in 1975, Busey appeared on three tracks of Russell's *Will O' the Wisp* album, credited as Teddy Jack Eddy, and also later played drums for Kris Kristofferson and Willie Nelson. Incidentally, the actor who portrayed Mazeppa in the show is Gailard Sartain who also played the Big Bopper in *The Buddy Holly Story*.

While Busey is better known to the general public as an actor in over 100 films, he is also an activist for awareness of Traumatic Brain Injury after his 1988 motorcycle accident. He was not wearing a helmet in the accident, in which he hit his head on a curb, nearly costing him his life. For Oklahomans who were alive to see Mazeppa's broadcasts in the early 1970s, however, he will always be Teddy Jack Eddy, and for any fan of Buddy Holly's legacy, Busey's Oscar-nominated portrayal of the primary 50s rocker will stand as the definitive filmic statement on Holly's short but impactful life. Along with manically mesmeriazing appearances on NBC's *All-Star Celebrity Apprentice* in 2012 and 2013, Busey had plans to record some Buddy Holly songs that were never recorded, to be included in an as-yet-to-named film.

Gary Busey

Recommended Reading

For more insight into the eclectic nature of the 1970s Mazeppa television show, see the site emphasizing the Mazeppa show's preservation, www.mazeppa.com ; also see this site dedicated to preserving Tulsa television history: tulsatvmemories.com/mazeppa

Gary Busey's myspace.com site: www.myspace.com/therealbusey

Byas, Don

(b. October 21, 1912 - d. August 24, 1972)

Born in the regional hotbed of Southwestern jazz, Muskogee, Oklahoma, Carlos Wesley "Don" Byas is considered one of the few musicians with enough musical abilities to cross the bridge from the swing era of the 1920s and 30s, to the bebop period of the 1940s, before moving to Europe in the 1950s where he remained for the rest of his life. Although certainly a part of the Kansas City blues-based "riff" style, itself imbedded in Oklahoma territory band traditions, Don Byas also negotiated the flurried notes of bebop with a full-bodied tone that ranks him with his closest comparisons, Coleman Hawkins and Charlie Parker, as one of the more important tenor saxophone players of 20th-century jazz.

Don Byas began his career gigging out of his hometown of Muskogee, Oklahoma, a jazz rich city founded out of wilderness hunted by the Osage when Muscogee (Creek) Indians were removed to the area in 1828. Many Muscogee people, having based their "civilized society" on European models of the South, kept slaves of African descent but allowed them relatively more freedoms than non-Indian slave owners. Subsequent to the Civil War when freed slaves were incorporated into the tribe and given allotments in Indian Territory, Muskogee developed a thriving African-American business district, school system where students learned music and Shakespeare, and an entertainment center that served as a social and economic center for the all-Black towns around Muskogee. The town that produced **Claude "Fiddler" Williams**, **Jay McShann**, **Barney Kessel**, and several other notable jazz figures also served as a railroad nexus for the entire Southwest, which kept new musicians coming to town all the time. This environment provided many performance and learning opportunities for young musicians. For example, Don Byas recruited Jay McShann on his first gigs when McShann was not even that good of a piano player. After playing as a teenager with the most influential territory bands of the Southwest, i.e., Walter Pages's Blue Devils from Oklahoma City, Bennie Moten out of Kansas City, and a group led by transplanted Muskogeeite Terrence Holder call the Dark Clouds of Joy, Byas formed his own group, The Collegiate Ramblers, while in college at Langston University, the historically African-American university in Langston, Oklahoma. In the 1930s, Byas played with some of the West Coast's biggest orchestras, to include Lionel Hampton (1935) and Buck Clayton (1936) before heading to Kansas City to join up with Andy Kirk and his Mighty Clouds of Joy (1939-40).

In Kansas City, Byas became part of the now legendary jam session scene that would go all night long and, ultimately, by most critics' opinions, where Byas's style developed in relation to Coleman Hawkins. Gutarist Eddie Durham remembers a night when Ben Webster, with whom Byas is also connected critically, Coleman Hawkins and Byas had a battle of the tenor saxophones: "They started at eight o'clock and they finished at eight o'clock the next morning." Jazz critics often explain Don Byas in the context of Hawkins, who was eleven years older than Byas and had been playing professionally since age 16 in Kansas City. Hawkins was obviously a mentor for Byas, and the experience explains one of the reasons Byas was able to fit in with the new generation of beboppers who felt the basic big band formulas in which they had been forced to operate were stifling and bereft of creative allowances. With Byas able to play fast and melodically, Byas once told the story about Charlie Parker getting him out of bed to jam because "I was the only one who could play fast enough." By 1941 Byas moved to New York City play in the Count Basie Orchestra as Lester Young's replacement. It was then he recorded "Harvard Blues" with the Basie band, the song most widely used in demonstrating Byas's input on Basie's sound and the changing style of jazz at that time. Byas's solo on "Harvard Blues" practically set the standard for smooth saxophonists of the 1940s with its lilting flow and and warm, round tone. Gunther Schuller, the classical composer and noted jazz scholar, is so enamored with the Byas solo that opens the record, which Schuller calls "flawless," and believes the recording is one of the early Basie band's best.

Another noted aspect of Don's ability is his capacity for spanning the styles between slow ballads and the breakneck speed of bop. Byas is indebted to Hawkins for his big sound, but Byas also added flutter-phrasing and harmonic scale experiments, the sound

By Hugh Foley

most commonly associated with bop via Charlie Parker. While he was in New York City with Jay McShann's orchestra, Parker checked on the burgeoning bop scene at Clark Monroe's Uptown House, one of the two Harlem clubs generally acknowledged as the birthplaces of bop, and recalled, "Don Byas was there, playing everything there was to be played." Oklahoma trumpeter **Howard McGhee**, a player Miles Davis praised as a major influence, remembered telling trumpeter Roy Eldridge, "You're staying too traditional. You ought to come and hang out with Don Byas and learn to play." Subsequently, Eldridge went from playing in the Louis Armstrong style to delivering a rapid fire delivery of harmonic phrases.

Instead of being locked into past jazz styles, Byas moved forward stylistically in the 1940s. An excellent early example of this fluttering, fast-paced phrasing mixed with smooth, soulful melodies, is available on record and CD as *The Harlem Jazz Scene-1941*, featuring Dizzy Gillespie on trumpet, Thelonious Monk on piano, Oklahoma-raised **Charlie Christian** on guitar, and Don Byas on tenor saxophone. Leonard Feather wrote the liner notes for the album and says it is a representative session showing the genesis of bop. Feather, however, focuses on the interchange between Christian and Gillespie, whereas, other critics claim Byas is already a confident player in the idiom while Gillespie is still feeling his way into an identity within the bop movement. From a distance of sixty years hence, Don Byas appears to have been influencing not only one of jazz's and bebop's great trumpeters in Gillespie, but also bop's most monumental saxophonist, Charlie Parker. Even one of Parker's biographers, Ross Russell in *Bird Lives!* (Charterhouse, 1973), describes Parker's style as "a variation of Don Byas out of Coleman Hawkins." Between 1941 and 1944, Byas recorded a number of sessions with Basie, some tracks with Billie Holiday, others with Buck Clayton, did several sessions with other small jazz groups yet to be seen or heard as a result of the World War II vinyl ban and musicians union strike, and was part of the Coleman Hawkins Sax Ensemble, which recorded for Keynote Records.

Don Byas

In 1944, Dizzy Gillespie hired Byas, Oklahoma bassist **Oscar Pettiford**, drummer Max Roach, and pianist George Wallington for a job that opened up on 52nd Street in New York City. The group is known variously as the first modern jazz group or the first working bebop group in jazz. Their music, with its halting rhythmic regularity and exploration of the unfamiliar dissonance of chromatics, soon became the talk of the jazz world. The music was controversial and for some time was just known 52nd Street Jazz. As jazz's next evolution developed, Don Byas blew on the front lines and left the interpretation of his true "bopness" up to the critics, some of whom always felt that Byas was more lyrical than Coleman Hawkins, Dexter Gordon, or Charlie Parker which kept him from fully representing the often frenetic jazz subgenre. However, Gordon was not even into the style until he came to New York and heard Hawkins and Byas. On the 1944 recordings with Gillespie,

Byas seems the most comfortable with adapting his fluid, full-toned sound developed in the swing era to the faster and more melodically complicated aspects of bop. By remaining with his blues and ballad roots, and still adapting to the new style, Byas was able to maintain his individuality and creative progression. Other strong evidence suggesting Byas should certainly be classified as a modern comes from Benny Goodman's biographer, musician James Collier, who says in 1989's *Benny Goodman and the Swing Era* (Oxford): "To my mind, the only swing musician who managed to cross the line [to bop] was Don Byas." Quite often, Don Byas is classified as both swing and bebop in any number of jazz reference materials. During the period of 1944 to 1946, Byas recorded a number of titles for Savoy which demonstrate his trademark style of his big-toned, beautiful ballad style: "Sweet and Lovely" (1944), "September in the Rain" (1945), and "They Say It's Wonderful" (1946). Don's influence on the bop era is more than evident when the music migrated to Los Angeles. By 1947, when Oklahoman **Wardell Gray** and Dexter Gordon picked another song besides "The Hunt" for a live recording session at Billy Berg's, they chose Don's "Byas-A-Drink," which not only featured a Gray/Gordon sax duel, but an extended bop guitar solo by Muskogee, Oklahoma native, **Barney Kessel**.

In 1946, Byas reached his critical apex when he recorded again with Dizzy Gillespie on "Anthropology," "52nd Street Theme," "Ol' Man Bebop," and the now standard jazz classic "Night in Tunisia." The album on which the songs were released also included four songs by a Coleman Hawkins-led group and was an immediate success and sold very that year. Byas left Gillespie for a short job with Duke Ellington that did not work out, but the misfire did not discourage Ellington from hiring Byas on a 1950 tour of Europe, or saying in his memoirs Byas "definitely influenced the avant-garde." Byas left the U.S. for Europe in 1946 with the Don Redman band and took up residence there, finding European audiences more appreciative of his work than those back in United States. Byas toured intermittently with American jazz titans such as Dizzy Gillespie, Stan Getz, Art Blakey, and Ben Webster on their tours throughout Europe where he was widely known. As a result of being in Europe, however, Don never regained the status he held in the U. S during the 1940s. Nonetheless, Byas recorded and released several critically acclaimed albums in the 1950s and early 1960s, *Don Byas [Inner City]* (1953), *A Tribute to* Cannonball (1961), and *A Night in Tunisia* (1963), but he was not recorded often through the late 1960s. He returned to the United States only once in 1970 when he appeared at the Newport Jazz Festival largely because of Dutch documentary being made about him. Byas died of lung cancer August 24, 1972 in Amsterdam, leaving his wife, Jopie, to care for their four young children: Dotty Mae, Ellie Mae, Carlotta, and Carlos, Jr.

In retrospect, Don Byas's most prolific and influential period of playing happened between 1940 and 1946 when he was making the transition from his solid background in the earthy blues of the Southwest and the smooth swing of the big band era into the oncoming bebop era. Although nearly forgotten in the late 1900s by popular jazz history, with the exception of living contemporaries, or modern saxophonist Stanley Turrentine who credits Byas as a precursor to Turrentine's own fame that resulted from the ability to play sensuous ballads. By the beginning of the 21st century jazz critics and historians, such as Jeroen de Valk in his 2001 biography of Ben Webster (Berkeley Books), began to realize and write that Don Byas's tenor saxophone was a vital bridge between the swing and bebop eras, and Don's huge tone grew out of the foundation set by Coleman Hawkins into a lulling, romantic flow equal to any of the greatest tenor saxophone players in jazz history.

By Hugh Foley

More recordings of Byas' music became available in the early 2000s, to include *Don Byas Quartet featuring Sir Charles Thompson Live* (Storyville, 2001), *Vogue* (RCA Victor, 2001), *En Ce Temps-La* (Gitanes Jazz/Universal, 2002), *Riffin and Jivin* (Past Perfect, 2002), and *Americans Swinging in Paris* (EMI 2002), and *Savoy Jam Party: The Savoy Sessions* (Universal, 2009).

C

Caddo Nation of Oklahoma

(In the region that became Oklahoma since since at least 700 A.D.)

As one of thirty-nine federally recognized American Indian tribes, bands, tribal towns, or nations in Oklahoma, the Caddo are one of the first known tribes to have called the state home, along with their historic and current neighbors, the **Wichita** and their affiliated tribes. Along with Caddo people who sing in Native American Church services with specific Caddo songs, and others who are members of other denominations of Christian churches where hymns are sung in the Caddo language, the tribe's annual observation of their traditional Turkey Dance, with all of its associated social and ceremonial songs and dances, is the tribe's most significant and unique contribution to world music from its original ways prior to its contact and conflict with Europeans, Texans, and then the colonial-minded Americans.

The annual Turkey Dance is held each year where the Caddo perform many ceremonial and social dances such as the Swing Dance, the Bell Dance, the Cherokee dance, the Bear Dance, the Drum Dance, the Duck Dance, and the Fish Dance. The music of the Turkey Dance, and its accompanying social and ceremonial songs, has been preserved by Canyon Records on the compact disc re-release of recordings made in 1975 at the Hasinai Cultural Center near Hinton, Oklahoma. *Songs of the Caddo: Ceremonial and Social Dance Music Volume I & II* (Canyon, 1999) provides a stellar recording of Caddo songs that are still being performed each year by the tribe at their annual dances. Along with the "Turkey Dance Songs," the album features the "Caddo Flag Song," "Bell Dance Songs," "Duck Dance Songs," "Fish Dance Songs," "Bear Dance Songs," and "Morning Songs." Long-time powwow attendees also remember the Caddo hosted some of the very first intertribal powwows in Oklahoma at Murrow's Dance Ground near Binger in southwestern Oklahoma around the time of World War I, long before any of the head staff, parade in, or contesting elements were introduced to the powwow arena. The Caddo also still have a strong Native American Church musical tradition because of their proximity to its late 19th century development in southwestern Oklahoma, and the continued practice of the ceremony with all of its accompanying music through the present era. Some Caddo people follow a distinctive denomination of the Native American Church that emerged in the late 19th century known as the Big Moon ceremony. The music of the Native American Church is meditative and mesmerizing, essentially consisting of a simple phrase that is repeated in song or chant by the singer, usually referencing some spiritual aspect of the ceremony, and accompanied by a gourd rattle shaken in unison with a designated drummer playing a small water drum. The drum is usually a small cooking kettle covered in an animal hide and filled partially with water to get a unique percussive sound. Songs are sung in a round, with participants taking turns singing as the drum and the rattle go around the tipi circle for most of the all-night ceremony that lasts until just after sunrise. The Caddo also have a legacy of music associated with the Ghost Dance movement of 1889 and 1890 that was a last attempt by Native some Plains Native people to turn back the tide of white encroachment through song and dance. While the ceremony was ultimately outlawed by the United States government in 1890, some of the music from that period has never been forgotten. In 1989, Caddo singer Randlett Edmonds recorded four songs for The State Arts Council of Oklahoma's Songs of Indian Territory Project. Three of the songs are Caddo Ghost Dance songs with Randlett accompanied by Wimpy Edmonds, one of which can be translated into English as "In the end the Caddos will go to the land above." Also on the cassette release of the project is a Bell Dance song on which Randlett Edmonds is accompanied by Margie Deer, Geneva Edmonds, and Donna Edmonds Williams.

Currently, two organizations, the Caddo Culture Club and the Hasinai Cultural Preservation Organization actively pursue the maintenance of Caddo life ways and traditions. As of 2010, the Hasinai Society sponsored weekly practice of drumming and singing Caddo songs at the tribe's cultural building. According to the tribe's website, "Everyone is welcome to attend, from beginners to advanced, all ages. Snacks are served." Along with weekly Caddo language classes sponsored by the tribe, both the Hasinai Society and Caddo Culture Club have weekly meetings at the tribal complex. Additionally, due to intermarriage between Caddo people and members of other tribes, the Caddo also sponsor yearly stomp dances, the traditional song and dance of the **Muscogee (Creek)** people. While participation in stomp dances is relatively new compared to their other music, some Caddo people enjoy this musical tradition for its cultural connection to their relatives, as well as the general good feeling that comes from the social experience of a non-ceremonial stomp dance.

As part of its efforts to recognize the vast and historic American Indian musical traditions from the state, in 2001 the Oklahoma Music Hall of Fame in Muskogee, OK, inducted the Caddo Nation into the hall of fame for the tribe's persistence in keeping their musical traditions alive in the face of overwhelming circumstances. Even after the death of many tribal members in the 19th century due to illness and the harsh conditions of several relocations, the ensuing boarding school movement of the 20th century that suppressed the practice of traditional music and dance among youth, as well as the general social pressures of integrating into mainstream American society, the Caddo have persisted in maintaining as much of their ancient music as possible. When the former

Caddo Singers, circa 2001

chairperson of the Caddo Nation, LaRue Parker, accepted the induction award for the Caddo into the Oklahoma Music Hall of Fame, she said the award was "for all the singers we left behind, and the wonderful singers who carry on our traditions today."

In 2010, Chairperson Brenda Edwards led the Caddo Nation of roughly 5,000 people. Contemporarily, the tribe maintains a number of programs for its citizens, operates its own art gallery and cultural center, and has its own fire brigade, as well as all the standard governmental departments necessary to running a nation state and tribal community. While many Caddo people have entered the intertribal powwow world, and others maintain unique Caddo Native American Church songs, Caddo singers continue ancient musical traditions such as the Turkey Dance that occur nowhere else in the world of music.

Caddo Nation of Oklahoma: www.caddonation-nsn.gov

Caldwell, Chuck

(b. April 10, 1934)

Known by musicians with whom he has played as the "Man Who Tamed the Steel Guitar", Chuck Caldwell has worked with a number of Western swing and country music luminaries from his long-time base of Lawton, Oklahoma, where he was born and where he started playing guitar at age five or six when he picked up a guitar his mother owned and on which she could play a few chords. While he never learned to read music formally, Chuck began picking out melodies by ear, took a few guitar lessons, and joined his first band by age 12. As a result of Lawton being a military town due to the presence of Fort Sill Army Base, plenty of work for musicians existed in the town to entertain troops on R and R. By the time he was sixteen, Caldwell was playing professionally throughout Oklahoma and Texas with the Southern Aires, led by Western swing and rockabilly legend, **Tommy Allsup**, a gig he kept from 1950 to 1964, during which time he saw his first pedal steel guitar in about 1950. After trying to make his own pedal steel with mixed results, he acquired a Gibson Electraharp in the late 1950s, and began mastering the instrument which led Chuck to become known in Oklahoma Western swing circles as a fine player. That status garnered him his most extended touring dates with **Merl Lindsay** and his Oklahoma Night Riders who were based in Oklahoma City, but traveled from Nashville to North Dakota, and from Las Vegas to Anchorage, Alaska, playing with Lindsay. Throughout his career, Caldwell worked with a number of significant musicians on stage, to include Loretta Lynn, Marty Robbins, Tex Ritter, Don Gibson, Webb Pierce, Chuck also did eight tours with the Grand Old Opry, backing up Little Jimmy Dickens, and also toured with Pee Wee King. With the Southern

Aires, he experienced opening for Elvis Presley's combo seven times in 1955, just before Elvis exploded on the national scene with "Heartbreak Hotel" in 1956.

Caldwell has one independent CD to his credit, *Johnny Case Presents Chuck Caldwell: Country Music Legacy* (Priority Records), recorded from 1974 to 1977, and demonstrates his complete grasp of the instrument on a collection of country music classics, as well as his own composition, "Lawton Blues". While his overall career might be relegated to the good memories of musicians with whom he played, and who obviously appreciated his skillful abilities on the steel, he is also remembered for a unique footnote in rock and roll history due to his presence at Clovis, New Mexico recording session in May of 1957 where Buddy Holly was laying down his first big hit, "Peggy Sue". Needing a little more rhythmic texture, Caldwell was asked to jingle a set of keys during the recording, which he did, and which can be heard on a close listen to the song, especially during the song's choruses.

Cale, Johnny "J. J."

(b. December 5, 1938)

With a recording career that spans more than fifty years that is filled with the fusion of country, blues, and rockabilly for which he has become critically revered and widely covered by other musicians, J. J. Cale is singer, guitarist, songwriter, and studio engineer who may be the most iconoclastic artist to emerge from the 1950s rock scene in Tulsa. While has remained popular in Europe since the 1970s, his actual name is lesser known by many music fans in the U.S. who may know his songs, but not him. Cale's music still receives regular airplay in the states as done by such notable artists as Eric Clapton, Lynyrd Skynyrd, Deep Purple, Johnny Cash, Santana, the Allman Brothers and Widespread Panic. Exhibiting his broad appeal to musicians of many genres, a wide-ranging but partial list of additional artists who have covered Cale's material include Chet Atkins, Kansas, Dr. John, Nazareth, Larry Carlton, Captain Beefheart, Freddie King, Deep Purple, and Waylon Jennings.

Born in Oklahoma City, but reared in Tulsa, he began playing a friend's guitar in the pre-rock era when **Bob** and **Johnnie Lee Wills** still held sway over Oklahoma's popular music scene. After scraping together enough money to get his own guitar, Cale's earliest musical influences included the Elvis Presley Sun rockabilly records with Scotty Moore on guitar, Clarence "Gatemouth Brown, Chuck Berry, and Chet Atkins, along with other 1950s rock icons such as Buddy Holly, Chuck Little Richard, and Fats Domino. In trying to play like those musicians, J.J. (a stage name he created that has been wrongly

J.J. Cale, 1970s publicity shot

By Hugh Foley / 99

interpreted by French writers as Jean Jacque) remembered in a 1990s interview, "I missed it and came up with my own kind of thing."

As a teenager in Tulsa whose age collided perfectly with the first wave of classic rock and roll in the 1950s, he formed his own group, Johnny Cale and the Valentines, and played in clubs for "ten dollars a night and all the beer you could drink," alongside Russell Bridges (aka **Leon Russell)**, Leo Feathers, **Carl Radle**, **Chuck Blackwell**, **Jimmy Karstein**, **David Gates** (who would later form Bread), and **Jack Dunham,** before Cale moved to Nashville in 1959 and was hired by the Grand Ole Opry's touring company. He returned to Tulsa after a few years, reunited with Leon Russell, and in 1964 moved to Los Angeles with Russell and Radle. Once in Los Angeles, Cale fulfilled engineering duties for Leon Russell at Leon's home studio, where he met Snuff Garrett who signed Cale to Viva Records in 1965, and who would also record Cale for Liberty Records. Cale's Viva album with fellow Oklahoman, **Roger Tillison**, *Take a Trip Down Sunset Strip* (1967), released under the group name The Leathercoated Minds, is primarily a collector's vinyl album, and a curiosity to Cale that so many people are interested in it as it sounds extremely dated to him. In co-operation with Snuff Garrett, the project was re-released on CD by Sundazed Records in 2006. The album is primarily a collection of psychedelic era cover songs, plus four Cale instrumentals and some sound effects recorded around the Sunset Strip in Los Angeles. After the Leathercoated Minds, Garrett also recorded Cale for Liberty Records. One "audition record" single was went out to radio stations from the sessions, featuring a Cale/Russell composition, "It's a Go-Go Place", essentially a party song. The B-side was a cover of a novelty tune about the comic book detective, "Dick Tracy", wherein Cale's vocals sound a lot like the wry approach of another Oklahoma song jokester, **Roger Miller,** who had just had #1 hits with "Dang Me" (1964), and the iconic "King of the Road" (1965). The most significant recording to come out of the Liberty Sessions was a grooving rock song with a rolling-down-the-road snare drum, Cale's casual voice extolling the early morning hours, country rock guitars, and a complimenting horn section that launches the song like a Stax Records soul number. While the song did not even seem significant enough to release, the first recording of "After Midnight", popularized by Eric Clapton as his first solo hit in 1970, illustrates a musical arranging formula, tempo, lyrical theme, and stylistic aesthetic that would inform all of Cale's music after that. Essentially, the artistic palate appears to have been set for J.J. Cale as he was recording the Liberty sessions, even if nobody really knew it yet. Not enough seemed to be happening for him at the time in Los Angeles, so he went back to Tulsa and started working the club circuit where he had started out in the 1950s.

After a trip to Nashville where he worked as a recording engineer, Cale signed with Leon Russell's Shelter Records in 1969. Cale was still putting his solo career together when he heard Clapton's version of "After Midnight" on a Tulsa radio station. The song was Cale's first hit as a songwriter and provided him with some much needed exposure and income from royalties. Encouraged by the success of "After Midnight," J.J. released his first album, *Naturally* (1971) which provided the Top 40 hit "Crazy Mama", as well as his own version of "After Midnight", and "Call Me the Breeze", later covered in a five- minute-plus version on Lynyrd Skynyrd's mega-platinum *Second Helping* (MCA, 1974). Skynyrd's version of "Call Me the Breeze" appeared again in 2002 on the *Sunshine State* soundtrack. A particularly interesting element of "Crazy Mama" and "Call Me the Breeze" is J.J.'s use of an Acetone drum machine he had obtained by trading an old banjo for it. Continuing to experiment with recording, Cale ran the drum machine through an old Fender amplifier, turned it up and recorded it, which may be one of the first uses of a drum machine on a pop record, now considered standard practice for many of the manufactured artists of the contemporary era. Cale followed *Naturally* with *Really* (1972) which furthered his recording style of letting the soloing instruments be equal to his vocals on the tracks, produced the minor hit "Lies," and offered a low-key, two-minute song named after his home state, "If You're Ever in Oklahoma."

Cale continued his Oklahoma theme by naming his third album *Okie* (1974), and also persisted in his lo-fi recording techniques by recording the title track on the back porch of his house in Tulsa, and laying down other tracks for the album, such as "Anyway the Wind Blows", inside the house. *Okie* also provided more inspiration for Lynyrd Skynyrd who recorded "I Got the Same Old Blues Again" on *Gimme Back My Bullets* (MCA, 1976). With more royalties coming in from other people's versions of his songs, in 1975 Cale moved to Tennessee and bought a home in Hermitage which was far enough outside of town so people "would not just drop by all the time." In 1976, Cale released *Troubadour* featuring his last chart hit, "Hey Baby", but more significantly included the would-be drug anthem, "Cocaine", covered by Clapton on his 1977 album, *Slowhand* (Polydor). The entire album *Slowhand* is a nod to J.J. Cale and the influence of his trademark bluesy-shuffle on Clapton's musical aesthetic of the time. Clapton once said the album *Lay Down Sally* was as close as an Englishman could get to being J.J. Cale. On the strength of the single "Cocaine", Cale could have gone back out on the road in support of new album. Instead, he headed back to Nashville where he barely stayed busy, playing on an album by a French singer, Eddy Mitchell, and working on Neil Young's *Comes a Time* (1978).

Cale's next album, *5* (1979), with appearances by old friends **Carl Radle** and **Jimmy Karstein**, who has played on practically every J.J. Cale session and show since the early 1970s, as well as his guitarist and wife, Christine Lakeland, on vocals and various instruments. Lakeland, originally from Kalamazoo, Michigan, met J.J. at a prison benefit show in Nashville after she had just come off the road playing with **Merle Haggard**. Cale hired her for his band and Lakeland has been with him ever since. *5*'s sound reaffirmed the source of Dire Straits' style, who had a hit the year before with "Sultans of Swing" from their self-titled album of Cale clone songs. While radio ignored *5*'s single, "The Sensitive Kind", Carlos Santana "got it" and took the tune to the middle of the *Billboard* Hot 100. In 1980 Cale left Nashville and returned to California where he promptly sold what he did not want, and packed the rest into a gleaming Airstream trailer and moved into an Anaheim trailer park where he was notoriously reclusive. Cale released his final Shelter album, *Shades*, in 1981 to very little fanfare although it had songs with his subtle humor, "I Wish I Had Not Said That," and his penchant for straight ahead back porch jams on "Mama Don't". 1982's album, *Grasshopper*, found success in Europe, but not in the U.S., and 1983's album, *#8*, became his first not to chart at all. Following that disconcerting experience after more than twenty-five years of playing and recording music, Cale went into a lengthy seclusion. A pop culture reminder of Cale surfaced when "After Midnight" surfaced on a 1988 Michelob commercial featuring Clapton in the commercial.

During his six-year release hiatus, Cale recorded songs that finally emerged in 1989 on *Travel-Log*, an album that featured **Hoyt Axton** on backing vocals, James Burton (Elvis Presley's touring guitarist from the 1970s) on one track, and long-time drummer and fellow Oklahoman, Jim Karstein. When he started to tour for the album, Cale told an interviewer quoted in a press release for the album that he had spent the previous six years mowing the lawn, cycling, and listening to rap and Van Halen. *Travel-Log* snuck into the lower half of *Billboard*'s Top 200 for about 10 weeks, peaking at #136, his last chart album until the 2000s.

J.J. released his tenth album, *Number 10*, in 1992 to his fans' delight, but not many others, and in 1994 released *Closer to You*, an album featuring his wry take on the music industry, "Sho-Biz Blues". *Closer to You* garnered the same cultish admiration from long-time Cale devotees, as did his 1996 release, *Guitar Man* that contained solemn, dire predictions of general environmental and cultural disaster in "Death in the Wilderness," as well as the usual misfit and social outsider characters that fill Cale's songs. Mercury released two "Best of" compilations in 1997 and 1998, *Anyway the Wind Blows: Anthology*, and *The Very Best of J.J. Cale*. In 2001, Cale released his first live album, *Live*, recorded at Carnegie Hall and other venues around the U.S. and Germany. Again, the CD featured stalwart Cale sidemen **Bill Raffensperger**, **Rocky Frisco**, and **Jim Karstein**, with "newer" additions to his comfort zone of players, Christine Lakeland and Jim Cruce, who began playing with him in the 1980s. Cale also joined Eric Clapton in 2001 to perform on an album by the Crickets, Buddy Holly's band. Clapton's admiration for Cale has existed since he first heard "After Midnight." Asked by an interviewer for a press release which musician he would want to be other than himself, Clapton named J.J. Cale. "I like his philosophy, writing skills, and musicianship," Clapton explained, "He's a fine, superior musician, one of the masters of the last three decades of music." Those comments explain why Clapton covered another Cale tune, "Travelin' Light," on his 2001 *Reptile* CD. Also re-surfacing in 2001 was Cale's "Long Way Home" from *Closer to You*, which appeared in the film *Bandits*, starring Billy Bob Thornton and Bruce Willis. In 2002, Mercury Records released another "Best of" J.J. Cale as part of its *20th Century Masters* collection. Also in 2002, Classic Pictures released a DVD of a 1979 Cale performance as *J.J. Cale: the Lost Session*.

J.J. Cale (right) with the author, New York City, circa 1989.

Cale toured in 2002 with a host of Oklahoma musicians with whom he has long been comfortable, to include Tulsa-based pianist Rocky Frisco and bassist Bill Raffensperger, as well as musicians long known for their association with the Tulsa music scene, **David Teegarden** (drums), Don White (guitar/vocals), and **Walt Richmond** (keyboards). In June of 2003, Cale returned to Tulsa to record with those same musicians *and some* for an album that became *To Tulsa and Back* (Sanctuary, 2004). Recorded at his friend David Teegarden's Natura Studios near Beggs, Oklahoma, the album included what amounted to a reunion of Cale's old Tulsa buddies. Along with old regulars such as Richmond (keyboard), Teegarden and White, the album also features other long-time accomplices: **Jimmy "Junior" Markham** (harmonica), Bill Raffensberger (bass), Rocky Frisco (keyboard), Gary Gilmore (bass), Jimmy Karstein (drums), and Shelby Eicher (fiddle, mandolin). Full of Cale's now instantly recognizable vocals singing wearily or in subtle exaltation about life's variables, *To Tulsa and Back* clips along with a bouncy tempo that first emerged on "After Midnight", alternately ranging through the overlapping zones of country, blues, and rock. Just like his earliest style-defining recordings, the album's texture is flush with subtle horn, keyboard and fiddle fills, rhythmically led by finger-picked electric guitar and a loping bass, all of which is accented by sharp electric guitars played with a breezy touch. Hit the record button, start up the musicians, and, presto, you get a J.J. Cale record.

A slight difference on this one is Cale's maturing lyrical bent, in that he wrote one song for the environmental Earthjustice campaign ("Stone River"), and two with more than casual socio-political commentary ("The Problem" and "Homeless"). Cale toured for only the second time since 1996 to support the album released by an unusual amalgamation of labels, Sanctuary, Blue Note, and Capitol's EMI France division, as Cale has remained a consistent seller in Europe.

Along with a stop at Eric Clapton's *Crossroads Guitar Festival* in Dallas that was chronicled in a DVD of the event, J.J.'s 2004 concerts were frequently sold out, and enhanced further by Clapton joining him during the tour.

J.J. Cale, 2001

To Tulsa and Back mostly found favor with his most ardent fans and always-supportive journalistic reviewers, but did not sell well enough to chart, serving to make him only that much more enigmatic, an image furthered by the filming of a documentary about Cale's life by German director, Jorg Bundschuh, released in 2008 as *To Tulsa and Back: On Tour with J.J. Cale*. While the film was being completed, all Cale did was appear on a sparkling blues album with Eric Clapton, *The Road to Escondido* (Reprise, 2006), a Top 25 album that won a GRAMMY for Best Contemporary Blues Album in 2008. Cale's sixteenth studio album, *Roll On* (Rounder, 2009), features twelve more new songs, plus the title track with Clapton left over from *Escondido*, and sounds very much like other J.J. Cale music, which is to say each new album is like getting a visit from an old friend who has some new stories to tell. Cale calls on David Teegarden and Jim Keltner for most of the album's percussion, but being the iconoclast he is, J.J. plays multiple tracks of guitars, pedal steel, bass, drums, and synthesizers by himself on the CD, which landed reverent reviews by critics such as Austin Scaggs in *Rolling Stone* (March 5, 2009), but the album was embraced primarily by his loyal fans in the U.S., and just barely cracked into the European album charts. The Rounder Records press release for the album hinted it might be the last new studio album for a while from Cale, who turned 72 in 2010.

J.J. Cale's nonchalant rock songs and overall sound have been embraced and popularized by several artists since Eric Clapton's hit with "After Midnight". Clapton convinced Cale to get back in the studio, however, with several vocal and guitar contributions to Clapton's self-titled 2010 CD. Along with filling a niche in American popular culture reserved for rustic musical sages and wizened blues men, his larger relationship to Oklahoma's music history is his particular representation of the state's place as a musical crossroads where country and blues have coexisted and nourished each other since colliding in the late 19th century within the state's boundaries, and coalescing in Tulsa with a bunch musically gifted teenagers in the 1950s, of which J.J. Cale is one of the most celebrated.

www.jjcale.com

By Hugh Foley / 103

The Call

(formed 1980, Santa Barbara, California)

With primary hits "The Walls Came Down", "I Still Believe", and "Let the Day Begin", The Call was a moderately successful 1980s modern rock band started by two men with shared Oklahoma backgrounds who met in California, neither of them knowing their grandfathers had been best friends in college. While not on par commercially with U2, The Call's sound was equally ambitious with aggressive rock guitar, swirling keyboards, funky and decorative bass lines, constant double time drumming, and Been's soaring vocals with lyrics more in tune with U2's anthems and existentialism than American pop love themes. Vocalist Michael Been is highly regarded by some of rock's truly stratospheric voices, such U2's Bono and Simple Minds' Jim Kerr, both of whom did guest vocal appearances on Call albums, as did rock iconoclast Peter Gabriel. According to the band's myspace page, singer/songwriter/bassist Michael Been lived in Oklahoma City where he "grew up on rock and roll: Elvis, Little Richard, Chuck Berry, The Beatles, The Stones, and Yardbirds." Been started playing guitar as child, and "as soon as I was old enough, I had a band." Been then moved to Chicago where he was impacted by blues greats still alive at the time, such as Muddy Waters and Jimmy Reed, while absorbing Bob Dylan and The Band on recordings. Co-founder and drummer of The Call, Scott Emerick, also explains his Oklahoma musical foundation on the band's myspace page: "I've been playing since I was a kid. I grew up in a musical environment. My dad was a musician so we always had music in our home. He played drums, trumpet, and guitar and sang in combos. My other brother also sang in local bands around Tulsa. I played in the jazz band at school, and it was about the same time I began drumming for a rock band." As well as his favorite rock drummers Charlie Watts and Levon Helm of The Band, Emerick listened to the great jazz drummers Buddy Rich, Max Roach, and Art Blakey. "They all had a tough sound," he writes, admiringly, adding, "Being from Oklahoma I suppose I was influenced by country and Western music."

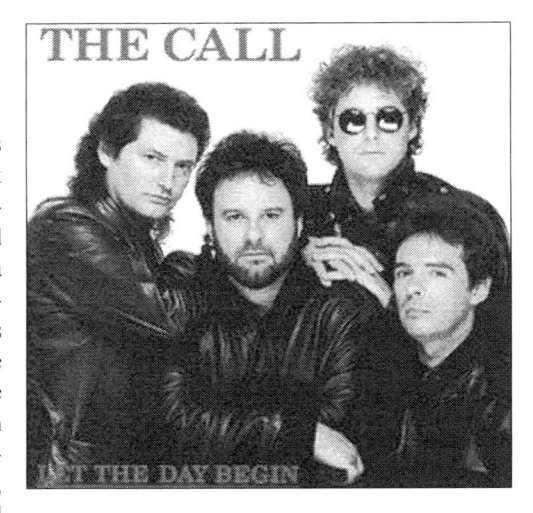

After high school, Scott followed a well-worn path of Oklahoma musicians heading out to California to look for work and a music career. After playing in a couple of bands around Los Angeles, and getting a house band gig in Las Vegas for six months, he returned to Tulsa where he heard about Michael Been. As he recalls, "I saw this guy I had known in California who suggested I go back and look up this singer named Michael Been who had this really great voice. I did and Michael and I have been playing music together since then." After meeting in 1972, the two played in a few bands together before locating to Santa Cruz, California where they formed Moving Pictures with Bay Area musicians Tom Ferrier (guitar) and Greg Freeman (bass). In 1980, renamed The Call, they signed with Mercury/Polygram, launching an-year major label career (1982-1990). While the self-titled first album barely caused a blip on the pop music landscape, 1983's *Modern*

Romans (Mercury) landed just as MTV was programming music videos as the cornerstone of their channel. With a catchy melodic hook played on guitar, Emerick's galloping drums, Been's confrontational but magnetic vocals, The Band's Garth Hudson on keyboards, and a group sing-a-long chorus, "When the Walls Come Down" fit right into an MTV or modern rock radio rotation of Talking Heads, U2, Simple Minds, Big Country, and Tears for Fears. While the song only reached #74 on the *Billboard* Hot 100, the band's popularity via MTV and recognition by British pop singers earned them a 1983 tour of the U.S. and Europe opening for Peter Gabriel, on the road due to his popular hit, "Shock the Monkey", also an MTV favorite of that period. After one more album for Mercury, *Scene Beyond Dreams* (1984), did not achieve label expectations, The Call moved to Elektra. Altering their line-up with Jim Goodwin keyboards when Hudson left, and Been switching to bass when Freeman departed, the result was *Reconciled*, which stayed on the *Billboard* album charts for thirty weeks in 1986.

With its historic Oklahoma photographs of a baby in an open leather carrying bag on the front cover, and a serious Oklahoma twister kicking up dust on the back cover, *Reconciled* revealed The Call at its most quintessential distillation as a pop band, both for better and for worse. The band was certainly as good a group of musicians as any of the UK pop rockers, and live television performances from the period now archived on youtube.com bear that out. Been's voice was equal to any of the major male pop singers of the time. However, while Been's singing and lyrics were gripping on a recording, he was not the same type of mercurial performer as Bono, nor as telegenic as Kerr, Gabriel, or Byrne, a hindrance in the new video-driven era of the 1980s as flashier West Coast pop metal acts began to dominate more video air time. Additionally, the band got caught in the grey area between a fragmenting radio spectrum, as Top 40 radio and more traditional album rock stations tried to define themselves in contrast to the new modern rock format the mid 1980s born out of the audience who leaned more toward R.E.M. and U2, as opposed to the aging classic rockers or Jackson family/Whitney Houston pop of the era. While The Call had a sound appropriate for pop radio stations that also played Simple Minds, Been's lyrics and vocal delivery were closer to Bono's or David Byrne's, placing the group more in a modern rock radio context, which kept it away from the mainstream rock stations. Nonetheless, the album garnered immediate interest due to the presence of Jim Kerr of Simple Minds and Peter Gabriel on background vocals, and The Band's Robbie Robertson playing guitar on one track. Along with Kerr being a fan of Michael Been, the album produced one legitimate single, *"I Still Believe (Grand Design)"* that garnered enough airplay to justify Simple Minds, then at a peak of their success, to invite The Call out to open for their North American tour. 1987's *Into the Woods* (Elektra/Asylum) generated no interest from any of those camps as it had none of the inspired spark of *Reconciled*. Another label change, this time to MCA, provided the band its last surge of contemporary popularity with the 1989 album, *Let the Day Begin*, the title track of which was finally a #1 hit on *Billboard*'s Mainstream Rock Chart. However, "Let the Day Begin" rose no higher than #51 on the pop singles chart.

Ironically, at about the same time as the decade waxed into the 1990s, modern rock radio began shifting away from the big production sound embraced by The Call and Simple Minds, and started transitioning into the harder-edged grunge era led by Nirvana, Soundgarden, the Red Hot Chili Peppers. Therefore, The Call had by default become a retro-rock sound that no longer fit "alternative" radio, was too alternative for pop radio, and too commercial for college radio. Their final album, *Red Moon*, could not even be saved by a guest shot by Bono himself on "What's Happened to You", which was issued as a single, but only received minimum notice in the mainstream radio rock market, and barely more in the modern rock format due to the U2 connection. In 1990, the Call announced their disbanding. After a few years of regrouping, Michael Been released a solo album in 1994, *On the Verge of a Nervous Breakthrough* (Qwest/Reprise), and continued recording bass and vocals in sessions for other artists. In 2000, The Call, with Been, Ferrier, and Musick, returned with a live album, *Live Under the Red Moon*, and a supporting tour that carried them through most of 2001. At least three greatest hits collections have been released for the band, the most recent being the Millenium Collection: 20th Century Masters Collection (Hip-0, 2000). In 2009, the Oklahoma History Center used the phrase "Another Hot Oklahoma Night" from lyrics in The Call's song, "Oklahoma", released on *Reconciled*, to carry the theme and name of their exhibits and a book on rock history in the state of Oklahoma. With a shock to everyone, singer Michael Been died of an apparent heart attack at a music festival in Belgium, 8/20/2010. Been was working as a sound man for Black Rebel Motorcycle Club, for whom his son was the lead singer and bassist.

Sources
http://the-call-band.com
www.myspace.com/thecallband

The Cannons

(Larry – b. September 15, 1955)

(Darla and Karla – b. October 17, 1961)

With perfect harmonies that only seem to come from family acts, The Cannons recorded for Mercury Records and landed two songs on the *Billboard* Hot Country Chart in 1986 and 1987. While all three siblings were born in Muskogee, Oklahoma, they grew up in Wagoner just fifteen miles to the east. Karla and Darla started singing together at age three, and

The Cannons (l-r): Karla, Larry, and Darla.

followed a familiar show business path of singing in church and for civic clubs, playing in the Wagoner Public Schools band program, and then joining brother, Larry, for performances as a group at Western Hills Lodge when they were juniors in high school. Larry plays trumpet, played in the Pride of Oklahoma Marching Band, and also served as the band's drum major, as well as playing rhythm guitar on all non-horn focused songs by the group in concert. Both twins are multi-instrumentalists; Karla plays trumpet, piano, and several other instruments, while Darla plays saxophone primarily.[1]

Highly enjoyable entertainers who featured country, gospel, classic rock and roll, and vocal music specialty numbers that allowed the trio to highlight their harmonies, the group performed in a number of impressive forums, such as The Grand Ole Opry, at The White House in 1983, on several Nashville Network television specials, and multiple appearances on the nationally syndicated country music and comedy program, *Hee Haw*. They played Academy of Country Music and Country Music Association showcases, in Las Vegas and Switzerland respectively, and performed with a long list of significant performers: Johnny Cash, Marty Robbins, Reba McEntire, Barbara and Louise Mandrell (whose father, Irby, managed The Cannons), The Oak Ridge Boys, The Statler Brothers, Vince Gill, Kitty Wells, Dottie West, Kathy Mattea, Ricky Skaggs, Lynn Anderson, Mel Tillis, Hank Thompson, Donna Fargo, The Whites, and Wanda Jackson.

In 1986, The Cannons charted "Do You Mind If I Step In Your Dreams", on the *Billboard* Hot Country Chart, peaking at #73, and followed with "Love'll Come Looking for You" in 1987, peaking at #73, not major hits, but indications of their professional status in the music industry, more than many people who try to make a career out of music can say. In 2010, Karla (Cannon) Shelby was the Director of Choral Activities and Musical Theater at Western Oklahoma College in Altus; Darla was a financial associate in the budget office at the University of Oklahoma and owned a restaurant with her husbnd. As chief legal counsel, Larry was the corporate secretary and direrctor of legal services for Life Way of Nashville, TN.

Note

1. The author played trombone in the Wagoner Junior High Band with the Cannon twins in the mid-1970s.

Cantrell, Jerry (guitarist for Alice in Chains)

(b. March 18, 1966)

Primarily known as the lead guitarist, songwriter, and harmony vocalist for the Seattle rock group, Alice in Chains, who emerged from that scene just after Nirvana and Pearl Jam, Jerry Cantrell is not a native-born Oklahoman; however, he often does spend quality time in the state on a family ranch, called the Double J, in southeast Oklahoma in Atoka County. Cantrell was born in Tacomah, Washington, and raised by his mother, Gloria Jean. As of 2010 he lived in Los Angeles, but has been drawn to Oklahoma since he was a child by his father, Jerry Cantrell, Sr., and other close family members who live in the general area of Boggy Depot, a long faded pre-Civil War trading post. Around 2005, Cantrell and his father, about whom he composed the Alice in Chains 1992 hit, "Rooster", began building a ranch house on

Jerry Cantrell, 2010

land that has been in the family since prior to Oklahoma's statehood in 1907. According to Cantrell when he showed the place off in an episode of *MTV Cribs*, it is a part-time residence, rehearsal spot, and family gathering spot for the guitarist, but otherwise a full time cattle ranching operation run by his father. In the MTV feature, Jerry indicated he considered the ranch his "family place" now and forever, to be passed on to his children, a sentiment that pretty much locks him into state lore from now on. Cantrell's body of work with Alice in Chains contains some of the defining guitar riffs and melodic hooks of 1990s rock music (think "Down in a Hole", "Man in a Box" or "Would"). Cantrell also has two solo albums, the first one named after his father's childhood home, *Boggy Depot* (Sony, 1998), and *Degradation Trip* (Roadrunner, 2002). In 2012, Cantrell started working on the next Alice in Chains album, tentatively slated for a 2013 or 2014 release.

Sources

www.aliceinchains.com
www.jerrycantrell.com
MTV Cribs, Episode 605, (New York: MTV Networks, 2009).

Card, Hank

(b. March 31, 1955)

Rhythm guitarist, primary songwriter, and one of the founding members of the Austin Lounge Lizards, a neo-traditionalist bluegrass band with uproarious comic and satirical tendencies, Hank Card was born to William L. and Alva M. Card in Caldwell, Kansas, because his hometown of Medford, Oklahoma, lacked hospital facilities. He, however, lived in Medford, the county seat of Grant County, located in the north central part of the state, until age six. Hank has one brother, Lee A. Card, a long-time associate district judge in Ardmore. His father was raised in Medford, and was an attorney there until the Card family moved to Oklahoma City, where Hank's father died in 1961. Hank's mother was raised in southeastern Oklahoma, taught high school and college English for many years, obtained her doctorate at age sixty, and died in 2002. Within a career of over thirty years, the Austin Lounge Lizards have recorded a number of critically praised and laughed at bluegrass albums of social and political comedy songs.

Hank Card

Upon graduation from Putnam City High School in Oklahoma City in 1973, Hank chose to attend Princeton, the prestigious Ivy League university, which had always appealed to him, and, as Hank said in a recent interview, he was fortunate to be admitted and his mother somehow managed to pay the expenses. Graduating with a history degree from Princeton University, Hank headed to Austin, where he completed his law degree at the University of Texas, and became an administrative law judge for the state of Texas, a position he currently retains.

While at Princeton, Hank met Conrad Deisler, and the two combined their folk and country music interests to perform in numerous folk-oriented bands, including Canyon City Limits. Prior to college, Hank had little interest in guitar and songwriting. When both moved to Austin in 1980 to attend law school at the University of Texas, they met Tom Pittman, a philosophy graduate student from Georgia, who played banjo and steel guitar, and the Austin Lounge Lizards were born that year. Soon they added a bass player (Tom Ellis and then Mike Stevens) and mandolinist (Tim Wilson then Paul Sweeney). After playing bluegrass in local venues, the band took Best Band honors at the 1983 Kerrville Folk Festival. Rather than cover country and folk tunes, the group discovered they had the ability to write political and social theme songs tinged with humor, irony, and satire, a feat accomplished over the past twenty-two years. Hank, along with Deisler, became the primary songwriter for the eight albums released over that time period. Deisler once described their commentary as "guerilla warfare on the conventions of country music." According to Card, his influences in writing satirical songs came from Frank Zappa, Homer & Jethro, and Brave Combo.

The Austin Lounge Lizards cut their first album, *Creatures from the Black Saloon*, in 1984 on Watermelon Records, which features Hank's songs, "Swingin' From Your Crystal Chandeliers", "Didn't Go to College", and "The Golden Triangle", It was followed by *The Highway Café of the Damned*, released in 1988 on the Watermelon label.

Hank's songwriting is highlighted with the title track, as well as "Ballad of Ronald Reagan", "Acid Rain", and "Cornhusker Refugee". Their third album, *Lizard Vision*, was recorded live at the Waterloo Ice House in Austin. Released in 1991 on the Flying Fish label, it includes several of Hank's songs, such as "A Case of Coors Beer", "Bust the High School Students", "Pizza on the Ground", and "George Jones is Playin' in the City". After their fourth album for Flying Fish, *Paint Me on Velvet*, the Lizards released *Small Minds* (Watermelon), another connection of folk music comedy with kooky Card songs like the political satire of "Gingrich the Newt" or the discussion of general human folly in "Bonfire of the Inanities". High accolades followed when the Lizards brought home the *Austin Chronicle*'s Best None of the Above Band, and Kerrville's Band of the Year in 1994. The *Live Bait* EP album, including some of the group's favorites, such as Hank's "The Highway Café of the Damned", was released in 1996 by Watermelon and re-released in 1998 by Sugar Hill.

In 1998, the group produced *Employee of the Month* on the Sugar Hill label. Nine of the thirteen tracks are written or co-written by Hank, including "Stupid Little Texas Song", "Hey, Little Minivan", "The Dogs, They Really Miss You", "Love in a Refrigerator Box", and "Leonard Cohen's Day Job". To promote the album, the band traveled to Great Britain, their first overseas tour, and received warmly by 3,000 fans at the Ironbridge Bluegrass and Roots Festival in Shropshire. They also performed a live two-hour show in London, broadcast via satellite to thirty-one countries. The Lizards continued their satirical torment, I mean, torrent, in 2000 with *Never an Adult Moment* (Sugar Hill) featuring Card's songwriting on seven tracks, including "Forty Years Old and I'm Living in My Mom's House," "Big Rio Grande River," "The Me I Used To Be," "Waitin' on a Call from Don," "The Illusion Travels by Stock Car," and "Ashville/Crashville". While a lot of writers work for days and weeks to come up with a funny song title, song concept, or one good line that will crack a smile on listeners' faces, Card just seems to wake up and barely have time to get them all down. 2003's *Strange Noises in the Dark* (Blue Corn) starts smiling as soon as the laser hits the ones and zeros in the audio file. Card contributes the album's title track, and co-authors a few other goofy numbers: "Tastes Like Chicken", "The Lonely Yodeler", and "Banana Slugs! Racing Down the Field (Proposed UC-Santa Cruz Fight Song)". The Lizards slithered back in 2006 with more hilarity on *The Drugs I Need* (Blue Corn), the title track of which is co-written by Card as a biting look at prescription drug prices. Along a tune written by himself "One True God" questioning who gets to call God what, his other co-writes include laughers like "Xmas Time for Visa", "Buenos Dias, Budweiser", "Toast the Earth with Exxonmobil", and "We've Been Through Some Crappy Times Before". Festival Records also released a live set of some of their better known tunes in 2006.

Described on their website as "The Most Laughable Band in Show Business," the group is funny and not shy about exploring controversial political subjects through the prism of folk songs, but they do it "clean", a show business ethos of not incorporating profanity into their performances. Additionally, their up tempo bluegrass often belies the seriousness of the political commentary contained within the songs, an old trick for musicians, to beguile listeners with happy music and create contrasting tension within the lyrics. If listeners do get uncomfortable while listening, then at least we know the art is engaging enough to challenge our own perceptions, long a primary goal of satirical folk music, created to magnify some of life's absurd contradictions. The Austin Lounge Lizards were already scheduled to continue doing just that through at least the spring of 2011.

www.austinloungelizards.com

Cargill, Henson

(b. February 5, 1941 – d. March 27, 2007)

Known for his 1968 No. 1 somewhat controversial and unorthodox country hit, "Skip a Rope," singer and songwriter Henson Cargill was born in Oklahoma City. Although he learned to play the guitar as a youngster, Henson's career plans focused on ranching. His family background, however, was in law and politics as his father was a well-known trial lawyer, and his grandfather was a former mayor of Oklahoma City. He attended Colorado State University in Fort Collins, where he studied animal husbandry, and married in his final year of school. Following graduation, he returned to the family ranch in Oklahoma, but began playing music at local clubs in the Oklahoma City area, and serving as a deputy sheriff in Oklahoma County.

When a country music group, The Kimberlys, came through Oklahoma City, their leader Harold Gay convinced Henson to join them. After touring the Pacific Northwest and playing the Las Vegas nightclub circuit via his smooth baritone, Henson moved to Nashville in 1966, where producer Don Law helped him sign a five-year ecord deal with the Monument label in 1967. With a voice similar to the smooth ballad style of Marty Robbins, Cargill's debut single, "Skip a Rope," written by blind songwriter Jack Moran, reached #1 on the country charts in 1968 and remained there for five weeks, as well as crossing over to the pop charts, rising to #25. Given the blindness of the composer, the song is interesting because it's about listening, not seeing, children skipping rope and talking about what their parents do and say. The lyrics of this song raised a few eyebrows in country music circles because of its protest nature, condemning parents who set a bad example for their children by evading income tax and practicing racial discrimination, remembering again in 1968 all kinds of social unrest kept the US roiling internally. The song's popularity certainly came from Cargill's crooning ability, and the easygoing country music accompaniment, but the lyrics resonated across social lines, as the song was later recorded by soul singer Joe Tex, famous for "I Gotcha" and "Ain't Gonna Bump No More (with No Big Fat Woman)". Henson surged a little more with "Row, Row, Row, a minor hit in 1968 with the theme of pulling together and getting on up the river collectively, certainly a positive "response record" to any perceived negativity on his part in "Skip a Rope". 1968's "None of My Business", perhaps just throwing up his hands thematically at the entire mess, ended his early country chart run at #8. In 1968, he became host of Avco Broadcasting's *Midwestern Hayride* on WLWT-TV in Cincinnati, which was syndicated as *Country Hayride*. After a two year hiatus, Henson recorded a 1971 album, *The Uncomplicated Henson Cargill* with "The Most Uncomplicated Goodbye I've Ever Heard" charting in the country Top 20. In 1972, Henson moved to Mega Records with little success, and then moved again to the Atlantic Records in 1973, remaining with the label until 1975 when they closed their country music operations in

Henson Cargill, circa 1972

Nashville. With Atlantic, he produced two Top 30 hits, "Same Old California Memory" and "Stop and Smell the Roses," a Mac Davis song. He also cut his first album with the new label, *This is Henson Cargill Country*, in 1974, notable for a Kris Kristofferson cover, "Jody and the Kid". Henson did not record again until 1979 when he scored a top 30 country hit with "Silence on the Line" for the independent label, Copper Mountain. His follow-up on Copper Mountain, *Have a Good Day,* provided another minor chart success with the title track, but Cargill's chart motion ended there. Two albums collecting his more memorable recordings were re-issued in the 1980s, *In The Shadows* (West Q, 1984), a collection of country music classics, and *All American Cowboy* (Amethyst, 1988), containing his best known songs. In 2009, Omni Records released a twenty-six track collection of Cargill's recording for Mega Records from the 1972-73 era, including "Oklahoma Hell", where the lyrics lament that "all Daddy raised was sweat and dust", but the family was happy to have what they did, and happy to live in their Oklahoma hell, which ultimately proved to have oil under it. Indeed, as Carson sings, "God smiled down from heaven on Dad's Oklahoma hell." In the 1980s, Henson retired from recording and returned to his Oklahoma ranch, eventually marrying Sharon Simms on September 8, 1988. Cargill died March 24, 2007 during surgery. While Cargill's career will ultimately be thought of a one-hit wonder, with "Skip A Rope" representing that legacy, his smooth baritone and easy delivery are hall marks of Oklahoma crooners, as opposed to the more nasal delivery of a Southeastern US mountain man or country singer. Additionally, "Skip A Rope" provides an opportunity for a valuable pop and country music object lesson about the year 1968 in American history, when generational and racial tensions were at such a fever pitch that even pleasant sounding country music could not avoid reflecting some of the acrimonious and frightening tenor in society.

Larry Carlton

(b. March 2, 1948)

Winner of three GRAMMY awards, widely recognized jazz fusion guitarist Larry Carlton is often associated with Oklahoma by a lot of earnest music fans. On his website bioography, Carlton indicates he was raised in Southern California, where he first began playing a guitar as a young child. And while Carlton does not appear to have been born in Oklahoma, his first guitar was. The old acoustic he found at his grandmother's house had been brought to California from Oklahoma by his mother who played when she was a teenager, accompanying her fiddling father. In an interview published on his website, Carlton remembers the duo

Larry Carlton

played in southeastern Oklahoma, "They used to play for little barn dances and at church for the gospel singing." As a result of this musical background in the family, an acoustic guitar was always present at one of his relatives' house, and he became fascinated with the

instrument. Enter his mother again, who said he could only start taking lessons when he was big enough to hold the instrument in his lap, which happened when he was six-and-a-half years old. Those lessons certainly provided the springboard for a recording career of more than thirty years, and led to Carlton's acclaim as one of the primary modern smooth jazz, fusion, and popular music session guitarists since his emergence in 1968; however, the ubiquitous presence of a family guitar and musical sensibility from Oklahoma came even before that. "I've never had another kind of job," Carlton says, "I've always been a guitar player." Of course, he was born into it.
www.larrycarlton.com

Caroline's Spine

(Formed 1993 in San Diego, CA)

Scrolling out a moody and meditative pop metal to appreciative audiences throughout North America and Europe, Caroline's Spine has always considered Oklahoma "home" since two of its primary musicians are from Tulsa and the band has based its operations there since 1995. Guitarist and vocalist Mark Haugh, a 1988 Tulsa Bishop Kelly graduate, moved to California where he attended Loyola Marymount University and met singer and guitarist Jimmy Newquist. Newquist, born in Framingham, MA, and reared in Phoenix, AZ, was going to film school at Loyola Marymount and had already signed with an independent label, ANZA Records. Mark Haugh recorded some guitar tracks on the singer's first recordings, called *Caroline's Spine* (ANZA, 1993) after the band name on which Newquist had already decided. With some success on college stations, the two musicians quit their day jobs, acquired a rusty old van, a drummer - native Californian, Jason Gilardi (b. October 21, 1974, Los Angeles) – and began picking up gigs. In the spring of 1994, Jason, Mark, and Jimmy recorded their second album, *So Good Afternoon* (ANZA). The album won the group "Top 5 Unsigned" status in a Yamaha Music Showcase that year, and the band continued touring until the final piece of the band's plan came together when they came through Tulsa in 1995 to recruit Bishop Kelly graduate and Tulsa native, Scott Jones (b. July 30, 1970), to play bass.

Jones had known Haugh since high school when the two had an ill-fated band that got booed off the stage in Tulsa; that and the usual "creative differences" split the group. After graduating high school, Jones attended St. Mary's University in Texas before transferring to Oklahoma State University in Stillwater where he graduated with a degree in psychology. Jones had not heard from Haugh for five years until receiving a phone call from the guitarist who asked Jones to book a show in Tulsa for Caroline's Spine. After the show, the group

Caroline's Spine, circa 1999: (left to right) JimmyNewquist, Jason Gilardi, Scott Jones, and Mark Haugh.

asked Jones to play bass, knowing he had never played bass, but Scott agreed and the band solidified to what it remains in 2003. With a solid lineup in place, the group began breaking as an independent act in Oklahoma, Utah, and Arizona when they recorded their third independent album, *Ignore the Ants* (ANZA, 1995), where the cult favorite and college radio standard, "Hippie Boy", made its first appearance. The song's appeal to Caroline Spine fans owed to its sentimental interpretation of the relationship between a conservative father and his rock musician son. In the fall of 1995, the group recorded some acoustic tracks that later surfaced on their final ANZA CD *Huge*, an album that sold well enough to get the attention of Hollywood Records who signed the band to a four-album deal.

The band's first release on Hollywood, *Monsoon* (1997), is really a re-mixed greatest hits record taken from the band's four previous independent albums, plus the addition of one new song, "You and Me". Radio picked up on "Sullivan" from the album, about the same time as other similar sounding bands, such as Creed, were starting to make waves in commercial pop rock. The group's next releases came in the form of a single on the soundtrack to *An American Werewolf in Paris* (Hollywood, 1997), "Turned Blue", really a preview of their formal Hollywood Records debut, and first formal studio production, *Attention Please* (1999). *Attention Please* is the band's peak period album with two songs spiking into mainstream rock radio's chart consciousness, the title track of the album as Creed was at the top of the charts in 1999, and "Nothing to Prove" in 2000. According to Mark Haugh, "No other record had utilized the kind of time and measures we did with this one. For this undertaking, the pre-production, recording, post-production, and artwork took all of eight months to complete, about seven and a half months longer than we were used to spending on any other project." For help throughout the recording process, they worked with well-known producer Roy Thomas Baker (Queen, The Cars, Ozzy Osbourne, et. al.), and enlisted engineer Nick Didia, who amped up their material for *Monsoon* and who has worked with Pearl Jam, Rage Against the Machine, and Stone Temple Pilots, to mix the album. The influences of both rock professionals is obvious throughout the album's careful song construction, and big, pop metal sound that relies on a prominent kick-drum-snare drive, just-this-side-of metal guitar riffs, and dramatic, at times soaring, vocals. The album took so long to work out, Hollywood released "Wallflower" as a single, previously included on *Monsoon*, but dating back to 1994's independently released *So Good Afternoon*. Eventually, the album produced three hits on the nationwide active rock radio format charts, and Caroline's Spine toured North America with everyone from KISS and Aerosmith to Bush and New Model Army.

Even with the beginning success that many bands never even reach, the group came to loggerheads with Hollywood Records, and the two parted ways, freeing the band to tour and record on its own. Like many artists who have been less than pleased with their corporate contracts that sometimes deliver as little as eleven cents per CD sold, after production and promotional costs of an album have been paid back, Caroline's Spine turned to their own website and fans to embrace their 2000 self-released and produced album, *Like It or Not*. The album contains new songs, re-mastered tracks from the four out-of-print ANZA CDs, live recordings, and demos, but is only available from the website and considered by the band to be an "extra" for the fans. Continuing to perform regularly throughout the U.S. during 2001 and 2002, the band released two more independent albums in 2002, *Live,* a collection of concert recordings, and *Overlooked*, their first proper studio album since *Attention Please*. In 2003, the band took a break while Jimmy Newquist released a solo album and played some shows to promote it, Gilardi and Jones worked on a side project, New

Science. In 2007, the primary members of Caroline Spine regrouped to record *Captured*, which mined their earlier emotionally-laden pop metal style, but was embraced primarily by fans of their peak work. In 2008, Caroline's Spine released a new set of recordings in the same style, *Work It Out*, available primarily as a downloadable CD, with only Jimmy Newquist remaining from the original group. As of 2013, Newquist continued to tour with new band members as Caroline Spine, and the band's major releases were available for streaming on the group's website.

www.carolinespine.com

Carson, Jeff

(b. December 16, 1963)

Charting a #1 smooth Nashville pop country hit on his first album, "Not On Your Love," singer, songwriter, and bass/harmonica player, Jeff Carson was born in Tulsa, Oklahoma but moved at a very early age to the small northwest Arkansas town of Gravette, about ten miles east of the Oklahoma border, and about five miles south of the Missouri border. Like other eventual musicians who grew up elsewhere after starting life in Oklahoma, Jeff emerged from a musical family with his sister playing piano, brother on bass, and his grandfather Ernest, who taught Jeff to play the harmonica. He began his musical career singing in church, playing guitar and harmonica, with self-proclaimed influences of Merle Haggard (first concert), George Jones, and James Taylor. After signing with Curb Records and releasing his self-titled debut in 1995, the first single, "Yeah Buddy", failed to chart; however, the second single, a sentimental Nashville country pop love ballad, "Not On Your Love", zipped to #1 on *Billboard*'s Hot Country chart, even slipping into the lower reaches of the pop Hot 100 for a couple of weeks. To capitalize on the success of the first single, Curb followed with a similar sounding follow-up about a loving but strained relationship between a father and son, "The Car", which climbed to #3 on the Hot Country Chart, and stalled (*couldn't resist that*). Carson reached the top ten of the Hot Country Chart only one more time with 1996's "Holdin' On To Something". After the #1 hit, Carson had three more albums on the Curb label, including *Butterfly Kisses* (1997), *Shine On* (1998), and *Real Life* (2001), but none propelled him back to the top of the country charts. According to his website, as of 2010 Carson had plans to release a greatest hits package, and was a commissioned police officer for the Franklin, Tennessee Police Department. He graduated from the Tennessee Law Enforcement Training Academy in December, 2009, with a shooting average of 99.6%, only 0.004 away from being the Academy's 'Top Gun'."

Jeff Carson

www.jeffcarson.net

www.myspace/jeffcarson

Carter, Rose
(vocalist for The Chuck Wagon Gang, 1935 – 1950s)
(b. December 31, 1914 – Snyder, OK)[1]
(b. December 31, no year – Altus, OK)[2]
(b. December 31, 1915 – Noel, Missouri)[3]
(b. December 31, 1915 – No birthplace listed)[4]

Rose Lola Lee "Rose" Carter was the original soprano of The Chuck Wagon Gang, a harmonizing family gospel singing group who eventually sold millions of records for Columbia from the 1930s through the 1950s. Scholarly confusion exists over her birth date and place, with two different possibilities being in Oklahoma, Altus and Snyder. In his essay on the group, Colin Larkin reports Rose's father, D.P. "Dad" Carter, was a railroad brakeman on the Rock Island Line, eventually being located in Calumet, Oklahoma, where son Roy was born March 1, 1926. The fact Dad moved around with available work on the railroad may also add to the confusion about Rose's birthplace. Her two listed Oklahoma birthplaces of Snyder and Altus are just about fifteen miles apart from one another in southwestern Oklahoma, and connected by the Burlington Northern Rail Line; however, her other listed birthplace is in Noel, Missouri just a few miles east of the Oklahoma border in northeastern Oklahoma, or the opposite side of the state. Interestingly, the one commonality between both areas is, you guessed it, the Burlington Northern Rail Line.[5] In any case, after moving to Lubbock, Texas, Dad formed the quartet in 1935 out of desperation by the family to earn money for medical care to help cure one of his and wife Carrie's eight children. After gaining a paid local radio spot in Lubbock that met with positive results, Dad moved the family to Fort Worth where they began a popular program on WBAP, first singing country favorites and gospel tunes, and then focusing primarily on singing harmonized Southern Gospel due to audience demand. They began recording for Columbia in 1936, and later added subtle instrumental elements of country music such as an electric, which helped their music crossover to secular country radio stations, and tacitly endorsed electric guitars in gospel music.

According to allmusic.

The Chuck Wagon Gang, circa 1955, with Dad (inset), then l to r: Eddie, Rose, Anna, Roy, and Howard.

By Hugh Foley / 115

com author, Sandra Brennan, the group "spent a few months at a Tulsa radio" station in 1942 before disbanding due to World War II. The group would go on to sell over thirty-seven million records, a major one of which was the first commercially licensed recording of "I'll Fly Away", written by Spiro's **Albert E. Brumley**, and released to great popularity in 1949. Another ironic, yet sad, connection to Oklahoma for the family is that Dad Carter collapsed and died in an Oklahoma City theatre, just before going onstage for a special concert, as he had retired in 1955 due to heart trouble. That same year the group was awarded the status of "#1 Gospel Act in America" by the National Disc Jockeys Association, the first of many awards received by the group for annual and cumulative achievement in the music industry during their now seventy-five year career. Several lineup changes occurred over the years due to the natural attrition of show business, but The Chuckwagon Gang remained active as of 2010.

www.thechuckwagongang.net

Endnotes
[1] Paul Kingsbury, ed. Encyclopedia of Country Music Compiled by the Staff of the CountryMusic Hall of Fame. (New York: Oxford University Press, 1998).
[2] Copperfield Records, "Chuck Wagon Gang Biography", www.copperfieldmusic.com.
[3] Barry McCloud, Definitive Country: Ultimate Encyclopedia of Country Music and Its Performers. (New York: Perigree, 1995); this birth date is also listed by allmusic.com.
[4] Colin Larkin, Virgin Encyclopedia of Country Music. London: Muze/Virgin, 1998).
[5] For a more detailed look at railroad lines in the state, see John Morris, Charles R. Goins, and Edwin C. McReynolds, "Railroads in Oklahoma, 1870 to 1985", Historical Atlas of Oklahoma, 4th ed. (Norman: OU Press, 2006).

Carter, Roy (vocalist for The Chuck Wagon Gang, 1955 – 1980s)

(b. March 21, 1926)

Often confused in online databases with the rhythm guitarist of the 1970s disco/funk group, Heatwave, and/or the British oboist with numerous recording credits, both of whom have the same name, Roy Carter (the Oklahoman) was born in Calumet, Oklahoma, on March 1, 1926, apparently because his father was working on the railroad there (*see previous entry on Rose Carter*). Brother to **Rose Carter**, Roy was a "middle-period" member of the multi-million-selling Southern Gospel group, The Chuck Wagon Gang, founded by his father in 1935 after the family moved to Lubbock, Texas and needed the money for his sister's health care. Roy joined the group in the mid-1950s as they experienced their last flash of major success, and as original members, and their replacements, began to weary from the fatigues of a show business lifestyle, Roy performed and recorded with the family group through the 1980s. He is also credited with overseeing The Chuck Wagon Gang's resurgence in the sacred music industry with Copperfield Records, starting in 1979, which led to the group's continued busy schedule from that point up to the series of bookings listed on their website through 2010.

www.thechuckwagongang.net

Recommended Reading
Terrell, Bob. The Chuck Wagon Gang Lives On (New York: St. Martin's 1990).

Chainsaw Kittens

(formed 1989 in Norman, OK – played reunion gig as recently as 2008)

Formed after the demise of his first band to land a recording contract, Defenstration[1], Tyson Meade started and fronted The Chainsaw Kittens, a dynamic alternative rock group with just enough quirk via Meade's immediately identifiable vocals and poetic lyrics, and plenty drums/bass/guitar power to ride the new rock sound that washed over American popular culture in the wake of Nirvana's upturning of the national pop and rock music charts in 1991. Not unlike other bands and musicians out of Oklahoma who have been widely admired by critics, fans, and musician peers, The Chainsaw Kittens' unique sound did not meet with enough commercial success after ten years of releases to warrant pressing on. The band forever becomes a paradigm for originality, hard work, excellent musicianship, dynamic live shows, and in-studio creativity that often goes unrecognized by the mainstream public, while music scene insiders and enthusiasts shake their collective heads (and ears) at what does make it on to the charts.

Meade formed the group Defenestration about 1980 with his friend Todd Walker, in what Tyson called early in his career "the uptight capital of the world," Bartlesville, OK, his hometown. Of Bartlesville, Tyson describes an environment not unfamiliar to any teenager operating outside of the norm in the peer pressure-heavy environment of teenagedom. "If you weren't a junior high football player, or kissed up to them, you were a freak," Tyson remembers in an early 1990s video interview available on youtube.com, "and I was kind of freak anyway. But, the conservative environment made for good writing." Meade and Walker continued their band project, the name of which means to throw something or someone out of a window, in Norman, home of the University of Oklahoma, and all the college town elements that make it one of the slightly more progressive art and music communities in the state. Once there, the duo built the rest of the group, and recorded an independent EP in 1986 funded mostly by Meade's mother, while playing everywhere possible in a scene that included the developing **Flaming Lips** who had yet to release their first LP by that point. Defenestration released one album for Relativity Records, *Dali Does Windows* (1987), who was no doubt drawn to the group's uniqueness when all labels were trying to find bands for the nationwide college radio scene of the 1980s that provided a successful business model of both airplay and promotion for local gigs, a trail first figured out by Black Flag in the early part of that decade. In any case, just as the tour to support the album was to start, the old friends, Walker and Meade, had disagreements which ended in Walker leaving the group to tour shorthanded, effectively tossing the band's future out the window.

At the same time Meade returned to Norman to sort through the ashes of Defenestra-

The Chainsaw Kittens

tion in 1989, **Trent Bell** was playing in a band his senior year at Norman High School. Being in the same musician circles, Bell suggested to Meade that the vocalist should connect with some other high school students he knew at Norman High. Even though Meade was a few years older and reluctant to join up with a high school band, he did, and the band evolved into the Chainsaw Kittens while Bell continued playing with another band that made the rounds of Austin, Dallas, and back to Norman, often opening up for bigger bands. Just as the first Chainsaw Kittens album, *Violent Religion* (Mammoth, 1990), was about to be recorded, Bell was asked to join the band he had been partially responsible for getting together in the first place.

Recorded in Tulsa by **Steve Ripley** and Ron Getman while Ripley still owned the historic Church Studio, *Violent Religion* set the musical template for the Kittens: Tyson's sometimes growling and screaming, sometimes melodic vocal delivery of his way-beyond-average lyrical abilities; a driving, rolling, rack-tom heavy drum sound; gritty, powerful rhythm guitars, and unashamed-to-be-good-lead-guitar-work; and enough noise, distortion, and other added-on multi-track elements (Ripley's input?) to qualify as psychedelic art rock. While the group proper does not include Bell in the Kittens line-up, he is listed as playing guitar as an "additional kitty", along with the heavyweight local talent, Steve Ripley on ebotron and **Phil Seymour** on background vocals. The entire album is indicative of a collective harder, progressive rock sound emanating out of college radio markets in the late 1980s that led to the new, so-called "alternative", commercial rock of the first half of the 1990s, as opposed to the pop metal that had devolved into power ballads by that same period. Concluding a frenetic set of twelve tracks on *Violent Religion* that toss the listener around in an aural dryer, "She's Gone Mad" is as tough a rock song as you will ever hear.

With all the promise of *Violent Religion,* a dynamic live show with Meade at the mic, and a market place urgently seeking "the next Nirvana", producer Butch Vig, who had produced Nirvana's game changing *Nevermind* album, and would go on to produce the Smashing Pumpkins' *Siamese Dream,* signed on to oversee the recording of the Kittens' second album, *Flipped Out in Singapore* (Mammoth, 1992). While continuing the palate established by *Violent Religion*, Vig's production corralled some of the first album's reckless splendor, and added the signature equalization he'd attached to Kurt Cobain's guitar on *Nevermind*. Tyson still shrieks like John Lennon in scream therapy, terrorizes listeners with a Johnny Rotten razor voice, and soars like David Bowie on his most introspective lyrics, all of which is supported by spot-on rock music by the band (now with Trent Bell and Mark Metzger (guitars), Clint McBay (bass), Aaron Preston (drums), and singer Meade), however, in retrospect, with twenty years' hindsight, Vig's production makes the group sound like Nirvana with a different vocalist (listen to the opening of "High in High School"), perhaps not enough to distinguish them as something entirely different, which they were because of Meade's theatrics, lyrics, and really, better rock guitar work by Bell as Cobain was not a lead player, but the album nor singles charted anywhere but in college radio.

The band's third album on *Mammoth*, 1993's *Angel on the Range*, just featured seven songs, short by LP standards, but kept the band's catalogue and touring base growing. *Angel on the Range* finds the band (adding Eric Harmon (drums) and Matt Johnson (bass), and minus Metzger on guitar) continued the group's earlier stated melodic and arty punk rock musical ethos ("Kick Kid"), but also introduces a slightly different direction for the group as they infuse the collection with a couple of ballads that emphasize an acoustic guitar on rhythm ("Angel on the Range"/"Mary's Belated Wedding Song"). The recording seems to be a transitional moment for the band, as they had brought in a new rhythm section and were going with just Bell as the guitarist in a traditional four-member rock band set up. While *Angel* contains their earlier stylistic touchstones, it also is a harbinger of their forthcoming work that emphasized contrasting loud and soft dynamics (a Nirvana influence on most rock bands at the time), unusual for rock rhythms, and Meade's inspirational vocal and lyrical directions delivered with more singing and less screaming. Their final album for Mammoth, 1994's *Pop Heiress* with its Cure-like melodic opening of the first single, "Pop Heiress Dies", should have been their pop rock moment as the song quantifies all that made them an excellent band, however, due to Kurt Cobain's death that year, the alterna-rock movement lost its leader. Also, Weezer released their first, clean-cut geek rock album, and Korn initiated the nu-metal movement with their first album, effectively changing the rock music landscape that year. Nonetheless, the Smashing Pumpkins, also a leading pop rock group at the time following their substantive 1993 *Siamese Dream* album, were fans of the Kittens and signed the band to a label started in part by Pumpkins James Iha and D'arcy, Scratchy Records. Distributed with heavy market presence by Mercury in 1996, the self-titled CD was recorded primarily in Norman at Trent Bell's Bell Labs Studio over a seven month period at Bell's studio, and launched with the hopes it would be the band's major breakthrough. Mercury's anonymous press release for the album touted the Kittens' "unique combination of fragile melodies, twisted lyrics, raw and powerful guitars, and lovely, hummable pop choruses." With all the studio time necessary, the Kittens' created what would be a final testament (although not last album) to their unacknowledged prowess as one of the 1990s most original rock bands. With choruses that sounded very much like Smashing Pumpkins choruses on songs such as "Tongue Trick", but had already been sounding that way with their first album, causing one's critical imagination to wonder how much the Pumpkins were really influenced by the Chainsaw Kittens (check out "Mother", "I'm Waiting" or "Violent Religion" from 1990 with the Pumpkins more popular songs in mind, not to mention Meade's alternating screaming and singing, a noticeable element of Pumpkins' front man Billy Corgan's vocal style, not mention Kurt Cobain's, but Meade had already evolved to that point by 1990). In any case, the album features several extremely catchy tracks, "Dorothy's Last Fling" and "Heartcatchthump", as well as "Bones in My Teeth", notable also for the appearance of one of Oklahoma's most underrated guitarists, songwriters, and performers, Mike Hosty, on lap steel. However the album did not register at alternative radio, and certainly not at mainstream rock radio that had turned the harder edged music of Slipknot and Korn. Finding its only real acceptance at college radio, from which they never really did graduate format-wise, the band toured to support the CD, but it generated no hits. Incredibly, with all the press and peer accolades the band received through their career, according to *Billboard* chart archives, none of their albums or singles charted, ever. After an additional four-song EP on Scratchyy, and an independent disc, *All American* (Four Alarm, 2000), the band called it quits. Getting his Bachelor's degree from OU in the midst of his band work in the late 1990s, Tyson has released one solo album, *Motorcycle Childhood* (Echostatic, 1996), and had plans to offer up another when he gets ready.[2] Meade continued creating art, traveling abroad to teach English, working in advertising, and occasionally returning to Oklahoma to perform solo shows or reunion gigs with his old bands, most recently with The Chainsaw Kittens in 2008 in Norman. His band mate and co-writer of the lion's share of Kittens' tunes, guitarist **Trent Bell,** has enjoyed mountains of success as an engineer and producer at his Bell Labs Recording Studio in Norman.

Endnotes
1. For more insight into the history of Tyson Meade's first group, Defenestration, who recorded one major label album, Dali Does Windows (Relativity, 1987), see the very informative and thorough insider's fan website on the band at http://defenestrationfan.tripod.com.
2. For more background on Tyson Meade, see two stories published in the state's major newspapers: Thomas Conner, "The Year of the Cat?" Tulsa World, 25 August, 1996, section H, p. 1; and Gene Triplett, "The 9 Lives of Tyson Meade," Daily Oklahoman, 9 January, 2004: section D, p.1.

Chance, Greyson

(b. August 16, 1997)

An ultra-example of how fast a music career can get going in the Internet era, Greyson Michael Chance parlayed an uploaded video recording of his 2010 middle-school talent show performance of "Paparazzi", by modern mega-pop star Lady Gaga, into an appearance on the top-rated television show, *Ellen*, and a recording contract with Ellen DeGeneres' planned recording label, eleveneleven, reportedly named as such because she saw Greyson's video on May 11th. Additionally, his home-made videos have been watched over forty *million* times via his youtube.com site, driven by his appearance on *Ellen*, and also by a wide variety of media observers who embedded the video into stories about Chance's meteoric rise into the national popular culture consciousness. The youngest child of Scott and Lisa Chance, Greyson was

Greyson Chance, 2011

born in Wichita Falls, Texas, but was resident of Edmond, Oklahoma, in 2010, when he finished the sixth grade at Cheyenne Middle School. In April, 2010, Greyson, who had three years of piano lessons up to that point, participated in the annual school choir concert and talent show, a common activity at public schools as the year starts to wind down. Because of his enormous affinity for Lady Gaga's individualistic nature, he chose to perform her pleading ode to a failed lover, or to paparazzi she wants to love her, depending on one's reading of the song. While the camera work is shaky on the video, looking like a typical parent, hand-held video of their child performing at a talent show, Greyson's pure talent interpreting the song instantly captivates one's attention. Faces of the female students sitting and watching the performance mirror our own amazement at the vocal range and expressive abilities of Greyson on the song, no doubt the same amazement *Ellen*'s producers saw when they were sent the video by Greyson's older brother, Tanner. A whirlwind followed at the Edmond youngster was flown to L.A., appeared on *Ellen* where he spoke to Lady Gaga by phone while on the show, and then performed a shortened rendition of the song, every bit as expressive as his youtube.com version, but with network caliber camera work allowing viewers to concentrate even more on his considerable talents.

With Ellen's interest and the public's vote via repeated viewings of his music videos, as well as a co-management team of the men who manage Madonna (Guy Oseary) and Lady Gaga (Troy Carter), Greyson is poised to have a longer biographical entry in a future *Oklahoma Music Guide*. Or, as popular culture moves faster and faster, turning this week's viral video star into next year's "whatever happened to feature," he could also be the "kid who did that Lady Gaga video." Either way, his astounding recognition thus far speaks for itself. As of July 10, 2010, the "Paparazi" video had been viewed 27, 782, 733 times; his original songs, "Singing Stars" and "Broken", had been viewed 3,918,562 and 5,041, 853 times respectively. Additionally, after joining youtube.com and opening his user account in April, 2010, three months later Greyson Chance was already the #30 Most Subscribed (All Time) Musician, poetically placed between his idol, Lady Gaga, and his teen nemesis, Justin Bieber, who may just have to make some room pretty soon for the new kid on the block. His first single, "Waiting Outside the Lines", was released in 2011, after which he appeared on Jimmy Fallon and the Disney Channel to build momentum for the release of his first album, *Hold On 'til the Night* , on Ellen's Degeneres' label (eleveneleven), which peaked at #29 on the US album charts. His second album, *Truth Be Told, Part 1* (Geffen) was released as a digital download only. While commercial success has been somewhat elusive at home, Chance was named Most Popular New International Artist of the Year in 2012 by the MTV-CCTV Mandarin Music Awards on China Central Television (CCTV).

www.youtube.com/user/greyson97

www.myspace.com/greysonchance

Chenoweth, Kristin

(b. July 23, 1968)[1]

An outrageous vocal and performing talent with a truly stratospheric voice, Kristin Chenoweth sings opera and Broadway tunes with shared facility, portrays roles brassy and diminutive with equal aplomb on film, television, and stage, and has garnered a number of substantial awards since her debut on Broadway in 1997. Born Kristi Dawn Chenoweth in Broken Arrow, Oklahoma, a suburb just south of Tulsa, she was adopted at birth by an engineer father, Jerry, and a homemaker mother, June. By her own description, Chenoweth has indicated she is one-quarter **Cherokee**. After a childhood of singing in her and other churches, as well singing for thousands at a Southern Baptist Convention by age

Kristin Chenoweth

twelve, Kristin studied drama at Broken Arrow High School under Billie Sue Thompson. She then earned her earned a bachelor of fine arts in musical theater and a master's degree in opera performance from the prestigious vocal music program at Oklahoma City University. While at OCU, she studied under noted voice teacher, Florence Birdwell, won the title of "Miss OCU", and was a second runner-up at the 1991 Miss Oklahoma pageant, a fact she jokes about in her 2009 memoir.[2]

After graduation, she won the "Most Talented Up-and-Coming Singer" award the Metropolitan Opera National Council auditions, receiving a full scholarship to the Academy of Vocal Arts in Philadelphia. Before beginning her studies in Philadelphia, she auditioned for an off-Broadway production of *Animal Crackers*, and when awarded the leading role, decided to turn professional in 1994. After a stint in the off-Broadway musical, *The Fantasticks*, and a 1997 Broadway debut role in Moliere's 17th century farce, *Scapin,* she received the Theater World Award for Outstanding Broadway Debut in 1997 for her role in the musical, *Steel Pier*, which ran from March to June of 1997. Kristin's next role, however, would elevate her to status as Broadway's newest and brightest star, one that has not stopped shining bright across the entertainment sky since she won several major awards in 1999 for her role as Sally Brown in *You're a Good Man, Charlie Brown*. For that role, she won a a Tony Award for Best Featured Actress in a Musical, Drama Desk and Outer Critics Circle Awards for Outstanding Featured Actress in a Musical, Antoinette Perry Award for Best Featured Actress in a Musical, and the Clarence Derwent Award for Most Promising Female Performer. By then, a known, sterling performer, Kristin continued working, first in the comedy, *Epic Proportions* (1999), followed by off-Broadway productions include *A New Brain* (1998), *Strike Up the Band* (1998), and *On a Clear Day You Can See Forever* (2000).

With her undeniable stage presence, magnetism, and commanding personality, all contained within a petite four foot eleven frame, both television and film entities pursued Chenoweth as a wide-ranging character actress and voiceover specialist. Among several television performances, she has appeared in thirteen episodes of her own show, *Kristin* (2001), as well working on *Frasier* (2001), *The West Wing* (2004 to 2006), *Sesame Street* and *Elmo's World* (as Ms. Noodle from 2001 to 2007), *Ugly Betty* (2007), *Pushing Daisies* (2007-2009: for which she won an Emmy in 2009), and *Glee* (2009-2010), a show meant for her if there ever were one. Film opportunities have also presented themselves to Kristin, a representative list including acting or voice roles in *Bewitched* (2005), *The Pink Panther, Deck the Halls,* and *RV* (2006), *A Sesame Street Christmas Carol* (2007), *Space Chimps* (2008), *Tinker Bell and the Lost Treasure* (2009), and *Tinker Bell and the Great Fairy Rescue* (2010).

Sony Classical released her first CD, *Let Yourself Go*, in 2001. A collection of standards from the great American songbook (Gershwin, Berlin, Rodgers and Hart, etc.), Kristin's performance of "The Girl in 14G" is the gem of this disc. Admittedly a bit of a novelty number, the song's lyrics, about a girl in New York City who just wants some peace and quiet, but keeps hearing her neighbors singing all the time, allows Chenoweth to demonstrate and have fun with her opera training and Broadway panache. Within the song, she switches effortlessly from the mousey delivery that has made her popular as a character actress and voiceover specialist, into the powerful opera singer she was trained to be at OCU. With the CD out, she headed out on her first national tour (accompanied by the Seattle Men's Chorus), with concerts at the Hollywood Bowl and in New York's Central Park accompanied by the New York Philharmonic. Her 2002 tour schedule included appearances with the Virginia Symphony, Kansas City Symphony, Washington, D.C. National Symphony, as well as performances at such venues as Wolf Trap, Hollywood Bowl, and the New Amsterdam Theatre. She was also one of the featured native Oklahoma performers who participated in the grand opening of the newly renovated Civic Center Music Hall in Oklahoma City. Chenoweth was featured in 2002 on the A & E television special, *Richard Rodgers: Falling in Love*, a celebration of the 100th anniversary of one of the greatest American songwriters, performing "My Funny Valentine", accompanied by violinist Joshua Bell, and was also part of a star-studded lineup for the *Richard Rodgers: A Centennial Celebration* held at the Kennedy Center for the Performing Arts in Washington, D.C. in 2002. As one of the headliners of the Worth Street Theater Company's Tribeca Playhouse Stage-Door Canteen, she also performed for personnel who worked at Ground Zero following the events if September 11, 2001 in New York City. She performed with the Signature Symphony in Tulsa at the Tulsa Performing Arts Center for Education in 2003

In 2003, Kristin returned to Broadway in *Wicked: The Life and Times of the Wicked Witch of the West*, in which she played the role of Glenda the Good, for which she was nominated for a basket full of awards in 2004: Drama Desk Award for Outstanding Actress in a Musical; Drama League Award for Distinguished Performance; Outer Critics Circle Award for Outstanding Actress in a Musical; Tony Award for Best Leading Actress in a Musical. With all this acclaim in the media and entertainment capital of the world, one wondered the Oklahoma would come out in Kristin. That question answered itself in 2005 with Sony's release of her second album, *As I Am*, a collection of contemporary Christian songs, many (but not all) with a Nashville pop country production quality. Of the set, her version of "Poor Wayfaring Stranger" stands out, but the collection barely landed on the *Billboard* Contemporary Christian Album Chart, topping out at #31. In 2007, Chenoweth was only second musical theater performer to be presented by New York City's Metropolitan Opera in one night show, *Kristin Chenoweth: Live at the Met*, in which she performed signature songs, new selections, and opera arias, supported by dancers and a twelve-piece orchestra.

Following a tried and true sales strategy since the beginning of popular music's specialty marketing, Chenoweth released a lushly produced holiday set, *A Love Way to Spend Christmas* (Sony, 2008), which met with a little more success, charting on the Billboard album chart (peaking at #77), and #7 on the Holiday Chart. Given her meteoric career and ultra-star status, fans also enjoyed her 2009 memoir of her career so far in *A Little Bit Wicked: Life, Love, and Faith in Stages* (Touchstone Press). The ensuing book tour brought her to Oklahoma City's Full Circle Books for a signing of the book, about which the publisher's press release gushed, "Kristin shares her journey from Oklahoma beauty queen to Broadway leading lady, reflecting on how faith and family have kept her grounded in the dysfunctional rodeo of show biz." That rodeo included shooting a television pilot in 2009 for with spending time shooting the television pilot for the proposed NBC legal drama, *Legally Mad*, in which she was to play "Skippy Pylon", "a cheerful and brilliant attorney who nonetheless exhibits flashes of psychosis", according to her website. However, NBC decided not to go ahead with the show. Along with being the guest artist for the Grand Finale Concert at Bartlesville's OK Mozart Festival in June, 2009, she joined the voice cast of Fox's animated comedy *Sit Down, Shut Up,* as the voice of the science teacher, but that show was cancelled after four episodes. Undeterred, in 2010 she took her multiple skills back to the Broadway stage boards in the musical *Promises, Promises*, receiving a broadway.com Audience Award for Best Leading Actress and Best Diva Performance. She also was nominated for 2010 Emmy Award as Outstanding Guest Actress in a Comedy Series for her role in the television musical comedy series, *Glee*.

In November, 2010, she was to be inducted into the Oklahoma Hall of Fame, with her name and likeness to be displayed at the Gaylord-Pickens Oklahoma Heritage Museum in Oklahoma City, and her name recognized on a granite monument in the Heritage Plaza at the Oklahoma State Fairgrounds. After two concerts in Los Angeles on New Year's Eve, 2010, her 2011 schedule included an April performance of *Defying Gravity: The Music of Stephen Schwartz* in New York City. Along with being inducted into the Oklahoma

Music Hall of Fame in 2011, she also released a country music album that year, *Some Lesson Learned* (Sony Masterworks) featuring songs by some of country music's leading songwriters.

Kristin endured a frightening experience in 2012 when a lighting rig fell on her during the filming of the CBS legal drama, *The Good Wife*. After recovering from extremely serious injuries, she picked back her busy schedule right back up, co-hosting *Red Carpet Live* prior to the 85th Academy Awards, performing concerts, and prepping for providing the voice for a character in the 2014 animated film, *Rio 2*. Kristin Chenoweth is truly one of the performing gems of Oklahoma music who has few, if any, rivals for vocal range, dynamic showmanship, and endearing stage presence.

www.kristin-chenoweth.com

Endnote

1. While Kristin Chenoweth's birthday is listed as July 23, 1968 on her official website, her alumni profile on the Oklahoma City University website lists July 24, 1968 (as of 3/3/2013), as did an article in Parade Magazine, "In Step With Kristin" (May 15, 2005), and her wikipedia.org biography reflects the same thing (as of 3/13/2013). This is classic example of how challenging it can be to try and figure out which way to go with a fact about an artist's career when their own material contradicts reputable press coverage or biographical material.

Cherokee

(Cherokees began arriving in Indian Territory in 1828)

In the same way the tribe has fragmented during the continued transitional period all American Indians encountered in the twentieth century, Cherokee musical styles have both eroded and grown in the same way the tribe has over the last 200 years, with some traditions dying out completely, some preserved in very small pockets, and some musical traditions evolving with Christianity, technology, and the interaction with other tribes and U.S. popular culture. As a result, the most prominent contemporary Cherokee musical styles include the traditional ceremonial songs and dances, often called "stomp dances", that are part of the original ceremonial traditions of the Cherokee still being practiced in the Cherokee Nation; river cane flute music; Cherokee fiddle music; and the Christian-influenced harmonized Cherokee hymns.

Demonstration Stomp Dance, 2002

Cherokee people are also active in the intertribal powwow traditions of Oklahoma and have ranged successfully into every musical sphere of American popular and classical music.

Ancient as the tribe itself, the Cherokee stomp dance is sung in the "original language of God," according to UKB elder Dave Whitekiller, and persists as part of Cherokee social dancing and ceremonial activities. Within the dance circle and its layer of rings, Whitekiller explains that many Cherokee religious and social order concepts can be explained, however, the stomp dances were one of the first activities missionaries found southeastern tribes doing that ran contrary to the concept of fire as a symbol of the Biblical destination of sinners. Missionaries found the Cherokee, and neighboring tribes such as the **Muscogee**, dancing in a counter-clockwise circle around a fire, men singing and women shaking leg rattles made out of turtles. Because of the use of the fire as spiritual center for the ceremonies, some missionaries misperceived the dance as a pagan ritual in which participants are worshipping Satan and his environment. However, Whitekiller explains the fire at the center of the dance is a symbol for not only for cooking and for heating, but also a symbol for God and used as a focal point for the religion to worship by: "that is to say that the heat rises [from the fire], and as you sing the songs of merriment, or you sing the songs of thanks, or whatever with regards to religion, the sound of your voice carries over the fire and is spiraled up into the beyond to the giver of all things."

One can currently find (if you know where to go) as many as eight active Cherokee ceremonial grounds. Redbird Smith Grounds near the Vian/Gore area is the oldest Cherokee ceremonial grounds in Oklahoma. Redbird Smith's youngest son, Stoke Smith, broke away from his father's grounds and formed his own ground closer to the Vian/Sallisaw area. The father and son split over philosophical differences, again beyond the scope of this essay. For many years Stoke's Grounds have been the most highly attended with large crowds each year during the Cherokee Nation Labor Day celebration. Smaller active Cherokee dance grounds include Wolf Grounds near Stillwell, Oklahoma; New Echota Grounds near Tahlequah has been active for over five years; Chewey Grounds near Chewey, Oklahoma died out in the 1950s, but has been revived in tandem with a Christian church; Sugar Mountain Ground near Welling, Oklahoma held one meeting per year for many years through the 2000s, as did Rocky Ford Grounds south of Oaks, Oklahoma; a recent startup grounds, active in 2010, is near Kenwood, Oklahoma, a community of many Cherokee speakers . Acquiring recordings of Cherokee traditional dance music is problematic, but not impossible. Recorded and produced by Willard Rhodes, the vinyl-only *Delaware, Cherokee, Choctaw, Creek* (AFS L-37) features Cherokee stomp dance songs as well as a Cherokee lullaby, a Christian hymn, the "Horse Dance Song," "Quail Dance Song," and "Pumpkin Dance Song," all performed by Tom Handle in Jay, Oklahoma. While these appear to be the only commercially released songs by the federal Archive of Folk Song, other recordings do exist in the collection, to include 1951 recordings of Christian hymns sung by the Ross Quartet, led by Field Ross in Pryor, Oklahoma, a reading of the Cherokee alphabet by Ross, and his recitation of the Lord's Prayer in Cherokee. Additional Cherokee field recordings housed in the Franz Olbrechts Collection at the Library of Congress, originally from the Frances Densmore/Smithsonian Institution collection of wax cylinders, include a medicine song for protection, a speech in the Cherokee about the allotment of Cherokee lands, a "Mask Dance," "Bear dance," war cry, and "Ball Game Dance." Also from the set of original cylinder recordings are the "Ground Hog Dance," "Eagle Dance," "Pipe Dance," "Bear Hunting Song," "Hymn in Honor of the Rising Sun," "Medicine Song to Cure Wounds," "Medicine Song Against Witchcraft Diseases," and hunting songs for the bear and for the turkey.

The national archive's Artur Moses Collection also holds several 1946 recordings made in North Carolina at the Eastern Cherokee's reservation. Will Weste Long performs several Cherokee dance tunes, although they are not enumerated, along with Christian hymns "The Son of God," and "Meeting of Christians." In 1949, the Smithsonian recorded more traditional dances in North Carolina such as the "Victory Dance," "Friendship Dance," "Snake Dance," "Corn Dance," and "Bear Dance." While these are recordings are well documented, one set of recordings has yet to be explicated. Titled simply "Cherokee Indian

Recordings," two reels of sound originating from discs in the Smithsonian's Bureau of American Ethnology have yet to be translated or determined as the collector and contents are unidentified. Interested researchers should consult the widely published work of Dr. Charlotte Heth, a noted Cherokee ethnomusicologist, who recorded sixteen reels of Cherokee music for her dissertation, "The Stomp Dance of the Oklahoma Cherokee: A Study of Contemporary Practice with Special Reference to the Illinois District Ground" (1975), the audio and video field recordings of which are now located in the Museum of the Cherokee Indian in Cherokee, North Carolina.

Contemporary recordings include Kevin Lewis's *Ceremonial Songs and Dances of the Cherokee, Vol. 1 and 2*, and *Cherokee Stomp Dance*, recorded and produced by American Indian rapper Litefoot, and led by Tom Wildcat, Tommy Wildcat, Lucas Wildcat, and Ladney Keener. While all of these recordings are representative of the Cherokee stomp dance tradition, one can only truly appreciate the dance live in its intended environment, as part of ceremonials that are often remote and hard to find for the person who has no close association with the traditional Cherokee community. However, opportunities do exist to see and participate in the dances at the increasing number of public, social dances that are being performed in gymnasiums and community centers in and around Tahlequah throughout the year, and the previously mentioned Cherokee National Holiday, held over Labor Day Weekend in Tahlequah, provides ample opportunity for learning more.

Another Cherokee traditional music form currently experiencing a renaissance of interest is the Cherokee cane flute. Victor Wildcat, a public school educator in Fort Gibson, and a cultural preservationist of traditional Cherokee arts and crafts who has taught hundreds, if not thousands, of school children and adults in northeastern Oklahoma how to make and play the river can flute since 1998. Wildcat explains the instruments were used traditionally as courting instruments to impress would-be lovers and gain their hearts. The historical record also reflects the flutes being used by Cherokees to greet visitors coming into a village, perhaps, to soothe any would-be attacker. Made from river cane abundant in the Illinois River area of the contemporary Cherokee Nation, Wildcat also notes the flutes are also played "just for the enjoyment of music." He regularly demonstrates Cherokee and Muscogee hymns, traditional songs, and Anglo-Christmas music on the flute for school functions, educational workshops, and other public demonstrations, but has not made an official recording. National recognition for the Cherokee cane flute came in 2002 when the annual Native American Music Awards voted Cherokee Tommy Wildcat "Flutist of the Year" for his album *Pow-Wow Flutes* (2001). Wildcat, only distantly related to Victor Wildcat, has released a number of albums through Warrior Spirit productions, a company organized by Wildcat and his twin sister, Tammy, to include *Warrior's Spirit* (Cherokee River Cane Flute), *Cherokee*

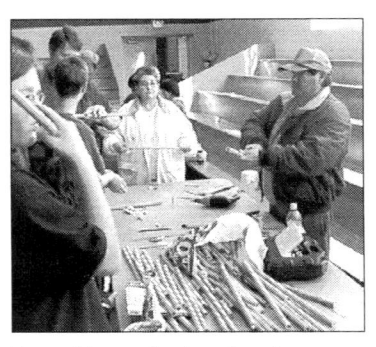

Perry Ummerteskee teaches how to make and play Cherokee river cane flutes at Rogers State University, 2002.

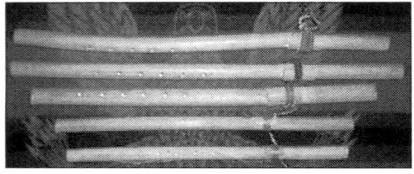

Cherokee river cane flutes made or taught by Victor Wildcat.

Flute Songs and Voices, *GWY* (Stomp Dances), and *Cherokee Songs and Flute* (featuring "Amazing Grace"). Both Tammy and Tommy have become well-known performers with their dance troupe, Dancers of Fire, appearing in the Discovery Channel's *How the West Was Lost* series and several other video productions. Tommy, who also appeared in TNT's *Tecumseh: The Last Warrior*, completed two European tours in 1995 and 1997, performs yearly at powwows in Hawaii, and travels extensively across mainland America each year performing at cultural festivals, powwows, historic museum sites, and colleges as a featured artist.

Gospel music and Christian-influenced hymns continue to play an important part of contemporary Cherokee cultural and religious activities. The songs mix tribal history, often relating to the removal of the Cherokee from their homelands in North Carolina, Protestant Christian elements of harmony and lyrical content, and sometimes scales more related to American Indian music than the European musical system. The first major name in contemporary Cherokee gospel music is J.B. Dreadfulwater (b. January 12, 1932 – d. March 9, 2002), who performed for more than fifty years with a gospel group, the Osceola Trio. Dreadfulwater was also the director of the Cherokee Choir that traveled the United States for many years under his direction. Collectors can still find vinyl copies of his music on albums such as *Squan-ti-ni-se-sti Ye-ho-wah* (*Guide Me Jehovah*), a representative collection of piano and organ-heavy gospel music. Dreadfulwater also led the Cherokee Indian Baptist Choir on two Cherokee Hymns for the State Arts Council of Oklahoma's 1989 Songs of Indian Territory project, available on cassette. In 2002, the Native American Music Awards nominated his album with the Cherokee Choir, *A Wonderful Place*, as "Best Gospel/Christian Recording," but the album lost out to the Cherokee National Children's Choir which probably would not have disappointed the elder Cherokee singer.

J.B. Dreadfulwater

Sponsored by the Cherokee Nation of Oklahoma, the Cherokee National Children's Choir has been featured on several excellent recordings since 2000, the first of which was *Cherokee Gospel Music* (CNRC, 2000). Recorded at Jeffrey Parker's Cimarron Labs near Tahlequah, and featuring the Cherokee National Children's Choir singing in the Cherokee language, *Cherokee Gospel Music* is a collection of traditional Cherokee hymns such as "Orphan Child" which has its sources in the Cherokee "Trail of Tears" when many children became orphans as a result of their parents' deaths on the journey. In 2001, the Cherokee Cultural Resource Center made its second gospel CD, again featuring the children's choir with the additional voice of noted Cherokee pop and country singer Rita Coolidge, whose own group, Walela (after the word in Cherokee for butterfly), also has recorded

Mary Kay Henderson leads the Cherokee National Youth Choir in a 2006 performance at the Oklahoma Music Hall of Fame Induction and Concert.

contemporary versions of traditional Cherokee songs. Voted the Best Gospel/Christian Recording in the 2002 Native American Music Awards, the album has both traditional Southern gospel songs such as "Amazing Grace" and "What a Friend We Have in Jesus" as well as songs related to the specific experiences of the Cherokee: "On the Road Where They Cried," "One Drop of Blood," "North Wind," and "Evening Song." In 2002, the Cherokee Nation released a third album of the Cherokee National Youth Choir, *Building One Fire*, featuring Gil Silverbird. The album again follows the formula of the first two collections by featuring the Cherokee Youth Choir singing hymns in the Cherokee language. Along with the traditional hymns, the group also recorded native-Oklahoman **Albert E. Brumley**'s "I'll Fly Away," featuring **Red Dirt Music** luminary, and the album's producer, Jeffrey Gray Parker on acoustic guitar, mandolin, and bass. The album also includes two live performances by the choir at the Museum of the American Indian in New York City and the Department of Interior in Washington D.C. to commemorate the events of September 11, 2001 in those two cities; sung in the Cherokee language, the choir performs "America" and "The Star Spangled Banner."

Leo Feathers

Also in 2001, the Cherokee Nation Cultural Resource Center released, *Children's Songs in the Cherokee Language* (CNCR 002). The CD includes several well-known children's songs, "I'm a Little Terrapin," "Twinkle, Twinkle, Little Star," "Baa Baa Black Sheep," sung Cherokee with instrumental accompaniment. The disc was designed to help young Cherokee school children learn their language in a familiar musical environment, and are available as free downloads through the Cherokee Nation of Oklahoma's website. Although the choir's makeup evolves as young people mature out of the group, several more CDs have been released in the 2000s. A holiday flavored release, *Jesus is Born Today* (2003), coincided with the choir being recognized by Harvard University's Kennedy School of Government as an outstanding tribal program. In 2004, the released another album, *Cherokee Sunday Morning*, and a DVD, *Live from Washington D.C.: First Americans Festival* (Cimarron Multi-Media), filmed on location in the nation's capitol in 2004. The DVD features the choir in performance for President George W. Bush at the White House, in concert at the prestigious Kennedy Center, and stirring rendition of the traditional Cherokee song of comfort, "Orphan Child", which was born out of the suffering of removal, sung at the Vietnam Memorial Wall. In 2007, the choir, now recognized as the pre-eminent tribal choir in the United States, released *Precious Memories*, another collection of traditional gospel songs in English and Cherokee.

Like many of their tribal counterparts throughout the United States, the Cherokee have embraced the "pan-Indian" tradition of the intertribal powwow for social, commemorative, and fund-raising purposes. Both the United Keetoowah Band and the Cherokee Nation sponsor powwows throughout the year at tribal facilities, the Tahlequah Community Center, and other locations in the Tahlequah area. The Cherokee Gourd Society, a dance based largely on **Kiowa** traditions, has organized an annual Christmas powwow since 1992, and a full-blown competition powwow is part of the annual Cherokee National Holiday held since 1952. Additionally, each year a number of smaller competition, benefit, and honor dances are held throughout the Cherokee Nation at public schools, colleges, community centers, fairgrounds, and just about any other place big enough where a dance can be held. While some Cherokees have adopted the intertribal powwow traditions based largely on plains tribes' celebrations, several Cherokees from Oklahoma have also made and continue to make substantial contributions outside of the traditional music realm.

Cherokee-Quapaw **Louis W. Ballard**, a Pulitzer Prize nominee for music, is a versatile composer who has written music for ballet and choral arrangements as well as chamber and orchestral works. Another successful classical music artist is Cherokee mezzo-soprano Barbara McAlister, born in Muskogee, who has performed with prominent opera companies around the globe. In the popular music genre, pioneering electric guitarist **Nokie Edwards** of the Ventures is Cherokee, and Leo Feathers, born in Stilwell, played guitar in primary **Tulsa Sound** bands, and with Jerry Lee Lewis, Bonnie Raitt, Willie Nelson, Leon Russell, and Dickie Betts. Western swing guitarist Jimmie Rivers, born in Hockerville, plays a wonderfully bright jazz/blues style of electric guitar, available on Jimmie Rivers and the Cherokees, *Western Swing 1961-1964* (Joaquin, 1995). is an enrolled Cherokee, and the well-known Cherokee actor Wes Studi plays bass and rhythm guitar with Firecat of Discord, who released a self-titled album in 1998. Cherokee Blues guitarist James "Ace" Moreland (b. Miami, OK, d. Feb. 8, 2003) recorded four searing albums of blues for Ichiban, Wild Dog, and King Snake Records, playing with and opening shows for Bonnie Raitt, Taj Mahal, .38 Special, George Thorogood, John Hammond, and **Steve Gaines** (of Lynyrd Skynyrd). Included in Moreland's catalogue is the Cherokee history based song "Indian Giver" on the CD *Give It To Get It* (King Snake, 2000), an album title taken from a Steve Gaines song. Tahlequah-based **Jeffrey Gray Parker**, a Cherokee Nation citizen, is a composer, musician, producer, and studio engineer, also associated with **Red Dirt Music**, has received worldwide airplay and critical praise for his ambient blend of traditional and contemporary instruments. Finally, Broadway star Kristin Chenoweth has indicated on repeated occasions that she is ¼ Cherokee.

According to Elvis Presley's official website, his maternal great-great-grandmother, Morning Dove White (b. 1800 – d. 1835), was a full-blooded Cherokee. However, particular difficulties come into play when differentiating between enrolled and non-enrolled Cherokee citizens, also beyond the range of this discussion, but any publicly acknowledged claim of Cherokee heritage, such as that of Presley, rock guitarist Jimi Hendrix, country singers Hank Williams, Willie Nelson, and Loretta Lynn, exemplifies the deep, intertwined connections between Cherokee history and the developing music of American mainstream popular culture. While scholars have been primarily concerned with the music of "the old ones," as Dave Whitekiller called the ancient Keetoowah people,

Cherokee fiddler Sam O'Fields

By Hugh Foley / 129

more work is now being done on both the evolving Cherokee Christian music and popular music created by both enrolled and non-enrolled Cherokee people. Additionally, more appreciation has evolved both among Cherokees and scholars for traditional fiddling among the Cherokee, an instrument introduced to the Cherokee by Aglo and Scot traders in 18th and 19th centuries. Along with learning to play various religious and social songs of the new Cherokee country immigrants, the portable instrument came with some Cherokees on the removal to Indian Territory where its presence remained a musical tradition until the present day. While much discussion has occurred regarding a specific "Cherokee fiddle" style, and whether or not its earlier players incorporated unique tunings familiar to their own tribal music ears, or bowing styles due to their proximity to other traditional Anglo fiddlers, the Cherokee Nation has continued to hold fiddle contests and performances for several years at their annual Labor Day Holiday, and the United Keetoowah Band of Cherokees has held fiddling contests for nearly forty years.[1]

Any conversation about music in Oklahoma that leaves out traditional and contemporary American Indian music is missing a huge part of the melodic, rhythmic, and historic mosaic of the state. While not as readily available as popular music, ancient songs expressing the deepest connections between the Cherokee people and their creator are still being sung in a worshipful manner each year at Cherokee ceremonial grounds.

More accessibly, tribal children are recording and singing Christian hymns in the Cherokee language for appreciative audiences nationwide, and the Cherokee flute and fiddle traditions are active and being cared for by dedicated individuals, all of which bodes well for the continued vitalization of Cherokee heritage, language, and music into the infinite future.

Cherokee Nation of Oklahoma: www.cherokee.org

United Keetoowah Band of Cherokee Indians: www.keetoowah.org

Eastern Band of Cherokee Indians: www.cherokee-nc.com

Note

1. For an extensively researched essay on the history of the fiddle among Cherokees, see Justin C. Castro, "Cherokee Fiddling," *The Chronicles of Oklahoma*, 87, no. 4 (2009-10): 388 – 407.

Cherry, Don(ald) Eugene

(b. November 18, 1936 – d. October 19, 1995)

Most often declared a leader of the free jazz movement for his work with Ornette Coleman, Don Cherry was also the first to use the pocket trumpet in jazz, and spent his later years exploring, composing, and learning the instruments of non-Western, world music. In terms of his significance to Oklahoma music and history, Don's family serves the same symbolic history lesson as that of many Oklahomans who left the economically depressed state in the 1930s and 40s. Born in Oklahoma City, Don's grandfather played piano, his grandmother played piano for silent movies, and his father owned the 1920s-era Cherry Blossom Club in Tulsa. Don's mother, Daisy McKee, was a parlor piano player, was reportedly half-Choctaw, the same tribe as the mothers of both Charlie Parker and Oklahoma blues man **Lowell Fulson.** When Don was four-years-old, the family's move to the West Coast in 1940 coincided with the general migration of Oklahomans who went to California to find work during The Depression and World War II. In the Watts section of Los Angeles, Don played trumpet in junior high band, and trumpet in both the Jefferson

High marching and dance band. The band director at the time, Samuel Brown, who also taught jazz musicians **Wardell Gray** and Art Farmer, was a significant inspiration.

While Cherry began his professional career as a teen, playing piano in an R & B group led by Billy Higgins, jazz critics and fans began to notice Don playing pocket trumpet as a regular member of Ornette Coleman's L.A. groups from 1957 through Coleman's most influential recording period of the 1960s. The smaller, pocket cornet which Cherry called a pocket trumpet provided a distinctive tone which differentiated him from other jazz trumpeters. Cherry moved to New York with Coleman in 1959 and played with him on many of the seminal albums of free jazz: *Something Else!!!!* (1958), *Change of the Century* (1959), and *Free Jazz* (1960). The free jazz movement drew as many detractors as the twentieth century classical music of Stravinsky did from classical purists in the early 1900s. Free jazz was frenetic with whirling, improvised solos intertwining with one another, a Dixieland band for the turbulent era of the civil rights movement of the 1950s and 1960s. In fact, the music was a conscious effort by Coleman, John Coltrane, and Don Cherry to expand the stylistic elements of jazz when hard bop, with its aim of making jazz palatable to mainstream audiences, did not appeal to the free jazz players specifically because of the style's commercial intent. Free jazz embodied the essential elements of jazz: improvisation, rhythmic vibrancy, knowledge of standard tunes, and a virtuoso's command of an instrument.

Cherry left Coleman in the early 1960s, played with Sonny Rollins and Albert Ayler, and co-led The New York Contemporary Five in 1963-4. Afterwards, like many other American jazz men who were left with little work during the early rock era, Cherry went to Europe where he recorded his first albums as a band leader, two of which became his most highly praised albums, *Complete Communion* (1965) and *Symphony for Improvisers* (1966). The albums were one of the earliest recorded appearances for the Argentinian tenor saxophonist Gato Barbieri, who Cherry discovered in Italy. During this period Cherry switched to a traditional-sized cornet. Cherry taught at Dartmouth College in 1970, moved to Sweden where he was based until 1974, and recorded with the Jazz Composer's Orchestra Association in 1973. During the 1970s, Cherry became increasingly interested in non-Western, world music and traveled extensively through Europe and the Middle East studying ethnic instruments, melodies, and musical contexts. In the late 1970s, Cherry worked with rock singer Lou Reed, and into the early 1980s he led a cooperative trio, Codona, through three albums of jazz incorporating African, East Indian, Asian, and other ethnic music forms. Cherry also acquired another pocket trumpet in 1983 and began to reincorporate it into his repertoire. After Codona ceased as a unit, Cherry formed the group Nu which toured Europe in 1987, and recorded *Art Deco* in 1988, which served as a reunion of sorts from the early Ornette Coleman Quartet. The session reunites Cherry with bassist Charlie Haden and drummer Billy Higgins from the early Coleman group, and provides new opportunities for saxophonist James Clay who had been in obscurity for many years. "Body and Soul", three Ornette Coleman tunes, and some originals make this a fitting representation of mature and experienced musicians who ushered in the free jazz era. *Art Deco* also serves as Cherry's only chart success, reaching #9 on *Billboard*'s Jazz Album Chart.

Up until the time of his death in Malaga, Spain in 1995, Cherry continued learning new instruments from around the world such as sitar, gamelan, conch, trumpet, and wood flutes, and composing music for them. These multi-ethnic musical elements are apparent on 1990's *Multi Kulti*. While critics report Cherry had an uneven live career, none disagree that he was a major force in the free jazz movement which was the form's final evolution before merging with rock in the fusion period of the 1960s. Cherry even fulfilled that role by playing his pocket trumpet on a recording by the very underground New York group, Bongwater, released on their 1998 collection, *Box of Bongwater* (Shimmy Disc). Throughout his career, Cherry attempted to stretch the boundaries of jazz and learn as much as he could about the music of the world. Cherry's musical legacy is primarily that of a free jazz originator, and a unique and unpredictable improviser who can be placed at the very top of the list of innovative jazz artists. He is survived in the music industry by son, Eagle Eye Cherry, who has recorded four albums of alternative pop from 1997 through 2006, and his step-daughter, dance music artist, Neneh Cherry, who has several releases from 1989 through 2008. Like many other musicians who were born in the state and left at an early age, Don Cherry is still representative of the musical environment of Oklahoma City where both his parents and grandparents were either casual or professional players, a family background that facilitated his interest and pursuit of a musical career.[1]

Note

1. One can easily learn more about Don Cherry by searching the Internet (allmusic.com or wikipedia.org), however, for fantastic video recordings of Cherry playing live, search his name on youtube.com; for extensive recordings and a bibliography of writing dedicated to Cherry's career, see Mark C. Gridley, "Don Cherry," *The New Grove Encyclopedia of Jazz* (New York: St. Martin's, 1994).

Cheyenne & Arapaho Tribes of Oklahoma

(Assigned to reservation in Indian Territory in 1869)

After the reservation era of 1869 to 1890, during which time Cheyenne and Arapaho lands were held in common, the tribe experienced the same difficult timeline as other tribes in Oklahoma who saw their lands carved up into 160 acre allotments for individual tribal members (1890), followed by the opportunistic land runs for "surplus" tribal lands that had not been allotted (1892), and then the abolishment of their tribal status with the formation of the state in 1907. Subsequently, tribal children were carted off to boarding schools where they were prevented from speaking their tribal languages or practicing traditional ceremonies, causing a ripple effect when they returned home when they did not teach their own children songs or language for fear it would get them into trouble, or it was of no use to them. Additionally, missionaries, in concert with the Federal government, believed the tribal ceremonies and dances were heathenish and had to be stopped if the Native people were going to be Americanized, and Christianized. Therefore, many songs and traditions "went underground", as Cheyenne and Arapaho people kept them alive in private, which is where many of those traditions remain today, and partly explains the caution with which tribal members approach outsiders. Active musical traditions among the Cheyenne and Arapaho tribes include war dance music and warrior society songs, Peyote Songs for the Native American Church, lullabies and Christian hymns in the Cheyenne and Arapaho languages, as well as extremely private music that goes along with the Cheyenne Sun Dance or Arapaho Sacred Pipe Ceremonies.[1]

More often than not, most American Indian music does not register with non-Indian people. Either the music is inaccessible because of complexity of the contextual relationship between tribal people and traditional music, or non-Indian ears just don't hear the dynamics and subtleties within what appears to be simple percussion (a drum and/or rattle), and monophonic vocals repeating the same verbal sounds over and over, some of which may be words and some of which may be vocables invested with meaning. [INSERT Cheyenne 3 with caption "Welcome sign at Cheyenne Cultural Center near Clinton, OK"] Upon closer examination to the body of Cheyenne music, listeners will find a great variety meanings and purposes for songs that can often illuminate one's understanding of tribal history and life, both as it was "back there when", as well as how it is today. Listeners can begin by placing the tribe's music in a wider Great Plains singing tradition on *The Great Plains: Indian Singers and Songs* (Canyon-6052), containing the Cheyenne Dave Group of the Southern Cheyenne, the Philip Whiteman Group of the Northern Cheyenne, and the Otto Hungary Group of the Northern Arapaho, along with Kiowa, Oglalla, and Arikara singers. Those unaccustomed to listening to Plains Indian music should begin to note a pitch difference in singers from the northern or southern Plains. Typically, southern singers produce a lower pitched singing, and northern singers produce a higher pitched tone to their singing. So, just within differing current geographical origins of the same tribes, one hears a difference in singing style. That alone helps people to begin to understand the wide-ranging differences among Native people as a whole, as well as how differences can occur within tribal entities themselves. This relates to the modern intertribal powwow world in which often both a northern, higher-pitched, drum group is present to alternate with the southern, lower-pitched, drum group. As a result, most Cheyenne and Arapaho powwow singing in Oklahoma tends to fall into the lower, southern style of war dance and powwow singing, as opposed to the northern branches of the tribes who sing more in the higher-pitched northern style.

Numerous recordings have been made of Southern Cheyenne Peyote Songs, or the music of the Native American Church that evolved in the late 19th century in Indian Territory as an acceptable synthesis of American Indian southern Plains religious beliefs merged with Christianity, and using Peyote as the church's sacrament. The ceremonies occur in a tipi and last throughout the night until daybreak, and are the true unification of American Indian spirituality and Christianity as a religious concept. Several Cheyenne people were instrumental in protecting the church from legislative attempts by the Oklahoma territorial government to ban it late in the 19th century, and were also some of the first to witness its incorporation as a governmentally validated religion, to include the use of the sacred medicine, peyote, as a sacrament.[2] Native American Church music is fast, mesmerizing, and incantatory with songs often relating to the relationship between worshippers and the creator, or to mark significant points in the ceremony, such as an "Opening Song" to begin the service, a "Midnight Water Song" to mark the admittance of holy water into the ceremony at midnight in the service, a "Morning Water Song" to mark the drinking of water at sunrise after a full night of prayer, and "Closing Song" to mark the end of the service when worshippers leave the tipi at sunrise. Canyon Records features two recordings with Cheyenne songs. Alfred Armstrong (Cheyenne-Caddo) sings several Peyote Songs on *Indian Lord's Prayer Songs* (CR-8025), and Warren Van Horn (Cheyenne) does the same thing on Van Horn, Barker & Clark, *Peyote Prayer Songs* (CR-8019). Indian House Records also has recordings of Cheyenne Peyote Songs in its catalogue: *Cheyenne Peyote Songs – Vol. 1* (IH 2201) and *Vol. 2* (IH 2202) feature Arthur Madbull, Lee R. Chouteau, Toby Starr, and Allen Bushyhead. A more obscure, but extremely beautiful set of twenty four Southern Cheyenne Peyote Songs were released on the independent Indian Records label (not to be confused with Indian House Records), and only issued on vinyl to this writer's knowledge. Recorded at Fay, Oklahoma at an unknown date, the recording was sung by Grover Turtle and Arthur Madbull, a name now familiar to researchers because of his Indian House recordings. Additionally, Indian House also has two different titles with Northern Cheyenne Warrior Dance Songs (SC112) and Northern Cheyenne Warrior Sun Dance Songs (SC 700).

The contemporary Cheyenne and Arapaho Tribes of Oklahoma are based in Concho, Oklahoma, just about six miles north of El Reno. Along with all the governmental aspects of operating a nation-state and all the services that implies, the tribes have a culture and heritage program that, according to the C & A website is designed to "promote tribal content, foster cultural participation, active citizenship within the tribe and participation in tribal life." Within that context, activities include traditional hand games (which have many songs that go along with them), traditional singing of Cheyenne and Arapaho songs, and education about cultural and traditional dance, as well as other traditional ceremonies mentioned earlier, such as the Sun Dance (Cheyenne) or Pipe Ceremony (Arapaho). [insert Cheyenne image 4 of powwow sign with no caption necessary]Interested parties not connected to the tribes might want to start with the basics, which would be the Annual Oklahoma Indian Nation Powwow, held the first weekend of August since 1989 at the Concho Powwow Grounds behind the tribal complex.

www.c-a-tribes.org

Endnotes
1. For a helpful, but non-Indian, scholarly survey of traditional music among the Cheyenne and Arapaho, see the noted earlier 20th century American Indian ethnographer, see Frances Densmore (1867-1957), *Cheyenne and Arapaho Music: Southwest Papers No. Ten* . originally published in 1937 by the Southwest Museum in Los Angeles, but recently reprinted by Kessinger Publishing in Whitefish, MT, in 2008.
2. To begin understanding more about the history of the Native American Church in Oklahoma, see Daniel C. Swan, *Peyote Religious Art: Symbols of Faith and Belief* (Jackson, MS: University Press of Mississippi, 1999).

Chickasaw Nation

(Arrived in Oklahoma via forced removal from their homelands in 1837)

As one of the five major tribal groups from the southeastern United States who were removed over what is well-known as the "Trail of Tears" in the 1830s[1], the Chickasaw Nation is headquartered in Ada, Oklahoma, with a jurisdictional territory that includes more than seven thousand square miles of south-central Oklahoma, encompassing all or part of thirteen Oklahoma counties. Musically, the tribe does not presently have any active ceremonial grounds practicing the pre-removal dances or songs of their ancestors, however, the tribe does sponsor a Chickasaw Nation Dance Troupe that demonstrates traditional Chickasaw dances such as the Friendship Dance or Stomp Dances at various Chickasaw events. Prior to leaving their homelands in the lower Mississippi Valley, the tribe practiced a similar style of music and dance worship as other peoples in the Southeast, informally known as the stomp dance, a slight difference being that men and women served as singers, instead of women only keeping the rhythm with their turtle shell leg rattles.[2] While somewhat difficult to find, two undated albums of Choctaw-Chickasaw Dance Songs were released on vinyl by the Choctaw-Chickasaw Heritage Commitee, likely in the 1970s. Out of sixteen songs on the two albums, only one is noted as Chickasaw specific, "Hard Fish". The song is a call and response type song that is familiar to those who know stomp dance music, however, the singers in this particular song use a drum and bells as their accompaniment. Typically, bells are not typically heard in other Southeastern traditional music, but are part of Chickasaw and Choctaw traditions. With regard to the development of Christian music within the Chickasaw realm, because of the close proximity of the Chickasaws geographically, culturally, and linguistically, Chickasaw people often sing **Choctaw** Christian hymns.[3]

Chickasaw and Choctaw singers and dancers circa 1970s.

Notable musicians from the tribal citizenry include Tessie Mobley, and opera singer who attended school in Ardmore, Oklahoma, where the tribal website indicates she "lived on a family farm… learned to break horses, shoot a rifle, and, in contrast, studied piano from age six." After attending various universities in the United States, she studied opera in Berlin before performing in major opera companies across the US and Europe. Nicknamed the "Songbird of the Chickasaws", she was inducted into the Oklahoma Hall of Fame in 1964. Another Chickasaw Nation citizen who has made significant contributions to contemporary classical music is Jerod Tate, whose seeks to broaden the range of American Indian classical composition. He received favorable reviews in *The Washington Post* for his performance of "Iholba (The Vision)", for solo flute, orchestra, and chorus, commissioned by the National Symphony Orchestra and premiered at the Kennedy Center for the Performing Arts. He has received commissions for his compositions which have been performed by the Minnesota Orchestra, the Buffalo Philharmonic Orchestra, the Colorado Ballet, The New Mexico Symphony, Oklahoma City Wind Philharmonic, and many others. Tate is the Artistic Director for the Chickasaw Chamber Music Festival, and Composer-in-Residence for the Chickasaw Summer Arts Academy, and has several other composer-in-residence credits. Of particular note is his work at the Chickasaw Summer Arts Academy which produced a CD, *Oshtali* ("divide into four parts"), showcasing a sixteen-song collection of compositions created by students of the Academy. Recorded at the Wanda L. Bass School of Music at Oklahoma City University by the GRAMMY nominated string quartet, ETHEL, and released by Thunderbird Records in 2010.

According to a press release about the project, the Chickasaw Nation is the only tribe in the United States that sponsors its own fine arts academy. Chickasaw and other American Indian students, ages 8-19, major in art, dance, literature, music composition, theatre, and video production, culminating in a grand public performance at the academy. Additionally, the tribe has instituted a Chickasaw Chamber Music Festival, with its inaugural event slated for 2011. In 2012, the tribe inducted famed Chickasaw opera star of the 1930s and '40s, Tessie Mobley, known as the "Songbird of the Chickasaws", into the Chickasaw Nation Hall of Fame

www.chickasaw.net

Endnotes
1. Other tribes removed from their Southeastern homelands to Indian Territory in the 1930s included the Cherokee, Muscogee (Creek), Euchee, Seminole, Natchez, and Choctaw.
2. In a very short note on Chickasaw music included in the "Culture" section of the Chickasaw Nation's website, an unknown author indicates women served as singers, which is unusual among American Indian religious music traditions, but not unheard of, and also relates the tribe used clay pot drums, rattles, and cane flutes.
3. When the Chickasaw were moved to Indian Territory, they were resettled among their former neighbors prior to removal, the Choctaws, with whom they shared many cultural traits. In 1856, the Chickasaws separated from the Choctaws to form their own independent government, but this close association is still felt today as many Choctaw and Chickasaw traditions are often considered one in the same, even though tribally distinctive subtleties are present to those aware enough to discern them.

Childers, Robert "Bob" Wayne

(b. November 20, 1946 – d. April 22, 2008)

Born in West Union, West Virginia to Howard and Rhea Childers, Bob Childers is often called the godfather of **red dirt music**, or the "Dylan of the dust" for his primary role in establishing the red dirt genre of Oklahoma music, a combination of folk, blues, rock, and country that has a unique Oklahoma lyrical sensibility, usually focused on better times in the past, humorous endurance of hardship, or meditations on contemporary rural or small town life. After beginning guitar at age 16, Bob graduated high school in Ponca City, Oklahoma, and studied music at the University of California – Berkeley. After leaving California, Childers began traveling the country before settling in Stillwater upon hearing a local musician, Chuck Dunlap, one of the first Stillwater musicians to release music that embraces the multi-genre facets of what has grown into a full-fledged genre that allows for all kinds of wiggle room for a musician stylistically and lyrically.

Childers emerged nationally in 1979 with his debut album titled *I Ain't No Jukebox*, which he recorded with help from his friend, another red dirt luminary, Jimmy LaFave. The album received many positive reviews and led Childers to touring nation-wide. Released

Robert Childers

in 1982, his second album, *Singing Trees, Dancing Waters* gained him enough critical attention for a gig at the White House in Washington, D.C., and enough confidence to move to Nashville in 1986. Initial successes in Music City convinced Bob to encourage some of his friends to make the same move, and several other Stillwater musicians followed, including Tom Skinner and Garth Brooks.

Childers released two albums that year. *Four Horsemen* was another strong effort, quickly followed by the all-instrumental *King David's Lament*. The gypsy in Bob led him to the burgeoning music scene of Austin, Texas where he recorded *Circles Toward the Sun* (1990). By 1991 Childers had relocated again, back to Stillwater where he released *Nothin' More Natural* (1996,) *Hat Trick* (1999), and a fan club collection of rarities, *La Vita e Bella - Outtakes, Demos and Jams 1980 - 1988* (2000). His return to Oklahoma facilitated collaboration with other red dirt artists, to include *Dirt & Spirit* with The Great Divide (1999), *Two Buffalos Walking - Live At The Blue Door* with Terry Buffalo Ware (2003), *Kindred Spirits* with Randy Crouch (2004), and *Ride for the Cimarron* with Jason Boland and the Stragglers (2006).

Beginning in 2004, Childers' health was in decline. Compiled as a benefit to assist Childers, the three-CD album, *Restless Spirit*, features tracks from over 50 performers who donated their own versions of Childers' songs, to include a who's who of red dirt artists, such as Jimmy LaFave, No Justice, Steve Ripley, Mike McClure, Brandon Jenkins, Greg Jacobs, Tom Skinner, Cross Canadian Ragweed, and several others.

Childers' influence on Oklahoma music and musicians cannot be underestimated. Childers was inducted into both the Oklahoma Music Awards "Red Dirt" Hall of Fame and the Woody Guthrie Festival Hall of Fame. in 2008, Bob was inducted posthumously into the Oklahoma Music Hall of Fame. In his honor, the Red Dirt Rangers and Tom Skinner and The Science Project played several of songs at the induction ceremony and concert. As of 2010, his various writings and unrecorded lyrics were still being catalogued by his friends and heirs, who included his two sons, Zach and Jesse. In total, more than 200 different artists have recorded his songs, a fitting legacy for the godfather.
www.binkyrecords.com/artists/childers

Choctaw Nation

(Arrived in Indian Territory via forced removal from their homelands, 1831 - 1833)

As one of the five major tribal groups from the southeastern United States who were removed over what is well-known as the "Trail of Tears" in the 1830s[1], the Choctaw Nation is headquartered in Durant, Oklahoma with a tribal membership of over 200,000 as of 2010. Musically, the tribe does not presently have any active ceremonial grounds practicing the pre-removal dances or songs of their ancestors. In the recent past at Choctaw events and gatherings, traditional dancers and singers from the Mississippi Choctaw are invited to make cultural demonstrations of the old songs and dances. However, the tribe does indicate on its website that it is teaching young people traditional Native dances through its culture and heritage program. Choctaw songs and dance are quite different than the stomp dances of their linguistic relatives, the Muscogee (Creek). Instead of men leading songs in a call and response fashion while going around a fire in a circle with women keeping the dance's rhythm with turtle shell rattles, Choctaw percussion consists of a drum, bells, and sometimes a rattle, and women also sometimes sing the responses, which is never the case with traditional Muscogee (Creek) songs. However, listeners familiar with Muscogee (Creek) ceremonial songs will hear many similarities between the melodies in Choctaw traditional songs and those that are heard typically during the Muscogee (Creek) Ribbon Dances during the annual Green Corn Celebration. Perhaps the songs sung by the medicine man at the Creek Green Corn where a rattle and/or small drum and the traditional Choctaw songs are some of the older songs for both groups that are obvious indicators of ancient tribal links between the two.

While somewhat difficult to find, two undated albums of Choctaw-Chickasaw Dance Songs were released on vinyl by the Choctaw-Chickasaw Heritage Committee, likely in the 1970s. Several songs on the albums indicate the seriousness and fun with which Choctaw people honored the animals of their world, as well as the new things presented to them by the Europeans. According to the liner notes on the album by Buster Ned, Chairman of the Choctaw-Chickasaw Heritage Committee who released the albums, "These songs were sung at stomp dances and stickball games in the Oklahoma counties of Marshall, Carter, and Bryan from 1890 to 1937." Volume I of the two-disc set includes the "Jump Dance", "Tick Dance", "Drunk Dance", "Drum Dance", "Snake Dance", and "Duck Dance", the last one of which uses a duck call as part of the instrumentation. Along with the use of bells on these songs as a percussive instrument, one can glean that the Choctaws were willing to incorporate anything new they felt fit the songs. Volume II records another "Jump Dance", along with a "Double Header", "Stealing Partners", two "Drunk Dances", two "Drum Dances" and a "Memorial Song", which is not explained, but is much slower and somber than the other songs.[2]

Additional active musical traditions within the Choctaw Nation include flute makers and players, such as Presley Byington, who keep the ancient traditional courting instrument alive as a modern instrument.

Choctaw flute maker, Presley Byington, of Idabel, OK.

In fact, the Native American flute may be the most widely appreciated American Indian instrument, as it does not require non-Native listeners to stretch their ears out quite so much to grasp what is going within the tribal music tradition. The whispery quality of a cane flute is pleasant and soothing, as well as being fairly easy to play. With regard to the development of Christian music among the Choctaws, more than a hundred hymns exist in the Choctaw language, and probably more. The Choctaw Nation online bookstore carries several different collections of Choctaw singing, the most recent being *A Choctaw Christmas*, which is a collection of holiday favorites sung in Choctaw, and *Talhohoah Momah* (translation: "They Are Still Singing"), in which Choctaw Councilman Charley Jones sings Choctaw hymns. in the range of modern music, Choctaw hip-hop singer and Oklahoma City resident, Jesse Robbins, a.k.a. Red Eagle, has started to build a performance reputation around Oklahoma and Texas with protest songs like "Ain't Your Mascot" and "Seventh Generation". One of the more interesting historic Choctaw music stories is Big Chief Henry's Indian String Band. Comprised of the Choctaw family of Henry Hall, the group recorded at least six novelty songs for RCA-Victor in a 1929

Dallas, Texas, to include "Choctaw Waltz", "The Indian's Dream", and "On the Banks of the Kaney".

Like most tribes in Oklahoma, the Choctaw also sponsor a huge intertribal powwow at their annual Labor Day Celebration at the national capitol, Tushka Homma, where visitors are also most likely to see traditional Choctaw music demonstrations and hear Choctaw hymns, as well intertribal powwow muisc and country music. www.choctawnation.com

Endnotes
1. Other tribes removed from their Southeastern homelands to Indian Territory in the 1930s included the Cherokee, Muscogee (Creek), Euchee, Seminole, Natchez, and Chickasaw.
2. For more information on Choctaw musical traditions, see James H. Howard and Victoria Lindsay Levine, *Choctaw Music and Dance* (Norman: OU Press, 1990).

Christian, Charlie

(b. July 29, 1916 - d. March 2, 1942)

The first significant soloist on the electric guitar in any music genre and one of the major role models for all jazz guitarists from 1940 onward, including **Barney Kessel,** Herb Ellis, Wes Montgomery, and George Benson, Charles Henry Christian was born in Bonham, Texas, but the family moved when Charlie was age two to Oklahoma City, where he was raised in an atmosphere of Kansas City style jazz and country music.

Charlie's first love was baseball, taught to him by his father. During his early childhood, Charlie was "off to hit the stick," as he would say. He had aspirations of playing in the Negro baseball league, and the sport remained one of his greatest passions throughout his life. However, he came from a musical family. His blind father, Clarence "Henry" Christian, was an itinerant trumpeter-guitarist-vocalist, while his mother was a pianist and his brothers were also musicians, including Clarence, who played violin and mandolin, and Edward, a string bass player. The three sons would often accompany their father into the wealthy white neighborhoods of Oklahoma City and serenade residents in return for cash, clothing, or food.

Charlie's first instrument was the trumpet, which he learned in elementary school under the tutelage of Ms. Zelia Page Breaux, noted Oklahoma City music educator. However, he switched to the guitar at about age twelve, and began studying the instrument under local musicians, guitarist Ralph "Bigfoot Chuck" Hamilton and trumpeter James Simpson, who taught Charlie three songs: "Rose Room," "Tea for Two," and "Sweet Georgia Brown." Because the family was poor, Charlie constructed his first guitar out of cigar boxes in a manual training class. By the time Charlie was thirteen, his father had died and older brother, Edward, ten years his senior, had organized his own band, the Jolly Harmony Boys.

Charlie Christian

After graduating from Douglass High School in Oklahoma City, Charlie toured as a bass player with several territorial bands, including Anna Mae Winburn, Nat Towles, and Alphonso Trent. Eddie Durham, a trombonist and guitarist in Jimmy Lunceford's band, is credited with influencing Charlie's renewed interest in the guitar, and he began performing in Trent's sextet on his $77.50 Gibson ES-150 guitar with magnetic pickup and electric amplifier. By 1937 Christian was leading his own combo in Oklahoma City and continuing to experiment with electrical amplification on his guitar. Two years later, it is reported that Mary Lou Williams, eminent jazz pianist and member of Andy Kirk's Clouds of Joy, suggested to jazz promoter John Hammond that he come by to hear Charlie who was playing at the Ritz Ballroom in downtown Oklahoma City. Hammond liked what he heard and contacted Benny Goodman about an audition for Charlie in Los Angeles, where Goodman was recording his first sessions for Columbia Records. Christian and Hammond traveled to the West Coast, but Goodman was turned off by Charlie's attire and concept of an electric guitar. One source states that for the audition, Charlie wore a ten-gallon cowboy hat, pointed yellow shoes, a green suit over a purple shirt, and a string bow tie. Despite Goodman's attitude, Hammond persisted and helped Charlie set up his amplifiers on the stage of the Victor Hugo Restaurant in Beverly Hills, where Goodman was performing. With the instigation of Goodman, his band began jamming on "Rose Room," a piece that the leader figured Charlie would not know, but it was one of the first tunes he learned in Oklahoma City. When it was Charlie's turn to solo, he played some twenty-five impressive choruses to the excitement of Goodman, his band, and the audience. That night Goodman hired Charlie to become a member of his entourage, and for the next two years, was featured soloist with the Benny Goodman Sextet. In October of 1939, Goodman played Carnegie Hall, where he introduced Charlie on a sextet number "Flying Home" saying "with Charlie Christian on the electric guitar. I really think he is one of the most terrific musicians that has been produced in years."

While in New York with the Goodman ensemble, Christian became interested in the new developments in jazz taking place on 52nd Street. He began jamming with leaders in the bebop movement, such as Dizzy Gillespie and Thelonious Monk, at such venues as The Savoy and Minton's Playhouse, and became a fellow pioneer in the development of this subgenre of jazz. The late night sessions proved to be part of his undoing, however, as the late nights (sometimes until daybreak) and bouts with alcoholism affected Charlie's health. March 13, 1941, would turn out to be Christian's last record date with the Goodman Sextet. Three months later, on a tour of the Midwest in June, he collapsed onstage. He was rushed back to New York, where doctors at Bellevue Hospital determined that his TB had returned. By July, he had been transferred to the Seaview sanatorium in Staten Island to get his health back. Rumors persist that he was smuggled out to Minton's on occasion, or that friends smuggled in female company and marijuana, hastening his demise. At age twenty-five, younger than Robert Johnson or Jimi Hendrix, the founding father and primary architect of the modern jazz guitar style died at Seaview Sanatorium on Staten Island. He is buried in Gates Hill Cemetery in Bonham, Texas.

Native Oklahoman Barney Kessel, one of the major figures in jazz guitar during the twentieth century, paid tribute to Charlie in 1975 at the Concord Jazz Festival: "I would venture to say that there is not a guitarist alive today, whether he knows it or not, who is playing jazz, amplified or unamplified, who doesn't owe something to and have some of Charlie Christian in his playing."

Christian was one of the first inductees into the Oklahoma Jazz Hall of Fame in

1989, was inducted into the Rock and Roll Hall of Fame in 1990 in the category of "Early Influences," and inducted into the Oklahoma Music Hall of Fame in October of 2002. In November of 2002, he was the subject of a NRP story, "Revisiting the Sound of Guitar Pioneer Charlie Christian" by Tom Vitale.

In 2002, Columbia/Legacy Jazz released *Charlie Christian: The Genius of the Electric Guitar*, a four-CD boxed set that is the first comprehensive of the Columbia Recordings with the Benny Goodman Sextet and Orchestra (1939-41), plus the Metronome All Star Nine. The set includes 98 tracks – 17 of which are previously unreleased in the United States, and encompasses master and alternate takes, breakdowns, false starts and rehearsal sequences, and an uncut twenty-minute jam session. A new liner note essay by British biographer Peter Broadbent is included, and it is complemented by in-depth track-by-track sessionography researched by Loren Schoenberg. Also in the liner notes is a memoir from close friend Les Paul that tops list of testimonials from B.B. King, George Benson, Jimmie Vaughan, John Scofield, T-Bone Walker, Wes Montgomery, Brian Setzer, Joe Satriani, Barney Kessel, Herb Ellis, Tal Farlow, Bill Frisell, and more.

Vernon Reid, the lead guitarist for Living Colour, says "It all starts with him: Charlie Christian is The Father. In his all-too-brief time, Charlie changed the world of jazz, blues, and everything else besides. It is literally impossible to overstate the importance of his contribution to the development of jazz. His limitless stream of melodic ideas; the many blue shades of his pungently sad, sweet tone; and his irrepressible swing all continue to influence generations of guitarists. From Wes Montgomery to James Blood Ulmer, from Tal Farlow to Charlie Hunter: It all began with the first master of the electric guitar, Mr. Charlie Christian."

According to a Columbia/Legacy jazz press release to promote the collection in 2002, *Genius* tracks Christian's 14 extant Columbia studio dates spanning 17 months through March 1941 (one year before his death), when he recorded "Solo Flight" with the orchestra, the signature by which the famed Gibson ES150 guitarist would be known forever. The first Goodman feature actually built around Christian (though not issued until nearly two years after his death), "Solo Flight" found him in transition to the nascent Be-bop movement, upon which fellow conspirator Thelonious Monk and others considered him a primal force.

54 tracks on *Genius* were first issued on Columbia Records in the U.S. between 1939 and 1989, during the 78 rpm, LP and CD eras. One track, the alternate of "Flying Home," was issued (for the first time) as a 1948 Armed Forces V-Disc. Another number, 1939's "I'm Confessin'," was issued (for the first time) by Time-Life in 1978. The five tracks recorded in 1940 by Goodman and Christian in the company of Count Basie and five of his key band members (including Lester Young, whose long tenor saxophone solo lines were a primary influence on Christian) were secreted away by Hammond and didn't surface until 1972, when they were issued by Jazz Archives.

"[Christian's] name is ranked alongside those of Louis Armstrong, Earl Hines, Lester Young, and Charlie Parker," Broadbent concludes in the boxed set's liner notes. "Each elevated music to a new level of achievement, whilst establishing a new vocabulary that made them the premier voice on their chosen instrument." Musicologist Loren Schoenberg has contributed invaluable in-depth interpolations of every individual recording session on *Genius*, incorporating track-by-track analyses that carefully trace the evolution of Christian's music and the development of the Sextet. "Hearing these recordings in such superb fidelity is like seeing a newly minted print of a classic film," Schoenberg writes,

"All sorts of details appear that were lost in the poorly copied transfers that comprised the great majority of LP and CD issues available until now."

A saxophonist, conductor and educator who played in Goodman's big band, Schoenberg is the executive director of the Jazz Museum in Harlem and the author of The NPR Curious Listener's Guide To Jazz. "[Christian] learned from Eddie Durham and Django Reinhardt and others who brought something new to the guitar," he notes, "but in Christian's hands it became an altogether new instrument. With just a few exceptions, he eschewed the chorded solos that were such a large part of the guitar's legacy. It was all about the line and about how rhythm could extend the line and give it all sorts of new and unexpected shapes." The liner notes in the set are rounded out by a series of testimonials from various practitioners of the guitar spanning more than six decades, spearheaded by "My Friend Charlie Christian," an evocative reminiscence by Les Paul. The Gibson guitar legend, already a star on radio in 1938, recalls an odyssey that brought him from New York to a gig in Tulsa starring **Bob Wills & His Texas Playboys**. That is where Les Paul met Christian, and one can only imagine the jam session onstage that night described by Paul. His story segues to befriending Christian sometime later on his first trip to New York. Paul ordered matching blond Gibson electric guitars and custom-made tube amplifiers for the two of them from Eddie Bell's 46th Street store — but the rigs proved too heavy for either of them to schlep down the street so they returned them. In his testimonial, Les Paul writes, "*What I'm doing was so much harder than what he's doing* — that's what I thought back then. But over time, through being with Charlie, I realized how tough it is to come down on that one note in the right place, and how much more of a *drive* he had. He had that ability, like Lionel Hampton, to take a note, to take one 'A' and just pound it into your head until it was the greatest note you'd ever heard. He didn't play beyond himself. He didn't think, 'What the hell, no one's listening. Why don't I try this?' Charlie wasn't one to go out over his head. The beat came first. He locked himself into that driving sound." Among the numerous guitarists whose thoughts are included in the booklet with their testimonials to Christian's towering influence are (alphabetically, not in order of appearance): Walter Becker (Steely Dan), George Benson, Herb Ellis, Tal Farlow, Bill Frisell, Warren Haynes (Allman Brothers Band, Government Mule), Barney Kessel, B.B. King, Russell Malone, Wes Montgomery, Vernon Reid (Living Colour), Duke Robillard, Joe Satriani, John Scofield, Brian Setzer, Derek Trucks (Allman Brothers Band, Derek Trucks Band), Jimmie Vaughan, and T-Bone Walker. As John Scofield testifies, "Miles Davis told me that he thought Charlie Christian was the original instigator of the bebop movement, Bird and Diz's main influence. When you listen to his playing today, it's still inspiring, fresh,

Charlie Christian's last guitar, a Gibson ES 250 electric, displayed at the Oklahoma History Center, 2010.

harmonically and rhythmically advanced. I love the fact that the modern jazz movement seems to have been started by an electric guitarist!"

In 2007, Oklahoma City officials renamed a section a street near downtown, Charlie Christian Avenue, and the Charlie Christian Jazz Festival entered its twenty-seventh consecutive year in 2012.

www.charlie-christian.com

www.charliechristianfestival.com

Clark, Roy

(b. April 15, 1933)

One of the most multi-talented entertainers in American music and inductee into the Oklahoma Hall of Fame, Oklahoma Music Hall of Fame, and Gibson Guitar Hall of Fame, singer, songwriter, guitarist, banjoist, fiddler, trombonist, pianist, trumpeter, actor, and comedian, Roy Linwood Clark was born in Meherrin, Virginia, although he has resided in Tulsa for the past twenty-five plus years, where an elementary school and airport bears his name. His father, Hester, worked at various jobs including cotton picker, tobacco grower, and sawmill worker before the family moved to Washington, D.C., where his father worked as a computer programmer for the

Roy Clark

Department of Health, Education, and Welfare. Both his father and mother, Lillian, were amateur musicians with father competent on banjo, fiddle, and guitar; and his mother on piano. Roy's first instrument was a cigar box with a ukulele neck and four strings crafted by his father for a school band at Meherrin Elementary. Both parents took an interest in Roy's music, especially his father who tutored him on the banjo. He made his first public appearance in 1948 at a military service club with his father's square dance band. Roy won back-to-back National Music Banjo Championships in 1949-50, garnering his first appearance on the Grand Ole Opry, and later was guest on Arthur Godrey's Talent Scouts Show.

In addition to music, Roy excelled in sports, especially baseball and boxing. At age sixteen, he was offered a tryout with the St. Louis Browns baseball team, but could not afford the fare to the workout. When he was seventeen, he boxed in the light-heavyweight division in and around Washington, D.C., and won fifteen consecutive bouts before opting for a career in music.

Clark's first break came in 1955 when he became a regular on the Jimmy Dean television show, *Country Style*. After Dean left for New York, Clark was given the show, and during the next five years, established himself as a versatile entertainer through his musicianship and comedy. In 1960, he joined **Wanda Jackson** as lead guitarist and front man during which time she recorded one of her biggest hits, "Let's Have a Party," as well as playing concerts with her in Las Vegas. Although Jackson dissolved her band about a year later, Roy continued to play Las Vegas, including the Frontier Hotel. During this time, Jim Halsey, Jackson's former manager, became Roy's manager and landed him a role on the popular television show, *The Beverly Hillbillies*, where he played the dual roles of Cousin Roy and Big Mama Halsey.

In 1963, Roy debuted on *The Tonight Show* and later became the first country artist to host the show. Although he had recorded singles for Four Star, Coral and Debbie, Roy's first contract with a major label, Capitol, was signed in 1962. His first Capitol album was *The Lightning Fingers of Roy Clark*, and his fourth single, "Tips of My Fingers," reached Top 10 on the country charts and achieved Top 50 on the pop charts; his first crossover recording. After recording "Through the Eyes of a Fool" (1964) and "When the Blows in Chicago" (1965) for Capitol, he switched to the Dot label in 1967. In 1969, he scored with Charles Aznavour's "Yesterday, When I Was Young" and "September Song." The former was Roy's second crossover hit; charting Top 10 in country and Top 20 in popular.

In 1969, CBS invited Roy and Bakersfield country star Buck Owens to co-host a new country music and comedy show *Hee Haw*, a country version of *Laugh In*. For the next two years, it became one of the highest rated shows television shows in the U.S. But CBS decided to drop the program because it created an unfavorable image for the network, however, the show's producers syndicated it and began reaching some thirty million viewers weekly on some 200 stations. Roy co-hosted the show for more than twenty-five years.

The decade of the 1970s proved productive for Clark. He continued headlining at Las Vegas' Caesar's Palace with Petula Clark; launched a twenty-one day tour to Russia in 1976 with eighteen sold out concerts in Moscow, Leningrad, and Riga, which resulted in the CMA's "Friendship Ambassador" award (he returned to Russia in 1988 to sold out venues); performed in 1976 with Arthur Fiedler and the Boston Pops Orchestra; appeared at Carnegie Hall in 1977; and recorded several hits, including "Thank God for Greyhound" (1970), "I Never Picked Cotton" (1970), "The Lawrence Welk-Hee Haw Counter-Revolution Polka" (1972), "Come Live With Me" (1973), a #1 hit, "Riders in the Sky" (1973), one of his first instrumental hits, "Somewhere Between Love and Goodbye" (1973), "Honeymoon Feelin'" (1974), "The Great Divide" (1974), "Heart to Heart" (1975), and "If I Had to Do It All Over Again" (1976), the song most identified with him.

By the end of the 1970s, Clark's recording career began to slow. He left ABC/Dot for MCA, and had one hit, "Chain Gang of Love." In 1981, he recorded an inspirational album for Songbird, *The Last Word in Jesus is Us*. By 1982, he had switched to Churchill Records, long time manager Jim Halsey's label. Roy, Grandpa Jones, Buck Owens, and Kenny Price formed the Hee Haw Gospel Quartet in 1984, and recorded an eponymous album on the Hee Haw label.

Roy's career was rejuvenated in 1983 when he was the first nationally recognized artist to build a theater in Branson, Missouri, The Roy Clark Celebrity Theater. His name recognition was responsible for attracting guest appearances by several Nashville stars, including **Roger Miller**, Johnny Cash, **Merle Haggard**, Oak Ridge Boys, Willie Nelson, and a host of others, and to make Branson a new "mecca" for country music performers.

The list of honors, awards, and accolades for Clark are overwhelming, including many firsts. He was the first star to take an act to the Soviet Union, first country artist to headline a night at the Montreaux International Jazz Festival, first country performer to headline at MIDEM, the music industry fair at Cannes, first country artist to receive a five star rating in the jazz periodical *Downbeat*, first national ambassador for UNICEF, and the first country performer to appear as a guest on the *Tom Jones Show* in London.

Roy's awards include ACM Comedy Act of the Year (1969, 1970, and 1971), ACM Entertainer of the Year (1972 and 1973), CMA Comedian of the Year and Entertainer of the Year (1970 and 1973, respectively), CMA Instrumental Group of the Year with Buck Trent (1975 and 1976), CMA Instrumentalist of the Year (1977, 1978, and 1980), and *Guitar Player* magazine's Best Country Guitarist (1976 through 1980). He was also a finalist for the CMA for Entertainer of the Year (1969, 1970, and 1974) and Instrumentalist of the Year for the years 1967 through 1976, and again in 1979 and 1984.

Clark is an inductee in the Oklahoma Hall of Fame (1982), Gibson Guitar Hall of Fame (1982), and the Oklahoma Music Hall of Fame (2000). In 1987, he was belatedly made a member of the Grand Ole Opry.

His humanitarian efforts are noteworthy. He has received the Minnie Pearl Award from the CMA, donated millions of dollars to the Children's Medical Center in Tulsa and St. Jude's Children's Hospital in Memphis, and sponsors the Roy Clark Celebrity Golf Tournament that annually raises funds for charities.

Roy and his wife, Barbara of more than 50 years, currently reside in Tulsa and own a ranch in northeastern Oklahoma where he raises cattle and horses. He has invested in a wide spectrum of projects, including the Tulsa Drillers, a minor league baseball team affiliated with the Colorado Rockies. In 2010, Clark again signed with his long time fried, business associate and agent, Jim Halsey, to continue booking Clark for perforances far and wide. In 2011, the Oklahoma History Center produced an exhibit celebrating Clark's long standing presence on the country music comedy and variety show, *Hee Haw*. The exhibit also chronicled the extensive impact Oklahomans had on the show, and also the impact the show had on the careers of Reba McEntire, Garth Brooks, Sheb Wooley, **Jana Jae**, and Gailard Sartain. In 2012, Northeast Technology Center in Claremore, OK named its music school after Clark.

www.roy-clark.com

Clark, Sanford

(b. 1935)

A minor rockabilly artist who had one notable song, "The Fool", Sanford Clark was born in Tulsa, Oklahoma, but moved to Phoenix, Arizona at an early age. Of particular interest in Sanford's career is his only hit was written, recorded and produced by Mannford native, **Lee Hazlewood**, who also wrote another song Clark recorded later, "Houston", but Hazlewood then recorded and produced another version with Dean Martin that knocked Clark off the radio deejay turntables. One thing Sanford did not record that he should have, and that was Roger Miller's "Dang Me". Apparently, Clark met Miller who asked the one hit wonder boy to record Roger's latest jokester tune. Clark declined, and while he continued performing as a country and rockabilly artist as late as 2002, he never had a hit after "The Fool". He could, however, be heard walking the halls after shows, saying, "Dang ME." Just kidding about that part. "The Fool" reappeared on a UK rockabilly compilation 1999, *Magnum Rockabilly*, which also included "Big"Al Downing's "Down on the Farm".

By Hugh Foley / 145

www.rockabillyhall.com/sanfordclark.html

Clauser, Al (and his Oklahoma Outlaws)
(b. 1911 – d. March 3, 1989)

Leader of one of the most popular western swing bands in the 1940s and 1950s and one of the first bandleaders to use the term "western swing" in the 1920s, Henry Alfred "Al" Clauser was born in Manitoba, Illinois. He began his musical career in his native state of Illinois, where he played in local clubs in the Peoria area while in high school. Starting first with a trio, Al expanded his band to six pieces, and the group performed over radio station WMBD.

Al Clauser and his Oklahoma Outlaws.

Although none of the band members had ever visited Oklahoma, Al needed a "western" name for the group, when they began appearing on radio station WHO in Des Moines, Iowa, in 1934. While on WHO, Al's group was heard by **Gene Autry**, and hired them to perform in one of Autry's movies, *Rootin' Tootin' Rhythm*. During their time in Hollywood, the band recorded twelve sides for the ARA label in Los Angeles. By 1938, the band had signed with radio station WCKY in Cincinnati, Ohio, however, after about a year, they returned to KHBF in Rock Island, Illinois, where the Mutual Broadcasting Network began carrying their show to some 272 stations in the Midwest.

During World War II, Al and the band, sometimes referred to as the Oklahoma Outlaws or Oklahoma Cowboys, when they played western swing, or The Serenaders, when they played pop music, relocated to Tulsa, where the band members worked in the air defense factories.

By the end of World War II, Al had expanded his band to nine members, and they gained regular daily broadcasts on radio station KTUL in Tulsa. Al's band competed with other western swing bands in Oklahoma, such as **Johnnie Lee Wills** and Leon McAuliffe. Later, during the 1950s, the group also performed on KTUL-TV. It is reported that Clara Ann Fowler (**Patti Page**) received her first major break on the Al Clauser show on KTUL-TV when she was twelve years old, and cut her first record with Al's Oklahoma Outlaws.

Al and the Oklahoma Outlaws disbanded in the late 1950s, but Al continued to work on KTUL-TV on his popular children's show in which he starred as "Uncle Zeke." He also built a recording studio west of Tulsa in the Lake Keystone area. Al died in Tulsa on March 3, 1989.

A 2000 compilation entitled *The Golden Age of Al Clauser and his Oklahoma Outlaws*, was issued by Binge Discs, a German company. It consisted of twenty-two tracks, including several pop tunes ("Little Brown Jug" and "Bill Bailey"), traditional western and cowboy tunes ("Little Old Sod Shanty on the Claim" and "Sweet Betsy From Pike"), and three songs co-written by Al ("The Little Black Bronc," "Lonesome Cowboy Song," and "Tired Little Wrangler"). Al and the group also appear on two other recent overseas company releases: Varese's *Gene Autry With the Legendary Singing Groups of the West (1936-1949)*, on which they perform "The Old Home Place," and Bear Family's eight

Cletro, Eddie

(b. October 28, 1918)

A noted Western music performer, singer, and guitarist based in Los Angeles who played with Oklahoman Spade Cooley for about a year in 1946 and '47, Eddie Cletro was born in Trenton, New Jersey, not in Oklahoma, as has been noted in various publications over the year due to his management's early decision to claim he was from Coalgate, Oklahoma. Therefore, while Cletro is not from the state, the idea he needed to be in order to be a credible Western performer can be further discussed in terms of the state's identity as a rootsy, authentic environment. Other 20th century performers who claimed to be from Oklahoma, or associate with the state, but were not, included Cowboy Copas, Eddie Cochran (although his family had Oklahoma ties), and Al Clauser, and for some reason, their last names all begin with the letter "C". Nonetheless, Cletro's "Flying Saucer Boogie" is still a classic, and he was still performing as of 2005.

Eddie Cletro

Note

1. For an extensive review of Cletro's career, see his complete profile at www.hillbilly-music.com.

Coburn, Sarah

(b. forthcoming?)

Praised as "blissfully sublime" by Opera News, Sarah Coburn is captivating audiences with her "precision placement, mercury speed, and a gorgeous liquid gold tone, gilded by a thrilling top and bottom register" (The Globe and Mail). Following her performances as Lucie de Lammermoor at Glimmerglass Opera, the New York Observer noted "she turns out to have qualities that have made legends out of so many of her predecessors, from Adelina Patti to Maria Callas: stage charisma, a thrilling upper register and, crucially, a fearlessness about abandoning herself to opera's most abandoned heroine ... this is a palpably exciting voice ... Ms. Coburn is a budding prima donna of exceptional promise." Daughter of Oklahoma Senator Tom Coburn and former Miss Oklahoma, Carolyn Denton Coburn, Sarah was born and raised in Muskogee, Oklahoma, and attended Oklahoma State University where she received a Bachelor of Music Education degree, followed by studies at Oklahoma City University's prestigious Wanda Bass School of Music where she earned a Master of Music degree.

Coburn's many successes performing bel canto repertoire include Asteria in Tamerlano with Washington National Opera, Elvira in I puritani with Washington Concert Opera, the title role in Lakmé with Tulsa Opera, the title role in Lucie de Lammermoor, with both Cincinnati Opera and Glimmerglass Opera, the title role in Linda di Chamounix at the Caramoor Festival, Giulietta in I Capuleti e i Montecchi with Glimmerglass Opera, the title role in Lucia di Lammermoor with Utah Opera, and Norina in Don Pasquale with Florida Grand Opera. She also performed the role of Princess Yue-Yang in the world premiere production of Tan Dun's The First Emperor at the Metropolitan Opera opposite Placido Domingo, which she returned the following season to reprise in the production's revival, and created the role of Kitty in the world premiere of Anna Karenina at Florida Grand Opera, later reprising the role with Opera Theatre of Saint Louis. Ms. Coburn has also appeared as Adele in Die Fledermaus with both Seattle Opera and Michigan Opera Theatre, Oscar in Un ballo in maschera and Olympia in Les Contes d'Hoffmann with Cincinnati Opera, and both Sandrina in La finta giardiniera and Susanna in Le nozze di Figaro with Florida Grand Opera.

Sarah Coburn

On the concert stage, Ms. Coburn has sung Bach's Mass in B Minor and Mozart's Mass in C Minor with the Seattle Symphony as well as Carmina Burana with the National Chorale at Avery Fisher Hall, the National Symphony Orchestra, Haddonfield Symphony at Philadelphia's Kimmel Center for the Performing Arts, and the Dallas Wind Symphony. Sarah Coburn is a winner of the 2004 George London Foundation Awards, a 2004 recipient of a Sara Tucker Study Grant from the Richard Tucker Foundation, a 2004 Jensen Foundation Award Winner, a 2003 Liederkranz Foundation Award Winner, a 2002 Opera Index Career Grant recipient, and was a National Grand Finalist in the 2001 Metropolitan Opera National Council Auditions.

In 2009-10, Sarah sang Asteria in Tamerlano and Rosina in Il barbiere di Siviglia with Los Angeles Opera; Rosina with Florida Grand Opera; the title role in Lucia di Lammermoor with Tulsa Opera; Gilda in Rigoletto with Welsh National Opera; and appeared as the featured artist in an evening of bel canto arias with both the Canterbury Choral Society and the Bartlesville Symphony Orchestra. Other highlights over the last ten years include include Vittoria in Pedrotti's Tutti in maschera at Wexford Festival Opera, Euridice in Haydn's L'anima del filosofo under the baton of Sir Roger Norrington at the Handel & Haydn Society, and Gilda in Rigoletto with Portland Opera. She also appeared as soloist in Messiah with both the Seattle Symphony Orchestra and the Philadelphia Orchestra, in Carmina Burana with the New Jersey Symphony Orchestra, in concert with Bryn Terfel in Florida Grand Opera's Superstar Series, and in recital with Lawrence Brownlee for the Vocal Arts Society.[1]

Coburn has been featured on one recording, Anna Karenina (Signum, 2009), and has multiple videos on youtube.com demonstrating her incredible vocal range and expressive ability. Having experienced quite a dramatic rise from starring in a Muskogee Little Theatre production of Grease, in April, 2010, she wrote in her website's blog: "As I look back on the past few years, I am amazed at how many things have changed in my life and how blessed I am. 2007 brought the mutt and the man; 2008, the marriage; 2009, motherhood; and in 2010, I hope to master the management of it all! As I type this, I am on a small break from performing, and it has been a wonderful time of focusing on being a wife and mother. I love my job and feel so fortunate to sing for a living, but right now, I think that being a stay-at-home mom could be the best job in the universe. (Not that I would really know, as I have only been home for six weeks.) Ah, well. We will soon be on the road again, and I am truly thankful for my many blessings: a refreshing time at home, a healthy baby, a wonderful husband, and more beautiful music in the near future."

Her engagements in the 2010-11 season included her debuts with Wiener Staatsoper as Amina in La sonnambula and Opéra de Montréal as Gilda in Rigoletto, as well as reengagements to sing Gilda with Los Angeles Opera and Rosina in Il barbiere di Siviglia with Seattle Opera. Also for Los Angeles Opera she sings Handel's "L'allegro, il pensoroso, ed il moderato."In 2011, she returned to Oklahoma for a Christmas concert with Tulsa Community College's Signature Symphony.
www.sarah-coburn.com

Note
1. The majority of this entry's information is courtesy of Sarah Coburn's official biography from her publicists at Barret Vantage Artists (www.barrettvantage.com).

Cochran, Edward "Eddie" Ray

(b. October 3, 1938 – d. April 17, 1960)

Recognizable for all time in rock history for the anthem, "Summertime Blues", and to a lesser extent for his other hits, "C'mon Everybody" and "Twenty Flight Rock", Eddie Cochran was born in Albert Lea, Minnesota, not in Oklahoma as has been printed for many years in countless reputable rock and pop music reference works[1]. The confusion stems from Cochran's early responses in interviews where he said he was from Oklahoma in order to give himself a more authentic background for a career as a country and/or rock and roll performer. Unlike claims by Cowboy Copas, Al Clauser, or Eddie Cletro, who made similar statements for publicity purposes, Cochran's story is based in a little more reality as his grandparents lived in Oklahoma City, and his parents lived there before moving to Minnesota, and then on to California. According to excellent research done by Graham Pugh and published at www.eddiecochran.net, Cochran's family did move to Oklahoma City for a brief period in 1953 in order to be

Eddie (left) and Hank Cochran (unrelated) performed as the Cochran Brothers in the mid-1950s.

By Hugh Foley / 149

closer to Cochran's grandmother, Corda. The Cochrans lived in the Darliene Apartments on 215 Northwest 4th Street, the present site of the Oklahoma City National Memorial where the Alfred P. Murrah Building stood prior to its bombing. Pugh found proof of Cochran's residency in Oklahoma City for those months through interviewing Cochran's cousins and a close friend, as well as finding Cochran's picture in the 1953 Albert Lea and Bell Gardens school yearbooks. 2

Notes
1. Not to call anyone out, because compiling factual information on popular music can be fraught with misinformation, randomly copied facts without attribution, and a willful misrepresentation by artists for all sorts of reasons, but as of July, 2010, *Rolling Stone*'s online biography of Eddie Cochran, as taken from the *Rolling Stone Encyclopedia of Rock* (New York: Fireside, 2001), still lists Cochran as born in Oklahoma but raised in Minnesota.
2. For a complete overview of the connections between Eddie Cochran's family and Oklahoma City, see Graham Pugh's extremely thorough website dedicated to clearing up the whole story, complete with images, maps, and all kinds of historical details at www.eddiecochran.net.

Coffey, Kellie

(b. April 22, 1971)

Merging lyrics that often speak from a woman's point of view with a strong, full voice that is intimate, warm, and confidently expressive, singer/songwriter Kellie Coffey charted five country singles between 2002 and 2004, and saw her first album, When You Lie Next to Me, rise to #5 on the country album chart. Largely due to the success of the album's title track which went Top 10 country and also crossed over to the pop charts, Kellie won the ACM's Top New Female Vocalist of 2003.

Raised in Moore, Oklahoma, where the water tower says "Home of Toby Keith," Kellie actually was born at the Baylor University Hospital in Waco, Texas, because her father was in dental school at that time. After completion of dental school, the family, headed by Bob and Roseann who are native Oklahomans, returned to Oklahoma in 1974 when Kellie was about three years old. She recalls that singing has been a part of her life since childhood, although her immediate family was not especially musical. Her father, a dentist in Moore, occasionally played by ear an upright piano, located in the den of their home, her grandfather played the clarinet, and her two brothers (Rob and John) sang.

Kellie Coffey

Her first public singing took place in church, and she took piano and voice lessons from Barbara Ramsey, a local music teacher in Moore.

Kelly's first professional performance came at the age of nine, when her parents encouraged her to participate in the Oklahoma Opry, where she sang "Pecos Promenad", the Tanya Tucker hit, and "Dancing Your Memory Away", a Charley McClain recording. After graduating from Westmoore High School, she enrolled at the University of Oklahoma in Norman, from which the entire Coffee family graduated from. At OU, Kellie majored in vocal performance and participated in such campus activities as Sooner Scandals, an annual musical. During these events Kellie realized she wanted to become a professional vocalist.

Following graduation from OU, Kellie headed for Los Angeles, where she roomed with a friend from college. She began to search for entertainment jobs while working as a singing waitress, writing songs, and taking lessons in a singing/performance class. About this period, she explained in 2010 on her website's biography, "All through high school and college, I led a pretty typical, Midwestern, all-American life. When I graduated from OU with a vocal performance degree, it felt like it was time to fly. My goal was to make a living as a singer. I had a friend from OU who had moved to L.A. the year before and had an extra room. So, I packed up my car and headed west. Leaving Oklahoma was very difficult for me and for my whole family, especially my mom. She was a stay at home mom. We are very close but my parents were very supportive. They always believed in me."

After making ends meet in L.A. by being a singing waitress, she began to get work as a demo singer, and was writing songs. "When I first started writing, it was because of a break-up," she explains on her site, "So all of my early songs were about love lost. I discovered that song-writing for me was therapeutic." After making several demo tapes and obtaining work as a demo singer, Kellie met Geoff Koch, who wrote songs for television shows, including Walker Texas Ranger. Through this contact, she was hired to sing and write songs for the hit show, and began to garner additional jobs in radio, television, and film. The friendship between Kellie and Koch blossomed into a marriage. While in Los Angeles, Kellie secured a job singing at Disneyland in Anaheim that resulted in further work at Disney World in Orlando, as well as recording, "Sharing a Dream Come True," which was the corporate entertainment giant's theme song for several years both in its theme parks and on its advertising campaigns.

Kellie continued her songwriting endeavors and began to make trips from Los Angeles to Nashville because her songs were primarily country oriented. Through the efforts of Judy Stakee, she signed a contract with Warner-Chappell in Nashville to write country songs for herself and others. By 1998, she had written or co-written five songs suitable for a demo tape to pitch to the A&R personnel in Nashville, and soon signed a recording contract with Joe Galante, head of the RCA label. Kellie's debut album includes eleven tracks, of which she co-wrote seven. Brett James, from Oklahoma City and family a friend, co-wrote two of the songs, one with Kellie. During its first week of release, Kellie's CD sales broke Leann Rimes' country music record held since 1996. During the summer of 2002, she opened for the Kenny Chesney on his Senorita's and Margaritas tour. Over the next two years, three more singles she co-wrote charted on Billboard's Hot Country Songs chart, "At the End of the Day", (#18), "Whatever It Takes" (#44), and "Texas Plates" (#24), the last of which is a saucy tune about three Oklahoma girls chasing a car with Texas plates, presumably in pursuit of the driver and/or other occupants. Her last chart single, "Dance with My Father" (#41), is a cover of 2003 Luther Vandross pop hit, recorded for a planned second album that did not happen until she released her own independent CD in 2007. Continuing to tour as an opening act, she toured with George Strait on his 2004 tour, and made additional tour dates with Keith Urban, Brooks & Dunn, Montgomery Gentry, Trace Adkins, Wynonna Judd, Martina McBride, Lone Star, and Alan Jackson.

After four years performing live for over one million people, Kellie and BNA Records parted ways. She continued to write, but put her recording career on hold to focus on having a family, starting with a son, Jackson Geoffrey. Subsequently she teamed with GRAMMY Award winning songwriter/producer Wayne Kirkpatrick (Little Big Town),

and again with Judy Stakee as Executive Producer, co-writing all but one of the 12 songs on her independent CD, Walk On. With the modern era's distribution opportunities being wide open for an artist's controlled exploitation, the first video off the album, "I Would Die for That", a song dealing with infertility and a working woman's desire to have a child, reached over 500,000 views on youtube.com. Coffey's second child, Maggie Rose, was born in 2008, Kellie focused on mom duties, but, according to her website, "She still finds the time to write songs, record and release new music." Interested listeners should check out the songs on her website's jukebox, especially "Dream You Hear", a single from Walk On that did not chart but is a beautiful, heartbreaking song about love and loss with several moments where her voice exhibits why it has attracted so much attention since she was a child.
www.kelliecoffey.com

The Collins Kids (Larry and Lorrie)
Lawrence Albert Collins [b. October 4, 1944]
Lawrencine May Collins [b. May 7, 1942]

Reared on a dairy farm and attending a one-room school in the Pretty Water community near Tahlequah, Oklahoma, Larry and Lorrie Collins were among the most influential rockabilly acts of the 1950s. Lorrie was born in Tahlequah, and Larry was born in Tulsa General Hospital before being hauled back out to Pretty Water. Their father, Lawrence, farmed in Oklahoma, and later worked in the wrought iron steel business. Their mother, Hazel, a gospel singer and mandolin player, had come from a musical family in which her father played fiddle and all of her sisters played instruments. As a result, Hazel encouraged both Larry and Lorrie to sing, especially in church and at socials afterwards on Sundays. At the age of eight, Hazel took Lorrie to Tulsa where Western swing steel guitarist Leon McAuliffe was playing at the Cimarron Ballroom. McAuliffe complimented Lorrie,

The Collins Kids

and told Lorrie's parents if they were going to help her have a career they need to relocate to California, or Tennessee, to develop her talents. Their mother had a sister who lived in Redondo Beach, California. Lorrie and her mother went out to California by themselves on a Greyhound Bus, while Larry, their older sister, and father stayed on the dairy farm in 1953. Once in California, Lorrie went to a few auditions, received encouragement, and then returned to Oklahoma. About a month later, their mom convinced their father to sell his cows and make the move to California. In the meantime, Larry had received a guitar a $12 Stella guitar from Sears and Roebuck as his Christmas present in 1952. According to Larry in an interview with Jeff Moore and Larry O'Dell for the Oklahoma History Center's 2009 exhibit on rock music in the state of Oklahoma, he could play the instrument as soon as he opened it up. "It's just the gift of my musical ability," he remembers, "My mom showed me a couple of chords, but I was playing and singing "Kaw-Liga" by the end of the day, and I could not sit still doing it." Collins also explained he source of their rockabilly sound and energy: "As far as us and our music, it was Pentecostal music, blues, and country music."

With Lorrie's growling rock and roll voice, and Larry's rapidly evolving guitar skills, the duo won a Town Hall Party talent contest in February of 1954. The next day, the Collins Kids landed a spot on the Los Angeles television show, Town Hall Party, broadcast over KFI radio and KTTV-TV, and later carried by a network of NBC radio stations. Televised every Saturday night from Compton, California, it was hosted by Tex Ritter. This breakthrough gave the Collins Kids major television and radio exposure before they were teenagers, and they appeared in every episode of the show following their first appearance. Larry often jammed on the show with guitarist Joe Maphis, known as "King of the Double-Necked Mosrite," and who became his mentor. Maphis, who played a sunburst double neck electric guitar designed and constructed by Oklahoman Semie Moseley, arranged for Moseley to build a similar model for Larry with his name inlaid on one neck. Thereafter on the show, Larry and Joe, playing their twin-necked Mosrites, would lay down some exciting instrumentals, such as "Hurricane," "Fire on the Strings," and "The Rockin' Gypsy." The Maphis-Collins synergy was so solid that the pair recorded four instrumentals in 1957. As a guitarist, Larry in turn influenced Dick Dale, the "king of surfer guitarists."

On Larry's eleventh birthday in 1955, the Collins Kids recorded their first releases for Columbia—"Hush Money" and "Beetle Bug Bop." During their tenure with Columbia and Epic Records, they were showcased in their "hopped-up hillbilly" style with such releases as "Whistle Bait," "Hot Rod," "Soda Poppin' Around," "In My Teens," "Hop, Skip, and Jump," "Rock Boppin' Baby," "Hoy Hoy," "Mercy," and their version of Wanda Jackson's "Let's Have a Party," all of which spoke directly to the teen generation of the fifties. Generally, Lorrie sang lead and Larry contributed the high harmony vocals and breath-taking guitar licks, and Maphis worked on most of their recording sessions.

Lorrie and teen heartthrob Ricky Nelson dated during the 1950s, after meeting on the Town Hall Party show. Lorrie appeared on The Adventures of Ozzie and Harriet as Ricky's girlfriend, and the couple sang the Collins Kids' version of "Just Because" on one episode. The romance, however, cooled and Lorrie eventually eloped in 1959 and married Stu Carnall, road manager for Johnny Cash, with whom the Collins Kids toured.

The Collins Kids popularity resulted in appearances on the Steve Allen Show, Ed Sullivan Show, Jackie Gleason Show, Dinah Shore Show, Art Linkletter's House Party, Merv Griffin Show, Ozark Jubilee, and Grand Ole Opry, and in the 1960 Universal Pictures movie, Music Around the World, where they were noted for their colorful costumes. The duo won the Best New Instrumental Group Award from the Country Music Disc Jockey's Poll, presented at one of their appearances on the Grand Ole Opry stage in the mid-1950s.

Dissolving their act in 1961 after the birth of Lorrie's first child, Larry continued to write music and is best known as co-composer of "Pecos Promenade" (1980), "Delta Dawn" (1972), and "You're the Reason God Made Oklahoma" (1981), the latter two nominated for Grammy awards. "You're the Reason God Made Oklahoma" was the ACM and Nashville Songwriters Association Song of the Year in 1982, and was nominated for the same award by the CMA. Artists who have recorded Larry's songs include Helen Reddy, Bette Midler, Waylon Jennings, Mac Davis, Three Dog Night, Willie Nelson, Lacy J. Dalton,

The Collins Kids perform at 2009 at the Oklahoma History Center in Oklahoma City.

Lou Rawls, Sonny James, Nancy Sinatra, Merle Haggard, and Ann Margaret. Larry also recorded his sister singing duets with longtime associates like Haggard and Nelson. The latter teamed with Lorrie on the unreleased sequel to Larry's hit, "Daughter of Delta Dawn." [insert image of Collins Kids 2 Larry plays guitar with caption "Larry Collins, 2008")

Although Lorrie retired, Larry continued to record as a solo artist for Columbia Records, primarily in Nashville. In later years, he earned his living as a golf pro. Lorrie became an at-home mother and raised thoroughbred horses. In 1993, Larry and Lorrie reunited for the Hemsby-on-Thames Rockabilly Festival in the U.K., drawing some 3,000 avid followers. Following the success of the Hemsby festival, they returned to the U.S., and played sold out dates at Bimbo's in San Francisco and the Palamino nightclub in Hollywood. The duo returned to the U.K. festival again in 1995 and 1998, both of which attracted sell-out crowds, and they remain intensely popular in Europe. Larry and Lorrie were inducted into the Rockabilly Hall of Fame in 1997 as the 43rd and 44th members.

Several of their recordings have been reissued in the United States and Europe, especially by Bear Family Records, a German company. The best are the 1991 Hop, Skip & Jump, a 2-CD box set with 59 tracks, including several songs the two co-wrote, such as "Mercy," "Whistle Bait," "Hot Rod," "I'm in My Teens," "Heart Beat," "My First Love," and "What About Tomorrow," and the 1998 Rockin'est, a 22-track collection containing all their favorites. They are also featured on two other Bear Family compilations—Ain't I'm A Dog: CBS Rockabilly and Whistle Bait: CBS Rockabilly, Vol. 2. On the former, Larry and Lorrie perform "Hop, Skip & Jump" and "Party." On the same recording, Larry and Joe Maphis present their lickety-split guitar licks on "Hurricane". Larry's jagged electric guitar work is also highlighted as the title track ("Whistle Bait") of the second compilation. Lorrie was featured as one of the four pioneers of rockabilly in the Welcome to the Club of Women of Rockabilly telecast in 2002 on PBS. In 2009, the Collins Kids returned to Oklahoma to participate in a special concert at the Oklahoma History Center to open the "Another Hot Oklahoma Night" exhibit about the history of rock music in the state.

Collins, Tommy

(b. September 28, 1930 – d. March 14, 2000)

One of the pioneers of the Bakersfield Sound in country music, composer of some twenty songs for Merle Haggard, including "The Roots of My Raising", "Hello Hag", and "Carolyn", and a 1999 inductee into the Nashville Songwriters Hall of Fame, Leonard Raymond Sipes was born the youngest of six childen to Leslie Raymond and Willie Etta Sipes on a farm near Bethany, Oklahoma, a northwestern suburb of Oklahoma City. During his childhood, Collins listened to Jimmie Rodgers and Ernest Tubb recordings, and learned to play the guitar and sing with encouragement from his mother.

Leonard attended Carson Elementary School, graduated from Putnam City High School in Oklahoma City in 1948, and spent two years at Central State (now University of Central Oklahoma) in Edmond (1949-51). During his stint in college, Collins entered talent contests, worked as a disc jockey, and appeared on Cousin Jay Davis' radio program on station KLPR in Oklahoma City. He won his first talent contest in 1951 on KLPR, which resulted in his own regular show on the station, accompanied by his first band called the Rhythm Okies, consisting of Collins on rhythm guitar and vocals, Billy Porter on lead guitar, Johnny Gilchrist on steel guitar, Russell O'Neill on fiddle, and R.M. Bradshaw on bass. While in Oklahoma City, the Morgan Brothers, a Fresno, California, based group, heard Tommy on radio, and assisted him in obtaining a recording contract. Four songs, three of which were composed by Collins ("Campus Boogie," "Smooth Sailin'," and "Fool's Gold"), were recorded in an Oklahoma City studio, and issued on the Morgan Brothers record label in 1951.

During the Korean War conflict, Tommy enlisted in the Marine Corps, but was discharged due to an injury he suffered during his college days. He, therefore, headed back to Oklahoma to resume his musical career. He met Wanda Jackson in Oklahoma City and they started dating, and when the Jackson family visited friends in Bakersfield, California, in 1952, Tommy accompanied them. Although the Jacksons returned to Oklahoma, Tommy decided to remain in Bakersfield.

Tommy soon began making contacts in Bakersfield and became friends and eventual roommates with a young recording artist and disc jockey named Terry Preston, whose given name was Ferlin Husky. Husky recorded some of Leonard's songs for his record company, Capitol, and helped him obtain a recording contract with Capitol in 1953. It was during one of these recording sessions that Husky named Leonard, "Tommy Collins," when one of the musicians ordered a Tom Collins cocktail, and thereafter became Leonard's stage name. Also in 1953, Tommy signed with Cliffie Stone's Central Songs publishing firm as a songwriter, and performed on Stone's Town Hall Party show.

Husky played lead guitar in the back-up band on Tommy's first recording session with Capitol on June 25, 1953, but was replaced with a then unknown Buck Owens, who continued with Tommy through 1957. Four of Tommy's songs were cut during that first session, "You Gotta Have a License," "Let Me Love You," "There Will Be No Other," and "I Love You More and More Each Day." The second session on September 8, 1953, included five songs, all written by Tommy, including "Boob-I-Lak," "I Always Get a Souvenir," "High on a Hill Top," and "You Better Not Do That." The latter became Tommy's first successful single, a 1954 release that remained on the country charts for seven weeks and peaked at #2. He made his first appearance on the Grand Ole Opry in 1954, one of the first West Coast artists to grace the stage of the "mother lode" of country music. He performed two of his self-penned songs, "You Gotta Have a License" and "You Better Not Do That," accompanied by the young Buck Owens. During the mid-1950s, Tommy recorded three Top 10 hits ("What'cha Gonna Do Now," "Untied," and "It Tickles") and two Top 15 cuts ("I Guess I'm Crazy" and "You Oughta See Pickles Now"), all of which possessed a light-hearted narrative, but significantly influenced the Bakersfield Sound. One of Tommy's songs "If You Ain't Lovin' (You Ain't Livin')," was a major hit for Faron Young in 1954, and was included on seven of Young's subsequent albums.

In 1956, Tommy's life changed as he underwent a religious conversion and began to devote his songwriting to sacred music. Some the songs he wrote were recorded as duets with his wife, Wanda Lucille Shahan. During the late 1950s and early 1960s, he attended Golden Gate Baptist Seminary, served as an ordained Southern Baptist minister for about five years, and spent two years at Sacramento State College taking courses. His contract with Capitol Records expired in 1960 because Tommy had not produced any hits.

In 1963, Tommy missed writing songs and recording country music, and decided to reenter the secular side of the music business. Capitol was willing to resign him to a contract, but he charted only one more song with the label, "I Can Do That," a duet with his wife Wanda.

Following his Marine duty in Vietnam in the early 1960s, Tommy was assisted in 1965 by Johnny Cash. The latter was instrumental in Tommy's switch to the Columbia label. He reentered the Top 10 in 1966 with "If You Can't Bite, Don't Growl." He also recorded several minor hits over the next few years, including "I Made the Prison Band." He soon sought out Merle Haggard after hearing his "Sing a Sad Song" on the radio. Tommy and Merle became instant friends and were soon fishing in the Kern River, when not on tour or in the recording studio. Haggard recorded Tommy's "Sam Hill" in 1964. In addition to Haggard, Tommy also toured as an opening act with old time friend Buck Owens during the late 1960s.

In 1971, Wanda filed for divorce because of Tommy's increasing dependency on alcohol and drugs, and he suffered from severe depression for about a year, although he continued writing songs, especially for Haggard. In 1972, Tommy's song, "Carolyn," was recorded by Haggard and became a #1 hit, although Haggard had reservations about recording it because he felt it was not country. The lyrics of the song were a coded message to his former wife, Wanda.

In 1976, Collins headed for Nashville and signed a recording contract with the Starday label, which released an album of Tommy's compositions that he had written for other artists entitled Tommy Collins Callin' (1976). Thereafter, he devoted the remainder of his career to songwriting after signing a contract with Sawgrass Music. After Tommy wrote "Hello Hag," Haggard responded with his hit single, "Leonard," a 1980 song that immortalized Tommy. In 1984, Tommy's "New Patches" was recorded by Mel Tillis and became a Top 10 hit.

Throughout the 1980s and up to the mid-1990s, Tommy continued to write songs, and in 1993, signed a contract with Ricky Skaggs Music. In 1988, he performed at the Wembley Country Music Festival in England based on reissues of several of his songs by the German label, Bear Family.

Honors over the years were showered upon Tommy, including BMI Awards in 1954 ("You Better Not Do That"), 1955 ("What'cha Gonna Do Now"), 1972 ("Carolyn"), and 1977 ("The Roots of My Raising"), one of Haggard's hits in 1976. In addition to the Opry, he also performed on the Ozark Jubilee and the Louisiana Hayride.

Tommy's songs have been recorded and rerecorded by a host of varied artists ranging from Faron Young ("If You Ain't Lovin' (You Ain't Livin'") to BR5-49 ("You're a Hum-Dinger"), including Bobby Bare and the Collins Kids ("What'cha You Gonna Do Now"),

Tommy Cash ("Roll Truck Roll"), Jimmy Dean ("Sam Hill"), Little Jimmy Dickens and Dion and the Belmonts ("You Better Not Do That"), George Jones ("New Patches"), Rose Maddox ("Let Me Love You" and "Down, Down, Down"), Johnny Duncan ("All of the Monkeys Ain't in the Zoo"), Johnny Paycheck ("Carolyn"), Jim Reeves ("Just Married"), Jean Shepard ("It Tickles," "Just Give Me Love," "I Learned It All From You," and "Did I Turn Down a Better Deal"), Skeets McDonald ("You Talk About Me, I'll Talk About You," "You're Too Late," and "But I Do"), Conway Twitty ("The Roots of My Raising"), The Farmer Boys ("Oh! How It Hurts"), Charley Pride ("After All This Time"), Osborne Brothers and Seldom Scene ("High on a Hilltop"), Hot Rize ("If You Ain't Lovin' (You Ain't Livin'"), Mark Chesnutt ("Goodbye Comes Hard For Me"), Rick Trevino ("Poor, Broke, Mixed Up Mess of a Heart"), and George Strait's No. 1 hit in 1988, "If You Ain't Lovin' (You Ain't Livin')," which is included on five of Strait's albums.

Perhaps the greatest tribute to Tommy's songwriting came in 1963 when Buck Owens recorded an entire album (twelve tracks) entitled Buck Owens Sings Tommy Collins, including "If You Ain't Lovin' (You Ain't Livin')," "But I Do," "It Tickles," "I Always Get a Souvenir," "My Last Chance With You," "Smooth Sailing," "You Gotta Have a License," "High on a Hilltop," "There'll Be No Other," "What'cha Gonna Do Now," "No Love Have I," and "Down, Down, Down." Collins is included in the 1996 Heroes of Country Music, Vol. 4: Legends of the West Coast (Rhino) with "You Better Not Do That."

Tommy's humorous and intelligent songwriting style, his impact on the development of the Bakersfield Sound, and his influence on other songwriters were his most significant contributions to the field of country music. His song, "The Roots of My Raising," reflects his roots in Oklahoma, and is included in the five-box CD set, Leonard, issued by Bear Family in 1992. Roger Miller, another Oklahoman who wrote many songs in the Tommy Collins style, once told Tommy: "I got my attitude for songwriting from you." Collins died at his home in Ashland, Tennessee, on March 14, 2000.

Color Me Badd

(Formed 1987, Oklahoma City, OK)

Combining tight vocal harmonies with origins in doo-wop and 1960s R & B, and the thumping bass lines and beats of 1980s hip hop, Color Me Badd emerged in the early 1990s during a revival of pop vocal groups such as Boyz II Men and En Vogue. The group's catchy, romantic ballads and made-for-video dance moves foretold the "boy band" trend of American popular music in the late 1990s exemplified by N'Sync and Backstreet Boys. Before disbanding, the group won two American Music Awards and two Soul Train awards, as well as earning a pair of Grammy nominations. All four members, Bryan Adams (b. November 16, 1969, Oklahoma City), Mark Calderon (b. September 27, 1970, Oklahoma City), Sam Watters (b. July 23, 1970, Camp Springs, MD), and Kevin "KT" Thornton (b. June 17,

1969, Amarillo, Texas), attended Northwest Classen High School in Oklahoma City. The four school friends harmonized in the hallways between classes, formed a quartet called Take One, and made their debut at a high school talent show singing a song from a Levi's 501 commercial.

When Kevin Thornton saw Jon Bon Jovi walk into a movie theater where Thornton worked, "KT" assembled the group and convinced Bon Jovi to listen to them for sixty seconds. The pop rocker liked what he heard and gave the group an opening slot in front of the band slated to open for Bon Jovi that night, Skid Row, and the group performed in front of 15,000 people in Oklahoma City. In 1987, Robert "Kool" Bell of Kool and the Gang heard the group and persuaded them to move to New York City and helped them find a manager. The group landed a deal with Giant Records in 1990, and their performance of "I Wanna Sex You Up" was featured on the New Jack City soundtrack. The song helped the soundtrack rack up double platinum sales, and then, to everyone's surprise, went Top 5. The complete album was not even finished when the group hit with "I Wanna Sex You Up," so the group worked overtime to produce the full-length collection. Still lacking a complete album, the group released a follow-up single, "I Adore Mi Amor," which became a crossover #1 hit on both the pop and R & B charts in 1991. The song illustrates the group's multi-cultural background when they sing in both English and Spanish which certainly contributed to its international success. This good fortune set the stage for the group's first album, C.M.B. (1991), which sold over three million copies. C.M.B. also included another number one hit, "All 4 Love," and two more Top 20 hits, "Thinkin' Back" and "Slow Motion" in 1992. Color Me Badd's next single, "Forever Love," was released on the Mo' Money film soundtrack and was their sixth consecutive single to reach the Top 20. In 1992, they finished second only to Boyz II Men as the top pop singles act of the year. At the height of their popularity, the group was recruited by Billy Joel and Jermaine Jackson as a backing vocal group, and appeared on such top-rated television programs as The Tonight Show, Saturday Night Live, Live with Regis and Cathy Lee, In Living Color, Beverly Hills 90210, and Oprah. After releasing a collection of remixes of their hit singles, Young, Gifted, and Badd – The Remixes (1992), Color Me Badd released their sophomore effort, Time and Chance (1993). The album sported two Top 20 pop singles, "Time and Chance," and "Choose," and sold more than 500,000 copies, but those numbers did not impress record company executives who had been spoiled by the success of the first album. The third Color Me Badd album, Now and Forever (1996), provided their final showing in the Top 20 with "The Earth, the Sun, and the Rain." Having completed their contractual obligations with Giant Records, Color Me Badd signed with Sony for their final album, Awakening (1998). The group reworked one song, "Remember When," from the album to benefit the victims of the 1995 Oklahoma City bombing of the Alfred P. Murrah Federal Building. The Oklahoma City Philharmonic Orchestra and the Oklahoma Public Schools Honor Choir appeared on the song, but the album did not sell well and the group decided to call it quits. In 2000, Giant Records released Best of Color Me Badd that included the group's biggest hits, as well as two previously unreleased tracks, "Got 2 Have U" and "Where the Lovers Go," both recorded during the Time and Chance sessions.

Color Me Badd lasted over ten years as a group, foretold the oncoming late 1990s pop movement with their tight harmonies, coordinated dance moves, and hip hop beats, and experienced success at the very top of the music industry. Subsequently, some of the members of the group continued in the music business and some left for good. Sam Watters has worked as a producer and arranger for Anastacia and 98 Degrees, written and produced songs for

Jessica Simpson, and provided background vocals for Paula Abdul, and Patti Austin. Since 2000, Watters has also produced several greatest hits packages, such as UK More Wicked Hits (2001), and Funky Divas Vol. 2 (2002), a compilation of dance-pop songs featuring female vocalists. In 2002, Watters co-wrote and sang background vocals on Celine Dion's "I Surrender," from the album A New Day Has Gone, a song made even more famous when covered by American Idol's 2002 winner, Kelly Clarkson. Bryan Abrams released a 2001 independent solo album, Welcome to Me, and Kevin Thornton released Conversion in 2008, a solo hip hop/rap album with gospel and soul music flavors. In 2010, Mark Calderon resided in Cincinnati, Ohio, selling insurance. In 2010, Color Me Badd reunited as a trio without Watters, and appeared on a game show, Rock and a Hard Place, hosted by Meatloaf, to raise funds for a charity group in Los Angeles. Color Me Badd was inducted into the The Oklahoma Music Hall of Fame in 2000.

Colourmusic

(formed 2003, Stillwater, OK)

Embracing a 1960s "happy pop" sound with the release of their CD, Red, in 2005, and evolving to their most recent 2010 recordings, self-described as "proto-industrial," founding Colourmusic members Ryan Hendrix and Nick Turner met in 1999 as students at Oklahoma State University. Hendrix (b. Oklahoma City, September 1, 1977) grew up in Piedmont, Oklahoma, before moving to Stillwater to attend OSU, where he met Turner, from Danby, England, who was spending a semester as an OSU international student. During Turner's first time in Stillwater, the two became friends and began experimenting with music, but nothing formal beyond making fake soundtracks to movies they both admired. Turner went back to England after his semester in Stillwater, graduating from Keele University in Staffordshire with a degree in English literature and American studies in 2000. Hendrix continued his studies at OSU, earning a bachelor's degree in broadcast journalism, and a master's in English in 2006. Within that period, Turner returned to Stillwater and the two formed Colourmusic around 2003, taking their name from the concept of sound being organized around the color spectrum (the color spectrum is made up of seven colors, and the major Western scale, DO-RE-MI-FA-SO-LA-TI- and back to DO an octave higher, also has seven notes).

Colourmusic, 2006 in Stillwater

Self-described "absurdists," early Colourmusic shows were spectacles with all kinds of stage theatrics, costumed participants, and themes, such as a 2006 show in Stillwater where they "gave birth" to their new CD on stage. Subsequently they progressed to wearing all white outfits in front of a multi-colored backdrop with streamers and confetti showering the stage, and various "assistants" dancing or interacting with the audience and band. Adding Nick Ley and Colin Fleishacher (Fleishacker?), both from Ponca City, Colourmusic shows became "events", not eagerly missed by Oklahoma alternative music fans interested in the next progressive pop group to bubble up out of the state, a concept not lost on Flaming Lips long-time manager, Scott Booker, who signed on as Colourmusic's manager, a move that helped their first two EPs, the Red EP (2005) and the Yellow EP (2006), garner college radio and MTV airplay. Booker's connections to the Flaming Lips also helped the group land a spot in a segment with the Lips' Wayne Coyne on NBC's Tonight Show in 2007. In 2008, the group's first two EPS were combined into 2008's Orange (Great Society) album, both a merging of the first two EP's colors, and serendipitously representing the primary school color of OSU.

Listening to the first album (or the first two EPs), one hears a variety of 1960s and early 1970s pop influences, everything from the Mamas and Papas ("Motherfather"), maybe even the Banana Splits ("The Gospel Song"), harmonies akin to The Byrds ("Winter Song" or "Circles"), and other vocal and instrumental elements hinting they could be The Cowsills of their era. While

Colourmusic, 2006 in Stillwater

the band has not had what one would necessarily call a hit outside of college radio attention for the first releases, the band's energetic sounds on "Yes!", with its big drum kit pounding, raggedy guitar sound, repetitive keyboard riffs, and happy-to-the-point-of-smile-hurt-choruses, exemplify their early period aesthetic. The band has also embraced new media methods of promoting their music, to wit several videos featuring the band's music can be found on youtube.com. Of particular distinction is the popular video for "Yes!" (15,000 views as of July, 2010), which was shot in various locations around Oklahoma, but mostly in many familiar Stillwater spots.

While Colourmusic's early material embraces a jovial-to-the-point-of-sugary texture, according to Hendrix in a July, 2010, interview, their new material has taken on darker hues. Influenced by Iggy Pop's first solo LP, 1977's The Idiot, and David Bowie's mid-nineties black-techno work with Trent Reznor, Hendrix indicates the band was interested in exploring some ugliness on their latest set of recordings, expected out in 2011 as an album with the word "pink" in the title. The group also had plans for fall, 2010 recordings for another album to be ready in 2011 so they could stay on the road as a working band without having to stop to do another album. To keep from falling into a rut artistically, Hendrix describing their self-monitoring technique: "If what we are working on the at the time fits into any kind of box, then we think that is wrong for us, and try to move on to make it something new."
www.colourmsic.net
www.myspace.com/colourmusic

Colton, Graham

An Oklahoma City-born singer/songwriter best known nationally for the 2008 single "Best Days", Graham Colton has parlayed his sensitive lyrics and emotive singing voice into national television appearances, tours and opening slots for Counting Crows, John Mayer, Dave Matthews Band, Kelly Clarkson, John Mellencamp, and Sheryl Crow, as well as significant Internet success where his songs and albums have sold well as downloads from his own and other online music sales points, such as iTunes. Colton's father, who still plays in the 60s and 70s cover band, Wise Guys, he started in college, encouraged Graham who spent a childhood listening to his father's group, as well as the music from the 60s and 70s played around the house. He began writing songs while attending Heritage Hall High School, where he also quarterbacked a state championship team throwing passes to now-professional football player, Wes Welker. He's influenced heavily by Oklahoma alternative groups Wakeland and the Nixons; later, he would write songs with Nixons lead singer Zac Malloy.

As for Oklahoma's influence on his music, he told interviewers Larry O'Dell and Jeff Moore, who interviewed him for the 2009 exhibit on rock history at the Oklahoma History Center, "Oklahoma is a lot of things. It's somewhat rootsy and organic, but then there's the Americana influence, and I like to think that I pull from a lot of that stuff. I also think because I had the ultimate Friday Night Lights experience here in Oklahoma [referring to his football experience], that also finds its way into my music as well." Indeed, Graham had a dual lifestyle in high school, playing football on Friday nights and then playing music on Saturday nights at a Mexican restaurant in Oklahoma City. During his senior year he gave some friends some discs of his songs, and by the time he reached Southern Methodist University in the fall, he was received e-mails from people he didn't know wanting to know where they could get his music or see him perform live. "I had fans and I didn't even know I was a real musician yet," he told the Oklahoma History Center researchers. Loaned a fifteen-passenger van by his grandfather, Jackie Cooper, a well-known car salesman in Oklahoma City, Colton and his band hit the road, touring Texas and Oklahoma his freshman year, leaving school on Thursday returning late on Sunday.

Graham Colton

After a couple of years touring around Texas and Oklahoma, his CD made its way to Adam Duritz of Counting Crows who engaged Graham as an opening act on their 2002 tour, which immediately broadened Colton's fan base, and opened up a wider world of opportunities. With Duritz's mentorship, as well as a friendship with Better than Ezra's Kevin Griffin, Colton began negotiating the hazards of starting a music industry career. In 2004, Colton and his band signed a deal with Universal Records, resulting in their first album, Drive (2005). With a pop rock sound that doesn't distinguish itself as much as it fits into contemporary popular music, the album notched attention on Billboard's various regional, Internet, and "artists to watch" charts, the songs registered with a variety of audiences, leading to the band's opening for the previously mentioned artists. Of the album's twelve songs, "All the World Tonight", "Morning Light", and "Cut" all match the ballad-y palate biggest hit so far, "Best Days", from his 2007 solo follow-up album, Here Right Now, which blasted on to iTunes single (#4) and album (11) charts in October, prompting iTunes editors to tag Colton as Top New Pop Artist for that year. The song received considerable attention, selected for use by Fox's American Idol, and earned Colton 2008 performances on NBC's Tonight Show, CBS' Late Show with David Letterman, NBC's Today Show, ABC's Live with Regis and Kelly, and The Ellen DeGeneres Show. In 2009, he released three EPs independently through his website, and three more in 2010. Continuing to climb the national pop culture ladder, his song "Twenty Something" was featured on the ABC drama, Boston Medical. He has colloborated with

Flaming Lips front-man, Wayne Coyne, and in 2012 released his full-length album, *All Because of You* under the name, Sooner the Sunset.

www.grahamcolton.com

Comanche Nation

By the early 1700s, the Comanche tribe cast a vast sphere of influence over a huge swath of the American southwest. Known as the Comancheriá to the Spanish colonizers and explorers, Comanche country included parts of what is now the western half of Oklahoma, southeastern Kansas, much of north central and northwest Texas, and the eastern half of New Mexico. Their moniker, Lords of the Plains, derived from their horsemanship, battlefield acumen, and vast trade networking influence throughout their empire through the 1860s. Subsequently, the tribe was consigned to a reservation in pre-statehood southwestern Oklahoma (then still Indian Territory) by the Medicine Lodge Treaty of 1867.

Following the standard late 19th century pattern of government enrollment of American Indian tribal people, individual Comanche lands were allotted to tribal members, with the "surplus" being opened to boomer land grabs in the final run of Oklahoma Territory on formerly Indian Land in 1906. In the span of only forty years, the Comanche transitioned from a feared and respected nomadic Plains tribe at war with foreign invaders of their country, to landed tenants of farms and ranches.[1] After enduring a full century of radical changes to their lifestyle, and grappling with a new social structure courtesy of the evolving United States, the Comanche have evolved with their surroundings and grown to a population of nearly 15,000 tribal members, about half of which live in the Lawton, Oklahoma area, the location of their tribal headquarters.[2] Like many tribes who survived the reservation era, boarding school movement, and missionary influences, the Comanche not only have a large body of traditional music for a variety of ceremonial purposes, but have also made significant contributions to the modern development of the Plains flute, created many original Christian hymns in the Comanche language, and added scores of singers to the modern powwow world. Traditional music still plays an important role in modern Comanche veteran's organizations, many of which have songs specifically to represent them, such as the Comanche Little Ponies, Comanche Indian Veterans Association, or the Comanche Code Talkers. Historically, among traditional songs recorded throughout the early 20th century, determined listeners can find a Comanche Raid Song, Comanche Round Dance Song, and Comanche 49 Song (recorded in 1901), Comanche Dance Songs (recorded from 1927 to 1928), and a Comanche War Song (circa late 1920s).[3] The tribe has also encouraged many newer children's songs that are Comanche translations of traditional English songs for kids, the purpose for which is to teach the Comanche language with familiar and simple melodies. Comanche children learn the "Comanche Alphabet Song", "Old MacDonald", "Happy Birthday", and "Our Numbers". In fact, the Comanche Language and Preservation Project includes songs as part of its mission statement. Historically, however, the tribe has many, many songs related to its particular world view, and its singers made some of the very first recordings in Oklahoma music history.

In 1893 and '94, celebrated ethnologist James Mooney made the earliest known recording of Comanche songs, a Ghost Dance Song, and songs related to the peyotism that evolved into the modern Native American Church via Comanche absorption of the religion. The Red Road or Peyote Way had been part of Comanche life for at least 200 years prior to Mooney's arrival. After the Comanche received the horse in the last 1600s, numerous sources indicate the tribe began ranging into south Texas where the peyote religion began for tribes such as the Lipan Apache and Tonkawa east of the Rio Grande, due to the presence there of the sacred medicine, Peyote, used as a sacrament, healing tool, and visionary aid in the church's ceremonies. Further archaeological evidence indicates peyote has been used by humans in the area for as many as 8,000 years B.C.E. However, Comanche leader Quanah Parker is largely credited for bringing the religion north to Oklahoma and into the 20th century by incorporating elements of Christianity into the ceremony and belief system, which essentially saved it from being completely outlawed by state and federal governments.[4] A massive body of Comanche Peyote Songs has come forward to the present day via more than a century of singers who have recognized the importance of preserving the songs. As a result of their alliances in the mid-19th century with the **Kiowa** due to shared interests in protecting their lands, and then by proximity when the Comanche were assigned to the same southwestern Oklahoma reservation area in 1867 with the Kiowa and Apache, many recordings of Comanche Peyote Songs are compiled with Kiowa Peyote Songs. The first major commercial release of Peyote Songs was issued by Smithsonian Folkways as *The Kiowa Peyote Meeting* (Folkways FE 4601) in 1973. While the recordings were made in 1964 and '65, the release is an ultimate package of explanations about the Kiowa Native American Church meeting, which is very close to the Comanche version, and the collection includes one Comanche Peyote Song. A highly sought collectible on vinyl, a compact disc containing all the recordings is available to diligent Internet searchers. For a full set of Comanche Native American Church songs, seek out *Comanche Peyote Songs Vol. 1 & Vol. 2* on Indian House Records (IH 2401 and IH 2402). Recorded in 1969 by one of the primary commercial recorders and producers of American Indian music in the second half of the 20th century, Tony Isaacs, the disc features notes by Isaacs on the recordings, and translations and comments on the songs by singer Roy Wockmetooah. Indian House also released *Kiowa-Comanche Peyote Songs* (SC 507 and SC 591) which were part of the legendary Soundchief imprint, a catalogue of records mostly recorded, sequenced, and produced by Rev. Linn D. Pauahty, a Kiowa Methodist minister from Carnegie, OK. Indian House also released Kiowa *Spiritual Peyote Songs Vol.1, 2,* and *3,* which contain many

Charles Chibitty, the last living Comanche Code Talker in 2003, sings the Comanche Code Talker Song for a class at Rogers State University in Claremore, OK.

By Hugh Foley / 163

Comanche songs, as do the releases *Faith, Hope, and Charity, Vol. 1* and 2. The other primary North American commercial outlet for American Indian music is Canyon Records in Phoenix, Arizona. Canyon released forty-two Kiowa and Comanche Peyote Songs sung by Horace Daukei and accompanied by Lee Chester, drummer, on the album *Peyote Early Morning Chants* (CR-6158).

Mostly because ethnomusicologists long dismissed the Christian music of American Indians as just a Native language version of missionary-taught songs, Christian hymns of all tribes are often difficult to track down prior to the 1950s. While others recordings may exist, the first Comanche hymn of note was led by Lee Motah and recorded in 1954 by Willard Rhodes for the Library of Congress albums titled *Music of the American Indian*. The hymn led by Motah is the only Christian hymn out of twenty-two songs included on the album featuring several tribes in Oklahoma (AAFS L39), to include the Comanche, as well as Cheyenne, Kiowa, Caddo, Wichita, and Pawnee songs. In 2004, Smithsonian Folkways finally released a collection of Christian songs in Native languages, *Beautiful Beyond* (SFW 40480), including two Comanche Hymns recorded by members of Petarsey Church. Also in 2004, Millard Clark (Comanche/Cheyenne), another important producer of Native music from Oklahoma from the 1980s to the present, released a 1985 recording of Comanche Church Hymns on his independent Indian Sound label. Most recently, Comanche/Seneca singer, **Marla Nauni,** has released two independent albums of Comanche Hymns which have received wide recognition and kept her touring the U.S. to perform the songs and many different educational functions, institutions, museums, and gatherings. Another new singer of Comanche hymns is Quannah Kennedy who has received more than 21,000 plays of four songs she has posted on her playlist at www.myspace.com/mizzquanahkennedy.

Another important musical style on which the Comanche have had an important influence is the Plains flute, the haunting and peaceful sound of which has become extremely popular among non-Indians as tool for relaxation and meditation tool via recordings that use tremendous amounts of echo to generation peaceful overtones. While originally used as a courting instrument among the Comanche, the Plains flute was revived and re-popularized by "Doc" Tate **Nevaquaya**, whose re-introduction of the Plains flute inspired hugely popular non-Comanche performers such as R. Carlos Nakai, Kevin Locke, and **Andrew Vasquez**. Comanche flutists who continue the tradition of Plains flute include **Cornel Pewewardy** and Kevin Connywerdy. Interested listeners can pursue Nevaquaya's accessible 2004 release on Smithsonian Folkways, *Doc Tate Nevaquaya: Comanche Flute*, or track down Tom Mauchahty-Ware's 1978 Indian House release, *Flute Songs of the Kiowa and Comanche* (IH 2512), recorded by Tony Isaacs.

Comanche music is just another example of the tremendous depth of artistic and musical expression in the American Indian world. From the very first recordings in the 1890s that depict the serious transition the Comanche people were navigating in the shift from a nomadic, warrior lifestyle, Comanche music chronicles that experience. From the War Dance Songs that would not fulfill their purpose until Comanche people began serving in the U.S. armed forces,[5] and Ghost Dance Songs that were performed as a last gasp against the encroaching tide of Americans and prayer to maintain their ancient way of life, like most American Indian music, Comanche songs had a purpose beyond entertainment, literally to help the people survive. Whether hearing the syncretic songs of the Native American Church that combine Native musical traditions and prayer concepts with Christianity, or Christian hymns borne out of a belief that the old days were gone and a new era must be embraced, the music is serious and important. Not to say one can't find humor in the music, however, as Comanche Hand Game Songs carry whimsical titles such as "A Man Standing on a Hill", "Flirt Song", and "Flapping Sleeves Song". Additionally, all the splendor and pageantry of a contemporary powwow where many Comanche songs are rendered can be seen each year at Sultan Park in Walters, Oklahoma at the annual Comanche Homecoming Powwow in mid-July, as it has been since 1952, an era in which many tribal celebrations began to re-surface after a period of dormancy due to governmental restrictions.[6] While some ethnomusicologists decry the powwow as a Pan-Indian activity that has moved from its original tribally specific intent, Comanche Nation Tribal Chairman, Mike Burgess, said in a 2009 speech opening an exhibit about powwows at the Comanche Nation Museum, "The powwow, as it is called, is a misnomer to our people. It embodies our culture, our history, our knowledge of who we are, and where we've come from. Putting those together gives us designs of where we are going."

www.comanchenation.com

Endnotes
1. The most recent re-telling of the Comanche story from their days as rulers of the high plains known as the Comancheria, see Sam C. Gwynne, *Empire of the SummerMoon, Quanah Parker, and the Rise and Fall of the Comanches, the Most Powerful Indian Tribe in American History*, (New York: Scribner, 2010).
2. See the Comanche Nation's website at www.comanchenation.com for more extensive background on the tribe, its history, cultural components, and contemporary status and concerns.
3. All of the recordings referenced from 1894 through the late 1920s are archived at the Indiana University, Bloomington, Archives of Traditional Music. The citations, source recording information, and track listings are available to the public through the library's search engine at www.iucat.iu.edu.
4. For an extensive history of the Native American Church, see Omer C. Stewart, *Peyote Religion: A History* (Norman: OU Press, 1993).
5. While many American Indians served with distinction throughout the 20th century in the United States Armed Forces, few tribes are as stories as the Comanche for the Code Talkers who used the Comanche language in World War II to send coded messages behind enemy lines in Europe, saving thousands of lives. While the Navajo are well known for their work in the Pacific Theater in World War II, not as many people know about the Comanche's work in helping defeat Hitler.
6. For further understanding of the governmental oppression of American Indian music from the reservation era through the Federal Indian Reorganization Act of 1934, see John W. Troutman, *Indian Blues: American Indians and the Politics of Music, 1879-1934*. Norman: University of Oklahoma Press (2009).

Convertino, John

Having lived in Stillwater and Tulsa, where he graduated from Tulsa Edison High School in the 1980s, John Convertino is one of contemporary alternative rock's most enduring, versatile, and widely-respected drummers. While in Oklahoma he played with family members (his older brother was a guitar teacher in Stillwater) in cover bands Stand Clear and Circus.1 Subsequently, he made his way to Los Angeles where he played drums with Howe Gelb, a long-time folk/poet/troubadour, in the group Giant Sand, which is where Convertino met future music partner, guitarist JoeyBurns. In 1994, Giant Sand moved their base of operations to Arizona, with Convertino and Burns taking on various rhythm section gigs, to include forming Friends of Dean Martinez, a deserty-space music Western lounge band, but left after one album, 1995's The Shadow of Your Smile (Sub Pop). Subsequently, the duo worked as a rhythm section for various artists, such as Victoria Williams, Barbara Manning, and Richard Buckner, then wrangled together Calexico, an evolving group of guitarristas, musicos, mariachis, horn players, and percussionists, with Burns and Convertino at the core.

After their first recordings as a duo under the name Spoke for an independent German label in 1996, they changed to Calexico, focusing on the traditional Anglo and Latino music of the American Southwest. Since then, the group has expanded and contracted like a button accordion, recording six albums through 2008. They have released several tour-only CDs, often live albums or collaborations, been on several soundtrack compilations, and recorded with alternative country artist, Neko Case, on three of her critically acclaimed albums. Their collaboration with independent folk band, Iron & Wine, In the Reins, gave Calexico its only appearance thus far on the US Billboard charts, but several of their albums have charted in the UK. Their website indicated they were booked solidly through 2010, with a European tour in September of that year.
www.casadecalexico.com

John Convertino, New York City, 1988

Note
1. Convertino's Tulsa background was mentioned in an article by Thomas Conner, "Musical Crossing Guards" Tulsa World, 9 November, 2002, section D, p. 5.

Cook, David

(b. December 20, 1982)

Born in Houston, Texas, and raised in Blue Springs, Missouri, instant pop star David Cook moved to Tulsa in 2006 to pursue a career in music, after graduating the University of Central Missouri with a graphic design degree. Prior to being crowned the seventh American Idol winner because of his gripping rock star voice, David Cook played guitar in the Midwest Kings, a regional college town party band adventuring out in a 500-mile radius of Tulsa. Along with playing local singer/songwriter/cover gigs wherever he could, Cook recorded an independent album, Analog Heart, and tended bar at Capellas Lounge in downtown Tulsa at 230 E. 1st Street. In 2007, Cook accompanied his brother to an American Idol audition in Nebraska, only trying out after his brother didn't make it, and urged on by their mother who was present. Cook sang Bon

David Cook

Jovi's "Livin' on a Prayer" (that fine cover bar tune), taking advantage of Idol's new rules allowing self-accompaniment, got his ticket punched to Hollywood, and "poof" he was gone out of Tulsa's musical milieu.

Nonetheless, David Cook's story is very interesting for several reasons. For starters, Cook felt Tulsa was a place a person could come to get started in the music business, and he was right. By getting a regular paying musician's gig with the Midwest Kings, developing his show business acumen within the (mostly) music friendly nightclubs and bars of Tulsa, and recording his first album which he would give away at his bartending job and try to sell at gigs, David Cook lived a show business life in Tulsa, Oklahoma, and that experience helped him prepare for the rigors in American Idol. What is Idol but determining who the best karaoke or cover band singer in a given year, anyway? Speaking of which, Cook's rise to pop culture stardom happened very quickly, and the timeline is also interesting for how fast it can all happen for someone with the right talent, discipline, and motivation at the right moment.

On May 4, Cook was one of three finalists on Idol; May 18, he was one of the final two; May 21, Cook wins, breaking American Idol voting records by 23 million; May 25, Cook breaks several Billboard chart records with eleven songs on the Hot 100 (the most since the Beatles in 1964!) and 14 songs on the Hot Digital Songs chart; May 31 Cook travels the familiar round of pop star appearances on the Today Show, Ellen, Live with Regis and Kelly, soon thereafter signing his deal with 19 Recordings/RCA Records. Instantly, "The Time of My Life" goes #1 on iTunes and #3 on the Hot 100; In June, Cook starts recording his forthcoming album; July 1 he starts the American Idol tour; September 14 Cook plays BOK Center to roars of kudos and pride; September 22 he models Skechers in national marketing campaign print advertisements (People, Star, US Weekly, etc.); November 18 releases his self-titled solo album, many of the songs of which have already charted anyway (and three of which are co-written by Oklahoman Zac Malloy, known for his work with the Nixons); December 21 appears on the cover of TV World with Goofy promoting the Walt Disney World Christmas Day Parade; January, 2009 his album is certified Platinum certifying one million physical units sold by the Recording Industry Association for America; February, 2009 launches a national tour with two of his former Midwest King band mates along for the ride, Neal Tiemann on lead guitar, and Andy Skib on rhythm guitar/keyboards; from then on, David Cook is no longer a resident of Tulsa. And that's how fast it can happen.

www.davidcookofficial.com

Cooley, Spade

(b. December 17, 1910 - d. November 23, 1969)

Often referred to as the "King of Western Swing" and the first to popularize the phrase, "Western swing," fiddler-bandleader Clyde Donnell Cooley was born in a storm cellar near Pack Saddle Creek near Grand, Oklahoma in western Oklahoma near the Texas line. Born to parents, Emma and John, Donnell was raised in an impoverished home. As Cooley once said, "I was born poor and raised poor."

Spade's first exposure to music was through his father and grandfather who enjoyed playing the fiddle, and, according to several sources, was playing fiddle for dances at eight years old. After moves to Oregon and California, young Donnell was given violin lessons by one of this father's friends. Classically trained, Spade later played violin and cello in his school orchestra. Not caring much for farm labor, Spade began playing fiddle at local dances in the Modesto, California area c. 1930. He then jumped a freight train "with nothing but my fiddle and three cents in my pocket" to Los Angeles, where he met Roy Rogers, who needed a stand-in for his motion pictures at Republic studios and because several of his friends thought he resembled Rogers. This work allowed him to make a reasonable living during the day so he could play his fiddle at night in various clubs around town, including jobs with Stuart Hamblen and Jimmy Wakely. Donnell's poker playing skills soon earned him the nickname ("Spade") that was to stick with him the remainder of his life.

Because of his reputation as an excellent fiddler, Spade was hired by promoter Foreman Phillips in 1942 to play with bands at the Venice Pier Ballroom in Venice, California. Management suggested he form his own swing band that included such notables as guitarist Noel Boggs, another native Oklahoman; guitarist Smokey Rogers; and crooner Tex Williams. His popularity soared and Cooley's band was soon packing them in by the hundreds at the Pier, Riverside Rancho, and Santa Monica Ballroom, and rivaling Bob Wills' outfit that had just moved to southern California. With his boundless energy and aggressive fiddling, Spade soon landed a recording contract with Okeh Records (a subsidiary of Columbia) in 1943. The next year, Spade and his band recorded "Shame, Shame on You," which hit #1 on the country charts and was adopted as his theme song. Two years later, another Okeh recording, "Detour," was also a major hit in 1946. By this time, Spade's band had reached headliner status at the prestigious Santa Monica Ballroom, and he and the band were invited to appear in their film debut, The Singing Sheriff, a 1944 Bob Crosby movie. They later performed in several films, including Chatterbox, The Singing Bandit, Outlaws of the Rockies, and Texas Panhandle. In 1946, Spade and his band left Okeh and signed with RCA in 1947, recording such favorites as "Spanish Fandango," "Hillbilly Fever," and "Wagon Wheels."

In 1947 Spade was poised to enter the new medium—television. He headed his own show on station KTLA, the first commercially licensed television station in Los Angeles. Called the "Hoffman Hayride" (named after the sponsor who was a television manufacturer), it quickly attracted an audience and became the top-rated program in the area in the late 1940s, however, ratings declined and the show was cancelled in the early 1950s, even though Spade attempted several innovations, such as replacing his old band with an all-female ensemble. The stress of remaining a top performer began to tell on Spade as he was sidelined in the early 1950s with a series of heart attacks.

Still popular in southern California, Spade recovered from his heart problems, and toured the region during the mid-and-late 1950s, performing at various venues. Plagued by alcohol, drugs, and marital problems, Spade was faced with separation from his second wife, Ella Mae. He wavered between divorce and reconciliation that continued for several years, until 1961 when he was living in the Mojave area where he has purchased some land for an amusement park. On April 3, he lost control of his senses, if he had any, and killed his wife, forcing his fourteen-year-old daughter, Melody, to watch the horrible even unfold. After a sensational trial at the Kern County Courthouse in Bakersfield during which his daughter testified, Spade was convicted of murder and sentenced to life in prison. During the trial he suffered another heart attack and afterward was sent to a medical detention center at Vacaville rather than a high-security prison. While confined, Spade taught inmates the rudiments of fiddle playing, and performed for them. Due for review by the California Parole Board in 1970, Spade was granted leave from Vacaville to participate in a police benefit concert in Oakland in 1969. After a well-received performance of three songs before a crowd of some 3,000, he went backstage and suffered a fatal heart attack at the age of fifty-nine.

Several recent CD releases of Cooley's material include Spadella: The Essential Spade Cooley (1994-Sony), a collection of Spade's singles, including all his hits in its twenty-nine tracks; Heroes of Country Music, Vol. 4: Legends of the West Coast (Rhino-1996), presenting Spade on "Shame on You"; Spade Cooley Big Band, 1950-1952 (1999), a thirty-three track album from Harlequin Records; Shame on You, a Bloodshot Records release in 1999, including twenty-five tracks of previous unreleased radio transcriptions; Spade Cooley, 1941-1947 (2000), released by the Country Routes label and featuring Oklahoman Noel Boggs; A Western Swing Dance Date with Spade & Tex (Spade Cooley and Tex Williams), twenty-seven tracks released in 2000 by Jasmine Music; and in 2005, Fidoodlin' (Collector's Choice), a collection of some of his final recordings in 1959, for Raynote Records.

Copas, Lloyd "Cowboy"

(July 15, 1913 – March 5, 1963)

With fifteen charted country hits, the highest being 1960's #1, "Alabam", Lloyd Cowboy Copas looked, sang, and played the part of an Oklahoma cowboy music star, claiming all his adult life he grew up on a ranch near Muskogee, Oklahoma1. As an example of Copas' claims, his 1961 album, Inspirational Songs (Starday), features liner notes written by Starday Records president, Don Pierce, who says, "On the personal side, Cowboy Copas, is a tall, slender man from the state of Oklahoma, who has resided for many years in Nashville with his family." While Copas did live in Nashville, he was not from Oklahoma. Similar to other country, Western, or rockabilly stars who claimed to be from the state but were not (Al Clauser, Eddie Cletro, and Eddie Cochran), Copas believed his native Ohio background was not sufficient credibility for the career he had chosen as cowboy singer. So, he lived out the myth he created for himself, until he met his unfortunate demise in a plane crash on March 5, 1963, the same plane crash that killed country stars Hawkshaw Hawkins, and Nashville Sound chanteuse extraordinaire, Patsy Cline.

Lloyd "Cowboy" Copas

Note
1. While the entry for Cowboy Copas on www.wikipdia.org tells his story solidly and accurately enough, for more details on Copas' Ohio background, see rockabilly researcher Randy McNutt,

We Wanna Boogie: An Illustrated History of the American Rockabilly Movement (Hamilton, OH: HHP Books, 1988).

Crain, Samantha

(b. August 15, 1986)

Lionized by music critics for her first two albums in 2009 and 2010, adored by ardent fans who have spun her songs a quarter of a million times on her myspace.com site, and kept her on the road solidly as much as she wants, Shawnee native Samantha Crain balances a winsome and melancholy lyrical sensibility in some songs, with one that verges on happy-go-lucky-life's-not-so-bad-after-all pieces. Born in Shawnee and raised in the surrounding rural area where she attended Dale High School, some of Crain's songs sound like they were whispered to her by a ghost who lives in an abandoned clapboard house out in the country; others are deeply sensitive to life's peculiarities and inevitable tragedies, romantic and otherwise; still others are hopeful, encouraging the listener to enjoy the blessings of another sunrise.

Samantha Crain

Her first gig at age 17 in a Shawnee coffeehouse preceded her attending Oklahoma Baptist University in Shawnee and majoring in English lit. While in school, she applied for and was accepted into a songwriting retreat at Martha's Vineyard in Massachusetts, where she first started writing and getting into music seriously. Leaving home proved to be inspirational for her, as she mined the experience for songs that later appeared on her first full-length album, Songs in the Night (Ramseur). Covertly, Crain refers to her father, Rickey Dale Crain, a world champion power lifter, in "Devils in Boston", saying he was "not strong enough to keep me from runnin' off to Boston." Even though she was able to get out of Oklahoma, the state in no way could get out of her. In several interviews she has credited Oklahoma folk king, Woody Guthrie, and Oklahoma freak kings, the Flaming Lips, as her dichotomous musical inspirations from the state. Songs in the Night nods to her home state with "Scissor Tales" [scissor tails are the OK state bird, ed.], mentions "Tornado Alley", and named her publishing company Green Corn Rebellion Music, a reference to the 1917 uprising in rural Oklahoma protesting the Federal government's disproportionate military drafting of Seminoles, Muscogee (Creeks), African-Americans, and European-American farmers in the build up to World War I.

Crain's first recording, The Confiscation: A Musical Novella, is a self-released EP of five songs derived from some short stories she'd written, and organized in chapters on the disc, exploring the dynamics of loss in romantic, family, or otherwise close relationships. Aside from listening yourself to the music, the album's thematic material may be best hinted at by chapter titles, "Beloved, We Have Expired", "In Smithereens, the Search for Affinity", and "The Last Stanchion Goes Belly Up". Given its immediate notice in new-folk circles, and Crain's constant touring to support it and herself after returning home from Martha's Vineyard, North Carolina's Ramseur Records offered to re-release the CD in 2008, and enlisted her for a full-length album for the following year. Produced by Danny Kadar (Avett Brothers, My Morning Jacket), and recorded in Asheville, North Carolina, Songs in the Night features an assembled band working under the name the Midnight Shivers. The musicians embellish her readily identifiable voice with twang-y space guitars, banjos, distant percussion, organs, and trombone. After seeing Crain and the Shivers at a Brooklyn, NY, show in March, 2009, about a month before the first album came out, New York Times writer Jon Caramanica reveled in her performance (3/31/2009), a harbinger of the positive impression she would make made on other music critics who crowed about her in Performing Songwriter (March/April, 2009, and again in May's issue), Rolling Stone (April 30, 2009), and Paste (May, 2009). The tidal wave of attention also coincided with a collaboration between Crain and noted film director Sterlin Harjo (Barking Water), who produced a short film intended to be an introduction to her austere hometown life in Shawnee, showing where she worked at a Wall's Discount Store sorting clothes, a local movie theater, and a coffee trailer. Available on youtube.com, the video features her music and Harjo's recognizable cinematic style of highlighting everyday Oklahoma as an iconic American landscape, and manipulation of video colors digitally for dramatic artistic effect. In the video she explains why she likes Oklahoma so much, that it "still feels wild, like it's an old Western movie," and is not at all like the cities she spends so much time in on tour. Harjo, who is Seminole and Muscogee (Creek), also features Crain's music prominently, especially "Scissor Tales", in his critically lauded film, *Barking Water* (2009).

In 2010, Ramseur Records released Crains' second album, You (Understood), which abandoned the Shivers for some closer-to-home folks, including Eric Nauni from the Oklahoma City band, Student Film, on drums/percussion, Stillwater singer Sherree Chamberlain on some background vocals ("We Are the Same"), and recording in Wichita, Kansas, with old friend Joey Lemon who recorded and produced her first EP. According to the Ramseur Records press release for the album, within its songs Crain depicts her experiences with sixteen different people who affected her during the writing and recording of material, which follows her familiar loping melodic and vocal template, although she stretches her voice out a little more than on the first disc, perhaps because of the familiar surroundings and friends; however, You (Understood) glistens with a different musical palate than the first album. Gone is the top-of-the-mountain remote music ambience of Songs in the Night, replaced by alternating point on and stutter-step rhythms courtesy of Nauni, more focus on Crain's rolling rhythm acoustic or electric guitar, and occasionally winding up to full scale rock music. The music is not as crowded as it sounds, with spaces empty as the stretch between Oklahoma City and Wichita on I-35, notably captured in "Wichitalright". Crain teamed up with Harjo again to create the video for "Santa Fe" from the album, filmed artfully in New Mexico and available on youtube.com She began touring the US and Canada in May, 2010. Before the summer was even over, she had a glowing review in the Washington Post (6/18/2010), heard the lead-off track to You (Understood), "Lions", featured on HBO's Hung, and received notice her Songs in the Night album had been nominated in five categories by the Native American Music Awards (NAMMYS) due to her citizenship status in the Choctaw Nation of Oklahoma. She released her third studio album, *Kid Face* in 2012 to solid reviews.

Crain has said repeatedly she believes she has been able to develop her own sound because she has evolved artistically outside of mainstream music centers; that Oklahoma's semi-remoteness, mythical qualities, and cost of living, all provide for intense artistic exploration without the financial pressures of living in an urban center.

www.samanthacrain.com

www.myspace.com/samanthacrain

Crook, Tommy

(b. February 16, 1944)

One musician who has foregone touring the country to remain in Tulsa, where "in-the-know" music enthusiasts recognize him as one of the premier guitarists in the United States, if not the world, is Tommy Crook. While not widely recognized as part of the Tulsa Sound per se, Crook typifies its multiple elements in his musical inspiration, and played in bands with some of its primary movers and shakers in the early 1960s. However, with his uncanny, encyclopedic chord voicings, and a unique finger picking style where he sometimes places bass strings on the bottom two positions (B and E) on his guitar, Crook's sound is inspirational in its ability to re-envision any familiar tune he plays, a hallmark itself of a jazz great.

A native Oklahoman, Tommy Crook started playing guitar at age four when his father, Buck Crook, gave him his first guitar, and taught him to play rhythm and lead. With Chet Atkins and Les Paul as his major influences, by age eleven Crook became a featured solo act on Porter Wagoner's touring show, and was soon a regular on Hank Thompson's live TV show from Oklahoma City, and Leon McAuliffe's TV show in Tulsa. While Tommy attended Tulsa's Central High School in the early 1960s, he played in bands with David Gates, Jimmy Karstein, Carl Radle, Leon Russell, J.J. Cale, Gene Crose, and Jimmy Markham, a blues vocalist and harmonica player who has recorded with .38 Special and A.C. Reed. After graduating Central in 1962, Crook tried pharmacy school for a while at Southwestern Oklahoma State University, but tired of the academic environment and returned to Tulsa where he worked as guitar salesman with Eldon Shamblin at The Guitar House, and later a traveling factory rep for Ampeg Amplifiers. Giving up the retail business after a few years, Tommy turned to playing full time, touring Southeast Asia with the USO, and then taking jobs around Tulsa before landing a 12 ½ year gig at the Tulsa Airport Sheraton where he accompanied himself with a drum machine, leading to his first album, Mr. Guitar and Mr. Drums in 1968.

Tommy Crook, 2002

Tommy Crook has played with a cadre of great musicians (Chet Atkins, Merle Haggard, Leon Russell, Pat Boone, Lou Rawls, Chuck Berry, Charlie Daniels, and Jerry Lee Lewis). It was Chet Atkins who provided the most regularly repeated praise of Crook when Chet answered Johnny Carson's question of whether or not "anyone, anywhere played guitar as well or better" than Atkins. Atkins said, "Yes, Johnny, Tommy Crook in Tulsa, Oklahoma."

In 1989, Tommy Crook recorded a self-titled album with David Teegarden that wound up in the hands of Asleep at the Wheel's Ray Benson who has said, "Tommy Crook is the most unique and talented guitar player I have seen in my life." Benson passed the album on to Willie Nelson, who in turn gave the tape to Guitar Magazine, and the internationally recognized publication featured Tommy in its March, 1989 issue. Since then, he has continued playing a steady series of gigs at restaurants and clubs in Tulsa, as he does not like to travel and has no desire to tour. In 2002, he recorded a CD, 110 Degrees in the Shade – Guitar Duets with Anthony Weller, and is available primarily from him or via the Internet. Also in 2002, he performed in honor of Charlie Christian at the 2002 Oklahoma Music Hall of Fame induction ceremony and concert. In 2003, Tommy was featured in a Vestapol DVD, World of Fingerstyle Jazz Guitar, in which he is shown playing "Melody of Birdland", "All The Things You Are", and "It Had To Be You". In 2007, Crook himself was inducted into the Oklahoma Music Hall of Fame for his incredible musical talent, recognized by all who have heard or seen him play. A quiet, humble, and unassuming man, as of 2013, Crook played played every Friday night at Lanna Thai Restaurant on Memorial Boulevard in Tulsa.

Crooked X
(Formed circa 2007 in Coweta)

With self-proclaimed influences of Shinedown, Black Label Society, and Pantera, and equally obvious references to Metallica and Iron Maiden, Coweta's Crooked X is Oklahoma's most recent musical volley into the heavy metal world, with the only real precedents being Enid's Oliver Mangum, and Tulsa's Agony Scene, both disbanded. The earliest members of Crooked X to play together were Forrest French (lead vocals/rhythm guitar), who began playing guitar at age 4, and Boomer Simpson (drums), who joined up after both faltering on the 5th grade football team. They heard about Jesse Cooper (lead guitar/backing vocals), who has been playing since he was three, and then added Josh McDowell (bass) after meeting him at the Guitar Center.

The band's career jolted in early 2007 when they won second place on the CBS Early Show "Living Room… Live" talent competition as a result of Boomer's father, Bill Simpson, sending the show's producers a video of the group playing one of their original songs, "Death of Me". The young musicians had several songs by that point, having started when they were all mostly eleven, beginning with their first ever song, "Nightmare", which does appear on their debut CD. Their age

Crooked X, the first version (from left): Cooper, French, McDowell, and Simpson.

By Hugh Foley / 173

Live in Stockholm, 2008

Roll Dream" also just peeking into the Hot Mainstream Rock Track charts for one week. Their early song, "Nightmare", was placed in the *Rock Band* video game, and they were the subject of a television documentary telling the story of them going from a Coweta garage to playing for thousands of people in Europe opening for Kiss. The album showed the promise and the limitations of a group of fourteen-year-olds. The band does rock out, with chugging metal riffs and zippy solos, tasteful double kick drum work by Simpson, and how a metal singer is supposed to sound vocally. They juxtapose melodic choruses with rumbling metal riffs ("Time is Now"), have a power ballad ("Fade"), imitate 70s stage metal ("Rock N Roll Dream"), and even merge metal with grunge, sort of Nirvanica ("Lost Control"). Had "Lost Control" been the first single, it would have defined the band completely differently, instead of essentially giving them an old-fashioned, 70s metal rocker with "Rock N Roll Dream", they could have come out with a sound that merged two more recent hard rock developments in Metallica and Nirvana. While Crooked X's music does occasionally *get there*, the lyrics of the songs are what one would expect from junior high students, simple rhymes, mock horror and gothic lyrics, and the rambunctiousness of being that age. At some point, the novelty of their age wore off, or never stuck, on adult rock radio programmers or older adult metal fans. The group did tour in 2009, as part of Disturbed's Music as a Weapon Tour, but according to the wikipedia.org profile for the group, in June, 2010, the band's vocalist and co-founder, French, "parted ways with Crooked X, as did bassist Josh McDowell. The band, which has not performed since September of 2009, has been auditioning new members." That left rhythm guitarist, Cooper, and drummer, Simpson, to decide what to do next, after graduating high school, that is. When they do, they'll have more great rock music memories than any guitar video game player will ever know.

Crooked X at Rocklahoma, 2011

www.crookedx.com

www.myspace.com/crookedx

Cross Canadian Ragweed
(formed in Yukon, 1994)

Emerging from the often over-generalized **Red Dirt Music** scene of Stillwater, home of Oklahoma State University and regularly referred to as West Nashville or North Austin by alternative and contemporary country insiders, Cross Canadian Ragweed (CCR) has sold more than a million copies combined of their eleven roots-rocking poetic albums, been concert fan favorites at venues throughout the U.S. since 1995, and finally took a family-focused hiatus for an undetermined length of time in the spring of 2010. With a self-proclaimed slogan, "Smells like country, tastes like rock and roll", CCR is comprised of front man and lead guitarist Cody Canada (b. Pampa, TX, May 25, 1976), drummer Randy Ragsdale (b. Enid, June 27, 1977), rhythm guitarist Grady Cross (b. St. Louis, MO, August 4, 1975), and bassist Jeremy Plato (b. Oklahoma City, February 13, 1976). The group's name derives from combining the names of band members who have played together since they were in Yukon's middle and high schools. The latter is where Canada and Cross met drummer Ragsdale, two years younger than the rest of the band, but also the son of Johnny C. Ragsdale (b. 1951- d. 1997) who had played guitar with **Bob Wills** and **Reba McEntire.** The elder Ragsdale elevated the group's professionalism through discipline and practice, and its musicianship by passing on his lead guitar skills to Canada. Before leaving Yukon for Stillwater, the group played any and everywhere they could get a show.

After Cross, Canada, and Ragsdale graduated Yukon High School in 1993, '94, and '96 respectively, and Plato graduated from Calumet in 1994, each moved to Stillwater ostensibly to attend Oklahoma State University, but more importantly to regroup. By the middle 1990s, Stillwater's music scene teemed with young bands like the **Great Divide**, Medicine Show, **Jason Boland**, and the **Red Dirt Rangers**, among others, who played local Stillwater outlets such as the Tumbleweed, Willie's Saloon, where Garth Brooks started playing on open mic nights, and the Wormy Dog Saloon, a college bar with saddles for barstools. Before long, the band was filling Stillwater, Tulsa, and Norman bars and clubs for four years before getting their first Texas gigs in Amarillo and Lubbock, followed by shows in Fort Worth, Dallas, and Austin. CCR's successful shows began developing a fan base that resulted in tens of thousands of independent albums sold, no mean feat for a young band with little to no commercial airplay.

Released on the band's independent label, Underground Sounds, the first Cross Canadian Ragweed album, *Carney* (1998), features a who's who of red dirt musicians as players and co-songwriters.

Cross Canadian Ragweed, circa 1999

By Hugh Foley

Recorded and mastered by Jeffrey Parker at his Cimarron Sound Lab in Tahlequah, *Carney* is both the perfect introduction to Cross Canadian Ragweed and a further example of red dirt music's hybrid combination of country, folk, blues, and rock. The album is full of acoustic strumming, electric leads, twangy steel accents, and introspective lyrics written or co-written by Cody Canada and a full of cadre of red dirt singer/songwriters such as **Jason Boland**, Mike McClure of **The Great Divide**, **Bob Childers**, and Tom Skinner. Additionally, keyboardist Corey Mauser (Big Head Todd and the Monster) and drummer Jimmy Karstein (**Leon Russell**, Eric Clapton, **J.J. Cale**, et. al.) flesh out the expert musicians prominent throughout the disc. CCR's second disc, *Live and Loud at the Wormy Dog Saloon* (Underground Sounds, 1999), was recorded in the club where the band enjoyed their first big crowds in Stillwater, and a window into CCR's multiple influences and live show. While not a sonic masterpiece, the album is an excellent illustration of red dirt music's ethos of country, rock, and folk by including Jerry Reed's "Amos Moses," a Bob Childers and Tom Skinner collaboration, "Headed South," that appeared on *Carney*, Neil Young's "Hey, Hey, My, My," Mike McClure's "Down at the Harbor," and Bob Dylan's "Rainy Day Women." *Live and Loud at the Wormy Dog* also is a witness to Canada's developing songwriting skills and guitar abilities ("Bang My Head" and "Workin' on OK"), some everyman political leanings ("The President Song"), and the very popular Gene Collier song, "Boys from Oklahoma," that takes a particularly strong swipe at Stillwater's rivals to the south in Norman.

With a couple of years to play a plethora of shows, practice, and write more songs, CCR released *Highway 377*, an album that really brings out the rock side of the band with power chords ("Back Around" and "Time to Move On"), choogling Grateful Dead riffs ("42 Miles"), and plenty of gritty lead guitar work. The album also represents a spiritual rejuvenation of sorts for Canada as a result of a near disastrous wreck Canada and two friends experienced driving down Highway 377 while working in the oil fields near Wolf, Oklahoma. Driving a company truck depicted on the album's cover (post-crash), the old '82 Chevy suddenly veered off the road and fell sixty feet down a drainage ditch, but Canada and his two friends walked away with only minor injuries. While Jesus appears regularly in the band's liner notes, *Highway 377* marks the first appearance of the chosen one as the subject of a song. The collection is full of outcast characters ("Look at Me"), broken dreamers ("Back Around"), Vietnam vets ("Long Way Home"), and, or course, Jesus ("Highway 377"). Early hints of commercial potential also resulted from the disc when Dodge picked up "Long Way Home" for a nationwide Dodge truck commercial, and subsequently used "42 Miles" for another nationwide spot in 2003.

Given the relatively lo-fi but fun filled *Live and Loud at the Wormy Dog*, fans eagerly embraced 2002's *Live at Billy Bob's Texas* (Smith Music). Recorded at the famous honky tonk in Fort Worth that boasts over 15 million visitors and a monthly electric bill of more than $15,000.00, *Live at Billy Bob's Texas* finds the band slinging through their best known songs to that point, a new one co-written by Canada and Mike McClure ("Hey, Hey"), and a few covers ("Crazy Eddie's Last Hurrah," and "Mexican Sky"), along with a toned down "Boys from Oklahoma" in front of a very vocal and obviously appreciative crowd. With an accelerating fan base and selling thousands of records without the assistance of a major, or even minor, record label, the group soon found themselves at the forefront of the rowdy country music coming out of Texas (by way of Oklahoma), and major labels started to notice the band's popularity growing like, ahem, weeds.

Having heard about the band from people as diverse as Radney Foster, Dallas Cowboys' special teams coach Joe Avezzano, Texas club owners and other bands' managers,

Oklahoma native and Universal-South executive **Tim Dubois**, one of Nashville's most important music industry types, and his business partner Tony Brown began courting the group with the old "We don't want to change a thing about you" line that often predates haircuts, fashion advice, and hottie-laden videos that have little or nothing to do with a band's original vision of themselves. Universal-South was true to its word, however, and the band delivered the self-titled album known as *Purple* or *The Purple Album* (2002). Dedicated to Randy Ragsdale's younger sister, Mandi, who died at age nine on the way home from a CCR show in 2001 and whose favorite color was purple, the album is a mature work of songwriting and musicianship. As opposed to the band's first album on which they received a mountain of help from red dirt elders, *Purple* features only two songs co-written by old friend and co-producer Mike McClure, who also adds some guitars and piano to the album. Nodding more toward rock than country, the album is a coming of age collection for many reasons, as Cody Canada's songwriting voice was obviously getting stronger and more reflective with age. His usual downtrodden, marginalized and lovelorn characters are all present in "Brooklyn Kid," "Don't Need You," "Walls of Huntsville," "Broken," and "Suicide Blues." However, a deeper, more metaphysical side is emerged from Canada's pen with "On a Cloud," an homage to the ten men associated with OSU's basketball program who died in a plane crash on the way back from a game with the University of Colorado January 27, 2001, and "Carry You Home," an extremely personal take on the relevance of Jesus in the speaker of the song's life. The song that gained the group national attention, "17," is a watershed moment in the band's career, earning a #1 spot on The Texas Music Chart for seven straight weeks in January of 2003 (and further illustrating Oklahoma's significance in Texas music). CMT's regular rotation of "17," a video shot completely in Stillwater and around Payne County, lifted the band to national familiarity. Co-written by Canada and Jason Boland, the song's classic line, "You're always 17 in your hometown," rings with experience of small town life and how one never really gets away from the image they cut as a high school senior in their hometown. Either the town wonders what ever happened to you since then because you've never gone back, or knows everything that's happened because you never left, and that's how small towns are. Bolstered by "17", and the album's second single, "Constantly", both of which were medium-sized hits on the *Billboard* Country Charts, their debut major label album made it to #70 on the Country Album chart.

With their musical template of soft strumming, introspective pieces juxtaposed with country rock party songs in place, the band enjoyed a torrid career track on critically lauded and commercially successful album releases: *Soul Gravy* (Universal, 2004)(#5 country album), *Garage* (Universal South, 2005) (#6 country album), *Back to Tulsa – Live and Loud at Cain's Ballroom* (Universal South, 2006)(#27 country album), *Mission California* (Universal South, 2007) (#6 country album), and *Happiness and All Other Things* (Universal South, 2009) (#10 country album). While the band's albums did well across the board commercially, the band's singles did not fare as strongly at country radio, with only "Fightin' For", from *Garage*, cracking the Country Top 40, a phenomenon that either says more about contemporary country radio being out of touch with the album buying public, or, perhaps the band's rock-tinged sound did not resonate fully with pop country radio programmers. CCR was too country for rock programmers, ultimately placing the band in the alternative country, or Americana music radio format where there's a high musical quality and aesthetic toward singer/songwriters, but not as many large markets and radio coverage as mainstream country radio.

Aside from getting any and all of their discs to fully appreciate the group's career in total, an interested listener who likes to a see band live should track down the limited edition copy of the *Garage*, containing a live concert DVD recorded in College Station, Texas. From there, one derives the insight as to why the band's fans came out in droves to see and hear the group that can sock a fan in the solar plexus with their music, or drop heartfelt and meaningful lyrics that never get too sentimental via Canada's tough Oklahoma "Talking Blues" vocal delivery. The band frequently opened for other established acts that enjoyed the atmosphere set by crowd-stirring CCR shows, to include Willie Nelson, Kid Rock, ZZ Top, George Thorogood, Johnny Lang, Lynyrd Skynyrd, Keith Urban, Dierks Bentley, and Miranda Lambert. Ragweed headlined absolutely packed concert venues from coast to coast through 2010, selling out 41 venues in 2005, and their 2004 Red Dirt Round Up and Family Jam in Oklahoma City brought 60,000 people to the Zoo Amphitheater to hear a number of red dirt music luminaries, notably the first appearance of the **Red Dirt Rangers** after their terrifying 2004 helicopter crash on the Cimarron River. CCR has also played several benefit concerts for one of many sincere and positive causes over the years, such as Mandi's Ministries, a seat belt safety awareness organization name after Randy Ragsdale's earlier mentioned sister. In the summer of 2005, the band broke an attendance record at Lone Star Park, a horse racing track, in Grand Prairie, TX, drawing 23,656 fans to see their show, causing a giant traffic jam on I-35 for miles in each direction toward the cities of Dallas and Fort Worth. The band's own bus got held up by traffic and had to be extracted by the police and given an escort to the show, while fans drank 3,000 gallons of beer, draining the vendors just into the start of the Ragweed set. Previous records had been set by Willie Nelson, the Beach Boys and Texas favorites Pat Green and Charlie Robison. If that didn't quell any and all questions existed about the band's popularity, their next CD, *Garage* (Universal South) did.

After being released October 4, CCR's third studio album for Universal South debuted at #6 on *Billboard*'s Country Album Chart with almost 30,000 copies sold immediately. Among the songs on the album, their highest charting single, "Fightin' For", a song co-written with Mike McClure, about which Canada said in a 2005 press release for the album, "is just one of those marriage songs – about when you call home late and your wife's mad at you because she knows you've been partying and she can't be out partying with you." Also, deeply affected by the murder of the former Pantera guitarist, Darrell "Dimebag" Abbot, Canada wrote "Dimebag" as a tribute to the widely admired fallen guitarist who was killed on stage by an angry "fan" in 2004 playing while Abbot with his post-Pantera group, Damageplan. The song was picked up by some rock radio stations and impressed Abbot's brother and Pantera drummer, Vinnie Paul, enough to sit in with the band on the song at a CD release party in Fort Worth. With an extra DVD that comes with the disc, *Garage* also gives fans access to several videos and a great collage of early period photos of the band to mark their ten-year anniversary. Produced along with Mike McClure, the album brought forth an avalanche of acclaim in articles by regional publications (*Daily Oklahoman, Fort Worth Star-Telegram, Tulsa World, Dallas Morning News*) as well as national pubs like the *Washington Post, Billboard, Country Music Today*, and *Pollstar*. In 2007, the band released their third live disc, *Back to Tulsa: Live and Loud at Cain's Ballroom* (Universal South), a CD and DVD culled from two shows in 2005 at the legendary Cain's Ballroom in Tulsa. Hitting #27 on the *Billboard* Country Album Chart, the discs are another excellent window into the musical reasons for their live success with most of their fan favorites included as a result of online fan voting, only leaving off ones they had recorded live before. Their 2007 album, *Mission California*, told the same story again, success on the album charts (#6), but no real hit single, and 2009's *Happiness and All the Other Things* (Universal South) maintained that tradition with their loyal fan based pushing it up to #10 on the Country Album Chart.

In May, 2010, the band came to a stopping point. Drummer Randy Ragsdale told the boys he needed to be at home with his family, especially to help with his autistic son. Without much discussion, the group decided to take a hiatus. Canada explained in a press release, "We've always said from the start, we're Ragweed as the four of us, or not Ragweed at all." Grady Cross added, "These guys, they're my brothers. I love playing with them. I'm sure we'll be back on the road soon." And Jeremy Plato closed out the statement by saying, "We've been at this for a long time. We've all had to spend time away from home missing birthdays, holidays... It'll be good for us to have a breather."

While Cross and Ragsdale did decide to take some time off, Cody Canada is driven by the artist's need to stay out there and keep doing the things that make them who they are. To that end, Canada has taken to the studio and road as a solo artist with CCR bassist, Jeremy Plato, hopping on for the ride. Billed as Cody Canada and the Departed, a quick Oklahoma tribute album, *This is Indian Land*, featuring songs by many Oklahoma music artists, hit the streets in 2011, followed by their CD of originals, *Adventus*, in 2012. Meanwhile, Grady Cross opened Grady's 66 Pub in Yukon where the live music always sounds like you hope it will from a joint run by a veteran of more than a thousand performances of his own.

www.crosscanadianragweed.com; www.gradys.66.com

Crow, Alvin
(b. September 29, 1950)

Before being one of the first artists to make Austin a center for live music in the early 1970s, playing a significant role in the "cosmic cowboy" movement, and helping to revive Western swing at the same time, fiddler, guitarist, and bandleader Alvin Crow was born in Oklahoma City. At the age of four, Alvin learned to play the fiddle on his grandfather's lap, and started playing in country bands when he was seven. He took classical violin lessons for fifteen years before advancing to a seat as the youngest violinist with the Oklahoma City Symphony. His interest in the fiddle was stimulated by growing up in a family of musicians who lived in the Sweetwater community near the Oklahoma-Texas border. His absorption of fiddle music from his family exposed him to a variety of fiddle tunes, including waltzes, polkas, and breakdowns. Crow continued his love for other genres of music, including Cajun, rock-and-roll, and country, which expanded his music repertoire before leaving Oklahoma.

In 1968 Alvin moved to Amarillo, Texas, where for the next three years, he experimented with combinations of various styles of music, such as blues, jazz, and western swing, all that al-

Alvin Crow

low improvisation on the fiddle. He organized the Pleasant Valley Boys in 1969, and moved in 1971 to Austin, where the band became an integral part of the "progressive country" movement during the 1970s. Since basing his operations in Austin, Alvin has fronted other Austin-based bands, such as The Broken Spoke Cowboys, The Neon Angels, and the Route 66 Playboys.

Alvin's touring circuit includes all of Texas and Oklahoma, as well as other neighboring states. His music has taken him to other American venues in New York City, where he played Carnegie Hall, and Washington, D.C. and European countries such as England, France, and Germany. He also performed for President Jimmy Carter at the White House during the late 1970s.

Crow has recorded several albums, primarily with Polydor Records and the independent label, Broken Spoke. The first Polydor recording, *High Riding*, was produced in 1977, and received an award from *Country Music* magazine as the Best Album by a New Artist. The magazine also named Alvin as Best New Male Vocalist in 1978. Additional albums include *Cowboy*, *Honky Tonk Trail*, *Alvin Crow Sings Pure Country*, *Alvin Crow with the Pleasant Valley Boys*, and *Texas Classics*. He has played session fiddle with a number of artists and bands, including Ed Burleson, Doug Sahm, Sir Douglas Quintet, and the **Red Dirt Rangers**.

Alvin Crow

Alvin's more popular singles include "Yes She Do, No She Don't", "Crazy Little Mama at My Front Door", and "Nyquil Blues", the last of which was included on a compilation album of *Texas Music, Vol. 2: Western Swing and Honky Tonk*, released in 1994. Alvin and his band were selected for another compilation of artists who appeared at the Kerrville Folk Festival (*Early Years 1972-1981*) where he performed "Take Me Back to Tulsa" and "Milk Cow Blues", released in 1998. An active participant in artist residency programs, Crow has worked with the Texas Commission on the Arts and the Texas Folklife Resources program in which he performs and teaches K-12 students throughout the state, and continues making regular appearances at various venues around Austin where he is held in the highest regard my musicians and Texas music fans alike. Past, present, and future fans can hear live tracks and keep up with Alvin via his myspace.com site.

www.myspace.com/alvincrow

Cruz, Edgar
(b. March, 1962)

Absolutely one of Oklahoma's most talented and versatile guitarists, Edgar Cruz plays Classical, pop, rock, jazz, and a variety of world music styles, especially traditional Latin or Mexican music, with equal grace, facility, and technical complexity. Born and raised in Oklahoma City into an extremely musical family, Cruz first picked up a guitar at age fourteen when he and his brother were excited by rock music while growing up surrounded by the music of his father, Manuel Cruz, an Oklahoma City mariachi and Latin music legend. At the same time Edgar and his brother were playing classic rock covers and name their band, Relayer, after an album by Yes, Manuel was playing at Mexican restaurants and for private mariachi jobs. Once Edgar picked up the guitar and bass, Cruz's father introduced him to the *guitarron*, or "big guitar" of mariachi music, and Edgar began accompanying his father at gigs while still in high school. After high school, he received an associate's degree in music from Oklahoma City Community College, began doing solo acoustic gigs around Oklahoma City, notably a long-running gig at Crystal's Restaurant in OKC, and then graduated from Oklahoma City University with bachelor of music in guitar, after studying with Michael Millard at OCU.

After several years of performing solo shows, Cruz released three independent cassettes in 1989 duplicated on his own cassette recorder that sold well, *Best of Edgar Cruz Vol. 1 and 2,* and a very popular Christmas collection, *Throw another Tape on the Fire.* In 1990, he released his first CD, *Classical Demands*, followed up by his popular Christmas tape on CD, and was off to the races performing and producing new CDs ever since. As of fall, 2010, Edgar has produced 17 CDs and two DVDs which have sold more than 15,000 copies combined worldwide. As of 2010, Cruz performs over 200 concerts per year on average, and has played throughout the United States, Europe, and South America. He has been a headliner at The Chet Atkins Festival in Nashville, TN since 1995 and is a regular performer at many Oklahoma festivals in Oklahoma, to include Festival of the Arts, Paseo Festival, Sunfest, and Global Oklahoma. Those who have witnessed Cruz's performance are instantly impressed with precision, speed and complexity with which his fingers strike the strings of his guitar to create a symphony of sound unusual to just one instrument. As part of his signature style, while playing a tune in his own arrangement, he might start with the song's basic chords and rhythm, then evolve to the point where he is keeping the rhythm and chord progression going while also picking out the melody of the song, and/or the lyrical phrasing. He truly is as much fun to watch as he is to hear. Cruz offers a widely diverse live repertoire of classical, jazz, rock, Latin, pop, rock, and music for young audiences, such as "The Greatest Hits of the Guitar", "Malagueña", "Classical Gas", "Bohemian Rhapsody", "In the Mood", "Dueling Banjos", "Hotel California", "A Classical Medley", and "Wipeout", as well as many classical or Latin favorites depending on the venue and audience.

Edgar has been named Oklahoma's Top Performing Artist and/or Acoustic Guitarist for over ten years by the *Oklahoma Gazette*. He has received numerous civic acknowledgments for his contributions to various charitable events. A true working musician who has created his own niche, Cruz not only performs for concerts and festivals, but according to his website, he is open for weddings, receptions, banquets, anniversaries, birthdays, schools events, churches, conventions, fiestas, memorials, and restaurants, as well as guitar master classes, lessons, lectures on the history of guitar styles or techniques, or any special occa-

Edgar Cruz

sion; and most any gig by Edgar Cruz is a special occasion by any musical standard.
www.edgarcruz.com

Cunningham, Agnes
(b. February 19, 1909 – d. June 27, 2004)

A founding member of Oklahoma's Red Dust Players, singer and accordionist with The Almanac Singers, and co-founder and editor of *Broadside: The Topical Folk Song Magazine*, Agnes "Sis" Cunningham was born on a farm near Watonga, Oklahoma, about thirty miles northeast of Weatherford, where her future husband lived and where she would attend college. Agnes' parents had homesteaded on the former Cheyenne-Arapaho Indian Reservation and began farming on the banks of the North Canadian River, however, the soil was sandy, and they moved to another farm with better land closer to Watonga. The middle of five children (two older brothers and a younger brother and sister), Agnes helped her mother raise chickens, tend the vegetable garden, and clean house. When Agnes was six, her father, William "Chick" Wallace Cunningham, taught her to play chords on the piano, and she

The Almanac Singers, circa 1941: Woody Guthrie (far left); Pete Seeger (tallest at center); Agnes Cunningham with accordion (far right).

would stop to practice at her grandmother's house after school in Watonga. Her father, who had made the 1893 Cherokee Strip land run, was an old-time fiddler and claimed to know more than 500 fiddle tunes. Politically, he was a Debs Socialist, not surprising given their hard scrabble farm existence. One of her brothers, William, a 1925 journalism graduate of the University of Oklahoma, became state director of the Oklahoma's Writers Project in 1935.

A voracious reader, while in high school Agnes joined the debate team and started a school newspaper, *The Shotgun*, which gave her some journalistic experience that served her well later as an editor. Since her mother, Ada (Boyce) Cunningham was a schoolteacher, when Agnes graduated high school she enrolled at Weatherford Teachers' College (later Southwestern Oklahoma State University) in 1927 to become a teacher. She completed two years, and began teaching music at age twenty. In the summer of 1931 Agnes attended the Commonwealth College near Mena, Arkansas, an unaccredited labor college with socialist tendencies. Her brother Bill was director of the college and his wife was on the faculty. It was here that Agnes began writing songs, such as "Sundown" and "There are Strange Things Happening in This Land", which her father helped compose. She also began collecting songs in this period, such as "Song of the Evicted Tenant", written by an eleven-year-old named Icie Jewell Lawrence. Following Commonwealth, Agnes became an organizer for the Southern Tenant Farmers' Union, and served as a delegate to its convention in Muskogee, Oklahoma, in 1937. She left Oklahoma for the next two years, and taught music and directed the singing of labor songs at the Southern Labor School for Women near Asheville, North Carolina.

In 1939 Cunningham returned to her native state to help organize the Red Dust Players, a musical and acting troupe formed to present topical skits and songs for sharecroppers and union workers around Oklahoma. She continued to write songs during her two years with the Red Dust Players, such as "The Oil Derrick Out by West Tulsa", reflecting the oil workers strike at the Mid-Continent Refinery of the DX Oil Company near Tulsa. It was during her two-year tenure with the Red Dust Players that she met **Woody Guthrie** and Pete Seeger when they came through Oklahoma City to visit Woody's wife and children, a trip that also manifested Guthrie's "Union Maid" after he attended a union meeting in Oklahoma City.

Sis met Gordon Friesen of Weatherford in March, 1941, through their association with the Communist Party, and married on July 23 of that year. Fearing repercussions from their Communist activities, Sis and Gordon moved to New York City the following November. Pete Seeger invited them to move into the Almanac House at 130 West Tenth Street. A year earlier, Seeger, Lee Hays, and Millard Lampell had formed the Almanac Singers, the first urban folk singing group in America, and invited Sis to join.

The Almanac Singers consisted of several musicians, including at various times, Woody Guthrie, Bess Lomax, Peter Hawes, Cisco Houston, Arthur Stern, Josh White, and Burl Ives. Sis appeared on the Almanac Singers 1942 album *Dear Mr. President* (Keynote) with her contribution, "Belt Line Girls", a song she had written to highlight women's work in the war effort. In the song, she sings; "…When a thousand hard working girls step in and take a hand, out roll the tanks and the planes and guns, and there's freedom in the land." Several of the Almanac Singers either enlisted or were drafted into the military services as the U.S. entered World War II.

In late 1942 Sis and Gordon moved to Detroit to assist Bess Lomax and others to organize another branch of the Almanac Singers, but the attempt failed. Subsequently, Sis went to work in a war plant and Gordon became a reporter for the *Detroit Times*. In 1944 they returned to New York, where daughters Agnes and Jane were born in 1945 and 1949, respectively. By this time Gordon was blacklisted and could find no steady employment. Both were investigated by the U.S. House Un-American Activites Committee. During that difficult period, he and Sis took turns taking care of their daughters and worked part time jobs. Also during this time, Sis wrote two of her most remembered songs, "Mister Congressman", and "Fayette County". In "Mr. Congressman", she wrote lyrics that would fit to the children's tune, "Little Brown Jug": "Congressman, Mr. Congressman, Sittin' up there in Washington, If you don't listen to our song, You ain't a-gonna be in Congress long."

In 1961 Pete Seeger returned from a tour of England where he had witnessed a renewed interest in writing songs dealing with the political and social issues of the day. He visited with West Coast folksinger Malvina Reynolds about starting a publication that would print new folks songs concerned with current topics. When Reynolds decided to concentrate on her own singing and writing career, Seeger turned to Sis and Gordon, and in 1962 the first mimeographed issue of *Broadside* was printed. The first edition contained six songs, including "Talking John Birch Society", by a yet unknown Bob Dylan. It was the first Dylan song to appear in print.

Broadside continued to showcase the work of Dylan. "Blowin' in the Wind", for example, appeared in the magazine nearly a year before Peter, Paul, and Mary recorded it. Other young folk songwriters followed, including Phil Ochs, Janis Ian, **Tom Paxton**, Buffy Ste. Marie, and Peter LaFarge. *Broadside* published not only the songs of the new generation of songwriters, but also those of the older writers, such as Pete Seeger and Malvina Reynolds. With financial assistance from Pete and Toshi Seeger, *Broadside* continued until 1988, sometimes publishing irregularly, monthly, bimonthly, or quarterly, but for twenty-six years it provided an opportunity for folk music enthusiasts to learn the songs of both new and old songwriters. Throughout those years, it was Sis who transcribed the music in order to print the music notations into the magazine, and Sis who took part in hootenannies to help support the magazine. Finally, she recorded a full album of her songs, *Sundown,* released by Folkways Records in 1976 as *Broadside Ballads, Volume 9* that has been re-issued by Smithsonian Folkways Recordings as *Agnes "Sis" Cunningham Sings Her Own Songs and A Few Old Favorites* (Smithsonian Folkways, 2004). *The Original Talking Union with the Almanac Singers* was originally released by Folkways Records in 1955, since re-issued by Smithsonian Folkways in 2004.

Three of her tracks appeared on the five-CD compilation *Best of Broadside, (1962 to 1988)* (Smithsonian Folkways, 2004), to include "Sundown", "My Oklahoma Home (It Blowed Away)", and "But If I Ask Them". Of those three, "My Oklahoma Home (It Blowed Away)" will resonate with Oklahomans not only for its rural diction, but also for its comical take on what happens when twister comes rolling down tornado alley in Oklahoma. After the speaker of the song loses their home, they exclaim, "My home is always near, it's in the atmosphere, and it may be that I'll go there when I die, and stake me out a new claim in the sky." While he did change the lyrics for his own delivery and lyrical rhythmic sensibility, Bruce Springsteen revived the song with reckless energy on his 2006 CD, *We Shall Overcome: The Seeger Sessions* (Sony).

In 1999, Ronald Cohen, historian and folk music scholar, edited *Red Dust and Broadsides: A Joint Autobiography* (Amherst: University of Massachusetts Press) of Agnes "Sis" Cunningham and Gordon Friesen, written primarily by the both of them in their later years. Gordon died in 1996, and Agnes passed on in 2004 in New York City. An undated article on the event of her death, published in the *Watonga Republican* and forwarded to the author, called Sis "one of Watonga's most notable and controversial former residents." Indeed she is one of Oklahoma's most notable female musical figures, and one of its very few true folk song writers of her era, with only Woody Guthrie as a counterpart and peer. Additionally, her work publishing *Brodside* preserves a vital era in American folk music history.

References

Encyclopedia of Oklahoma History and Culture, 1st ed., s.v. "Cunningham, Agnes."

Sisario, Ben. "Agnes Cunningham, 95, Dies; Sowed the Seeds of Folk Music." *New York Times*, online edition, 30 June, 2004, http://www.nytimes.com/2004/06/30/arts/agnes-cunningham-95-dies-sowed-the-seeds-of-folk-music.html (accessed July 19, 2010).

D

Gail Davies
(b. June 5, 1948)

Not only an influential country singer and songwriter, an in-demand session vocalist as a background singer or harmony vocalist, Gail Davies is also extremely notable for her role as a female pioneer behind the studio mixing board as the first woman to produce her own records, and record for others as well. Additionally, her songs are often written from the point of view of a strong woman making decisions based on *her* best interests, honky-tonk heartbreak songs from the wronged woman's perspective, or as an aggressor in starting or terminating a romantic releationship. Born in Broken Bow in the Ouachita Mountains of southeastern Oklahoma, known as "Little Dixie" because of its Southern cultural traditions, Patricia Gail Dickerson was the daughter of William "Tex" Dickerson, a pioneer performer on the Louisiana Hayride. After her parents' divorced, Gail, her mother, and two brothers, migrated to the Point Orchard, Washington, near Seattle. By the age of nine she was already singing harmony with her brother Ron, patterning themselves after the Everly Brothers. The sibling duo recorded an album, but it was never released. Her mother remarried and the children were adopted by their stepfather, Darby Alan Davies.

Gail Davies

Following graduation from South Kitsap High School in 1966, Gail moved to Los Angeles and married jazz musician Robert Hubener, who encouraged her to try singing jazz styles. That did not work out, her marriage to Hubener dissolved, and she became a session singer at A & M Records studio. During her career in Los Angeles, Gail recorded with such artists as Neil Young and **Hoyt Axton**, another Oklahoman. She also met singer-songwriter Joni Mitchell, sparking her initial interest in record production began. Gail cites Joni as a major influence in her life but it was A&M's top recording engineer, Henry Lewy, who spent hours in the studio teaching Gail how to produce her own music. During her days at A&M (late 60's to mid 70s), Gail was invited to sit in on a number of landmark sessions including one with ex-Beatle, John Lennon. "Sitting at the board between Lennon and Phil Spector was the most incredible thing that happened to me at A&M," Gail recalls in the biography posted on her website in 2010, "Everyone was recording there back in those days. Joe Cocker, The Carpenters and Carole King. It was a great learning experience. I was lucky to be a part of it all."

While on the L. A. music scene, Frank Zappa heard Gail sing at The Troubadour, a folk music club in Los Angeles, and invited her to join his European tour, but Gail declined because of an opportunity to duet with **Roger Miller** on the *Merv Griffin Show*, her television debut. While the jobs were few, her vocal cords felt the strain and were not responding well. Advised by physicians to give her voice a rest, Gail purchased a guitar in a pawnshop and began writing songs, and before long she began channeling the honky-tonk sadness from her childhood and failed marriage into songs that resonated with country music fans going through similar issues. She had plenty of mentorship close by, not only from her multiple contacts in the music industry, but her older brother, Ron Davies, also enjoy songwriting success as the composer of "It Ain't Easy" for Three Dog Night and David Bowie.

Gail signed with EMI Publishing in 1975 and moved to Nashville, where she met her second husband, Richard Allen, a staff writer for Screen Gems Music. Her first composition, "Bucket to the South", was a hit single for Ava Barber in 1978, and later recorded by Lynn Anderson and Mitzi Gaynor. Because of this writing success, Gail was signed in 1978 to a recording contract with CBS/Lifesong. Her first album was *Gail Davies*, and resulted in two Top 30 singles, "No Love Have I" and "Poison Love". A follow-up single, "Someone is Looking for Someone Like You", one of her own compositions, reached #11, remained on the country charts for more than four months, and was eventually translated into seven languages. In 1979, Davies moved to Warner Brothers where she began producing her own albums, including *The Game*, her first such effort.

During the 1980s, Gail amassed a string of successful singles and LPs, including "I'll Be There (If You Ever Want Me)" (from the 1980 album of the same name), "It's a Lovely, Lovely World" (which featured a duet with Emmylou Harris), "Grandma's Song", "Are You Teasing Me", "Singing the Blues", and "Blue Heartache", which was her first venture into bluegrass, climbing to #7 on the *Billboard* Country Single chart. Gail also produced her 1982 album, *Givin' Herself Away*, a "feminist oriented collection," according to Robert K. Oermann, co-author of *Finding Her Voice*: *The Saga of Women in Country Music*. Able to define a strong woman in either catastrophic emotional situations, or as an aggressor in either staring or terminating a relationship, Davies writes songs that men can't. *Givin' Herself Away* included such songs as "Round the Clock Lovin'" and "You Turn Me On I'm a Radio", both of which charted in the Top 10 on the Country Singles chart. In 1983, Gail gave birth to Christopher Alan Scruggs, son of songwriter and instrumentalist Gary Scruggs, and grandson of the legendary bluegrass banjoist Earl Scruggs. When Christopher was five months old, she began preparation for her last album with Warner Brothers, *What Can I Say*, producing two singles, "Boys Like You" and "You're a Hard Dog to Keep Under the Porch". Her move to RCA in 1984 led to the *Where Is A Woman to Go* album featuring a number of significant songs, such as "Break Away", "It's You Alone" (written by her brother Ron and featuring Ricky Skaggs on the mandolin and singing harmony with Gail), "Jagged Edge of a Broken Heart", and "Unwed Fathers". Throughout her career, the speakers of her songs are often from the point-of-view of a woman speaking out about the harshness of their domestic situations, or at least verbalizing their displeasure with how their man was acting. By 1984, she had garnered ten Top 20 country hits.

Well-known and highly praised in the UK, Gail performed at the 1985 Wembley Festival of Country Music in London, and upon her return, she formed Wild Choir, a country rock group. The band released a self-titled album in 1986 on RCA that included two moderately successful singles, "Next Time" and "Heart to Heart". One of the other tracks on the album was "Safe in the Arms of Love", which became a Top 5 Country hit for Martina McBride in 1995. The same year, Davies felt women songwriters had gone largely unappreciated as Nashville songwriting force. To promote and recognize women composers, she organized "Writers in the Round", featuring only women songwriters and airing on *Austin City Limits*, the long-running PBS music program. Among the women writers to participate in the landmark program were Emmylou Harris, Rosanne Cash, and Lacy J. Dalton. In 1989, Gail again switched labels to MCA, and released *Pretty Words*, an album that failed to produce any hit singles, but by that point she had charted fifteen songs on the *Billboard* Country Singles Chart between 1981 and 1989. One year later, she moved to Capitol/EMI and produced *The Other Side of Love* and *The Best of Gail Davies*. Then, when Capitol became Liberty, Gail was hired by Liberty Records to become the first female staff producer in country music. From 1990 to 1993, she worked with several new country music talents, such as The Kinleys and Mandy Barnett. After leaving Liberty, Gail toured Europe as a member of the songwriting group Nashville Unplugged. In the mid-1990s, Davies formed her own label, Little Chickadee Productions, which resulted in several albums, including *Eclectic* (an album she wrote), *Gail Davies Greatest Hits* (an album assisted by her new husband Rob Price), and *Live and Unplugged at the Station Inn*, a bluegrass-oriented album released in 2001. Her *Greatest Hits* (Little Chickadee/KOCH) includes twenty of her best-known hits. Guest appearances on the album include Emmylou Harris, Ricky Skaggs, **Kevin Welch**, Mandy Barnett, and Kathy Mattea. Continuing to tour in England, she consistently received great reviews for her performances there. Ever able to morph in and out of various country music styles, Gail recorded a notable duet with bluegrass stalwart Ralph Stanley on his 2001 GRAMMY nominated album, *Clinch Mountain Sweethearts*.

A long-time fan of perhaps *the* classic honky-tonk artist, Webb Pierce, Gail produced a tribute album to Pierce in 2002. Davies remembers Pierce performing alongside her father on the Louisiana Hayride when she was a child, watching her parents dance to his records, and finally her first hit was in 1978 was a cover of his 1960 hit, "No Love Have I". Recorded by Davies live over two days for only about $5,000.00, with the only expense being studio time, the album features some of country's best-known singers and Nashville's best studio musicians on Pierce's classics. Also a benefit CD with all proceeds from the album going to the Minnie Pearl Cancer Foundation (Pierce died of cancer in 1991) and the Country Music Hall of Fame and Museum, *Caught in the Webb*, featured such traditional artists as Billy Walker, Willie Nelson, George Jones, Charley Pride, Del McCoury, Dwight Yoakum, and Pam Tillis, as well as younger acts like Mandy Barnett, Allison Moorer, and Robbie Fulks. BR549'S cover of what really is the "honky-tonk anthem" in country music history, "There Stands the Glass" is worth the disc by itself. 2003 witnessed the release of Gail' newest CD, *The Songwriter Sessions* (a double disc featuring 45 of her original compositions), and she continued through 2010 with shows planned across the US and back in England and Ireland. Finally, in 2010 she planned to release her autobiography, *The Last of the Outlaws*.

Why then, at the end, give so much space in the *Oklahoma Music Guide* to a woman who left the state at an early age? For a few reasons: 1) she was born into a musical family in Oklahoma, and it was that same musician lifestyle led by her father that wound up breaking up their family, while at the same time making primary musical imprints on her as exemplified by her life-long affinity Webb Pierce, as well launching the lyrical content of much of her more successful music (i.e., breakups); 2) she also stands as one of several examples of Oklahoma folk/country music singers (Samantha Crain, Agnes "Sis" Cunningham, Kellie Coffey, Gus Hardin, Reba McEntire, Carrie Underwood) who take a no-

nonsense approach to their sense of independence in society, as well as their vocal criticism of a "male-centric" family structure and governed workplace; 3) Davies should also be a primary example of a woman excelling in the studio production and technology area of the music business where the music is made; 4) Finally, Gail Davies' most powerful songs are ones in which she expresses what everyone feels at one time or another as they endure the peaks and valleys of romantic relationships, and offers consolation by commiseration, with an indication that whoever goes through honky-tonk heartbreak is not the first, not alone, and never will be, due to the presence of cathartic country music like hers.

www.gaildavies.com

Davis, Jesse Edwin III
(b. September 21, 1944 – d. June 22, 1988)

Gifted enough to be mentioned in the same breath as John Lennon, Eric Clapton, and B.B. King, Jesse Ed Davis was one of rock and pop's primary session guitarists from 1966 to 1977. The last ten years of Davis's life were marred by drug and alcohol addiction. However, his career and recordings with major rock figures testify to his abilities and status as a multifaceted guitarist known for his fluidity in the idioms of classic rock and roll and the blues, especially on slide guitar. According to the Kiowa Tribe of Oklahoma's enrollment office, Davis was an enrolled Kiowa, but also had Comanche and **Muscogee** (Creek) heritage. He is often misrepresented as a full-blood Kiowa. Born in Norman at the U.S. Naval Hospital, Davis's mother, Vivian Saunkeah Davis, started Jesse Ed on the piano, but his father, Jesse Edwin Davis II, himself a Dixieland drummer who played with many local musicians, brought home an old Stella guitar for the budding musician. Davis took lessons from a local guitar teacher, practiced long hours, and exhausted the instructor's knowledge. Soon after, at sixteen-years-old, Davis toured with Dick Clark of American Bandstand on a 30-city tour. Also along for the tour were Ronnie Hawkins and the Hawks, with Levon Helm who befriended the young guitarist. After completing a degree in literature from the University of Oklahoma, and doing time as a guitar teacher at a music store in Norman, where **Moon Martin** also taught, Davis toured briefly with country crooner Conway Twitty in the early-1960s. Afterwards, Jesse Ed moved to Los Angeles and re-connected with Levon Helm who introduced him to fellow Oklahoman **Leon Russell**. Russell was then at the center of studio session work in Los Angeles and was able to get Davis his first session work with Gary Lewis and the Playboys. While un-credited on the Leon Russell-produced recordings by the Monkees, Davis played guitar on the Monkees' 1966 #1 hit, "Last Train to Clarksville."

In 1967, Davis recorded live for the first time with John Lee Hooker for an

Jesse Ed Davis

album released under Hooker's name as *Live at Café Au Go Go*. During the same year, Jesse Ed started his four-album association with blues man Taj Majal, during which time Davis contributed lead electric and acoustic guitar, bass guitar, piano and organ to Majal's recordings from 1967 to 1971. The impact of Jesse Ed's playing during this period cannot be underestimated as it established him as "the" slide guitar player of American popular music. Not only did the Taj Majal recordings endear Davis to his British contemporaries and the L.A. studio scene, Duane Allman appears to have gleaned his interest in and ability to play slide guitar from Jesse Ed's recording of "Statesboro Blues" with Majal. Stories vary as to how Duane Allman heard Davis. Some say it was via a Taj Mahal's album given to Duane by brother Greg Allman while Duane was recuperating from a horse riding injury, and others say it was when Duane saw Davis with Majal in an L.A. club. Nonetheless, the fact remains the Allman Brothers' version of "Statesboro Blues," appearing on the landmark 1971 live album, *At Fillmore East*, features a near carbon copy of Jesse Ed's slide work on Taj Majal's version of the song released in 1968.

Also in 1968 Jesse Ed traveled to England with Majal and performed in the Rolling Stones' *Rock and Roll Circus* film. Playing a purple paisley Fender Telecaster, Davis is featured prominently in the song "Ain't That a Lot of Love," also including Tulsa's Chuck Blackwell on drums. During the sessions for the film, Jesse Ed was warming up backstage on Gene Vincent's "Be-Bop-A-Lula" when John Lennon, the former Beatle and avid 1950s rock fan who was also in the film, noticed Davis and spontaneously joined in with him on the tune. The two musicians became friends, and Lennon later featured Davis heavily on the solo albums *Walls and Bridges* (1974) and *Rock and Roll* (1975), after which the two remained friends until Lennon's death. Additional indicators of Davis's prowess as a blues player are his inclusion on Michael Bloomfield's *Live at Fillmore West* (1969), and another album with John Lee Hooker, *Endless Boogie*, in 1970.

Also in 1970, Jesse Ed recorded his first solo album in London at Olympic Sound Studio. On the self-titled release featuring a cover painting by Davis of an American Indian smoking a pipe in the artistic style of the well-known group of Kiowa painters, the Kiowa Six, Jesse Ed used many Oklahoma images and place names on the album, such as "Reno Street Incident," "Tulsa County," and "Washita Love Child," a song that may best describe Jesse Ed's perspective of his youth and turn to rock and roll. Davis sings, "I was born on the bank of the Washita River in a Kiowa-Comanche tipi. Daddy had a hard time, mama made his eyes shine. Lord, it was just us three. . . . I did that powwow thing, Daddy showed up with a standard guitar and I knew right then I'd leave. Mama said, 'Son, what about your schoolbooks? . . . What about the draft?' Dad said, 'Honey, don't worry about the boy. (He's) got a guitar and a pen to write.'"

Available only as a Japanese import, Jesse Ed's first album exhibits his distinctive, ringing telecaster guitar work, strong sense of blues and boogie, and the party-all-the-time attitude that ultimately served to be his demise. In "Every Night is Saturday Night" Davis sings, "Every night is Saturday night for me, boogie time for me and all my friends. Rock-n-roll and lovin' one another, never gonna let the party end." Among other stalwart players on the album, Jesse Ed enlisted Eric Clapton and Leon Russell. Having finished his own album, Jesse Ed played a variety of session dates in 1971, to include work on Albert King's *Lovejoy*, Leon Russell's *And the Shelter People*, and American Indian folksinger Buffy Saint-Marie's *She Used to Wanna Be a Ballerina*. He also replaced an ailing Eric Clapton during part of the *Concert for Bangladesh*, a benefit concert in New York City organized by another ex-Beatle, George Harrison, to whom Davis had been introduced by Lennon. Davis and Clapton had obvious simpatico and respect for one another in the usually uptight and highly competitive world of lead guitarists.

The next year, 1972, followed the same hectic pace Davis had established the year before. He recorded another solo album, *Ululu*, named after the cry some Plains tribe women will make as an acknowledgement of a special occasion, or as a celebratory complement to a traditional American Indian song. Long before the **Red Dirt Music** movement of the 1980s and '90s centered in Stillwater, Jesse Ed recorded "Red Dirt Boogie, Brother" for *Ululu*, as well as songs by the Band, George Harrison, Leon Russell, and **Merle Haggard**. "Red Dirt Boogie Brother" also gives an indication of Davis's opinion of his place in the pantheon of the rock stars with whom he was associating, as well as the perceived clichés that went along with him being from Oklahoma. As the "Red Dirt Boogie Brother" begins, Davis sings, "Ain't no Beatle, ain't no Rolling Stone, ain't but just one thing. Can't get next to jazz, just plain old rock 'n' roll, ain't got no such dream." Later in the song he emphasizes he is not an Okie from Muskogee, but "just a red dirt boogie, brother, all the time." Also of interest on the album is his cover of Leon Russell's "Alcatraz," largely about the American Indian occupation of Alcatraz Island in San Francisco Bay in late 1960s and early 1970s. To hear the most visible American Indian in American popular music during that time period sing a song critical of the U.S. government's policies toward American Indians places Jesse Ed in a more political context, and a deeper one than the constant partying mode he espouses much of the time. Overall, *Ululu*, also available only as Japanese import, may be his most contemplative album with "Farther On Down the Road" and "Make a Joyful Noise" exploring his philosophical side about life and its purposes. Studio musicians on the album include bassist Donald "Duck" Dunn, of Booker T. and the MG's fame, and Tulsa's Jim Keltner, along with Leon Russell on keyboards.

Also in 1972, Jesse Ed played on the million-selling, first official Jackson Browne album, *Jackson Browne*, and can be heard on the album's hit single, "Doctor My Eyes." Davis also appeared on B.B. King's *L.A. Midnight,* Arlo Guthrie's self-titled album that included many of **Woody Guthrie**'s songs, and the Steve Miller Band's *Recall the Beginning*, all released in 1972. In 1973, Jesse Ed recorded again with Arlo Guthrie on *Last of the Brooklyn Cowboys*, Roxy Music front man Bryan Ferry on *These Foolish Things*, and released his third and final solo album *Keep Me Comin'*.

Jesse Ed's last solo album, *Keep Me Comin'*, opens with the instrumental "Big Dipper," and features the Albert King-style lead blues guitar Davis favored so often. *Keep Me Comin'* continues with his usual slide guitar work ("She's a Pain") and funky blues ("Natural Anthem" and "Bacon Fat"). The album also features a number of oblique references to Davis's consumption with drug use ("Keep Me Comin'", "Bacon Fat," "No Diga Mas," and "She's a Pain"). The usual all-star suspects are present on the record (Jim Keltner, Leon Russell), and some less clear appearances by "Bonnie, Mick, Rod, and El Mysterioso" which are only indicated by those

Jesse Ed Davis, circa 1965, Oklahoma City, backing up Conway Twitty.

names in the liner notes. Overall the album is a long party in a studio full of musicians who like funky grooves, sharp horn riffs, and are all enamored with Jesse Ed's world weary Oklahoma-accented vocals, and attitude-laden guitar work, often more convincing because of his confident authority than the originality of the licks.

A less than stellar, but obviously interesting, live performance by Jesse Ed Davis in the Santa Monica Civic Center in 1973 has surfaced on the Internet as *Sue Me Sue You Blues* and is obtainable by those diligent enough to pursue it. Made in Spain, and having sold for as much as $140.00 through the online auction site, E-Bay, the album is a very uneven performance in which Jesse Ed loses his voice after only a couple of songs, to which he credits the flu. He plays through seven songs from his three solo albums, and closes with a cover of Chuck Berry's "Roll Over Beethoven," none of which adds much to his overall legend. Of particular interest on the disc are four studio sessions demo tracks with John Lennon where the two are working out the songs that will be on Lennon's *Walls and Bridges*, to include "Going Down on Love," "Surprise Surprise," "Whatever Gets You Through the Night," and "Nobody Loves You When You Are Down and Out."

Whatever ideas Jesse Ed had for more of his own music, he was subsumed by the work other people wanted him to do for them. In 1974, he recorded with **Brewer** and Shipley on their self-titled album of that year, Harry Nilsson on *Pussy Cats*, the Pointer Sisters on *There's a Plenty,* Ringo Starr on *Goodnight Vienna*, and John Lennon on *Walls and Bridges*. Davis's guitar is featured throughout *Walls and Bridges*, to include slide guitar on "No. 9 Dream" and "Nobody Loves You (When You're Down and Out)," and lead guitar on the instrumental "Beef Jerky." The American Indian presence through Davis is obvious on the album from the "Little Big Horns" horn section, to "Scared," a song that begins with two wolf cries and proceeds with a mock-Hollywood western musical motif while Davis solos. Davis continued working with rock royalty in 1975 when he recorded with The Who's Keith Moon on *Two Sides of Moon*, George Harrison on *Extra Texture*, and John Lennon's "contractual fulfillment" record of 1950s and 1960s standards, *Rock and Roll*. Also that same year, Davis recorded again with Arlo Guthrie (*Together in Concert*) and Harry Nilsson *(Duit On Mon Dei)*, David Bromberg (*Midnight on the Water*), Rod Stewart (*Atlantic Crossing*), the 5th Dimension (*Earth Bound*), and Mac Davis (*Burnin' Thing*).

The significance of Jesse Ed playing on albums by rock artists, R & B artists, and country artists all in the same year serves as further proof of his overall talent which seems to have known no boundaries in popular music. Davis's last prolific year as a sideman was 1976.

By Hugh Foley / 191

Along with repeat customers Ringo Starr (*Ringo's Rotogravure*) and Harry Nilsson (*Sandman*), Davis recorded with Neil Diamond (*Beautiful Noise*), and Eric Clapton on *No Reason to Cry* and Clapton's 1976 birthday sessions that have only been released as the bootleg *Happy, Happy Birthday Eric* (Dandelion, 1998). Davis also added his guitar to recordings by several other lesser, second-tier artists such as David Cassidy, Van Dyke Parks, and Geoff Muldaur. Disenchanted with the session scene in Los Angeles, Davis moved to Hawaii in 1977. During that year, he only did two sessions, one for Long John Baldry (*Welcome to the Club*), and one for Leonard Cohen (*Death of a Ladies Man*). At the end of the 1970s, as popular music tastes shifted toward disco and the more youth-oriented punk and new wave scene, Jesse Ed's blues rock expertise was less and less in demand. His own personal demons of alcohol and drugs also led to his seclusion and lack of activity. According to his obituary in the *Los Angeles Times*, he returned to Los Angeles from Hawaii in 1981 broke and ravaged by drug addiction.

By 1985, Davis formed the Graffiti Man band with American Indian activist and poet, John Trudell. The duo recorded *a.k.a. Grafitti Man*, first released as an independent cassette available only by mail order. When a copy reached Bob Dylan, he called it the "album of the year" and played it over the public address system before his concerts. Trudell openly credits Davis with the encouragement he needed to put his poetry to music, and Jesse Ed explained to an interviewer in 1986 that the opportunity to play with John Trudell was a saving grace at a time in his career when he had nowhere to play and nothing more than his addictions to keep him busy. Trudell also has connections to Tulsa where he met his wife, Tina Manning, who was pregnant with their fourth child when she and their three children were killed in an arsonist's fire on the Duck Valley Reservation in Nevada. The event largely ended Trudell's activism in the American Indian Movement, in which he served as chairman from 1973 to 1979, and for which he felt his family was targeted, and turned him to writing poetry for therapeutic purposes. Ultimately writing became Trudell's primary artistic activity and led him to the collaboration with Jesse Ed Davis that would become Davis's last creative effort as a musician.

As a final attempt at reconciling his substance abuse problems, Davis checked into a chemical treatment program, and served as an alcohol and drug counselor at the American Indian Free Clinic in Long Beach, California. He also began appearing at club dates on the West Coast with John Trudell and the Grafitti Man Band. When the group appeared in Los Angeles in 1987, George Harrison, Bob Dylan, and John Fogerty joined them onstage. Davis was not able to overcome his personal issues, however, and only a few days before a scheduled appearance at the Palomino Club in North Hollywood, Davis died of an apparent drug overdose in Venice, California on June 22, 1988. Ironically, Davis's work resurfaced that year on Eric Clapton's *Crossroads*, a boxed set retrospective. Since then, his work has re-emerged on several re-issues by Neil Diamond, Emmylou Harris, Jackson Browne, Lightnin' Hopkins, John Lennon, Taj Mahal, Harry Nilsson, The Rolling Stones, and Ringo Starr. His work has also appeared on film soundtracks such as *Blue Collar* (1995) and *Kent State* (1995), as well as on Sony's *Story of the Blues* and *Guitar Player Presents Rock*, a compilation of significant rock tracks assembled by *Guitar Player* magazine that included Taj Majal's "Six Days on the Road," on which Davis is featured. His first three albums were re-issued in Japan in 1998, and in 2002 the Oklahoma Jazz Hall of Fame inducted Davis in the blues category. At the ceremony, attended by Jesse Ed's widow, Kelly Brady Davis, and his mother Vivian Davis, Taj Mahal performed in Jesse Ed's honor, and said, "It's about time people started paying attention to what Davis played and how he played it. He was a great player." In 2011, Jesse Ed Davis was inducted into the Oklahoma Music Hall of Fame in Muskogee for his work as one of rock's primary session guitarists from the late 1960s through the 1970s.

Dean, Ester

Growing up around her church-singing mom who also played blues around the house, Muskogee, Oklahoma native Ester Dean is the first significant major R&B/hip hop artist from Oklahoma since the **GAP Band**, with her 2009 Top 40 hit, "Drop it Low", featuring Chris Brown, and multiple songwriting credits for major R&B artists. After getting her first experience in Muskogee studios she called cold out of the phone book while still in middle school, her family moved to Omaha, Nebraska where she skipped finishing high school, earned her GED, and moved to Atlanta where she experienced the usual music industry newcomer trials before getting a writing gig with various producers, Chris "Tricky" Stewart and Jazze Pha (Girlicious' "Like Me"), Ciara ("Never Ever"), and the Pussycat Dolls ("Whatcha Think About That"). After getting her to write some hooks for Young Jeezy, Polow Da Don signed Dean to his Zone 4 label. Her first single, "Drop It Low", received instant notoriety for its association with the film *More Than a Game* about NBA basketball star LeBron James' high school career. However, because of its catchy beats, memorable melodic hooks, Ester's confident female delivery, and an edited version for airplay, "Drop It Low" was propelled by the magnification, reaching #38 on the *Billboard* Hot 100 and #33 on *Billboard*'s Hot R&B, both in October of 2009. The song had staying power, and was still on the pop chart five months later in March 2010 as re-current, or popular song that radio has continued to play long after its release date and peak position.

Ester Dean

Having moved to Los Angeles in 2008, Ester has written all or part of songs for Christina Aguilera, Soulja Boy Tell 'Em, Rihanna, Monica, T.I., Usher, Mary J. Blige, Dr. Dre featuring Jay-Z, Katy Perry, and R. Kelly. Along with writing "We Are" for the 2012 U.S. Olympic Team's official video, Dean is working on her debut full-length album, reportedly due in 2013.

www.esterdean.com

www.myspace.com/esterdean

Debris

(formed Chickasha, OK, 1975)

Oklahoma's only real entry into the punk rock/art rock world of the mid-1970s, Debris recorded one gloriously ramshackle album, *Static Disposal* (1976), is at various points reflective of the proto-punk of the Velvet Underground or Iggy and the Stooges, and at other moments descended from early 1970s glam rock of David Bowie or T Rex. Occasionally, the music ranges into its own brand of psychedelic rock with keyboard sound effects, progressive jazz accents, massive reverb and echo, and stutter step rhythms that are also obvious references to their self-proclaimed Captain Beefheart influences (hear "Witness"), and at other points is a talking punk rock rave-up that later emerges in hundreds, if not thousands, of punk and hardcore bands throughout the present era, even though those bands are likely never to have heard of Debris. This is music that probably could only have emerged in mid-1970s Oklahoma. In a 2009 conversation with founding member, Chuck Ivey, at the Oklahoma History Center's opening of "Another Hot Oklahoma Night," an exhibit based on rock music history in the state, Ivey said he thought their unique blend of rock influences probably could have only occurred in their "scene of one" in 1975-era Chickasha.

Emerging from the disintegration of another Chickasha band, Victoria Vein and the Thunderpunks,[1] bassist/vocalist Ivey and multi-instrumentalist/guitarist Oliver Powers linked up with drummer Johnny Gregg, also from Chickasha, and formed in the summer of 1975. According to their myspace.com site, "Their chaotic performance style, and dark, quirky sound did not endear them to their Oklahoma City audiences. At one such show, a Battle of the Bands, competition where 50 bands vied for a new sound system, Debris cam in dead last while a cover band took home the prize." Undaunted and driven by their independent artistic ideals, the band made the most of a promotional deal offered by Benson Sound Studios in Oklahoma City for ten hours of studio time and a 1,000-LP pressing of an album for $1,590.00. Recorded in two mid-December sessions, the album was pressed and released in 1976 when the band began sending it out to record labels and rock music magazines. Listening to "One Way Spit" one can instantly see the punk and glam rock appeal the song would have had in New York music circles of the mid-1970s. The song opens with the leader barely able to get the 1-2-3-4 count-off out of his mouth before the band slices in with crashing, furious rock that calls up the New York Dolls and swirls with energy and conviction, if not direction. Given the immediacy with which the songs were recorded, Debris' *Static Disposal* exhibits all those earlier mentioned influences, but also reeks with the impact of the *Rocky Horror Picture Show*, which had its nationwide US release in September, 1975, the fall after the band formed. Since that film would have been about the freakiest thing going on in accessible popular culture in Oklahoma, the band certainly would have

Debris at Bill and Dee's in Norman, OK, 2010.

seen it. That being the case, the vocals on *Static Disposal* frequently drift into a spot-on channeling of Tim Curry's character, *Frank-N-Furter*, from *Rocky Horror*, and yet at other times are somewhere between Richard Hell, David Byrne, and Don Van Vliet (Captain Beefheart). The music did not emerge from a vacuum, nor did it break particularly new ground that had not been covered by earlier artists. As a nod to those earlier sounds, the group covered "Real Cool Time" by their obvious forefather, Iggy Pop, on *Static Disposal* . In any case, what the band did do with limited resources, boundless energy, wreckless talent on a variety of instruments, and the ability to literally do whatever seemed right at the time, Debris created some timeless rock art that is only now being recognized by the wider rock music history world for the group's innovation, experimentation, and just downright bizarreness.

Music fans will also take note that Debris recorded their album three months before the Ramones, generally considered the first American punk rock band, set up in the studio to record their Sire Records debut in February, 1976.[2] While not a complete punk album, just with its lead off track, "One Way Spit" earns Debris cult status among rock music aficionados for its chaotic, raw frenzy. Unfortunately for Debris, all that of that contemporary understanding only comes with thirty-five years of historical hindsight. With only negative responses, the group called it quits after only three shows in 1976. However, within a year, East coast critics and fans came around to the extremely original recording, and Debris was even offered a gig at the legendary CBGB/OMFUG nightclub in New York City, already deep into the burgeoning punk and new wave era with bands like Talking Heads, Television, Blondie, and, of course, The Ramones.

The influential *Static Disposal* has been re-issued on Anopheles Records, first in 1999 as a faithful reproduction of the original LP on compact disc, then again re-issued the LP on clear vinyl as a collector's copy in 2002. Given the demand for the disc, Anopheles pressed a second edition of the CD in 2007 with a detailed, twenty-eight page booklet with extensive historical notes, and an additional forty minutes of basement recordings from the band's Subterraneous Static Disposal office in Chickasha, circa 1975-76. Additionally, the band reunited with original members Ivey and Gregg for several gigs from 2005 to 2010, adding both Charlie Harrison (keyboards) and Robb Hayes (guitar) of the Thunderpunks from back there when. Hayes was also present at the recording of the *Static Disposal*, and made adjustments to the EQ on Ivey's bass amp at the end of "One Way Spit". The band serves as a further paradigm for how the relative isolation and slow pop culture evolution of the state (prior to the Internet era) has actually helped Oklahoma musicians develop unique styles, such as **Chainsaw Kittens**, **Flaming Lips**, and **Samantha Crain**, all of whom have said as much several times. Add Debris to that list, right at the top.

www.myspace.com/debris1975

Endnotes
1. A 1975 video of Victoria Vein and the Thunderpunks' appearance on Ronnie Kaye's 1970s *American Bandstand*-esque Oklahoma City TV show can be seen on the Debris myspace.com page.
2. For insight into the wide variety of antecedents to what became known as punk rock, ee Tim Sommer, "Who Invented Punk," *Big Takeover,* Fall, 2010, Issue 66, Volume 1: 1, pp 12, 14. While Sommer mentions many of the standard references for punk's ancestors, he can be said to have included Debris in a roundabout way, writing "many, many others were all playing simple hard-driving music that was remarkably smiliar to '76/'77 British, American and Australian punk rock."

Delta Rhythm Boys
(formed at Langston University, 1934)

One of the shimmering harmony vocal groups of the late 1930s, 1940s, and early 1950s in the US, and still popular in Europe throughout their ultimate disbanding in 1987, the Delta Rhythm Boys formed in 1934 at Langston University in Langston, Oklahoma. While their individual origins are unknown as of this writing, the original members who formed at the then primarily African-American college consisted of bass singer Lee Gaines, baritone Kelsey Pharr, first tenor lead Carl Jones, second tenor Traverse Crawford, and pianist/arranger Rene DeKnight. According to multiple sources, often whom are just repeating each other, general agreement exists that in 1936 the group transferred to Dillard University in New Orleans, changing their name to the Frederick Hall Quintet, a nod to the school's music director.[1] By 1938, the group had relocated to New York, appeared in Broadway shows as the Delta Rhythm Boys, and made their first recordings for Decca Records in 1940. The group benefitted from a shifting music industry paradigm in the early 1940s of emphasis on vocalists and vocal groups, instead of big bands led by recognizable names, many of whom, along with their musicians, were drafted to be part of the war effort. Another factor that helped magnify their status was the musicians strike of 1942 to 1944, during which time the American Federation of Musicians union instigated a recording strike against record companies over a royalty payment dispute. Subsequently, vocal groups that did not need instrumental accompaniment enjoyed a brief boon, such as the Mills Brothers, the Andrews Sisters, and the **Dinning Sisters**. The group appeared on network radio shows, in several films, and many film shorts.

Interested listeners can find numerous video recordings of the Delta Rhythm Boys smooth harmonies and urbane presentations on youtube.com, including their most often-cited recordings, "Dry Bones" and "Take the A Train", as well as many others, to include a delightful up tempo version of "St. Louis Blues", a harbinger of the doo wop vocal groups of the 1950s.[2] As a diametric opposite to the loud and raucous jump and jive style of 1940s made popular by Louis Jordan and Oklahoman **Roy Milton**, the Delta Rhythm Boys' sophisticated vocal harmonies did not resonate with the changing popular music tastes of the early 1950s. Overwhelmed by the musical groundswell of gritty urban blues out of Chicago, and the first wave of Anglo rockabilly singers emerging out of Memphis, the group depended on its European following for the rest of its career, permanently locating

Delta Rhythm Boys original lineup (from left) Rene DeKnight (piano), Kelsey Pharr, Traverse Crawford, Carl Jones, Lee Gaines.

there in 1956. Lee Gaines and Traverse Crawford continued performing with added members, with Gaines dying in 1975, and Crawford following later in 1987, ending the group's fifty-year career. Along with saxophonist **Don Byas,** who also attended Langston after his youth in Muskogee, and where he played in a group called the Collegiate Ramblers, the Delta Rhythm Boys appear to shine further musical glory on the historically African-American college, and further illustrates the wide and diverse impact of musicians with Oklahoma ties on major periods in American popular music history.

Endnotes
1. For more details of the Delta Rhythm Boys' recording and performer career, see Colin Larkin, "Delta Rhythm Boys," *Virgin Encyclopedia of R&B and Soul.* (London: Muze/Virgin, 1998).
2. For insightful thoughts on the Delta Rhythm Boys' place in the linear continuum of American popular music, see Craig Harris, "The Delta Rhythm Boys," (allmusic.com; accessed July 21, 2010).

Denver, John
(b. December 31, 1943 – October 12, 1997)

As one of the 1970s most popular artists whose songs crossed over from pop to country and adult contemporary charts, John Denver is still known internationally for his major hits of that period, "Take Me Home Country Roads", "Leavin' on a Jet Plane", "Rocky Mountain High", "Thank God I'm a Country Boy", and "Sunshine on My Shoulders". While all major music references agree John Denver was born in Roswell, New Mexico as Henry John Deutschendorf, Jr., none of those sources, such as the *Rolling Stone Encyclopedia of Rock and Roll* or allmusic.com, nor the biography in his 2007 *Essential John Denver* (RCA/Legacy) collection, go beyond saying he lived in different Southwestern regions or towns in his youth, or that his family settled in Texas after his birth. However, when this author began compiling information on Oklahoma musical figures in the late 1980s, John Denver's name came up over and over again anecdotally from various people who like to talk about Oklahoma music, but they could rarely go further than a vague reference to Corn, Oklahoma, or that his father was in the Air Force in the state, both of which turned out to be more or less accurate. Denver himself clears up those vagaries about his family's close connection to the state in his autobiography, *Take Me Home* (Harmony, 1994), writing, "Dad was a plowboy from western Oklahoma; Mom was a hometown (Tulsa) girl," and goes on to explain his father was in the Army Air Corps studying at the Spartan School of Aeronautics when his parents (Henry and Erma) met in Tulsa.[1] The first long-form explanation of Denver's Oklahoma ties emerged in Victoria Lee's *Distinguished Oklahomans* on Touch of Heart Press in 2002. In her essay on John Denver, she explains in detail how far the family's ties go back in the state, with grandpa Deutschendorf immigrating to the state at age eighteen prior to World War I, and moving out to Bessie in western Oklahoma, just south of Clinton, where he met his future wife. After marrying, scrapping it out on a rented and then government managed farm, and having a family of eleven children, the Deutschendorfs bought their own farm in 1942 in Cordell. John's father, Henry John, was the second oldest child, joined the Army Air Corps, and wound up in Tulsa for training, as mentioned by Denver himself, where he met Denver's mother, Erma, who was born in Beggs. Due to his father's military service, Henry "Dutch" and Erma moved to Roswell, New Mexico in 1943 where John was born in December of that year. Lee goes on to explain that Erma often would visit her relatives back in Tulsa when Henry was on military assignment, service that would ultimately place "Dutch" in the Oklahoma Aerospace Hall of Fame. On one of those trips when he was eleven, his grandmother, Kate Swope, bought him his first guitar, a 1910 Gibson acoustic, and he began to take some lessons arranged by his mother. Also according to Lee, who gathered a number of disparate resources via e-mail for her esssay, John's father thought it would be a good idea for John to spend some time finding out what growing up on his family's farm in Bessie, Oklahoma would be like, especially the hard work of harvesting wheat. However, a 2010 *Tulsa World* obituary on Erma's death by staff writer, Tim Stanley, indicates that Erma's mother had a farm in Corn, Oklahoma, where "Denver spent many summers growing up."[2] Either both families had farms in the area, or the truth may lie somewhere in the middle as Bessie and Corn are about ten miles apart from one another, and separated by mostly by wheat fields. So, in either case Denver spent many impressionable summers walking down country roads with sunshine on his shoulders around Corn, or sitting on a tractor in the wheat fields around Bessie thanking God he was a country boy until he enrolled at Texas Tech University in 1961. Once in college, he began writing songs and singing in Lubbock's local clubs, left for L.A. in 1964 after dropping out of school, and began his ascent into the stratosphere of popular music stardom, While he may not have been born in the state, John Denver received his first guitar in Oklahoma, learned about country living from its wheat fields in western Oklahoma, and never forgot that in many ways Oklahoma would always represent going home to him, a lyrical trope he mined for four #1 singles and two #1 albums, one of which was, naturally, *Back Home Again* (RCA, 1974).

John Denver

Endnotes

1. See John Denver, *Take Me Home: An Autobiography* (Harmony, 1994), pp X.

2. For complete details of her research into Denver's Oklahoma background collected via a variety of e-mail messages from varying sources, See Victoria Lee, *Distinguished Oklahomans* (Tulsa: A Touch of Heart Publishing, 2002), pp 68-69.

3. For Erma Deutschendorf-Davis' obituary, see Tim Stanley, "Sooner native, John Denver's mother dies," *Tulsa World*, 21 January, 2010, section A, p. 13.

DeVaney, Yvonne McGowan
(b. December 25, 1925)

With a lush voice that recalls Patsy Cline, and having recorded for several labels (Capitol, Columbia, Decca, et al.) under various stage names, (Yvonne O'Day, Vonnie Taylor, Vonnie Mack, and Jean Dee), Yvonne DeVaney's professional music career as a singer and songwriter spans more than sixty years. Her best-known song, "A Million and One," was a Top 10 hit for Dean Martin in 1968, and recorded by Pat Boone, David Allan Coe, and Hank Snow. Artists such as Dottie West, **Wanda Jackson**, The Wilburn Brothers, and the U.K.-based Cheltenham Singers have also recorded songs by DeVaney. Born as one of six children in Retrop, a tiny crossroads community eighteen miles south of Elk City in southwestern Oklahoma, Yvonne McGowan began singing at age two, won a classical piano contest at age eleven, and by age fifteen played guitar in a song and tap dance duet act with her accordion-toting sister, Mary Nell. First billed as The McGowan Sisters, and then known as the Oklahoma Sweethearts, the duo had their own show on Elk City's KASA radio after winning an amateur talent contest, and also made a public appearance with Roy rogers and Trigger in 1943. After high school, Yvonne and Mary Nell joined an all-girl Western troupe, Billye Gale and the Hollywood Cowgirls, touring the Orpheum Theater Circuit and the Fox Intermountain Circuit in 1944. Ending her professional partnership with Mary who left the duo for marriage and a family, Yvonne began appearing with Art Perry and His All Girl Band in Kansas City, Missouri in 1945, as well as with the Cumberland Mountain Folks on KWFT Radio in Wichita Falls, Texas in 1947.

Returning to Oklahoma in 1948, Yvonne became a featured vocalist with Merl Lindsay's popular Western swing dance band in 1951. In '52 she was invited to join WKY-TV as a featured vocalist with the Chuck Wagon Gang in Oklahoma City on WKY-TV's *Chuckwagon Show*, and a featured singing spot on the station's *Sooner Shindig*. During her stint on the *Chuckwagon Show*, she met honky tong singer Webb Pierce who urged her to send him some recordings so he could play them for record company executives. In 1953, unknown to Yvonne, Capitol Records A&R executive Ken Nelson flrew into Oklahoma City to watch Yvonne perform on the *Chuckwagon Show*. Nelson had some to offer a contract to Yvonne, and immediately after the show signed Yvonne to Capitol Records, one of the first female country singers to receive an individual contract, largely due to the success of pioneering female honky tonker, Kitty Wells, and pop crossover artist **Kay Starr**.

Yvonne DeVaney

By Hugh Foley

After signing Yvonne, Capitol changed her name to Yvonne O'Day, under which she recorded her first minor country hit, "Snowflakes," along with several other country singles, "I Just Want to Be With You," "Kisses on Paper," and "Baby I Go For You." Given **Patti Page**'s massive multi-format success, Capitol decided to move Yvonne into the pop field, changing her name to Vonnie Taylor and recording her backed by the Van Alexander Orchestra in Hollywood in 1954. Singles released under her new show biz moniker included "Love Is a Gamble," "This Is the Thanks I Get," "When You're Making Love to Me," and "Does It Hurt You to Remember." In 1955, as Vonnie, she joined Red Foley on the *The ABC-TV Ozark Jubilee* broadcasts out of Springfield, MO, a program that was one of the foundational commercial music successes in Missouri that led to the development of Branson, MO, as a country music tourist mecca.

In 1956 Yvonne moved to Columbia Records where her name was again changed, this time to Vonnie Mack, and she made several recordings with backing by the Jordanaires and the Anita Kerr Singers, including "I Live For You," "Please Forgive Me," "Blue Mountain Waltz," and "Slowly I'm Losing You." In 1960, Columbia tried a different approach by again creating a new persona for Yvonne, Jean Dee, under which she recorded "Open Arms," "If You Don't Somebody Else Will," "Hey Punkin'," and "You Don't Have To Tell Me." With some strong name recognition as Jean Dee, Yvonne moved to Decca Records that same year (1960) where she again recorded with the Jordanaires on "Sweethearts on Parade" and "Day By Day Your Love Grows Sweeter." During this period she also toured with **Bob Wills and His Texas Playboys**, with whom she performed during Wills' first engagement at the Golden Nugget in Las Vegas in 1962. Yvonne continued recording throughout the 1960s as Jean Dee for Phillips ("My Greatest Hurt" and "Nothing Down"), and for King Records as Jean Dee ("Dim the Car Lights" and "You're the Only Thing That Really Matters to Me"). She also recorded for Spar ("Rome Wasn't Built in a Day", "Step into My World," "We'll Make It This time," and "You'll Come Home to Mama"), Chart Records, and, eventually her own label, Compo Records. In 1967, Yvonne received a BMI Citation of Achievement for her songwriting, notably, for "A Million and One."

Given her lengthy songwriting, recording, and performing background, Yvonne formed her own recording and publishing companies in 1972, to include The YMD Music Group, Sunny Lane Music Publishing (ASCAP), Country Classics Music Publishing (BMI), Compo! Publishing (BMI), and Compo Records. Her first release on Compo, "Sitting in the Amen Seat" (1973) was a hit in Canada, and began a series of charted songs for Country Classics Music Publishing, to include recordings of Yvonne's songs by Billy Walker, Hank Snow, Dottie West, and Wanda Jackson. DeVaney's "Wine from My Table" reached #1 in Ireland, England, France, and Germany. Her BMI catalogue lists over 75 songs she has written.

Yvonne continued releasing music through 2001, notably *A Good Thing* (2001) featuring ten songs she wrote and recorded. By 2003, the album received worldwide airplay on radio stations in the U.S., Australia, Denmark, France, Kenya, Malta, Poland, Russia, Switzerland, and Wales, just to name a few of the twenty-seven known countries where Yvonne's music has been broadcast since the beginning of this century. Additionally, Yvonne embraced the new technology of the Internet, distributing her songs electronically on various "aggregators," or web distribution portals, and appearing on Internet "radio" spin charts as late as 2004.

www.ymdmusic.com

Diffie, Joe

(b. December 28, 1958)

Once described by Tammy Wynette as all her favorite vocalists rolled into one, and recognized by the music industry as one of the 1990s' most commercially successful country music stars (hi songs have been played on radio 25 million times since 1994 and album sales exceeding five million), singer/songwriter Joe Logan Diffie was born at St. John's Hospital in Tulsa, Oklahoma, the son of Joe R. and Flora (Lowrance) Diffie. His first music instrument was a guitar, his father's F-hole Airline from Sears & Roebuck, on which his father taught him to play. Joe recalls his father playing not only guitar, but also banjo and piano. His dad was also a major influence in Joe's listening habits, primarily the songs of George Jones, Lefty Frizzell, **Merle Haggard**, and Johnny Cash. The family often sang country and gospel songs while riding in the family pickup, and Joe harmonized on such songs as "Peace in the Valley" and "Amazing Grace." He made his public debut at age four, singing "You Are My Sunshine," accompanied by his Aunt Dawn Anita's country band in Duncan, Oklahoma. Joe also sang in church with his mother and sisters Meg and Monica. All this background provided Diffie with the perfect baritone blend of honky-tonk melancholy or up tempo party songs, then switch to good or bad romance storyteller, all accompanied by more than enough twang and fiddles to remove any doubt about his country music identity, as opposed to worrying about being pop enough to crossover to marginal country listeners.

Although Joe was based in Oklahoma during his youth, the family did relocate to various other places, including San Antonio, Texas (1st grade); Washington state (4th and 5th grade); and Wisconsin (6th though sophomore year of high school). Joe liked sports, and in high school, lettered in football, baseball, golf, and track; and was named Best All-Around Male Athlete his senior year at Velma-Alma High School in Oklahoma. Both his mother and father and two sisters were also graduates of the same high school

Joe Diffie, 2010.

After high school graduation, Joe attended Cameron University in Lawton, Oklahoma, with the intention of pursuing sports and working toward earning credits for medical school. Competition was keen on Cameron's football team, and he decided against following his athletic dreams. He fell in love with a girl who became his first wife in 1977, and abandoned ambitions of

By Hugh Foley

medical school. Faced with supporting a family, Joe left college and began work in the Oklahoma oil fields, and later drove a truck in Alice, Texas, used to pump cement into oil wells. Finding the long hours and hard work associated with this job too much, Joe returned to Oklahoma and began work in an iron foundry (Westran) in Duncan, Oklahoma, and started playing music on the side. His music activities during the 1970s and 1980s included participation in two gospel groups, Genesis II and Higher Purpose; a rock band, Blitz; and a bluegrass band, The Special Edition. But it was the bluegrass group that proved most satisfying to Joe as he played clubs and festivals in Oklahoma and surrounding states, including **Bill Grant**'s bluegrass festival in Hugo. Joe began to write music, and set up an eight-track studio in Duncan to produce demos for him-self and other musicians in the area.

Not by choice, but life left its sometimes harsh marks on Joe in 1986 when he lost his job at the foundry, was forced to close his studio because of a lack of money, and went through a divorce. While none of those are desirable events in and of themselves, they served as Joe's grad school for country music lyrics. After re-balancing, Joe borrowed money from his parents, and decided to move to a different environment, namely Nashville, in hopes of making it as a songwriter. Before he left for Nashville, Joe had forwarded some demos to "Music Row," where **Hank Thompson** had recorded one of his songs, "Love on the Rocks", one that his mother had sent Thompson, and while Randy Travis came close to recording another, "Love's a Hurtin' Game".

In Nashville, Joe secured a job with Gibson Guitars through one of his bluegrass friends, Charlie Derington, and began making contacts in the country music arena, including Johnny Neel, his next-door neighbor and songwriter with Forest Hills Music. The two began composing when Joe provided transportation for the sight impaired Neel. Soon Joe was given a staff songwriter position with Forest Hills, where his demo tapes attracted the attention of the Nashville crowd, one of which ("There Goes My Heart Again") was recorded by Holly Dunn (Joe sang back-up vocal harmonies) in 1989 and reached #4 on the *Billboard* Country Chart. Joe had co-written the song with Wayne Perry and Lonnie Wilson, who became Joe's producer and drummer. Diffie recalls his first royalty check for $16,000, and that figure prompted him to compose more songs. By then, he had also remarried (tempting the country music lyrical muses).

Diffie's demos eventually resulted in a recording contract with Epic Records in 1990. His debut album, *A Thousand Winding Roads*, produced four #1 hit singles, including his first, "Home", as well as "If You Want Me To", "If the Devil Danced (In Empty Pockets)", and "New Way (To Light Up an Old Flame)". The latter was his first composition released as a single. He also debuted on the Grand Ole Opry in 1990 backed by his seven-piece band, Heartbreak Highway, was nominated for the CMA Horizon Award in 1991, ACM nomination for Best New Male Artist in 1992, CMA nomination for Best Male Vocalist in 1992, and *Music City News* Star of Tomorrow nomination in 1992.

Diffie's second album, 1992's *Regular Joe*, contained several hit singles, such as "Is It Cold in Here", "Ships That Don't Come In", and "Next Thing Smokin'". In 1993, a third album, *Honky Tonk Attitude*," yielded two major hits, "Prop Me Up Beside the Jukebox" and "John Deere Green", followed by *Third Rock from the Sun* with two more hit singles, "Third Rock from the Sun" and the crazy popular "Pickup Man". He followed in 1995 with two more Top 10 singles, "So Help Me Girl" and "I'm in Love with a Capital 'U'". Joe also earned several awards and honors in the early 1990s, including the CMA Award in 1993 for Best Vocal Collaboration with George Jones, **Vince Gill**, and **Garth**

Brooks (among others) on "I Don't Need Your Rockin' Chair"; became the seventy-first member of the Grand Ole Opry cast in 1993; was inducted into the Country Music Hall of Fame Walkway of Stars in 1995. In 1999 Joe captured his first GRAMMY Award as one of several country music stars, including **Merle Haggard**, who collaborated on the "Same Old Train" song written by Marty Stuart for the *Tribute to Tradition* album

Acknowledged as a major country music star, Joe experienced more personal challenges in the 1990s. His second son, Tyler, was diagnosed with Down's Syndrome, urging Joe to help establish First Steps, Inc., an organization to raise funds for educating the physically and mentally handicapped. Diffie has held many fund raising events for First Steps, including Country Steps In for First Steps and the Joe Diffie Charity Golf Classic. For these charitable causes, Joe received the first Honorary Unsung Hero Award presented by the Nashville Council of Community Services and the Country Radio Broadcasters' Artist Humanitarian Award in 1997.

Joe continued to make waves in Nashville. In 1995, he released two successful albums, *Mr. Christmas* and *Life's So Funny*. The latter included "Bigger Than the Beatles," a *Billboard* #1 Country Chart hit in 1996, and a new song from his first *Greatest Hits* album produced another chart single, "Texas Size Heartache" in 1998. Diffie charted in the Country Top 10 again in 2001 with the title track from *In Another World*, and produced four more Country Chart singles through 2004. In 2002, Joe was joined by Mark Chesnutt and Tracy Lawrence for their Rockin' Roadhouse tour that included stops in seventy-five cities, including Stillwater, Oklahoma. More than 350,000 country music fans attended shows on the tour. The tour won the 2002 International Entertainment Buyers Association All Access Award in the category of "Festival, Fair or Special Event of the Year."

Overall, the "Pickup Man," as Joe is affectionately called in Nashville, has charted numerous Top 10 hits, twelve of which have reached #1. His *A Thousand Winding Roads*, *Life's So Funny*, and *Regular Joe* albums were certified gold, while *Honky Tonk Attitude* was platinum and *Third Rock from the Sun* reached double platinum status. An easy call, The Oklahoma Music Hall of Fame and Museum inducted Diffie into the Hall of Fame, and after purchasing an abandoned water tower, erected it outside the museum with had "Billy Bob loves Charlene" in green paint on the tower, as inspired by Diffie's hit song "John Deere Green". In 2009, Rounder Records released *The Ultimate Collection*, comprised of a long-term project of Diffie's to re-record his memorable songs, to include a personal favorite of this author, "Prop Me Up Beside the Jukebox (If I Die)". In 2010 Rounder brought Joe full circle with *Homecoming: The Blue Grass Album*, giving Diffie a chance to return to the bluegrass sounds that elevated his status initially twenty-five years prior in his native Oklahoma before he became one country music's biggest stars of the last twenty years. Sounding good on the radio,

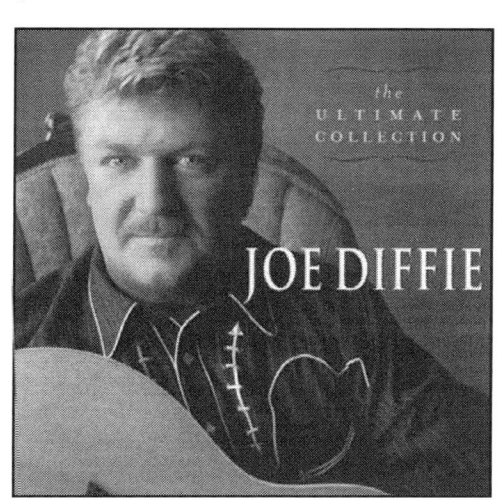

The Oklahoma Music Hall of Fame commemorated lyrics from inductee Diffie's "John Deere Green" on a water tower outside the museum in Muskogee, OK.

By Hugh Foley / 203

in the beer joint, or just playing in a work truck, Joe's music is instantly familiar and comfortable, with lyrics steeped in real life experience and vocal tones that either roll out easy as a bass (the low end, not the fish), or manipulate the subtle nasal twangflips of masters such as George Jones, Randy Travis, and all the Hanks, magnifying Tammy Wynette's praise of Diffie being so many good things rolled up into one. According to his website, his fans still agree, as Joe was booked solidly for performances through 2013.

www.joediffie.com

Dillard, Ernestine
(b. 1941)

Born in Nesbitt, Mississippi, but a resident of the Tulsa area since 1990, Ernestine Dillard is a singer of sacred and secular music, a motivational speaker, and a minister. However, she may always best be remembered by a defining moment, singing "God Bless America" at the Oklahoma City Memorial Service held five days after the bombing of the Alfred P. Murrah Federal Building. With distinguished guests such as President and Mrs. Clinton, Billy Graham, Governor and Mrs. Keating, and 20,000 people in the Oklahoma City Fairgrounds Arena, ballpark, and surrounding buildings, the atmosphere was beautified by 150 symphony and philharmonic level musicians, and amplified to a worldwide live television audience via CNN. After a highly emotional service in which the 168 deaths of April 19, 1995 were eulogized, and comfort was offered to the injured, the survivors, and the more than 200 children who were either new orphans or suddenly in single parent families, Ernestine Dillard stepped to the podium to conclude the prayer service program with "God Bless America", accompanied by the Oklahoma City Philharmonic and conducted by Joel Levine. The following moments can only partially be described as sublime, melancholy, and inspiring all at the same time. Mere adjectives will forever fall short of the speed with which every listener's spirits lifted, buoyed by

Ernestine Dillard

each ascending glissando of Dillard's voice as she reached the song's apex, with each repeat of the word "America" going inexplicably higher and higher. Her final phrasing of the song's last words "my home sweet home" is transcendent, and for that moment the world seemed stronger from our shared humanity than weaker because of one inhumane act. During the weeks following the service, the Oklahoma City Philharmonic received calls and letters from across the country wanting a recording of the all the music in the service, but certainly driven by Dillard's vocal and emotional powerhouse finale. As a result, Warner/Reprise Nashville produced a compact disc of the event's music, including "God Bless America", on *Oklahoma City Relief: A Time of Healing* (1995), with a portion of the proceeds benefitting Project Recovery OKC. While not the performance of the actual service (the CD was recorded June 2, 1995 in Oklahoma City), Dillard's rendition is just as beautifully sung, and really more balanced as an audio document than the live performance, which was driven by the intense feelings of everyone present that day. Interested parties are well-advised to seek out the live version on youtube.com by just searching Ernestine Dillard's name.

While the version of "God Bless America" will probably be what Dillard is most remembered for musically by the wider public for many years, people closer to her, or who have benefitted from her tremendously selfless charity work, know she is much more than one performance of a patriotic standard, no matter the widespread impact of that one moment in time. After a 30-year nursing career, Ernestine has traveled the world on missions trips, participated in a wide variety of memorial services, Christian events and concerts, and maintained a ministry she calls "Moments of Truth" in which she uses the power of music to heal hurting and troubled souls.

According to her website, Mrs. Dillard is the winner of several awards for musical performances, to include the W.C. Handy Heritage Award, and is also an Oklahoma Jazz Hall of Fame Inductee. She has performed for two Presidents of the United States, multiple governors, state senators, and was selected out of 145 entrants to compete with professionally trained female vocalists in the prestigious Savannah on Stage "American Traditions" competition. Her 30-minute musical presentation, including her "God Bless America" medley received a standing ovation and she was awarded the gold medal first prize. With the honor came the opportunity to tour with Della Reese, and perform at the Kennedy Center in Washington D.C. where she has also performed in the National Cathedral. As of 2010, she made her home in Bixby with her husband, Reverend Loomus Dillard.

www.ernestinedillard.org

Dinning Sisters
Lou (b. September 29, 1922)
Ginger and Jean (b. March 29, 1924)
Jean (d. Feb. 22, 2011)

A hallmark of Oklahoma musicians is their adaptability to different styles through various popular music eras. With the naturally sweet harmonies of musically gifted siblings, the Dinning Sisters sang cowboy, Western swing, and country songs on national radio programs like WLS's *National Barn Dance*, and popular songs with big band orchestras as part of that era's "sweet swing" recordings, a style noted for its smooth and easy listening qualities, as opposed to some of the earthier swing groups of **Jay McShann** and Count Basie, or the more complicated and musically sophisticated compositions of Duke Ellington. In a case of being in the right place at the right time and having the talent to take advantage of an opportunity, the trio also benefitted from the musicians strike of 1942 when record labels could only record vocalists, an event that helped established the Dinning Sisters as one of popular music's highest quality vocal groups of the 1940s. Only the Andrews Sisters, and to a lesser extent the Boswell Sisters, rivaled the Dinnings' notoriety on radio and records during their most popular era.

Reared in or near Wichita, Oklahoma, in southwestern Oklahoma's Comanche County, their father, John Dinning, was musical director in their church, and their mother played organ. The Dinning Family consisted of nine childrent: (Don, Vern [Ace], Wade, Marvis, Lucille [Lou], twins Eugenia [Jean] and Virginia [Ginger], Dolores [Tootsie], and

Mark], all of whom, except one brother went into the music business. They all sang in their father's church choir at an early age. Brothers Ace and Vern formed a band, eventually recruiting sisters Jean, Gingers, and Lou to sing in the group, a move that proved fruitful with multiple successes at area talent shows in the girls' pre-teen years. By their mid-teens, Ginger, Jean, Lou were performing as The Dinning Sisters and progressed to their own fifteen-minute show on local radio, and had performed with brother Ace's Orchestra in Illinois. By 1935, the trio was touring clubs and theaters in the Midwest with the Herbie Holmes Orchestra. With their brother, Wade, as manager, in 1940 the trio re-located to Wichita, Kansas, where they were featured daily on KFH Radio's *Ark Valley Boys* program and *Tea Time Jamboree*. With a solid background of performing experience under their belt, the trio and their brother went to Chicago in 1941 to audition for the NBC Radio Network, and were promptly signed to a five-year contract. During the early 1940s, the Dinning Sisters were regulars on Chicago radio programs, to include the *Bowman Musical Milkwagon* and the WLS Barn Dance where they backed up stars such as Perry Como and Kate Smith. Along with reportedly being Chicago's highest-paid radio act in the early 1940s, Hollywood came calling and signed the ladies to a movie contract to sing with Ozzie Nelson's Orchestra in the film, *Strictly in the Groove* (1942). While on the West Coast recording their first film tracks, the Dinning Sisters auditioned for Capitol Records, resulting in a seven-year contract with the label. With a tremendous amount of confidence the trio's harmonious and unified sound, and a need for product in the midst of the musicians' strike of 1942, Capitol released an entire album, *Songs by the Dinning Sisters*, in 1943 that established the group as major music industry figures in the 1940s. Lou left the group in 1946 to get married and pursue a solo career that lasted for ten more years on Capitol with moderate success.

Dinning Sisters original lineup, 1942, (from left): Lou, Ginger, and Jean.

After a three-year stint by Jayne Bundesen, during which time The Dinning Sisters' enjoyed their major hit, the million-selling, and Oscar-winning, "Buttons and Bows." The song appeared in the Bob Hope and Jane Russell film, *Paleface* (1948), a production rife with American Indian stereotypes of the time, but a favorite among Hope fans, and which did propel The Dinning Sisters to platinum status. During this period, the Dinning Sisters also provided vocals for two Disney films, *Fun and Fancy* (1947), and *Melody Time* (1948).

Jean, Boyd, Ginger, and Dolores Dinning, circa 1952 on the 25th Anniversary of the Grand Ole Opry.

Tired of the road life, Jayne retired from the group, and sister Dolores [Tootsie] was called in as a replacement through 1952. While the trio recorded with notable musicians such as Tennessee Ernie Ford, Tex Ritter, and Bob Crosby (Bing's brother) in the 1950s, the sisters' popularity faded as rock and roll rose to dominance in popular music. Two of the sisters continued songwriting and singing projects, notably Jean's composition, "Teen Angel," a #1 hit for their younger brother, **Mark Dinning**, in 1960, on which Dolores sang harmony vocals, leading to her status as one of Nashville's foremost background singers as part of the Nashville Edition. Along with a twenty-five year stint on Hee Haw as a backup singer and performer, Dolores also worked in the 1960s with the Anita Kerr Singers and Jordanaires, a period in which her list of recording credits is extremely impressive, with sessions on recordings by Jim Reeves, Perry Como, Bobby Bare, Patti Page, and Andy Williams.

The Nashville Edition (Dolores second from right) recording Hee Haw Theme in 1968.

During this period, she married Bill Edgin in 1962, and so her background vocal credits appear as Dolores Edgin from that point forward. Dolores is the yodeler of record on the **Merle Kilgore** composition, "Wolverton Mountain," a 1962 hit for Claude King, and Dolores sings multiple back up parts on Bob Dylan's *Self-Portrait* (Columbia, 1970). Additional extremely well-known songs featuring vocals by Dolores include Lynn Anderson's "Rose Garden," Tanya Tucker's "Delta Dawn," and Dolly Parton's "I Will Always Love You," with additional supporting roles on recordings by Elvis Presley, Marty Robbins, George Jones, Tammy Wynette, Barbara Mandrell, Waylon Jennings, Charlie Pride, and many others.

Bill and Dolores (Dinning) Edgin, circa, 2008, Nashville, TN.

According to her website, Dolores has appeared on approximately 10,000 recorded songs, and has received numerous NARAS awards for background vocals, and is BMI Songwriting Award Winner. The family's musical traditions continue with the sisters' nephew, Dean Dinning, who is a bassist with the alternative rock band, Toad the Wet Sprocket. With their outstanding vocal harmonies, charming presentation, and ability to sing various musical styles, the Dinning Sisters are remembered for their sparkling1940s recordings, but should also be thought of as an outstanding training ground for Dolores, who became one of country music's most respected and in-demand session vocalists.

Recommended Listening

For Western swing, rockabilly, and country recordings, see The Dinning Sisters, *Back in Country Style* (Jasmine, 2002); for big band era recordings, see The Dinning Sisters, *Almost Sweet and Gentle* (Jasmine, 2001);

for the greatest hits overview of the sisters' career, to include the Disney tracks, "Buttons and Bows," and their cover of Jack and Woody Guthrie's "Oklahoma Hills," see *The Best of the Dinning Sisters* (Collector's Choice, 1998).

Sources

www.doloresdinningedgin.com

www.singers.com/jazz/vintage/dinning

Dinning, Mark

(b. August 17, 1933 – d. March 22, 1986)

Remembered most for his 1960 #1 pop hit, "Teen Angel," Mark Dinning was born in Grant, Oklahoma, a tiny hamlet with less than 100 residents located in southern Choctaw County. One of nine children (Don, Vern, Wade, Marvis, Lucille, twins Eugenia and Virginia, and Dolores), who all pursued a musical career except one of his brothers, Mark was surrounded by music during his youth. His father was a farmer, but musical director in the local church, his baby sitter was Clara Ann Fowler (later known as **Patti Page**), and three of his sisters formed a vocal group in the 1940s, the **Dinning Sisters**, who had Top 10 single in 1948 with "Buttons and Bows," which won an Oscar. Mark raised turkeys as a child and won first prize in a local 4H club contest.

At seventeen, Mark learned the electric guitar and began performing in local clubs with his brother Ace. After high school, he was drafted and while in the army, he decided to seek a recording contract after his discharge in 1957. He headed to Nashville and auditioned for publisher Wesley Rose, who liked what he heard. Rose phoned Mitch Miller, his friend in New York, who was with Columbia Records. But Miller had just signed a new artist (Johnny Mathis) and rejected Rose's proposition. Rose within six weeks had signed Mark to MGM Records. His early country music career is almost forgotten, however, Germany's Binge Records released *I'm Just a Country Boy* (Binge 1012), which includes songs like "Ramblin' Man", "The Streets of Laredo", "Lost Highway", and "The Black-Eyed Gypsy".

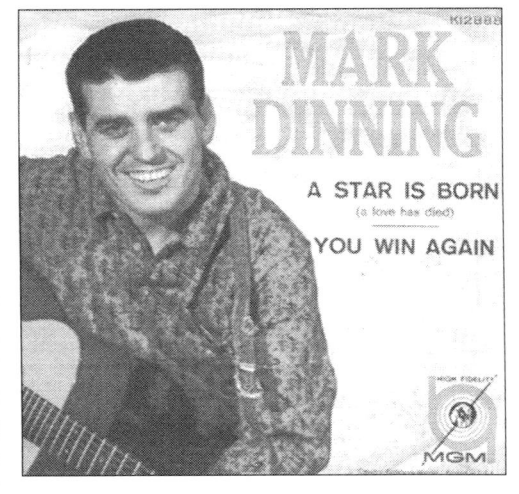

In 1959, Jean, Mark's sister, was reading a magazine article related to juvenile delinquency. The author of the article offered a new name for good teenagers, and suggested "teen angels." As a songwriter, Jean took the phrase and began writing lyrics that evening, and then woke up in the middle of the night and completed the song. At a family dinner shortly thereafter, Jean played several demos for Mark while he was eating, and one of them was "Teen Angel". He liked it so much that before the dinner was concluded, a microphone and tape recorder was set up on the dinner table and he recorded it.

Jean made some 45s of the recording and mailed one to Mark. She did not hear from him for about a month and then called him to find out what had happened to the record. According to Mark, he had not opened the package because he did not have a record player. Jean encouraged Mark to take it to the nearest record shop and play it. He complied with Jean's request and a crowd gathered around the listening booth and asked where they could buy the record. This convinced Mark to take the song to Rose, who was immediately enthralled with it. A change was made from "are you flying up above" to "are you somewhere up above?" Rose called Jean, now Jean Surrey, after her marriage to Red Surrey, and invited her to the recording session to sing backup vocals, but she declined as she had just given birth to a daughter and could not make the trip, so sister Dolores (Dinning) Edgin stepped in and added the harmony vocals.

The teenage death ballad, in which a girl is killed by a train when she goes to get her boyfriend's ring out of a stalled car, rose to the top of the pop charts in the U.S. and cracked the Top 40 in the U.K, despite the fact that many radio stations in both the U.S. and U.K. banned it because of its morbid nature. One British trade paper ran a headline concerning the song, which read "Blood Runs in the Grooves." Had the Brits thought a little about their own musical history, perhaps they would have placed in a tradition of murder and tragic death ballads that go back to the 1600s English broadside ballads.[1] In terms of writing credits on the song, Jean made an agreement with her husband, Red Surrey, that both names would go on any songs either one of them wrote. When Jean and Red were divorced, ownership of "Teen Angel" returned to her as part of the divorce settlement.

By the mid-1960s, Mark felt his time as a pop artist had passed, saying "groups were in and singles were out" once the British Invasion took American popular culture by the throat. He had three chart singles after "Teen Angel", to include both "A Star is Born (A Love Has Died)" and "The Lovin' Touch" in 1960, and "Top Forty News, Weather, and Sports" in 1961, but none came close to his biggest success. Even though his best-known song was a 1960 hit, and as such is one of the early 1960s most recognizable pop songs, "Teen Angel" appears on numerous compilations commemorating the 1950s and 1960s, including the *American Graffiti* movie soundtrack (1993), *Billboard Top Pop Hits: 1960* (1994), *Please Don't Take the Girl* (1996), *Rock N Roll Relix 1954-1959* (1997), *Music That Changed Our Lives: 50s, 60s, and 70s* (1998), *Last Kiss* (2000), *Rock Revival* (2000), *Teenagers in Love* (2001), *Pop Hits of 1950-1967 I* (2005), and is also a karaoke favorite through the modern era. One hit wonders do not go quietly in the U.S. Dinning performed sporadically through 1986 when he died of a heart attack, ironically while driving home in his car from a club appearance in Jefferson City, Missouri, after which he headed up above to join the rest of the teen angels for whom he had been singing for twenty-six years. Sister Jean died at age 86, February 22, 2011, in Garden Grove, California.

Note

1. To begin learning more about British Isles murder and tragic death ballads, as well the larger British ballad tradition, see those collected by Francis Child in *English and Scottish Popular Ballads* (Boston: Houghton Mifflin, 1904), and MacEdward Leach, *The Ballad Book* (New York: Harper, 1955).

Downing, Big Al

(b. January 9, 1940 – d. July 4, 2005)

The only African-American artist to span the musical spectrum from rockabilly, R&B, pop, soul, disco, and country music, country-soul pioneer Big Al Downing is best remembered for his booming voice and joyous live performances, constantly blurring the lines between country, pop, and R&B, as well as compositions, "Mr. Jones", "Touch Me (I'll Be Your Fool Once More)", and "Bring It on Home", all Top 20 country chart hits.

Downing also played piano for such legendary country artists as **Wanda Jackson** and Marty Robbins in some of the first bi-racial American rock and roll bands.

Born in the small Craig County community of Centralia, northwest of Vinita, Downing was one of eleven children. When Al was eight, the family of sharecroppers moved fifteen miles west to Lenapah where the family worked hard on their farm, no doubt building Al into "Big Al" as he and his brothers were paid fifty cents a ton for loading hay onto trailers for the King Ranch of Texas, with thirty bales of hay to the ton. Then, while driving the truckloads of hay and alfalfa from Oklahoma to Texas, Downing listened to country music radio stations all the way, such as KVOO in Tulsa where they would have heard various incarnations of the Wills bands in the late 1940s, as well as KLAC, Nashville, where the family could listen to the Grand Ol' Opry. In a 1992 interview, Downing said, "All they played all day long was country and I just grew to love it." Al also remembered the program after the Opry signed off, John Richbourg's "From Way Down South in Dixie", where host John R played R&B, then called "race" music, as well as "a mix of Gospel, Delta blues, and rock and roll thrown in for good measure. Al's first musical experience was at age ten when he joined his father and eleven siblings to sing in a gospel choir at area churches. He was strongly influenced by a wide array of music genres, including gospel, country, and rhythm and blues. By age ten, Al taught himself to play the piano on an instrument with only forty working keys he found in a trash dump while returning home from cutting hay. The Downing boys loaded the piano onto the back of a hay truck and took it home to use for firewood, only to find it was still playable. "I was about 13 when we brought that piano home," Al laughed in a 2003 interview, "For awhile it was just a stand for the radio. But eventually, I started picking out Fats Domino tunes. Before you knew it, the kids in school were asking if I could play tunes at recess. I never dreamed that it would take me to the places I've been." Domino later recorded two of Downing's compositions, "Mary, Oh Mary" and "Heartbreak Hill."

Big Al Downing

During his teenage years, he began to perform at community functions and high school proms, and won a talent contest at age fourteen sponsored by radio station KGGF in Coffeyville, Kansas, just across the Oklahoma/Kansas border. He played and sang Domino's hit at the time, "Blueberry Hill." Downing's performance impressed Bobby Poe, a Vinita, Oklahoma-born rockabilly bandleader who was in the audience that night, and asked him to join his all-white group, the Poe Kats. Of course, during the 1950s race mixing was still largely unheard of outside of major urban centers on the coasts and in Midwest music towns such as Chicago and Kansas City. However, Poe believed the group could attract more dates if Al would play piano and sing Fats Domino, Little Richard, Chuck Berry, and B.B. King songs, while Bobby and the Poe Cats would cover Elvis, Jerry Lee Lewis and Buddy Holly. After turning down a basketball scholarship offer from Kansas State University, Downing accepted Poe's offer and at age sixteen left Oklahoma for his first tour. The group landed a regular gig in Boston, Massachusetts playing seven nights a week where Al was paid $90.00 weekly. In a 2003 press release for his *One of a Kind* album released that year, he remembered, "It was a crazy time; a time of change. There wasn't much money but the music was great. I wouldn't have missed it for the world."

From 1957 to 1964, Big Al played piano with the group, which recorded several singles on the Dallas-based White Rock label promoted by Lelan Rogers, Kenny Rogers' brother. At a January, 1958 session, the band recorded "Oh Babe" "Rock 'n' Roll Boogie," "Rock 'n' Roll Record Girl," and 1958's "Down on the Farm." The latter was picked up by Challenge Records and narrowly missed the charts, but has become a rock and roll classic, and clocks in at only one minute and thirty seconds, predating brief tunes by punk and hardcore groups of the 1970s (Ramones) and 80s (Minutemen) with their own microscopically short songs. After an electric guitar plucking out the notes to "Old Mac-Donald", the song kicks off with Downing exhibiting a Little Richard-esque command of the band, piano, and his vocals shouting about doing a rock and roll jig down on the farm, then stirs in some fierce electric rockabilly guitar that makes "Down on the Farm" primary in the rock canon of that period with its obvious merging of R&B and rockabilly styling, not necessarily new by 1958, but by that time still adventurous to openly mix the two styles. By '58, Black and White music was growing further apart with the classic rock and roll period starting to close out with Little Richard's religious conversion, Elvis Presley's Army service, Chuck Berry's arrest, Buddy Holly's death, Jerry Lee Lewis' publicity troubles, and Carl Perkins' motorcycle wreck. In any case, The Poe Kats also toured Kansas and Oklahoma during the late 1950s, playing in V.F.W. halls and honky tonks performing the entire gamut of rock and roll. It was during these tours that Big Al first experienced racial segregation by hiding under a blanket while the band booked hotel rooms and eating in a separate dining area in restaurants. **Jim Halsey**, a native of Independence, Kansas, and booking agent for the emerging rockabilly queen **Wanda Jackson**, also from Oklahoma, noticed the group and signed them as her back-up band. While touring with Jackson, the Poe Kats opened shows for such country luminaries as Marty Robbins, Bobby Bare, Red Sovine, Dottie West, and Don Gibson. But the most memorable time for Downing was when he backed Jackson on her Capitol Record sessions in Hollywood, including "Let's Have a Party", her biggest hit, released as a single in 1960.

Big Al Downing, early 1960s

In 2003, Capitol-Nashville re-issued both of Wanda Jackson's albums that feature the Poe Kats, the self-titled first album from 1958, and *Rockin' with Wanda* (1960). In the liner notes of Jackson's recordings, she recalled that the group would have to smuggle Downing into a motel room in a bass fiddle body bag. In the meantime, another session for the Poe Kats at White Rock resulted in interest from several larger record firms, including Carlton and Atlantic. Carlton's Jack Scott released Big Al's "Miss Lucy" and "Just Around the Corner" for national distribution, while "Piano Nellie" was sold to the Atlantic subsidiary, East West. Downing's first pop hit, a duet with Little Esther on Lenox Records, "You Never Miss Your Water (Til the Well Runs Dry)", splashed on the lower half of the Hot 100, peaking at #73, but making the pop chart nonetheless. A straight R&B number, Big Al goes back and forth with Little Esther, urging her on as the two are the straight soul of an over-produced session with strings and a full horn section.

Big Al Downing, circa 2003

As a solo recording artist in the late 1960s, Downing found modest success with his recording of the Marty Robbins song, "Story of My Life," however, he scored another Hot 100 pop chart hit with 1975's "I'll Be Holding On" (#85), a song that fulfills Downing's often positive lyrical aesthetic, in this case affirming the solidity of long-term, committed, romantic relationships. Also his first charting R&B single, "I'll Be Holdin' On" landed on what were then Disco Charts at the time in the United States and Europe, now known at dance music charts. "I'll Be Holding On" is also notable for its merging of the fervor of soul with the steady dance beat (played on a drum kit not by a machine), but filled with strings and wind instruments, a big background chorus, really sounding over produced like a of late 60s Motown music, more designed for non-urban audiences, but when it comes time for an instrumental solo we hear a *banjo* enter the mix, clearly a sensibility that this music was linked to the country, and not the city at all. Once again, an Oklahoma musician merges different genres to establish their own identity. This ability made Downing popular around the world. During the decade of the 1970's, he toured the internationally, performing concerts in England, Spain, Switzerland, Holland, Germany, Italy, France, Greece, Philippines, Japan, Singapore, and Thailand, where he played for The Thai king. In the late 1970s, Downing signed with the Warner Brothers label and released additional popular soul and R&B singles, including "Mr. Jones," "I'll Be Your Fool Once More", "Bring It on Home", "Midnight Lace", "I Ain't No Fool", and "The Story Behind the Story", leading to Downing receiving *Billboard* magazine's New Artist of the Year and Single of the Year Awards in 1979. After Warner Brothers would not sponsor a complete album of only his songs, Downing moved from one "indie" to another in the 1980s, including Team, Vine Street, Jumble, Door Knob, and Rollercoaster. Other minor hits for these labels included 1984's "The Best of Families" (#69 Hot Country Singles); "There'll Never Be a Better Night for Being Wrong"; 1987's "Oh How Beautiful You Are To Me" (#69 Hot Country Singles); 1987's "Just One Night Won't Do It" (#67 Hot Country Singles). In total, Big Al Downing appeared on various national record charts twenty seven times, a feat that must be viewed in terms of him being an African-American who scored singles and enjoyed concert access for both R&B and country music audiences. His only Black peers during his peak years of the 1970s would have been Charley Pride and **Stoney Edwards**, another Oklahoman. With Darius Rucker's recent solo departure to country music stardom after a pop career in Hootie and the Blowfish, and keeping in mind African-American DeFord Bailey, the pioneering harmonica player and entertainer of the Grand Ole Opry, Big Al Downing is really one of only five highly visible and successful African-American men in the country music field, not including crossover R&B artists Solomon Burke, Aaron Neville, or Fats Domino who some enjoyed country music success, or the mountainous genre duality of Ray Charles' "Cryin' Time".[1] Big Al Downing scored 15 singles on the *Billboard* Hot Country Singles chart from 1978 to 1989, with his 1983 self-titled release on Team Records reaching #22 on the Country Album Chart. His 1987 album brought back members of his first band for *Big Al Downing and the Poe Kats*, showing that he still felt strongly about his professional music beginnings and never forgot how he started in the business.

After his last chart success, several labels released both new recordings and compilations of Downing's early music through the 1990s and 2000s. In 2003, the Cayman Islands' based Platinum Express Records released *One of a Kind*, an album that exhibits Downing's multiple influences, running the gamut from country to R&B. On *One of Kind*, Big Al salutes truckers in "Joe's Truck Stop," goes country all the way in "A Cigarette, a Bottle, and a Jukebox," throws down some of his piano pounding roots on "Boogie Woogie Roll," gets as honky-tonk as one can on "I'm Raisin' Hell," and rolls out some gritty urban blues on "Rock Me Baby." Also in 2003, Big Al crossed over into the digital broadcasting age with a national live broadcast from the XM Satellite Studios in Washington, D.C. The live performance on XM Radio was the first-ever live broadcast for the channel. He was enthusiastic and excited about the performance, exclaiming, "I love this – it is so cool." While still performing seventy five shows per year, Big Al was struck with the effects and diagnosis of Acute Lymphoblastic Leukemia in late June, 2005, hospitalized for chemotherapy immediately, and died in Massachusetts just about a week later on July 4, 2005, with his wife of twenty-seven years, Beverly, and many other family members by his side.

Crazy Music Austria Records released two discs posthumously, 2007's *Live at XM Radio* chronicles his satellite radio performance, and a retrospective, 2008's *Best of the Early Years*. A member of the Rockabilly Hall of Fame, his songs were also recorded by Fats Domino, Bobby "Blue" Bland, Tom Jones, and contemporary alternative country artist, Webb Wilder, an overall testament to his music's range and appeal. Quoted in a 2005 press release from Moore Media, Downing said he "loves to hit the stage," adding, "I get a thrill out of making the audience feel good. It's not about me; it's about the people who are listening and making them happy." At the end of the press release, he indicated "the rewards have been many" for choosing a life in music, but his only regret was "not keeping track of that ol' upright piano" where it all started, down on the farm in Lenapah, Oklahoma.

www.bigaldowning.com

Note

1. For those interested in learning more about the contributions of African-Americans' contributions to country music, see the 1998 historical booklet and hear the 3-CD set in *From Where I Stand: The Black Experience in Country Music* (Warner Brothers, 946428-2), which contains Al Downing's "Down on the Farm" and "Touch Me (I'll Be Your Fool Once More)".

DuBois, Tim

(b. May 4, 1948)

One of the most successful music industry executives, producers, managers and songwriters in of the modern era, Tim Dubois' name may not be instantly recognizable to the general public, but they are aware of him unconsciously through hit songs he has written, artists he discovered, signed, or produced, and record labels he led to massive commercial success with extremely popular artists. Along with producing a gold and platinum albums by significant country music artists, just a few of which are Brooks & **Dunn**, BlackHawk, and Diamond Rio, he had five #1 country hits. His songs were recorded also recorded by Alabama, Asleep at the Wheel, Glen Campbell, **Vince Gill**, Ricky Skaggs, Jerry Reed, **Bryan White**, and **Restless Heart,** among others. Additionally, during his tenure as vice president and then president of Arista Records, Nashville (1989-2000), he oversaw record sales of eighty million by artists on the label.

James Timothy DuBois was born in Grove, Oklahoma to school teachers Everett and Jessie DuBois. His father could chord around on piano and play harmonica, but was not supportive of his choice to be a musician, and his mother was not musical. His older brother, Edward, played trombone and sang; Tim started to pick up the guitar at age 14 in 1962, which obviously impacted his younger brother, Randy who also played guitar and later wrote songs with Tim. With a fire really lit under DuBois by the Beatles, he joined various bands while in Grove High School. According to DuBois, in a July, 2010 telephone interview, he never thought about writing songs, or even where they came from, until he went to a student council conference summer camp in Edmond at what is now the University of Central Oklahoma (then Central State College). When a roommate played a song he had written himself, Tim was struck with the idea that he could do that, and became obsessed by the idea of being a songwriter. That led to one music theory class with the high school band director in Grove, James Rowe. In that class Tim learned more about how songs work, chord structure, and how music resolves, among other basic aspects of music terminology and technique.

Tim DuBois

After high school, Tim continued to play in folk and rock and roll bands, namely the New Avengers, when he enrolled at Oklahoma State University in 1966. The group started as the Avengers, but had to be re-named after one year due to half the band being drafted right in the middle of President Lyndon B. Johnson heightening of the Vietnam War. A ten-piece band, The New Avengers played a variety of styles, but focused on R&B with a horn section, playing fraternities, or occasional shows in the dorms without the horn section. DuBois remembers the New Avengers as being average to mediocre, and not nearly as good as the #1 group in Stillwater at the time, Mag 7. Even though he was playing music and living a musician's lifestyle, he did not cease his academic goals. After earning his B.S. and M.S. in accounting in 1971 and '72, respectively, he moved to Dallas where he worked in the financial industry, to discover his executive peers were fans of the outlaw country movement rising up out of Texas at the time, led by Willie Nelson, Waylon Jennings, Michael Martin Murphy, Jerry Jeff Walker, etc. According to Victoria Lee in a feature on DuBois in *Distinguished Oklahomans*, a compilation of well-known Oklahomans' bios, this spurred him on to start checking out books in the Dallas Public Library on the music industry, specifically, Clyde Davis' *Inside the Record Business* (Ballantine, 1976), a prescient choice as DuBois would later work for Davis.[1]

After working for the Federal Reserve Bank of Dallas from 1973 to 1974, Tim moved back to Oklahoma where he pursued doctoral studies at Tulsa University and OSU, and taught as an instructor of accounting at TU (1974-76) and OSU (1976-77), during which time he met fellow OSU student, **Scott Hendricks**, in 1974, and the two began writing songs together, along with other friends in Stillwater. In the winter of 1975 DuBois and Hendricks made their first attempt at pitching songs in Nashville, setting up meetings with publishers before they left as a result of Tim's research on the music industry, and sold one song written by Tim and his younger brother, Randy. The experience started a series of road trips between Nashville and Oklahoma that struck pay dirt in 1977 when Verne Oxford recorded Tim's "Good Old Fashioned Saturday Night Honky Tonk Bar Room Brawl", and had a moderate hit with it at #55 on the *Billboard* Hot Country Chart. With that much encouragement, Tim loaded up the family, and moved to Music City in 1977. Unlike many young dreamers who move to Nashville in hopes of a career, Tim Dubois had the advantage of his professional accounting skills, as well as the academic credentials to teach that subject. With his degrees and teaching experience, Tim was able to land almost immediately, and work consistently as an instructor of accounting at the University of Tennessee-Nashville from 1977 to 1980, Tennessee State University, Nashville (1980-81), and at Vanderbilt University from (1981 to 1985). The academic lifestyle provided DuBois with the malleable time schedule needed for the creative work of his songwriting, and he took full advantage of it.

From 1977 to 1985, Tim Dubois exploited his musical abilities and life experiences for more than twenty Hot Country Chart singles, contributing music, lyrics, production, or all three. This period began to peak in the fall of 1981, when Razzy Bailey scored a #1 *Billboard* Hot Country single with "Midnight Hauler", a song for which DuBois wrote the lyrics after driving on Highway 51 between Stillwater and Tulsa while traveling to teach a class at TU. While heading east outside of Yale on what can be a lonely stretch of two-lane state highway that cuts a path through the scrub oaks of the Cross Timbers and bridging the Cimarron River, an 18-wheeler with a bumper sticker reading "Midnight Hauller" (sic) blasted by him way above the legal limit of 65 mph. With that title as a beginning inspiration he wrote more on the way back from Tulsa, and eventually added the music with Wood Newton, the song's co-author. Along with the story of its creation, "Midnight Hauler" is interesting for several reasons as a DuBois project: 1) Tim's location in Oklahoma busts out of the song when Razzy the trucker can't wait to get home because he's "got a little woman waiting back in OKC." 2) One can also place the song in the "Okie Boogie" tradition that dates back to early statehood era boogie-woogie piano players, and the boogie numbers played by territory and swing bands of the 20 and 30s, to the "**Bob Wills** Boogie" (1946), or **Jack Guthrie**'s "Oakie Boogie" (1947), then followed much later by the Tractors, who had their biggest success in 1994 on DuBois' label, Arista-Nashville. After listening to the Razzy Bailey tune, one can hear a boogie continuum template that surfaces on The Tractors' "Baby Likes to Rock It" with the train rhythm snare, boogie bass, knife sharp electric guitars, and a near-talking singer (**Steve Ripley**) commanding the story in a confident regional accent. Not to say one inspired the other, as both come from the same well spring of regional and musical inspiration, but comparing the two with the previously mentioned antecedents is interesting stylistically, and the two songs "Midnight Hauler" and "Baby Likes to Rock It" do have Dubois in common. 3) Finally, the song uses the highway setting or driving/traveling motif, an element of many of DuBois' songs. Dubois explains that when he would get writer's block, he would get in his car and drive until he figured out what was missing in the song, or would often come up with lyrics in his extensive business travels. Obviously, his techniques worked, as he would have two more #1 singles within the next year after "Midnight Hauler" was #1.

By December of 1981, Alabama struck #1 on the country singles chart with another

DuBois co-write, "Love in the First Degree", and also made it as far as #15 on the *Billboard* Hot 100 pop chart. Flash forward to the next summer (1982), when Dubois' has another hit with the hilarious divorce song (if divorce can ever be hilarious) recorded by Jerry Reed, "She Got the Goldmine (I Got the Shaft)". The song resonated instantly with a country music audience all-too-familiar with the subject *not* to get a laugh out of Reed's delivery, and the song's narrative of starting out a marriage innocently enough, and then realizing at the end that one is going to come out of it out worse than when going in. The song was #1 on the country singles chart in September 1982, and even inched up the pop charts to #57. That capped a twelve-month period in which DuBois was the writer or co-writer of three hit singles, for which he received the CMA Triple Play Award, recognizing such an accomplishment.

Songs that are popular enough to register as crossover songs are always an attention-getter in the music industry which constantly seeks to broaden its base marketing appeal. Nominated for six awards for the three #1 songs of 1981 and 1982, and given the Award of Merit for "Goldmine" by the Nashville Songwriters Association International that year, Tim Dubois had more than arrived, he had started a whole new party. He continued teaching, songwriting and producing through 1985 when he was able to become a full time music industry executive as a Partner at the talent management firm of Fitzgerald/Hartley. That evolved after he put together the band Restless Heart, got them their contract with RCA, and began looking around for suitable management for the group. Not finding any, he approached Fitzgerald/Hartley, then in Los Angeles without any presence in Nashville, and convinced them into letting him open a Nashville office with first client Restless Heart, followed by Foster & Lloyd (forecasting another famous duo with "&" in the name that would occur later). During three years of heading the Nashville office from 1986 to 1989, DuBois would oversee three gold albums for Restless Heart and co-write their 1988 #1 single, "Bluest Eyes in Texas". Also as a result of his connection with Fitzgerald/Hartley, he became acquainted with their already established client, **Vince Gill**, a new natural fit for the Nashville office. Dubois began partnering with **Vince Gill**, and the two co-wrote "Oklahoma Swing", a 1990 #13 country single featuring a Gill duet with **Reba McEntire**. In the meantime, legendary record producer and executive, Clive Davis, contacted DuBois in 1989 about opening a Nashville division of Arista Records, all of which swirled around the heady country music business years of the late 1980s and early 1990s as **Garth Brooks** re-energized Nashville as an American popular music center. As much as Garth Brooks did at the time, DuBois' contributions to the country music industry are also prolific.

As the head of Nashville's Arista's office, DuBois continued tremendous success for himself, his boss, and his acts. After starting cold in 1989 as vice president and general manager of Arista-Nashville, DuBois led the label to being the #2 label in the industry within 18 months, and after four years had overseen seventy-five million record sales for the company. By 1993, Tim was promoted to president of the company, and served in that role until 2000. With extreme fiscal acumen, and a firm ideological grip on country music as a popular music product, DuBois discovered and/or signed Alan Jackson, Brooks & **Dunn**, Brad Paisley, **The Tractors**, Lee Roy Parnell, BlackHawk, Pam Tillis, BR-549, and Diamond Rio. Then, produced hugely successful albums by Steve Wariner (Gold), Diamond Rio (Gold (2) & Platinum (2)), and BlackHawk (Gold & Double Platinum).[2] All told, Arista-Nashville sold eighty million-plus albums under his leadership. However, he did not leave behind his songwriting just because he was in the executive's chair.

In 1991, Vince Gill's recording of another co-write with Dubois, "When I Call Your

Name," bounced to #2 on the *Billboard* Hot Country Chart, and #1 on *Radio & Records'* country singles chart; via the song's popularity and its repeated awards, "When I Call Your Name" rose to #1 on the Recurrent Chart, a *Billboard* chart that tracks songs that have had their initial chart run but return as a result of sales and airplay. As DuBois' fifth #1 single, "When I Call Your Name" received the CMA Song of the Year, *Music City News* Single of the Year, and the Songwriters Assn, (NSAI) Award of Merit. The song appeared on another *Billboard* chart in 2010 as a most streamed video clip on the America Online web streaming service, again displaying its popular longevity.

After leaving Arista-Nashville in 2000, DuBois endured a brief, one-year term as President of Creative Content at Gaylord Entertainment Group, before transitioning to senior partner of Universal South Records from 2002 to 2006. Along with established popular country artists Phil Vassar, Joe Nichols, and Marty Stuart, Universal South branched into alternative country, red dirt music, and the Americana radio format by signing Waylon Jennings' son, Shooter Jennings, and home-state heroes, **Cross Canadian Ragweed**. In 2008, with titanic amounts of success and practical experience in the music industry, and still holding the degrees he earned almost forty years before at Oklahoma State, he returned to academia, joining the faculty at Vanderbilt University's Owen Graduate School of Management where he had taught twenty-two years before; in 2010, he taught Business Models in Music Publishing, Artist Management, and Entrepreneurship in the Entertainment Industry. Among multiple recognitions for his work, in 1996 *Business Nashville* touted DuBois as the most powerful person in the music industry; in 1992, *Pollstar* tagged him as Record Executive of the Year; in 1994 and '95, *Entertainment Weekly* included him on its list of the 101 Most Powerful People in the Music Industry. He sits or has served on boards of directors at the highest levels of the music industry in Nashville (ACM, CMA), as well boards serving songwriters, the Country Music Foundation, AND the National Academy of Recording Arts and Sciences. If that weren't enough meetings, in 2010 he also chaired the Nashville Convention and Visitors Bureau, and was a board member at Sun Trust Bank in Nashville.

Also in 2010, he served as the vice president and managing executive of the American Society of Composers, Authors, and Publishers (ASCAP), in Nashville. In that role, he says, "I can protect my profession, and help songwriters." After so much success, he feels it is important to "play a role in helping the industry redefine itself," and in doing so can give back to the business that has provided him with so much. Regarding the next evolutions in the music business, DuBois says he has "no vision for what he thinks it will be", and can only seeing it changing more quickly than slow-moving corporate giants can track.

Tim DuBois is one of Oklahoma's most interesting music stories. Not only did he write and produce #1 hits as a musician and lyricist, because of his degrees in accounting and practical experience in the field, he became a valuable manager, producer, and record label executive. Additionally, a firm lesson is present in his story that indicates having a college degree in a marketable subject can buy a person creative time to pursue their individual goals, whatever those goals may be. That makes him a good and valuable teacher. With regard to lyrical elements of his songs, Dubois mined the gold out of his life experiences of small town Grove, Oklahoma, as well as the cowboy and college town sensibility of Stillwater, and the evolution of his evolving roles as a young man and college student, to husband, father, provider, and professional; often those songs, such as "Big Dreams in a Small Town", "Hummingbird", or "Midnight Hauler", are vibrant with the rhythmic or scenic palate of all the highway traveling, thinking, and dreaming he did between Stillwater, Dallas, Tulsa, and Tennessee, on his way to the top of Mount Nashville.

www.madmanager.com/TimDuBoisSite.html

Note

1. For more details on DuBois' life experience before moving to Nashville, see the essay written by Victoria Lee, who profiled DuBois for her biographical collection, *Distinguished Oklahomans* (Tulsa: A Touch of Heart Publishing, 2002), pp. 77-78.
2. Established by the Recording Industry Association of America, Gold equals 500,000 albums sold, Platinum equals 1,000,000 copies sold, and Double Platinum equals 2,000,000 albums sold.

Jack Dunham

(b. August 31, 1939)

Like many people who are part of history but don't know it at the time, Jack Dunham, a growling rock and roll singer schooled in the 1950s Tulsa music scene, remembered about that era in a 2003 interview, "We were carrying on like crazy wild people. We didn't realize we were making the tracks that Tulsa's rock and roll musicians would be following to this day." Known in the music industry as a talented songwriter who penned Conway Twitty's 1979 #1 single, "Your Love Has Taken Me That High," Jack Dunham was one of the first of the 1950s-era Tulsa musicians to migrate to Los Angeles, where he recorded for Imperial Records in the early 1960s. Dunham is also thought of as the man who introduced rhythm and blues to many young Oklahoma musicians who apprenticed in his Tulsa-based bands in the late 1950s, thereby helping to spawn the combination of rockabilly, blues, and rock and roll that has come to be known as the Tulsa Sound.

An enrolled Cherokee whose Grandmother Dunham was a full blood Cherokee and Grandmother Shoemake was ¾ Cherokee, Jack Dunham was born August 31, 1939 in Albuquerque, New Mexico, to Blanche and Ray Dunham. He moved to Tulsa with his parents when he was one-year-old where he attended Longfellow and Emerson Elementary Schools, Roosevelt and Wilson Junior High Schools, and Tulsa Central High School. Dunham's first musical memories in Tulsa are of riding his bicycle to the Cain's Ballroom and peering through the windows at Johnnie Lee Wills and his Western swing bands in 1949. Dunham also remembers how the pre-rock country boogie of the Wills bands on the radio got his mother's feet tapping in the kitchen while she washed dishes. "Everything that came out of Tulsa in those days came out of Western Swing," Jack says, "we were just another branch of it." In 1951 Blanche gave young Jack a record player and cardboard box full of old 78 rpm records, from which he promptly learned all the words to songs by artists such as Bob Wills and Nat King Cole, among others.

Jack Dunham

While at Central High School from 1955 to 1957, during the peak of the classic period of rock and roll with Elvis Presley as its anointed king, Jack performed with Chuck Fourneir, Bill Ragan, and Bill Miller as the Tri-Lads at various school dances and parties around Tulsa. The first time Jack and his friends heard Elvis was at Chris's restaurant, a lunch hangout across the street from Tulsa Central. Jack remembers, "'Heartbreak Hotel' came on and there was this hush after it. I had to hit my face with the fork I was using to snap me out of it. It was like a bomb went off. Everyone was racing each other after school to the record store to get a copy." After graduating high school, Jack enrolled at Oklahoma State University for a year, and then returned to Tulsa in 1959, ostensibly to attend Tulsa University, but a desire to create the music that was electrifying the 1950s quickly overwhelmed his studies.

Leaping into the 1958 Tulsa music scene already roiling with vocal talents such as Bobby Taylor, Gene Crose, David Gates and Flash Terry, Jack assembled the now legendary Upsetters, named after Little Richard's band. The flamboyant 1950s front man provided a model for outrageous "Jumpin' Jack" Dunham who walked on tables during shows while screaming out rock and roll and R & B. Jack's first band in 1958 featured John "J.J." Cale (guitar), George "Valentine" Metzel (upright bass), and Jimmy Turley (drums). Also during that year, the band evolved into Jackie Dunham and the Upsetters, to include Russell "Leon" Bridges (piano), Cherokee Leo Feathers (guitar), Chuck Blackwell (drums), Ron Ryle (electric bass), and Johnny Williams (saxophone). At various gigs throughout the '59 and early 1960, practically every musician who is noted for participating in the Tulsa Sound made their way through The Upsetters. Guitarists included Lee Weir, Tommy Rush, and Tommy Crook; bassists were Bill Raffensberger, Jack Cox, Gerald Goodwin, Carl Radle, and Ralph Brumett; Bill Boatman and Sammy Dodge played saxophone; Jimmy Karstein, Buddy Jones, Chuck Farmer, and C.B. Glasby were drummers for the group at various times; and pianists Jimmy Manry, Eddie Spraker, Rocky Frisco, and Doug Cunningham also saw playing time. The rotating group of musicians performed regularly throughout Tulsa on the stages of the Pla-mor Ballroom, Casa-Del, Cain's Ballroom, Cimarron Ballroom, the Sheridan Club, the Tropicana Club, Danceland, and the Paradise Club.

It was during these shows that Jack acquired his stage name, "Jumpin' Jack" Dunham, due to his tendency to bound from the tops of pianos and tables, as well as from the stage into the audience, founded in his admiration for the crowd pleasing antics of Little Richard, Jerry Lee Lewis, and Elvis Presley. "It started down at the V.F.W. on 6th Street in Tulsa with that stage that is really dangerously high. I jumped off of it while I was singing and the people went insane. After a while I got tired of crawling back up there." In June 2005, Jack was re-visiting the V.F.W. for the first time in years to set up a show for Oklahoma City rocker Wes Reynolds. "I wouldn't even consider jumping off that stage now," Jack laughed. The Upsetters was just one of many Tulsa groups playing rock and R & B for Tulsa crowds whose tastes were changing during the period just after the classic rock period and just prior to the surf music and Motown successes of the early 1960s. Their set list featured covers by Little Richard, Chuck Berry, Jackie Wilson, the Del Vikings, and occasionally one of Jack's own songs.

Dunham made his first recordings in 1959 while working at KVOO radio and television. Setting up Johnny Cale on guitar, Bill Boatman on bass, Jim Turley on drums, and (Leon) Russell Bridges on organ, Jack provided vocals for "Lonely Girl," written by Dunham and Boatman, and "You Don't Need a Man Like Me," a bluesy love ballad. With the experience of getting their music down on an acetate master, the group headed down to Oklahoma City to record at Gene Sullivan's studio, then just about the primary non-radio station recording studio in the state. They re-did "Lonely Girl," and a new blues tune penned by Dunham, "I'll Leave It Up To You," both of which were released in 1959 on a 45rpm single by a vanity label out of Shawnee, Dixie Records, but the single generated little interest outside of their hometown.

Continuing to perform and get tighter as they played on a regular basis in early 1959 at the Tropicana Club in south Tulsa, the Upsetters featured Feathers on guitar, Williams on sax, Russell on piano, Ryle on bass, Blackwell on drums, and Jack on vocals. In early '60, Dunham booked the group back into Sullivan's studio with Cale sitting in for an ailing Leo Feathers. The group recorded Cecil McNeely's "Something on Your Mind" and Titus Turner's "All Around the World," not released until Jack moved to California in May of 1960 and struck a deal with Dondee Records. Close listeners to the song will hear Jack say, "Go, John", referring to Cale, when the now-famous guitarist starts to take his solo. Dunham bought the master for $35.00 from Sullivan and took it back to Tulsa.

Not long after the "All Around the World" session, Jack's life-long buddy Bill Miller, who had moved to Los Angeles in 1959 to work in the film industry, called Jack to offer a low-level job at KTLA-TV, Jack loaded up wife Bobbie and Jack Jr. into a 1950 Ford and headed west on Route 66, making him one of the first of his generation of Tulsa musicians to migrate to the West Coast, making the trip in 1960.

At work by the following Monday via Miller's connections, Jack watched job postings on the KTLA mailroom bulletin board and soon took a job in the mailroom at Paramount Pictures. While running mail during the bulk of the day to Paramount offices and stars such as Yul Brynner, Jack switched his lunch hours to be able to try to bend the ears of record industry executives, finally getting "Something On Your Mind" and "All Around the World" out on Dondee Records under the name "Jackie Dunham and the Hollywood Weekends." The song received some moderate West Coast airplay, but more importantly proved his abilities and potential as a vocalist to the public and the Hollywood music industry. While working in Paramount's purchasing department, Jack parlayed an acquaintance with Bobby Darin into a meeting with movie star and radio personality, Pat Buttram, largely known as Gene Autry's movie sidekick and Mr. Haney on television's *Green Acres*. Buttram introduced Dunham to Al Joslow, who had managed Tommy and Jimmy Dorsey, and Joslow landed Jack an audition at Imperial Records, then featuring Fats Domino, Ricky Nelson, and Slim Whitman. By the following week he signed with Imperial as "Jackie Dunham" and within two months had recorded four songs.

Jack Dunham's 1961 Imperial Sessions sit at the crossroads of the 1950s rock and roll sound that by then had been completely commercialized by singers such as Frankie Avalon, Fabian, and Bobby Rydell, and prior to the oncoming British invasion that served up grittier American R&B back to the land of its origin. Dunham recorded two of his own songs at the sessions, "Slow Down Your Life," and "My Yearbook," both of which have a decided 1950s flair musically and lyrically. Of particular interest is his recording of "Early in the Morning," previously recorded by Buddy Holly and co-written by Bobby Darin. Jack's vocal style on the record is very reminiscent of what becomes Mick Jagger's early style: the scratchy blues shout, the mix of a soulful croon, and the deliberate swagger of Elvis Presley.

Also of note on the recording is Muskogee native, Barney Kessel, as the guitarist on the session. Kicking off "Early in the Morning" with a blues riff that further illustrates Kessel's own musical diversity as a session player, the track also how Oklahomans had already infiltrated the Southern California studio scene by the time the young Tulsa musi-

Jack Dunham, circa 2000, Bixby OK.

cians started arriving in the early 1960s. Already nervous before the session, Jack really butterflied up when he was introduced to Barney Kessel, whom Jack knew from Kessel's work on Julie London's records, but didn't actually know what the famous jazz and session guitarist looked like. "He was real nice to me," Dunham remembers about Barney, "and he just said, 'you go on over to the microphone and sing. You'll do all right or Al (Joslow) wouldn't have signed you in the first place." The Imperial session closed out with a cover of Fats Domino's "I Think of You," on which Jack shows influences of Domino and Jerry Lee Lewis, but exhibits a gutsier vocal style than any of the highly packaged East Coast singers of the early 1960s could achieve convincingly.

On the strength of his Imperial singles and their success in the western and southwestern United States, Jack assembled a band and began touring those regions, as well as making TV appearances on the Wink Martindale Show, Steve Allen Show, and Lloyd Thaxton Show in Hollywood. After strain on his family urged Jack to come off the road, he met Bob Keane, founder of Del-Fi Records, and the man who discovered, produced, and recorded Ritchie Valens. Keane introduced Jack to Gene Autry and Joe Johnson, respectively the principal owner and operator of Autry's 4-Star Music Publishing Company, and they signed Jack to a one-year songwriting contract. While writing songs for 4-Star he met another young vocalist and songwriter, Glenn Campbell, who recorded five of Jack's songs as demonstration recordings. One of the songs, "Hurry Up Sundown," was recorded by Ricky Nelson for Imperial, but never saw the light of day after Nelson's death. Also at 4-Star, Jack met Glen Kastner with whom he co-wrote songs for Lonzo and Oscar, who were the opening comedy act at the time for country singer Eddy Arnold, as well as a song recorded by Hank Snow, "Listen." With limited success and his contract up at Imperial, Dunham began looking back across the country for opportunities, and found them in Clovis, New Mexico.

While also visiting family in Clovis in 1964, Jack checked out the Norman Petty Recording Studios. At the time, Petty happened to be recording Jimmy Gilmer and the Fireballs. After introducing himself to Petty, Jack was invited to stay around for the sessions, and on the second day met Ray (Ruffin) Ruff, then playing with his own band, the Checkmates, but who had also played with Buddy Holly's Crickets in the 1950s. Ruff operated a studio and booking agency in Amarillo, Checkmate Productions, and after an invitation from Ruff, in 1964 the Dunham family took up residence in Amarillo so Jack could write songs and work in Ruff's studio. In 1965, Jack's second son, Damon Ray Mills, was born, and over the next two years, twenty of Jack's songs appeared on the Checkmate label, to include recordings by Red Steagall, Buddy Knox, the Checkmates, and J. Frank Wilson, known for his million seller, "Last Kiss." Jack wrote Wilson's follow-up, "Unmarked and Covered with Sand." In 1966, Jack wrote "Rebound to Tulsa," a song that garnered him significant enough attention from Capitol Records for them to release it through their Tower Records label. Subsequently, Jack and Ray Ruff put a band together to support the single and toured through Texas, Colorado, Arizona, and Louisiana. The most fortuitous product of the tour was not the single's success, but Jack's meeting with Conway Twitty at a tour stop in Dallas.

When Dunham met the then-successful rocker, Twitty indicated he was changing from rock to country and was aware of Jack's songwriting through "Big" Joe Lewis, then the bassist for Twitty's band and a friend of Ray Ruff's. Twitty encouraged Jack to call if he ever made it out to Nashville. After a move back to Tulsa to unsuccessfully try and save his marriage in 1967, Dunham took Twitty up on the offer, and by 1968 Dunham was writing for Conway's Twitty Bird Music in Nashville. After two years of songwriting and attempting to manage single parenthood, however, Jack had yet to have any of his songs recorded or released. In a major decision, Jack moved with his two boys to Atlanta, Georgia, supporting himself outside of show business for the first time since 1959 by learning to install wallpaper, and later marrying a girlfriend he'd known before he left Tulsa, Ruth Carnes, and with whom he had his third son, Derek. Jack didn't stop writing, however, and sent "The Memory of Your Sweet Love" to Conway, which he recorded in 1971 for his album, *How Much More Can She Stand* (Decca), and began a decade-long relationship between Jack and Conway wherein the country crooner recorded over thirty of Dunham's songs, eighteen of which still remain unissued after Twitty's death.

In 1972 Conway recorded "Back When Judy Loved Me," Jack's song about his first wife, Diane. Twitty recorded two more of Jack's songs in 1973, "When the Final Change is Made," included on Conway's album, *You've Never Been This Far Before* (MCA), and "Lead Us Back to Love," which surfaced on Twitty's only gospel album, *Clinging to a Saving Hand* (MCA). Using memories of his first wife, Diane, and his second wife, Bobbie, Jack wrote "On My Way to Losing You," manifesting on Conway's 1975 Top 10 album, *This Time I've Hurt Her More* (MCA). In 1976, *Music City News* awarded Jack its "Horizon Award" for being one of country music's most promising "new country songwriters," even though he had been writing songs for almost twenty years by that point. Also that same year, he wrote "At Least One Time," recorded by Conway for his album *Now and Then* (MCA), and recorded by a Texas country singer, Nat Stuckey, for his album, *Independence* (MCA). By 1977, Central Songs Publishing offered Jack a job as staff writer and head of their writing department in Los Angeles, but Dunham did not want to uproot his sons from their schools in Atlanta, so he stayed at home and kept writing, a choice that proved to be the right move when he churned out "Your Love Had Taken Me That High," a song that Conway recorded and took to #1 on *Billboard*'s country singles chart. The album containing the song, *Conway* (1978), reached #13 on the *Billboard* country albums chart. "Your Love Had Taken Me That High" also received a nomination as CMA Single of the Year, but lost out to Kenny Rogers' "The Gambler."

Marking his career in the music industry, Dunham has received several BMI songwriting awards, two CMA awards, and a BMI #1 song award for "Your Love Had Taken Me That High." With this success, Dunham focused more on family and his commercial wallpaper business than songwriting over throughout the 1980s, and returned to Tulsa permanently in the 1990s.

In 2002, Classics Records of Sweden released the compilation, *Rock Til You Drop*, featuring a number of 1950s rockers, to include "Jackie" Dunham on the now legendary "All Around the World". By 2005, Dunham was still writing songs, working with multi-instrumentalist Jim Blair (Neverly Brothers/City Moon). In the early 2000s, Jack also served on the board of directors of the Oklahoma Music Hall of Fame and Museum.

Starting his career with inspirations from the upbeat music of Western Swing and the ebullient rock and roll of the 1950s, Jack Dunham evolved into an R & B showman by 1959 along with some of Tulsa's most prominent musicians as his supporting group, and flirted with regional pop stardom on the West Coast in the early 1960s. Turning to country music songwriting to achieve his greatest professional success, much of which was based lyrically on his real life experiences of trying to keep a family together while providing for them via show business, he experienced the extreme highs and lows of following one's dreams of a music career and lived to tell the story through his songs. Jack Dunham's life in music also amply illustrates the multi-genre background that was nurtured in his hometown of Tulsa, and represents the cross-cultural elements of what is commonly referred to as the Tulsa Sound, but whose roots also are intertwined with the Wills Brothers multi-faceted "Okie Jazz," the country boogie of Jack Guthrie prominent throughout Oklahoma in the late 1940s and early 1950s, and the popular rock and roll of the middle and late 1950s. Jackie Dunham and the Upsetters were a significant catalyst for the musical mélange of blues, rock, and country elements known as the Tulsa Sound that echoed through popular music well into the 1970s via Eric Clapton, and into the 1980s by way of Dire Straits, but had its beginnings in the local clubs of Tulsa's music scene in 1959 and 1960 with "Jumpin' Jack" Dunham stage diving into American popular music history he didn't even know he was making. As of 2011, Jack was retired and living in the Tulsa area.

Dunn, Robert Lee "Bob"

(b. February 8, 1908 – d. May 27, 1971)

Known as *the* number one western swing electric steel guitar player, Bob Dunn was a top-flight musician who serves as the model for all steel guitar players after him in Western swing, and other sub-genres of country music that feature the instrument. Although he may not have been the very first to use the amplified electric guitar, he may be credited with being the father of the electric steel guitar in country music.[1] He is known for his jazz-tinged, single string ad-libs in the pioneering the 1930s Western swing outfit, Milton Brown and his Musical Brownies. Born into poverty either in the rural farm town of Braggs, Oklahoma, just south of Muskogee, or in Fort Gibson which is just twelve miles north of Braggs, Bob Dunn, like many musicians of the early twentieth century, found his ticket out of those dire circumstances by turning to music and excelling in it. Bob's first musical experiences came by accompanying his father, Silas B. Dunn, on fiddle breakdowns in the old time country tradition. One of four brothers born by Iva (Pruitt) Dunn, Bob was the only one who aspired to be a musician. As a child he heard a group of musicians traveling through and became entranced by their use of the steel guitar. He eventually came into possession of one and began to take lessons through correspondence with a Hawaiian native, Walter Kolomoku, who lived in Oklahoma City. Listening to his early recordings, one can hear the influence this training had on Bob's playing. However, many other influences existed in the area where Bob grew up. The family is known to have lived in Fort Gibson during

Bob's youth, the town that also produced jazz singer **Lee Wiley**. Known as Three Forks, where the Verdigris, Grand, and Arkansas Rivers meet, Bob's geographic location placed him just across the river from the music rich town of Muskogee, a regional entertainment center which also produced jazz musicians such as **Barney Kessel**, **Jay McShann**, **Don Byas**, and **Claude "Fiddler" Williams**.

Along with being exposed to all the potential live sources of musical influence, Bob also came of age during the 1920s when phonograph recordings and radio made learning about new styles and players more convenient. Quitting school in the eighth grade, Bob was soon playing professionally in his early teens during the early to mid 1920s. The first known bands Bob played with were the Panhandle Cowboys and Indians, and California Curley and his Cowboy Band. By 1930, Bob was working in Paul Perkins's band at KFKB in Milford, Kansas, voted the most popular radio station in America the previous year. The band played for a quack doctor, J.R. Brinkley, famous for selling "goat gland" to cure all kinds of ailments. During Bob's time in Kansas, he met his wife, and when Brinkley had trouble with the Kansas authorities, the show moved to Texas. To avoid the same troubles he had in Kansas, Brinkley constructed the 75,000 watt station XER in Mexico, just across the Rio Grande River where he was outside the influence of U.S. authorities. After a while with Brinkley, Bob worked and traveled with several western bands, vaudeville tours, and jazz bands. During those years, the early 1930s, Bob began playing trombone, and recorded a few sides with Jimmie Davis. With its slide action, the brass instrument's musical elements found their way into Bob's steel guitar playing technique. Many of his famous ad-libs derived from moving the slide-bar on the steel up and down one string, similar to the way in which a trombone works with its slide. Also about the same time, while Dunn was in New York working wherever he could find jobs on Coney Island, he saw an African-American man playing a slide guitar that had been rigged with a homemade pickup and became inspired to learn more about the instrument.

Many people were experimenting with electric guitars in the early to mid-1930s. During this time, Adolph Rickenbacker and George Beauchamp created one of the first electric guitars, known as the "frying pan," because it looked a frying pan with a long handle, but the instrument did not catch on commercially. Bob Dunn created his own version of the electric steel guitar when he began playing with Milton Brown and & his Musical Brownies. A vaudeville tour landed Bob in Fort Worth in 1934, then the epicenter of the western swing movement, where he went to the studios of KTAT to visit the Brownies who featured a Hawaiian steel number in each one of their broadcasts. After demonstrating his

Bob Dunn

Bob Dunn

style, Dunn became a Musical Brownie and told Milton Brown what he wanted to do with the instrument. Brown procured an amplifier and Dunn attached a homemade pickup, perhaps modeled after the one he had seen in Coney Island, onto a big guitar he bought in Mexico. An admirer of jazz trombonist Jack Teagarden, Dunn began experimenting with the instrument in order to replicate the sounds of brass instruments played in a jazz style. This technique gave him his unique tone and attack. Dunn's addition to the Musical Brownies substantiated the strong foundation of the first western swing group to gain prominence in the Southwest, even before **Bob Wills and his Texas Playboys**. In 1935, the group's popularity led to their first recording sessions for Decca in Chicago. At these sessions, Dunn recorded "Taking Off," his signature tune and country music's first important steel guitar number, available on Rhino Records' *History of Country Music, Vol.1: Legends of Western Swing*. Dunn also recorded important solos on "Cheesy Breeze," "You're Tired of Me," and others during the sessions which had wide ranging implications by virtue of the records being sold by the thousands as a result of the Brownies' fame. Dunn's sound became emulated throughout the Southwest and had influence on everyone from other steel players like Leon McAuliffe, to Texas-born, but Oklahoma raised, jazz guitarist **Charlie Christian**, both of whom would have certainly heard Dunn at least on radio. Don Tolle, a guitar player who recorded with **Johnnie Lee Wills** in the 1950s and had a short stint with Bob Wills, remembered listening to Dunn as a child on the radio, and said, "Dunn played some things nobody ever got, but the man who came closest to replicating his style was Paul Mattingly."

Mattingly, born in Sand Springs, Oklahoma on January 12, 1921, was a career military man who had bands in Colorado and Wyoming, and played with The Alabama Boys in Muskogee, Oklahoma, after his retirement from the Army in 1975. Although Mattingly was only recorded informally, he is recognized as an excellent imitator of Bob Dunn. Because Mattingly would have been at the very impressionable age of fifteen or sixteen when Dunn's recordings with Decca were released, he is a good indication of their impact on young musicians of the era. Additional indications of the popularity of the electric steel guitar included the Gibson guitar company's rush to commercialize the instrument, which they did when the first one shipped from their factory in May of 1936.

In 1936, the Brownies recorded again in a New Orleans hotel room with Dunn turning in more spectacular performances on good time tunes such as "Somebody's Been Using That Thing," blues like "Fan It," and the ballad "An Old Water Mill by a Waterfall." About a month after the New Orleans sessions, Milton Brown suffered fatal injuries in an automobile accident and the band broke up not long after. By 1937, Dunn joined former Brownie Cecil Brower in a western swing band led by Roy Newman on WRR radio in Dallas. Dunn did record with Newman for Vocalion Records in June of 1937, but left soon thereafter to join another ex-Brownie, Cliff Bruner, who had moved his Texas Wanderers to the new home base of Beaumont, Texas. Already recording for Decca, Dunn joined the band of future stars such as Moon Mullican on piano and vocals, and pioneering amplified mandolin player, Leo Raley. Due to internal strife that often afflicts musical groups,

Dunn left the Wanderers and returned to Del Rio and spent the winter of 1937-38 playing over another high-powered border radio station, XEPN. By the spring of 1938, Dunn was in Houston playing on radio shows and joined back up with the Texas Wanderers who had returned to their original base of Houston, and reformed with many of their original stars such as Mullican and Bruner. In September of 1937, the group recorded an excellent session of songs that again demonstrated Bob Dunn's high flying, jazz-tinged solos, but the band broke up again over the winter of 1938-39. Most of the highlights of Dunn's recordings with Bruner were reissued by Texas Rose Records under Bruner's name in 1983 and are still in print.

After leaving Bruner, Dunn formed a short-lived group, Bob Dunn's Vagabonds and recorded a solid session for Decca wherein Dunn even sang one song, "When Night Falls." Soon after the sessions, Dunn broke up the Vagabonds and traveled extensively throughout the Southwest and Southeast, to include a stop in Nashville at the Grand Ole Opry that he did not care for at all. Distinctions have long existed between the schooled Western swing musicians who could read music, and the less formally trained old time country musicians of the Southeast who the Western swing musicians considered mountain musicians cut of a lesser musical cloth. Dunn returned to Houston, reformed the Vagabonds for one lackluster recording session for Decca in 1940, recorded another less-than-stellar set with Bruner, and traveled to Dallas where he recorded with Bill Mounce. The second of these sessions with Mounce is significant because Dunn played with Jimmy Wyble, a nineteen-year-old electric guitarist, who played with Bob Wills and **Spade Cooley** before moving gaining prominent jazz status with Benny Goodman, and who has stated Dunn was a significant early influence on his playing. Also during this time, Bob's alcohol consumption, legendary among his peers who often felt he played better after a few belts, began to take its toll on his patience and playing. He did not like having to play commercial melodies that were essentially lesser versions of his original, unique style. With the arrival of World War II, Dunn served three years in the Navy and returned a somewhat changed person. His drinking problem appears to have abated during the war, and when he returned to Houston he took advantage of the GI Bill by successfully completing his high school equivalency requirements, and enrolling in the Southern College of Fine Arts. Eventually, he earned a master's degree in music. He continued playing in the Houston area and formed the Blue Serenaders, a pop and jazz band, with some of the horn players at the college, and, interestingly, Bob played a lot of trombone with the band. Dunn also joined a couple of Western swing bands in 1948 and 1949, but country music was changing and honky style was becoming more prominent in Texas. Dunn sat in on a few more recordings in 1949 and 1950, but by the fall of 1950 Dunn had opened a music store and focused primarily on his business and teaching. Dunn's sister-in-law, Nina, remembered 1950 as the year Dunn stopped drinking for good and became "the kindest person you would ever want to meet." Bob Dunn's story has gone largely unnoticed in the last fifty years, but some of country music's leading scholars, such as Bill Malone and Nick Tosches, have been partly responsible for keeping Dunn's name in the forefront of record collectors and country music aficionados. In 1995, Kevin Coffey wrote Dunn's life story in *The Journal of Country Music*, as a result of interviews with many of Dunn's relatives and contemporaries.[2] Subsequently, Dunn's legacy is being recognized more and more for his innovation and contributions to country music, such as his induction into The Steel Guitar Hall of Fame. His hall of fame plaque highlights Bob Dunn as "The first steel guitarist to introduce jazz licks into country and western music." On the larger scale of Oklahoma music history, Dunn's ability to combine elements of jazz, blues, and country is a testament to the multiple, multi-cultural influences to which he was exposed as a youth, along with their wide-ranging musical identities and influences.

Notes

1. See the history of the first Gibson electric guitars at the Gibson guitars website, www.gibson.com/products/Gibson/Stories/FirstElectrics, (accessed July 28, 2010).

2. Used primarily for this essay as a confirmation timeline to coordinate dates and events of Bob Dunn's life from multiple sources, many of which conflict so they are not listed here, see the thorough and detailed accounting of Bob Dunn's life by Kevin Reed Coffey, "Steel Colossus: The Bob Dunn Story." *The Journal of Country Music* 17, no. 2: pp. 46-56. No date is listed on the mimeographed copy of the article sent to the author by relatives of Bob Dunn. Additional correspondence with family members, such as Dale Dunn Jeffers in a letter written to the Oklahoma Music Hall of Fame, 30 March 2000, and forwarded to the author in his role on the board of the hall of fame were also consulted in the creation of this entry on Bob Dunn,

Dunn, Ronnie

(b. June 1, 1953)

With their duo harmonies on up-tempo dance hall country and honky tonk rock songs aimed at the high-pocketed jeans set still boot scootin' and two-steppin across the well-worn dance floors of country music-oriented clubs and venues of Oklahoma, Kix Brooks and Ronnie Dunn are still members of contemporary pop country's superstar elite, even though they decided to disband in 2010. With thirty million-plus albums sold, twenty-three #1 country hits, and a score of music industry awards since their debut album, *Brand New Man* (Arista), debuted on the *Billboard* charts in August, 1991, Brooks and Dunn were known as country hit makers and dynamic live entertainers with their raucous and elaborately stage tour, *The Neon Circus and Wild West Show*. While neither musician is an Oklahoma native, Ronnie Dunn lived in Tulsa and Grove for most of the period between the early 1970s and the early 1990s when he moved to Nashville for good. During that time he experienced **Leon Russell**'s Shelter Records milieu of the '70s, led the house band at two popular urban Tulsa honky tonks during the 1970s and 1980s, had two records with Jim Halsey's Tulsa-based Churchill label in the early '80s, and won one first place in national talent contest in 1988 while still based in Oklahoma. The prize for winning included $30,000 and a $25,000 recording session with producer and Oklahoma native Scott Hendricks, who ultimately alerted Arista Records' head Tim Dubois, also an Oklahoman (see a trend here?), to Ronnie Dunn's material. It was also Dubois who introduced Dunn to Brooks and then signed them as a duo to Arista's Nashville label. The rest, as they say, is a long story written over a short amount of time.

Ronnie Dunn, 2005

By Hugh Foley / 227

While Kix Brooks was born in Shreveport, Louisiana (b. May 12, 1955), and started playing guitar as a child, Ronnie Gene Dunn was born in Coleman, Texas, where his pipefitting and truck-driving father, Jessie Dunn, also a hopeful country music artist, played guitar and sang in a country band called the Fox Four Five. The traditional country music Ronnie's dad played did not have enough appeal for the younger Dunn, however, as he indicates on the Brooks and Dunn website: "My mother [Gladys] and father listened to hillbilly music all the time," Dunn remembers, "[but] the music just didn't rock hard enough for me. If the music had been as hard as the feelings, it'd've been perfect. So, when it was our turn, I was intent on making country *rock*." Before getting to rock, however, Ronnie spent a few years learning the lessons of one of country music's primary themes: traveling. Both through their moves and the elder Dunn's work as long haul truck driver, the Dunns accepted geographical transitions as an economic necessity.

Ronnie's first brush with Oklahoma was when the elder Dunn's work brought them to Tulsa and Ronnie attended Skiatook High School for a year, but the family moved back to south Texas, where Ronnie attended Port Isabel High School, and started playing bass in bands around local nightspots. After high school he majored in psychiatry at Abilene Christian College, which he attended with the goal of becoming a Baptist minister, but couldn't stop playing the honky tonks. Before long Ronnie had to decide between Bible college and country music, and helping him to make the choice was Ronnie's mother, then living in Tulsa since his father started working for Arrow Trucking, the largest state-based trucking operation in Oklahoma. Gladys sent Ronnie a newspaper clipping about Tulsa-based music promoter and entrepreneur Jim Halsey, thinking the young musician could find opportunities in the early 1970s Tulsa music scene of which Halsey was part. After making the move from Texas, Dunn found a Tulsa music community swirling around the Church Studio. Dunn remembers the years around the Shelter Records on the Brooks and Dunn website: "The Shelter crowd was the *most* soulful. You get around those kinds of people and it makes you think because you've witnessed the difference. It certainly set the bar for me – and you can't clear it every time, but it sure sets a standard you can feel good about."

While working a string of odd jobs during the 1970s, Ronnie Dunn led the house band at Duke's Country, then Tulsa's top-notch live music country nightclub. Later, Ronnie and his band opened for touring headliners at Tulsa City Limits, the popular urban honky tonk open from 1985 to 2000 that inspired Brooks and Dunn's first major hit, "Boot Scootin' Boogie." On the band's website in 2002, Dunn remembered how playing in those clubs inspired his overall understanding of how a group succeeds at the club level: "From playing in bands and watching the patterns of what people would like to dance to – because in Oklahoma and Texas, if they don't dance, you're dead… it's like a honky tonk education. You have to stand and deliver just to get in."

After records in 1983 and 1984 with Churchill records failed to boost his career beyond regional status, Dunn continued to work outside of the music business during the week, while playing on the weekends. Around the time he had moved to Grove by 1988, where he was working in a liquor store, Ronnie's friend and **Tulsa Sound** veteran, Jamie Oldaker, who has played drums for Eric Clapton, entered Dunn's name in the 1988 Marlboro Talent Roundup. With a demo tape featuring the musicians that essentially became The Tractors, minus **Steve Ripley,** who was then working as the band's recording engineer since he owned the Church Studio in which they rehearsed and made the demo, Dunn's band won the Tulsa regional competition and earned the right to compete in Nashville at the finals, which they also won. Along with the prize money the group split, they also received $25,000 worth of studio time with Oklahoma native Scott Hendricks who recorded three songs: "Boot Scootin' Boogie," "You Don't Know Me," and "The Dean Dillon Song." Hendricks passed the songs along to another Oklahoman, Tim Dubois, who had just cranked up Arista's Nashville label, and who liked the songs so much he flew to Tulsa to see the band play at Joey's Bar and then advised Ronnie to move to Nashville. Unsure of relocating, Dunn had still not moved to Music City in 1990 when Dubois called to get permission to include "Boot Scootin' Boogie" on Asleep at the Wheel's *Keepin' Me Up Nights* (Arista, 1990). Dunn finally signed with Dubois in 1990. However, Ronnie had not yet moved to Tennessee and preferred to commute back and forth from Oklahoma while seeing how things would turn out in Nashville.

With Alan Jackson as the lead act on Arista at the time, Dubois did not want to introduce another solo performer through the label too soon, so Dubois suggested Ronnie work out some songs with another young guitarist, singer, and songwriter, Kix Brooks. When the two started working on demos together, Dubois recognized the easy chemistry between the two singers, and suggested they work as a duo. Both blanched at first, sure they could have careers on their own, but Dubois offered them a contract and they signed to Arista as "two-show." Within a year, *Brand New Man* (Arista, 1991) hit the shelves and set the course for the musical brand of Brooks and Dunn. Dunn's memories of the era were on the Brooks and Dunn website in 2002: "I remember driving back and forth from Tulsa to Nashville all the time. We had a Ford Explorer and I put 100,000 miles on it that year. In 1991, I heard "Brand New Man" for the first time on the radio when I was coming into Nashville. That was one of the last trips."

Certified in 2002 for sales of six million units, with three million of those coming between 1991 and 1993, *Brand New Man* set a steady course for Brooks and Dunn that continued unabated throughout the 1990s and into the 2000s. The album's title track opens the disc and features the two singers' now instantly recognizable harmonies, along with lyrics that speak of a character's conversion from a disposition of "a wild side a country mile wide" into a brand new man who can settle down and love a woman right. The song was the first of four from the album to reach #1 on the country charts (a feat never accomplished by a duo or group in successive fashion), also to include "My Next Broken Heart," a fatalistic weeper about not being able to stay in love, and "Neon Moon," a perennial slow dance favorite when the hour gets late and last minute intimate deals are being struck in the glow of beer joint neon signs.

Ronnie Dunn (left) with Kix Brooks, 2005

While those three songs were hits, none had more cultural impact than "Boot Scootin' Boogie" that remained at the #1 spot on the country charts for four weeks and crossed over into

By Hugh Foley / 229

the pop Top 50 while spawning a national resurgence in country line dancing. Written by Dunn to both commemorate and provide a tune for the country line dancing at Oklahoma and Texas honky tonks, the song does not mention the Tulsa City Limits club specifically, but the opening line gives plenty of references for those who frequented the place "Out in the country past the city limits sign," while making the song generic enough for dance halls throughout the region. Traceable to the pop culture group dancing of the 1970s disco period known as the Bus Stop, then filtered through the urban cowboy flash of the early 1980s, line dancing is still one of the most popular group activities in Oklahoma honky-tonks. While some dancers participate nonchalantly, others concentrate hard to keep up, and others, buoyed by their choice of adult beverages, laugh through the whole process. More often than not, however, Brooks and Dunn's "Boot Scootin' Boogie" is still the song of choice for the dance that doesn't leave anyone in the house out, except the bartenders and bouncers, most of the time. The duo magnified the whole trend by releasing a six-and-a-half-minute club mix of the song on their second album, *Hard Workin' Man* (Arista, 1993). Before it was all said and done for *Brand New Man*, however, the album stayed on the charts for an incredible three years straight.

Before *Hard Workin' Man* really got underway, Brooks and Dunn started receiving what would be steady string of awards for their recordings and live performances. Kix Brooks explained on a 2005 Brooks & Dunn promotional radio disc for *Greatest Hits II* that **Garth Brooks**' impact on the country music concerts influenced their live shows. Brooks says, "I think Garth had a lot to do with that, and the big explosion around him. His thing opened up the live aspect of it, the production aspect, where we could broaden all that to a younger audience and take off with more of rock live approach, use instrumentation with more force to reach audiences." Accolades started piling up for their performances. B&D were named CMA's Vocal Duo of the Year in 1992 and 1993, and started headlining shows in 1993 as *Hard Workin' Man* produced more hit singles to bolster their already hit-filled set. The Top 5 title track featured Ronnie belting out a sympathetic tune for the hard working men and women who like to let it loose on the weekends. The single also earned the pair their first GRAMMY in 1993 for Best Country Performance by a Duo or Group. Also taken from *Hard Workin' Man*, "We'll Burn That Bridge When We Get There", a song about rebound love, made it to #2 on *Billboard*'s Hot Country Chart, and a slow ballad lamenting a lost love, "She Used To Be Mine", crested the top of the *Radio and Records* country charts in 1993. Still pulling singles from the album, Brooks and Dunn hit the Top 5 again in 1994 with Kix singing "Rock My World (Little Country Girl), and had another #1 country hit via "That Ain't No Way to Go", both from *Hard Workin' Man*, an album that sold more than four million copies. Not

Brooks and Dunn with Reba McEntire, 1998

surprisingly, Brooks and Dunn were named CMA's "Vocal Duo of the Year" in 1994 (and again in 1995, 1996, 1997, 1998, 1999, 2001, and 2002).

The third Brooks and Dunn album, *Waitin' on Sundown* (Arista, 1994) continued their formula for success: lovelorn characters and general social desolation that has long been a prominent country music theme ("She's Not the Cheatin' Kind", "You're Gonna Miss Me When I'm Gone", and "A Few Good Rides Away); tight harmonies between the two men on almost every song, and at least a few of tunes about embracing the rowdier side of Saturday night ("Whiskey Under the Bridge", "She's the Kind of Trouble I Don't Mind", and "My Kind of Crazy"). The up-tempo "Whiskey Under the Bridge" landed the group another Top 5 hit in 1995, and "If That's the Way You Want It" recalled the easy crooning style of Western swing, emphasized by Dunn's imitation of a **Bob Wills** call during the guitar solo. Major awards followed their career's success with Brooks and Dunn being the ACM Entertainer of the Year in 1995 and 1996, along with holding the ACM's title of Best Vocal Duo from 1991 to 1997.

Brooks and Dunn, Red Dirt Tour poster,

A month after Brooks and Dunn released their fourth album, *Borderline* (Arista, 1996), CMA awarded the duo Entertainer of the Year and they promptly scored a number one hit from *Borderline*, "My Maria", a cover of B.W. Stevenson's 1972 pop hit that earned them a GRAMMY Award for Best Country Performance by a Duo or Group in 1996. The remainder of the album often sounds like a lesser imitation of the duo's stellar earlier material, with the exception of Ronnie's obvious homage to his trucker dad, "White Line Casanova", that starts out with the line "I'm dead headin' down from Tulsa." One has to wonder if the constant grind of the music business caused Brooks and Dunn to rely more on formula than inspiration for *Borderline*, but hardcore fans didn't seem to mind as the album sold over two million copies. With enough scores to justify it, the duo released a *Greatest Hits* (Arista) package collection in 1997 that sold more than three million copies and included three new songs, one of which was a hit, "Honky Tonk Truth", that relied on their trademark danceable twang-rock. With no reason to rush, they took two years to release their next album, 1998's double platinum *If You See Her* (Arista), featuring an ace cover by Dunn of **Roger Miller**'s "Husbands and Wives" (#1), showing why that song's universality is timeless, a collaboration with **Reba McEntire** that also charted #1, "If You See Him/If You See Her", and a third #1 country single, "How Long Gone". The album is a also an interesting marketing partner with Reba's album, *If You See Him*, (also released in 1998), and sharing the single "If You See Him/If You See Her". The duo change their sound somewhat on *Tight Rope* (Arista, 1999) by enlisting the talents of producer Byron Gallimore (Faith Hill, Tim McGraw), but dug back for another familiar pop hit for perhaps the album's strongest track, John Waite's 1984 pop hit, "Missing You." While most artists would be satisfied with a gold record, 500,000 copies sold of *Tight Rope* seemed like the group's fan base was holding strong, but the casual country listener and more youthful spender that makes up a lot of the music industry's purchasing element was not embracing the group on that CD.

By Hugh Foley / 231

"Bouncing back" in 2001 with *Steers & Stripes* (Arista) that debuted at #1 on the *Billboard* country album charts and eventually sold a million copies, Brooks and Dunn sounded familiar and professional, if a little bit too safe on the smooth country side for traditional honky-tonk rockers. The album also marked the first one by the duo that did not feature songs mostly written by themselves, with Ronnie only contributing to one, "Good Girls Go to Heaven," that either borrows, or consciously exhibits, a guitar riff from the Kinks' "(Wish I Could Fly Like) Superman," a lyrical motif from the Rolling Stones' "Some Girls," and a vocal delivery from Dire Straits "Money for Nothing." Dunn acknowledges an inspirational drought of sorts when he thanks producer Mark Wright on CD's liner notes for "bringing a whirlwind of much needed creativity and energy to the table."

While *Steers and Stripes* often coasts on the massive production qualities for which Nashville country music has come to be known, the album still produced three #1 singles in the national emotionally and psychologically draining time after September 11th, 2001: "The Long Goodbye," a heartbreaking ballad about the end of a love affair; "Only in America," a pluralistic song by Brooks about diversity in the United States; and "There Ain't Nothing 'Bout You" which became *Billboard*'s Most Played Country Song of 2001, and stayed at the #1 spot for six consecutive weeks on the Hot Country Singles chart. While their own songwriting may have slowed to some extent, Brooks and Dunn's ability to pick hits aimed at their working class fan-base, and tailor made for the duo's familiar, and one would have to say, comforting, voices jettisoned them into the twenty-first century as top-of-the-line country superstars.

Confirmation of this fact came in 2001 and 2002 when they were named CMA's Entertainer of the Year both years. By the end of 2002 the duo released their first holiday album, *It Won't Be Christmas Without You* (Arista), and had been awarded the Country Radio Board's Humanitarian of the Year award in recognition of their public work for the Monroe Harding Children's Home, Ronald McDonald House, St. Jude Children's Hospital, and the Women's Hospital at St. Thomas Moor where they financed breast cancer imaging machines. Additionally in 2002, Brooks and Dunn won the American Music Award as Favorite Country Duo or Group, the CMT Flameworthy Award for Duo of the Year, and the CMA's Duo of the Year for the 10th time. In February, 2003, Brooks and Dunn received the Inaugural Elvis Presley Patriotic Song Award for "Only in America," the video for which won CMT'S Duo Video of the Year Award. Also in 2003, they planned the next leg of their highly successful *Neon Circus and Wild West Show* that continues to elevate their reputation as dominant live showmen. The show gained such a reputation for rowdy hard country that *USA Today* did a photo essay on the tour in 2002, and CBS Television's *Sunday Morning* chronicled the fervent fans that follow the tour across the country in the manner of the Grateful Dead's "Deadheads." By spring, 2003 Brooks and Dunn again found themselves winning Duo of the Year at the 38th Academy of Country Music Awards.

Released in July 2003, *Red Dirt Road* (Arista) provided the group with yet another #1 country hit. Appealing to nationwide country music audiences with its chiming mandolin and instantly familiar, sing-along chorus, the album's title track is about learning life's lessons out on the red dirt back roads of the rural south. While the album is much rootsier than their recent outings with a prevalence of dobros courtesy of Jerry Douglas ("Caroline" and "That's What She Gets for Loving Me"), acoustic guitars ("When We Were Kings"), mandolins ("Red Dirt Roads"), fiddles ("My Baby's Everything I Love"), and harmonicas ("That's What She Gets for Loving Me"), the collection also ranges into softer ballads ("I Used to Know This Song By Heart," and "Memory Town"). Also included on the album is a Brooks and Dunn composition, "My Baby's Everything I Love", that pulls out every stop on a honky-tonk stomper that features most of the previously mentioned instruments taking a solo on a guaranteed two-stepping favorite. Much of the album centers on the concept of redemption through trial, especially the up tempo gospel-tinged "hidden" track at the end of the collection. Overall, the album sees Brooks and Dunn foregoing much of their more polished latter 90s sound for a grittier approach that befits their origins in the dance halls of Oklahoma, Texas, and Louisiana, and was rowdy enough for thousands to bounce around to in stadiums and arenas throughout North America.

The Oklahoma Music Hall of Fame and Museum inducted Ronnie Dunn into the Oklahoma Music Hall of Fame in 2003. "Had it not been for Oklahoma," Dunn said in a press release acknowledging the induction, "and the abundance of places to play... well, it's where I honed everything I do for the most part. The lion's share of what I know, I learned in Oklahoma and the clubs around there, because it was such a rich musical environment. From **Bob Wills** to **Leon Russell**, the **GAP Band**... the spectrum was so broad, it really gave you an appreciation of what music could be. And nobody worried about what it was, beyond good, so you picked stuff up from every kind of music being played and brought it to what you did." About Tulsa, Ronnie Dunn explained, "Tulsa is also a huge part of who I am musically. We'd play clubs and end up at the Caravan Ballroom, with a lot of the original Bob Wills players – people like Eldon Shamblin."

In August, 2003, B&D's spot-on cover of Waylon Jennings' "I Ain't Living Long Like This" appeared on RCA's *I've Always Been Crazy: A Tribute to Waylon Jennings*, and the group continued touring to massive audiences. Two years later, their next collection, *Hillbilly Deluxe* (Arista, 2005) was a #1 smash Platinum album with a #1 single, "Play Something Country", and three other chart singles. Bolstered by their continued the success, Brooks and Dunn hit the road again with their most elaborate show yet, working with noted visual director Marcia Kapustin who has worked with U2, Metallica, Paul McCartney, KISS, Elton John and the Rolling Stones.

They followed with their tenth and final studio album in 2007, *Cowboy Town*, charting four more singles on the country chart in or near the top ten, and re-issued one track, "Cowgirls Don't Cry", a song inspired by their friend and colleague, Reba McEntire. After B&D performed the song with Reba McEntire at the CMA Awards in 2008, the sound was so popular it was re-issued to radio stations with her vocals and on subsequent pressings of the CD, crediting all three of them. While the album did not provide #1 hits in the US, Canadian radio and the public sent three of the tracks to the top of their country chart, "Proud of the House We Built", "Put a Girl In It", and "Cowgirls Don't Cry" (with Reba). The title track of the CD, "Cowboy Town", was also chosen as the National Finals Rodeo's official song from 2007 to 2009.

In August of 2009, the most awarded act in Country Music Association history announced on their website they were going to "call it a day," planning to tour one final time through 2010 to thank their fans. By 2011, Dunn announced he would be working more as a solo act, and he released his first solo album, *Ronnie Dunn*, in June, 2011. And to think, half of all that success started out side of Tulsa past the city limits sign. Oklahoma made a significant impact on Ronnie Dunn for the reasons it has on many musicians learning their trade in the state. On his induction into the Oklahoma Music Hall of Fame, he said, "[Oklahomans] never lose sight of their musical heritage there – the music always moves forward from the roots, and I carry it with me to this day."

www.ronniedunn.com

Durrill, John
(See Five Americans entry)

E

Edwards, Nokie
(b. May 9th, 1935)

While lead guitarist for the most significant instrumental combo in the history of rock music, The Ventures, Nokie Edwards established himself as a fleet soloist and important stylist during The Ventures' peak of popularity in the 1960s and '70s. Playing with fellow Oklahoman and co-founding member of The Ventures, bassist **Bob Bogle**, and the other two Ventures, co-founder and rhythm guitarist Don Wilson (b. February 10, 1937, Tacoma, Washington), and primary drummer Howie Johnson (b. WA, 1938 - d. 1988), Edwards helped redefine and re-popularize the electric guitar combo in the midst of the late 1950s and early 1960s pop music era with its homogenized and watered-down rock and roll. Their drum-driven, fast dance music, featuring Nokie's speedy electric guitar work, inspired countless surf music groups and garage bands from the 1960s, not the least of which were several major British Invasion bands like the Beatles and Kinks. The Ventures' influence continued into the punk rock movement of the 1970s, and the alternative country music of the 1980s through the 2000s. Musicians who are on record as being inspired by the group include Jimmy Page, Stanley Clarke, Steve Miller, George Harrison, The Ramones, Jeff "Skunk" Baxter of Steely Dan, and all-world guitarist Larry Carlton. Additionally, their success in Japan opened up the American music market in that country. According to his website's publicity page, "During the 1960s alone, Nokie Edwards and The Ventures had no less than 33 albums to hit the US charts. In addition to The Ventures albums, Nokie has performed as a guest on over three dozen CD's and recorded over two dozen solo albums - seven of which he produced of his own."

While the group had admirable success on the single charts in the 1960s with fourteen Top 100 singles, The Ventures' thematic LP collections drove their notoriety. According to The Ventures' website, thirty-seven of their albums made the US charts. More than 150 albums have been released in Japan alone, and their 1960s-era *Play Guitar with The Ventures* series was the first and only set of musical instructional records ever to make the album charts. The group had five gold albums, was named *Billboard's* Most Promising Instrumental Group of 1960, sold an unprecedented one million albums per year from 1961 to 1966, and have sold over one hundred million albums through 2003. While Bob Bogle and Don Wilson started the band under the name of The Versatones, the addition of Nokie Edwards on bass in 1959 before he switched permanently to guitar, ensured the group will be exalted be forever in popular and rock

Nokie Edwards, 2002

music's Valhalla, to include the Rock and Roll Hall of Fame in Cleveland, who inducted the group in 2008.

Born in the tiny western Oklahoma agricultural community of Lahoma smack in the middle of Oklahoma's famous dustbowl, Nole ("Nokie" is a combination of Nole and Okie) Floyd Edwards joined a musical brood where his father played violin and guitar, and most of his twelve brothers and sisters were also musically inclined. His brothers, uncles, and father spun out bluegrass, country and western, "Everything," as Nokie said in a 2003 telephone interview. Like many other Oklahomans did in the 1930s due to drought and the Depression, the Edwards were forced into moving west when Nokie was not even a year old. Surrounded by music and musicians, by the time he was five, Nokie began teaching himself the guitar, and when he was eleven he could play all string instruments, but decided to concentrate on just guitar. Also at eleven, Nokie made his first radio performance in Idaho, and by the middle 1950s he played with the Grand Ole Opry when they toured the Northwest. Eventually he played with well-known country artists such as Lefty Frizzell, **Cal Smith**, Ferlin Husky, and Buck Owens, with whom Bob Bogle and Don Wilson first saw Edwards play lead guitar.

In a 2002 interview posted on his website, Nokie remembered how he came to be with The Ventures: "It started with Don Wilson and Bob Bogle performing in Washington. Bob came into a club where he heard me playing with Buck Owens in 1959. The next night Don joined Bob and returned to hear me perform on lead with Buck. Don and Bob talked to me about playing with them. Skip Moore was performing on drums where I was playing and I introduced Skip to Bob and Don. As a result they asked Skip to work on some jobs with them. We played around the Tacoma, Washington area in a few clubs, and then went into the studio to record 'Walk, Don't Run' in 1959." By the next year Don's mother, Josie, produced "Walk Don't Run" on her own Blue Horizon label when the demo was turned down by various labels. The song surged regionally on radio and was picked up by Dolton Records for distribution where it peaked at #2 on the national pop charts, kept off the top spot by Elvis Presley, Chubby Checker, and Bryan Hyland's "Itsy Bittsy Teeny Weeny Yellow Polka Dot Bikini".

Nokie Edwards played lead guitar with The Ventures from 1959 to 1968. While he is often thought of as the early bassist of the group, Nokie explained to an interviewer in 2003, "When we first started recording, I played bass on about five songs, and I was holding the bass when the picture was taken, so everybody assumed I was the bass player. When we did shows, Bob would start playing [guitar] on "Walk Don't Run", "Perfidia", and some of those, then I would change off and finish the evening." During the 1960s Nokie played on nearly fifty albums, usually as the lead guitarist, on all The Ventures' best-known songs: "2000 Pound Bee" (the first song to use a fuzz box effect on a guitar), "Hawaii Five-O", "Fugitive", "Surf Rider", "Lullaby of the Leaves", "Yellow Jacket", "Walk Don't Run '64",

The Ventures with Nokie Edwards holding bass guitar.

By Hugh Foley / 235

"Sleep Walk", "Pedal Pusher", "Ghost Riders in the Sky", "Wipe Out" by the Surfaris, "Pipeline" by Spickard and Carmen, and "Driving Guitars".

Along with Nokie's impact on The Ventures, his guitar playing inspired numerous young people in the United States, Europe, and, especially Japan to take up electric guitar. The demand created a market for Ventures guitar-related products, to include their 1960s-era *Play Guitar with The Ventures* series in which the albums featured Ventures songs with out the respective musical parts. That four-album series was the first and only set of musical instruction records to ever make the pop album charts. Additionally, from 1962 to 1968, Nokie and The Ventures popularized Mosrite guitars designed and made by native Oklahomans whose parents were also part of the great Okie migration west, **Semie Moseley** (b. Durant, 1935), and his brother **Andy Moseley** (b. Durant, 1933). The Ventures signed an exclusive distribution agreement with Moseley, and featured the guitar on their album covers. The publicity spurred orders from around the world, especially Japan, for the Mosrites, many of which are now considered collector's items by guitar enthusiasts.

Edwards left The Ventures in 1968, replaced by Gerry McGee who has continued an amicable off-again, on-again musical relationship with the group. Ironically, The Ventures had their last major hit, the theme to the TV series *Hawaii Five-0*, on which he plays, after Nokie left the group. Legend holds that a Hawaiian disc-jockey decided to use the Ventures recording of the theme song to back ads for the program on local radio stations, and listeners kept calling to see who was playing the theme on the ad. The song was released as a single in 1969 and reached #4 on the pop charts, practically pulling the TV show into popularity with it. While the song was the biggest instrumental hit of the year, it could not be nominated for a GRAMMY because it had actually been released in the year previous to its commercial success. Nonetheless, *Hawaii Five-0* and its theme song kept The Ventures sound in front of the American public until 1980 when just about anyone who watched television could sing at least the first few measures of the song's melody, and instantly visualize the Hawaiian natives rowing through the surf when the song played over the show's title credits.

After a four-year hiatus in which he recorded three solo albums, Nokie re-entered the fold from 1972 to 1984 when The Ventures recorded another twenty-plus albums both in the states and in Japan. After 1984, Edwards left for a steady career of solo engagements, but still joined The Ventures for occasional shows (and recordings) in the U.S. and Japan. Aside from his work with The Ventures, Nokie has performed as a guest on twenty-one CDs, and recorded thirteen solo CDs. He released a solo album in 2002, *Hitchhiker*, available through his website, a lovely, lyrical album of instrumentals available only through his website. Also in 2002, Nokie made his first tour of Europe where The Ventures never traveled, even though they recorded several albums specifically for the European market. By 2003 The Ventures had sold more than 100 million albums worldwide.

Additional honors the band received include two gold singles for "Walk, Don't Run", the only time a cover of a song by the same band has ever achieved that status (1960 and 1964); *Billboard*'s Favorite Single Instrumental Record for "Walk, Don't Run" in 1960; the First Gold Eight Track Award from Japan; and the only foreign group to ever receive the prestigious Japanese Grand Prix Award. Nokie received individual recognition in 1994 when his composition, "Ginza Lights," was voted the All-Time #1 Song in Japan, and he has also received a Platinum Sales Award for his composition, "Surf Rider (a.k.a. Spudnick)" that appeared on the million-selling soundtrack for the film *Pulp Fiction* in 1994.

Since 2000, Nokie received two GRAMMY nominations (2004 and 2005) for his instrumental work on a Gospel albums by the Jordanaires and the Light Crust Doughboys, and has continued touring the world to appreciative audiences, no more so than in Japan where he is considered a musical icon. In the decade prior to 2010, he performed for the Chet Atkins Association Society, Nashville, Tennessee; Mesquite, TX Guitar Festival; Muriel Anderson's "All Star Guitar Night" in Tennessee and California; "Guitar's For Life" Concert, New York; Japan nearly thirty times from 2000 to 2010; with The Ventures in Soave, Italy and the Seattle's Experience Music Project; Guitar Extravaganza, Edmonton, Canada; and North Carolina and Ohio's Thumb and Finger Style Guitar Conventions. Perhaps no performance was more gratifying than The Ventures' 2008 induction into the Rock and Roll Hall of Fame in Cleveland, Ohio, a final validation of the legendary group's place in the pantheon of rock history. The group had already been inducted into the GRAMMY Hall of Fame in 2006 for "Walk Don't Run". Adding to that accolade, Edwards received the *Guitar Player* magazine Certified Legend Award in 2009. In 2010, Nokie showed little sign of slowing his performing and recording pace since the world's popular music audiences are always eager to see and hear one of rock and roll's true guitar legends. Like Bob Bogle who moved away from Oklahoma at a young age, the state's influence on Nokie may have been minimal, but like Merle Haggard whose parents also moved from Oklahoma during the 1930s, Nokie grew up around Okies and their music which imprinted a permanent twang on just about everything he has ever played.

www.nokieedwards.com

Edwards, Frenchy "Stoney"

(b. December 24, 1929 - d. April 5, 1997)

With his strong baritone and obvious country accent, Stoney Edwards was one of a handful African-Americans, along with DeFord Bailey, Charley Pride, O.B. McClinton, and **Big Al Downing**, who made significant contributions to the country music field as a singer, songwriter, instrumentalist, and honky tonk stylist in the tradition of Lefty Frizzell. Born on a farm near Seminole, Oklahoma, Stoney was raised on bootlegging and country music. Of mixed ethnic background which he felt made him a perennial outsider, his father's ancestors were African-American, American Indian, and Irish, while his mother's background was African-American and American Indian. When Stoney was young, his father left home leaving Stoney's mother to raise the seven children. As a teenager, he became interested in country music, especially **Bob Wills** via radio station KVOO in nearby Tulsa, and by listening to the Grand Old Opry. His dream was to perform on the Opry, therefore, he taught himself to play the guitar and fiddle while in high school, mentored by his uncles who played in a local string band, and began experimenting with songwriting.

For a short period he was reunited with his father in Oklahoma City, where Stoney worked as a dishwasher. He later moved to California to live with an uncle and was employed at various jobs, including janitor, truck driver, and cowboy, which resulted in several moves around the country. In the early 1950s, he met Rosemary in California and they were married and settled in the San Francisco Bay area. With a family to support, Edwards retained only part-time interest in music as he worked for the next fifteen years as a blue-collar laborer. An accident in 1969 in Richmond, California, forced Stoney to change occupations. Because of severe carbon dioxide poisoning and a broken back, he turned exclusively to singing and songwriting. His first song, "A Two Dollar Toy," based on his little daughter's windup toy, became his first charted single reaching #68 on *Billboard*'s country charts in 1971. This convinced Stoney to become a serious musician, both in terms of writing and playing the guitar.

The next major turn of events included an invitation to open a concert in Oakland for his childhood idol, Bob Wills. An attorney in the audience heard Edwards' version of "Mama's Hungry Eyes", and suggested he contact Capitol Records and provide them a demo, as many labels were looking for the next Charley Pride. Within a week, he had signed with Capitol, a recording company he remained with for six years, using the then unknown Asleep at the Wheel as one of his backup bands. He released six albums on Capitol, including *Stoney Edwards, A Country Singer*; *She's My Rock*, producing a 1973 top 20 hit by the same title as the album; *Down Home in the Country*; *Mississippi You're On My Mind*, from which the title track yielded another Top 20 single; *Blackbird*, and *Hank and Lefty Raised My Country Soul*. The latter album's title track also became not only a Top 40 hit, but also has become a country music classic. Stoney's son, Kenneth, relayed a story about Stoney finding Lefty Frizzell sitting in a Nashville bar crying while listening to "Hank and Lefty Raised My Country Soul". Frizzell explained he didn't think anyone remembered or cared about him, and it took a black man (Stoney) to remind everyone. "It was a kind of off," the younger Edwards wrote in a 2003 e-mail, but still "a great compliment." Stoney's additional Top 20 hits included "Don't Be Angry" and "I Bought the Shoes That Just Walked Out on Me".

The 1976 "Blackbird (Hold Your Head Up High)" song created enough controversy that Stoney was banned from some country music radio stations in the United States because of its racial connotations. In the song, he mentions the "n" word, creating enough potential trouble with the song to keep it off of the airwaves. While Sly Stone or Parliament-Funkadelic might be able to get away with it, Stoney would not in a white dominated country music field. Compounding the point, in 1977 Capitol released Edwards because his albums were "unprofitable," and he signed on in 1978 with JMI Records for whom he had a minor hit, "If I Had to Do it All Over Again". In 1981, he recorded *No Way to Drown a Memory* (Music America/MCA), an album interesting in itself as it was recorded at the Benson Sound Studio in Oklahoma City, and includes songs by **Tommy Collins**, **Merle Haggard**, and a co-write between Collins and **Bobby Barnett**. Also the cover

Stoney Edwards, 1981

features Stoney leaning over a bar at the Last Chance Saloon at the Frontier City Amusement Park in Oklahoma City.

During the 1980s, Edwards' health deteriorated because of diabetes, costing him one leg, however, he continued recording, and his songs kept being recorded by other artists. George Jones had a #2 country single hit with a re-recording of "She's My Rock". In 1986, he collaborated with several country stars to produce an album that featured Johnny Gimble, Ray Benson, Leon Rausch, and **Ralph Mooney**, another Oklahoman. *Just for Old Time's Sake*, recorded in 1991, was Edwards' first solo album in a decade, and featured several notable country artists, such as Johnny Gimble, Leon Rausch, and Ray Benson. Finally, in 1998, *Poor Folks Stick Together: The Best of Stoney Edwards* was released by the Razor and Tie label, and included a number of his best-known recordings, including "She's My Rock", "Hank and Lefty Raised My Country Soul", as well as "Head Bootlegger Man", a tribute to his early days in Oklahoma, and "I Bought the Shoes That Just Walked Out on Me", one of his personal favorites, according to the press release for the CD.

Stoney Edwards is another musical example of the cultural and ethnic blending that occurred in Oklahoma from its first settling by American Indians, and people of African and European descent, joining Big Al Downing and Charley Pride as one of the few African-Americans who made careers as country music stars (prior to Darius Rucker), while we might also add one of the few American Indians to have done the same thing. While he never had what one would consider a major hit, Stoney had a solid career in the music business, and his warm, knowing voice reflects of life of triumphs and tragedies as expressed through his honky-tonk music that seeks healing through commiseration and cathartic expression, the essence of the blues and the hardest of country music. Edwards died from stomach cancer on April 5, 1997 at the age of 67.

Egerton, Stephen

(b. September 2, 1974)

An aggressively melodic guitarist with elevated rock dexterity, Stephen Egerton is well-known in punk rock, hardcore, and progressive pop rock circles for his lead guitar sound imprint and compositional abilities via the Descendents from 1987-2004, and that band's alter ego, All, through 2010. Not originally from Oklahoma (born as Stephen Patrick O'Reilly in Fort Bragg, North Carolina), Egerton was raised in Salt Lake City, Utah, where he became part of the punk and hardcore scene as a guitarist and drummer, notably playing with bassist Karl Alvarez from 1980 to 1985 in bands such as Massacre Guys. In 1985, Egerton expanded his guitar range when he moved to Virginia, studied classical guitar, and joined the Washinton D.C. group, Auto Da Fé. When the Descendents' guitarist and bassist left in the summer of 1986, Egerton and Alvarez joined their friend, drummer Bill Stevenson, in the group. By September of 1986 they began recording perhaps *the* primary punk pop album of 1987, *All* for SST Records, the label operated by Black Flag's guitarist, Greg Ginn.

Stephen Egerton in a 2009 performance will All.

With the group's most well-known antecedents, the Minutemen (varying rhythms/ guitar virtuosity/social commentary lyrics), Black Flag (speed, ferocity, snide and indicting vocals), and Husker Dü (harmonized vocals/melodic chord progressions), the Descendents refined hardcore into "Rush on caffeine", referring to the Canadian progressive rock group known for its complicated song constructions. On fast melodic songs with multiple tempo changes, ripping guitar solos, harmonized vocal parts, and smart-alecky lyrical content, the Descendents forecast later successful punk pop groups such as Green Day and Blink 182, although neither are as musically advanced as The Descendents nor All. Just before the release of the final Descendents album, *Cool to Be You* (Fat Wreck Chords), Stephen and his wife, Nat, moved to Oklahoma in March, 2003, so their kids could be close to her family. Once in place, the Egertons started Armstrong Recording Studio in Tulsa where Stephen says he "records and mixes bands from all over," and makes his own music.

Listening to the first Descendents album to feature Egerton, one can hear his ability to play heavy rhythmic power chords strong as any pop metal guitarists of the late 1980s, and lickety-split leads that ignite Descendents songs, but also layers the music's texture with his classical scales and influences ("Impressions" or "Iceman" from *All*), and subtle counterpoint riffs to vocals throughout his oeuvre of recordings. As a guitarist one might call "the George Lynch of punk rock," Egerton's established musical template recurs and evolves through his multiple sessions for both the Descendents and All, up through the release of his 2010 solo album, *7 Degrees of Stephen Egerton* on Paper and Plastick Records. The CD's title is a smiling comment on how many people in rock circles can connect their trajectory to Egerton by a band, recording, studio, tour, song, etc. Egerton played all instruments on his solo collection, and asked sixteen friends from different bands he has played in, toured with, or recorded, to contribute vocals, notably Milo Aukerman, the best-known Descendents vocalist, Scott Reynolds of All, Mike Herrera of MXPX, and Chris DeMakes of Less than Jake. Alongside the Descendents' recording and touring career for eighteen years before the group disbanded, Egerton plays on every All album from 1988 through 2000, and according to Egerton, All is still doing occasional shows as of 2010. After being in Oklahoma for seven years, Stephen is still excited about the artistic opportunities in his adopted home state, saying, "I'm still exploring the Oklahoma music scene, which is excellent! There are some extremely talented people here, and a great music history. I think many musicians are here that have, and will continue to make, a lasting impression."

www.stephenegerton.com

www.descendentsonline.com

www.myspace.com/armstrongrecording

Eicher, Shelby

A composer, teacher, and recording artist as a great fiddler and multi-instrumentalist who was a member of Roy Clark's touring band for fifteen years, Shelby Eicher grew up in Northern Ohio playing square dances with his mom, dad and grandmother. The band consisted of his grandmother and the Fulton County Sand Shifters. In 2010, Eicher lived in Tulsa, a base from which he performed about twenty times a year, and gave lessons to about thirty students on fiddle, mandolin, and guitar. As an instrumentalist, he is equally adept at Fiddle, Viola, Chin-cello, Mandolin, Mandola, Mando-cello, Alto Guitar and Guitar.

Of his many professional accomplishments, he recorded five albums with Roy

Clark during his fifteen years as part of Roy's band. While with Clark, Eicher fiddled his way onto national television programs such as *Hee Haw* (ten years), *The Tonight Show* (four times), *Grand Ole Opry, Nashville Now, Merv Griffin*, and internationally with Clark on a tour of Russia where they were also featured on a television special on Russian TV. One of the Clark albums featuring Eicher merges TV and the live performance, *The Roy Clark Show Live from Austin City Limits* (MCA, 1982). As a session musician, his work can be heard on J.J. Cale's CDs *Roll On* (2009) and *To Tulsa and Back* (2004), as well as the Tractors' *Fast Girl* (2001), Hank Thompson's *My Personal Favorites* (2006), and a Roy D. Mercer CD playing the "Fishin' Report" theme. Along with doing a commercial studio work for advertising jingles and film soundtracks, Shelby has been in a number of groups: Shelby Eicher Hot Gypsy Trio, Cafe' Jazz, The Grasshoppers, The Kings of Western Swing, Riders of the Cimarron, Cowbop, and the duo of Mark Bruner & Shelby Eicher, with whom he has released two independent CDs. In 2009, Shelby released a CD of traditional fiddle tunes he's known most of his life. One recording preserves a performance with Eicher's grandmother when he was ten-years-old and playing with her on stage.

Shelby Eicher

Eicher is also a well-known educator and professional music instructor. He has served as a Harwelden Repertory Artist (2006/2007/2008), a Harwelden Artist in the Schools, an instructor and performer at the Roanoke Bluegrass Weekend, and as a judge for Oklahoma State Fiddle Championship (since 2002). He also directs education the National Fiddler's Hall of Fame in Tulsa, and sits on the Tulsa Symphony Orchestra education committee.

www.shelbyeicher.com

Elam, Katrina

(b. December 12, 1983)

Initially via the Oklahoma Opry and Oklahoma Country Music Association for her vocal prowess, as she knocked people out at private events, state fair shows, and OK Opry Events. By sixteen she'd shared the stage with **Vince Gill** and **Reba McEntire**, and rapturous words started to sound off in Nashville about the powerful young Oklahoma singer and developed-beyond-her-years songwriter. Katrina started home schooling by the 10th grade so she could focus on her performing schedule and songwriting aspirations, and received the writing deal with Warner, providing her a paycheck and encouragement she needed to move to Nashville at age eighteen.

Within a short period of time, she was being courted by RCA, Capitol, Sony, and Universal South, the label then headed by Oklahoman **Tim DuBois**, and his partner Tony Brown, with whom Elam had wanted to work since she was about ten due to associating Brown with Reba McEntire. Universal South had the inside track as DuBois had already known Elam for several years, and Brown was her dream producer, all of which ended up in her 2004 self-titled debut album, released when Katrina was just twenty-years-old. Even with her excellent voice and original lyrics, some of country music's best session musicians (Bryan Sutton-acoustic guitar, Jerry Douglas-dobro, Aubrey Haynie-fiddle/

mandolin), beautiful packaging, and powerful marketing, Elam's album barely dented *Billboard*'s Top Country Album chart, staying for only a week at #42 and dropping off in October, 2004. Co-writing nine of the album's eleven songs, Elam's first single, "No End in Sight", peaked at #29 on *Billboard*'s Hot Country Songs chart. The follow-up singles, "I Won't Say Goodbye", did not chart while she toured with Keith Urban, and "I Want a Cowboy", barely bucked up to #59 (out of 60 places) for one week in March, 2005. Listening to the album, one wonders why "Drop Dead Gorgeous" was not picked as a single. A hot, up tempo number with tough singing, Elam puts a conceited man in his place with one of the album's best lines, "Nobody loves you like you do." The song struts with a full-on rock-out by the ace studio musicians, but has a couple of creative studio sound tricks that may have made it sound "too creative" for mainstream country radio. However, one should remember that 2004 is also the year Gretchen Wilson hit the scene with her extra-trashy girlneck image and song style, so perhaps the thinking was for Elam to be the anti-Gretchen, and "Drop Dead Gorgeous" seemed too close to Wilson's sound at the time. Katrina's lyrics are what really get a listener's attention on the album, whether the convincing and hard-to-listen-to heartache of "The Breakup Song", or her thoughts on a small town's limited expectations of teenage women in "Normal". In any case, Elam began readying her sophomore album in 2005, while another perfect country music storm was brewing on the American Idol talent show. In May, 2005, another Oklahoma singer born the same year as Katrina, Carrie Underwood, won the national talent search, and was just a few months away from releasing her record-smashing first album, *Some Hearts*.

Katrina Elam, 2006

The first single from Elam's never-released second album, "Love Is", landed in the fall of 2006, peaking at #47 on the Hot Country Songs chart. Even with Elam's pure voice singing a about the conflicting tensions of love backed by lush, if melodramatic, Nashville production complete with strings, the song did not really stand a chance with Underwood's "Before He Cheats" parked at #1 on the Hot Country Songs chart and setting the modern tone for women singing country music. Additionally, Universal South Records experienced a shake up as Tim DuBois left the company, leaving one of her main champions on the outside while the new leadership decided what to do, which wound up being to not release the album. Once again, Elam was a victim of timing, at first not being as brassy as Gretchen Wilson, and then not able to outsoar Underwood's rocket, and finally by her record label swirling in uncertainty.

The trajectories of Elam and Underwood began to intertwine when Elam's second single, not co-written by her, but obviously angling for a tougher image, "Flat on the Floor", had just barely entered the Hot Country Songs chart at #52 when Carrie Underwood expressed interest in it. With promotion for the song pulled by Universal South, Underwood made "Flat on the Floor" the leadoff track to her #1 2007 *Carnival Ride* album, sounding a little more robust than Elam did on the tune. However, Carrie also recognized Elam's lyrical abilities, including a song co-written by Katrina, "Change", on the 2009 #1 Underwood album, *Play On*. Also in 2009, Reba McEntire thought a lot of Elam's "I Want a Cowboy", as she reached back to the song and recorded it for the 2009 #1 album, *Keep on Loving You*, essentially giving Elam a pay raise to sooth any stress she may have had about her own music's initial lukewarm reception by radio and the general country music market. Very few songwriters as young as Elam can claim co-authorship of two songs on concurrent #1 albums by major stars, but the connection here is obvious, the Oklahoma night.

As of 2010, Katrina Elam's official website was still hosted by Universal South, but had not been updated by her or the label since 2006. She has two myspace.com sites: myspace.com/katrinaelam has not been updated since 2008, but indicated she would be giving in to her camera friendly visage, and starring in a film, *The Perfect Country Gift*, to be released in 2011. Her second site, myspace.com/katrinaelamsmusic had been updated as recently as July, 2010, where she wrote in her blog: "Just wanted to thank everyone for all the kind thoughts and words while I have gone through a few stumbling blocks in my career recently. I have a new outlook and I am now working on new material. Stay tuned, stay in touch and once again thank you for all your love and support. Y'all mean so much to me."

Katrina Elam performs, 2006

www.myspace.com/katrinaelamsmusic

Ellison, Scott

(b. June 13, 1954)

A salty, veteran blues guitarist with impeccable chops, Scott Ellison is one of Tulsa's most respected guitarists, equally adept at blues, R&B, or rock. Waking up musically like many other young people on February 13, 1964, the Tulsa native witnessed the Beatles on *Ed Sullivan* and was guitar love-struck. Within days he was taking lessons, learning Beatles songs, and by age 12 was making money on guitar in a teen cover band, the Knight Riders. According to his myspace.com website, Ellison says he was influenced equally by the British Invasion bands, the sounds of Motown, and the R&B coming out of Stax Records in Memphis in the early 1970s. Scott started his own band in the mid-1970s, and after moving to Nashville he began touring with Jessica James (Conway Twitty's daughter) in 1975. By 1981 Clarence "Gatemouth" Brown picked Ellison to accompany him on tour as a rhythm guitarist, and Ellison immediately knew the life of touring musician was for him. He watched and learned a great deal

Scott Ellison

from playing with "Gatemouth," saying "What impressed me so much was not only his musicianship - he was a big influence on my guitar playing, but also his energy. He just had so much fun doing it. I told myself I want to have fun like that when I'm doing my own thing."

By the mid-1980s, Ellison was doing his own thing. A move to Los Angeles proved fortuitous as Scott began playing and touring with the likes of The Box Tops, The Shirelles, J.J. Jackson, The Drifters, The Coasters, Peaches and Herb, and Gary "U.S." Bonds. By the early 1990s Scott had formed his own blues band and opened up shows for such legends as Joe Cocker, Roy Orbison, The Fabulous T-Birds, Leon Russell, Bobby Bland, Buddy Guy, and B.B. King. Ellison has also released a number of blues oriented CDs featuring his original music: *Cold Hard Cash* (Burnside, 2001), produced by Dennis Walker (Robert Clay); *Live at Joey's*; *Chains of Love*; *Bad Case of the Blues* (2003) featuring Tulsa Sound musicians **Jimmy Karstein** and **Rocky Frisco**; and *Ice Storm* (Earwig, 2008). Scott has had his songs featured on the TV shows *Sister, Sister*, *Eye on LA*, and the soap opera *Santa Barbara*. Scott's version of "Down Down Baby" was played regularly on the cultish TV show *Buffy The Vampire Slayer*, and the MTV movie *Love Song* included three of Scott's songs.. In 2007, he scored another film credit in *Feast of Love*, starring Morgan Freeman, in which Ellison's "Don't Push Your Luck" played in the film's opening scene. As of 2013, Scott continued touring the US and Canada, often playing the Hard Rock Casino in Catoosa with his band consisting of Scott on guitars/vocals, Billy Estes or Robbie Armstrong on drums, and Jon Parris on bass.

www.myspace.com/scottellisonband

England, Ty

(b. December 5, 1963)

Mining Oklahoma swing for his first and best-known song, "Should've Asked Her Faster", Gary Tyrone England was born in Oklahoma City. His grandfather, who played the harmonica, first introduced Ty to country music by giving him his first guitar and teaching him some basic chords, as well as introducing him to traditional country music. On his official website, England remembers, "My grandpa taught me to play the old country songs on guitar, and it was through him I started listening to guys like Hank Williams and Lefty Frizzell. I grew up on it." Whenever Ty and his grandfather would get together, Ty would play the guitar and his grandfather, the harmonica. England's first musical performance was at a junior high talent show, and during high school, he sang with the chorus. Continuing to develop his acoustic guitar skills in the 1970s, he played with a number of local bands in Oklahoma City where he also worked a variety of jobs: restaurant busboy, grocery sacker, and automotive painter.

After high school graduation, he attended Oklahoma State University in Stillwater, where he began playing sets at Aunt Molly's, a coffeehouse in the basement of the OSU Student Union. One night, Ted Larkin, a student, approached Ty and told him he should meet another musician attending OSU, **Garth Brooks**. He joined Garth in 1982, and the two began making music while rooming together. The two made a pact that if one of them found success, he would help the other. Focusing more on music than classes, he withdrew him from college and found a job back in Oklahoma City, completing his marketing degree through courses at night, while working a day job at the automotive paint plant.

In 1988 England received a call from his old buddy Garth Brooks, who had just signed with Capitol Records, and called to honor their pact. Garth invited Ty to join him in Nashville for the wildest music industry ride in American popular culture history since Elvis Presley or the Beatles changed the music of their eras in the 1950s and 1960s. Garth Brooks' massive popularity, accompanied by his "rock concert energy" live shows, changed country music from that point forward, and England picked his way through the whole thing as Garth's guitarist and backup vocalist on *No Fences* (1989), *Ropin' the Wind* (1990), and *The Chase* (1991), which have sold a combined *forty million* copies. Ty toured and recorded with Garth for six years, the visibility certainly helping him gain his own chance for a solo career, signing with RCA Records in 1995. With a pleasant singing voice, good looks for video, and fun live performances, plenty of space existed in the country music industry for England at the time, especially having been so close to Garth's gold dust.

A common theme in these kinds of stories is that the record label signs someone young and exciting, gives them songs to sing, musicians to record with, and a marketing team that understands the time logistics of recording, producing, packaging, promoting, and distributing the music. Occasionally, someone will break through that stale process with their energy and talent, and then get oppressed artistically by marketers trying to make the whole system work too quickly. If no results, i.e., airplay, sales, occur within the cyclical time frame of label's production schedule, the idea is either to exploit as fast as possible, or toss just as quickly once the artist falters.

Right out of the box, Ty's first single became his signature tune. An Oklahoma swing song about a shy guy who loses out on the girls, "Should've Asked Her Faster" bounced off of Ty's self-titled debut album right up to #3 on *Billboard*'s Hot Country Songs chart. Instead of capitalizing on the momentum of England's "feel good" swing vibe, letting his identity settle in with another feel good song, RCA wanted to do too much too fast and changed what he had become known for, trotting out a ballad, "Smoke in Her Eyes," which did not register because it didn't sound anything like the first single, creeping up only to #44. The album had other swing numbers ("A Swing Like That"), Haggard-esque tonkers ("Her Only Bad Habit Was Me"), and even blues ("The Blues Ain't News to Me), but the common record promotion sensibility is to broaden an artist's appeal before they even really get established as who they are known for. In any, case RCA got the message and released another up tempo single from the album, a rural lifestyle novelty tune, "Redneck Song", but the South couldn't even save it and the rednecks only made it into the fringe of the Hot Country Songs chart at #55 in March, 1996. In the meantime, England toured and readied his second album for RCA, *Two Ways to Fall* released in the fall of 1996.

By Hugh Foley / 245

Two Ways to Fall followed the goofy promotional pattern at RCA. Instead of releasing "Kick Back", a Swing tune reminiscent of "Should Have Asked Her Faster" with some great fiddle, electric guitar, and steel playing, would have instantly established the new album as Ty England album. RCA went with "Irresistible You", a sweet enough honky-tonk love song, leaning more toward Southern rock with its Allman Brothers slide work references, rather than Oklahoma swing, but the song did make it to #22 on the Hot Country Songs chart, better than the last two singles from the first album. Unbelievably, RCA did not follow up with "Kick Back", or even the album's punchy opening track, "It Starts with 'L'", but "All of the Above", a very generic country rock song that did not exhibit England at his potential best, and the chart reflected it with #46 showing in January, 1997. RCA seemed to forget what kind of environment England emerged from: Garth's fun, swinging, energetic shows, not ballad singing school. However, since England did not write any of the songs on the album, one can understand why the label would try him out in a variety of styles to see what might stick at radio or retail. Criticizing single release choices is easy in hindsight, but logic would seem to indicate if a label has a Top 5 hit by an artist, they would release one more single by the artist that sounds like the first hit before cutting the artist loose, which is what happened after the album did not meet expectations commercially. Ty returned to Oklahoma, where he could get off the music industry merry-go-around and spend time with his family, wife Shanna and four children, Aspen, Ty, Levi, and Mattie. Re-grouping, England signed with Capitol for a 2000 release, *Highways & Dancehalls*, produced by his old friend Garth Brooks. Capitol revised England's image, as the cover of the album showed Ty with no hat, and the name Tyler, ostensibly to separate him from Ty Herndon with whom he often shared the charts (around the same chart positions) in the middle 1990s. The album witnesses Ty relaxing his voice, singing ballads and story songs, singing some tenor parts recognizable from his early harmonies with Garth on all those million sellers. Only one of three singles released from the album, the slow "Drove Her to Dallas", dented the charted at #54, getting no higher in the seven weeks it sat there. Fans and radio might have been way confused by that point, not only was there no Oklahoma swing on the album, the artist's name was different, and that was his only Capitol release.

In 2006, Oklahoma-based Triple T Records released England's *Alive and Well and Livin' the Dream*, with two singles, "Redneck Anthem" and "Perfect Girl" registering regionally, but not on the national chart. Nonetheless, the independent release let England stretch out more vocally than he had on his last two major label projects, and the recordings sound like he's enjoying himself more as a result of getting to be himself. In 2010, he made a concert stop at Perkins Fest, in Perkins, Oklahoma, just ten miles south of Stillwater where Ty England's dream started with a friend who kept his word.
www.tyengland.com

Ester Drang

(formed Broken Arrow, 1995)

With layered vocal parts and harmonies, spacious and floating keyboard and lines, looping guitar melodies, and drums alternating tempo and timbre in their compositions, Ester Drang is another of Oklahoma's modern pop groups such as **Starlight Mints**, **Colourmusic**, and **Other Lives**, who are probably better known outside of the state than they are too far from their own front doors. The band is comprised of original members James McAlister (drums/pianos/synths), Bryce Chambers (vocals,guitars, pianos, synths), and Kyle Winner (bass guitar/bass synths), with the addition of Jeff Shoop (guitars/synths) after their first full-length album, *Goldenwest* for Burnt Toast Vinyl in 2001.

Comfortable with a slow, lyrical meditations surrounded by keyboards and atmospheric percussion, Ester Drang is so subtle about their religious convictions, the contemporary Christian tag is not often applied to their music as its appeal goes beyond the perceived limitations of sacred pop music. After signing with Jade Tree Records the group released 2003's *Infinite Keys* and 2006's *Rocinate*, both of which followed the space vibe template with roots in 1980s Brit atmospheric pop of the Durutti Column or Chameleons UK. Some of the groups Ester Drang has played with include The American Analog Set, Starflyer 59, The Get Up Kids, Styrofoam, and Unwed Sailor. In 2005, Shoop and McAlister moved to Seattle, Washington, where McAlister added drums to Sufjan Stevens' *Illinois* album, joined Pedro the Lion on several live dates as part-time member, and teamed up with **Aqueduct**'s David Terry. After a two-week European tour in 2005, and a home-town gig at the Cain's Ballroom lat in that same year, the band toured through much of 2006 to support *Rocinate*. The group's last listed performances were in 2007, according to their official website, and they had not posted anything on their myspace.com website since the same year. However, the band did play a Tulsa show in 2013, and announced via facebook that upcoming activities would be announced soon.

www.esterdrang.com

www.myspace.com/esterdrang

www.jadetree.com

Estes, Toni

(b. February 8, 1978)

Tulsa native Toni Estes is one of Oklahoma's most accomplished R & B artists with her soaring and sultry vocal skills. With a GRAMMY nomination for co-writing Whitney Houston's million selling single, "It's Not Right, but It's OK", and her self-assured, hybrid R & B meets rap album, *211*, released in 2000 on Priority Records, Toni has already enjoyed a high profile career as a vocalist and songwriter. Growing up in a house filled with music, Toni's father, Billy, is long time session drummer who has worked primarily on commercials and industrial recordings in Tulsa. Her mother, Lachelle (Owens)

Estes, reportedly has a fine singing voice, and her brother is a budding record producer. Estes began appearing in television commercials at six as a result of her father's work in that industry, opened for Natalie Cole and Gladys Knight when she was only fourteen, and was in chorus both at Tulsa Booker T. Washington and Tulsa Central High Schools. Through a friend in Tulsa, Toni met producer Jon-John, known for his work with Kenneth "Babyface" Nelson. After hearing her tape, Nelson encouraged Toni to move to Los Angeles after graduating from Tulsa Central High School to begin singing demos and support vocals. This process got her noticed in the highly competitive L.A. music scene and, at seventeen-years-old, she was signed to a major label.

In 1997, Toni provided backup vocals for R & B artists Jon B., Immature, and Laurneá. Although an album was not released through the major label contract, she did connect with Rodney Jerkins who was writing songs and producing for Whitney Houston. The professional relationship grew when Jerkins invited Toni to write songs for a new Whitney Houston album. Estes wrote eight songs, "It's Not Right, but It's Ok" being one of them, and the producers used Toni to record the songs because her voice sounds similar to Houston's. Along with "It's Not Right," Houston picked two more of Toni's songs, "Get It Back," and "If I Told You That" for her 1998 album *My Love Is Your Love*. Not only did Estes get co-writing credits, she also sang background vocals on the three songs. When an album still did not materialize for Estes, she gained a release from her contract and began looking for a new deal that she ultimately found at Priority Records, a label known primarily for rap artists. This led to the inclusion of her song "Hot" on the *Next Friday* soundtrack in 1999, and her subsequent album, *211*, named after the address of the north Tulsa home where she grew up.

Toni Estes

Toni Estes describes her sound as "hard core R & B with some real singing on top." Listing influences such as old school artists like Maze and Bobby Womack, the album features several slow jams such as "I Adore," "Let Me Know," and "She's Already," which exhibit Toni's powerful R & B ballad abilities. She co-wrote eight of the songs on the album and collaborated on the album with a number of well-known producers such as Teddy Riley, Warryn Campbell, and Teddy Bishop. Her brother Angelo, then seventeen, produced two of the songs on *211*. As of 2010, she lived in Texas, according to her myspace.com site, on which interested listeners can find a new track, "Goin' Back" that exhibits her still smooth vocal skills meshed with an easy-going R&B track.

www.myspace.com/toniestes

Evangelicals

(Founded Norman, 2005)

Another example of quirky Oklapop, the Evangelicals are one of several modern pop and rock bands from the state that follows a familiar template of elevated and distant vocals with non-sequitur lyrics held up, hidden, and swirled around by a texture of melodic keyboards, guitar arpeggios, and kooky sound effects. Consisting in 2010 of Norman North High School graduate, Josh Jones (vocals), Kyle Davis (bass/keyboards), Austin Stephens (drums), and Todd Jackson (guitars), the Evangelicals started out as a solo act in Jones bedroom with the recording of early tracks that evolved into the band's first album, *So Gone* (2006). Once Jones had enough to work with and add to, he recruited his OU chum Davis and long-time friend, Austin Stephens, to help fill in some of the music's blank spaces.

After completing the demos, Johnson shopped them to **Scott Booker** at Hellfire Management who helped the band get in front of Misra Records pen and contract carriers at the South by Southwest Music Festival and Conference in Austin.[1] As a result, the Evangelicals released *The Evening Descends* (2008), much of which was recorded in **Trent Bell**'s studios in Norman where chimey toy piano music with layered, harmonized vocals must waft out of the air conditioning vents, picked up by the live microphones. Throughout the album, the Evangelicals show a mix of whimsical influences from the Beach Boys, Pink Floyd, the Association, and old B-movie horror soundtracks to their obvious Norman forbears, the **Flaming Lips**, **Chainsaw Kittens**, and **Starlight Mints**. Additionally, due to being relatively isolated from a massive urban music scene with pressures to sound one way or another, the Evangelicals are following a muse that led the Beatles through Sgt. Pepper, **Debris** through *Static Disposal*, and the Flaming Lips through all kinds of transcendent psychedelic circus rock, incorporating any and all sounds, musical textures, instruments, time signatures, and accidentally recorded phrases into a fluffy brew of modern pop that one would not know is from Oklahoma unless they were told, and now you have been. The Evangelicals were booked for several performances into 2011.

www.myspace.com/evangelicals

The Evangelicals are from left to right Austin Stephens, Kyle Davis, Josh Jones, and Todd Jackson, 2008.

Note

1. One can follow the development of the Evangelicals in a series of articles published in the *Daily Oklahoman*: Daniel Lapham, "Local Band Q&A: The Evangelicals," Daily Oklahoman, 11 April, 2005; Gene Triplett, "CD debut has Evangelicals founder singing praises," *Daily Oklahoman,* 9 June, 2006: section D, p.7; Gene Triplett, "Evangelicals will answer the call to return home," Daily Oklahoman, 7, March, 2008: section D, p. 1; Brandy McDonnell, "Halloween fosters Evangelicals' seal," Daily Oklahoman, 30 October, 2009: section D: pp 1, 6.

F

Fields, Ernie

(b. August 26, 1905 – d. May 11, 1997)

A smooth, lyrical trombonist and territory band leader whose home base was Tulsa starting in the 1930s and continuing through his death in 1997, Ernie Fields was born in Nacogdoches, Texas, but raised in the one-time all-black town of Taft, Oklahoma. Fields was known for his 1960 R&B-sized rendition of Glen Miller's big band classic, "In the Mood", which Fields rode all the way up to #4 on *Billboard's* Hot 100 pop songs chart. Long before that, however, he led one of the Southwest's most consistent and durable territory bands starting in the early 1930s and kept playing dates through the mid-1960s. Territory bands were usually hot-blowing blues and jazz bands with mostly African-American musicians who toured the Midwest, or territories, often playing for pockets of black people in various cities, or for whites in more progressive cities. According to historian Albert McCarthy in *Big Band Jazz*, Fields' group in 1931 contained two notable figures, eventual jump bandleader **Roy Milton** on drums, and legendary Muskogee pianist Hobart Banks, of whom **Jay McShann** spoke highly when remembering a Muskogee jazz musician who could have been successful internationally, but chose to stay close to home. By 1933, both of those musicians had been replaced in the Fields band, according to a lineup of the group printed in *The Chicago Defender* that year as listed by McCarthy, and the group continued gigging the Midwest and Southwest before being discovered in Dallas by John Hammond in June, 1939. Writing about *Down Beat* magazine's response to the signing of Fields, McCarthy indicates *Down Beat* told its readers that Ernie and the orchestra had been tumbling around the region in a beat up Dodge truck, and mentioned consecutive one-nighters in a town "forty miles east of Tulsa", Wichita, Kansas, and then back down to Dallas, grueling by any standards, but that was the standard of the time for touring bands.[1]

Fields took his orchestra to New York in 1939 to record, notably "T-Town Blues", played in the area for a while, and headed back to T-Town itself, Tulsa. For the next twenty years, Fields kept a group on the road, not easy to do as work for big bands slowed down to a halt after the arrival of the rock era, however, because of his R&B and blues-based sound, he fit in with audiences keen for authentic dance and listening music of that type. Ironically, it was a big band song, Glen Miller's "In the Mood" that propelled Fields to the Top 5 of the Hot 100 in January, 1960. Field's version hops like a novelty version of Boots Randoph's "Yakety Sax", also showing what a

Ernie Fields Orchestra, circa 1940s

vacuum US popular music was experiencing in 1960: Motown had yet to really take off, the Beach Boys and surf were just waxing up their boards, **The Ventures** had kept guitars on the pop charts, and Bob Dylan had just moved to New York's Greenwich Village. Fields tried to follow up four months later with a similar R&B take on another Glen Miller hit, "Chattanooga Choo Choo", but the song stalled at #54, and 1961's attempted update on "The Charleston" went nowhere as the slickly produced new sounds coming out of Motown were starting to represent a new era in African-American popular music. When Fields retired in 1966, his son, Ernie Jr. continued the family musical tradition as a saxophonist who played with the bands of Marvin Gaye and Rick James.[2] McCarthy notes Fields' band was really the last of the territory groups to stop working as a unit, and just for lasting so long, not to mention actually having a pop hit, which McCarthy does not mention because he didn't consider Fields' hits jazz, Ernie Fields should be recognized by jazz historians. For his ability to keep a big band going for so long, changing with the times by incorporating rock and roll and R&B into his repertoire, and for being a primary representative of the bluesy and swinging territory band tradition while based in Tulsa for most of career, it's no surprise he was one of the Oklahoma Jazz Hall of Fame's initial inductees in 1989. In 2013, OK POP announced it had acquired Fields' personal photos, recordings, posters, and other artifacts for display in the museum planned for Tulsa by the Oklahoma History Center.

Recommended Listening
Big Band Jazz Tulsa to Harlem: Featuring Cab Calloway, Ernie Fields, and Jimmy Hamilton (Delmark, DL-4390).

Notes
1. For a thorough overview of Fields' bands and their personnel from 1931 to 1960, see Albert McCarthy, *Big Band Jazz* (New York: Putnam, 1974): pp. 112. 2. For a delightful appraisal of Fields' career from a progressive musician's point of view, see the biographical entry for Ernie Fields written by multi-instrumentalist Eugene Chadbourne at www.allmusic.com (accessed July 28, 2010).

Fisher, Shug (George Clinton)

(b. September 26, 1907 – d. March 16, 1984)

Bassist for three extended periods with one of Western music's emblematic groups, the Sons of the Pioneers, a cast member of two of the earliest country music radio shows (*WWVA Wheeling Jamboree* and *WLW Boone County Jamboree*), and one of the first to use a stand up bass in country music, George Clinton Fisher was born in Tabler, Oklahoma, a tiny hamlet four miles east of Chickasha. He received his sugar-shortened nickname, "Shug", from his mother. Fisher's father was Scotch-Irish, whereas, his mother is reportedly one-quarter Choctaw.[1] His musical background propelled him into show business in Los Angeles, where he parlayed his Oklahoma knowledge and ability to speak in a strong western or country accent into roles in fifty films from 1943 to 1981, and on twenty-eight television shows or continuing TV series from 1954 to 1981.

At age ten, the family moved to coal country of Pittsburgh County, Oklahoma, in a covered wagon. Shug's first instrument was mandolin, then the fiddle which has the same G-D-A-E string configuration, and then the guitar to back his father, also a fiddler, although that was unbeknownst to Shug until he found his father playing the instrument after Shug brought it home and set it down. The two played square dances with the elder Fisher on lead, and Shug "seconding", or providing rhythmic chord changes to support the fiddle.

One can only search the imagination for an image of the mythic medicine show that rolled through Pittsburgh County in 1924, when a seventeen-year-old Shug watched the wagon's "Toby" character, usually a comedian with red wig and blacked-out tooth performing cornpone comedy with music.[2] As a result of the traveling show sparking his show business dreams, he decided to make a combination of music and comedy his career. No report of what happened to his mother, but Fisher and his father drove their model T Ford in a move to California in 1925, where Shug worked various jobs in the oil fields before landing a job on radio station KMS in Fresno. After appearing on the "Hollywood Breakfast Club" show doing his songs and humor, he was approached by Tom Murray to join his group, the Hollywood Hillbillies, which he did. With a stash of fiddlers, guitar players, and vocalists in abundance, Fisher learned to play the stand-up bass, adding it to the combo as his contribution to instrumentation in country music. By that point, the stand up bass occurred primarily in jazz, but early cowboy groups such as **Otto Gray and His Oklahoma Cowboys** tended to use the smaller viol. With this ability, Fisher became more desirable, and jumped ship for the Beverly Hill Billies on a regular gig in San Francisco before returning to Los Angeles for a spot on the the "Covered Wagon Show".

In 1935, Fisher teamed with Roy Faulkner, "The Lonesome Cowboy," broadcasting from the first of the X-Border stations (XERA) in Del Rio, Texas, owned and operated by Dr. J. R. Brinkley, who advertised his various medical remedies. The "X" stations could operate with tremendous power since their transmitters were often in Mexico, often covering major portions of the western, mid west, and southwestern United States. While touring on this widespread popularity and radio promotion, he met Hugh Cross, composer of "Back to the Old Smokey Mountains," and the two formed a duet called Hugh and Shug's Radio Pals. The duet became regulars on the *WWVA Wheeling Jamboree* and the *WLW Boone County Jamboree* during the 1930s.

At the outbreak of World War II, Shug returned to Los Angeles, where he worked for the

Shug Fisher

Lockheed Aircraft plant in Burbank, and entertained defense workers for the Victory Committee. Upon the invitation of Pat Brady, Roy Roger's comic sidekick who played bass and did comedy for the Sons of the Pioneers, one of Western and cowboy music's most successful group acts ever, Shug joined the group the Pioneers in 1943 and stayed for three years. From 1946 to '49, he played with Stuart Hamblen, and began playing character roles in films, such as *The Man from Oklahoma* (1945), but returned to the Sons of the Pioneers when Brady left the group to re-join Roy Rogers for movie and television work. During this stint with the Sons of the Pioneers, Shug and the group performed at Carnegie Hall in 1951, probably his peak moment with the group. A year later, he was back with Hamblen.

In 1953, Shug met Ken Curtis, best known for his role as Festus on the *Gunsmoke* television series, and worked with him in movies, television, and radio for the next two years. In 1957, he rejoined the Sons of the Pioneers for the last time and stayed with them until 1959, during which he appeared on several of their RCA recordings, many of which are crystallized and in the re-mastered 2004 released, RCA Country Legends: *Son's of the Pioneers* (RCA). Along with appearing in the critically missed B-Movie, The Giant Gila Monster in 1959, he performed as part of Red Foley's Ozark Jubilee cast from 1959 to 1961, and enjoyed an extremely fulfilling film and TV career through his retirement in 1981. In 1962, he appeared in the iconic John Ford Western, *The Man Who Shot Liberty Valance,* pairing Jimmy Stewart and John Wayne for the first time. Among many television shows, mostly with a Western or country setting, Fisher appeared in *Bonanza* (1961, '69, '70), *Gunsmoke* (1962 to '74), and brought his career full circle with regular appearances as "Shorty Kellums" on the *Beverly Hillbillies* (1969-70), an ironic return to some of his first professional music work with the group with that name in San Francisco. In addition to his music, Shug appeared in sixteen movies with Roy Rogers, played the role of Shorty Kellums in nineteen episodes of *The Beverly Hillbillies* television series, and performed on several *Gunsmoke* shows with his old friend, Ken Curtis, who was at his side when Shug died in March of 1984, after a long illness.

Son of the Pioneers, circa 1940s; Shug Fisher, (bottom right).

Along with his highly successful entertainment career, Fisher indicates a few things about Oklahoma culture, and is actually one of the reinforcements for the mid-twentieth century popular concept of authentic Western characters coming from Oklahoma. Fisher learned music traditionally in the state, moved to California as so many Oklahomans did in the 1920s and 30s, and succeeded in turning his Oklahoma dialect, rural sensibility, and musical talent by into notable career in music, movies, and television. Being from Oklahoma actually benefitted Shug Fisher as it provided him a life of authentic experience from which to draw for a notable show business resumé. After ceasing his professional work in 1981, he endured a lingering illness before dying in Los Angeles with his long-time friend, Ken Curtis, at his side.

Shug Fisher, actor

Notes

1. Information regarding Fisher's mother's American Indian (Choctaw) heritage, and other facts that can be confirmed in this essay, derive from a biographical entry for Fisher from an undeterminable published reference work, as the page has been separated from the original text, and is in the author's individual file for Fisher. No author, publisher or title may be determined from the page itself, only that the information printed on the page is cogently arranged, professionally laid out, and thorough in its narrative of his life. No original part of it has been duplicated here without corroboration from other public sources.

2. For insight into the medicine shows of 1920s rural Oklahoma, see Robert Lee Wyatt III, "Traveling Shows", *Encyclopedia of Oklahoma History and Culture* (Oklahoma City: Oklahoma Historical Society, 2009). One may also access the online version of the entry at http://digital.library.okstate.edu/encyclopedia/index.html (accessed July 31, 2010).

The Five Americans

Mike Rabon (b. April 16, 1943)
John Durrill (b. August 29, 1940)
Jimmy Wright (b. December 2, 1950)
Jim Grant (b. July 29, 1943 – d. November 29, 2004)
Norman Ezell (b. October 22, 1943 – d. May 8, 2010)

Originally formed in Durant at Southeastern Oklahoma State University in 1962 as The Mutineers, The Five Americans (5As) became perennial Top 40 chart dwellers for a two-year period (1966 to 1968) with their harmonized garage pop singles, "I See the Light", "Zip Code", "Sound of Love", "Evol-Not Love", and their signature song, "Western Union", a #5 hit on *Billboard*'s Hot 100 in May, 1967. Mike Rabon, lead guitarist, vocalist, and leader of the group, was born in Port Arthur, Texas, but moved to Hugo at one month of age; his parents were both schoolteachers and native Oklahomans when they moved to Spencerville, Oklahoma, a very small community in southeastern Oklahoma. While there, Rabon became a self-taught guitarists, and by age twelve joined a local group called The Buckaroos. Bassist Grant was born in Hugo; drummer Wright in Durant; and keyboardist Durrill in Bartlesville. The only non-Oklahoman was guitarist Ezell, who was born in Albuquerque, New Mexico. While many Oklahoma rock and pop musicians of the 1960s made their careers in Los Angeles, the Five Americans bounced out of the Dallas, Texas scene with their tight harmonies, electric guitars, melodic bass, and drum-kit heavy sound perfect for a market ready to embrace an American Beatles.

Durant's geographic location in southern Oklahoma exposed all of the musicians to Dallas radio stations playing the new pop and rock music ushered in by the British Invasion, as well hearing the Oklahoma City Top 40 wars of the 1960s between KOMA and WKY always trying to beat the other with the latest big thing. After playing local venues in and around Durant until the summer of 1964, and knowing they had "the sound", Rabon proposed the band play some gigs in Dallas in order to pay for tuition the next college semester. In Dallas, the group developed a local following in such nightspots as the Pirate's Nook, where they were noticed by John Abdnor, president of Abnak Records, who began to support the group, allowing them to write songs and providing space for them to practice. In the summer of 1965, Abdnor Records released one of the group's original songs, "I See the Light", and it climbed to a respectable #26 on *Billboard*'s Hot 100 pop songs chart. The next single, "Evol – Not Love" (#52/1966) rolled out with a militaristic drum cadence, and (saying something in itself as the Vietnam War escalated at the sametime), and seemingly conscious Beatle-esque harmonies, even to the point of imitating John Lennon's unique vocal waivers, all tried to embrace the transition in popular music of the mid-1960s in reaction to Beatles'

albums *Rubber Soul* (1965) *Revolver* (1966), and the Beach Boys' *Pet Sounds* (1966), moving most pop rock groups to a more mod, psychedelic sound with distorted guitars, multi-tracked vocals, and heavier keyboard accents and fills. Jumping right in the fray, the Five Americans released their biggest hit and signpost tune, "Western Union," co-written by Rabon, Ezell, and Durrill in the spring of 1967. Exhibiting the magic moments of a hit single, the song breaks open with a catchy keyboard riff that is later replicated by the song's memorable a cappella vocal breaks, all around the subject of getting a high-tech Dear John letter via Western Union. The success of song prompted invitations to appear twice on *American Bandstand*, four times on *Where the Action Is*, and as guests on *The Steve Allen Show*. While introducing the band on his show, Allen says, "They have a very good sound. They are one of the groups that even the old squares like. You know there's certain groups the old squares don't like; then there are other groups that they'll describe, 'Now, they sing kind of nice.'"[1]

Since American popular culture does not let go of its one (or a few) hit wonders easily, "Western Union" has enjoyed steady remembrances. Included as part of the highly praised musical template of Cameron Crow's film, *Vanilla Sky* (2001), "Western Union" has remained a favorite on classic oldies radio in the U.S. and Canada, reaching the one million airplay status mark as certified by BMI in 1998. The Five Americans' peak moment is May 20, 1967, when "Western Union" sat at #5 on *Billboard*'s Hot 100 pop singles chart. Unfortunately for everyone making popular music at the time, the Beatles released *Sgt. Pepper's Lonely Hearts Club Band* in June, 1967 and changed the game for everyone. With its highly crafted studio sound, concept album song arrangement, varied instrumentation, and elaborate song construction, *Sgt. Pepper* became the new standard for commercial and artistic pop rock music. While the Five Americans cracked the top 40 again with "Sound of Love" (#36), an obvious nod to the Summer of Love happening at the time, the band's sound by that point was more related to the previous four years in pop, not what was happening at the moment. Their fall release, "Zip Code", tried to capitalize on their previous "communication theme," and received exactly the same response from their supporters at radio and retail, inching the song inside the top 40 at #36, the same spot as the previous single. After one more attempt, "7:30 Guided Tour", just stuck a toe in *Billboard*'s Hot 100 at #96 in February of 1968, the group began to fracture under the stress of touring and creating a another communication song to please radio and their label. After Durrill and Ezell left, the group used San Franciscans Bobby Rambo (guitarist) and Lenny Goldsmith (keyboards) to fulfill tour obligations and record their final album, *Now and Then*, the band broke up in 1969. Along with *Now and Then*, The Five Americans recorded four albums: *I See the Light* (#136/1966), *Western Union/ Sound of Love* (#121/1967), *Progressions* (1967).

United Artists released John Durrill solo album in 1978, *Just for the Record*, with a leadoff track of "Oklahoma City Nights", but the album did not distinguish itself enough to divert the label's weighty attention to its only other signee, Elton John. Rabon later organized a band called Michael Rabon and Choctaw, which successfully toured the Southwest in the mid-1970s, but returned to college for his Master's degree and currently teaches music in Hugo, his hometown. Jim Grant launched his own logo company in Dallas before his death in 2004, and Norman Ezell was a teacher and preacher in northern California before his death of cancer in 2010. Jimmy Wright lives in Ohio and is a videographer for Breakthrough Ministries. Of the group, Durrill had the most post-5As music industry success. He went on to play organ and write songs for The Ventures, and penned the 1973 #1 hit single for Cher, "Dark Lady", as well as a 1980 #3 *Billboard* Hot Country Song for Merle Haggard, "Misery and Gin" and "Charlotte's Web," recorded by the Statler Brothers, which also made it #5 on the country charts.

For several years, the members of the Five Americans could not actually re-group under that name due to a bad management contract the group signed when they were young and naïve about the music industry. Once all of legalities were sorted out, all five original members reunited in 2002 to rerecord all of their 1960s hits. The motivation behind the re-recordings, according to Rabon, was based on the use of "Western Union" in the *Vanilla Sky* film. Paramount Studios bought the right to use the song from Sundazed Records, which owns the original masters, and has not paid the Five Americans any royalties for their sales in Europe, or anywhere else. By rerecording their songs in the same studio with all original members and the same engineer, the group now owns a second original master of all their hits. Rabon states that one cannot tell the difference between the 1967 and 2002 masters, and planned an eventual release of those re-recorded songs as well as some lost masters that have never been released. In 2003, the group performed at a sold out show for the annual Southeastern Oklahoma State University Arts Gala scholarship benefit (minus drummer Jim Wright who had a scheduling conflict), their first public appearance since 1988. The re-formed group played several gigs throughout 2003 at Six Flags amusement parks across the country, and ocean cruises with a rock music theme, and continued shows when the conditions were right throughout the 2000s; Rabon and Durrill re-united for a 2009 show at the Oklahoma History Center to commemorate deejay Ronnie Kaye's *The Scene* as part of the Another Hot Oklahoma Night Rock Exhibit in place from 2009 to 2011, an exhibit made possible in part by successful Oklahoma groups like The Five Americans.
www.thefiveamericans.com

Flaming Lips
Coyne, Wayne (multi-instrumentalist, vocalist, b. Pittsburgh, PA, March 17, 1965)
Drozd, Stephen (multi-instrumentalist/guitarist, b. Houston, TX, June 11, 1969)
Ivins, Michael (bassist, engineer, b. Omaha, Nebraska, March 17, 1963)
Scurlock, Kliph (drums and percussion since 2002)
(Formed in 1983, Oklahoma City, OK)

Flourishing in their third decade of making rock music under the leadership of Wayne M. Coyne, the Flaming Lips are Oklahoma's most significant rock group ever. For over twenty five years of lush popular music, sonic experiments, rambling extended tracks of mythical and mystical musings, rough edged rock outs, and occasional bouts with commercial success, the Flaming Lips have enjoyed the four bounties of music industry success: critical acclaim in the press, public adoration for concerts and their multiple audio/visual products, enough commercial success to keep their contract with Warner Brothers, and industry recognition with three GRAMMY Awards. Born in Pennsylvania but raised in northwest Oklahoma City, Wayne Coyne grew up in a large family of "four brothers, a sister, a dog, two cats, and a snake," according to the band's website. Along with nurturing his ample artistic talents as a painter at Oklahoma City's Classen High School, Wayne began working as a fry-cook at the local Long John Silver's, a job he kept for several years until signing with Warner Brothers records in 1992.[1] After buying his first guitar at age fifteen, he allegedly stole a collection of musical instruments from an area church hall and convinced his brother Mark and bassist Michael Ivins to start the band (or so goes one of the legends about the group). The group began their career with either an intentionally nonsensical psychedelic name that vaguely references an erotic film, an obscure drug reference, or a dream in which a fiery Virgin Mary kissed Wayne in the backseat of his car, depending on who is telling the story. Of course, rock music (and all of show business) is filled with embellished or creative press releases in order to create a good story or band image, and the origin of band/song/album name is not as significant as the shape it takes artistically and in the minds of listeners or viewers. In any case, after wearing out (or frustrating) a long line of drummers, percussionist Richard English agreed to take on the task of keeping time for the group's initial outings locally in Norman and Oklahoma City. The group released their self-titled debut, a five-song EP on green vinyl, through their own label, Lovely Sorts of Death, in 1985. The album is an earnest first rock album that brought them to the attention of college radio nationwide as a result of its reissue on Pink Dust Records, and sounds like a punk rock group playing Pink Floyd songs as the group wrestled with what kind identity they would have, a sonic template they have carried on subconsciously since, and eventually elevating to a fine rock art with a full on cover of Pink Floyd's *Dark Side of the Moon* album in 2010. With books, films, and columns of writing filled with critical applause for the Flaming Lips, the following narrative hits some of the band's highlights, leaving the reader to journey on his or her own through their sonic and visual labyrinth, kee"ping in mind things may not always be what they seem or sound like.

Soon after the group's initial EP, Mark Coyne left the group to get married and Wayne took over the lead vocal role. As a trio, the group released *Hear It Is* in 1986, which hinted at the band's stylistic future on songs that featured Wayne Coyne's sincerely off key vocals and personal lyrics, fairly straight ahead garage rock songs founded in The Who and Stooges, and the occasional noisy ramble by the whole group. Fans can certainly discern Coyne's penchant for musical drama in the album's songs, as well as the early signals of his interest in layering echo-laden vocals, a la Brian Wilson, and adding esoteric sounds on multiple tracks for an ethereal effect in the music. In 1987, the group released *Oh My Gawd...The Flaming Lips*, featuring more refined developments of the style on *Hear It Is*, as well as examples of Coyne's interest in sound effects and "noise" as part of his sonic soundscape. The influence of classic rock such as the Beatles and The Who is also readily apparent on songs such as "Everything's Exploding." The band's upbringing in Oklahoma City where mainstream rock has long dominated rock radio might be a partial explanation for this element of their sound. Additionally, close listeners to songs like "One Million Billionth of a Millisecond" can hear riffs and vocals that are eerie harbingers of the future sounds of Seattle groups like Nirvana.

After recording 1988's *Telepathic Surgery*, a continuation of the studio experimentation with multi-tracking and further development of Coyne as a singer and songwriter, English left the band, and the group added drummer Nathan Roberts, while Donahue became a

The Flaming Lips, left of right: Steven Drozd, Wayne Coyne, and Michael Ivins.

full-time member of the group under the pseudonym Dingus. The new lineup recorded 1990s *In a Priest Driven Ambulance*, marking the band's evolution into a very competent rock band with more to offer than studio experiments, musical kookiness, and classic rock references. The album also continued Coyne's long interest in religious imagery and plenty of guitar mania. After *In a Priest Driven Ambulance*, which bolstered the Lips' solidly entrenched cult status on college radio, the band signed a major label deal with Warner Brothers, and released *Hit to Death in the Future Head* that outsold all the Lips' albums before it with the backing of the corporate music industry. The contract also allowed Wayne to purchase the first fireproof house in Oklahoma City that became the Flaming Lips Compound where Coyne still lives in the neighborhood where he grew up in the northwest part of town. After *Hit to Death*, Donahue left to focus on his group, Mercury Rev, and drummer Roberts left shortly after that.

Wayne Coyne, 2006

In 1993, the Lips released *Transmissions from the Satellite Heart* with new guitarist Ronald Jones and multi-instrumentalist, Steven Drozd, who entered the band as drummer. Son of musician, Vernon Drozd, Steven spent his early life in Houston, where he played keyboards in his father's polka band before moving to Lawton where he attended Eisenhower High School. He played in many of the schools musical ensembles, to include the symphony and jazz groups. With Drozd's contributions to the band, the group took on slightly more elevated musical tone, and *Tranmissions from the Satellite Heart* registered commercially in ways that previous releases had not. The group supported the album by playing the second stage on the Lollapalooza tour, but the album did not sell well until the single "She Don't Use Jelly" surprisingly found its way on to the pop charts after becoming a nationwide college radio favorite. As a result of the unlikely success of their album selling beyond their (and Warner Brothers') wildest expectations, the group landed an opening slot for the mainstream pop rock group, Candlebox, and created more of a sensation with their lip-synched performance of the hit on *Beverly Hills 90210*. With an unanticipated national notoriety, thereby creating new found pop expectations for the band, the Lips pursued their own non-pop vision with the eight-song compilation, *Providing Needles for Your Balloons* (Warner Bros., 1994), consisting of live recordings, four-track demos, a Christmas song, and a radio broadcast on KJ-103 in Oklahoma City. Then, baring the process behind their hit, the band released a three-song EP, *Turn It On*, in 1995 that included the demo version of the song.

In spite of the success of *Transmissions*, the Lips did not try to replicate the album with another hit, but continued their exploration of the studio with multi-layered pop on *Clouds Taste Metallic* that is roundly felt by critics as the band's most mature and important work up until 1995. Elevated comparisons to the epic Beach Boys' album *Pet Sounds* started to roll forth from the rock press, and song titles on the album such as "This Here Giraffe" and "Christmas at the Zoo" do not hinder the analogies at all. In 1996, the band frayed at the ends when Jones vanished on a spiritual journey from which he did

Stephen Drozd, 2009

not return, Drozd's hand was rendered inoperative for a time when he was bitten by a spider (later memorialized in "The Spiderbite Song"), and Ivins was the victim of a strange hit-and-run accident when another vehicle's wheel came loose and hit Ivins' car, trapping him inside (mentioned in the same song). Also in '96, Coyne started his famous "parking lot experiments" in Oklahoma City where he produced about forty tapes and invited various people to bring their cars to the lot where they would all play the tapes simultaneously in the cavernous confines of the parking garage. This led to similar displays with multiple boom boxes around the country where Wayne passed out cassette players of all types and had audience members start tapes on cue. Subsequently, Coyne talked Warner Brothers into letting him try one of the most experimental audio projects since John Lennon convinced George Martin to include Revolution #9 on the Beatles' so-called *White Album*.

Zaireeka (Warner Bros., 1997) is a four CD set designed to be played in four different CD players at the same time, individually, and/or in any combination thereof, and was overwhelmingly approved of by rock critics who were probably more stunned by the whole thing than able to dissect it with any relevance whatsoever. At the same time they had been working on *Zaireeka*, the band had been developing songs for their 1999 release, *The Soft Bulletin*, a peaceful and lush album sounding like Neil Young backed by the Salsoul Orchestra. Coyne's vocals continue as a warble, his lyrics are introspectively deep without losing their sense of humor, and the heavy use of synthesized strings often make the record sound like a soul or disco album of the 1970s. On *The Soft Bulletin*, the group also continues to borrow riffs, consciously or unconsciously, from all the rock and pop that has drifted through their ears since their childhood. Beach Boys critical comparisons abounded as Coyne somehow builds up to almost replicating the delicacy of Brian Wilson's most inspired moments while maintaining the Lips' own powerful originality in a song like "Buggin'". Following *The Soft Bulletin*, the group worked on soundtrack music for a documentary on Oklahomans who catch giant flathead catfish using their wiggling fingers for bait. The film, *Okie Noodling*, produced an entire Lips album, *The Southern Oklahoma Cosmic Trigger Contest*, consisting of music Wayne calls "epic country and western," further adding the album features, "harmonica, banjo, upright bass, strings, and occasional hiccups." At the same time, the group also worked on songs for a holiday score called *Christmas on Mars*, which Wayne dubbed "cosmic and religious," and began working on their 2002 release, *Yoshimi Battles the Pink Robots*, which he says was influenced by both of the other projects.

According to Coyne, *Yoshimi's* "theme of sunshine funerals will render its listeners powerless to study or analyze it, and enable them to sit back and –hopefully for a couple of minutes at a time – just simply be … entertained." While the album is not a concept album per se, it does have several "sound story" compositions connected throughout the record and loosely based on the fictional character of a singer, Yoshimi, who fights robots that are programmed with synthetic emotions. Other songs on the album further Coyne's examination of life's intricacies and dichotomies in songs such as "All We Have is Now" and "Do You Realize??" To derive one's happiness only from specific moments in time is "to miss out on the cosmic accident that is all of life's moments," according to Coyne, and the inspiration for "Ego Tripping at the Gates of Hell." While early Lips material seemed to always be some derivative of what had gone before it, *Yoshimi* offered more much originality and mature artistic production than it is a result of its musical forebears.

"Do You Realize" resonated with fans because of its lyrical theme of telling people that you love them before it's too late, and eventually wound up being chosen as the state rock song for Oklahoma in 2009, but not without some controversy, to be discussed later.

The Flaming Lips are also become well known for their elaborate stage shows that exhibit Wayne Coyne's enduring influence of the Butthole Surfers who also provided over-the-top, multi-media stage shows during the 1980s and early 1990s, and with whom the Lips toured in the 1980s. In their 2002 *Yoshimi* tour, the Lips used the standard rock format of bass, drums, and guitar, but also added several sequencers and other machines. On stage Wayne and other band members had at their disposal several bags of glitter, a dry ice machine, four huge disco balls in the back of the stage, another disco ball hanging from the ceiling, a dozen beach-ball-sized balloons they throw to the audience, and three people standing on stage in stuffed animal costumes resembling public television's Teletubbies. In the tradition of both the Surfers and 1960s psychedelic rock concerts, the Flaming Lips project bizarre combinations of videos on the screen behind them, to include Shannon Doherty introducing the band on their *90210* appearance, a short film featuring Yoshimi of the Boredoms fighting Japanese girls in school-girl outfits, and a sequence of a naked woman playing Frisbee at a nudist colony. In August, 2002, the group worked with noted video director Mark Pellington on the video for "Do You Realize??" in which Coyne, clad in all white, strums a white guitar while tutu-wearing dancing girls and two giant rabbits hover about him in Las Vegas. Also in the fall of 2002, along with their own live performances, the Lips toured as the backing band for alternative folk rock hero Beck. *Yoshimi* found its way to the top of the college radio charts that year, and was a finalist in the second annual Shortlist Prize for Achievement in Music, an award given to an album of artist merit that has sold less than 500,000 copies.

Wayne Coyne, Lollapalooza, 2006

In September of 2002, Restless and Rykodisc records released two deluxe, multi-disc packages providing a comprehensive look at Flaming Lips material from 1983 to 1991, *The Shambolic Birth* and *Early Life of the Flaming Lips*. Comprised of the band's debut EP, first four full-length albums, and a wealth of previously unreleased or hard-to-find material, *Finally, the Punk Rockers are Taking Acid 1983-1988*, and *The Day They Shot a Hole in the Jesus Egg 1989-1991*, are essential releases for Flaming Lips completists. All previously issued material was re-mastered by the Lips' long-time producer Dave Fridmann, while the band's bassist, Michael Ivins, and Wayne Coyne wrote extensive liner notes for each release. In October of 2002, the group recorded the video for "Yoshimi Battles the Pink Robots, Pt. 1" in the Samurai Japanese Restaurant and Saki House in Oklahoma City. The group also appeared on national television several times in the fall and winter of 2002, to include NBC television's *Late Night with Conan O'Brien*, the WB Network's *Charmed*, CBS television's *Late Late Show with Craig Kilborn*, and PBS's *Austin City Limits*.

Through the winter of 2002 and 2003, the group played a series of dates in Spain, Scotland, and England, with a New Year's Eve show sandwiched in between at Chicago's Metro. To coincide with the British appearances, the group released two different CDs of Lips music, plus a DVD. British CD 1 included the *Yoshimi* album and a couple of remixes, British CD 2 contained the *Yoshimi* album and two different versions of songs from the CD, and the DVD included the *Yoshimi* album's audio, the video for the single, a tune from the *Okie Noodling* soundtrack, and a track from the *Christmas on Mars* soundtrack. By the time of its release in Britain, the album had garnered the following accolades: *Uncut* magazine's #1 album of the year, *Mirror* magazine's #1 album of the year, *Mojo* magazine's #2 album of the year, *Esquire* magazine's top 6 albums of the year, *Record Collector* albums of the year, *Time Out* critics' album of the year, *Time Out* readers' album of the year, *GQ* albums of the year, and several other top ten and best of lists from around the world. The recognition crested in February when the group won a GRAMMY Award for Best Rock Instrumental Performance via *Yoshimi*'s "Approaching Pavonis Mons by Balloon (Utopia Planitia)". When all-everything rock group Coldplay performed in Oklahoma City that same month, singer Chris Martin changed the lyrics of the band's "Everything's Not Lost" to "because you live in the same town as the Flaming Lips, the greatest band in the world. .

Through March of 2003, the Lips toured Europe, playing Austria, Germany, Sweden, Holland, France, Italy, and Greece, among other countries, and followed that up with a steady stream of performances across the U.S. and Canada in major markets. In May, 2003, the group released the *Fight Test* EP CD, and a "Fight Test" 7" vinyl picture disc. The EP covers Beck and Kylie Minogue songs, and two new Lips songs. The CD version included two videos, one for "Fight Test", and the other a trailer for the band's feature length film, *Christmas on Mars*, eventually released in 2005.

In 2004, the Lips co-headlined the Lollapalooza Tour, and played the giant Coachella Festival. Also by that point, the DVD-Audio disc of *Yoshimi Battles the Pink Robots* became the #3 selling DVD-Audio disc of all time, behind the extremely iconic LPs of Fleetwood Mac's *Rumours* and the Eagles' *Hotel California*. As another mark of the respect the group had earned by that point from musical peers, the *Tallywood Strings* released *The String Quartet Tribute to the Flaming Lips* (Vitamin), as well as being requested to re-mix tracks

Flaming Lips at Lollapalooza, 2006

by Thievery Corporation, Chumbawamba, Modest Mouse, and Yoko Ono. By 2004, the group had more history than most bands ever will, and found time to collaborate on a collector's edition coffee table book, *Waking Up with a Placebo Head Wound: Images of the Flaming Lips from the Archives of Jay Blakesberg and J. Michelle Martin-Coyne (1987-2004)*. Unavailable unless purchased on the collector's market, the limited edition book features 375 images from photographers Jay Blakesberg and Martin-Coyne, Wayne's spouse, and includes a foreword by Wayne, as well as essays by Ivins, Drozd, Martin-Coyne, and band manager **Scott Booker**.

Flaming Lips, OKC Zoo Amphitheater, 2007

2005 found the band contributing to the *SpongeBob SquarePants Movie* soundtrack, and assembling a compilation of dissimilar songs by other artists in one compilation, *Late Night Tales* (Azuli), which did include their own version of the White Stripes' "Seven Nation Army". After a documentary about the band, *The Fearless Freaks*, shot by long-time Coyne friend, Bradley Beesley, testified that the group is not short on real bizarreness (never mind the imagined), and that the group has had severe trials in maintaining themselves as a unit, that summer the Lips also released all nineteen of their videos in surround sound in a video collection titled *V.O.I.D. (Video Overview in Deceleration), 1992-2005* (Warner Brothers), and worked fearlessly on their next album, *At War with the Mystics*.

Released April 4, 2005, *At War with the Mystics*, glistened with the Flaming Lips' decade-plus of learning themselves musically, Coyne continued to challenge listeners to think beyond the typical pop lyrical box (sneaking in some political commentary behind his circus barker's smile), and with the mad scientist engineer, David Fridmann, raised the bar on their own kooky production standards that always fill a Lips with recording with sounds that only become apparent after repeated listening. The album's first single, "The W.A.N.D." emerges more than it starts, building on the song's "click track" or the metronome rhythm track often used on studio recordings to keep musicians in time, moves through sparse and lush parts, big rock drum beats, sound effects, curses at the ones abusing their power in society, layers harmonized vocals that now sound like a familiar sonic palate for the group, and emphasizes Wayne's now recognizable vocal imprint. While a minor chart maker on *Billboard*'s Hot 100, the album itself began a climb to #11 on the album charts, recalling 1970s super group, Led Zeppelin, who had many successful albums, but never enjoyed a #1 single (Zep's "Black Dog" made it to #4 in 1969). The Lips' follow up single, the "Yeah, Yeah Song", did a little better than "The W.A.N.D.", inching up to #48 on the Hot 100, both of which helped the album reach Gold status (500,000 sold) in the U.K. Overall, the album is a sonically diverse collection of songs that exhibits the Flaming Lips in their territorial glory of studio experimentation. One can hear a range of influences on the album, such as the movement towards the free-jazz/funk, and/or soul soundscape of the "The Wizard Turns On..." that sounds like it could have been on Funkadelic's 1971 funk rock masterpiece, *Maggot Brain*. The GRAMMY voters acknowledged the song's unique qualities, awarding the "The Wizard Turns On..." with the GRAMMY for Best Rock Instrumental Performance in 2007. Other tunes on the album bounce along like the modern pop with a Liptwist they were in 1996 ("It Overtakes Me"), build around sound effects such as the siren's foundation of "Mr. Ambulance Driver", or genuinely invoke disco tunes from Wayne's imagination of what the Beach Boys's serrated alter-egos might sound like, while poking comically at uninformed leaders ("Haven't Got a Clue"), a song whose basic track was started by Lips friend Greg Kurstin and forward to the band for completion. As a whole, the album rewards encore listening as the sum of its many parts is equal to its many interesting parts. Peer audio engineers agreed, voting to award *At War with the Mystics* Best Engineered Album, Non-Classical in 2007.

Michael Ivins, 2007

In 2006, Broadway Books released a Lips biography, *Staring at Sound: The True Story of Oklahoma's Fabulous Flaming Lips*, written by *Chicago Sun-Times* pop critic Jim DeRogatis. An exceptional work of rock journalism and popular music the book is based on hundreds of hours of interviews with the band. According to a Broadway Books press release for the tome, "The narrative follows the Flaming Lips through the thriving indie-rock underground of the 1980s and the alternative-rock movement of the early '90s, during which they found fans in such rock legends as Paul McCartney, the Rolling Stones, Robert Plant, and Devo, and respected peers in such acts as the White Stripes, Radiohead, and Beck." Also in 2006, the group recorded a live concert at the Oklahoma City Zoo Amphitheater in front of a manic hometown crowd dressed in all sorts of fuzzy, funny, and funky outfits, released in 2007 at *U.F.O's At The Zoo: The Legendary Concert in Oklahoma City*, and embarked on a full American tour in the summer of 2006. By 2007, the fine art quotient of the Lips' oeuvre reached another high point when the group announced they would be working with noted screenwriter and playwright, Aaron Sorkinn (*A Few Good Men*, *The West Wing*), on a Broadway musical version of *Yoshimi Battles the Pink Robots*. If that weren't strange enough to fans that have followed the band since the 1980s, Oklahoma City recognized the band in 2007 by naming an alley in the Bricktown entertainment district after the psychedelic art rock group, and in the same year, the Oklahoma City Public Schools placed Coyne on their Wall of Fame, recognizing prominent alumni from the district.

In 2008, the Flaming Lips (finally) released their film that had been announced for a 2003 release, *Christmas on Mars* (Warner Bros.), and on which Coyne had been working since 2001. A rock and roll fantasy from Coyne's original idea, and featuring band members as well as many of their friends, the film explores themes of isolation, panic, and human compassion, one of Wayne's most recurring artistic elements. Also in 2008, the Lips performed on national television during VH1's concert honoring The Who, and rang in the 2009 with their second annual New Year's Eve Freak Out concert in Oklahoma City's Cox Convention Center. Even the Lips couldn't imagine how freak 2009 would be not too far from downtown at the state Capitol.

Chronicled somewhat in the introductory essay to the *Oklahoma Music Guide II*, in the summer of 2008 an advisory panel was assembled by the Oklahoma History Center's Larry O'Dell and Jeff Moore to establish a state rock song in tandem with the exhibit they assembled on rock music history in the state. After whittling the list down to ten songs that can teach anyone a lot about rock music from the state, an internet voting process ended up with the Flaming Lips' "Do You Realize??" as the top vote-getter out of 21,000 votes. What followed could only have happened in Oklahoma.

After a fairly benign Senate vote on March 2, 2009, in which it passed Senate Joint Resolution 24 (46-0), naming "Do You Realize??" as the Official Oklahoma Rock Song, Coyne rejoiced in the Senate chambers, and beamed at a news conference afterwards, reveling and forgetting all at the same time that he was in Oklahoma, a conservative and politically carnivalesque state that has not voted for a Democratic Presidential candidate since Eisenhower, yet elected a Democratic governor on several occasions since then, to include Governor Brad Henry, then in the penultimate year of his second term, 2009. When the trio of Coyne, Drozd, and Ivins arrived at the House chamber on April 23, 2009, fresh from band practice where they had been working on the Lips' next album, *Embryonic*, original member Ivins was wearing a t-shirt with the iconic hammer and sickle logo that has long been associated with communism. Let's remember for a second that **Woody Guthrie** was vilified up until really just the last decade for his purported communist tendencies, so much so that his home town of Okemah would barely even recognize him until older town leaders died off. Coupled with the memory by some representatives of Coyne's exuberance during the 2007 Flaming Lips Alley ceremony in which he used some PG-13 language, thirty-nine house members voted against the song and the band, leaving the total vote short of the required 51 majority votes for passing the measure at 48-39. While many elements of state government were aghast at the vote's failure as many plans had been based around it, especially at the Oklahoma History Center in coordination with the Another Hot Oklahoma Night exhibit, Governor Henry stepped in to sign an executive order by the following week to make "Do You Realize??" the official state rock song, although that act stops just short of the law it almost became. Hysteria careened through the state's newspapers, the story made CNN and late night comedy shows, and Coyne tossed a little nitro on the fire by saying the whole process was stopped by "small-minded religious wackos" and the "smart, normal, rational people of Oklahoma know better", a phrase that was repeated in so many publications it's now folkloric instead of bibliographic.[2] All of a sudden, the band practice space and recording studio did not seem so boring after all, and the Lips got right back to work on their next album, *Embryonic*.

Recorded in New York and Oklahoma City between February and July, 2009, again with sound machinist Dave Fridmann at the helm, *Embryonic* stretches out a number Lips tropes unveiled over the second half of their career into a soundtrack for a rave party hosted by Darth Vader on the Death Star. Any writer who tried to encapsulate the album had to pull out similar things that have been said before about Lips music, but this writer will try by saying that *Embryonic* is a rock art boxing match between Brian Wilson and Sonic Youth refereed and scored by corrupt referees and punch counters, the Flaming Lips. *Embryonic* is really soundscape architecture, as much an aural building as musical form. Merging deep house beats, distortion, random clips and sound effects, the music swirls around the stereo, as the band (including Fridmann) is extremely sophisticated in manipulation of sound placement in the electronic audio spectrum.

Flaming Lips, 2009

264 / Oklahoma Music Guide II

Embryonic also appears to be partly influenced by Drozd's progressive jazz background at Lawton Ike High School, as the album occasionally mirrors sonic textures of Miles Davis' *Bitches Brew*, and other jazz/rock fusion such as Chick Corea's Return to Forever ("The Sparrow Looks Up at the Machine", "Gemini Syringes", "Powerless"). Other songs are just Flaming Lips songs that do not fit any category or influence as the group really has become its own genre, the goal of transcending one's influences and becoming original ("Your Bats", "Sagittarius Silver Announcement"), or stay original but add references to their influences in interesting ways, such as the riffing on Led Zeppelin's "Kashmir" in "Scorpio Sword"). Juxtaposed against the musical tension on *Embryonic* are Coyne's existentialist vocals winsomely questioning, challenging and cathartically expressing life's challenges ("Evil", "If", "Silver Trembling Hands", "Watching the Planets"), and offering more urgent vocals on relationship songs ("Convinced of the Hex", "See the Leaves"). The group has given over to the idea that they create albums, much like rock artists did in the late 1960s and early 1970s. Coyne must know Lips fans are not waiting to hear their new song on Top 40 or even modern rock radio, but waiting for the next album to come out as a digital download or disc. That strategy worked as *Embryonic* had no single on any commercial radio chart, but the buying public popped the CD to #5 on *Billboard*'s Top Internet Albums chart, and #8 on their top 200 Albums chart, a successful charting by any record label's standards. The sessions also spawned a short film documenting the project, *Blastula: The Making of Embryonic*.

After the *Embryonic* sessions, the group embarked on recording a complete version of the classic 1973 Pink Floyd album in **Trent Bell**'s Norman studio, Bell Labs, cementing Floyd's long influence on the band which original fans have talked about since the group's initial releases. To complete the album, the Lips enlisted local freakrock understudies, **Stardeath and White Dwarfs**, the German electronica singer and performance artist, Peaches, to fulfill Chaka Khan's voice parts, and also brought in hardcore icon, Henry Rollins, the former lead singer of pioneering punk and hardcore outfit, Black Flag, also well known as a spoken word artist, television host, writer, ranter, publisher, actor, and activist.[3] Regarding the recording and release of *Dark Side of the Moon*, one can only say the Lips' version is not a tribute, but revisionary; honorable, but not honoring. The recording sifts the original songs through the Lips' colander, throws them in a blender, and really sounds like the band is finally able to open up and play through their influences, channeling the sources of their inspirations into something all together new. Throughout the album, a listener often forgets they are traveling in a rock space time machine, and just thinks they are listening to a new Flaming Lips album, until one of the familiar melodies or lyrical phrases appears as a reminder. Commercially, the album splashed into the Top Internet Album chart (#12), symbolizing the high-tech comfort of

Wayne Coyne, 2002

many Lips fans, but did not fare as well on the Top Rock Album chart (#42), or the top 200 Album chart (#157). As an addition to their catalogue, however, hearing the band play and record such a seminal album by one of their primary musical inspirations, all through the aural spectrum of the band's studio gizmos, a zip loc of honky funk, and their familiar psychedelic textures, gives listeners a rare glimpse into a band's viewpoint of their musical foundations, and, subsequently, how those foundations helped form the group. Following up on their New Year's Eve Freak-Out Tradition, the Lips staged another concert in Oklahoma City in 2009 where they not only played a so-called standard Flaming Lips show, but added on a complete performance of *Dark Side of the Moon*, a performance they repeated at the Bonnaroo Festival in June, 2010. What's next, the Flaming Lips re-record *The Beatles* (a.k.a. *"The White Album"*)? Who wouldn't want to hear Wayne's "cover" of "Revolution #9"? Okay, maybe a few people might not, but *OMG* would.

With over thirty years of a music career behind them, to include three GRAMMY Awards, multiple albums, films, and mixed-media projects, as well as elaborate circus-like concerts, and nothing but critical raves surrounding their every move contemporarily, The Flaming Lips are more proof that Oklahoma's supposedly isolated environment can produce innovative and enduring music for the global environment, and the musicians do not have to leave the state to create it; but they do have to travel to support it. In 2010, the Lips toured England's Isle of Wight, Portugal, Poland, Norway, France, Belgium, and upon returning to the US played a few Midwest shows before touring Canada, the US West Coast, then Austin and Florida.

Along with multiple releases in all kinds of crazy promotional packages, in 2011 The Lips recorded a six-hour song to raise money for the Central Oklahoma Humane Society and the University of Central Oklahoma's Academy of Contemporary Music. They also rang in the new year with a concert in which they teamed up with Yoko Ono for their annual New Year's Eve freakout in Oklahoma City. Along with a single featuring Ms.Ono in 2012, The Flaming Lips also released an album of collaborations, *The Flaming Lips and Heady Fwends* (Warmer Bros), featuring Nick Cave, Bon Iver, and Erykah Badu, among others. If all that weren't enough in 2012, the band also set a Guinness World Record for most live shows in a 24-hour period, which Wayne termed an "absurd joy" in a press release by the band.

www.flaminglips.com

Endnotes

1. To get a very solid overview of the Flaming Lips' career from a local Oklahoma City point of view see Gene Triplett's coverage in the *Daily Oklahoman*: "Wayne Coyne's teen dedication sign of future," *Daily Oklahoman,* 5 November, 2004: section D, p.1. ; "Flaming Lips open wide for *Freaks* film," *Daily Oklahoman,* 22 April 2005: section D, p.1.; "Flaming Lips front man Wayne Coyne: master performer or space cadet?" *Daily Oklahoman,* 22 April 2006: section D, p.1. ; "Making their own mythological path; surreal grandeur belies band's origins," *Daily Oklahoman,* 22 April 2007: section D, p.1. ; "Wayne Coyne, Flaming Lips to ring in 2009 in city with concert, *Daily Oklahoman,* 29 December 2008: section C, p.1.; "Flaming Lips and friends ready to light up *Dark Side of Moon*," *Daily Oklahoman,* 29 December 2009: section D, p.1.;"Flaming Lips' documentary to be screened," *Daily Oklahoman,* 11 June 2010: section D, p.1.

2. To follow the mostly amusing paper trail of the Oklahoma State Rock Song saga involving the Flaming Lips, see stories in Oklahoma's two major urban dailies, the *Tulsa World* and *Daily Oklahoman*: George Lang, "For Lips, a 'beautiful' moment," *Daily Oklahoman*, 3 March, 2009: section A, p. 11; George Lang, "Flaming Lips celebrate Sooner roots; now state returns favor," *Daily Oklahoman,* 3 March 2009: Section D, p. 4; Michael McNutt and George Lang, "Singing Lips' Praise Despite Opposition," 24 April, 2009: Section A, p.1; Jennifer Chancellor, "Coyne: Lips song targeted by 'wackos'," *Tulsa World* , 25 April, 2009: Section A; p. 1; Gene Triplett, "Song fight isn't rocking Flaming Lips' world," *Daily Oklahoman,* 25 April, 2009: Section A; p. 15;

Bruce Plante, editorial cartoon: "Cast Your Vote for the Official State Doofus: Michael Ivins of the Flaming Lips or the Oklahoma House of Representatives," *Tulsa World*, 26 April, 2009: Section G; p. 6; Editorial, "House of Cards: These folks are funny (not really)", *Daily Oklahoman*, 27 April, 2009: Section A; p. 12; George Lang, "After House snub, Lips are all smiles," *Daily Oklahoman*, 29 April, 2009: Section A; p. 12.

3. In many ways, Rollins' participation in the *Dark Side* project brought Coyne all the way back to his early 1980s days in Norman when he saw Black Flag as really *the* hardcore band of the time, which they were; not punk and not metal, but hardcore, the new, fast, and angry music coming out of southern California in the early 1980s. Significant to the Lips development, Black Flag pioneered the college radio circuit around America, creating a tour of towns with college radio stations and clubs that supported that music, which ultimately became the alternative rock market circuit in the late 1980s that embraced the Flaming Lips and set the stage for rock's next evolution with Nirvana and others who followed them. Rollins, Greg Ginn, and company are not often given enough credit for figuring out the whole "alternative" touring system at that time which allowed many bands to follow the path that Black Flag whacked out across America.

Flash Terry (Verbie Gene Terry)
(b. June 17, 1934 – d. March 18, 2004)

Born into a musical family in the small country town of Inola, Oklahoma, about 15 miles west of Tulsa, Verbie Gene "Flash" Terry started playing guitar professionally at age seventeen. His first gig was with Jimmy "Cry Cry" Hawkins and the Teardrops in Tulsa. After several years as a local back-up musician in the 1950s, Flash began recording with Tulsa recording pioneer, Hugh Whitlow, in 1958. The collaboration produced Terry's first and most well known recording, "Her Name is Lou," which was an R & B chart hit for Indigo/Lavendar Records. Through his retirement in 2003, Flash Terry represented the 1940s heyday sound of horn pumped R&B that presaged the rock and roll movement of the 1950s. He supported blues stalwarts Aaron "T-Bone" Walker and Little Johnny Taylor, as well as R&B vocal groups such as The Impressions. His music has been released on a number of specialty and collector labels such as Relic, Wheel, Indigo, and Lavendar. Flash's songs have also been included on retrospectives of 1950s and 1960s R&B recordings, to include *All Night Long They Play the Blues* (Specialty), *West Coast Modern Blues: The 60s* (P-Vine), *West Coast Winners* (Moonshine), and *Cruisin' the Drag* (Wheel).

In 1966, Flash began a thirty-year career as a bus driver for the Tulsa Metropolitan Transit Authority while continuing to play locally in Tulsa and regionally with his group, the Uptown Blues Band. In 1972, he toured nationally with Bobby "Blue" Bland. In 1974, Flash recorded an album for **Leon Russell**'s Shelter Records, at the Church Studio in Tulsa, which was finally released by Visionary Records as *Enough Troubles of My Own* in 1986. Visionary also released *A Night on the Town* in 1988, and the independent *Live at the El'Ray with Flash Terry and Sam Franklin* was available by 1992. In 1994, the Oklahoma Jazz Hall of Fame inducted Flash under the blues category and has placed his early records on permanent display in the Greenwood Cultural Center and Jazz Hall of Fame in downtown Tulsa.

In the late 1990s, Flash released two solo albums on his own JFT label: *Backdoor Man* (1996) and *Mr. Bluesman* (1998). *Mr. Bluesman* features some tracks featuring **Bob Wills**' steel guitarist Leon McAuliffe, and

Flash Terry

By Hugh Foley

features appearances by **Tulsa Sound** veteran and bassist for Eric Clapton, **Carl Radle**. The album included recordings from the **Leon Russell**'s Shelter Studio in Tulsa (better known as The Church Studio later when **Steve Ripley** owned it), the Rogers State College (now Rogers State University) studios in the defunct **Hank Thompson** School of Country Music, and at the Lodestone Studio in Broken Arrow. Highlights on the album include the funky "Open Your Heart," and several songs that exhibit Flash's fine guitar work ("Enough Troubles of My Own" and "Call Me Anything"). An extra bonus is "Milk Cow Blues" featuring McAuliffe on steel guitar. In 1998, Flash Terry and the Uptown Blues Band received a "State of Excellence" award as "Oklahoma's Favorite Blues Band from then Oklahoma governor Henry Bellmon." Flash Terry was also active involved in many charitable community causes throughout his career, often playing for benefits and fundraisers for organizations like Special Olympics of Tulsa, Junior League of Tulsa, Women's Business League, the Helena Blues Society, and Fire, Accident, and Trauma Victims in Need of Assistance. Major feature articles about his career have appeared in *Living Blues*, *Juke Blues, Blues Gazette*, and *Real Blues Magazine*. He continued playing regionally with the Uptown Horns at many concerts, club dates, and several festivals, and was an annual part of the Dusk 'til Dawn Blues Festival in Rentiesville from 1990 to 2003 where his group often backed up the headliner of the show, after Flash played a complete set earlier in the evening. Recorded in 1997 and released commercially in 2002 on **DC Minner**'s Texas Road Recordings, *Guitar Showdown at Dusk 'til Dawn Blues Festival* features Flash on Willie Dixon's "Back Door Man", and a song written by and featuring the guitar style Flash learned from his father, "More and More'" Until announcing his retirement in 2003, Flash and his full-throttled horn section were probably the only group in Oklahoma that could really bring back the brass and reed bolstered R & B of **Lowell Fulson** and **Roy Milton**. That group included Kevin Pharris on rhythm guitar, Ron Martin on bass, Harry Williams on drums, Daryl McGee on trombone and horns, and Mike Sanders on trumpet and horns, collectively known as the Uptown Horns. In 2003, the Oklahoma Music Hall of Fame inducted Flash, and after a series of strokes in early 2004, he died in Tulsa on March 18, 2004.

For Love Not Lisa
(Formed Oklahoma City, 1990)
Lewis, Mike (vocals, guitar)
Miles (guitar)
McBay, Clint (bassist)
Preston, Aaron (drummer)

After solidifying their group in Oklahoma City, hard rocking outfit For Love Not Lisa moved to Los Angeles in 1991 where they released an independent, self-titled EP in 1992 on Indivision Records, showing both metal and punk influences, and including several live tracks. Within a short time, FLNL landed a deal with Elektra/East West Records, who released the band's 1993 album, *Merge*. While the album held up a rock flag pretty well, the mixture of ballady-punk/metal and more aggressive, riff based songs made the collection imbalanced for purists of either style, and likely kept off the radio that already had Nirvana, Pearl Jam, Soundgarden, Alice in Chains, etc., for the former sound on "alternative" rock radio, and Metallica for the latter on harder rock stations. However, one song from *Merge*, "Slip Slide Melting", was included on 1994's film soundtrack for *The*

Crow, which brought the band more notoriety, helping them land tours with Fugazi, Green Day, and Rage Against the Machine. A second album, *Information Superdriveway* (Elektra/Asylum), hit the shelves in 1995, with an even more polished sound, but could not achieve any notoriety in a very crowded rock music marketplace in the mid-1990s. Unfortunately, For Love Not Lisa had punk overtones that kept it from being too pop, and rocked too hard for pop and modern rock stations before the sensitive commercial metal of groups like Creed enjoyed Gold album success with a similar formula in the late 1990s, or the so-called "emo" (or emotional) pop rock groups like Fall Out Boy became popular in the 2000s. Tooth and Nail Records wrapped up For Love Not Lisa's catalogue by releasing *The Lost Elephant*,

For Love Not Lisa

which continued the group's noncommittal rock style, and also the too-familiar tepid response from radio and record buying public. Since then, guitarist Miles started a band, Echo Division, in 2005, and released *Under the California Stars* on Interleague Records, an album with more melody, calm rock, and instrumental restraint than any of the FLNL releases. Vocalist Lewis has ventured into music merchandising with the online store, www.zambooie.com.

www.myspace.com/forlovenotlisa

Frazier, Dallas

(b. October 27, 1939)

One of the most prolific songwriters in the 1960s and 1970s, with songs as "Alley Oop", "Mohair Sam", "There Goes My Everything", and "Elvira" to his credit, singer and songwriter Dallas Frazier was born in Spiro, Oklahoma, a community of around 2,000 people located in far eastern Oklahoma near the Arkansas border. Dallas' family moved to California when he was about four years old, and settled on a ranch near Bakersfield, a hotbed of country music. One of Dallas' songs, "California Cottonfields", recorded by **Merle Haggard**, realistically portrays the family move to California. He attended elementary school in East Bakersfield and graduated from McFarland High School in 1957. In 1988, Dallas received a bachelor's degree in Christian education from Emmanuel Bible College, and a graduate degree in theology from the same institution in 1989.

By age twelve, Dallas had become proficient on several instruments, including the guitar, trumpet, and piano. He won a children's talent contest in 1952 hosted by Ferlin Husky, then a Bakersfield disc jockey. Held at Bakersfield's Rainbow Gardens dance hall, Dallas sang a Little Jimmy Dickens song that so impressed Husky that he signed him to sing in his traveling band, the Termites. Dallas moved in with the Husky family and roomed with another Oklahoman, **Tommy Collins**. It was Collins who taught Dallas his first chords on a $10 guitar.

Husky introduced Frazier to Capitol Records executive Ken Nelson in 1953, but it was not until 1954 that Nelson signed him to a recording contract. At age fourteen, he published his first song and recorded his first Capitol single, "Ain't You Had No Bringin' Up at All", followed by another one of his songs, "Love Life at 14". At about the same time, he started singing off and on with Cousin Herb Henson on a local television show.

At age fifteen, Dallas joined Cliffie Stone's *Hometown Jamboree*, a Los Angeles-based television show, often teaming up for duets with another native Oklahoman, **Molly Bee**. Stone, who headed the country music operations for Capitol Records, had been impressed with Dallas and made him a regular cast member on the show. After four years the show folded, and Dallas married his girlfriend, Sharon Carpani.

During his early singing career, Frazier was writing songs, and in 1960, his pop novelty tune, "Alley Oop", recorded by the Hollywood Argyles, hit #1 on the *Billboard*'s pop charts and eventually sold more than a million copies. He wrote the song while working at a cotton gin in Pond, California. Gary Paxton, member of the Hollywood Argyles, met Dallas at a filling station at two in the morning when he had stopped to ask for directions to Hollywood. The story goes that Dallas, after getting off work, led Gary into Hollywood, and the two of them hit it off. The song was covered by a number of diverse groups: the Beach Boys, Dante and the Evergreens, Brian Poole and the Tremeloes, the Bonzo Dog Doo-Dah Band, and the Dynasores. Following this major hit, Dallas was concerned that the music business was a negative influence, and he and Sharon moved to various locales in the late 1950s and early 1960s, including Phoenix, then back to McFarland, California (where Dallas' family lived), and on to Portland, Oregon, where he decided to renew his songwriting career when Husky came through town on a concert tour.

Dallas Frazier

In 1963, Dallas and Sharon moved to Nashville, where he began to work for Husky's publishing house, continued to perform on radio and television, and expanded his songwriting list. He had a minor hit with Husky in 1964, "Timber I'm Falling", and then scored in 1965 when Charlie Rich and Peggy Lee recorded his "Mohair Sam", which he had penned for Jim Reeves' Acclaim Music.

After moving to Blue Crest Music publishing, Frazier wrote three of the best-selling songs in 1966: Jack Greene's "There Goes My Everything" (#1), which also captured the CMA Song of the Year Award in 1967, Connie Smith's "Ain't Had No Lovin'" (# 3), and George Jones' "I'm a People" (Top 10), all on the country charts. Finally, he penned and recorded "Elvira", which would become a #1 hit for the Oak Ridge Boys in 1981, and also recorded by Kenny Rogers and Rodney Crowell. The Oak Ridge Boys recording sold a million copies and was nominated for the CMA Song of the Year in 1981 and 1982. As an aside, a street named Elvira in east Nashville gave Dallas the idea for the song.

In 1967, George Jones scored with two more of Dallas' songs, including "I Can't Get There from Here" and "If My Heart Had Windows", later recorded by Patty Loveless. Moreover, Engelbert Humperdinck had a huge hit with his recording of Dallas' "There Goes My Everything". Other artists to record this song included Elvis Presley and Jack Greene. As a result, Dallas received in 1967 a host of awards, including the BMI Certificate of Achievement for "There Goes My Everything" in both pop and country categories, Songwriter of the Year by the Nashville Songwriters Association, CMA and *Music City News* awards for Song of the Year, and a GRAMMY Award for Best Country Song. According to Dallas, "There Goes My Everything" was inspired by the divorce of a close friend.

Success for Dallas' songwriting talents continued in 1968 with George Jones recording "Say It's Not You" (Top 10), Connie Smith's "Run Away Little Tears" (Top 10), and O.C. Smith's "Son of Hickory Holler's Tramp" (Top 40 on the pop charts), which was also made a country hit by Johnny Darrell. Moreover, George Jones paid tribute to Dallas' songwriting talents with his *Sings the Songs of Dallas Frazier* in 1968. Finally, Merle Haggard used three of Dallas' songs on his *The Legend of Bonnie and Clyde* album, and Willie Nelson and Brenda Lee both recorded "Johnnie One-Time".

The next year also proved productive for Dallas with two Charley Pride hits, "All I Have to Offer You (Is Me)" and "I'm So Afraid of Loving You Again", as well as another hit for Jack Greene, "Back in the Arms of Love". In 1969, he won the CMA Triple Play Award for the three hits on the charts in one year. By the end of the decade, Dallas had written more than 300 songs.

During the 1970s, songs continued to flow from Dallas' very creative mind, including Charley Pride's "I Can't Believe That You've Stopped Lovin' Me", Jack Greene's "Lord Is That Me", Diana Trask's "Beneath Still Waters", Connie Smith's "If It Ain't Love (Let's Leave It Alone)", Jerry Lee Lewis' "Touching Home", Elvis Presley's "Where Did They Go Lord", Johnny Russell's "Baptism of Jesse Taylor", **Carl Smith's** "The Way I Lose My Mind", and Tanya Tucker's first #1 hit, "What's Your Mama's Name". This string of songs earned Dallas' induction into the Nashville Songwriters Association International Hall of Fame in 1976. By this time, he had signed on as a writer with Acuff-Rose publishing house.

By the 1980s, Dallas' songwriting credits slowed down, but his hits didn't. Emmylou Harris scored a #1 hit with "Beneath Still Waters", Gene Watson topped the charts with "Fourteen Carat Mind", and the aforementioned success of "Elvira" by the Oak Ridge Boys crossed over to the pop charts as a Top 5 pop hit. Several new country artists also began recording Dallas' songs, including George Strait ("Honky Tonk Down Stairs"), Patty Loveless' ("If My Heart Had Windows") a song Dallas wrote for his wife Sharon, and Randy Travis ("When Your World Was Turning for Me"). In 1982, Dallas was again honored as *Music City News* Songwriter of the Year, and won the Robert J. Burton BMI Award for "Elvira". Frazier is one of several Mercury Records recording artists featured on *50 Years of Country Music from Mercury*, a 1995 collection of seventy-three tracks, on which he performs "Shooby Dooby Sue".

In 1988, Dallas retired from songwriting and decided to pursue a career in the ministry, and little has been heard from him since in the secular world, but the songs he wrote before leaving it continue airing on country and oldies radio stations.

Frisco, Don Roscoe Joseph III "Rocky"

(b. July 27, 1937, St. Louis, MO)

Having been involved with music professionally in Tulsa since the late 1950s, pianist/keyboardist Rocky Frisco is best known for his work with J.J. Cale on a number of concert tours, and their derivative albums and films, as well as studio work with Cale whom Rocky has known since the two went to Tulsa Central High School in the mid-1950s. Frisco began playing accordion and ukulele at eight-years-old, and by age fifteen had played melophone in the school band, and began playing guitar. By 1957, he began jamming with various black and white groups in Tulsa, to include joining Gene Crose's band in which J.J. (then Johnny) Cale was playing guitar. In 1958 he received a recording contract from Mercury Records and began performing as Rocky Curtiss. That same year, while working for Oklahoma City radio station KOME, Rocky participated in a publicity stunt of riding a bicycle for seven days across Texas to meet Elvis Presley, whose mother, Gladys, Frisco met and had cookies with, as well as meeting and jamming privately with Elvis. In 1959, he appeared on a Columbia Harmony album, *The Big Ten*, as Rocky Curtiss on vocals and piano, and toured New England and Canada in the Four Flames. After souring on the music industry to money being stolen from him by unscrupulous agents, Rocky retired from music from 1961 to 1969, a period in which he worked in radio, for IBM, and raced Mini Grand Prix cars in Canada.

Rocky Frisco, 2008

In 1969, Frisco began playing in bands again around Tulsa. He contributed tracks to the 1970s nuclear protest album that supported those who opposed the proposed Black Fox Nuclear Power Plant near Inola, Oklahoma, and played in Betsy Smittle's band through the 1980s until she left to play in the band led by her brother, **Garth Brooks**. In 1985, he played with the Tommy Overstreet Band, and from 1986 to 1988 he performed as pianist, vocalist, MC, and comedian for the Ozark Country Express. Along with playing for other local Tulsa groups, Frisco accompanied J.J. Cale on his 1994 world tour, and played with Cale at Carnegie Hall and the rest of his U.S. tour in 1996. By the late 1990s, he began acting, appearing in commercials that aired on the Nashville Network, and in a film made in Oklahoma, *Melvin*; in both roles, he played an "old codger." In 1998, he recorded three tracks on Steve Pryor's *El Nino Chickendog* CD, and played piano for local Tulsa favorites, Barton

Rocky Frisco with Elvis Presley, 1958.

Rocky Frisco playing with Eric Clapton and J.J. Cale.

and Sweeney, on their *Timeline* CD. In 1999, Rocky added piano to another local Tulsa music stalwart's CD, Scott Aycock's *Pennies on the Track*, and continued acting in Biblical roles for *The Zion Severn Report* produced by Willie George Ministries. His most notable acting role thus far is appearing in Disney's remake of *Where the Red Fern Grows*, shot mostly around Tahlequah in 2003. Rocky has played or recorded with many Oklahoma musicians, to include **Flash Terry**, **Tom Skinner**'s Science Project, the **Red Dirt Rangers (*Starin' Down the Sun*, 2002)**, Clyde Stacy, Brad Absher, and Susan Herndon. Rocky has appeared on a number of J.J. Cale releases: *JJ Cale Live* (Delabel/Virgin, 2001) and a 2002 video by the same name. Along with appearing on five tracks from J.J. Cale's *To Tulsa and Back* CD (Sanctuary), also in 2004, he played with Cale and Eric Clapton at the Crossroads Guitar Festival, immortalized on a DVD by that name. And, in 2006, Frisco was featured prominently in the J.J. Cale tour film, *To Tulsa and Back: On Tour with JJ Cale*. For his long contributions to the Tulsa music scene, as well as his elegant and wizened keyboard work that appears on significant nationally released recordings and concert films, Rocky Frisco was inducted into the Oklahoma Blues Hall of Fame in 2008, and the Oklahoma Music Hall of Fame in 2009.

www.rockyfrisco.com

Fulson, Lowell

(b. March 31, 1921 – d. March 6, 1999)

As the author of classic blues songs such as "Everyday I Have the Blues", "Three O'Clock Blues", and "Reconsider Baby", Lowell Fulson's brand of post-war urban blues helped define the West Coast blues style in the late 1940s with the addition of a horn section to the standard electric blues combo of bass, guitar, and drums. Born in Tulsa, Oklahoma, to parents of Choctaw and African-American descent, Fulson grew up around Ada, Oklahoma in south central Oklahoma. Lowell's grandfather played violin, and two of his uncles played guitar. He listened to Blind Lemon Jefferson records as a child and started playing guitar in the Pentecostal Holiness Church in one key, "G." The first blues he learned to play was in the key of "A." By 1938, Fulson was playing around little clubs in Ada singing everything he had to, such as "Beer Barrel Polka", "Silvery Moon", and other songs whites liked at the time. Given his relatively rural location in southeastern Oklahoma, he was not exposed to the more urban jazz developments in Oklahoma City, Muskogee, and Tulsa.

Around 1939, Fulson played with Dan Wright in a twelve to fifteen piece string band at picnics and other social gatherings. Fulson remembered, "There was a place they called the Bottom where black people gathered together to drink, gamble, play the blues, whatever, and I'd go don there afterward and pick me up some change picking my guitar." That is where Lowell met Algernon "Texas" Alexander, who had recorded as early as 1927, and started playing with him throughout Texas in 1940. Fulson modeled his vocal style after Alexander who had a rambling, low-key vocal technique that played heavily on his rural drawl. Fulson's vocals exhibit this technique throughout his career even though he tried different styles at different times, often at the behest of producers trying to update his sound and image. Fulson played with Alexander for a summer throughout Texas and Oklahoma, but left the elder blues man in 1941 when Lowell moved with his first wife and son to Gainesville, Texas, where he worked as a cook and played mostly in church. In 1943, he was drafted into the Navy, as a cook, but also entertained troops in the U.S. and Guam until the war's end. After being discharged from the military in 1945, he returned to Oklahoma where he worked as cook at the Wade Hotel in Duncan, Oklahoma, but wanted to go to the West Coast to try to find a musical career. As a result of the migration of many African-Americans to the San Francisco Bay area in World War II to work in the shipping and munitions industry, Oakland had a thriving blues scene of nightclubs, bars, and independent record labels. Since Fulson had been stationed in Oakland during part of his Navy stint, Lowell knew about the scene there and decided to make it his home in 1946 when he made his first recordings for a hundred dollars.

Fulson's first release was "Cryin' Blues"/"You're Going to Miss Me When I'm Gone" with his brother Martin Fulson backing him up on guitar. In 1947, Fulson established a solid backing band of bass, drums, and piano and recorded several more songs for various labels in Oakland where he had an R & B hit with "Three O'Clock Blues", later covered by B.B. King. Playing primarily around San Francisco and Oakland, Fulson moved to Los Angeles in 1949 where he recorded with fellow Oklahoman **Jay McShann** on the Swing Time label. Because McShann was more advanced musically than Fulson, Lowell preferred pianist Lloyd Glenn who had played with T-Bone Walker. Fulson and Glenn decided to add horns to their sound to fatten it up and the hits started to follow, as well as the moniker of uptown blues, sometimes called West Coast blues, or California blues.

Uptown blues is a hybrid form of blues that combines the riffing horn section elements of jazz with the electric blues combo of drums, bass, and guitar. In 1950, Lowell had solid success on the Swing Time label with "Everyday I Have the Blues", an R & B hit that reached #5 on the charts, and became B.B. King's theme song for many years. Fulson followed up with "Blue Shadows" (#1 R & B) and "Lonesome Christmas" (#7 R & B) in 1950. With several children in school, pianist Glenn did not want to tour behind Fulson's growing popularity, but continued playing on the recording sessions. Fulson then teamed up with Ray Charles who played with Fulson's rocking big band until 1953, as did saxophonist Stanley Turrentine. In October of 1950, the group's show at the Elks hall in Los Angeles broke a ten-year standing attendance record for the hall. Once Swing Time folded, Lowell's music was released through the Aladdin Record label that had purchased the masters from Swing Time in order to sell the records throughout the Midwest and South. Aladdin had particular success with Fulson's "I'm a Night Owl."

In 1952, Fulson played a packed Apollo Theater in New York, then toured with Ruth Brown and Joe Turner. In 1953, with Aladdin still releasing his music, Fulson toured with T-Bone Walker when Swing Time officially went bankrupt. Wasting little time, however, Lowell signed with Chess's Checker label in Chicago where he had a major hit with "Reconsider Baby" in 1954. The single reached #3 on the R & B charts and became a blues standard, covered by artists such as Elvis Presley, Ray Charles, and, eventually, Eric Clapton. However, Fulson did not fit in with the Chicago studio environment where his horn section made him stand out from Chess stable of Howlin' Wolf and Muddy Waters. Subsequently, uptown blues became a somewhat snide commentary by Chicago musicians about Fulson's music, which prompted him to move back to the West Coast and mail in all his studio recordings to Chess. The strained relationship did not prove fruitful overall, and Lowell left the label in 1962.

Lowell Fulson, circa 1990

After continuously playing one-nighters and assorted club dates in the early 1960s, Fulson signed with the Kent label and had a minor R & B hit with "Black Nights" in 1965. In 1967, he had two more R & B hits with "Make a Little Love" and "Tramp", which almost broke into the Top 50 on the pop charts. Otis Redding and Carla Thomas also recorded "Tramp" and their version sold much better than Fulson's. During the 1970s, Fulson moved from the Kent label to Jewel Records, owned by Stan Lewis and based in Shreveport, Louisiana, but Lowell's commercial success was relegated to American popular music history. In the 1980s, Fulson "laid low," in his own words, while his classic recordings were reissued to demanding blues collectors. His 1988 recording for Rounder Records, *It's a Good Day*, was well received critically, but garnered only modest sales. In the 1990s, Fulson recorded for Bullseye Records in the same style for which he had become famous, and continued to tour when he was healthy. In 1993 he received five W.C. Handy Awards, was inducted into the Rhythm and Blues Hall of Fame, and the Blues Hall of Fame both for his career and his song, "Reconsider Baby". Fulson's 1996 album, *Them Update Blues (Rounder), was nominated for Grammy in the "Best Traditional Blues" category. By the time of his death in an assisted care facility near Seal Beach, California, Fulson symbolized yet another Oklahoman who had absorbed the deep musical influences of his youth, and subsequently made major innovative contributions to his art form which came to be known as uptown or West Coast blues.*

By Hugh Foley

G

Gaines, Cassie LaRue
(b. January 9, 1948 – d. October 20, 1977)

Gaines, Steve Earl
(b. September 14, 1949 – d. October 20, 1977)

As members of southern rock group Lynyrd Skynyrd, guitarist Steve and vocalist Cassie Gaines contributed significantly to the group's live concerts and recordings from 1976 to their tragic demise in 1977 when the band's plane crashed outside Gillsburg, Mississippi, on the way to a concert in Baton Rouge, Louisiana. Both Cassie and Steve were born in the northeastern corner of Oklahoma, in Miami, to Bud and LaRue Gaines. Even though she attended NEO A & M in Miami for two years, Cassie did not start singing professionally until she went to Memphis State University where she graduated with a degree in physical education in 1975. Steve began playing guitar at fifteen, inspired after his father took him to see a 1965 performance by the Beatles in Kansas City. Upon returning to Miami, Steve's father bought him a guitar and Steve started his first group, the Ravens, in 1966, while still in high school. That group consisted of Steve on guitar and vocals, Archie Osborn (bass and vocals), Jerry Sanders (drums and vocals), and Johnny Burrows (guitar and vocals).

After high school, Steve majored in art, first at Northeastern Oklahoma A & M, and then at Pittsburgh State College in Kansas. During this period, Steve joined Pink Peach Mob, a psychedelic outfit, in 1967, with Don Malchi (guitar), John Moss (drums), Jerry Carpenter (bass), Dee Poole (lead vocals), Mike Rivers (keyboards), and Jim Poole (organ). Next, in 1968 Steve formed Manalive that recorded one single, "Boogie", in the Memphis Sun Studios made famous by Elvis Presley and many other blues and country artists in the 1950s. In 1970 Steve joined RIO Smokehouse, then featuring the three-guitar attack for which Lynyrd Skynyrd would later become famous when Gaines joined that group, but also performed and recorded again with Manalive, notably in Memphis where Jerry Phillips, son of Sun Records impresario Sam Phillips, signed the group to Hot Water Records, a subsidiary of the famous soul label, Stax.

In early 1972, Steve joined Detroit, essentially the Detroit Wheels without Mitch Ryder, which followed in the same blues rock mold popular among groups

Cassie and Steve with Lynyrd Skynyrd.

of the period, i.e., the Allman Brothers, the Marshall Tucker Band, and Skynyrd. After leaving the band Detroit, Steve and his wife, Teresa, moved to a farm in Seneca, Missouri, just across the Oklahoma border and not far from their home base of Miami, where they had their only child Corrina, named after a Taj Majal version of the song on which Oklahoma native **Jesse Ed Davis** played guitar.

In 1973 Steve formed Crawdad with John Seaburg (bass guitar and vocals), John Moss (guitar and vocals), Terry Emery (keyboards), and Ron Brooks (drums), performing everywhere from high school dances to the clubs and honky tonks in Oklahoma, Kansas, Arkansas, and Missouri. Steve's widow, now Teresa Gaines Rapp, has released two very insightful posthumous recordings from this period, *Okie Special* and *I Know A Little – Live*, both available though the Steve Gaines's website. *Okie Special* demonstrates Steve's varied influences, from Motown (Jr. Walker's "Road Runner") and funky fusion (Billy Cobham's "Crosswinds"), to grooving blues (Chuck Willis's "Snatch it Back and Hold It") and classic rock and roll (Chuck Berry's "No Money Down"). Two songs are also included on *Okie Special* from the Detroit group. Gaines's original composition, "Ain't No Good Life", later found on Skynyrd's *Street Survivors*, is also on *Okie Special*.

Cassie Gaines

Another family-released disc indicating Steve Gaines's ultimate impact on Lynyrd Skynyrd can be found on *I Know a Little-Live*, recordings made by Gaines's groups Crawdad and Manalive in the early-to-mid-1970s. No dates are included on the compact disc, so determining their place in Gaines' development is difficult. However, the group's sound is so rooted in the popular Southern rock of the time that Gaines's composition "I Know a Little" appears to have been written for Lynyrd Skynyrd even before they knew who he was. Again, Gaines' influences are prominent on the disc with cover versions of songs by Freddie King, Big Joe Turner, Curtis Mayfield, and Bob Dylan. Cassie also makes a vocal appearance on one of Steve's songs, "People Comin' At Me".

In 1975 one of Cassie's friends from Memphis State, Jo Jo Billingsley, was a backup singer for Skynyrd. When the group told Billingsley they were looking for another singer, she asked Cassie to audition for the gig and she got it. Once on the job, Cassie found out Skynyrd also wanted to hire another guitarist to fatten up their sound after the relatively disappointing sales of their 1976 album, *Gimme Back My Bullets* (MCA). She suggested her younger brother, and when the group was playing in Kansas City, Cassie convinced them to let Steve sit in for one song. Singer Ronnie Van Zant agreed and instructed the soundman to cut Steve out of the mix if he could not keep up well enough. Gaines played

Steve Gaines

slide on Jimmie Rodgers "T for Texas", impressed the whole band, and was invited to join the group.

The first Skynyrd recording to feature both Steve and Cassie Gaines is the Top 10 live album *One More for the Road* (MCA, 1976), which includes the famous fourteen-minute jamathon version of "Free Bird". Back in the studio with a renewed sense of purpose and a fresh injection from Steve Gaines's guitar work and compositions, Skynyrd recorded the Top 5 album, *Street Survivors* (MCA, 1977). Two of Steve's songs he had been playing for years with his other groups, "Ain't No Good Life" and "I Know a Little", appear on the album, and he co-wrote two new songs with vocalist Van Zant, "I Never Dreamed", and "You Got That Right", the latter of which made it to #69 on the *Billboard* Hot 100. Steve's trademark "popping Stratocaster" style can be heard on the band's cover of **Merle Haggard**'s "Honky Tonk Night Time Man", and Cassie's backup vocals are also prominent on one of the best-selling Lynyrd Skynyrd albums. While *Street Survivors* returned the group to the international stardom, three days after the album's release, the band's plane crashed due to a seemingly negligent decision by the pilot to have enough fuel in the aircraft, killing Cassie, Steve, Ronnie Van Zant, and the band's manager, Dean Kilpatrick. Ironically, the album cover for *Street Survivors* included a picture of the group Steve engulfed in flames, and the record was taken off the market in the U.S. to have the cover photo replaced, however, European releases maintained the original cover.

Steve Gaines

Periodically, more material from Gaines's career has been made available. In 1988, MCA Records released a Steve Gaines solo album, *One in the Sun*, culled from tapes he had recorded with producer John Ryan at the Capricorn Studio in Macon, Georgia, and **Leon Russell**'s Church Studio in Tulsa. Enlisting his old band mates from Crawdad to back him up, the out-of-print album is clearly a work in progress with the Capricorn tracks recorded "live," and the Church tracks pieced together track-by-track. Steve's promise as a guitarist and vocalist in the southern rock boogie blues genre is obvious on the album's lead-off track, "Give It to Get It", a song later covered by **Cherokee** guitarist Ace Moreland (also from Miami) and used as the title for Moreland's 2000 album on Icehouse Records. In 2001, the neo-Rebel rock outfit, Drive-By Truckers, dedicated their 2001 *album, Southern Rock Opera*, to Skynyrd, with "Cassie's Brother" featuring some tribute guitar work in Gaines' style. Also in 2001, Mercury re-released both *One More for the Road: the Rarities Version* and *Street Survivors*, the latter of which included an alternate remixed version of "You Got That Right" including Steve's guitar way up front in the mix. Released in 2003, the Manalive recordings made by Steve at the Sun Studios in Memphis are available only through the Steve Gaines website.

As a final testament to the band's staying power and significance in the rock music canon, in 2006 Lynyrd Skynyrd was inducted into the Rock and Roll Hall of Fame in Cleveland, Ohio, where Steve's Fender Stratocaster guitar is part of the Lynyrd Skynyrd exhibit. While Steve Gaines' name was part of the group inducted into the hall, Cassie and the other Honkettes were left off of that list, but not this one.

www.stevegaines.com

www.lynyrdskynyrdhistory.com

The GAP Band
(Formed in 1967, Tulsa, OK)

Leaning on influences ranging from Parliament-Funkadelic and Sly and the Family Stone to Earth, Wind, and Fire, The GAP Band, comprised of multi-instrumentalist brothers Ronnie, Charlie, and Robert Wilson (all Tulsa natives), surfaced as one of the most popular R & B groups of all time with four of the band's nine albums certified as Platinum plus (platinum is one million sold). With fifteen Top 10 R & B hits, the group has become a perennial favorite of sample-happy hip hop and R & B artists looking for a fat bass lines, smooth vocal hooks, and funky beats. Their song "Outstanding" remains one of the most sampled songs in history, having been renewed by over 150 artists in their tracks.

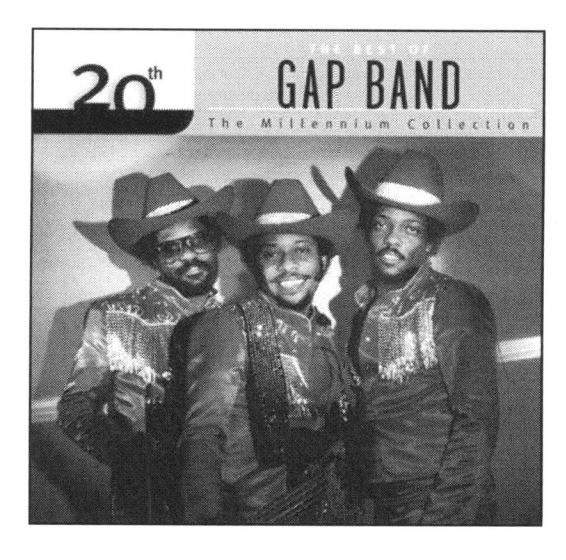

The Wilson brothers grew up performing in their father's Pentecostal church in Tulsa where their mother was a pianist, and where they sang every Sunday before their father's sermon. All three brothers took piano lessons, and their parents demanded they practice at home. Ronnie, the oldest, started a group when he was fourteen and eventually recruited his younger brothers to play in the band they named after streets in the heart of Tulsa's historic African-American business district — Greenwood, Archer and Pine. After a typographical error changed their name from the G.A.P. Street Band to The GAP Band, the name stuck. The group played various clubs around Tulsa and got their break in 1974 when they provided bass, horns, and vocals to **Leon Russell**'s album, *All That Jazz* (Shelter/MCA). Subsequently, Russell signed the band to record their first album for his Shelter label, *Magician's Holiday* (1974). The group moved to Los Angeles shortly thereafter and recorded a gospel single for A & M, "This Place Called Heaven", and a slightly noticed self-titled album for Tattoo in 1977.

The GAP Band's success really took flight in 1979 via *The Gap Band II* (Mercury), now a gold album, from which the group scored a Top 5 R & B hit "Shake," followed by other 1980 R & B Top 10 hits, "Steppin' Out" and "I Don't Believe You Want to Get Up and Dance (Oops, Up Side Your Head)." Their 1980 platinum-selling album, *The Gap Band III* (Mercury), sported more R&B hits, including the #1 "Burn Rubber (Why You Wanna Hurt Me)" and 1981's #5 R&B hit, "Yearning for Your Love", which sealed their status top recording stars. Their 1982 album, *Gap Band IV* (Total Experience), provided their biggest pop hit, "You Dropped a Bomb On Me", exhibiting their trademark bass-heavy style and the silky smooth vocals of Charlie Wilson. The song is still played at Allie P. Reynolds Stadium in Stillwater when an Oklahoma State baseball player hits a home run. The group continued a string of R&B hits through the 1980s, including "Party Train" (1983), "Jam the Motha" (1983), "Beep a Freak" (1984), "Big Fun" (1986), "I'm Gonna Git You Sucka" (1988), "All of My Love" (#1 R&B, 1989), and "We Can Make it Alright" (1990).

By Hugh Foley

While Ronnie Wilson became a born-again Christian and began pastoring in 1984, Charlie Wilson is one of the most in-demand vocalists in the R & B, urban contemporary, and rap music industry. His vocals have appeared on albums by Ray Charles, Snoop Dogg ("Snoops Upside Ya Head," et al.), Zapp, Quincy Jones, Master P, Mia X, and Mystikal. Charlie also continues working with some of the top producers and young performers in the music industry: Steve Huff, Terry Lewis, Shekspeare, Tricky, D.J. Quik, Dr. Dre, D.J. Pooh, and Daz Dilinger. Through his publicist, Charlie Wilson says, "I feel very fortunate to be able to return musically to somewhere I never really left, and it's flattering to know that the younger generation of musicians still fill their tracks with the sounds my brothers and I created years ago." After scoring a 2000 #1 R&B hit, "Without You", Charlie Wilson also enjoyed watching his 2009 solo effort, *Uncle Charlie* (Jive), enter the *Billboard* Top 200 album charts at #2, and debut on the Top R&B/Hip-Hop Album chart at #1. In 2010, *Billboard* named Charlie Wilson the #1 Adult Contemporary Artist of 2009, and *Uncle Charlie*'s single, "There Goes My Baby", the #1 Urban Adult Contemporary Single of 2009.

Numerous compilations have documented The GAP Band's career, from *Gap Gold: the Best of the Gap Band* (Mercury, 1985), to a best-of collection through Mercury's 20th Century Masters Series (2000). In 2001 Hip-O released *Ultimate Collection*, a thorough collection of their greatest hits with extensive liner notes, while Ark 21 released *Love at Your Fingertips*, featuring a few new tunes, live recordings, and several remixes of "You Dropped a Bomb On Me." After enduring several years of hardship due to being taken advantage of by unscrupulous music industry managers and executives, the GAP Band were honored in 2005 by BMI as one of the most influential R&B groups of all time. Proof of that status is in the names of major R&B/Hip-Hop artists who have sampled the group, to include Nas, Snoop Dogg, Warren G., Jermaine Dupri, Da Brat, Notorious B.I.G., Blackstreet, Mia X, and Mary J. Blige. "Outstanding" was sampled for a 1990s malt liquor commercial, and "You Dropped a Bomb on Me" was featured in the 2004 video game *Grand Theft Auto: San Andreas*. Universal Music re-released GAP Band II, III, IV in the 2000s, and several of their more popular songs became successful ring tone downloads through 2010. The group has continued making occasional concert appearances, performing in Tulsa in 2007, and in Oklahoma City in 2010, as well as periodic performances for nationally syndicated urban radio host Tom Joyner on his cruises or benefit shows for charities such as the

The GAP Band Receives BMI Music Award, 2005

280 / Oklahoma Music Guide II

United Negro College Fund. On August, 15, 2010, bassist Robert Wilson died at his home in Los Angeles. Robert had recorded much of a new album that has yet to be released, while **Charlie Wilson** has continued an extremely successful solo R&B recording career through 2013.

www.gapband.com

Garcia, Benny, Jr.
(b. March 20, 1926 – d. September 17, 2005)

    Highly regarded by jazz fans and Western swing musicians for his vibrant melodic ability and full-bodied sound that derives from his idols, **Charlie Christian** and **Barney Kessel,** Benny Garcia may not have garnered the same critical acclaim as those two Oklahomans, but his performances and/or recordings with bandleaders such as **Bob** and **Johnnie Lee Wills,** Benny Goodman, and singing cowboy Tex Williams, as well as playing with Merl Lindsay, **Jimmy Wakely**, **Johnny Bond**, and Patsy Cline, cement his stature as an important Oklahoma musician.

    Born in Oklahoma City of Mexican-American ancestry, Benny started taking guitar lessons at age fourteen. He listened intently to Benny Goodman records with Charlie Christian playing lead guitar, trying to pick out the melody lines. Later, Garcia met Christian's mother who became fond of the young guitarist, and let Benny play Charlie's amp and guitar. Benny still owns one of Charlie's tortoise shell picks given to him by Mrs. Christian. As a teenager he played live broadcasts on WKY radio with local buddies, tenor saxophonist Fred Beatty, pianist Al Good, singer/guitarist Jimmy Wakely, and singer/guitarist Johnny Bond. By his early 20s, Benny played regular gigs with Merl Lindsay and the Oklahoma Night Riders at Oklahoma City's Elmwood Ballroom and the Warner Theater. Later, he joined the staff band at KOMA radio in the Biltmore Hotel that was right across the street a movie theater where singing cowboy star Tex Williams, then at the height of his fame with the million-selling hit, "Smoke, Smoke, Smoke That Cigarette," stopped to play and promote one of his movies in 1948. Tex also took in the KOMA broadcast and offered Benny a job in his traveling Caravan of three long, black Packards and an equipment truck. Garcia accepted and was officially a touring musician in Williams' ten-piece Western swing band, alongside the great pedal-steel player, Earl "Joaquin" Murphey, traveling across the U.S. and Canada for three years before settling in Burbank, California.

    Once in California, Benny recorded on several sessions for Capitol and Columbia Records, and in 1950 joined the Hank Penny jazz band. He also took guitar lessons from jazz guitar giant, and heir to Charlie Christian's throne, Oklahoma native Barney Kessel who was also living in the Los Angeles area at the time. Before Benny became too immersed in the L.A. music scene, however, he was drafted during the Korean

Benny Garcia

Benny Garcia and Don Tolle

War and wound up at the Camp Desert Rock atomic bomb test site in Nevada. Once out of the Army, Benny headed back to Oklahoma where Johnnie Lee Wills hired him for regular performances at Cain's Ballroom and on KVOO radio in Tulsa through 1957. Garcia also toured with Bob Wills in 1958, traveling throughout the United States, again, and then picked up work with Patsy Cline for several of her live performances. Returning to Oklahoma City in the early 1960s, Benny played regularly with the Al Tell Quartet and Wayne Nichols Orchestra until getting a call from Benny Goodman who recruited Garcia to record on *Hello Benny* (Capitol, 1968). Subsequently, he joined the Benny Goodman band and hit the road for several U.S. and Canadian tours into the 1970s.

Settling down in Oklahoma City, Benny has been a fixture on the jazz club, lounge, and restaurant circuit for the last 30 years. He has also been featured in a German concert video, *Legends of Western Swing Guitar* where he duets with Eldon Shamblin on "Stay a Little Longer." In 1999, Benny was asked by Barney Kessel to play for the ailing Kessel who was unable to play for his induction into the Oklahoma Music Hall of Fame. Garcia has also been a regular at reunion gigs of remaining members of Bob and Johnnie Lee Wills' bands, most recently in March, 2003 at the Cain's Ballroom. Playing with a Latin-tinged jazz group, Los Locos, Benny recorded a self-titled album on Lunacy Records in 2001, sound samples of which are available on MP3.com.

In 2002, Benny played on a Western swing-styled album by Oklahoma vocalist and fiddler Harvey "Preacher" Davis, *Harvey Davis and Friends* (Lunacy), on which former Wills drummer Tommy Perkins also appears. In 2002, Garcia was inducted into the Western Swing Hall of Fame, and in 2003, was inducted into the Oklahoma Music Hall of Fame. Continuing the family tradition of fine guitar playing, Benny Garcia, Jr. has performed with **Vince Gill,** as well as served as Gill's guitar technician, and also played with the Dixie Chicks.

Gaston, Lyle

A native of Woodward, Oklahoma, Lyle Gaston co-wrote a number of songs recorded by **Hank Thompson**, the most notable of which is "How Do You Hold a Memory?", a #11 country hit for Thompson in 1958. Gaston worked at a local radio station in Woodward, KSIW, where he was known for his pleasant speaking voice and singing ability, and where he recorded a number of demo tapes. Somewhere along the way he made friends with honky-tonk star, Hank Thompson, and the two collaborated on several songs: "Blackboard of My Heart", "Mr. and Mrs. Snowman", "How Do You Hold a Memory?", "Two Hearts Deep in the Blues", "You'll Be the One", and "My Old Flame" which was included on Thompson's 1961 Capitol release, *An Old Love Affair*. 1950s rockabilly artist **Eddie Cochran** also recorded Gaston's "Stocking and Shoes" for his 1957 LP. *Singin'* to *My Baby*. Gaston's memory held on through the beginning of the twenty-first century as "Blackboard of My Heart" appeared on a Russian 2008 compilation of country music, *Wanted Country Memories*, by Australian country music artist, Ellie Lavelle, and on Hank Thompson's *Twenty Greatest Hits* (Gusto) in 2009.

Gates, David
(b. December 11, 1940)

Best known for his work with Bread, and as a songwriter whose songs have been hits around the world, David Gates helped define the genre of "soft rock" in the 1970s with Bread hits such as "Make it With You", "If", and "The Guitar Man," as well as his solo single "Goodbye Girl." At last count, Bread and Gates have sold more than 17 million records. Born to a band teacher and band director in Tulsa, Oklahoma, Gates was surrounded by the classical music of his parents and the big band sounds of his older siblings. Encouraged and instructed by his father, Gates could read music by age five, and was proficient on bass, guitar, and piano by his high school years at Tulsa Rogers. He formed his first rock band in 1957 and backed Chuck Berry. In 1958, he wrote, recorded and released his first single, "Jo-Baby", named after his high school sweetheart, Jo Rita. An indication of his romantic hits to follow, "Jo-Baby" was recorded to sway Jo Rita away from another boy. Gates paid to press 500 copies of the single and it became a local hit, as well as winning over Jo Rita whom he married and started family with while enrolled at Oklahoma University.

Eager to continue his musical career, Gates loaded his wife and two children into a ten-year-old Cadillac, and moved the family to Los Angeles in 1961. Soon thereafter, in early 1962, Chuck Blackwell and Gates's Tulsa Rogers classmate **Leon Russell** arrived and the three formed a trio, worked clubs at night, and did some session work during the day. One of the clubs was called the Crossroads in the San Fernando Valley. Jam sessions there included a young Glen Campbell, Russell, Elvis Presley's future guitarist James Burton, and future super session men Hal Blaine and Jim Horn. What set Gates apart from the rest, however, was his classical music background, which provided opportunities for him to write arrangements for other artists. Gates remembers, "I had an advantage. I knew rock and roll, country, and rhythm and blues. I could read and write music. I could do arrangements. I could produce. I could play bass. I could do a lot of different things to make a living." By 1963, Gates had his first hit as a songwriter, "Popsicles and Icicles", a #3 pop hit for The Murmaids. Throughout the 1960s, Gates arranged music for Elvis Presley, Duane Eddy, The Nitty Gritty Dirt Band, **Merle Haggard**, **Hoyt Axton**, Buck Owens, Captain Beefheart, Ann-Margret, and Bobby Darin. Gates also produced the movie theme to *Baby the Rain Must Fall* in 1965 that became a Grammy-nominated top ten hit for Glenn Yarbrough.

David Gates

By Hugh Foley / 283

By the late 1960s, Gates decided he wanted to record his own songs and founded the group Bread in 1968. Released in 1969, the group's first album, *Bread*, featured strong songs such as "Dismal Day", "London Bridge", and "It Don't Matter to Me" which became a hit later when the group's second album was released. The album *Bread* was not an overwhelming success, as the group had not yet established their signature sound of soft, acoustic guitar based songs with a supporting string section that would surface on 1970's *On the Waters*. By adding an occasional electric guitar solo, *On the Waters* established the sound known as "soft rock" and in many ways launched the adult contemporary radio format. The album featured the #1 hit, "Make It with You", and caused enough interest in the band to bring back "It Don't Matter to Me", from the first album, which went to #10 on the pop charts. *Manna* (1971) continued the group's smooth studio pop sound and produced more hits, "Let Your Love Go" (#28), and the mega-hit, "If" (#1). *Baby I'm-a Want You* (1972) followed up on the group's string of chart hits with the album's title track (#3), "Mother Freedom" (#37) which was the closest the group really ever got to rocking out, "Everything I Own" (#5), and "Diary" (#15). The band followed up this success with another 1972 album, *Guitar Man*, with three more Gates-penned hits, "Sweet Surrender" (#15), "Aubrey" (#15), and "The Guitar Man" (#11). 1972 also saw the albums *Manna, Baby I'm-a Want You,* and *Guitar Man* go gold (500,000 in sales), and *Baby I'm a Want You* was nominated for a Grammy. In 1974, reggae artist Ken Boothe scored a #1 UK hit with "Everything I Own", and back in the states and *The Best of Bread Vol. 2* went gold.

With a tremendous amount of success under their belts, but a less than perfect working relationship, the group decided to call it quits in 1973. Bread reunited briefly in 1977, and produced another hit written by Gates, "Lost Without Your Love", the title track of an album that became the group's seventh consecutive gold record, and final project as a group. David Gates released a series of solo albums throughout the 1970s that produced consistent hits in the adult contemporary format, the biggest of which was the theme song to the Oscar-winning film *Goodbye Girl* (1977). Also in 1977, Joe Stampley had hit on the country charts with his version of "Everything I Own"; later, in 1987, Boy George had #1 one international hit with his own rendition of the song.

After 1981's modestly selling solo album, *Take Me Now*, Gates withdrew from the music industry to spend more time with his family on a Northern California ranch he purchased in 1974 just after the height of Bread's success. Even though Gates went into semi-retirement, his song "If" was recorded by Julio Iglesias in 1984 and became a worldwide hit in a bilingual version of the song. In 1992, Gates built his own studio at the ranch and collaborated with country artist Billy Dean in 1993. In 1994, the Warner Brothers subsidiary, Discovery Records, released a Gates solo album, *Love Is Always Seventeen*, and in 1996 Gates joined a world tour with three original members of Bread to play their hits in South Africa, Australia, Southeast Asia, England, and various other countries.

In 1998, Gates also began a trend of playing with symphony orchestras, an idea based on the heavy string arrangements in Bread's hit material, when he played with Tulsa Symphony and debuted an original song, "Tulsa, My Hometown". Also in 1998, Gates was inducted into the Oklahoma Music Hall of Fame. In 2002, Gates performed with the Tulsa Community College Signature Symphony for a benefit concert and returned to perform for a celebration of the 50th anniversary party for the Utica Square Shopping Center. Further indicating David's widespread appeal, his composition "If", now covered by more than one hundred artists, was included on Dolly Parton's 2002 traditional country album, *Halos and Horns* (Sanctuary). To support the release of the retrospective *David*

Gates Songbook (Zomba/Jive) in 2002, which included five new songs, Gates performed on a successful 2003 spring tour of England. Gates' has continued to surface in the 2000s with many of his songs appearing on television shows (*Late Show with Craig Ferguson, House M.D. The Simpsons*), film soundtracks (*Bandslam, Snow Angels, Happy Feet, Stuck On You, Maid in Manhattan, Ash Wednesday*, et. Al.), Dolly Parton's *Live and Well* concert DVD in 2004. Also in 2004, the alternative rock band, Cake, covered "The Guitar Man", and Ray Parker Jr. recorded the same song in 2006. While David Gates has not been active as a live performer of late, he continues to write and produce in his own studio at his California ranch.

Gill, Vince
(b. April 12, 1957)

With an instantly recognizable voice, stringed instrumental skills that allow him to fit alongside the fastest bluegrass bands or the most subtle blues and country pickers, Vince Gill is on the short list of Oklahoma musicians known by only their first name. He has sold more than twenty-six million albums, earned eighteen CMA Awards, including Entertainer of the Year in 1993 and 1994, is tied with George Strait for having won the most CMA Male Vocalist Awards (five), and is currently second only to Brooks and Dunn for accumulating the most CMA Awards in history. Gill is a member of the Grand Ole Opry, and has received 20 GRAMMY Awards to date, the most of any male country music artist.

Born to Stan and Jerene Gill, the youngest of three children, in Norman, Oklahoma, home of the University of Oklahoma and now a southern suburb of Oklahoma City. Vince was raised around music as his father, Stan, a lawyer and judge, played banjo part time in a country band, and encouraged his son to consider a career in country music. His brother Bob was a blues fan, while his sister Gina followed folk music. Early on, Vince learned the banjo from his father, but a neighbor, Bobby Clark, introduced Vince to acoustic guitar, which became his instrument of choice. Vince and Clark formed a teenage bluegrass group called The Bluegrass Review that later became Mountain Smoke, both of which played at **Bill Grant's** Old-Time Country and Bluegrass Festival in Hugo, opened for Pure Prairie League, and demonstrating their string pulling prowess, warmed up the stage for KISS at The Myriad in Oklahoma City.

Following graduation from Northwest Classen High School in Oklahoma City in 1975, Gill headed to Louisville to join the Bluegrass Alliance that featured Dan Crary and Sam Bush. Following the Bluegrass Alliance stint, he was a member of Ricky Skaggs' Boone Creek bluegrass band. Perhaps his biggest break was in 1976 when **Byron Berline** contacted Vince to

Vince Gill

become a member of Sundance, based in Los Angeles. After two years with Berline, he auditioned for Pure Prairie League, who remembered him from their previous encounter when Mountain Smoke opened up for PPL. Some fifty guitarists were auditioned, but Vince was hired in 1979 because of his versatility on other instruments, such as the banjo and fiddle, as well as his vocal talents. He became their lead singer for the next three years and appeared on their albums *Can't Hold Back*, *Something in the Night*, and *Firin' Up*, the latter included six of Vince's compositions, one of which became a Top 40 single in 1980, "I'm Almost Ready".

After leaving Pure Prairie League in 1981, Vince joined Rodney Crowell's Cherry Bombs as a harmony singer and guitarist, often backing Rosanne Cash. Before too long, Tony Brown, former keyboard player for the Cherry Bombs and then A & R man for RCA (later MCA Nashville and Universal South), signed Vince to a contract in 1984, and Vince moved to Nashville. Later that year, he recorded a mini-album, *Turn Me Loose*, including six of the eight tracks written or co-written by him, two of which reached *Billboard*'s Hot Country Songs chart, "Victim of Life's Circumstances" and "Oh Carolina." He was named ACM's Top New Male Vocalist for 1984.

In 1984, Vince switched record companies and recorded two albums for the Buddha label, *The Things That Matter* (1985) and *The Way Back Home* (1987) with a majority of the tracks written by him. The 1985 album included the modest hit "True Love", and two top ten charters, "Oklahoma Borderline", and "If It Weren't for Him". The latter single featured Rosanne Cash singing harmonies with Vince. The 1987 album produced a top five hit, "Cinderella" and a top twenty hit, "Let's Do Something". During this time, Vince also became an in-demand studio harmony vocalist and guitarist, recording on more than 120 records, and began focusing heavily on songwriting.

While he had enjoyed phenomenal success to that point commercially, his guitar playing was so well known that he received an offer from Mark Knopfler of Dire Straits to join that group. While flattered, he decided to persist in his country music career, which began to really pay off in 1989 when he joined the MCA-Nashville roster. He was reunited with Tony Brown, who had originally signed him. The first album for MCA, *When I Call Your Name*, yielded two important singles that launched Vince to stardom, the title track with Patty Loveless singing harmonies, and "Oklahoma Swing", featuring a duet with fellow Oklahoman, **Reba McEntire**. These two songs also highlighted Vince's talents as a songwriter, both of which he collaborated on with another Oklahoman, **Tim Dubois**. "When I Call Your Name" won the CMA Single and Song of the Year for 1990, a GRAMMY for Best Country Vocal Performance by a Male in 1990, and *TNN/Music City News* Award for Single of the Year for 1991. The album was later certified double platinum (two million sold).

Vince continued his successes in 1991 with the release of *Pocket Full of Gold*, a bluegrass-oriented album that went double platinum a year later, and featured three strong singles, "Lisa Jane", "Look at Us", and the title track. The 1991 release was followed with two highly acclaimed 1992 albums, *I Never Knew Lonely* and *I Still Believe in You*. The latter album produced two #1 hits, "Don't Let Our Love Start Slippin' Away" and the title track, both co-written by Vince, and reached double-platinum status in 1993.

Honors and awards were showered on Vince during the 1990s, beginning with his invitation to become a Grand Ole Opry member (1991); CMA Entertainer of the Year (1993/1994); CMA Male Vocalist of the Year (1991/1992/1993/1994/1995); CMA Songs of the Year for "When I Call Your Name" (1991), "Look At Us" (1992), and "I

Still Believe in You" (1993); CMA Album of the Year-*I Still Believe In You* (1993) and *Common Threads: The Songs of the Eagles* (1994); CMA Vocal Events of the Year with Mark O'Conner and the New Nashville Cats for *Restless* (1991), George Jones and two other Oklahomans **Garth Brooks** and **Joe Diffie** for "I Don't Need Your Rockin' Chair, *TNN-Music City News* Award for Instrumentalist of the Year (1991/1992/1993/1994)), as well as their awards for Album of the Year-*I Still Believe In You* and Single of the Year –"I Still Believe In You" (1993), and Best Vocal Collaboration for "Go Rest On That Mountain" with Patty Loveless and Ricky Skaggs, GRAMMY Awards for Best Country Vocal Performance by Male (1990/1992/1994/1996/1997/1998), Best Country Song for "I Still Believe in You" (1992), Best Country Instrumental Performance Collaboration with Asleep at the Wheel for "Red Wing" (1993), Best Country Vocal Collaboration for "Restless" (1991), Top Male Vocalist Award from the ACM (1992/1993), and the Minnie Pearl Award for Humanitarian Efforts from *TNN/Music City News* (1993).

In 1993, Vince released *Let There Be Peace on Earth*, a platinum seasonal album, s followed by two albums in 1994, *Vince Gill & Friends* and *When Love Finds You*, which later went triple platinum. The *Friends* tracks included vocals by such notables as Emmy-lou Harris, Bonnie Rait, and the Sweethearts of the Rodeo. In 1994, the *When Love Finds You* production soared to near the top of the country album chart, crossing over to the top ten of the pop album charts. The album garnered GRAMMYs for Vince for Best Country Vocal Performance Male for "Go Rest High on That Mountain" and Best Country Song for "Go Rest High on That Mountain" (1995), and CMA top honors for Song of the Year in 1996. Vince had written the song in memory of his half-brother, Bob, who had died of a heart attack in 1993. Gill appeared on television with Gladys Knight at the American Music Awards to inaugurate promotion of an ambitious project teaming the legends of R & B with the legends of country in an MCA album that offered an innovating blend of these two American music genres.

In 1996, Gill released *High Lonesome Sound*, a platinum album that featured his high tenor vocals and bluegrass instrumentation. The album soon went platinum and earned Vince three more GRAMMY Awards, including Best Male Country Vocal Performance for "World's Apart" (1996), Best Male Country Vocal Performance for "Pretty Little Adriana" (1997), and Best Country Collaboration with Vocals for "High Lonesome Sound" featuring Alison Krauss and Union Station (1996). In addition, he was given the Vocal Event of the Year by the CMA for his duet with Dolly Parton on "I Will Always Love You," and Song of the Year for 1996, "Go Rest High on That Mountain." Finally, 1996 was capped off with the *TNN-Music City News* Award for Best Vocal Collaboration with Patty Loveless and Ricky Skaggs for "Go Rest High on That Mountain."

In 1998, Vince released *The Key*, a highly acclaimed gold album with ten of the thirteen tracks written by him, including "My Kind of Woman/My Kind of Man," a duet with Patty Loveless, which captured the 1999 CMA Vocal Event of the Year, "Hills of Caroline," featuring Alison Krauss; "The Key to Life," a tribute to his late father; "Kindly Keep It Country," a duet with Lee Ann Womack; and "What They All Call Love," with harmony sung by Faith Hill. The album highlights Vince's talents on the guitar and mandolin with instrumental contributions by such legendary Nashville session artists as guitarist Randy Scruggs, pianist Hargus "Pig" Robbins, and fiddler Stuart Duncan. "If You Ever Have Forever in Mind", the second track on the album, won Vince a GRAMMY Award for Best Country Vocal Performance by Male in 1998. Vince's instrumental greatness was showcased on "A Soldier's Joy" in the Randy Scruggs' album *Crown of Jewels*, and won him a 1998 GRAMMY for Best Country Instrumental Performance. *Breath of Heaven: A Christmas Collection*, a seasonal album, was released in 1998. Finally Vince's most recent contribution is "All Prayed Up", one of the tracks on the *Will the Circle Be Unbroken, Vol. III*, released in 2002 on Capitol Records.

Vince has also been a finalist for several other CMA Awards, including Song of the Year ("When I Call Your Name') and Vocal Event of the Year ("The Heart Won't Lie") with **Reba McEntire** (1990), Entertainer of the Year (1991/1992/1995/1996/1997/1998) , Album and Single of the Year for *Pocket Full of Gold* (1991), Single of the Year ("Look at Us") in 1992, Single and Music Video of the Year ("Don't Let Our Love Start Slippin' Away") in 1993, Single and Video of the Year ("Look At Us") in 1992, Singles of the Year for ("Don't Let Our Love Start Slippin' Away") in 1993, ("When Love Finds You") in 1995, and ("Go Rest High On That Mountain") in 1996, Albums of the Year for (*Rhythm, Country & Blues*-1994), (*When Love Finds You*-1995), (*High Lonesome Sound*-1996), and (*The Key*-1999), Male Vocalist of the Year (1997/1998/1999/2000), Song of the Year ("If You Ever Have Forever in Mind") and Vocal Event of the Year for "No Place That Far" with Sara Evans, both in 1999. He has also earned twenty BMI Songwriter Awards and nine *Music City News* Songwriter Awards for such compositions as "Pretty Little Adriana", God Rest High on That Mountain", "I Still Believe in You", and "When I Call Your Name".

In 2000, Vince released *Let's Make Sure We Kiss Goodbye*, a thirteen-track album with twelve written or co-written by him. It was recorded just months before his marriage to CCM artist Amy Grant on March 10, 2000, and contains several romantic songs, such as "When I Look Into Your Heart", a duet with Grant; "The Luckiest Guy in the World", and "Little Things". It also features Vince's daughter, Jenny, on harmony vocals for "That Friend of Mine". Also in 2000, Vince released a children's album, *The Emperor's New Clothes*, and received a GRAMMY for his instrumental performance on "Foggy Mountain Breakdown", a collaboration with Earl Scruggs, Randy Scruggs, **Leon Russell**, Steve Martin, and several others. Vince and Amy were made proud parents on March 12, 2001, when Corrina Grant Gill was born. Finally, Vince teamed with pop diva Barbara Streisand on her latest album, *Duets* (Columbia, 2002) on which they perform "If You Ever Leave Me".

After inductions into the Oklahoma Hall of Fame, National Cowboy Hall of Fame, and Oklahoma Music Hall of Fame, Vince was elected president of the Country Music Hall of Fame and Museum in Nashville in 2002. He also hosted the Country Music Association Awards from 1992 to 2004. He has made frequent trips back to Oklahoma to support various state causes. For instance, in 2002 he served as master of ceremonies for the dedication of the new Capitol building dome in Oklahoma City. He opened the ceremonies by singing "Oklahoma Hills" co-written by **Woody** and **Jack Guthrie**. Gill's self-produced his 2003 release, *The Next Big Thing* (MCA), reached #4 on the country album charts, #14 on the *Billboard* Top 200 album charts, and the album's title track made the Top 20 of the country singles charts. The follow up single, "Someday," was a Top 40 country track, and Vince played more than sixty dates in 2003 to support the album. Also in 2003, two of Gill's songs, "When I Call Your Name," and "Go Rest High on That Mountain," landed at 44 and 66 respectively on CMT's 100 Greatest Country Songs of All Time. In 2004, Vince reunited with Rodney Crowell, Tony Brown, Richard Bennett and Hank Devito (as well as new additions Eddie Bayers, John Hobbs and Michael Rhodes) as the Notorious Cherry Bombs, releasing a rootsy, grit-filled album on Universal South Records containing the

Vince Gill performing at the 2007 Crossroads Guitar Festival.

hilarious Gill/Crowell co-write "It's Hard to Kiss the Lips at Night that Chew Your Ass Out All Day Long", and the home-state homage, "Oklahoma Dust". Also in 2004, indicating his continued status as one of America's most respected guitar pickers, Gill appeared at Eric Clapton's Crossroads Guitar Festival, two tracks of which were included on the DVD released to document the festival. In the subsequent year, 2005, Gill achieved the highest recognitions in country music for a songwriter and performer, including induction into the Nashville Songwriters Hall of Fame and the Country Music Hall of Fame.

In 2006, Gill released *These Days*, a groundbreaking, four-CD set featuring forty three new recordings of diverse musical stylings. Each album in the set explored a different musical mood: *Workin' on a Big Chill* is filled with up tempo jams good for any truck speakers are the stereo field party; *Some Things Never Get Old* is filled with traditional country that your grandpa would like; *Little Brother* exhibits Vince's long-time association with, and excellence in performing, bluegrass and folk numbers; and *The Reason Why* is full of Gill's trademark winsome ballads that few voices in country music can really pull off like he can. The set features a variety of guest performers including John Anderson, Guy Clark, Sheryl Crow, Phil Everly, daughter Jenny Gill, wife Amy Grant, Emmylou Harris, Diana Krall, Michael McDonald, Bonnie Raitt, Leann Rimes, Gretchen Wilson, Lee Ann Womack, and Trisha Yearwood. Considered a far-reaching and adventurous project for a country musician, *These Days* won a GRAMMY Award for Best Country Album of 2007 at the 2008 GRAMMY Awards. Also in 2007, Gill collaborated with Oklahoman **Jimmy Webb** on "Oklahoma Rising" a song to commemorate the state's centennial celebration. Starting with a nod to Oklahoma's American Indian heritage by including a Plains flute and Native chant, the song extols the state's history in beautifully metaphoric terms, and was included on a benefit CD, *Oklahoma Rising: A Salute to the Artists and Music of Oklahoma* (Oklahoma Centennial Commission, 2006). Profits from the CD were designated to benefit Habitat for Humanity in Oklahoma, apropos as Gill has been associated with many benevolent causes over the years.

Besides being known for his talent as a performer, musician and songwriter, Gill is regarded as one of Country Music's best known humanitarians, participating in hundreds of charitable events throughout his career. An avid golfer, Vince helped create the annual Vince Gill Pro-Celebrity Invitational Golf Tournament ("The Vinny") in 1993, which has raised around three million dollars thus far to support junior golf programs throughout Tennessee. As a result, the PGA of America awarded him its Distinguished Service Award in 2003. Continuing his record-setting GRAMMY Award receptions, Gill accepted his twentieth GRAMMY Award for participating on the track "Cluster Pluck", included on Brad Paisley's 2008 album for Arista-Nashville, *Play: The Guitar Album*, which received the

GRAMMY nod as Best Country Instrumental Performance. Also in 2008, CMH Records released a children's album in their *Rockaby Baby!* series with a collection of Gill's songs performed as instrumental lullabies, *Hushabye Baby! Lullaby Renditions of Vince Gill.* Also that year, he continued his home state charitable ways by performing a benefit at his old elementary school, now the Cleveland Elementary Arts and Science Specialty School on NW 23rd Street in Oklahoma City, to help refurbish the school's auditorium, raising nearly $95,000 in the process. Also during the concert, he was awarded the *Oklahoma Today* magazine's Oklahoman of the Year Award for 2007.

Without picking or singing another note, Vince Gill has created a stellar legacy matched by few other artists in country music history. However, one can also glean that Vince cares about more than just his personal wealth and accomplishments as he has demonstrated by contributing to charities in his adult home of Tennessee, while never forgetting his roots in Oklahoma and how they contributed to his success. While Gill has not had a major country single since the late 1990s, his bold musical production such as the multi-disc, multi-genre discs released under the title of *These Days*, now a platinum album with over a million copies sold, indicates his audience has matured with him, and wants to hear what he is up to artistically, not necessarily concerned with how he fits into Nashville's start of the moment treadmill. Since his 2010 compilation, *Love Songs*, is comprised of previously released material, itself reaching the Top 40 of the country album charts, one can only imagine the new material he has been developing since the GRAMMY winning *These Days*. In 2011, Gill released his first album since 2006, the critically acclaimed and commercially successful, *Guitar Slinger* (MCA), which peaked at #4 on the *Billboard* Top Country Album charts, and rose to #14 on the *Billboard* Top 200 Albums, showing Gill's popularity flows beyond country music's borders. Also in 2011, he celebrated 20 years as a member of the Grand Ole Opry,

In 2012, Gill continued high-profile appearances as he joined a Western swing retro group, the Time Jumpers, a Nashville live group that plays mostly for benefits and has a rotating lineup, eventually releasing a self-titled album in the fall of 2012. Also in 2012, Vince received his star on the Hollywood Walk of Fame, played a whole bushel of gigs all over the place, to include the Guthrie International Bluegrass Festival run by his old buddy, **Byron Berline**. With so many one-off studio sessions, guest shots, live performances, benefits, awards (20 GRAMMYS and counting), the file is still open (and bulging) on Vince Gill, with much more to be

Vince Gill at his 2002 Oklahoma Music Hall of Fame Induction with fellow inductees Barney Kessel (center) and Byron Berline.

heard from this over-the-top-talent. His website is an extremely active and thorough documentation of his total accomplishments and current happenings.

www.vincegill.com

Gilliam, Les

Recognized as "Oklahoma's Balladeer" since 1998 by the state legislature, an accomplished presenter of cowboy, Western, and traditional folk and country music from Oklahoma with sixteen albums to his credit, Les Gilliam was born October 18, 1934, in an Ardmore Hospital, the only member of his family born in a medical facility. However, his hometown is Gene Autry, Oklahoma where he and his family lived until he was fifteen. Subsequently, the Gilliams moved to Ardmore where Les started singing on KVSO Radio in Ardmore and KTEN Television in Ada. He worked his way through Murray Jr. College (now Murray State) playing with the Arbuckle Mountain Boys, and with basically the same band at Oklahoma A&M (now Oklahoma State), where he eventually graduated with a mathematics degree. After graduation, Gilliam moved to Dallas where he was a cast member of the Big D Jamboree for several years. Music then became more of an avocation while he spent thirty eight years in the computer business, and he and his wife, Martha, raised their family.

After retiring from the high tech world, he went into the music business full time, presenting a solo show of cowboy/country music on acoustic guitar, and performing as many as one hundred performances per year. Within that format, he presents the highly acclaimed "Cowboy Hit Parade Show", counting down the top cowboy hits of the singing cowboy era, and the "Oklahoma Pride Show", where he takes listeners on a history trip of Oklahoma country music, performing songs by Woody Guthrie, Gene Autry, Bob Wills, Patti Page, Merle Haggard, Roger Miller, Garth Brooks and Vince Gill, all Oklahoma Music Hall of Fame inductees. Along with his band, Silver Lake, Les has given numerous concerts and Western style dances across the five-state-region contiguous to Oklahoma, the International Country Music Festival in Vienna, Austria, and in several states across the U.S., including a series of dates for Silver Dollar City in Branson, Missouri, since 1997. Additionally, Gilliam has represented the state in Washington D.C. at the Kennedy Center's Millennium Celebration which featured music from each of the fifty states. Gilliam was chosen by Senator James Inhofe's office to represent Oklahoma in the prestigious 1999 event.

With his comforting and smooth baritone voice, humorous and thoughtful delivery, as well as his bright and fluent cowboy guitar picking style, Gilliam has recorded sixteen

Les Gilliam

independent albums of well-known and original country, Western, and gospel music. Along with the previously mentioned Wrangler Award, Gilliam received the Oklahoma Governor's Arts Award in 2006 for his many years of keeping Western music alive and informing Oklahomans of their musical heritage through his entertaining and informative performances. In 2011, Les was inducted into the Oklahoma Music Hal of Fame in Muskogee, Oklahoma.

www.lesgilliam.com

Gilmore, Gary

A primary contributor to American blues rock from 1968 to the present era, Gary Gilmore is one of the most significant bassists to come out of Tulsa, along with peers **Bill Raffensperger** and **Carl Radle**. He is also a photographer and artist with some of his work appearing on album covers and posters for various bands. Emerging on the national scene in 1968 with **Chuck Blackwell** and **Jesse Ed Davis** in Taj Mahal's blues band, Gilmore's easy, loping bass work appears on three Mahal albums of the late 1960s, *Natch'l Blues* (1968), *Taj Mahal* (1968), and *Giant Step/De Old Folks at Home* (1969). During Gilmore's time with Mahal, he appeared in the Rolling Stones' *Rock and Roll Circus* television special, released as a DVD in 1996. Gilmore 's soulful rhythm also bounces around **J.J. Cale**'s second album, *Naturally*, in 1972, an association that continued through Cale's 2004 album, *To Tulsa and Back*, and Cale's collaboration with Eric Clapton in 2006 for the GRAMMY winning contemporary blues album, *Road to Escondido*.

Gilmore's bass work transfers easily between rock, blues, and country, all significant signposts for Tulsa musicians who have worked within groups or for artists in each of those genres, such as his tracks on the cultish 1981 Tulsa Sound album, Rockin' Jimmy and the Brothers of the Night *By the Light of the Moon*, perhaps the best example of the Tulsa Sound without any of the usual famous names attached to such a project, unless one is familiar with the musicians, like Gilmore, on the record. Gary also appears on the lead track, "The Tulsa Shuffle", from the Tractors' multi-platinum 1994 self-titled album, as does Jim Byfield, of the previously mentioned Rockin' Jimmy and the Brothers of the Night. Gilmore's illustrations, photography, and art work have been part of album CD packages or posters for The Casualties, No Redeeming Social Value, Madball, and Awkward Thought. His bass style, often a light hop that might be best described aesthetically (if not specifically) as the rhythm to the kids' song "Shortin' Bread", also appears on the Oklahoma supergroup album put together by **Jamie Oldaker**, *Mad Dogs & Okies* in 2005. Additionally, his work with Mahal and Cale has resurfaced several times on anthologies and "Best

Gary Gilmore, performing in 2006 at the Oklahoma Music Hall of Fame Induction Ceremony in Muskogee, OK, on behalf of inductee, Carl Radle.

of" collections by both artists, as well as on the soundtrack for *Martin Scorsese Presents the Blues: A Musical Journey* (2003), and compilations such as *Story of the Blues* (1995) and *Blues Gold* (2006).

Good, Al
(b. 1917 – d. March 5, 2003)

The last of the big band leaders from Oklahoma who maintained at least a ten to twelve-piece ensemble through the early 2000s, Al Good and his musicians performed for thousands of dances, broadcast programs, and other high-profile events over his fifty-year career centered in Oklahoma City. An energetic and good natured bandleader who always seemed to be having a good time in front of the orchestra, Good started out in Morgantown, West Virginia, played in groups there, and then Atlantic City and New York City, before moving to Oklahoma City in 1945 to work for WKY Radio, where he did several live radio shows per day, and formed his band a year later.[1]

Al Good and his Orchestra began playing for state-wide events in the late 1940s, to include Governors Balls from Roy Turner (1947) through Brad Henry (2003), and appearing on one of the state's first television shows, *Sooner Shindig*, in 1949. Good's orchestras accompanied national celebrities and performers who came to Oklahoma, including Lena Horne, John Wayne, Roy Clark, Frankie Avalon, Mike Douglas, Bob Hope, Danny Thomas, Roy Rogers and Dale Evans. His band was the featured group on a weekly television show, *A Good Time for Music*, on KWTV, Channel 9, in Oklahoma City. He was also the leading musical contractor in Oklahoma for many musicals, to include *Hello Dolly*, *Cabaret*, *Carousel*, and others. Additionally, his bands featured guest vocalists such as **Anita Bryant**, **Garth Brooks**' mother, Colleen, as well as Brian White's mother, Anita Wilson, and country vocalist, Sammi Smith. Given his experience in the entertainment business, Good worked for many years as a booking agent, bringing many jazz and big band stars to the state, such as Count Basie, Woody Herman, Stan Kenton, Harry James, Al Hirt, Buddy Rich, The Tommy Dorsey Orchestra, and the Glenn Miller Orchestra. Good's band served as the original orchestra for the Western Heritage Awards at the Cowboy Hall of Fame, and also was the bandleader for many years at the National Finals Rodeo in Oklahoma City, during which time Clem McSpadden introduced Reba McEntire to rodeo fans as a teenager in 1974 to sing "The Star Spangled Banner", garnering instant attention at what was just the beginning of her career. According to a 2003 article in the *Daily Oklahoman*, once Good heard McEntire sing, he suggested she perform a capella.[2] In the early 2000s, his group performed regularly in Yukon at Ernie's Palace. On a personal note, this writer had a

Al Good

Al Good Orchestra, 1997, video screen grab.

chance to work with Al Good in the spring of 1997, booking his orchestra for a swing dance in Stillwater. Scheduled for the OSU Student Union Ballroom, the dance helped the Memory Music Club of KSPI-AM, Stillwater, to celebrate fifty years of the station playing big band music, only to be followed a year later when the station converted to sports and news talk. In any case, the entire working experience with Al Good was how a professional booking should happen: the artist was clear and up front about their fees and needs; a contract arrived in a timely manner from the artist and was promptly returned; the group arrived early, looked spiffy and professional in stage clothes appropriate for their musical genre, and played an evening of big band hits that had the crowd dancing and happy for the entire time they played. Good was personable and friendly, kindly and casually elegant in demeanor, and congenial as a host and bandleader, dancing around in front of the orchestra almost the entire evening. Working with Al was better than good, the experience was a great lesson in the professionalism necessary for a of long-lasting musical entertainment career.

Notes
1. For more background on Al Good, see the article written on the event of his death: Sandy Davis and Gene Triplett, "Beloved bandleader dies, leaves legacy of good will," *Daily Oklahoman,*7 March, 2003: section A, p.1.
2. Ibid.

Grant, Bill
(b. May 9, 1929)

As part of the perfect bluegrass duo with long-time musical partner Delia Bell, Billy Joe Grant is Oklahoma's highest profile bluegrass musician, having traveled to perform in thirty-four states while recording thirty-two albums. A singer, songwriter, mulit-instrumentalist with mandolin specialty, bluegrass promoter, and member of the Choctaw Nation of Oklahoma, Billy Joe Grant was born raised, and as of 2010 still resides on the 360-acre ranch that has been in his family for more than a century near Hugo, Oklahoma, a community of about 6,000 residents, county seat of Choctaw County, and the site for the oldest bluegrass festival west of the Mississippi, Grant's Bluegrass Festival. Growing up as a Grand Ole Opry listener (Grant family purchased their first radio in 1937 and Bill began tuning in to WSM-Nashville), Bill considers Bill Monroe and the Stanley Brothers as his bluegrass idols. While listening to the Opry in the 1940s, Bill began singing some of the songs broadcast over the airwaves. The beginning of Bill's interest in music was sparked when he began learning a few chords on his mother's piano, and then a friend loaned him a guitar.

After high school, Bill devoted more time to his cattle business, and his music hobby occupied less of his time. But in 1959, Bill met Delia Bell, a native Texan, whose husband had been a friend of Bill's since childhood. The

Circa 1982

two musicians discovered their voices blended well together, and they began to sing at local functions. Grant had already been singing on KIHN radio in Hugo, and Bell began joining him in about 1960. After singing together sporadically throughout the 1960s, Bill and Delia formed the Kiamichi Mountain Boys in 1969, and continued performing as Bill Grant and Delia Bell for several years and albums.

After a visit in 1969 to Bill Monroe's bluegrass festival in Beanblossom, Indiana, where Bill and Delia were invited to sing a number with Monroe, often thought of as the "father of bluegrass", Bill decided to establish an outdoor bluegrass festival site on his ranch (about two miles east of Hugo) in 1969 calling it the Salt Creek Park Old-Time Country and Bluegrass Festival. The first festival line-up was a virtual "Who's Who in Bluegrass", including Bill Monroe and the Bluegrass Boys, Ralph Stanley and the Clinch Mountain Boys, The Country Gentlemen, and Mac Wiseman. Following the first festival, bluegrass fans in Oklahoma launched the first bluegrass club in the state, Oklahoma Bluegrass Club, based in Oklahoma City. Because of Grant's festival and formation of the Oklahoma Bluegrass Club, Governor David Hall proclaimed a "Bluegrass Week in Oklahoma" in 1973, while also naming Grant the state's "Ambassador of Bluegrass Music", a title revived under subsequent Governors, Frank Keating and Brad Henry.

Bill Grant and Delia Bell, circa 1976.

Since its inception, Grant's festival has added a variety of amateur contests, including those that focus on old-time fiddling, mandolin, banjo, guitar, dobro, and bands. Notable winners in the amateur contests who have achieved national and international stature include **Vince Gill** and **Joe Diffie**. In 1997 the Oklahoma state legislature recognized Grant's festival as the "oldest bluegrass festival in the world under original management and name."

In 1971, Bill launched his own Kiamichi Records and released several albums featuring hot picking on all stringed instruments associated with bluegrass, sacred and secular songs in the style of traditional "old time" country, and the requisite high lonesome harmonies. Collectors enjoy tracking down the vinyl LP copies of *My Kiamichi Mountain Home* (1972), *Kiamichi Country* (1973), *There Is a Fountain* (1973), *The Last Christmas Tree* (1976), *My Pathway Leads to Oklahoma* (1978), *The Blues-Mountain Style* (1979), and *The Man in the Middle* (1979), most of which have been re-released on as Old Homestead compact discs.

Bill's songwriting talents have focused on his home area, the Kiamichi Mountains of southeastern Oklahoma, and include such compositions as "Stairway to Heaven," "Cheer of the Home Fires," "A Few Dollars More," "My Kiamichi Mountain Home," "Where the Old Kiamichi Flows," "Beneath the Old Pine Tree," "When the Angels Come For Me," "Bluer Than Midnight," "I Know the Time Has Come For Me," and "Kiamichi Moon." He and Delia are internationally recognized for their vocal harmonies in the old-time mountain style, closer to the nasality of mountain music of Tennessee or Virginia that distinguishes bluegrass singing from the crooning of guitar-toting cowboys or Western swing love singers, and is the aural antecedent of the hard country of honky-tonk singers such as Hank Williams, Sr., Webb Pierce, or George Jones. Grant's Kiamichi Mountain home is the Oklahoma aural equivalent to the Blue Ridge, Appalachian, or Ozark Mountains in the southeastern United States.

With this authentic American sound in tow, Bill and Delia toured the U.K. in 1979, where they recorded *Bill Grant and Delia Bell in England* on the U.K. label, Kama. The Kiamichi Mountain Boys, comprised of the Bonham Family with Delia and Bill, disbanded in 1980 because the Bonhams did not want to travel as much as Bill and Delia were getting ready to do as they cut four albums for Rounder Records, *The Cheer of the Home Fires* (1983), *A Few Dollars More* (1985), and *Following a Feeling* (1988), backed by the Johnson Mountain Boys. Consistent touring supported the releases as Bill and Delia Bell became known as the premier bluegrass duo of the period. Recognizing the duo's special moment in bluegrass music, Rounder released a "best of" compilation in 1997, *Dreaming*, with highlights culled from the three albums, and available forever as an mp3 download.

In the 1990s, Bill and Delia recorded for the Old Homestead independent record label, specializing in old-time country, gospel, and bluegrass, a process by which their music could also get out to their fans and other bluegrass performers. With more than eighty compositions to his credit, Bill's songs have been recorded by artists such as Ralph Stanley ("Stairway to Heaven"), and Alice Stuart.

Bill Grant, circa 2008.

Grant also added bass guitar to Kid Rock's *Polyfuze Method* album in 1993. The duo appeared on 1992's *Stained Glass Hour: Bluegrass & Old-Timey Gospel Songs* with Ricky Skaggs, as well as *Rebel Records: 35 Years of the Best in Bluegrass (1960-1995)* released in 1996. Although he retired from running the festival and promoting bluegrass in 2004, Grant has continued to receive recognition for his outstanding career in music. In 2006, the International Bluegrass Music Association (IBMA) gave Bill its Distinguished Achievement Award, granted to five individuals per year for their contribution to bluegrass music – singing, playing, or promoting – and Grant is all three. In 2007, he received a Special Recognition Award for his support of arts in the state of Oklahoma by the Oklahoma Arts Council, and released his first solo album, a sixteen-track CD, *Turned Loose*. In 2008, he was again recognized by the IBMA with induction into the International Bluegrass Music Hall of Fame Owensboro, Kentucky, where its accompanying museum educates the public about bluegrass by celebrating it via its greatest creators and players. Also in 2008, at age 79, he released the CD, *Bill Grant on the Kiamichi Trace*, and a live DVD.

www.myspace.com/billgrantmusic

Grantham, George

Called the "Ringo of country rock" by the Nitty Gritty Dirt Band's John McEuen, drummer and harmony singer George Edwin Grantham, was an original member of 1970s country rock group, Poco, from 1969 to 1978, and again through their reunion years. Grantham was born in Cordell, Oklahoma, a community of roughly 3,000 residents located in southwestern Oklahoma. Along with the Byrds, Flying Burrito Brothers, and Dillard & Clark, Poco helped pioneer the synthesis of country and rock, but it is Poco that is considered the most "countrified" of the country rock groups. Its whiney steel guitar and mountain-style banjo picking anticipated the coming of country rock as popular music in the form of the Eagles, as well as the neo-traditionalist movement in the 1990s.

Poco was formed in Los Angeles by two former members of Buffalo Springfield, Richie Furay and Jim Messina, as well as Rusty Young. Young, steel guitarist with Poco, had known George since he was sixteen because they had performed together in a band called Boenzee Cryque in Colorado. When Poco was organized, Young contacted George for his percussion and vocal skills. George played on twelve albums with Poco, including the seminal country rock album, *Pickin' Up the Pieces* (1969), which contains "Calico Lady", on which Grantham sings lead vocals. Grantham also drums and sings on Poco's first Epic album, *Crazy Eyes* (1973), where Grantham subtle and steady drum work opens the album's title track. The group's 1974 release, *Seven*, highlights George's drum skills with a solo on "Drivin' Wheel". Poco's most notable singles on which George played and sang include "You Better Think Twice", "C'mon", and "Rose of Cimarron". George again performed with Poco in 1984 on the *Inamorta* album. In 1989, Poco reunited (Messina, Furay, Meisner, Young, and Grantham) for the 20th anniversary of the group's founding to record an RCA album, *Legacy*, charting two pop singles, "Call It Love" and "Nothin' To Hide". Three collections featuring the best of Poco, with George on drums and vocals, are MCA's *Crazy Loving: The Best of Poco 1975-1982* (1989), Sony/Columbia's *Forgotten Trail (1969-1974)*, released in 1990, and *Best of Poco: 20th Century Masters* (MCA, 2000).

After leaving Poco, Grantham joined a band called Secrets, and has recorded backup vocals and played drums with the Flying Burrito Brothers, The Gaithers, Rick Roberts, Ricky Skaggs, Sylvia, Steve Wariner, and Ronnie McDowell, with whom he played for four years. Grantham formed a new band in 1998 called Hoopla and the group released an album entitled *It's Always Something* on the Spoon label. At a Poco reunion show in 2004, Grantham suffered a stroke while playing which has prevented him from further music since that time. A number of musicians have worked on his behalf to raise money for his medical expenses, an account being established as the George Grantham Benefit Fund at Suntrust Bank in Nashville, Tennessee. As an example of his respected status among his musical peers, donors to the fund have included Timothy Schmit, Kentucky

George Grantham (far left) with Poco.

By Hugh Foley

Headhunters, Scotty Moore, Steve Wariner, DJ Fontana, Don Henley, Richie Furay, Chris Hillman, Graham Nash, the Orleans Band, John McEuen (of Nitty Gritty Dirt Band), Jim Messina, Kenny Loggins, Charlie Daniels, and R.E.M.

Gray, Otto (and his Oklahoma Cowboys)
(b. March 2, 1844 - d. November 8, 1967)

Leader of the first nationally known band to perform western music, to appear on radio and stage, to tour the U.S., to wear cowboy attire, to appear on the cover of *Billboard* magazine, to present the first female singer in country music, and to become a model for other cowboy and western music ensembles, Otto Gray was born in Lincoln County, South Dakota. Although born in South Dakota, Gray's parents homesteaded in Payne County, Oklahoma, in 1889 during the first land run into Oklahoma Territory. Gray was raised on a farm near Ripley, Oklahoma, where he became adept at roping skills, and eventually joined "Wild West" shows in Wyoming, Oklahoma, and other western states. He married Florence Opal Powell, a native Kansan, in 1905, and the marriage resulted in one son, Owen. Otto never became a musician (he tried his hand at the fiddle on occasion), but both "Mommie" (Florence's nickname) and Owen both sang, and their son played several musical instruments and wrote songs.

According to a 1930 Otto Gray songbook with an unknown publisher found at a Stillwater yard sale in the early 2000s by *OMG II* scouts, the band's early history is both celebrated and mythologized by an unknown, highly enthusiastic author:

> Early in 1924, Billy McGinty, one of the Colonel Roosevelt's famous "Rough Riders," organized an Oklahoma Cowboy Band as a fiddlin', singin', and dancin' unit for the purpose of bringing back to the present generation the music and songs of the early days in the West.
>
> The boys were recruited from the ranches and, with Otto Gray as manager and leader, they soon became the vogue at all local gatherings and on amateur programs in the nearby towns. Their fame quickly spread, and their reputations as entertainers and musicians soon brought them to the attention of radio station managers: and it was over KFRU, a

The Billy McGinty Cowboy Band (1925). Back row, left or right: Henry Hackney, Grank Sherrill, Roy Munday, Guy Messecar, and Paul Harrison. Front Row, left to right: Marie Mitchell, Norma (last name unknown), Molly McGinty, Paul Sharum, and Ulyss Moore. Sitting in front: Ernest Bevins.

small broadcasting station in Bristow, near Stillwater, Oklahoma, Mr. Gray's home town, that they made their debut on the air.

About this time, Otto Gray, part owner of the Schultz and Gray Ranch near Wynona, took over complete charge of the band, Billy McGinty retiring to devote his entire attention to this ranch and postmatership at Ripley, Oklahoma. With Mr. Gray in charge, the group now known as "Otto Gray and His Oklahoma Cowboys," entered the big broadcasting studios in the West and Middle West, and he and his cowboys had much to do with making the plaintive and rollicking cowboy songs famous and giving them a permanent place in the list of American Folk Songs.[1]

As noted above, in 1926 Gray assumed management of Billy McGinty's Cowboy Band, a Ripley, Oklahoma-based outfit that had appeared on radio station KFRU in Bristow, Oklahoma, which eventually became the famous country music blowtorch AM station, KVOO, when KFRU switched its location to Tulsa, and which also indicates the nascent stage of American broadcasting where a station could just change town locations. In any case, the band, under Gray, continued to broadcast over radio, and gained sponsorship from an Oklahoma hosiery company, an extremely early instance of a country music band's commercial potential demonstrated through endorsements over radio, a concept manifesting itself in extreme ways during the flour power Western swing radio years of the 1930s Texas broadcasting with **Bob Wills** or the Light Crust Doughboys. Bolstered by their success, the band traveled in Gray's $20,000 customized Cadillac which could accommodate all the band members, was equipped with a two-way radio transmitter, and featured a set of longhorns on the hood. The band toured the Midwest like cowboys with their chaps on fire, traveling some 2,000 miles to cities, such as Kansas City, Jefferson City, and St. Louis, Missouri, where they performed on radio station KMOX.

In 1928, Gray changed the name of the band from its original name to Otto Gray and his Oklahoma Cowboys, and moved operations of the band from Ripley to Stillwater, home of Oklahoma A & M College, some fifteen miles to the northwest. During the next two years, Gray led the band on tour again through the Midwest and on to the East. Gray's group began to gain national attention, especially when *Billboard* magazine carried an article on them in 1929, and they broadcast over the Columbia Broadcasting System later that year. This network included the largest stations in the Midwest, such as WBBM (Chicago), WCCO (Minneapolis-St. Paul), MKBC (Kansas City, KMOX (St. Louis), KOIL (Omaha), and KFH (Wichita). Reports indicated that Gray and the Oklahoma Cowboys performed in such cities as Schenectady, Buffalo, and Binghamton, New York; Pittsburgh, Pennsylvania; and Cincinnati, Ohio, traveling the RKO and Orpheum vaudeville theater circuit. While traveling the East Coast, Gray signed a contract with the National Broadcasting Company in New York, and in 1930, *Billboard* again carried feature articles on the band, raving about their shows.

But the major breakthrough for the band was in 1931 when Otto Gray and his Oklahoma Cowboys were featured on the front cover of *Billboard*, the first country or western band to appear on the magazine's cover. Gray himself appeared on the front cover again in 1934, and would later use the magazine to advertise the act. After seeing the Oklahoma Cowboys in *Billboard*, other acts around the country began to emulate their western fashion, which included ten-gallon hats, chaps, and boots, as well as playing western music.

Between 1926 and 1931, Gray's band recorded on such labels as Gennett, Champion, Savoy, Superior, Fast, Bell, Okeh, Supertone, Vocalion, Meltone, Polk, and Pana. The band's repertoire included old-time fiddle tunes, ballads, novelty songs, and original pieces, such as "She'll Be Comin' Round the Mountain," "Suckin' Cider Through a Straw," "Plant a Watermelon on My Grave," "I Had But Fifty Cents," "The Cowboy's Lament," "Pistol Pete's Midnight Special," "Who Stole the Lock from the Hen House Door?" "Cowboy's Dream," and "Where Is My Wandering Boy Tonight." In 1931 Otto and Mommie were signed by Film Exchange, a New York-based company, to appear in several short films.

Otto Gray and His Oklahoma Cowboys (Early 1930s). From left to right: Otto Gray, Florence "Mommie" Gray, Lee Allen, Wade Allen, Owen Gray, and "Chief" Sanders. Rex, "The Bark of the Air," sits on teh floor.

Over the years, the Oklahoma Cowboys Band personnel changed. The lineup generally consisted of Otto (emcee), Mommie (vocals), Owen, their son, who assumed the moniker "Zeb" in the act, played banjo, Wade "Hy" Allen (cello), "Zeke" Clements (vocals and guitar) and Chief Sanders (fiddle). Other members at one or another included Whitey Ford, vocalist and banjo player, who later appeared on the Grand Ole Opry as the "Duke of Paducah." The act also included Rex, a dog who barked when Otto entered or departed the stage, rope tricks performed by Otto and Mommie, and Owen singing his signature song, "It Can't Be Done," a novelty number that included lyrics such as "you can't hit a ball with a bat of your eye" and "you can't raise a cow from the calf of your leg." Only Otto, Mommie, and Owen remained with the band from its inception. It should be noted that Gray's band was the first country music act to use a cello in its ensemble.

Of particular interest is a film of Otto Gray's Oklahoma Cowobys released by Yazoo Records on DVD, *Times Ain't Like They Used To Be: Early American Rural and Popular Music (1928-35)* (Yazoo DVD512, 1992). The performance by the band is a hilarious and corny vaudeville effort with multiple musical styles, comedy bits with Western rope gags, and moments where the musicians trade instruments during and in-between songs. Of even more interest is the patter delivered by members of the band, which is an obvious source reference for **Woody Guthrie**'s "stage voice" in rhythm, tone, accent, and lilt. Because of Okemah's proximity to Bristow, Guthrie would have heard Otto Gray comingo out of KFRU in Bristow. Guthrie acknowledges seeing Gray in an Okemah theater when the future folk-singer was a youth. A knowledgable listener of Guthrie's vocal timre and delivery is instantly recognizable in this important film.

After their last tour in 1935, the band disbanded with Otto Gray's retirement from music. He returned to his ranch near Stillwater and later became a real estate entrepreneur. Otto died in Springdale, Arkansas, where his second wife resided, while Mommie died on November 14, 1950 in Stillwater. Both Otto and Mommie Gray are buried in Fairlawn

Otto Gray and His Oklahoma Cowboys broadcasting from the General Electric station, WGY, Schenectady, New York, early 1930s.

Cemetery in Stillwater. For an outstanding and fascinating look into the career of Otto Gray, music fans should make the trek to the Washington Irving Trail Museum near Ripley, Oklahoma, about 10 miles east of Stillwater.[2] At the museum one can see posters, phonograph records, and several historic photos of the famous cowboy band that was Oklahoma's first major country music export to the world. The group's commercial success also represents the beginning recognition by American popular culture that authentic cowboy, country, and Western music may come from a lot of different places in the South, Southwest, Midwest, and Western United States, but the one place all of those locales have in common is Oklahoma specifically, easily considered a well-spring of the tributaries running throughout the musical geography of early twentieth century American popular music.

Notes

1. *Songs: Otto Gray and his Oklahoma Cowboys*, published in 1930 with several images of Otto Gray and His Oklahoma Cowboys, the short biographical entry quoted in this entry, and a collection of their songs, is missing its cover, but the folio may have been printed by Otto Gray himself, as the back page indicates, "Additional copies of this book may be obtained at fifty cents per copy by addressing Otto Gray and his Oklahoma Cowboys, Stillwater, Oklahoma." The book was found in a box of sheet music at a Stillwater yard sale not far from OMG II author's home, and purchased for a dime.

2. Washington Irving Trail Museum: www.cowboy.net/non-profit/irving

Gray, Wardell
(b. February 13, 1921 - d. May 25, 1955)

A primary bebop tenor saxophonist perhaps best known for his amped up sax battles with Dexter Gordon's on jazz classics, "The Chase" and "The Hunt," Wardell Gray was born in Oklahoma City, but left the state at an early age. The youngest of four children, Gray's family moved in 1929 to Detroit, where his first music lessons were on the clarinet which he played when he entered high school at Northeastern High School. After transferring to Cass Technical High School in 1935, he dropped out in 1936, wanting to focus on jazz. His brother-in-law and noted Detroit musician, Junior Warren, advised him to stay with the clarinet, but once Wardell heard the restrained wild mind and playing of Lester "Prez" Young on record, he switched to tenor saxophone. His first job was with Isaac Goodwin's small band, a part-time ensemble that played local dances. Thereafter, he played with the Dorothy Patton combo in Flint, Jimmy Raschel's band in Detroit, and Benny Carew's group in Grand Rapids. At about this time, he met Jeanne Goings and they had one daughter, Anita, born in 1941.

In 1940, Wardell took a tenor chair at the Congo Club, a popular nightspot in Detroit's black entertainment area. At one time or another, the club featured such well-known jazz artists, such as **Howard McGhee** and Teddy Edwards. He and Jeanne were separated and he met Jeri Walker, a young dancer in the chorus line at the Three Sixes, a club near the Congo. Jeri, who he eventually married in 1945, knew Earl "Fatha" Hines, and when he came to Detroit in 1943, she persuaded Hines to hire Wardell. He doubled on tenor and clarinet with Hines until 1945. He also joined Billy Eckstine's big band for a short period before working with Benny Carter in 1946.

In 1947, Gray relocated with Carter's band to the West Coast where he was active in the growing bebop revolution, playing with Dexter Gordon in the South Central Los Angeles jazz clubs, such as The Bird in the Basket, Lovejoy's, and Club Alabam. To truly understand the L.A. jazz scene in this period, one must not only re-visit the seminal recordings with Gordon and Gray of 1947, but take a wider look at the Central Avenue scene which was being infused by additional Oklahoma talent such as **Barney Kessel, Jay McShann, Joe Liggins, Howard McGhee** and **Don Byas**. Instant listener success for the task of learning more about the South Central's jazz scene of the 20th century's middle years can happen by acquiring the essential 1999 four-disc set on Rhino, *Central Avenue Sounds: Jazz in Los Angeles (1921-1956)*. Among the 101 tracks on the disc, "The Chase" is a great example of the sax battles between Gray and Gordon that delighted jazz fans and critics. Ross Russell arranged to record a simulation of one of their competitions on "The Chase", Wardell's first nationally recognized recording. For a live sense of what was going on at the time and just how dynamic the playing was between not only Gray and Gordon, but also Oklahoma natives, guitarist Barney Kessel and trumpeter Howard McGhee who were also right in the middle of it all, fans of this music *must* hear the live Savoy recordings of July 6, 1947. Released as *The Hunt* (Arista, 1977), the original two-LP set included four songs, one per side of vinyl. The eighteen-minute title track, "The Hunt" is also known as "Rocks n Shoals" as denoted on the album label. The track is a free-wheeling, kaleidoscopic ramble through all that was lionized in bop, not only by jazz critics, but fans and writers such as Jack Kerouac who cites "The Hunt" twice in his beat manifesto, *On the Road*, as well as "The Chase". One can easily imagine Dean Moriarty hurtling through the western night in a hulking 1940s vehicle, headlights barely illuminating the road, with the song only in his head because no radio would have been playing it, and no other way existed to hear it until he arrived in the smoky West Coast jazz clubs where the music twirled into the cool Cali mornings.

With his newly gained national fame, Wardell joined the Just Jazz series for which he recorded "Just You, Just Me" and "Sweet Georgia Brown," often noted as essential recordings in his canon. Also during this time, the "King of Swing", Benny Goodman heard Gray's melodic sax shouting at a concert in 1947, and was so impressed he hired Wardell immediately; Gray played his first gig with Goodman at the Click Club in Philadelphia in 1948, but the group met the fate of many bop groups in the late 1940s. Not even Goodman's

Wardell Gray

name could bring enough people out to support the group as the generation of Big Band lovers was back from World War II and ready to settle down with their families, not go sit in a club and listen to extended jazz rambles. Financially unsuccessful, Goodman eventually dissolved the group, but Wardell had no trouble picking up work on the East Coast jazz circuit, first with Tadd Dameron and then Count Basie's band.

In 1949, Gray returned to Goodman, this time in Benny's big band, but life with Goodman was an unhappy one for Wardell with the constant traveling and his marriage to Jeri breaking up. On leaving Goodman, he rejoined Count Basie around 1950, however, Basie's group was downsized to a septet, including Clark Terry and Buddy DeFranco, rather than the big band. He played with Basie, both with the septet and big band, intermittently until 1951 when he decided to return to the West Coast and

Wardell Gray

remarried after divorcing Jeri. By this time, jobs in the Los Angeles area were scarce and recording sessions were few. Although his home life was going well, he seemed disillusioned with the music business. In 1952, he did make another live recording session with Dexter Gordon that proved that he was still capable of playing superbly, as did the recordings with Wardell's septet in Los Angeles that same year. Unfortunately, substance abuse affected his playing during this time, reflected in his last studio session in 1955. When Benny Carter opened the Moulin Rouge in Las Vegas in 1955, he called upon Wardell to join his band, but when the show opened on May 25, Wardell was absent. The next day he was found with a broken neck on a stretch of desert on the outskirts of Las Vegas. Wardell Gray was mysteriously dead at age thirty-four. Gray's solo work on such numbers as "Twisted" (1949), "Farmer's Market" (1952), and "Little Pony" (1950) have become classics, and his *Memorial Albums, Vols. 1 and 2* are among the best collections of his work, released on CD in 1992 on Fantasy Records. A biographical film, *The Forgotten Tenor*, was made in 1994 by Abraham Ravett, and in 2002 the U.K. label Proper Records released a four-CD set of Gray's music, *Blue Lou*, featuring a retrospective of Gray's work from 1947 to 1952. Contemporarily, the essence of Gray's saxophone excellence is available on many recordings under his own name and on tracks by the numerous notable artists with whom he recorded.

The Great Divide
(formed in 1992, Stillwater, OK)
Green, Kelley (b. January 22, 1968)
Lester, J.J. (b. July 16, 1968)
Lester, Scotte (January 1, 1964)
McClure, Mike (b. July 7, 1971)

Surfacing in the college town of Stillwater, Oklahoma, in the early 1990s, The Great Divide were the first group of red dirt musicians classified solidly as such to have been signed to a major label when Atlantic Records picked up the band's second independent album for re-release. The Great Divide's music combines traditional honky-tonk dance numbers, beach party music, Southern rock, and the lyrical smirk of Oklahoma singer-songwriters. Called "Texas Music" south of the Red River, The Great Divide developed a wide following in the Lone Star State which brought them to the ultimate attention of major label talent scouts. With first practices in an old Quonset hut south of Stillwater in 1992, the Great Divide evolved in Stillwater's college town multi-taste music environment, playing beach party songs, country covers, and their own refinement of the red dirt singer-songwriter style. Led by vocalist, guitarist, and primary songwriter **Mike McClure** (b. Shawnee), The Great Divide's defining "Stillwater country" sound is buoyed by brothers Scotte (b. Stillwater) and J.J. Lester (b. Edmond), on guitar and drums respectively, and bassist Kelley Green (b. Little Rock, AR). With their refined red dirt pop, introspective lyrics, and breezy instrumental techniques, the Great Divide's most popular sound is equally at home in a honky-tonk dance hall or a college town party with the best of friends.

Raised in Tecumseh where he began playing guitar at age ten and writing songs in high school, Mike McClure attended Seminole Junior College in 1989, and after two years transferred to Oklahoma State University in Stillwater where he met Scotte Lester, a former bull rider and firefighter, along with Kelley Green, an agricultural economics major at the time, and J.J. Lester, also a former bull rider. As with many other singer-songwriters associated with Stillwater and the Red Dirt scene, McClure had the opportunity to hone his songwriting skills locally at the "The Farm," a house rented by John Cooper of **Red Dirt Rangers** outside Stillwater where a lot of local musicians and songwriters would gather and jam from 1979 to 1999. McClure had the chance to be around many songwriters, but took an obvious lyrical and vocal inspiration from **Jimmy LaFave**. In some respects, and with all respect, McClure elevated LaFave's vocal style into a more commercially viable entity. While maintaining LaFave's plaintiveness and lyrical insight, McClure's melodic voice sounds like LaFave minus the barbed wire chirp at the top of LaFave's voice. LaFave's endearing musical signature and unique raspy twang is one of the reasons he's a unique and beloved artist, but his sound is not going to be embraced by corporate country, which is where McClure and the Divide enter the picture. After practicing in a Quonset hut on the Lesters' family farm, the band played their first gig in 1992 on the back of flat bed trailer at a steer-roping event in Perry, Oklahoma. The group also played often at the Wormy Dog Saloon near the Oklahoma State University campus, released their first CD, *Goin' for Broke*, independently in 1994. By touring the Texas college towns and major cities eager for the band's bouncy honky-tonk, *Goin' for Broke* sold more than 10,000 copies.

With repeated trips to south of the Oklahoma border, The Great Divide developed a strong fan base. The group's status

The Great Divide

elevated quickly as they began opening for artists like Willie Nelson, Tracy Lawrence, the Dixie Chicks, the Charlie Daniels Band, and Chris LeDoux. The Great Divide also served as harbinger for other Oklahoma red dirt artists who have gone on to make Texas a working market for their music (Cross Canadian Ragweed, No Justice, etc.). Interestingly once the music goes south of the Red River (the border between Oklahoma's southern border and Texas), the red dirt style transmogrifies into "Texas Music" where it can be heard from Lubbock to Padre Island. Therefore, when red dirt artists wind up on the Texas Music Chart, the larger country music industry often takes notice. As a result of their growing popularity The Great Divide landed a dreamed-for major label deal, and signed over their second already released independent CD, *Break in the Storm*, to Atlantic Records who re-released it in 1998. Defining their sound of sandy floored honky-tonks, the album was produced by Lloyd Maines, the Texas steel guitar player and father of Dixie Chick Natalie Maines, who has produced projects for Jerry Jeff Walker, Robert Earl Keen, Red Dirt Rangers, Charlie Robison, and many other notable country music figures. The result was a national coming out party for red dirt music in which The Great Divide acknowledged all those musicians who had in many ways developed the style, such as **Bob Childers**, Tom Skinner, and **Jimmy LaFave**. The album launches with a quintessential Great Divide sound rooted in their college town country music ethos ("Never Could"), and plops the listener right down at an island bar ("Pour Me a Vacation"), but overall did not perform nationally as record company executives hoped or expected. "Never Could" only ascended to #74 on the *Billboard* Country Singles chart, but it did create enough action for radio to embrace ""Pour Me a Vacation" a little more, propelling the "beach tonk" single #60 after eight weeks on thet, but that was the extent of the band's national singles chart action outside of the Texas Music Chart. Atlantic Records had difficulty in marketing the album nationwide as pop country, and the CD did not succeed outside of The Great Divide's traditional base of Oklahoma and Texas, and parts of the Midwest. Nonetheless, the album features LaFave on guest vocal on "Used to Be", an archetypal red dirt song co-written by Tom Skinner, another red dirt stalwart. Along with a being a perfect vehicle to hear McClure and LaFave's voices on the same track, the song has an up tempo and happy melody, but melancholy lyrics of better times in a decaying small town root the song in red dirt's linkage to folk singing from Oklahoma.

Hoping to develop the band, Atlantic went ahead with a second album, *Revolution* (1999), and brought back by Lloyd Maines to guide the sessions. The album does have some defining Great Divide music on it ("San Isabella" and "College Days"), and also keeps flying the red dirt flag with two Bob Childers songs, but the disc was not successful enough by company terms, just blipping into the *Billboard* Hot Country Album chart for one week at #73. As a result, The Great Divide left the corporate music industry machine to go back to their independent ways. After leaving Atlantic, the group released a compilation of red dirt artists on their own Broken Records label, *Dirt and Spirit*. In an attempt to rekindle earlier fires, the group loaded their gear into the historic Will Rogers Theatre in Oklahoma City where they recorded *Afterglow: The Will Rogers Sessions* a re-visiting of the band's highlights as a popular regional touring act. In their final attempt to make the band work outside of their traditional geographic base, in September, 2002, The Great Divide released *Remain* on their own label.

Recorded in Nashville and featuring vocalist and songwriter McClure for the final time on a Great Divide release, *Remain* included more introspective McClure songs ("Moon is Almost Full" and "If Not for You"), bolstered by the hybrid country rock sound on which

The Great Divide built their early following. The album also features a hidden track at the end of the collection that features the band really enjoying what sounds like a mostly live acoustic take, a reminder the guys in the band were united artistically and could make very good music together. The album enjoyed success on the Texas Music Chart, reaching #3 south of the Red River while the group toured heavily throughout the Southwest; however, it did not rekindle major label interest in the group. Also, over the winter months of 2002 and '03, Mike McClure played a string of solo acoustic shows through Texas and Oklahoma, and released his first solo CD, *Twelve Pieces* (Compadre), featuring acoustic songs McClure did not consider Great Divide songs. By enlisting guest vocalists Cody Canada of **Cross Canadian Ragweed,** and Susan Gibson, known for writing the Dixie Chicks' hit, "Wide Open Spaces", the album's release and McClure's solo performances led fans to speculate that he would leave the group. Those rumors were confirmed when The Great Divide announced they would perform their last show with McClure on March 28, 2003 at the Tumbleweed dance hall near Stillwater. The performance was recorded and released as *The Great Divide Absolutely Live at Tumbleweed Vol. 1*. With his compositions recorded by **Cross Canadian Ragweed**, **Jason Boland and the Stragglers**, **Garth Brooks,** and **Tyler England,** and having produced albums for Ragweed and Boland, McClure seemed content to work things out on his own as a solo singer-songwriter and American music entrepreneur. Given his lyrical gift for songwriting, and further abilities as a singer and producer, McClure's future seemed ripe with possibilities when he left The Great Divide.

The post-McClure Great Divide decided to soldier on since they had a recognizable name and strong fan base through the Southwest and Midwest. J.J. Lester took time out in the spring of 2003 to produce another new Stillwater act, **No Justice**. By the end of the summer of that year, the group added a new lead singer and guitarist from Ohio, Micah Aills, with whom they recorded one album, 2005's *Under Your Own Sun*. Two singles, "Freedom" and "Crazy in California", were released to radio, but neither recaptured the band's earlier and better-known sound, and in 2007, the band officially called it quits for the time being. .By 2011, the old friends and original lineup decided they could play again for a few gigs just to enjoy the comraderie they had developed for so many years on the road in the studio. They and the fans enjoyed it so much, the band did it again in the fall of 2012, festival style with a weekend of like-minded souls and billed as The Great Divide's College Days to kick off the new school year for Oklahoma State (and whoever else) at the Tumbleweed Dancehall in Stillwater. Probably won't be the last time time, either.

Griffiths, Barrick Jonathan
(b. 1958)

A 1977 graduate of Broken Arrow High School who studied music education at Oklahoma State University before pursuing a professional career in music, Barrick Griffiths has become one of the most respected and sought-out arrangers, proofreaders, and copyists in the Los Angeles music industry. Along with being a gifted trumpet player who has worked as a side musician for a number of significant top-tier acts, the list of artists he has worked with as an arranger is a "who's who" of the American popular music world, just a partial listing of which includes Barry Manilow, Marc Anthony, Michael Jackson, Whitney Houston, Mariah Carey, En Vogue, Monica, Michael Bolton, George Strait, Dionne Warwick, Bobby Brown, Bette Midler, Amy Grant, the London Symphony Orchestra, and

Diana Ross. Griffiths arranged music for Michael Jackson's still popular 30th anniversary television special in 2001, and Marc Anthony's HBO special, "The Concert from Madison Square Garden". Griffiths came from a musical family in which both his parents were musicians (Howard, a trumpeter, and Karen, a pianist). Born in Independence, Kansas, Barrick attended grade school and junior high school in Coffeyville, Kansas, after which the Griffiths moved to Broken Arrow where he was the band president, lead trumpet, and student conductor at Broken Arrow High School. Following graduation in 1977, he attended Oklahoma State University in Stillwater where he studied music education, as well as furthering his trumpet abilities with trumpet instructor Paul A. Montemurro. Not only did Griffiths develop his abilities as an instrumentalist at OSU, he also began producing and arranging for the school's musical productions.

Leaving Oklahoma State just prior to completing his degree, Barrick went on the road as music director, trumpeter, keyboardist and music arranger with the Overtons, a Stillwater-based singing group who toured cross-country as an opening act for Bob Hope until 1983. After returning to Stillwater, Griffiths was hired to create string arrangements for the demo production of two songs, "Blue Rose" and "Heaven's Got a Hell of a Band", for a young unknown singer-songwriter named **Garth Brooks** who was trying to make headway in Nashville with the demo tape and some help from **Reba McEntire**. During the mid-1980s in Oklahoma, Griffiths had stints with the Oklahoma Symphonia as a substitute trumpet player, and performed the same function for the Oral Roberts University television program before heading to Los Angeles in 1988. Not long after arriving in L.A., he was able to land a job with Terry Woodson Music, where he continues to work as an arranger, orchestrator, music copyist, and proofreader. The job of orchestrator requires extensive understanding of musical notation and theory, as well as the specific nuances of different musical genres, in order to write down music for recording sessions, and provide notation of musical ideas by performers or songwriters. His first gig was on the film, *Shadows in the Storm* (1988), starring Ned Beatty, instigating an extensive film soundtrack career, to include composing the highly praised musical score for the short film, *Cover-Up '62: The Final Days of Marilyn Monroe* (2004). Along with working on music for twenty albums with "his idol", Barry Manilow, Barrick has provided arrangements for musical stars such as Liza Minnelli, Peggy Lee, and Mel Torme, and worked as a music copyist for Sammy Davis, Jr., and Frank Sinatra. Via his time with Torme and Lee, Barrick was tagged with the moniker "J.B. Griffiths", a sobriquet under which he has appeared on albums by Barry Manilow, Frank Sinatra, Jr., Amy Grant, Vince Gill, and many, many others. Manilow gives "J.B. Griffiths" a "special thanks" on the liner notes of *Scores* (Concord, 2004), an album comprised of songs from Manilow's musical theatre pro-

Barrick Griffiths conducts at Capitol Records in Los Angeles.

ductions of 1994 and 1997. "J.B." also had a ten-year run with the American Cinema Awards, during which he collaborated with Dionne Warwick, Stevie Wonder, Olivia Newton-John, Al Jarreau, Henry Mancini, Whitney Houston, Christina Aguilera, and Mariah Carey.[1]

Another highlight for Griffiths was being the chief arranger for Michael Jackson's 30th Anniversary Celebration, recorded for CBS the night before 9/11 at Madison Square Garden in New York City, a program that still airs in many countries. A viewing of the program indicates Barrick's wide-ranging abilities as he scored and arranged music for the non-Jackson performances, such as hip-hop, reggae, rock, lush pop ballads, R&B, gospel, quiet storm soul, and disco. By listening to the music of the whole show, keeping in mind how many different styles and kinds of performers appear on stage, one can easily understand why Griffiths is a highly-desired music professional for his versatile abilities. Griffiths also had to do a last minute string arrangement for the final number by Michael Jackson and rock guitarist, **Slash**, as well as a full arrangement of another duet that was going to feature Michael and Whitney Houston, but was cut due to personal issues Houston was going through at the time. Barrick was also hired to create brass and woodwind arrangements for the live orchestra parts on a few of the songs performed by Jackson for the special that still re-airs internationally on the anniversary of Michael's death, and probably always will. Along with his impressive background of arranging all sorts of music for the myriad artists mentioned already, Griffiths has also proofread or worked on music for films such as *Blackhawk Down*, *The Notebook*, *Bridge to Terabithia*, *Bridget Jones' Diary*, *Flicka* and several Adam Sandler films such as *50 First Dates*, *Mr. Deeds*, and others. Additionally, he has performed as a side musician on trumpet for acts such as Jim Nabors, Rosemary Clooney, Dionne Warwick, Mitzi Gaynor, Shirley Jones, Billy Eckstine, Roger Williams, and the Lettermen.

With all of his success, Griffiths felt one of his greatest honors was when his hometown of Broken Arrow asked him to arrange music and conduct the live orchestra for the first performance ever in their then new Performing Arts Center in 2009. At Barrick's request, he, along with Broken Arrow band directors Scott Tomlinson and Darrin Davis, founded the Broken Arrow Studio Orchestra. The orchestra is comprised of the high school jazz band, the high school string section, as well as additional French horns, woodwinds, and percussion in an effort to provide the school's music students with the opportunity to perform in a "Hollywood-style" studio orchestra setting. The evening was especially important for Griffiths as it was the last show his then-ailing father was able to see Barrick perform in just a few short months prior to Howard's passing. Barrick has always stressed that both of his parents were his earliest and most formative music instructors, always encouraging him in every step of his career. His mother taught him the basic foundations of theory, harmony, and gave him his first few years of piano lessons, while his father taught him to play the cornet and

Barrick Griffiths and Stevie Wonder

trumpet beginning in the 5th grade and continuing for life. After Barrick's graduation from high school in 1977, he enjoyed sitting side-by-side with his father as fellow trumpeters in the Tulsa-based big band, The Sounds of Music Orchestra, for the next thirty years.

In 2011, Barrick continued working for Terry Woodson Music in Los Angeles, his twenty-third year at the company. He also provided work for other Los Angeles music offices such as Disney Music, Paramount Music, and Sony Music. By mid-summer, 2011, Barrick finished work on preparing the music soundtrack for Sony's planned end-of-summer blockbuster, *The Rise of the Planet of the Apes*, the prequel to the original *Planet of the Apes*. As for Oklahoma's place in Griffiths' heart, in a 2011 e-mail to the author fact-checking this entry, Barrick wrote how much the state means to him: "I may live in Los Angeles, but Broken Arrow will always be my home."

Barrick Griffiths

Endnotes
1. Barrick Griffiths was profiled in Oklahoma State University's alumni magazine by Matt Elliot. "The Arrangement of a Lifetime." *State Magazine*, (Spring, 2008): 36-39.

Guthrie, Jack
(b. November 13, 1915 - d. January 15, 1948)

Best known as co-composer of "Oklahoma Hills," cousin of famed folksinger **Woody Guthrie,** and producer a distinctive style of singing and yodeling based on his idol, Jimmie Rodgers, Jack Guthrie was born Leon Jerry Guthrie in Olive, Oklahoma, a tiny hamlet southwest of Tulsa in Creek County. Jack disliked the names of Leon and Jerry and assumed "Jack" when he cut his first record. When he moved to California, he was also known as "Oklahoma" or "Oke," monikers given to him by folks in "Cali" because of his roots in Oklahoma. His father was John Camel Guthrie, younger brother of Charley Guthrie, the father of the noted folksinger Woody Guthrie.

Jack was influenced by his father, a blacksmith by trade, but also an old-time fiddler, as well as by several of his relatives, such as Woody, who were musicians. As a result, Jack learned several instruments, including the guitar, fiddle, and bass fiddle. Jack's family moved to Amarillo, Texas, when he was eight, but returned to Oklahoma City in 1929. They then relocated to Texas once again, but returned to Sapulpa, Oklahoma when Jack was fifteen. According to noted Oklahoma music expert, Guy Logsdon, who wrote the liner notes to the Bear Family re-issues of Jack Guthrie's music in 1999, Jack's sister, Wava, indicated that Jack learned some guitar chords from **Gene Autry** while Autry was working as a telegraph operator in Sapulpa. Logsdon also notes that Wava indicated Jack was not infatuated with schoolwork, and would enter the front door of school, only to head out the back door. Apparently, the last school Jack attended was seventh grade in tiny Midlothian, Oklahoma, located in Lincoln County.

As many other Oklahomans did, the family moved to California in the mid-1930s finally settling in Sacramento. Prior to their residence in Sacramento, Jack worked several jobs in the Los Angeles area, including a laborer for construction companies, driving a truck, and working for the WPA and U.S. Forest Service. Following a rodeo accident in which he broke his back, Jack began serious pursuit of a career in music.

At age nineteen, Jack married Ruth Henderson in 1934, resulting in a chaotic marriage in which they were iften separated. Shortly after they were married, Jack developed a rodeo act that included trick roping and bullwhip performances during which Ruth assisted him. During the act, Jack would always sing and play several songs.

In 1937, Jack's cousin Woody moved to Los Angeles, and the two of them formed a musical team. Because their singing styles varied, the two rarely sang together; Jack played the guitar or fiddle when Woody sang, while Woody would pick the guitar and play the harmonica when Jack sang. After several successful performances, they auditioned for radio station KFVD in Hollywood, and on July 19, 1937, made their debut as the *Oke & Woody Show*. Shortly thereafter in 1937, Woody penned "Oklahoma Hills," which they used during their shows. But after two months of the show, Jack left because of family responsibilities, including a new baby son, and the program became the Woody and Lefty Lou Show. Maxine "Lefty Lou" Crissman was introduced to Woody through Jack, and Woody soon discovered the two harmonized well; hence, she became his new singing partner on the KFVD show. In 1939, Woody left the West Coast for New York City, but Jack remained as construction worker, rodeo performer, and played music at beer joints and nightclubs, where he was dubbed "Oklahoma's Yodeling Cowboy."

After meeting several musicians who worked as session personnel for Capitol Records, and Ruth Crissman, a friend who had joined his rodeo act and provided funding for his venture into the recording field, Jack recorded "Oklahoma Hills" for Capitol Records in 1944, his first for the recording company.. The famed song was released by Capitol in 1945, and soon became a #1 country music hit across the nation. When Woody heard the recording over a jukebox, he contacted Capitol and declared it was his composition. After negotiations between Jack and Woody, the two compromised and decided to share the copyright.

In 1945-46, Jack served a short period in the US Army. When "Oklahoma Hills' was released, he was stationed in the Pacific. After discharge, Jack formed a band called the "Oklahomans," and the group played dances along the West Coast and did some touring with Ernest Tubb. His health began to decline and his family suggested that he check into a sanitarium because his sister had suffered with tuberculosis; however, Jack refused and kept writing songs, performing with his band, and recording for Capitol, including eight sessions between 1944 and 1947 that included thirty-three songs. Among these sessions were two more of Jack's compositions, "Oklahoma's Calling" and "For Oklahoma, I'm Yearning", the latter he co-wrote with his sister, Wava.

In 1947, Tubb arranged for Jack to appear in the film, *Hollywood Barn Dance*, in which he sang another one of his hit songs, "Oakie Boogie", a song that is particularly important for its representation of the hybrid style of music known as country boogie, itself an outgrowth of Western swing and a musical forebear to the rockabilly movement of the 1950s. His last recording session was similar to the last Jimmie Rodgers session. A cot was set up in the studio on which he could rest between songs. He died a few weeks later at the Livermore Veteran's Hospital, located near Sacramento, shortly after his 32nd birthday. Buried in Memorial Cemetery in Sacramento, Jack Guthrie is often overlooked in the popularization of such songs as "Oklahoma Hills" and "Oakie Boogie".

In 1996 Rhino Records released *Heroes of Country Music, Vol. 4: Legends of the West Coast*, which featured Jack and His Oklahomans performing "Oklahoma Hills". Bear Family, a German company, released a thirty-track CD entitled *Milk Cow Blues* in 2001, which features Jack singing some of his Jimmy Rodgers' favorites like "Muleskinner Blues" and "Peach Pickin' Time in Georgia". Additionally, Bear Family has released *Oklahoma Hills*, which features most of Guthrie's better known tunes, and *When the World Has Turned You Down,* that includes the remainder of Guthrie's Capitol session recordings, as well as the remainder of his radio transcriptions. Exhibiting his wide-ranging interests, *When the World Has Turned You Down* finds Guthrie performing Roy Acuff's "Low and Lonely", Ernest Tubb's "You Nearly Lose Your Mind", Red Foley's "Freight Train Blues", as well as **Bob Wills**' "Time Changes Everything" and "Take Me Back to Tulsa", and several traditional blues numbers.

All Bear Family discs feature extensive notes from Tulsa's Guy Logsdon, who has carried out more than 40 years of research into the hard-to-track Jack Guthrie, and is also one of the absolute foremost experts on Woody Guthrie's life and career. While not nearly as significant as his cousin, Jack Guthrie did popularize "Oklahoma Hills", and was one of many forerunners of the burgeoning rockabilly movement with his own brand of country boogie that both pre-dated and influenced the early rock and roll movement of the 1950s. Like Bob Wills said when asked what he thought about rock and roll, "Man, we were playing that back in the '30s." So was Jack Guthrie.

Guthrie, Woodrow Wilson "Woody"
(July 14, 1912 – October 3, 1967)

Because of the volume and historical significance of his work, Woody Guthrie is the single most important Anglo-American folk singer of the twentieth century. His most enduring song in the popular consciousness is "This Land is Your Land," however, his songs about the dust bowl and Great Depression in the 1930s, and the union movement of the 1940s, are important documents of life and politics in those times. By writing and singing about current events from his perspective, Guthrie recast the folk ballad into medium for social protest, observation, and contemplation of political activism. Born in Okemah, Oklahoma and named after President Woodrow Wilson, Guthrie's enduring music continues to influence countless musicians and singer songwriters to the present day. Of the thousands of songs he wrote but never recorded, new interpretations by contemporary artists are constantly reviving Woody, and his children's songs are still valuable and fun experiences for young people, parents, and teachers.

Woody Guthrie's family first came to Indian Territory sometime in the early 1890s when his maternal grandfather moved with his schoolteacher wife and five daughters to a farm outside Welty, a speck of a town now in Okfuskee County, but then in the **Muscogee (Creek)** Nation. Around the same time, Woody's paternal grandfather, Jeremiah Guthrie, came in from Texas to start a cattle ranch on the Deep Fork of the Canadian River. Guthrie's father, Charles Edward Guthrie, met Woody's mother, Nora Belle Tanner, in the rural society of northeastern Okfuskee County, and the two were married in 1904. Born five years after Oklahoma's statehood, Woody heard old-time ballads his mother sang to him as a child, and started playing a harmonica as a young boy by imitating an African-American man who shined shoes in a barber shop and also played the mouth organ. Woody wrote in his autobiography that his father played guitar and banjo, and sang, "Negro and Indian square dances and bluses." Guthrie also remembered hearing black men making up songs every day as they built his grandparents' new house, and Indians, most likely Creeks, singing and chanting as they walked the backtrails in the woods. Woody's tragedy-filled family life is an important part of his story and is covered thoroughly in Joe Klein's authorized 1980 biography, *Woody Guthrie: A Life* (Delta). His sister died in a fire accident, and his mother wound up in a state asylum as a result of the socially and medically misunderstood Huntington's Disease that Woody also later developed. With little supervision at home, Woody lived on the fringes of Okemah's rough and tumble social elements in his early teens. However, he also continued going to high school where he started drawing cartoons, and was on the high school newspaper and yearbook staff. His classmates thought him entertaining enough to put him on the back of flatbed truck for a show on Main Street in hopes of raising money for the junior prom.

After the family with whom he had been staying moved to Arizona in 1928, Woody quit school and traveled to Texas where he worked odd jobs of all types. He picked grapes, helped carpenters, drilled water and oil wells, and hauled wood, all the while carrying his harmonica and playing with everyone he could wherever he could. After making it as far south as the Gulf of Mexico in the summer of 1929, he tired of the migrant farm lifestyle and headed

Woody Guthrie

back to Okemah. When he arrived, a letter from his father was waiting that asked Woody to head west to the oil-boom town of Pampa in the Texas panhandle. Seventeen when he arrived in Pampa, Woody worked at various odd jobs before getting a job at a drugstore across the street from his father's rooming house. In the back of the drugstore, he found an old guitar and started to learn some chords from his father's brother, Jeff. Next to the store, an African-American shoe shine man knew how to play the blues, and showed Woody the rudiments of the form on guitar which would influence many of his greatest songs with blues in the titles. Although Woody did not finish high school in Pampa, he attended for a short while and during that time met Matt Jennings who had purchased a pawn shop fiddle but did not really know how to play it. The two struck up a friendship, learn to play together, and before long met another boy, Cluster Baker, who played guitar, and they formed the Corncob Trio. Matt also connected Woody to his first wife, Mary (Jennings) Guthrie, with whom Guthrie had three children – Gwen, Sue, and Bill.

The group got their first taste of being paid musicians at a dance at the local skating rink, and continued playing mostly at people's houses and local functions. By 1934, the Corncob Trio started getting better gigs and Woody started writing his own songs. Then, the event that would shape Woody's identity as a musician and folksinger occurred on April 14, 1935. As a result of a long drought, thousands of tons of topsoil roared through the Oklahoma and Texas panhandles and covered Pampa in a heavy dirt blanket. Following the dust were migrants, fliers in their hands that promised work in the verdant fields and valleys in California. The stories they told and the experiences of living through the dust storm and the Great Depression caused Woody to start writing the first of his dust bowl songs. Woody began to ramble from Pampa and his young wife more and more in 1936. He wrote and sang about what he saw on the roads and highways of the Southwest. He sang to the dispossessed, repossessed, and depressed. He sang songs about the lives he heard about and witnessed while traveling, songs from past lives he remembered from his mother's old time ballads, and the cowboy and country songs that were popular on the radio.

Woody Guthrie's childhood home in Okemah, circa mid-1970s.

After a lot of traveling around the Midwest, Southwest, West, and back to Pampa, Woody decided to go to California in 1936. He arrived in Glendale, California, a gathering place for migrant Okies, a negative term in the national jargon at that time. Several other Guthries had made their way to Glendale, including Woody's cousin, Jack Guthrie, who would later have a hit with "Oklahoma Hills," written by Woody but made popular by Jack. Already working as a would-be cowboy singer, Jack found work for them in a cowboy vaudeville show that led to the *Oke and Woody* radio show on KFVD, a Los Angeles station. Due to financial difficulties (they were not being paid for the show), Jack left, and Woody continued on the show with Maxine "Lefty Lou" Crissman. The homespun show appealed to the thousands of former farm dwellers who inhabited Los Angeles in the late 1930s, and in late 1937 Woody and Maxine signed a one-year contract with Standard Broadcasting. In 1938, Woody took an offer to assemble a hillbilly musical troupe to perform on powerful Mexican radio station XELO, but it did not work out and he and Maxine wound up back in Los Angeles on KFVD. Exhausted, Maxine's interest and ability in performing faded and the show ended in June of 1938. Woody began traveling through California and seeing the destitution of the people who lived in the farm camps, under bridges, and on the streets. His songs started to become more political and even more of a document of the people's hard lives he was witnessing. Guthrie became an active supporter of worker's rights and labor unions. Songs like "Vigilante Man," "Do-Re-Mi," and "Dust Bowl Refugee" entertained thousands of people at labor rallies, communist related meetings, and organized meetings touting unions, good wages, and government assistance for the economically disadvantaged, also known as "the poor." This status led to his interaction with Ed Robbin, a reporter for the *People's World*, the West Coast's Communist newspaper, and began a long misunderstood musical and authorial connection between Woody and the Communist Party detailed fully in the previously mentioned Klein biography.

In 1940, Guthrie moved to New York where he met and sang with Pete Seeger, Burl Ives, and **Agnes "Sis" Cunningham**. He traveled the East Coast performing widely for both folk music fans and gatherings of workers who were trying to upgrade their rights. During this time he also wrote his first version of "This Land Is Your Land" under a working title of "God Blessed America", and made an important connection with noted folklorist Alan Lomax who recorded Woody in Washington D.C. in March of 1940. During these sessions, Woody recorded some of his best known songs: "Talking Dust Bowl Blues", "Do-Re-Mi", "Hard Times", "Pretty Boy Floyd", "They Laid Jesus Christ in His Grave", and "I'm Going Down the Road Feeling Bad", among others. In addition to singing on the Library of Congress sessions, Guthrie talked a lot. Tracks such as "Monologue on the Youth of Woody Guthrie" and "Dialogue on the Dust Bowl" serve as very informative oral histories of both Guthrie's life to that point and of his time in Oklahoma and California. Subsequent to the sessions, Lomax convinced RCA to record Woody's dust bowl songs in their studios, which they did in April, 1940, and released them on Victor as *Dust Bowl Ballads Volume 1 and 2* in sets of 78 rpm 10" records, again in 1950 as *Talking Dust Bowl* (Folkways), and in 1964 as *Dust Bowl Ballads*. Critics often cite these recordings as his most important works and are primary listening for students of Guthrie. Songs from *Dust Bowl Ballads* include "Talking Dust Storm Blues", "Dust Bowl Refugee", "Dust Cain't Kill Me", and "So Long, It's Been Good to Know You". The songs are not only important documents of Woody's lyrical delivery in his strong Oklahoma dialect, they are also novellas of the rough life many people endured in the 1930s. His knowledge of the realities in the Depression-era dust bowl is as important as any history book on the period. Collectors should note that all the *Dust Bowl Ballad* releases have subtle track differences, which is why Guy Logsdon's discography in *Hard Travelin': The Life and Legacy of Woody Guthrie* (Wesleyan University Press, 1999) is a primary source for understanding the complexities and details of Woody Guthrie's recording career.

Woody's New York years in the early 1940s were busy with performances on radio, concerts, and recordings. In 1941, Guthrie began touring the United States with Lee Hays, Pete Seeger, and Millard Lampell in a group called the Almanac Singers whose core members went onto form The Weavers, sans Woody, that became the most commercially successful folk group of the late 1940s and early 1950s. They appeared alternately at concerts, charity affairs, radical meetings, and union gatherings. In addition to traditional folk songs, the group performed topical Guthrie compositions such as "Union Maid," "Talking Union", and "Union Train a Comin'". Woody's period with the Almanac Singers is explored in some detail by Richard A. Reuss with JoAnne C. Reuss in *American Folk Music & Left Wing Politics: 1927 to 1957* (Scarecrow Press, 2000). Between stints with the Almanac Singers, Woody was commissioned by the U.S. Interior Department to travel to Oregon and write songs in support of the Bonneville Dam's construction in Oregon, which he did by writing twenty-eight songs in twenty-eight days for the Bonneville Power Authority. The end product of the project culminated as *The Columbia River Songs*, to include "Roll on Columbia" and "Grand Coulee Dam." In 1942, he divorced Mary, and began a relationship with Marjorie Mazia, a dancer in the Martha Graham troupe, whom he married in 1946 and with whom he had four children – Cathy, Arlo, Joady, and Nora. In 1943, his novel, the semi-autobiographical, sometimes philosophical, and all Woodysized *Bound for Glory* appeared on bookshelves. With World War II in full swing, and Woody

Woody Guthrie

all of thirty-one-years old, he joined the U.S. Merchant Marine and traveled from the British Isles to Russia, a journey that provided the lyrics for several anti-fascist songs. After the war ended, Guthrie returned to New York where he settled in New York with Marjorie and continued writing songs of all types, especially children's songs that manifested on the album *Songs to Grow On* (1946). Tragically, their first child was killed in a fire. Their other children included Arlo, who is a noted folk singer in his own right, Joady, and Nora.

In the years after 1946, Guthrie performed as a soloist and in concerts with other well-known folk singers of those years, such as Ramblin' Jack Elliot, Leadbelly, Pete Seeger and the Weavers. He also began to experience the first symptoms of the Huntington's disease that plagued his mother many years before in Oklahoma. Recordings followed for Moses Asch's Folkways Records that provided material for many albums throughout the late 1940s. Smithsonian Folkways Records made previously unreleased recordings from this period (1944-1949) available in 1994 on *Long Ways to Travel* which included the whole diversity of Woody's repertoire. The collection contains union songs, tragic ballads, nonsensical fun songs for children, and talking blues. By 1950, however, Woody's life started to unravel due to his illness, and his recordings of the early 1950s are not indicative of his genius. He did marry again in 1952, to Anneke Van Kirk, but his condition and the age difference between the two doomed the union. His health deteriorated to such a point in the 1950s he could not play guitar, type, nor hold a pen anymore.

In 1954, Guthrie entered Greystone Hospital in New Jersey by his own choice, the first of thirteen hospitals in which he would stay until his death. During the 1960s, Guthrie only degenerated slowly due to Huntington's, a disease of the muscles that leaves the mind active but slowly robs the body of its ability to move, and for which no known cure exists. Ironically, Guthrie was not able to participate in the resurgent folk music scene of the 1960s when artists such as Bob Dylan modeled themselves after his iconoclastic ideals, image, and Okie delivery. Dylan made repeated visits to Guthrie's hospital room in the years before Guthrie died, and did much to maintain Guthrie's songs and style before the public. Issued on Columbia Legacy in 2010, Bob Dylan's *The Witmark Demos: 1962-1964* provides a new lens into both Dylan's early modeling of Guthrie, as well as how important Guthrie's vocal delivery and lyrical observations impacted on the young folk singer from Minnesota. In 1965, a collection of Woody's stories, drawings, poems, new songs, articles, and reminiscences were published as *Born to Win*. After his death in 1967 at the Creedmoor State Hospital in Queens, New York, Guthrie was honored by many memorial concerts to raise money and awareness for Huntington's disease. Woody Guthrie's legacy has not gone unnoticed nationally, nor locally in Oklahoma. In 1971 Woody was inducted into the Songwriters Hall of Fame, and the Nashville Songwriters Hall of Fame followed suit in 1977. In 1988, Guthrie was inducted into the national Rock and Roll Hall of Fame for his pioneering work in using the folk song as an agent for social change.

In 1990, *Pastures of Plenty: A Self-Portrait*, edited by Dave Marsh, provided the public with many excellent photos of Guthrie, and also printed drawings and other unpublished writings by him. In 1996, the year he was awarded a posthumous Lifetime Achievement Award by the Folk Alliance, Woody's daughter, Nora Guthrie, opened the Woody Guthrie Archives in New York City. The collection of Guthrie's personal papers, to include letters, notebooks, diaries, photographs, drawings, and thousands of songs, is open to the public by appointment. As a benefit to the archives, in 1996 a live concert was organized in honor of Woody at the Rock and Roll Hall of Fame and Museum that became the CD, *'Til We Outnumber Them*, released on Ani Difranco's Righteous Babe Records in 2000. On the album, Arlo Guthrie, Billy Bragg, the Indigo Girls, Bruce Springsteen, Ramblin' Jack Elliot, and Dave Pirner of Soul Asylum play Woody's songs. The Woody Guthrie Archives also served as the foundation for alternative folk rockers Billy Bragg and Wilco to collaborate on songs for which Woody left lyrics but only the slightest musical notation. The result of the project became two albums, Mermaid Avenue (1998) and Mermaid Avenue Volume II (2000). In 1997, Rounder Records released *This Land Is Your Land*, a collection of Woody's children's songs performed by Woody and Arlo to accompany the video *This Land Is Your Land: The Animated Kids' Songs of Woody Guthrie* (LIVE Enterntainment). In 1999, the aforementioned *Hard Travelin': The Life and Legacy of Woody Guthrie*, edited by Rock and Roll Hall of Fame staffers Robert Santelli and Emily Davidson, brought together friends, family, and scholars to celebrate the life and achievements of America's foremost folk singer, to include the excellent discography and bibliography by Oklahoma cowboy singer and music historian, Guy Logsdon.

While Oklahoma has had a somewhat uneven love affair with its celebrated son, Woody is becoming more and more revered in his home state. In 1997, the newly founded Oklahoma Music Hall of Fame made Woody its first inductee, and in 1998, Woody's hometown of Okemah became the site for the annual Woody Guthrie Free Folk Festival, still active on each year on the weekend nearest Woody's birthday of July 14. Singer-songwriters come from around the country to play in Woody's memory, scholars assemble to talk about his legacy, and seminars raise awareness about Huntington's disease. By 2010, the numbers of visitors from all over the U.S. and the world had swelled to 8,000 people. While the city of Okemah regularly celebrates the event with banners along the street, and businesses welcome Guthrie fans from around the world, some people have still not gotten beyond their deeply set opinions of Guthrie. As late as 2002, an enlarged article appeared in one Okemah business window during festival week titled "Woody Was No Hero," wherein the author speaks negatively of Woody, and one local church greeted festival goers with the maxim, "Words without deeds is like a garden with weeds," perhaps referring to Guthrie's incredible volume of writing but perceived lack of moral character by townsfolk. In 2001, The Friends of Libraries in Oklahoma, a local extension of the national organization, made Woody's birthplace of Okemah the state's first Literary Landmark, and placed a plaque in his honor by the statue of the folk-poet in his home town.

New books in the 2000s by and about Woody's include those targeted toward preschoolers, *Howdi Do*. In 2002, five-time GRAMMY nominees, Cathy Fink and Marcy Marxer covered the Guthrie/Billy Bragg song "Birds and Ships," gleaned from *Mermaid Avenue, Volume I*, and released it on their CD, *Postcards* (Community Music). In 2003, the

Woody Guthrie Free Folk Festival Program, 1998.

National Folk Alliance's Nashville Local Committee helped sponsor The Woody Guthrie 90th Year Celebration in Music City. A concert featured Arlo Guthrie, Nanci Griffith, Gillian Welch and David Rawlings, **James Talley**, Jimmy LaFave, Ramblin' Jack Elliott, Slaid Cleaves, Ellis Paul, Janis Ian, Corey Harris, and others, and the month-long celebration also included a photo exhibit from the Woody Guthrie Archives, a Woody Guthrie film festival, and outreach into the Nashville schools with Woody's music. As part of the celebration, the Country Music Hall of Fame sponsored an exhibit of Woody Guthrie-themed paintings by renowned folk artist Kathy Jakobsen, and presented a panel discussion led by pop music journalist and historian Dave Marsh. The panel, entitled "Can You Get from the Dust Bowl to Music Row?", discussed how Guthrie's songs relate to the great populist tradition of country music in the manner of Jimmie Rodgers, Merle Haggard, and Steve Earle. The hall of fame's museum also displayed Guthrie's 1930s model Slingerland guitar.

Multiple recordings of Woody's songs, or songs about Woody, have materialized since 2003's publication of *OMG 1*. In 2004, Rounder Records released Guthrie contemporary and co-hort Ramblin Jack Elliot's *The Lost Topic Tapes: Isle of Wight 1957*, containing five WG songs. That same year, Boulder, Colorado jam band, Leftover Salmon wrote a song to Woody telling him how much things have changed since he rambled the American highways. Also in 2004, Smithsonian Folkways opened their *Classic Folk Music* compilation with Guthrie's "Pastures of Plenty", and the family tradition continued with Woody's granddaughter/Arlo's daughter, Sarah Lee Guthrie, made her major label debut no New West Records with her collaborator, husband, and musical partner, Johnny Irion on *Exploration*. The two forged their own path, however, avoiding the easy temptation of covering one of her grandpa's songs, choosing instead to do Pete Seeger's "Dr. King". In 2005, perhaps Woody's best known song, "This Land is Your Land", was re-recorded by Art Alexakis, front-man for the alternative rock group, Everclear, for use in the 2004 Presidential election where it was used at rallies and the Democratic Convention that year. However, Sharon Jones and the Dap Kings' R&B funky workup of the same song on their CD, *Naturally* (Daptone, 2005), revives the tune in a way that few covers of Woody's material every have, and probably qualifies on the Top 10 or 20 of any compilation from this point forward of his songs as re-interpreted by new artists. In 2005, the rough hewn Americana tunesmith, Jay Farrar, led his band, Son Volt, through an atmospheric nod to Woody's hometown in *Okemah and the Melody of Riot* (Sony Legacy). Also in 2005, the Joel Rafael Band recorded a whole album of Woody's songs on *Woodyboye* (Appleseed), but perhaps the most extremely irreverent but hilarious recording from the Guthrie universe emerged under the name Folk Uke, a collaboration between Arlo's other daughter Cathy Guthrie and Willie Nelson's daughter, Cahty Nelson. Both dads join in on some song titles readers will just have to look up because we hope this book winds up in some elementary school libraries somewhere, and the album's song titles might just get it taken out. In 2006, the Woody Guthrie foundation released some of Woody Guthrie's Jewish lyrics that were recorded by the Klezmatics, a spun-around-sideways klezmer band from New York City on *Happy Joyous Hanuka* (Shout Factory), and Ramblin Jack Elliot bounced back into focus with *I Stand Alone* (Anti) with an ode to his old pal, "Woody's Last Ride". In 2008, Music Road Records released a two-disc tribute CD, *Ribbon of Highway/Endless Skyway*, to accompany a tribute tour for Woody across America. Narrated by red dirt luminary, **Bob Childers**, the set features the music of Slaid Cleaves, Eliza Gilkyson, **Jimmy LaFave**, Kevin Welch, Ellis Paul, and Pete Seeger. To explain the purpose of the disc and tour, Jimmy LaFave, explained in a press release, "We're trying to showcase all facets of Woody Guthrie. He was so many things beside a songwriter; a painter, a philosopher, a soldier, a poet, and a supporter of the disenfranchised. His songs were just the tip of the iceberg. He was the spirit of America." Also in 2008, smooth folk chanteuse, Johnatha Brooke, immersed herself in the Woody Guthrie archives with permission to record whatever she wanted sitting in the mountains of Guthrie lyrics, recorded or unrecorded. After enlisting some ace players, to include Keb' Mo, Derek Trucks, Mitchell Froom, Joe Sample, Brooke interprets Woody's lyrics as if they came from her own gut, but so smoothly the polish on the songs belies the winsome melancholy that permeates the story telling that is at once familiar and brand new at the same time. Hear why Woody Guthrie could have just as easily been a Nashville songwriter of the last thirty years on *The Works, Words: Woody Guthrie, Music: Jonatha Brooke* (Bad Dog). As for a modern version of Guthrie's true sense of humor, lyrical pacing, irreverence for the status quo's concepts of decorum, and a true descendent of Woody's observationally dead-on social commentary storytelling, track down Todd Snider's 2011 disc, *Live: The Storyteller* (Aimless/Thirty Tigers). All one has to do is hear "The Ballad of the Kingsmen",

Ribbon of Highway, Endless Skyway (Shout Factory, 2008).

"America's Favorite Pastime" and "Mushroom Story" to recognize the spirit of Woody Guthrie is alive and well in today's next generation of entertaining musical storytellers who can get up in front of an audience with just a guitar in tow, and teach us about ourselves by getting us to laugh before we realize on reflection the powerful points that are being made about modern life, a Guthrie hallmark indeed.

To Mark the 100th anniversary of Woody's birth, the George Kaiser Family Foundation purchased the Woody Guthrie archives in order to move them to Tulsa. Also in 2012, Tulsa University hosted a highly-attended academic conference and symposium on the life and work of Woody Guthrie, which was capped off by an all-star tribute concert at the Brady Theater. Tribute performers included the Flaming Lips, John Mellencamp, Hanson, Arlo Guthrie, and several others. In 2013, Woody's unreleased 1947 novel, *House of Earth*, became available to the public for the first time. Those readers who have gone through all available Guthrie writings will not be surprised by the frank sexuality in the story, but those who are more casual admirers of Woody's work might be surprised by the explicit detail with which he describes his characters intimacy. The book further stands as Guthrie's attempt to really set down the diction of 1930s Okies and panhandle Texans, along with a major metaphor in the house made of earth as a symbol of a long lasting home that will not suffer the temporality of wooden floorboards, walls, and roofs. Like his characters, the house made of earth is made to weather the worst conditions, and remain standing.

Okemah city limit sign, 2010.

Along with everything else in 2012, Woody Guthrie was inducted into the Songwriters Hall of Fame in New Yok City, the Gilcrease Museum of Tulsa put together a traveling Woody Guthrie exhibit for Oklahoma schools, and Smithsonian Folkways released a three-CD box set of primary Guthriie recordings, along with 21 previously unreleased recordings, along with a 150-page large cofee table book.Of particular interest in the set are Woody's first known - and recently discovered - recordings, from 1939. *Woody at 100: The Woody Guthrie Centennial Collection* won a GRAMMY in 2012 for Best Boxed or Special Limited Edition Package.

While a multitude of musical albums, exhibits, books, films, articles, and experts continue to tell the story of Woody Guthrie, the best place to learn about his legacy is through the music he produced and the books he wrote, or volumes that have been compiled from his writing. While historical context and critical explanation can help one gain deeper insight into the complicated and rich life of Woody Guthrie, no one tells his story better than he has through his songs and words. The Woody Guthrie Archives has put together an excellent website that directs students, teachers, scholars, musicians, and fans to multiple resources for further study and appreciation of Woody Guthrie's life, legacy, and music, all of which add up to a primary canon of American folk music that surfaced from the most traditional sources of Anglo-American balladry, play-party songs, and talking blues, and wriggled out through the prism and sieve of small town Oklahoma, big time Depression, World War weariness, hollering protests, and glaring harbingers of the Civil Rights era and Vietnam-era expressions of discontent. His significance continues to resound in the legions of folksingers who followed Woody's calloused fingertips and tireless storytelling into the modern era to re-interpret our own world with a sense of humor, wry cynicism, and insight born of gritty experiences that can only be gained on the road, among the people, and from reading anything and everything about this world, its contradictions, and its glories.

www.woodyguthrie.org

H

Haggard, Merle
(b. April 6, 1937)

Having written, co-written, and recorded several classic country music standards, such as "Okie from Muskogee", "The Bottle Let Me Down", "Today I Started Loving You Again", and "Working Man's Blues", Merle Haggard parlayed a strong understanding of the lives and musical ethos of hard core country music fans into thirty-nine #1 singles, a presence on the country album charts from 1965 through 2011, and bucket loads of awards, honors, and inductions to various musical halls of fame. While Haggard was not a native-born Oklahoman, his mother, Flossie (Harp) Haggard, and his father, James Haggard, lived in Checotah, Oklahoma, about fifteen miles south of Oklahoma. On land that is now under Lake Eufau, the Haggards were getting by as tenant farmers in the 1930s until their barn caught fire and they lost all of their livestock and farm tools. As a result, in 1934 the Haggards followed the stream of "Dust Bowlers" heading west in the great Okie migration during the Great Depression to find work and sustenance for their families.[1] As a result, Merle Haggard was born into a transplanted Oklahoma culture, emerging into the world from the family's converted boxcar home in Bakersfield, California. Haggard's father played fiddle, but his mother was the inspiration behind his taking violin lessons at an early age. The fiddle has remained an important part of Haggards' career, evident both when he still pulled a "sawbox" on stage for at least one song through 2011, as well as in his life-long affinity for the music of Bob Wills and Western swing that consistently informed his musical identity.

When Merle was nine-years-old, his

Merle Haggard

father died, which began an unruly and rebellious childhood that led to a rocky adult life. By 1957, Merle earned a publicly funded vacation in San Quentin Prison. Not only did he have a chance to reflect on his life, he was allowed a guitar to pick on as he had since high school. He began writing songs in the vein of his heroes Jimmie Rodgers and Jimmie Davis, and also saw Johnny Cash perform twice at the prison, which led Haggard to believe he could have a career in country music once he was released in 1960. Once out of prison, Merle received help from Buck Owens and Bonnie Owens in getting his career started. Haggard eventually married the Blanchard, OK native, Bonnie Owens, in 1965. The couple divorced in 1978, but he continued to feature her as a backup vocalist as part of his live concerts into the 2000s until she retired from performing.

In the early 1960s, Merle formed his backing group, the Strangers, who began playing a diverse range of country songs to please the patrons of various geographic origins in the oil field bars and honky-tonks around Bakersfield. In doing so, Haggard is identify with a loose country music subgenre known as the "Bakersfield Sound," known for the pin-point picking bite of a Fender telecaster, the supporting twang of a steel guitar, and lyrical focus on the interpersonal relationships between men and women ("Today I Started Loving You Again", "Things Aren't Funny Anymore", "Someday We'll Look Back", and "She Ain't Hooked On My Anymore" with Toby Keith). Some of Haggard's most successful songs are from the socio-political points-of-view based on a working class perspective ("Workin' Man Blues", "Big City", "The Fightin' Side of Me", "I Take A Lot of Pride in Who I Am", and "That's the News"). Haggard also mined his prison experiences for successful songs ("Branded Man", "Sing Me Back Home"), as well as his knowledge of outlaws ("I'm a Lonesome Fugitive", "Bonnie and Clyed", and "Pancho and Lefty" with Willie Nelson and written by Townes Van Zandt), the honky-tonk lifestyle ("The Bottle Let Me Down", "I Think I'll Just Stay Here and Drink", "Honky Tonk Night Time Man"), a tough upbringing ("Mama Tried", "Hungry Eyes"), and life on the road ("Silver Wings"). Perhaps none of his music has had the impact on both Oklahoma and the image of Oklahomans in popular culture as his number one country hit in 1970, "Okie from Muskogee".

According to Merle himself, "Okie from Muskogee" was originally a tongue-in-cheek espousing of red, white, and blue values written as an antithetical lyrical stance to the 1960s counterculture still present in 1970. As a member of the initial Oklahoma Music Hall of Fame Board of Directors, the author had the chance to visit with Merle prior to his induction into the Oklahoma Music Hall of Fame at its first induction in 1997. Ironically, the concert and induction was held in the Muskogee Civic Center, the same building where the original demo version of "Okie from Muskogee" was recorded, and then sent back to Capitol Records headquarters. Before Merle knew it, the actual demo became the hit recording. Merle indicated that their tour bus was on the way to a prison show in McAlester,

Muskogee Chamber of Commerce promotional bookmark, circa 2010.

By Hugh Foley / 321

Merle Haggard, circa 2000

and someone on the bus was rolling a cannabis cigarette as they passed a sign for Muskogee, a town he'd heard about all his life since it was the "big town" for people from Checotah, near where his parents farmed. He said to himself, "I bet they don't smoke marijuana in Muskogee," and the song began to take shape. Also credited with developing the lyrics as a co-writer is native-Oklahoman, Eddie Burris, then Merle's drummer, who stayed with Haggard for many years as both drummer and bus driver. Burris indicated that the Strangers liked to go through Muskogee when they could because a Western clothier carried a particular brand of shirt they liked wearing. The song itself uses a variety of stereotypes about mythological small town, flag-waving America. As a result, right-wing conservatives, who felt their country's ideals and image were being unfairly assailed by the anti-war and anti-establishment elements of the United States, propelled the song to #1 status on the country charts. The song became popular enough to just peek at the *Billboard* Top 40, inching up to #41 in 1970. Not only did the song give the city of Muskogee worldwide recognition, "Okie From Muskogee" also began turning the term "Okie" into a positive image. Throughout the 1930s and forward, the image of the Okie as a poor, white, migrant farm worker was one with which established Oklahomans did not want to be associated. With one song, however, Merle converted the image into one of traditional values whereby the Okie could be proud to represent a purer form of American idealism. The song's satire was often lost on its fans, however, and embraced as fervent truth instead of cynical social commentary, a hallmark of many Haggard songs.[2] By the early 2000s, the city of Muskogee's chamber of commerce capitalized on the city's worldwide recognition as a result of the song, and launched an advertising campaign to capitalize on the town's notoriety as a result of the hit.

Haggard continued producing hits through the 1970s and '80s; however, much of his star quality faded among the younger country music fans driving the Nashville country music machine by the 1990s. While Merle could still pull a faithful, though smaller, crowd than he had during the peak of his popular success, after more than thirty-five years of working with major labels, Haggard signed on the independent label, Anti, a subsidiary of Epitaph Records, primarily know for punk rock and hardcore rock recordings. The resulting album, *If Only I Could Fly* (Anti, 2000), is a stripped-down, back to basics country music effort that put Haggard back on the road to old and new fans. Quoted in a 2000 press release from Anti Records, Haggard said, "I feel at home with young punk rebels." Along with recognizing his historical status (he donated some of his family's heirlooms to the Smithsonian Institution in 2003), he continued recording and performing through the 2000s. In 2003, he released *Haggard Like Never Before* on his own label, Hag Records. The album's primary single, "That's the News", generated national press and media appearances for the song's critique of the news media's lack of focus on the collateral damage of war in the form of continued human suffering, after the dust of hostility has cleared, when service men and women return home stunned to their friends and families. He continued similar sounds and lyrical ways on 2005's reunion with Capitol Records, *Chicago Wind*, containing an anti-Iraq war song ("America First"), and two Oklahoma-related tunes, a duet with Toby Keith on more of Haggard's world-weary perspective ("Some of Us Fly"), and a Roger Miller song, "Leavin's Not the Only Way to Go". Haggard's 2007 disc, *The Bluegrass Sessions*, continued his social commentary ("Where Did America Go?"), along with some "bluegrass-ish" versions of his some of his hits ("Big City", "Hungry Eyes"), and included a medley of songs made famous by his idol, Jimmie Rodgers, all set off by outstanding bluegrass players. In 2010, Haggard released yet another disc, *I Am What I Am* (Hag/ Vanguard), which showed him in a confident, but easy swinging, form. His music has continued the country music trope of retrospective wisdom, a.k.a. hindsight, and his weathered view of love manifests itself perfectly in "Pretty When It's New". The album received enough positive attention to warrant Haggard performing its title track on *The Tonight Show with Jay Leno* in February, 2011.

Haggard on fiddle, 1973

Merle Haggard is one of country music's most significant singers, songwriters, and bandleaders from his entry onto the scene in 1963 ("Sing a Sad Song") through his continued work in the current era as an American music icon.[3] Along with many awards for millions of on-air performances of songs, and millions of albums and singles sold, Haggard received the prestigious Lifetime Achievement Award for his outstanding contributions to American culture from the John F. Kennedy Center for the Performing Arts in 2010. While Merle was not born in the state, he can claim much of its musical and sociological heritage due to his parents being part of one primary historical period of Oklahoma's development as state, namely the Dust Bowl and the Okie migration west. In 2004, the historic Cain's Ballroom in Tulsa added his portrait to its display of country music giants, the first new once since the group of images of country music giants were placed there in 1950. As mentioned earlier, he was one of the first inductees into the Oklahoma Music Hall of Fame. In many ways, his multiple hit singles and albums, Academy of Country Music and Country Music Association Awards, 1984 GRAMMY Award (for "That's the Way Love Goes"), and inductions into the Country Music Hall of Fame (1994) and Nashville Songwriters Hall of Fame (1977), are all due to his Oklahoma parents, especially his mother, who carried their love for music from Oklahoma to their new home in California. Once there, Flossie Haggard made sure her son knew the basics of music by arranging for his first lessons, providing him the foundation for picking his way out of prison, and ultimately into the ears, hearts, and thinking caps of millions. Health permitting, Haggard continued touring through 2012.

Endnotes

1. For more insight to the Haggard family's Oklahoma experience before moving to California, as well as Merle Haggard's accounting for a large portion of his most successful years in music, see Merle Haggard with Peggy Russell, *Sing Me Back Home: My Story*. (New York: Pocket, 1989).

2. Haggard tells one version of the story behind "Okie from Muskogee" in the "Story Behind the Song" feature in *Performing Songwriter* (September/October, 2007).

3. Demonstrating his iconic status in American music as of 2009, and deftly encapsulating his full life and career, see the feature profile by Jason Fine, "The Fighter: The Life & Times of Merle Haggard," *Rolling Stone*, 1 October 2009: pp. 56-65, 86-88, 94-96.

Halley, David
(b. 1950)

Most associated with the west Texas sounds of Jimmie Dale Gilmore, Joe Ely, and Butch Hancock and the Austin progressive country scene in the 1990s, songwriter and guitarist David Halley was born in Oklahoma City, although he was raised in Lubbock, Texas. He first became interested in music when he saw Elvis Presley on the Ed Sullivan Show in 1958 or '59. With music surrounding him in the home where his mother played piano, and the family stereo had stacks of records around it, Halley began writing songs while attending Coronado High School.

By 2000, David had composed songs for such artists as Stacy Dean Campbell, Katy Moffatt, Jerry Jeff Walker, Joe Ely, Jimmie Dale Gilmore, Mickey Newbury, and Keith Whitley. His most notable song is "Hard Livin'", recorded by Whitley on several of his albums, and was a Top 10 *Billboard* country singles hit for Whitley in 1987. David also wrote "Fair and Square", which was the title of Gilmore's 1988 release. Additional songs of note include "Rain Just Falls", recorded by Campbell on his 1999 album, *Ashes of Old Love*, and "Further" on her *Cowboy Girl* album of 2001. David has played session guitar for several artists, including Gilmore, Hancock, Dick Hamilton, Jo Carol Pierce, and Darden Smith. He appeared with Townes Van Zandt, Gilmore, Ely, and Hancock on an *Austin City Limits* special in 1983 entitled "West Texas Songwriters".

David Halley, Stray Dog Talk, 1990

Halley's first album, *Stray Dog Talk*, released in 1990 by Elvis Costello's Demon Records, included eleven tracks all written by him, and featured a duet with Syd Straw on "Dreamlife". The album also included "Hard Livin'", "Rain Just Falls", and "Further", all of which demonstrate his sensitive style that belies the grittiness of his lyrics. His second album, *Broken Spell*, released in 1994 on the now defunct DOS label, included eleven tracks all composed by Halley. Halley's is featured performing his composition "Further" on the compilation, *Horse Songs*, and contributes "Swiss Cottage Place" to the 2000 Mickey Newbury tribute album, *Frisco Mabel Joy Revisited*. In 2010, *American Songwriter* included his "Rain Just Falls" as one of the "50 Country Songs Every Songwriter Should Know". While David Halley did not grow up in Oklahoma, his mother's musical ability is another example of the state exporting its music with parents who passed it on to their children once they arrived in their new locations.

As of 2013, Halley continues to perform in clubs around Austin, Texas, where he lives.

Halsey, Jim
(b. October 7, 1930)

With a career spanning more than sixty years as a premier artist manager, agent and impresario, Jim Halsey discovered and/or guided the careers of a staggering list of country and popular music figures from 1949 through 2011. Born 1930 in Independence, Kansas where his family owned the Halsey Brothers Department Store, the young Halsey learned important business lessons, namely how to put on an enthusiastic and positive face for customers, but be serious-minded about the economics involved with business, skills tailor-made for a show business promoter. Independence is barely 90 miles north of Tulsa, giving Jim easy access to performances venues such as the Cain's Ballroom, but also close enough for bands from Oklahoma to perform in Independence, both of which initiated a lifelong

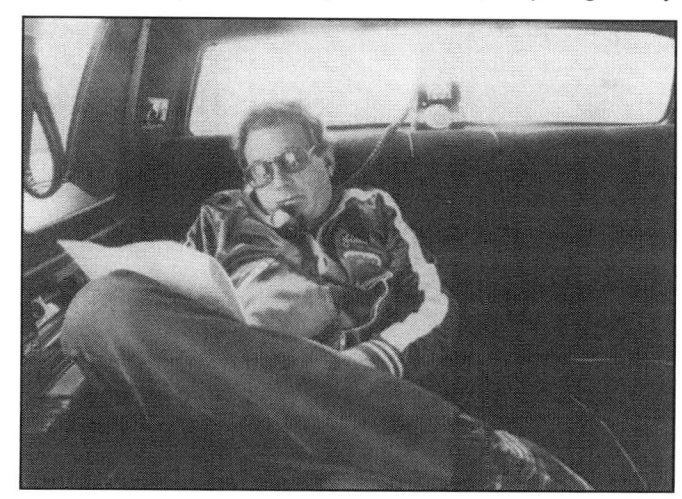

Jim Halsey, the "Starmaker," taking care of business in a limousine, circa 1970s.

association for Halsey with music in Oklahoma. While in high school, Halsey became inspired after learning about Russian talent and entertainment impresario, Sol Hurok, who managed major Russian and American performance artists, and eventually brought the Russian Bolshoi Ballet to the United States in 1959. By reading about the grandeur of Hurok's career, Halsey dreamed of being a show business promoter, sales and talent agent, marketer, and producer. After taking some business and marketing classes at Independence Community College, Halsey promoted his first concert at age 18, a successful Western swing dance featuring Leon McAuliffe, which led to promoting other shows in southeast Kansas. After promoting Hank Thompson shows in the area in 1950, Thompson approached Halsey about being his agent, which led Halsey to forming the Jim Halsey Co. Talent Agency with Thompson as his first client in 1951.[1] As a result, Halsey opened his Oklahoma City office in 1952 after convincing Thompson to relocate his base of operations from Dallas, Texas, to Oklahoma. Through Thompson, Halsey met the first lady of rock and roll, Wanda Jackson in 1956, whom Halsey guided though her late 1950s and 1960s major label career. Then, through Jackson, Halsey met superpicker and grinner, Roy Clark in 1959, as a result of Jackson hiring Roy Clark to play for a string of high-profile Las Vegas gigs Halsey was promoting for Jackson in 1960. Due to this meeting and their ensuing friendship, Halsey became Clark's manager in late 1961 and guided him to popular music/television stardom, a professional relationship that continued through 2011 when the two still had several projects in the works. But the fun business had only started for Jim Halsey, who proceeded to manage or book more than 150 name artists throughout his extensive career. Beginning with an office in Los Angeles in 1962, and then a Tulsa office in 1971, the Jim Halsey Company ultimately had fixed bases in those cities, as well as Nashville, New York, and London, from 1971 to 1990. After growing to between forty and fifty stars, dependent on their various career tracks, the Jim Halsey Company was the largest country music agency in the world. Along with his fifty years working with Roy Clark, Halsey managed or booked the following artists: Waylon Jennings, Reba McEntire, Minnie Pearl, Wanda Jackson, Clint Black, Tammy Wynette, Mel Tillis, Merle Haggard, Dwight Yoakum, The Judds, Jerry Reed, Clarence "Gatemouth" Brown, Glen Campbell, Ronnie Dunn, Ray Wylie Hubbard, Roy Orbison, Willie Nelson, the Osmond Brothers, Tammy Wynette, Bob and Johnnie Lee Wills' Texas Playboys, Bob Hope, Jerry Jeff Walker, George Jones, and many, many others. As of 2011, alongside his half a century of work with Roy Clark, Halsey remained the personal manager of the Oak Ridge Boys after more than thirty-six years, continuing to supervise their career, and often sold-out performances for around 160 dates a year.

Like his hero Sol Hurok, who brought Russian performers to the United States with diplomatic intent, Jim Halsey has organized and presented country music performances all over the world, in many places, for the first time. The result of this work expanded the horizons of country music into Europe, Asia, Africa, and South America. "Even in the late 1950s," Halsey wrote in a 2011 e-mail to the author, "We were pioneering Southeast Asia and the European markets with Wanda Jackson and Hank Thompson. Our specialty was taking country music to locations and venues where it had never been presented before." Halsey's 1976 tour, presenting Roy Clark and The Oak Ridge Boys in the Soviet Union won praise both culturally and in diplomatic circles.

In 1990, the booking agency division of The Jim Halsey Company, Inc., was sold to the William Morris Agency where he remained a consultant for several years. Since the mid-1990s, much of Jim Halsey's professional focus has been directed toward education. From 1995-1999 Halsey created and served as director of the award-winning Music and Entertainment Business Program at Oklahoma City University in Oklahoma City, Oklahoma. Additionally, Halsey is a Visiting Professor at HED Music College in Yehud, Israel. In 2011, he focused on sharing and preserving the knowledge of his vast career through The Halsey Learning Institute of Music & Entertainment Business, an online internet school, but also lectures and teaches extensively at colleges and universities around the world. In spring, 2010, Halsey brought his experiences full circle by instigating The Jim Halsey Institute of Music and Entertainment Business at Independence Community College. Through this coursework, students may take online classes in the music and entertainment business, talent development, and creative artist management, with future courses planned in songwriting, music publishing, artist promotion, video production, and every aspect of being a music industry professional.[3] Halsey is also the co-creator of the *Billboard*/Starmaker Song Contest, in its 19th year in 2011, with contest awards in cash, merchandise and recognition for songs in several categories of popular music.

Halsey's expertise encompasses more than just successful talent management and booking. His business experience includes broadcasting (he has owned several radio stations), owning and running a record label (Churchill Records, distributed through MCA), and banking (he has served on the Board of Directors of three banks). Halsey also manages his various ranching, real estate operations, and other investment interests, along with being a successful music publisher. With such massive experience and expertise in sales and marketing, he also conducts a popular seminar series, "How To Make It In The Music Business". Halsey's presentations and lectures explain the important functions of managers, agents, record companies, press and PR, producers, specialized music/entertainment attorneys, music publishers, promoters, performing rights organizations, copyright protection, and other components that make up the "star team", his reference to the total organization needed for music business success. Organizing the materials for the lectures encouraged Halsey to produce an accompanying text for his talks and courses, *Starmaker: How To Make It in the Music Business* (Tate, 2010), a must-read for any future music industry professional.

Halsey's avid interest in the arts is shared by his wife, Minisa Crumbo Halsey, the daughter of world renowned Potawatomi artist, Woody Crumbo, and Muscogee (Creek) educator Lillian Hogue Crumbo. Halsey has featured a Woody Crumbo painting of an eagle dancer on the reverse side of his company's business cards for several years. Together, Jim and Minisa have amassed an extensive American Indian art collection. Minisa, of Muscogee (Creek) heritage and enrolled with the Citizen Potawatomi Nation, is also considered an important Native American artist in her own right. She has exhibited her works worldwide in galleries and museums. The Halseys have lived in multiple locations around the U.S. due to the demands of their business, occasionally maintaining several residences at the same time in locations such as Independence, Kansas; Malibu, Santa Monica, and Beverly Hills, CA; Taos and Santa Fe, NM; Oklahoma City; Nashville; Tulsa, and New York City. Since 1998, the Halsey's have lived in the Tulsa, Oklahoma area. Their four children are Sherman, a MTV award-winning television and video producer, director, artist manager and promoter; Gina, a licensed acupuncturist/herbalist; Crissy, a ski instructor and realtor; and Woody, a pilot for United Airlines. Considered an expert in many fields of the music business, and business "period", Halsey has served on the following Boards of Directors: The Country Music Association (CMA); The Academy of Country Music (ACM); National Academy of Recording Arts and Sciences (NARAS, Austin Chapter); Mercantile Bank and Trust, Tulsa; Citizens National Bank, Independence, KS; Farmers & Merchants Bank, Mound City, KS; Southwestern School of Law; Tulsa Philharmonic; National Music Council; Nashville Symphony Orchestra; Tulsa Symphony Orchestra; Philbrook Art Museum, Tulsa; Thomas Gilcrease Museum, Tulsa; U.S. Committee for UNICEF; MEIEA (Music and Entertainment Industry Educators Assoc.); and the William Inge Theatre Festival and Foundation. He is listed in the "Who's Who in the World",

Jim Hasley (right) with Oklahoma Historical Society executive director, Dr. Bob Blackburn, Tulsa, 2009.

By Hugh Foley / 327

"Who's Who in America", "Who's Who in the Entertainment Business", "Who's Who in the Southwest", "Who's Who in Business and Finance", and the "International Directory of Distinguished Leadership". In 1984, Halsey was elected president of FIDOF (International Federation of Festival Organizations - UNESCO). Upon completion of eight years of the presidency, he was elected President of Honour. This internationally recognized organization has a membership of 360 major music festivals in 187 countries, fulfilling a vision Halsey has to bring global peace and harmony through international music festivals where people of multiple backgrounds can enjoy and learn from their common ground in music.

Halsey has received multiple awards and recognition from many prestigious music industry organizations, such as the Academy of Country Music, *Billboard* Magazine, and the performer's rights organization, SESAC, as well as the one-time (pre-internet) important music industry publication, *Cashbox*. However, Halsey has also received many awards for his international service to the world by promoting American country and popular music abroad, and helping develop the concept of international music festivals.[4] He has been honored in Bulgaria, Poland, Austria, Germany, Spain, and Japan for his work in those countries and around the world, as well as in the United States for his global efforts. In 1986, he received the Commendation for Outstanding Leadership in Promoting World Peace and Harmony Through the Medium of Visual and Performing Arts from the Mayor of Los Angeles, Tom Bradley. He received a Lifetime Achievement Award from the International Entertainment Buyers Association in Nashville, the Oklahoma Governor's Award in Arts & Education in 1998, and the Cherokee Honor Society Medal of Honor from the Cherokee Nation of Oklahoma in 1999. While not an enrolled member of the Cherokee Nation, Halsey can trace his lineage back to the well-known Cherokee leader and scholar, Sequoyah. As a result, he says, "My Cherokee award is one of which I am the most proud."[5] Halsey was inducted into the Oklahoma Music Hall of Fame in 2000 with his old friends and colleagues, Roy Clark and Wanda Jackson. As a surprise to him (maybe), and to all those who witnessed the concert in Muskogee on the night of his induction into the Oklahoma Music Hall of Fame, the Oak Ridge Boys provided an impromptu and unbilled performance in Jim's honor. As part of the Oklahoma Historical Society's plans to fully document the history of popular music from Oklahoma, The Oklahoma History Center produced a 2010 exhibit about Halsey's career and those it shaped in "Starmaker: Jim Halsey and the Legends of Country Music". In 2011, Oklahoma History Center produced another Halsey-influenced exhibit, "Pickin' and Grinnin': Roy Clark, *Hee Haw*, and Country Humor".

www.jimhalsey.com

Endnotes

1. Halsey's early life in Kansas and the development of his career as a promoter from 1949 through 1960 is covered by Victoria Lee in her collection of essays published as *Distinguished Oklahomans*. (Tulsa: Touch of Heart, 2002).

2. Aside from engineer Steve Ripley who is seated to the immediate left of Halsey looking at the printed image, the personnel of the *Reunion* recording session is detailed in the Wills brothers' entry of this guide.

3. For more about the Jim Halsey Institute of Music and Entertainment Business at Independence Community College in Independence, Kansas, see http://indycc.edu/halsey/index.html.

4. For a complete list of Jim Halsey's extensive awards in the U.S. and internationally, see his website.

5. Halsey, Jim, e-mail to the author, 28 June, 2011.

Hanson, Clarke Isaac
(b. November 17, 1980)

Hanson, Jordan Taylor
(b. March 14, 1983)

Hanson, Zachary Walker
(b. October 22, 1985)

Riding their tight, three-part harmonies and songs inspired by classic late 1950s rock and roll, Motown, and 1960s R & B, Hanson became Oklahoma's biggest pop stars of the 1990s, Garth Brooks not included. While Isaac and Taylor were born in Tulsa to musical parents, Walker and Diana, who met when they attended Nathan Hale High School, Zach was born in Arlington, Virginia. The group rocketed to the top of the international pop music charts in 1997 with their single, "MMMBop," from the GRAMMY nominated album *Middle of Nowhere* that reached #2 on the *Billboard* album charts. The song was one of the biggest debut singles of all time. The group's breakthrough sound featured well-blended harmonies that seem to only come from musical siblings, while their melodic sense easily channeled Motown without sounding too derivative. As opposed to many pre-manufactured teen pop stars, they can play their instruments, and are indeed a band, which allows them create, record, and tour behind music they are able to replicate as a group. Their musically inclined parents provided a nurturing environment for the supportive production of music by the gifted, if not prodigious, young musicians. While the three brothers projected a carefree, happy-just-being-alive teen image when they first emerged, they have transformed one major hit into mature music business people in control of their own product and industry destiny. Whether Hanson will ever recapture the dynamic and frenzied pop music moment they experienced in 1997 remains to be seen; however, the group has maintained their career by marshalling the power of the Internet to interact directly with their fans worldwide, cutting out the industry's cut of their business, so to speak, and marketing themselves exclusively through their own management of a label to release their music and videos. As a result of their fans maturing with the evolving communication and music distribution technologies, Hanson has had significant internet sales success. The group's website offers premium access to many special recordings, images, and video for "subscribing" fans. Additionally, the worldwide success of their initial hit single has allowed them to continue performing both music and charitable acts around the globe.

The Hanson brothers' parents, Diana and Walker, performed together in high school musicals and continued to pursue their musical interests at the University of Oklahoma. While Diana majored in music, they both sang with a Christian group called The Horizons that performed across the United States. After college, the two went back to their hometown of Tulsa, started a family, and Walker began working for Helmerich & Payne Inc., an international oil drilling and gas exploration company. As the Hanson family grew in the 1980s, Walker progressed through management at the company and in 1989 began a series of transfers that led the Hansons to Ecuador, Venezuela, and Trinidad-Tobago. Eager to give their kids a taste of home, the parents ordered a *Time/Life* collection of classic rock roll from 1957-1969. The boys started listening to the music and singing along with it, which became a primary musical influence. The family returned to Tulsa in 1990 and settled in a rural section of West Tulsa where they were home-schooled by Diana. After hearing the boys harmonize on songs they had learned from the *Time/Life* set, Walker and Diana taught them to sing "Amen" after saying a prayer at the dinner table, reflecting both the musical acumen and spiritual focus of the parents. From there, the boys (then aged six, nine, and eleven) took piano lessons and decided to form a group called the Hanson Brothers, which they changed to The Hansons, and, finally, Hanson.

In 1990, the boys began singing *a capella* (without instruments) at private

Hanson's Best of *Collection*, 2006

parties, local events, clubs, and made their first major appearance at Tulsa's Mayfest in 1992. That performance led to many others and for the next few years the group traveled throughout the Midwest doing shows, with Walker as their roadie, and Diana as their publicist and t-shirt vendor. The group started working with a manager, Christopher Sabec, as a result of an impromptu performance on the street at the South by Southwest Music Conference in Austin, Texas. Then, in 1995, the boys decided to add instruments to the group. Although all three had already been taking piano lessons, Taylor stayed on keyboards, Isaac picked up a Gibson Les Paul guitar at a Tulsa pawnshop and began learning how to play the instrument, and Zac borrowed a set of Ludwig drums from a friend who had them in the attic, later replaced by a set of Pearl drums (both the Les Paul and the Pearl drum set have appeared on display at the Rock and Roll Hall of Fame in Cleveland, Ohio). Later in 1995, as the group became more proficient, Diana and Walker put together the resources necessary to record and release Hanson's debut CD, *Boomerang*. In addition to five songs they wrote, the band also included covers by obviously primary influences, the Jackson 5, to whom they have been compared vocally, and the rhythm and blues standard, "Poison Ivy."

Hanson released their second independent CD, *MMMBop*, in May of 1996 with the first version of "MMMBop", a very catchy pop tune in the mold of early Jackson 5 records. Not long after, Hanson's manager, Christopher Sabec, sent a copy of the album to Steve Greenberg of Mercury Records. Greenberg made a trip out to Coffeyville, Kansas, where the group was playing, and immediately signed them. Greenberg wanted to get Hanson into the studio immediately, but felt the group's sound needed fattening, and their songs needed tightening, so he enlisted studio remix kings the Dust Brothers who had produced Beck's multi-platinum album, *Odelay*, as well as Steve Lironi who had worked with Black Grape, and Mark Hudson who had some 1970s pop success with his own family act, The Hudson Brothers. After six months in a Los Angeles studio, the group finished the album, *Middle of Nowhere*, in January, 1997.

While the album was being scheduled for a March release, the group made the video for "MMMBop" with noted video director Tamra Davis, and the promotion machine was set to make whatever it could out of the group's debut major label release. With the album due to hit stores in May, "MMMBop" was released to radio nationwide in late March and the song caused an immediate stir on the charts, entering at #16. With this success, the Mercury promotions department went into hyper-drive and began setting up interviews, performances, photo shoots, CD signings at record stores, and mall performances. Within days of the album's release, Hanson appeared on the *Rosie O'Donnell Show*, *The Late Show with David Letterman*, *CBS This Morning, The Today Show,* and *Live with Regis and Kathy Lee*. With all of this exposure, and the upbeat sound of "MMMBop", reminiscent of early Jackson 5 Motown songs like "Rockin' Robin", the single went to #1 on the *Billboard* Hot 100, and has kept their name in popular music consciousness ever since.

Hanson, 2011

Acclaim back home soon followed when Oklahoma governor Frank Keating declared May 26, 1997 Hanson Day in the state. In June, Hanson presented an award at the MTV Movie Awards, performed live in Oklahoma City to a frenzied audience, appeared on Jay Leno's *Tonight Show*, and their video for "MMMBop" was in heavy rotation on MTV. In July, the group had a cover story in *Entertainment Weekly*, and continued making promotional appearances in the U.S., Europe, Canada, Asia, Australia, and Indonesia throughout the year. If any doubt existed about Hanson's significance beyond pop, *SPIN* magazine, which typically focuses on music outside of the mainstream, featured the group in a September article. By the time the swell of Hansonmania crested, "MMMBop", the catchy feel-good single that introduced the band to the world, went #1 in twenty-seven countries. In June, 2011, the official video for the song had more than 6.7 million views on youtube, the popular online video service.

Critical accolades coincided with the song's success. New York's *Village Voice* named "MMMBop" best single of 1997. *Rolling Stone* named *Middle of Nowhere* one of the "Essential Albums" of the decade, and *SPIN* noted, "Hanson [is] perhaps the only band in recent history beloved by both hormonally crazed 12-year-olds and their Motown loving parents, by both *Tiger Beat* and the *New York Times*." In October of 1997, the group sang the National Anthem at the opening game of the World Series. After building up so much momentum, what could Hanson possibly do for an encore? Other singles followed from *Middle of Nowhere,* "Where Is the Love?" and "I Will Come to You", both of which made the Top 40, but failed to achieve the success of the debut single. Wanting to satisfy the clamoring for more material by Hanson fans, Mercury rushed out a Christmas album, *Snowed In*, just in time for the 1997 holiday season, and was elated to see it become the

#1 Holiday Album of 1997. The group debuted songs from the album on a Saturday morning Fox broadcast of *Hanson's Jingle Bell Jam*, directly targeted toward the cartoon-aged audience. They also played the Jingle Ball at Madison Square Garden on the same bill as Aerosmith, The Wallflowers, and Fiona Apple, among others.

By the end of 1997, *Oklahoma Today* magazine name Hanson its Oklahomans of the Year, and they were awarded Best Song and Best Breakthrough Act by the MTV Europe Music Awards. The frenetic pace of Hanson's life and the way in which their fans reacted to them is well documented in *Tulsa, Tokyo and The Middle of Nowhere* (Polygram Video, 1997), which became the #1 Music Video in the U.S. In 1998, Hanson was nominated for three Grammy awards, to include Record of the Year, Pop Performance by Duo or Group with Vocal, and Best New Artist. In February of 1998, they taped an episode of VH-1's *Storytellers* concert series, and in May of 1998, Mercury released the group's earlier independent recordings as *3 Car Garage: The Indie Recordings '95-'96*. The album included the earlier version of "MMMBop" that ultimately got the band signed. Also in 1998, the group went on a three-month North American tour and took along Tulsa pop group Admiral Twin as their opening act. As a result of the tour, Mercury released a concert recording, *Live from Albertane*, which had a decent showing of #32 on the album chart in November, 1998, but the concert video zoomed up to #1 on the Billboard Top Music Video charts, ostensibly because their fans (legions of teenage girls) wanted to *see* them.

After a tremendous amount of success in such a short amount of time, the group returned to their Tulsa home, continued their home schooling, and started writing songs for their next album. 2000's *This Time Around* retains the undeniably catchy melodies and exuberant singing that distinguished *Middle of Nowhere*, and finds the boys exploring new sonic avenues, however, it did not achieve the momentous success of their previous studio outing. "Our songwriting and musical style have developed in a lot of ways," observed Isaac in a Mercury press release, "The guitar sound is heavier in points than before. But there are also more soft moments, more piano- and keyboard-driven material than on the last record. There's been an overall evolution within the band." Taylor added, "We just felt that song best represented where the music was going, and the genre we want to be associated with. It's a little more rock and roll; the chord structure is more complex." Musical guests on the album included such notables as Beck cohort DJ Swamp and John Popper (of Blues Traveler) on harmonica. Guitar prodigy Jonny Lang lends a hand on three tracks, including "This Time Around". With a not-so-subtle reference to a strong religious conviction that can be heard through much of Hanson's catalogue, "Dying to Be Alive" augments its inspirational message about living life to the fullest with backing vocals from a gospel choir led by Rose Stone of Sly & the Family Stone fame. The album also suffered from bad timing as the music industry was going through massive changes in 2000 due to the new era in music distribution through the internet. Their label, Mercury Records, was merged with Island/Def Jam, a label more known for hip hop, and funding dried up for both promoting the album, as well as supporting their tour. When the album peaked at "only" #19 on the *Billboard* Top 200 album chart, and the title track single stalled at #20 on the Hot 100, and with the band's primary allies at their label already gone, the band's employment with Island/Def Jam teetered on instability.

After *This Time Around* did not measure up to the group's previous critical and sales success, Isaac explained he and his brothers were not worried. "Getting to make the music, and having a good time doing it, is the most important thing to us," he said in a 2000 interview. An important harbinger of things to come surfaced through *This Time*

Around: internet sales. While the label was not happy with the traditional sales and airplay charts, the CD reached #3 on the *Billboard* Top Internet Album chart, created to track sales from online retailers. Given that many Hanson fans were in their teens when they became fans of the band in 1997, those same teens became heavy users of the internet, and were in perfect position to become online Hanson fans, a trend that continued from *This Time Around* through the 2010's *Shout it Out* (3CG), but we are getting ahead of ourselves.

In 2001, Hanson released another concert recording, *At the Fillmore*, and the group contributed their voices to a recording of John Lennon's "Imagine" to benefit children who lost parents in the September 11 terrorist attacks. Throughout 2001 and 2002, local Tulsa music fans were treated to unscheduled, impromptu appearances around town when different members of the group tried out new material, or appeared with their friends in Admiral Twin. In 2002, Hanson appeared on an episode of *Sabrina, the Teenage Witch*, wherein the group debuted "Strong Enough to Break," from their expected 2003 release, *Underneath*, and were featured in a documentary by VH1, *Bubblegum Babylon*, that discussed the darker sides of the teen pop industry. Starting in 2001, the band began recording demos for songs they thought would make a good album for Island/Def Jam. However, the head of their new label who did not have a history with the band, Jeff Fenster, was not convinced the songs were marketable, which began a process of back and forth that ultimately ended in the band's departure from the label. The band skewered the experience in the film, *Strong Enough to Break* (3CG, 2004), a self-made documentary about being stonewalled by their label on any decision to plan for the acceptance of material for a new album, and chronicled the challenges they experienced internally trying to fulfill some perception of creating the next Hanson "hit" for a label that was less and less supportive. As a result of leaving the label in 2003, formed their own label, 3CG Records, and then turned to the internet and their fans, wherein Hanson demonstrated that Island/Def Jam did not understand their music, and the label missed a golden opportunity when *Underneath* hit the e-streets.

A game-changer in many ways, their 2004 release, *Underneath*, on their own 3CG Records, hit #1 on *Billboard*'s Independent Album Chart, as well as #2 on the Top Internet Album chart, making it one of the most successful self-released albums of all time. The album features work with Danny Kortchmar (known for his work with Billy Joel, Bon Jovi, and James Taylor), vocals by Michelle Branch, and a Matthew Sweet composition as the title track. *Underneath* also provided a single, "Penny & Me", that was #2 in Singles Sales, although it didn't receive much U.S. airplay, proving their fans were going to buy their music whether it was on the radio or not. Houston, we have a paradigm shift. Their 2005 release, *Best of Hanson: Live and Electric*, met slightly lower success on the *Billboard* Top Independent Albums chart (#15) and the Top Internet Albums chart (#14), but live albums are usually bought just by fans who want to hear new versions of

Hanson, 2001

older songs. Also in the summer of 2005, "Penny & Me" was still charting in the U.K.

While heavily promoted via touring and their internet site, their 2007 album, *The Walk*, met with moderate success among fans, but did not reach the success levels of any previous work commercially or critically on the independent or internet sales charts. One of the album's songs, "The Ugly Truth", was included on the *Van Wilder* film soundtrack (Eleven Seven, 2006). The album's title, the themes of the songs, and its surrounding promotion did indicate a shifting understanding of Hanson's potential impact on the world via their status as internationally known pop musicians. During the previous years to *The Walk*, one has to imagine the band members maturing in their family lives (Taylor married in 2002 and has four children; Isaac married in 2006 and has two sons; Zac married in 2006 and has two children). That maturity also manifested itself with their charitable work to benefit AIDS research in Africa, participating in the TOMS shoe project to provide shoes for African children, and to further raise awareness about poverty through their website and on-stage announcements to their fans during 2008's "Walk Around the World Tour", all of which surrounded the theme of walks for charity and heightened awareness of the band's philanthropic interests, detailed fully at hanson.net. In 2009, Taylor branched outside of Hanson proper with members of Smashing Pumpkins (James Iha-guitar), Fountains of Wayne (Adam Schlesinger-bass/vocals/songwriting), and Cheap Trick (Bun E. Carlos-drums) to form Tinted Windows, a power pop collective that released a self-titled album in 2009 that peaked at #18 on *Billboard*'s Top Rock Album chart, and #59 on the Top 200 Album chart. In between sessions and gigs for Tinted Windows, the Hanson brothers worked on their next album, *Shout it Out*, returned to Africa to deliver 50,000 donated shoes, continued to highlight the HIV/AIDS and poverty crisis in Africa, and furthered their other goodwill projects of building schools and drilling water wells in impoverished areas. Hanson's 2010 album, *Shout It Out* (3CG) demonstrates the group's artistic growth as they have matured into a soulful rock group without losing the hummability of their signature sound. With the resources to accomplish their creative desires, and also a return to the music that inspired them in the first place, the group brought in pop music arranger Jerry Hey (known for work with Frank Sinatra, Michael Jackson, George Benson, Quincy Jones, and with whom they had worked on *Underneath*), as well as Motown bassist Bob Babbit who played on classics for that label such as Stevie Wonder's "Signed, Sealed, Delivered, I'm Yours", and Smokey Robinson and the Miracles' "Tears of a Clown". The result is a full on R&B powerhouse of Hanson's recognizable harmonies, lyrics that continue to probe the timeless interpersonal relationship themes of pop music, and the band's increasing technical facility with more instruments for a richer texture to their sound. The album's single, "Give a Little", fulfills the promise of their earlier work to provide feel-good, up tempo pop songs peppered with R&B influences, their perfect harmonies on sing-along choruses, and Taylor's blue-eyed soul crooning. The song continued receiving airplay as of June, 2011, on loyal Hanson radio stations nationwide, but also in the band's home state, such as KISS-FM, Oklahoma City. While the song did not impact the national radio charts of *Billboard*, the song did continue appearing on internet and international radio charts, in essence confirming their continued strength in the independent and world pop e-consciousness. *Shout it Out* performed respectably on the *Billboard* Top 200 Albums chart, peaking at #30, but trends that began in 2000 with *This Time Around* continued for Hanson's 2010 album. *Shout it Out* hit #5 on the Top Internet Album chart, #15 on the Top Digital Albums chart, and #2 on the Top Independent Albums chart, final proof that Hanson's fans are waiting for new music, and the band knows how to get it to them via modern technology that puts the band in control of their music. As if they were finally fully embracing and capitalizing on their pop moment of 1997, instead of almost trying to live it down on every recording since, they performed "Mmmbop" live on the U.S. version of *Dancing with the Stars* in April, 2011. In a demonstration of their contemporary status as fun band to be remembered by today's teen poppers, in June, 2011, the group made a cameo as a party band in the video for Katy Perry's then Top 5 *Billboard* Hot 100 hit, "Last Friday Night (T.G.I.F.)". Their 2011 EP, *Facing the Blank Page*, was only available through membership on their website mid-year, and the band had shows scheduled in England and the U.S. through November of that year. In 2013, Hanson continued communicating with their fans via their website, playing a variety of special performances, and doing what most musicians wind up doing in their thirties, raising families - in harmony, no doubt.

www.hanson.net

Hardin, Gus
(b. April 9, 1945 – d. February 17, 1996)

Named as Top New Female Vocalist in 1983 by the ACM, Carolyn Ann Blankenship was born in Tulsa, Oklahoma. Nicknamed "Gus" as a teenager, she was also called "Red" and "Cookie" because of her red hair. Gus was the daughter of Mikey O'Malley, who she never knew, and was raised by her mother, Hopie, a Cherokee photographer. She began singing in church as a child, and sang in talent contests while in junior high and graduated from Nathan Hale High School in Tulsa. A soulful singer able to command blues, rock, and country styles, Hardin ultimately recorded five albums, and appeared on at least three compilations. In 1974, Gus was plagued with cataracts on her eyes after taking steroids and cortisone derivatives for her allergies, and for five years was legally blind (1979-84), having to take eye drops to see much of anything at all. As a recording artist and performer, she kept the surname of keyboardist, Steve Hardin, whom she met and married in Tulsa, and then divorced, only to run into him again in Nashville during the height of her success there circa 1983-84, after which he became her keyboardist and music for about a year during her watershed moments on the country music charts.

Gus Hardin

After performing in Tulsa nightclubs for fifteen years, Gus became the project of GPC (Giant Petroleum Company) Entertainment (an agency primarily consisting of oilmen from Tulsa, including Fred Williams, Rick Loewenherz, and Mike Kimbrel) who formed in 1979 with the intention of making her a star. She opened for several big name country acts, including Johnny Paycheck and the Oak Ridge Boys, during the next three years.

In 1982, Gus signed with RCA Records and began working under the tutelage of Rick Hall at Fame Studios in Muscle Shoals, Alabama, where she recorded her debut album, *Gus Hardin*, in 1983, featuring the Top 10 country hit, "After the Last Goodbye". Via that success, Hardin garnered that year's ACM 's Top New Female Vocalist, as well as recognition by *Billboard* and *Cashbox* as New Country Artist of the Year. In 1984, Gus underwent two intraocular lens transplant operations in Tulsa, which provided full sight. The same year, she released her second album, *Fallen Angel*, which reached #63 on the *Billboard* Country Album Chart, and spawned three minor country chart singles, to include the title track, as well as "I Pass", and "How Are You Spending My Nights". Marketed as tough woman mistreated emotionally in romantic relationships, her songs often mined the country music trope of lost or wronged-love, such as "If I Didn't Love You", "My Mind Is on You", and "Loving You Hurts". Her third album, *Wall of Tears* (RCA, 1985), replicated the success of her first album, yielding another hit single, a duet with Earl Thomas Conley, "All Tangled Up in Love," which rose to #8 on Billboard's Hot Country Songs chart, and earned her nominations for Best Performance by a Duet from CMA, ACM, and *Music City News*. Hardin's follow-up singles, a non-LP duet with Dave Loggins (of Loggins and Messina), "Just As Long As I Have You", and "What We Gonna Do?" from the Wall of Tears LP, did not succeed to industry expectations. However, her 1985 video for "I Pass" did get notice by the American Music Awards for a nomination as Favorite Country Music Female Vocalist Video.

According to published reports, while she was respected (if not marketed) for her plucky and assertive personality, Hardin's manner impressed some others as "abrasive", resulting in her being bounced from RCA once the hits dried up, and she returned to Tulsa in the late 1980s to perform in clubs there.[1] She appeared on the 1993 compilation, *Sounds of Tulsa*, produced by radio station KMOD, and a 1995 holiday album, *Classic Tulsa Christmas*. In 2001, some of her unpublished recordings were made available through Rainy Day Records on the album *I'm Dancing as Fast as I Can*, available primarily as on online down load as of 2011. Divorced six times, she became known as the "Elizabeth Taylor of Country Music", and publicists often made that fact part of her image. With a voice most often described as "whiskey-soaked", which is really a euphemism for the honest honky-tonk pain that Gus manifested in her voice, she never achieved the great potential that many people saw in her. Fellow Oklahoman Leon Russell said, she "sounds like a combination of Tammy Wynette, Otis Redding, and a truck driver." Tragically, Gus Hardin died in a 1996 automobile accident on Highway 20 east of Claremore, Oklahoma, on the way back from a singing engagement at Grand Lake, Oklahoma.

Endnote

1. The reason for Hardin's departure from RCA derive from a biographical entry for Hardin from an undeterminable published reference work, as the page has been separated from the original text, and is in the author's individual file for Hardin that has evolved over many years through donations and inheritances of information to *OMG*. No author, publisher or title may be determined from the page itself. No other part of it has been cited unless corroborated by other sources, and is used only here as reference for the point mentioned.

Hardin, Steve

(b. October 27, 1946)

A songwriter, keyboardist, harmonica, and clavinet player, Steve Hardin wrote two Top 10 country hits, "I Love My Truck" for Glen Campbell, and "Breakin' Down" for Waylon Jennings. Born in Bartlesville, Oklahoma, where he graduated Bartlesville's College

High School in 1964, Hardin played in a variety of bands in Tulsa (Johnny Fisher in 1967, Bill Davis Band in 1968), toured Canada with Arkansan Tommy Landon and the Emcees, and returned to more gigs in Tulsa, Oklahoma City, and Dallas. Hardin launched a fact-finding tour to Los Angeles in 1977, resulting in gigs with Delaney Bramlett (of Delaney and Bonnie – think "Layla"), Jimi Hendrix's drummer, Mitch Mitchell, and many other prominent live performance situations, before he joined the hard Southern rock boogie band, Point Blank, in 1979. While in Point Blank for only about a year, he wrote the song "Mean to Your Queenie" which appeared on the album, *Airplay*, for MCA Records, the song remains a staple high point of Point Blank's contemporary concert performances. While in Point Blank, Hardin met John Kay of Steppenwolf due to Point Blank opening for Steppenwolf, and accepted a position as the keyboard player for Steppenwolf. In retrospect, one has to consider this a very significant indication of Hardin's abilities playing abilities, especially since he would be tasked with replicating the iconic Steppenwolf keyboard parts on their major hits, such as "Magic Carpet Ride" and "Born to be Wild". After touring with Steppenwolf around the country, Hardin found himself in Los Angeles with the band, and became aware through a friend of country pop singer Glen Campbell's desire to hire a writer for his albums, tours, and TV appearances. After interviewing with Campbell, Hardin was hired and spent five years working with Glen on tour, writing songs (under the name Joe Rainey), and performing on *The Glen Campbell Music Show*. After his years with Campbell, Hardin moved to Nashville. Not long after arriving in town, Steve began frequenting Nashville's Hall of Fame Club, where he happened upon his ex-wife, Gus Hardin, to whom he'd been married back in Tulsa when they played music together, including her first public appearances. By 1984 and 1985, Gus was experiencing what would be her biggest success in country music, and Steve became her keyboardist and music director for a year before moving to south Florida and joining a reggae band.

Steve Hardin

After about seven years of being the only non-African descendant in the reggae group, (as well as having the longest hair among the musicians, both of which earned Hardin the band nickname of "Okiedread", he moved back to Nashville and started playing in a house band at The Bourbon Street Club. Among others who sat in on an irregular basis with the players was a bartender at the club, a then unknown future star of redneck honky-tonk, Gretchen Wilson. Wilson appeared on two songs Hardin cut as demos for Tulsa's all-world drummer, Jamie Oldaker, who was set to produced Hardin's 1998 CD, *Rhythmgypsy*. The album did not meet with commercial success, however, Hardin's wordplay skills are evident in songs like "I Ain't Even Breakin' Even", and "Okie Dread", a reggae number in which he answers challengers to being the only white boy present by singing, "My heart is black but my neck is red."

At the time of an August, 2010 article by Jim Hess in the Tahlequah-based music and arts publication, *The Current*, Steve Hardin was living back in the city of his birth, Bartlesville, awaiting some eye surgeries and only able to play his instruments about forty-five minutes a day due to arthritis derived from 40 years of constant playing.[1] Those forty years took him all over the world, and by 2011 he had played with Taj Mahal, Willie Nelson, Steve Perry (Journey), Freddie King, Dickie Betts, Jerry Reed, Jimmy Webb, Eric Burdon, Jody Miller, Henson Gargill, Doug Kershaw, Tanya Tucker, War, and Glen Campbell, among many others (and we mean it when we say "many"). As for a hallmark of his "Oklahoma-ness", one instantly notices the diversity of musicians with whom Hardin performed and toured, from R&B, rock, and blues, to country, reggae, Cajun, and funk. This musical diversity and adaptability is a consistent thematic element of Oklahoma musicians that surfaces again and again throughout this work. Oklahoma musicians either have to be able to play various styles to accommodate Oklahoma audiences with diverse expectations, or are able to "genre-shift" because they understand the close proximity of popular music's boundary lines, especially those between gospel, blues, country, and rock. Hardin exemplifies this through his tours with Point Blank (Southern boogie rock), Glen Campbell (pop country), Lonnie Mack (blues), Delaney Bramlett (blues rock), Steppenwolf (classic rock), Percy Sledge (R&B), and Black Oak Arkansas (redneck rock). As a session musician and songwriter, he recorded and wrote songs on albums for Point Blank *(Airplay* in 1979), Tanya Tucker ("Somebody's Trying to Tell You Something" and "My Song" from *Dreamlovers* in 1980, and "Heartache #3" and "Rodeo Girls" from *Should I Do It* in 1981); Glen Campbell ("Rollin'" and "It's Your World" from *It's the World Gone Crazy*, and "I Love My Truck" from *The Nights the Lights Went Out in Georgia*, both from 1981); and Waylon Jennings "Breakin' Down" from 1983's *It's Only Rock and Roll*. Hardin also appeared on numerous television shows, such as *The Tonight Show with Johnny Carson, Midnight Special, Tom Snyder Show, Merv Griffin, Inaugural Ball 1980,* and *The Glen Campbell Music Show.* Hardin is one of the many excellent musicians and successful songwriters who have come from the state, but often go under the radar due to Oklahoma's more well-known frontline performers. However, also represents the diversity of Oklahoma musicians and how many of them have risen to the highest levels of the professional music industry because of their ability to navigate various genres with musical expertise, often born out of the multi-faceted requirements of being a musician in the state during the 1960s and 1970s where one stood squarely at the national crossroads of the blues, country, and rock.

Endnote
1. For an extensive interview with Steve Hardin and full details on many of his career moves, see Jim Hess, "Established Artist Extra – Steve Hardin," *The Current*, August, 2010, pages 32-34.

Harris, Roy
(b. February 12, 1898 – d. October 1, 1979)

One of the most important figures in the establishment of American symphonic music, or that music which reflects a sense of American national identity, Leroy Ellsworth Harris was born of Scottish, Irish, and Welsh ancestry near Chandler in Lincoln County, Oklahoma, where his family (father, Elmer and mother, Laura) claimed land during one of the historic land rushes, most likely the one of 1895 that absorbed "excess" Kickapoo lands. According to Harris' primary contemporary biographer, Dan Stehman, Harris' parents actually moved from California to take part in the land grabs that are a controversial aspect of Oklahoma history.[1] The death in infancy of three of the five Harris children, combined with Laura's respiratory issues, de-glamorized frontier life for Elmer in the developing Oklahoma Territory. After a gambling windfall in his favor, Roy's father, a farmer, took his family to the San Gabriel Valley in California in 1903.[2] While Harris did not grow up in Oklahoma, he is still an example of music exported by the state to other places, especially California. Harris, however, is not part of the Great Depression migration of Okie farmers in the 1930s, but an earlier generation of people who saw Oklahoma as an opportunity to start a new. At the time of Harris' birth, the developing United States experienced a "piano boom" as part of its popular music culture. With the success of Scott Joplin's ragtime and sheet music distribution of Tin Pan Alley hits, a middle class home was not considered complete without a piano on which to play popular, classical, or religious music. Leroy was born into such a home. His first music instruction was from his mother who gave him piano lessons, although he later learned the clarinet. Additionally, Harris biographer Stehman also notes that Harris remembered hearing his mother and father accompanying themselves while singing various folk songs, ones he obviously never forgot about as American folk music became an important part of his creative aesthetic.[3] By career's end, Harris composed thirteen symphonies, such as *Farewell to Pioneers*, *Symphony No. 3*, and *Folksong Symphony*, as well as more than two hundred works in a variety of genres, such as quartets, concertos, program music, suites, themes and variations, song cycles, folk music variations, etc.

Harris shortened his name to Roy when he was a teenager, and enlisted in the U.S. armed services in 1916 to fight in World War I. Following his discharge, Roy enrolled at U.C.L.A. in 1917, continuing his music studies at the University of California-Berkeley from 1918 to 1921. As a student, he earned his tuition by driving a dairy cart. During 1924-25, Roy studied with Arthur Farwell, who introduced him to Walt Whitman's poetry, which became one of his inspirations for musical composition, including the *Whitman Suite*. Among his other early teachers and advisers were Clifford Demorest, Ernest Douglas, Alec Anderson, Fannie Charles Dillon, Henry Schoenfeld, Modeste Altschuler, and Arthur Bliss.

In 1926 Roy traveled to the East Coast for the premier of his "Andante for Orchestra" by the New York Philharmonic. While staying at the MacDowell Colony, he met Aaron Copeland, who encouraged Roy to study under Nadia Boulanger in Paris. With financial assistance from Alma Wertheim and two Guggenheim fellowships, he spent 1927 through 1929 under Boulanger's tutelage. During this time, he wrote the "Concerto for Piano, Clarinet, and String Quartet", which premiered in Paris. This established him as one of the promising young American composers. In 1929 Harris returned to the U.S. only to injure his spine in a fall that immobilized him following surgery. During this time of convalescence, he learned to compose on the piano and devoted his recovery period to refinement of his concepts of melody, harmony, and texture. Following his recuperation, he joined the Julliard School of Music summer faculty in 1934, and married Beula Duffey in 1936, his fourth marriage. Roy renamed his bride Johana, after J.S. Bach, and the couple had five children. Johana was an integral part of Roy's musical career thereafter, and served as consultant on many of his piano compositions, including "American Ballads" and the "Fantasy for Organ, Brass, and Timpani".

Roy's first national recognition came through Serge Koussevitzky, for whom he wrote his first symphony, *Symphony 1933*. His most successful work was *Symphony No. 3*, which premiered under Koussevitsky in Boston in 1939. Additional works for which he is noted include *Chorale* and *Prelude and Fugue* for string orchestra, *Song for Occupation*, *Story of Noah*, *Symphony for Voices*, *Three Symphonic Essays*, *Memories of a Child's Sunday*,

Variations on a Theme for flute and string quartet, and *4 Minutes 20 Seconds* for flute and string quartet, and *Children's Suite*.

Roy's teaching positions included Mills College in Oakland, California (1933), Westminster Choir College of Rider University in Princeton, New Jersey (1934-38), Juilliard School of Music in New York City (summers only from 1934-38), Cornell University in Ithaca, New York (1941-43), Colorado College in Colorado Springs (1943-48), Utah State Agricultural College (1948-49), Peabody College for Teachers in Nashville (1949-50), Chatham College in Pittsburgh (1951-56), Southern Illinois University (1956-57), Indiana University (1957-60), *Universidad Interamerican de Puerto Rico* in San German (1960-61), and California State University-Los Angeles (1970-76). His best-known pupils were William Schuman, who later was president of the Juilliard School of Music and director of the Chamber Music Society of Lincoln Center, Peter Schickele, an extremely versatile composer of American art music, and George Lynn, who became director of the Westminister Choir College.

Roy's other accomplishments include the organization of numerous music festivals, such as the Pittsburgh International Festival of Contemporary Music. Moreover, he founded the International Congress of Strings (1959), served as chief of music programming for the overseas branch of the Office of War Information (1945-48), elected to the American Institute and Academy of Arts and Letters, received the title of Composer Laureate of the State of California, awarded the Elizabeth Sprague Coolidge Medal, given the Naumburg Award for his *Symphony No. 7*, and visited the U.S.S.R in a delegation of American composers sponsored by the U.S. State Department (1958).

Roy Harris, circa 1935

During the 1970s, several tributes were established for Harris, including the Roy Harris Archive at California State University-Los Angeles (1973) and the Roy Harris Society (1979). The latter organization was formed to promote performances, recordings, and research contextualizing Roy's long and noteworthy career. While he did not grow up in Oklahoma, the Anglo-Saxon folk musical ethos of his parents certainly had its impact on him. The Harrises illuminate for modern Oklahomans some insight into the lives of the land runners; that they were people of all locales, including from the West who came to the state seeking opportunity, but then also departed due to frontier hardships. Invariably, those who left Oklahoma went west, bound for the promise of California, with the folk songs of their lives to pass the time on the trip, and then entertain themselves when they got there. Although he met with some criticism for his inclusion of American folk melodies (such as "When Johnny Comes Marching Home") into his music, as critics felt it simplistic. However, just listening to that overture of 1935, *When Johnny Comes Marching Home*, one can hear the dissonant explorations of modern classical music (such as the impressionist music of Claude Debussy in a piece like *La Mer*) filled with the rambunctious optimism and grandeur of Harris's American idealism (akin to the music of Aaron

Copland in *Fanfare for the Common Man*). However, instead of being one or the other of those influences, Harris also recognizes the tension of a growing and developing country both from his parents' turbulent times, and the Depression in which the piece was being performed. As a result, the piece swells with confidence and happy renditions of the primary theme, and then fragments into the musical equivalent of a battered American flag flapping in the wind. By using counterpoint within the orchestra to develop two contrary themes of possibility and danger, Harris resolves with a quick conclusion, almost a symphonic rim shot, the conjectural meaning of which might be interpreted as steely resolve to go forward with confidence in uneasy circumstances.[4] After an extremely iconoclastic life in which he produced one of the most profound bodies of original art music of the 20th century, Roy Harris died in Santa Monica, California on October 1, 1979.

Endnotes

1. The Oklahoma land runs are mythic for some Oklahomans who trace their ancestry to those immigrants into Oklahoma from 1889 to 1895 when "excess" lands were opened for settlement by the U.S. Government. In fact, the lands were obtained via the remainder of land left in Oklahoma Territory after American Indians were enrolled and allotted sections of land based prior to the eventual dissolution of tribal governments. This aspect of the history remains controversial in public schools where mock land runs are routinely carried out, but the American Indian point of view or an explanation of how the land was available in the first place is often left out of lesson plans for the students, as well as the "feel-good" reporting about the land runs in the electronic and traditional press.

2. For a detailed review of Roy Harris' life and catalogue of his complete output of works and performances, as well as extensive scholarly writing about Harris, and critical reviews of his work in annotated bibliographic form, see Dan Stehman, *Roy Harris* (New York: Greenwood Press, 1991).

3. Ibid, page 1.

4. For perfectly representative examples of Harris' American nationalistic music, see the CD, *Portraits of Freedom: Music Aaron Copland and Roy Harris* (Delos, 1993) for his *American Creed* symphony and the overture, *When Johnny Comes Marching Home*.

Harris, Samuel "Sam" Kent

(b. June 4, 1961)

Along with having gained substantial attention for his acting, songwriting, producing, screen writing, photography and directing, Sam Harris is one of the most successful singing stars to ascend from Oklahoma to a fixed place among the brightest lights of Broadway in New York City. His full singing range, his showmanship, and his choreographic expertise make him an in-demand concert performer and hot ticket in contemporary musical theater, as well as a respected director and performance consultant. Born in Cushing, Oklahoma, but raised in Sand Springs just west of Tulsa, Sam's earliest musical performance was at two-years-old singing "The Star Spangled Banner" at a football game in Oklahoma. Exposed to gospel music at an early age and musical theater before he moved from Oklahoma at fifteen, Sam's first national exposure was on the television talent program, *Star Search* in 1983. After winning his first competition on the program by singing "Somewhere Over the Rainbow", Sam continued as "Grand Champion" on the show for sixteen weeks during its inaugural season.

The success on *Star Search* led to a two-record deal with Motown, producing *Sam Harris* (1984) and *Sam-I-Am* (1986), both now out of print. His only minor R & B hit, "Sugar Don't Bite", came from the first album and peaked at #36. Sam's limited chart success was not reflected in album sales, however, as *Sam Harris* went on to be a million-selling album. The album included his version of "Somewhere Over the Rainbow", now a signature piece of his live performances. *Sam-I-Am* featured several original songs co-authored by Sam and his brother, Matt Harris. Even though the album had no hit to speak of, and was released only on vinyl and cassette as the CD revolution was taking place, *Sam-I-Am* also sold over a million copies. After having sales success with his first two albums, Sam turned to other show business challenges of writing and directing for television and Broadway. Harris wrote the TBS sitcom, *Down to Earth*, that lasted four years, the Los Angeles produced musical *Hurry! Hurry! Hollywood!*, and the stage production of *Hard Copy*.

In addition to touring the country in concert, Harris has played to sold-out audiences at New York City's Carnegie Hall, Los Angeles' Universal Amphitheatre, and London's West End. On Broadway in New York, Sam received strong critical notices and a Drama Desk nomination for his work in *Grease*. He received a Drama League award for his performance in *The Life*, in addition to Tony, Outer Critic's Circle and Drama Desk nominations for the role. Off Broadway and regionally, Sam starred as Al Jolson in *The Jazz Singer*, played the lead role in the Broadway musical revue *Revival*, which he wrote, performed in *Jesus Christ Superstar*, *Different Hats*, *Hair*, *Cabaret*, and toured nationally in Andrew Lloyd Weber's *Joseph and the Amazing Technicolor Dreamcoat*. Harris has also appeared on numerous television shows and specials, working with Stevie Wonder, George Michael, Liza Minnelli, Madonna, Elizabeth Taylor, Whitney Houston, Roberta Flack, and Elton John. After working with Sam, Liza Minnelli waxed rhapsodic about his work: "When Sam sings, I'm perfectly all right, except for the fact that I can't breathe! I find myself crying and laughing and applauding and knowing why I went into this business." He has also made guest appearances on major talk shows such as *The Tonight Show* with Jay Leno, *Oprah*, *Rosie*, *Arsenio*, *Geraldo*, and others.

Sam has continued releasing albums, mostly of standards and songs he has written, to include *Different Stages* (1994), *Standard Time* (1997), *Revival* (1999), and the popular Christmas collection, *On This Night* (2000). Some highlights from his Motown career were released on *The Best of the Motown Sessions* in 1994, and various compilations have included his music, such as *Being Out Rocks*, *Tap Your Troubles Away: Words and Music of Jerry Herman*, and *George and Ira Gershwin: A Musical Celebration*. Along with his recordings throughout the 1990s, he also ranged into the realm of photographer, shooting cover images for Eagle-Eye Cherry, D*Note, and Beth Orton. In 2001, Sam worked behind the scenes at the Michael Jackson anniversary concert where he supervised Liza Minnelli's segment by arranging her songs with a 400-person gospel choir, and directed and arranged songs for Deborah Cox and Missy Elliot on the show. In late September of 2001, Sam appeared on Oprah Winfrey's *Music to Heal Our Hearts*, a show to comfort those affected by the events of September 11th of that year. In December

Sam Harris performing at the 2010 Oklahoma Music Hall of Fame Induction Ceremony and Concert in Muskogee, Oklahoma.

of 2001, he returned to Tulsa for sold out Christmas shows at the Van Trease Performing Arts Center for Education, and his solo cabaret show in New York City garnered him a Manhattan Association of Cabaret and Clubs Award (MAC) as Major Male Vocalist of 2002.

By the fall of 2002, Sam gained rave critical reviews for his starring role of Carmen Ghia in the Mel Brooks Broadway production of *The Producers* that extended through December 15th of the year. In early 2003, Harris began performing his one-man show, *Sam*, to wowed reviews from the *Los Angeles Time*, *Variety*, and several other West Coast publications. Harris brought the show to Tulsa in April, 2003 when he performed at the VanTrease Performing Arts Center and delighted the crowd with his eclectic repertoire of songs ranging from pop standards to Broadway songs and his own music. He has appeared in three feature films, *In the Weeds* (2000), *Little Man* (2005), and *Elena Undone* (2010). Additionally, in 2010 he was inducted into the Oklahoma Music Hall of Fame in Muskogee.

Even with all of this success, Sam repeatedly says his greatest accomplishment is his family, consisting of partner, Danny Jacobsen, a film producer and presentation coach, and adopted son, Cooper. To see Harris perform is to witness an inspirational and edifying example a human being's power to captivate audiences with forceful expression supported by innate talent, long hours of practice, and the confidence of someone who knows they are being enjoyed for what they do best. Along with Kristin Chenoweth, and Muskogee-born pianist and arranger Linda Twine, Sam Harris is not only one of the brightest lights on Broadway whose switch flicked "on" in Oklahoma, his multi-faceted impact on the entertainment industry guarantees his name will remain on marquees, liner notes, and end credits for many years to come.

www.samharris.com

Harter, Ali
(b. June 20, 1984)

With a memorable voice that can be either breezy or full of gritty soul, and the musical ability to accompany herself with guitar work that is both technically and harmonically interesting, Ali Harter is one of Oklahoma's more promising progressive pop music artists, having developed a strong following in Europe. A current resident of Choctaw, Harter started her musical career on fiddle, but started playing it like a guitar, so her parents switched her to that instrument. She has played in local bands and as a solo musician in the Oklahoma City area since her initial public appearance in 1999. While Ali started playing more rock music early on, she gravitated toward her mother's affection for Bonnie Raitt, who became a primary inspiration. Her first album, *Worry the Bone*, released in mid-2007 on the OKC-based Little Mafia Records, generated significant interest in Europe where it was re-released in 2008. As a result, Ali has been able to tour France, Belgium, Italy, and Switzerland consistently since 2007, having made thirteen European tours through mid-2011. With a spritely and percussive guitar style, accompanied by her lilting and melodic voice, Harter has become a playlist favorite on European stations like Radio 3FACH in Luzerne, Switzerland. Given her expressive voice and syncopated guitar style, Harter traveled to Switzerland in 2010 to play the prestigious, Montreaux Jazz Festival. As for recognition in the U.S., two songs from Harter's *Worry the Bone* CD appeared on a season six episode of ABC Television's popular show, *Grey's Anatomy* ("Untitled No. 3" and

"You Can Keep 'Em"). Her songs have appeared in a number of independent films, such as Oklahoma filmmaker Sterlin Harjo's *Barking Water*, and Mickey Reeses', *Le Corndog Du Desespoir*.

Harter's 2010 CD, *No Bees, No Honey* (Little Mafia) can be heard in its entirety on her myspace.com site.[1] With no pop genre outside of her boundary, Harter is equally comfortable with a horn-laden stage band ("The Girl Who Sings"), 21st century rockabilly ("Lonely Man"), multi-textured modern rock ("That Place is Gone"), honky-tonk sing-a-longs ("Close Up the House"), country ballads filled with steel guitar ("On My Own") or the subtle bounce of carnivalesque Dixieland music that is a sparse but respectable neighbor to hot club jazz, itself based on the music of Paris in the 1930s ("The Best Mess"). At times her voice is broad and emotive as U.K. powerhouse Joss Stone, or as light and carefree as Malibu, California pop star, Colbie Caillat. With an admitted affinity for Bonnie Raitt and Joe Cocker, her closest Oklahoma musical cousin is most likely Samantha Crain, as both mine a similar musical aesthetic with their voices.[2] However, while Crain's lyrics tend to draw in the listener as much as her singing, Harter seems to be the other way around, whereby just the sound of her voice can substantiate its presence. People just like to hear Ali Harter sing.

Ali Harter at the Conservatory, Oklahoma City, 2010.

In 2009, Ali's European reputation continued to climb, bolstered by collaborating that year with Wax Tailor, the alias of French trip hop/hip hop producer, Jean-Christophe Le Saout, on his album *In The Mood For Life*. Harter co-wrote and sang on the album's first single, "This Train", helping propel the CD to *Billboard* Top 10 album status in France, as well as just breaking into the *Billboard*'s European Top 100 Albums in October, 2009. As an end result, Harter received a gold record in France, marking sales of at least 50,000, for her work on *In The Mood For Life*. A popular festival and opening act due to the diversity of her set list that she just calls "roots music", Harter has opened for a wide variety country, blues, and rock artists, such as Miranda Lambert, John Mayall, and Dierks Bentley, and shared festival billing with The Flaming Lips, Leon Russell, Ben Harper, Tori Amos, PJ Harvey, The Black Crowes, and Cake. Constantly touring, to see her one-woman show in a local setting is the best way to appreciate her singing and songwriting skills. As of 2013, she was planning to record her next album.

www.aliharter.com

Endnotes

1. To hear Ali Harter's second album, *No Bees No Honey* (Little Mafia, 2010), visit www.myspace.com/aliharter. As of June 2011, fans could also download four, free re-mixes of Harter's songs on her website that demonstrate how her voice fits a variety of genres.

2. For a more in-depth interview with Ali Harter, see Jeremy Bigelow's online interview with Harter in Okie Magazine at www.okiemagazine.com (last accessed June 28, 2011).

Hayes, Wade

(b. April 20, 1969)

With a smooth baritone naturally inflected with home-state-Oklahoma twang, a versatile lead and rhythm guitar ability, and hit songwriting abilities that likely evolved from repeatedly playing country music covers in his father's country dance and bar band, Tony Wade Hayes emerged on the national country music stage in 1994 with his first hit, and a #1 *Billboard* Hot Country Singles hit at that, "Old Enough to Know Better", co-written by fellow Oklahoman and Nashville mentor, Chick Rains. The song's namesake album on Columbia Records was also certified gold in 1995, an impressive accomplishment for a new artist's first album. Born in Bethel Acres, Oklahoma, a community of about 2,500 residents southeast of Oklahoma City, Wade grew up in a country music atmosphere. Wade's grandfather was a fiddle player and his instrument was passed on to Wade by his father, Don. Don was a professional country musician, who also moon lighted as a carpenter, while his mother, Trisha, was a hairdresser. The Hayes household listened to a variety of country music from the "outlaw country" of Waylon Jennings and Willie Nelson to the "Bakersfield Sound" of Merle Haggard and Buck Owens, along with the traditional honky-tonk twang of Lefty Frizzell. Wade's first instrument was mandolin, perhaps influenced by another one of his idols, Ricky Skaggs, but by the time he was a teenager, he was playing lead guitar with his father's band, Country Heritage, in honky tonks around Oklahoma. Around the same time, Wade's father signed a contract with an independent record company in Nashville, where he took the family for about a year. The Nashville label folded, leaving the Hayes family broke. Upon returning to Oklahoma, Wade continued to play in his father's band during high school, after which he attended three different colleges, including the University of Central Oklahoma in Edmond, where he declared business as his major, but left college after about a year to pursue professional music opportunities.

Wade Hayes

In 1991, while watching Ricky Skaggs emotional speech at the CMA awards suggesting young artists should follow their dreams, Wade decided to make the move to Nashville. With about $450.00 in his billfold and all that he could pack in his truck, he arrived in "Music City" in the fall of 1992. Working construction in the daytime, primarily roofing houses, he performed at amateur nights on Music Row, primarily Gilley's nightclub, where he was offered a regular job singing at night. In 1993, country artist Johnny Lee heard Wade at Gilley's, and was impressed enough to hire him as lead guitarist for his backup band. While in Nashville, Wade had begun to cutting demo tapes, as well as honing his songwriting skills. A veteran songwriter and vice-president for Sony/Tree publishing house, as well as a Muskogee, Oklahoma native, Chick Rains invited Wade to write some songs and eventually arranged an audition with record producer Don Cook, who had produced Brooks and Dunn. Within a 72-hour period in 1994, Wade had landed a deal to write songs for Tree and a seven-album recording contract with Columbia.

Released in 1994, Wade's debut album, *Old Enough to Know Better*, generated four singles that kept Hayes' voice and guitar work in constant rotation throughout 1994 and 1995, "Old Enough to Know Better" (#1), "I'm Still Dancin' With You" (#4), "Don't Stop" (#10), and "What I Meant To Say" (#5). The "Don't Stop" video racked up some extra press and attention when it was deemed overcharged in sexual innuendo by Country Music Television, who originally threatened to ban it; only three months later fan support had pushed it to #1. Co-writer on the first two hit songs from the album "Old Enough to Know Better", "I'm Still Dancin' With You", Hayes enjoyed watching the album achieve gold status, or 500,000 units sold, a rare accomplishment for a first recording. Label and artist alike relished the album's success as the best-selling debut record of the year. As a result of the sales recognition for Hayes, he was named *Billboard* magazine's Top New Country Artist and was an ACM nominee for Top New Male Vocalist of the Year for 1995. His second album, *On a Good Night*, peaked at #19 on the *Billboard*'s Hot Country Album Charts, and sported three singles; the first, "On a Good Night", an up tempo redneck party rocker reached #2 on the Hot Country Singles chart, but Hayes' co-writes did not register as well: "Where Do I Go To Start All Over" (#42) and ""It's Over My Head" (#46). In any case, Hayes and Columbia Nashville smiled at the record's gold status, bolstering both artist and label to continue his "bad cowboy" honk-tonk party and womanizing image, which also resonated with CMA who nominated him for their Horizon Award in 1996.

Hayes stutter-stepped out of the gate in 1997 with an ill-received cover of "Wichita Lineman", the classic 1968 pop country tune popularized by Glen Campbell and written by Elk City native, Jimmy Webb. The song was considered a pre-release for Wade's new album with a devil-may-care party ethos, *Tore Up from the Floor Up*, but became more tempered on final CD release as *When the Wrong One Loves You Right* in 1998 (which did not include "Wichita Lineman"). The album's first single, heralded Hayes' Oklahoma connections, "The Day She Left Tulsa (In a Chevy), and witnessed him shifting into more of a contemplative ballad singer than a country bar party maniac. The label saved that for the follow up single, "When the Wrong One Loves You Right", preserving Hayes' initial successful formula of an up tempo country rocker about honky-tonk love affairs, but it only reached #50 on the Hot Country Singles chart. Interestingly, the third single reverted to Hayes' developing ballad style, and scored a respectable Top 15 hit with "How Do You Sleep at Night". As a last attempt to capitalize on the early ideas for the album, Columbia released "Tore Up From the Floor Up" that attempted to replicate Hayes' earlier beer joint ruckus aesthetic, but was Hayes' lowest charting single thus far (#57). As a whole the album was a success, reaching #9 on the Hot Country Album charts. The "Don't Stop" video was controversial, and CMT originally threatened to ban it, however, three months later fan support had pushed it to #1.

Honors and awards continued for Wade in the late 1990s. At the TNN/*Music City News* Country Awards show, Wade was presented with the Male Star of Tomorrow honor, followed by the Blockbuster Entertainment Award for Favorite New Country Artist, and *Entertainment Tonight* named him the "Hottest Face to Watch" in country music. However, that was not enough to keep him on Columbia. In 1999, Hayes signed with Monument Records who released his fourth album, *Highways and Heartaches*, producing two singles that did not break the top forty on the Hot Country Singles chart, and Hayes parted ways with Monument. In 2003, Wade teamed up for a duo act with Claremore native Mark Mc-

Clurg, a twelve-year veteran of Alan Jackson's band, the Strayhorns, as well the long-standing country group out of Claremore, Stonehorse. The two released their first single, "It Doesn't Mean I Don't Love You," in the spring of 2003, which charted at #41, not enough to keep them together as an act, nor convince Universal South to release an album. After nine years of working the country music industry hard from every angle of performing, writing, recording, video-making, and promotional work, Hayes went on hiatus.[1] After re-charging, Wade returned the way many artists work today, and that is in control of his own recordings. In 2009, he released *Place To Turn Around* independently, with ten of his own songs on the CD, and made it available both at his regular concerts throughout the U.S., and on his website as an electronic honky-tonk download. Through the fall of 2011, he had scheduled concerts in Oklahoma, Texas, Kansas, New Mexico, and North Carolina.

Wade's 1952 reissue of Fender Telecaster guitar that he occasionally still plays on stage bears the signatures of his three country music idols—Merle Haggard, Willie Nelson, and Waylon Jennings. The latter, who died in 2002, was one of Wade's obvious vocal influences, as Hayes is able to channel Jennings big voice that comes from the top of the throat, somewhere between the nasal singing of traditional country, and the diaphragm source of torchy ballad singers. Hayes did get to meet his idol when he played lead guitar for Jennings on the NASCAR-sponsored album, *Hotter Than Asphalt* (Columbia, 1996). With regard to Oklahoma music, Wade Hayes is another example of the state exporting its musical talent to the world. Of course, a thousand lessons had to be learned playing for the people in country bars and dance halls of Oklahoma with his father's band before he was ready, but Hayes still had to marshal up the courage to pack up his dreams and head to the country music kingdom of Nashville, where he found the great and powerful Oz of Tennessee is fickle and plays favorites, heavily. For a period of about five years, Hayes was a heavy favorite. Now, he is own bandleader, often back in Oklahoma, with a thousand more experiences to write and sing about for his fans who are old enough to know better now, but still get a little tore up and every now and then, and need a musician who commiserates with them on that level. Wade Hayes is that musician.

www.wadehayes.com

Endnote

1. For extremely enlightening insight into the period of Wade Hayes' sudden ascension in the country music world, and the ensuing pressures he experienced, see Bruce Feilter, *Dreaming Out Loud: Garth Brooks, Wynonna Judd, Wade Hayes, and the Changing Face of Nashville*. (New York: Avon, 1998).

Wade Hayes performs at the Oklahoma Music Hall of Fame to honor his Nashville mentor, Chick Rains, 2008.

Hazlewood, Lee

(b. July 9, 1929 – d. August 4, 2007)

Best remembered for his compositions "These Boots Are Made for Walking" and "Jackson" major hits for Nancy Sinatra in the 1960s, as well as creating the "big twang" guitar sound for Duane Eddy, Barton Lee Hazlewood was born in Mannford, Oklahoma, a community of roughly 2,000 inhabitants west of Tulsa. The first child of Eva Lee and Gabe Hazlewood, his father was a wildcatter in the Oklahoma oil fields and occasionally promoted dances as a part-time booking agent. One of Lee's fondest memories is being lifted onto the shoulders of Bob Wills at a show booked by his father. Oil field wildcatters travel wherever the new oil strikes occur and, when Lee was twelve, the family moved to McClain, Texas; Ft. Smith, Arkansas; Paris, Arkansas; and eventually to Port Neches, Texas where he spent his teen years on the Gulf Coast. Lee attended high school in Huntsville, Texas, and gave Southern Methodist University in Dallas a shot in an attempt to study medicine, but was soon called to the armed services, after which he received his basic training at Colleen, Texas, was stationed at Ft. Hood, Texas, and later played drums in Alaska for the 4th Army Division band.

Lee was again called into military duty during the Korean War, and served as a disc jockey for the AFRS radio in Korea and Japan. After this stint in the service, Lee decided not to return to college and moved to Los Angeles, where he attended Spears Broadcasting School to develop his skills at deejaying. He was hired as country DJ at KCKY radio in Coolidge, Arizona, where he earned $40 a week. A newly arrived young New Yorker by the name of Duane Eddy began to visit Lee at the station, and they soon struck up a friendship. They would drive to Phoenix for country music shows and met 17-year-old Al Casey. By 1953 Lee was honing his songwriting skills and registered his first song with BMI, "Four Bell Love Alarm". Lee's first record production came in mid-1955 when he took Duane Eddy and Al Casey to Phoenix to cut "I Want Some Lovin' Baby" and "Soda Fountain Girl", two of Lee's songs.

Lee Hazlewood with Nancy Sinatra at a Nashville recording session, circa 1968.

In 1955, Lee was fired at KCKY and took another DJ job on KRUX in Phoenix, where he also organized his own Viv Record label and Debra Publishing House. He penned several songs for Sanford Clark, another Oklahoman, including "Run Boy Run" "Son of a Gun" and "The Fool". Lee asked Clark to record "The Fool" on a Phoenix-based label, MCI. Some 500 promotional copies were distributed throughout the U.S., and a Cleveland DJ sent it to Dot Records, who immediately signed Clark and released it on the Dot label. "The Fool" hit #7 on the *Billboard* charts and sold more than 800,000 copies. Because of his success with "The Fool," Lee was offered a producer position with Dot Records, and the family moved to Los Angeles. It was here that Lee met publisher Lester Sill and Dick Clark, the TV host of *American Bandstand*, after which the trio formed Jamie Records. Another break came for Lee when he began writing songs with his old Coolidge friend, Duane Eddy. Lee is also credited with the "big reverb twang" sound of Eddy's guitar due to Hazlewood's use of a silo for an echo chamber during the recording process. They also collaborated on "Rebel Rouser", "Cannon Ball", "Shazam", and "Dance with the Guitar Man", all released on the Jamie label. Much of Eddy's success also stemmed from his regular appearances on Clark's *American Bandstand*.

Moving to the Reprise label in 1965, Lee wrote and produced U.S. hits by Dean Martin ("Houston") and Dino, Desi, and Billy ("I'm A Fool"). Lee was introduced to Nancy Sinatra, who had recorded several unsuccessful singles with Reprise. He charged Nancy with developing a new sound that would appeal to truck drivers, and nicknamed her "Nasty Jones". Lee's "These Boots Are Made for Walkin'" made Nancy an international star, and she followed with more of Lee's songs, including "How Does That Grab You, Darlin'", "Sugartown", and "Lightning's Girl". Lee and Nancy cut the following duets, "Jackson," "Some Velvet Morning," and "Lady Bird," all released on the *Nancy and Lee* album (1968). The pair recorded a follow-up album in 1972, *Nancy and Lee Again*. The partnership ended because Nancy grew tired of singing Lee's songs, although her career plummeted thereafter.

Lee's own recordings in the 1960s, which appeared on various labels, included *Trouble Is A Lonesome Town* (1963), *The N.S.V.I.P. [Not So Very Important People]* (1965), *Friday's Child* (1966), *The Very Special World of Lee Hazlewood* (1966), which featured his own version of "Boots", *Love and Other Crimes* (1968), and *The Cowboy and the Lady*, a duet with Ann Margaret (1969). Lee's only album in the 1970s, *Poet, Fool, or Bum* (1973), was panned by critics and included one track, "The Performer," which expressed his disillusionment with the music business.

Hazlewood moved to Sweden and continued making records for the Scandinavian market, although remained in relative obscurity in the U.S. during the late 1970s and 1980s. He resurfaced in the U.S. in 1995, touring with Sinatra after her comeback album, *One More Time*, was released. Lee contributed two vocal tracks to his old friend Al Casey's *Sidewinder* album, released by the German Bear Family label in 1999, and the same year, released his first album in twenty-five years, *Farmisht, Flatulence, Origami, ARF!!! and me*, a collection of standard pop tunes, such as "Honeysuckle Rose", "It Had To Be You", and "Don't Get Around Much Anymore". Glad to hear his vintage pop baritone, critics applauded his voice which had remained powerful to that point.

In the late 1990s, Sonic Youth drummer Steve Shelly and his Smells Like Records began to release a series of Lee's classic albums, including *Cowboy in Sweden*, *Requiem for an Almost Lady*, and *The Cowboy and the Lady*. In 2002, German label, City Slang, released *Total Lee! The Songs of Lee Hazlewood* with a host of college radio types, i.e., Lambchop, St. Etienne, Jarvis Cocker, Tindersticks, and Evan Dando, covering some of Hazlewood's most famous material. Also in 2002, Xlibris published Hazlewood first book, *The Pope's Daughter*, described on his website as a "surreal combination of biblical imagery and his time with Nancy Sinatra." The Hazlewood/Sinatra tour de force, "These Boots are Made for Walkin'" also surfaced with a heavy, hip-hop beat, when Jessica Simpson covered the song in a highly suggestive video promo for the film, *Dukes of Hazzard* (2005). Lee's final album, Cake or Death (Ever Records, 2007) featured various guest artists from throughout his career, to include Duane Eddy.

Hazlewood's final work, a spoken word project, "Hilli (At The Top Of The World)" was recorded with Icelandic fans, admirers amiina, best known as collaborators with atmospheric music wonders, Sigur Ros, and released in December, 2007, about four months after his death August 4, 2007. In 2012, Light in the Attic Records released a 17-track album comprised of the best of Hazlewood's work right after the Nancy Sinatra success, to include a variety of space cowboy tunes by Ry Cooder, Hazlewood himself, and some breathy cooing by Ann Margaret.

An iconoclastic figure of American popular music, Lee Hazlewood was born in Oklahoma, and gauging its impact on his life is conjectural at this point. However, one can imagine his father's wildcatting optimism and show business side projects in Oklahoma re-enforced the independent and visionary aspects of Lee's character, while the diverse and full music of the Texas Playboys, as well as the personal flamboyance of Bob Wills, who once hoisted the youngster on his shoulders, was never that far away from his consciousness. One doesn't have to guess too much about Oklahoma's verifiable impact on Hazlewood; look no further than the image of boots walking and the sound of twangy guitar, both intrinsic aspects of his biggest successes, and, both are also an incontrovertible aspect of Oklahoma's iconic imagery and aural identity (ok, Texas' too), which he encountered first as childhood experiences around Mannford, Oklahoma.

www.leehazlewoodmusic.com

Hedges, Michael
(b. December 31, 1953 – d. December 1, 1997)

Regarded by critics and musicians as one of the 20th century's most technically complicated and stylistically advanced acoustic guitarists, Michael Hedges combined several unusual guitar techniques, such as personal tunings, fret board tapping, and percussive plucking styles, to achieve a musically dense and harmonically rich texture in his playing and compositions which he called "violent acoustic," "heavy mental," and "acoustic thrash." Although born in Sacramento, California, Hedges grew up in Enid, Oklahoma, a town of 45,000 people in north central Oklahoma. His mother, Ruth, who was from Marshall, Oklahoma and a cornet player, and his father, Thayne, a piccolo player from Enid, met in the band at Phillips University in Enid.

After a series of moves for academic reasons, the family wound up back in Enid in 1955 at 1323 W. Broadway. Michael had his own record player from the time he could turn it on, and his musically oriented parents started

Michael Hedges

him with piano lessons at age five. However, they discontinued the lessons after a couple of years because Michael would not practice once he had a piece of music committed to memory. When Hedges was in the fifth grade, he came home from the YMCA and told his mother that one could rent a guitar and have lessons for $5 a month at the Y, and the Hedges agreed to the lessons. Also while in grade school, Michael began playing cello in the school orchestra. During his junior high years, his parents gave him the red electric guitar he asked for on Christmas and he began playing it in the Enid High School Stage Band. However, in order to be in the band he had to play something else besides guitar, so he started playing flute and took lessons from Dr. Milburn Carey.

The Hedges family spent one year at Humboldt State in Arcata, California, where Michael spent his junior year playing flute and guitar in the high school band. The Hedges returned to Enid for Michael's senior year, where he was graduated in 1972. He continued in the band, and, after high school, Hedges enrolled at Phillips University where his father was a director of the Community Speech and Hearing Center. At Phillips he studied flute and classical guitar, as well as composition and music theory under Dr. Eugene Ulrich, whom Hedges repeatedly cited as an important mentor. According to his mother Ruth, during his time at Phillips he also formed various trios and dance bands, and spent countless hours in the university practice rooms. Not able to get any significant guitar instruction in Enid, Michael drove to St. Louis periodically for lessons. After his third year at Phillips, Hedges transferred to the Peabody Conservatory in Baltimore, Maryland, where he earned his degree in composition. He started Peabody as a guitar major, but switched to composition, and then continued at Stanford University's Center for Computer Research and Musical Acoustics. While enrolled at both universities, Michael would study and practice during the day and play area clubs, bars, and cafes at night.

During a gig at the Varsity Theater in Palo Alto, California in 1980, Windham Hill Records founder Will Ackerman discovered Hedges and offered him a recording contract on the spot. Ackerman later recalled about the night, "Michael tore my head off. It was like watching the guitar being reinvented." Just before meeting Ackerman, Michael had already started playing with bassist Michael Manring and, subsequently, Hedges and Manring began their recording careers on Hedges' first Windham Hill release, *Breakfast in the Field* (1981). The album established Hedges as a unique force in the acoustic guitar world and began his journey to significant notoriety for his innovative style of sounding like several guitars playing at once, what he called his "man-band." The technique was produced by his left hand tapping notes while his right hand picked the remaining strings. 1984's Grammy-nominated *Aerial Boundaries* manifested the diverse array of Hedges' performance and compositional developments, as well as the technical innovations in acoustic amplification for which he also gained his elevated reputation. According to Windham Hill press materials, *Aerial Boundaries* is considered one of the most important acoustic guitar albums ever.

In 1985, Hedges increasingly became known as a new age artist, primarily because of his association with Windham Hill, which had essentially created the genre and received substantial credibility by Hedges' success. Realizing the "new age" tag did not totally describe Hedges' eclectic musical inspirations, Windham Hill created a new subsidiary label, Open Air, to release Michael's 1986 album, *Watching My Life Go By*, featuring Michael's vocals for the first time, chanting by Bobby McFerrin, and music played on wine glasses. Also released in 1986 was a holiday album, *Santa Bear's First Christmas*, containing background music performed, arranged, and composed by Hedges. *Santa Bear* also marked the first appearance of the rare harp guitar Michael favored for several recordings and performances throughout the remainder of his career. Displaying both his incredible abilities to sound like an accompanying and a solo guitar at the same time, as well as his improving vocal style, 1987's *Live on the Double Planet* was recorded at various concerts across the U.S. and Canada. The album also features two compositions for the harp-guitar, covers of Bob Dylan's "All Along the Watchtower" and the Beatles' "Come Together," and several more original compositions recorded live.

In 1988, Hedges released *Strings of Steel,* furthering the style for which he has become praised by such jazz and rock notables as Steve Vai, Crosby, Stills, and Nash, Pat Martino, and Pete Townshend. Rock virtuoso Vai said about Michael, "The first time I heard him play, I was stunned into silence." The Who's guitarist, Pete Townshend, explained, "Michael will never by forgotten as one of those who respected, absorbed, and yet rose above all trends to create accessible and commercial music for a new age."

In 1990, Michael released the Grammy-nominated *Taproot*, featuring instrumental pieces and one vocal composition set to the lyrics of poet e.e. cummings. The album was Michael's first recording in his Northern California recording studio, The Speech and Hearing Clinic, and furthered his interest in the metaphorical and symbolic potential of instrumental compositions by basing some of the music on writings by poet Robert Bly and mythologist Joseph Campbell. Hedges also experimented with more varied sound textures by including woodwinds, drum programs, synthesizers and percussion on the album, as well as harmony vocals by David Crosby and Graham Nash. In addition, on *Taproot* Michael started creating his own labels for his playing, such as "savage myth guitar" and "transterm guitar." In the years following the release of *Taproot*, Hedges received accolades such as *Guitar Player*'s readers' poll awards for "best acoustic guitarist" five years in a row, and was also named by the same magazine as one of "25 Guitarists Who Shook the World." In 1992, Michael wrote and played all the music for the children's animated video, *Princess Scargo and the Birth Day Pumpkin* (BMG Kidz). Eager to remain outside of the standard categories of New Age and solo guitarist, Hedges released 1994's *The Road to Return*, featuring more of his vocals, and an astonishing array of instruments played by Hedges on the album, to include drums, flutes, synthesizers, harmonica, and electric guitar. The only other musician on the album is Janeen Rae Heller who plays musical saw. In 1995, Michael wrote an autobiography of sorts, *Michael Hedges: Rhythm, Sonority, Silence* (Stropes Editions), which included an introduction by him about his life, some of his more famous tunings, and tablatures of popular Hedges tunes such as "Aerial Boundaries" and "Rickover's Dream." That year he also went back out on the road with Michael Manring in support of *The Road to Return*, and then began performing solo as he developed new material that would become the Grammy Award-winning *Oracle* album in 1996. *Oracle* featured the return of a guitar to him that had been stolen back in 1982 when he was opening for Jerry Garcia in Palo Alto, California in support of *Breakfast in the Field*, on which he had

Michael Hedges

played the same custom-built guitar. The guitar reenergized Michael, and also signaled his return to purely instrumental music. Along with another Beatles cover, "Tomorrow Never Knows," and a solo guitar interpretation of Frank Zappa's "Sofa #1," Michael ranges expertly through his dramatic fingerings and unique tunings on *Oracle*. The album won a Grammy for "Best New Age Album" in 1998. Sadly, it would be his last full-fledged release as Michael Hedges was killed in an automobile accident over Thanksgiving weekend in 1997 near Medocino, California. Subsequently, in 1998 Phillips University renamed its music building in honor of Hedges, and in 1999 Windham Hill released material recorded shortly before his death on *Torched*. The album included six original instrumentals, eight vocal tracks, and a live track from 1994. Intended as "sketches" for the album *Torched*, the label left them just as they were recorded and mixed by Michael. Included on the CD is his only song that is directly titled after the state in which he grew up, "Rough Wind in Oklahoma." In 2000, Windham Hill released a *Best of Michael Hedges* CD that contains many of the highlights of his career, and in 2001 duplicated much of that set with some additional live tracks on *Beyond Boundaries: Guitar Solos*. In 2006, RCA Victor released a four-CD set, *A Quiet Revolution: 30 Years of Windham Hill*. The collection contained three of Michael's pieces, "When I Was Four", "Rickover's Dream", and "Because It's There", placed in the appropriate context of both the label and genre he instigated with the unique expression of his talent on guitar. He website features many interesting articles, interviews, lyrics, images, and a complete discography that provide a new fan tremendous insight into his career. The site also is rewarding for long-timer aficionados who just cannot hear from, or enough about, the innovative musical mind and the ear-blowing works of art Hedges produced.

www.nomadland.com

Hendricks, Scott

As of June, 2011, producer, recording engineer, talent scout, music publisher, and record company executive, Scott Hendricks, could be credited with the instigation, oversight, or actual production of eighty-two top ten country hits, with forty-five of those reaching #1 status. Not bad for a farm boy born to parents Inez (a secretary) and Howard (a police officer) Hendricks in Clinton, Oklahoma, where Scott began writing songs and playing in bands as a youth. According to the bio published on his website, Hendricks was obsessed with music from an early age, and picked up the guitar when he was 8 years old. Though he'd never even seen a recording studio, he knew he wanted to work in one. Hendricks started playing in local bands in junior high, began writing songs as a teen and was an all-state stage-band guitarist at Clinton High School. After graduation, Scott headed to Stillwater where he enrolled at Oklahoma State University. Once there, Hendricks joined a band that played covers of Top 40 hits of rock, pop and funk bands. He supplemented his education by working at a local studio. He also met another future Nashville industry giant in Stillwater, Tim DuBois, who at the time (1974-75) was teaching accounting at OSU while playing music and writing songs with friends in the college town. Hendricks hit it off with DuBois, and the rest, as they say, is country music history.

With a desire to make it in country music as songwriters, in the winter of 1975 DuBois and Hendricks made their first attempt at pitching songs in Nashville, setting up meetings with publishers before they left as a result of DuBois' research on the music industry, and sold one song written by Tim and his younger brother, Randy. This inspired

DuBois to relocate to Nashville while Hendricks stayed at OSU to finish his degree, which he did in 1978. Immediately thereafter, Hendricks headed to Nashville, moved in DuBous' basement, and began looking for work with some of the experience he had gained in Stillwater and at Oklahoma State, which he found by landing a job as a salesman for Nashville Sound Systems, a studio-design company that had him designing and selling gear to recording studios. He also picked up a part-time role teaching studio engineering classes for the famed music business program at Belmont University. During a sales call at Glaser Sound Studios, the studio engineer lobbed an invitation for Hendricks to drop by and hang out at sessions any time he wanted. "Little did he know how seriously I took his offer," Hendricks laughs. "Every day when I got off work, I would go there and hang out while Jimmy Bowen would make all these incredible records." Hendricks was an unpaid gopher at Glaser Sound—and got very little sleep. He taught Belmont classes in the morning, worked his day job, then hung at the studio into the early morning hours. It was at Glaser that he witnessed sessions by the likes of Merle Haggard and Hank Williams Jr. and became familiar with some of Music City's A-list session players. After nine months the Glaser Brothers hired Hendricks as a full-time engineer. He was officially "in," but it was just the start. From Glaser Sound Hendricks moved to Bullet Recording Studios, where he was chief engineer. Once established, Hendricks teamed with Tim DuBois and became one of the most (if not THE most) significant producing and management teams in country music during the 1980s and early 1990s, with Scott Hendricks becoming an important record company executive and producer in his own right from the mid-1990s through 2011.

Scott Hendricks

Beginning with the group assembled in 1985 around a college friend of Hendricks and Dubois, Oklahoman Greg Jennings, Scott produced thirteen Top 10 hits Restless Heart, six of which rose to the coveted #1 status ("That Rock Won't Roll" and "I'll Still Be Loving You", 1986; "Wheels" and "Why Does It Have to Be", 1987; "Bluest Eyes In Texas" and "A Tender Lie", 1988). These successes increased focus on Hendricks as a go-to engineer as well as an up and coming producer. Wayne Watson asked Scott to produce/engineer his next project, which became a No. 1 album in Contemporary Christian Music. Hendricks also mixed and/or engineered albums by Alabama, Anne Murray, Lorrie Morgan and Tanya Tucker, among others. He recorded Lee Greenwood's "Holdin' a Good Hand", which earned a GRAMMY nomination for Best Engineered Recording for 1990. Scott also engineered seven Hank Williams Jr. albums, including the award-winning album, Born to Boogie (Warner Bros., 1989). During the partnership with Hank Jr., Hendricks combined Hank Williams' vocals from a 1951 acetate recording with new tracks to create "There's A Tear In My Beer", a honky-tonk number with a foot in two different generations. It won a GRAMMY and trophies from both the CMA and the ACM. Also starting in 1989, Hendricks co-produced the first two Alan Jackson albums and a No. 1 single from

Alan's third album, which combined sold over 12 million copies. Hendricks followed with an astounding string of #1 successes as producer for the likes of Alan Jackson, a partial list of which includes "Wanted", 1990; "Here in the Real World", 1990; "Chasin' That Neon Rainbow", 1990; "Don't Rock the Jukebox", 1991, "Dallas", 1992; and "Tonight I Climbed the Wall", 1993.

Along with Tim DuBois, Hendricks was instrumental in pairing newcomers Ronnie Dunn and Kix Brooks, co-producing three albums by the most successful duo in country music history, Brooks & Dunn on Arista-Nashville, the label being run by DuBois. Hendricks' recordings of Brooks & Dunn produced multiple #1 hits ("My Next Broken Heart" and "Brand New Man", 1991; "Neon Moon" and "Boot Scootin' Boogie" (1992); "We'll Burn That Bridge" and "She Used To Be Mine", 1993; "She's Not the Cheatin' Kind", 1994; "Little Miss Honky Tonk" and "You're Gonna Miss Me When I'm Gone", 1995). More success followed as Hendricks produced albums by his one-time fiancé, Faith Hill, Lee Roy Parnell, Steve Wariner and John Michael Montgomery, including John Michael's mega-hits "I Swear" and "I Can Love You Like That"; #1 hit singles by Faith Hill ("Wild One", 1993; "Piece of My Heart", 1994; and "It Matters To Me", 1995); #1s by Lee Roy Parnell ("Tender Moment", 1993 and "A Little Bit of You", 1995); and #1 hits by John Michael Montgomery ("I Swear", 1993; "Be My Baby Tonight", 1994; "I Can Love You Like That" and "Sold", 1995). Hendricks won a Country Music Association award for Single of the Year (Production) for "I Swear", and six trophies from the Academy of Country Music, plus one more from the CMA for his production skills. He also won an Emmy for his production of Hank Williams Jr.'s *Monday Night Football* theme. In 1991, Hendricks founded Big Tractor, a music publishing company. Starting with just one writer, Big Tractor has matured into a successful and respected independent publishing company with song credits that include George Strait's "I Saw God Today" and Lonestar's "Amazed", the No. 1 country song in the history of the BDS monitoring system, which is part of the Nielsen ratings system that monitors airplay in at least 140 U.S. markets, on the internet, and on television.

In 1995 Hendricks took over as President/CEO of Capitol Records Nashville and restructured the label, dropping a staggering 25 acts and focusing the efforts of the label around mega-seller Garth Brooks and an unknown artist, Trace Adkins. Brooks' career had in many ways pumped new and major popular music life into Nashville, creating new expectations for new artists, and giving Garth an unparalleled amount of power. As a result, many published reports in industry publications indicated Brooks was not happy with the way his album *Fresh Horses* was handled by Capitol in 1995, pinning the blame on the label's leadership.[2] No one was questioning Hendricks' supervision of Trace Adkins' career, however, as Adkins' 1996 Capitol album, *Dreamin' Out Loud*, glistened with two #1 singles, "I Left Something Turned On At Home" and "This Ain't No Thinkin' Thing", but hits in 1997. Hendricks fortuitously met Adkins when he was introduced by a friend at the Nashville airport. I heard him say 'Hello' and immediately asked him if he sang," Hendricks remembers. "I went to see him play the next night at a local bar, and I signed him on the spot." That began a relationship which continued through 2010 when Adkins was featured on another Hendricks production of an Oklahoma artist, Blake Shelton's #1 hit, "Hillbilly Bone". Back in 1997, however, Hendricks exited Capitol later took over as president of Virgin Records' Nashville division from its establishment in 1998 until its dissolution in 2001, a period in which he went through a ten-year stretch without a Top Ten hit to his credit, until Blake Shelton's 2008 #1, "She Wouldn't Be Gone".

Also during Scott's time at Capitol, he was instrumental in shaping Deana Carter's multi-platinum album, *Did I Shave My Legs For This?* After making some significant changes to its content, Hendricks then broke numerous accepted rules by releasing a four-and-a-half minute ballad as the first single on a new artist. That single, "Strawberry Wine," teamed with two other No. 1 singles from the album, led to sales of more than 5 million copies. Another unconventional move was Hendricks' signing of Roy D. Mercer, who became one of the most successful comedy acts in history, selling millions of records. "Determining good from bad is really pretty easy," Hendricks says. "Determining good from great is not as easy." Hendricks' Capitol Nashville success is also signified by his signing an unknown Australian artist, Keith Urban, to the label as part of the band The Ranch. Urban has gone on to become one of country's best-known talents. "Signing Keith was a no-brainer," Hendricks recalls. "He is a world-class guitarist and entertainer. It just seemed like it was only a matter of time before it all came to together for him as an artist." Hendricks' tenure at Capitol Nashville lasted less than three years, but his impact while at the label just further cemented his prominent industry status in Nashville.

After leaving Capitol, in 1998 Hendricks was asked to establish a separate EMI label and founded a Nashville division of Virgin Records, where he signed Chris Cagle and worked with Ronnie Milsap. In 2001, Hendricks went back to his first love, independent production, producing a new round of hits by Trace Adkins, Jeff Bates and others. In 2007, Hendricks joined Warner Bros. Records Nashville as the head of its A&R department, coordinating the musical efforts of Blake Shelton, John Rich, James Otto, the Jane Dear girls and Hunter Hayes, among others. In addition to his A&R duties at Warner Bros., Hendricks' producing efforts have been instrumental in Blake Shelton's ascent from mid-level act to bona fide star with three #1 singles, including "Hillbilly Bone," as well as two more #1s, "She Wouldn't Be Gone" (2008) and "All About Tonight" (2010). By his own tally, Hendricks has spent 73 weeks—almost a year and a half—at the top of the country charts. While not a performer or front line name that country fans recognize, they are subconscious recipients of his business acumen and music industry savvy. "I've always just had a passion to be a part of making music," Hendricks observes. "If anything, I'm more passionate about making music than I ever was. I can't wait to get up and go to work every day and find the next great song or the next great artist." As of 2011, Hendricks was Senior VP of A&R for Warner Music Nashville, where he has a primary voice in who gets signed to a recording contract and what songs they record. Hendricks resides in Brentwood, Tennessee with his wife, Teri, and his two daughters, Keely and Shaye.[3]

www.scotthendricksproduction.com

Endnotes
1. Hendricks' early life in Clinton, college years as Oklahoma State, and first work in Nashville is covered by Victoria Lee in her collection of essays published as *Distinguished Oklahomans*. (Tulsa: Touch of Heart, 2002).
2. For more insight into the period of Hendricks' appointment to the head of Capitol Nashville and the ensuing tension between the label and Garth Brooks, see Bruce Feilter, *Dreaming Out Loud: Garth Brooks, Wynonna Judd, Wade Hayes, and the Changing Face of Nashville*. (New York: Avon, 1998).
3. Some of the historical information in this essay, including the quoted remarks by Hendricks, came directly from his published at www.scotthendricks.info. For a complete discography of Hendricks' #1 hits, see www.scotthendricks.info/discography.html

Herron, John

As a member of the last incarnation of The Electric Prunes (mid-1968 through 1970), known best for their 1966 psychedelic garage classic, "I Had Too Much to Dream Last Night", John Herron (born in Elk City, Oklahoma), plays keyboards on the band's final two albums, *Release of an Oath: The Kol Nidre* (Reprise, 1968) and *Just Good Old Rock 'n' Roll* (Reprise).

According to an interview aired on WRVU, Vanderbilt University's college radio station, David Whetstone, the final vocalist and drummer The Electric Prunes, said he was in a Colorado-based band with John Herron (organ) called Climax when Whetstone received a call from a fellow musician in Denver whose manager also worked with The Electric Prunes. In order to fulfill a production contract, but with no actual members of the original band, Herron moved to California, where he recorded more or less as a session musician on the final two albums under the name of The Electric Prunes. The first recording was *Release of an Oath: The Kol Nidre*, a sprawling mess of an album arranged by David Axelrod (a former Capitol Records A&R man known for production of artists such as Herb Adderly and Lou Rawls who was hired by Warner Brothers to complete the project). The album has lyrically religious overtones, but zero liner notes to indicate who is doing what on the dated sounding tracks filled with plodding and swelling strings, blues-rock guitar solos, occasional keyboard fills and accents, and melodramatic religious pontifications.

The Electric Prunes, circa 1968, with John Herron, second from left.

Before disbanding, the "Not Really The Electric Prunes", Herron added keys to another album, *Just Good Old Rock and Roll*, re-released by Collector's Choice in 2006, and featuring songs that are every bit as bad as their titles, "Giant Sunhorse", "Thorjon", "Silver Passion Mine", and "14 Year Old Fun". Throughout the recordings, however, Herron's keyboard work is suitable for the period, yet rarely has the opportunity to rise above support status in the music's texture.

Hinder

(formed 2001 in Edmond, Jones, and Oklahoma City)

A swaggering rock group in the tradition of Aerosmith and Guns N' Roses, Hinder features way better than average rock vocal harmonies, grind-it-out rhythm arrangements, and enough swirling guitars to provide throaty singer Austin Winkler a suitable musical palate for his emotive vocal style. In live performances, the band sounds like a group of good friends who know what each other is going to say (or play) next, and unify heartily under the Hinder hard rock banner. After meeting vocalist Austin Winkler who was fronting a cover band hired to play a party for drummer Cody Hanson and guitarist Joe Garvey when they were students at the University of Central Oklahoma, the three struck up a friendship, started jamming at Hanson's house in Jones, and figured out a band name related to their frustration in finding a suitable moniker (check the first word suggested after "frustrate" in a thesaurus, and one will see "hinder"). They had their first gigs in 2001, began playing at the Samurai Sake House in Oklahoma City, and then the Blue Note as their honed their sound. The band's final formation consisted of guitarist/vocalist Garvey (from Oklahoma City), drummer Hanson (from Jones), lead vocalist Winkler (from Oklahoma City), bassist/vocalist Mike Rodden (from Oklahoma City), and guitarist Mark King (from Guymon).

In 2003 the group recorded their first independent EP, *Far From Close*, on the independent label, Brickden, which sold about 5,000 copies. Off to produce a more polished demo, labels began hearing about the band when checking on other projects at the studio in Vancouver, where Hinder was recording. The ensuing competition between Roadrunner, Atlantic, and Universal ended with the band signing to Universal, who released their first album, *Extreme Behavior*, in 2005. With four singles that charted on *Billboard*'s Hot Mainstream Rock chart, to include the massively popular swaying rock ballad, "Lips of an Angel", which also nearly crested the Hot 100 pop singles chart, lodging at #3 in 2006. As a result of triple platinum sales (three million units sold) driven largely by "Lips of Angel", Universal was able to milk the album for five singles total through 2007. That same year, the Oklahoma Music Hall of Fame honored Hinder with its Rising Star Award.

The band's second album, *Take It to the Limit* (Universal, 2008), kept the band active on *Billboard*'s Mainstream Rock Chart ("Use Me" #3, "Without You" #32, "Up All Night" #16, and "Loaded and Alone" (37), and was certified gold with 500,000 units sold, but the group did not register as solidly on the pop charts (even though they tried with "Without You", "Thing for You" and "Far From Home" in the power ballad tradition of "Lips of an Angel"). Additionally, the album sounded a little more like an 80s pop metal project than the grittier first album, perhaps owing to the dreaded sophomore slump wherein a band pours years of writing and preparation into their first album, and then has to turn around and churn out a new one in a much shorter time than took the first one to evolve. In 2010, Hinder released *All American Nightmare*, which produced two more Mainstream Rock tracks, the album's title track made it to #6 on the Mainstream Rock Chart in the early part of 2011 with swirling guitars, heavy guitar and bass rhythm riffs, quiet passages building tension for Winkler to launch into his screaming lyrical tirades, and powerful drumming by Hanson. In June, 2011 the band's second single from *All American Nightmare*, "What Ya Gonna Do" neared the Top Twenty of the Mainstream Rock chart, again looking for the success of their earlier major hit by releasing a sing-along ballad. While recapturing a moment of massive pop music awareness is always tricky, Hinder has established a loyal fan base through consistent touring, and is filling a niche for modern rock music fans who are not as interested in thinking so much as they are in having a good time, which

Hinder, 2011, (l-r): Joe Garvey, Mike Rodden, Austin Winkler, Cody Hanson, Mark King.

Hinder certainly celebrates unashamedly in their songs, along with the occasional reflection on the travails of love common to so much popular music. Touring constantly, the band released its fourth studio album in late 2012, *Welcome to the Freakshow* (Republic). Rock on dudes.

www.hindermusic.com

Hinton, Sam

(b. March 21, 1917 – d. September 10, 2009)

One of the first professional musicians to use the term *folk music* in describing his performances and claimed to know more than a 1,000 songs, singer, guitarist, accordionist, and dulcimer player Samuel Duffie Hinton was born in Tulsa, Oklahoma. His mother, Nell Duffie Hinton, was a talented musician and taught both ragtime and classical piano, while encouraging Sam to pursue music. When Sam was five years old, she took him to Jenkins Music Store in Tulsa and purchased a harmonica for him. According to Sam's mother, he was playing "Turkey in the Straw" before they left the store, and, when he was eight or nine years old, won an amateur contest on the harmonica at the Strand Theater in Tulsa, receiving two dollars for first prize. His grandfather presented Sam with a push-button diatonic accordion for his eighth birthday. During his youth Sam often sang for pleasure, usually for family and friends. He learned many folk songs from his mother who had learned them from Sam's great-grandfather, and from the time she spent as a child in Texas, where she learned several cowboy songs. Sam's father, Allan F. Hinton was interested in art, but his parents discouraged this avenue, and he became a civil engineer.

Sam was also interested in nature and devoted many hours exploring the natural environment around him, especially snakes. When Sam was about twelve years old, his family moved to Crockett, an east Texas community rich in wildlife and folklore, and from where he graduated from high school. One of the graduation gifts he received in 1929 was a copy of Carl Sandburg's *American Songbag*, a gift from his older sister Mary Jo, which was to have a tremendous influence on his musical direction as he read it from cover to cover while in college.

In 1934 Sam enrolled at Texas A&M University as a zoology major. While in college, he learned the guitar and continued to sing the songs that he had learned as a boy, what he discovered people called folk music. He supported himself during the two years at College Station working as a musician, calligrapher, scientific illustrator, sign painter, and selling snake venom to Sharp and Dohm pharmaceutical company in Pennsylvania. The venom came from sixty water moccasins that he raised as a hobby. During his sophomore year at A&M, Sam made friends with Professor J. Frank Dobie at the University of Texas-Austin, a noted folk scholar. Dr. Dobie invited Sam to do a lecture-recital of East Texas folk songs, his first professional performance, for the Texas Folklore Society.

Sam Hinton

By Hugh Foley

After two years at A&M, Sam traveled to the East coast to join his family in 1935, when his brother and sister-in-law were killed in an auto accident, which also seriously injured his mother who never fully recovered from the accident. His father had identified a better paying civil service job in the Washington, D.C. area (Riverdale, Maryland) and went to work for the U.S. Department of Interior. During the summer of 1935, Sam and his two teenage sisters, Nell and Ann, formed a group called the Texas Trio, which performed in and around the D.C. area. Sam's father promoted the trio, acting as chauffeur and was able to get them on local radio. In early 1937, he also drove them to New York City, where they auditioned for the Major Bowes Original Amateur Hour, a popular radio program during the late 1930s. Sam was also working part time as a window decorator and sign painter for a department store, as well as scientific illustrator in the Department of Herpetology at the National Museum.

On January 18, 1937 the Texas Trio won The Major Bowes Amateur Hour. The winners were expected to travel with one of the Bowes units around the country. His sisters were too young, but Sam fulfilled the requirement and toured for the next two years with various troupes under the names of Major Bowes and Ted Mack, playing in forty-six states and Canada. When the troupe completed its visit to Los Angeles, Sam dropped out and went back to U.C.L.A. as the Department of Interior had relocated his father to Los Angeles. Hinton graduated with a degree in zoology from U.C.L.A. in 1941. During the last two years of college, Sam continued to sing as a part-time job to help pay for his tuition. One of those jobs (1939-40) was a part in the musical comedy *Meet the People*, in which he worked alongside such budding stars as Nanette Fabray, Virginia O'Brien, and Doodles Weaver. While at U.C.L.A. he met and married Leslie Forster, a violinist and soloist with the university's *a capella* choir, who taught Sam the more classical side of music.

After gaining his degree, Sam worked for three years as director of the Desert Museum in nearby Palm Springs, California. In 1944 he served as editor-illustrator for the University of California, Division of War Research, in San Diego, and worked there through the end of World War II. He then took a position as curator with the famed Scripps Institution of Oceanography at the University of California in San Diego. While there, he taught courses in music, folklore, geography, and biology for the University of California extension service. He was also a lecturer in folklore in the University of California-San Diego Department of Literature. In 1965 he was appointed as assistant director of Relations with Schools at U.C.S.D. Two years later, he became associate director, and remained in that position until his retirement in 1980.

While in the D.C. area in the mid-1930s, Sam visited the Library of Congress and met Dr. John Lomax and his son Alan. Alan suggested at the time that Sam record some of his East Texas folk songs, but it was not until some ten years later, while Sam was in Washington on business that he approached Dr. Duncan Enrich, who had become the curator of the Archive of Folk Song at the Library of Congress. Thus, in 1947 Sam made his first recording for the Library of Congress Archive of American Folk Song, *Buffalo Boy and the Barnyard Song*, an album of Anglo-Irish songs and ballads. On the recordings Sam played a steel stringed Washburn guitar. Three years later, Hinton made his first commercial recording, a 78-rpm single, "Old Man Atom" (later known as "Talking Atomic Blues") for Columbia Records. It became his most requested number and was later covered by The Weavers and several other folk groups. He also sang it at the Newport Folk Festival on many occasions. In 1952, he teamed with Ben Cruz, a singer of Spanish and Mexican folk songs, to record an album on the Bowmar label, *Folk Songs of California and the Old West*.

Sam moved to the Decca label in the early 1950s to record several children's folk songs in their Children's Series including "The Barnyard Song", "Country Critters", "The Frog Song", and "The Greatest Sound Around". He participated in a two-record album, *How the West Was Won*, in which he helped Alan Lomax and Si Rady select the songs, write the liner notes, and sang nine of the songs. Other luminaries to record on this RCA album included Bing Crosby, Rosemary Clooney, Jimmy Driftwood, and the Salt Lake City Mormon Tabernacle Choir. Continuing his relationship with Decca, Sam recorded three more albums in the 1950s, including *Singing Across the Land* (1955), *A Family Tree of Folk Songs* (1956), and *The Real McCoy* (1957).

In the 1960s Sam was featured on several albums, including *American Folk Songs and Balladeers* (1964), *Newport Folk Festival, 1963* (performed "Barnyard Song" and "Arkansas Traveler"), *The Songs of Men: All Sorts and Kinds* (1961), *Whoever Shall Have Some Peanuts* (1961), *The Wandering Folksong* (1966), and *I'll Sing You a Story: Folk Ballads for the Young* (1972). The latter four collections appeared on Folkways Records in association with his good friend, Moe Asch. The Folkways recordings have all been reissued under the Smithsonian/Folkways series of compact discs. Finally, in 1976, Sam recorded *Cowboy Songs* for the National Geographic Society.

After his retirement in 1980, Sam devoted full time to performing, particularly to schoolchildren in the San Diego area. His programs, such as "Old Songs for Young Folks" and "Singing Through History," were presented to more than one million children over a sixty-year span. He continued actively in folk music circles, including performances at the Newport Folk Festival, Berkeley Folk Festival, and Topanga Folk Festival, service on the Board of Directors of *Sing Out: The Topical Folk Song Magazine*, founding member of the San Diego Folk Song Society, anchorperson for National Public Radio's coverage of the Smithsonian Festival of American Folklife in Washington, D.C., and host of a thirteen-part series on folk music for the National Education Television network.[1] The 2002 Sam Hinton Folk Heritage Festival, held in La Jolla, California, featured Sam at age eighty-five as one of its performers in what appears to be his final public performance.

Endnote

1. Much of the biographical material in this essay is summarized from liner notes included in the CD booklet published with *Sam Hinton: The Library of Congress Recordings, Marcy 25, 1947* (Bear Family, 1999). Additional notes were made from the first-hand account of Sam's musical career, as he discusses it in the oral history interview archived at www.sandiegohistory.org/audio/hinton.

Hobbs, Becky

(b. January 24, 1950)

An extremely prolific songwriter of country music, Becky Hobbs has composed hits for such luminaries as Alabama, Emmylou Harris, Moe Bandy, George Jones, Glen Campbell, John Anderson, Janie Fricke, Shelly West, Helen Reddy, and Loretta Lynn. Born Rebecca Ann Hobbs in Bartlesville, Oklahoma, she began writing songs and playing piano before she was ten years old. Bill Hobbs, her father, was a violinist and loved Big Band music, while her mother preferred country music. By fourteen, Becky was playing the guitar and writing protest songs, influenced by Bob Dylan, and formed a folk duo with her friend, Beth Morrison. While in high school, she formed her first all-female band, The Four Faces of Eve, as age fifteen. As a student at the University of Tulsa, she performed in miniskirts and go-go boots in her second all-female band, The Sir Prize Package.

By 1971, Becky had moved to Baton Rouge, Louisiana, where she was performing with a bar band called Swamp Fox. The band then settled in Los Angeles and Becky remained with the group until 1973, when she began to write songs on a serious basis. Signing with MCA Records, she released her first album, *Becky Hobbs*, in 1974. Canadian vocalist Helen Reddy heard the album and recorded four of Becky's compositions, "I'll Be Your Audience", "I Don't Know Why I Love that Guy", "I Can't Say Goodbye to You", and "Long Distance Love". Hobbs then moved to Nashville and recorded two albums for the Tatoo label, *From the Heartland* (1975) and *Everyday* (1977). She also began to write songs for Al Gallico, who was considered one of the top country music independent song publishers in Nashville at the time. Gallico introduced Becky to Jerry Kennedy, who signed her to a Mercury Records contract. In 1978, she recorded "The More I Get the More I Want", which reached the Top 100 and gave her first feel of recording success. She followed with a second single, "I Can't Say Goodbye to You", which made the Top 50, and won the American Song Festival Award. She then cut three more singles with limited success. During the 1980s, Becky continued to write with her songs recorded by Lacy J. Dalton ("Feedin' the Fire"), John Anderson ("Look What Followed Me Home"), and the Tennessee Valley Boys ("Lo and Behold").

In 1983, Becky teamed with Moe Bandy for a Top 10 hit, "Let's Get Over Them Together", and during the next two years, she had two hit singles for Liberty/EMI-America, "Oklahoma Heart" and "Hottest 'Ex' in Texas". In 1984, Loretta Lynn and George Jones recorded Becky's "We Sure Made Good Love", to be included on Jones' *Ladies Choice* album.

1985 was a watershed year for Hobbs, starting with the Alabama recording "I Want to Know You Before We Make Love", released on the group's quadruple-platinum album (four million units sold), *Forty Hour Week*. Co-written with Candy Parton, the song had already gone #1 with Conway Twitty. Alabama also recorded Becky's "Christmas Memories" for their Christmas album, which was certified double platinum (two million units sold). Moe Bandy and Joe Stampley recorded Becky's "Still on a Roll", and Shelly West released two more of Becky's compositions, "I'll Dance the Two Step" and "How It All Went Wrong". Finally, Becky was invited to join the Grand Ole Opry cast.

Two years later, Becky's songs were picked up by several more country music artists, including Glen Campbell and Emmylou Harris ("You Are") and Moe Bandy ("Rodeo Song"). The Campbell-Harris duet was nominated for a GRAMMY.

In 1988, Becky released one of her best albums, *All Keyed Up,* originally on the MTM label, but her contract and album were picked up by RCA after MTM's demise. It included three hit singles, "Jones on the Jukebox", recognized widely as one of the best musical tributes to George Jones, "Are There Any More Like You", and "Do You Feel the Same Way Too". Two years later, she released "Talk Back Tremblin' Lips", an old Ernest Ashworth hit, on the Curb label, but it did not fare well on the charts.

Becky Hobbs

In 1992, "The Beckaroo," a nickname bestowed upon her by friends, and her band,

The Heartthrobs, toured Africa as part of the U.S. Government Arts America, performing in nine countries. Returning to the studio in 1994, Becky released *The Boots I Came to Town In* on Intersound, which included "Pale Moon", "Mama's Green Eyes (And Daddy's Wild Hair)", and her own version of "Angels Among Us", previously recorded by Alabama, which was then picked up by two television programs with angels as their main theme. She was named *Cashbox* magazine's Independent Country Music Female Artist of the Year for 1994, and additional honors include a BMI Performance Award for "I Want to Know You Before We Make Love", a Gold Album for Helen Reddy's *Live at the Palladium* recording, and the Most Promising Act of 1989 by the British Academy of Country Music. For her spritely performances, Becky earned the title "Das Energie Bundel" for her shows in Switzerland.

In 1996, Becky married Duane Sciacqua, guitarist who played with Glenn Frey, formerly of The Eagles. Duane produced Becky's 1998 album, *From Oklahoma With Love* with all tracks written by Becky, including "Yellow Pages Under Blue", "God's Gift to This Woman", and "Rockin' and Rollin' and Raisin' Hell", and released on Hobbs' record label, Beckaroo. She released another album of songs all written or co-written by her in 2004, *Songs from the Road of Life* (Beckaroo). Often referred to and promoted as the "female Jerry Lee Lewis," Becky's style has been described as a fusion of hard-hitting honky-tonk songs with an electrifying rockabilly sound. An enrolled Cherokee and great grand-daughter of the somewhat controversial Cherokee woman leader, Mary Ward, Becky has also recorded a three-song EP, *Let There Be Peace: Tribute to Mary Ward, Beloved Woman of the Cherokee*. The inspiration to tell Mary Ward's complete story urged Becky to write a full musical about Ward, with seventeen songs depicting key moments in Nancy Ward's life, which she hoped would be produced by 2011, initially somewhere in the Cherokee Nation in Oklahoma. The songs for the musical were released by Becky in 2011 on the album *Nanyehi: Beloved Woman of the Cherokees* (Beckaroo).

www.beckyhobbs.com

Hockensmith, Hadley

(b. November 14, 1949)

A lead guitarist with a deft blues feel and who has toured with Neil Diamond for twenty-seven years as of 2011, Hadley Hockensmith was born in Atlanta while his father was stationed there in the Air Force. He learned to play the basic chords of the guitar from his dad, who preferred country and western, and began playing in a junior high band with friends. Before too long he was introduced to the blues, which he preferred to country, and he began traveling to Edmond on weekends where he played with older and more experienced musicians in after-hours clubs, and played with other bands around Oklahoma City at live gigs and in recordings at places like Gene Sullivan's studio in Oklahoma City. Hadley continued playing multiple gigs in his mid-teens, to include a live performance with the Righteous Brothers when they were touring with their massive hit, "You've Lost That Loving Feeling", and needed a good guitarist, a position for which Hadley came highly recommended. After playing in a variety of blues bands around Oklahoma and Dallas, in 1978 he and his wife, Deby, Hadley moved to Los Angeles for the promise of work by friends who were already in California working in the Christian music industry.

Upon arrival in L.A., he began working studio sessions and meeting numerous excellent musicians and songwriters. During his esteemed career, Hadley has played live or recorded with Andre Crouch, David Gates, America, Michael McDonald, Jeff Beck, Gordon Lightfoot, Ray Charles, Johnny Rivers, Glen Campbell, and, ultimately, Neil Diamond. In the early 1980s, Hockensmith began working with Ron Tutt, a drummer known for his 1970s work with Elvis Presley, who had begun working with Neil Diamond on tour, but was still doing various recording sessions where he met Hadley. When Diamond needed a touring guitar player in 1982, Tutt recommended Hockensmith who got the job, staying with Diamond until the present day, now totaling twenty-seven years of playing live on stage around the world. In addition to his work with Diamond, Hadley was a member of a jazz fusion group, Koinonia, from 1981 through 1988, with whom he recorded three albums, and has released one album of his own solo guitar, which found favor with jazz and new age radio programs in the U.S., Canada, and Europe.

Hadley Hockensmith on stage as part of Neil Diamond's band, 2010.

Source
Video interview with Hadley Hockensmith by Jeff Moore and Larry O'Dell from the Oklahoma Historical Society, recorded , 2010.

Holly, Doyle
(b. June 30, 1936 – d. January 13, 2007)

As bass guitarist, harmony singer, comedian, and soloist for Buck Owens' Buckaroos from 1963 to 1970, Doyle Floyd Hendricks was born in Perkins, Oklahoma, a community of around 2,000 residents located south of Stillwater. Doyle learned the bass guitar at an early age, and formed a band with his older brothers, which performed at rodeos. As a child, his musical influences included Bob Wills, Tommy Duncan, and Ernest Tubb, and considered the Texas Playboys the best band ever assembled. As a teenager, he worked in the Kansas, Oklahoma, and California oil fields. Following high school graduation, he joined the U.S. Army and was stationed in Okinawa and Japan. After his four-year stint in the armed services, he returned to the oilfields around Bakersfield, California, where he performed on a part time basis with Johnny Burnette's band, alongside Fuzzy Owen and Merle Haggard, played bass for Jimmy Wakely, and worked for Joe and Rosalee Maphis.

Doyle joined Buck Owens and the Buckaroos in 1963. During his seven-year career with the group, he played bass guitar and sang on some nine albums with Owens, including *I've Got a Tiger by the Tail* (1965) and *Carnegie Hall Live Concert* (1966). On the former album, Doyle sings a fine rendition of "Streets of Laredo", and on the latter, he adds "Fun 'N' Games with Don (Rich) and Doyle." He also toured the U.S., Canada and Europe with the group, performing at such venues as the White House and the Palladium in London. After leaving the Buckaroos in 1970, Doyle formed his own band, the Vanishing Breed. Two years later, he signed a recording contract with the Barnaby label for which he cut two albums, *Doyle Holly* (1973) and *Just Another Cowboy Song* (1974). In 1972, Doyle was named Bass Player of the Year by the ACM, considered one of the top session men in Nashville. During the 1970s, Holly had two minor hits "Queen of the Silver Dollar" (Top 30), "Lila" (Top 20), and several other barely noticed, but well-titled, releases "Lord How Long Has This Been Going On", "A Rainbow in My Hand", "Woman Truck Drivin' Fool", "I'll Be All Right Tomorrow". His tune, "Richard and the Cadillac Kings" garnered him an ASCAP award.

Doyle Holly

Holly appeared on the Grand Ole Opry and the Opry Gospel Show, as well as on several televisions shows, including *Dean Martin Presents*, *Music Country USA*, *Hee Haw*, and *Nashville Now*. Doyle and his band have opened for numerous artists, such as Conway Twitty, The Whites, Gene Watson, and Randy Travis. Doyle also served on the Board of Directors of R.O.P.E. (Reunion of Professional Entertainers), an organization devoted to artists who have remained in the music business for more than twenty-five years. He was also honored in 1980 with induction into the Walkway of Stars at the Country Music Hall of Fame in Nashville.

In the early 1990s, Doyle left country music, and opened Doyle Holly's Music Store in Hendersonville, Tennessee. He also drove a customized entertainer bus, for stars such as Shania Twain. Several Buck Owens and the Buckaroos albums were released in the 1990s, including *The Buck Owens Collection* (1992) and *The Very Best of Buck Owens, Vols. 1 and 2* (1994), which include Holly playing the bass guitar. In 2002, OMS Records released *Together Again*, a bluegrass-oriented tribute to Buck Owens that features all the living Buckaroos, including Tom Brumley, Willy Cantu, and Holly. He died January 13, 2007 in Tennessee, and requested no services be held, only that everyone celebrate his life in their own way.

www.doyleholly.com

Mike Hosty/Hosty Duo
(formed roughly, but righteously, in Norman, OK, about 1994)

Guitarist extraordinaire, songwriter of many insights, droll but wry vocalist, pedal bass player, one-man-band drummer, and between-song-patter-and-joke specialist, Mike Hosty, has been playing bars and multiple genre events around Oklahoma City since 1990. Around 1994, he teamed up with drummer Mike Byars (b. Noble, 12/15/69) to form the Hosty Duo, one of Oklahoma's most cherished contemporary live music acts for fans of blues, rock, hilarious songs that often reference the state, and music that can bound from polka and disco to country and right back to rock in the span of two-minute Hosty spiel in

Mike Hosty in Stillwater, 2011

between tunes during a show. While he has received some national and regional attention (a song made it on Jimmy Kimmel, his "Molokai Cowboy" is a hit in Hawaii, and his "Oklahoma Breakdown" notched Stoney LaRue a #1 spot on the Texas Music Chart for April, 2007 – and becoming that chart's #1 song for the year), Mike Hosty toils on a constant basis through the college towns and other appreciative spots he has developed through consistent touring in Texas, Arkansas, Oklahoma, and Colorado.

Often, Hosty tours with Byars (noted as Tic Tac) on Hosty albums, who provides a steady, hypnotic, beat on a stripped down kit of kick drum, snare, high hat, and ride cymbal. Byars is ready to take any turn with Hosty, able to provide a perfectly metered disco beat, a boom-chuck cowboy beat, a hard-driving blues-rock pulse, or the tougher rhythms of off-beat polka or reggae, not to mention the often-needed rim shot to accent Hosty jokes. When Byars is not present, Hosty keeps his foot-pedal bass in the truck and unpacks his own one-man band drum set, with kick, snare, hat, and tambourine all controlled by Hosty as he keeps time for himself. Both are superbly entertaining versions of Hosty-time, revered by the fans who go to shows, calling out the names of their favorite songs, and singing along loudly to choruses (verses often change on the spot). The most regular fans of Hosty's antics show up like they are on a pilgrimage every Sunday night for his long-time weekly performances at The Deli, in Norman.

Hosty's albums are musical journeys through corn mazes of the wildly imaginative singer/songwriter's mind and unique lens through which he views society, especially in Oklahoma. Mostly available from a cardboard box that sits at the side of the stage at Hosty shows, or his website, there are at least eight Hosty CDs released independently by himself with investments by Discover Card. While he doesn't do as many of the songs from his first anthology (1992 to 1996), the second anthology *Un Hombre Malo* is a perfect place to begin getting to know his guitar work and lyrical adeptness on songs such as "Mr. T", "U, Me and B.E.T.", "Corndog", "James Brown", and "Chicken Bone 99". The songs pack an added punch as recorded by Trent Bell at Bell Labs in Norman. Recorded by the duo, and just released on their name, Hosty Duo, the 2003 brown bag wrapper CD contains his clever song about being a married man working in bars all the time, "Married Man", crowd favorites "Fraidy Hole" (the Oklahoma tornado song), "Fried Pie", and the now legendary "Oklahoma Breakdown", a song that encapsulates a novel of Oklahoma ethos in its 4:46 length. Stoney LaRue liked it so much he made a staple of his Texas shows, causing some Texas fans to accost Hosty south of the Red River and confront

Hosty Duo dummer Mike Byars

him as to why he's doing Stoney's song. In any case, the song's slide guitar vibe, lyrical focus on forbidden (or at least past curfew) love down by the river bed in the back of a friend's truck endears it to many fans. Hosty's other 2003 disc, a sort-of stab at a country music album that starts laughing at itself halfway through, preserves live tracks from a Phoenix, Arizona show of 2002, and the standard crowd call outs "Truck Stop Shower Stall" and "Johnny Cash".

Hosty released two live discs in 2006 with many of his best-known songs as fans are used to hearing them, in a live environment, along with some new favorites developed to that point, "Linda Cavanaugh", about an unusual affinity for an Oklahoma City television news personality, "Spamoramathon", and "Disco Truck/Pole". In 2008, he continued the disheveled guitar comedy with "Eat Yer Mac & Chees", "Pterodactyl", "Please Don't Make Me Love You", and, finally, a song titled after one of his more recognizable catch phrases when a joke between songs fall flat or just get missed due to general bar noise, "Tough Crowd". With a quick wit as close to Groucho Marx as you might find alive today, Mike Hosty's songs are intrinsically Oklahoman yet transcend their local connections into broad-based and humorous insights into society, his in-between song banter and jokes with instrumental examples are tear-inducing funny, and his musical skill is parallel to any others in the blues-rock world playing the stages of the Oklahoma in the current era. Local publications agree, as *Oklahoma Magazine* voted Hosty Duo one of "Oklahoma's Best Bands in 2010" after being the magazine's "Best Band" in 2009; the *Oklahoma City Gazette* voted Hosty 2010's "Best Singer Songwriter"; and in 2012 Hosty was voted "Best Musician" by the *Norman Transcript*. National prominence has escaped Hosty for the most part, except getting mentioned on the *Tonight Show with Jay Leno* in the "Dumb Ads" segment for a bar called Taboma that promoted a show with the ad, "Mike Hosty Plays With Himself." Also in 2012, Hosty released *Hosty Duo II* (HossTone Music), probably the most subtle of all his discs without as much of the humorous calamity as others. *Hosty Duo II* has a few more love songs than usual, along with the usual varied guitar textures and danceable rhythms that make Hosty Duo such a fun band for so many "Hostyfarians" throughout the mid and southwest. The disc closes out with a trademark "Hosty talker" where Mike tells a story of one of the many highways he has traveled many times crisscrossing the region as one of the most entertaining acts that not enough people know about. Whether it's the duo when just the two guys can get a whole house moving, or by himself when fans eagerly shout out request for their favorite Hosty obscurities, every Oklahoma music fan should see one or both at least one time. In 2013, Hosty continued fulfilling a slew of regional dates, and promoting his teen girl group, The Sopapillas, on his own independent label.

Mike Hosty's one-man band, Stillwater, 2011.

www.hosty.com

By Hugh Foley / 367

Hubbard, Ray Wylie

(b. November 13, 1946)

Hubbard is best known for his early classic "Up Against the Wall, Redneck Mother," which became the impromptu rallying call for the "outlaw country" rebellion against the Nashville Sound of the 1970s. Born in Soper, Oklahoma, a small town of about 500 residents west of Hugo in Choctaw County, singer-songwriter-guitarist Hubbard and his family moved during the mid-1950s to Oak Cliff near Dallas where his father served as high school principal. During high school years at Adamson High School, which also produced such future stars as B.W. Stephenson ("My Maria") and Steve Fromholz ("Hondo's Song"), he learned the guitar and became acquainted with Michael Martin Murphey. The two formed a folk duo that performed in a coffee house, The Rubaiyat, where he met the legendary Ramblin' Jack Elliott and "folkie" newcomer Jerry Jeff Walker. Following high school, he attended the University of Texas-Arlington and North Texas State University, where he was an English major. After leaving college, he assembled several folk groups, including The Coachmen, Three Faces West, and Texas Fever. While traveling the folk music circuit, Hubbard performed at such venues as The Bottom Line in New York City and Freight and Salvage in Berkeley.

Hubbard then moved to Red River, New Mexico, and performed in his own club, The Outpost, where he renewed friendships with Walker, who sold him a 1938 Roy Smeck Stage Deluxe guitar complete with an angel painted on the side. He performed at the first Kerrville Folk Festival in 1972, as well as other noted folk music festivals held in Napa Valley, Mariposa, Newport, and Philadelphia. Upon his return to the Dallas area in the early 1970s, Hubbard spent most of his time writing and performing with Walker, and in 1973 Walker recorded Hubbard's notable anthem for the progressive country music movement in Austin, "Up Against the Wall, Redneck Mother", on his highly acclaimed Viva Terlingua album. The album was a phenomenal success and brought Hubbard instant cult status within the progressive country community. About the same time, Hubbard formed a back-up band he dubbed The Cowboy Twinkies, considered by many the first "cowpunk" band, which included fellow Oklahoman Terry "Buffalo" Ware, guitarist who played with Hubbard from 1972 to 1978 and again from 1986 to 1997. The band's repertoire included an array of music forms ranging from Merle Haggard to Led Zeppelin.

In 1975, Hubbard's band released a self-titled debut album, Ray Wylie Hubbard and the Cowboy Twinkies, for Warner Brothers' Reprise label. The album sold poorly and resulted in the break up of the band. Hubbard did not reappear again until 1978 when he recorded his debut solo album, Off the Wall, on the Willie Nelson short-lived label, Lone Star, which included his own rendition of

Ray Wylie Hubbard

"Redneck Mother" as well as "Bittersweet Funky Tuesday" and "Freeway Church of Christ". A year later, Hubbard began performing with Jerry Jeff Walker's old back-up band (Lost Gonzo Band), which he renamed the Ray Wylie Hubbard Band. During the early 1980s, Hubbard released two live albums, Caught in the Act (Waterloo), recorded at the Soap Creek Saloon in Austin, and Something About the Night (Renegade), which featured Walker and a different back-up band, Bugs Henderson Trio. Although Hubbard made news headlines in 1987 when his 1954 Martin guitar was stolen from a pawn shop in Dallas, he did not record again until 1992 when Lost Train of Thought was released by his own record label, Misery Loves Company. The 1992 release included a duet with Willie Nelson on "These Eyes" as well as several other Hubbard songs such as "When She Sang Amazing Grace". Loco Gringo's Lament (Dejadisc) followed in 1995. Produced by the veteran Lloyd Maines, father of the Dixie Chicks' Natalie Maines, it received rave reviews from such publications as Rolling Stone magazine. Two years later, Hubbard recorded Dangerous Spirits (Philo), which included guest artists Lucinda Williams and Tony Joe White. Hubbard returned with Crusades of the Restless Nights in 1999, Live at Cibelo Creek Country Club in 2000, and Eternal and Lowdown in 2001, all on the Philo label. These albums reflect Hubbard's turbulent lifestyle and flair for storytelling. After a period of substance abuse in his early career,

Hubbard has remained sober in the 1990s, and is a strong supporter of charities, including benefit performances for Vietnam Veterans and Clown Ministry, an agency that provides clowns for terminally ill children. In 2003, Hubbard's album, Growl, displayed a return to roots, of sorts. Aside from the classic, experienced take on the music industry on "Rock and Roll is a Vicious Game", the album is heavy on blues constructs, themes, and instrumentations, and includes what may be Ray Wylie's next anthem for musicians south of the Red River, "Screw You, We're From Texas", which Ray Wylie points out in the liner notes of the album, "is not screw you, Oklahoma or Arkansas or any other state. It's screw you, people who don't appreciate cool music, because we're from Texas, and this is the kind of music we do." Hubbard has continued exploring the dark myths disguised as truths in Southern, rural, and swampy environments of the South and southwest. His music is filled with ragged percussion, searing blues licks, and his own world-weary insight, often talking as much as singing. His last album for Rounder, Delirium Tremolos (2005), exhibited these musical and lyrical themes in "This Mornin' I am Born Again", "Roll and I Tumble", "Cooler-n-Hell", and "Choctaw Bingo". His 2006 disc for Sustain Records, Snake Farm, stumbled half-blind down many of the same mossy and dark paths with "Snake Farm", "Mother Hubbard's Blues", "Life and Die Rock and Roll" and "Resurrection". His 2010 disc, A. Enlightenment B. Endarkenment featured more of the previously mentioned rattletrap talking blues, "Whoop and Hollar", "Every Day is the Day of the Dead", "Pots and Pans", and "Down Home Country Blues". Of particular note was a song co-written with Houston troubadour/smart aleck, Hayes Carll, on a splendid homage to the woman who inspires a singer-songwriter to pick up a pen again, "Drunken Poet's Dream". In 2012, Hubbard released The Grifter's Hymnal, with the absolutely timeless "Mother Blues," as personal a song a singer/songwriter could every pull off without sounding too sentimental. Not settling for anything pretty or trite, The Grifter's Hymnal is full of the churning blues, sardonic lyrics, and rapier wit that has fans looking forward to seeing him perform and record some more. Hubbard was booked solidly across the U.S. through December, 2013.

www.raywylie.com

Huff, Charlie

A fairly obscure rockabilly artist, Charlie Huff is an Oklahoma singer, songwriter, and guitarist who recorded more than forty of his own songs between 1947 and roughly 1958. In 1947, Huff recorded in Los Angeles "Oklahoma's Own Cowboy Singer", accompanying himself on guitar as a solo act on tunes such as "Conversation with a Mule", "Maybe Next Week Sometime", "Bad Brahma Bull", "Stuck Up Blues", and "Sad Sack". Huff recorded for 4 Star, North Star, his own Huff Records, and Arlo Records. He may have recorded some of his records at KBYE Radio in Oklahoma City, where he was also known as Cowboy Huff.

Additional Huff titles include "High Hat Blues", "They Talked About Peace", "I'm Sure You Belong To Me" and "No Two-Timin' Me". Huff's records are considered collectibles, and are valued especially by European rockabilly enthusiasts. The Oklahoma Historical Society has eight recordings of Huff in its archives (OHS-1004), apparently recorded circa July, 1953 in Oklahoma City as Charlie Huff and His Sons of the Plains featuring twin bass fiddle accompaniment on the recording by two unknown players.

Charlie Huff, circa 1950s

Hughes, Billy

(b. September 14, 1908 – d. May 6, 1995)

Composer of "Tennessee Saturday Night", a #1 hit for Red Foley, as well as songwriter for such notables as Eddy Arnold, Ernest Tubb, and Spade Cooley, singer, fiddler, and songwriter Everette Ishmael "Billy" Hughes was born in Sallisaw, Oklahoma, an eastern Oklahoma community of roughly 7,000 population, near the Arkansas border. He was first noticed as a fiddler and singer with "Pop" Moore in Oklahoma City, and later performed with Johnny Bond in the same city.

In 1938, Hughes moved to southern California, where he performed at a Los Angeles club called Murphy's with his band, the Pals of the Pecos. To record his band, he formed his own label, Fargo Records. He also recorded for several labels, including Four Star, King, Mutual, in which he displayed an exceptional voice for western swing and blues music. In addition to "Tennessee Saturday Night", Billy composed such songs as "Rose of the Alamo", and several novelty songs ripe with double entendre, such as "Take Your Hands Off of It", and "Stop That Stuff" while verging on social commentary with his "Atomic Sermon". While in California, Billy played fiddle and wrote songs for Jack Guthrie and sang on some of Luke Wills' recordings.

Additional recording artists who used Hughes' songs include a wide range of vocalists such as Rosalie Allen, Tex Williams, Jerry Lee Lewis, Hank Locklin, Ella Mae Morse, and Pat Boone. Finally, his talents as a fiddler and vocalist were demonstrated on two of pop singer Barry Manilow's recordings in the early 1990s, just before Hughes died in 1995.

370 / *Oklahoma Music Guide II*

Iowa Tribe of Oklahoma

As a member of the Siouian linguistic family, the Iowa pronounce the tribal term for which they are known as "Ioway" and are located today primarily in two geographic areas: southern Payne County, Oklahoma (near Perkins, OK), and on the border area of northeast Kansas (Brown County) and southeast Nebraska (Richardson County). The tribal term *Ayavois*, roughly translated as "marrow", is the name for which the tribe was known by French traders, and the source of the state of Iowa's name. The people call themselves *Bah-kho-je*, a term deriving from their relatives, the **Otoe-Missouria**, with whom the Iowa share very similar language and cultural traditions. According to Iowa tribal oral history, "when the Otoe saw our village in the winter it was covered with gray snow from the fire-smoked snow, and in the Ioway language they called us BAH-KHO-JE, (Snow Grey)." Archaeologists surmise the Iowas are descended from the agricultural Oneota people of the Woodland culture, and became allies with the Winnebago, later developing some aspects of Plains life when they acquired the horse about 1800.[1] Before that happened however, somewhere in the mist of ancient history, a group separated from the Winnebago and traveled south toward the Iowa River, and separated again. The group that remained near the Mississippi became the Iowa, and the other group became the Otoe and Missouria Tribes, which is why one often learns about Iowa history and language through Otoe-Missouria sources, and vice-versa.[2] A series of migrations led the Iowa through present-day Illinois where they lived along the Upper Iowa River, then in Iowa at what is now known as Council Bluffs. They also are known to have been in southern Minnesota, where they were first observed at the mouth of Blue Earth River by the French explorer Le Sueur in 1701.

Along with early eighteenth century recognition for agriculture, the Iowa were also known for their skills in making pipes out of the pipestone quarries about 130 miles west of Blue Earth. The Iowa people were skilled in dressing buffalo skins and pelts which encouraged their early trade with the French. After acquiring horses, the tribe developed some aspects of Plains Indian life (such as the war bonnet that is part of their modern tribal seal), and began vying for control of more territory with the Dakota, Sauk, and Fox, in order to continue hunting trading with the French. This interaction with the French also accelerated the tribe's assimilation into a European lifestyle. By 1824, the Iowa ceded all of their lands in Iowa and Missouri to the U.S. and were forced onto a reservation in Kansas they would share with the Sac and Fox. Conditions were terrible, however, and in 1838 some members of the Iowa moved on to Indian Territory where they settled with their former enemies, now friends, the Sac and Fox. When allotment of tribal lands in Kansas as proposed in 1876, even more Iowa people moved south to Indian Territory.

In 1883, the U.S. government provided the Iowa with their own reservation in Indian Territory, now Oklahoma. The reservation placed them directly west of the Sac and Fox, north of the Kickapoo, and not far from their ancient relatives, the Otoe-Missouria. As with all Indian lands in Oklahoma, however, once individual Iowa tribal members received allotments in 1890, the remaining lands were opened for white settlement in the famous Oklahoma land runs, and the Iowa people began the 20th century trudge through American history in which they suffered similar fates to other tribes: discouragement by governmental authorities of practicing ceremonies and their accompanying music, Christianization, the Boarding School movement in which they were prevented from speaking their tribal language, then the opportunity to reorganize under the Oklahoma Indian Welfare Act of 1936.

Iowa people who remained in Kansas ultimately coalesced into the Iowa Tribe of Kansas and Nebraska under the Indian Reorganization Act of 1934, adopting a constitution and bylaws in 1978. Currently, the Iowa in Kansas and Nebraska raises cattle, operates a grain-processing center, and engages in gaming, as well as providing social and security services for its people. Iowa people in Oklahoma reorganized under the Oklahoma Indian Welfare Act of 1936, forming a constitution and bylaws as the Iowa Nation of Oklahoma in 1937.[3]

With regard to Iowa music, the tribe suffered the same cultural oppression as all other American Indians starting in 1889 with Court of Indian Offenses that made the participation in traditional ceremonies illegal (which by nature included music of the most tribally specific type). Traditional Iowa music is not well-known by scholars or the usual archives of traditional American music, such as Indiana University at Bloomington's Archives of Traditional Music, nor the Smithsonian Institution. Native American history author, Barry Pritzker, indicates the Iowa practiced a version of the "Grand Medicine Dance", also known to other Woodland Tribes, but details no particular music resulting from his research.[4] The tribe's interaction with Christian missionaries and obvious acceptance of those religious tenets is indicated by an 1843 Iowa Hymnal, preserving both the phonetics and some phraseology of the Iowa language, as well as a firm date with which to begin exploring Christian music within the Iowa tribe. This acceptance of Christianity played an important part in the development of Iowa music and religion as some Iowa people became members of the **Native American Church**, the pan-Indian religion that merged Christianity with Peyote-ism (to varying degrees depending on the tribe) at the end of the 19th century, and which appealed to many Native people, especially on the Plains and in the southwest who were discouraged from practicing their ancient ceremonial ways in the late 19th century. Within a Christian context or pre-text, the Native American Church provides a traditional American Indian religious format (inside a tipi, around a fire, with singing and praying all night for the purposes of healing, comfort, and meditative reflection).[5] Ceremonies typically last from about 9 p.m. on a Friday or Saturday night through Sunday morning, during which time music is performed almost throughout except during specifically set breaks for prayer and/or personal expressions. Native American Church songs are typified by a fast-paced drumming on a small "kettle-sized" water drum, a hand rattle, usually made of a gourd filled with pebbles, played in time with the drum, and lyrics with either literal or symbolic meaning, depending on whether or not words or "vocables" are used.[6] As with other tribes who "put down" their traditional religions (such as the Kiowa and their Sun

Dance), American Indian tribal people infused Native American Church songs with their tribal language and worldview, and the Iowa were no exception. A relatively early adherent to the Native American Church outside of its origins in Oklahoma with the Comanche and Kiowa, Joseph Springer is probably the first Iowa Peyotist, likely receiving the ceremony from none other than from **Comanche** leader, Quanah Parker, around 1879. And, because of many tribal members' acceptance of Christianity as far back as the 1840s (per the date of the hymnal), the Iowa were also serious about the Christian element of the church, similar to their Otoe relatives, and Springer was their leader.[7] Also well respected among leaders of the Native American Church in Oklahoma, Springer spoke to the Oklahoma legislature in 1908 to defend the religion, along with Quanah Parker. As a result, the Iowa developed a strong body of Native American Church music, alongside that of the Otoe-Missouria.[8] Given this history, one should not be surprised to find Native American Church songs and recordings to be the primary contribution of Iowa musicians to the catalogue of world music.

The first "release" of Iowa music appears as a tribal library project, a 1967 recording, *BAH KHO JE Prayer Songs*, consisting of 16 Native American Church Prayer Songs with Ioway, Otoe, and Pawnee singers, recorded in Perkins, Oklahoma, circa 1967, and available only through the Iowa Tribal Library. Further confirmation of the close cultural and tribal kinship between the Otoe and Iowa people, as well as neighboring Pawnee and Sac & Fox tribes, can be determined by the list of the singers on the cassette-only release: Howard (Ioway) and Ruth (Sac & Fox) Springer, Franklin (Iowa) and Martha (Otoe) Murray, Ned and Maggie BigSoldier (Ioway), JoRita BigSoldier (Ioway), Dan Murray (Ioway), Alice Sine (Ioway), Esther (Otoe/Ioway) and Ezra Fields (Pawnee), Elsie (Ioway) and Mark (Otoe) Whitehorn, Art and Angeline Lightfoot (Otoe), and Rev. John and Mrs. Stoneroad (Otoe/Pawnee). The most notable Iowa singer at the turn of the 21st century was Billy McClellan, Sr., of Sac and Fox, Otoe, and Iowa descent (b. 5/15/1954 – d. 9/3/2004), who recorded five albums of Native American Church songs. A member of the Iowa Chapter of the Native American Church, McClellan's first two albums, *Songs of the Native American Church Volumes I and II*, were issued on cassette only through the Oklahoma-based Indian Sounds label by long-time American Indian music entrepreneur, Millard Clark. Subsequently, McClellan's third album was issued on compact disc as *From the Heart: Native American Church Songs* (Cool Runnings), and his fourth album, *Songs of Life* (Cool Runnings, 2001). Finally, McClellan recorded thirty-six new songs in 2002, released as *Our Songs* (Cool Runnings), just after his untimely death in 2004, at age 50. An accomplished fancy dancer, feather and bead worker, McClellan wrote that his "songs

Billy McClellan, Sr.

By Hugh Foley

were composed with love and compassion, to help everyone live in a good way, to have a good life, and to be able to live in harmony and peace."[8]

Continuing the long tradition of Native American Church singers with Iowa heritage, Jeff McClellan, who is also of Sac & Fox, Otoe, Shawnee, and Seneca heritage, recorded an album of Peyote songs with two other young Oklahoma singers, Kyle Robedeaux (Otoe/Seminole) and Brian Stoner (Ponca/Cherokee). Released on the prestigious Canyon label in 2005, *For Our Loved Ones: Peyote Songs of the Native American Church* includes songs from the Comanche, Otoe, Cree, Ponca, Sac and Fox, and Kiowa, as well as several "straight", or standard songs that do not necessarily have a specific tribal origin, but have evolved as a result of people from several different tribes worshipping together for over 100 years in the Native American Church in Oklahoma and throughout North America. Jeff McClellan has also released one album through the Cool Runnings label, *Down South*, a collection of 40 Native American Church songs, many in the Sac and Fox language, and some other old songs passed down to him as he grew up in the church with many members of his family participating all their lives.

Jeff McClellan

With roughly 500 tribal members in 2012, the Iowa in Oklahoma are also involved in gaming, as well as economic enterprises such as a convenience store and smoke shop, the proceeds from which provide tribal services and environmental operations, to include a tribal ground and surface water program, buffalo and cattle program, eagle aviary program for injured eagles, and Wetlands Nature Center. As part of their participation in the larger community of tribes in Oklahoma, the Iowa Tribe sponsors many intertribal dances based on the Southern Plains **powwow** model at its tribal dance grounds, to include honor dances, graduation dances, birthday dances, various holiday dances, and the annual Iowa Tribal Powwow, held the third weekend in June, since 1985.

2012 Iowa powwow singers (l-r): Geoff White (Kiowa/Cherokee), Head Singer John Arkeketa (Iowa/Otoe/Muscogee), and Joel Deerinwater (Cherokee/Muscogee).

Endnotes

1. Oral and tribal history from Iowa Tribe of Oklahoma, *26th Annual Iowa Tribal Powwow Program, 2011*. (Perkins, OK: Iowa Tribe of Oklahoma, 2011).

2. For more information on the historical connections between the Iowa and Otoe-Missouria, as well as a good general history on the Iowa prior to their relocation to pre-statehood Oklahoma, see Greg Olson, The Ioway in Missouri. (Columbia: Columbia University Press, 2008). For solid contemporary overviews of both tribes, see Blue Clark's Indian Tribes of Oklahoma: A Guide. (Norman: University of Oklahoma Press, 2009).

3. Some historical information presented here is gleaned from the tribe's website: Iowa Nation of Oklahoma, "History", http://www.iowanation.org, (accessed July 5, 2011).

4. For Pritzker's complete essay on the Iowa Tribe, see his writing about them in *A Native American Encyclopedia: History, Culture, and Peoples*. (New York: Oxford University Press, 2000). However, readers should note that Pritzker's entry begins with his version of the Iowa's name, which does not match the tribe's version, so that might indicate other inaccuracies in the entry.

5. The author is very careful about explaining how much Christianity is or is not part of a particular tribe or chapter's individual theology regarding the incorporation of Christianity into their songs, liturgy, and belief system. While some tribes and chapters have made Christianity a fundamental part of the Native American Church faith, others incorporated Christianity into the songs, prayers, and iconography of the church to convince government agents it was a Christian religion, just the "Indian Way" of doing it. As the religion spread north and southwest, differing elements of Christianity were included or excluded, depending on the leaders of those tribal chapters.

5. Vocables in American Indian music are vocal sounds that may or may not have a literal meaning; vocables may carry a melody that has meaning, such as representing a time of night or morning during the service, or derive from the earlier periods, to include the 19th century reservation era, when vocables allowed tribes an opportunity to sing together, even if they did not speak the same language.

6. For more about Joseph Springer and the development of the Iowa specific elements of the Native American Church, see Omer C. Stewart's *Peyote Religion: A History*. (Norman: University of Oklahoma Press, 1987), pp. 123-24.

7. For more discussion the early Native American Church music of these two tribes, see Truman W. Daily and Jill D. Hopkins, "Native American Church Songs of the Otoe" in *Proceedings of the 1992 Mid-America Linguistics Conference and Conference on Siouan/Caddoan Languages*. Eds. Evan Smith and Flore Zephir (Columbia: University of Missouri Press), 303-317. For some history on the church among these tribes, and a more detailed examination of the music in the church, see Jill Dee Davidson's Ph.D. dissertation, *Prayer Songs to Our Elder Brother: Native American Church Songs of the Otoe-Missouria and Iowa*. (Columbia: University of Missouri, 1997).

8. Billy McClellan Sr.'s quote about his songs is inscribed on the compact disc, *From the Heart: Native American Church Songs* (Cool Runnings, circa late 1990s).

J

Jackson, Wanda

(b. October 20, 1937)

With a fiery growl of a rock and roll voice that made her the undisputed "First Lady of Rockabilly", Wanda Jackson is a singer and hit songwriter who was one of the first women (if not *the* first) to break the male-dominated performance barrier in mainstream rock and roll during its emergence into the American popular music consciousness in the mid-1950s. After the commercial rock and roll music industry waned in the late 1950s[1], Wanda shifted easily back into country music where her authentic Oklahoma honky-tonk twang, understanding of the blues, and commanding vocal presence garnered chart success and international bookings into the 1970s. Subsequently, Jackson became a cult figure in worldwide rockabilly, rebel rock, and girl power circles through the 1980s and '90s. By the 2000s, Wanda enjoyed a full-scale celebration of her life in music with various awards, hall of fame inductions, special recordings, films, articles, and books released to acknowledge, commend, and historicize her role as an American pop music pioneer, especially for women. Born as the only child of Tom and Nellie Jackson in Maud, Oklahoma, a community of roughly 1,000 residents located southeast of Oklahoma City, Wanda learned how to yodel at age nine from an older cousin, Betty Lou Ledbetter, an older cousin. After working in a bakery during the day and pumping gas at night, Tom Jackson headed for

California in 1942 looking for more steady work. Leaving Nellie and Wanda at Nellie's parents' house in Roff, Oklahoma, Tom found work for North American Aviation in Los Angeles and moved the family to the West coast. Following World War II, Tom left the aviation company and completed schooling to become a barber. Nellie became homesick and the Jackson family returned to Oklahoma in 1948.

Renting an apartment in the Capitol Hill neighborhood in Oklahoma City, Tom began driving a taxicab. A musician who knew enough to teach Wanda basic guitar and piano chords starting when she was six-years-old, her father bought her a small Stella guitar on which to practice, and purchased an upright piano so she could take lessons. Around this time, Wanda heard the first record that made an indelible impression upon her: Hank Williams' "Lovesick Blues". Noticing the development of Wanda's singing and playing skills, Nellie entered the young singer in local talent contests. By singing one of her father's faves, and using her yodeling skills on Jimmie Rodgers' "Blue Yodel #6", Wanda won a fifteen-minute slot on radio station KLPR in March of 1953, where she began performing regularly while still a student at Capitol Hill High School, only a few blocks from the station. Demonstrating her resourcefulness as a teenager, Wanda gained her own sponsors and wrote her own ad copy. Carrying her guitar from home to school to the studio each day, she was eventually given a slot on two of the station's local broadcasts, Cousin Jay's Mountain Jamboree and Uncle Willie's Country Show. During her teenage years, she wrote her first songs: "If You Knew What I Know" and "You'd Be the First One to Know".

The first major break of Wanda's early career dates to meeting country music legend, who became her self-avowed mentor, Hank Thompson, then leading the Brazos Valley Boys on-stage at the Trianon Ballroom in Oklahoma City, as well as performing over WKY-TV between 1952 and 1954. Having heard Wanda's KLPR program, Thompson invited her to perform at the Trianon Ballroom with the Brazos Valley Boys. She had already been well-aware of Thompson due to his massive 1951 hit, "Wild Side of Life", and also the possibilities for women in country music when Kitty Wells released her answer song to Thompson, "Honky Tonk Angels", which also spoke from the woman's perspective. Before too long, KWTV in Oklahoma City invited Jackson to perform each week before a live audience. Soon thereafter, Wanda cut a demo tape at Thompson's studio on North May that was sent to Capitol Records who passed on Wanda because they perceived her voice too immature. Undaunted, Thompson forwarded the tape to Decca which promptly signed her in 1954. Thus, Wanda was a Decca recording artist before she left high school. The five songs that Wanda first recorded with Decca included straight ahead country tunes: her own "If You Knew What I Know", "The Heart You Could Have Had", "The Right to Love", and "Lovin' Country Style". One of her Decca Records, "You Can't Have My Love", a duet with Billy Gray, made the country Top 10. This success prompted a call from the Grand Ole Opry for a

Wanda Jackson's 1957 Capitol Records publicity photo.

guest performance that ended on a negative note—she was asked to cover her shoulder-less dress that her mother had made especially for the Opry. Wanda did not return to the Opry stage for forty years, although Nellie continued designing Wanda's dresses for years.

After high school graduation in 1955, Wanda joined the *Ozark Jubilee*, an ABC television network show based in Springfield, Missouri, and hosted by the venerable Red Foley. While performing on the Jubilee from 1955 to 1957, she also hit the tour circuit with her father, Tom, serving as her manager. Also during this period, Wanda met Elvis Presley at a radio station promotional appearance when they began to work on the same tours in 1955. A close friendship developed between the two, and Elvis advised Wanda to consider changing her style to the new music they didn't really even have a name for yet ("rock 'n roll"). While Elvis was beginning to have success at that time, his national breakthrough, "Heartbreak Hotel", had not yet been recorded. Presley was still touring the Southwest and South on the strength of his Sun Records releases. One must think Elvis heard Wanda with her angry-sounding, if not sexually dangerous voice, and heard a commonality with what he knew he was doing with his voice to audiences. After giving Wanda his ring that she wore around her neck for years, she and Elvis continued as good friends and colleagues through 1957 when Presley moved to Hollywood in order to focus on his movie career. In the meantime, Capitol made up for their earlier A&R error and signed the ferocious (and precocious) queen in waiting.

With the help of Jim Halsey, who had been managing Hank Thompson from an Oklahoma City base, Wanda signed a contract with Capitol Records in 1956, a company with which she would remain for eighteen years. When signed, Capitol felt they need to market her as strictly country, or as an artist of the "new music". At the time, Jackson felt more than anything she was singer, and desired to sing the songs she liked and let the label figure out how to market them. At the time, songs were not being written from the woman's perspective to give girls a chance to scream through a rockabilly number. Since all of rock's primary figures were men, songs didn't exist with a speaker (or singer) of the song explaining a woman's point of view. To compensate, Wanda would change the gender of figures in songs to provide a female sensibility singing the song. In need of new material, Wanda turned to her hometown contacts. Jackson's first Capitol single, "I Gotta Know", was written specially for Wanda by a friend in Oklahoma City, Thelma Blackmon, peaking at #15 on Cashbox's country single chart. Backed with outrageous guitar dexterity by Joe Maphis and Buck Owens, musically the song jokes with the whole idea of the boundaries between country music and rock, shifting tempos between verses and chorus from a honky-tonk slow dance to an up tempo rockabilly pace. Lyrically, "I Gotta Know" centers on the female singer/speaker questioning the good intent of a man who is making a lot of promises to her in hopes of furthering his amorous goals.

Her second Capitol single was a song she had been performing (with some objections from the principal) since her days at Capitol Hill, "Hot Dog! That Made Him Mad". The song features Wanda giving her man a hard time on purpose just for the fun of it. With encouragement from her father, Wanda decided to write her own "girl power" rock and roll songs. "Mean, Mean, Man" indicates her full commitment to the unique vocal imprint that typifies her celebrated 1950s sound, and is the vocal harbinger of Janis Joplin's hyper-sexualized blues screaming of the 1960s. In 1956, *Cash Box* magazine agreed on her individuality, voting Jackson the "Most Promising Female Vocalist". Even with this acknowledgment, American audiences did not seem commercially ready for a sexually threatening woman singing rock and roll songs from a woman's point of view. Not only was her sensuous growl the first American popular music vocal equivalent of Mae West, the 1930s stage and film star who capitalized on the all the theatrical tropes of a confident woman, or her late 1950s Hollywood contemporary, Marilyn Monroe, Jackson's voice emanated from an Anglo woman. American popular culture had supported African-American women in the music industry who were singing sexually confident songs alongside "wronged woman" songs. Examples abound with Bessie Smith (1930s), Billie Holliday (1940s), and especially Jackson's Black contemporary of the 1950s, Ruth Brown. However, put a really cute white girl on a stage and then listen to her sing the blues of a confident woman, and it scared people in 1954, the same year of Brown v. Board of Education (the Supreme Court case that ruled "separate but equal" was unconstitutional). Wanda Jackson and her primary rock and roll contemporaries were the aural signifiers of a cultural shift in challenging establishment racial, gender, and sexual roles, as challenging the authority by which those roles had been established. In the same way that Elvis Presley's Sun Records music of 1954 demonstrates the complete cultural diffusion of southern Black music into southern White homes that could produce a Presley, Wanda Jackson's occasionally sexually threatening music symbolizes the evolution of differing and evolving sexual mores for women in the 1950s, as well as furthering the long-standing practice of cloaking sexual terminology in euphemistic terms for country, blues, and, therefore, early rock music. To go for it completely, in 1958, she recorded "Fujiyama Mama", with all of its obvious innuendo and double entendre. While not a success in the United States (due to the previously mentioned gender and lyrical issues in the song), the Armed Forces Radio Network (FEN) began spinning it in Japan. During the song's climb to monumental hit status in that country, a #1 hit for as long as six months, one wonders if that many 1950s Japanese fans understood enough English to realize the first line of the songs refers to war-ending U.S. actions to end the war against Japan at Hiroshima and Nagasaki in 1945. The song's success resulted in a sensational tour of Japan in 1959 with thousands of fans greeting her at every stop on the two-month tour. Shortly before she departed for the Japanese tour, Wanda and Halsey decided to hire her own band. Known to Halsey because of his regional connections in northeastern Oklahoma, Bobby Poe and the Poe Kats was an integrated band led by Vinita native, Bobby Poe, and featuring Big Al Downing, as pianist.

After her return from Japan, Wanda and the Poe Kats traveled to Los Angeles to cut an album entitled simply, *Wanda Jackson*, for which she recorded "Let's Have a Party", a song that remained in obscurity for another two years before it became more recognized, and one of her signature songs.

Jackson's 1958 debut album, *Wanda Jackson* (Capitol), establishes her as an important American popular music singer of her era. Not only does she have a unique and singularly identifiable voice, Wanda's ability to move effortlessly between rock and country music demonstrates the important connections between the two styles, and also challenged the American popular music world to accept her sexual bravado in the same way male rock and roll artists of the 1950s were reward for theirs with hits laden with double entendre. Capitol did their best to showcase Wanda as both a country artist and rock and roll artist, something that had not really been done with a female artist by a major label. The promotion team at Capitol was not quite how to couch it, but they studiously avoided the term "rock 'n roll". The un-credited liner notes on the back of the album say the collection is "a brightly styled collection of her own and everybody's favorite ballads, country and rhythm tunes."[2] Both sides of the vinyl LP version of *Wanda Jackson* begin with a slower country ballad ("Day Dreaming"/"Just Call Me Lonesome") and end with an up tempo rocker ("Long Tall Sally" (a Little Richard hit)/"Let's Have a Party"). Along with its bipolar musical aesthetic, the album also features Wanda on a cover of "Money, Honey", originally a song popularized by the Drifters in 1953, and again Elvis Presley in 1956, but the song takes on a whole new meaning when sung furiously by Wanda, a straightforward attempt at subverting and capitalizing on the gender reversal concept. What also strikes a listener to her first album is how close she and the Poe Cats sound to early Beatles music, especially when John Lennon's number is called and he attacks a 1950s American rock standard with a razored voice, sounding more like Wanda Jackson in her vocally sizzling moments than he does like any other American rock and roll singer. Given Capitol's prominence in the U.K. in the 1950s, one would not be surprised to find out Lennon had heard Jackson's Capitol 1958 album as by all counts that year represents the coalescence of his band, The Quarrymen, basing their set on skiffle[3] and 1950s American rock and roll. Whether or not Lennon heard her 1958 album, the industry was listening. Based on the "Fujiyama Mama" recording, *Disc Jockey* magazine named Wanda as "Best New Female Singer" in 1958. By late 1958, however, Wanda took a break from recording in order to prepare for and complete the Japanese tour in early 1959. Later that year, Capitol released *There's a Party Goin' On* (Capitol 1959), featuring an unknown guitarist Wanda had seen perform in Washington D.C. and invited him to be her bandleader. By 1960, the declining popularity of rock nationwide, coupled with Wanda's Oklahoma authentic country music background, magnified overtures to her for performances in Las Vegas where country music had been introduced by Hank Thompson and Bob Wills. The Vegas shows coincided with a fortunate bump to Wanda's career in 1960 after a Des Moine, Iowa, disc jockey began using the exultant "Let's Have a Party" as his theme song and, after many requests, contacted Capitol Records to let them know kids wanted to purchase it. Issued as a single by Capitol in mid-summer of 1960, by October it was a modest, but certain, Top 40 hit on the *Billboard* Hot 100 (#37). With a new hit and Vegas calling, Jackson put together a band featuring Roy Clark as band leader and guitarist. By joining Wanda in Vegas, Clark also came to meet his long-time business partner, Jim Halsey, for the first time. With "Let's Have a Party" as a hit, Jackson began calling her newly formed band The Partytimers when they opened at the Golden Nugget in Las Vegas in late 1960. Capitol rushed out and album composed of her earlier 1950s vintage rockabilly tracks as *Rockin' with Wanda* (Capitol, 1960), but the LP did not include "Let's Have a Party"[4].

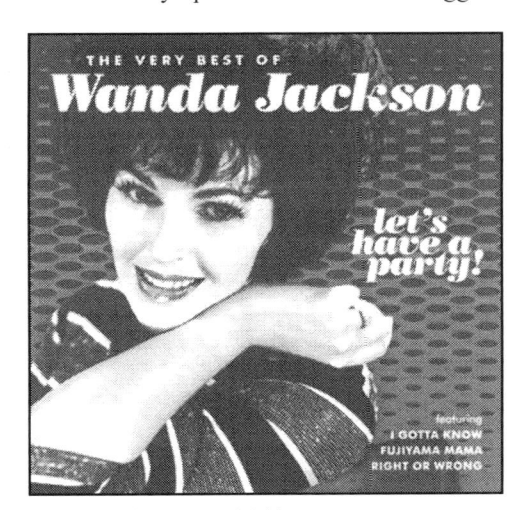

Universal/Fontana 2011

In 1961, Jackson recorded the first of four singles that charted as "crossover" hits (songs that succeed in more than one genre format) between 1961 and 1962. Interestingly, the first hit of the four charting singles on the pop charts, "Right or Wrong", is a Jackson composition from a different point of view, bouncing the scornful woman perspective, and singing from the viewpoint of a woman who is willing to put up with whatever to be with her lover. As opposed to the earlier single, "I Gotta Know", in which the singer asks for real proof of a man's love, all the speaker wants to hear in "Right or Wrong" is for the man to say "I love you," and that is proof enough for her satisfaction. The honky-tonk slow dance classic resonated with the public more than any of her previous confrontational "equal love rights" songs, and peaked at #9 on the country charts. One might feel Jackson's lyrical stance in "Right or Wrong" is a weakened sign of resignation by the speaker that an imperfect relationship is better than none. However, only twenty-four at the time, Jackson had already been on the major label whirlwind for five years where she saw practically no women in leadership of the music industry. After recording music intended to start fires under people that never really caught on the U.S., and recognizing show business was still a man's dominion for the most part in 1961. She had first-hand experience in the gender hypocrisy by having a dear friendship with the most famous rock star of them all, Elvis, who was able to capitalize in an extreme commercial way on his sexuality. However, Jackson's attempt at the same stance was not met favorably by the larger public on her 1950s recordings. So, "Right or Wrong" took the alternative path, a traditional point of view from a woman resigned to her less than perfect love life, the larger allegory of which symbolizes a person who stays with whatever it is that really matters to them, even through turbulent times. Editorial interpretations of the lyrics aside, a better and more important indication of their significance to the general public is represented by #29 on the *Billboard* Hot 100, a significant stab into the pop mainstream for a country artist of the time, increasingly a goal of the Chet Atkins-inspired Nashville Sound, a smoothed out country meant for urban audiences. Jackson's follow-up fits the "countrypolitan" sound perfectly, with its harmonized background singers, string section accompaniment, soft electric guitar, and her echo-laden vocals. As a result of its "elevator country" motif, "In the Middle of a Heartache" not only reached Top 10 country status in 1961, it also crossed over to the pop charts where it notched a #27 position on the *Billboard* Hot 100. By the end of 1961, "Right or Wrong" was the #45 country single of the year, and one of her signature songs from that point forward; however, her biggest hit seems to be her one and only marriage, a rarity for country music artists. Wanda married "outside of the industry" to IBM programmer, Wendell Goodman, in 1961. Eventually, Goodman became her manager, and with whom she reared two children, Gina and Greg.

  Building on her success in the United States and Japan, coupled with Jim Halsey's rising international presence and goals for promoting country music worldwide, Wanda's music has truly had global impact. She was Capitol Records' biggest selling female in the German language, a result of her recording German language versions of her songs from 1965 through 1970, a process she repeated in the Dutch and Japanese languages. Back in the U.S., she had two Top 20 country hits, "Tears Will Be the Chaser for Your Wine" and "The Box It Came In", and hosted *Music Village*, her own syndicated TV show in 1967 and 1968. In 1969, she re-visited her tough woman stance in a few singles during those years, notably with "My Big Iron Skillet", a song which threatened death for a cheating spouse by way of a skillet bashing, but by that time the women's movement was in full swing and a song like Aretha Franklin's "R-E-S-P-E-C-T" more accurately reflected the pop culture ethos of the time. Musically, Jackson enjoyed more success in Germany with her #5 German hit of 1965 "Santo Domingo", the reverse "B" side of which included the German language song "Morgen, Ja Morgen" (translation: "Tomorrow is Tomorrow"). With eight more German singles, which comprised most of a 1968 album, *Made in Germany* (Electrola), she was an obvious member and anchor of the Capitol Caravan that toured Europe in 1970, and was voted Favorite Female Country Music Singer in Scandinavian countries in the early 1970s. While experiencing commercial success in the late 1960s with her TV show, country hits, and European tours, Wanda also felt she had lost her personal direction in life. In most of her performances through the current era, Jackson stops and takes a moment to note "the most important day of her life", June 6, 1971, when she became a Christian. She also had her final Top 20 country hits that year, "A Woman Lives for Love", for which she received another GRAMMY nomination, and "Fancy Satin Pillows". By that year, Wanda had been a country music professional for 17 years, had multiple rock and country hits, performed around the world, hosted TV shows, won awards, gained a lot of recognition, sold a fair amount of records, and felt her faith and status afforded her the opportunity to record a Gospel album for Capitol, *Praise the Lord*, in 1972, which turned out to be her last for the financially conscious label, and which precipitated a journey through a series of independent Gospel albums and evangelizing across the U.S. through the 1970s, performing almost exclusively in churches and at church events.

By the early 1980s, Wanda became an icon for rockabilly enthusiasts from Europe who sought her out and arranged for regular tours in Scandinavia, England, and Germany throughout that decade. She recorded an album of mostly rockabilly standards in Sweden with Swedish musicians for Rounder Records in 1986, *Rock 'n' Roll Away Your Blues* (Varrick/Rounder VR025), and continued working regularly in the rockabilly genre. The German label, Bear Family Records, responsible for historicizing so much quality American roots music, has released two box sets of her music, the four-CD set, *Right or Wrong* (1954 – 1963) (BCD 15629), and the eight-CD set, *Tears Will Be the Chaser for Your Wine* (BCD 16114). In 1995, Wanda recorded two songs for the modern honky-tonk and rockabilly artist, Rosie Flores, for whom Wanda would obviously be a role model. On a promotional tour with Flores for the album, Jackson was surprised to find so many fans who knew her music, inspiring her get back on the road again in the 1990s, foreboding the 21st century, which came calling on her iconic status, historic significance, and continued ability to rock a joint with her trademark voice.

The new century began with her 2000 induction into the Oklahoma Hall of Fame in Muskogee, Oklahoma, and continued with inductions into the Rockabilly Hall of Fame and the International Gospel Music Hall of Fame. She was one of four rockkabilly pioneers, along with Oklahoman Lorrie Collins, on the PBS special, *Welcome to the Club of Women of Rockabilly* telecast in 2002. In 2002, she was back to performing in Germany, Austria, and Sweden, and in August of 2002, she performed at the "Red Hot Rockabilly Party", an outdoor concert at Damrosch Park at Lincoln Center in New York City.

Wanda Jackson in the 1960s.

Several labels have found a ready market for Wanda's catalogue and newer material. In 2000, the Ace label released *Queen of Rockabilly* containing thirty tracks of her major rockabilly hits. In December, 2002 Wanda's performance at the Village Underground in New York City was recorded for a live album on DCN Records, *Live and Still Kickin'*. The album features Wanda talking the audience through her career, telling the appreciative New York City audience the stories behind the most influential songs in her life and her best known hits, as well as

Wanda Jackson, 1986.

many personal anecdotes about herself.[5] In 2003, Capitol Nashville re-released her first two Capitol LPs, *Wanda* (1958) and *Rockin' with Wanda* (1960). In late 2003, Wanda recorded a new album for CMH Records, signed by a woman A&R executive (times have changed). *Heart Trouble* featured many A-list roots rockers eager to be part of a legend's new project featuring familiar standards and some new songs. Backed by Tom Waits' core rhythm section and guitarist, and featuring appearances by Elvis Costello, Dave Alvin, Lee Rocker (Stray Cats), Rosie Flores, the Cramps, along with her own return to the industry of which she had been such a big part fifty years prior, insured excellent press attention for the disc, as well as surrounding her string of shows to support the album, even if all the press was not perfectly complimentary. In a November 7, 2003, issue of *Entertainment Weekly*, critic Ken Tucker calls the album "uneven" due to the "well-intentioned guest stars" that shift the focus away from Jackson. However, the *Detroit Free Press*' Martin Bandyke touts the album as "energetic and vital", as well as "one of the most fun listens of the year", in a December 6, 2003 review published in the *Tulsa World* (D4). Either way, the album only heightened Jackson's historic profile, and the very next year (2004) she was nominated for induction into the Rock and Roll Hall of Fame in Cleveland, Ohio, championed by Elvis Costello, but Wanda did not receive the necessary votes, much to the dismay of fans. However, additional attention was not in short supply for Jackson in the upcoming years. In 2004, the long-established Midwest purveyor of roots music with a twist (mostly a maniacal, wild-eyed twist), Bloodshot Records released a tribute album, *Hard-Headed Woman: A Celebration of Wanda Jackson*, with multiple modern alternative country artists recording her best known songs. Artists/disciples who signed on for the project included Neko Case, Robbie Fulks, Rose Flores, Laura Cantrell, Bottle Rockets, and Wayne Hancock, among others. In 2005, Wanda received a prestigious National Heritage Fellowship, the National Endowment for the Arts' highest honor in the folk and traditional arts. In 2006, she recorded an album of songs closely associated with Elvis Presley, along with one about the ring he gave her all those years before. On *I Remember Elvis* (Goldenlane Records), Jackson does a lot of Presley's earliest material she would have remembered him singing from his pre-stardom Sun Records days ("Mystery Train", "Good Rockin' Tonight", "Baby, Let's Play House", etc.) as well as songs from his breakthrough period ("Heartbreak Hotel" and "Love Me Tender"). Also in 2006, K.P.I., a New York City-based television and new media company, traveled across the U.S. and Europe, following Wanda and Wendell from honky-tonks to New York City's Lincoln Center, and then to Sweden and Finland to shoot documentary for a film about Wanda Jackson's life and career. The film's title went through various revisions, ending with 2007's version, *Wanda Jackson: The Sweet Lady with the Nasty Voice*.

More than 500 Rock and Roll Hall of Fame ballots were again sent to voters in 2009. Subsequently, fifty-five years after signing with Decca Records while still in high school,

Wanda Jackson became a member of the institution she had a part in creating. While not quite equal in pop culture status, but equally as permanent, The Oklahoma City Council voted in 2009 to re-name a Bricktown alley as Wanda Jackson Way, the fourth music star associated with Oklahoma City to have a thoroughfare named for her (the others being Charlie Christian, Vince Gill, and Flaming Lips). Also in 2009, Wanda's career was further documented by the Oklahoma History Center for its exhibit on rock music from the state of Oklahoma, *Another Hot Oklahoma Night*. By the end of 2009, Jack White (best-known to casual pop music fans for his stripped-down blues-rock duo, The White Stripes), jumped at the chance to record Jackson for his label Third Man Records, having had previous success with Loretta Lynn on the *Van Lear Rose* project that gained Lynn so much new attention by her association with White and his fans. Seemingly smitten by working with one of his own rough-and-tumble rock music forbears, White's recording of Jackson for *The Party Ain't Over* (Third Man/Nonesuch, 2010), joyously shrouds her still tough-as-nails voice with his sparkling grit production and raggedy-rock guitar work on some 1950s rock standards ("Shakin' All Over", "Rip It Up"). But, where the album gets progressive, even post-modern with its collision of similar aural aspects from different eras combined in a new context, is with Jackson's interpretation of contemporary tough pop music girl, Amy Winehouse, on a meaner-than-Amy version of Winehouse's hit single, "You Know I'm No Good". More prophetic, however, may be the last track on the album, a re-visit to Jimmie Rodgers "Blue Yodel #6", the song that started it all at an Oklahoma City talent show, the perfect bookend to an extraordinary and historic rock, country, gospel, and popular career that actually shows no signs of slowing. [Insert image Jackson Wanda, image 5 with caption "Wanda Jackson sings at the Oklahoma History Center in 2009 backed by Larry Collins"] Due to Jackson's association with White, and then merged with her own legendary status, she appeared on *Conan* and the *The Late Show with David Letterman*, and gained bookings at highly notable music festivals such as Stagecoach, Bonnaroo, and Newport Folk Festival.

In 2010, Jackson also received the Lifetime Achievement Award from the Americana Music Association, presented by Jack White at the Ryman Auditorium in Nashville. In 2011, Universal Music released *Let's Have a Party: The Best of Wanda Jackson* internationally on its Fontana label, and she was an intrinsic part of the Rock and Roll Hall of Fame's exhibit, *Women Who Rock: Vision, Power, and Passion*, promoted as the first major museum exhibit to recognize, showcase, and contextualize important roles played by women in rock music. Starting with blues shouters, such as Ma Rainey and Bessie Smith, right up through to contemporary provocateur, Lady Gaga, the exhibit must position Jackson squarely in the middle of those artists as rock and roll's first commercial female success and, arguably, its first threatening woman to challenge established gender roles lyrically and delivery-wise in rock's nascent stages. Before settling into a smoothly produced

Wanda Jackson's 2011 album, The Party Ain't Over, produced by Jack White for his label, Third Man Records.

and highly active professional country music career in the 1960s and early 1970s, along with her Gospel period of the remaining 1970s, Jackson subverted the sexuality that had been the sole domain of male artists to that point in the mid-1950s, grabbed it, and snarled about it to her audiences in a voice both distinctive and memorable. Additionally, her songs from a woman's perspective continued a tradition in country music with Kitty Wells as its instigator; however, Jackson was the spark for female rockers to scream about their own issues with love and life. Finally, Wanda Jackson's music shows the close inter-relationships between country, blues, rock, and gospel music of 20th century American popular music, indicated further by her songs "crossing over" from country to pop charts in the early 1960s; and, not only did she appeal to various fan bases in the U.S. during her career, her music overcame language and geographical boundaries to gain fans in Europe and Japan. From an Oklahoma music point of view, Jackson further illustrates a common touchstone of successful Oklahoma musicians: being able to transition to more than one style of music, which she was able to do when the first wave of rock and roll began to dry up, and she returned to the honky-tonk music she'd been singing before Elvis suggested she shake it up some. In 2011, Universal Music Group released *Let's Have a Party: The Best of Wanda Jackson* on its Fontana label, and in 2012 Sugar Hill Records released *Unfinished Business*, produced by Steve Earle's son, Justin Townes Earle. The project included Wanda giving her spin on several great songs by Townes Van Zandt, Steve Earle, Justin Earle, and a set of WoodyGutrie lyrics from the projects helmed by Jay Benney and Jeff Tweety. In 2013, Wanda continued touring from her home base of Edmond, Oklahoma, where she resides with her husband and long-time manager, Wendell Goodman.

www.wandajackson.com

Endnotes

1. The first primary era of rock music as an important commercial pop music phenomenon is between the years 1954 (when Bill Haley's "Rock Around the Clock" topped the charts) and 1958 (by which time Elvis Presley was in the Army, Buddy Holly had died in a plane crash, Carl Perkins had been injured in a motorcycle accident, Jerry Lee Lewis had fallen from public grace due to an ill-perceived marriage, Little Richard had become a minister, and Chuck Berry was incarcerated for indiscretions with a minor). After 1958, the primary popular music became doo-wop (The Drifters), industry-created teen pop stars with watered-down rock music imitations (Pat Boone), and smooth, commercial folk (The Lettermen). In 1960, the next movements in rock music surface in the Pacific Northwest with electric combo guitar groups like The Ventures, southern California surf bands who merge The Ventures' riffing with the harmonies of commercial folk music (The Beach Boys), and the new urban gospel-influenced R&B out of Detroit (Motown). During this shift in the American popular music continuum, many country stars who had been working either in rockabilly or Elvis-style rock and roll (Conway Twitty, Johnny Cash, and Wanda Jackson), turned to country as the next market for their music. Given that "billy" was part of the rockabilly term, the transition was not a stretch for the musically nor aesthetically for the artists.

2. As European and American releases of albums often differ, liner notes quoted from back cover of *Wanda Jackson* (Capitol, 1958) printed in France through EMI Pathé Marconi (PM 231).

3. Skiffle is a British popular music of the mid-20th century that channeled a variety of musical styles, including that of traditional folk music of the British Isles, popular music of the British musical theater from the first half of the 20th century, and rapidly embraced both African-American and Anglo-American musical styles such as the blues and country music. As a result, new artists like John Lennon and his Quarrymen had to play skiffle songs known to their audiences, but at eighteen-years-old in 1958, Lennon also wanted to play the rock and roll music of his generation. Wanda Jackson's first album emerged during that year.

4. Releasing a compilation of an artist's material due to a hit single, but not including the hit single on the compilation (presumably due to record buyers already owning it as a single or from a previous album) was a common tactic by Capitol (and other labels) to get consumers to buy as much vinyl as possible to get more distance out of an artist's material. In this case, if fans wanted "Let's Have a Party" and more music from this new singer they'd just heard about, the label knew that meant two purchases instead of one, a pattern

furthered during Capitol's Beatles era, when they culled British releases for a few songs each before releasing the removed songs on another album, one of the reasons why Beatles fans collect European releases in order to hear the full complement of songs as released originally in England.

5. Wanda tells stories behind most of her best-known songs, as well as discusses various life experiences to include the date she converted to Christianity, in between the live performances of her music on The Wanda Jackson Show, *Still Alive and Kickin'* (DCN CD1013, 2003).

Jacob Fred Jazz Odyssey
(Formed in 1994 in Tulsa, OK)

Named after a combination of pianist Brian Haas' life-long infatuation with the name Fred, and a scene in the rock satire film *Spinal Tap* when the fake band members talk about performing a "free form jazz odyssey," Jacob Fred Jazz Odyssey (JFJO) is not only Oklahoma's most significant jazz group, but also one of the foremost contemporary jazz groups in the world, with Haas as one of the genre's most lionized modern keyboard visionaries. Along with easily referencing any jazz sub-genre, especially those related to both bebop of the late 1940s and progressive jazz of the 1960s, JFJO'S extended improvisational jams meld funk, rock, European art music, hip-hop, and jazz into a distinctive fusion that is both entertaining for casual jazz fans, if there is such a thing, and intensely rewarding for more advanced listeners who appreciate JFJO's dazzling display of instrumental skill, complicated shifting tempos, varied dynamics, and rich textures of the group's music. As its sole remaining original member in 2011, who plays at least 150 dates a year around the world, Haas has led JFJO as a quartet since 2008, after nine years of working within the trio format with bassist Reed Mathis from 1999 through late 2009. Before the trio period, JFJO operated as a multi-genre octet complete with hip-hop style MCs and a horn section. Members of the quartet-sized JFJO in 2011 were Haas (piano), extremely gifted and accomplished bassist from Kansas City, Jeff Harsbarger (double bass), Tulsan Chris Combs (lap steel), and Josh Raymer (drums). With Combs on lap steel, the group's most recent incarnation takes on a spacey Western twang, a 21st century descendant of Okie jazz, Nashville's derisive term for the multi-genre Western swing of Bob Wills and his Texas Playboys, which became famous operating out of Tulsa in the 1930s, '40s, and '50s. Not to say that JFJO is in any way a Western swing band, but their iconoclastic pursuit of an individual musical identity and voice harkens back to Wills own visionary ideals of playing jazz on stringed instruments, to include the lap and pedal steel guitars. With regard to that past as part of their consciousness, the band's own website nods to an idea of "Red Dirt Jazz" that is "equal parts earthy and nimble, pastoral and sweeping, elegant and rollicking." JFJO also emerged from the outrageously rich jazz tradition of Tulsa, and Oklahoma as a whole, that provided a training ground, performance opportunity, and milieu for the development of twentieth century jazz and some of its great practitioners. While Muskogee (Barney Kessel, Jay McShann, Don Byas) and Oklahoma City (Charlie Christian, Jimmy Rushing) also produced their share of jazz greats, Tulsa is where Count Basie joined up with the Oklahoma City Blue Devils, as well as the birthplace of trumpeter Howard McGhee, saxophonist Earl Bostic, and bassists Cecil McBee, and Wayman Tisdale, along with many good players who filled the Wills' brothers bands operating out of Tulsa from the 1930s through the early 1960s.

As a result of this history, excellent jazz musicians were still around town in the 1990s and some of them were playing in jazz ensembles at the University of Tulsa (TU), where Brian Haas was studying classical piano on a full music scholarship. Needing a break from his extensive solitary practices, he began scouting out musicians he felt matched his own zeal for music and started calling them together. The first version of JFJO formed around very talented trombonist Matt Leland, guitarist Dove McHargue, drummer Sean Layton, who served as mentor for many young musicians in the Tulsa scene at the time, and Haas playing bass lines on the piano. After playing around Tulsa at small clubs and restaurants, the group recruited percussionist Matt Edwards (b. June 6, 1976, Norman, OK), and seventeen-year-old Reed Mathis (b. September 27, 1976, Saginaw, Michigan). With Mathis and different drummers, JFJO toured the U.S. from 1999 through most of 2008, selling out major venues across the country. Reed met Haas because the two had musician friends in common at TU and those friends told Haas he needed to check out the young bass player from Booker T., then only a junior who agreed to be part of the band. Once assembled, JFJO started as an eight-piece, free form group with a full horn section, and immediately started drawing large crowds around Tulsa with their combination of hip hop beats and melodic anchors of Prince, Thelonious Monk, Wayne Shorter, and John Zorn. Based on the success of their energetic live shows, the group recorded and released two live albums that are now out of print: *Live at the Lincoln Continental* (1995), released while Mathis was still a senior in high school, and *Live in Tokyo* (1996). Both album titles are jokes and early indications of the band's whimsical sense of humor, as no Lincoln Continental Club exists, and the group recorded *Live in Tokyo* at the Tulsa punk/rock club, Eclipse. With these releases placing the group way out into the "We are going to do what we want" realm, Oklahoma music fans began to think of JFJO as Tulsa's freaky jazz cousin to Oklahoma City's psychedelic posters, the Flaming Lips. Jacob Fred Jazz Odyssey began delving further into improvisation and extended jams, in which Haas and Mathis flew through sets as musical trapeze artists, engaging audiences with their instrumental skill, musical "conversations" and harmonic experimentation, both individually and as a counterpoints to each other. Always propelled and punctuated by enormously capable and trusted drummers Matt Edwards, Richard Haas (Bryan's younger brother), and Jason Smart, JFJO's trio configuration excelled at jazz's primary requirement

Jacob Fred Jazz Odyssey 2011, left to right: Harshbarger, Combs, Haas, and Raymer

of being able to state a musical theme, and then elaborating on that theme via instrumental improvisation while retaining primary aesthetic elements of the original theme's melody or chord progressions; ultimately, the standard jazz composition resolves by returning to "the head", or start of the piece to conclude. Via these skills, and the strength of their second album, JFJO started getting gigs around the United States.

After a couple of well-received shows in Boston, Accurate Records, the label that launched other new-jazz experimentalists such as Medeski, Martin, and Wood, Morphine, and Jazz Mandolin Project, offered the group a deal to release another album. The resulting disc, *Welcome Home*, was recorded during two sold out shows at Club One in Tulsa in September of 1998, and included a couple of studio tracks from April, 1998. Received well critically in both jazz and progressive music circles in the U.S., the album opened doors for more gigs around the U.S. outside of their base to that time of the Midwest with Oklahoma as its center. With a heavy touring schedule getting more and more intense with every passing month, JFJO started showing the haggard signs of an independent band touring the country in a van. First, ace trombonist Matt Leland left the group in the spring of 1999, and original JFJO drummer Sean Layton was replaced with Matt Edwards who had already been playing percussion with the group. Under similar circumstances of touring duress, guitarist Dove McHargue and trumpeter Kyle Wright played their last show with JFJO in July of 1999. Pared to a trio formally, as they had already been experimenting with the three-man format, Haas, Mathis, and Edwards began an intense touring schedule of more than 500 shows over the next two years, selling out venues in Boston, San Francisco, Atlanta, Washington, D.C., and Austin, Texas. The primary document from this period as a trio with Matt Edwards on drums is the very independently produced CD, *The Jacob Fred Trio: Live at Your Mama's House Volume 1*, recorded on two dates in January 2000 at the Bowery in Tulsa. Given the relative lo-fi quality of *Live at Your Mama's House* and being eager to get something else out the group could sell at its shows, JFJO also released *Bloom 1996 to 1998* in 2000. According to the JFJO website, *"Bloom* is a retrospective release covering Spring '96 to Spring '98. [It] includes some live material from the opening for Medeski, Martin, and Wood days of '96, and JFJO's first time in the studio without an audience later that summer (producing the hauntingly beautiful 'Hymn 1008'). *Bloom* also included some 1997 live recordings from San Francisco's Elbo Room, and two never-before-heard Sean Layton vocal tunes from '98 that represent Fred's only venture into the land of multiple overdubs… Some of the material was originally released on 1996's *Live in Tokyo* and is back, re-mastered and all polished up."

JFJO spent the latter half of 2000 and the early part of 2001 recording, mixing, and mastering *Self Is Gone*, named after a *Tulsa World* headline about then TU basketball coach Bill Self leaving the university. Recorded in Los Angeles and Chicago, *Self Is Gone* contains recordings of ten, first-take, improvised songs highlighting the incredibly facile players. Having pretty much worn out drummer Edwards by 2001, Brian Haas' younger brother, Richard, joined the group. Richard's presence brought the polyrhythmic traditions of African drumming to the group's sound, which can be heard and seen online via the band's website at a concert recorded live at Tipitina's in New Orleans. Since the two brothers had played together since grade school, the interplay between the two was a natural symbiosis, however, the constant touring took its toll on the younger Haas, and Richard only lasted until October of 2001. Subsequently, JFJO hired on Jason Smart, a drummer from Cincinnati who had been working at a Tulsa music store, and who is featured on JFJO's most recent recording, 2002's *All Is One: Live in New York City*. *All Is One*. *All is One* was recorded live in New York City at the well-known experimental music venue, the Knitting Factory, and for the Knitting Factory label that has grown out of the club's extensive history with avant-garde music. The group also released two limited edition live discs on their own, one recorded at the High Sierra Music Festival in July of 2002, and one recorded at the Telluride Acoustic Festival. Still to be released is an album recorded live for the New York independent label, Phoenix Presents, which specializes in improvisational music. In 2003, Jacob Fred Jazz Odyssey enjoyed regularly scheduled residencies at jazz clubs in New York and Boston, and returned to Oklahoma where they played a few select shows in Tulsa and Stillwater. In the summer of 2003, JFJO was honored by the Oklahoma Jazz Hall of Fame with the Legacy Tribute Award, and Bryan Haas linked up with former JFJO drummer Matt Edwards as The Void, a vehicle for long form improvisation, and called their show "Lab One featuring Return of the Void." Reed Mathis has also performed with Matt Edwards and other friends outside of JFJO, notably in 2002 where he was able to play other instruments on which specializes: cello, sitar, and acoustic guitar, a harbinger of his departure several years later in 2009 to join the San Francisco-based more rock and groove oriented jam band, Tea Leaf Green. Between 2003 and 2009 with Jason Smart on drums, however, the trio worked at an extremely high level, releasing at least nine albums proper, each one receiving more praise than the last for their sonic experimentation, boundary stretching music, and virtuosic technical abilities. As a bonus to fans, the group also made available many free recordings of JFJO one-of-kind-every-night shows via download from their official website. As they performed around the country and world for much of the first decade of the 21st century, the band garnered the highest praise possible from major music industry jazz critics who all raced to their thesauri to take their best shot at using word symbols to describe JFJO's music, to include the likes of *Downbeat*, *Jazz Times*, *Village Voice*, *San Francisco Chronicle*, and "industry Bible", *Billboard*. After hearing the 2010 release, *Ludwig*, on which the quartet performed re-arranged movements from Beethoven's 3rd and 6th Symphonies, completely modernizing them, *Billboard* touted JFJO as "one of the finest and most exciting jazz groups around," and *Downbeat* called *Ludwig* "a tour de force of jazz melded with classical."[1] The group successfully premiered the piece in concert at the annual OK Mozart Festival in Bartlesville, Oklahoma, in June, 2010, accompanied by the 50-piece Bartlesville Symphony Orchestra, led by music director Lauren Green. According to Haas, the work took years to complete with the goal of transforming the two-hundred-old music of Beethoven in "modern music for today's audiences," perhaps the most noticeable attempt by a contemporary artist with national status since, dare we say, Walter Murphy's 1976 #1 disco hit, "A Fifth of Beethoven"? JFJO's versions of Beethoven's "Eroica" and "Pastoral" movements are buoyed into a new existence by Haas' calamitous precision on piano informed by his classically trained musical roots, Combs' spaghetti Western space twang, Harshbarger using a bow on his double bass, and Raymer providing jazzbang percussive accents and passionate rolls around the drumkit's rack toms between important phrases and sections of the pieces. Creating program music for a new age, JFJO continued upping the musical ante in 2011 with a dynamic composition by Combs based on the Tulsa Race Riot of 1921. Incorporating all the musical genre elements of Tulsa's history, JFJO uses both the celebratory nature of jazz, as well as its funereal qualities, along with quotes from blues, Western swing, bluegrass, pop, and classical music to depict the before, during, and after of the Tulsa Race Riot, much like the Program Music of 19th century Romantic composers who sought to depict images, events, or ideals through the tone, texture, and tempo of their compositions. Interest-

Brian Haas, circa 2003

ingly, Jacob Fred Jazz Odyssey also typifies in their own way a primary hallmark of Oklahoma's most successful musicians, and that is being diverse musically in order to have a broader base for one's talents and further opportunities to reach one's professional and/or artistic goals, namely surviving as a musician and not anything else, which is what the members of JFJO clearly seem both designed and destined to do. Brian Haas made his solo album, *Petting Sounds*, recorded in one continuous session and engineered by Leon Russell's son on the mixing board used to record the Beach Boys' classic *Pet Sounds*, available as a free download via his website (still up as of July, 2011). JFJO was booked throughout 2011 and into 2012 at venues across the United States for in-demand performances of their challenging, worldly jazz and their contemporary and innovative classically-based art music. As of early 2013, the group was taking some time off to re-charge, write, and get ready for the next steps in their storied career.

JFJO drummer, Matt Edwards, circa 2003.

www.jfjo.com

www.brianroyhaas.com

www.chriscombsmusic.com

Jana Jae

(b. August 30, 1942)

After moving to Tulsa in order to better centralize her base of performing operations, and later to property she purchased near Grove, Oklahoma, the "Queen of the Country Fiddle", Jana Jae, has become an important musical, educational, tourism and community fixture in Oklahoma's arts community, but she is also widely regarded as a traditional fiddler and classical violinist of the first order both in the U.S. and around the world where she still tours as of 2011. After moving to Grove, she started a non-profit organization dedicated to the preservation of traditional American music, and has hosted music festivals in the area since 1995. Beginning in 1997 under her non-profit umbrella, Jae started hosting the American Heritage Music Festival in June, the Cajun Festival in July, and the National Fiddle Camp in July, bringing in musicians and tourists from as many as forty states each year to the Grand Lake area. As a result of her long time residency in the state, her acclaim as an internationally recognized classical violinist, and her prominence on the television program, *Hee Haw*, she is easily one of Oklahoma's two most prominent fiddlers recognized on a national scale, the other being her long-time friend, Byron Berline.

Born Janet Margaret Myer in Great Falls, Montana, "Jana" first learned about the violin at age two via a 1/8-sized instrument while living with her parents who were studying at the Juilliard School of Music in New York City. She was later introduced to traditional American "Old Time" fiddling by her grandfather in Idaho when she moved there at age seven with her mother. Jae's grandpa was a one-time northeastern Oklahoma fiddler and fiddle contest champion, who taught her the reels, waltzes, and other country dances popular during the barn square dance era of the late 19th and early 20th centuries in Indian Territory and Oklahoma. The fiddle still held sway in the northeastern part of the state where the Ozark Mountains begin their craggy grey crawl to isolated mountain homes across northern Arkansas and southern Missouri, homes where a fiddle was traditionally a ubiquitous instrument for self-made music due to its portability and affordability. With assistance from her grandfather who helped her to learn to play by ear, Jana began performing in public at a very young age, appearing on the Ted Mack Original Amateur Hour at age four, and continuing to amaze audiences throughout her childhood with her re-call knowledge of traditional fiddle tunes. With folk training supreme in her pocket, Jae elevated her skills to a point where several times she won the highly-competitive National Old Time Fiddlers' Contest in the Ladies National Championship Division in Weiser, Idaho, before continuing her classical training on violin. After winning scholarships to Interlochen, a well-known Arts Academy for youth in Interlochen, Michigan, as well as to the International String Congress, an organization formed by Oklahoma-born classical composer, Roy Harris, due to his perception that formally trained string players were becoming harder to find in the 1950s, she studied abroad at the Vienna Academy of Music, and earned her degree in music while studying in Denver, Colorado. Jae taught for several years, until she began performing concerts in which she merged her knowledge and abilities in classical and bluegrass music, much to the delight of her audiences.

Jana Jae plays fiddle with her 90-year-old mother, Grove, OK, 2011.

While on the West Coast, Jae met Buck Owens who had already heard about her fiddling abilities. After hearing her play "Orange Blossom Special", Owens offered Jana a job as the first female member of his band, the Buckaroos, at a time when women typically were not lead instrumentalists in country music combos. With that connection, however, and with her abilities to play so many styles of music, she began to network with the Who's Who of country music during the 1960s and early 70s, leading to a management deal with Jim Halsey. Ultimately, it was Halsey who encouraged her to move to Tulsa so she could have a central base of operations from which to travel the country and world, instead of being stuck out on the West Coast with heaps of added travel to the middle, southern, or eastern parts of the U.S. After taking Halsey's advice (which seems to have worked for a lot of significant artists), Jae moved to Tulsa where she lived for several years as a touring base before purchasing property near Grove, Oklahoma. Ironically, she found out later from her mother that the grandfather who had taught her so much about the fiddle had lived in nearby Vinita for a time while courting her grandmother. As a result, she brought some traditional Oklahoma music full circle back to the state after it had departed many years earlier in the mind, ears, and fingers of her grandfather.

Due to Jae's varied musical abilities, she has played a wide range of classical, jazz, folk, and country music festivals and events, both in the U.S. and abroad. Jae has performed at the Montreux Jazz Festival in Switzerland, the Wembley Festival in England, and the New Orleans Jazz Festival. She has also continued to tour consistently in Australia, the Philippines, Australia, Africa Brazil, and throughout Europe. Through her connection to Buck Owens (to whom she was even married for a few days before she had the marriage annulled), and Owens' broad swath of country music friendships and business relationships, to include Halsey, Jana eventually became part of the regular cast of the popular 1960s and '70s corny TV show filled with great country music, *Hee-Haw*, eventually appearing on more than a hundred episodes with her bright and effervescent personality, mountainous fiddle skills, and the ability to pull off a professional vocal rendition of traditional country songs. She has also performed with many country music notables, such as Chet Atkins, Roy Clark, Ray Stevens, The Oak Ridge Boys, Mel Tillis, Rocky Skaggs, Tammy Wynette, Asleep at the Wheel, and the Nitty Gritty Dirt Band. She has produced many independent albums of both traditional tunes and music educational materials, such as DVD lessons an instruction books. Jae's Lark Records released, *The Devil You Say*, in 2006, on which she performs traditional tunes such as "Orange Blossom Special", "Cotton Eyed Joe", and "Sally Goodin", about as traditional as an old time fiddler can get, but also adds a couple of Oklahoma-themed tracks, "Bob Wills Medley" and "The Devil Went On To Tulsa". In 2008, Lark Records released *Ashokan Farewell*, an album of more traditional tunes, mostly waltzes, and including another nod to Bob Wills with the state of Oklahoma's official country and western song, "Faded Love". Jae also released a fiddling instructional DVD through her website to teach bowing techniques, and how to play harmony, standard and advanced song endings, and improvisational strategies, along with training on several standard fiddle tunes.

Watching a Jana Jae performance, whether in the classical or traditional American music modes, is to see and hear an effortless musician who is in ultimate command of both her instrument, and musical idioms she learned both the formal and old-fashioned ways, combining to create a unique performer who can play bluegrass or Bach with equal distinction. For readers who have made it through several of the entries in this text, she also illustrates a major commonality of successful musicians as a whole: those who can do or play more than one thing in the music industry seem to be the ones who have the most enduring success. Additionally, Jae has made significant contributions to both musical tourism and traditional music education in Oklahoma through her festivals, exhibits, concerts, workshops, and other aspects of her non-profit foundation. In 2011, she continued hosting her traditional music festivals at Grand Lake, but had also expanded the concept to her first home-state of Idaho.

w ww.janajae.com

James, Brett
(b. June 5, 1968)

An extremely successful songwriter who was written or co-written several #1 country hits, Brett James Cornelius was born to parents, Carolyn and Dr. Sam Cornelius, in Columbia, Missouri, but raised in Oklahoma City and Cordell, Oklahoma. While in college at Baylor University, his parents gave him a pawn shop guitar, on which he learned three chords, and began writing songs. After recording a demo while still studying medicine at the University of Oklahoma Medical School, James made a spring break journey to Nashville where he had been able to arrange some meetings with labels there.[1]

After signing with Tim DuBois' at Arista Records, James opted out of medical school and relocated to Nashville where his self-titled debut album was released in 1995 on Arista. Only one single, "Female Bonding", blipped into the *Billboard* Hot Country Singles chart, and the album did not even register on the chart at all. After seven years of trying to make country music career, James lost his record and publishing deal, and in 1999 he headed back to Oklahoma and medical school, but continued writing songs. Not long after school started, Faith Hill recorded a song he co-wrote, "Love is a Sweet Thing", for her album *Breathe*, and over the next nine months thirty-three of his songs were recorded by artists such as Martina McBride and Tim McGraw. As James' co-writes, Jessica Andrews scored a 2001 #1 *Billboard* Hot Country Single with "Who I Am", written with Troy Verges in the back office of parents' house, and Martina McBride took "Blessed" to #1 on the *Billboard* Hot Country Singles chart in March, 2002. With this success, James again signed a record deal with Arista in 2002, releasing two singles of his own, "Chasin' Amy" (2002) and "After All" (2003), both of which inched into the country Top 40 at #34 and #39 respectively, not enough to inspire enough confidence for the label to release an album, urging James to focus primarily on songwriting, an extremely good choice in retrospect, as he now has become one of Nashville's leading songwriters.

Brett James

In 2004, another James co-write, "When the Sun Goes Down", notched #1 status on the *Billboard* Hot Country Singles chart for Kenny Chesney and Uncle Kracker, and his 2006 co-write, "Jesus Take the Wheel", did the same as Carrie Underwood's breakout song after winning *American Idol*. "Jesus Take the Wheel" also earned James' (and his two co-writers) notice with a Grammy Award for Best Country Song of 2006, and ASCAP's Country Songwriter of the Year. In 2009, four more of James' co-writes topped the Hot Country Singles chart: Rodney Atkins/"It's America"; Kenny Chesney/"Out Last Night"; Rascal Flatts/"Summer Nights"; and Carrie Underwood/"Cowboy Casanova". The next year, 2010, witnessed even more accolades for James. Two songs he co-wrote, Jason Aldean's "The Truth" and Chris Young's "The Man I Want to Be", achieved #1 status on the *Billboard* Hot Country Singles chart, and pop artist Daughtry gained another Top 40 hit with a James co-write, "Life After You". Also in 2010, ASCAP again awarded James its Country Songwriter of the Year Award.

Along with close to a hundred credits on songs for country artists such as Rhonda Vincent, Billy Ray Cyrus, Faith Hill, LeAnn Rimes, Pat Green, among many others, he has had songs recorded by pop artists The Backstreet Boys/"Helpless When She Smiles", Jewel "One True Thing", Bon Jovi/"Til We Ain't Strangers Anymore", as well as Latin artist Paulina Rubio "Todo Me Amor". James has an outrageous 750-plus songs listed on his ASCAP songwriters' database. Throughout his career, James' songs have appeared on country, pop, Canadian, rock, and Latin charts, indicating the widespread appeal of his lyrics, and the further benefits of looking outside of one's immediate interests for music industry success. Along those lines, James also began working as a record producer in

2008, with credits on the reissue of Taylor Swift's self-titled debut album (Big Machine, 2008), which also included a bonus track co-written by James, "A Perfectly Good Heart". He also co-produced Jessica Simpson's #1 country album, *Do You Know* (Sony, 2008), adding two other co-writes with Simpson, "Man Enough" and "Still Beautiful".

Notes
1. Of all the online articles about Brett James available, the only mention of James' songwriting start and entry into the Nashville fray is in Brandy McDonnell's article, "Doctor of songwriting," *Daily Oklahoman*, December 2, 2009, D6.

Jernigan, Dennis
(b. circa 1959)

Born in Sapulpa to parents Robert and Peggy Jernigan, but raised on a farm near Boynton where he attend the public schools, Dennis Jernigan is best known as a contemporary Christian pianist, singer and songwriter with three charting singles on *Billboard*'s Top Contemporary Christian chart. As a pianist, Jernigan's abilities were opened up when his Grandmother Jernigan moved next to the family, bringing along a piano in her trailer home on which he practiced almost daily. Without a music teacher out in the country, Jernigan learned to play by ear. He began playing publicly at age nine in church, where his grandfather, Herman Everett Johnson, was the pastor, and his father, Robert, was the song leader. After high school, Jernigan attended Oklahoma Baptist University to study musically formally, and graduated in 1981. Since that time, Jernigan has recorded more than thirty-five albums of his original Christian music, some of which has charted nationally: "Break My Heart" (#39/1994); "Celebrate Living" (#37/1996); and "This is My Destiny" (#35/1999). His success within the realm of the Christian music and service is better gauged by the national and worldwide demand for his performances and personal testimony through his ministry which is based in Muskogee, Oklahoma, where he lives with his wife, Melinda, with whom he has nine children. His most recent recording, *Here in Your Presence – Dennis Jernigan Live from San Antonio*, captures his concert ministry performances "as they are", with his songs backed by a large choir and excellent musicianship, along with the core messages of encouragement and ministerial wisdom for which he has become known.

www.dennisjernigan.com

Dennis Jernigan

Johns, William
(b. October 2, 1936)

An internationally renowned operatic tenor who has performed throughout Europe and the United States, especially in roles developed by Richard Wagner, Dr. William Johns is also widely recognized as significant teacher who has worked with many contemporary opera performers, and was born in Tulsa. With a full and expressive voice expected of opera singers, William made his American debut in 1965 at the Metropolitan Opera House in New York at the National Council Concert. In 1967, he appeared at the Lake George Opera in Saratoga Springs, New York, in the role of Rodolfo in Puccini's *La Boheme*. His European debut in the early 1970s was with the Bremen Opera (Germany), followed by the Welsh National Opera (Cardiff, Wales) in the roles of Radames in Verdi's *Aida* and Calaf in Puccini's *Turandot*.

Johns' Royal Opera House (Covent Garden in London) debut was in 1987 as Bacchus in Strauss' *Ariadne auf naxos*. This was followed by the role of Florestan in Beethoven's only opera, *Fidelio*, in Philadelphia in 1988, and the role of Tristan in Wagner's *Tristan und Isolde* in San Francisco in 1991, where he has performed since 1967 in a number of significant operatic roles. Additional roles played by William include Siegfried in Wagner's *Siegfried*, Lohengrin in Wagner's *Lohengrin*, Tannhauser in Wagner's *Tannhauser*, as well as the Emperor in Strauss' *Die Frau ohne Schatten*. Johns has also performed with the Hamburg Opera, Vienna Opera, Houston Opera, and Dallas Opera. He has also performed at the Australian Opera, and as of 2010, lived there.

William Johns

Johnson, Cecil
Johnson, Herman (b. May 10, 1920)

Fiddling brothers Herman and Cecil were born on the Johnson family farm near Sparks, Oklahoma, a small community in Lincoln County near Chandler. Two of thirteen children, both began playing around age eight, as they were surrounded by fiddlers in the form of their grandfather, father, two uncles, and other brothers who played, all by ear. While Cecil was a National Champion fiddler, he was also a fiddle maker and repairer, as well as an in-demand restoration expert on a variety of stringed instruments. Cecil Johnson's primary championship year was 1977 when he placed first in the Senior Division at the Oklahoma State Fair fiddling contest, fourth place in the Senior Division at the extremely competitive Weiser, Idaho National Championship Fiddlers' Contest, and first place in the Senior Division at the Ogden, Utah National Championship Fiddlers' Contest. Both brothers were invited to Washington D.C. in 1976 to perform old time fiddle tunes at the Smithsonian Institute's Bicentennial American Folklife Festival, some of which was recorded for the National Archives. Cecil did make one recording at the peak of his performing success, *Country Style Fiddling* (John's, 1978), an album released on his own label recorded at Gillian Music Studio in Chandler. Along with Cecil on lead fiddle for all tunes, the album includes Ralph McGraw

Cecil Johnson

(guitar), Steve Gillian (2nd fiddle, mandolin), and Russell Gillian (banjo, guitar). Russell Gillian also became a National Champion guitarist. While Cecil tended to remain around Chandler where he played for church events, home fiddling sessions, social gatherings, family reunions, and the like, Herman extended the Johnson family's fiddling fame to even greater heights.

In liner notes accompanying Herman Johnson's 1978 independent album, *National Champion* (John's), also recorded at Gillian Recording Studio in Chandler, noted Oklahoma folk and country music historian, Guy Logsdon, chronicles Johnson's career through 1977. By age nineteen, Herman played with the Oklahoma Ragtimers on KGFF radio out of Shawnee before moving to Sherman, Texas in 1940, where he and his Harmony Boys played regularly on KRRV, Sherman. Like many lives at that time, his was interrupted by World War II. After his service time, he wound up back in Shawnee in 1946 where he and his wife, Mary Jane (Bartosh), raised four children, and where he continued playing in various Western swing dance bands in the area as Bob Wills had created a huge demand for that style of music throughout the Southwest and West in the 1930s, 40s, and 50s. Working as machinist at Tinker Air Force Base until his retirement in 1974, Herman began competing at various local and national fiddle contests starting about 1960, and winning a lot of them. He won the National Championship at the previously mentioned mountaintop of fiddle contests in Weiser, Idaho, five times (1968, 1969, 1973, 1977, and 1978), and is the only person to be undefeated in that contest, He is also enshrined in Weiser's National Fiddlers Hall of Fame. After winning the Grand Masters' Championship in Nashville in 1974, he appeared on *Hee Haw*, *The Porter Wagoner Show*, and *The Grand Ole Opry*. Accompanying Herman on guitar for many of the championship competitions was Ralph McGraw of Tecumseh, who is also featured on Cecil Johnson's previously discussed album. Besides Herman and McGraw, Steve Gillian is the only other musician on Herman's album, playing second fiddle, but Gillian became a National Champion fiddler himself, no doubt learning what it took partially from Herman. Another fiddler who learned a lot from Herman Johnson is Jeanine R. Orme of Ogden, Utah, who studied with Herman for twenty-five years, ultimately transcribing many of Herman Johnson's tunes and publishing the collection as *Herman Johnson Master Fiddler: 39 Solos by America's Legendary Fiddler* (Mel Bay, 1999).

Herman Johnson

Jones, Claude
(b. February 11, 1901 – d. January 17, 1962)

One of the jazz trombonists who helped free the instrument from its traditional role as a rhythm and accent instrument with his melodic improvisations, Claude B. Jones was born in Boley, Oklahoma, one of Oklahoma's National Historic Landmarks due to its status as the prominent all-Black town from that movement and period of Oklahoma history in the late 19th and early 20th centuries. Claude attended Langston High School in Langston, Oklahoma, another one of the all-Black communities in the state and home of Langston

University. During high school, he played drums and trumpet in the band, but was influenced by a carnival parade with a trombonist leading the band. At around twelve years of age, Claude's parents gave him a Wurlitzer trombone, took lessons on the instrument from a local teacher, and eventually played trombone in the community band.

Following high school, Claude served a two-year stint with the U.S. Army band, in which he played bass horn, trumpet, and trombone. After discharge from the armed services in 1922, he attended Wilberforce College in Wilberforce, Ohio, where he played in the Wilberforce College Band, but soon dropped out and joined the Synco Jazz Band, a forerunner of McKinney's Cotton Pickers, based in Springfield, Ohio, with whom he later performed at the Greystone Ballroom in Detroit and various nightclubs in Harlem, as well as recording with McKinney intermittently in the 1920s. Tightly scripted and arranged, McKinney's music is both a descendant of Dixieland and a forerunner to the closely formatted big bands of the 1930s, requiring musicians to be adept readers of music, as well as competent soloists when called upon. Through those performances and recordings, Jones came to the attention of major bandleaders of the day due to the melodic dynamics of his solos.

Jones gained attention for his work with Fletcher Henderson during the late 1920s and early 1930s. Then, he both recorded and played through the 1930s with big bands led by Don Redman, Chick Webb, Alex Hill, Jelly Roll Morton, and Cab Callaway. In the 1940s, he was part of Duke Ellington's esteemed post-war orchestra from 1944 to 1948. Additional bandleaders for whom Claude played include Coleman Hawkins at the Golden Gate Ballrooom in New York City, Zutty Singleton, Joe Sullivan, Benny Carter, Louis Armstrong, and second periods with Callaway and Redman. During the 1940s, he left full-time music to manage his own sausage manufacturing company. In the early 1950s Claude was back with the Fletcher Henderson Sextet, and again with Ellington for about six months, but in 1952 he left music completely, becoming a mess steward aboard the S.S. United States upon which he died at sea on January 17, 1962.

Claude Jones, 1946

To hear some of the practically "proto-bop" playing by Jones, track down the 1931 Don Redman recording, "Shakin' the Africann", in which Jones concludes the piece with a joyous sequence of syncopated slurs up and down the scale, pinching out blue notes as perfect accents to the counterpoint by the orchestra. Jones was a highly respected contemporary all jazz musicians of his era, even of Louis Armstrong, and is featured with the king of all jazz trumpeters on "Down in Honky Tonk Town" in 1940 on the Decca label, available on *Louis Armstrong 1940-1942* (Melodie Jazz Classics, 1996). Jones also recorded with such luminaries as Henry "Red" Allen, Sidney Bechet, Lionel Hampton, and Ben Webster, and should be considered one of Oklahoma's most important jazz musicians.

Jones, Norah
(b. March 30, 1979)

Oklahoma music fans often mistakenly claim the multi-instrumentalist, singer, and songwriter known expecially for her Grammy Award-winning and multi-platinum 2002 album, Come Away With Me (Blue Note), and its massive hit single, "Don't Know Why"; however, the singer was not born in the state and has never lived in Oklahoma, although her mother, Sue Jones, is from Oklahoma, and the most likely source of this confusion. Norah was born in Brooklyn, New York, and then moved to Grapevine, Texas, after her parents' separation. Her father is the famous sitar player Ravi Shankar. Nora attended public school in Grapevine and Dallas, then studied jazz at the University of North Texas before returning to New York where she launched her career. Jones is so disconnected from the state, that when she announced during a 2010 Tulsa performance that her mother is from Oklahoma, she could make no sense of fans yelling "Boomer" and "Sooner" back to her. "All I hear is 'Pooh-Bear'", she said from the stage, to the chuckles of Oklahoma State fans in the audience..

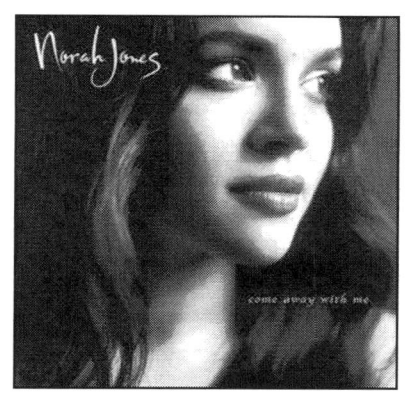

Jones, Stacy
(b. circa 1970)

Lead singer for the alternative pop rock group, American Hi-Fi, Stacy Jones was born in Tulsa. Prior to being in American Hi-Fi, Jones was a drummer for successful alternative rock bands, Letters to Cleo and Veruca Salt. Formed in Los Angeles in 2001, American Hi-Fi's most successful single "Flavor of the Weak", reached #5 on *Billboard*'s Modern Rock chart, and #41 on the Hot 100, *almost* making them a Top 40 band. The band's first two albums made it into the *Billboard* Top 200 album charts, *American Hi-Fi* (#81/2001) and *The Art of Losing* (#80/2003). However, their third album, 2005's *Hearts on Parade* (Maverick), peaked at #129 on the album charts, and 2010's *Fight the Frequency* (RED) did not chart at all.

Stacy Jones, 2002

Noted in various reviews for his snarky attitude and lyrics (befitting a punk rock frontman), when asked via a Q and A section of the band's website about his Oklahoma connections, Jones' replied with a terse but clear phrase: "Zero musical experiences growing up, cuz I moved when I was 1." Enough said.

www.americanhi-fi.com

By Hugh Foley

Joplin, Scott
(b. circa 1867 – d. April 1, 1917)

The most notable figure of the late 19th and early 20th centuries piano style known as ragtime, Scott Joplin, was not born in Oklahoma, although his birth in extreme northeast Texas outside of Texarkana puts him about thirty miles outside of the state. What makes Joplin an interesting figure in Oklahoma music history is first his "wandering years" as an itinerant pianist in the 1880s, a period in which life for African-Americans was both promising and prosperous in the pre-statehood Oklahoma and Indian Territories, and also a time of relative lawlessness in both places that provided an ample amount of work for musicians in saloons, hotels, and other venues where such entertainment was welcome, if not a necessary diversion. Oklahoma would have been a likely place for Joplin to find work in developing railroad towns, all-Black towns, and the "wet" towns of Oklahoma Territory. According to okblues.org, a website dedicated to preserving blues history in the state, "Joplin was known to have performed in the "sporting houses and saloons of late 19th century Indian Territory before moving on to Sedalia, Missouri," at which point his career is documented meticulously through his death. Many published biographies and websites repeat this vague historical note about Scott Joplin without any documentation to back it up. However, scholars do know that Joplin was very aware of, and most likely rode, the Missouri-Kansas-and Texas railroad line, known as the KATY, which also went east from Dallas to Texarkana, and north through Indian Territory to get to Kansas and Missouri, to include a stop at his future home of Sedalia, Missouri. He commemorated the joining of the KATY Railway (when two locomotives were crashed together as a publicity stunt in Texas) with "The Great Crush Collision March", dedicated to the Missouri-Kansas-Texas Railway. He would also have certainly known the most significant Black town between Texas and Kansas or Missouri, which was Muskogee, a town that produced a number of significant jazz musicians (Jay McShann, Don Byas, Claude "Fiddler" Williams, and Don Byas), and was very hospitable to African-Americans via its significant Black business district of South Second Street, which featured a number of "joints" and other performance opporunities during Joplin's era. Additionally, the KATY was his direct route to Sedalia. More information about Joplin's time in Indian Territory is a good scholarly detective quest, as a few leads have already been turned up.

Scott Joplin

One of the most often repeated stories is about a ragtime era pianist, Brun Campbell, born in Kansas in 1884 to a father who took off on one of the Oklahoma land runs, but was not able to get there fast enough to acquire any land. As a result, however, he saw the multiple sales opportunities and hauled his family down to Oklahoma Territory where Brun received piano lessons in Oklahoma City. According to an online essay by ragtime scholar and transcriber, Richard Egan, Campbell was playing piano in an Oklahoma City music store and was noticed by Otis Saunders, "a pianist and close friend of Scott Joplin," who challenged the precocious Campbell with an inked manuscript of "Maple Leaf Rag", Joplin's famous composition. After learning about Joplin and ragtime, Campbell headed to Sedalia where Joplin is supposedly to have named him "The Ragtime Kid".[1] A further known fact linking Joplin to Oklahoma City is a touring production of his opera, *A Guest of Honor*, broke up in Oklahoma City, leaving the surviving members of the troupe to either form or join a minstrel show to get back home. Oklahoma City had two vaudeville houses targeted toward the sizable African-American audiences in Oklahoma City, both operated by TOBA, the notorious Theater Owners Booking Association that booked Black acts across the country, and a scattered association of Black vaudeville houses in the city.[2] Little else is known about the opera's appearance in the city, and whether or not it was even performed, but Joplin was aware of the opportunities for his work in the Oklahoma Territory, and apparently had both friends and business associates in the state from his earlier time there. Little is really known about Scott Joplin's time in Indian Territory or Oklahoma Territory, but his developmental years as a performer are repeatedly linked with the pre-statehood territories in the 1880s and early 1890s, even though they are not well-documented to this time.

Notes
1. For more discussion on Brun Campbell's career and the mention of Joplin's friend, Otis Saunders, in Oklahoma City, see Richard Egan, "Brun Campbell: The Rag-Time-Warp", http://stlouis.missouri.org/501c/fsjoplin/euphony/9405campbell.htm (accessed July 10, 2011).   2. E-mail to the author from Oklahoma ragtime scholar, John Wilson, September 21, 2002.

K

Karstein, Jimmy
(b. 1943)

With perhaps the lightest light touch of the various talented drummers from Tulsa[1], as well as being well known for his jazz-influenced rhythms, subtle off beat accents, and tidy rolls added to the musical changes in a song that bind a tune together, Jimmy Karstein defines the subtlety of drummers who play the low-key blues rock sometimes known as the **Tulsa Sound**. While the Tulsa Sound is a misnomer for some musicians with whom it is associated, saying the two words do not fully encompass the whole style that is a sum of many parts, the rock "subgenre" is primarily associated with **J.J. Cale** in the 1970s, as well as Eric Clapton who has openly praised Cale with emulation and respectful reverence. The easy, laid back rocking blues that first appealed to Clapton when he was introduced to it by Delaney Bramlett (of Delaney and Bonnie) has largely defined J.J. Cale's style since his first significant album recorded in Los Angeles under the name the Leathercoated Minds, a 1966 studio project engineered by **Leon Russell** on which Karstein plays drums. Leon Russell first encouraged Karstein (and several other Tulsa musicians) to head out to Los Angeles for studio work, and Karstein began with Gary Lewis and the Playboys in 1965 when Gary Lewis was peaking in popularity, but not necessarily writing or playing the music on his records; that was left up to Russell. Karstein also recorded with J.J. Cale in 1966 on Cale's first significant LP project under the name the Leathercoated Minds, continuing an association between the two that began when the two were teenage musicians in Tulsa, and exists to the present day. Karstein appears no less than ten J.J. Cale albums over a thirty-year span in which he has been part of Cale's "A-Team" of support musicians, often drawing tracks with complex rhythms befitting his considerable abilities, which alone could indicate Karstein's noteworthy embedded status as one of rock's important drummers; however, his additional work with Leon Russell, Eric Clapton, Joe Cocker, **The Tractors**, and Stephen Stills, along with local Oklahoma recordings by the Red Dirt Rangers and Susan Herndon, seals the deal.

Along with some pretty cheesy attempts to cash in on the psychedelic pop sounds of the moment, the 1966 Leathercoated Minds recording is still important for understanding J.J. Cale's defining aesthetic early in his career, as well as Jimmy Karstein's style that appears to be fully formed at the time. The future of both musicians can be heard on the sessions. Along with a few tunes featuring Cale's droll delivery for which he becomes known, one can also hear Karstein playing the easy shuffle rhythm often applied as a musical descriptor for the Tulsa Sound. Karstein also shows his facility with the jazz-influenced counterpoint and poly-rhythmic approach on which Cale continued to call for his albums from 1972's *Really* (Shelter) through 2009's *Roll On* (Rounder), and which also obviously appealed to Eric Clapton, who first heard Karstein's work through the Leathercoated Minds' recording of "After Midnight", which Clapton had been introduced to Delaney Bramlett (of Delaney and Bonnie – think "Layla"], with whom Clapton had been writing and recording in the late 1960s. Eventually, "After Midnight" became Cale's first hit as songwriter when Clapton's version zipped up to #18 on *Billboard*'s Hot 100 in 1970. While his reverence for J.J. Cale's relaxed vocal and guitar style is obvious, Clapton also obviously appreciated Karstein's tempo and drum work on the original version. Not only did Clapton recruit Karstein for the 1973 post-heroin addiction "comeback" shows in London, recorded and released as *Eric Clapton's Rainbow Concert* (RSO), in which "After Midnight" is a featured track, Clapton also appears to have directed Jamie Oldaker on at least a couple of occasions to provide a drum track in the ballpark of what Karstein had been doing as early as 1966, but was again noticeable on Cale's 1972 album, *Really* (Shelter).

Jimmy Karstein

For ear insight to Karstein's quiet intensity and easily identifiable rhythmic imprint, put on Cale's "Going Down" from the *Really* album. Notice Karstein's deft snare work that keeps the track settled down, and serves as the anchor between the song's sections, a hallmark of the hushed ballast often present in Cale's music. From the same album, one hears the quiet intensity of Karstein's jazz-influenced timekeeping via his ride cymbal work on the choruses of Cale's version of Muddy Waters' "Mo Jo". Cale seems to just "hear" Karstein on some of his music, and it is usually on songs with faster tempos or with more complicated rhythmic requirements than a basic kick/snare/hat accompaniment. In 1975, Eric Clapton features another Tulsa drummer, Jamie Oldaker, on *There's One in Every Crowd* (RSO). Introduced to Clapton by Tulsa bassist, Carl Radle, with whom Clapton had been playing since the Delaney and Bonnie days, Jamie Oldaker plays a complicated part reminiscent of Karstein's early work with Cale on Clapton's "We've Been Told (Jesus is Coming Soon)". The next year, Cale bounces one right back to Clapton with "I'm a Gypsy Man" from the 1976 *Troubadour* LP, on which Karstein mirrors the rhythm work on "Mo Jo", but this time he freshens the moment by alternating heavily between the kick drum and high hat on "I'm a Gypsy Man" instead of the snare and ride cymbal he favors for accents and meter on "Mo Jo". As for influences and inspirations, a writer who is not a drummer has to be careful, but just listen to the previously mentioned cymbal work by Karstein on Cale's two albums from '72 and '76, and then check Jamie Oldaker's work on "The Core" from Eric Clapton's triple platinum 1977 album, *Slowhand* (RSO). While not the exact same rhythm nor tempo, Oldaker hits the ride with one less tap in the choruses to make it his own, but the aggressive restraint Karstein applies to the ride cymbal in "Going Down", and the high hat in "I'm a Gypsy Man", is an obvious stylistic harbinger of Oldaker's foundation in "The Core". Therefore, as much as J.J. Cale's vocal delivery, guitar style, and lyrical content influenced some of Clapton's music in the middle 1970s and beyond, Karstein's more complicated rhythms that would not be out of place in a bebop combo from the late 1940s can be heard in Oldaker's drumming on both "We've Been Told (Jesus is Coming Soon)" and "The Core", either by design (Clapton wanting a track like that for himself), or osmosis as a result of being from the same musical environment (Tulsa) that produced both drummers. Clapton makes connecting the dots a little easier when he mentions a "gypsy woman" in "The Core", which starts off the side 2 of the *Slowhand* vinyl LP from 1977, just as "I'm a Gypsy Man" opens side 2 of Cale's *Troubadour* vinyl LP from 1976, which also includes Cale's version of "Cocaine" that Clapton covered so notoriously for *Slowhand*, by which we can infer Clapton also heard "I'm a Gypsy Man" since it was on the same Cale album. A key difference between the two drummers (Karstein and Oldaker) is that Cale used up to five or more different drummers or percussionists (including himself) for his multiple-styled songs on albums recorded on his own time schedule in the varying locations of California, Nashville, and Oklahoma, whereas, Clapton used one drummer for the bulk of his 1970s period, Jamie Oldaker, who is as adept at reggae and the Tulsa shuffle as he is at rock or blues. Up until the 1990s, Cale tended to bring in Karstein for either tunes with complex rhythmic structures or the straight ahead shuffle he has been playing with J.J. Cale since 1966. Karstein continued providing much of the same on on Cale's 1979 LP, *5* (Shelter): (hear "Lou-Easy-Ann" or "Fate of a Fool), and Karstein's unobtrusive but intrinsic drumming secures "If You Leave Her", from the 1981 Cale LP, *Shades* (Shelter). Karstein's signature feats are repeated again on Cale's 1994 Virgin Records release, *Closer to You*, but Cale seems to be going to his trusted accomplice for even more tracks (five on this album), a trend that will continue Cale's 2004 album, *To Tulsa and Back* (Sanctuary), on which Karstein is featured on six songs. Finally, on Cale's 2009 Rounder Records disc, Karstein appears on two songs, a straight-ahead 50s rocker, "Oh Mary", and the aptly titled low-key homage to the best acquaintances from the past, "Old Friend".

Notes
1. Along with Jimmy Karstein, other drummers from Tulsa who are also recognized with significant distinction for their contributions to rock music include **Jim Keltner**, **Chuck Blackwell**, **Jamie Oldaker**, and **David Teegarden**.

Kaw Nation (Kanza)
(Arrived in Indian Territory, 1873)

Tribal oral history indicates ancient presence among the great mass of Siouan speaking people in the northern Great Plains and Great Lakes regions prior to their first contact with Euro-Americans in the 1800s when the tribe had migrated south and controlled most of the present-day state of Kansas, which took its name *and* land from the tribe. Known as the "People of the South Wind" due to their geographic location within the Siouan sphere of influence, the Kanza are part of the "Dhegiha" branch of the Siouan speakers that includes the Osage, Quapaw, Ponca, and Omaha. According to the tribe's website, www.kawnation.com, an 1825 treaty reduced the tribe's domain in what is now Kansas from twenty million acres to two million. Then, due to unlawful settlers, railroad dollars, politicians who wanted more of Kaw territory for expansion, an 1846 treaty chopped that down to 256,000 acres near present-day Topeka (a Kansa word for "a good place to grow potatoes"). An 1872 federal act the Kaw vehemently opposed foretold the removal of the tribe to Indian Territory in 1873, where the tribe was placed on a 100,137 acre site next to their relatives, the Osage, with whom they share the same language. By that point, the Kaw had been reduced from several thousand, prior to contact with the newcomers in 1800, down to 533 people after disease and starvation devastated the Kansa people. Often, promised annuities and supplies never arrived, frequently being shortcut by unscrupulous government agents. By 1888, only 194 Kaw people remained on the reservation they purchased, but did not get to keep, as the Kaw Allotment Act of 1902 enrolled tribal citizens, allotted lands to members, then dissolved the Kaw Tribe, and opened up the "excess lands" for settlement.

Having maintained a small, but consistent community since tribal dissolution by the federal government, the tribe was allowed to re-organize as a functioning government in 1959, which they did in present-day northeastern Kay County, Oklahoma. After establishing a tribal headquarters, they had to move it again when part of the former reservation was flooded to form Kaw Reservoir, what is now Kaw Lake. In the last fifty years, the tribe has grown to a population of 3, 167 tribal citizens, according to their official website in July, 2011. As one of the thirty-nine federally recognized American Indian tribes in the state of Oklahoma, the Kaw Nation operates many economic development enterprises, such as Southwind Energy, discount tobacco shops, the Kanza Travel Plaza, and the Southwind Casino. The tribe also provides all the basic governmental aspects of a tribal nation, to include health care, housing, daycare, social service and education programs, emergency assistance. and a tribal court system. While the history of the Kanza people between 1800 and the present is well-documented, what is less known about is their traditional music, very little of which is part of the general body of knowledge about American Indian music. Ironically, Kaw musical influences represent the single biggest emergence of traditional Native American music within an American popular music or jazz context.

The story of Kaw music appears to follow the path of many other Native American tribes, who saw their long-held traditions fade in the 19th century through attrition with the loss of so many tribal members due to the previously mentioned history. Alongside those developments, government policies prohibited any visible maintenance of those traditions beginning in 1889 with the Federal Court of Indian Offenses that could punish participants of traditional ceremonies. Kaw historian, Ron Parks, reports the Kaw people were firm about the relevance of their dances before removing to Oklahoma, even trying to share them in public with hopes of engendering some non-Indian public understanding of the Kaw people's humanity. Again cited on the tribe's website, Parks quotes a local Topeka,

Kansas newspaper from 1860, where the writer tries his best to describe what he doesn't really understand: "about twenty Kanzas 'gave a war dance' in Topeka. The dance was conducted in a circle, with ten or twelve 'musicians' seated the center keeping time and making a "sort of music" by beating upon drums constructed of raw hide while the dancers moved around them in slow procession." Just before and after removal , however, the tribe lost elders, leaders, song keepers, and ceremonial people responsible for the knowledge of such traditional ceremonies. Combined with federal policies preventing their old ways, and a lessening population, the remaining Kaw and other Plains tribes looked to new spiritual pathways in the late 19th.[1] Initially, some Plains tribes drifted toward the Ghost Dance, however, the Kanza took on a dance from their relatives, the Omaha. With this ceremony known as The Grass Dance, the people wore the traditional clothing of their ancestors, lined out a circle as holy ground, put a big drum in the center, and then sang, prayed, and danced clockwise around the drum, an obvious forerunner of the contemporary Oklahoma powwow. First to take up the Grass Dance (not to be confused with the contemporary powwow dance by the same name) were the Sauk (modern Sac and Fox), Potawatomi, and Kickapoo tribes, followed by the Otoe and Ponca, from whom the Kaw most likely learned the ways of the ceremony. However, the Kaw did not have the staying power necessary to maintain the tradition, leading them to pass their drum and the ceremony to their other Dhegiha relatives to the east, the Osage, who maintain it contemporarily as the annual summer Osage ceremonials known as the I'n-Lon-Schka.[2] The closest modern dance to linked to those days is the men's Southern Straight Dance of the contemporary powwow world, in which a man tells a story of a hunt or successful quest in war with his dance. As a result, many Kaw are straight dancers today, and often dance with their Osage relatives in the traditional I'n-Lon-Schka dances which are not the same as an intertribal powwow. Also during the transitional period for the Kaw between their arrival in 1873 and Oklahoma statehood in 1907, many Kaws turned to the Native American Church as a traditional way of worship that was spreading northward through the Plains, although not yet having that official name yet by charter, as it would later. The ceremonies evolved from the Peyote rituals and religions from southwest Texas where Peyote exists naturally (one of only two regions in the world where the plant grows – the other being a similar geographic region in Mexico). Some of the earliest tribes still in existence who are associated with the religion include the Tonkawa and Lipan Apache, for whom it was already part of their traditions in that part of Texas. Once the Tonkawa with some Lipan were finally settled on the Fort Oakland reservation just west of present-day Ponca City, members of both the nearby Otoe-Missouria and Ponca tribes became practitioners, as early as the 1880s. No clear explanations are obvious in the massive amounts of research that has been on the development of the Native American Church as to how the Kaw first began to practice the Peyote faith, but their proximity to the Tonkawa, Ponca, and Otoe-Missouria would have provided plenty of connections for the Native American Church to enter the Kansa worldview.

Without detailing the whole ceremony of the Native American Church which has many elements and purposes for the health and well-being for its adherents, services are conducted inside a Plains tipi with a fire going all night inside the tipi. Sung throughout the service that can go from 8 to 10 hours, even longer in the Osage version of religion, Native American Church songs feature a drummer who is responsible for the assembling and all-night use of a steel kettle with water inside of it, and a hide stretched across to provide the fast rhythm for songs. Participants who sing shake a gourd rattle to the fast tempo of the water drum, and offer prayer songs that provide participants a direct communication through the medicine to the creator in order to give thanks, offer praise, or petition for health and general well-being. The songs may use either words or vocables.[3] As the Native American Church gained momentum in the early 20th century, especially among Plains tribes in Oklahoma, skeptical state and federal legislators viewed the church's sacred use of Peyote as unnecessary drug use, instead of a healing medicine and prayer catalyst as it is understood within the church .[4] Subsequent legislative hearings and court cases resolved the right of Native people to practice the religion, and therein it began the focus and repository of much creative, artistic and musical energy of the church participants. As for the Kaw's participation in Peyotism, Native American Church scholar Thomas C. Maroukis notes a 1919 government report in which as much as 60% of tribal members were practicing Peyotists, which means some music must have existed in the Kaw language, but so far no record of any songs appear in the usual American Indian music archives or commercial resources, which includes Canyon Records, Indian House Records, Smithsonian, or Indiana University Archives of Traditional Music. Some Kaw music may have been recorded but just hasn't been documented as such since many field recordings from early 19th century in Oklahoma are under-identified.[5] Therein lies the irony of the Kaw tribe's impact on American popular music. While no Kaw-specific Native American Church songs seem to have made it to the various common repositories of traditional American Indian music, a Kaw/Muscogee (Creek) jazz musician is responsible for the most prominent appearance in American popular music of anything resembling authentic American Indian music.

Saxophonist, singer, and composer, **Jim Pepper**, (born June 18, 1941 in Salem. Oregon), is descended from the traditional chief line of the Pepper family on his father's Kaw side, and from the Muscogee (Creek) Nation via his mother, Floy Pepper. He grew up in Portland, Oregon, where he began playing saxophone, but also traveled back and forth to Oklahoma to visit his relatives from both tribes. As a result, Pepper was exposed to the traditional ceremonial music of the **Muscogee (Creek),** often called "stomp dances", which occur ceremonially in the summer as part of the Green Corn Celebration, or the traditional Muscogee (Creek) person's New Year's. Additionally, he was further introduced to the big drum songs of the Plains-based powwow (a true tradition of the Kaw back to the Grass Dance). Finally, he became acquainted with the prayer songs of the Native American Church from his Kaw relatives. Ultimately, he absorbed a Native American Church song from his grandfather, Ralph Pepper, described by Jim as a **Comanche** song used when water is brought into the tipi at midnight or dawn. The song evolved a into "Wichi-Tai-To", first recorded in 1969 on an album under the group name of Everything is Everything, with Jim Pepper on lead vocals and saxophone. The song merges Pepper's "pre-Kenny G" smooth sax work with authentic Native American church vocals. Also included the songs are English lyrics describing imagery of Native American Church elements such as the water spirits, which are commonly reflected in Peyote art, jewelry, and design as water birds. The implication in the song is that the water spirit circling the speaker's head makes him glad that he is alive, and, therefore, heals him, the primary traditional purpose of the Peyote religion. The impressionistic and improvisatory nature of the song is completed when Pepper adds trills with chimes and swirling sax scales to aurally depict the water spirits circling him with their positive blessings. While the general public certainly did not understand the references, Americans as a whole liked the feel of the song enough to propel it onto the *Billboard* U.S. Hot 100 singles chart for five weeks, peaking at #69 in the

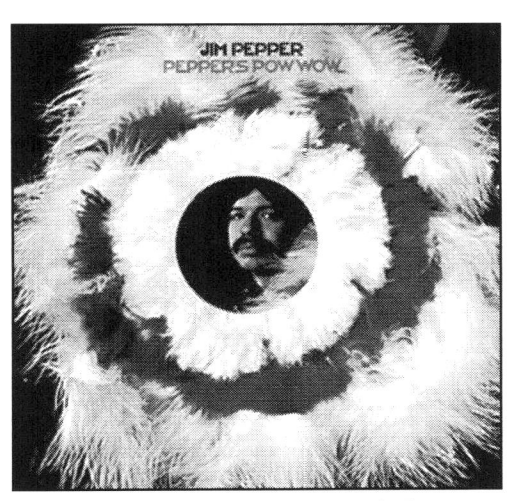

Jim Pepper's 1971 album, Pepper's Powwow

March, 1969. Many bloggers and online responders to various Pepper fan sites remember the song was popular well into the 1970s on FM album rock radio stations, underground stations, and abroad, as the song was popular in England when it was released there on Vanguard Records. The folk rock duo **Brewer** & Shipley covered the song on their 1969 *Weeds* album, adding more acoustic guitars and harmonies for a version that remained part of their "Best of" repertoire from that point on, and was also played quite heavily on FM rock radio stations. "Witchi-Tai-To" is the first significant example of traditional American Indian music that appears anywhere in American popular music. Therefore, at least two Kaw men can be said to have had the first significant influence of traditional Native music on American popular music and jazz: Ralph Pepper, who taught the song to his grandson; and Jim, who forged it into an unlikely mid-range pop hit and early 1970s underground rock and jazz radio standard. Additionally, Pepper's use of the unhurried jazz saxophone is also a pre-cursor to other smooth jazz pop successes of George Benson, Chuck Mangione, and Kenny G in the 1970s and 1980s.

Jim Pepper appeared on as many as thirteen albums, seven of which were solo albums, starting with *Pepper's Powwow* (Embryo, 1971). The album includes several songs with traditional American Indian music as their foundation, to include a different version of "Wichi-Tai-To" than the one that became a hit, as well as songs based on fast and slow war dances of the powwow, and one track which is a Muscogee (Creek) stomp dance. On live versions of "Witchi-Tai-To", widely available via online video sites, Pepper can often be heard yelling out "Hohmbucks-che" during the free-form vocalizing part of the song he always included, which is a Muscogee (Creek) phrase (spelled "Hompvksce" in the tribal alphabet) which translates more or less into "Let's eat!" Pepper also played with renowned jazz artists, often some of its most visionary and experimental figures, such as **Don Cherry** (also from Oklahoma), modern jazz guitarist, Bill Frisell, and John Scofield (perhaps, *the* jazz fusion guitarist). All three appeared on Pepper's most lionized solo album, *Comin' and Going* (Island, 1983), which is considered the manifesto of his "American Indian jazz" with nine songs that merge American Indian traditional music and jazz, perfecting what he had started with *Pepper's Powwow*. Although Pepper died in Portland, Oregon, February 10, 1992 of lymphoma at only age 50, his music and life continues to be celebrated with concerts, festivals, posthumous awards, and new recordings of his music, such as the 2008 version of Witchi-Tai-To recorded by Muscogee (Creek) poet and saxophonist, Joy Harjo, and included on her album, *Winding Through the Milky Way* (Fast Horse).

As for other Kaw contemporary music, tribal member Derek Mccubbin (b. 1978 in Stillwater) is a singer, songwriter, drummer and guitarist who has recorded with blues artists Watermelon Slim and Fried Okra Jones, as well as the Delicious Militia (which also included Oklahoma State Rhodes Scholar Blaine Greteman), and the Stillwater-based folk rock duo, Slapout. With Slapout, Mccubbin honors his Kaw heritage with "South Wind", a song he composed and sang for the independently released CD, *Benched* (Rock House, 2008). The song details how the south winds put the Kanza into motion as part of their natural place and movement in nature's universe.

The Kanza Nation hosts an annual intertribal powwow on the first weekend of each year at the Washunga Bay Powwow Grounds, with Thursday nights of the four day gathering usually reserved for traditional Kaw songs and dances the tribe is trying to maintain, and the weekend operating as a traditional three-day powwow with contesting in the standard powwow dance categories, and gourd dancing every day and/or evening before the main war dance starts. Typically, youth dancers contest on Friday night, ladies compete on Saturday night, and men dance against one another on Sunday, which is also when Kaw people have special activities related to their place in the circle. The dances are always free and open to the public. One of the more beautiful tribal dance sites in the state of Oklahoma, the Kaw Powwow is held by the lake named after the tribe that now covers a huge cut of their former reservation. The first week of August in Oklahoma is usually extremely hot, but the breezes always seem favorable to the Kanza at Washunga Bay, especially southern ones glancing off the lake toward the annual dance. Water spirits, indeed.

www.kawnation.com

Notes

1. For further understanding of the governmental oppression of American Indian music from the reservation era through the Federal Indian Reorganization Act of 1934, see John W. Troutman, *Indian Blues: American Indians and the Politics of Music, 1879-1934*. Norman: University of Oklahoma Press (2009).

2. A good coalescence of multiple ethnographic materials related to the precursors and diffusion of the The Grass Dance appears in Gloria Young's essay, "The Dream Dance and Ghost Dance in Oklahoma", from *Songs of Indian Territory: Native American Music Traditions of Oklahoma*. (Oklahoma City: Center for the American Indian, 1989), pp. 18-25/

3. Vocables in American Indian music are vocal sounds that may or may not have a literal meaning, such as the "hey-ya-nay-nay" of Native American Church songs, or the drawn out "hey-ya" in Plains Indian or contemporary powwow singing; vocables may carry a melody that has meaning, such as representing a certain family, or signifying a particular element of a ceremony; vocables also derive from the earlier periods, to include the 19th century reservation era, when vocables allowed tribes an opportunity to sing together, even if they did not speak the same language.

4. For more information regarding the Kaw-specific elements of the Native American Church, as well as an authoritative history on the church's formal origins in Oklahoma, see Omer C. Stewart's *Peyote Religion: A History*. (Norman: University of Oklahoma Press, 1987), pp. 117-18.

5. Maroukis cites a 1919 U.S. federal government questionnaire sent out to tribal agencies for superintendents to report on the use of Peyote by tribal members. See the full details of his analysis in Thomas C. Maroukis, *The Peyote Road: Religious Freedom and the Native American Church*(Norman: University of Oklahoma Press, 2010), pp. 109-110.

Keith, Jeff
(b. October 12, 1958)

With a wailing and cutting raspy tenor voice as the lead singer of the bluesy heavy metal group, Tesla, Jeff Keith makes a power ballad sing-along sound painful and heartwarming all at the same time. Keith's archetypal pop metal voice has fronted Tesla since it formed in 1985 in Sacramento, California, through its contemporary existence as a touring and recording band in 2011. Born Jeffrey Lynn Keith in Texarkana, Texas, the singer spent his childhood years in California, but came to terms with life as a teenager of a single mom (Anita) in Idabel and Broken Bow, Oklahoma, both about seventy miles from his birthplace. Determining where some of the grit in Keith's vocal delivery originates, as well his tougher-that-your-average-80s-glam-rock-star image, look no further than Southeastern Oklahoma's "Little Dixie", where Texas, Arkansas, Louisiana and Oklahoma almost form a "four corners" meeting place. The American South, with all of its cultural implications, really does begin when getting into that part of Oklahoma, or leaving the state from that direction (if it hadn't already started around Idabel or Broken Bow). Certainly, Keith, who was still skinny at 53 in 2011 and most likely a similar wiry teen, had to develop a confident attitude moving into Broken Bow for the 7th grade as the new kid from California in 1970. Perhaps Oklahoma's biggest contribution to Keith's musical career is just the rugged milieu where he came of age in the mid-1970s. February 23, 2001, *Daily Oklahoman* interview with music writer George Lang to promote a performance in Oklahoma City, Keith explained he was the only one of his friends to graduate Idabel High School in 1976. That environment also likely explains why he got out of town after graduation, and headed back to California where his father still lived. Within a few years he was singing in a band with his brother, and by 1983 was fronting a group known locally in Sacramento as City Kidd beginning in 1982, but evolved into Tesla by 1985 due to a name-change suggestion by their manager when they were recording their first album, *Mechanical Resonance* (Geffen, 1986).

Jeff Keith, Tesla lead singer, 2009.

Known as a hard rock and heavy metal band with more than casual blues influences, and with a tougher image than Los Angeles glam metal groups of the 1980s, Tesla features Keith's plaintive, razor-edged vocals surrounded by hard riffing and acrobatic electric guitars. According to the band's website in 2011, calling them just glam or heavy is inaccurate because of the blues base to their music. Their first single, 1987's "Little Suzi", was only a minor pop hit, just barely dipping into the pop charts at #91, but it did get them noticed at mainstream rock radio, with enough play to go Top Ten on *Billboard*'s Mainstream Rock chart, and prime the publicity pump for single number two. The band's follow up, "Modern Day Cowboy", exhibits all the touchstones of pop metal for that period: big snares, biting blues-based electric guitar counterpoints and solos, and Keith's melodic screeching, all of which notched the first Top 10 *Billboard* Mainstream Rock hit in their belt. Ironically, given their primary musical style, the group's two biggest pop hits were a power ballad and an acoustic cover of a rebelliously-stanced folk rock song, "Signs", originally a Top 5 hit by the Five Man Electrical in 1971. The band's biggest original song was 1989's "Love Song" (#10 on *Billboard*'s Hot 100), a sway-along rock concert favorite for 80s metal fans featuring Keith's voice riding the razor's edge between the pretty high melodies of Journey's Steve Perry and the raggedy piercings of Axl Rose from Guns 'n Roses.

Summing up Tesla's chart career is an impressive list of commercial and chart successes no matter what genre is being discussed. Between 1987 and 2008, the band had fourteen Top Ten songs on the *Billboard* Mainstream Rock chart. Also during that time, the band released ten studio albums, three of which went Platinum (a million units sold) or better: *Mechanical Resonance* (Geffen, 1986); *The Great Radio Controversy* (Geffen, 1989, 2X Platinum); *Psychotic Supper* (Geffen, 1991). The group also had one Gold al-

Tesla with lead singer Jeff Keith in cowboy hat.

bum, 1994's *Bust a Nut* (Geffen), and produced four live albums, one of which, *Five Man Acoustical Jam* (Geffen, 1990), reached #12 on the album chart and provided their hit single cover of "Signs", recognizable to just about any about thirty or over at the time, and which reached #8 on the *Billboard* Hot 100 twenty years after the original was a hit. Their fourth Platinum sales success, *Five Man Acoustical Jam* was criticized by heavy rock purists for softening up metal even more than power ballads already had; however, the project was also lionized by popular music critics and the band's label, who heard the album as a broadening for metal at the turn of the 1990s. Not only that, but a metal band had just not gone acoustic before with such total conviction. Some Tesla fans also enjoyed hearing the songs stripped of the electronic devices and effects for which metal is known, in essence converting them to kind of a folk metal. Interestingly, Keith's voice maintains its clarity, tunefulness, and soul whether acoustic or electric guitars swirl about him.

Tesla called it quits for a couple of years in the mid 1990s as the mainstream rock environment/industry shifted to differing musical aesthetics (Grunge, Rap 'n Rock, Riot Grrl Rock), but the 1995 CD, *Times Makin' Changes: Best of Tesla* become a Gold Record anyway. After taking a break to work on personal projects and issues within the band, the group began patching up differences and drifting back together through the late 1990s, and reunited in 2000. Since then, three more Tesla albums have hit *Billboard*'s Top 200 LP charts:ts: *Into the Now* (Sanctuary, 204)(#31); *Real to Reel* (Ryko, 2007); and *Forever More* (Ryko, 2008)(#29). After releasing 2010 live album recorded at concerts in Europe, in 2011 the group released *Twisted Wires and the Acoustic Sessions*, and continued touring (they played the heavy metal retro-fest, Rocklahoma, in 2010). As for Oklahoma's impact on Jeff Keith, it's just a home state, graduated-high-school-there-kind-of-thing. He said as much to music writer Jennifer Chancellor in a July, 6, 2008 interview published in the *Tulsa World*, proclaiming himself as the same Idabel boy he has "always been."

www.teslatheband.com

Keith, Toby
(b. July 8, 1961)

Perhaps the most polarizing country music artist in American popular music history due to his unabashed flag waving and ruffian philosophies, singer, songwriter, and guitarist Toby Keith has parlayed his warm baritone, half singing/half talking vocal style, and working class lyrics embedded with humor and social commentary into several millionselling albums (8 hit #1), twenty-five #1 country singles, monster grosses at the box office for his sold out tours, and a successful chain of restaurants across the United States. Keith recorded twelve studio albums between 1996 and 2010, two Christmas albums (1995 and 2007), and had four greatest hits packages released (1998, 2003, 2004, and 2008). In 2005, Keith started his own record label (Show Dog) when his label at the time, Dreamworks, folded, and now releases all of his music through the collaborative Show Dog – Universal label, to include his 2010 album, *Bullets in the Gun*, which debuted at

#1 on *Billboard*'s Top 200 album chart, produced two Top 20 country singles, and went Gold with more than 627,000 sold in 2010 alone. While Toby Keith's public persona is one of a patriotic, working class, truck-driving, football-watching, honky-tonkin' good ole' boy, he is a dedicated family man (one wife (Tricia) – three kids (Shelley, Krystal, and Stelen), politically active (for both sides, it seems), philanthropic for charities such as Children's Hospital in Oklahoma City, and public service-oriented, to include nine USO tours of combat zones in the Middle East as of 2011, with some of those tours venturing out to remote and dangerous forward operating bases (FOBs).

Born Toby Keith Covel and raised on a farm near Clinton, Oklahoma, a community of about 10,000 residents west of Oklahoma City on Interstate 40, to Hubert K. and Joan Covel, Toby chased varied interests while growing up, such as rodeo, football, and music. His self-proclaimed musical influences start with his father's affinity for classic country music, and after that he has listed artists ranging from Merle Haggard, Jimmy Buffet, Billy Joel, and John Prine, to Steve Goodman (folk), Elton John, and Lionel Richie, all of whom are united by strong songwriting skills. Fascinated with the musicians who played his grandmother's supper club in Fort Smith, Toby learned to play the guitar when he was about eight years old (later some mandolin), and began writing songs when he was in the sixth grade. Occasionally, he would sit in with bands playing at his grandmother's club. While in high school, Toby worked for a rodeo company (test rode bulls and broncos for rodeos) adjacent to his parent's farm, but was too tall (6' 4") to become a professional rodeo rider, and played high school football at Moore High School. He was an avid Oklahoma Sooners football fan, and during his youth, worked as a vendor for Saturday games in nearby Norman. After lettering at defensive end in high school, he gave college football a thought, but felt he needed to make some money to support himself, so he followed his father into oilfield work.

Toby Keith, 2010

When Toby wasn't working tough and dirty jobs in the oilfield, he formed a band with a few friends in 1981 and began playing local bars under the name, Easy Money, still the name of his band. When the Oklahoma oil industry dipped in 1982, Keith gave his pro football dreams a shot, making the cut with the Oklahoma City Drillers (defensive end) where he crashed pads and helmets for two seasons in the short-lived United States Football League. All the while, he kept gigging away when the opportunity presented itself, primarily for tips and beer. One of the band's first paying gigs was at a stock car track and, according to Toby, not one note could be heard over the roaring, bored-out engines.

By the mid-1980s, Keith and his band, Easy Money, had purchased a Silver Eagle bus, and began playing fifty-one weeks a year in the major dance halls around the southwest, especially Dallas' Top Rail. Keith and the band recorded several of his original songs on an independent label, and after placing second for Oklahoma in the Dodge-Wrangler band competition, the band made a series of demo tapes that Keith peddled in Nashville, but no one took him up on his sound at the time. One of Toby's fans, an airline stewardess, had given Harold Shedd, Mercury Records/Nashville president and former Alabama producer, a demo tape on one of his flights, and, after he had listened to the tape, flew to Oklahoma City to see Toby and the band perform. Toby signed with Shedd in 1991, and his self-titled debut album, released in 1993, eventually went platinum. Eight of the ten tracks on the album were written by Toby, and included "Should've Been a Cowboy" (#1 on *Billboard* chart), "He Ain't Worth Missing" (#5 on *Radio & Records* chart), "A Little Less Talk and a Lot More Action" (#2 on *Billboard*), and "Wish I Didn't Know Now" (#1 on *Radio & Records*). To promote his first album, Toby went on a "Triple Play Tour" with two then relatively unknowns, Jon Brannen and Shania Twain. Finally, *Billboard* magazine named Toby as Top New Country Artist for 1993, and at the end of the decade reported that "Should've Been a Cowboy" received the most airplay of any song in the 1990s. According to various printed legends, Toby wrote "Should've Been a Cowboy" after an attractive woman at a dance hall spurned one of his band members for a dance, but later accepted a dance proposal from a man dressed in cowboy attire. Someone in the club who was watching yelled, "Should've Been a Cowboy". Back in Oklahoma, the song was used immediately after every home Oklahoma State University Cowboys football game for years (into the early 2000s), until Keith's obvious allegiance to the University of Oklahoma Sooners, and comments related to that preference surfaced in the press. Ah, Bedlam (the nickname for the OSU/OU rivalry). Keith's debut album sold more than a million copies and was certified gold, earning him several awards for 1993: *Billboard*'s Top New Country Artist; BMI Songwriter Awards (6); and BMI Publisher Awards (6). However, the Country Music Association just looked the other way as if Keith had tried to make it an failed, just the beginning of the uneasy relationship between Nashville and the perceived "Okie Rogue" who often said what a lot of people think, but don't necessarily say.

In early 1996, Shedd left Mercury to become president of Polydor, Mercury's sister label. He took Toby with him to become the flagship artist of the new label, and they released Toby's second album *Boomtown* with seven of the ten tracks written or co-written by Toby, including four hit singles: "Who's That Man" (#1), "You Ain't Much Fun" (#2), "Big Ol' Truck" (#15), and "Upstairs Downtown" (#10). According to Toby's press machine at the time, *Boomtown*'s themes were spawned by Toby's experiences in the western Oklahoma oil patch, where he watched several towns, including Elk City, realize overnight growth with 1,500 oil rigs pumping crude, and then go fallow once the oil bust hit Oklahoma in the early 1980s. He also entered the common pattern of successful artists releasing holiday albums, recording *Christmas to Christmas* in 1995, featuring songs from top Nashville songwriters and reaching #7 on the *Billboard* Holiday Chart.

In 1995, Keith received the CMA Triple Play Award recognized for composers who had attained three #1 songs during the past year in *Billboard*, *Radio & Records*, or *The Gavin Report*. He also made his film debut in 1996 when he appeared in *Burning Bridges* with Tanya Tucker and Vanessa Williams. By the time Toby had recorded his third album, Polydor had merged with A & M Records/Nashville. Released in 1996, the same year the Country Music Hall of Fame inducted him into its Walkway of Stars, Keith's next album, *Blue Moon*, on which he wrote or co-wrote eight of the ten tracks, featured several relationship-oriented hits songs: "Does That Blue Moon Ever Shine on You" (#2); "A Woman's Touch" (#6); and "Me Too" (#1). A & M closed its Nashville division and Toby moved back to Mercury in 1997, where he released his fifth album, *Dream Walkin'* which charted four more *Billboard* country hits: "We Were In Love" (#2); the Grammy-nominated collaboration with Sting, "I'm So Happy That I Can't Stop Crying" (#2); "Dream

Walkin'" (#5); "Double Wide Paradise" (#40). By 1997, Toby became frustrated with the music industry and wrote a poignant ballad entitled "Tired," reflecting his dissatisfaction with all the corporate shuffles and label changes. Mercury jammed out
"Best of" album in 1998, *Greatest Hits: Volume I*, which went platinum, and produced a Top 20 single, "Getcha Some". In 1999 Keith approached the new president of Mercury, Luke Lewis, a New York City business executive, concerning an album project which included "How Do You Like Me Now" as one of its tracks. Lewis was concerned about the "political correctness" of the lyrics, questioned the recording quality of the album, suggested Toby re-cut the whole thing, minus "How Do You Like Me Now". Disgusted, Toby parted ways with Mercury, and purchased the album's tracks for a $100,000. Keith new of new label in town, Dreamworks Nashville headed by James Stroud, and sold it to Dreamworks for $120,000, and then promptly signed with the label for a multi-album deal that included a large degree of creative freedom on Keith's part.

Released in 1999, *How Do You Like Me Now?* became a bona fide *tour de force* with nine of the twelve tracks written or co-written by him. Both the title track and "You Shouldn't Kiss Me Like This" scored #1 positions on the *Billboard* Hot Country Singles chart. This seventh album was his most successful, capturing a number of awards, including CMT's #1 Video of the Year ("How Do You Like Me Now?") and Male Video Artist of the Year, ACM's Male Vocalist and Album of the Year, CMA's Male Vocalist of the Year (2001), and nominations for CMA's Single, Song, and Music Video of the Year, and American Music Award nominee for Favorite Country Album. Also in early 2001, Keith performed at the White House, singing a medley of Stephen Foster songs, such as "Oh! Susanna," which aired on PBS' *In Performance at the White House* the same year.

Toby Keith's music can really be divided up into the pre and post 9/11 era. The "pre-911 era" ended with his 2001 CD, *Pull My Chain*, featuring nine of the thirteen tracks co-written by Keith, and scoring a "hat trick" of three #1 singles: "I'm Just Talkin' About Tonight", "I Wanna Talk About Me," one of the first rap-like singles in country music, and "My List". *Pull My Chain* was certified double platinum in 2002, and Keith was the only country vocalist to have three #1 hits during the year. The "My List" video was also used by the New York police and fire departments for a training video as it depicted a firefighter going off to do his duty, presumably on 9/11 as the song about appreciating the smaller things of life had already been out before the attack on New June, 2003, and which became the title for a 2008 film co-written and starring Keith and comedian Rodney Carrington. "Rodeo Moon" (co-written with Chris LeDoux), "Rock You Baby" (co-written with Scotty Emerick, one of Toby's background vocalists, rhythm guitarist, and his primary co-writer for several years), and another #1 single, "Who's Your Daddy?" The album continued an outrageous string of Multi-Platinum and Gold albums that topped or scored near the top of the US Country and *Billboard* Top 200 album charts: Shock'n Y'all (Dreamworks, 2003) (#1 Country/#1 Top 200) (ACM Album of the Year/Entertainer of the year/Male Vocalist of the Year for 2003); the

Toby Keith, 1993 Publicity Photo.

autobiographical tale of his experiences in his grandmother's Fort Smith supper club. *Honky Tonk University* (Dreamworks, 2005) (#1 Country/#2 Top 200) (*Billboard* Country Album Artist of the Year, Country Artist of the Year, and Country Male Artist of the Year, 2005); *White Trash with Money* (Show Dog, 2006) (#2 Country/#2 Top 200); *Big Dog Daddy* (#1 Country/#1 Top 200); *That Don't Make Me a Bad Guy* (Show Dog, 2008) (#1 Country/#5 Top 200); *American Ride* (#1 Country/#3 Top 200); and *Bullets in the Gun* (#1 Country/#1 Top 200). Additionally, his 2008 Show Dog "Best of" compilation, *35 Biggest Hits*, also notched #1 Country Album status and hit #2 on the Top 200. As one might imagine, the popular albums notched a number of hit singles. Just the #1 hits in 2003 included "I Love This Bar", "American Soldier", and "Whiskey Girl". His ever-popular "As Good as I Once Was" hit #1 in 2005; "Love Me If You Can" spiked the top spot in 2007; "She Never Cried in Front of Me" and "God Love Her" both rose to #1 in 2008; and "American Ride" was his most recent #1 hit in 2009, a year for which he was named Most Successful Country Artist by *Billboard*. As mentioned earlier, his 2010 album, *Bullets in the Gun*, was also a significant sales success, as was 2011's *Clancy's Tavern,* (#1 *Billboard Country Albums*/#5 on *Billboard* Top 200), with the #1 country single, "Made in America," the kegger singalong favorite and now entrenched karaoke standard, "Red Solo Cup" (*Billboard* #5 Country Single), and another Top Ten Country Single, the memory loss memorial song, "Beers Ago." 2012's *Hope on theRocks* followed the now familar honky-tonk thematic and musical formula for Toby's records and enjoyed similar success with the album hitting #3 on *Billboard*'s Country Albums chart and #6 on *Billboard*'s Top 200 pop albums chart.

Along with his extensive recording and concert successes, as well as his successful chain of restaurants (Toby Keith's I Love This Bar and Grill), the first of which opened in Oklahoma City's Bricktown entertainment district, Keith is extremely committed to philanthropic and public service causes.

Though it received little media attention, Toby personally loaded and delivered rescue equipment in his pickup following the 1995 bombing of the Alfred P. Murrah Federal Building in Oklahoma City that killed 168 people. In 1999, he performed a benefit concert for victims following the tornado that devastated his high school hometown of Moore, Oklahoma. As of 2011, he had toured combat zones in the Middle East nine times for the United Service Organizations (USO), entertaining troops who are enduring hazardous duty in extremely hostile areas on land, as well as at sea aboard US Navy ships. He has also contributed mightily to charitable causes back home, to include the annual Toby Keith and Friends Golf Classic which he began in 2007 to raise money to pay for housing for pediatric cancer patients and families seeking care at Children's Hospital in Oklahoma City. In 2008, he raised $709,000, in 2009 he tallied $555,000, and in 2011 he added $650,000 to aid children and their families who are battling cancer. Keith also looked outward, appearing

Toby Keith performs for troops in Afghanistan, 2009.

in the 2008 Live 8 Concerts to raise world awareness about poverty in Africa. While Toby Keith has received criticism from both sides of the political spectrum for being too far left or right, depending on the critic's individual agenda, one cannot dispute his commercial success, industry recognition, and popularity among country music fans due to songs that speak to their experience. Additionally, while he is occasionally perceived as a mindless "flag waver" with some of his music, Toby Keith does not use patriotism as a marketing tool, but backs it up by putting his own life, and his band's life, in some very real harm's way to show his appreciation for the very American aesthetic of being a volunteer military professional in the U.S. Armed Forces. While Keith's music has verged on the jingoistic, his songs are often about the very real relationships, life trials, weekend celebrations, and dualistic relationships (boyfriend/girlfriend, husband/wife, city slicker/country boy, preacher/sinner, worker/boss, and patriot/pacifist) that have always been part of country music and its most successful songwriters and performers. In fact, Toby Keith may be viewed in terms of a folksinger who has chronicled the real experiences of service members at war in the 21st century ("I'm an American Soldier", "Ballad of Balad"). Heretical as it may sound for folk music pacifist/purists, by the strict terms of folk music, Keith qualifies as a folksinger on several fronts: 1) he is not a classically trained musician, having learned the basics among other musicians and then refined his craft through live performances; 2) Along songs about occupations, relationships, and the dichotomies of contemporary life, some of Keith's songs are about the authentic experiences of service people and their families living in the post-9/11 era; 3) he writes both lyric and narrative ballads, the former telling of experiences impressionistically, and the latter telling a straight-ahead story in a linear fashion. 4) and finally, he uses very basic accompaniment for his songs, wherein the song is really more important than any stratospheric musical skills. Therefore, aside from being a multi-million dollar commercial country artist, he fulfills the long tradition of patriotic song in American popular music, as well as telling stories average people can relate to in a simple manner. To hear and see how his knowledge of the environment and terminology of the military environment touches nerves with the military people for whom he performs, just do a a basic review of videos made by service members on cell phones or personal video cameras, and uploaded to commercial video hosting sites such as youtube.com. Therein, viewers/listeners will learn how he connects those serving abroad at war.

Toby Keith, 2003

Inducted into the Oklahoma Music Hall of Fame in 2005, Toby explained his professional philosophy on his website that year, a quote no longer present there in 2011: "I just did my own thing. I am what I am. I wasn't afraid of attitude . . . I'm a big boy, and I can shoulder any criticism I might get for doing things differently. I talk Southern; I sing stone-cold country—my roots are there . . . I see compromise all the time, and in the end, you lose with that. Most successful people are not afraid, and they don't compromise to please whoever." Toby continued, "You have to go do what you do best, and not what somebody else tells you. You've got to fight the system a little bit."

www.tobykeith.com

Keltner, Jim
(b. April 27, 1942)

The session drummer of the rock era from the mid-1960s forward through the present day, Jim Keltner was born in Tulsa and went through at least the 7th grade there before his family relocated to Pasadena, California where he spent all of his teen years and attended high school. It was in Pasadena where he fell in love with jazz, attended Pasadena City College, taking one semester of piano, and played in his first bands. After marrying right out of high school and working many types of gigs in the Pasadena area to support his family, Keltner landed a studio gig as the session drummer for Gary Lewis and Playboys Top 5 single, "She's Just My Style", produced by **Leon Russell**, which began a career-long relationship with Russell, and by extension, many other players commonly associated with Tulsa. By century's end, Keltner had recorded or performed with a staggering list of popular music icons, musicians, singers, and songwriters. While Keltner never studied drums or percussion formally, he told drumchannel.com in an interview published on youtube.com as "How Does Jim Keltner Earn a Living?" that he learned the basics of reading music in Tulsa as a 7th grade orchestra member. Keltner is known for laying down sturdy and steady rock beats, funky R & B grooves, complicated poly-rhythms associated with Latin or African music, and unobtrusive stability with signature to any style of pop music

Professional drummers discuss Keltner in the most reverent terms, placing him in the context of significant Big Band-era jazz drummers Buddy Rich and Gene Krupa, as well as comparable in distinctive technique along the lines of the modern jazz wizard, Elvin Jones, known for his progressive work with John Coltrane. With regard to rock music, Keltner is simply considered the absolute best session percussionist one can hope to have on their project, easily placed in the frontline company of rock drummers known for the subtleties and accents of a jazz drummer (Charlie Watts), and precise timekeeping with strategic fills (Ringo Starr). Some of Keltner's work in rock music is part of the genre's standard canon: Bob Dylan's "Knockin' on Heaven's Door"; John Lennon's *Imagine* LP ("Jealous Guy" and "I Don't Want to Be a Soldier"); Steely Dan's "Josie"; Gary Wright's "Dream Weaver"; and Ringo Starr's "Photograph".

A partial list of additional musical artists with whom Keltner has recorded and/or performed looks like the table of contents for a who's who of popular and world music for the second half of the 20th century: Roy Orbison, George Harrison, Jerry Garcia, Eric Clapton, Joe Cocker, **Hoyt Axton**, Barbara Streisand, the Rolling Stones (and many of the individual member's solo projects), Joni Mitchell, Seals and Crofts, Neil Young, Elvis Costello, The Bee Gees, Jackson Browne, Jesse Ed Davis, Ry Cooder, Randy Newman, Los Lobos, Pink Floyd, Warren Zevon, Tom Petty, Willie Nelson, Lucinda Williams, Sheryl Crow, Mavis Staples, B.B. King, John Lee Hooker, J.J. Cale, Porter Wagoner, Dolly Parton, Arlo Guthrie, Joe Walsh, John Hiatt, Flaco Jiminez, Leo Kotke, Rod Stewart, Yoko Ono, Ali Farka Toure,

Jim Keltner

Earl Scruggs, Roberta Flack, Harry Nilsson, **Tractors**, Freddie King, Leonard Cohen, Albert Collins, Neil Diamond, **Roy Clark**, Keith Moon, Jerry Lee Lewis, the Traveling Wilburys and T Bone Burnett. In addition to hundreds of recording sessions for multiple popular music artists, Keltner has also recorded for several film soundtracks, notably the drums for Randy Newman's songs heard in the popular animated Pixar feature, *Toy Story* (1995), as well as tracks for *Meet the Fockers* (2005), and *Charlie Wilson's War* (2007). For a contemporary representative sample of Keltner's elite skills, listeners can do no better than check out his work on the 2009 T Bone Burnett 2009 project, *The True False Identity* (Columbia), or Eric Clapton's 2010 self-titled album on Reprise Records. While Jim Keltner did not emerge from the late 1950s and early 1960s Tulsa music scene that produced many of the peers from Oklahoma with whom he eventually worked, such as his long-time playing cohort and friend, **Carl Radle**, Keltner did at least learn the basics of learning to read music in Tulsa as a 7th grader, which indicates the all-world drummer's career caught fire first in Oklahoma before it spread throughout some of popular music's most recognized performances from 1965 through the present day.

Kemp, Wayne
(b. June 1, 1941)

With multiple artists having recorded his witty songs that can make a person smile just hearing the titles, Wayne Kemp is one of country music's most successful songwriters. A 1999 inductee into the Nashville Songwriters Hall of Fame, Wayne Kemp was born in Muldrow, Oklahoma, and lived in Greenwood, Arkansas as child where he played mandolin in his family's band at churches, high school, and other local functions until 1953 when his family sold their farm and moved to California. While attending high school in Stockton, Wayne played in a band until his family moved back to Oklahoma in 1956. That year, Wayne hired on with Benny Ketchum as a lead guitar player and toured the Southwest backing up star like Jimmy Dickens, Red Sovine, and **Wanda Jackson**.

Wayne moved back to California in 1961 where he performed in night clubs and on local TV shows with artists such as Glen Campbell and Jeannie Seely. By 1964, he returned to Oklahoma where he settled in the southwestern town of Cache. With nearby Fort Sill as a resource for a party-ready clientele, Kemp played regularly at the Bonanza Club, and had a weekly TV show in Lawton. This visibility translated into a meeting with L.D. Allen who introduced Wayne to George Jones, who quickly recognized Kemp's flair for good country songwriting.

In 1965, Jones took Wayne to Nashville and recorded nine of Kemp's songs, to include the classic #1 hit, "Love Bug," and featured Kemp on lead guitar. Kemp also went on to play guitar for Patsy Cline, Red Sovine, and Conway Twitty. In 1967, Wayne recovered from a horrendous automobile accident to play guitar again. A year later, when Conway Twitty recorded Wayne's "The Image of Me," Kemp was signed by Tree Publishing in Nashville. He recorded for a variety of labels, first with Dial in 1963 and later with MCA, United Artists, Mercury, and Door Knob. From the late 1960s through the

Wayne Kemp

late 1980s, he charted twenty-four singles, including "Honky Tonk Wine" (Top 20 hit in 1973), "Won't You Come Home", "Don't Send Me No Angels", and "Who'll Turn Out the Lights (In Your World Tonight)". His last charted single, "Red Neck and Over Thirty", was a duet with Bobby G. Rice in 1986. Two of Kemp's albums are available, including *Kentucky Sunshine*, a MCA release in 1974, and *The Alcohall of Fame* from Country News, a Swedish company. The latter album contains several of Kemp's lesser known compositions such as the title track as well as "Leavin's Been Comin'", "I'm Gonna Get a Whippin'", "Daddy's Livin' off the Memories of Mama", and "Love Comes Here to Die".

Kemp's songwriting talents earned him lofty status in Nashville's country music circles. His song, "Darling, You Know I Wouldn't Lie", was nominated in 1969 for CMA Song of the Year, and Johnny Cash included Kemp's "One Piece at a Time" (a #1 hit in 1976) on more than twenty of his albums, using it as the title track for a 1976 collection. George Strait has recorded Kemp's songs on more than ten albums, including such compositions as "My Old Flame Burnin' Another Honky Tonk", "She Knows When You're On My Mind", "The Fireman" (Top 5 in 1985), "Won't You Come Home", "I Should Have Watched That First Step", "That's Where My Baby Feels at Home", "Hot Burning Flames", and "Love Bug" (Top Ten in 1994). In addition to "The Image of Me", Twitty scored with such Kemp songs as "Next In Line", "Darling, You Know I Wouldn't Lie", and "That's When She Started to Stop Loving You" (Top 5 in 1970).

Kemp's "Love Bug" appeared on no less than eight George Jones albums, while Ricky Van Shelton's favorite Kemp songs were "I'll Leave This World Loving You", which reached #1 in 1988, and "Who'll Turn Out the Lights", released on at least six Shelton albums. "I'm the Only Hell (Mama Ever Raised)" was a Top 10 hit for Johnny Paycheck in 1977, and two contemporary country vocalists, Emmylou Harris and Chely Wright, have recorded the Kemp song, "Feelin' Single, Seein' Double" while Jason Allen recorded "Next In Line" and "Cryin' for Their Mamas". Several traditional country artists have also recorded his tunes: the Ernest Tubb and Loretta Lynn duet ("Won't You Come Home"), Hank Williams, Jr. ("Waitin' on the Tables to Turn"), Faron Young ("I Just Came By to Get My Baby"), Ronnie McDowell ("Hot Burning Flames" and "Who'll Turn Out the Lights"), Ronnie Milsap ("Who'll Turn Out the Lights" and "I'll Leave This World Loving You"), Carmol Taylor ("I Really Had a Ball Last Night"), and Darrell McCall ("Here We Go Again"). Outside country music, Elvis Costello & the Attractions recorded "Darling, You Know I Wouldn't Lie". Although "Darling, You Know I Wouldn't Lie" was a CMA nomination, it was Kemp's "The Image of Me" that was recorded the most times and by a vast array of artists, including **Bob Wills** and the Texas Playboys, Charley Pride, Ernest Tubb, Jim Reeves, Conway Twitty, Tom Petty & the Heartbreakers, Flying Burrito Brothers, Doug Sahm, and The Country Rockers.

In 2005, Country Country Records released a CD of Kemp singing some of his hits on an album produced by Wayne and his son, Robert Kemp. The CD also includes some new songs written by Wayne, to include "Somehow Without You" and "Pretty Boy Floyd". While Kemp has not had a hit in several years as of 2011, the memory of his honky tonk classics is clear among contemporary artists. In 2011, Matraca Berg released an answer song to Kemp's "Your Wife's Been Cheating on Us" from the female perspective on her hit Americana CD, *The Dreaming Fields*, flipping the concept around with "Your Husband's Been Cheating On Us".

Kessel, Barney

(b. October 17, 1923 – d. May 6, 2004)

    In a 1960s interview, B.B. King recounted seeing and hearing Barney Kessel for the first time at a 1950s after-hours session on the West Coast: "I heard Barney Kessel, and he shamed me. It made me want to study hard to better myself as a person and a musician." Not only did blues and jazz guitarists respect Kessel, but those players in the country music world were also very aware of Kessel. Don Tolle, recording guitarist for Western swing band leader **Johnnie Lee Wills** in the early 1950s, also explained what it was like to be playing in a club when Kessel walked in: "He would come around when we were playing as the Texas Playboys. Hell, he didn't know who we were. He was so damn far above the rest of us we just knew who he was. I always felt humbled when he walked in." Born in Muskogee, a town with a vibrant jazz scene in the first third of the twentieth century that also produced other acclaimed jazz musicians such as **Don Byas**, **Jay McShann**, and **Claude Williams**, Barney Kessel is known and celebrated for his stylistic versatility and improvisational genius on the guitar from the 1940s through the 1980s on over fifty albums and in worldwide concerts when health problems curtailed his playing. A revered musician and composer who shaped the sound of jazz guitar for all time, perhaps his best-known tune is the jazz classic, "Swedish Pastry".

    Barney spent his early years surrounded by the thriving jazz scene of Muskogee in the 1930s. His Eastern European Jewish father owned a shoe store at 110 S. 2nd across the street from the black theater in Muskogee, right in the heart of the African-American commercial and entertainment district on South 2nd Street in Muskogee. As a result, Barney Kessel was significantly exposed to the deep jazz tradition in Muskogee. Not only was his father's shop on South 2nd Street, a few doors down at 128 S. 2nd was the family residence which doubled as a clothiers, and both were nestled between night clubs, theaters, pool halls, and what the maps of early Muskogee only call "Negro joints." Kessel was literally reared in the shadow of, and eventually took the spotlight in, Muskogee's

Barney Kessel

and Oklahoma's jazz scene in the 1930s. His subsequent success in jazz further emphasizes the importance of Muskogee's jazz scene, because if Barney Kessel could grow up and absorb the music he did in Muskogee, and then become an original, innovative, and highly regarded jazz guitarist, one must say that Muskogee was genuinely a primary development center of American jazz, wherein the traditions of jazz were relayed from one generation to the next.

    Barney's first musical memories of Muskogee echo from the box cars and hobos who played Jimmie Rogers songs as they rolled along the tracks just a couple of blocks from South Second Street. He began guitar lessons when he was twelve from a Hawaiian man who taught for the WPA. Barney remembers never having to unlearn the lessons in chords, harmonies, and reading music that he learned in the six months he took lessons from the Hawaiian. At thirteen, Kessel played on the local radio station, KBIX, with his friend Cobal Parker. By fourteen, Barney worked regularly in three bands that played dances at places like Honor Heights park, then a "whites only" social hall. While he played in two primarily white bands, Barney was also the only white player in a group led by Ellis Ezell from 1937 to 1939. Ezell's group required Barney to play horn lines in the manner of **Charlie Christian** who, at the time, was the featured guitarist in the Benny Goodman Orchestra, and is commonly acknowledged by scholars and Kessel alike as his major influence. Other influences drifted into Barney's ears when he worked in Muskogee movie theaters and heard all the Hollywood musicals, the songs of which later became pop standards and foundation melodies for jazz. Kessel has also cited Lester Young, Nat King Cole, Duke Ellington, Charlie Parker, and Bill Evans as influences, but acknowledges the Christian influence is deepest because it is on the guitar.

Barney left Muskogee in the fall of 1939 where he attended high school in Stillwater and played with the Varsitonians, an OSU dance band. In the spring of 1940, he moved to Norman and played with the Varsity Club, but did not graduate from high school. Also that spring Kessel met Charlie Christian in Oklahoma City, and jammed with him on three separate occasions. However, Barney told himself at that time he would not take licks from Christian, but would play his own way and develop his own style. Nonetheless, Kessel's most common stylistic touchstone is found in the work of, and the connection to, Christian, and is an important starting point for any newcomer to Barney Kessel's music. While it is true Christian provided the foundation for Kessel, Barney built a musical structure unique to his own vision on it.

Arriving in Los Angeles with a guitar, an amplifier, a bag of clothes and a nickel, Barney started his career on the West Coast with the Chico Marx big band in 1942 and '43. In 1944, Barney was featured in the award-winning jazz documentary, *Jammin' the Blues*; however, because of racist sensitivities in Hollywood, and Barney being the only white musician in the production, Warner Brothers died his skin black and put him in the film's shadows. Through 1945 and '46 Barney played with Artie Shaw in a group with significant bop leanings as the style had migrated across the country from 52nd Street in New York City. Kessel also stared playing with Charlie Barnet in 1945 and continued through 1947 while picking up significant studio gigs like those with Charlie Parker in '47 that are considered jazz classics. Parker and Kessel jammed that year, and afterwards Parker called Kessel for the now legendary Dial Records session. While some critics are divided on the significance of Kessel's contributions to the Dial sessions, he is clearly making significant bop statements in "Cheers, Cheers," "Barbados," and "Relaxin' at Camarillo." By Kessel's own account, he was also learning a great deal from the acknowledged architect of bebop in Parker. In 1948, Barney purchased two guitars from guitarist George M. Smith, who owned the 1933 Gibson L-5 and 1937 Gibson L-5 since they were made. As a staff musician at the time, Smith played with 20th Century Fox movie studio in Hollywood in the 1930s and '40s. After purchasing the two guitars from Smith, Kessel played them from July 1948 through March 1969 for all his work. This included movies for all the major Hollywood studios, to include four Elvis Presley movie soundtrack sessions, Barbara Streisand's *On A Clear Day You Can See Forever* (1970), two movies with Dean Martin and Jerry Lewis, and another with Jerry Lewis alone. He also played the guitar on numerous recordings, including those with the Righteous Brothers, Sarah Vaughan, Ella Fitzgerald, Billie Holliday, Sonny & Cher, the Beach Boys, and records produced by Phil Spector. Barney also played the guitars for numerous television shows, including *Hollywood Palace*, *The Judy Garland Show*, a Bing Crosby Christmas Special with Paul Weston's orchestra, *The Bob Crosby Show*, and Jack Smith's radio show five days a week for two years.

In 1952, Kessel joined the trio led by Oscar Peterson, one of the most recorded pianists of the 1950s. It was with Kessel when the trio, including Ray Brown on bass, helped usher in both the hard bop movement and the laid back West Coast cool jazz of the 1950s. After Peterson, Kessel's concept of replacing the piano with guitar in a jazz trio set new standards for the guitar as a lead instrument in jazz combos. As a result of his elevating status among musicians, critics, and fans in the 1950s, Barney was a regular winner of critic and fan polls. Along with Ray Brown and drummer Shelly Manne, Kessel recorded the historic *Poll Winners* albums from 1957 to 1960, considered some of his finest and most representative moments. Kessel won numerous awards for his work with Lionel Hampton, Ben Webster, Roy Eldridge, Woody Herman, Lester Young and Billie Holliday, as well as his own solo albums starting with 1953's *Barney Kessel, Volume I* (Contemporary).

Among the accolades bestowed on Barney are the *Esquire* Silver Award (1947), Best Guitarist in *Down Beat*'s Readers' Poll (1956-1959), the Jazz Critics' Poll (1953 through 1959), the *Metronome* Readers' Poll (1958 through 1960), and the *Playboy* Readers' Poll (1957 through 1960). Exhibiting his diverse talent, Barney also composed, arranged, and recorded a jazz rendition of the opera *Carmen* in which André Previn played piano.

Barney Kessel

Kessel did not limit himself to the jazz idiom, however, as he became one of Hollywood's top session for artists from many different genres throughout the 1950s and '60s. Along with recordings for the Elvis Presley films, *Girls, Girls, Girls* (1962) and *Fun In Acapulco* (1963), and two other Presley sessions in July and August of 1965, Kessel played guitar for the Righteous Brothers' 1965 hit "You've Lost That Lovin' Feelin'," and on the Beach Boys' "Good Vibrations" from the *Pet Sounds* session of 1966. He recorded with a dizzying array of artists, to include Judy Garland, Barbara Streisand, Marlene Dietrich, Gene Autry, Tex Ritter, Ike and Tina Turner, Fred Astaire, The Coasters, Stan Kenton, Same Cooke, Duane Eddy, Dexter Gordon, Woody Herman, Frank Sinatra, Big Joe Turner, Lester Young, Johnny "Guitar" Watson, T-Bone Walker, Dinah Shore, and Dinah Washington. Kessel's session work could also be heard on television shows such as *Man from UNCLE*, *The Odd Couple*, *Love American Style,* and *I Spy.*

In all, Barney worked for almost forty years in Hollywood as an arranger and freelance musician for radio, hundreds of films, and TV music for many commercials, including Der Wiener Schnitzel and Rice Krispies. Outside of a few pop and rock guitar players, Barney Kessel may be the most heard American guitarist of the 1950s, '60s, and '70s, even if the majority of the listening public did not know his name. Kessel was also a musical ambassador for the U.S. State Department during the Carter administration, touring Europe, Asia, the Balkans, Egypt, and South America. Barney released several guitar and music instruction videos, lesson books, and sheet music through his esteemed career, in addition to a steady stream of solid, and sometimes brilliant, albums until 1988.

A respected and in-demand educator, Barney he gave guitar seminars and workshops throughout the world in conjunction with his performances. He continued touring consistently throughout the world with successful performances in the U.S., Canada, Portugal, Sweden, Italy, Germany, the British Isles, and Japan in 1991. Also in 1991, Kessel was inducted into the Oklahoma Jazz Hall of Fame along with **Chet Baker**. In early 1992, Barney received rave reviews when he played in Australia, New Zealand, and across the U.S. Later in 1992, Barney had his first major health problems when he suffered a massive stroke that incapacitated his right arm, ending his playing career.

Through the 1990s Kessel was feted around the world with honorary concerts and awards. In 1995, Vestapol Videos released a one-hour video, *Barney Kessel: Rare Performances 1962-1991* which includes his acceptance speech at the Oklahoma Jazz Hall of Fame Induction Ceremony. Additional film clips of Kessel are included on Vestapol's *Legends of Jazz Guitar* series. In 1996, the University of Oklahoma awarded Barney an honorary doctorate for his great contributions to the world of jazz. In 1997, *Just Jazz Guitar* dedicated an entire collectors' issue to honor Kessel's work. The magazine, now out of print, features several photos provided by Barney and Phyllis Kessel, interviews with Barney from around the world, and scores of some of his compositions. In 1999, Barney was inducted into the Oklahoma Music Hall of Fame in his hometown of Muskogee. Also in 1999, in the rush of end of the decade/century/millennium lists, *The Daily Oklahoman* named Barney as one of the top ten musicians from the state in the twentieth century behind **Woody Guthrie, Charlie Christian, Oklahoma City Blue Devils, Bob Wills,** and **Roger Miller**. Additionally, the Beach Boys' "Good Vibrations," on which Kessel plays, was chosen as one of the top ten rock songs ever by a panel of 700 music industry people in another end-of-century list. Upon his death at home of a brain tumor in 2004, *Guitar Player* magazine honored the guitar master in their September issue by republishing some of his wisdom from the columns he wrote for that magazine over the years. In 2012, young musicians were still being inspired by Barney Kessel. One of the new generation's best jazz guitarists, Graham Dechter of Los Angeles, openly names Kessel as a major influence. Dechter include's his version of Barney's "Be Deedle Dee Do" on the 2012 release, *Takin' It There,* for Capri Records. Interested viewers/listeners may find several excellent Barney Kessel video performances by Kessel on the video sharing website, youtube.com.

Looking back at the twentieth century and the musicians who pioneered jazz as an art form, Barney Kessel stands third in the holy trinity of jazz guitarists, next in line after Django Reinhardt and Charlie Christian. Barney Kessel's playing is intellectual and effortless. While challenging for a musician, a joy for the jazz fan, and a simple pleasure for the casual listener, Barney's music is in many ways the story of jazz told in melody, harmony, rhythm, tone, and texture. If the narrative of jazz is its improvisation, Barney Kessel can be claimed as one the form's master storytellers, and that story is best told through his elegant recordings that will delight fans for generations to come with his fifty-seven years of excellence in harmonic elaboration, superior improvisation on the electric guitar, progressive arrangements, and sparkling original compositions.

Kilgore, Merle

(b. August 9, 1934 – d. February 6, 2005)

A member of the Nashville Songwriter's Hall of Fame and composer or co-composer of more than 330 songs, including "More and More", "Wolverton Mountain", and "Ring of Fire", singer, songwriter, guitarist, disc jockey, actor, and talent manager Wyatt Merle Kilgore was born in Chickasha, Oklahoma, a community of about 15,000 residents located southwest of Oklahoma City. Multitalented Merle also recorded songs for more than twenty-five years. His family moved to Shreveport, Louisiana, when Merle was about four or five, and from 1940 to 1947, he attended Creswell Elementary School. As a fourteen year old, he started carrying Hank Williams, Sr.'s guitar at the Louisiana Hayride, and two years later, was performing on the show as principal guitar accompanist, while still in high school. He was also working for the American Optical Company delivering glasses during his after school hours. He graduated from Byrd High School in Shreveport in 1952, and attended Louisiana Tech University in Ruston for a year.

While in college, Merle gained his first job as a disc jockey at radio station KRUS in Ruston, and a year later was appearing on television shows as "The Tall Texan" (Merle is 6' 4" in height) on KFAZ (Ouachita Valley Jamboree) and KNOE in Monroe. During his late teens, he teamed with Webb Pierce to co-write, "More and More", a #1 hit for Pierce for ten weeks and a million-seller, later recorded by Guy Lombardo, Johnny Duncan, and Charley Pride. Merle also signed his first recording contract with Imperial Records, and his first single was a version of "More and More", for which he also received a BMI songwriters award.

From 1955 to 1960, Kilgore worked as a disc jockey for several Louisiana radio stations, including KBSF (Springhill), KCU (Shreveport), KENT (Shreveport), and KZEA (Shreveport). During this time, he penned and recorded his first Top 10 hit, "Dear Mama," on the Starday label, continued to perform on the Louisiana Hayride, and wrote several more songs, including "I Can't Rain all the Time" and "Seeing Double" (1954); "Funny Feeling" (1955); "I've Got a Good Thing Going", "Tom Dooley, Jr.", and "Hang Doll" (1958); "Baby Rocked Her Dolly", "I Will Be My First Time", and "Jimmie Bring Sunshine" (1959). To close out the decade, Merle wrote "Johnny Reb," recorded by Johnny Horton, a Top 10 hit, which eventually sold more than fifteen million records.

During the early1960s, Kilgore hosted the Big Ten Jamboree in Eldorado, Arkansas (1960), made his debut on the Grand Ole Opry (1960), received the WSM Nashville "Mr. DJ" award (1960), signed a contract with Mercury Records (1961), moved to Nashville to become manager of Shapiro-Bernstein Music (1961), joined the Johnny Cash road show (1962), performed at Carnegie Hall (1962), and co-wrote the million seller No. 1 country hit, "Wolverton Mountain", with Claude King, who recorded it for Columbia in 1962. Written for Merle's uncle who introduced him to the mountain in Arkansas, the song crossed over to become a

Merle Kilgore

By Hugh Foley / 421

Top 10 hit on the *Billboard* Hot 100 for King, as well as for Jo Ann Campbell who recorded a version that made the Top 40.

In 1963, Merle teamed with June Carter to write "Love's Burning Ring of Fire", first recorded by Anita Carter, and later revived as "Ring of Fire," which became a No. 1 hit on the country charts for Johnny Cash, June's future husband. For his many songs, Merle was named one of *Billboard* magazine's Top 10 Songwriters in 1963.

After performing at the Hollywood Bowl in 1962, Kilgore appeared in his first feature film, *Country Music on Broadway*, in 1963. His other acting credits include *Second Fiddle to a Steel Guitar* (1965), *Sing as Song for Heaven's Sake* (1966), *Nevada Smith* (1966), *Five Card Stud* (1968), *Educated Heart* (1970), *W.W. and the Dixie Dance Kings* (1974), *Nashville* (1975), *Roadie* (1979), *Coal Miner's Daughter* (1980), and played himself in the NBC television movie, *Living Proof*, the story of Hank Williams, Jr. (1981). He released two more albums with Starday, *There's Gold in Them Thar Hills* (1963) and *Merle Kilgore* (1964), before he switched to the Mercury label to record *Merle Kilgore, The Tall Texan* (1966). He signed with Ashley Records in 1968 and released *Ring of Fire*, and then resigned with Starday for one of his last albums, *Big Merle Kilgore* (1973).

In 1969, Kilgore became general manager of Hank Williams, Jr.'s publishing companies, and was Hank, Jr.'s opening act for more than twenty years. In 1986, he was named executive vice-president and head of management of Hank Williams, Jr. Enterprises. He performed on and managed a majority of Hank, Jr.'s biggest albums in the 1970s and 1980s, including *Habits Old and New, Rowdy, Strong Stuff, Man of Steel,* and *Hog Wild,* as well as negotiated the deal for Hank, Jr.'s performance of the *ABC Monday Night Football* theme song in 1989. Kilgore was elected to the CMA Board of Directors in 1989, and still served in that capacity for several years, and in 1990, was elected president of the Nashville Songwriter's Association Board of Directors. The same year, he was voted the first CMA Manager of the Year. In 1998, he was inducted into the Nashville Songwriters Hall of Fame (Connie Smith and Marty Stuart provided the musical tributes to Merle) and the North American Country Music Association Hall of Fame.

Kilgore's songs have been recorded by a host of artists representing a wide variety of musicalgenres, including The Animals, George Benson, Brothers Four, Ray Charles, Country Joe McDonald, Country Gentlemen, Bing Crosby, Dick Dale, Lefty Frizzell, Mickey Gilley, Bill Haley and the Comets, Tom Jones, Burl Ives, Jerry Lee Lewis, Rick Nelson, Willie Nelson, Olivia Newton-John, Nitty Gritty Dirt Band, Carl Smith, Blondie, Carlene Carter, Hank Snow, Joe Stampley, Ray Stevens, Ernest Tubb, Tammy Wynette, Dwight Yoakum, Faron Young, Frank Zappa, Van Morrison, and Bob Dylan. In 1995, Bear Family, the German company, released Teenager's Holiday, a CD that included all the classics written by Merle. In 1994, Merle opened Merle Kilgore Management in Nashville, representing Hank, Jr., as well as several other artists. In 2004, Kilgore was inducted into the Oklahoma Music Hall of Fame in Muskogee, and in 2005 he died of complications from treatments for lung cancer at age 70. A couple of years before that, Merle was nice enough to send a personal letter to the Oklahoma Music Guide to compliment our staff (i.e., HF)" on a job well done. Upon receiving it, the author called the number on the letterhead to ask permission to quote it on the back of the next book (as it is now). He answered the phone in a bassy, good-old-show-bizness-boy-tone, and after being asked to use his words for our promotion, he knew perrfectly well why, and belted, "Son, you can do whatever you want with that letter. I'm proud to be from Oklahoma. Good luck with anything it can do for you." Thanks for **everything**, Merle.

www.merlekilgore.com

Kings of Leon
(formed 1999, Nashville, Tennessee)
Anthony Caleb Followill (b. January 14, 1982) (vocals, rhythm guitar)
Ivan Nathan Followill (b. June 26, 1979) (drums, percussion, backing vocals)
Michael Jared Followill (b. November 20, 1986) (bass guitar, backing vocals)
Cameron Matthew Followill (b. September 10, 1984) (lead guitar, backing vocals

Formally united about 1999 in Nashville, Tennessee, Kings of Leon have really been a band their whole lives as a result of being comprised of three brothers (Caleb, Nathan, and Jared) and a first cousin (Matthew). The tight symbiosis of the group on stage, genetic harmonies, and easy coalescence on recordings shows it. Equal parts gritty Southern blues rock, energetic punk rock, and chimey, anthemic British rock of the 1980s, Kings of Leon feature easy on the ear vocals, a lot counterpoint between vocalist and all the other instruments to create a popular rock style that has really hit the charts harder and higher around the world than in the U.S. As for their Oklahoma connections, they are linked to the state by family, birthright, and a youthful understanding of the rural environment, as well as experiencing the extreme religious environment of the Pentecostal Church, for which their father was a traveling preacher. Nathan and Matthew were born in Oklahoma City while Caleb and Jared were born in Mt. Juliet, Tennessee. Their childhood and teen years are now the stuff rock and roll myths are made of, riding around the South with their parents to different Pentecostal churches where they would sleep where they could, were mostly home schooled by their mother (except about four years when they attended a small Pentecostal parochial school outside of Memphis), and had to attend church services no questions asked.

Kings of Leon, 2010, (L-R) Nathan Followill, Matthew Followill, Caleb Followill, Jared Followill.

As for turning into rockers, a couple of points should be made: 1) Pentecostal people are not called "holy rollers" for nothing. Services are about being taken over by the Holy Spirit, being filled with it to the point of speaking in tongues. The faithful are used to an environment where there is a lot of yelling and wailing going on. Pentecostal music moves, has electric instruments and drum sets, meant to develop a fervored environment that is practically hypnotic, and that's where the boys learned to play. And the preaching is loud, shouting loud, filled with gestures and expeted responses from the congregation to urge on the message from the pulpit. No wonder Kings of Leon called their first EP *Holy Roller Novocaine* with all of the double meanings that title implies. 2) Rock fans might remember that four of the biggest white rockers in the 1950s, Elvis Presley, Jerry Lee Lewis, Johnny Cash, and Carl Perkins, all came from Pentecostal family backgrounds, and look how they turned out. Understanding those two things (the vigor of Pentecostal worship and the first generation of major rockers coming out of that environment), sets one up for understanding a lot of the breakout party rock ethos of the Kings of Leon. About 1997, their parents divorced. At that point, the boys were old enough to decide on whether they wanted to go church or not (*not*), and set up about forming their vent machine (the band), and went about letting out anything they had kept bottled up for years (like buying Led Zeppelin albums). And purge they did, in ways that put them in a long tradition of public excess for highly visible rockers, and they were already used to a spirit-filled, turn-it-loose musical environment for practically their whole lives. So, here come the unholy rock and rollers.

As for Oklahoma, drummer Nathan Followill is closely connected to the state, and keeps a miniature University of Oklahoma football helmet on his drum set in concert just as a reminder. Regarding the Sooner blood that runs in his veins, Nathan told *Daily Oklahoman* entertainment editor Gene Triplett as much in an interview published March 11, 2005. Followill just had to say "Boomer Sooner" for the story, and indicates he'd spent about as much time in Oklahoma as Tennessee up to that point, and still has a lot of family in the state. However, the scales have mostly tipped back toward Tennessee as the band really has their headquarters set up there. Even Matthew, who was born in Oklahoma City, was living in Mississippi and going to high school when the brothers drafted him to come up to Tennessee and join the band.

Kings of Leon drummer, Nathan Followill, 2004.

By 2002, Kings of Leon had a record deal after writing and rehearsing in Nashville, and by 2003 released *Holy Roller Novocaine* through RCA Records, causing immediate notice in England where the band was instantly embraced, a trend that has repeated itself globally throughout their subsequent releases until 2010's *Come Around Sundown*. Their first full-length, an energetic punch in the gut, *Youth and Young Manhood* (RCA, 2003), sold 750,000 copies-plus around the world (Australia, England, and the Netherlands being key markets), whereas, the disc "only" moved about 100,000 back in the U.S. Their second album, *Aha Shake Heartbreak* (RCA, 2004), with an equal amount of Southern rock tropes and style, but with the best harmonies since 38 Special, notched a Top 20 album spot in England, and picked up a lot of high-profile fans as the group toured with Bob Dylan and Pearl Jam in 2005 and 2006. *Aha Shake Heartbreak* made a little noise on the *Billboard* Top 200, peaking at #55 after nine weeks on the album chart. The band's third album, *Because of the Times* (RCA, 2007), was their most polished effort yet, and did o.k. in Europe with their fans in picking up about 70,000 copies. However, pop critics are a fickle bunch, and the album did not receive favorable reviews, mainly because the lyrics were drummed up out of their rock and roll bacchanalia experiences, and it sounded different than the first three records. The critics did not note that Jared was only twenty-one at the time and had only been playing bass a few years, and lead guitarist Matt was also just twenty-two at the time. I mean, write about what you know, right? The boys were writing about their crazy rock and roll life while learning their instruments, and critics sit in their offices with their free copies of the album and nothing to do but write about how they don't want to hear about younger kids having so much fun with their major label rock star status. Some conundrum isn't it, from both points of view. While the critics got on the boys living like the Rolling

Matthew Followill, Australia, 2004.

Stones forty years prior, the album didn't do badly on the charts, rising to #25 on the *Billboard* Top 200, and surging to the upper reaches of the Top Internet Album, Top Digital Album, and Top Rock album charts, and further bouncing around the various European and Internet charts for another year. Their next album, *Only by the Night* (2008) took care of all that "nobody knows in your own hometown" business.

The band's fourth album, *Only by the Night*, entered the U.K. Album Charts at #1, debuted on the *Billboard* Top 200 at #4, flew up the *Billboard* U.S. Alternative Rock Chart to #1, and reached #5 on the *Billboard* Comprehensive Album chart, #4 on the Current Album chart, and #1 on the Digital Album chart. The band also enjoyed a trend again in Europe and back in the U.S. whereby their previous albums received return chart action due to the success of the current one. The album was the third biggest album in the U.K. for 2008, and the #1 album in Australia for that year. All of this success was both to their large following abroad, but they finally got a bona fide hit single out of the deal, "Sex on Fire" (#1 UK, #1 US Hot Modern Rock, #1 Ireland). The single continued to smooth out the formula they'd been perfecting since their earliest records. That chiming guitar has always been popular in England and Ireland, whether it came from U2's the Edge, the Chameleons UK, or even new wave pop acts like Big Country. In that context, Kings of Leon fit the UK's pop aesthetic up until they put the word "sex" in the title of their song. Do that, and you have America's attention, which they did, and it happened. More importantly, the success of "Sex on Fire" set up the worldwide media system for the second single from *Only by the Night*, "Use Somebody". A hit song around the world, "Use Somebody" ratcheted Top 10 slots in the U.S., Australia, Ireland, New Zealand, and peaked at #2 in the U.K. While *Only the Night* did give in to come country music trappings the guys had to have soaked up from all those years rolling around the South, "Use Somebody" fits the formula of many early U2 successful singles with a ballad-y intro, and a loud rocking sing along chorus with repetitive guitar picking on the same chord or string, galloping drums, and nothing really that fancy, just a catchy song about needing someone to love. Bingo! *Only the Night* was certified Platinum in the U.S. for selling a million copies in the year after it was released, "Use Somebody" won a 2010 Grammy for Best Rock Performance by a Duo or Group with Vocal, one for Best Rock Song, and one for Record of the Year. Along with the making of the album, Kings of Leon had several videos made that were loaded to the video file sharing service, youtube.com. For fans who want to see how deep their Oklahoma roots really run, get a good look and listen at their Oklahoma family down in southeastern Oklahoma, complete with family sings, some good and bad memories told, wading in the creek catching crawdads and eating them, and just a lot of plain old goofy country fun. Just enter "Kings of Leon home movies" to get the pictures. They also released a live DVD in 2009, *Live at the O2 in London, England*, filmed in front of 18,000 of the fans who took them to heart first, and viewers/listeners can see why they are so popular there.

Jared Followill, 2004

Kings of Leon lead singer Caleb Followill, 2004.

By Hugh Foley / 425

In 2010, the band released their fifth studio album, *Come Around Sundown*, and took off on a fifty city North American and European tour, watching as their album climbed to at #2 on the *Billboard* Top 200 album chart in November, 2010. In 2011, they were named the Oklahoma Music Hall of Fame's Rising Stars, released a documentary on their lives and careers, *Talihina Sky: The Story of the Kings of Leon*, and received another GRAMMY nomination for one of the songs on *Come Around Sundown*, "Radioactive". One listen to "Radioactive" for anyone with a country church background would know that the band's own country church background is not too far out of mind, as Caleb quotes the old gospel standard they must have heard thousands of times, "When the Roll is Called Up Yonder". After singing the famous opening line of the chorus, he then wonders aloud if he will be there, and if it really will be a moment that separates those born of the water and those not. Either way, the singer can't stop thinking about it because the whole question is embedded in where he came from, and becomes a contemporary metaphor for how one is living life from day to day. What is interesting is watching and listening to Kings of Leon mature from a butt-kicking rock band bent on the hedonism of finally being free to do whatever on the tour bus, into more contemplative artists musically and lyrically. This might just show they may have learned more about meditating on life's principles than they thought, and that is what most likely comes out of the country church and rural family background they absorbed being in Oklahoma for formative parts of their lives.

The group remains a little dangerous, if not reckless, however, having to cancel its U.S. tour in 2011 due to "vocal issues and exhaustion," but stories bounded out of the mouths of train wreck watchers, tattle tails, and journalists who witnessed some of the excesses endemic to the lifestyle. After re-collecting themselves, the group went back into the studio in 2012 to begin working on their next album.

Kiowa Tribe

(In the area of Oklahoma since at least the late 1700s)

With their tribal administration offices located in Carnegie, Oklahoma, the Kiowa are one of the thirty-nine federally recognized American Indian tribes that maintain their contemporary headquarters in Oklahoma, and one of six tribes currently based in the Southwestern quadrant of the state that was all once known as Indian Territory. Considered a menace to Spaniards, Mexicans, and Anglo-Americans traveling the Santa Fe Trail, the Kiowa gave the U.S. Government fits in trying to corral the nomadic Plains tribe with thousands of years of traditions. The Kiowa also provided lively copy for sensationalized western pulp fiction of the 19th century with their constant raiding, or defending, depending which side you were on, and the Kiowa's image of a chief with an eagle feather war bonnet has become one of America's iconic if not stereotypic images of the American Indian. While exact locations differ according to individual oral and scholarly historic perspectives, the Kiowa traditionally trace their origins as a tribe to the mountainous regions of western Montana at the sources of the Yellowstone and Missouri River. Recent

Kiowa Gourd Clan Encampment, Carnegie, OK, 2003.

linguistic studies have also suggested the tribe may have come from as far south as what became Mexico before arriving in Montana. The Kiowa are the only tribe classed in their linguistic family.

An extremely truncated version of Kiowa history includes the oral history of their entrance into the above world through a hole in the ground, some of the tribe being left behind when a pregnant woman could not get through. Not knowing what glacial period that might have been, modern history begins when the Kiowa are known to have migrated into the Black Hills from Montana after acquiring the horse in the 1600s. Devil's Tower, in eastern Wyoming near Sundance, is still an important identity marker for the Kiowa. Expelled from the Black Hills by the Lakota and the Cheyenne around 1750, the group headed south beyond the Arkansas River where they subsequently fought with the Comanche until about 1790 in the southern plains region of what is now Kansas, Texas, Oklahoma, Colorado and New Mexico. Realizing friends would be important and necessary during the oncoming Plains Indian Wars with the U. S. government, the Kiowa, and their allies the Na-I-Sha Apache, made peace with the Comanche about 1790 and began harassing travelers together who were on their way west through Kiowa, Comanche, and Apache (KCA) land, then known as Indian Territory. After the Civil War finished, the U.S. government turned its attention to the "Indian problem," and sent troops out to Indian Territory, what is now Oklahoma, and began to round up Plains tribes. Some Kiowa begrudgingly accepted reservation life in 1865, while others opposed it violently and resisted colonization until the Medicine Lodge Treaty of 1867.

The Medicine Lodge Treaty attempted a peace agreement in return for future paternal care of the Cheyenne, Arapaho, Comanche, Na-I-Sha Apache (then known as the Kiowa-Apache because of historical alliances with the Kiowa), and the Kiowa. The sternest elements of the warrior societies did not give in, however, and maintained combat through the Battle of the Washita (1868-1869) and the Battle of Palo Duro Canyon (1874) until the U.S. Army forced the Kiowa onto reservations where diseases caused many deaths and ultimate resignation to reservation life. By 1879, the systematic elimination of the buffalo had also been successful by government and commercial enterprises to deprive the Kiowa, and other Plains tribes, of their traditional subsistence lifestyle. The end of the Kiowa reservation period began with the planned allotment of "excess" tribal lands in the 1892, but did not actually happen until 1901 when the remaining land could be opened to homesteaders, or Oklahoma's legendary "boomers." With the complete eradication of their ancient lifestyle in just about fifty years, the 20th century provided many hardships for tribal members as they attempted to adjust to mainstream society all around them, and maintain significant elements of their traditional life. While the Kiowa made significant contributions in the areas of art (the Kiowa Six) and literature (N. Scott Momaday) throughout the 20th century, the maintenance of their tribal musical traditions of the Black Leggins Society, the Oh-Ho-Mah Lodge, the Kiowa Gourd Clan, Peyote songs, and sacred Kiowa hymns is one of their most significant contributions to world culture. Many of the Kiowa songs and ceremonies are related to warrior societies that provided Kiowa people with both identity and purpose throughout the 20th century. Men and women of the Kiowa, as well as all American Indians, served in greater proportional capacities in the U.S. Armed Services than any other ethnic group through the Vietnam War. This provided another century's worth of music related to war expeditions, coming home, and the remembrance of those who never returned from any wars in which the Kiowa have ever participated.

In a 2002 presentation at the annual American Indian Sovereignty Symposium in

Oklahoma City, Jim Anquoe, a Kiowa singer who is also a acultural preservationist and historian with the Oklahoma Historical Society, explained the Omaha gave many Plains tribes the war dance songs that still exist today among tribes such as the Kiowa and Cheyenne. Many tribes have acquired the war dance songs through the Ponca via the Omaha, according to Anquoe, to include the Kiowa who have adopted the songs of many different tribes, and their memorial song from the Cheyenne. In fact, the Cheyenne gave Kiowas the dance bustle one sees in the Kiowa O-Ho-Mah Lodge warrior society, representing a long tradition of interconnectedness between Plains tribes.

Kiowa music is one of the most heavily recorded American Indian musical traditions. Due to the foresight of the Smithsonian Institution's concern for American folk life in the 1930s, '40s, and '50s, several recordings exist of Kiowa singers from that period who were still closely related to the 19th century. Indian House Records and Canyon Records took up the Kiowa commercial recording flag from the 1960s forward to 2003 with several excellent releases. Some independent recordings were made for vinyl release throughout the 1960s and 1970s, and have long been out of print, such as *16 Kiowa Songs* (Indian Records) sung by Roland Horse, Bruce Haumpy, and Billy Hunting Horse.

Founded in the 1940s by the late Rev. Linn D. Pauahty, a Kiowa Methodist minister from Carnegie, Oklahoma, Soundchief recorded and released extensive recordings of the best singers throughout the northern and southern plains. The American Soundchief label introduced the popular in-depth approach to recording American Indian music. Whereas early albums of Indian music often presented several tribal groups and types of songs on one album, Rev. Pauahty was the first to publish albums where one tribal group sang one set of songs such as war dance, grass dance, peyote, or round dance songs. The format was more enjoyable for the experienced listener of American Indian music. While most of the original vinyl releases are now out of print, Indian House Records in Taos has made the recordings available through cassette reissues. Kiowa recordings on the Soundchief label include war dance songs, war expedition songs, circle songs, two-step songs, several recordings of Peyote songs, and Kiowa Black Leggings Warriors Society songs.

Along with Indian House Records, Canyon Records is one of the longest-standing companies devoted to releasing American Indian music. Canyon's albums of significance to the Kiowa include 1972's *Kiowa: Forty-Nine and Round Dance Songs* sung by Mr. and Mrs. Vincent Bointy, Raymond White Buffalo, Mr. and Mrs. Bruce Haumpy, Mr. and Mrs. Bill Botone, Herschel Kaulaity, Mr and Mrs. John Emhoolah, Jr., and Ted Creeping Bear. Several stories exist for the origin of "49" songs, to include the story of fifty men who went to war and only 49 returned, or a second version with only one returning. The songs might also be connected to a famous Sioux war expedition of 1849, or dances that were held by Plains Indians to disrupt the Army's sleep during the gold rush year of 1849.

Cozad Family singers, Red Earth, 1999.

Kiowa singer Jack V. Anquoe (1933-2006).

A story on the back of the *Kiowa: Forty-Nine and Round Dance Songs* recounts the appearance at a 1920s Oklahoma county fair of a dancing-girl-show themed after the California Gold Rush of '49. Later that night, Kiowas and other Indians went off to a social dance where they started making fun of the barker from the show, including English lyrics, and the imitation became a standing joke and name for Kiowa social dances. According to Kiowa elder Evans Ray Satepauhoodle, the songs now known as "49" songs were originally called "Goo Daw Gee", or "Wisdom Songs" that were sung when men were going off to war or a hunting party, or returning. The songs held the wisdom of the tribe, and so were called as such. Another commonly known story also has the songs deriving from Kiowa round dances in the late 1940s to accompany the social gatherings of returning soldiers from World War II. As many American Indian veterans had difficulty in adjusting to second class life back in the states after they had just enjoyed full status as important men in extremely difficult combat situations, 49 dances also developed a reputation for alcohol consumption. While in the 1940s the term "Goo Daw" was used by Kiowas of the day for a late night social dance, terms such as the "49", or now just "the nine," have since evolved into a standard term for songs that are sung "after the powwow" in a field or someone's backyard to wind down from a day and night's dancing in the rule-laden powwow arena where alcohol is forbidden. Jim Anquoe says Bill Koomsa, Jr. is the undisputed best singer of "49" songs. A spirited set of 49 songs were released as *"49" at Hog Creek* by Millard Clark on his Indian Sound label in 2002. The album has no titles, a few English lyrics relating to beer and the pizza delivery man, and includes many singers whose names are mentioned on other Kiowa albums. Clark has released at least three other volumes of "Round Dance Songs with English Lyrics", or "49" songs, with Millard and Tom Ware as lead singers. Contemporarily, Round Dance songs are still being recorded with new themes. Glen Ahhaitty (Kiowa/Comanche/Cherokee) has recorded two albums of social Round Dance Songs for Canyon Records, *True Lies from the Road* and *No More Lies*, both released in 2010.

In 1975, Canyon released *Kiowa Scalp and Victory Dance Songs* sung by Bill Koomsa, Sr., Billy Hunting Horse, Wilbur Kodaseet, Bill Koomsa, Jr., and Lonnie Tsotaddle. Women singers on the album are Georgia Dupoint, Ann Koomsa, Martha Koomsa Perez, and Pearl Woodard. Bill Koomsa, Sr. remembers in the album's liner notes that the scalp dance songs were sung when a war party returned from its destination, as were victory songs. He also explained that victory dances are danced in a circle like a round dance except in the opposite direction – counter clockwise. Koomsa's father, Bob Koomsa, was a prominent Kiowa singer who was on the committee that adopted the Kiowa Flag song after World War I. Some of the material from *Kiowa Scalp and Victory Songs* was reissued on Canyon's 1998 CD, *Traditional Kiowa Songs*. Serious scholars, enthusiasts, and preservationists will want to research the Library of Congress Music Division in Washington, D.C. where many recordings remain unissued, and the Oklahoma Historical Society where the important collections of Jim Anquoe and Edwin Chapabitty, Sr. are housed.

The Smithsonian released an important early album under the title of *Folk Music for the United States: Kiowa* (AAFS L35). The songs were recorded from 1936 to 1951 and included Sun Dance Songs, Death Songs, Ghost Dance Songs, Legend Songs, Peyote

Songs, Christian hymns, Round Dances, two steps, War Dance songs, Rabbit Society songs, and a Flag song. Singers include George Hunt, Matthew Whitehorse (leader), and Kiowa Singers at the Big Tent on the Christian Hymns. In 1964, Folkways Records, now part of the Smithsonian Institution, released *Kiowa Songs* (FE 4393) featuring brothers Kenneth Anquoe and Jack Anquoe, Sr. on Gourd Dance songs, War Dance Songs, Round Dance songs, Trot Dance songs, Buffalo Dance songs, and a Flag Song. Also singing on *Kiowa Songs* were Nick Webster (Arapaho), Oscar Tahlo, Adam Kaulaity, Laura Tahlo, and 71-year-old chorus leader Sally Kaulaity.

Descending from one of the Kiowa's most significant song-making families, Kenneth Anquoe is also important for starting one of the first urban powwows in the U.S. in Tulsa in 1946 with his brother, Jack Anquoe, Sr. As a family, to include Jim Anquoe (b. Mountain View, 1933 - d. Tulsa, 2006), Mary Ann Anquoe (b. Mountain View, OK, July 19, 1930 –d. 2002, Tulsa, OK), and Jack Anquoe Jr. (b. Claremore, OK, September 17, 1956), who have also been featured on several recordings, the Anquoes have also released important independent recordings such as 1985's *Original Kiowa War Mother Songs Volume 1* on cassette, and Jack Anquoe, Sr. has recorded albums with his drum group under the name Grayhorse, such as *Spirits Who Dance* (1996), on Sound of America Records. According to his obituary, Anquoe composed more than 100 ceremonial songs and was a member of the Kiowa Black Leggins. He also originated the "three-tailed fancy dance song" that allows dancers to exhibit their skills to varying rhythms and speeds. His singing groups recorded as many as twenty albums worth of recordings, six of which are cassette releases, the rest on vinyl and CD. His performance group of dancers and singers performed across the United States, and in Europe, Canada, and Japan. The Anquoe family is one of the Kiowa's original singing families, according to Jim Anquoe, which has been documented by the family back to the 19th century when the drum was only a flat hide on the ground. Mary Ann Anquoe's "War Mothers Song" is featured on the 1995 Smithsonian Folkways release, *Heartbeat 2:More Voices of First Nations Women*.

War Mother songs are an important part of 20th century Kiowa musical heritage. The songs emerged from the clubs formed by Kiowa mothers who had sons in the service during World War II. Forty seven known war mother songs exist, according to Jim Anquoe, and were composed by his father James Anquoe and Louis Toyebo. The family now maintains those songs with a different family member able to sing a group of them. A few these songs were released on a 1997 Rykodisc album, *American Warriors: Songs for Indian Veterans*. The recordings were made on the World War II era radio program, *Indians for Indians Hour*, on the University of Oklahoma's radio station, WNAD, in Norman.

Another series of songs called hand game songs go along with the "hide and guess" games that many Plains tribes play. The team that is "hiding" the bones or sticks in their hands will sing songs and generally cause confusion for the team who is guessing where the marked bones or sticks are. Two albums of hand game songs were recorded in 1968 by Indian House Records and subsequently released as *Handgame of the Kiowa, Kiowa Apache, and Comanche – Volume 1 and 2: Carnegie Roadrunners vs. Billy Goat Hill*. A few of these songs resurfaced on a 1996 compilation CD released by Indian House called *Proud Heritage: A Celebration of Traditional American Indian Music*. Indian House also recorded war journey songs in 1969 and released them as *Kiowa 49 – War Expedition Songs*, which featured singers Gregory Haumpy, Billy Hunting Horse, Ralph Kotay, Bill Koomsa, Jr., Barbara Ahaitty, Pearl Kerche, Angeline Koomsa, Nan B. Koomsa, and Wilda Koomsa. The uptempo war expedition, or war journey, songs were sung to get warriors up

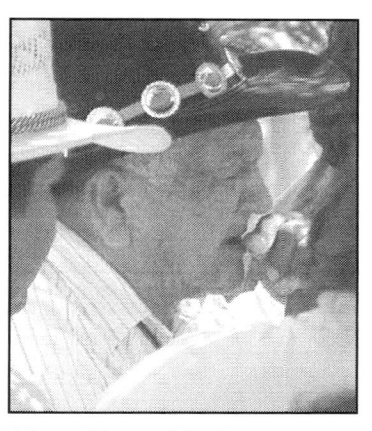

Kiowa Singer, Billy Evans Horse

before going off to battle and date to the Plains period. While some Kiowa songs may be borrowed or part of larger Plains singing traditions, Jim Anquoe made clear in his 2002 presentation that songs the Kiowa "own" are the songs that go along with the war dance society known as the Black Leggins Ceremonies, sometimes called "Black Legs," to indicate the black leggings members of the war dance society wear in the ceremonies. Pronounced "Tone Kone Go" in roughly Anglicized Kiowa, the ceremonies are conducted each year in May at Lone Bear's Dance Ground in Carnegie. Two accessible recordings exist of the Black Leggings Society: one is available on the Indian Soundchief reissues through Indian House Records, the second is by Bill Kaulaity, James Cozad, and Daniel Cozad: *Kiowa Black Leggings Society Songs* (Canyon).

Music is highly personal in Kiowa society and ceremonies. Many families and individuals have songs that are restricted in their use by that family or individual. In a 2000 oral history interview with Dr. Mary Jane Warde and Jim Anquoe of the Oklahoma Historical Society, Parker Emhoola provides a good example of how the Kiowa feel about their individual songs. As a member of the O-Ho-Mah Lodge, a Kiowa war dance society centered around a pipe dance ceremonial held until the mid-20th century at the Whitehorse family dance grounds, Emhoola was given a song he liked by the leader of the O-Ho-Mah Lodge at the time, Charlie "Old Man" Whitehorse. According to Jim Anquoe, Parker's song is one of the few remaining individual songs in the O-Ho-Mah lodge. Parker Emhoolah explained in his oral history, "The song came from the north, as did other songs in the O-Ho-Mah. It's a special occasion song and is not meant to be sung just as a pow wow song." This distinction between commercial popular music, or even intertribal pow wow music, and the intensely personal and often spiritual nature of American Indian music is further detailed by Emhoolah in the interview: "We have a song called the 'tagging song.' This is when we are taking new members and recruits into the organization. We only sing it once a year, and that song is being used by other tribes as a regular intertribal song and it is not. It is an O-Ho-Mah song. You are not supposed to use that song. It is a ceremonial song. One day is set aside during the ceremonial to use that song. It is forbidden to use the song outside of the Oh-Ho-Mah ceremony. There are special songs for special reasons and special occasions and some of those songs are restricted. If you want to use a song, you go through the family and ask before you sing anything that is not yours."

Two excellent sets of Oh-Ho-Mah Lodge recordings exist thanks to Indian House Records and members of the Oh-Ho-Mah Lodge who permitted the preservation enterprises to take place. The first two volumes were accomplished in Anadarko, Oklahoma in 1975 and are titled *War Dance Songs of the Kiowa: O-Ho-Mah Lodge Singers*. These recordings include singers Ralph Kotay, Dixon Palmer, Rusty Wahkinney, Bill Ware, Tom Ware, Truman Ware, Mac Whitehorse, Mildred Kotay, Maxine Wahkinney, Florene Whitehorse, and Lucille Whitehorse. The second set were made in 1994 at Stecker, Oklahoma, and subsequently released by Indian House Records as *Songs of the O-Ho-Mah Lodge: Kiowa War Dance Society Volume 1 and 2*. Singers on these releases included Parker Emhoolah, Ralph Kotay, Bill Ware, Mac Whitehorse, Roland Whitehorse, and Florene Whitehorse

Taylor. *Songs of the O-Ho-Mah Lodge: Kiowa War Dance Society Volume 3 and 4* feature different singers than the first two volumes and were recorded October 2000. Released in 2001, Volumes 3 and 4 include singers Joe Fish Dupoint, Bill Ware, Stony Ware, and Mac Whitehorse. "Oh-Ho-Mah songs were sung for warriors who were going away," according to 2001 Oklahoma Historical Society interview with full-blood Kiowa, Alice Jones Littleman, "so they would come back in a good way." In World War II –era Oh-Ho-Mah ceremonials, Littleman remembers, "They prayed for all the soldiers, not only the Indians. They prayed for all the young people."

Another example of Kiowa musical traditions that has influenced intertribal powwows throughout the U.S., Canada, and Europe is the music of the Kiowa Gourd Clan (Tia-Pah), or "Tdiepeigah" as it is known in Kiowa. Pronounced roughly as "Thigh-a-pay-go" in English, and now usually shortened to just "Thia-pay," the Kiowa Gourd Clan is a primary identity marker for the Kiowa and major source of traditional music and language preservation. According to Jim Anquoe, Tia-pah is also the Kiowa word for the dialect of Kiowa spoken east of Fort Cobb, whereas, Tone-kon-go (Black Leggins) is the Kiowa word for the Kiowa dialect west of Fort Cobb. Two accessible recordings exist of Kiowa Gourd Dance Songs: one set was released by Canyon Records as *Gourd Dance Songs of the Kiowa* (CR-6148), and Tony Isaacs and Indian House Records recorded a 1974 set entitled *Kiowa Gourd Dance Volume 1 and 2*, featuring singers Daniel Cozad, Joe Cozad, Larry Cozad, Leonard Cozad, Sr., Billy Hunting Horse, Adam Kaulaity, Vincent Spotted Bird, Yale Spotted Bird, Velma Cozad, Barbara Ahhaitty Monoessy, Dobbin Monoessy, and Naomi Svitak. The Gourd Dance songs' origins are traced by the Kiowa to the red wolf that gave them the songs, which is why one will hear what sounds like "yelps" at the end of some Gourd Dance songs, in honor of that red wolf. These yelps are an excellent example of how the uninitiated listener of American Indian music might consider elements of Indian songs as just vocables, or sounds with no meaning, whereas, the so-called vocables in these Kiowa songs are directly related to the oral history behind their origin. Additional accounts have been offered to the origins of the Kiowa Gourd Clan. An August 17, 1991 issue of the Anadarko Daily News carried an article regarding Kiowa Tia-piah Society Origins, linking the origin of the organization to an 1838 battle with the Cheyenne on Wolf Creek near Camp Supply, Oklahoma, the result of which was many dead warriors on both sides. The resulting peace agreement between the tribes instigated the forming of the group that became an intrinsic part of the Sun

Kiowa Gourd Clan singers in 2003(l-r): Cletus Gayton, Sidney Toppah, and Earnest "Iron" Toppah.

Dance. Currently, three Gourd Dance organizations meet on the 4th of July weekend, one at Carnegie, one south of Carnegie, and one in Lawton. A lot of music has come out of the tradition, and much of it has been recorded.

According to the liner notes by Tony Isaacs in *Kiowa Gourd Dance Volume I*, the meaning of "Tia-pah-go" refers remotely to the words meaning skunkberry and brave, the translation of which has become obscure, and now is specifically the name of the war dance society known as the Kiowa Gourd Clan. The English name of "gourd dance" comes from the rattles used by the dancers, which at one time were made out of gourd or rawhide, but now consist of baking powder cans or metal saltshakers. Even though these rattles have been used since the revival of the dance in the 1950s, they are still called gourds when speaking in English. The origin of the dance itself is imbedded in the Kiowa ceremonial traditions of the sun dance, shut down in the latter 19th century by the U.S. Government out of fear and ignorance of American Indian rituals and religion. The sun dance was "put away" by the tribe in exchange for badly needed rations and clothing from the government, and a buffalo hunting party could no longer be held which eliminated an important part of the ceremony. Jim Anquoe pointed out in his presentation that gourd dance songs grew out of the Kiowa's sun dance and brush dance songs, and the Kiowa Gourd Dance is the traditional dance of Thia-pah-go warrior society.

Leonard Cozad, Sr., who is generally considered *the* Kiowa elder singer in 2003, told Tony Isaacs his memories of the gourd dance's origins in a 1974 interview included on *Kiowa Gourd Dance Volume 1*: "The Kiowas had bands or societies, I don't know how far back. From what I got from a few of my elders, they had these dances only once a year in the summertime. In those days we had a sun dance – a bigger place to go for all the societies and organizations; and these sun dances were put on by different societies, such as the Young Colts, the Mustangs, the Gourd Society, the Black Leggins, and the Elite Warriors. Each of these societies had their own songs. When they are going to put up a sun dance lodge, each society has a brush dance, from gourd dance and Black Leggins on down, except for the Elite Warriors, we never heard anything about that. But these others are the ones, the people who have work to do to put up the lodge. When it's done, that's when the sun dance begins. In the meantime, all these different societies have their own places in the circle – a big circle with the lodge in the center, and they put on dances as time goes on."

Evans Ray Satepauhoodle (1931-2004) Kiowa singer, educator, and mentor.

After the last Kiowa sun dance was held in 1887 at Oak Creek, members of the original "Gourd Clan," or Tia-pah-go, continued dances until 1927 when the last dance was held a few miles south of Carnegie. The Gourd Dance was not held again until Armistice Day of 1946 when it was again performed in Carnegie. In 1956, some of the descendants of the original members began working out the songs for the Kiowa Gourd Clan. A recent treasure trove of reel-to-reel tapes, donated to the Oklahoma Historical Society by the Edwin Chapabitty, Sr. family, document the singings when the gourd dance songs were formed, as well as many other Kiowa songs and songs from surrounding tribes such as the Cheyenne, Arapaho, and Comanche. The cataloguing of these significant recordings, and other important work on the American Indian music of Oklahoma, is ongoing through the Oklahoma Historical Society and its Oklahoma Folklife Council's Tribal Songs Project. As for the Kiowa Gourd Dance, those who revived the dance in the 1950s and formed the Kiowa Gourd Clan have now essentially split into three different organizations, discussed in detail by Luke E. Lassiter in his 1998 book, *The Power of Kiowa Song*. Regardless of factionalism, the public is welcome to attend the annual Kiowa Gourd Clan Ceremonies held in Carnegie Park next to the rodeo grounds every year on July 4th. While the event does not feature the usual trappings and vendors of intertribal powwows, the event is one of tremendous depth and significance for both the Kiowa and American culture in general. As Leonard Cozad, Sr., the original drum keeper of the revived Kiowa Gourd Clan, explained to Tony Isaacs, "It's just like prayers songs, it just makes you happy, and makes people feel good. . . . When they hear the drum and the song, then they want to live – they want to go on to hear these good things among the homes and their children." Many singers have been recorded throughout the years, but even more have not. The Kiowa Gourd Clan's 1996 program mentions some of the common family names known around the Gourd Clan drum: Whitefox, Daugomah, Ahhaitty, Koomsa, Tenedooah, Kaulaity, Lone Bear, Doyeto, Cozad, Toyebo, Lone Wolf, Anquoe, Bointy, Botone, Emhoolah, Red Bird, Tsoodle, Satepauhoodle, Horse, Gayton, and Tenequoot.

In addition to the Gourd Dance itself, The Little Rabbit Society is a Kiowa children's organization and has its own set of songs that are sung during morning ceremonies on the last two days of the encampment. An added element of bittersweet fun and irony has also been present for several years in the presence of a bugler dressed in authentic 19th century U.S. cavalry regalia. The bugler, most recently Bill Bartee of Bethany who married into the Tsoodle family, plays cavalry calls during some of the Gourd Clan's songs. The history behind the bugler lies with Kiowa chief Standing Bear's military strategy. During the Plains Indian Wars, the Kiowa captured a bugler. Chief Satanta, "Sate-I-tay" or White Bear, an obvious military genius, learned how to play the cavalry's bugle calls. When the cavalry played charge or retreat on the battlefield, White Bear would play the opposite call and confuse the mounted troops. During one portion of the Kiowa Gourd Clan Ceremonies, a bugle and other war trophies are mounted on staffs in the center of the arena. While humorous, the Kiowa do not forget White Bear refused life under U.S. government rule, and continued raiding off the reservation because of meager rations and the intrusion of the railroad into traditional buffalo country. Taken to a Texas prison, he committed suicide rather than conforming. This episode in Kiowa history only adds to the reverence of the annual and open-to-the-public Kiowa Gourd Clan proceedings.

Contemporarily, Sacred singing is not limited to the warrior societies in Kiowa life. Kiowa singers have made significant contributions to both the Peyote religion's music, and the sacred hymn singing of the Kiowa Christian church. Bill Kaulaity and Daniel Cozad, as well as Joe Fish Dupoint and Dewayne Tofpi have each recorded sets of Kiowa peyote songs for Canyon Records, and Indian House Records has released several sets of Kiowa peyote songs, each one

Kiowa Gourd Clan bugler, Bill Bartee.

different from the other. The first set on Indian House, recorded and released in 1997 and 1998, is called *Kiowa Spiritual Peyote Songs Volume 1, 2, and 3*. Volumes 1 and 2 feature Kiowa, Apache, and Comanche peyote songs sung by Nelson Big Bow and Kenneth L. Cozad. Volume 3 of *Kiowa Spiritual Peyote Songs* consists of 28 Kiowa and Comanche peyote songs sung by Nelson Big Bow, and assisted by Howard Cozad. In 1998, Indian House recorded and released *Faith, Hope, and Charity: Kiowa Native American Church Prayer Songs, Volume 1 and 2*, recorded at Medicine Park, Oklahoma. Both volumes of *Faith, Hope, and Charity* contain 32 Kiowa and Comanche peyote songs sung by Daniel

K. Cozad, Sr., Joe Fish Dupoint, Kenneth L. Cozad, and Howard Cozad. Finally, Indian House released the first of a four-volume set of *Kiowa Peyote Songs* in 2002 recorded at Hog Creek, Oklahoma, and featuring singers Joe Fish Dupoint, Howard and Kenneth Cozad, Lonnie Emhoolah, and Herbert Redbird, with Volumes 2 and 3 being released in the summer of 2003. In 2009 and 2010, Grammy-nominated Kiowa singer Cheevers Toppah teamed up with Diné (Navajo) singer for two albums of Peyote Songs of the Native American Church, *First Light* (Canyon) and *Awakening of Life* (Canyon).

Cheevers Toppah (Kiowa/Navajo) also released a beautiful album of harmonized church hymns of the Kiowa, *Renewed Spirit* (Canyon, 2010), representing the traditional (non-Peyote) Christian side of Kiowa religious life. Indian House also recorded two sets of sacred hymns in 1971, *Kiowa Church Songs – Volume 1 and 2*. Singers on the albums of church songs, both available on cassette, include David Apekaum, Ray Cozad, Harry Domebo, Walter Geionety, Tom Tointigh, Ruby Beaver, Kathleen Redbone, Joyce Robinson, and Nancy Tointich. Fred Tsoodle, a Kiowa sacred hymn singer, won a 2001 National Heritage Fellowship award from the National Endowment for the Arts for his preservation of Kiowa hymns. As of 2003, Tsoodle was the song leader at the Rainy Mountain Kiowa Indian Baptist Church in southwestern Oklahoma. Another public source of Kiowa hymns is the *Songs of Indian Territory* cassette produced by the State Arts Council of Oklahoma in 1989. Ralph and Mildred Kotay and Vivian Komartly sang two hymns for that project to preserve the Native American music traditions of Oklahoma. Also on the cassette are Kiowa Gourd Dance, Round Dance, and War Dance songs by Ernest "Iron" Toppah, Tommy Ware, Joe Fish Dupont, and Stoney Ware.

The Kiowa have also played an important role in the development and preservation of the Plains flute tradition. As part of the Smithsonian's Folk Music Series of American Indian music, Belo Cozad (1864-1950), seventy-seven at the time of the 1941 recording by Willard Rhodes in Anadarko, explained the story of the Kiowa flute which is included on *Plains: Comanche, Cheyenne, Kiowa, Caddo, Wichita, Pawnee* (AAFS L39), later released on *A Treasury of Library of Congress Field Recordings* (Rounder, 1997). Belo said he got the music from "way back in Montana," when a poor boy went up on a mountain for four nights, and learned this music from "some kind of spirit" who told the boy to "make good music this way, keep it as long as you live, and it will give you a good living." The boy got the flute from a great cedar tree on the mountain, and with the music he became well off, had a good home, good wives, and good children. Belo considered himself one of those children. Cozad then plays a short rendition of the song that can be considered at the root of the Kiowa flute tradition. Also on the album, Cozad sings and plays a Kiowa love song on the flute.

Contemporarily, artists such as Terry Tsotigh, Tom Mauchahty-Ware and **Cornel Pewewardy** maintain the Kiowa flute tradition. Both Ware and Pewewardy are of Kiowa and Comanche descent, and both tribes' music influences the musical output of both artists. One of Mauchahty-Ware's several recordings includes *Flute Songs of the Kiowa and Comanche* (Indian House, 1978). The album includes the "Kiowa Flag Song," love songs,

Blues Nation, 1990

and Comanche hymns. Additionally Ware has also recorded on albums of previously discussed Oh-Ho-Mah recordings from 1975, "49" songs with Millard Clark, and is also a vocalist and guitarist with the American Indian blues group, Blues Nation. Furthering the obvious connection between blues and "49" songs, Blues Nation records and performs electric blues with lyrics reflecting Indian themes and subjects like "Empty Tipi Blues," and "Can't See the Signs" on their 1999 self-titled album. Other Kiowas in the group have included Terry Tsotigh on drums and harmonica, and bassist Sonny Klinekole who is of Kiowa, Comanche, and Apache descent. Along with Comanche guitarist Dusty Miller and Muscogee (Creek) keyboardist Obie Sullivan, Blues Nation was still active in Oklahoma City nightclubs in 2013. The group is part of a substantial blues tradition among the Kiowa spearheaded by Kiowa/Comanche/Muscogee guitarist **Jesse Ed Davis** who made significant contributions to rock, pop, and blues music in the 1960s and 1970s. Another recognized Kiowa guitarist is Cecil Gray who plays with the all-Native group, the Blackhawk Blues Band, nominated for a Native American Music Award in 2002 for "Debut Group of the Year," even though they have been playing together since 1990.

Phillip "Yogie" Bread, also Comanche and Kiowa, has been recognized for both his musical abilities on the traditional flute and as a blues harmonica player. He has been playing harmonica since he was ten, and travels the country playing festivals, tribal affairs, and other special occasions. Bread toured Europe and was featured at the Budapest Hungary Blues Festival in 1994 and 1995. Bread has also contributed music to a video documentary, *Oklahoma*, and in 1997 released an independent CD, *Thon-Gya!*, Kiowa for "This is what they say." *Thon-Gya* is a spoken word and traditional-meets-contemporary music release that explores various aspects of Kiowa and lifestyle and tradition.

While Kiowa musicians have ranged into the realm of popular music and blues, the majority of Kiowa singers carry on ancient traditions of which they are the contemporary representatives. While many tribes throughout the United States have lost their musical traditions and converted to either Anglo-influenced Christian music or the intertribal pow-wow tradition, the Kiowa continue to preserve and practice music that existed before the Europeans ever arrived in North America, and continue singing those songs as a primary component of what makes them Kiowa.

Recommended Reading
1. Lassiter, Luke. The Power of Kiowa Song: A Collaborative Ethnography. Tucson: University of Arizona Press, 1998.

Kottke, Leo
(b. September 11, 1945)

One of the great fingerpicking acoustic guitarists of the second half of the 20th century whose music focused primarily on his interpretations of blues and folk music, Leo Kottke was born in Athens, Georgia, but lived in Muskogee as a youth and teenager where he played trombone in the West Junior High Band, competing with future Muskogee District Attorney, Julian Fite, for first chair, and led by legendary Muskogee band instructor, Lowell Lehman, who Kottke calls "inspirational". When he was 13, Kottke fell ill and became bed-ridden. As a result,, he could not play the trombone lying down, so his folks brought him an inexpensive guitar, which he liked, and began to play it, as well picking up the banjo around the same time after he recovered. In an essay posted on his website in 2011, Leo indicates he took trombone lessons for a total of eight years while in Muskogee, but it is unclear whether or not he graduated from Muskogee's Central High School before he joined the U.S. Navy Reserve. The bulk of this story is recalled by the author due to being asked by then Cain's Ballroom owner, Larry Shaeffer, to give Mr. Kottke a ride from his hotel to the Cain's for a sound check. As part of our small talk during the ride, Kottke volunteered the Muskogee information. An extremely successful guitarist, Kottke changed styles late in life due to tendinitis, forcing him to create a new way to play with to compensate for the injury. Early in his career, Leo was known for using open and unconventional tunings to create a unique musical identity. He has recorded twenty-three studio albums, the most successful commercially of which is *That's What* (Private Music, 1990), which peaked at #24 on *Billboard*'s Top 200 Album chart. Many of his albums are highly praised by guitar aficionados and critics. In 2011, he was booked solidly all year at performances across the U.S. Like **Jim Keltner,** Leo Kottke had his first musical education in Oklahoma, but may not have been influenced by the actual music scene that would become his area of artistic expertise (acoustic guitar), although he does cover **Bob Wills**' "San Antonio Rose" on *Dreams and All That Stuff* (Capitol, 1974), and he has said in various interviews Muskogee is where he first heard the blues on a Mississippi John Hurt record.

Leo Kottke

www.leokottke.com

Kubik, Gail

(b. September 5, 1914 – d. July 20, 1984)

One of the youngest American composers to garner a Pulitzer Prize for music, Gail Kubik was an extremely prolific composer, and most often associated with 20th century modernism in classical music, the adherence to which occasionally put him at odds with the commercial film industry who wanted lighter fare. The relevance of his work was validated when his *Symphony Concertante* won a Pulitzer in 1952. Composer and violinist Gail Thompson Kubik was born in South Coffeyville, Oklahoma, a community of approximately 800 residents, located near the Oklahoma-Kansas border in the northeastern part of the state. An obvious child prodigy, he was awarded a full scholarship to study at the Eastman School of Music at age fifteen. While at Eastman from 1930 to 1934, Gail studied violin with Samuel Belov and composition with Bernard Rogers and Edward Royce. He continued compositional study with Leo Sowerby at the American Conservatory in Chicago in 1935 and with Walter Piston and Nadia Boulanger at Harvard University in 1937-38. Known as an excellent composer and orchestrator for film, radio, and television, he often drew from his commercial work for his concert music, the most recognized of which are his vocal compositions and chamber music.

During the early 1940s, Kubik served as staff composer and program adviser for NBC Radio in New York City, music consultant for the Office of War Information Film Bureau, and coordinator of the First Motion Picture Unit of the U.S. Army Air Corps. During the mid-1940s, he was considered one of the best composers for wartime documentaries. Following World War II, Gail spent considerable time in Europe after capturing in 1950 the Rome Prize, a coveted fellowship that provides residency in Italy for gifted American artists and scholars. He was in Europe from 1950 to 1955 and again from 1959 to 1967. From 1970 until his retirement in 1980, he was composer-in-residence at Scripps College in Claremont, California.

Kubik's honors include two Guggenheim Fellowships in 1944 and 1965, and the Pulitzer Prize for his *Symphony Concertante* in 1952. At that time, he was the youngest recipient to win that award. His second and third symphonies were commissioned, respectively, by the Louisville Orchestra and the New York Philharmonic. Gail's varied works include *Frankie and Johnnie*, composed in 1946 for dance band and folksong; *In Praise of Johnny Appleseed*, originally written in 1938, but revised in 1961, for chorus and orchestra; *Trivialities* for flute, horn, and string quartet (1934-36) *Variations on a Thirteenth Century Troubadour Song* (1935-37); *Folk Song Suite* (1941-44) for orchestra; *Memphis Belle* (1944) for orchestra; *Thunderbolt Overture* (1953) for orchestra; *Pastorale and Spring Valley Overture* (1947) for orchestra; *Boston Baked Beans: A New England Fable* (1950) for chorus and orchestra; *Magic, Magic, Magic!* (1973-76) for chorus and chamber orchestra; *A Christmas Set* (1968) for chorus and chamber orchestra; *A Record of our Time* (1970) for chorus and orchestra; *Litany and Prayer* (1943-45) for male chorus; *Prayer and Toccata* (1969) for chamber orchestra; *Fables in Song* (1950-69) for voice; *Stewball* (1942) for band; *Fanfare and March* (1945) for band; and *Fanfare for One World* (1947) for band.

Gail Kubik

Gail also completed numerous radio, television, and film scores, including *Puck: A Legend of Bethlehem* (1940) for radio; *Thunderbolt* (1945) for film; *C-Man* (1949) for film; *Gerald McBoing-Boing* (1950) for film and also for accompaniment to Dr. Seuss as the piece was created for an animated short based on a story by Dr. Seuss; *The Miner's Daughter* (1950) for film. His composition work for the film, *The Desperate Hours* (1955), was largely cut by the film company, Paramount, due to their perception of its inaccessibility for average audiences. He also scored *The Silent Sentinel* (1958) for television. Finally, Kubik worked as an arranger with a number of chorale groups, including the Robert Shaw Chorale (*Amazing Grace*), Atlanta Singers (*American Sampler*), Dale Warland Singers (*Blue Wheat*), and Westminister Abbey Choir (*Folk Songs*). A CD entitled *Gail Kubik*, recorded in 1960, is available on the Contemporary label, and in the early 2000s, Kubik's Pulitzer Prize-winning *Symphony Concertante* was re-issued on compact disc through Composers Recordings as part of an ongoing series of making important classical compositions available to the public after being re-mastered for better sound quality. The recording was made in 1971 as Kubik also conducted the orchestra through his most notable work. Gail died at his home in West Covina, California, on July 20, 1984.

L

LaFave, Jimmy
(b. July 12, 1955)

With a self-described major songwriting influences of Bob Dylan and Chuck Berry, Jimmy LaFave is an earthy singer-songwriter with a plaintive voice that is both dire and hopeful, and who uses the familiar American musical forms of folk, blues, rock and country to provide a musical palate for his stories learned from thousands of conversations on the road, loves bitter and sweet, and insightful observations about the social paradoxes of our time. Born in Wills Point, Texas (about thirty miles east of Dallas), LaFave attended junior high and some of high school in Mesquite, Texas, where he started his musical career playing on a Sears & Roebuck drum set. Shortly thereafter, his mother cashed in some green stamps for Jimmy's first guitar, and he wrote his first song in junior high school, which was "something about traveling around and being a hobo." Jimmy's mother was a devout country music fan, listening to such artists as Hank Williams, Sr., and **Merle Haggard**, and lead to Jimmy being to primarily being exposed to country music during his childhood. In 1970, when Jimmy was about fifteen, his family moved to Stillwater, Oklahoma, the college town known both for being the home of Oklahoma State University, and a multi-genre form of folk rock often called "**Red Dirt Music**", but usually referred to as "Texas music" south of the Red River border between Oklahoma and Texas. During this time, Jimmy came of age, discovering Bob Dylan's records, and then wanting to know where Dylan's inspirations lie, led LaFave to Woody Guthrie, which became a career-long kindred spirit connection. Also during the 1970s, LaFave experienced the nascent period of Stillwater's incubation as *the* red dirt music town when musicians like **Steve Ripley** and Chuck Dunlap churned up the first dust of the movement in the early and mid-1970s. By 1979, LaFave was very much part of the scene that began to evolve a few miles west of Stillwater in a rural farm house rented by John Cooper of the Red Dirt Rangers known by just about everyone during that for about twenty years as "The Farm". Understanding the collective environment where people could jam, socialize (party), and crash is really the first place for a person to get a sense of Jimmy LaFave's beginnings. He says as much on his "Ramblin Sky" from the 1997 Bohemia Beat CD, *Road Novel*, when he sings, "I know a farm down in the red dirt country where magnetic properties reside". The Farm was a weekly draw for Stillwater musicians, but also many of their friends travelling the north/south I-35 corridor to and from Texas,

Jimmy LaFave performing at Woody Guthrie Folk Festival, Okemah, OK, 2010.

who knew they could just drive about 10 miles or so off the interstate, park their van at the Farm, rest in peace and safety, maybe play some, and get back on the road the next morning. That kept a constant flow of new stories and musical ideas coming into town, and re-charged the camaraderie that kept the scene vibrant. LaFave pretty much sums up the genre's musical vibe in his "Red Dirt Roads at Night" on his 1997 compilation, *Trait* (Bohemia Beat), on which he sings about driving red dirt road section lines in Payne County (Stillwater's location), and enjoying life with a companion, all the while pulling out some old-pickup-tough blues to a joy ride tempo.

During his time in Stillwater, Jimmy became well acquainted with **Garth Brooks**, then a student at Oklahoma State University. The two shared band members and both played at Willie's, a college hangout on "The Strip" (an area of shops and bars south of the campus on Washington Street). According to Jimmy, Garth was the Wednesday night "happy hour" performer passing the hat for tips, while LaFave played the better-paying Friday and Saturday night gigs. Jimmy says Garth was performing a lot of cover songs, mostly George Strait and Dan Fogelberg material. LaFave's favorite Garth story is when the OSU Cowboys played the Nebraska Cornhuskers in a home football game, and Brooks cut his own version of "Devil Went Down to Georgia" replacing the original lyrics with "when the Cornhuskers come down to Stillwater". Subsequent to making a quick set of cassettes featuring the song, Garth then proceeded to sell them all out in front of the stadium before the game. Brooks aside, LaFave acknowledges he was strongly influenced by the music of Oklahoma. While in Oklahoma, Jimmy began to define his sound which, he states, was "based on a combination of his experiences [in Stillwater] among authentic songwriters from the tradition of Woody Guthrie."

In the early 1980s, Jimmy toured the Southwest out of Stillwater with Night Tribe, his original band, and then moved to Austin, Texas in 1985 to find a larger audience, locate a recording studio, and rub elbows with singer-songwriters like Joe Ely, Butch Hancock, and Guy Clark. He soon became identified with a new venue, Chicago House, an Austin coffeehouse. For the next eight years, he devoted his time to songwriting, improving his performance skills as a solo artist, working in other Austin clubs, and assembling a new version of Night Tribe. By 1991, LaFave had been voted Vocalist of the Year, and his group was named Band of the Year in the Music City Poll of Austin Insiders. While his songwriting talents were recognized, resulting in a publishing agreement with Polygram Music, he became frustrated with not being able to get his music out, so in 1992 Jimmy released a self-produced live album, *Austin Skyline*, containing four Dylan covers and eleven of Jimmy's songs. Furthering the Dylan connection, the liner notes for *Austin Skyline* are written by Bob Johnson, who produced Dylan's *Nashville Skyline* and *Blonde on Blonde* albums, among other Dylan projects. LaFave's second album, *Highway Trance*, was released in 1994 with fifteen of the sixteen tracks composed by Jimmy, five or six of which, he says, were written during his Stillwater days. A third album, *Buffalo Return to the Plains*, was recorded in 1995 with all fourteen tracks written by Jimmy, and further endeared him to the Austin music scene, as well as rapidly developing fan base. As a result of both, in 1996 LaFave was invited to perform on the PBS *Austin City Limits* series, but the highlight of the year was when Nora Guthrie, Woody's daughter, requested Jimmy represent Woody Guthrie's music by performing the "Tribute to Woody Guthrie." for the induction ceremonies when Woody was inducted into the Rock and Roll Hall of Fame in Cleveland. Also in 1996, he was again awarded The Austin Music Awards' Best Singer-Songwriter of the Year. When the Oklahoma Music Hall of Fame in Muskogee named Woody Guthrie as their inaugural inductee in 1997, the Guthrie family again chose Jimmy to perform on Woody's behalf, which was the first musical performance of the first induction ceremony and concert for the hall of fame. Guthrie has been a beacon for

LaFave, and the Guthrie family feels the ultimate trust in LaFave's sensitivity and respect for energizing Woody's legacy.

Along with "Ramblin Sky" where he sings about the Farm in Stillwater, LaFave's fourth Bohemia Beat album, the previously mentioned *Road Novel* (1997), was recorded in Austin and produced by Jimmy. The CD includes a nicely worn cover of **Leon Russell**'s "Home Sweet Oklahoma" in Jimmy's inimitable squeaky rasp of a voice, and a primary example of LaFave's allegiance to Chuck Berry-esque rock and roll is also present on the album ("Vast Stretches of a Broken Heart"), a musical form to which Jimmy has returned again and again throughout his recording and performing career, seemingly at least once an album and/or once a show. To cap off 1997, Jimmy toured Europe twice (where he is hugely popular) and made several stops around the U.S. and Canada where he has also developed a strong following for his poignant and personal songs of the human experience. Unsurprisingly, many of LaFave's songs are about the place where he has spent a lot of time between shows, the road. Not only is that evident on *Road Novel* (duh!), but he was also happy to be a part of two compilations of songs recognizing the iconic American highway, U.S. Route 66, the most original miles of which are still evident in Oklahoma. He contributed "Route 66 Revisited to the compilation, *Songs of Route 66: All-American Highway* (1998), covered the Woody/Jack Guthrie song, "Oklahoma Hills" on *More Songs of Route 66: Roadside Attractions* (2001).

In 1999, Bohemia Beat released a two-CD set, *Trail*, highlighting many previously unreleased LaFave tracks from the 1980s and 1990s, many of which were recorded live and off the air from his varied promotional radio appearances, to include the quintessential "Red Dirt Roads at Night". Interestingly, the disc includes twelve Bob Dylan songs as done by LaFave, a further reflection of Dylan's major impact on Jimmy as a songwriter. Two years later, he released the critically acclaimed *Texoma*, a sixteen-track collection is highlighted by wonderful tribute to the Okemah kid, "Woody Guthrie", as well as a personalized interpretation of **Jimmy Webb**'s "The Moon is a Harsh Mistress". Overall, *Texoma*, and obvious reference to Jimmy's dual Oklahoma/Texas allegiances, is "just" another album of LaFave's observationally astute American music, with no real filler. LaFave has appeared at least three times on NPR's *Mountain Stage*, was a featured performer at the first Woody Guthrie Festival in Okemah, Oklahoma in 1998, to which he returns every year, and has performed numerous times at the Kerrville Folk Festival, including the 1995 festival that was made into a *Kerrville Folk Festival: 1995 Highlights* album, on which Jimmy sings "When the Tears Fall Down". He has produced and hosted a benefit for the American Indian College Fund in Austin, which featured twenty of Austin's best singers and songwriters. Moreover, he has sung back-up vocals for such artists as **Ray Wylie Hubbard**, **Tom Russell**, and Bob Childers, and in 2000 added half a duet to the Burns Sisters' Philo/Rounder disc, *Out of the Blue* ("Never Be Mine".

On a 2002 tour stop in New York City, LaFave again connected with Nora Guthrie, who

Jimmy LaFave, publicity image Bohemia Beat Records, circa 1999.

By Hugh Foley / 441

was looking for Oklahoma and Texas musicians to put new music and life to more than 50 sets of Woody Guthrie lyrics. She turned the project over to LaFave who coordinated the *Ribbon of Highway – Endless Skyway* album and tour. Recorded and released in 2008 as the first issue of LaFave's Music Road records, *Ribbon of Highway – Endless Skyway* merges the new/old songs Guthrie left unrecorded and with no music, along with some of his best known songs, all linked by narration from Woody's writings by red dirt music luminary, **Bob Childers.** The 2003 tour made the rounds of major cities in the U.S. with a rotating cast of characters, allowing LaFave multiple opportunities to talk about the man, the myth, the mind, and the lyrical mountain maker, Woodrow Wilson Guthrie. Stops on the tour included Old Town School of Folk Music (Chicago), Ryman Auditorium (Nashville), The Ark (Ann Arbor, MI), Westport Arts Center (Westport, CT), Sommerville Theater (Sommerville, MA), Palladium Theater (St. Petersburg, FL), as well as performances in New York City and Los Angeles.

In 2005, LaFave was signed by Red House Records, the first release for which was *Blue Nightfall*, an often contemplative album, save the necessary Chuck Berry-styled homage to Oklahoma's bountiful music scene, "Music from the Motor Court", the continued resurrection of his long-time road ghost buddy, Jack Kerouac ("Bohemian Cowboy Blues") and the album's up tempo "movin' on" closer, "Gotta Ramble". Outside of those three which provide solid artistic balance to the album, the collection is often a very quiet affair texturally, perhaps due to the birth of a son, Jackson, to Jimmy and his spouse, Barb, in 2002 ("I Wish for You"). Additionally, he received the news that his mother was diagnosed with cancer as he was working his way through songs that would become *Blue Nightfall*, the result of which are several spacious, melancholy ruminations ("Blue Nightfall", "Rain Falling Down", "When You Were Mine"), as well as a song his mom liked for its faith affirmations, "Revival". While LaFave's fans are many and want to see him perform, why he is often thought of as a "road dog", he has not made a lot of impact on sales charts nationally; however, his 2007 Red House release, *Cimarron Manifesto,* did scored a #1 slot on the Americana Music Association's radio chart, indicating significant national airplay on stations that feature alternative country, singer-songwriters, and more acoustically based music, a format tailor-made for Jimmy LaFave, if there ever were one. *Cimarron Manifesto* is yet another collection of leaving songs ("Car Outside"), road songs ("Catch the Wind"), Woody inspiration and Red Dirt trope of a degraded society ("This Land"), a little country character study ("Hideaway Girl"), Chuck Berry with a twist of LaFave re: the job's aging rockers have to take if their peak time has passed ("That's the Way it Goes"), and a getting-back-to-the family-tune ("Home Once Again"), before closing out with "These Blues".

In 2010, Jimmy self-released what is essentially the songs his fans request the most at live shows, *Favorites 1992 – 2001* (Music Road), and in 2011 appeared on the compilation of artists performing Sara Hickman songs, *The Best of Times* (Sleeveless), on which he contributes a version of her "Standing Ground". Also in 2012, Jimmy made his fifteenth consecutive appearance at the Annual Woody Guthrie Folk Festival in Okemah, and released his tenth album, *Depending on the Distance* (Music Road). Along with the usual contemplative tunes, a Springsteen cover, two by Bob Dylan, and the unexpected cover of John Waite's 1984 hit, "Missing You", the long-lasting tune on this one is "Red Dirt Nights", a great ramble through Oklahoma's mythic/poetic town names accompanied by the riding-down-the-road rhythm that is at the heart of traveling music. And Jimmy knows a thing or two about traveling, both his own road and Woody's.

www.jimmylafave.com

Lambert, Miranda Leigh
(b. November 10, 1983)

With a don't-mess-with-me persona that comes partially from being comfortable around firearms since age five (her father was career law enforcement officer), along with the attitude that derives from just being born and raised in east Texas, Miranda Lambert also has extremely strong musical abilities of songwriting, playing (acoustic guitar), and delivering her own hit country songs from an independent woman's point of view. Lambert's solo compositions or co-writes have also been widely embraced by the non-country media and music worlds due to the crossover nature of some of her best-known songs, many of which verge on pop rock with heavy snare drum beats and electric guitar solos, even if the melancholy, mad, or tough-talking lyrics are delivered in Lambert's flattened Texas twang ("Kerosene", "Gunpowder and Lead", "Crazy Ex-Girlfriend", "Famous in a Small Town", and "White Liar"). Up until her 2010 status as a "must add to the playlist" country music radio power rotation artist, several of Miranda's singles peaked on the *Billboard* popular music charts before they peaked on the country song charts, indicating the appeal of her music outside of the country music world. Not to say she does not understand nor produce country music in the traditional mode of examining the dynamics of interpersonal relationships, such as charting country singles about young love ("Me and Charlie Talking"), love lost ("Bring Me Down", "More Like Her", and "Dead Flowers"), or leaving town to start over ("New Strings"). Lambert resolved many of her own relationship questions when she bought a farm near Tishomingo that just happened to sit right next to one owned by her then boyfriend, Oklahoma country music star, **Blake Shelton.** The two married May 14, 2011, and enjoy the collective spread of their permanent residence in southern Oklahoma's Johnston County.

Miranda Lambert, 2007

Lambert's first #1 single, 2010's "The House That Built Me", is a nostalgic ballad she did not have a hand in writing, but the song is suited to her desire to perform songs that mean something to her. In her official press materials for the song, Lambert explains, "That's another one of those songs where I think, 'Dang it, why didn't I think of that?' I grew up on an old dairy farm in the country. We had older ladies knock on the door all the time and ask if they could come in because they were raised there, or their husband lived there when they got married. My mom would give them tea, and I would just sit there and listen to their stories." Given her relatively fast and massive success, (all three of her albums have gone #1 on *Billboard*'s Country Album charts), Lambert makes extra efforts to write and/or record songs that fit her concepts of herself as an artist, and the messages she wants to get out to her listeners. Taking a cue from the success of a quieter Miranda on "The House that Built Me", after a cover of Loretta Lynn's "Coal Miner's Daughter" recorded for a Lynn tribute album reached #14 on the Hot Country Songs chart in December, 2010, Lambert released the introspective "Heart Like Mine", another co-write she considers autobiographical because of its rumination on her upbringing in church, compared to what she saw in the world after joining a country band, and how she feels about her Christian walk in the midst of balancing social expectations with her realities as an individual. As does happen occasionally when Jesus makes a cameo in the right country song, "Heart Like Mine" floated right up to *Billboard* Country Songs chart heaven and landed on the #1 cloud in May, 2011, and was still hovering in the top ten of that chart after twenty-three weeks in late July, 2011. Additionally, continuing a trend of pop recognition for Lambert, "Heart Like Mine" reached #44 on the *Billboard* Hot 100, and was still a re-current on radio at the end of summer, 2011; however, as a point of interest, the song did not appear on the *Billboard* Contemporary Christian Music (CCM) charts, although "Heart Like Mine" is a more salient and questioning theological discussion than one typically hears in CCM, which is often based more on redemption after personal trials, or just downright celebration as if there is no trouble on the horizon, as there always is. Lambert's "Heart Like Mine" discusses the idea of what a Christian should or shouldn't do, and acknowledges congregational perceptions of having a drink, smoking a cigarette, or getting a tattoo as flaws to be avoided. However, the speaker/singer in Lambert's song knows that Jesus is powerful enough to part waters and raise the dead, so He would certainly be able to understand the modern heart of a country singer. Not only that, since Jesus actually advocates having a glass of wine in his memory, Lambert thinks He would be cool to hang out with, as she indicates in an introduction to an acoustic performance of "Heart Like Mine" released as the official video for the song. Miranda and her co-writers should have also gotten CCM points for referencing Gospel standards "I'll Fly Away" (by Oklahoman Albert E. Brumley, by the way), and "When the Roll is Called Up Yonder" (now alluded to twice in 2011 by major OK artists, as **Kings of Leon** use a line from it on their song "Radioactive"). However, add a wailing rock guitar solo to "Heart Like Me", and never mind the overall confrontational element of responding to sneering church folks by saying "God Bless," and, well, you've got a #1 country song, but not one that's going to be received like Carrie Underwood's "Jesus, Take the Wheel", which went #1 on the Hot Country Songs chart, made it to #25 on the Hot 100, and landed respectably on both the *Billboard* Hot Christian/Adult Contemporary chart and the Hot Christian Songs chart, due to its trouble/redemption-by-faith model. The power of Lambert's song is only increased by its absence from those the CCM charts. In fact, her song has reached and will reach many more people than any #1 song on either CCM chart. Furthermore, since she is elevating a discussion of Jesus' understanding and good heart into the forefront of her music, she is both fulfilling a primary Christian tenet of sharing her Christian faith, and also embodying another tried and true approach to reaching country music's core audience, a tradition extending all the way back to the first giants of the genre, the Carter Family, who released singles like "Let's Be Lovers Again", "Kissing is a Crime", "Gospel Ship", "God Gave Noah the Rainbow Sign" and "Meet Me By Moonlight Alone" within a two year span from 1935 to 1937. Amen, indeed, and now back to our story.

Arriving to parents Richard and Beverly Lambert in Longview, Texas, and then maturing in nearby Linville, pretty close to the midway point between Dallas and Shreveport, Louisiana, Miranda's father was also a musician in addition to his police and detective work. He shared a strong affinity with Amanda for classic country (Merle Haggard), outlaw country (David Allan Coe (irony noted) and JerryJeff Walker), and good songwriters like John Prine. She saw her first country concert at age nine, a Garth Brooks performance around 1992 when Brooks had converted country music arena shows into cowboy rock concerts, and her interest was piqued. Under her father's watchful eye, she began singing at local talent shows, and then the Johnny High Country Music Review in Arlington, Texas, which had also launched LeAnn Rimes. Before too long, she had landed a coveted deal while still in high school, but after experiencing Nashville's do-this, do-that, we-know-what's-best-for-you bossarama, she headed back home to Linville, got her dad to teach her how to play guitar, and started writing her own songs. Before graduating high school, she was fronting a bar band locally in Longview, just thirty minutes east by car on I-20, and began the process of acquiring the stage savvy and crowd command she would need in years to come on rowdy tours as the opening act for the likes of Keith Urban, George Strait, **Toby Keith**, Kenny Chesney, Brad Paisley, and Brooks and **Dunn**'s *Last Rodeo Tour*, a sequence that began with a talent contest in Nashville.

In 2003, at age twenty, Miranda auditioned and came in third for the *Nashville Star* talent show, which led directly to her deal with Epic Records. With eleven of the twelve songs co-written by her, Lambert's first album, *Kerosene* (2005), debuted on the *Billboard* Country Album chart at #1, a rare feat by a debut artist. Placed on various top ten lists for 2005 (*New York Times*, *Rolling Stone*, *CMT.com*), the album spawned four singles that registered in the top forty of *Billboard*'s Hot Country Songs chart, and sold a million copies to become a Platinum album. Each of her subsequent albums, *Crazy Ex-Girlfriend* (2007), on which she wrote or co-wrote eight of the albums eleven cuts, and *Revolution* (2009), featuring eleven of fifteen songs written or co-written by Lambert, both speared the #1 slot on *Billboard*'s Country Album chart. *Revolution* also provided the previously mentioned #1 singles, "House that Built Me" and "Heart Like Mine". As a result of these successes, Miranda appeared on a multitude of magazine covers, morning and prime time television shows, and in many newspaper and magazine feature articles (all viewable on her website), alternately depicted as an elegant, red-carpet award nominee/recipient, or posing with a shotgun over her shoulders for *Rolling Stone*, a challenging visual dichotomy for a non-country music press trying to figure her out as bully, babe, basketcase, or important new country music brain and voice. Miranda Lambert is perceived by some of the press as a rebel figure of country music for her mud-boot wearing, Christian swearing, firearm-toting honky-tonk swagger. In fact, she is in the role of what the most romanticized country music artists have always been, a little bit dangerous, but down to earth, and willing to sing things that aren't always pleasant to hear because of the painful memories they can invoke. She understands country music can act as a soul cleanser through the artist/listener commiseration of shared experiences, the essence really of any music's potential cathartic qualities. People don't sing the blues to feel worse; they sing the blues to get the pain out of their system, to have a good cry, so to speak, and Miranda Lambert understands that a meditative reflection on life's melancholies can have as much power as a vicarious gut punch to a lover who is acting like a jerk. In the tradition of country's most successful artists, she gives listeners both while embodying an image closer to the crowd side of the barrier between audience and stage. Not only have country, pop, and rock fans embraced her songs, music industry awards voters have also recognized her splendorous abilities and sparkling successes.

Miranda Lambert

Among many awards and award nominations she has received since 2007, all of which are listed on her website, a few stand out indicating her contemporary status as *the* female country singer since 2010: Academy of Country Music's Top Female Vocalist (2010, 2011); GRAMMY Award for Best Female Country Performance for "The House That Built Me" (2011); Country Music Association Female Vocalist of the Year (2010); Academy of Country Music's Album of the Year (*Crazy Ex-Girlfriend,* 2008,and *Revolution,* 2010); Country Music Association Album of the Year (*Revolution,* 2010). With her last single from *Revolution,* "Heart Like Mine", adding another #1 single to her already familiar set list parading around the U.S. as a headliner on Lambert's *The Revolution Continues Tour,* fans, critics, promoters, merchandise vendors, publicity machines, record label executives, music video makers, media schedulers, and all types of tour support could only try to prepare for the popularity avalanche she enjoyed with the release of her fourth studio album, *Four the Record,* in 2011. The album body slammedt he charts (#1 *Billboard* Country Album,/#3 *Billboard* Top 200), and topped the Hot County Single chart with "Over You," as well as charting two more TopTen singles ("Baggage Claim" and "Fastest Girl in Town". On top of that, Lambert slapped everybody around with another hit album featuring herself, Ashley Monroe, and Angaleena Presley as the Pistol Annies with *Hell on Heels* (Columbia), an album full of hard country songs that debuted at #1 on *Billboard*'s Country Album chart.

To the point of her place in the *Oklahoma Music Guide,* however, what about Oklahoma will impact Miranda Lambert, and how might it surface in her music? She has already made an impact on her local community in by performing benefits to raise nearly $140,000 in 2009 and 2010 to launch the building of a new animal shelter in Tishomingo, which goes along with her other work for the Humane Society of East Texas, and support of St. Jude Children's Research Hospital of Memphis, Tennessee, and the Catch a Dream Foundation, which provides outdoor adventure experiences for youth under eighteen who are experiencing life threatening illnesses. On the music front, what will definitely be worth listening to is how Miranda Lambert matures as a songwriter, and how that evolution merges with the expectations and experiences of her fans. She has already provided a contemporary country rock soundtrack for strong women who can do a lot of work by themselves, but ultimately want a companion they can trust to share the load, and she has provided thoughtful contemplations on the place of a remembered past and how it shape's one's current mindset.

While Miranda Lambert may have been born and raised in Texas, where she learned how to shoot, what traditional country music is from her dad's point of view, and how to strum a "D" chord followed by a "G" and an "A" (about all you need to get going in country music). In Texas, she was able to observe small town life that connects her to country music's small town and rural majority, saw her first country concert (by an Oklahoman , Garth Brooks) and gained her first musical performance experiences that provided the skills she needed to progress. Oklahoma is now her "second home state", as she has said on numerous occasions. In return, Oklahoma has provided her farm living a comfortable distance (about three hours drive) from her first hometown in Longview, close enough to visit, but too far just to pop in. In Oklahoma she has also found a husband who understands her professional challenges and issues because he has more or less the same ones. Finally, as a result of being a land and vehicle owner in the state, she pays property taxes to Johnston County for her farm, and state fees to the local tag agency for her Oklahoma license plate, which will be about the last thing anyone from Texas sees of her when she's heading north back across the Red River, going home.

www.mirandalambert.com

Lamond, Don

(b. August 18, 1920)

Referred to as a "drummer's drummer" by Steve Allen on a 1950s television performance in a contest with two other significant jazz drummers, Louis Bellson and Lionel Hampton, and lionized mostly drummer for Woody Herman's Herd and George Wein's Newport Festival All-Stars, jazz percussionist Donald Douglas Lamond was born in Oklahoma City, although he was raised in Washington, D.C. His lawyer father took an interest in Don's early grade school music by renovating the home basement so Don could practice his drums downstairs. In high school Don took percussion lessons from Horace Butterworth, and upon completion of high school, he studied all percussion instruments at the Peabody Institute in Baltimore.

Lamond made his professional debut with Sonny Dunham in 1943, and then worked with Boyd Raeburn in 1944. He joined Woody Herman's First Herd in 1945 and remained until it disbanded in 1946. Thereafter, he freelanced in 1947, including studio work with the famed bop jazz artist Charlie Parker, including the well known "Relaxin' at Camarillo," which included three other Oklahomans in the session (**Wardell Gray**, **Barney Kessel**, and **Howard McGhee**). Hearing Lamond on "Relaxin' at Camarillo" is to hear his perfect time keeping, "swinging the eights" on the big ride ride cymbal to drive the track, but adding snare shots and syncopated accents that indicate why he was respected as drummer by major peers such as Buddy Rich. Lamond knew the importance of consistent meter and yet was able to add his own personality within the windows of opportunity on a given track. He also recorded with other noted bop artists such as Coleman Hawkins and Dizzy Gillispie. He rejoined Herman's Second Herd and stayed with the band for two years until it dissolved in 1949; overall, he appeared on more than a dozen recordings with Herman's ensembles.

Around 1953, Don settled in New York, and for the next two decades vacillated between big bands and small combos. He worked primarily as a television show and studio drummer. He played on several television shows, such as Steve Allen, Gary Moore, and Ed Sullivan, and recorded with such bands as Stan Getz (five albums), Benny Goodman (six albums), Sonny Stitt, **Jack Teagarden**, Quincy Jones, Eddie Condon, Al Cohn, Miles Davis, Duke Ellington, Bud Freeman, Maynard Ferguson, Stan Kenton, and Bob Crosby. He also recorded with such popular vocalists as Billie Holiday (five albums), Perry Como, Lena Horne, June Christy, Anita O'Day, Harry Belafonte, Carmen McCrae, and another Oklahoman **Lee Wiley** on her *Back Home Again* album in 1971. In the late 1960s he was drummer for George Wein's Newport Jazz Festival All-Stars, and toured Europe with the group. By the late 1970s Lamond was leading his own ensemble, Big Swing Band, in Florida, as well as working with Harry Wuest's Top of the

Slingerland advertisement featuring Don Lamond on drums with bandleader Woody Herman in the background.

By Hugh Foley

World Band at Disney World. By this time Don had become a resident of Florida, where he helped young musicians by giving them an opportunity to play in his big band. Don's discography as bandleader includes a 1962 Command Records LP *Off Beat Percussion* featuring *Tonight Show* bandleader, Doc Severinsen, on trumpet, and *Extraordinary* (Circle, 1996 re-issue).

Reference
Scott Yanow, "Lamond, Don(ald Douglas)" in *The New Grove Dictionary of Jazz*, ed. Barry Kernfeld. (New York: St. Martin's Press, 1994), 675.

Lay, Rodney
(b. February 13, 1940)

    Born into a musical family where his grandfather and father were part-time musicians, singer, songwriter, radio DJ, band manager, and show business entrepreneur, Rodney Lay was born in Coffeyville, Kansas, which is all of three miles from the northern Oklahoma border, and not far from where he has lived for many years in Dewey, Oklahoma on a horse farm. As his father played guitar for square dances, Rodney learned to play guitar at an early age and debuted publicly at his school at age nine. He and his sister, Sue, formed a double act, performing at talent shows, and when he was fifteen, Rodney joined Tommy Joe Ryan and the **Country Rhythm Boys, where he did not** get paid, but did get some valuable on-the-job training. By 1957, as rock 'n roll swept the nation's popular music landscape, Lay formed the Off Beats, which by 1960 had become the rock 'n roll band, the Blazers. Lay then took the band to Kansas City where the group recorded "Teenage Cinderella" for their own Kampus label, making a profit of 35 cents per record. Johnny Tillotson's manager purchased a copy of the disc for his young singing star, but an executive with Dore Records in Hollywood heard the disc, and released it under the banner of Rodney and the Blazers. Dore also released their follow-up, "Snow White" backed with (b/w) "Tell Me Baby". At the suggestion of Joey Dee, who led the Starliters, Rodney moved the band to New York City in 1962, where they played the famous Peppermint Lounge, and criss-crossed the country playing high-energy rock 'n roll shows reminiscent of the previous decade's style, as pop music had shifted form a focus on rock music to the new folk movement, Motown, and West coast surf sounds. The Blazers headed back home to Coffeyville where they picked up tours with Jerry Lee Lewis who was still recovering from his overall blacklisting by the music world due to his social indiscretions. However, Lay's fortunes changed in late 1962 when he met and played with Roy Clark in Las Vegas, who at the time was leading Wanda Jackson's band, and who would also later play a major part in the Lay's career. Lay's Blazers toured with Wanda Jackson from 1964 to 1966, but by that time the Beatles and a complete new style of rock music had overwhelmed the 1950s pop stars and classic rock 'n roll style, causing Rodney to alter his image from the silver hair and wraparound glasses of his Blazers years to denim and boots as many rockers from the 1950s (to include Wanda Jackson) reverted to their country roots, or just played similar music, slowed it down, and called it country.

    In 1966, Rodney became a DJ on station KGGF Coffeyville and stayed with the he stayed with the station as a solid gig while he put together a new band, Rodney Lay and the Wild West. Working as a disc-jockey also gave him the opportunity to hear massive amounts of music sent to him as promos. With his experience as a musician, he could analyze trends in new country music, and figured he could do the same thing. With his connections to **Jim Halsey** from his time with Wanda Jackson, Lay was able to get his songs to a number of artists. In 1967, Hank Thompson had a Top 20 country hit with Rodney's "He's Got a Way with Women", a bluesy song about a Casanova who steals the singer's woman. In 1969, Waylon Jennings hit the Top 20 with Lay's "Something's Wrong in California", the lyrics are from the point of view of lover who regrets not fulfilling his promises, and feels he needs to get back to California. Interestingly, Lay flips the geography and writes a tune The Hagers take to #41 on the country chart, "Gotta Get to Oklahoma ('cause California's Getting' To Me)".

Lay's radio gig led to his next break when Buck Owens was on his radio show that led to Owens arranging a record deal with Owens' Blue Book label, and then with Capitol. Lay released two singles for the label, "Georgia Boy" b/w "I Don't Wanna Make It" and "Tennessee Woman/I Don't Know Enough". While the singles did not chart, Rodney's show business connections led to a brief appearance in Sam Peckinpah's film starring James Coburn and Kris Kristofferson, *Pat Garrett & Billy the Kid* (1973). Music had been first in Lay's life, however, and so he took the opportunity for his band to back Freddy Fender for eighteen months between 1975-1976, which were the biggest years for Fender who toured behind the Top Ten hit "Wasted Days and Wasted Nights". His next show business opportunity arrived after the Fender tours when he became Roy Clark's bandleader, which exposed him to an international audience via performances with Clark on the *Hee Haw* variety television show, and as a result of touring. By 1979, Rodney had signed to Sun Records, and his 1980 album, *Rockabilly Nuggets*, provided a minor country chart single, "Seven Days Come Sunday". By the end of that year, Rodney had moved to Halsey's Churchill label, as Rodney Lay & the Wild West, and in 1982, had another splash into the country charts with "Happy Country Birthday Darling", followed by "I Wish I Had a Job to Shove", a humorous answer song to Johnny Paycheck's "Take This Job and Shove It", which also received significant airplay. Lay enjoyed a another mild chart successes with "You Could've Heard a Heart Break"; however, Johnny Lee took the song to #9 on *Billboard*'s Hot Country Songs chart in January, 1985, giving Lay his first *Billboard* top ten country single. Lay's version of Bill Haley's seminal 1954 classic, "Rock Around the Clock", which is the song that is typically thought of as beginning the rock 'n roll era in the national mindset, and which appeared on the *Rockabilly Nuggets* LP, was featured in the Tom Cruise vehicle, *Born On The Fourth Of July* (1989). Rodney also managed Roy Clark's band in the 1990s, and jointly owns the Roy Clark Celebrity Theater in Branson, Missouri, with Roy.

Through the years, Rodney's second love has been horses, leading to his current residence on a ranch in Dewey, about 30 miles south of where he was born. In total, Rodney Lay's career is a good example of the multi-faceted skills often required to succeed in show business. Having been able to play music as a front man, bandleader, or

Rodney Lay and the Blazers, circa 1961, with Rodney Lay in light-colored suit.

By Hugh Foley / 449

sideman, work as a disc-jockey by which he met valuable connections, as well as being able to write songs and even take acting jobs when offered, Rodney Lay was able to enjoy a long and steady career in show business, an experience many hope to accomplish, but few really get to do for a lifetime. Rodney Lay is one of those people.

www.rodneylay.com

Lewis, Edward A.
(b. January 22, 1909 – d. September 18, 1985)

Trumpeter with such jazz bands as Bennie Moten, **Jay McShann**, and Count Basie, trumpeter, bandleader, and composer Edward ("Big Ed") Lewis was born in Eagle City, Oklahoma, a tiny hamlet northwest of Oklahoma City in Blaine County. Prior to starting school, Ed's family moved to Kansas City, Missouri, where he learned baritone horn from his father, trumpeter Oscar Lewis, and marched alongside him in Shelly Bradford's Brass Band.

Ed Lewis, 1940s

Lewis made his professional debut with Jerry Westbrook's ensemble in 1924, playing baritone horn, but soon switched to trumpet. After brief stints with groups led by Paul Banks and Oklahoman Laura Rucker, he was hired by Bennie Moten, for whom he played lead trumpet from 1926 to 1931, and left after Moten fired some other musicians to whom Lewis was loyal. Following a short stay with the Thamon Hayes band, Ed joined Harlan Leonard's Kansas City Rockets from 1934 to 1936, and then became lead trumpeter with Jay "Hootie" McShann's Orchestra in 1937 before joining the Count Basie Orchestra later that year, auditioning on the same day as Billie Holliday. He was a member of Basie's ensemble until 1948 when jazz shifted from the big band unit to a smaller combo popular with bebop artists. During his tenure with Basie, he appeared on more than a dozen albums Basie recorded in the 1930s and 1940s, although was never a major soloist with the band. He was a member of the Basie ensemble at the same time as several other Oklahomans, such as **Jimmy Rushing** and **Ted Donnelly**. During this time, Ed composed several songs, including "Justrite" and "It's Sand, Man!" The latter was Lambert, Hendricks, and Ross.

Once Basie's style changed to accommodate the shifting commercial concerns of jazz artists, their labels and promoters, as well as audience tastes, Lewis retired from music and drove a taxicab in New York City. However, he returned in the mid-1950s to lead his own band playing local club dates. A year before his death, Ed toured Europe with The Countsmen, a group of former Basie band members. Although Ed never cut an album of his own, his recording credits, in addition to the Basie albums, included trumpet work for such diverse artists as Chuck Berry, **Charlie Christian**, Dave Brubeck, Buck Clayton, Coleman Hawkins, Billie Holiday, Jimmy Rushing, Lester Young, and Johnny Otis. Ed died in Blooming Grove, New York, on September 18, 1985.

Reference
Frank Driggs, "Lewis, (Big) Ed," in *The New Grove Dictionary of Jazz*, ed. Barry Kernfeld. (New York: St. Martin's Press, 1994), 693.

Liggins, Joe (b. July 9, 1915 - d. August 1, 1987)
Liggins, Jimmy (b. October 14, 1922 - d. July 18, 1983)

Along with Louis Jordan and **Roy Milton,** the Liggins brothers were among the top rhythm and blues artists in the late 1940s and early 1950s, totaling more than fifteen Top 10 hits on various *Billboard* charts between them. The more successful commercially of the two brothers, Joe Liggins was a pianist, vocalist, songwriter, and bandleader, who was born in Guthrie, Oklahoma, located about thirty miles north of Oklahoma City. Not much is known about the Liggins brothers experiences in Oklahoma before they both relocated to California. Little brother Jimmy became a guitarist when his parents (Dad was a minister) disapproved of his boxing under the name "Kid Zulu", urging him to get a guitar and learn how to play it with Joe's group, which he did, before working as a vocalist and bandleader on his rugged R&B recordings for Specialty Records. Jimmy was born in Newby, Oklahoma, a tiny hamlet southwest of Tulsa, and his recordings were a little rougher-edged than Joe's.

Already a solid boogie-woogie piano player, Joe moved to San Diego in 1932, and later in 1939 to Los Angeles, where he performed with various groups, including Sammy Franklin's California Rhythm Rascals. Franklin rejected Joe's rolling boogie tune, "The Honeydripper", leading Joe to organize his own combo dubbed The Honeydrippers, and recorded it on the Exclusive label. At the peak of R&B's surge onto the national pop music chart scene, "The Honeydripper" hit #1 in 1945 (staying for eighteen weeks in the top position) and eventually became the first million selling instrumental in R & B history. An up tempo number that kicks off with sax solos, a peppy baritone sax counter point rhythm riff, Joe Liggins' piano guides the tune through a good feeling that would have resonated with the post-World War II euphoria enshrouding the U.S. at the time. The Honeydrippers, a sextet that included saxophonists Willie Jackson and James Jackson, Jr., developed a sound based on a mixture of pop, big band swing, and blues, featuring Joe's rhythmic piano and smooth vocals, a sound often referred to as either jump blues, commonly considered the precursor to the first wave of rock 'n roll in the 1950s, as well as the the early version of West Coast blues before **Lowell Fulson** began recording with his own combo, and adding an electric guitar to create "uptown blues". Joe and the group

Joe Liggins

registered nine more hits with Exclusive from 1945 to 1948, including "I Got a Right to Cry", "Roll'em", "Dripper's Boogie", and "Dripper's Blues". In 1949 the Exclusive label folded because of financial difficulties and Joe sought a new recording home.

Art Rupe at Specialty Records had already signed Joe, whose professionalism and quality were top rate, and and acquiesced to Joe's requests for a deal after checking with older brother, Jimmy, who approved, thus Jimmy joined his olderr brother at th label in 1950. Joe's debut with Specialty was his version of "Rag Mop", followed by the No. 1 rhythm and blues hit in 1950, "Pink Champagne", was voted R & B record of the year by *Billboard* magazine. Because of the national success of their recordings, The Honeydrippers toured the Midwest and East Coast, including Chicago (Pershing Ballroom) and New York City (Apollo Theater). Joe returned to California and teamed with Amos Milburn to draw more than 6,000 fans in Oakland. To conclude 1950, Joe recorded "Little Joe's Boogie" and "Daddy on My Mind," his first 45 rpm.

In 1951, Joe signed a three-year contract with Specialty, and recorded "Frankie Lee," "I Just Can't Help Myself," "This One's For Me," "Bob Is My Guy," "That's the One for Me," and "Whiskey, Gin, and Wine," with vocals by Candy Rivers, an ex-gospel singer from Indianapolis. The first all-Black radio network developed by Mutual Broadcasting Company went on the air in 1951, and Joe and his Honeydrippers were featured that year.

Joe continued to tour in 1952-53 with stops in Chicago, Cincinnati, St. Louis, Kansas City, and Denver, playing at such venues as Wrigley Field. He recorded several more sides for Specialty in the early 1950s, including "Tanya," "The Big Dipper," and "Boogie Woogie Lou," but the rock and roll era was launched and Specialty dropped Joe from its roster in 1954. In 1954, Joe moved to the Mercury label, then to Aladdin, then back to Mercury in 1962, but never matched the success he had with Specialty or Exclusive. "The Honeydripper" continued to play dates on the West Coast through the mid-1980s, always promoting the jump blues sound that bridged the gap between swing and rock and roll.

Jimmy's entry into the rhythm and blues field was attributed primarily to older brother Joe's success. He moved from Oklahoma to San Diego in 1932, and after giving up boxing, worked as a radio DJ, then helped Joe as his chauffeur and right hand man for more than a year (1945-46). Jimmy taught himself to play guitar while standing on the side of the stage with his amp turned down, playing along with Joe's band until he knew enough to join.

Jimmy dubbed his octet ensemble with three reeds (Harold Land, Charlie "Little Jazz" Ferguson, and Maxwell Davis) and himself on guitar as The Drops of Joy, after Joe's Honeydrippers, and the famous territory band, the Mighty Clouds of Joy. Grittier than Joe's ensemble, The Drops of Joy signed with Specialty Records in 1947 recording "I Can't Stop It" and "Troubles", which did not get much attention. Released in 1948, the second single, "Teardrop Blues" b/w "Cadillac Boogie" became Jimmy's first successes with "Teardrop Blues" jumping into the Top 10 of the R & B charts. The B-side, "Cadillac Boogie" is a perfect example of how jump blues was leading to the evolution of rock 'n roll, embodying boogie-woogie, a little wilder sax solo based more in bebop than Joe's more sedate and sophisticated sound, and was about driving a nice car around to pick up girls. All of these stylistic touchstones, along with the addition of Jimmy's just good enough electric guitar hint at the upcoming rock 'n roll era of the 1950s.

Jimmy Liggins

In 1949, Jimmy scored a hit with "Careful Love" and "Don't Put Me Down", both of which broke into Top 10 on the R & B charts. The Drops of Joy toured the Southwest, primarily Oklahoma and Texas, and remained a favorite in their southern California base. While on tour, Jimmy was shot in the face in Jackson, Mississippi. The bullet broke his jaw and severed his tongue, however, he recovered and resumed his career. Jimmy's last hit recording for Specialty was "Drunk", a novelty tune about the travails of alcohol that was based on other R&B drinking songs such as "Drinkin' Wine Spo-Dee-O-Dee" and Joe's "Pink Champagne". By 1954, Specialty's emphasis was on other artists, such as Guitar Slim, and Jimmy's seven-year association with the label ended. He moved to a rival Los Angeles company, Aladdin, where he recorded an answer tune to "Drunk" entitled "I

Ain't Drunk (I'm Just Drinkin'"), a classic later covered by bluesman Albert Collins, as well as Ike Turner. Turner's cover is significant because it shows that he was aware of Liggins' work. Many rock music historians have credited Ike Turner with being an important "precursor" to rock with his "Rocket 88", which sounds quite a bit like "Cadillac Boogie". Both songs feature a similar musical aesthetic in tempo and use of saxophones, and both songs are both about cars, but Turner uses a guitar played through a broken amplifier to achieve the distorted sound that many rock aficionados say makes it more toward rock than "Cadillac Boogie". Most rock historians don't refer back to Liggins, just lumping him in with other jump blues artists, but they usually don't bring up the electric guitar proto-rock of "**Bob Wills** Boogie" either. Liggins stuck with the boogie-woogie as long as he could. His his last hit with Aladdin was "Boogie Woogie King" in the jump blues tradition. In 1958, Jimmy formed his own record label, Duplex, which he retained until 1978. His recording popularity had almost completely fallen off, and the handful of sides he recorded for his own label never achieved the success of his work with Specialty and Aladdin. In the mid-1970s, Jimmy moved from Los Angeles to Durham, North Carolina, where he opened a music school, and the "Boogie King" died there in 1983.

References

John Broven, Liner Notes, *Joe and Jimmy Liggins: Saturday Night Boogie Woogie Man*, (Specialty, UK).

Bill Dahl, "Jimmy Liggins" and "Joe Liggins", *All Music Guide to the Blues*, (Emeryville, CA: Miller Freeman, 1996).

Lindsay, Merl
(b. December 12, 1915 – d. October 12, 1965)

One of Western swing's best-known band leaders outside of the Wills Brothers, Merle Lindsay Salathiel was born into a musical family in Oklahoma City and began playing fiddle at age ten in Salathiel's Barn, a ballroom owned by his father, C.E. Salathiel. Many Oklahoma artists performed with Lindsay during his time in Oklahoma, to include singers **Wanda Jackson**, **Norma Jean,** and **Yvonne DeVaney**, as well as lead guitarists **Benny Garcia** and Don Tolle.

In 1937, Lindsay formed his first band, the Barnyard Boys, filling a strong need for Western swing in Oklahoma City as Bob Wills and his Texas Playboys created a huge demand through their broadcasts on Tulsa 50,000 watt blowtorch, KVOO, for the music that combines jazz, blues, country, and pop elements into danceable swing music. Lindsay's group expanded to eight members in 1941, was renamed the Night Riders, and moved to California, eventually performing in thirty-five states, as well as entertaining troops who were deployed abroad during World War II.[1]

Merl Lindsay

Large numbers of transplanted people from the Oklahoma region moved to California during the great Okie migration of the 1930s, when poverty, unemployment, and drought led droves to relocate in the West. The upside for Oklahoma bandleaders was a market for their music in California. For a period in the 1940s, Lindsay performed live on a network of stations from Long Beach to Los Angeles, California, and then performed throughout the region, as well at a ballroom he owned in

Compton, California. Also while in California, he followed Bob Wills' lead and began appearing in films, mostly with Jimmy Wakely as a member of a band or trio appearing in Western B-movies. When fans of Western swing began going to and returning from World War II, if they returned, they began to settle down and not go out as much, which lessened audiences for the music in the late 1940s. With the advent of television as an entertainment alternative, and the oncoming rock 'n roll youth movement of the 1950s, Western swing's popularity began to decline, leading Lindsay to head back toward the music's cultural hearth, Oklahoma and Texas, in 1947. Once back in Oklahoma City, he broadcast a daily television and radio show on WKY, Oklahoma City, and continued playing regionally into the 1950s.[2]

In 1957, Lindsay assumed leadership of the Ozark Jubilee Band on Red Foley's ABC-TV show, by that point called *Country Music Jubilee*, and broadcast from Springfield, Missouri. Not only was the show the first national television program to focus solely on country music when started as the *Ozark Jubilee* in 1955, the show was also the catalyst for the development of the country music entertainment Mecca of Branson, Missouri. Given the exposure and publicity surrounding Lindsay's stint on ABC, he maintained the band's name as "The Ozark Jubilee Band" when they eventually returned to Oklahoma City to "Lindsay-Land", which served as the band's home bandstand and headquarters for arranging their performances throughout the southwest in the first half of the 1960s.[1] In 1965, Merl Lindsay was diagnosed with cancer, and died in the fall of that year just shy of his 50th birthday. Lindsay's brother, Doyle Salathiel (1920-1976), played with Merl's bands, and wrote their theme song, "Water Baby Blues", that was also covered by Eddie Cochran, and Maddox Brothers and Rose. Lindsay's nephew, Max Salathiel (1935 – 2006), who appeared with Merl in the 1950s, became a recognized guitarist in Oklahoma City and played with many local groups through the early 2000s.

Merl Lindsay's Night Riders embodied the most intrinsic elements of Western swing, to include danceable music, swing versions of popular songs played largely on stringed instruments with horn section accompaniment, and improvisation by soloists in the best traditions of jazz. During Lindsay's career, he and his bands recorded for Cormac, 4 Star, Bullett, MGM, and Mercury Records. His best known songs are the previously mentioned "Water Baby Blues", as well as "Slidin' Steel", co-written with steel guitarist Gene Crownover, and another one many displaced Oklahomans could related to in California, "Lonesome Okie Goin' Home". Lindsay's recordings have appeared on several European compilations both on vinyl and CD, to include *Boppin' Hillbilly Vol. 7* (Collector, WLP 2807), *Rockabilly Shakeout* (Ace, CH 191), and Bear Family, *That'll Flat Git It, Vol. 19* (D/Dart). Most recently, Krazy Kat Records released the most significant recordings of Lindsay's peak period on *Merl Lindsay and His Oklahoma Night Riders 1946 – 1952*.

Notes

1. Material regarding Merl Lindsay's early life in Oklahoma City is repeated wholesale online, whereas, Guy Logsdon's essay on Lindsay is the only one that discusses his siblings and parents being musicians. Accessed July 21, 2001, the essay, "Merl Lindsay" can be found at http://digital.library.okstate.edu/encyclopedia/entries/L/LI009.html in the Oklahoma Historical Society's online *Oklahoma Encyclopedia of Music and Culture*.

2. Some first-hand history about about Merl Lindsay's transition from the Night Riders to the Ozark Jubilee Band was written by Gene Jones, one of Lindsay's steel players in the 1950s and 1960s, and which can be seen at www.genejones.com (accessed July 20, 2011).

Lindsey, Ryan

The Tulsa Sound, Red Dirt Music, and Western swing have all been quantified by many American music experts to the point where only a few semantic elements of each are up for discussion or disagreement. However, we have enough ethereal examples to create a new state music genre for a more subjective dialogue, Okie Pop. With introspective existential lyrics surrounded by spacious music full of subtle textures, wide-ranging dynamics, and atypical instrumentation, Okie Pop features candy cane melodies that are hard to forget, and rhythms that are more stutter steps than grooves, but make a listener fall in lock step to the song's grand design where the narrative purpose is often deeper self or social awareness. Ryan Lindsey is the latest in a line of cool-as-anybody bands from the state to embody all of these stylistic touchstones that started with the first generation of these groups such as the **Chainsaw Kittens** and **Flaming Lips,** and continue with contemporary groups such as **Starlight Mints, Colourmusic, Other Lives**, and **Cheyenne,** all of which have emerged from the college towns of Norman or Stillwater. The youngest of three brothers, Ryan Lindsey surfaced in Stillwater, home of Oklahoma State University, where he bought a bass guitar with money from his paper route and at age fourteen joined his older brothers in the band Kids Eat Free (Nick Wheeler of **All-American Rejects** was also in the band). When his siblings moved away to college, Ryan was asked to join Cheyenne, a band then more alt-country, but now qualifying as Okie Pop based on the previous description, who moved to Brooklyn, New York, in hopes of furthering their opportunities nationally after positive reviews for their first releases in the progressive music press and webosphere. Along with his work for Cheyenne, Lindsey is also a performing and recording keyboardist with Starlight Mints, and continued working with both bands when the stars lined up for all involved.

Ryan Lindsey

In 2006, Ryan moved to Norman to attend the University of Oklahoma, and continue playing with Cheyenne and Starlight Mints. After performing his own songs solo for a year between Cheyenne and Mints gigs, he recorded his debut album *White Paper Beds*. Of the album, Ryan's website describes the collection music as "guilt-free pop confections that echo the multi-instrumentalist's varied influences (Paul Simon, James Taylor and Ben Folds)." Regarding the album's lyrical stance, his website touts the singer-songwriter's unique blend of observational wit, emotional poignancy and whimsical melody." Legendary composer, arranger, producer Van Dyke Parks heard the finished product and introduced Ryan to the president of Bug Music, David Hirshland, who saw Ryan in concert at the South by Southwest Music Festival in Austin, Texas, and signed the young musician to a publishing deal with Bug. Subsequently, powerhouse progressive radio station, KCRW, in Los Angeles, began playing Ryan's music where Chris Douridas, influential National Public Radio music supervisor and host of *NPR*'s *New Ground*, used two of Ryan's songs in the Sundance Award Winning motion picture *American Teen* (2008). According to Ryan's publicity materials, no less than the *Los Angeles Times* touted his song that appeared on *American Teen*, "Let's Go Out", as "the perfect teenage love song." Lindsey's music has also been heard on CWTV's *One Tree Hill* ("Open Late") and the CBS-TV show, *Welcome to the Captain* ("Introspective Personality"). Additional mainstream sources for his music may even hit unwitting listeners subconsciously, with Lindsey's songs appearing on internal music systems nationwide in Starbucks coffee shops ("Put Your Trust in Ross"), the Gap and Old Navy clothing stores, and on a Pay Less Shoes commercial.

In 2008, he collaborated with Grammy-winning songwriter and Semisonic front man Dan Wilson to write a handful of songs for the Ballas Hough Band, an up-and-coming pop-rock outfit featuring Mark Ballas and Derek Hough of the hit television show *Dancing With the Stars*. Also in 2008, Bug Digital re-released *White Paper Beds* on Bug Digital. In 2009, he continued writing songs, touring around the country working out his new material, and keeping up with his duties as the touring and recording keyboardist for Starlight Mints. In 2011, he appeared on a local Oklahoma City Christmas compilation of original holiday songs, *A Blackwatch Christmas*, also featuring Samantha Crain and Colourmusic, and produced by Blackwatch Studios in Norman. Once listeners become familiar with Lindsay's voice they will start to hear it more and more in the stores they visit and the commercials they watch.

http://ryanlindsey.net or www.myspace.com/ryanlindsey

Little Texas
(Formed 1988, Nashville)

As a country music group with two native Oklahomans as founding members, Little Texas enjoyed a string of eighteen straight singles appearing on the *Billboard* Hot Country Songs chart from 1992 to 1997. At their peak, the group had a successful, double barreled approach, alternately featuring their lush harmonies on sentimental and melancholy ballads, to include "What Might Have Been" (#2), "Amy's Back in Austin" (#4), and "My Love" (#1). Little Texas also had a punchy, honky-tonk rocking quotient that factored into to more Top 5 songs, "Kick a Little" (#4) and "God Blessed Texas" (#5), that helped pile up a total of eight Top 10 hits from their first three albums. Rhythm guitarist and backing vocalist, Dwayne O'Brien, was born and attended high school in Ada. Rhythm guitarist and lead vocalist, **Tim Rushlow,** was born in Midwest City while his father was stationed at Tinker Air Force Base before moving to Arlington, Texas, where Rushlow and O'Brien met in 1984 while the two went to James Martin High School and were in choir together, Finding their voices blended well together, they began playing in garage bands locally. After developing more professional skills, they started gigging around northern Texas and southern Oklahoma, and performed in the live music shows at Six Flags Over Texas, which led to a job offer in 1986 imitating country music legends at Opryland in Nashville, a job

Dwayne O'Brien of Little Texas

Rushlow took, but O'Brien did not, choosing instead to finish a chemistry degree at East Central State University in Ada. After graduation, O'Brien headed to Nashville to catch up with Rushlow where they formed Little Texas with Rushlow's high school buddies, lead guitarist Porter Howell and bassist Duane Propes who were attending Nashville's Belmont University. They added Howell's wife and Rushlow's first wife as backup singers, plus two more musicians, and started touring the country by booking themselves as The Varsities and being their own roadies for about 300 dates a year (which means week-long gigs at bars playing covers, college shows, parties, fairs, and a hundred other dates they probably don't remember). The band met keyboardist Brady Seals and drummer Del Gray in Massachusetts, who joined the band shortly thereafter when the other two musicians left the group. Impressed by their talent and work ethic, Warner Brothers signed the group in 1989, at which point they came up with the name Little Texas, after Little Texas Boulevard where they practiced in Nashville. Buying a 1972 Chevy van for $300 and building a trailer themselves, the group played clubs around the country, appeared on *Star Search* (they didn't win), and by 1990 had developed enough material to record their first, *First Time for Everything* (Warner Brothers, 1991), which did launch a number of firsts for the musicians.

Little Texas' debut album reached #6 on the *Billboard* Country Album chart, and gained gold status with the aid of its Top Ten hit, "Some Guys Have All the Love", which established their pleasant vocal meshing, and set up the album's third single "You and Forever and Me" that climbed to #5, and launched the band on a six-year ride of top ten hits, million-selling albums, and sold out concerts. Merging glam rock looks (and some music not that far from the genre), earthy lyrics about Daddy, high school football games, hayfields, and plenty of references to Texas, the group continued its meteoric rise in 1993 when their second album *Big Time* (Warner Brothers), stomped up to #6 on the Country Album chart, and *sold* big time, to the tune of more than 2 million copies, or double platinum status. With hit singles "My Love", "What Might Have Been" and "God Blessed Texas" hoisting the band into rarified air, but also pumping air into the head one of the lead vocalists, Brady Seals, whose was primary vocal was on all three hits and started him thinking solo career. The band's third album, *Kick a Little* (Warner Brothers, 1994), also went platinum with boosts from another Texas-themed track, "Amy's Back in Austin" and the group's parking lot party anthem, "Kick a Little", but was also the end for Seals who signed with Reprise to go be a star on his own in late 1994.

After Seals left, he was replaced with another vocalist and multi-instrumentalist, Jeff Huskins, for two songs the label added to a greatest hits package released in 1995. *Greatest Hits* did go gold due to the many fan favorites on the disc. After Seals' departure, the group tried to shrug it off with "Life Goes On", but that was the band's final Top 10 hit. Their 1997 self-titled album started out of the gate with an ominously titled first single, "Bad for Us", which turned out to be a harbinger for the group, as none of the three singles released from the album made the top 40 of the Hot Country Songs chart. After a ten-year run as Little Texas, comprised of thousands of performances, recording four studio albums, and trying to hold the band bus together after one of the wheels fell off, the group took a hiatus with no real expectation of re-uniting.

After the split, Tim Rushlow formed a group under his own name, and signed with Atlantic Records who released his conservative 2001 effort with all of the safe studio trappings of extremely polished, but a little sterile, pop country. The album can only be heard as Rushlow stretching out to find out who he was outside of Little Texas. While some of the songs are about inspirational people who make sacrificial choices in life ("In the Meantime"), and love their partners through something so difficult as Alzheimer's disease ("She Misses Him"), which did make the Hot Country Songs Top Ten, the album was so far away from the rowdy rural insights or heavenly harmonies of Little Texas that only the most ardent fans picked it up. Rushlow put together a group by 2003, including Tishomingo native (and Rushlow's cousin) Doni Harris on acoustic guitar and vocals. In March, 2003, the group signed to Lyric Street Records, the label that has released debut albums by SheDaisy and Rascal Flatts. The band's first single, "I Can't Be Your Friend", forced fans to read between the lines a little due to the song's title, but still reached #29 on the *Billboard* Hot Country Song chart. However, the parent album of the single, *Right Now*, never hit the market due to the label's reorganization, and after the cousins formed a duo called Rushlow Harris, they split after two singles on Toby Keith's Show Dog Nashville label in 2006 and 2007. Meanwhile, sitting around the house was starting to get old for the four original members of Little Texas minus Rushlow and Seals, and talk turned to getting back out on the road and stage. Rushlow was not thrilled apparently, and he, along with newcomer Huskins, made a legal volley to keep their former bandmates (and one would think, friends) from using the name Little Texas, a ploy that did not work. In 2007, Little Texas signed with Montage Music Group and released a live album featuring their hits in the context of a performance to show they were still a working band, which includes O'Brien (rhythm guitar and backing vocals), Porter Howell (lead guitar and lead vocals), Del Gray (drums), and Duane Propes (bass guitar and backing vocals). About a month later, they released the studio album, *Missing Years*, the title track of which peaked at #45 on the *Billboard* Hot Country Song chart. You can't keep a band with several recognizable songs down though, and according to the band's website, the band who knows what working hard is all about had was bookings from California to Florida at truck shows, county fairs, festivals, stadiums, private events, casinos, opening slots and headlining concerts through 2011, and they were already lining up shows for 2012 to kick a little more you know what.

www.littletexasonline.com

Logsdon, Guy
(b. May 31, 1934)

A primary scholar, cataloguer, and authority on **Woody Guthrie**, Western swing, **Bob Wills**, American cowboy music and poetry, as well as the wide variety of traditional music and folklife in Oklahoma, Dr. Guy Logsdon was born in Ada, Oklahoma, to Guy and Mattie Logsdon, where he also graduated high school and East Central University. His father encouraged all of his children to play music, urging Guy to take up the bass fiddle in their family band plus a few locals, The Western Seven. As a teenager, Guy taught himself to play guitar, and joined up with some high school friends to form the Diamond D Boys.[1] Since then, he has continued playing music throughout his life, primarily focusing on cowboy songs, faithful interpretations of Woody Guthrie's music, and other Anglo-American music of Oklahoma for a multitude of performances and scholarly presentations across the United States. Logsdon has also released a CD, *Traditional Cowboy Songs* (Logsdon, 1999), featuring cowboy songs as they were often traditionally sung on the cattle trails, with no accompaniment. While he is widely recognized and enjoyed for his musical abilities in the context of his informative and entertaining performances, Guy

Guy Logsdon

Logsdon's scholarly work on the life, career, and music of Woody Guthrie, as well as his work cataloguing American cowboy songs and Western swing music, are some of his most important contributions to American music history and the collective memory of Oklahoma's traditional culture.

After graduating East Central University, Logsdon taught English in California, Oklahoma, and Arizona from 1956 through 1963 before becoming the reference librarian at Oklahoma State University in 1964. His next professional role was Director of Libraries at the University of Tulsa from 1967 through 1981, and then taught as a professor of education and American folklife at TU from 1981 through 1989 when he retired to begin his free lance life as a scholar, writer, and entertainer. He has been accompanied through his life by his wife, Phyllis (born in Okemah, November 17, 1935), who is an accomplished musician who is trained on piano, but also plays several instruments and sings, proving a delightfully diverse texture to their performances. As a performer and presenter in a musical context, Logsdon has given and/or participated in numerous Woody Guthrie programs across the United States, appearing with Arlo Guthrie, Pete Seeger, and Ramblin' Jack Elliot, among others. He has appeared widely as a cowboy singer, folk song performer, and music history presenter at some of the country's most prestigious locations for such occasions, to include Central Park, New York City; Cowboy Poetry Gathering, Elko, Nevada; Smithsonian Folklife Festival and the National Museum of Art, Washington D.C.; National Cowboy and Western Heritage Museum, Oklahoma City; Gene Autry Museum, Los Angeles.

With regard to Logsdon's scholarly work, his list of academic accomplishments, album liner notes, and popular culture publications is impressive both for its quantity, quality, and historic significance. He has written liner notes or annotations for at least forty album and CD projects, to include many high-profile productions for Smithsonian/Folkways for the releases of historic recordings of Woody Guthrie, Pete Seeger, and cowboy songs, as well as multiple liner notes for albums on the prestigious Bear Family Records label in Germany that has licensed and produced a tremendous amount of American roots music, in addition to many releases related to cowboy music, Western music, and traditional Anglo folk music. Logsdon's scholarly writing includes a high volume of publications on traditional Anglo-American music and musicians, especially related to his stated specialties of Woody Guthrie, Western swing, and cowboy music. He has also published articles and essays about the American Indian history in Oklahoma, Dust Bowl and its migrants, Oklahoma's Theatrical and Movie Stars, and Oklahoma's Classical, Pop, Rock, and Blues Musicians, and a history of his hometown, Ada, Oklahoma.

Of particular significance to Oklahoma music researchers are five articles for the journal, *Oklahoma Librarian*, between 1973 and 1976 that detail an abundance of primary Oklahoma music materials for building an Oklahoma music collection from his perspective at that time. The only challenge with some of the obscure materials mentioned in those articles is that many of them are contemporarily out of print, or highly collectible, which make them expensive acquisitions, but significant, nonetheless. Logsdon's books about music are also extremely interesting and pertinent to American and Oklahoma music history. He compiled a collection of bawdy cowboy lyrics in *"The Whorehouse Bells Were Ringing" and Other Songs Sung by Cowboys* (University of Illinois Press, 1989), and contributed biographical essays of various Western and cowboy performers to *Saddle Serenaders* (Gibbs Smith, 1995). His most recent work *The Flip of a Coin: The Story of Tommy Allsup* (Logsdon Books, 2010) is a collaboration with historic rock, country, and Western swing guitarist and producer, **Tommy Allsup**. The biography is titled as an allusion to Allsup's famous loss of a coin flip that kept him from getting on the plane that ultimately crashed and killed Buddy Holly, for whom Allsup was playing guitar at the time. Also in the works is Logsdon's long-awaited full-length text on Woody Guthrie, *Woody Guthrie and His Oklahoma Hills*. Given Guy's extensive labor of love with the primary materials related to Guthrie's life and music, the book should be a definitive and quintessential work on Woody Guthrie.[2]

Logsdon has also won numerous awards for his writing, work as a librarian, and service to the preservation and vitalization of cowboy culture, American folklife and the traditional arts. Among several awards, he received the Stanley Draper Award for Contributions to Oklahoma's Folk and Musical Heritage in 1977 from the Oklahoma Heritage Association; the American Cowboy Culture Award for Contributions to Western Music by the National Cowboy Symposium in 1997; the Chester A. Reynolds Memorial Award for Interpretation of Western Heritage by the National Cowboy and Western Heritage Museum in 2006; and was inducted into the Oklahoma Historians Hall of Fame by the Oklahoma Historical Society in 2007. He has also received several important research grants for his work on Woody Guthrie's complete biblio-discography from the Smithsonian Institution (1990-1991) and National Endowment for the Humanities (1993-1995). In 2011, he continued work as the BMI Woody Guthrie Research Fellow for further study in the Woody Guthrie Archives in New York City for his forthcoming book on the legendary folk singer. In 2012, Nine Lives Music published Guy's collaborative book project with Woody's sister, Mary Jo Guthrie Edgmon, *Woody's Road: Woody Guthrie's Letters Home, Drawings, Photos, and Other Unburied Treasures*.

www.guylogsdon.com

Notes

1. For a detailed and enlightening oral history of Guy Logsdon's life and family background, see Stan Peregien Sr.'s published interviews with Logsdon that appear at www.paregien.net/articles/Logsdon-Guy/Logsdon-Guy-Part1.html (accessed July 21, 2011). However, researchers should note that some dates in Paregien's interviews do not align with Logsdon's own published resume at www.guylogsdon.com.

2. For a compete discography of Logsdon's liner notes and annotations, as well as his scholarly publications, and books, see his website at www.guylogsdon.com/about-guy (accessed July 21, 2011).

Los Reactors

(Formed 1979 in Tulsa – Disbanded, 1983 – Reunited, 2005 – Renamed The Adaptors, 2010)

Aside from Oklahoma's other punk rock contribution, **Debris,** whose album predates both the Ramones and the Sex Pistols' recordings that tend to be thought of as the beginning of the genre (after its primary influence Iggy Pop), Los Reactors are the lone success story from the Tulsa punk rock scene of the late 1970s and early 1980s. After various configurations beginning in 1978, and solidifying as The Reactors in 1979, the group's initial line-up featured Roger Scott (guitar), Dale Lawton (guitar), Tommy Gunn Waggoner (bass), and Darrell Smith (drums). Lawton left in 1980, after which keyboardist Joe Danger, a.k.a. Joe Christ, whose given name was Joseph Linhart (b. June 18, 1957 – d. June 21, 2009), joined the band, and they changed their name to Los Reactors. Along with his witty lyrics that fell right in line with punk's acidic commentary on accepted social norms, Linhart's keyboard is a primary distinguishing factor of Los Reactors' sound imprint, as punk rock groups typically did not use a keyboard given the instrument's association with the overproduced commercial music that punk sought to avoid. However, Linhart's swirling, calliope-esque keyboards harkened back to the rougher melodic sounds of 1960s proto-punk garage groups such as ? and the Mysterians (think "96 Tears"), and actually provided the band with its signature sound for their only two official singles, "Dead in the Suburbs" and "Be a Zombie", both of which were independently released, and can be heard on youtube.com or the band's myspace.com site (as of July, 2011).

Los Reactors, circa 1982

The punk rock scene in Tulsa has a special distinction because England's Sex Pistols actually played in Tulsa at the Cain's Ballroom in 1978. For years, musicians who cared would go behind the stage where Pistols' bassist, Sid Vicious, punched a hole in the wall and pay appropriate homage to it. The reason the Sex Pistols were even in Tulsa was their management's strategy to avoid major urban areas and only play smaller, out-of-the-way markets to generate even more interest in the band when they finally got to the big cities, which never happened due to the group's implosion. In a subtle way, the Sex Pistols' appearance in Tulsa, one of only seven shows in the U.S., created an awareness of punk rock in town, and a small scene grew out of that interest, to include the first rumblings of Los Reactors that year. In a 2005 interview by Troy Canady of the internet fanzine website, terminal-boredom.com, Los Reactors' keyboardist Linhart remembers several Tulsa punk rock groups, such as The Automatic Fathers, NOTA, The Insects, and The Bridgeclimbers, as well bands from Dallas (The Nervebreakers and the Ralphs), and Oklahoma City's contributions, The Randys and The Hostages, all of whom created a regular rotation of bands in town necessary to create a regular clientele of fans that is the core of any music "scene". According to a fan posting on the band's myspace.com site on the occasion of Linharts death in 2009, Linhart's additional contributions to the Tulsa punk rock milieu came through his management of the Bleu Grotto club where he booked regional punk bands like the Embarrassment, the Ralphs, Brave Combo, Hitler Youth, and Mutant Fish that helped nourish the exchange of ideas among bands, and nourished the do-it-yourself (DIY) aesthetic so important in the punk rock and hardcore music worlds when no record company support was ever expected. The connections also allowed Linhart to get additional bookings for Los Reactors who played most of their shows in the states contiguous to Oklahoma, and regularly drew solid crowds for that time in Tulsa, Oklahoma City, and Norman, as well as Dallas, Fort Worth, Wichita, and Kansas City. The band played and played but hit a ceiling after doing the same thing over and over. In 1983, Linhart decided it was time to move on, which he did, moving to Dallas where he continued booking bands at the Empire Club's "Bigger Than God" band nights, named after one of the bands he formed after Los Reactors; other groups included G Spot and The Healing Faith. He later moved to Atlanta and began making independent films with a punk rock ethos, such as *That's Just Wrong*, and documentaries about the practice of self-mutilation, often producing the music soundtracks for his films by either recording new music or using music from his various bands.

After Los Reactors disbanded in 1983, bootlegs were the only place to get the Los Reactors records. As limited, 7" vinyl pressings, Los Reactors singles were no longer available until Righteous Death Records compiled a collection of tracks culled from rare live performance and rehearsal tapes, which was released as a *Best of* cassette in 1995. In 2000, an Italian label, Rave Up Records, took some of the cuts from Righteous Death's *Best of* compilation, as well as some studio unreleased studio recordings, and issued *Dead in the Suburbs* on vinyl, which sold out quickly online and is no longer available. In 2004, San Francisco-based Rip Off Records reissued the album on CD, and included rare video footage of the band. Also in 2004, Seattle punk band, The Briefs, included "Dead in the Suburbs" on their compilation of singles and covers, *Singles Only*, generating new interest in Los Reactors. As a result, the group reunited for a show in June, 2005 at The Venue in Tulsa, and played again at the Dot-Dash Festival in New York City. The Tulsa performance was recorded for a DVD by Linhart's Dept. 13 Films, and released as *Alive in the City* (2007), which also features interviews with both Joe Linhart and Roger Scott. Given the tremendous positive reaction to the group's reunion shows, the group played again at the Cain's Ballroom in 2007. The resurgence was not to continue. By all counts a healthy and vigorous person, Linhart died unexpectedly in his sleep on Father's Day, 2009. Out of respect for his memory, the surviving members of the group permanently changed their name to The Adaptors, a name they had used previously when playing without Linhart.

www.myspace.com/losreactors

Love, Clarence
(b. January 26, 1908 – d. January 18, 1998)

Never really known for his own musicianship, and his bands never recorded, Clarence Love will be remembered as a no-nonsense, professional band leader whose groups inspired others and whose various oral histories and short biographies help flesh out the jazz traditions of Oklahoma, Kansas City, and the Southwest. Although Clarence Love was born in Muskogee, the Love family moved to Kansas City in 1912, but not because of Oklahoma's segregation laws that were enacted at statehood in 1907. As he told the author for an interview conducted for my dissertation on the significant jazz musicians from Muskogee, Love spoke about his family's solid financial status, representing some of the prosperity experienced by early 20th century African-Americans in Muskogee.[1] Love's father took the family to Kansas City where, as Love says, "He had a better arrangement."

Love's story is significant because of its basic facts: born in Muskogee, moved to Kansas City, received a musical education, began forming bands after high school, kept forming bands with young musicians who would later take off such as Bill "Count" Basie, Billie Holliday, J.J. Johnson, and Eddie Heywood, discovered guitarist Wes Montgomery, and toured with an all-woman orchestra, the Darlings of Rhythm, during the World War

II years when most of the male musicians were in uniform. Since no recordings exist for the Clarence Love's Band, critical information is scant on the groups he did lead. Often, Love is simply listed as one of the many territory bands of the late 1920s and early 1930s. One of the pianists who worked with Love, Eddie Heywood told jazz writer Stanley Dance, "I went with Clarence Love's band for a couple of years. There was nobody well known in it, but I would say it was the best band I ever worked in. The musicians played wonderfully together, and were great overall so far as tone and everything were concerned. That was when I found out stock [arrangements] could sound very well if they were played very well."[2]

Clarence Love

Clearly, all the hallmarks of which Heywood speaks are directly attributable to the band leader, Clarence Love. Muskogee jazz pianist and bandleader, Jay McShann, told the author he saw Love's group at a Manual Training High School assembly, and it inspired him to keep pursuing music. Many mentions of Love in jazz histories are in lists of groups, or lists of bands someone famous played with at one time, or as examples for bigger issues. Having spoken with Mr. Love personally three or four times before his death, it was his anecdotes that made him so interesting and enjoyable as a conversationalist. He spoke with a tone of incredulity that not many people know his story, even though he was inducted into the Oklahoma Jazz Hall of Fame in 1990 alongside Jimmy Rushing, the Blue Devils, and fellow Tulsan Al Dennie. (When he found out I had a copy of McCarthy's *Big Band Jazz*, the book that gives Love the most attention, he let me know he was still mad at McCarthy for not returning his photos after they were published.) Clarence Love's words made me smile every time I talked with him. For that reason, parts of an unpublished letter from Love are included here to let him give his own final statement regarding his historical significance: "My folks moved to K.C. in 1912, where I attended school. . . . My band play[ed] only sweet, jazz, swing - in our part, and always blues. The question always asked [is] why so many Black and White musicians come from Muskogee? Why: No liquor in Oklahoma is number one cause. Kansas City in Missouri was wet and Pendergrass (sic)[referring to Kansas City mayor "Boss" Tom Pendergrast] liked music and fun. Muskogee had only three Black big bands but all three leaders, Clarence Love, T. Holder, and Jay McShann bands were formed in Kansas City. T. Holder's big band was later Andy Kirk's Clouds of Joy, which was formed in Tulsa. I am now the oldest (in time) not age, of the bands we called Road Bands. These were several big bands like us in K.C. on the road daily. They were called Territory Bands. If you want to know more about me, go to the library and read McCarthy's Big Band story.[3] I am the only traveling band leader that had two big bands, one male and one female: Clarence Love Male with Count Basie and Lester Young; and Female Darlings of Rhythm with Billy (sic) Holiday as vocalist. I formed a band at age 14 in high school. I managed Wes Montgomery. Eddie Heywood was my pianist and many others [worked for me] who made it to the top, like Aunt Esther [Lawanda Page] with Redd Foxx. Well, that's my story. Musically yours, Clarence Love, the Legend".[4]

By Hugh Foley / 463

Notes

1. The author's dissertation examined the cultural milieu of Muskogee, Oklahoma to explain why Muskogee produced so many nationally recognized jazz musicians (JayMcShann, Don Byas, Barney Kessel, Walter and Joe Thomas, Claude "Fiddler" Williams, and Clarence Love). The text is listed in the dissertation index as Hugh W. Foley, Jr., "Jazz from Muskogee: Eastern Oklahoma as a Hearth of Musical Culture" (PhD diss., Oklahoma State University, 2000).
2. Eddie Haywood is quoted in Stanley Dance's *The World of Swing*, (New York: Scribners, 1974), 320.
3. Love is referring to Albert McCarthy's *Big Band Jazz* (New York: G.P Putnam's Sons, 1974).
4. Undated letter from Clarence Love to the Oklahoma Music Hall of Fame, of which the author is a founder, circa 1996.

Lunceford, James Melving "Jimmie"
(b. June 6, 1902 – d. July 12, 1947)

Jimmie Lunceford was one of the primary bandleaders of the swing era, known for his energetic showmanship, as well as for the polish and professional of his orchestra. Later, the band was known for novelty interplays between his soloists and a variety of atypical rhythmic and novelty sound effects in arrangements created by his trumpet player, Sy Oliver.[1] While every jazz encyclopedia or reference published lists Lunceford as having been born in Fulton, Missouri (likely a confusion between the abbreviations for Missouri (MO) and Mississippi (MI), or even Denver, Colorado (where Lunceford came into his musical maturity), the author received a 2005 e-mail from jazz history author, Eddie Determeyer, in the Netherlands indicating Lunceford was born in the Evergreen Community near Fulton, Mississippi on June 6, 1902, the accepted date of his birth. However, what is interesting and had not yet been revealed in jazz histoy is Determeyer's further revelations. According to his research, Lunceford was born to James Riley Lunceford (born April 14, 1869 or 1870 in Abney Mississippi) and Idella "Ida" Shumpert (or Shumper) (born March 1, 1883 in Oklahoma City), the daughter of Samuel and Matilda Williams Shumpert of Oklahoma City. Furthermore, Determeyer explains the Luncefords moved to Oklahoma City in 1902 or 1903, shortly after Jimmie's birth. His younger brother, Cornelius "Connie" Lunceford was born in Oklahoma City in 1904.[2] One can only guess at this point about the whole story, however, a well-known aspect of Oklahoma's African-American history is that the state was marketed to Blacks in the late 19th century as a promising place to escape the Jim Crow racism of the South.[3] Like many African-Americans who came to Indian Territory or Oklahoma Territory hoping for the Black Utopia to be as advertised, thousands left Oklahoma after the first statehood legislature enacted segregation laws. Saying anything for sure about why the Luncefords left is pure conjecture. According to Determeyer, the Luncefords moved to Denver, Colorado in 1915, which is where the narrative of Jimmie Lunceford's musical story picks up in typical essays about his

Jimmie Lunceford, 1946

life in music. Nothing more is known by the author at the time of this writing about the Luncefords' experience in Oklahoma City.

Notes

1. For more details for the style of Lunceford's orchestra, as well as further discography and selected readings on Lunceford, see J. Bradford Robinson's biographical essay, "Jimmie Lunceford," *The New Grove Dictionary of Jazz*, ed. Barry Kerfeld, (New York: MacMillan, 1994), 720.

2. Eddy Determeyer's research was ultimately published in *Rhythm is Our Business: Jimmie Lunceford and the Harlem Express* (Ann Arbor: University of Michigan Press, 2006).

3. For a good overview of expectations for those who left the South for Oklahoma in the late 19th century, see Jimmie Franklin's "Black Oklahomans: An Essay on the Quest for Freedom" Alternative Oklahoma: Contrarian Views of the Sooner State, ed. Davis Joyce, (Norman: University of Oklahoma Press, 2007), 36-51.

M

Maloy, Zac

While many Oklahoma modern rock music fans know Zac Maloy by voice better than name as a result of him fronting the 1990s rock group, **The Nixon**s, he has since become one of popular music's top songwriters and producers. After growing up in Ada and graduating from Ada High School, Maloy moved to Norman City where he formed The Nixons with guitarist Jesse Davis, bassist Ricky Brooks, drummer Tye Robinson, and himself on vocals and guitar. Touring incessantly, The Nixons established themselves regionally as Oklahoma's version of the Seattle group, Pearl Jam, with Maloy's expressive vocals, repetitive riffing guitars, and loping rhythms ready-made for rock concert swaying. Girls liked the band because of Maloy's vocal performances, and guys like the group because they rocked out, making them the perfect date band for rocking couples of that period. After a self-released album in 1990, a six-song EP, *Six* (Dragon Street, 1992), and the full-length independent CD, *Halo* (Rainmaker, 1994), the group signed to MCA Records as labels were still trying to find the next Nirvana, or Pearl Jam. The group released two fairly successful albums, *Foma* (MCA, 1996) and *The Nixons* (MCA, 1997). *Foma* provided the band its most significant single, "Sister", which was embraced by modern rock (*Billboard* #11), mainstream rock (*Billboard* #6), and some Top 40 stations (*Billboard* #39). Always a strong live act due to Maloy's commanding vocal presence and the tight start and stops that come only with years of rehearsals and performing together on the road, the band toured incessantly during the MCA years, performing as many as 300 shows a year on tour with Soul Asylum, No Doubt, Kiss, Bush, and Radiohead. A later single from their self-titled release, "Baton Rouge", received signifi-

Zac Maloy, 2010

cant mainstream rock attention, however, modern rock and Top 40 had already moved away from the grunge sound by the late 1990s, tending to focus more on either rock 'n rap hybrids (Rage Against the Machine), riot grrl rock (Ani Difranco), geek rock (Weezer) or more dance oriented pop (No Doubt). The Nixons released one more disc through Koch Records, *Latest Thing* (2000), producing a minor chart single, "First Trip", but chose not to sustain the group after touring to support *Latest Thing*. Following the band's demise ("hiatus"), Maloy began writing songs with his friend Jaret Reddick of the Texas pop/punk band, Bowling for Soup, thus beginning his transition to songwriter.

Throughout the 2000s, Maloy lived in Tulsa and worked with a variety of artists who recorded songs he either wrote or co-wrote. An early major success was "Used To", which appeared on American Idol-winner Daughtry's 2007 #1 *Billboard* album that stayed on the charts for three years and eventually sold more than five million copies. This success energized his name in the music industry and artists began flying in and out of Tulsa to work with him.

The list of artists with whom he has worked is not only significant because of their success, but also because of their diversity, to include James Blunt, Train, Jonas Brothers, Theory of a Deadman, A Rocket to the Moon, Our Lady Peace, Hanson, and Jason Castro. As for hits, he co-wrote **David Cook**'s "Come Back to Me" which notched a 2009 Top 15 *Billboard* Hot Adult Contemporary chart spot, **Carrie Underwood**'s 2010 #1 country hit, "Temporary Home", Cavo's 2010 Top Ten rock single "Crash". Continuing his good fortune working the Oklahoma artists, Maloy also has co-write credit on "Get Some" from another Ada High School alumnus, **Blake Shelton**, whose 2011 album, *Red River Blue* (Warner Brothers), debuted at #1 on the *Billboard* Hot Country Album charts in July of that year. As a producer, Zac has had success with Burn Halo, the southern California hard rock band, with whom he co-wrote several tracks, and also produced material for his old friends in Bowling for Soup.

In 2009, Maloy relocated his family to Nashville where he has a studio, and where he collaborates and records with various songwriters and performers.

www.zacmaloymusic.com

Manning, Kim
(Born 1978)[1]

A native of Ponca City, Oklahoma, Kim Manning is blessed with an incredible five-octave voice and began studying classical music at age six, earned a theater degree from the University of Tulsa in 2000, studied rock music at Paul McCartney's performing arts school in Liverpool, England, and began working for an opera company in what seemed to be a sure shot for a career in that field. However, with money she earned at the company, she and friend loaded up her Volkswagen bus and headed to Canada where they worked as street performers. Through that experience, they met a woman who knew funk bandleader and icon, George Clinton, leading Kim to seeing a performance of the P-Funk All-Stars in San Francisco where she got to meet and hang out with people in the band. Subsequently, as a result of being in Los Angeles to audition for a musical theater company, she went to a late-night jam session where people were impressed and passed her number, really her mom Kathryn's phone number back in Ponca City, to George Clinton. Clinton himself starts calling Kim's mom and asking how to find the singer, which her mother then relayed back to Kim. As a result, Manning got her audition with Clinton, using her recorded senior opera recital piece as a demo of her singing. According to an interview published on her website, Clinton asked, "Can you still sing like this?" Of course, she could, and the next day she was in the studio with funk bass master, Bootsy Collins, and Buckethead, the extremely significant rock, funk, and fusion guitarist. From that point forward, she has been a featured vocalist for George Clinton and the P-Funk All-Stars, still performing with the group as of 2009 when they appeared in Tulsa and she sported at University of Tulsa t-shirt on stage.

By singing with George Clinton, Manning has toured the world and appeared on numerous television appearances, to include the Grammy Awards, *The David Letterman Show*, *Jay Leno*, and as Peaches on VH1's *Flavor of Love*. In 2006, she released her first solo album, *The Love and Light Activation* (Pseudohippie), which has been praised for its multi-genre approach with reggae, funk, and rock, all infused with her unarguably powerful voice. She can be heard on George Clinton's 2008 album, *Gangsters of Love* (Shanachie), alongside the Red Hot Chili Peppers on a remake of Shirley and Lee's "Let the Good Times Roll", which appeared on *Billboard*'s Top R&B/Hip Hop Album chart. She has also added vocals to tracks by Snoop Dogg, Fishbone, and Sly Stone, several other tracks by George Clinton ("Booty", "Bounce to This", and "Electrofunk"), and is heard throughout the 2004 concert DVD, *George Clinton Live at Montreux* (Eagle Rock, 2005). Most recently, she formed a group known as Wahnderlust with Sacramento, California vocalist, guitarist, and keyboardist, Lantz Lazwell. With ambitious plans for a double album that was scheduled for released sometime in 2011, preview songs released through their website indicate her influences from working with George Clinton since 2000. On the Wahnderlust songs, Manning's voice is just flat nice to listen to as it fills the tracks that bump around the borders of soul, R&B, and funk rock.

Kim Manning sings with GeorgeCinton & the P-Funk All-Stars in Tulsa, 2009.

www.kimmanning.com; www.wahnderlust.com; www.myspace.com/wahnderlust

Note
1. Matt Gleason cited Manning's age in his article "Bring in the funk", *Tulsa World*, May 6, 2006.

Markham, Jimmy "Junior"

A primary figure of what has become known as the **Tulsa Sound**, Jimmy "Junior" Markham is Oklahoma's best known harmonica player. Markham graduated from Tulsa Central High School, and like many other teenagers of the era, was jump started into rock 'n roll by seeing Elvis Presley in 1956 at the Tulsa Fairgrounds Pavilion in 1956.[1] Markham played in many local Tulsa bands starting around 1959. Instrumentally, Markham first played trumpet which is how he originally met up with **Leon Russell** (then Leon Bridges), leading Markham to travel out to Los Angeles in the early 1960s where he recorded an album for Capitol, *Chuck Meets Bo*, an album featuring six Chuck Berry tunes and six Bo Diddley tunes that featured James Burton on guitar. Along with witnessing what seemed like the whole popular music world of the mid-1960s visiting or recording at Leon Russell's house/studio on L.A. at the time, he also became half of the Flying Burrito Burrito Broth-

Jimmy "Junior" Markham, 2009

ers' horn section with well-known Texas saxophonist, Bobby Keyes (think the sax solo on the Rolling Stones' "Brown Sugar"). Markham returned to Tulsa in 1969 and opened the Paradise Club, switching to harmonica which gave him a chance to sit in with many blues artists who played the Paradise. Junior has performed live with Muddy Waters, John Lee Hooker, Charlie Musselwhite, Sonny Terry and Brownie McGhee, Delbert McClinton, Leon Russell, J.J. Cale, Jerry Lee Lewis, A.C. Reed, Waylon Jennings, and Willie Nelson.

In 1987, Markham relocated to Nashville and quickly made a name for himself as a harmonica player and vocalist both in Nashville nightclubs, played on some minor country sessions, and led a blues band. Junior Markham and the Jukes on many college gigs throughout the southeast. He has recorded tracks for A.C. Reed's Alligator Records CD, *I'm in the Wrong Business*, The Tractor's platinum debut CD, *The Tractors*, David Onley's *High Wide & Lonesome*, and he had a track on the Taxim Records compilation of Tennessee blues bands, *Whiskey Blues*. Leon Russell included Junior's song, "Soul Food", on *Asylum Choir II* (Shelter, 1971). Markham recorded an album for King Snake Records titled *Wound Up Tight* (1999). As of 2011, Markham could be seen jamming with any number of old friends around Tulsa, notably at the Oklahoma Jazz Hall of Fame's Tulsa Harmonica Summit in February of that year. One performance from that show, "I Found Love", could be seen on youtube.com featuring Markham on vocals and harmonica with his old friend, **Chuck Blackwell**, on drums.

Note

1. Matt S. Alcott details Junior Markham's early musical experiences and career in online essay, "A Harper's Bizarre Journey" on his website at http://members.cox.net/j.markham/about.htm (accessed July 21, 2011).

Martin, John David "Moon"
(b. October 31, 1945)

Not nearly as popular in his home country as he is in Europe, with notable exceptions among musicians, quirky rock music fans, and smiling Oklahoma music historians, Moon Martin is a talented multi-instrumentalist, vocalist, and songwriter whose own rockabilly-tinged power pop, usually linked to the 1970s new wave era, has gained him cult-like status in Europe, much like another power popper from Oklahoma, **Dwight Twilley**, with whom Moon shared a manager. Martin also has broad respect throughout the music industry from artists such as B.B. King, Linda Ronstadt, and **Steve Ripley** who have featured him on their recordings. He is also a prolific songwriter. Robert Palmer had a hit with Moon's "Bad Case of Love You (Doctor, Doctor)" in 1979, and other singers who picked his songs to record include Bette Midler, the Mamas and the Papas, the Association, Nick Lowe, Mink DeVille, Koko Taylor, and Paul Rodgers of Bad Company. Martin's music exhibits many stylistic elements of late 1970s new wave rock, but the constant presence of the blues, and the ease with which twang seeps into some of his songs, also display common elements of Oklahoma's influence on his generation of musicians, such as **Steve Gaines** and **Jesse Ed Davis**. Additionally, his nods to 1950s rock conventions he learned from second-hand records, and his propensity for Beatles covers all indicate the broader context of his teenage years and musical influences in the United States during the 1960s.

Nicknamed "Moon" as an adult because of his tendency to put the moon in song lyrics, John David Martin was born in extreme southwestern Oklahoma in Altus where he spent his childhood and teen years in Altus, the home of Altus Air Force Base, and just fourteen miles north of the Red River and the Texas border. Being so close to Texas and Mexico had its advantages. namely blues blasting out of the radio from Big Joe Turner, Bo Diddley, and Louis Prima, all coming from Texas and Mexico border stations (mega-watt stations that didn't have to adhere to U.S. broadcast power regulations). In Altus, a friend's father was a jukebox distributor, and Moon would go to the warehouse where stacks and stacks of worn-out 45's and 78's sat after coming out of jukeboxes. He was able to buy a lot of the records cheaply, and began to play his guitar along with them, the first being Buddy Holly's "Peggy Sue" and then several Chuck Berry records. After taking some lessons from a local musician, Lou Vargas, to whom all his records are dedicated, Moon first joined a country outfit in the mid-60s, Cece Wilson and the Panhandle Ramblers. Then, caught up in the general excitement of the British Bands Invasion, he formed a Beatles tribute group with some high school friends to earn money by playing at school dances.

After high school graduation in 1963, and that means the night of graduation, Martin had his car loaded with his clothes and a hotel room reserved in Duncan, Oklahoma where he had a job lined up to play in a band with bassist David Dickey, who went on to be the bass player for America. The band's first gig was in Lawton, where Ft. Sill supported a number of bars and the necessary musicians to entertain in them. Unfortunately, when the club was raided authorities discovered he was underage, and that put him out of a job.

Re-strategizing, Moon headed north for Norman to enroll at the University of Oklahoma, and joined a band with Paul Blaylock who needed a bass player. In the fall of '63, he started teaching guitar alongside **Jesse Ed Davis** at a music store owned by the booking agent for a local rockabilly band, The Disciples, who regularly toured the Midwest and Gulf South. When The Disciples guitar player left, the group auditioned both Martin and Davis, and Martin got the gig, a point of ribbing between Davis and Martin for years.

John "Moon" Martin

During the years between 1963 and 1967, The Disciples toured colleges as far south as Louisiana and Mississippi and as far north as Illinois and Michigan. In 1967, at a club in Detroit, The Disciples played with another group in which Bob Seger played keyboards, and Fontaine Brown, a strong-voiced blues singer, was on vocals. Before long, Brown had moved to California and was working as a producer at Blue Thumb Records when he called Martin and suggested they bring out The Disciples to make a recording. Fifteen credits short of a degree from the pharmacy school at OU, Martin decided to give it a whirl. The experiment barely worked out when the group was not really able to get their dynamic live sound down on tape. So, Fontaine Brown joined the band as a singer and the group changed their name to Southwind. Under that moniker and as the only white band on the label, they recorded two fairly obscure country-rock albums, a self-titled one, *Ready to*

Ride (Blue Thumb, 1969), and *What a Place to Land* (Blue Thumb, 1973). As an opening act, the group shared stages with Jimi Hendrix, Janis Joplin, Creedence Clearwater Revival, Spirit, Sly Stone, Tower of Power, Chicago Transit Authority, Jethro Tull, Canned Heat, John Lee Hooker, David Lindley, and Linda Ronstadt, but Southwind's recordings received little attention from radio or the buying public. While Martin had been splitting his time between Oklahoma and California, when the group split in 1972 Moon moved to Los Angeles permanently where he worked as a truck driver, wrote songs in his spare time, and continued doing studio work.

Along with session work for Linda Ronstadt on her third solo album in 1971, during which Moon turned down an offer from Glenn Frey to try out for the just-forming Eagles, Martin has also recorded with Gram Parsons, blues giant B.B. King, Michelle Phillips of the Mamas & the Papas. Also during the '70s, while plans for a solo album never materialized, his songs were being covered by the wide array of artists mentioned earlier. Mink DeVille's cover of Martin's "Cadillac Walk" on the punky soul crooner's 1977 LP, *Cabretta* (Capitol), finally brought Moon to the attention of Capitol executives as a potential solo artist. Like every other label trying to catch up with the British punk movement, the label needed artists it could market as new wave, a more palatable term for the new music coming out of New York's CBGB's, Boston, Los Angeles, and Great Britain. Sire Records had the Ramones and Talking Heads, Chrysalis had Blondie, Epic had the Clash, A&M had the Police, Columbia had Billy Burnette, Elektra had the Cars. Warner Brothers had to deal with the Sex Pistols, and Capitol, well, had The Knack, The Motels, and Moon Martin. While Martin didn't exactly fit the mold musically with his Oklahoma country-rock background, he looked the part in horn-rimmed glasses, foofy Sgt. Pepper-period Beatles hair, and seemingly sullen disposition. Also, his songs were smart enough, and catchy enough, that he was often compared to Elvis Costello when Moon's first two albums set a high standard of radio friendly pop songs about desperate subjects of the human condition.

Eager to get something out, Moon released a five song EP, *Victim of Romance* (Capitol, 1978), containing his studio version of "Victim of Romance" that had been recorded and released by Michelle Phillips in 1977 on her A&M Records release by the same name. The EP also had four live songs, recorded at the El Mocambo in Toronto, Moon's own version of "Cadillac Walk"; a Lennon and McCartney cover, "I Saw Her Standing There", indicating his Beatles tribute days still weren't over; and the song that would become his signature piece, "Bad Case of Loving You (Doctor, Doctor)". Another fan favorite, "Hot Nite in Dallas", also made its first appearance on the EP. With exception of the Beatles cover (which he changed to Lennon and McCartney's "All I've Got to Do") the other four songs became the core of his debut solo album, *Shots From a Cold Nightmare* (Capitol, 1979). While the record did not generate much commercial or radio interest, it did energize music critics in the U.K and in the U.S. who admired Martin's holistic perspective of rock, able to incorporate his rootsy Oklahoma background with the smarty pants pop of new wave L.A. and beyond. As Moon described it in an interview on his official website, "Being from that part of the country, all the players were more blues-oriented. My hero was Freddie King."

In the same year Robert Palmer's version of "Bad Case of Loving You" reached #14 on the pop charts, Moon Martin's second album of 1979, *Escape from Domination* (Capitol), proved to be his greatest commercial success as a solo artist. Produced by Craig Leon, who produced the first Ramones album, *The Ramones* (Sire, 1976), *Escape from*

Domination provided Moon with his biggest hit single, "Rolene", that landed at #30 on the pop singles charts and spurred enough interest to have commercial sheet music published for it. During this period, he toured internationally as an opening act for Blondie, Joe Jackson, The Kinks, The Police and Rockpile. A second single, "No Chance," made the Top 50, and the album apexed at a modest #80 on the album charts. Also, Rachel Sweet was inspired enough by "I've Got a Reason" to include it on her 1980 album for Stiff Records, *Protect the Innocent*. Martin's third album, *Street Fever* (Capitol, 1980), did not produce a hit single, and made it to a humble #138 on the U.S. album charts, but splashed the Top 20 in both Sweden and France. Subsequently, according to Martin, he "made some bad decisions" with his next outing. While recording the album *Mystery Ticket*, with Robert Palmer producing, or overproducing, Martin had to return from the recording studio in Nassau to do promotion for the first album. That left Palmer to create what he felt was the first American techno record by using Gary Numan and people from Tangerine Dream. With its heavy synthesizer sound, Martin's final album for Capitol, who really just wanted to capitalize on the success of the first record, *Mystery Ticket*, released the album with all of its warts. While the album gave Moon his last American chart success when "X-Ray Vision" made the dance club charts, and the album again hit the Top 20 in Sweden, it confounded fans, radio, and critics in the U.S. Perhaps the record was just too much of a shift too soon, as the Human League hit ninth months later with the same sound to receptive ears throughout the music media.

Having played professionally for almost twenty years, and being lucky enough to together a Los Angeles studio in the mid-1980s where he recorded *Mixed Emotions*, but Capitol did not want to promote the album that was almost completely created on a sampler and sequencer. Moon turned to his enthusiastic European fan base for its primary acceptance, and *Mixed Emotions*, released on vinyl only in France, with little notice in the United States. Moon popped back up in the early 1990s with two albums on small, independent labels, *Dreams on File* (FNAC, 1992), which not only saw his return to roots rock guitar, but also marked Moon's public appearance in a cowboy hat (an Oklahoma birthright). *Bad News Live* (1993), recorded over three nights in Paris, preceded two compilations of older songs, *Cement Monkey* (Core), and *Lunar Samples* (Core).

In 1995, the British label, Eidsel, repackaged Martin's first four albums as double CD packages: *Shots from a Cold Nightmare/Escape from Domination* and *Street Fever/Mystery Ticket*. Also in '95, Moon settled in a Nashville-area log cabin and built Ponyboy Studio, where he recorded and engineered a solo album in 1999, *Louisiana Jukebox* (Eagle), recorded without the use of any "music machines." The album's rowdy brew exhibits some of Nashville's best session players on new songs like "Get Hot or Go Home," "Pictures of Pain", and "Good Mornin' Policeman", Martin enjoyed working with session players in Nashville. He said in a 2002 interview with the author, "In Nashville it was the first time that guys came up with musical ideas that weren't clichés." The album also served as the impetus for several European tours of France, Germany, Holland, and Belgium.

Also in 1999, EMI released a twenty-two track compilation, *The Very Best of Moon Martin*, and Moon again toured Europe, where he could be seen on tour in France wearing a flannel shirt with cut off sleeves and an OU baseball cap. He returned to France again in the spring of 2000 for more enthusiastically received shows. In 2002, Moon sold his Nashville house and studio (without the gear) to Steve Earle and moved back to L.A. where he has recorded 15 songs that are "all over the place – ballads, blues, nice songs." He planned on recording the album in French and English to satisfy both fan bases, and as of 2002 thought he would move to France where he could work and record steadily.

Since then, Martin has not yet released the album, and has not been heard from much since. Asked what Oklahoma gave him musically, Moon replied, "experience in live music situations, an understanding of the mixture of country and Black music that is rock and roll, and the fact that a lot of good musicians came from the state challenged me to be better. At this stage, I realize the only satisfaction I'm going to get out of music is to get better, and I think I have."

www.moonmartin.com

Marvin, Frank James "Frankie"
(b. January 27, 1904 – d. January 18, 1985)

Marvin, John Senator "Johnny"
(b. July 11, 1897 – d. December 20, 1944)

Starting in the 1920s vaudeville era, Frankie and Johnny Marvin both enjoyed multiple successes in show business as performers, songwriters, and musicians. According to a 1932 songbook issued under their name, Johnny Marvin emerged into the world in a covered wagon somewhere on the Ozark Mountain Trail as the family made their way to the newly established land opportunities in the Indian and Oklahoma "Twin" Territories, finally settling in Butler, a small farming community in what became extreme western Oklahoma's Custer County. Johnny's little brother, Frankie, was born in Butler seven years later. By age ten, Johnny "seconded" or played accompaniment on guitar while his father played fiddle at local square dances. As the legend goes, Johnny left home at age twelve, intent on joining the circus, but after "roaming around" for a couple of years, went back to Butler an opened a barber shop at age fourteen. After cutting hair for an undefined period of time, he left the barber shop to join a group called the Royal Hawaiians because he could play guitar, learning to play ukulele and steel guitar while with the troupe. Johnny went into the Navy during World War I, while brother Frankie ran the barber shop Johnny had started. After being discharged from the service, Johnny went into vaudeville, eventually winding up in New York City where he began writing songs for he called "down home folks."[1]

Within a few years, Johnny began making records and evolved into a very popular ukulele player and crooner in the 1920s, enjoying success in vaudeville as "Honey Duke and His Uke", and later as "Johnny Marvin, the Ukulele Ace". Johnny Marvin had several hits in the 1920s, to include "Happy Days Are Here Again", "There's Something Nice About Everyone (But There's Everything Nice About You", and "Red Lips, Kiss My Blues Away", among many others. So well known was Johnny Marvin that he had a ukulele marketed under his name, sporting his face on it, and appeared in a 1927 Warner Brothers film depicting his vaudeville performance which included playing musical saw. 1929 was extremely busy for Johnny as he made more films and recordings, continued to be a top-rated vaudeville performer, and traveled to London for highly touted performances.[1] Ironically, he recorded

Johnny Marvin

"Happy Days Are Here Again" in 1929, but lost much of his savings in the stock market crash of that year. Many recordings of Johnny Marvin are available online due to the majority of his material now being in the public domain. Johnny is representative of the crooners of the 1920s and early 1930s that evolved due to advances in microphone technology that allowed singers a more expressive style of singing. Johnny Marvin was one of the most popular singers of the l920s, reportedly selling as many as eighteen million records.[2]

On a return visit to Butler, Johnny found that Frankie had been buying all of Johnny's records, and learning the songs. So, Johnny took Frankie back to New York, and within six months Frankie was also making records and performing on New York's vaudeville stages. Both Johnny and Frankie Marvin were working in New York City when a young singer named **Gene Autry** showed up who had met the brothers' parents back in Oklahoma. Autry hoped the Marvins would aid him in getting into the business, which they did by helping him get work.

Frankie Marvin

Gene Autry began his career more in the vein of the singing brakeman, Jimmie Rodgers, whose yodeling blues were the model for many guitar slinging country singers of the period. Some of Autry's first recordings were linked to the Marvin brothers, and the style of Rodgers. One of Autry's first recordings, "Slu-Foot Lou", was recorded in December 1929, and is a Frankie Marvin song featuring Gene Autry on vocal, yodeling, and guitar. On the same session he recorded a song credited to Frankie and Johnny Marvin, "Stay Away from My Chicken House", on which Frank Marvin is credited with "animal imitations". By 1931, Frank Marvin is credited with steel guitar on two Autry recordings, "Bear Cat Papa Blues" (co-written by Frank Marvin), and "I've Always Been A Rambler". Given Autry's success, in 1932, the brothers released a songbook, *Frankie and Johnny Marvin Folio of Down Home Songs with Guitar Chords* (Southern Music Publishing, 1932), which included both "Stay Away from My Chicken House" and "Bear Cat Papa Blues" (with a note of its recording by Autry), Jimmie Rodgers "Yodeling Cowboy", and their own "Oklahoma, Land of the Sunny West". The interaction between Autry and the Marvins proved serendipitous as Johnny had lost most of his savings in the stock market crash, and was able to benefit from their work with him. As Autry began to take off as a performer, he went to California and the Marvins followed.

Frankie Marvin continued playing with Autry, and began appearing in Autry's films starting in 1934. Frankie continued to appear with the famous singing cowboy through Gene's television years in 1950. Johnny continued performing, notably as an entertainer through much of World War II in remote locations around the world. He died at his North Hollywood, California home in 1947 of a heart attack.[3] Frankie continued living in Valencia, California until his death at age eighty. In 2000, Binge Records released *The Golden Age of Frankie Marvin*, a mix of all the different styles Marvin had played throughout the vaudeville era, to include jazz, blues, old time Western songs, through his later post-war cowboy songs. In 2002, BACM released Frankie Marvin, *Early Recordings by Gene Autry's #1 Sideman*, a collection of Marvin's early yodeling and blues recordings from

1929 to 1932 in the vein of Jimmie Rodgers, and obviously served as an influence on Autry's early direction as well. While the memory of these two brothers may be fading from contemporary popular culture consciousness, their story is one of the earliest examples of the success Oklahomans had in American popular music on a national, and in the case of Johnny, an international level.

Notes
1. The biography of the early years of Frankie and Johnny Marvin is published in *Frankie and Johnny Marvin Folio of Down Home Songs* (New York: Southern Publishing, 1932).
2. For details about Johnny Marvin's vaudeville career, his film work, recordings, and ads related to his appearances in London, see Jeff Cohen's fan page for the elder Marvin brother, probably the most detailed research available on the career of Johnny Marvin, although the information in it does clash with other internet databases on the brothers, at http://vitaphone.blogspot.com/2006/12/so-long-sad-times-go-along-bad-times.html.
3. For a solid review of Johnny Marvin's career, as well his work in the context of the development of the crooner as a singing style in American popular music, see Michael R. Pitts, *The Rise of the Crooners: Gene Austin, Russ Columbo, Bing Crosby, Nick Lucas, Johnny Marvin, and Rudy Valley*, (Lanham, MD: Scarecrow Press, 2002).

Mathews, Arthur "Tony"
(b. November 4, 1941)

Born into a family of gospel singers in Checotah, Oklahoma, Tony Mathews toured the world and recorded with Ray Charles and Little Richard, released a highly praised solo album of his own on Alligator Records in 1981, *Condition: Blue*, and continues playing in Los Angeles at clubs, private parties, and various recording sessions. He is one of a handful of Oklahoma's most accomplished blues guitarists, the others being **Lowell Fulson**, **J.J. Cale**, **Jesse Ed Davis**, and **Elvin Bishop**. Inspired by gospel groups such as the Soul Stirrers with RH Harris, his own family of multi-racial (African/Muscogee/Choctaw/Cherokee/Anglo) gospel singers, and by local guitarist Herbie Welch, Mathews started playing guitar at age 14, and served an apprenticeship with a self-destructive blues man from Rentiesville, Oklahoma, Tim Gilkey. He also sang with gospel quartets on local radio shows in Muskogee, and during the 1950s, Mathews made several recordings with his uncle, vocalist Robert Love, for Chess Records in Chicago, to include "Good Morning Little School Girl", "Shy Guy", and "Another Night Alone".

At 17, Mathews traveled to Dallas where he backed up musicians like Joe Turner, the Five Royals, and the Upsetters, but returned to Checotah to finish high school at the urging of his parents. In 1962, Arthur left Checotah for California, changed his name on arrival to avoid confusion with another Arthur Mathews, and wound up touring with the Simms Twins, forerunners of Sam and Dave, with whom he appeared on the *Jackie Wilson Show* in 1963. From 1964 to 1966, Tony toured with Little Johnny Taylor during Taylor's hit period with "Part Time Love," did studio work for Motown in L.A. on tapes that were sent to Detroit where vocals were added, and recorded for Convoy Records. In 1966 he landed a job with Ray Charles who picked out Matthews because of his "gospel feel." In 1967, Tony left Ray Charles and started touring with Little Richard, staying on the road with the 1950s rocker until 1970, with an intermittent gig supporting shows by Billy Preston.

After starting a family and staying close to home until 1972, Tony hit the road again with Ray Charles from 1973 until 1976. He played sessions and live dates around Los Angeles through the late 1970s, and recorded with Louisiana blues man Lonesome Down in 1977. The next couple of years he played guitar on Chicago blues man Louis Myer's *I'm a Southern Man*, on Rudy Love's disco album, *This Song Is for You*, and Prince Dixon's Gospel albums that were reissued as the Best of Prince Dixon by Hightone Records in 1999. Tony spent 1980 through 1982 touring again with Ray Charles, taking a break in 1981 to record *Condition: Blue*, originally released on Alligator in 1981, and subsequently released through Hightone where it is currently available. An album that has not received the credit it deserves for predicting the development of smooth, studio blues that became popular via Robert Cray in the 1980s, the album features Tony's unmistakably gospel-influenced vocals and his guitar work that is deeply rooted in Oklahoma's rural blues traditions. In 1983, Tony sang background vocals for one of Robert Cray's finest early albums, *Bad Influence*, and in 1984 recorded guitar tracks for Frankie Lee's 1984 Hightone album, *Ladies & Babies*. Tony went back out with Ray Charles briefly in 1988, but primarily continued playing private parties, occasional club dates, and various sessions as a sideman.

Tony Mathews performs at the Down Home Blues Club, Rentiesville, OK, 2007.

In 1990, S.D.E.G. records released Tony's *Alien in My Own Hometown*. Featuring his stinging lead guitar, his soulful vocal delivery, the album is smooth, uptown recording with horns, gospel influence background vocals, his sense of humor in songs like the album's title track and "Too Many People in My Bed". In 1994, Tony played guitar for Bobby McClure's *Younger Man Blues*, and added some work to a comedy album, *Outrageous Radio*. Matthews was one of the featured guitarists on *Guitar Showdown at the Dusk 'til Dawn Blues Fetival*, recorded in 1997 at **DC Minner**'s festival just a couple of miles from Tony's childhood home, and where he is an annual performer. Hear him at his most relaxed and easy going in this recording of Elmore James' "Dust My Blues" and Jimmy Rogers' "You Told Me Baby". Also in 1997, he was inducted into the Oklahoma Jazz Hall of Fame in Tulsa.

In 2000, Tony played on the Broadway soundtrack for a revue of African-American musical styles that traced the evolution of blues from Africa and slavery through the end of the 20th century, *It Ain't Nothin but the Blues*. Tony has also had some minor roles on television, such as in *Matlock* and *Mannix*, and played in the film *Lost Highway*, a movie about Hank Williams learning his trade from black musicians. In 2001, he produced an album by saxophonist Hollis Gilmore. In 2003, some of his work with Ray Charles resurfaced on a Rhino Records compilation, *Ray Charles in Concert*, on which Tony appears on the 1975 recordings of Charles and his band in Tokyo and Yokohama, originally released as *Ray Charles: Live in Japan* on vinyl, but released again in 2009 by Concord Records as an MP3 download through Amazon.com. In 2005, Mattews continued on as Hightone Records' "go to" guitarist, appearing on most of Floyd Dixon's *Fine! Fine! Thing!*

Throughout the 2000s, Tony Mathews continued playing around Los Angeles, and returned home several times to visit his family in Checotah and play yearly at the Dusk 'til Dawn Blues Festival, being inducted into its Oklahoma Blues Hall of Fame in 2007.

Mathis, Reed
(b. September 27, 1976)

A member of San Francisco rock band, Tea Leaf Green, since 2008, but a fifteen-year member of Tulsa modern jazz group, **Jacob Fred Jazz Odyssey (JFJO),** Reed Mathis is recognized as one of the most gifted and exploratory bassists in modern music. Mathis grew up in a musical family in Tulsa, and began playing bass at age eleven. By age fifteen, he played mandolin with members of the Tulsa Philharmonic on Vivaldi's "Mandolin Concerto in D", and at sixteen he attended the prestigious Interlochen Center for the Arts in Michigan where he was the top-ranked bassist during his time there. At seventeen, while still enrolled at Tulsa's Booker T. Washington High School, he joined Brian Haas in Jacob Fred Jazz Odyssey, certainly the most significant jazz group to emerge from Oklahoma, but also recognized as one of the primary jazz groups of the modern era nationally. Reed met Haas because the two had musician friends in common at Tulsa University and those friends told Haas he needed to check out the young bass player from Booker T., then only a junior who agreed to be part of the band. Once assembled, JFJO started as an eight-piece, free form group with a full horn section, and through the years had as many as sixteen different members, before settling on the bass, drums, piano format that achieved critical accolades, important residencies, and recorded sixteen albums, nine of which Mathis produced.

JFJO toured the U.S. from 1999 through most of 2008, selling out major venues across the country. Throughout his career, Mathis has taken opportunities to record with other musicians. He appears on two discs by Tulsa guitarist, Jared Tyler (*Blue Alleluia*, 2002 and *Here with You*, 2006), and three with Tulsa blues guitarist, Steve Pryor (*El Niño Chickendog*, 1997; *The Neighbors*, 1999; and *Life's Ladder*, 2006). Mathis teamed with New York-based experimental and jazz pianist/organist Marco Benevento, and appeared on three releases with Benevento's trio (piano and two drummers), as well as performing with them at Carnegie Hall in 2009. In 2007, Mathis began playing with the San Francisco rock band, Tea Leaf Green, and appears on Tea Leaf Green's 2008 CD, *Raise Up the Tent*. He tried to split time between the two groups (JFJO AND TLG), producing JFJO's *Winterwood* album in 2008. However, before that album's release in 2009, he announced his departure from JFJO citing the desire to experience some other musical opportunities with Tea Leaf Green. In 2009, he told interviewer Dennis Cook with the online music journal, www.jambase.com, that he hoped to work again with Brian Haas and JFJO because he is still good friends with

Reed Mathis, circa 2002

them and has tremendous respect for them musically and personally. In 2012, he was still in Tea Leaf Green and touring nationally.

One would be hard-pressed to find a more creative and interesting bassist to listen to in any setting he chooses, whether it is jazz, jam bands, hard rock, classical, free form free-form progressive music, or any other setting. With his classical training, jazz back ground, rock foundations, and willingness to take himself way out on a limb musically, Reed Mathis is one of the few musicians the author has ever heard that rewards a listener for extended and repeated listening. He is just one of those musicians a fan of challenging and interesting music wants to follow. As for Oklahoma, he is on a very short list of bassists from the state who have achieved such national acclaim, the others being fellow Booker T. Washington alumni, Cecil McBee and Wayman Tisdale, as well as Tulsa's Carl Radle and Okmulgee's Oscar Pettiford.

www.tealeafgreen.com or www.jfjo.com

McAlister, Barbara

Barbara McAlister is a world-renowned opera singer, and was born in Muskogee, Oklahoma. She is also an enrolled member of the Cherokee Nation of Oklahoma. The *Tulsa World* wrote of the mezzo soprano dramatic singer, "The power of her voice and presence elevates every scene in which she appears."[1] Barbara's mother, Clare, was of German heritage (born in Maryland in 1905), and an excellent pianist. She also indulged in stamp collecting on a serious level, beginning the *Fine Arts Philatelist* magazine, which chronicled art as depicted on stamps, which endured as an international publication from 1955 to 1999. Barbara's father, Lawrence, was a Cherokee born in Indian Territory in 1905, and also a long-time radiologist in Muskogee. In addition, Lawrence was a classical singer. As a result of her parents' musical background, McAlister was raised in a musical environment where many musicians visited her home, especially vocalists as her father was also in a barbershop quartet. She remembers many times when people would gather in the home and sing away an evening. Barbara's first voice teacher in Muskogee was Jeanne Parker. Her brothers have both lived impressive lives, with John McAlister serving in the Air Force and retiring as a psychiatrist; her other brother, Lawrence, Jr., retired in Salem, Oregon, after an engineering career including work at Redstone Arsenal in Alabama that was an early 1950s incubator for rockets and ballistic missiles, and later managed the manufacturing of a computer for the Apollo 13 lunar module. After high school, Barbara attended the University of Tulsa, and then transferred to Oklahoma City University, where she studied with Inez Silberg, and graduated with a degree in music/voice. During summers of her college years at Oklahoma City University, she studied for one summer at the American Institute of Musical Studies in Graz, Austria, and performed in summer stock musicals back in the states, through which she made a connection with Oklahoma actor, Clu Gulager. Gulager encouraged her to go to California,

Barbara McAlister

which she did after graduating OCU. While living in Los Angeles and Hollywood for nine years, she studied privately with voice teachers Lee and Sally Sweetland.[2]

McAlister's break came when she won the prestigious Loren Zachary Competition in Los Angeles in 1974 and 1975. The Zachary Competition is the one of the most valuable prizes in the world for a young opera singer, providing opportunities internationally. After her wins, she auditioned for the German Repertory Theater and performed for that company for ten years, singing the mezzo-soprano repertoire in German for the appreciative opera houses of Passau, Koblenz, Bremerhaven, and Flensburg in Germany, in Monte Carlo where she performed the role of Meg in *Falstaff*, Cannes, Modena, Ferrara, Paris, Lisbon and Hong Kong. In some summers, she traveled to Italy and worked with Pavarotti's coach, Ettore Campogalliani, and Rainaldo Zamboni, learning opera roles), and in other summers ('79 and '80) she was in Bayreuth, Germany at the Wagner Festival. She made her debut as Azucena in a Hong Kong performance of *Il Trovatore* under the direction of Kingman Lo. Along with performing with the Düsseldorf Symphony, and the Symphony in Ulm, she toured much of France, and some of Spain and Portugal in the last 1990s with the New Bulgarian Opera as Ortrud in *Lohengrin*, as well as in performances of Beethoven's 9th, and Verdi's *Requiem*. After her ten years in Europe, she lived in New York City for about twenty years, where she continued to receive wide acclaim for her rich voice and expressive interpretive skills of librettos (text or lyrics of an opera).

A recipient of a New York Wagner Society grant, Barbara has been heard as a soloist in concert at Carnegie Hall (the works of Mark Hayes), Alice Tully Hall, and Weill Recital Hall. She sang with the New York Grand Opera in three roles with famed New York City opera director Vincent La Selva: Pucceini's *Suor Angelica* with soprano Gabriella Tucci; Verdi's *Masked Ball* in the role of Ulrica, also with Tucci, repeating *Masked Ball* several summers later. Appearing in the New York Grand Opera, which performs in the middle of Central Park, she remembers vividly the great experience of performing in New York City's famous park: "I cannot forget the first time I sang there, looking out on the sea of faces, with the background of the beautiful trees, and the New York skyline rising above." She also apprenticed with the Santa Fe Opera Company and Central City Opera Company in Colorado, and has appeared with many symphonies, to include those in Houston, Dusseldorf, Hamburg, Bremerhaven, and Ulm. She has also performed with the Washington Opera Company, Cherokee Heritage Center, Arizona Opera, San Diego Opera, Tulsa Opera, Florentine Opera, New York Grand Opera and Opera New England. Living a "dream come true," McAlister performed as Vera Boronel with Gian Carlo Menotti staging his own material for The Washington Opera's 50th Anniversary performance of *The Consul*, at the Kennedy Center for Performing Arts in Washington D.C.

McAlister has also given recitals for the Oklahoma State Arts Council Touring Program, singing opera arias and Native American songs in the Cherokee language. In 1996, Barbara created the role of Qualla in Lindor Chlarsson's opera *Mountain Windsong*, based on Cherokee author Robert Conley's novel by the same name, detailing the Cherokee removal from their homelands in the 1830s. She has also played Selu, or Corn Woman, in the Trail of Tears drama/musical at Tsa-la-gi outdoor amphitheater in Tahlequah, Oklahoma, fulfilled the role of Mary in *Der fliegende Hollander* (The Flying Dutchman) for the Anchorage Opera in Alaska, and has portrayed Amneris in Verdi's *Aida*. A complete list of roles Barbara has performed is available on her website under the link, "Repertoire".

In addition to her career as an opera and concert soloist, Barbara is a renowned Native American visual artist, inspired by Jerome and John Tiger, and studied one semester at Bacone College with Dick West. Her paintings have been shown at the Five Civilized Tribes Museum and Jacobson House in Oklahoma, the Wharton Art Gallery in Philadelphia, and Bullock's in Los Angeles. Many are now in private collections throughout the United States and Europe. In 2011, McAlister was a fine arts instructor/performer for the Cherokee Nation, and an adjunct professor teaching Broadway singing at Northeastern State University in Tahlequah. She was also a member of the 2010 - 2011 Oklahoma State Arts Council touring roster, singing programs across the state, including musical theater songs, opera, and traditional Cherokee songs. As a result of her vitalization of the Cherokee language through song, Barbara received the Cherokee Medal of Honor in 1999. Also in 2011, she received the Living Legend Award from the Bare Bones Film Festival in Muskogee, and sang for the First Annual Chickasaw Chamber Music Festival in Ada, for which she was scheduled to perform again in 2012. As of 2011, she continued singing for a wide variety of programs, recitals, and concerts across the United States. To make ready for those performances she "brushes up" once a year with voice coach Steve Sweetland, son of her L.A. coaches Lee and Sally, and her repertoire coach is Linda Hall in New York City. Recorded in Austin, Texas, and New York in 1998, Little Bear Productions released a compact disc, *Soul Journey*, in which Barbara recorded opera arias and art songs. According to her website, in the near future she planned on releasing a new CD, *Songs of the Nightengale*, consisting of Cherokee lullabies with a classical twist, accompanied by pianist, Maestro Tim Long (Choctaw/Muscogee), another native Oklahoman who is enjoying a flourishing classical music and opera career worldwide, and is an assistant professor of music, voice, and conducting at the State University of New York at Stony Brook. Clearly one of Oklahoma's most accomplished singers of any genre, Barbara McAlister is a sterling example that Oklahoma does not just produce notable country and rock music artists, but has also contributed performers who have excelled at classical music's highest levels on the world's most notable stages.

www.barbaramcalister.com

Notes
1. Both quotes are from the biography on Barbara McAlister's website and are not annotated.
2. Some details of Barbara McAlister's family and early life are discussed by Victoria Lee in her biographical sketch of McAlister in *Distinguished Oklahomans* (Touch of Heart Publishing, 2002), 177-78.

McAuliffe, Leon
(b. January 3, 1917 – d. August 20, 1988)

Born in Houston, Texas, William Leon McAuliffe was one of the 20th century's most significant steel guitarists, forever known for his 1936 recording of "Steel Guitar Rag" as a member of Bob Wills' Texas Playboys. An adaptation of Sylvester Weaver's 1923 blues tune, "Guitar Rag". McAuliffe only copyrighted his version, never claiming it to be an original composition. However, McAuliffe did co-write the classic, "San Antonio Rose", one of Bob Wills and the Texas Playboys best-known songs. McAuliffe is also recognized by Wills urging him to "Take it away, Leon" before a steel guitar solo.

While still in school in Houston, McAuliffe heard primary steel guitarist, **Bob Dunn**, who recorded and performed on an amplified electric steel guitar with Milton Brown and his Musical Brownies. McAuliffe took up the instrument, and after leaving high school in 1933, he played in Houston night clubs, primarily focusing on jazz as the Big Band Era began taking off. Around this time, the famous Texas entrepreneur and eventual politician, W. Lee "Pappy" O'Daniel, who formed the Light Crust Doughboys to promote the Burrus Mills Flour Company for whom he worked, heard McAuliffe and hired the sixteen-year-old McAuliffe to be part of the Doughboys. According to Bob Wills' biographer Charles Townsend, McAuliffe was only paid ten dollars per week because he was so young. In October, 1933, McAuliffe was put on a plane to Chicago where he recorded several tunes. By 1935 McAuliffe had a falling out with O'Daniel, and joined Bob Wills in Tulsa who had also left O'Daniel's dominion the year before. Wilth Wills, McAuliffe was raised to thirty dollars a week, and encouraged to take the steel guitar to new places, which he inevitably did. From 1935 to 1942 Leon made more than 200 recordings with Bob Wills becoming the ultimate steel guitarist, fusing jazz, blues and Western styles into his playing that helped the genre eventually become known as Western swing.[1]

Leon McAuliffe, circa 1964

After World War II and a U.S. Navy stint, McAuliffe returned to Tulsa but Bob Wills was touring nationally from his base in California. McAuliffe formed his own group in 1946, first known as Leon McAuliffe and his Western Swing Boys, but eventually becoming the Cimarron Boys. Making his home in the Cimarron Ballroom in Tulsa, a building he eventually owned, the Cimarron Boys played 400 consecutive weeks, or about eight years of shows, during which time the band also played regularly on KVOO radio out of Tulsa. During this period, he composed and recorded "Panhandle Rag", which made it to #6 on the Country/Western charts in 1949. During McAuliffe's recording career, he had releases by Starday, Majestic, Columbia, Dot and Capitol Records. In 1961, Floyd Cramer took "San Antonio Rose" to #8 on the *Billboard* Hot 100, but Leon did not a chart any songs beyond that. According to the Texas Playboys website (www.texasplayboys.net), McAuliffe was the one of the first musicians to have multi-neck steel guitars, with each neck featuring a different tuning. Furthermore, as Western swing went into decline, Leon purchased a radio station in Rogers, Arkansas, where he lived for a time, but also kept an apartment in Claremore where he taught at the Hank Thompson School of Country Music at Rogers State College until at least 1987. Throughout his professional career, he only lived in Tulsa, Rogers, Arkansas, and Claremore. McAuliffe's complete discography is available under his name at www.allmusic.com. However, two most recent releases of note include Leon McAuliffe, *Take it Away the Leon Way* (Jasmine, 2001), which includes recordings from Leon's big band in 1946, and rare recordings he made

Leon McAuliffe, circa 1950s

480 / Oklahoma Music Guide II

for Majestic Records in 1947-48. The most complete and modern compilation was produced by the label that has preserved and packaged so much important American roots music, Bear Family Records out of Germany. In 2009, Bear Family released Leon McAuliffe, *Tulsa Straight Ahead – Gonna Shake This Shack Tonight*, which includes more than half of his 59 Columbia recordings from 1949 to 1955, including his only real hit, "Panhandle Rag", and an outstanding historical overview of McAuliffe's career by Kevin Coffey.

Notes
1. While the time period of McAuliffe joining Wills is noted as March 25, 1935, much of McAuliffe's early career and time with Bob Wills is chronicled in extreme detail in Charles R. Townsend's primary biography of Wills, *San Antonio Rose: The Life and Times of Bob Wills*, (Urbana: University of Illinois Press, 1986), 99.

McBee, Cecil
(b. May 19, 1935)

One of the most significant double bassists of jazz for the last forty-five plus years, Cecil McBee is also considered a significant composer of jazz music, as well as a much-desired teacher for those who wish to play jazz bass on a serious level. Throughout most of his career he has been associated with the most progressive musicians in jazz, able to express himself as a unique sonic imprint while always maintaining tempo as a vital rhythm element. His bass work floats through pieces, unobtrusive, yet intrinsic, and when soloing McBee is interesting without being too ornate. Born in Tulsa, which he says on his website, was a town of "rich and varied musical roots – including country and western, rhythm and blues, classical and jazz."[1] He performed clarinet duets with his sister while in high school at Booker T. Washington in Tulsa, and played the same instrument in the high school marching band. At age seventeen, McBee switched to bass and performed at local Tulsa night clubs in the early 1950s.

After high school, Cecil studied bass and jazz composition at Central State University in Wilberforce, Ohio, where the deep jazz tradition there "inspired him to focus his attention on the bass, the classics, and jazz composition." He played bass professionally to support himself during his college years, and began his professional career with Dinah Washington in 1959. His college studies were interrupted for a two-year stint (1959-61) in the U.S. Army where he conducted and played clarinet in the 158th Band at Fort Knox, Kentucky. During that time, he says he developed a "personal study of bass composition and improvisation." After discharge, Cecil completed his bachelor's degree in clarinet and music education at CSU.

After training to become a music educator, McBee had become so enthralled with improvisation, he decided to give performance a try before committing to a teaching position, and moved to Detroit where he became involved in the intense jazz community present there in 1962. Within the next year, he joined the Paul Winter Sextet, and relocated to New York City with the group in 1964.

His performance and recording peers during the 1960s and 1970s are a testament to his outstanding abilities, when he played bass with a who's who of jazz musicians: Miles Davis, Grachan Moncur III, Elvin Jones, Jackie McLean, Wayne Shorter, Freddie Hubbard, Charles Lloyd, Yusef Lateef, **Sam Rivers**, Bobby Hutcherson, Pharoah Sanders, Alice Coltrane, Charles Tolliver, Lonnie Liston Smith, Sonny Rollins, Abdullah Ibrahim, Michael White, Jorace Tapscott, Anthony Braxton, Buddy Tate, Harry "Sweets" Edison, Wayne Shorter, **Chet Baker**, and Chico Freeman. His longest stint was with fellow Oklahoman

Sam Rivers (from El Reno, OK) from 1967 to 1973, during which time Cecil was bassist on such Rivers free-jazz recordings as *Involution, Dimensions and Extensions, Hues, Streams: Live at Montreux* (Blue Note), which was re-mastered and re-released in 2008; and *Sam Rivers Trio Live* (GRP, 1972 – re-released, 1998). He also recorded with Chet Baker on the sessions for *Blues for a Reason* (1984, re-released in 2011 on Criss Cross Records as an import). Among other musicians he played with, count Art Pepper (1978), McCoy Tyner (1980), Mal Waldron (1981), James Newton (1982-83), and Joanne Brackeen (1985). Also during the 1980s, McBee was bassist with free-jazz group, The Leaders, featuring trumpeter Lester Bowie, alto saxophonist Arthur Blythe, tenor saxophonist Chico Freeman, pianist Kirt Lightsey, and drummer Famoudou Don Moye. Cecil may be heard on The Leaders' albums, *Mudfoot* (1986), *Out Here Like This* (1986), *Heaven Dance* (1988), and *Unforeseen Blessings* (1988).

As bandleader, McBee has produced six albums. including *Mutima* (Strata East, 1974); *Music from the Source*, a live recording at New York's Sweet Basil Club in 1977, featuring Chico Freeman; *Alternate Spaces* (India Navigation,1977), which featured five of Cecil's original compositions ("Alternate Spaces", "Consequence", "Come Sunrise" "Sorta, Kinda Blues", and "Expression"); *Flying Out* (Indian Navigation), a chamber jazz collaboration with a mix of instruments such as piano, bass, cello, cornet, violin, and drums; *Compassion* (Enja, 1983); and *Unspoken* (Palmetto), featuring eight McBee works, including "Pantamime", "Unspoken", "Catfish", "Sleeping Giant", "Lucia", "Inside Out", "Slippin' and Slidin'", and "Tight Squeeze". From 1996 through 1998, Cecil fronted his own quintet that toured Europe.

Cecil McBee, circa 2010

In 2004, he was the bassist of record on *Gathering of Spirits* (Telarc, 2004), which commemorates the concerts by saxophonists Michael Brecker, Joe Lovano, and Dave Liebman known as the as the Saxophone Summit at concerts in the U.S. and Europe, which continued in 2011. In 2007, he reunited with The Leaders for another album, *Spirits Alike* (Double Moon), and in 2010, he played on Spigniew Seifert's *Man of the Light* (Promising Music). Overall, McBee has appeared on more than 200 recordings over the past forty-five years. In 2012, McBee appears with a jazz supergroup called The Cookers on *Believe* (Motema), playing bass on all tracks, two of which are his compositions ("Temptation(s)" and "Tight Squeeze").

Among McBee's other notable achievements are two NEA composition grants, and a Grammy award for his 1989 performance of "Blues for John Coltrane" with featuring Roy Haynes, David Murray, McCoy Tyner, and Pharoah Sanders. He served as a faculty member of the New School in New York City for fifteen years. As of 2011, Cecil had been a member of the Improvisation and Jazz Studies faculty at the New England Conservatory of Music for twenty-one years, and in 2010-2011, he was guest artist at Harvard University in their Jazz Band Program. He also published a series of highly praised educational texts,

Anthology of String Bass Improvisation, Books I, II, & III. The books provide technical, physical, musical, and theoretical methods for both self-instruction and teacher-assisted student learning. Still a very active player, in 2011 he played for concerts in Boston, New York, France, and Chicago. Cecil was a 1991 Oklahoma Jazz Hall of Fame inductee, and his often stated musical philosophy is "No tone unturned!"

www.cecilmcbeejazz.com

Notes

1. All quotes in the essay are from Cecil McBee's published press release biography on his website.
2. Cecil McBee's early years are detailed well by Ed Hazell in his essay on the bassist in *The New Grove Dictionary of Jazz*, ed. Barry Kerfeld, (New York: MacMillan, 1994), 725.

McBride, Laura Lee

(b. May 20, 1920 – d. January 25, 1989)

A brassy vocalist who exudes confidence and keen interpretive skills on her recordings, Laura Lee McBride was known as the "Queen of Western Swing" because she was the first female vocalist with a Western swing group, in this case **Bob Wills** and the Texas Playboys. Laura Frances Owens was born in Bridgeport, Oklahoma, a small community of just over 100 people west of Oklahoma City on U.S. Route 66 just west of the Canadian River bridge crossing. Laura was the daughter of Maude and D. H. "Tex" Owens, composer of the country classic, "Cattle Call". Her father gave up his occupation as a mechanic to devote his career to music, and the family moved to Kansas City, Missouri, where "Tex" launched his own radio show on KMBC. Laura Lee's first public performance was at age ten with her sister, teaming as "Joy and Jane" on their father's radio program.

Following high school graduation in 1938, Laura Lee organized her own band, the Prairie Pioneers, and the next year married Herb Kratoska, her father's guitarist. The band migrated to California, where they made thirteen movies with the legendary cowboy singer-actor, **Gene Autry**. She soon divorced Herb and returned to her native state of Oklahoma, where she began to perform with a reformulated band, Sons of the Range, on radio station KVOO in Tulsa. Influenced by her aunt, Texas Ruby Owens, who sang with W. Lee "Pappy" O'Daniel's Hillbilly Boys, Laura Lee was soon noticed by Wills, who was now based in Tulsa and also performing on KVOO. Because of her dynamic vocals, and because Wills needed a female vocalist, Wills hired her. She traveled with the Playboys to California, where they toured the West Coast and made several B-grade western films. She also married Cameron Hill, a guitarist with Wills.

Laura Lee McBride

In 1943 and 1944, Laura Lee recorded two programs with Wills on the Armed Forces Radio Transcriptions, including "I Betcha My Heart I Love You", which became her trademark song. During this period, she briefly toured with Tex Ritter. In 1945, Hill, her second husband, joined Dickie McBride's Village Boy's band in Houston, where Laura Lee sang with the band over radio station KTRH. This led to a divorce from Hill and she soon married McBride, who was known for his work with **Floyd Tillman**, Moon Mullican, and Cliff Bruner's Texas Wanderers, for whom he sang the first recording of "It Makes No Difference Now", a country standard. Dickie and Laura Lee developed a loyal following throughout Texas, Oklahoma, and Louisiana.

In 1950, Laura Lee returned to Bob Wills and rerecorded her signature song, "I Betcha My Heart I Love You", on the Kapp label. During the 1950s, she continued singing with McBride, did some disc jockey work, managed a restaurant, sold real estate in Bryan, Texas, and briefly worked with the legendary Hank Williams. When Dickie died in 1971, Laura Lee joined Ernest Tubb and toured with him for the next eight years. During the 1970s, she recorded *The Queen of Western Swing*, an album of western swing classics, on the Delta label, and participated in several Texas Playboys reunions following Wills' death in 1975.

In the 1980s, Laura Lee disc jockeyed in Farmington, New Mexico, and managed Grandpa and Ramona Jones' dinner theater in Mountain View, Arkansas. During this decade, she received several honors, including the Texas State Ambassador award and induction into the Western Swing Hall of Fame. She died of cancer in Bryan in 1989.

Mike McClure

(born July 6, 1971)

Coming into prominence as a result of fronting **The Great Divide** during their late 1990s major label run, Mike McClure is perhaps the most sensitive and self-reflexive of the singer-songwriters that have come out of the **Red Dirt** music scene. As opposed to commentary on the declining social environment of rural America, oppressive small town life, or humorous takes on society's paradoxes, all common Red Dirt lyrical themes, the Shawnee-born McClure focuses on interpersonal relationships and meditative reflections of the speakers in his songs, allying him with **Jimmy LaFave** as songwriting model. However, whereas Jimmy LaFave's unique raspy tenor is one of the endearing aspects of his voice that has made him a cult favorite, McClure's voice is closer to a mainstream version of LaFave's voice, a little smoother and slightly more radio friendly.[1] Essentially, The Great Divide with McClure on vocals was a more commercial sounding Jimmy LaFave, and the most mainstream version of Red Dirt music thus far (excluding **Garth Brooks**), even more so than the tougher growl of Cody Canada by himself or on the **Cross Canadian Ragweed** recordings. After leaving The Great Divide in 2003, McClure has released nine solo albums wherein listeners get easy-on-the-ears-vocals, contemplative songs that register with most common aspects of the human condition, and warm studio

Mike McClure, circa 2002

productions with plenty of good guitar picking. As of 2011, he led his three-piece band throughout the Southwest and Midwest. The Mike McClure band is made of McClure on vocals and guitar, long-time Red Dirt singer-songwriter, Tom Skinner (bass), and another Stillwater music scene veteran, Eric Hansen (drums), whom McClure has known since Hansen's membership in the Stillwater group, The Medicine Show.

Like many of the other musicians who came to maturity as songwriters in Stillwater during the 1980s and 1990s, McClure joined in the multitude of jams, song sharing sessions, and just general musical calamity that took place at the now famous "Farm" outside of Stillwater, a farmhouse rented by Red Dirt Rangers vocalist, from 1979 through 1999. In 1992, McClure formed The Great Divide with J.J. Lester, Scotte Lester, and Kelley Green, which led to six studio albums and one live disc before McClure went solo after ten years of gigs all over the country.

Along with his own solo albums, all of which are available through his website or on other online music stores such as www.amazon.com, McClure has also become known as an important studio production specialist. He produced several Cross Canadian Ragweed albums before their demise (co-writing their 2006 Top 40 Hot Country Song charting single, "Fightin' For"), and has worked with a number artists often associated with the Red Dirt sound, such as Stoney LaRue, Jason Boland & the Stragglers, Scott Copeland, Johnny Cooper, Whiskey Myers, and the Turnpike Troubadours. In 2005, Garth Brooks recorded McClure's "I'd Rather Have Nothing", originally done by The Great Divide in 1993, and included it on the 2005 Brooks Six-CD Limited Series Box set as part of the *Lost Sessions* disc, which went on to sell two million copies.

Mike McClure, circa 2003

In 2011 and 2012, McClure re-joined with The Great Divide for a shows in Stillwater, commenting on his website's blog how comfortable it felt and that they might do some more shows together if everyone could line up their schedules. For McClure's fans, a bonus of his website is that he often posts random thoughts, new song lyrics, and other commentary about his artistic and professional perspective on his blog, giving a real-time update on his music and industry work. While Mike McClure Band continues performing throughout Oklahoma, Texas, he also released another self-reflecting and contemplative solo album, *50 Billion* (2011), on his own 598 Recordings. Based in Shawnee, the label has also produced memorable new music from **Red Dirt** elder, Tom Skinner (*Tom Skinner*, 2012), as well as fast-rising newcomers The Damn Quails (*Down the Hatch*, 2011), and Roff, Oklahoma's Jessey General Thompson (in production, 2013)

www.mikemcclureband.com or www.598recordings.com

Note

1. For a great comparison of the similarity and subtle differences between the voices of Jimmy LaFave and Mike McClure, listen to their duet on "Used To Be" on The Great Divide's *Break in the Storm* (Atlantic, 1999).

By Hugh Foley / 485

McDaniel, Mel

(b. September 9, 1942 – d. March 31, 2011)

With his resonant baritone voice, and casual easy-going delivery, Mel McDaniel was a member of the Grand Ole Opry cast from 1986 until his death in 2011, and was best known for his #1 hit, "Baby's Got Her Blue Jeans On". Singer and songwriter Mel McDaniel was born in Checotah, a town of about 3,000 population located south of Muskogee, but was raised in other Oklahoma communities such as Okmulgee and Tulsa. Raised in Okmulgee, his first interest in music was when he learned the trumpet in the fourth grade, but soon learned the guitar. After seeing Elvis Presley on television, he decided to become a singer. He made his professional debut at age fifteen performing an Elvis song in a talent contest at Okmulgee High School. While in high school, Mel played in several local bands, and after graduation, began working as a musician in Tulsa clubs, and married his childhood sweetheart, Peggy. While in Tulsa, he recorded several singles for local labels (**J.J. Cale** wrote and produced his first single, "Lazy Me"), but he decided to leave Oklahoma and try his luck in other locations, first in Ohio and then in Alaska where he sang for oil field workers, and then in Nashville.

His acquaintance with record producer Johnny MacRae led to a recording contract with Capitol in 1976. During the next two years, he recorded several hits, such as "Have a Dream on Me", "I Thank God She Isn't Mine", "All the Sweet", "Soul of a Honky Tonk Woman", and "Gentle on Your Senses (Easy on Your Mind)", which became the title track of his first album. During this time, he was on tour with his newly formed band, A Little More Country, and made several television appearances. Based on this early success, Mel was nominated in 1977 as Most Promising Male Vocalist by the ACM.

Mel McDaniel

In 1978-79, Mel reached the Top 15 with "God Made Love," and hit the charts with such singles as "Border Town Woman," "Play Her Back to Yesterday," "Loved Lies." and "Lovin' Starts Where Friendship Ends". He also released his second album, *Mello*, in 1978.

Mel's third album, *I'm Countrified*, produced the title track single that reached the Top 20 in 1981. This was followed by his most successful releases to date, "Louisiana Saturday Night" and "Right in the Palm of Your Hand," both of which hit the Top 10. To round out the year, "Preaching Up a Storm", reached the Top 20. In 1982-83 McDaniel released his fourth and fifth albums, *Take Me to the Country* and *Naturally Country* with the title track of the former hitting the Top 10. It was followed by several other Top 20 singles, including "Big Ole Brew", "I Wish I Was in Nashville", "Old Man River (I've Come to Talk Again)", and "I Call It Love".

Mel McDaniel achieved a #1 hit in 1984 with "Baby's Got Her Blue Jeans On" from his *Let It Roll* album. The song stayed on the charts for twenty-eight weeks and garnered Mel several honors, including nominations for CMA Horizon Award and Single of the Year (1985), as well as a Grammy for Best Country Vocal Performance-Male. His 1985 output included the singles, "Let It Roll (Let It Rock)" and "Stand Up", both of which charted in the Top 10. During the late 1980s, Mel scored hits as "Shoe String", "Stand on It" (his version of the Bruce Springsteen hit), "Real Good Feel Good Song", "Ride This Train," Henrietta" "You Can't Play the Blues (In an Air-Conditioned Room)", and "Walk That Way". Capitol Nashville released *Rock-A-Billy Boy* (1989), a ten track CD, including "Blue Suede Shoes" and "Oklahoma Shines".

During the 1990s, Mel was still on the road with his six-piece band, Oklahoma Wind, completing some 200 dates a year. He also began performing at theaters in Branson, Missouri, and, after his break with Capitol Records in 1990, he signed with Intersound's new label, Branson Entertainment.

McDaniel's songwriting career is worthy of note. Fellow Oklahoman **Hoyt Axton** was the first to record one of his songs with "Roll Your Own", a hippie anthem later recorded by Commander Cody, Arlo Guthrie, and the Poodles. Recorded by Conway Twitty, Mel's "Grandest Lady of Them All" was used for the Grand Finale on the Grand Ole Opry's nationally televised 60th anniversary special. Additional artists who recorded Mel's songs include Kenny Rogers and Johnny Rodriguez, Earl Scruggs, and Doug Kershaw. In the mid-1990s, Mel was honored with a star in the Country Music Hall of Fame's Walkway of Stars. In 1996, McDaniel fell into an unmarked orchestra pit, nearly costing him his life. While he hurt multiple body parts, he fell on his guitar, which saved him, but did not prevent him from having to walk with a cane after that. Mel lived in the Stand Up Records released Mel's latest collection of songs with Oklahoma Wind, *Reloaded*, which celebrated 30 notable years in the country music industry. That same year, CMG Signature Series released a new album, *Cattle Bandits Bailey*. In 2006, Mel McDaniel was inducted into the Oklahoma Music Hall of Fame. After battling multiple health problems toward the end of his life (he had a heart attack in 2009), he finally succumbed to lung cancer in 2011.

McEntire, Del Stanley "Pake"
(b. June 23, 1958)

With a pleasing tenor and friendly cowboy demeanor deriving from his authentic rodeo background, Pake McEntire rode a 1986 RCA Records deal to seven singles hitting the *Billboard* Hot Country Songs chart between 1986 and 1988, three of which were in the Top 20. The biggest single, "Savin' My Love for You", made it to #3 on that chart, and its parent album, *Too Old to Grow Up*, reached #52 on the *Billboard* Country Album chart in 1987. Born in McAlester, he began singing while traveling in the car to rodeos with his dad, Clark. To keep Pake and his sisters, Alice, Reba, and Susie, from fussing and fighting while traveling the rodeo circuit, their mother, Jac, taught them to sing three and four part harmony in the back seat of their car.

Later in high school, Jac, who was the secretary for Kiowa High School, got together with teacher, singer, guitar, and fiddle player, Clark Rhyne, and approached the school's superintendent, Harold Toaz, about forming a school band. At that time, all three decided the school needed a country band class with the participating students receiving one credit. That was the beginning of the Kiowa Cowboy School Band of which six of the nine students are still making their living either totally or partially by playing and singing today. The class would play for country music events of all kinds for the school and the students would even borrow the instruments to go play gigs on weekends.

Clark Rhyne, who taught the class, wrote a song about Pake's grandfather, John

McEntire. On November 19, 1970, Clark took Pake, Susie and Reba to Oklahoma City where they recorded their first record, "The Ballad of John McEntire", which sold seventeen copies, and tapered off.

After graduation in 1971, Pake ran steers in Atoka and Pittsburg Counties in Oklahoma, roped in a bunch of rodeos, and continued to play music. Pake recorded his first album, a cassette-only release, *The Rodeo Man*, in 1980, and after competing at rodeos, Pake walked through the grand stands pedaling his music to the crowd like a hot dog vendor. Another cassette followed with sister Susie in 1983, the quality of which was good enough to land Pake an RCA contract for two albums, *Too Old to Grow Up* (1986), and *My Whole World* (1988). This period provided Pake his primary chart action on the *Billboard* Hot Country Songs chart, to include the singles "Every Night" (#20) and "Savin' My Love for You" (#3) in 1986; "Bad Love" (#12), "Heart vs. Heart" (#25), "Too Old to Grow Up" (#46), and "Good God I Had It Good" (#29), and "Life in the City (#62). As a result of his chart presence, Pake secured opening act slots for George Strait, sister Reba, Sawyer Brown, Alabama, The Judds, Eddy Raven, Keith Whitley, and Ronnie Milsap. After the second RCA album did not register on the charts, and its final single just barely blipped onto the Hot Country Songs chart, his contract was not renewed. After leaving RCA, Pake continued performing, ranching in Oklahoma, and raising his daughters, Autumn, Calamity, and Chism.

Pake McEntire

Released independently Pake's fourth album, *And The Danced* (2003), featured the title track co-written by Pake's daughter, Autumn. Since then, he has released three more independent albums, *Your Favorites and Mine* (2005), *Singin' Fiddlin' Cowboy* (2007), and *The Other Side of Me* (2008). He has made numerous television appearances on *Hee Haw*, *Nashville Now* and A&E's *Biography*. As of 2011, Pake performs throughout the Midwest at rodeos, fairs, dances, stage shows, and festivals of all kinds. He performs not only his own hits, but also features classic country songs, fiddle tunes, and other traditional country music that he says is "easy to understand".

www.pakemcentireband.com

McEntire, Reba
(b. March 28, 1955)

Calling Reba McEntire a superstar is not an exaggeration. She is the biggest-selling female country singer of all-time, having sold over fifty-five million albums. She has also had thirty-three *Billboard* #1 country songs, and overall has been on the *Billboard* country music charts from 1976 through 2011. Along with her long list of singing successes on recordings and in concert, she is an award-winning actress for her work on Broadway (*Annie Get Your Gun*, 2001, and *South Pacific*, 2005), starred in a popular television series, *Reba*, from 2001 through 2007, and has acted in eleven Hollywood films. A veteran producer who knows what she wants for her fans on albums, she is also a successful author, having published an autobiography, *Reba* (Bantam, 1995), and a personal memoir, *Comfort from a Country Quilt* (Bantam, 2000). With a brassy demeanor partially derived from independent ranch life and the individual confidence necessary for rodeo competition, her bigger than life voice that can growl, soar, or sob, and true-to-life Oklahoma country accent, Reba is one of a few popular music artists often recognized by just her first name. Reba Nell McEntire was born and raised on a 7,000 acre ranch near Chockie, Oklahoma, a tiny hamlet of approximately twenty residents, northeast of Atoka in the southeastern section of Oklahoma known as "Little Dixie" because of its Southern cultural traditions, including food, religion, and music. Her mother (Jacqueline, or "Jac") was an elementary schoolteacher, school secretary, and a gifted singer, who had her own dreams of a career as a country singer. Her father (Clark) was a rancher and champion rodeo steer roper (three time world champion), and her grandfather (John) was also an award winning rodeo steer roper. Her father's rodeo experience later influenced Reba to participate in rodeo competitions as a horseback barrel rider during which she started at age eleven and competed until she was twenty-one. Growing up on cattle ranch, Reba could brand a steer, castrate a calf, or vaccinate a cow. Her siblings consisted of Alice, an older sister; Del Stanley, or "Pake," an older brother who enjoyed country music chart success in the mid-1980s; and Martha Susan, "Susie," a younger sister, who eventually developed a stellar career in the field of contemporary country music. Two of Reba's earliest public performances were in the first grade when she sang "Away in a Manger" for a Christmas program, and at age seven when she sang "He" for the Kiowa High School commencement. One of her first honors was in the fifth grade when she won a trophy in a local 4-H talent show singing "My Sweet Little Alice Blue Gown". She also sang at the Kiowa Baptist Church after joining at age twelve. During her high school days at Kiowa High School (Kiowa is located northeast of Chockie and southwest of McAlester on U.S. Highway 69), Reba was a member of the Kiowa High School Cowboy Band led by Clark Rhyne, one of her teachers. While in high school, Reba, brother Pake, and sister Susie formed "The Singing McEntires." The trio was often booked into rodeos, clubs, and community centers by their mother. In 1971, the group recorded "The Ballad of John McEntire"; a song dedicated to their grandfather and distributed on a local label, Boss. Reba eventually included it on one of her albums.

In making future plans, Reba thought of following her mother in the teaching profession and enrolled as an elementary education major and music minor at Southeastern Oklahoma State University in Durant. While in college she was a member of a singing group known as the Chorvettes. During her college career, Reba was invited by rodeo announcer and Oklahoma politician Clem McSpadden to sing the national anthem at the National Finals Rodeo in Oklahoma City in 1974, televised on ABC's *Wide World of Sports*. Red Steagall, veteran cowboy and western music star, heard her sing the anthem and invited her to appear with him at a rodeo event for Justin Boots. Reba accepted the invitation and also did her rendition of Dolly

Reba McEntire

Parton's "Joshua". Steagall was impressed and arranged for McEntire to make a demo record in Nashville. First rejected by ABC Records because they did not need another girl singer, assistance from Steagall Reba signed with Mercury Records in 1975. Her first recording session was the 1950s song, "Invitation to the Blues", co-penned by **Roger Miller** and Ray Price.

Reba recorded her first chart song in 1976, "I Don't Want to Be a One Night Stand", which barely cracked the Top 100. The same year, she married Charlie Battles, a three time world steer wrestling champion and bulldogger ten years her senior, who gave up his rodeo career to help manage Reba's career. After their marriage, Reba and Charlie remained in Oklahoma where they operated a cattle business on a 225-acre ranch. After releasing three more unsuccessful singles, none of which charted in the Top 40, Reba completed her teaching degree, in case her musical career floundered. But in 1977, Reba cut her first album for Mercury, a self-titled release, which included the Miller/Price composition, "Invitation to the Blues", however, none of the tracks from this first album made much headway. She toured with Steagall's band in 1977, and made a guest appearance on the Grand Ole Opry, where she performed Patsy Cline's "Sweet Dream". Her recording of the Cline hit rose to #19 on the *Billboard* Hot Country Song charts.

In 1978 Reba cut a double-sided duet with Jacky Ward ("Three Sheets in the Wind"/"I'd Really Love to See You Tonight") that also entered the Top 20 on the country charts. Her second album for Mercury, *Out of a Dream*, released in 1979 produced five singles that cracked the country Top 40 charts, including "Last Night, Ev'ry Night", "Sweet Dreams", "(I Still Long to Hold You) Now and Then", "That Makes Two of Us" (another duet with Jacky Ward), and "Runaway Heart", perhaps the best of the songs.

McEntire's third Mercury album, *Feel the Fire*, released in 1980, spawned her first Top 10 hit, "(You Lift Me) Up to Heaven", reaching #8 on *Billboard*'s Hot Country Songs chart country charts, and remained on the charts for fifteen weeks. The album also yielded "I Can See Forever in Your Eyes" (Top 20) and "I Don't Think Love Ought to Be That Way" (Top 15). In 1981, she recorded her fourth album with Mercury, *Heart to Heart*, however, it failed to produce any notable singles. In 1982 Reba released her most successful album to that point—*Unlimited*. Beginning her stratospheric star ride, *Unlimited* included her first #1 single, "Can't Even Get the Blues" and a second #1 single, "You're the First Time I've Thought About Leaving". In addition, it spawned a #3 hit, "I'm Not That Lonely Yet". Her last Mercury album in 1983 was *Behind the Scene*, which produced "Why Do We Want (What We Know We Can't Have)", which cracked the Top 10, and "There Ain't No Future in This," which charted in the Top 15. For these successes, she received the CMA Horizon Award in 1983, and was a nominee for Female Vocalist of the Year.

One of the momentous occasions in Reba's career took place in 1980 when she added former Prudential insurance agent and steel guitar player Narvel Blackstock to her band. Shortly thereafter, Narvel became her bandleader and important adviser, and then progressed to become her road manager, tour manager, full manager (1988), and second husband in 1989 following the divorce from Charlie in 1987, when they split and she moved permanently to Nashville, a sequence which gives extra resonance to her selection of songs to record throughout the remainder of her career. In 1990, Reba gave birth to Shelby Steven McEntire Blackstock, who eventually became part of the family business, partnering with Narvel in their management company, Starstruck Entertainment.

In 1983, Reba decided to switch labels, leaving Mercury after seven albums to sign with MCA. During this change, Reba began to take more charge of her career, making significant decisions about its direction. In a step to broaden her audience and gain long-term visibility, she began appearing on the new cable television channel, *The Nashville Network*. During 1983, she made four appearances on the channel's live show, *Nashville Now*, hosted by Ralph Emery, WSM radio personality. These moves resulted in establishing herself as one of the decade's most popular artists, selling more than twenty million albums, winning four Female Vocalist of the Year awards from the CMA (1984-87), and five Female Vocalist of the Year awards from the ACM (1985-87 and 1990-91). Between 1985 and 1992, she had twenty-four straight Top 10 hits, including fourteen #1 singles. During this period, Reba was named *Music City News* Female Artist of the Year for the years 1985 through 1989, was acknowledged by *Rolling Stone* Critic's Choice Poll as one of the Top Five Country Artists, and received CMA's Entertainer of the Year Award for 1986, only the fourth female singer, after Loretta Lynn, Dolly Parton, and Barbara Mandrell, to win this highly coveted award. She also was nominated for the CMA's Entertainer of the Year (1985, 1987-89), Albums of the Year (*My Kind of Country*-1985), (*Whoever's in New England*-1986), and (*What Am I Gonna Do About You*-1987), Music Videos of the Year ("Whoever's in New England-1986) and ("What Am I Gonna Do About You"-1987), and Single of the Year ("Whoever's in New England"-1986). Finally, after making her debut on the Grand Ole Opry in 1977, she became a permanent cast member in 1986. The announcement was made on *Nashville Now*—the first artist to join the Grand Ole Opry during a televised broadcast. To complete the year, she made her first appearance at Carnegie Hall.

Reba's debut album with MCA, *My Kind of Country*, was released in 1984, and produced two #1 hits, "How Blue" and "Somebody Should Leave". The album eventually earned Reba's first gold record award from the Recording Industry Association of America (RIAA). The mid-1980s saw Reba release of string of noteworthy albums, including *Have I Got a Deal for You* (1985), *Reba Nell McEntire* (1986), *Whoever's in New England* (1986), *What Am I Gonna Do About You* (1986), *Reba McEntire's Greatest Hits* (1987), *The Last One to Know* (1987), and *Merry Christmas To You* (1987). The most successful of these was *Whoever's in New England*, which yielded two #1 hits, "Little Rock" and the title track, as well as *Music City News* and ACM's Video of the Year and a Grammy for Best Country Vocal Performance Female in 1987. "Whoever's in New England," Reba's first video, was filmed in Boston and premiered on the network television show *Entertainment Tonight*. As one of the most influential country collections of the 1980s, *Whoever's in New England* quickly reached platinum status and her *Greatest Hits* album eventually achieved triple platinum honors. *Have I Got a Deal for You* and *What Am I Gonna Do About You* scored as gold albums, and the latter's title track reached #1 on the country charts. *The Last One to Know* album was recorded during the divorce proceedings from Charlie Battles, and is understandably strong on songs about breakups and marital problems. The title track of the album charted at #1 in 1987 as did "Love Will Find Its Way to You" in 1988. The success of the album also indicated future song choices by Reba in which she would often record songs that spoke to the real issues impacting women, a decision which endeared her to fans.

Reba closed out the 1980s with three more hit albums she helped produce: *Reba* (1988), *Sweet Sixteen* (1989), and *Reba Live!* (1989). The *Reba Live!* collection features nineteen of her biggest hits and best known songs, including the single releases "Let the Music (Lift You Up)" (#3), "Sunday Kind of Love" (#5), "I Know How He Feels" (#1), "One Promise Too Late" (#1), and "New Fool at an Old Game" (#1). *Sweet Sixteen*, her sixteenth album, went to the top of the country album chart, where it stayed for thirteen weeks, and the single from the album "Cathy's Clown", Reba's rendition of an Everly Brothers song, reached #1 in 1989. The 1988 Reba album eventually reached platinum level in sales. More honors came Reba's way in the late 1980s in the form of American Music Awards Favorite Female Country Artist (1988/89), TNN Viewer's Choice Favorite Female Vocalist (1988/89), Gallup 1988 Youth Survey selection among the Top 10 Female Vocalists, and *People* magazine inclusion in the Top 3 Female Vocalists.

McEntire began the 1990s with another hit album, *Rumor Has It*, released in 1990, and it eventually reached triple platinum sales. Singles from the album included "Rumor Has It" (Top 5), "Fallin' Out of Love" (Top 3), and "You Lie" (#1). The CMA nominations for 1991 included Entertainer, Female Vocalist, Music Video ("Fancy"), and Album (*Rumor Has It*).

Reba McEntire, circa 1985

Reba has also experienced extreme personal/professional tragedy on what she says was the hardest day of her life when seven members of her band, her road manager, and the pilot and co-pilot of a chartered private jet were killed in a 1971 accident when the plane hit a mountainside during takeoff. Reba, Narvel, and two other band members were booked on other flights. Her 1991 album, *For My Broken Heart*, reflected some of the sorrow and sympathy for this tragic loss. The album quickly reached sales of more than two million, and eventually went quadruple platinum. "If I Had Only Known", a moving tribute to the deceased band members, provided a #1 single. Additional singles from the album that charted well included "Is There Life Out There" (#1) and "The Greatest Man I Ever Knew" (#1), a tribute to her father, who still actively ran his Oklahoma ranch in his mid-sixties. Reba's 1992 album, *It's Your Call*, eventually reached triple platinum sales, and produced two #1 hits, including "The Heart Won't Lie," a duet with label mate and fellow Oklahoman **Vince Gill**, and the title track. Reba had previously recorded a Top 15 single with Vince entitled "Oklahoma Swing," released in 1990. Her 1993 compilation of *Greatest Hits, Volume 2* reached triple platinum status, and spawned two new cuts, one of them a duet with Linda Davis, long time backup singer for Reba, "Does He Love You", which became a #1 hit. Reba was honored once again in 1992 with the *Music City News* Award for Female Artist of the Year and *People*'s Choice Award for Favorite Female Country Music Performer, a feat she would achieve for the years 1993 through 1998. Her CMA nominations for 1992 included Entertainer, Female Vocalist, Music Video ("Is There Life Out There"), and Album (*For My Broke Heart*). Her duet with Davis from the *Greatest Hits, Volume 2* album was named CMA Vocal Event of the Year in 1994, and received a 1994 Grammy for Best Country Vocal Collaboration.

In 1994, Reba released her twenty-second album, *Read My Mind*, which reached triple platinum sales, and another 1994 album, *Oklahoma Girl*, which included many of earlier singles, such as "I Don't Want to Be a One Night Stand", her first recording, "Invitation to the Blues", and "Runaway Heart". But it was her 1995 release, *Starting Over*, which cemented her 1990s mega-stardom. It peaked at #1 on the *Billboard* country chart and #5 on the pop list. It provided such singles as "On My Own," recorded with Trisha Yearwood, Martina McBride, and Linda Davis; "Ring on My Finger, Time on Her Hands," "You Keep Me Hanging On," and "By the Time I Get to Phoenix," Reba's version of native Oklahoman **Jimmy Webb**'s composition. Reba's next collection, *What If It's You*, was released in 1996, and contained such singles as "The Fear of Being Alone", "She's Calling it Love", and "I'd Rather Ride Around With You", and achieved double platinum sales. Her 1998 album, *Out of a Dream*, featured one of her own compositions, "Daddy," another tribute to her father. A second 1998 release, *If You See Him*, featured a duet with Brooks & **Dunn**, "If You See Him/If You See Her", another #1 hit *Billboard*'s country charts. Reba co-produced this album with Tony Brown, her long time producer, and native Oklahoman **Tim DuBois**. The album was supported by Reba's tour with Kix Brooks & Ronnie Dunn in 1998, which was the highest grossing tour in the history of country music at that time. Also in 1998, she received a star on the Hollywood Walk of Fame. The 1999 release, *So Good Together*, co-produced by Reba and Tony Brown, was acclaimed as her best album since *Starting Over*. It explored one of the consistent themes of country music, and many of Reba's most successful songs, interpersonal relationships, on songs like "We're So Good Together", "What Do You Say", "Where You End and I Begin", "She Wasn't Good Enough for Him". and "Nobody Dies from a Broken Heart".

2001 marked twenty-seven years since Reba was first discovered singing the national anthem in Oklahoma City. Appropriately, Reba released her twenty-seventh album, *Greatest Hits III-I'm a Survivor*. It included fifteen tracks supported by Alison Krauss vocals, and co-produced by Tony Brown, Tim DuBois, and Reba. The title track single, "I'm a Survivor" was one of the top country hits in 2002. She also organized a 2001 24-city tour of "Girls' Night Out", the first all female country tour, starring Reba, Martina McBride, Sara Evans, Jamie O'Neal, and Carolyn Dawn Johnson. Reba took Broadway by storm in 2001 with a six-month run as Annie Oakley in the revival of Irving Berlin's *Annie Get Your Gun*, for which she received both a Drama Desk Award and Outer Critics Award. In 2001, she partnered with WB-TV, and took on her first television sitcom, *Reba*, which focuses on the character Reba Hart and her trials and tribulations as a Texas "soccer mom." Fans elevated the program to a #1 position in her time slot for women 18-34. As a result, the half-hour show remained in production with Reba until 2007. The title track and first single from her *Greatest Hits, Volume III-I'm A Survivor* became the show's theme song. Finally, the *I'll Be* album was released in May of 2001. Co-produced by Reba and Jimmy Bowen, the fifteen tracks include the Lennon-McCartney composition, "If I Fell", and several old favorites such as "Starting Over Again", "Please Come to Boston", and "What Do You Say."

Called country music's "first video superstar", Reba ranked #6 on the CMT "Forty Greatest Women in Country Music" special aired in the summer of 2002. During the program, Carolyn Dawn Johnson, Lee Ann Womack, Trisha Yearwood, Sara Evans, Terri Clark, and Shania Twain all paid tribute to Reba as one of their major influences. In 2003, she received the Country Radio Broadcasters' Career Achievement Award, and hosted the Academy of Country Music Awards where the ACM bestowed upon her the title of Leading Lady of the Academy of Country Music in honor of her all-time leading wins in the Top Female Vocalist category. Also, two of her songs, "Fancy" and "Is There Life Out There," were included on CMT's 100 Greatest Songs of Country Music at #27 and #79, respectively. Also in 2002, she received the People's Choice Award for Favorite Female

Actress in a New Television Series for *Reba*. Her 2003 disc, *Room to Breathe*, which she co-produced, also went platinum (one million units sold), continued to show her crossover appeal by charting at #25 on *Billboard*'s Top 200 Album Chart, reached #3 on the *Billboard*'s Top Country Albums, and sported yet another #1 *Billboard* Hot Country Song, "Somebody", a top ten country single, "He Gets That From Me" (#7), and two more solid charting singles, "My Sister" (#16) and "I'm Gonna Take That Mountain" (#14).

With her television show taking up a lot of time, not to mention the introduction of her fashion line in 2005, MCA released two more greatest hits collections, one of which, 2005's compilation of #1 hits, *#1's*, achieved double platinum status. In 2007, MCA Nashville released a collection of duets between Reba and some of country and popular music's biggest vocal stars (LeAnn Rimes, Justin Timberlake, Vince Gill, Don Henley, Faith Hill, et.al). Her collaboration with *American Idol* winner, Kelly Clarkson, "Because of You", reached #2 on *Billboard*'s Hot Country Songs chart, and the duet with Kenny Chesney, "Every Other Weekend", notched a #15 slot on the same list. Overall, *Duets* was million-plus seller (platinum), smacking around the #1 slot on *Billboard*'s Top 200 Album chart and *Billboard* Top Country Album Chart, and also made it to the #4 slot on *Billboard*'s Top Canadian Album chart. After another Greatest Hits album in 2008, Reba signed with Valory Music (perhaps explaining the spate of best of collections prior to 2008). In the interim, she scored a #2 hit on the *Billboard* Hot Country Songs chart with "Cowgirls Don't Cry", a duet with Brooks and Dunn, and then released perhaps her most complete thematic album to date, *Keep on Loving You* (2009), a strong collection of songs directly related to meditating on her twenty-year marriage to Narvel at that point, and her first solo album since 2003. Quite possibly her most dramatic, heartfelt, and powerful collection of songs ever, the album featured "Consider Me Gone" which stayed at the #1 position on the Hot Country Songs chart for four weeks to begin 2010. The album debuted at the #1 position on the *Billboard* Top 200 Album chart where it stayed for two consecutive weeks, and slam dunked the #1 slot on *Billboard* Top Country Albums chart. The album also topped the Canadian Country Albums chart, and climbed #4 on the Canadian Albums chart.

A musical trend noticeable on the disc was the inclusion of a slightly more rock tone on guitar solos ("Strange" and "Pink Guitar"), perhaps reflecting that element that has been more and more prominent on Nashville studio albums over the last several years. Not to say there aren't plenty of steel guitars, fiddles, and cowboy songs on *Keep On Loving You*, but one can certainly hear trends in country music production by listening to one of country music's biggest stars. Either way, the album's songs were selected carefully to reflect the cycle of a relationship's ups ("I Keep on Loving You"), downs ("But Why"), endings ("Consider Me Gone"), sad reflections ("She's Turning 50 Today") and new beginnings ("I Want a Cowboy" and "I'll Have What She's Having). The rock and R&B tone of Reba's newest music continued with her 2010 album, *All The Women I Am*, which features another #1 single, "Turn on the Radio", allowing Reba to begin and end 2010 at the top of the charts. The album also is existentialist in nature from the point of view of examining the multiple aspects of life that go into making up one personality, symbolically depicting either Reba with all of her incarnations, or any listener who has multiple responsibilities life. Often, Rebe tells her song stories through a woman's point of view, such as experiencing the mundane aspects of life that often contextualize what seem like major moments at the time ("The Day She Got Divorced"), or when she also commits "If I Were a Boy" to her permanent catalogue on the album. Originally a hit for R&B star Beyonce, the song was received enthusiastically by Reba's fans when she covered it for a 2010 taping of *CMT Unplugged*. Songs about being a mom ("When You Have a Child"), when a woman says goodbye to a lover ("The Bridge You Burn"), and the desire to be someone's one and only ("Somebody's Chelsea") are also poignant songs on the album.

Throughout the first decade of the twenty-first century, Reba received multiple awards for both her contemporary status and her career achievements. In 2003, she received the Country Radio Broadcasters Career Achievement Award. In 2004, she was named AMA's Favorite Female Country Artist, and accepted the Prisim Award for Performance in a Comedy Series. In 2005, she was awarded an ACM Special Award for Most Female Vocalist Wins, and named Family Television's Top Actress. In 2007, she was named *Billboard* magazine's Woman of the Year, and in 2008 ASCAP presented her their Golden Note Award and Silver Circle Award. Also in 2009, with the success of *Keep On Loving You*, she became the sole record holder of the most #1 albums on the country chart for a female in the Soundscan era (since 1991), surpassing Loretta Lynn with whom she had been tied at 10. Of most significance in 2009, Reba was officially recognized by *Billboard*, Mediabase, and Country Aircheck as the biggest female hit-maker in country music history. In 2010, she received the National Artistic Achievement Award, and in 2011 was inducted into Nashville's Country Music Hall of Fame, alongside another Oklahoma country music legend, *Jean Shepard*.

One of Reba's greatest accomplishments as a business person is the building of Starstruck Entertainment in 1988, a conglomerate that contains her own booking, management, publishing company, transportation (jet charter service), and recording services. It is housed in a luxurious, 29,000 square foot office building on Music Row and includes a state-of-the-art music and broadcasting facility. As of 2011, Reba lived outside Nashville with her husband, Narvel, in a Civil War-era home. Their property is a large working ranch as Reba is still an avid horse breeder and trainer. Their son, Shelby, not only is working partner in Starstruck Entertainment, he has also begun racing cars at the professional level.

Blessed with so much success, she has also been extremely philanthropic. She has recorded a song specifically to benefit the Salvation Army, "What If", and has been active both behind the scenes and on stage for various causes. She has raised money through benefit concerts for the Texoma Medical Center in Denison, Texas, sponsored homes in the Nashville area for Habitat for Humanity, and hosted the Ben Johnson Celebrity Rodeo to raise money for Children's Hospital in Oklahoma City. Her own "Wrap a Little Love" program buys coats, clothing, and food for those in need, and receives support from the public through her fan club. She returned to Oklahoma in May, 2011, to Atoka Country where she teamed with another local country music success story, **Blake Shelton**, to perform two sold-out tornado-relief concerts for victims of the April 14, 2011, EF3 tornado that blasted tiny Tushka, Oklahoma. The concerts raised more than $500,000 to bring to the storm-stricken community in which two women were killed, more than forty were injured, and 150 homes, businesses, and public buildings, including the local school, were destroyed. Lyrics from the title track of *All the Women I Am* easily sum up her feelings about her home state: "I'm a daughter of the red dirt; Okie dust still in my bones." Not even an EF3 tornado can blow that away.

www.reba.com

McEntire, Susie
(b. November 8, 1957)

Winner of several awards in the 1990s from the Country Gospel Music Association and the Christian Country Music Association, and popular singer of contemporary Christian country music, who is also well-liked for her inspirational messages during concerts and performances, Martha Susan "Susie" McEntire was born in McAlester, Oklahoma, but

Susie McEntire, 2008

raised on a ranch near Chockie, some thirty miles south of McAlester and fifteen miles north of Atoka. The younger sister of country music megastar **Reba McEntire**, she was born to Clark Vincent and Jacqueline Smith McEntire. She has an older brother, Del Stanley, or "**Pake**," and another older sister, Alice Lynn Foran. Her father was a professional rodeo rider and rancher who taught the siblings how to ride, and her mother taught them music. Susie's Her first public performance was at a second grade Thanksgiving program. After forming the Singing McEntires, largely to get out of farm and ranch work, Susie, Reba, and Pake first performed as The Singing McEntires in Kiowa, Oklahoma. The band that also included Alan Jackson's long-time bass player, Roger Wills, who had just started playing bass, and the group recorded a song in 1971 entitled "The Ballad of John McEntire", a tribute to their grandfather. After graduating Kiowa High School, Susie headed to the farm-kid friendly Stillwater and received a bachelor's degree in personnel management (accounting minor) in 1980 from Oklahoma State University, and began work at J. D. Simmons in Oklahoma City.

With an expressive voice both distinctive and yet reminiscent of her famous sister's vocal imprint, Susie toured behind Reba as a back-up vocalist, appearing on Reba's 1981 album *Heart to Heart* and its 1982 follow-up *Unlimited*. During this time, she met Paul Luchsinger, a champion steer wrestler, and they were married in 1981, a marriage that was to be filled with challenges that ultimately could not be overcome, and they were divorced in 2008. After their marriage, Paul continued on the rodeo circuit, and she continued her touring with Reba, a situation that became untenable because of tensions within the marriage. After the birth of their first child, she stopped working for Reba and began singing with her brother, Pake, but that also presented problems for the marriage and she started traveling with Paul on the rodeo circuit. In 1984, she was invited to sing for the Cowboy Christian Fellowship at the National Finals Rodeo. Because her music was so well received by the group, Susie decided to launch a solo career based on both country music and contemporary Christian music, and released her debut album, *No Limit* (1985), produced by Psalms Ministries, an organization founded by Susie and Paul, which focused on ministering to rodeo people.[1] Unfortunately, as she shares in her modern testimonies, what people did not know was that a cycle of mental, verbal, and physical abuse had begun to take shape in their marriage by that point. In 1986, a second album was recorded, and for the next ten years, she would record an album per year. Based on these recordings, she was named Female Vocalist of the Year and Video of the Year for "So It Goes (With Everything But Love)" by the International Country Gospel Association and Country Gospel Artist of the Year by *Gospel Voice Magazine* Reader's Award. Her eighth album in 1993, *Real Love*, on the Integrity label, produced four #1 hits on the Positive Country charts, including "There is a Candle," "For Pete's Sake", "I Don't Love You Like I Used To", a duet with her husband Paul, and "I Saw Him in Your Eyes". As a result, Susie captured more honors in 1993 with Entertainer of the Year from the International Country GMA, Christian Country Female Artist of the Year from *Cashbox Magazine*, and Favorite Female Artist of the Year and Favorite Album of the also successful in reaching the #1 spot on the Positive Country charts with three singles, including "Two in the Saddle", "Take It to the Rock", and "You're It". In 1994, she garnered top honors as Female Vocalist of the Year and received the Vanguard Award from the Christian CMA, Christian Country Artist of the Year and Performance Excellence Album of the Year from *Gospel Voice* magazine, and was nominated for New Artist of the Year, Country Song of the Year, and Country Album of the Year for the GMA Dove Awards, and Christian Country Artist of the Year by *TNN/Music City News*. In 1995, she was given the *Gospel Voice* Diamond Award as Christian Country Artist of the Year and captured Female Vocalist of the Year from the Christian CMA, as well as nominations for Country Song of the Year ("For Pete's Sake') for the GMA Dove Award and Christian Country Artist of the Year by the *TNN/Music City News*. The next year, she was honored with another Diamond Award as Christian Country Artist of the Year, and was nominated for Christian Country Album of the Year (*Come As You Are*) for the GMA Dove Award, and Christian Country Artist of the Year by *TNN/Music City News*.

A Tender Road Home was released in 1997 on the New Haven label, and the single from the album, "Holy Heart", reached #1 on the Christian Country charts. In 1997, she was nominated as Christian Country Artist of the Year for the *TNN/Music City News* Award, and the next year received a nomination for Christian Country Artist of the Year for the GMA Dove Award. In 1999, Susie released the *Raised on Faith* album, which yielded two important singles, "My Kind of People", a #1 hit on the Christian Country charts, and "You Are the One", a #1 hit on the European Country Gospel charts. She was nominated for three more awards in 1999: Female Vocalist of the Year and Pioneer Award from the Christian CMA, and Christian Country Recorded Song of the Year ("Whispers in My Heart") by the GMA. Susie's 2001 album, *My Gospel Hymnal*, was nominated as Christian Country Album of the Year for the GMA Dove Award, and in 2003 she released *You've Got a Friend*, a thirteen-song album of contemporary Christian music and pop classics such as Bill Withers' "Lean On Me", James Taylor's "How Sweet It Is", and Carole King's "You've Got a Friend". Since then, she has four more albums *Count It All Joy* (New Haven, 2005), and *Let Go* (SLM, 2008), a title that hinted at the fact her divorce was finalized in May, 2008. In September of that year she began touring again, and sharing her faith, music, and the story of both her unhappy, abusive marriage, and how she has lived with the skin disease, psoriasis, since she was sixteen. She recorded a holiday album in 2009, *I'll Be Home for Christmas*, (SLM), and in December, 2009 married Mark Eaton, a professional fitness trainer and inspirational speaker. In 2010, she released another contemporary Christian country album, *Passages* (SM), and by 2011 had completely revamped her website to reflect her desire to emphasize "Susie" more than the powerful McEntire brand, although anyone who knows anything about her knows that she is Reba's sister. Legally speaking, she is Susie McEntire-Eaton. Susie continues her Psalms Ministries, and co-hosts *Cowboy Church* weekly on Rural TV, available through satellite television services. Her website reflects her personal ethos: "The music is country, the message is Christ." In a September, 2008 issue of *PowerSource* magazine, an industry trade magazine for Contemporary Christian Music radio stations, she wrote, "People are drawn to Christian Country music for much the same reason they are drawn to Country – true life stories. Today it's harder to draw a line between the two because they borrow from one another. Christian Country is palatable to people who may not believe; it stirs a yearning to learn more and gives them comfort." Able to share her powerful story of personal adversity that has ended positively with her current status as an extremely popular Christian speaker and musical performer whose songs really chronicle what has happened in her life, Susie was booked solidly through 2012 at a variety of faith-related events across the country.

www.susiemcentire.com

Notes
1. More details of the troubles Susie McEntire had within her marriage can be found in Victoria Lee's essay in *Distinguished Oklahomans* (Tulsa: A Touch of Heart, 2002), 172-174.

McGhee, Howard B. "Maggie"
(b. March 6, 1918 - d. July 17, 1987)

Known for his fast-fingered scales in the manner of other bebop players, such as Charlie Parker whom he admired, and the ability to hit the highest of notes on the trumpet with equal facility, Howard McGhee was one of the most talented instrumentalists, composers, arrangers, and bandleaders in jazz from the 1940s through his death in the 1980s in New York City. Born in Tulsa, his family moved to Detroit in 1921 when Howard was about three years old. Although his father was a physician, Howard learned the basics of music from his half-brother who played the guitar. In Detroit he attended Cass Technical High School, where he learned several instruments, including clarinet, piano, tenor saxophone, and trumpet, the latter being his final instrument of choice at age sixteen, after hearing Louis Armstrong and Roy Eldridge.

Howard McGhee performs in Rochester, New York, 1976.

At age sixteen, Howard quit high school and headed for the West Coast. After joining Lionel Hampton's band in 1941, he then became principal soloist for two years with Andy Kirk during which he was known for his "McGhee Special" solos. After Kirk, he joined Charlie Barnet (1942-43), returned to Kirk where he sat next to Fats Navarro in the trumpet section. Thereafter, he had brief stints with Georgie Auld and Count Basie, before moving to California with Coleman Hawkins in 1945. During the next two years on the West Coast, he recorded several swing-to-bop transitional numbers with Hawkins, such as "Stuffy", "Rifftide", and "Hollywood Stampede", and recorded "How High the Moon" with Jazz at the Philharmonic. He also recorded with Charlie Parker, including the famous *Lover Man* and *Relaxin' at Camarillo* sessions, the latter included fellow Oklahomans **Barney Kessel**, **Wardell Gray**, and **Don Lamond**.[1]

As one of the pioneers in the bebop movement in the early 1940s, McGhee performed at jam sessions at Minton's Playhouse and Monroe's Uptown House on 42nd Street in New York City. By the end of the 1940s, he was one of the most highly respected musicians in the bebop movement and was named Best Trumpet Player by the *Down Beat* poll in 1949. McGhee's late 1940s albums with such labels as Dial, Savoy, and Blue Note are among his best, including *Howard McGhee Sextet* (1947), *Maggie*, backed by vibraphonist Milt Jackson and trombonist J. J. Johnson (1948), and *Howard McGhee's All Stars* (1948).

Although relatively inactive during the 1950s due to substance abuse issues, he did complete a U.S.O. tour during the Korean War, and had recorded three albums on the

Bethlehem label, including *The Return of Howard McGhee*, which featured five of his own compositions, "Tweedles", "Oo-Wee But I Do", "Transpicious", "Tahitian Lullaby", and You're Teasing Me".

During his career, McGhee worked as an arranger for such notables as Billy Eckstine, Woody Herman, and Charlie Barnet. His most notable compositions include "McGhee Special", "Night Mist", "Midnight at Mintons", "Dorothy" and "Carvin' the Bird". Many of these compositions were recorded by the likes of Charlie Barnet, Wardell Gray, Freddie Hubbard, and Fats Navarro. He also appeared on sessions as trumpeter with such jazz artists as Gene Ammons, Kenny Clarke, Sonny Criss, and Miles Davis. McGhee's comeback in the 1960s and 1970s included formation of his own big band and recording dates with the Steeple Chase, Jazzcraft, Zim, Bethlehem, Contemporary, Black Lion, and Storyville labels. The latter label provided the last two recording sessions for Howard, including *Home Run* (1978) and *Wise in Time* (1979). *Home Run* included two of his compositions, "Get It On" and "Jonas", while *Wise In Time* contained a track by fellow native-born Oklahoman, **Oscar Pettiford**, "Blues in the Closet".

His final activities included touring Europe and Japan with George Wein, performing with Duke Ellington, and participating in jazz services at St. Peter's Lutheran Church in New York City, where he taught lessons both in classrooms and in his Manhattan apartment. He died in New York City in 1987. The Oklahoma Jazz Hall of Fame inducted McGhee in 2003. By 2011, many of McGhee's primary recordings had been re-mastered and made available as physical compact disc copies or as digital downloads.

Note
1. While many online databases exist that detail McGhee's career, and excellent biographical essay, bibliography, and list of selected recordings exists in Scott DeVeaux's essay, "Howard B. McGhee", *The New Grove Dictionary of Jazz*, ed. Barry Kerfeld, (New York: MacMillan, 1994), 731.

McGuire, Barry
(b. October 15, 1935)

Composer or co-composer of three of the biggest hits in the 1960s, "Greenback Dollar," "Green, Green" and "Eve of Destruction," as well as the gravelly-voiced lead singer with the New Christy Minstrels in their heyday, singer and songwriter Barry McGuire was born in Oklahoma City. According to his website, his parents were divorced when he was two-years-old, at which time he moved to California with his mother. He joined the U.S. Navy at age sixteen, but was discharged when the Navy found out his true age. Prior to his vocal and songwriting career, Barry was a minor actor in the television series *Route 66*. His first venture into professional singing came with Barry Kane in an act known as Barry and Barry.

In 1962 both Barry Kane and Barry McGuire joined the New Christy Minstrels, and McGuire was the group's lead singer on their fourth album, *Ramblin'*, released in 1963 by Columbia Records. It featured McGuire singing his own song "Green, Green," which became the group's first hit, peaking at #3 in 1963, and later covered by such artists as The Brothers Four, Glen Campbell, and Johnny Rivers. When Randy Sparks, the group's leader departed in 1963, he appointed McGuire as the new head of the New Christy Minstrels. In that same year Barry made his first major appearance before the national public on the *Andy Williams Show*. He was also the lead singer on several other Minstrel hits, including "Saturday Night" and "Three Wheels on My Wagon". While still a Minstrel, McGuire wrote "Greenback Dollar," which became a major hit for the Kingston Trio, and recorded his first solo album, *Barry Here and Now*, in 1962 on the Horizon label.

After leaving the Minstrels in 1965, McGuire signed with Lou Adler's Dunhill Records and was assigned as a staff writer with P.F. Sloan and Steve Barri. During the peak of the "protest song" movement during the Vietnam War, the trio wrote "Eve of Destruction," which McGuire recorded and which was a #1 *Billboard* hit in 1965, as well as reaching #3 in the U.K. The anti-establishment nature of the lyrics resulted in it becoming one of the most prominent protest songs during the 1960s as it questioned the Vietnam War and its civil rights connotations. The song was pulled from retail store shelves and banned on radio because of its anti-Vietnam lyrics. It even provoked an answer record, "Dawn of Correction." Ironically, it had been offered to the Byrds and was originally conceived as a flip-side selection. Barry's album, *Eve of Destruction*, was released in 1965 on the Ember label. The song resurfaced in 1979 when The Turtles inched it onto the *Billboard* Hot 100 at #100 for two weeks, and in 1998 as part of the soundtrack to Warren Beatty's political comedy film, *Bulworth*.

McGuire played a significant role in bringing the popular million selling quartet Mamas and Papas to the attention of producer Lou Adler at Dunhill Records in the mid-1960s. For that connection, he received a mention in their hit "Creeque Alley" (a hilarious song of how the group was formed), and they later offered their services as his back-up singers. McGuire was unable to follow-up his worldwide hit, although he released several singles and albums, including the highly acclaimed Sloan song, "Upon a Painted Ocean." He continued to pursue the protest song angle with the 1966 album *This Precious Time*, which featured the Mamas and Papas. It was followed with *World's Private Citizen* in 1967, which included assorted members from the Byrds and the Eagles. Both albums were released on the Dunhill label. The latter album generated such mediocre sales that McGuire stopped recording until 1971, when he returned with former Mamas and Papas sideman Dr. Eric Hord on *Barry McGuire and the Doctor* on the Ode label. The album featured such folk rock artists as the Byrd's Chris Hillman and Michael Clarke. During the 1960s, McGuire did some acting with a Broadway appearance in the musical *Hair*.

On Father's Day in 1971, McGuire was baptized and soon signed a record deal with Myrrh, a Christian music label. He recorded three albums in the mid-1970s associated with the "Jesus Movement," including *Seeds*, *Lighten Up*, *Narnia*, and *To the Bride*, all on Myrrh. The latter was a live recording with the 2nd Chapter of Acts group. When Billy Ray Hearn left Myrrh to launch Sparrow Records, McGuire followed and recorded three albums with Sparrow in the late 1970s, including *C'mon Along*, *Have You Heard*, and *Cosmic Cowboy*. In 1984 McGuire and his wife moved to New Zealand, her homeland, and lived there until 1990. While in New Zealand, he became involved in World Vision, a Christian international relief organization. Upon his return to the U.S., McGuire toured with Terry Talbot, doing about thirty-five to forty concerts per year. In 1994 his *Anthology* album was released by One Way Records, and included all of his hit songs, such as "Eve of Destruc-

Barry McGuire, New Zealand 1979.

tion". Overall, McGuire has recorded more than fifteen albums of Christian music for such labels as Myrrh, Sparrow, Word, and Maranatha. Steve McGuire (Barry's son) aka Peacemaker has recently released his version of "Eve of Destruction".

In 2002 McGuire participated in a PBS special, "This Land Is Your Land", during which he sang with several of the original New Christy Minstrels. In 2003, Barry publicly stated on his website that he was retiring from doing concerts, only available for engagements in which he and his son, Brennon, would play a few songs while Barry engaged in "a mixture of theological discourse, storytelling, and music." In 2006, Frogtown Records released two new McGuire songs, the anti-smoking "Mr. Hakk N' Koff" that was used for an anti-smoking animated short available as of July, 2011 on www.podcastplayhouse.net, and "I Pledge Allegiance", a jingoistic production celebrating the good old U.S.A. In 2008, he joined with former members of The Byrds for a live concert tour billed as "Trippin' the '60s", which features the group doing a variety of well-known 1960s songs. In 2011, the tour had made it to Australia, Germany, and various sites throughout the United States.

www.barrymcguire.com

McKinnon, Russ

A highly regarded session musicians and touring drummer, Russ McKinnon is repeatedly cited as being well-known in music circles for his six years of recording and touring with the horn-heavy R&B, funk and jazz group, Tower of Power, through the early 1990s. This period of his career led him to be honored for five consecutive years as one of the winners of *Modern Drummer* Magazine's prestigious Reader's Poll Award.[1] A Broken Arrow native, Russ McKinnon was band president at Sequoyah Middle School where he eventually became "student director", filling in for his instructor Harold Hance after Hance's heart surgery. Later, according to the Broken Arrow Public Schools website, he created drum cadences still in use by the Pride of Broken Arrow High School Band more than twenty years after his departure. Furthermore, while in school he played in every element of the school's music program, to include concert, marching, and jazz bands, as well as being named "1st Chair All State Drummer" of Oklahoma, among many other district and regional recognitions. After graduation from high school in 1977, Russ spent time in Boston, Massachusetts, with the 27th Lancers Drum and Bugle Corps, which he has indicated many times was a primary building block of his musicianship. During his years of studying music and the music business at Tulsa University, he coached the percussion section at Tulsa Union High School from 1978 to 1981, introducing the "Drum and Bugle" style of marching to the school's program.[2] After graduating Tulsa University in 1981, he attended graduate school at North Texas State University in Denton, known for its excellent music programs, especially in jazz. He began his professional career as a classical percussionist with the Tulsa Philharmonic Orchestra, later performing with the Fort Worth Symphony. Subsequently he moved to Los Angeles, California, where he became a staple session drummer with multiple recording and performance credits.

Along with his celebrated tenure as the funky motor for Tower of Power, McKinnon

Russ McKinnon

has displayed an extremely diverse ability to play with artists from many different musical genres. As a partial listing, Russ has performed or recorded with the following musical artists: Engelbert Humperdinck, Michelle Shocked, The GAP Band, Billy Vera, Donna Summer, Nicolette Larson, Joe Cocker, Marie Osmond, Bette Midler, Louis Miguel, Kenny G, David Foster, Phil Ramone, The 5th Dimension, and Melissa Manchester. Since 2001 Russ has been the only recording and touring drummer for pop balladeer Barry Manilow, with whom Russ has performed for sold-out audiences at prestigious venues worldwide, such as Madison Square Garden, Staples Center, Radio City Music Hall, the Wembly and O2 arenas in London, and the Las Vegas Hilton. As of 2011, his work has allowed him to travel to forty countries outside the United States. McKinnon has appeared on numerous recordings a sampling of which includes Tower of Power's *T.O.P.* (1993); Bette Midler *Sings the Peggy Lee Songbook* (2005); Barry Manilow's *2 Nights Live* (2004), *Scores: Songs from Copacabana and Harmony* (2004), *Greatest Songs of the Sixties* (2006), *Greatest Songs of the Seventies* (2007), and *Barry Manilow Sings the Peggy Lee Songbook* (2005). Russ has also made many television appearances, to include, *American Idol, Dancing with the Stars, The Tonight Show with Jay Leno,* NBC's *Today Show, Good Morning America,* A & E's *Music "By Request", The View, The Martha Stewart Show, The Rachael Ray Show, Late Night with Craig Ferguson, Beverly Hills 90210, Melrose Place, and Fame. Modern Drummer* magazine has also published a three-part series by Russ entitled, "Becoming A Working Drummer".

A longtime and active music educator, McKinnon is a popular drum set clinic leader across the U.S. and Canada, as well as in the United Kingdom and Continental Europe. As of 2011, McKinnon was still very active in the Los Angeles and U.S. West Coast music and recording scenes. His summers take him to Hawaii where he teaches percussion for the Kamehameha Schools in Honolulu. As for Oklahoma's influence on Russ, one can easily state the Broken Arrow Public Schools band program had a profound impact on the drummer's opportunities to play, compose, and conduct, a clear vote for supporting music education in public schools.

Notes
1. Russ McKinnon's biography as sketched out in this essay has been re-published at least ten times on various sites on the internet, always including basically the same information, but occasionally adding another musician with whom he has worked. This essay is a synthesis of that standard biography that has been re-distributed often.

2. For more details on McKinnon's career at Broken Arrow public schools, see the districts online newsletter, *BAPS WINS*, Volume 5, Issue 6, November 15, 2010, http://www.ba.k12.ok.us/WINS/greatgrad06.html (accessed July, 28, 2011).

He proudly plays and endorses Drum Workshop drums, SABIAN cymbals, Vic Firth sticks, Remo drum heads, Gibraltar rack systems, May drum mic systems, RhythmTech percussion, XL Specialty cases and HQ practice pads.

McPherson, J.D.

On his 2010 album, *Signs and Signifiers*, which became 2012's #1 Americana album, J.D. McPherson channels the rebel rock spirit of semi-Oklahoman, **Eddie Cochran,** and the hot honking jive of Louis Jordan without sounding like a 1950s cover band at the state fair. Surrounded by a highly skilled veteran combo providing expert counterpoint and blues complementing, McPherson yelps, twangs, and pleads through twelve tracks on his debut album for Chicago-based Hi-Style Records. The benefits mightily from McPherson's earnest adherence to the ethos of mid-1940s R&B and mid-1950s rockabilly, but also is time-coded by the Hi-Style Studio in Chicago, specifically configured to capture a warm analog sound with all ribbon, tube, and dynamic microphones passed through tube mixers and preamps onto 1/4 inch tape. As a result, the recordings have an "earthier" low end and rounder mid-range than a lot of hotly mastered contemporary popular music that singes the high end of a person's hearing after a while.

McPherson lets his inner-Okie go honestly. According to the profile on his website in 2011, he grew up in "southern Oklahoma, the progeny of an ex-military, farming father and "good word" preaching mother," which certainly qualifies regionally, religiously, and socio-economically. Southern Oklahoma in McPherson's world means Buffalo Valley, perched among the Talihina Mountains in the southeastern part of the state known to Oklahomans as Little Dixie, as depicted satirically (but with more than a little truth) in the 2009 film, *Leaves of Grass*, written and directed by Tulsan Tim Blake Nelson. McPherson is enthusiastic when people ask him about his Oklahoma background, as they often do in interviews, eager to talk about the state's rich musical history. According to an August 3, 2011, WNYC-FM, New York interview with Elliot Forrest, when McPherson is asked if he was born and raised in Oklahoma, the singer/guitarist replies, "yes, and I still live in Oklahoma too."[1] His 2011 Hi-Style Records publicity packet indicates McPherson's home is in now in Broken Arrow, a suburb just south of Tulsa.

McPherson's official publicity materials also indicate he was into both country and punk rock as a teenager, He learned **Conway Twitty** songs to join in with his best friend's father's country band, and would drive to Tulsa and Fort Smith, Arkansas to buy punk records by Stiff Little Finger and The Clash, and see hardcore acts like N.O.T.A. who played in the venerated "House that Bob (Wills) Built," the Cain's Ballroom in Tulsa (where the Sex Pistols also played in 1978, by the way). He also professes an affinity for 1980s alternative rockers the Smiths, Talking Heads, and the Pixies. The first album McPherson personally purchased was a cassette of Run D.M.C.'s 1986 commercially successful album, *Raisin' Hell*, with money earned from tearing up an old barn on the family's property. He really bought the tape deck the cassette just happened to be in, further indicating how hip hop music had permeated the interior U.S., but once J.D. heard the Kings of Queens he was convinced Run D.M.C. was every bit as much a part of the American music tradition as many important 1950s blues, rock, or R&B icons. Before too much longer, he landed a boxed set Decca Records compilation of Buddy Holly songs, after which he became entranced with Lubbock's bespectacled genius. That, in turn, pointed the wide-eyed rocker in the same direction that early American rock and R&B snagged the ears of British teens in the 1950s and 60s, who then went on to serve it right back up to U.S. teens in a more amplified, frenzied, virtuosic, and poetic fashion. Sing to yourself now, "And, the circle, was un-broken, by and by, Lord, by and by…"

J.D. McPherson, 2010

By Hugh Foley / 503

Another influential wallop for McPherson was getting kicked in the "wow" bone by discovering the 1940s-era Specialty label (home of Oklahoman R&B heavies **Roy Milton** and **Jimmy** and **Joe Liggins**), as well as Chicago's Chess Records, the nativity scene of urban blues and early rock and roll. J.D.'s father, a jazz and blues fanatic, and was happy to open up his collection once the punk-rocker took an interest, handing over Muddy Waters and John Lee Hooker records. As a result, McPherson's former band, The Stark Weather Boys, played sets alternating The Ramones with Bill Haley, The Stooges with Buddy Holly, and Nirvana with Carl Perkins.[2] It was through The Stark Weather Boys' www.myspace.com site that Hi-Style's Jim Sutton first heard McPherson, and invited J.D. to Chicago to talk about making a recording, which turned out to be *Signs and Signifiers*.[3] Once the songwriting and recording process got underway with the goal of making a traditional American rock 'n roll record, various influences began to surface.

On *Signs and Signifiers*, McPherson's unrestrained roots vocals on "North Side Gal", "Scratching Circles", and "Scandalous" rip right through the aural cloth woven by Specialty Records designers from back there when, while other tracks merge Chuck Berry rhythmic guitar riffs, Bo Diddley beats, and jump blues saxophone. J.D.'s earlier alternative rock roots do sneak out of the ground on a song like the album's title track where big reverb electric guitar waves wash through the song as an homage to the Smiths' guitarist Johnny Marr who used a similar sound in the 1984/85 Smiths favorite, "How Soon is Now?" Marr's own inspirations clearly have similar 1950s references, although taken to a 1980s post-modern rock sonic level and couched in the winsome gloom of Smiths' vocalist Morrissey. McPherson goes the opposite direction of the erudite rock poet, however, preferring the lyrical playground of jumpin' R&B and classic American rock and roll from its "golden age".

J.D. also seems to be dealing with the "educated hick syndrome" common to a lot of smart and educated people from Oklahoma. Upon leaving Oklahoma, a citizen traveler from the state is almost instantly perceived as a rural rube until they prove otherwise, or simply capitalize on the image to their own ends, i.e., **Frankie** and **Johnny Marvin, Woody Guthrie,** or **Sheb Wooley**. While he writes or co-writes eleven of the album's twelve tracks, McPherson understands the market drive of his genre enough to realize he can cover a song like Tiny Kennedy's 1955 single, "Country Boy", and can get away with it since he is from Oklahoma; most people outside of the state don't know the difference between Bartlesville and Bokchito, Sallisaw and Slapout, or Broken Bow and Broken Arrow. As **Eddie Cletro**, **Cowboy Copas**, and even **Eddie Cochran** before him all knew, the state represents a certain authentic, rural, and rootsy image in the national mindset, and J.D. is no stranger to the power of established symbolism, be it stereotypical or subtle. The re-born roots rocker also has an art degree in open media from Tulsa University, which led him to the reference for his album title, *Signs and Signifiers*, based on writings by French theorist, philosopher and critic, Roland Barthes, especially his essays on semiology, or the multiple layers of meanings within signs, symbols, or words. Judging by the remainder of his 2012-2013 tour schedule that included various U.S. gigs, as well as trips to Iceland and Europe, and many positive reviews appearing from various established and more proletariat corners of the internet, all signs point to a sustainable career for McPherson as long as he wants to keep up the image. Whether or not he will transcend his influences from the primordial stew of rock music, or just hold the line as a roots rock revitalizer, such as his forbears the Stray Cats, X, The Blasters, and The Cramps, remains to be seen. The answer likely depends on how insistent J.D. is on signifying himself as a musician born in the wrong era, or one who is a new sum of many parts torn out of the various American popular music tradition eras that have inspired him..

www.jdmcpherson.com

Notes

1. The Elliot Forrest interview with J.D. McPhersand Hi-Style Records owner, Jimmy Sutton, aired on the program, *Soundcheck*, over WNYC-FM, New York, August 3, 2011, and is archived as a podcast at http://www.wnyc.org/shows/soundcheck/2011/aug/03/studio-jd-mcpherson/ (accessed August 4, 2011).

2. For a fuller description of McPherson's early years of merging punk and rockabilly, see his interview with Dave Ashdown, "JD McPherson, rockin' down the plain," posted on Ashdown's online blog for Americana roots magazine, *No Depression*, November 19, 2010, at http://www.nodepression.com/profiles/blogs/jd-mcpherson-rockin-down-the.

3. After McPherson took off to Chicago, The Stark Weather Boys continued the tight combo rockabilly for which they are recognized in the Tulsa area. As recently as 2011, the group backed up **Tulsa Sound** veteran, Clyde Stacy, for whom the sound is not retro since he dates to the actual 1950s when the rollicking rhythms hit Tulsa teenagers the first time around. See and hear more about The Stark Weather Boys at www.myspace.com/thestarkweatherboys.

McShann, James Columbus "Jay"
(b. January 12, 1916 – d. December 7, 2006)

For many years among jazz critics, Jay McShann was often best known as the bandleader who provided saxophonist Charlie Parker with his first major professional gig and recording opportunities. By the early 21st century, however, McShann is recognized as an important transitional pianist whose style rose out of the ragtime and boogie-woogie-woogie traditions of the Southwest to foreshadow the oncoming swing and popular R & B eras. Jay McShann was also a progressive bandleader whose keen ear for musical talent encouraged the flourishing of the likes of Parker, Gene Ramey, Jimmy Witherspoon and Lowell Fulson. As an influence on other musicians, his songs have been covered by Count Basie, Chuck Berry, B.B. King, Maceo Parker, The Rolling Stones, and Buddy Tate. While his music is often categorized as Kansas City jazz, the music could just as easily be called Southwestern Jazz, Territory Jazz, or even Oklahoma jazz, since so many of its primary proponents moved up from Oklahoma to Kansas City. However, Kansas City was the epicenter of the movement and has the most logical claim to the genre title.

McShann's birthplace of Muskogee, Oklahoma, is now a known a source of tremendous jazz talent, producing more acclaimed musicians than its more populous neighbor Tulsa, fifty miles northwest. Factors included the city's well-educated, and economically thriving African-American population at the turn of the 20th century, the city's position as a travel nexus for several railroad lines, and Muskogee's location as the Indian Territory hub of the Black town movement in the late 19th century. This population provided solid music education for those who went to Manual Training High School, like Mc-

Jay McShann, circa 1940

By Hugh Foley / 505

Shann, and also offered multiple employment and mentoring opportunities for musicians. Muskogee's location and entertainment district also made the city a natural stopover for major touring artists such as Count Basie, Cab Calloway, or Louis Armstrong who were between Kansas City and Dallas. Additionally, Muskogee also became a dependable place for groups traveling through to pick up musicians, or for bandleaders like "T" Holder to use as a base for forming his hot blowing and hot swinging territory bands. Muskogee's South Second Street was a major Black business district for the entire Southwest, as major train lines, such as the M, K, & T, or the "Katy", made its way through Muskogee on runs from Texas to Kansas City in the 19th and early 20th centuries.[1]

Jay's father, Jess McShann, came to Oklahoma from Ratliff, Texas, about twenty miles east of Dallas, because he had an uncle living in the "Black friendly" town of Muskogee. His mother, Leona (McBee) McShann, came to Oklahoma from Alabama and settled around Chickasha before making her way to Muskogee in the early 1900s. As many families did as a result of the piano sales boom at the turn of the 20th century, the McShann's had an upright piano in their house on which his mother would play church songs. Devout Christians, McShann's mother took Jay to Central Baptist regularly, and his father took him to choir singing contests in neighboring small towns such as Redbird, Coweta, and Tullahassee where groups would come from various towns and have singing conventions. McShann had some of earliest musical impressions at these conventions, which he liked because of the variety of singing, as he remembered in a 1994 interview with the author: "Sometimes you'd be sitting on a bench with an old guy that sang bass and he could sing those low notes so low that it would almost shake the seat you're sitting on." His grandmother would take him to holiness churches in Muskogee where "They got in the groove," according to Jay.

Jay's first exposure to blues was through his father's job at Ferguson Brothers furniture in Muskogee when the elder McShann brought home a Victrola record player, and continued to bring home old records from the store that were being thrown out. "I remember I picked up a record and it was Bessie Smith and James P. Johnson backing her up," Jay said in 1994. "I put that record on and I really enjoyed it because the blues was good, [he sings], 'It thundered and it lightninged and the winds began to blow/And some poor folks didn't have no place to go.' Then she'd moan a little bit about it, making like it was so sad she couldn't sing no more. I knew then I liked that." McShann also began his interest in piano at a young age, picking up tips while his sister took piano lessons from Muskogee bassist Aaron Bell's mother, who was also the pianist at Central Baptist. He listened to Earl Hines secretly at night in the early 1930s on the radio from Chicago, and started sneaking out to see bands that were coming through Muskogee led by Bennie Moten or Muskogee native Clarence Love.

McShann also played in the band at Manual Training High School and first learned to "complement the blues" on piano from Russell when the high school director, a Texan named Kyle Collins, would put together small combos for area gigs. "I remember he took me on a gig with him, and I didn't know nothing," Jay said, "I thought you just played and played, and keep playing. So, he turned around to me and says, 'Complement the blues. Complement the blues.' I didn't what he was talking about, but when he starts doing his hands like this (ripples the fingers on his right hand), then I realized what he meant." Before long, he was playing with local musicians like Ellis Ezell, with whom **Barney Kessel** played, and also the great swing/be-bop transitional saxophonist, **Don Byas**.

"How I met Don Byas," Jay remembered in 1994, "was because of this Black lawyer in town who played tenor sax, Lawyer Kimble. He'd get together with Don Byas, another guy named Weaver, and Ellis Ezell. They would get that group together and get me to come play piano, but I couldn't. They'd say, 'We got to have somebody, so, come on, you got to play.' I was pretty young then." By age fourteen, Jay had his first paying gigs with Don Byas in Muskogee and nearby Wagoner, and those led to more performances in towns like Taft and Haskell. He also played with a family band out of Haskell called Professor Gray's band in places such as Shawnee, Wewoka, and Okmulgee, or "Dance towns" as McShann called them. The year was 1933, however, and those years were mean for just about everybody involved, so McShann left Muskogee at 17 for Tulsa where he had a stint with Al Denny's band before hooking up with some Kansas bootleggers looking for musicians to play in their south Kansas clubs. When that busted up, McShann headed for Kansas City, met a friend who gave him an apartment key, and within a few days he was working with a drummer named Hop on his first jobs in Kansas City.

As a result of Kansas City, Missouri's wide-open and free-flowing liquor atmosphere of the 1930s prohibition era, musicians from throughout the region went to Kansas City for work in the speakeasies, nightclubs, theaters, ballrooms, and other joints that existed there to support the good time center of the Midwest. Adding to his already formidable blues and jazz influences from Muskogee, Jay began listening to, and jamming with, master boogie-woogie player Pete Johnson who played the uptempo and vibrant precursor to rock and roll, and ultimately recorded its primary song, "Roll 'em Pete," with Joe Turner in 1938. Often noted for his percussive piano playing, McShann has been praised critically for his boogie-woogie style, and his original solo work that blends blues, boogie-woogie, and his major early influence, Earl Hines. Jay is often thought of as an important second generation boogie-woogie player who was more refined than the first round of rowdy players who grew out of the ragtime and honky tonk tradition. McShann played variously and regionally throughout Kansas City and the Midwest from 1934 to 1937. In 1937, McShann worked in a Kanas City group led by Buster Smith, of which seventeen-year-old Charlie Parker was also a member. Also in 1937, Jay formed his first group as a leader in Kansas City, which encouraged him to bring in new young players like Parker.

The beginning of this period are well documented on the compact disc *Charlie Parker with Jay McShann: Early Bird*, which features radio transcriptions from 1940 in Wichita, Kansas, and 1942 live performance at the Savoy Ballroom in New York City. The association with Parker became inescapable for McShann, as Jays' name comes up in 20th century jazz history books most often in reference to being the bandleader for Parker's first recordings and eventual debut appearance in New York City. However, more credit is being given to McShann as time has passed for leading one of the most progressive musical bands of the late 1930s and early 1940s. Even

Jay McShann performs at the Oklahoma Jazz Hall of Fame in Tulsa, OK, 1999.

By Hugh Foley / 507

though bop was a combo oriented jazz movement, the forebodings of the next era can be heard in McShann's recordings with Parker of 1941 and 42.

Instead of staying in the relatively safe confines of boogie-woogie, Jay explored more range and tonal possibilities within the form on his solos on "Hootie Blues" (1941) and "Vine Street Boogie" (1941). These transformations in his playing were natural developments as the big band era declined into small combo jazz that played more complex harmonic music, and perhaps also from the influence of having Charlie Parker in his band. Parker's first major calling card for his signature butterfly phrasing of bebop is on 1942's "Sepian Bounce" with McShann. For this reason alone, McShann is often regarded as an important leader in the evolution of big band musicians from the swing era into the bebop period.

McShann went to New York on the success of a national hit, "Confessin' the Blues," featuring Walter Brown on vocals and Parker on saxophone. The song was one of the biggest sellers for a Black group during the 1940s, even though it was not in the style the band preferred to play. The group's repertoire was largely made up of "riff tunes" on which the band could jam, but when the opportunity arose to record for Decca Records in 1941, the company's producer who had overseen earlier Count Basie Sessions, wanted a blues tune and so the group did it as an afterthought. Eventually, the record sold more than 500,000 copies and lit up the nation's jukeboxes in 1941 and 1942. From then on Jay McShann was considered a blues player, and in not too much more time Charlie Parker would leave the band for his own storied career.

Because so much has been made of Charlie Parker's life and career, the departure from McShann is a source of massive interpretation by Parker biographers and/or jazz historians. At least two critics say it was because of McShann's basic blues format Parker stayed behind in New York when the group planned on returning to Kansas City in 1942, whereas, others believe the McShann band offered Parker the right place to develop his ideas within the framework of a disciplined organization, and it was the McShann blues influence that provided Parker a foundation to progress through his dominant period of the mid 1940s when "Bird" showed a strong allegiance to the blues in his recordings. Without delving too far into the life of Parker, at least one of his biographers, Brian Priestley, and one very well known critic, Dave Dexter, report Parker's heroin addiction had worsened when he left McShann; so much so, Priestley says, Parker fell asleep on the bandstand and on a trip to Detroit with his next group, Parker overdosed and had to be left behind. Dexter reports more details of Parker's slip into heroin-addled oblivion, even though his most illustrious recordings were yet to be made, and McShann headed back to Kansas City.

Nineteen forty-three was the final year for the Jay McShann Orchestra as a large unit. While Kansas City bands were able to play through the depression, they could not play through World War II. The final blow came when McShann was accosted by federal agents as he came off the bandstand in New York and given his induction papers. Most critics define the demise of the McShann Orchestra as the end of the Kansas City era since so many of the New York bands were downsizing and replacing out-of-town members with New York musicians. On returning from the service, McShann led a number of small groups and recorded quite frequently throughout the rest of the 1940s and 1950s with small combos, and with the blues-jazz singer Jimmy Witherspoon, considered a leading jazz singer in league with Jimmy Rushing and Joe Turner. Witherspoon may have made his finest recordings with McShann in 1957. Also during the 1950s, McShann began working with fellow Muskogeean **Claude "Fiddler" Williams**, a relationship which continued at least through the summer of 2001 when both appeared at the Kansas City Jazz Festival. McShann continued recording in the 1960s for Capitol Records, began touring the United States and Europe, often with only a bassist and a drummer.

The 1966 Capitol LP, *McShann's Piano*, enjoyed solid worldwide success and brought him to the fore as the singer he needed to be in order to play his big hit of 1941 and 1942, "Confessin' the Blues." Jay recorded two albums with Eddy "Cleanhead" Vinson in 1969, and in 1972, and McShann's album *The Man from Muskogee*, not only boosted McShann's already noteworthy career, but also resurrected the career of Claude "Fiddler" Williams by featuring Williams on the album. Jay recorded two albums with Clarence "Gatemouth" Brown in 1973, recorded once with Helen Humes in 1974, with Ralph Sutton twice in 1979 and 1980, and Slim Gaillard in 1982, all of whom clearly benefited from his presence. In 1986, as a lot of music from the first half of the twentieth century began to be released on compact disc, Jay's music became more and more available through a series of reissues and jazz retrospectives. McShann had major associations with three albums in 1991, five in 1993, "only" one in 1994, five in 1995, eight in 1996, and seven in 1997. Included in the 1997 releases were his first work with Clint Eastwood on *Eastwood After Hours: Live at Carnegie Hall*, and a Stony Plain Records release, *Hootie's Jumpin' Blues*, which contained an oral history, as well as renewed versions of Jay's best-known songs with Duke Robillard's band. Six more albums with major credits for Jay appeared 1998.

McShann is the subject of the 1978 documentary film, *Hootie Blues*, and is also showcased in the TV documentary *Last of the Blue Devils*, even though he was never in the important territory group from Oklahoma after which the program is named. He has recorded for the Capitol, Atlantic, Master Jazz, Sackville, and Stony Plain labels in the United States, and the Black and Blue label in Europe. McShann has received many accolades, to include induction into the Oklahoma Music Hall of Fame, the Kansas City Hall of Fame, the Blues Foundation's Hall of Fame, and the Oklahoma Jazz Hall of Fame, the latter having named its Lifetime Achievement Award in his honor. He also received a number of awards: the Jazz Oral History Award from the Rutgers Institute of Jazz Studies, the Jass Master Award from the Afro-American Museum in Philadelphia, the National R & B Foundation Pioneer Award in Los Angeles, the Kansas City Jazz Heritage Award, the Jazz Era Pioneer Award from the National Association of Jazz Educators. The American Jazz Museum in Kansas City honored Jay's legacy by naming its outdoor performance pavilion for him in 2000.

As a result of consistently touring and recording in Europe from the 1960s through the early 90s when he intended to give up "going across the big pond" (but wound up back in Holland in 2003). McShann was widely considered a major pianist in Europe with a repertoire that encompasses the first half of the 20th century's popular music traditions of ragtime, boogie woogie, swing, jazz, and R & B. In 2001 and 2002, Jay traveled to Long Beach University in California, Detroit, Michigan, Atlanta, Georgia, and a jazz festival at Wichita Kansas, only to name a few gigs for the eighty-seven-year old pianist and singer at that time. Jay was also a featured element in *Piano Blues*, a PBS documentary directed by Clint Eastwood for the network's historic series, *The Blues*. In 2003, Stony Plain Records released *Goin' to Kansas City*, recorded by McShann over a couple of years in his adopted hometown from which the album takes its name. Containing a few of his compositions, including "The Fish Fry Boogie", "Some Kinda Crazy", as well as two of his famous co-writes, "Confessin' the Blues" and "'Fore Day Rider", along with an informative and personal 20-minute interview with McShann at home with his piano, the album received a Grammy nomination for Best Traditional Blues Album. Stony Plain also released *Hootie Blues* (2006), a 2001 live set that was recorded in Montreal, which also includes an interview with McShann recorded in 2003 in Holland when he performed at the North Sea Jazz Festival. The disc became the last released for the jazz legend while he was living. However, since his death in 2006 several re-issues have been made available, many of which are electronic downloads from a variety of online music sales points. The most complete discography online for McShann is under his name on the internet music database, www.allmusic.com.

Jay McShann must be considered an important jazz musician and bandleader who not only fostered the flourishing of Charlie Parker, but is also representative of several American piano styles, to include the barrelhouse, boogie-woogie, and blues traditions on piano. Additionally, Jay set off musical depth charges under jazz in the late 1930s and early 1940s that helped propel it into its next evolutionary period, known as bebop. With a foundation in Muskogee of African-American gospel music, formal music lessons, instruction in complementing the blues in high school, and having played with accomplished jazz musicians by the time he was eighteen, Jay McShann added boogie-woogie to his repertoire in 1930s Kansas City, formed a band with Charlie Parker as his lead saxophonist, and subsequently played and recorded his way to being one of the 20th century's major blues, jazz, and R & B pianists. By the beginning of the the 21st century, he and **Claude "Fiddler" Williams** were the primary living proponents of not only Kansas City jazz, but the respective precursor traditions from which they came in Muskogee. By the time of his death in 2006, Jay McShann was, more often than not, given due credit by jazz historians and fans for both defining Kansas City jazz, as well as for his own diverse abilities, techniques, foresight, and historic representation

Note

1. Many online and print texts feature profiles of Jay McShann. Along with surveying the critical context of McShann's work within the jazz literature canon, the author's dissertation examined the cultural milieu of Muskogee, Oklahoma to explain why Muskogee produced so many nationally recognized jazz musicians (JayMcShann, Don Byas, Barney Kessel, Walter and Joe Thomas, Claude "Fiddler" Williams, and Clarence Love). The text is listed in the *Dissertation Index* as Hugh W. Foley, Jr., "Jazz from Muskogee: Eastern Oklahoma as a Hearth of Musical Culture" (PhD diss., Oklahoma State University, 2000).

Meade, Tyson
(b. circa 1962)

With a unique vocal imprint that made him instantly distinguishable from all other alternative rock singers of the 1980s and 1990s, Tyson Meade is best known for his work in the **Chainsaw Kittens**, the progressive rock group for which he has been the lead vocalist and primary songwriter since its inception. Tyson's voice is hard to compare to anyone because of its sonic range. British singers such as Pete Shelley of the Buzzcocks or Morrissey of the Smiths might be the closest stylistic touchstones due to their high tenors. During the Kittens' peak, Meade was the closest Oklahoma came to a figure with the poetic and stage show sense of a Michael Stipe (the emotive and eccentric front man of R.E.M.).

Prior to Chainsaw Kittens, Meade was also in another Norman alternative rock outfit, Defenestration, and prior to that grew up in Bartlesville. The Chainsaw Kittens have never for-

Tyson Meade, 1996

mally broken up, and occasionally re-unite for one-off gigs, most recently in 2008 at the Norman Music Festival. Along with recording two solo albums, *Motorcycle Childhood* (Echostatic/Spacebaby, 1995) and the self-released, *Kitchens and Bathrooms* (2008), he has also worked as a disc-jockey at the rejuvenated Spy alternative music radio station in Oklahoma City when. Tyson has also exhibited his artwork in various locations, and has performed randomly scheduled solo shows in Dallas, Norman, and Stillwater up through at least 2008. While visiting frieds in Stillwater in January, 2012, Tyson recorded vocals on the independent recording, "Winter Boys Cutting the Rug" with Jesse Tabish of **Other Lives** on guitar and keyboards, Derek Brown on keybaords, and Aaron Frisby on percussion. Recorded in Frisby's Stillwater kitchen, the song is available only after a short run of collecti ble 7" records were released of the production. Meade continues the theme of recording in familiar spaces with his *Kitchens and Bathrooms* album, available as a free listen on his website.

Meade has also worked as an English teacher in Shanghai, People's Republic of China. While in China, Meade worked with students on a new album that was to be mixed in 2013 at old Chainsaw Kitten buddy **Trent Bell**'s recording studio in Norman known as Bell Labs. With lyrical skills that border between fascinating and oblique, leaving plenty of interpretive space for listeners to make their own meaning out of his songs, and an instantly identifiable voice, Tyson Meade is one of Oklahoma rock music's most iconic interpreters.

www.tysonmeade.com

Merritt, Chris Allan
(b. September 27, 1952)

With a voice praised widely for its versatility, emotion, and tonal color, Chris Merritt was not only the first American tenor to open at the famous La Scala Theater in Milan, Italy, since 1949 when he performed there in 1988, he also is the only singer in history to open the Milan opera season two years in a row (in *Rossini*'s *William Tell* in 1988 and Verdi's *I Vespri Siciliani* in 1989). With more than twenty different Gioachini Rossini roles to his credit (considered by several sources as a world record), Chris Allan Merritt was born in Oklahoma City. Yet another world-class product of Oklahoma City University, from which he has received an honorary Doctorate of Music, Chris Merritt is one of the world's most prominent opera Bel Canto tenors. Bel canto is an Italian musical term translating into "beautiful singing", and which requires an incredible vocal dexterity, such as demanded in the compositions by Rossini for which Merritt is known.[1]

Chris apprenticed at the Santa Fe Opera before making his professional debut in Santa Fe in 1975 as Fenton in Verdi's *Falstaff* under the direction of Edo de Waart. He made his European debut in 1978 at the Salzburg Landestheater, where he sang Lindoro (*L'italiana in Algeri*). From 1981 to 1984, he performed in Augsburg, where his repertory included Tamino, Idomeneo, Rodolfo, Julien, Faust, and Rossini's Otello. From the latter, he has developed an international reputation as a Rossini specialist, including Pyrrhus

Opera tenor, Chris Merritt

in *Ermione*, Erisso in *Maometto II*, James in *La donna del lago*, Contareno in *Bianca e Fallioero*, Arnoldo in *Guillaume Tell* (a role he has sung at La Scala, Paris, and Covent Garden), Argirio in *Trancredi*, Antenore in *Zelmira*, and Idreno in *Semiramide*. The latter was his debut at the world famous Covent Garden in London in 1985.

Additional tenor roles for which Chris is noted include Amenophis in *Moise et Pharaon*, Antenore in *Zelmira*, Argirio in *Rancredi*, Aeneas in *Les Troyens*, Admetus in *Alceste*, Leukippos in *Daphne*, Arturo in *I Puritani*, Nemorino in *La Juive*, Arrigo in *Vespri siciliani*, Sobinin in *A Life for the Tsar*, and Percy in *Anna Bolena*. He has portrayed a wide range of operatic heroes, ranging from the Mozartian classics like *Idomeneo*, *Mitridate*, *La Clemenza Di Tito*, *La Finta Giardiniera*, *Cosi Fan Tutte*, and *Die Zauberflote*, to Berlioz's *Benvenuto Cellini*, *Les Troyens*, and *The Damnation Faust*, to Puccini's *La Boheme*, *Madama Butterfly*, and *Il Trovatore*, as well as Meyerbeer's *Roberto le Diable* (Carnegie Hall) and Offenbach's *Les Contes d'Hoffman*.

Chris' illustrious career includes performances in the major operatic centers of the world, including the Metropolitan Opera (New York City), La Scala (Milan), Royal Opera House (London), State Opera (Vienna), San Francisco Opera, Paris Opera, Teatro Colon (Buenos Aires), as well as on stages in Barcelona, Madrid, Amsterdam, Hamburg, Munich, Rome, Geneva, and Venice. Merritt has opened many opera seasons for prestigious companies, considered a sign of his powerful abilities, and the respect he maintains in the opera world. In 1990, he opened the Chicago opera season at the with Gluck's Adméte.

Merritt also opened the 1990 Chicago opera season as Gluck's Admete. He performed again at the Met in New York City in 2005, in the principal role of *Kát'a Kabanová*, which he continued at the Royal Opera House in London during the 2007 season. Before heading off to London, however, he came full circle in 2006, appearing in *The Tempest* at the Santa Fe Opera. Merritt has appeared on a number of recordings. A good starting place for a representative sample of Merritt's work is on the CD, *The Heroic Bel Carto Tenor* (Phillips, 1995), which is more or less a "greatest hits" disc featuring a variety of his acclaimed work by Rossini. Released in 2007 on Bongiovanni Records, *Dal Vivo in Concerto* is a 1997 recording that shows the full tonal colors of his Merritt's voice and why he (and anyone singing Bel canto tenor) is considered "heroic". Merritt sails through the operatic scales as if buoyed by celestial powers, able to pull emotion out of his performance where some are only able to achieve the technical requirements of the pieces he sings. In 2006, BBC/Opus Arte released a DVD featuring Merritt in Wagner's *Das Rheingold*. Without acquiring the DVD, however, one can see and hear a variety of Chris Merritt's performances on www.youtube.com under his name in which audiences respond with thunderous applause and multiple shouts of "Bravo!"

Note
1. Elizabeth Forbes summarizes Merritt's career through 1995 in an un-sourced essay printed in 2001 and given to the author. However, she references R. Milne's' article "Chris Merritt" in the festival issue of *Opera* (1992), 6-12.

Meyer, Edgar
(b. November 24, 1960)

A three-time GRAMMY Award winner, and roundly considered one of the world's best and most versatile double bassists (a.k.a. "the stand-up bass"), Edgar Meyer is known for his work as classical performer, progressive bluegrass "NewGrass" artist, a country music session musician, and a classical composer who merges his multiple interests in the previously listed genres with jazz, folk, and world music. While he was born in Tulsa to his Oklahoma native mother, Anna Mary (Metzel) Meyer, and Tennessee-native music educator, Edgar Meyer, Sr., Edgar moved to Tennessee when he was four-years-old, and was reared in Oak Ridge. Additionally, he began playing bass at five-years-old, after he had left the state, so the impact of Oklahoma's musical environment is minimal, if present at all.[1] However, Meyer did get his first major break as country music session musician with Oklahoman **Vince Gill** on Gill's 1985 album for RCA, *The Things That Matter*, which includes "Oklahoma Borderline", the second top ten hit from the album on *Billboard*'s Hot Country Songs chart. Continuing the Oklahoma connections, Meyer plays with Muskogee-reared finger-picking luminary, Leo Kottke, on Kottke's 1989 album, *My Father's Face* (Private Music). Meyer also appears on **Garth Brooks**' second album, *No Fences* (Capitol, 1990), a #1 *Billboard* country album which also made it to #3 on the *Billboard* Top 200 Albums chart on its way to selling seventeen million plus copies, still Brooks' biggest selling album. Therefore, millions of people were hearing Edgar's work even if they did not know his name. The same year (1990), he recorded bass tracks for **Reba McEntire**'s album, *Rumor Has It* (MCA), and Oklahoma contemporary Christian artist, **Sandi Patty** on her album *Songs from the Hear* (Word). The following year he was back with Garth Brooks on his *Ropin' the Wind*

Edgar Meyer, circa 2010

(Capitol, 1991) album, and Garth is obviously a fan as Edgar returned for Brooks' 1997 album *Sevens*. Interestingly, Meyer also must have added tracks to a re-release of Roger Miller's hits on *Roger Miller's Classics* (Varese, 2002), as he is listed on the credits. As a result, Oklahoma musicians did have some influence in Meyer's success as a country music session player, but all that happened outside of the state, and sharing native state status with Gill, Patty, Brooks, and Reba, as well as move-ins Miller and Kottke, is more serendipitous than related to any kind of cause and effect. He was just the best player available at the time for those recordings; and, he remains the best player available for any recording in which he can be scheduled.

While Meyer may have moved from Oklahoma at an early age, he did emerge into the world within the state's boundaries, and that's all we need to know for him to be included here, as are several others who had the same experience (Oscar Pettiford, Howard McGhee, Nokie Edwards, Barry McGuire, et. Al). Aside from his birthplace, however, Meyer represents some larger issues in the field of music, and those include the influence a parent can have on a child's musical development, as well as a primary concept and very significant lesson that has surfaced throughout this text over and over, regarding long-term music-industry success: the more a musician can do beyond one genre, style, instrument, or industry function (producing, engineering, managing, publishing), the better chance that person has to make a career out of the music business. Edgar Meyer has parlayed his multi-faceted musical interests, coupled with an extraordinary talent, into exalted status among his peers, fans, and industry watchers. While the entertainment industry is often

By Hugh Foley / 513

built around exaggerated hyperbole, no one argues for a second with a publication like *The New Yorker*, who calls Meyer "The most remarkable virtuoso... in the history of the instrument."[2] Enough said.

Notes

1. To this point in the author's research, none of the vast amount of writing or press releases about Edgar Meyer indicates why his parents were in Oklahoma, other than his mother was a native of the state. Given that his father was a jazz bassist before he was a classical musician and string teacher, the author wonders if Oklahoma had any impact on Edgar Meyer Sr. as a jazz bassist, and through that influence jazz trickled down to Edgar. This is only conjecture at the time of this writing, but would be a good question for someone to ask Edgar as time goes on.
2. The undocumented quote from *The New Yorker* appears as part of several Sony Classical press releases for Edgar Meyer, but must have occurred before August 8, 2002, as that is the printer date on the Sony "Classical Notes" e-mal newsletter from which the quote is taken.

Mikaila (Dominique Enriquez)

(b. December 15, 1986)

Layering her soulful pop vocals over hip-hop beats, the Edmond-born, Mikaila enjoyed a sixteen-week run on the *Billboard* Hot 100 in early 2001 with "So In Love With Two", her one hit from the 2000 self-titled album on Island Records. Of French, Spanish, and Aztec Indian descent, Mikaila spent her early years in Edmond before relocating with her family to Dallas at age nine. It was in Oklahoma that her musical foundation was set, being reared in a musical family where she sang along with her mother who played piano in church. Musical families tend to not only encourage kids in musical directions, but also nurture and tolerate their development. In a 2000 Island Records press release for her only album, she explained her early childhood musical experiences: "I could sing before I could talk," she says. "At 3 years old, I'd stand in front of the mirror, singing into a candlestick, and tell my mother I want to be a star." According to the same release, her inspirations were primarily Mariah, Celine and Whitney Houston, as well as contemporary gospel music, and her mother's church music activities. When Mikaila was 9, her family moved to Dallas, and before too long she began showing off her velvety voice at sporting events. Soon she was something of a regular attraction at Texas Rangers games—belting out the National Anthem as easy as if it were the ABCs.

Enter talent scout and manager Marty Rendleman. Mikaila remembers, "Someone called Marty and said, 'You *have* to listen to this girl who sings at the Rangers games. "But [Marty] used to manage LeAnn Rimes—and she'd sworn off children. She was like, 'Call me when she gets her driver's license!'" Ultimately, Rendleman was persuaded to hear Mikaila perform—and she promptly lifted her ban on "minor" artists. Randleman began arranging high-profile appearances for Mikaila, including her Carnegie Hall debut as the sole featured vocalist with the U.S. Army Concert Band and at the 53rd Presidential Inaugural. With the exposure, the record company labels came calling, hoping for the next teen-sensation. "We came to New York and in one day had meetings with all the top record labels," Mikaila recalls. Island Records senior vice-president, Jeff Fenster, who'd come to the label from Jive Records, where he'd brought in Backstreet Boys and Britney Spears, punched her ticked for the teen pop idol bullet train.

Imagine being fourteen-years-old and having everything all the things one dreamed up of growing up singing into a candlestick. In the same press release, Mikaila almost seems stunned. "I always knew this would happen, but it's so much bigger than I ever imagined," she says. "You dream of it, and then one day you wake up and you have a meeting and photo session and a studio session and a dance class." There she is jet-setting from New York to LA, Norway to Sweden, hooking up with the hottest pop producers and writers on the scene at the time. Mikaila began working on her debut. "I told them about myself and what I wanted—hard drums, hip words that people can relate too, nothing too sappy," she says. After the album's completion, Island released the first single, "So in Love with Two". With its vocals that are someone where in between the acrobatics and soul of Mariah Carey or Whitney Houston (in her prime), and the breathy, talking songs of Britney Spears, and sparse keyboard instrumentation bounced around by hip hop beats, pop radio took some notice. The single made three of *Billboard*'s charts, the Hot 100, the Mainstream Top 40, and the Rhythmic Top 40, with its highest chart position (#25) occurring on the Hot 100. The single did earn her an opening spot, logically, for a Britney Spears tour of 2001, after which she appeared on Nickelodeon's *Slimetime* and Fox Family Channel's concert series, *Front Row Center*. She also landed a spot in NBC's broadcast of the 74th Annual Macy's Thanksgiving Day Parade, where she rode on the Fox Family Channel float and performed the charting single.

Pleasing as the rest of album really is for fans of soulful vocals and smooth rhythms, a second single "It's All Up To You" was not able to differentiate her from other more established artists, and the single did not chart. As a result, Island chose not to renew her deal. At fifteen-years-old, Mikaila's major label experience was over. As a chronological footnote that may or may not have had any impact on her success, her career attempted its takeoff just pre and post the events of September 11th, 2001, in which the economy and the public may just not have been ready to support another sugarpop teen singer. Mikaila has yet to resurface in the modern era where any scrap of detail someone wants to be known (and some they do not want to be known) can be revealed through the Internet. Regarding her age at the time of her chart success (15), Mikaila offers some perspective for parents and teens: "A lot of adults underestimate teenagers these days—we know more and have been through more than they may want to think," she says. She also offers some encouragement to future one-hit wonders: "I want young people, "I want young people, especially girls, to be able to relate to me. I want them to know you can do anything if you work hard."[1]

Note

1. All the facts and quotes in this essay are taken from an undated Island Records press release for Mikaila's debut album, presumably written in the summer of 2001 by an unknown author. Mikaila has no official website as of July, 2011. Her domain name of www.mikaila.com points to an Island Records web page that is "under construction," and her only other internet presence is via a website built by a fan and a fan group on www.facebook.com (accessed July, 2011).

Miller, Jody

(b. November 29, 1941)

With two distinctly different major periods and genres of music industry success (1963-68/pop and 1970-77/country), along with later bumps to her career via patriotic and Gospel music, Jody Miller enjoyed/endured more than forty active years in the music business, all powered by her strong, mostly self-trained voice, and her undeniable camera-friendly good looks. She is best known for the recording earned of "Queen of the House", an answer song to Roger Miller's #1 song of the same year, "King of the Road", and for which she earned a Grammy Award for Best Vocal Performance on a Country Record in 1965. Miller grew up in a transplanted Oklahoma family who had moved west in the 1930s. She was born in Phoenix, Arizona on a stopover during the car ride to California, and first arrived at an "Okie camp" where all people from Oklahoma gathered upon arriving in the state hoping for work. Eventually, the Millers got to Oakland, California where her father became employed as a mechanic, and music was everywhere in her house. "My whole family was musical," she says in 2004 press release issued as she was re-emerging in the music world with a contemporary Christian recording. Born Myrna Joy Miller, her father played the fiddle (even made them out of tree in their yard) and her mother sang, while she and her four older sisters learned to keep up and harmonize. The musically inclined family recognized her talent and began entering her in local talent shows at age seven, where she became known as "the little girl with the big voice." Also during this period, she got her first musical "training" from her sister, Pat, who taught her some basics of the guitar. In a powerful testimony on her website, she tells of how her father snuck her out to sing in bars. Ultimately, and unfortunately, his drinking and her mother's affair split up the family. So, at age eight, her parents split and she was sent back to Blanchard, Oklahoma to live with her grandmother. She also notes on her website that Blanchard's population was only about 750 at the time, when she arrived alone at age 8 to the town that didn't have any paved streets. On meeting her grandmother for the first time, she writes, "I'm not sure how I found her little house, but when I arrived, she hobbled down the front steps from the porch, She was 78 years old... wearing a bonnet and an apron and she was chewing a little stick. It was snuff. Squinting at me she croaked, "Who air you?" Miller also remembers her grandmother used to sit in her rocking chair and play the fiddle, which is, no doubt, where her dad picked up the instrument.

Being a teenager during the golden age of rock 'n roll in the mid-1950s, she (along with most other teens of the period) says her favorites of the time were Elvis Presley, Little Richard, and Fats Domino, but it was singing along with Mario Lanza's "La Donna Mobile" and Debbie Reynolds' "Tammy" over and over that really helped her develop her voice. At Blanchard High School, she received support from her teachers, and formed a group called the Melodies with her friends that impressed local audiences with their covers of songs by the McGuire Sisters, but the group did not exist beyond graduation, after which Myrna married her high school sweetheart, Monty Brooks.

Jody Miller, circa 1971

Following high school, Myrna worked at the Oklahoma state capital as a secretary, and memorized two hundred folk songs from books in the library, which she practiced in her YWCA room. Before too long, she was a paid singer at The Jester, a coffee house near the University of Oklahoma campus. When opening for local folk singer **Mike Settle** one night, a nationally known folk group, The Limelighters, had come to see their friend, Settle, but also wound up hearing Myrna sing. One of the members of The Limelighters, Lou Gottlieb, gave her his agent's name in Los Angeles and said she should head out there if she really wanted a music career. So, she and Monty did just that, borrowing money from his parents, and moving to L.A. where she met fellow Oklahoman Dale Robertson, who at the time was starring in a popular television program, *Wells Fargo*. She auditioned for him, and he, in turn, called a friend a Capitol Records who signed her that day after she walked over to the famous building that looks like a stack of records. Subsequently, they took her middle name, "Joy", added a "d" to it, and created "Jody", which sounded folkier, since that was how she was initially marketed. Her first album for Capitol, *Wednesday's Child Is Full of Woe* (1963), was her best shot at a folk album, but it did not garner much attention. However, the album is footnotable because it did include session recordings by guitarist Glen Campbell, and Cher, who sang some background vocals on the album. Her fortunes changed when Capitol called her to record a new song, "Queen of the House", that was written by a friend of Rogers Miller's as an answer to his "King of the Road".

According to Miller, "Queen of the House" sold half a million copies in five days, which got it up to #5 on *Billboard*'s Hot 100 in 1965. However, the chart was based on sales at the time, and the record pressing plant could not keep up with the demand at the song's peak, limiting its ascension to #5 on the country charts and #12 on the *Billboard* Hot 100. The song also had some tough competition at the time with The Beatles' "Ticket to Ride", The Beach Boys' "Help Me Rhonda", and The Four Tops "I Can't Help Myself" and a few others like Elvis Presley, Roger Miller, and the Supremes that kept "Queen of the House" from going much further on the pop charts. Nonetheless, the song was that moment most artists can only hope for, a bona fide hit, and it shot her into the limelight of television, tours, and more recordings. She also reached the pinnacle of a recording artist's industry recognition when she received the Grammy Award for Best Vocal Performance on a Country Record for "Queen of the House". Capitol continued releasing albums (six total including a "Best of" collection), but none provided another major hit single. The closest was her 1965 semi-protest song, "Home of the Brave", that reached #25 on the pop charts, but the musical tide was changing due to the British Invasion, and folk singers not named Bob Dylan, Joni Mitchell, or Joan Baez, were not doing as well as rock bands in popular music at the time. Capitol tried a collection of her singing Buck Owens' songs, and then seeing where she might fit best, made a "Nashville Sound of Jody Miller" album, but it only reached #42 on the country album charts. By the late 1960s, she and Monty returned to Blanchard where they lived until she heard Tammy Wynette's "Stand By Your Man" on the radio in 1968. She called the producer of the song, Billy Sherrill, said she would like for him to produce her. He invited her to Nashville where she began phase two of her career, this time in country music.

Jody's Nashville country years launched right out of the box with plenty of vigor, as her first two country singles, "He's So Fine" and "Baby I'm Yours", achieved #5 positions on the country charts, and earned her *Billboard*'s Artist Resurgence of the Year Award, setting up a country chart run of twenty more charting singles from 1971 to 1979. Of those years, 1971 to '73 were the most significant, with three more top ten hits ("There's a Party

Goin' On", "Good News", and "Darlin', You Can Always Come Back Home"), and three more top twenty hits on the country chart. Given her track record of notoriety starting in 1965 with "Queen of the House", her dynamic appearance vacillating between glamorous and sultry, and her further country hits that built a solid set list, Jody's performances were in demand for 250 shows a year through the 1970s. As the decade wore on and the anti-Nashville outlaw country began to take hold of country music (whether Nashville liked it or not), Jody's chart positions slid further and further down the numerical order of released singles. While she was performing more and more, she realized she was missing the childhood teen years of her daughter, Robin.

Jody was still living her dream when she had the revelation that her career was not going where she wanted it to be headed, and that she was missing out on some important aspects of her life. "I was either in Nashville cutting a new album, or traveling to a concert date somewhere. I was never home," she remembers in the 2004 press release. "Here I was on the road, my daughter is growing up and I'm missing her childhood." She had not had a hit in more than two years by 1981, and had an epiphany while performing: "I was on stage one night and looked out at the audience, all having fun and laughing and enjoying themselves. What was I doing? Working. I had been doing the same thing for eighteen years." When her Epic Records contract ended that year, she dismissed her band, and went back to Blanchard until Robin graduated high school and went to college at Oklahoma City University.

Re-inventing herself once again, Jody recorded an album of patriotic songs on the independent Oklahoma City label, Amethyst, which made its way to the George Bush (the first) presidential campaign. Consequently, not realizing (or caring) that she was a bona fide, 1960s folk-singing, Democrat; she toured with his campaign, singing the national anthem to rapturous applause. After Bush's victory in 1988, Jody sang at the inauguration in 1989. After that experience, and realizing the market for patriotic music was limited, Jody kept exploring other options, at which point she and daughter Robin formed a duo that gave them some time together performing, and doing some press, as

Jody Miller, circa 1965

Jody and Robin. That did get them on Ralph Emery's *Nashville Now* television program in 1990, but the mother-daughter act did not last too long. In the last stage of her career, she turned to Christian music, which has allowed her to share her beautiful voice and potent story to more audiences, which she continued to do through 2011. Of that genre, Jody says, "At this point in my life I've had hit records and traveled all over the world. My love these days is Gospel music. I know it's an old cliché, but if I can touch just one person with my song, then it's all worth it.

In 2000, Sony released the Jody Miller *Anthology,* a collection of her most recognizable songs from 1965 to 1977, which reminded a legion of classic country programmers about her American popular music legacy. In later years, she has been hailed a progressive, transitional figure that was able to alter her career's course based on the shifts in the music industry. She also confirms again that most successful musicians in this text have been adept at more than one style or aspect of the music business. By the 21st century, she reflected positively on her career: "I've been truly blessed," she says, "I've done folk, pop, country, patriotic, and gospel music. I've raised quarter horses, won a Grammy Award, and sung at the White House. But when I got to the supermarket here in Blanchard, folks still see me as 'Myrna Miller.' What more could you ask for?" After a nearly fifty-year career in which she toured the U.S., Europe, and the Far East (with Bob Hope), appeared on numerous nationally broadcast television shows, had two, long-term major label record contracts with thirty-one charting singles on the U.S. country or pop charts, enjoyed success in four different musical genres, and was still married to the same guy through it all, the answer is, not much.

www.jodymillermusic.com

Miller, Roger Dean
(b. January 2, 1936 – d. October 25, 1992)

The witty Roger Miller will always be known for his ability to bring light-hearted sensibility to heavy life subjects. His skills as a songwriter and singer culminated in the 1960s with major pop and country hits such as "Dang Me", "England Swings", "King of the Road", "Little Green Apples", and "Chug-a-Lug". Born in Fort Worth, Texas, Roger's father, Jean Miller, died at twenty-six when Roger was only a year old. As a result, Roger's mother, Laudene Holt Miller, sent her three boys to live with Jean's brothers, and Roger wound up with Armelia and Elmer Miller on a farm outside the tiny southwestern Oklahoma town of Erick.

Although fifteen years older than Roger, Erick native **Sheb Wooley**, who later had a hit with "The Purple People Eater", taught Roger his first chords on guitar, bought him his first fiddle, and spent a lot of time listening to the radio that brought them the Grand Ole Opry on Saturday nights and the Light Crust Doughboys from Fort Worth by day. The connection also provided Sheb the opportunity to meet his wife, Melva Miller, Roger's cousin, which probably explains some more of the closeness between the two. Filled with the hopes of youth, and desperate to escape Erick at the end of the Depression-ravaged 1930s, Roger traveled Oklahoma and Texas working where he could, and learning

Roger Miller

what he could in the honky tonks at night. He could not make enough money to buy a needed guitar, so he stole one in Texas and brought it back into Oklahoma. His conscience got the best of him though and he turned himself in to a judge who offered Miller an opportunity to enlist in the U.S. Army. After some hard lessons in Korea in 1952, Miller returned to the states and played fiddle in Special Services group at Fort McPherson, Georgia, called the Circle A Wranglers. After getting his discharge in 1956, Roger took off for Nashville where he had an unsuccessful audition with Chet Atkins and began washing dishes at the Andrew Jackson Hotel smack in the middle of Nashville's country music scene.

Roger's first break came as fiddler in Minnie Pearl's road band, and his second professional opportunity occurred when he met George Jones at WSM radio one night. Roger played George some songs, and Jones then introduced Miller to Don Pierce and Pappy Daily of Mercury-Starday Records. The meeting led to a record deal in which Miller recorded his first single, "My Pillow" b/w "Poor Little John". Although the single had no success, Roger rode to the Texas session with George Jones and the two co-wrote some songs along the way, to include "Tall, Tall Trees", which Jones recorded in 1957, and "Happy Child", which Jimmy Dean also recorded the same year. The lack of significant success urged Miller to move out to Amarillo, only a couple of hours west from Erick, with his wife and first child on the way. He joined the Amarillo Fire Department where he worked during the day, and played Amarillo nightspots to further his dreams. Miller certainly drew from the period for the opening lines of "Dang Me", but the relocation also proved fortuitous when Miller met Ray Price one night at a club in Amarillo. Several months later Price hired Roger to replace singer Van Howard in the Cherokee Cowboys, and the family was back on their way to Nashville. In the meantime, Miller had written "Invitation to the Blues", and the song made its way to singing cowboy Rex Allen, who had a hit with it in 1958. As Allen's version started to succeed, Miller suggested Ray Price cover the song and it became a #3 country hit. Roger also entered his first songwriting deal in 1958 with Tree Publishing and Buddy Killen, a Grand Ole Opry bassist Roger met in a Nashville bar. The two began a life-long friendship that saw Roger Miller rise to the heights of the country and pop music worlds.

With Killen getting his songs to artists, Roger began a string of country hits as a songwriter. Ernest Tubb hit with "Half a Mind" (#8), Faron Young made the Top Ten with "That's the Way I Feel", Jim Reeves took Miller's "Billy Bayou" to #1, and followed it a few months later with "Home" (#2). Even though Miller was having hits vicariously through other artists, he still wanted his own deal and landed one in 1958 on Decca Records for which he recorded an unsuccessful honky tonk single, "A Man Like Me", with Donny Little, later known as Johnny Paycheck, on harmony vocals. After leaving Ray Price's group, Roger joined Faron Young as drummer, and soon thereafter signed with RCA-Nashville, run by the legendary guitarist and architect of the Nashville pop sound, or, depending on one's perspective, the man who genericized country music, Chet Atkins.

In 1960, Miller's first single of that year was "You Don't Want My Love", later known as "In the Summertime", and defined much of what would follow from Roger Miller. The song is up tempo while the subject matter is about a man who has lost the love in his life, and features Roger's ad-libbed, bluesy scatting. The song made it to #14 on the country charts and was covered by pop crooner Andy Williams. "In the Summertime" also established Roger as a solo act. Less than a year later, Roger cracked the country top ten with "When Two Worlds Collide", a slow, weepy lament about what happens when people from different sides of life get together, and a title inspired by the sci-fi "B" film, *When Two Worlds Collide* (1951), a favorite of Miller's. Those two songs were the highlight of Roger's RCA career as he was dropped in 1963 by the label after "Lock, Stock, and Teardrops" failed to gain any chart response, and Atkins reportedly tired of Miller's celebratory lifestyle.

Even though he had some success with his songwriting and performing, Miller did not get remotely wealthy, or even stable, from his work to that point. His next break came from television when his old friend Jimmy Dean, then guest hosting *The Tonight Show*, called Roger whose walk-on performance of "I Walk the Line" with ad-libbed lyrics was an audience favorite. Appearances on other TV shows followed, and Roger decided he might have a better chance at a career in California than in Nashville. Smash Records entered the picture and picked up Roger in 1963. By January of 1964, Miller was ready for a session in which he cut fifteen songs with some of Nashville's top session musicians. Songs that came out of the session include 1964's million-selling Top Ten hit, "Dang Me", and the catchy popular drinking song, "Chug-a-Lug". However, the songs had not yet become hits, so Roger collected his $1,500 for doing the session, moved to California, and landed upstairs from the eccentric country and pop songwriter and producer from Mannford, OK, **Lee Hazlewood.** While Roger was scrounging for gigs in California, "Dang Me" became a #1 country hit, staying on the chart for twenty-five weeks, and peaked on the pop charts at #7. The song changed his fortunes for good and he became an in-demand performer on stage, TV, and in the recording studios. A few months later, "Chug-a-Lug" hit #3 on the country chart and #9 on the pop chart. By fall Miller was back in the studio for Smash Records, recording "Do-Wacka-Do", a solid #15 hit on the country chart in 1964. Later that year, Miller recorded the song for which he has become most known, "King of the Road".

Known by those close to Miller at the time as "the hobo song," "King of the Road" was released early in 1965 and in March hit #1 on the country charts where it remained for five weeks, made #4 on the pop charts, and by May had sold a million copies. In April 1965, Miller received five GRAMMY Awards for "Dang Me", to include Best Country Music Album, Single, Song, Vocal Performance, and, ironically, Best New Country and Western Artist. By the summer of 1965, Miller's career had reached its zenith, and he received his first royalty check for $168,000. Picked *Jukebox Magazine*'s Artist of the Year in 1965, Miller's crossover status inspired a number of mainstream press articles. *Life* magazine dubbed him a "cracker barrel philosopher," *Time* called him the "unhokey Okie," and in 1966 the *Saturday Evening Post* put him on the cover to represent a story chronicling the "Big boom in country music." The 1966 GRAMMY Awards also showered Miller with awards for the previous year's "King of the Road", to include Best Country and Western Album, Single, Song, and three Best Vocal Performance Awards: Country, Contemporary and Rock and Roll. The Academy of Country Music honored also honored him with Songwriter, Man, and Single of the Year Awards for 1965.

Roger Miller won five Grammy Awards in 1965 for "King of the Road".

Miller continued recording up tempo songs mixing sad topics with humorous lyrics such as "My Uncle Used to Love Me but She Died", as well as tear-in-your beer ballads like "The Last Word in Lonesome is Me" and "Don't We All Have the Right to Be Wrong". Roger also became known for the occasional pop song of pure, if not naïve, happiness as on "Walkin' in the Sunshine". One of his most ironic songs was the postcard view of London in 1965's "England Swings". The song presented a complete opposite view of

By Hugh Foley / 521

England from the one being represented by the British Invasion, and appealed to older Anglo-Americans from whom the "old country" had become a friendly, if not romantic, stereotype, whereas the upstart Beatles signified all the wrong things about popular culture at the time (long hair, irreverence toward authority, counter culture leanings, amplified rock music, etc.).

By 1966, Roger was everywhere. Starting with his national fame in 1965, Roger made television appearances on the *Andy Williams Show*, *Dean Martin Show*, *Hollywood Palace with Bing Crosby*, *Tonight Show with Johnny Carson,* and *The Glen Campbell Goodtime Hour*. The Roger Miller Special aired in January of 1966, and NBC gave him his own TV show that featured many big names but was not renewed at the end of its thirteen-week run in 1966. On his last show, he blew up the train set used on the program so no one else would use it. Early in 1967, Roger had his last crossover hit as a writer, "Walkin' in the Sunshine", and later in the year he recorded, but did not write, the western soundtrack for the film *Waterhole #3*. Subsequently, as a recognizable country music voice, Miller proved his good ear for commercial tunes and turned to recording other people's songs, to include Bobby Russell's "Little Green Apples" in 1968, his last Top 40 crossover hit as an artist, and Kris Kristofferson's "Me and Bobby McGhee, with Miller had a Top 20 country hit in 1969.

With his peak success years past, Miller recorded several country standards with honky-tonk arrangements in 1970 called *A Trip in the Country*. The album had no real impact, but "Don't We All Have the Right", which he had written in 1962 and included on the album, turned up on Ricky Van Shelton's first album, *Wild-Eyed Dream* (1987), indicating Roger's influence on young country singers (or their producers). Mercury folded the Smash label in 1970, but not before Miller had one more minor chart single with "Hoppy's Song", about the death of singing cowboy Hopalong Cassidy which Roger related to the end of an era in America. Columbia Records signed Miller after Smash folded, and Roger released *Dear Folks: Sorry I Haven't Written Lately*, which did not provide any hits.

In 1973, he wrote and sang songs for the Disney film, *Robin Hood*, and also appeared as the voice of Allan-A-Dale in the movie. That performance opened a new world of opportunities for his recognizable voiceovers and songs in productions aimed at children. He hosted and sang on *The Muppet Show* in the late 70s, and narrated several other youth-oriented features and specials throughout the remainder of his career. He also appeared in episodes of television programs such as *Love American Style*, *Daniel Boone* (as Johnny Appleseed), *Murder She Wrote*, and *Quincy* where he played a singer with a substance abuse problem. Along with operating his King of the Road hotel chain, and making regular concert appearances, Roger continued recording moderate hits for Mercury and Elektra through the 1970s until 1982's *Old Friends*, on which he teamed up with old friends Willie Nelson and Ray Price.

With *Old Friends*, Roger made it back into the country Top Ten with the album's title track, written for his folks back in Oklahoma. Miller also enjoyed a significant resurgence of interest in his work when he was commissioned in 1984 to write songs for a Broadway musical adaptation of Mark Twain's *Adventures of Huckleberry Finn* called *Big River*. Broadway producer and long-time fan had seen Miller at a live appearance at New York City's Lone Star Café, and knew Roger would be perfect to write the music and songs of the musical that opened in 1985 and was huge hit. When actor John Goodman left for a film role, Roger played the part of Pap, based on Miller's uncle in Oklahoma, for a few months on Broadway and in a national tour. Thanks to the show's success, Roger recorded a self-titled album for MCA in 1986, on which he sang several songs from the play, and *Big River* received seven Tony Awards, including Roger's for "Best Score." The extra attention induced the Academy of Country Music to give Roger their Pioneer Award for 1987, and *Big River* turned out to be the crowning achievement of his thirty-year career. The success of *Big River* led him to relax with his family until he was convinced by his manager and long-time friend, Stan Moress, to get back on the road, solo with guitar. The shows were met with enthusiastic response from critics and fans, but in the fall of 1991, Miller was diagnosed with lung cancer. His last performance was during CMA Week in Nashville, and after a year of treatment, with one remission, he died in Nashville at the relatively young age of 56. In 1995, Miller was inducted posthumously into the Country Music Hall of Fame. His third and final wife, Mary Miller, a former singer with Kenny Rogers and the First Edition, and backup vocalist for Roger from the 1970s forward, said the induction "would have been his ultimate dream come true." He is survived by seven children: Alan, Rhonda, Shari, Dean, Shannon, Taylor, and Adam. Roger's posthumous fame has been significant.

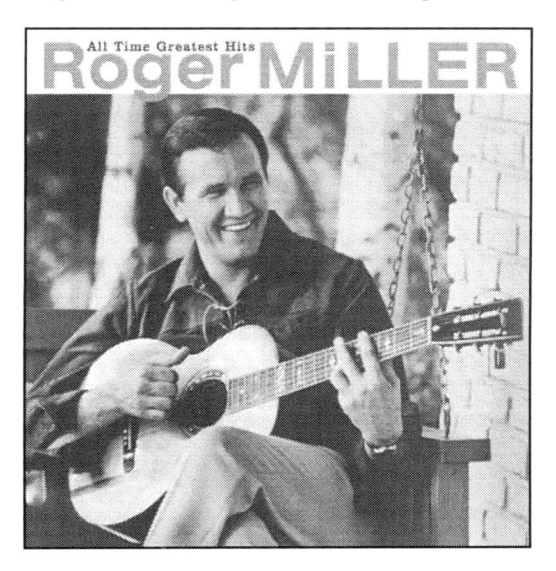

Since 1992, at least forty-four albums have been released devoted fully or in part to Miller's recorded output, The Nashville Network aired a two-hour television special remembering Roger's life and music featuring Reba McEntire, Willie Nelson, Trisha Yearwood and other country stars, and he received Grammy Hall of Fame Awards in 1997 and 1998. In 1999, his song "Husbands and Wives" was nominated as Song of the Year, and in one of the more significant "best of" lists produced in 2000, the Recording Industry of America and the National Endowment for the Arts listed "King of the Road" #84 on their combined "Songs of the Century" list. Roger's career sales included a platinum single (1,000,000 sold), six gold singles (500,000 sold each), and five gold albums (500,000 sold each). In 2003, CMT named "King of the Road" as one of the 100 Greatest Country Songs, placing it at #37 in the somewhat arbitrary list, and the musical, *Big River*, opened again on Broadway in November of that year. Also in 2003, Roger's son, Dean, released an album on Universal South Records, the first single from which was called "The Gun Ain't Loaded."

The people of Roger's hometown of Erick created the Roger Miller Museum Foundation in 2001 with the goal of building a museum to exhibit memorabilia from the life and career of yet another successful singing and songwriting Oklahoman, which happened in 2004, and has continued pulling motorists off I-40 going east or west into or out the western edge of the state. The museum also was able to release a unique Roger Miller album. In 1976, Miller performed a concert in Erick at the request of his mother, Armelia Miller, to benefit the Roger Miller Senior Citizen Center. Mary Miller discovered the tape of the performance, had it re-mastered, and is available only through the museum. In 2004, Miller

By Hugh Foley / 523

received Oklahoma's highest honor for a musician with ties to the state: induction into the Oklahoma Music Hall of Fame in Muskogee. In another appearance of Miller's songs, **Merle Haggard** included Roger's "Leavin's Not the Only Way to Go" on his 2005 disc, *Chicago Wind* (Capitol). Mary Miller has been very protective and proactive regarding Roger's career and copyrights. She successfully sued Sony/ATV Publishing for copyright infringement in 2007, finally being awarded nearly one million dollars in royalties and rights from Sony for songs Miller wrote in 1964.

With regard to Oklahoma, Miller certainly gained musical sense and his rural identity from the state. By all counts, however, he did want to get out of the state as soon as possible to succeed in show business, but his drive to accomplish his goals, regardless of the sacrifice to family and friends, produced lyrics that were at times melancholy and poignant, and other times celebratory and just downright silly, all of which evolved into country and pop hits to which many people could, and still do, relate. That was Roger Miller.

www.rogermiller.com

Milton, Roy

(b. July 31, 1907 – d. September 18, 1983)

As jump, jive, and rhythm and blues from the late 1930s to the early 1950s mowed a path for rock and roll in American popular music, bandleader, vocalist, and drummer Roy Milton, along with his contemporaries of Louis Jordan, Wynonie Harris, and **Lowell Fulson**, fronted one of the primary R&B combos that presaged the rock movement. Milton's top 5 R & B hit, "R.M. Blues", met the celebratory stateside mood in immediate post-World War II, and established Roy as an important small combo bandleader, rivaled only by Louis Jordan. At times, Milton was even more popular than Jordan, especially at the height of "R.M. Blues, which also established Specialty Records as an important source for R & B, blues, gospel, and primary influences on the first wave of rock and roll.

Born in the small, south central Oklahoma oil town of Wynnewood, Milton's father was a gospel singer, and his mother was reportedly American Indian. The family moved to Tulsa when Roy was four and he began singing in the local church choir as a child. By high school he played in his high school brass band, and in 1929 formed his own combo to play various social functions in the Tulsa area. From 1931 to 1933, Milton played with Tulsa bandleader Ernie Fields before moving to California in 1935 where he formed his Solid Senders orchestra. The Solid Senders mixed big band swing with gospel and blues and Milton released his first records independently before joining Hamptone, and then Juke Box Records.

Roy Milton

Under the entrepreneurship of Art Rupe, Milton recorded four songs for the newly formed Specialty label in 1945 to include "Groovy Blues", "Milton's Boogie", "Rhythm

Cocktail", and the 1946 Top Five R&B hit, "R.M. Blues", which placed Roy on a pedestal next to the king of jump blues, Louis Jordan. The success also allowed Specialty to attract other artists, such as Guthrie-born, **Jimmy Liggins.** Eventually, the label also released blues such as Guitar Slim's "The Things I Used to Do", and, ultimately, early rock and roll gems such as Lloyd Price's "Lawdy Miss Clawdy", Little Richard's major songs, "Tutti Fruiti," "Long Tall Sally", "Lucille", and "Rip it Up", in addition to Sam Cooke's early gospel recordings. Rupe recorded numerous Roy Milton songs through 1953, and scored nineteen Top Ten R&B hits with Roy such as "Thrill Me", "The Hucklebuck", "Information Blues", a cover of Louis Prima's "Oh Babe!" and, finally, "Night and Day" (1952) was Milton's last chart record for Specialty. The Specialty recordings featured Milton's earthy witticisms, such as "Keep a Dollar in Your Pocket" and "I've Had My Moments", as well as the pianist Camille Howard, and two bold saxophone players, Buddy Floyd and Benny Waters.

After leaving Specialty, Milton recorded for Dootoone and King throughout the 1950s with little success, and had a minor R & B hit for Warwick, "Red Light," in 1961. Milton worked one-nighters with his band throughout the 1950s and 1960s, but did not enjoy as much recognition from the British blues boom as other blues and R & B artists from the 1940s and 50s, primarily because Roy's group was not guitar based. Funky guitarist **Jimmy Nolen**, who provided James Brown's primary guitar licks, remembered seeing Roy's group in Oklahoma in the 1950s, and saxophonist Stanley Turrentine talked about running into Milton's bands in the "Blacks only" restaurants of the south during the same period. In 1970, Milton appeared with Johnny Otis at the Monterrey Jazz Festival and experienced a resurgence of sorts as he toured the U.S. and Europe, sometimes with Otis, but retired for all purposes at the end of the 1970s. Roy Milton is another Oklahoma musician who is credited with mixing several styles of music (gospel, swing, and blues) that were part of his primary musical experiences in the state. Subsequently, he not only crafted a sound tailored to his own identity that reached the masses as much as any post-World War II black artist of the late 1940s, but also is one of the forerunners of the multi-influenced hybrid popular music known as rock 'n roll.

Minner, D.C. & Selby
(b. January 24, 1935 – d. May 6, 2008)

No one did more in Oklahoma to keep the blues alive among young people and adult blues fans in the state at the turn of the 21st century than D.C. Minner and his bassist and wife, Selby, known collectively as Blues on the Move. A smooth vocalist and fluid blues guitarist with a sharp tone, Minner has written, recorded, and released his own "down home blues" since 1992 after playing through thirty years as a touring musician with only one minor break: when he did not speak for seven months in 1969 as his own form of social protest. The history of Minner's birthplace, Rentiesville, Oklahoma, stems from the collective stories of the **Muscogee (Creek) Nation**, a major Civil War battle at Honey Springs, and the Black town movement of late

D.C. and Selby Minner

19th century Indian Territory. Also the birthplace of esteemed African-American historian John Hope Franklin, Minner based his Texas Road Recording Company, the Annual Dusk 'til Dawn Blues Festival, and the Oklahoma Blues Hall of Fame in the rural Rentiesville nightclub where he entered the world and grew up.

D.C. Minner was the only child of Helen Pearson Minner and Clarence Minner, but was raised by his grandmother, Lura Drennan, on family land where she operated a juke joint, speak-easy, grocery, and after-hours blues club beginning in the early 20th century. His family came to Rentiesville from Alabama, with four Cherokee sisters and their black husbands settling in the Muscogee (Creek) Nation which was more hospitable to mixed-marriages between American Indians and African-Americans of the period. Rentiesville was close enough to the Cherokee Nation so the sisters did not have far to go to visit their relatives. As a youngster, D.C. spent hours listening to the acoustic blues played by various traveling musicians in the club, such as Al Freeman, a black man who played slide guitar with a pocketknife, and a white named Slim, eho played Delta blues and country dance tunes for customers. D.C. borrowed Al's guitar when the musician would pass out drunk, and then try to imitate what he saw on stage. Since the musicians turned the pegs on their instruments to get in tune, so did D.C., often breaking the strings before nervously setting the guitar back down and getting out the area quickly to avoid a scolding. As for other musical influences, his grandfather made everyone be quiet at noon so they could hear the broadcasts of **Bob Wills** and His Texas Playboys when they had come inside for lunch from working in the fields. Wills' music is also the first place D.C. recalled hearing horns in any music, and the source of the first song he learned, "Sitting on Top of the World," which his grandfather used to sing working behind the mules, and which Bob Wills made popular in Oklahoma through his broadcasts over KVOO. His grandmother, Lura, promoted large gospel sings in Muskogee, just twenty-eight miles to the north, and took D.C. to see major gospel groups like the Soul Stirrers.

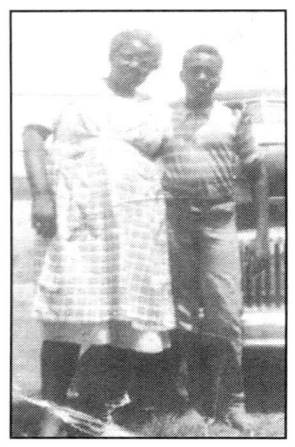

D.C. Minner's grandmother, Lura Drennan with D.C., circa 1945.

Minner's first instrument was an old front porch piano that became a pie safe after his family tired of him playing it, and he sang in gospel quartets when he was 14. D.C. explained the connection between gospel and blues in a 1998 interview published in *Living Blues* magazine: "I don't believe there's ever been any difference between church music and the blues in any area, except instead of saying 'Oh Lord' you say 'Oh baby'."[1] As a teenager, D.C. listened to R & B via Tennessee radio stations, Wolfman Jack out of Del Rio, Texas, and the X-border station, XERA, from Ciudad Acuna, Mexico. He left Rentiesville in 1953 to join the service where he learned to play flamenco guitar from two Army buddies, and returned to the states carrying a guitar. Not long after returning, he married his high school chorus teacher, and by 1961 was in Oklahoma City playing bass for Little Eddy Taylor. Soon thereafter, he played bass with Larry Johnson and the New Breed, a group that played independently through early 1967, but also made a living out of backing up blues stars like **Lowell Fulson**, Chuck Berry, Bo Diddley, Jimmy Reed, and Eddie Floyd when he had a hit with "Knock on Wood."

O.V. Wright, the gospel singer turned soul vocalist who epitomized the blend of gospel and R & B into 1960s soul music, kept New Breed working as his backup band for two years, and D.C. also played and led the band for two years with Freddy King, arguably his biggest influence on guitar. Minner has long used King's "Hideway" as his break song for starting and/or ending sets, and claims him "the best guitar player I've ever heard." When the group broke up about 1965, D.C. headed for California and played in a group with **Tony Mathews**. By 1969, D.C. opted for San Francisco and the Bay Area where he met Selby, his future bass player, wife, and business partner. Selby had worked her way to the West coast from Providence, Rhode Island where she was an art student and aspiring singer shocked into professional action by a four-hour Janis Joplin concert.

Traveling in a folk duo with Jim Donovan through Washington, D.C., Chicago, and New Orleans, Selby Minner heard about the blues scene in the Bay Area and headed west in the late 1960s. While working the coffeehouses and clubs as an acoustic blues and folk singer over the next few years, Selby eventually met D.C. in places where they crossed paths as musicians around 1973, and the two started performing together in 1976. The next year they left Berkeley in a step-van as Blues on the Move and stayed on the road for twelve years, marrying in 1979. With D.C. on guitar and vocals, Selby on bass and vocals, and a series of pick up drummers, they traveled the U.S., frequently in the Southwest and on the West Coast. They stayed in San Francisco for a year in 1984, and then in L.A. during 1986 and 1987 where they played regularly five nights a week throughout the metropolitan area.

Tiring of the road life and urban hassles, D.C. and Selby returned to Rentiesville in 1988 when they opened the Down Home Blues Club in the same house where he was reared. Saying nobody would ever come that far out in the country to hear music, neighbors and onlookers laughed as he started building the club, determined as Noah, and put the place together. At first, the club served the after hours clientele of the area who would bring beer in coolers, pay a cover, dance, or just listen to D.C., Selby, and/or various guests jam until dawn. Given the town's location and history, the club has an easy, relaxed feel of multicultural society where no one is above the blues. In 1991, the ethos escalated into the Dusk 'til Dawn Blues Festival, featuring a wide roster of local, regional, national, and international blues artists, many of whom D.C. and Selby met on their travels throughout the U.S. Claimed by the Blues Foundation in Memphis as a "must-see to say you are in touch with the blues scene in the country today," leg-

Larry Johnson and the New Breed, circa 1967, with D.C. Minner pictured far right with bass guitar.

By Hugh Foley / 527

endary artists such as Carey Bell, Eddie Kirkland, Magic Slim, and Nappy Brown have stunned blues fans with 4 a.m. sets at the festival, and up-and-coming artists like Indigenous and Rosie Ledet have played before they became national figures. Lesser-known, but extremely authentic artists, such as James Peterson and Drink Small have been to the festival, and a bevy of Oklahomans are featured each year.

The Minners also released a series of notable recordings in the 1990s on their Texas Road Recording label. Starting with the independent cult-favorite cassette, *Shake Hands & Make Friends with the Blues* (1992), D.C. and Selby released critically praised albums *Live 1991* (1994) and *Love Lost and Found* (1997), *Morning Train* (1998), *I Can Tell You Got Good Loving* (2001), and *Full Moon Over Rentiesville* (2003). The albums are full of D.C.'s experienced vocals merging soul, blues, and gospel with a rhythm and lead guitar style drenched in Freddy King, but filtered through a lifetime of exposure to R & B, country, and rock and roll. Selby also complements the albums with her own easy rolling bass work and warm singing, now seasoned by many years of playing with D.C. and backing up Little Johnny Taylor, Albert Collins, Lowell Fulson, Hubert Sumlin, and Smokey Wilson. Of particular interest from Texas Road Recording is the *Guitar Showdown* CD, recorded at the festival in 1996, the set sears through a battle of Oklahoma blues guitarists to include D.C., **Tony Matthews** (Checotah, OK), Larry Johnson (Muskogee, OK), **Flash Terry**, and Berry Harris (Stringtown, OK). Recorded live and released as an Oklahoma Blues Heritage CD free only to public schools in 1998, the album was reissued commercially by Texas Road in 2002.

D.C. Minner, circa 1995 Down Home Blues Club, Rentiesville, OK.

D.C. and Selby were also extremely active with the Blues in the Schools (BITS) program in which they did residencies with band programs and teach students how to play blues, R & B, and rock, as well passing on some valuable life lessons he had picked up along the way. D.C. began working with BITS on the West Coast in the 1970s, and has continued with Selby from kindergartens to colleges in Rhode Island, Massachusetts, California, and across Oklahoma until the present. One of Minner's students, Garrett Jacobson, already a classically trained pianist in his hometown of Edmond, Oklahoma, started playing with D.C. at age twelve in 1997 after meeting the elder blues man through BITS. After releasing two critically praised blues albums of his own by the time he was 18, Garrett now fronts his own blues-rock group regionally as "Big G" Jacobson. The Minners consistently supported youth getting involved in the blues, always making younger musicians a part of their annual festivals and open jams.

D.C. and Selby began participating on the Oklahoma Arts Council's Touring and Artist in Residence rosters since 1989, and worked with the Mid America Arts Alliance from 1993 through about 2007 in Kansas, Missouri, Texas, Nebraska, and Arkansas. The Minners' story did not go unnoticed on a local, nor national level. In 1998, D.C. was interviewed for *The Oprah Winfrey Show* about growing up in one of Oklahoma's original twenty-eight African-American towns. D.C. and Selby taped two songs in the club,

"Hideaway" and "Shade Tree Mechanic," recorded for the program airing March 6, 1998 on CBS. In 1999, The International Blues Foundation honored them in Memphis with a Keeping the Blues Alive Award, and featured them in a nationally distributed video about Blues in the Schools. In 1999, D.C. was inducted into the Oklahoma Jazz Hall of Fame in the blues category, and was the only one honored who actually lived in the state at the time of the award. The accolades of 1999 culminated with Rentiesville renaming the dirt road next to the Down Home Blues Club as D.C. Minner Street. ¼ mile north of the club, the street also borders the Honey Springs Civil War Battlefield where African-Americans, Anglo-Americans, American Indians, and Mexican-Americans fought against and among one another. As of 2011, friendly mix-raced crowds celebrate the blues together every Labor Day at the Dusk 'til Dawn Blues Festival.

In 2002, Texas Road Video released a 53-minute video documentary of the festival. Shot in the late 1990s and dedicated by D.C. to Oklahoma City native and former New Breed member Claude Williams, who led Ike and Tina Turner's band as a trumpeter in the 1970s, the video includes live music and interviews with Indigenous, Flash Terry, Blackhawk Blues Band, Michael Burton, Lem Shepard, Hiram Harvel, D.C. Minner and Selby. D.C. received his home state's highest musical honor when he was inducted into the Oklahoma Music Hall of Fame, along with his good friend, Flash Terry, in 2003, the year designated as the "Year of the Blues" by the U.S. Congress. Before and during his illness, up to his death on May 6, 2008, at home in Rentiesville, Minner made many recordings in his Texas Road Studio inside the house/club. Eventually, Selby Minner intends on releasing those recordings. As of 2011, Selby Minner continued performing, recording, and teaching the blues in Oklahoma, regionally, and nationally. She also maintained the Down Home Blues Club's as both a historic and active musical venue, and coordinates inductions and celebrations for Oklahoma Blues Hall of Fame. Founded and housed in the club by Selby and D.C., the Oklahoma Blues Hall of Fame seeks to create awareness about many lesser known Oklahoma blues musicians, as well as those who have made major contributions to the genre, none of which were as intrinsic to raising awareness of the blues in Oklahoma at the turn of the 21st century than D.C. and Selby Minner.

www.dcminnerblues.com

Note

1. For a complete oral history of D.C. Minner's early life, see the interview with Minner by Hugh Foley, published as "DC & Selby Minner: Oklahoma Down Home Blues" in *Living Blues* (# 139), May/June 1998, 40.

Mitchell, Leona

(b. October 13, 1948)

According to Mitchell family folklore, when a mother is carrying a child, she can make a wish for the baby growing inside of her. Pearl Mitchell made a wish that her tenth child would become a singer, and her wish was granted ten times over, as Leona Mitchell is one of opera's most acclaimed sopranos of the modern era. Born in Enid, where a street now bears her name, Leona Pearl Mitchell was one of fifteen children. At age four, Leona could sing "The Lord's Prayer" to perfection, and it appeared that her mother's wish was to become a reality. Leona recalls that during her early childhood, she dreamed of becoming a world-class vocalist, a dream that was to become true by all standards of operatic stardom (or any other musical genre). She received early vocal training in the choir at the Antioch Church of God in Christ in Enid, where her father, Reverend Hulon Mitchell, was the minister. Mitchell sang in her father's church choir from about age ten through high school, and during her teenage years was the choir director. The Mitchell household contained numerous musical instruments, including xylophone, bass violin, clarinet, saxophone, and guitars. Her father played several of these instruments by ear. Her mother, Pearl, was an excellent pianist, and young Leona took lessons from her. Because of the musical influences in the home, Leona's older siblings formed "The Musical Mitchells."

Leona attended Carver Elementary, Emerson Junior High, and Enid High School. During Leona's public school music education, her major influence was Maurine Priebe, director of choirs for the Enid school system. It was Priebe who discovered Leona's vocal talents while singing at Carver Elementary and Emerson Junior High. Mitchell played violin in the Enid High School orchestra, but had to drop it for choir as participation in both was disallowed at the time. Priebe played the Maria Callas and Leontyne Price recordings of *Aida* for Mitchell which inspired her future favorite role. Her most vivid recollection of high school performances under the direction of Priebe was the role of Aida in Verdi's *Aida*.

Leona Mitchell

With encouragement from Priebe, Mitchell auditioned for the music department at Oklahoma City University, and received a full scholarship (the first student to receive such an honor) to study music there following graduation from Enid High School. At OCU, she studied with Inez Silberg and performed several soprano roles in operas produced at the university. Her first was the role of Susanna in Mozart's *The Marriage of Figaro*. She obtained her B. A. in Music in 1971 from OCU.

During her post-college career, Mitchell completed graduate studies at the Julliard School of Music in New York, received the prestigious Kurt Herbert Adler Award of the San Francisco Opera, and was awarded the highly coveted $10,000 Opera America grant that enabled her to study with Ernest St. John Metz in Los Angeles. As a soprano, she debuted with the San Francisco Opera in 1973 as Micaela in Bizet's *Carmen*.

Mitchell's long and illustrious career as one of America's leading lyric-spinto sopranos has featured many extraordinary and riveting performances. Noteworthy among these are her 1975 debut as Micaela in Bizet's *Carmen* with New York City's Metropolitan Opera. She remained on the Met's roster in the 1980s and 1990s. It was an auspicious debut with Placido Domingo as her singing partner. A second highlight was also in 1975 when Mitchell received international acclaim for her selection to sing the role of Bess in the Decca-London complete stereo recording of the George Gershwin classic *Porgy and Bess* with the Cleveland Symphony Orchestra. A third highlight was in 1984 when Mitchell was pregnant with her son, she sang the role of Elvira in Verdi's *Ernani* with Luciano Pavarotti, the greatest lyric tenor of our time. Additional roles for which she has won international recognition include Donna Anna in Mozart's *Don Giovanni*, Mme. Lidoine in Poulenc's

Dialogues of the Carmelites, Pamina in Mozart's *Die Zauberflote*, Musetta in Puccini's *La Boheme*, Leonora in Verdi's *La Forza del destino*, Elvira in Verdi's *Ernani*, Amelia in Verdi's *Un Ballo in Maschera*, Butterfly in Puccini's *Madama Butterfly*, Leonora in Verdi's *Il Trovatore*, Elisabetta in Verdi's *Don Carlo*, Liu in Puccini's *Turandot*, and her favorite, the title role in Verdi's *Aida*. She has sung nearly 200 performances of this revered opera that has become so lovingly identified with her. Critical acclaim has rained down on her from the world's most significant opera observers and writers. The London *Daily Telegraph* exalted over Mitchell's for her unforgettable interpretation of *Aida*: "American Leona Mitchell produced a torrent of beautiful sound from one of world's greatest prima donnas. If Verdi were alive today, he would applaud Ms. Mitchell's performance as generously as did the opening night audience." The *Boston Globe* exclaimed she "revels in the one of the most gorgeous voices in the world." The *San Francisco Chronicle* proclaimed her voice as having "a rich, natural tone that possesses the listener as though her were producing it." The *Los Angeles Times* noted "she included as many gleaming high notes as most audiences could ever want… a performance of nobility, restraint, articulated warmth and vocal splendor." The *New York Times*, often tempered in any review due to the constant barrage of excellence to which the paper's critics are exposed, was officially smitten, saying, "[Mitchell] produces a creamy sound that remains smooth throughout her range, and her remarkable sense of the opera conveys the role's emotional resonance directly."[1] Her performances with the most prestigious opera companies have virtually spanned the globe with appearances on six of the seven continents, including Rio de Janeiro, Buenos Aires, Mexico City in South America; Paris, Nice, Bordeaux, Marseille, London, Edinburgh, Berlin, Frankfurt, Bonn, Hamburg, Rome, and Madrid in Europe; Tokyo and Hong Kong in Asia; Sydney and Melbourne in Australia; Cairo in Africa; and throughout North America from New York City to San Francisco. Her ravishing vocal opulence and commanding presence have resulted in recitals at some of the most important venues in North America, including Carnegie Hall, Lincoln Center, Kennedy Center, and the White House where she performed for Presidents Gerald Ford, Ronald Reagan, Jimmy Carter, and Bill Clinton. In 1985, Mitchell was honored in a joint session of the Oklahoma legislature where she was recognized for her achievements and named honorary chair of Black Heritage Month. She has also been recognized in her home state with honorary doctorates from OCU and OU. Other honors include grants from the Rockefeller Foundation and the National Opera Institute.

Along with several individual downloads available through internet music resources such as amazon.com or itunes.com, Mitchell is a featured performer on several albums: *Joy to the World* (Hallmark, 1988) featuring Mitchell and Placido Domingo on Christmas holiday songs; Puccini's *Turandot* (Gala, 2000); *Leona Mitchell Sings Favourite Soprano Arias* (Eloquence/Australia, 2002); and Puccini's *Greatest Hits* (Decca, 2003). Several of her performances are also available on DVD, to include one of her acclaimed roles with Luciano Pavarotti in the 1983 performance of Verdi's *Ernani* (Decca DVD, 2008); Puccini's *Turandot* (UMVD, 2003) featuring Mitchell and Placido Domingo as recorded at New York City's Metropolitan Opera in 1988; and *Verdi – Un Ballo in Maschera* (Kultur Video, 2006).[2] In 2008, she recorded a Christmas album, *A Classic Christmas*, with Oklahoma City's Windsong Chamber Choir, released that year, and primarily available at the choir's performances.

Residing in Houston as of 2011, Mitchell is married to Elmer Bush, her personal manager, and they have one son, Elmer "E.C." Bush IV. She performed in 2001 in her hometown of Enid as a fundraiser for the Martin Luther King, Jr. Scholarship program. In 2002, she performed for the 50th Anniversary of the OCU Musical Theater and Opera Company, sang a benefit concert for the Simon Estes Foundation in Tulsa, performed at the dedication of the new Capitol dome in Oklahoma City during which she sang the national anthem, and launched a concert tour with stops in her hometown performing with the Enid Symphony, as well as in Oklahoma City, Denver, Miami, St. Louis, and Washington, D.C. Extremely beneficent to her home state, Mitchell performed a benefit concert for the Tulsa Opera in 2004, and another benefit performance for the Oklahoma Jazz Hall of Fame in Tulsa in 2007. She also performed in 2008 in Oklahoma City with the 90-voice Chancel Choir and full orchestra in the renovated sanctuary of the Westminster Presbyterian Church. Leona was inducted into the Oklahoma Hall of Fame in 2001, and also the Oklahoma Hall of Fame in 2004, as well as the Oklahoma Jazz Hall of Fame and the Oklahoma Women's Hall of Fame.[3]

Notes
1. The critical review quotes are taken from Leona Mitchell's official press packet which does not document the specific issues from which the quotes are derived.
2. All of the recordings listed were available through www.amazon.com as of July, 2011.
3. The majority of this essay is derived from publicity materials provided by Leona Mitchell for the *Oklahoma Music Guide*.

Moeller, W.E. "Lucky"
(b. February 12, 1912 – d. June 15, 1992)

A primary country music booking agent from the late 1940s through the mid-1970s. Walter Ernest "Lucky" Moeller was born in the western Oklahoma town of Okarche. One of ten children, he herded cattle as a young man, and by the 1940s became a banker in Oklahoma City. With Western swing at its height of popularity, Moeller bought a ballroom owner in Clinton, Oklahoma, and led a band, Lucky Moeller and the Western Okies. By 1947, Moeller's group played regularly at the Trianon Ballroom in Oklahoma City, and by 1948 was broadcasting weekly over KOCY (OKC). Moeller eventually purchased the Trianon, booking major acts of the period, such as T. Texas Tyler, Hank Snow, Ernest Tubb, Eddie Arnold, and Roy Acuff, often backing them with the Western Okies.

By 1949, Lucky switched his band's name to the Rhythm Busters, and booked weekly radio broadcasts on Friday and Saturday nights over KTOK Radio (OKC) to promote the ballroom. By 1949 at least, Moeller began to manage **Bob Wills**, the famous Western swing artist, and two years later, honky-tonk king, Webb Pierce. Soon thereafter, Moeller moved to Nashville for the height of Pierce's success behind the 1953 classic barroom weeper, "There Stands the Glass".

W.E. "Lucky" Moeller

By 1956 Moeller relocated to Springfield, Missouri, becoming general manager of Top Talent Agency. There, he booked the Ozark Jubilee TV program, often featuring Pierce, and managed Red Foley, Brenda Lee, Smiley Burnette, Sonny James, **Wanda Jackson**, and a few other great show biz-names, Uncle Cyp and Aunt Sap, The Whirli-Jiggers, and Lennie and Goo-Goo.[1]

Returning to Nashville and employed by the Jim Denny Artist Bureau, Moeller managed many top country stars in the 1950s and 1960s, including Pierce, Hank Snow, Dottie West, Jimmie Dickens, **Norma Jean**, Lefty Frizzell, Minnie Pearl, and Porter Wagoner during Wagoner's notoriety for nationally syndicated Porter Wagoner TV show. Moeller also co-founded the Nashville Association of Talent Directors in 1958.

Moeller lived up to his nickname when he won half of the publishing rights to "Are You Sincere", a #3 hit for Andy Williams in 1958 (also covered by Elvis Presley, Trini Lopez, and Frank Sinatra). Originally written by another native Oklahoman, **Wayne Walker**, who was managed by the Denny Agency before the song was a hit, Moeller is usually listed as the song's co-author.[2] When Jim Denny died in 1963, Lucky changed the firm's name to Denny-Moeller, and soon, to Moeller Talent, Inc. which became a primary instigator in Waylon Jennings' career.[3] With son Larry (born in Oklahoma City, raised in Clinton), and son-in-law Jack Andrews helping run the show, Moeller Talent was "the world's largest country music talent agency" from the 1960s through 1974, when Lucky suffered a major stroke.[4] Returning to Okarche with Jack and daughter, Dixie, Moeller attempted to keep the agency going, but it closed within a year, and Lucky retired until his death in 1992. Staying in Nashville, Larry continued managing Waylon Jennings, and later, Willie Nelson out of an Austin office.[5] In 2011 Larry had retired in Lyles, Tennessee, while Jack and Dixie lived in Okarche.[6]

Notes
1. An advertisement in a March 23, 1957 issue of *Billboard* lists artists managed by Lucky Moeller at the Top Talent Agency (p.86).
2. This episode is discussed on a European rockabilly fan at website http://www.rockabilly.nl/references/messages/wayne_walker.htm (accessed July, 31, 2011), however, links to a Porter Wagoner website for clarification of the issue are not active.
3. Moeller is credited with being "one of the people instrumental in launching the career of Waylon Jennings" in a September 21, 1974 issue of *Billboard* magazine, (p. 42).
4. A rough sketch of Lucky Moeller's career up to through the mid-1960s occurs in an un-credited article that reads as much like a press release as it does a feature article, appears in the *The Oklahoman*, (p. 136), July, 10, 1966, but does include the quote about "the world's largest country music talent agency", citing a statistic that Moeller Talent arranged "exclusive personal appearances for about 75 percent of the world of entertainment."
5. Al Cunniff chronicled Moeller's career in an entry under Moeller's name in the *Encyclopedia of Country Music* (New York: Oxford University Press, 1998), 350.
6. Telephone interview between the author and Dixie (Moeller) Andrews, August 2, 2011.

Mooney, Ralph
(b. September 16, 1928 – d. March 20, 2011)

A forty-year veteran steel guitarist, who has backed such stars as **Merle Haggard**, Buck Owens, and Waylon Jennings, as well as a noted songwriter, including the much recorded "Crazy Arms," Ralph Mooney was born in Duncan, Oklahoma, a community of about 21,000 residents southwest of Oklahoma City. As a youngster, Ralph learned the fundamentals of guitar, mandolin, and fiddle from his brother-in-law. After hearing **Leon McAuliffe**, legendary steel guitar player for **Bob Wills** and the Texas Playboys, he chose that instrument and learned to play McAuliffe's "Steel Guitar Rag" employing an old knife to fret his flat-top guitar. During his early career, he crafted his own steel guitar composed of birch slabs for the body, coat hangers for pullers, and thick steel rods for legs.

As a teenager, Ralph followed his sisters to California, where they settled in Bell Gardens, a suburb of Los Angeles. According to all sources referenced for this essay, he didn't even see his first steel guitar until he was about thirteen years old.[1] After working as a machinist at Douglas Aircraft and Alcoa Aluminum, he finally decided to devote his life to music. Ralph discovered that his neighbor was **Merle Lindsay**, another native Oklahoman who had moved out to California in the wake of Western swing's popular wave of the late 1930s through the late 1940s. Lindsay gave Ralph his first professional job as a steel guitar player with his band, the Nightriders. Following this break, he began playing on weekends and doing session work for Skeets McDonald, known for his "Don't Let the Stars Get Into Your Eyes" composition. During this time, Jesse Ashlock, the fiddler with **Bob Wills' Texas Playboys**, helped Ralph out on an instrument Mooney had made himself.

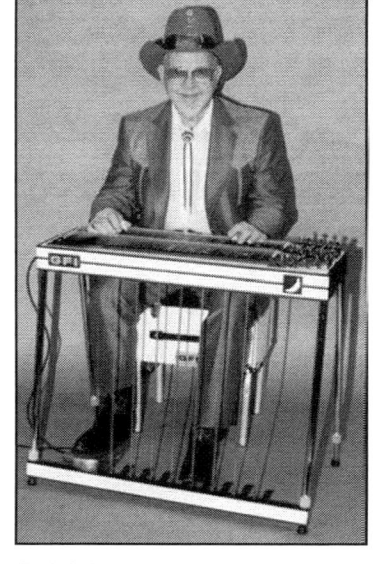

Around 1950, Mooney became a regular performer on Carl Moore's "Squeakin' Deacon" radio show on KXLA in Los Angeles where he met teenage singer Wynn Stewart, a consistent winner on the show's weekly talent programs. This acquaintance developed into a life long friendship, and when Ralph returned to the Los Angeles after a brief stint in Las Vegas, he began to play on a regular basis with Stewart, one of the pioneers in the development of the "Bakersfield Sound" in country music, of which the steel guitar was a primary instrumental imprint. Stewart's first Capitol sessions featured Mooney, and the friends opened the Nashville Nevada Club in Las Vegas.

Ralph Mooney, circa 2000

By the end of the 1950s, Mooney had created his signature multi-finger picking style, akin to the Earl Scrugg's three-fingered banjo style that is often described as "rolling", merged with a weepy steel guitar sound that sounds like someone crying. With this technique and his strong sense of melody, Mooeny become the go-to steel guitar player on the West Coast. He joined recording sessions of Bakersfield Sound luminaries, Merle Haggard, on which he played for Hag's first sessions on Talley Records in 1963, as well as on such Haggard hits as "Sing Me Back Home," "Swinging Doors," and one of *the* Honky-tonk anthems, "The Bottle Let Me Down". He also played on Buck Owens early Owens' hits such as "Foolin' Around" and "Under Your Spell Again", as well as on tracks by Johnny Cash, Neil Young, **Wanda Jackson**, Rose Maddox, **Hoyt Axton**, and Waylon Jennings. Mooney was a mainstay of Jennings' band from the late 1960s through the late 1980s.

Mooney's best-known recording is an album titled *Corn Pickin' and Slick Slidin'* (Capitol, 1968) on which he collaborated with guitarist extraordinaire James Burton. Burton is known for his tight-stringed Telecaster sound that cut through any environment with a signature imprint, as well as the ability to get a variety of sounds out of his guitar that implied he was playing a different instrument or through effects, which he wasn't. These abilities elevated Burton to primary session musician status and concert accompanist with Elvis Presley and Ricky Nelson, as well as country artists such as Merle Haggard and Emmylou Harris. The album is a joy as the two musicians comp for each other depending who is carrying the melody or soloing, and demonstrates the quintessential styles of both players, as well as their desire to let each other have their space on the recordings. Ralph played on recording sessions for more than seventy artists. He recorded several instrumentals for Challenge Records, including "Release Me" and "Moonshine", both of which later appeared on 4 Star Records releases, *Country Love* and *Tennessee Pride*, respectively. Mooney may also be heard with Waylon's band, the Waylors, on the soundtrack album from the 1975 film, *Mackintosh and T.J.*, as well as on *Wail Man Wail! Original Rockabilly & Chicken Bop, Vol. 3*, released by Sundazed Music in 1993. His contribution is "Moon's Boogie"m a previously unreleased number.

Throughout his career as an instrumentalist, Mooney was writing songs, including such standards as "Crazy Arms", "Falling for You", and "Foolin'". Ray Price had his first #1 hit in 1956 with "Crazy Arms", and the song later became a Top 20 hit for Willie Nelson. "Crazy Arms" typifies hard core country music as it depicts the loss of a lover to another, and the ensuing blue loneliness. Ray Price's version maintains the whiney steel guitar for which Mooney, and the Bakersfield Sound, was known as descended from the influence of Western swing's prominent use of the instrument. This was the opposite of the urban-aimed "Nashvilee Sound" of Chet Atkins whose goal it was to make country music more palatable to an urban audience in the wake of rock 'n roll's evolution in the mid-1950s. Atkins largely removed the steel guitar, but Mooney almost singlehandedly put it back. "Foolin'" was a Top 5 hit for Johnny Rodriguez in 1983. Ralph's compositions were recorded by a wide array of artists, such as Chuck Berry, the Andrews Sisters, Patsy Cline, Duane Eddy, Boxcar William, Elvis Presley, the Stanley Brothers, Bing Crosby, the Flying Burrito Brothers, Barbara Mandrell, and Ernest Tubb.

Inducted into the Steel Guitar Hall of Fame in 1983, Mooney was recognized for his innovative tuning (High G Sharp) and creating the "Mooney" take-off and "chicken pickin" before such styles had a name. According to the rationale for his induction into the St. Louis-based hall of fame, he is described by that site as "so uniquely original that he remains unduplicated." He was also named as Steel Guitar Player of the Year in 1966 by the Academy of Country Music. After retirement, Ralph has remained active by attending steel guitar conventions and seminars where he demonstrated his techniques. In 2002, he appeared at the Texas Steel Guitar Jamboree in Dallas, and as late as 2010 he was still making recording, being featured on four tracks on the Grammy Award-winning album, *Ghost Train: The Studio B Sessions* by Marty Stuart. Also in 2010, Ralph appeared in Nashville at a songwriting conference. He died at age 82 at home in Kennedale, Texas, of complications from cancer. While Ralph Mooney moved to California at a fairly young age (13), he did learn his musical rudiments in the state from a family member, and it was the KVOO, Tulsa, broadcasts of Bob Wills featuring Leon McAuliffe that had such a dramatic impact on his musical sense that it influenced both Mooney's entire musical career, as well as his intrinsic influence on the Bakersfield Sound. As a result, one may imply that Oklahoma's music scene had a fundamental effect on the development of the Bakersfield

Sound via Mooney's love for the steel guitar that he first heard and embraced aesthetically in the state.

Note
1. Determining where the primary information on Ralph Mooney derived is difficult from a scholarly point of view because at least four readily available sources all basically follow the same timeline and say more or less the same things, to include Mooney's un-credited biography on Country Music Television's website (www.cmt.com), an essay credited to Sandra Brennan under Mooney's name on the All Music Guide website (www.allmusic.com), an essay written by Cristin Maher published three days after Mooney's death on a website Taste of Country (tasteofcountry.com/ralph-mooney-dies-82/), and a printed essay by Dale Vinicur in *Definitive Country: The Ultimate Encyclopedia of Country Music and Its Performers* (New York: Perigreee, 1995), 559-560.

Moore, Marilyn
(b. June 6, 1931 – d. March, 1992)

A jazz vocal soloist with the Woody Herman, Ray McKinley, and Charlie Barnet Big Bands whose expressive abilities have been compared to Billie Holliday, jazz singer Marilyn Moore was born in Oklahoma City. Marilyn's parents worked in vaudeville, and she broke into the act at age three singing and dancing in the finale of the family's act. While attending high school in Oklahoma City, she sang with bands in local clubs.

After high school Marilyn moved to Chicago for a short while, singing in clubs in the Windy City, but, after serving as vocalist with Woody Herman and Charlie Ventura in 1949, she eventually landed in New York in the early 1950s. During this time, she was vocalist for Ray McKinley, Boyd Raeburn, and Al Cohn, whom she married in 1953. The couple had two children, Lisa and Joe Cohn. Joe is a talented jazz guitarist who has recorded an album, *Two Funky People*, and recorded with Muskogee's **Claude "Fiddler" Williams** on Williams' *Swingin' the Blues* album.

During the mid-1950s Marilyn concentrated on raising her family, but was invited to record for the Bethlehem label in 1957. The resulting album, *Moody Marilyn Moore*, was critically acclaimed due in part to the backing of such musicians as Al Cohn, Don Abney, Barry Galbraith, and Joe Wilder. However, her vocal phrasing and timbre so closely mirrored Holliday's that it sounded derivative. The next year she was cast in *Oh Captain!*, a jazz musical that was recorded by MGM Records, which also featured such legendary jazz artists as Coleman Hawkins, Art Farmer, Harry "Sweets" Edison, and Okmulgee's **Oscar Pettiford**.

Moody Marilyn Moore, Bethlehem, 1957.

Marilyn and Al were divorced in the late 1950s, and she focused on her children's upbringing. She never returned to professional singing or to the recording studio. The MGM record for *Oh Captain!* was never re-issued, however, *Moody Marilyn Moore* was re-mastered by Toshiba/EMI in 1990, and includes twelve tracks featuring a mix of Tin Pan Alley standards and torch songs suitable for her voice which is so close to Holliday's it loses any opportunity for a unique and recognizable imprint, an ironic curse that did not enable her to continue making further recordings. While some jazz aficionados relish Moore's simpatico with Holliday, and even though the two singers reportedly became friends, there will always only be one Billie Holliday, and there will always only be one Marilyn Marilyn Moore album.[1] From an Oklahoma point of view, however, one wonders if any other state could produce "a white Billie Holliday", as Moore has often been called by jazz reviewers, critics, and fans.

Note
1. Because she is considered a minor figure in jazz (she is not included in standard jazz reference works such as the *Grove Encyclopedia of Jazz*), the basic details of Marilyn Moore's life and career are scant at major music database websites such as www.allmusic.com, and have to be pieced together from press releases and fan reviews for her only album; however, her friendship with Billie Holliday is referenced by Will Friedwald in *Jazz Singing: America's Great Voices from Bessie Smith to Bebop and Beyond* (Cambridge, MA: Da Capo, 1996), 483.

Moseley, Andy (b. 1933)
Moseley, Semie (b. 1935 – d. August, 1992)

Founders and creators of the hand-crafted Mosrite Guitar line made famous by **Nokie Edwards** of The Ventures, and also played by notables such as Barbara Mandrell, Joe Maphis, Ronnie Sessions, Johnny Ramone of The Ramones, and Ricky Wilson of the B-52s, Andy and Semie Moseley were born in Durant, Oklahoma, smack dab in the middle of the Depresssion and Oklahoma's harsh dust bowl years. Like so many other significant Oklahoma musical figures who were born in the state but raised in California, the Moseley brothers moved with their family to Chandler, Arizona in 1938, and then on to Bakersfield, California in 1940. In the many biographical essays about the Moseley brothers, none indicate any kind of musical inspiration from their parents. Once in Bakersfield, their mother worked in a dry cleaner's shop, their father was an employee of the Southern Pacific Railroad, and they attended East Bakersfield High School. While in Bakersfield, Semie began playing in a Gospel group at age thirteen, and the two brothers began building guitars in their teens, experimenting with adding extra necks to the guitars. After successfully building a double necked guitar for Joe Maphis in 1954, while he was employed by Los Angeles-based guitar manufacturer Richenbacker, Semie and his brother Andy started Mosrite Guitars, in Bakersfield, with an investment from a Los Angeles preacher, Reverend Ray Boatright, in 1956.[1]

Boosted by the tremendous popularity of The Ventures in both the U.S. and Japan, as well as the general surge in American rock bands in the 1960s, the Moseley brothers' business peaked in 1968 when they were making 1,000 Mosrite guitars every month (acoustics and electrics), along with an assortment of multi-neck guitars, basses, dobros, and mandolins. In the mid-1960s, the brothers also started Mosrite Records, signing Barbara Mandrell, the daughter of a music store owner who sold Mosrite Guitars, and **Ronnie Sessions**,

The Moseley Brothers signing Ronnie Sessions to Mosrite Records, 1966.

Semie Moseley, 1953

who eventually charted several country singles for other labels in the 1970s. Fate turned against the Moseleys when they reached a marketing agreement with competitors that essentially put them out of business, causing Mosrite to go bankrupt in 1968.

In 1969, Andy Moseley moved to Nashville and marketed the hand-made guitars directly to studio musicians, entertainers looking for a stylish guitar to use on stage, and Nashville music stores, all of which helped keep the business afloat. Meanwhile, Semie opened a new factory near Bakersfield in 1970, before moving to Oklahoma City in the mid-1970s. The Oklahoma City shop led to a number of Mosrite guitars appearing in music stores and pawn shops throughout Oklahoma up until the late 1990s, creating a sort of folklore about the occasional discovery of one of the highly collectible instruments in obscure places throughout the state. Most likely, although unconfirmed at the time of this writing, Moseley chose to relocate to Oklahoma City due to the Bakersfield Sound's presence in the city via **Buck Owens'** syndicated television show, *Buck Owens Ranch*, on WKY-TV from 1969 to 1973. Moseley moved on to open shops in North Carolina in 1981, and then Boonville, Arkansas in 1991.[2]

About six months after moving to Arkansas, Semie died of bone cancer in August, 1992. Semie's daughter, Dana, built guitars for nearly thirty years for Ed Roman Guitars in Las Vegas. In 2011, she watched over the company's Mosrite production process, and continued building other guitars, as well as reportedly working on a history of her father's unique legacy, which started out in Oklahoma, and even returned for a short period in the 1970s, but ultimately cannot be said to have been influenced by anything more than the general economic and social history of the state in the 1930s, or the presence of Buck Owens and additional country music market that existed in Oklahoma City in the mid-1970s.

One might offer some conjecture that the Moseley brothers' parents came from a strong religious background, which certainly would have been present in Durant in the 1930s, and which may have led the boys to being involved in church music

Andy Moseley, 2010

early on, but that is only another guess at this time. As of 2011, Andy Moseley lived in Lebanon, Tennessee, enjoying the long-term continuation of Mosrite Records, and the Sound Source Studio in Nashville, which he started, and where his son, Mark Moseley has been a long-time engineer, producer, and partner in recordings for many artists, to include Oklahomans such as **Vince Gill**, **Joe Diffie**, **Nokie Edwards**, and **Garth Brooks**.

Notes

1. Robert Price's essay detailing the history of Semie Moseley and Mosrite guitars has been re-posted on several websites, to include http://www.bakersfield.com/static/FP/baksound/mosrite.htm and http://www.edroman.com/guitars/mosrite/moseley.htm (both accessed July, 2011)

2. An interesting amateur video of Semie Moseley's guitar shop in North Carolina is posted on www.youtube.com under the title "A Day with Semie Moseley 'Mosrite'" at http://www.youtube.com/watch?v=sSBEudhK8Ds (accessed July, 2011).

Mourning September
(formed Tulsa, circa 2001)

A Christian rock group formed in Tulsa, Mourning September released one album, *A Man Can Change His Stars*, in 2004 on Floodgate Records, an indie rock label in Costa Mesa, California distributed through Warner/Elektra/Asylum Records.[1] After gaining their deal with Floodgate via three-song demo, and then working with producer James Wisner, known for his work with Dashboard Confessional, the album is a fairly straightforward, highly energetic mainstream pop rock album with Tony Chavez's pleasing lead vocals, layered harmonies on up tempo choruses, and songs with a fairly typical "quiet verse/loud chorus" format. Josh Tipton's guitars are edgy without being abrasive, and a rhythm section of bassist Zach Tietsort and drummer David Walker solidly underpins the music as a whole. Lyrically, the group maintains the existential questioning common of much Christian rock that tries to reach its core audience with heavily coded imagery while hoping to crossover to mainstream audiences with generic lyrics than can also be applied to secular life.[2] After parting ways with drummer David Walker in 2004, by 2005 the group had gone on hiatus, according to its myspace.com web page, and its primary website had been taken down from the Internet.

Mourning September, circa 2005

Note
1. Confirmation of the band's Christian rock foundation is evidenced by a video interview with www.breathecast.com that is archived on www.youtube.com (
2. For a complete transcription of Mourning September's lyrics from *A Man Can Change His Starts* see, at one of the websites for such lyrics, www.christianrocklyrics.com, http://www.christianrocklyrics.com/mourning-september.php (accessed August 1, 2011).

Murray, Sunny
(b. September 21, 1937)

An incredibly creative and innovative jazz drummer who helped establish the instrument's role in free improvisation, drummer, composer, arranger, and bandleader James Marcellus Arthur "Sunny" Murray was born in Idabel, Oklahoma, a community of roughly 7,000 population located in the southeastern "Little Dixie" region of the state. Like so many others who escaped the state during the Depression, Murray's family moved to Philadelphia, Pennsylvania, where he began playing drums at age nine, often with his brother, but also learned the trumpet and trombone. Murray moved the role of drummer in jazz away from strictly being a metronome, and applied varied rhythmic elements and dynamics to recordings and live performances in which he was as much of an improviser as any of the other jazz musicians.[1]

In 1956, Sunny moved to New York City where he worked with diverse artists as Henry "Red" Allen, Willie "The Lion" Smith, Jackie McLean, Rocky Boyd, and Ted Curson. He moved closer to free jazz when he joined Cecil Taylor's group in 1959, and, after hearing John Coltrane's quartet and playing with Coltrane informally in 1963. While touring Europe with Taylor and Jimmy Lyons, he met Albert Ayler, and performed off and on with his group from 1965 to 1967. He was a member of the legendary trio that produced *Ghosts* and *Spiritual Unity*, as well as paying on several more Ayler albums, such as *New York Eye and Ear Control*, *Bells*, and *Spirits Rejoice*.

Murray made his first albums as leader in 1965 (*Sunny's Time Now*) and 1966 (*Sunny Murray Quintet*), and Ayler was guest performer on Murray's debut album. It was this album that garnered him the *Down Beat*'s Criteria Poll for Talent Deserving Wider Recognition in 1966 in the Drums category. From 1968 to 1971, he lived in France, where he played with Archie Shepp. In 1971, he returned to Philadelphia, and worked with Philly Joe Jones, an influential hard bop drummer, and also fronted his own group, The Untouchable Factor. His hard bop drumming style resulted in sessions with Ornette Coleman, John Tchicai, and another Oklahoman, **Don Cherry**.

Sunny's additional albums include *Big Chief* (1968) [Pathe-Marconi]; *Hard Cores* (1968) [Philly Jazz] on which **Cecil McBee**, another Oklahoman, plays bass; *Homage to Africa* (1969) [BYG] on which he joined by Shepp; *Sunshine* (1969) [BYG]; *An Even Break (Never Give a Sucker)* (1969) [Affinity]; *In Paris: Big Chief* (1970) [EMI]; *Charred Earth* (1978) [Kharma]; *Applecores* (1978-79) [Philly Jazz]; *Live at Moers Festival* (1979) [Moers Music]; *13 Steps on Glass* (1996) [Enja], which features a trio of tenor saxophonist Odean Pope and bassist Wayne Dockery; *Illuminators* (1996) [Audible Hiss]; and *We Are Not at the Opera* (1998) [Eremite], featuring Sabir Mateen on flute and alto/tenor sax. Murray's compositions include "R.I.P.," "Suns of Africa, Parts 1 & 2," "Flower Trane," "Real," "Red Cross," "An Even Break," "Giblets, Part 2," Complete Affection," and "Invisible Blues."[2] In 2008, Antoine Prum directed a 78-minute documentary on Sunny that not only re-counts his historical significance, but as the DVD's liner notes detail, "also follows him on several gigs to show the daily struggle to perpetuate a musical genre that is to a certain extend still ignored by the public at large." Additionally, several of the previously mentioned albums have been re-mastered and re-issued in years noted, to include *Sunny Murray* (2001), *We Are Not at the Opera* (2003), *Perles Noires 1 and 2* (2005), *Sonic Liberation Front Meets Sunny Murray* (2011). With regard to Oklahoma, no evidence exists it had any impact on him whatsoever, as he nonchalantly answers one interviewer's question about his birthplace by just saying, "Yeah, Idabel, Oklahoma", and then moves on, which is pretty much what his family did.

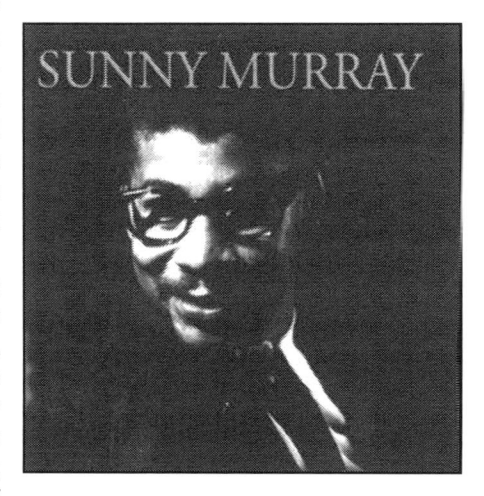

Notes
1. For an extremely revealing interview with Sunny Murray regarding his style and ethos, see his interview with Dan Warburton, published by www.parisatlantic.com at http://www.paristransatlantic.com/magazine/interviews/murray.html (accessed July, 2011). For a visual demonstration of Murray's active, complex style, see "Sunny Murray, Elvin Jones & Art Blakey" video on www.youtube.com at www.youtube.com.

Muscogee (Creek) Nation

(began arriving at Fort Gibson in Indian Territory, 1828)

With one traditional story explaining their origins in the West when the earth's mouth opened, and a subsequent journey toward the sunrise where they eventually created the highly evolved and structured mound building culture of the Southeastern United States, the tribe now known as the Muscogee (Creek) Nation, with its headquarters contemporarily in Okmulgee, was actually a confederation of towns along the creeks and rivers of Alabama and Georgia by at least the 1600s. Within this organization of independent towns, each community, or tribe, had political independence and quantified borders for their land. While individual languages and dialects also peppered the region, the Muskogean language was "the common tongue" for people who wanted to converse outside of their immediate geographic region. According to the *Dictionary of Creek/Muskogee* (University of Nebraska Press, 2000), "the terms *Creek* and *Muskogee* are used interchangeably by some people in English, though the term *Creek* is better known. Others retain a usage in which *Creek* is slightly broader in scope than *Muskogee*, sometimes referring to groups that are not ethnically Muskogee" but who do speak the language. Therefore, Creek may be used to describe a specific lifestyle of several groups of people from the Southeastern region of the U.S., while Muscogee may be used more commonly as an ethnic delineation connecting tribal people specifically to the pre-removal towns of the Muscogee Confederacy.[1]

Contemporary Muscogee (Creek) Council Mound, Okmulgee, OK.

After first encountering Europeans via the Spanish explorer, Hernando DeSoto, in 1539, the Creeks endured increasing European and American incursions for nearly 300 years before being expelled from their homelands in the 1820s and 1830s per the U.S. Indian Removal Act, which divested Southeastern tribes from their ancient territories and forcibly removed many of the people to Indian Territory, now Oklahoma. Currently, the Muscogee (Creek) people are represented in the United States by six, federally recognized tribal entities: four in Oklahoma, one in Texas, and one in Alabama. The largest group of the federally recognized Muscogee (Creek) people is the Muscogee (Creek) Nation, with its contemporary headquarters in Okmulgee, Oklahoma, and an enrollment of 71, 424 as of August, 2011. Three smaller Muscogee (Creek) tribal towns incorporated in 1936 under the Oklahoma Indian Welfare Act also maintain their federally recognized

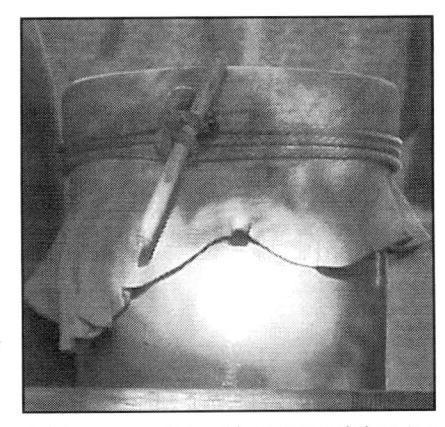

A Muscogee (Creek) ceremonial water drum.

tribal status in Oklahoma: Kialegee Tribal Town (Wetumka), Alabama-Quassarte Tribal Town (Wetmuka), and the Thloptholocco Tribal Town (Okfuskee County, near Okemah). Additionally, Creeks who fought on the side of the United States against Muscogee traditionalists in 1813 and 1814 are now federally recognized as the Poarch Creek Indians, located presently in southern Alabama on land granted to them by the U.S. Government. The Alabama-Coushatta also descended from Creek speaking people who continuously moved west to avoid white encroachment, finally settling in Texas near Livingston where their tribal headquarters is today. Bands of Creeks who relocated to Florida in order to escape removal were still seeking federal recognition in 2011.

According to the Muscogee (Creek) Nation's website, "the Muscogee people are descendents of a remarkable culture that, before 1500 AD, spanned most of the region known today as the American Southeast. Early ancestors of the Muscogee constructed magnificent earthen pyramids along the rivers of this region as part of their elaborate ceremonial complexes." John R. Swanton's *Social Organization and Social Usages of the Indians of the Creek Confederacy* (Washington: GPO, 1928) explains this early period of written Muscogee history well, as does Swanton's *Aboriginal Culture of the Southeast* (ibid.). Muscogee people lived in two major areas of what is now the Southeastern United States at the time of early European contact. According to the Muscogee (Creek) Nation's website, "The English called the Muscogee peoples occupying the towns on the *Coosa* and the *Tallapoosa* rivers, Upper Creeks, and those to the southeast, on the *Chattahoochee* and *Flint* rivers, the Lower Creeks. The distinction was purely geographical as was the fact that the Muscogee people lived along the creeks and rivers of Alabama, which earned the entire group of towns the term of 'Creek' Indians."[2]

After a long and violent sequence of armed conflicts, such as the Redstick War, or Creek Civil War of 1813-1814, and land cessions between the Creeks and the Americans, some Creeks began removing to Indian Territory as early as 1828.[3] President Andrew Jackson and the U.S. Army enforced the removal of the remaining 24,000 Muscogee to Indian Territory in 1836 and 1837, where they began arriving at Fort Gibson in those years after harsh travel, those who survived anyway. By conservative estimates, roughly forty percent of the tribe perished during the forced removals, effectively enacting genocide on the Creek people. The first council meeting of the new Creek Nation, most likely held in 1836, is marked in Tulsa by the Council Oak Tree at the intersection of 18th and Cheyenne in Tulsa, where an annual commemoration is held by the Muscogee (Creek) Nation each year. As many as forty-four tribal towns removed to the new land in Indian Territory, with as many as 100 different ceremonial grounds represented on arrival. In 1857, the Bureau of Indian Affairs counted 14,888 Creeks in Oklahoma. After these trials, the Muscogee people had to endure the "war between the whites."[4]

The American Civil War caused numerous troubles for the Creeks, some of whom fought for the Union, and others who fought for the Confederates out of distrust for the Northern government after the removal, and promises the South made to return Creek lands to the tribe. After the Civil War, the Reconstruction treaty of 1866 implicated the entire tribe with violating previous treaties in which the tribe agreed not to fight the United States. As a result, the Federal government took 3.2 million acres from the tribe, approximately half of the Muscogee domain, with a long-term plan of relocating tribes from other parts of the country in Indian Territory. Following the creation of a written constitution in 1867, the tribe established their new capital in what is present-day

Okmulgee, Oklahoma, created a constitution, government, and judiciary. The tribe also built a native rock capital building that still stands today in Okmulgee as a museum of Muscogee history and life ways.

Like all other Oklahoma tribes in the late 1800s, the Muscogee (Creek) people were forced to enroll as tribal members under the Dawes Commission and accept allotments. This process allowed the Federal government a chance to break up collectively-held land in an attempt to "detribalize" Native people and begin the assimilation process. While Muscogee (Creek) leaders like Chitto Harjo opposed the allotment, the end result was inevitable and Creeks had to accept their appointed lands. Additionally, with the creation of Oklahoma as a state in 1907, all tribal governments were abolished. However, the Muscogee (Creek) maintained a presidentially appointed Principal Chief during the period up until the 1970s when the tribe elected their own chief, and adopted a new constitution as a result of the Indian Self-Determination Act of 1975. For significant insight into many of the governmental processes that affected the Muscogee people, see Angie Debo's *And Still the Waters Run: The Betrayal of the Five Civilized Tribes* (OU Press, 1940), and also her important text, *The Road to Disappearance: A History of the Creek Indians* (OU Press, 1941). While imperfect in their description of Muscogee traditional activities, both books are substantive catalogues of the conflict between the Creeks and the U.S. Government. Finally, Jeffrey Burton's *Indian Territory and the United States 1866-1906* (OU Press, 1995) is a helpful contemporary text that rounds out the tribe's judicial experiences in the late 19th century as it was "subsumed" temporarily by the state of Oklahoma. While the Muscogee (Creeks) faced a similar set of cultural, social, geographic, and historical oppressions as other tribes in Indian Territory, unlike several American Indian groups who lost or gave up their traditional ways due to these forced harships, Muscogee people maintained their ancient religion, and many songs and dances that go along with it. While much has been written on Muscogee traditions by non-Indian anthropologists and historians, a contemporary person interested in traditional Muscogee spiritual values could do no better than seeking out *A Sacred Path: The Way of the Muscogee Creeks* (American Indian Studies Center, 2001). Written by a full-blood Muscogee, Jean (Hill) Chaudhuri, and her husband Joy Chaudhuri, a political science professor, *A Sacred Path* provides a knowledgeable viewpoint of traditional Muscogee history, values, philosophy, theology, and worldview, as well as insight into the Muscogee traditional ceremonial ways. John R. Swanton's *Religious Beliefs and Medical Practices of the Creek Indians* (Washington:

Muscogee (Creek) women often use condensed milk cans filled with small pebbles to provide the rhythm for Muscogee ceremonial songs popularly known as "stomp dances".

GPO, 1928), republished in 2000 by University of Nebraska Press as *Creek Religion and Medicine*, is also a foundational work in understanding the historical perspective of Muscogee ceremonial traditions, although it is laden with the usual non-Indian anthropological perspectives present in many works of its type from the 19th century. From a Muscogee (Creek) medicine man's point of view, interested readers should acquire David Lewis, Jr.'s *Creek Indian Medicine Ways: The Enduring Power of Mvskoke Religion* (University of New Mexico Press, 2008), an "as-told-to" book collated by anthropologist Ann T. Jordan. Lewis is a direct link back to Swanton's interviews with Lewis' great-grandfather, Jackson Lewis, whom Swanton quotes many times. As for an online resource, the excellent website created through William and Mary by Jack Martin, Margaret Mauldin, and Mary McCarty (www.wm.edu/linguistics/creek/) also provides easily accessible language lessons, music examples, and multiple websites for further studying Muscogee history and culture. From there, one can obtain the context to begin listening to traditional Muscogee music.

Muscogee (Creek) Ceremonial Leaders attend an annual memorial at the Council Oak Tree Park in Tulsa, Oklahoma, to commemorate the first Muscogee (Creek) Council meeting in 1836.

Muscogee Ceremonial Songs

With at least sixteen active ceremonial grounds where traditional Muscogee music is very much alive, a deep Christian hymn singing tradition that is more than two-hundred-years-old, and several contemporary musicians who have made significant contributions to the popular music and intertribal powwow music worlds, the Muscogee (Creek) Nation is a musically rich and diverse tribe whose contributions to world music illustrate both the preservation of ancient songs under oppressive circumstances, and more modern music that has evolved due to cross-cultural contact between Muscogee people and Americans of African and European descent.

The most traditional forms of music still practiced by Muscogee people are the ceremonial songs that go along with what are often called "stomp dances" that are part of the annual Green Corn Ceremonies to include the ribbon dance, feather dance, buffalo dance. All are still a vital part of the active ceremonial life of Creek people.

The oldest commercially available set of Muscogee ceremonial songs can be found through the Library of Congress Music Division, which released *Delaware, Cherokee, Choctaw, Creek* (AAFS L37) as part of its series, *Music of the American Indian*, recorded by Willard Rhodes between 1936 and 1951. Included on this vinyl LP are "Creek Ball Game Songs", a "Creek Lullaby" by Amanda Wesley, a "Creek Counting Song" by Victor and Amanda Wesley, "Creek Christian Hymns" led by Marcellus Williams, a "Creek Ribbon Dance Song" by Amanda Wesley, and "Creek Stomp Dance Songs" led by John Mulley. While this out-of-print record may prove difficult to track down, several excellent recordings of stomp dances and Muscogee ceremonial songs are available through Indian House Records. Although the term "stomp dance" is often less favorable than the term "ceremonial songs" by more traditional Muscogee people, stomp dance is a common term for the dance and songs practiced the Muscogee and their neighbors, the Euchee, Seminole, and Cherokee. Intrinsically linked to the yearly ceremonial dance cycle that reaches its high point during the Green Corn Ceremony, or "Creek New Year," when traditional people fast and perform purification ceremonies to clean out the "nasty things" that have built up over the previous year, the stomp dance is the vehicle by which prayers (included in the songs) are offered through the ceremonial fire that is the center of Muscogee traditional religion and ceremonies. Additionally, the songs and dances help the people who are taking medicine stay awake all night as is required of the ceremony's participants. According to liner notes on *Stomp Dance Songs of the Muscogee Nation* (IH 3009), the Green Corn Ceremony "is a time of coming together, purification, prayers for the people, the animals, all living things, for the world, and spiritual renewal for the coming year. It is a time of good feelings." Sam Proctor, a Muscogee medicine man at the Tallahassee (Wvkokye) Ceremonial Grounds, adds, "Our ancestors believed in the 'overseer,' or what they called 'Ofunga' (*Ofvnkv*). When we build the fire in the circle, they said the smoke goes up to 'Ofunga', and when he smells it, if it smells good, that's when the blessing will come."

Usually taking place during the overnight hours until past sunrise, "stomp dances", or Muscogee ceremonials, feature a song leader who guides the song in a call-and-response fashion while women shell shakers keep the rhythm of the song by shaking turtle shell rattles attached to their legs. Singers and dancers form a line that becomes several rows of circles around the fire with the leader and elderly people at the center of the dance near the fire, and younger dancers and singers in the outer circles. By singing and dancing around the sacred fire, the prayers are carried up to Ofunga via the smoke twirling out of the fire. As for the primary theology, Sam Proctor continues, "In order for the blessings to come, everyone has to come in unity, with one heart, one mind, and one love. The ceremonial ground is supposed to be built on love, run by love, and all the activities are supposed to be done by love." A former Baptist minister who gave up the pulpit to return to the ceremonial ways in which he was raised, Proctor adds, that based on his studies, the Bible and the ceremonial grounds have identical teachings where the two forms of worship are founded on the concepts of love and humility.

While the traditional ceremonies and their accompanying songs and dances have been performed for thousands of years, when European missionaries first encountered the Muscogee people worshiping through the fire, the symbolism of the fire and its relationship to the Christian hell proved to be an immediate focal point for reducing paganism within the Muscogee people, along with the Christian concept of no one entering the kingdom of heaven

Muscogee (Creek) Ceremonial Dance

but through Jesus. Compounding the problem is the contradictory nature of the Old and New Testaments. Traditional Muscogee people note the Bible itself claims in Ecclesiastes 3:1 "To every thing there is a season" and that includes "a time to dance" in Ecclesiastes 3:4. Historic and contemporary tensions and misunderstandings may also be gleaned from early-statehood newspaper accounts of "stomp dances" in Oklahoma that did not help matters. A February 16, 1910 article in *The Oklahoman* noted that a man new to the Territory, and interested in authentic western life, had killed "an old Indian named Rawlins" at a stomp dance and was paroled by then Oklahoma governor Haskell. A non-Indian witnessed claimed the accused was the only "sober person at the Indian dance when two squaws engaged in a fight. He started to separate them and brought all the redskins down on him." The man claimed self-defense and that he didn't meant to kill Rawlins. This played into a long standing belief among Native people that if "white" man killed an Indian, the charge was often manslaughter, whereas, if a Native person killed a "white" man, the charge was always murder. In any case, ceremonial grounds and "stomp dances" continued to get a bad reputation both from Christian ministers who believe the practice was wrong, and the way in which dances were often depicted in the mainstream Oklahoma press. An August 21, 1912 article in *The Oklahoman* printed this headline in all capital letters: INDIAN KILLED AT CREEK STOMP DANCE. The story details the "twenty-fourth murder in Creek County within the past six months took place at the Creek Indian stomp dance near [Bristow]. ...Every stomp dance held by the Creeks in the past two years has been featured by a shooting or cutting scrape." No wonder the dances started to get a bad name.

Coconut rattles are used during the Ribbon Dance of Muscogee (Creek) Ceremonials.

Not only were the dances portrayed negatively in the press, the dances' "paganism" did not fit into the 18th, 19th, 20th, and now some 21st century Christian visions of converting Muscogee people, which began largely in Georgia and Alabama when President George Washington appointed Benjamin Hawkins as the Indian superintendent of the Southeastern U.S. in 1796. Hawkins encouraged Muscogee leaders to allow Christian missionaries into Creek country. As a result, the missionary teachings and subsequent incorporation into the belief system by Muscogee Christians created divisions among Creek tribal towns, clans, and families that still exist today.

Reverend James Wesley, a Kialegee Tribal Town elder and long time Creek minister, explained in a 1998 interview, "All they knew back in those days was God, and that is good, but they did not know Jesus, and Jesus is our savior and Lord. When the Christianity came in, many ceremonial grounds people went into Christianity, and many Indians suffered. My mother told me, that in 1868, or so, when she was a young girl, an old preacher from Alabama Church north of Weleetka, the oldest Creek church, would come and have a meeting at somebody's house, and tell them about the gospel. While the Christians were there, sometimes the ceremonial people would come, some drinking, and chase these people off. They didn't do nothing to the women, but they would catch the men and whip them for listening. It was that way because at that time they all believed in the fire, but when Christianity started to take place, the ceremonial ground people said, 'That's not yours. Yours is the ceremonial ground. That's for the white people.' But the Christian people kept meeting and finally overcame some of these things. They established churches through all this persecuting, but they really had to sacrifice to build some of those churches. Many Christian people were beat up pretty bad because they believed in the Lord and were getting away from the ceremonial ground."

John Riley, a chairman for many years at Hutche Chuppa Indian Baptist where he grew up, told the *Muscogee Nation News* in 1999: "They used to be like one. The stompgrounds, they believed in God, they depended on him, just like the churches did. But they used the sacred medicine that was for the health of their bodies and the churches were for the spirit, so it was all one. But in this day and time, even the ministers that we are today, we kick at one another. I remember the older pastor, or minister, of our sister church across the river, Thewathlee. My mother used to tell me that when the pastor, who belonged to a certain stompground, used to fast, he would ask the church and get permission to go over there and use the medicine. They would let him go and he would fast and use the medicine. He didn't dance or anything, just use the medicine. After everything was over, he would report himself back in and they would take him back. He would get up there and lead the church."

John Riley, 1998

Given the complicated nature of this history, one can understand, appreciate, and respect the staunch determination with which traditional people maintain at least sixteen active Muscogee ceremonial grounds in the contemporary Muscogee (Creek) Nation of Oklahoma. After World War II, however, as many different tribes began reviving traditional dances around the state of Oklahoma, "Stomp Dances" also found a positive favor in the press. An August 8, 1947 article in *The Oklahoman* indicated the annual Seminole-Creek "stomp dance and ball game" would take place near Holdenville that weekend. A July 25, 1962 article ballyhooed the occurrence of a stomp dance with the headline "State Tribal Fete Planned in September," with an announcement that a "gigantic Indian powwow, council of the tribes, and stomp dance is on tap at the Del City American Legion Park." This trend continued into the 1980s with annual dances at the University of Oklahoma, followed by dances in the 1990s and early 2000s at Oklahoma State University, Rogers State University, Tulsa Community College, and Bacone College. By the first decade of the 21st century, the very active Muscogee ceremonial traditions that revolve around the "stomp dance" have become an accepted social dance outside of the ceremonial environment for many traditional Southeastern tribal people, now often included as educational presentations, social occasions, celebrations, or fundraisers. Long featured as the concluding element of some powwows in northeastern Oklahoma such

Muscogee (Creek) medicine man, Sam Proctor, leads a demonstration of a Muscogee ceremonial dance (a.k.a. "stomp dance") in 2006 at Rogers State University, Claremore, OK.

as the annual Copan Powwow hosted by the Eastern Delaware, and the Ottawa Powwow held each August, stomp dances are now being held at universities, public schools, community centers, and armories for reasons as diverse as financial benefits for ceremonial grounds or needy community members, substitute holiday activities for non-Christians or traditional people who do not celebrate "American" holidays, memorial dances, birthday dances, graduation dances, and educational exhibitions. Itself a point of controversy between traditionalists and "transitionalists," or those who are trying to preserve ancient traditions in contemporary times, the public, social stomp dance also provides an alternative to the pan-Indian powwow for descendants of the Southeastern tribes who have not been raised in the powwow world.

As a result of the stomp dance's increasingly public nature, Indian House Records, founded in 1966 by Tony Isaacs and his wife, Ida, began releasing Muscogee stomp dances on cassette in 1969, the first of which is *Songs of the Muskogee Creek – Part 1* (IH 3001). *Part 1*, recorded May 2, 1969 in Seminole, features "Buffalo Dance," "Long Dance," and five stomp dances. Lead singers include Harry Bell, James Deere, Netche Gray, Frank Jackson, Tema Tiger, and David Wind. Shell Shakers (women who wear turtle shell or milk can rattles on their legs) are Frances Deere, Stella Deere, Helen Tiger, and Eliza Wind. *Songs of the Muskogee Creek – Part 2* (IH 3002), recorded the same night and featuring the same singers and shell shakers, includes three stomp dances, a "Friendship Dance", "Gar Dance", "Guinea Dance", and "Morning Dance".

In 1978, Indian House released two more cassettes of stomp dances by Muscogee, Seminole, and Euchee singers and shell shakers. *Stomp Dance I: Muskogee, Seminole, Yuchi, Volumes 1 & II* (IH 3003 & 3004), feature twelve stomp dances between the two recordings made in Okemah, May 5, 1978. Lead singers are Jimmie Skeeter, Oscar Pigeon, Vernon D. Atkins, William M. Beaver, John McNac, and Harry Bell. Shell shakers for the recordings are Linda Alexander, Frances Cosar, Edna Deere, Caroline Harry, and Eliza Wind. New recordings of stomp dances released by Indian House in 1992 were *Stomp Dance – Volume 3 & 4* (IH 3005 & 3006), recorded in Bristow, March 8, 1991. *Volume 3* contains six stomp dances

Muscogee (Creek) Shell Shakers

and a traditional introduction by Spencer A. Frank. Lead singers are Eugene Thomas, George McNac, Sam Watson, Tema Tiger, Ralph Gray, and Spencer A. Frank. Shell shakers are Linda Alexander, Wenona Bunny, and Chumona Harjo. Along with detailed liner notes to explain the various dances, *Volume 4* features a "Double-Header Dance" led by Spencer A. Frank and Tema Tiger, a "Garfish Dance" led by Spencer A. Frank, and stomp dances led by Gary Bucktrot, Sonny Bucktrot, Joe Sulphur, and Billy J. Scott. Shell shakers are the same as on *Volume 3*.

In the 1990s, Indian House released two more cassettes of Muscogee stomp dances and ceremonial songs. Recorded October 22, 1994, at the Tallahassee Ceremonial Grounds, then near Wetumka, *Tallahassee Ceremonial Ground of the Mvskoke Nation* (IH 3007) includes a "Peace Dance," an "Old Dance," and six "Stomp Dances." Song leaders are John Proctor, Leon Bell, Jonas Harley, Eddie Lowe, Jimmy Gibson, and Thomas Yahola. By the following cassette's release, an expanded cultural sensitivity appeared on *Ceremonial Songs of the Muscogee* (IH 3008), recorded November 9, 1997 at the Tallahassee Ceremonial Ground. The words "stomp dance" do not appear anywhere but in the liner notes of the cassette: "The dances recorded in this album are often called 'stomp dance' in English, but since this name does not convey the real meaning of these dances, 'ceremonial dance' is preferred to be more accurate." Song leaders are from various ceremonial grounds: John Proctor (Tallahassee), Jimmy Gibson (Duck Creek), Eunice Hill (Nuyaka), Philip Deere (Nuyaka), Leon Bell (Tallahassee), Billy Joe "B.J." Jackson (Gar Creek), and Thomas Yahola (Tallahasee). Additional singers include Daniel Billie, Alfred Harley, Kelly Lowe, and Richard Williams. Shell shakers are Linda Alexander (who has appeared on Indian House stomp dance recordings since 1979), Frankie D'Ann Bell, Pat Bell, Marie BerryHill, Bonnie Gibson, Linda Grammer, Naomi Harjo, Shatota Harjo, Corina Lowe, Vivian Proctor, and Bertha Tilkens.

In 2000, Tony Isaacs and Indian House produced the first compact discs featuring only Muscogee stomp dances, *Stomp Dance Songs of the Muscogee Nation Vol. 1 & 2* (IH 3009 & 4000). Recorded at the Muscogee Nation Omniplex in Okmulgee, July 19, 1999, the two discs feature fourteen stomp dances reproduced beautifully by Isaacs' who by now has thirty years of experience recording stomp dances. Song leaders, with their home ceremonial grounds in parenthesis, include Wayland Gray (New Tulsa), Farron Culley (Okfuskee), Andy Butler (Peach Ground), Jimmy Gibson (Duck Creek), Russell Thompson (Nuyaka), Wendell Reschke (Peach Ground), Chapman Cloud (Nuyaka), Kevin Mack (Fish Pond), Roman Hill (Peach Ground), Vincent Butler (Kialegee), Darren Mack (Fish Pond), James Mosquito (Duck Creek), Joe Sulphur (Thlopthlocco), and Wesley Buter (Peach Ground). Shell shakers include the ageless Linda Alexander (New Tulsa), Alexis Crosley (New Tulsa), Irene Culley (Okfuskee), Lela Culley (Okfuskee), Bonnie Gibson (New Tulsa), Lee Harjo (Green Leaf), Sharon Harjo (Green Leaf), Sheila Harjo (Green Leaf), Dora Hill (Muddy Waters), Joann Hill (Okfuskee), Ella Mack (Fish Pond), Judy Proctor (Peach Ground), Irene Thompson (Kialegee), and Bertha Tilkens (New Tulsa). One other "Creek Stomp Dance Song" has been released through the Oklahoma State Arts Council's *Songs of Indian Territory*, and includes leader Thomas Yahola and members of the Tullahassee Ceremonial Grounds, the most recorded group of stomp dance singers and dancers.[7]

As a final element of significant interest to American music historians, the stomp dance's influence on the music of 18th and 19th century Muscogee slaves of African descent (or vice-versa) has yet to be fully detailed. For example, the "swinging" eighth notes of jazz are essentially the same rhythm of the Muscogee shell shakers during most of the stomp dances, and many of the vocal patterns of male singers exhibit the sliding pitches of African-American singing, as well as the call and response pattern of the dances being analagous to basic blues and gospel vocal patterns of African-American music. Given those possibilities, the Muscogee stomp dances are not only important elements of traditional Muscogee lifeways, but may also exemplify deeper connections between American Indian and African-American music, which in turn may lead to reinterpretations of the origins and development of some aspects of American popular music. Anecdotally, Muscogee "Stomp Dances" have been likened to African "Ring Shouts," and authors such as Gary Zellar, in his otherwise well-researched and important treatise on *African Creeks* (OU Press, 2007), offers a statement with no reference whatsoever that "Creeks likely adopted African dance and musical forms from the Africans who came among them" (11).

Sam Proctor leads the Ribbon Dance portion of the Green Corn Ceremony with Muscogee Ceremonial Songs, Tallahassee (Wvkokye), Creek Nation, OK, circa 2000.

Perhaps, some Africans picked up the swinging eighth notes of jazz from the wide tradition of stomp dancing among Muscogee Creeks which became the foundational rhythm of jazz. Muscogee medicine man Sam Proctor explains that the Creeks had a ceremonial song that mentions "the ones with kinky hair," in reference to the people of African descent who came into the Creek Nation as slaves, and some of whom rose to positions of governmental power in the early Creek Nation of Indian Territory. One thing for sure is that slaves of African descent had an important impact on the development of another unique aspect of Muscogee musical traditions, the Muscogee (Creek) hymns.

Muscogee (Creek) Hymns

The second most prominent form of Muscogee (Creek) musical expression is the Christian hymn tradition in existence just before, during, and since removal of the people from their original homelands. Both intermarriage and convincing missionaries introduced Christianity to Creek people via Benjamin Hawkins' encouragement in the late 18th century. Perhaps in order to ease the transition from ceremonial traditions to Christian services, many connections (with multiple exceptions) were allowed and still exist between the more traditional Muscogee Baptist and Methodist churches and the older, traditional ways of the ceremonial grounds: the number four plays prominently in both; "camps" are arranged in a circle around the center arbor or arbors; fasting is an important element for both religions; music is a core activity in both church services and ceremonials; the front church doors and the ceremonial arbor where the mekko (chief) sits both face east; men and women are segregated during services or ceremonies;

humility is a primary teaching; and both humility and love are intrinsic elements of both, as noted earlier by Sam Proctor. Additionally, most Muscogee (Creek) churches are named after tribal towns in the old Creek Nation of Alabama and Georgia. In fact, the oldest strictly Creek Baptist church is thought to be Alabama Baptist Church, north of Weleetka, dating to before the Civil War.

Most traditional Muscogee Baptist Christians forego any overt connections to the traditional ceremonial ways, as that would be contrary to Jesus's admonition in Matthew 6:24, that "no man can serve two masters: for either he will hate the one, and love the other; or else he will hold to the one, and despise the other." Another often quoted scripture by Muscogee preachers is John 14:6, where Jesus declares, "I am the way, the truth, and the life: no man cometh to the father but by me." With that as fuel, the argument has raged for two centuries now about whether or not a person can be traditional Creek and/or Christian, or even whether an Indian ceases to be Indian when they become Christian. Reverend Wesley did acknowledge that positive things do take place during the ceremonies: "At the ceremonial grounds, at the end of the main dance, the spokesman of the grounds would get up and tell people to have love toward one another, tell people to take care of their children and families, and to not commit adultery. There were some good things that came out of the ceremonial grounds and some good things that came out of the church. But years ago, a Christian man would go to the ceremonial ground and it was a sin, because they don't sing hymns, preach, don't pray, and don't know Jesus. The ceremonial ground is for the physical side, because that's where you clean yourself for the next year, but the church is for the spiritual side. For that reason, the Christian people were not allowed to go to the grounds. But today, it seems like there is no sin anymore. A lot of Christians go out there now. They say, 'I'm just going out to there look. I'm going out to observe,' so that kind of gives them an excuse. We don't have what we used to call sin anymore."

As separate areas of cultural interest, the ceremonial ground activities contain words, theological concepts, and songs that are not part of the Christian services, and vice-versa. For example, the "Giver of Breath" (Hesáketvmesé) is the word used for God at the churches, whereas, the previously mentioned

Muscogee (Creek) Baptist ministers, (l-r), Dorsey Nero, Wilbur Hobia, Kenneth Fixico, Alec Buck, David Mitchell, Franklin Harjo, Sr., John "Wayne" Tulsa, Wallace Gambler, Eugene Harjo.

Ofunga, or "overseer," is used for the creator at the ceremonial grounds. In *Sacred Path*, Chadhuri explains an important relationship exists between the two entities in Muscogee history, with Hesáketvmesé being a helper of sorts to Ofvnkv, which in turn may have made the acceptance of the term easier for early Muscogee Christians since it was already part of the belief system. Obviously, the connections and differences between the two Muscogee religious perspectives are extensively complicated, and could use more explanation for the benefit of all from a Muscogee point of view, but they are beyond the scope of this essay that is supposed to be focused on music.

Contemporarily, some of the more rural Muscogee Baptist churches maintain musical traditions linked not only to the 18th century Scottish and Anglo missionaries, 19th century rural Southern Baptists, but also to the 18th and 19th centuries when the Muscogee people, often mixed-bloods with Scottish and British intermarried husbands and fathers, owned slaves of African descent. After removal, since slaves could often speak both Muscogee and English, many early interpreters and preachers in Indian Territory were African-Creeks, often preaching to mixed audiences. When all missionaries were ejected from the Creek Nation in 1836 fgor upsetting the balance of participation in the traditional religion, African-Creeks became the de facto ministers until the missionaries were allowed to resume their work in the Nation in the mid to late 1840s. The first Baptist Church in Oklahoma, established in 1832 by a cooperative congregation of black, white, and Creek people near the north bank of the Arkansas River near Muskogee, illustrates this cross-cultural environment that led to the evolution of Muscogee hymns. By 1842, an Army officer witnesses a private home church meeting, likely held in secrecy, in which the colonel notes "the language and music were those of the Creeks and the whites, and the lyrics were apparently an old slave spiritual". Zellar notes that because Blacks often fostered the development of Christianity, they and other free blacks among the Creeks were allowed more latitude of movement up until the Civil War. One such African Creek, Monday Durant, was a prominent Baptist Church leader in Creek Country.[6]

After the Civil War, as slaves of African descent began to separate from their tribal owners and form their own churches, the Muscogee Christians maintained some of the older styles of singing African-American hymns and spirituals, as well as some songs directly from the earlier Scottish missionaries, and some common Southern Baptist hymns, often converted into the language. As a result, as of 2011, rural Muscogee Baptist and Methodist churches feature hymns in Muscogee and English, some of which are descended from the previously mentioned Scottish sources, but also spirituals reflective of 19th century African-American slaves. Interestingly, these hymns are not heard in Oklahoma's African-American rural churches. Therefore, the rural Muscogee Baptists and Methodists are the contemporary stewards of centuries-old African-hymn styles in the United States, as well as unique residual melodies left over from the historic political connections and inter-marriage of the Scottish immigrants. As a result, Muscogee hymns can be said to be tri-cultural in the least, as the lyrics display both Christian concepts and coded phrases that commemorate the painful and uncertain experience of removal, the songs exhibit both Scottish and African hymn styles, and they are sung in the Muscogee language. Researchers should listen to songs such as "Mekusape Fullana" for definite connections to the slidin pitches and blue notes of African-American spiritual traditions. Interestingly, the Creek hymn "Espoketis Omes Kerreskos" is the Muscogee language version of the African spiritual, "The Could Be the Last Time, We Don't Know". One hears the same melody of this hymn in the Staples Singers '1955 Gospel hit, "This May Be the Last Time", which Keith Richards of the Rolling Stones admittedly copied for the 1965 Stones' #1 UK hit, "The Last Time".

Recordings of Muscogee hymns are not widely available. In 1982, Canyon Records released a cassette of Muscogee hymns under the title *American Indian Hymn*

Singers: Special, Prayer, and Inspirational Songs, led by George Bunny, which has not been re-issued on CD. The State Arts Council of Oklahoma's 1989 release, *Songs of Indian Territory*, featured George Bunny leading Thewathlee Indian Baptist Church in "Must This Body Die", a song whose melody is linked to the Scottish hymn traditions still in existence in the most rural outposts of Northern Scotland. Clues to the form's origin can be found on the Smithsonian Folkways compilation, *Classic Mountain Songs* (SFW CD 40094). As sung by The Indian Bottom Association of the Defeated Creek Church in Linefork, Kentucky in 1997, "I am a Poor Pilgrim of Sorrow" exhibits the singing style of the Old Regular Baptist denomination that obviously had an impact on Muscogee hymn traditions prior to removal to Indian Territory. The song is a little faster than the Muscogee hymns, which are often slow and mournful, but still uses the "lining out" method of a singer starting individual lines with the congregation following, and has no instrumental accompaniment, a tradition brought by Scottish missionaries in the 18th century. A subtle difference exists in Muscogee hymns contemporarily in that the leader does not sing a whole line with the congregation responding, but the congregation quickly joins in once the line has started. Also "I am a Poor Pilgrim of Sorrow" has strong melodic similarities to the first hymn in all Muscogee hymnals, "Hesaketvmeset Likes," or "God, Our Creator and Preserver." Muscogee hymnals have no written music in them, only words. A singer must learn the melodies by the oral tradition and then apply the text, which can be typically found quickly by looking up the first few words of the song introduced by the singer. No song leader in a traditional Creek church says, "Now turn your hymnals to page so and so." People just have to learn the songs and/or learn how to look them up in a hymnal once the song has been introduced.

The oldest Muscogee Creek church is Alabama Church, north of Weleetka, often called a "Mother Church" to many others in the area. This image shows the diversity of their church membership, likely taken in the late 19th century.

Some small churches have released their own recordings of Muscogee hymns. In 1972, the Witt Memorial Indian United Methodist Church of Tulsa, founded in 1945, released two albums on vinyl of traditional Indian hymns that are now out-of-print. While not all of the songs or singers are Muscogee, *Volume I* includes two Creek-Seminole hymns, "Song of Hope" and "Help Me to Pray", and *Volume II* includes perhaps the best-known Creek hymn, "Heleluyvn", as well as "Hvlwen Heckvyofvn" (High where I am born"), and "Lord, Dismiss Us". Salt Creek Methodist Church has released two collections of Creek Hymns, recorded March 20 and 21, 1998. Available through Long and Scott Recordings based in Oklahoma City and Tuscon, *Yvhiketv Vhecicvlke* (The Song Keepers) *Volume 1 & 2* preserves nearly forty Muscogee hymns in the Methodist tradition with some insightful commentary on the recordings of the history of the hymns. Singers on *Volume 1* include Harry Long, Kenneth Fixico, Leonard J. Harjo, Amilia Deer, Molly Brown, and Imogene Harjo. Singers on *Volume 2* include Melissa Deer, Lizzie Bruner, Bessie Fixico, Amilia Deer, Imogene Harjo, Bessie Spencer, Molly Brown, Lora Ann Beaver, Semarian Fixico, Juanita Harjo, Harry Long, Leonard Harjo, and Kenneth Fixico. Most recently, since 2000, Concharty United Methodist Church has released two compact discs, *Ahesayecetv* and *Po-Ho-Sat-Ce*, available through their website at www.kvncate.com to help preserve and teach the Creek Methodist hymns.

While the music of Muscogee hymns provides all kinds of fodder for conversation about origins and influences, the texts of the hymns

Muscogee (Creek) singers recorded for Canyon Records' release of Muscogee (Creek) Hymns, 1982 (CR-611-C). Singers include George Bunny (leader), Jenny Bear, Delia Buckley, John Goat, Christie Hance, Harry Long, Rachel L. Pinezaddleby, Bob Pinezaddleby, Delma B. McClelland, Edna Mae Walker, Annie B. Washington, Alfred Wise, Allen Yargie, and Sammie Yargee.

offer ample opportunity for understanding the way in which Creek Christian music records both experience and spiritual expectation. While several hymnals exist in the Muscogee language, *Nakcokv Esyvhiketv* (*Song Book*), a hymnal translated by George Bunny, Woodrow Haney, Rev. James Wesley, and Morina Wildcat, provides non-speakers an interlinear translation of the songs wherein a lot can be learned about Muscogee Christianity, the general spirituality of Muscogee people, and how music provides both a vehicle for memory, celebration, and mourning for Muscogee Christians. With a clear link and opposition to the Muscogee traditional ceremonial ways that revolve around the taking of medicine for health and spiritual reasons, "Vc oh Vtes, Cv Kicetskes" ("Just as I am, without one plea") alludes to "the spirit's medicine." One can also relate a double meaning to many hymns that refer to a hard journey, or otherwise represent the removal of Creeks to Indian Territory, while at the same time representing the Christian spiritual journey from this world to heaven. "Cesvs em Vhakvn Pohis" ("Christian Triumph") refers to land that has been appointed for the singer, and after wickedness has been overcome, the singer will go and see that land. "Yvmv Estemerketvn" explains that "Here suffering, I pass." When sung, the song slows to a trudge in the repetition of "Tehoyvnvof," or

Muscogee (Creek) women at Arbeka Indian Baptist Church, 1999.

554 / Oklahoma Music Guide II

"I pass, I pass," before eventually getting to the "Elkv Hvtcen," or death river, thought of as either the metaphorical river of death and/or the literal Mississippi River or other rivers the Muscogee people crossed or otherwise died on during the removal period. A final example can be found in the Christian dismissal song, "Ce Mekusapeyvte," in which the lyrics plainly explain the thoughts of Christian Creeks on the "Long Walk" to Indian Territory: "Mohmen yvmv ekvnv, En kvpvkakeyofvt, Cen liketvn roricet, Fekvpetvn pu 'yaces" or "Now here land, We leave, Your place when we arrive, Rest we want." Of a particular solemn note, Muscogee people have relayed to the author that "Heleluyvn" ("Hallelujah") was often sung when a Creek person could go no further on the removal and perished. Not given time to bury the body, the people could only cover the fallen relative in leaves or a blanket, stand in a circle and sing "Heleluyvn", and then press on. Therefore, the hymns also act as permanent records of that tragic time, although fewer and fewer people seem to know the older songs, their sources, or their purpose today, which is why community singings have started to be organized to pass on that information.

Blown four times, a conch shell or a steer's horn is used to call worshippers into service at some Muscogee Baptist churches.

Along with fostering the tradition of these hymns that were given to the people for their spiritual sustenance in a Christian life, Muscogee (Creek) churches often act as tribal towns, or communities, in which traditional foods are shared, the tribal language is spoken, and tribal mores are conveyed through communal experience.

A considerable amount of interest evolved in the Muscogee (Creek) Hymns in 2006 as a result of a line-singing conference at Yale University in which Scottish line singers from remote northern Scotland, the Indian Bottom Baptist Association from eastern Kentucky, and the Sipsey River Baptist Association in northern Alabama were brought together by Yale music professor, Willie Ruff, to share their traditional line singing. As a result of a National Public Radio report on the line singing conference that aired in Tulsa, a woman with Muscogee (Creek) heritage, Jane Bardis, instantly recognized the hymns being sung at Yale as similar to Muscogee (Creek) Hymns. After Bardis contacted Professor Ruff, he contacted the author, and within a year a camera crew was in the Creek Nation recording hymns and interviewing knowledgeable people about the history of the songs. In 2007, members of Hutche Chuppa Indian Baptist Church were invited to Yale University to share the Creek hymns that were obvious musical relatives of the singing traditions from Scotland, Kentucky, and Alabama, but no one outside of the Creek Nation they existed. As a result, another chapter was told in relation to the development, maintenance, and significance of the Muscogee (Creek) Hymn tradition that is a model for cultural diffusion, influence, adaptation, and re-appropriation, evolving into what very well could be the first American music that embraces the three major cultures of the nascient United States: the Anglo-Scot European, the African, and the American Indian. In this author's opinion, no other American music has those three elements as early as Muscogee (Creek) hymns, which may make the hymns the first truly American music.

Aside from the ceremonial songs and Christian hymns, Muscogee people have made significant contributions to popular music, jazz, country, and to intertribal powwow singing. Country music star Hank Williams is said to have had Creek blood, and was inducted as such into the Native American Music Awards Hall of Fame. **Jim Pepper** (**Kaw**/Muscogee) successfully merged American Indian traditional music with jazz, most notably his "Witchi Tai To" which hit both the Top 40 and jazz charts in 1969. Pepper was born in June 18, 1941 in Portland, Oregon, where he also died February 10, 1992. Pepper spent part of his youth in Oklahoma, absorbing the music of the Muscogee (Creeks) via his mother's tribal affiliation, and the music of the Kaw due to his father's affiliation with that tribe. One can hear how he incorporates a Muscogee (Creek) "Stomp Dance" into his music on "Rock Stomp Indian Style" on *Pepper's Powwow* (Atlantic, 1971). Clearly Pepper's musical (and tribal) relative, award-winning poet, saxophonist, and writer, Joy Harjo (b. Tulsa, 1951) has released three albums of music with her own spoken word poetry, singing, and alto and soprano saxophone work. Performing with the genre-busting band, Poetic Justice, *Letter from the End of the Twentieth Century* (Silver Wave, 1997), combines rock, jazz, and multiple American Indian tribal music elements with Harjo's powerful poetry delivered with the confidence of someone who has given a thousand public readings of her work. Nominated for eight Native American Music Awards, and given the 1998 Outstanding Musical Achievement Award by the First Americans in the Arts, *Letter from the End of the Century* is an atmospheric, multi-styled musical album whose strength lies in the poems from Harjo's books: *She Had Some Horses* (Thunder's Mouth, 1983); *Secrets from the Center of the World* (University of Arizona, 1989); *In Mad Love and War* (Wesleyan University, 1990); and *The Woman Who Fell from the Sky* (Norton, 1994). While her poetry, and, therefore, the lyrics to her songs on *Letter from the End of the Century*, explores American Indian and world indigenous themes, Harjo only mentions being Muscogee once, in "Fear Poem." She also acknowledges her ceremonial participation in the album's title track, wherein she is haunted by a story she heard from a taxi driver that haunts her "from Tallahassee Grounds to Chicago, to my home near the Rio Grande."

In March, 2003, Joy Harjo received the Arrell Gibson Lifetime Achievement Award

Members of Hutche Chuppa Indian Baptist coordinated a trip for several Muscogee (Creek) singers to attend a line-singing comference at Yale University in 2007. Pictured are members of the church, associated family members, the documentary crew that filmed the conference, and Yale University professor of music, Willie Ruff, (third from left, second row from the bottom/front).

at the annual Oklahoma Book Awards, and the poetry award for her book *How We Became Human: New and Selected Poems* (Norton, 2002). Harjo released her second album, *Native Joy*, on her own independent label, Mekko Records, in the summer of 2003. While the CD featured her alto and soprano saxophone work, she also sang on the recording, whereas, up to that point she relied primarily on her poetry performance skills. According to Harjo, "I incorporated Muscogeean elements on the album. My favorite tune is 'Eagle Song,' and part of it is in the Mvskoke language." Helping her translate some of the lyrics for the song were elder traditionalist, Linda Alexander, and Ted Isham, Mvskoke language specialist and curator of the Creek Council House Museum in Okmulgee. Harjo released her most powerful disc yet in 2008, *Under the Milky Way* (Mekko), singing more than ever, telling stories in her powerful oratorical style developed through decades of live readings, all accented by a variety of percussive and stringed instruments, and her saxophone work which has progressed to a highly respectable style of subtle legato and stepwise self-assurance. When she pays tribute to Jim Pepper with her own version of his most notable recording, "Witchi Tai To", she is a convincing and respectful purveyor of Pepper's musical spirit. As an indication of her desire to further Pepper's merging of American musical traditions, Harjo features a variety of instruments on "Goin' Home", and brings Muscogee hip hop artist Julian B! in for some background vocals on the song she ends with phrases in the Muscogee language.[8]

Another Muscogee citizen who has enjoyed some success nationally is Muscogee rapper and R&B artist, Julian B!, who was born Julian B. Watson, September 26, 1970 in Okmulgee. A member of the Bear Clan, Julian has lived in South America, Colorado, and now Dewar, Oklahoma. He worked with the **GAP Band** in 1990, and has performed at the Apache Nation Unite concert, the American Indian Movement's anniversary celebrations, the Montreux Jazz Festival, the Denver March Powwow, and various universities, festivals, and Native gatherings around the country. Nominated for a Native American Music Award for Best Rap Artist in 1998, Julian B! has two albums, *Once Upon a Genocide* (Warrior, 1994), and *Injunuity* (Hot Commodity, 2002), with all songs written, produced, and "injuneered" by Julian B! Both albums feature a rebellious, yet insightful, Native lyrical stance supported by smooth R&B dance beats, but also vocals by Julian B! that range closer to soul singing than most hip hop.

Julian B!'s lyrics are deeply interwoven with the Muscogee identity, mentioning the Muscogee Nation and making "a ritual out of being humble" in "Revolution." Julian also ties his songs back to the previously mentioned concepts of love from both the Muscgoee Christian church and ceremonial grounds when he sings, "Vnokéckv" (love) in "Mother Earth." Additionally, the young rapper's music expresses a lot of things Indian people have been talking about for years, but have never had put to mu-

Joy Harjo

sic. "My Moccasins" discusses the Bureau of Indian Affairs, living in a racist society, and otherwise trying to maintain a spiritual outlook in the face of general societal apathy toward American Indians. Nominated as Best Rap/Hip Hop Recording at the 2002 Native American Music Awards, *Injunuity* as a whole is a much better than average rap album due to its use of additional smooth vocalists, horn riffs, harmonicas, and guest rappers like Shadowyze and Physics. The lyrics will be especially insightful to Muscogee citizens, and others who are generally aware of such insider Indian commentary as "Uncle Tomahawks," the history behind "Free Peltier," and the dangers of embracing non-Indian society ("Don't be Dancin' Wit Wolves in Sheep's Clothing"). By late 2002, Julian worked with Lord Tim Hinkley (The Who, The Rolling Stones, et al.) on new recordings, and in 2003 had made two videos to promote *Injunuity*, one of which received a Best Music Video Award at the 2003 Milwaukee Indian Summer Film Fest. Along with having a track included on a 2009 contemporary American Indian music compilation, *Indian Rezervation Blues and More* (Dixiefrog, 2009), Julian was tapped in 2012 by Muscogee (Creek) Nation Principal Chief, George Tiger, to begin formalizing a recording a studio for Muscogee (Creek) citizens to make recordings of their traditional or contemporary music.

Muscogee (Creek) hip hop artist, Julian B!

A widely recognized Muscogee (Creek) flutist, John "Yafke" Timothy (born in Muskogee, OK), was inspired by the legendary Creek-Seminole flutist, Woodrow William Haney, Sr., who, according to Timothy, "really re-invented the flute, the way it is played, and the dynamics he would incorporate into his notes." Haney won many awards for his flute work and played at the U.S. bicentennial celebration in 1976. As cultural resources assistant at the Five Civilized Tribes Museum in Muskogee, Timothy played for people from all over the world before 2000 when he became director of Ataloa Lodge Museum at Bacone College in Muskogee where the Native flute stayed alive on the eastern side of the state with help from Haney, Woody Crumbo, Vernon McNeal and others (with its obvious champions such as **"Doc" Tate Nevaquaya,** Tom Ware, Belo Cozad, **Andrew Vasquez**, and **Cornel Pewewardy** in the southwestern part of Oklahoma). Timothy has performed at various prestigious venues, to include ap-

Muscogee (Creek) Flutist John Timothy

pearances in Washington D.C., Georgia, New York City, Virginia, and across Oklahoma, strictly by request. He has released one CD of his atmospheric flute recordings, *Inutska*, in which every song has a Muscogee (Creek) and English title, and was recorded by Tulsa Sound veteran, **David Teegarden**.

Along with rap and jazz-fusion, several Muscogee musicians have taken the musical direction pointed out by the blues. Of course, guitarist **Jesse Ed Davis** (Kiowa/Comanche/Muscogee) made a strong impact on 1970s popular music specifically due to his ability to play bottleneck blues guitar. Obie Sullivan was a long-time keyboardist for the American Indian blues band, Blues Nation. Lead singer Vic Gutierrez of blues group Smilin' Vic and the Soul Monkeys is Muscogee/Euchee, and guitarist Chebon Tiger has been leading his own blues band since 1998. In the realm of country music, twelve-year-old Muscogee citizen Taylor Osborn won vocalist of the year in her age category at the 2003 North American Country Music Association's international competition at Pigeon Forge, Tennessee. Competing in the traditional country category, she sang "Blue" and "Walkin' After Midnight" to take the top honors. Country is also not out of the realm of the Muscogee (Creek) experience, as the fiddle was a ubiquitous instrument of the American west due to its portability. According to *The Fiddle Book* (New York: Oak, 1967), collected by Marion Thede, at least one traditional fiddle tune is known as "Creek Nation," and was said by Claude Keenan of Oklahoma County that it was based on "Creek song" and the tradition among fiddlers was that it was composed and played during the "Trail of Tears" (p. 30). Another young Muscogee (Creek) musician, Nokose "Blue Fire" Foley (b. 11/30/1994, Claremore, OK) has appeared regionally throughout Oklahoma, notably at the Dusk 'til Dawn Blues Festival in Rentiesville, Oklahoma where local bluesman **D.C. Minner** gave Foley his first paying gig as an interpreter of traditional Delta and modern electric blues. Also, Muscogee citizen Nicole Delpratt has achieved notoriety for her rendition of the United States National Anthem translated into the Muscogee (Creek) language.

Jamie Coon

In 2005, tribal citizen, Jamie Coon, a 1997 graduate of Okemah High School, received a Los Angeles Music Award Single of the Year nomination for her 2005 song, "Breathe", from her independently released album, *Everything So Far*. Her single, "Waiting", appeared in the CBS program *Ghost Whisperer*, and her music has been featured in several independent films. Jamie has performed at the Smithsonian National Museum of the American Indian, and the Kennedy Center, both in Washington D.C. She has been nominated for

Pete Coser (left) sings with Tony Arkeketa **(Ponca/Otoe)** in the Redland Singers, 2003.

Hugh W. Foley / 559

a number of awards in Southern California, Oklahoma, and by the Native American Music Awards.

Finally, Muscogee musicians have also made notable contributions to contemporary music of the powwow arena. Three brothers, Wayne Coser (b. Okmulgee), George Coser, Jr. (b. Tulsa), and Pete G. Coser (b. Okmulgee), have been members of the intertribal Redland Singers since the early 1970s, a drum group noted for being the one of the very first to bring the high-pitched style of northern powwow singing to Oklahoma. Pete joined Redlands in 1973, followed by his two brothers who had been singing with the Brave Scout Singers, the first northern-styled group from Oklahoma. Subsequently, Pete Coser's son, Pete "Petey" Robert George Coser, began singing with the Redland Singers as a youngster, and sang with Thunderhorse, a northern style powwow group who recorded two albums on the Arbor label, *Riding the Storm* (AR-113820) and *Native America* (AR-11592), and who have since morphed into Young Buffalo Horse in which both the younger Coser and the previously mentioned Nokose Foley are both touring members. In the southern singing style genre, G.C. Tsouhlarakis (Muscogee/Navajo) and Sam Cook (Muscogee/Pawnee) have recorded for Canyon Records with the Grammy-nominated drum group, **Young Bird**.

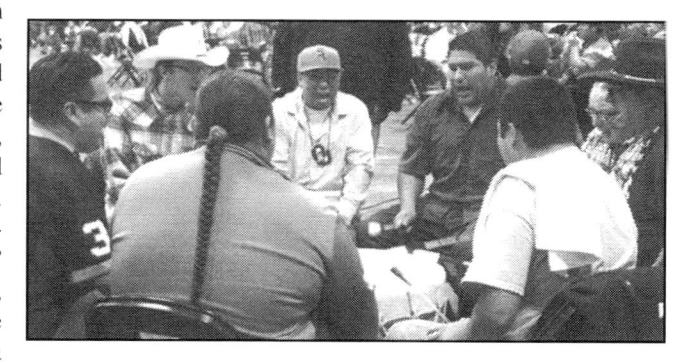

Muscogee (Creek) citizens Pete "Petey" Coser (far left #3) and Nokose Foley (in white cowboy hat) sing with Young Buffalo Horse at the 2012 Choctaw Nation Powwow. Powwow.

Given the extremely diverse history of music in the Muscogee (Creek) Nation and among its people, one can learn a lot in a short amount of time at the Annual Creek Nation Festival and Rodeo held the third weekend of June of each year. Along with the all-Indian rodeo and softball tournaments, the annual festival always features a Creek hymn singing, as well as an exhibition stomp dance held on the Thursday night of the festival.

www.muscogeecreeknation-nsn.gov

Notes

1. For a more detailed outline of Muscogee history from its own point of view, see the Muscogee (Creek) Nation's website at www.muscogeenation-nsn.gov.
2. For a look at the pre-removal Muscogee Creek world of the late 1790s and early 1800s from a U.S. governmental agent's point of view see, *The Collected Works of Benjamin Hawkins, 1796-1810* (Tuscaloosa: University of Alabama Press, 2003).
3. To understand more about the Muscogee (Creek) experience in the 1813-14 Creek Wars, see Joel Martin's, *Sacred Revolt: The Muskogee's Struggle for a New World* (Boston, MA: Beacon Press, 1991). For a solid history detailing the final years of the pre-removal domain of the Muscogee people, see Robbie Etheridge's *Creek Country: The Creek Indians and Their World* (Chapel Hill: University of North Carolina Press, 2003).
4. For insight into the challenges faced by the Muscogee during the Civil War, see Laurence M. Hauptman's *Between Two Fires: American Indians and the Civil War* (New York: Simon and Schuster, 1995), pages 52-57.

5. Notes in Daniel Littlefield's *Africans and Creeks: From the Colonial Period to the Civil War* (Westport: Greenwood, 1979), page 141.
6. For additional explication of the interaction between Africans and Creeks, and the important roles Blacks played in the development of Christianity, see *Gary Zellar*'s *African Creeks:Estelvste and the Creek Nation* (Norman: University of Oklahoma Press, 2007), in which he notes the significance of Monday Durant, page 36.
7. For additional catalogue information of Muscogee (Creek) music releases, see Indian House Records at www.indianhouse.com, Canyon Records at www.canyonrecords.com, or Arbor Records at www.arbor-records.com (all accessed July, 2011).
8. For more details on Muscogee poet and musicians, Joy Harjo, see www.joyharjo.com.

Musick, Scott
(also see **The Call**)

Drummer for the 1980s and '90s alternative rock band, **The Call**, Scott Musick was born in Tulsa in the early 1950s. His father was a musician who played big band music and jazz around the house, and Scott started playing drums when he was eleven, but had played trumpet for three years before that because there was one in the home. He took a summer school class on snare drum, and received an "A" for the class, causing the teacher to recommended Musick switch to drums, which he did, eventually playing in a state and national award-winning stage band at Edison High School under the baton of Mr. Ashley Alexander. Also during high school, Musick played in a band with guitarist **Tuck Andress**, and played other gigs with Oklahoma Music Hall of Fame inductee, **Tommy Crook.**

After graduating, Scott headed to California, played in a band, and came back to Tulsa for a few months. Before too long, keyboardist Danny Timms came through town on tour, and said he had a friend, Michael Been, with whom he was starting a band back in California. Timms encouraged Musick to return to San Francisco, which he did, and the group rehearsed for a couple of years in Timms' garage, but could never really get the band going beyond club gigs. Scott played with Michael Been and a couple of guys from Moby Grape for a while, and continued playing in bands through the mid to late 1970s. Tired of trying to keep personalities together in a band, Been decided to go off on his own, and Musick went along for the ride. With Been singing and playing his own songs, the new group wound up backing another Tulsan, **Phil Seymour**, who was working on his album, and wanted Musick and Been's tight group to play behind him for an audition for Shelter Records. While Seymour was taking a break, the A&R guy sent up to the gig by Shelter's Denny Cordell heard Michael Been and the band doing some of Been's songs. The talent scout went back to Cordell and said, "Been's band is the one you want to sign," which is what happened about 1979 when Cordell signed the band to a production deal with Mercury/Polygram. Sub-

Danny Timmus and Scott Musick (right) play at Lanna Thai Restaurant in Tulsa, 2010.

sequently, they began their career as The Call, enjoying the benefits of being major label artists, but never really breaking out of the cult level at college radio stations, or alternative, modern rock, stations during the 1980s and '90s. As the band's contract status waned in the mid-'90s, Musick began playing with Kris Kristofferson throughout the U.S. and Europe before returning to Tulsa to take care of family matters.

Since then, Musick has performed or recorded with Elvis Costello, Peter Gabriel, Smokey Robinson, Johnny Cash, **Hoyt Axton**, The Band, Delbert McClinton, David Cassidy, and Barry McGuire. Along with traveling to Nashville occasionally for studio sessions, and playing various gigs around Tulsa. In 2011 Scott also opened his own "Musick" school where he instructed private drum lessons .

Note
1. Much of the information regarding Scott Musick's early years came from a 2008 video interview conducted by Jeff Moore and Larry O'Dell for the Oklahoma Historical Society's oral history project to document the state's major contributors to the field of rock music. Additional information was gleaned from Musick's bio on the Lanna Thai Restaurant website at www.lannathai.com (accessed August 15, 2011).

N

Marla Nauni
(b. June 11, 1976)

Of **Comanche** & **Seneca** heritage, Marla Nauni was born in Lawton, Oklahoma, and is recognized nationally as premier performer of Comanche hymns. Released in 2004 with thirteen Comanche language Christian hymns, her first independent disc, *Comanche Hymns performed by Marla Nauni*, received a nomination from the 2004 Indian Summer Music Awards in the Best Traditional Vocal category. With a voice both plaintive and melodic, Nauni comfortably channels the natural rhythms of the Comanche language through her a cappella performances, and has full control of American Indian microtonal singing. Many ears have turned toward her powerful renditions of Comanche hymns, leading to prestigious performances at the National Museum of the American Indian, Washington, D.C., Red Earth in Oklahoma City, Turning Stone Resort Casino in New York, and Foxwoods Casino in Connecticut. Along with performing "Blessing Songs" at various nationwide events, along with multiple schools and university programs and presentations, she achieved radio airplay in Oklahoma, New Mexico, and Texas, as well as on high-profile public station, WPFW in Washington, D.C.

Marla Nauni

With a BA in Business Administration and an MBA from the University of Oklahoma, Marla is more than prepared to expand her sphere of influence into other entertainment business areas. She has modeled in Times Square and at the 2003 GRAMMY Awards, as well as for the Comanche Nation Casino in Lawton. She has also worked as an actress. Breaking in as extra in *American Indian Graffiti: This Thing Life* (2003) and *Contest* (2006), Marla also played a lead character in the 2005 independent short feature, *Okemah's Creek*. Filmed in Okemah, Marla portrays one of two best friends who decide to decide to rob a bingo hall due to their increasingly desperate situation in life. Luckily for Marla, her recording career is not nearly so desperate. Based in Cache, Oklahoma, Marla released her second CD, *Comanche Hymns II*, on her own label in September, 2010. Featuring eighteen songs in her unique vocal sound imprint, Nauni's sophomore disc highlights her confident studio singing, no doubt a result from several years of performing for large groups of people. *Comanche Hymns II* is also warmed nicely by several duets with her father Norman Nauni, Sr. Most recently she served in the capacity of Ms. Indian Lawton Woman, 2011, was scheduled for fall 2011 performances in Michigan, the Comanche Fair, Bacone College's Fall Powwow, and Lawton, Oklahoma's International Festival. Also in 2011, Marla received a nomination from the Indian Summer Music Awards in the Spiritual category for "Jesus is Coming" from her *Comanche Hymns II* album. The nomination earned Nauni a performance that year at the 24th Annual Indian Summer Music Awards Show in Milwaukee, Wisconsin.

www.myspace.com/marlanauni

Nevaquaya, "Doc" Tate
(b. July 3, 1932 – d. March 5, 1996)

Widely known as an award-winning artist who depicted many traditional elements of his native Comanche life and heritage, Doc Tate Nevaquaya is also generally credited with reviving the traditional American Indian Plains flute in the 1970s, and inspiring a generation of new players, including **Andrew Vasquez**, R. Carlos Nakai, Kevin Locke, and Tom Mauchahty Ware. Born as Joyce Lee Tate Nevaquaya in Apache, Oklahoma, "Doc" replaced "Joyce" due to his close friendship with Dr. C. W. Joyce. When Doc entered Fort Sill Indian School and was required to have a Christian name, the family arrived at Tate via a friend of Doc's grandfather's. Nevaquaya's parents died eight months apart, when he was thirteen, and he moved in with grandparents where he listened to their stories, and began drawing landscapes of the Wichita Mountains. He attended Haskell Indian Institute in 1950 and 1951, and taught himself to paint. By 1958 he was selling his work, and exhibiting his work extensively throughout the United States and abroad. Nevaquaya's work was purchased by Queen Elizabeth II and horror actor, Vincent Price, as well as for such important institutional collections as the Smithsonian Institution and the Indian Arts and Crafts Board, U.S. Department of the Interior in Washington, DC, San Francisco Museum of Modern Art, the Metropolitan Museum of Art in New York City, the Philbrook Museum of Art in Tulsa, and the Gilcrease Institute of American History and Art in Tulsa. While curious about the flute in his youth, Nevaquaya became increasingly interested in the 1960s when noted American Indian flute expert Richard W. Payne, M.D., of Oklahoma City, gave Doc Tate a traditional plains flute in 1967 as a trade for some artwork. Along with learning a tremendous amount from Dr. Payne, the flute inspired Nevaquaya to pursue remaining elder Comanche and other Plains flute players, and travel to the Smithsonian Institution and Library of Congress to listen to older American Indian flute recordings and study their flute collections. Nevaquaya lectured widely, to include workshops in his specialties at Brigham Young University and Georgetown University in 1972 and 1974, respectively. Along with creating a Comanche shield as tribute to the Tomb of the Unknown Soldier in 1973, by 1975 he was well known in non-Indian music circles for his playing abilities and shared the stage with Freddy Fender, Mel Tillis, and **Roy Clark** at the Roy Clark Ranch in Tulsa.[1] He also performed with Loretta Lynn, Sammy Davis, Jr., and Wayne Newton. In 1976, he recorded *Indian Flute Songs from Comanche Land*, the first modern commercial recording consisting entirely of American Indian flute music, and *Comanche Flute Music* (1979), available contemporarily through Smithsonian Folkways Records as compact disc under the title of Doc Tate Nevaquaya, *Comanche Flute* (SFW50403).

Perhaps the best-known contemporary American Indian flutist, R. Carlos Nakai, stated on his website, "When I began in the early 1970s the sum total of indigenous native flute players were "Doc" Tate Nevaquaya, Tom Mauchahty Ware, and Woodrow Haney, Sr. There were no others." Interestingly, all three of those players are native Oklahomans.

With his releases in the 1970s, Doc Tate furthered the repertoire for the American Indian flute by innovative use of melodies borrowed from traditionally vocal genres, such as war dance songs, victory songs, social dance songs, and Christian hymns. His notoriety stamped various countries on his passport with Asian tours in the 1970s, and multiple national television appearances on CBS with Charles Kuralt, and on ABC's *Good Morning America*, as well as performances on the British Broadcasting Corporation. In 1982 Doc Tate performed for the *Night of the First Americans* at the Kennedy Center for the Performing Arts in Washington, DC, and in 1986, he became the first American Indian to receive the National Endowment for the Arts Heritage Award, which recognized his contribution to Native American art forms and revival of the American Indian flute. He performed at the United Nations in New York City in 1985, and opened the archery competition at the 1989 U.S. Olympic Festival in Norman, Oklahoma with a flute song.

Named a "Living Legend" along with six other American Indian artists, he performed at Carnegie Hall in New York in 1990, and composed the song "Flight in Spirit" for the Oklahoma Arts Council in 1991 to honor the five famous American Indian ballerinas from Oklahoma. In 1992, he recorded another definitive album for Riversong Soundworks, *The Master*, including original songs and his trademark adaptations

"Doc" Tate Nevaquaya

of traditional music. From 1992 through 1995, he served in a variety of advisory and board positions, continued his performance-lectures, and received multiple national and statewide awards for his art and music, culminating in a "National Living Treasure" award in 1995 by the state of Oklahoma. In 1995, he played flute songs at the memorial service for renowned storyteller and the first "Oklahoma Treasure" award recipient, Te Ata, who died at age 99 in 1995. Although he died soon thereafter in 1996, footage of Doc Tate playing the flute and talking about its origins appeared posthumously in *Songkeepers* (1998), a video documentary about the history of the flute in American Indian music. *Songkeepers* also features Doc's eldest son, Sonny Nevaquaya (b. Apache, OK), who began playing and recording flute professionally in 1993 when he released *Spirit of the Flute*. In 1998 the younger Nevaquaya released *Viva Kokopelli!*, which blends contemporary instruments with traditional flute.

In 2000, the Red Earth Festival and Museum in Oklahoma City sponsored a major exhibit designed to interpret Doc Tate's life, *In the Realm of the Thirteen Feathers*. In 2001, his music lived on through his children, as Sonny Nevaquaya released *Doc Tate Nevaquaya – Legend and Legacy*, with four songs by Doc Tate, as well as songs from Sonny and three of his brothers. All but one of his sons play and make flutes as they were taught by their father. He and his wife, Charlotte, also had four daughters. As of 2011, Dr. Paula Conlon, a Patricia Deisenroth Presidential Professor of music at the University of Oklahoma, was the primary expert on the life, music, and art of Nevaquaya, and was under contract with OU Press to produce the definitive biography of Nevaquaya's life. According to her faculty website in 2011, she is focusing on his contributions to the flute from the various perspectives of his family, friends, and colleagues. The biography will also examine Doc Tate's impact on the history and development of Native American flute in the 20th century. An accomplished flutist herself, both formally trained as well as an expert on the American Indian Plains flute, Conlon writes, "The book also discusses the current transformation of the Native American flute form a private courtship ritual performed by young men to a more public expression of Native identity that no longer excludes female players."[2] Upon his death of a massive heart attack in 1996, he was survived by his wife, Charlotte, their nine children, seventeen grandchildren, and one great-granddaughter.[3]

Notes
1. A variety of biographies of Doc Tate Nevaquaya populate the Internet, however, one would be wise to stick with sources either written by or referenced by Paula Conlon, such as her biographical essay published online in the Oklahoma Historical Society's *Encyclopedia of Oklahoma History and Culture* under the title "Nevaquaya, Joyce Lee "Doc" Tate (1932-1996).
2. See Paula Conlon's faculty website (http://faculty-staff.ou.edu/C/Paula.J.Conlon-1/tateresearch.htm) for more details about her publication of Nevaquaya's biography, as well as her own extensive expertise in both the flute and additional Native American musical forms.
3. Additional details about Nevaquaya's life were gleaned from *Arts Oklahoma: The Newsletter of the State Arts Council of Oklahoma* (Spring, 1996), 1-15; and Doc Tate Nevaquaya's published obituary in the *Muskogee Phoenix*, April 6 and 7, 1996.

Nichols, Grady

A resident of Tulsa in 2011 who was raised in rural Siloam Springs, Arkansas, right on the Oklahoma border, Grady Nichols is very close to being the next significant jazz story from the state. Often classified as a smooth jazz saxophonist, Nichols incorporated funk, fusion, gospel, and even bop into his early compositions and performances, but has focused more on the smooth jazz sound with a consistent sprinkling of gospel and contemporary Christian themed tracks on each of his albums. While he has yet to hit the national jazz charts in *Billboard* magazine, Nichols has received significant attention on various smooth jazz websites, and critics wax rhapsodic about his saxofluency. His full energetic tone has landed him top opening spots for several "A-list" entertainers, and his music has been hard for the national media to deny as he has performed on BET On Jazz's *Jazz Scene*, been part of BET's *Sunday Night Live* house band, had his music featured on public service announcements for Coca-Cola, and made two appearances on the nationally syndicated *Hour of Power* program hosted by Dr. Robert Schuler. As a touring artist, Grady has opened for Ray Charles, Luciano Pavarotti, Jay Leno, The Temptations, The Righteous Brothers, Al Green, Huey Lewis & the News, The O'Jays, Jeffrey Osborne, Ellis Marsalis, Keiko Matsui, Stanley Turrentine, David Benoit, and Paul Taylor. He has also performed with The Beach Boys, Roy Clark, Bob James, Paul Brown, Kim Waters, Wayman Tisdale, and Marion Meadows. With five successful independent albums produced under his own supervision and label, as well as highly regarded live performances, and a sonic imprint appropriate for commercial media, as well as the nightclub and concert scene, Grady Nichols is a poised to create a long and substantial discography and performance dossier at the most respected levels of the smooth jazz and contemporary Christian music worlds.

While Grady matured in the very un-jazz countryside of rural Arkansas, the generic smooth saxophone of the Weather Channel perked his ears toward the instrument, which he began playing the sixth grade. While in Siloam Springs High School, he was able to study with an experienced player, Joe Davis, who had worked as a sax man for Sarah Vaughan and Mel Torme. After graduating John Brown University, he moved to Tulsa where he established himself as a significant regional player by releasing well-noticed independent albums, *Between You and Me* (1996), a rambunctious affair, and *Mysterious Intentions* (1997), both of which show his development as an artist who is finding his footing among the multiple choices offered by his youth, skill, and varied musical interests. His third independent album, *In the Fullness of Time* (2001), again exhibits his exploration through various modern jazz styles, focusing primarily on the softer and more melodic

Grady Nichols, 2010

tones that are not quite as kinetic as his first two efforts, pleasant though it may be for soft jazz listeners. The album also features Grammy award-winning singer/songwriter Bill Champlin, keyboardist / vocalist of the group jazz/rock fusion group, Chicago, alongside a 50 voice choir. Champlin praised Nichols by saying "This guy is really young. He's really positive and he's got maturity way beyond his years in his tone, his delivery, everything about him. A lot of guys are out there with chops. Grady uses the chops to get to his heart and from his heart it gets to you." The CD was recorded before a live studio audience and aired on television as "Grady Nichols Live." Quickly evident is the diversity of Grady's influences, using elements of jazz, reggae, Latin, blues and gospel. However, *Fullness of Time* seems to be more about Nichols trying to trying to figure out if he is going to mine Kenny G's gold shaft of easy listening jazz, or provide a guiding light to a new branch of contemporary Christian music, hesitatingly, but accurately termed Jesus jazz. On *Fullness of Time*, Nichols features titles such as "Heaven Help Us All", "Live for You", "Amazing Grace", and "First Corinthians Thirteen", a Biblical chapter devoted to the concept of charity conducted out of love. By delving into both the commercial smooth jazz world, as well as the modern Christian music world, Nichols replicates a repeated theme throughout this text: a majority of successful musical artists that achieve significant longevity in their careers have at least two different specialties. Herein, Nichols has already proven his music popular with two genre-specific fan bases, which bodes well for his long-term existence as an artist.

In 2003, Nichols released *Sophistication* through his own label, and on which his sound matured into a more confident and subtle approach composition and performing. Overt proselytizing and theological meditating aside on this collection, *Sophistication* was his most consistent album in tone to that point, reflecting the album's title. To enhance the whole project, Grady approached Grammy-nominated recording artist Jeff Lorber to produce, and Grammy Award-winning producer Paul Brown to mix. Other artists contributing to *Sophistication* include Grammy Award-winning Chris Botti (trumpet on "End of the Night") and Paul Pesco (rhythm guitar), who also has credits on albums by Madonna, Mariah Carey, Celine Dion and Jennifer Lopez. Every tune is a perfectly suitable display of his excellent sonic imprint that can accompany any dinner date ("Dinner and a Movie") or repeated plays on the Weather Channel. His adopted home state responded to the album with a Legacy Tribute Award from the Oklahoma Jazz Hall of Fame in 2004, and the **Charlie Christian** Jazz Music Award for Outstanding Achievements in Jazz in 2005. *Sophistication* also made a strong debut on internet stations and remained on the SmoothJazz.com charts for over 40 weeks. SmoothJazz.com also named *Sophistication* in the top 50 Smooth Jazz Albums of 2004 and gave it a Smoothie Award. With its rising popularity, Grady found himself sharing the stage with some of his musical idols and touring the country for club dates, multiple festival appearances, and select performances on the Norwegian Cruise Lines Smooth Jazz Cruise

In 2008, Nichols teamed with **Zac Maloy**, who produced *Take Me with You* (Grady Nichols, Ltd.), and co-wrote five of the songs with Nichols on the album. *Take Me with You* stretched Nichols into ranges of pop, R&B, and a more rhythmically textured sound with the addition of percussion accents, reverb-laden guitars, and spacey keyboard accents. With a long list of performances notched on his resume by that time, Nichols appears to have learned from his extensive live performing to find out more about who he wanted to be as an artist. *Take Me with You* bounces out of the box with a little more aggressive tone than his 2001 effort ("Bellisimo"), and grooves just a little harder than his previous album ("Runway"). Nichols also continued adding guest vocalists to his recordings, this time with former Sixpence None the Richer vocalist, Leigh Nash, on the jazzy pop number, "Every Kind of People", and Oklahomans Jenny Labow on the album's title track, as well as Tulsa's **Toni Estes** on "Give Love". Fulfilling a century of jazz tradition, Nichols also takes a familiar tune, in this case, Kylie Minogue's "Can't Get You Out of My Head", and riffs on the melody with his own inspired take. He also includes a song that fits the format of much contemporary Christian music that can be interpreted as either a love song, or tribute to Christ ("After the Rain"). Furthermore, Nichols also adds what a dance track with a "House Mix" of the album's title number, further indicating his willingness to sprawl out creatively. According to his website, Nichols' "goal was to record a CD that reflected his broad range of musical influences and tastes." On *Take Me with You*", Nichols further hoped to "capture something new and fun that is another layer of [his] musical personality." He also is grounded in his art's purpose for both himself and his fans. "Music is intimately connected to so many great moments in my life," Nichols says, "and to my way of thinking, that's the purpose of music, creating something that enhances memories and moments, binding them together. I am so blessed to have the opportunity to do that. That's my goal helping to create great moments and memories for people through music." Mission accomplished so far, with multiple exploits on the horizon at which to aim our ears, the most recent of which is 2012's *Destinations*, with an homage to his adopted hometown, "Tulsa".

www.gradynichols.com

Nitro

Mr. Nitro (Derrick Booker), with his associated rappers and production crew, is Oklahoma's only major label, nationally recognized hip-hop artist, outside of Muskogee's **Ester Dean**. The 2000 album, *Nitro Entertainment Presents... Hustlin' Pays* (Columbia) features a variety of rappers on fifteen tracks filled with urban references not uncommon on hundreds of rap albums since the mid-1980s when Run DMC launched hip-hop into the mainstream American popular music world. Several of the cuts are recorded in Oklahoma City and contain references to Spencer, Glencoe, and Oklahoma as a whole. Early responses to the album noted its beats being even slower than that of the hip-hop coming out of the southern United States, often referred to as the Dirty South style, as opposed to the rap from the East or West coasts of the U.S. Leave it to Oklahoma hip-hoppers to be even more laid back than Southern rappers, further indicating Oklahoma is not quite the South. Songs deal with standard rap topics: trying to survive on the streets ("Hustlin' Pays" and "Dodge the Sprinkle"), interpersonal relationships between men and women ("Don't Say Hi", "Watch Ya Girl", "Hennessey"), challenging other rappers to do better ("What's Up Now"), and partying because it's better than not partying ("Dippin'"). The album also features some sweet harmony vocals on a couple of tracks from a group noted as Mob Playas, and a smooth tribute cover of Eazy-E's "Boyz-in-the-Hood". An early vignette on the album says artists are from Oklahoma City, Lawton, and Tulsa, with monikers of the various contributors to the album including Mr. Nitro (a.k.a. Daddy D), Lady Ace, Young Fool, Boy Dogg, Buccett Loc, Mob Playas, Joe Cleezy, C.A.P., 2 Real, Piper, Mista Maze, Nfamous.

While released on the major label, Columbia, the album did not achieve widespread commercial success, although it has received a number of mentions as a "grassroots" album with "street cred" that represents Oklahoma well as hip-hop music. Language on the album keeps it squarely in the "parental advisory category."

Since the album, Nitro music has gotten its songs out via youtube.com, accompanied by very local music videos. The 2006 release, "I Wish You Would" is a spirited piece built around the common neighborhood challenge phrases, "Say somethin', try somethin', start somethin', do somethin', I wish you would", and goes on to reference Oklahoma, the Star Spencer Bobcats, being from the country, 23rd Street in OKC, the 4-0-5 (OKC's area code). Additional lyrics show Nitro's sense of humor, and the video features much of the crew in Oklahoma Sooners jerseys, as well as various shots around the city. Also in 2006, Nitro hosted a late night show television show, *Power Moves TV*, on Oklahoma City's Fox television affiliate. Good samples of Nitro's live, free-styling rap skills are available on a 2008 youtube.com video titled "Nitro/Gelly-That's My Song" (accessed August, 2011). According to scant information online about his career, Nitro is an Oklahoma City native, and started working professionally in 1994 when he produced some beats for Quean Latifah. For some of Nitro's early work, see the 1997 video, "Southside", shot in Oklahoma City for MCA Records that challenges East and Coast rappers who depend on the south for their record sales, but don't necessarily respect the rappers from the country. A very interesting take on the stereotypes in Oklahoma as a state, Nitro raps that people outside of the state think everyone "rides in horses and carriages with cowboys and Indians," and urges outsiders to take a closer look because "we're more than just Garth Brooks." Indeed.

In 2010, Nitro's "I Tried to Tell Y'all" featured more of the laid back beats for which he has become known, a "Tubular Bells"-like recurring riff on synthesizer, and even some bowling alley sound effects on the boasting song, a common rap lyrical trope. He hit his stride in the summer of 2010 with "The Greatest", sampling boxer Muhammad Ali, and rolling out a fast stream of rhymes that challenges other rappers with sharp humor and original taunts. With an obvious quick wit, live free-styling abilities, varied production skills, and wide network of rap and hip-hop connections, Mr. Nitro's name may not have yet seen its biggest font, nor widest distribution.

Derrick Booker (a.k.a Nitro)

www.myspace.com/nitro405

The Nixons
(Formed 1990, Oklahoma City)
Zac Maloy (lead vocals, guitars)
Jesse Davis (guitars, vocals)
Ricky Wolking (bass, vocals)
John Humphrey (drums, vocals)

Originally formed in 1990 by **Zac Maloy**, Jesse Davis, bassist Ricky Brooks (1990 to 1997), and drummer Tye Robinson (1990 to 1992) in Oklahoma City, all of whom appear on the band's first independent album in 1990, and subsequent six-song EP, *Six* (Dragon Street, 1992), The Nixons led the mainstream rock charge out of Oklahoma in the 1990s. Featuring Maloy's moving and forceful vocals, Davis' gut grabbing guitars, and an aggressive rhythm section more intent on providing a powerful palate than simply an accompanying tempo in the music's background, the band's lineup changed after their first two releases when drummer Humphrey was added in 1992. After recording the full-length independent CD, *Halo* (Rainmaker, 1994), and touring incessantly throughout the Midwest where they had developed a solid following, the group signed to MCA Records as labels were still trying to find the next successful alternative rock group. The Nixons released two fairly successful modern rock albums, *Foma* (MCA, 1996) and *The Nixons* (MCA, 1997). *Foma* provided the band its most significant single, "Sister", which was embraced by modern rock (*Billboard* #11), mainstream rock (*Billboard* #6), and some Top 40 stations (*Billboard* #39). Additional favorites from the album included "Happy Song", "Wire", and "Passion". Always a strong live act due to Maloy's commanding vocal presence and the tight start and stops that come only with years of rehearsals and performing together on the road, the band toured constantly during the MCA years, performing as many as 300 shows a year on tour with Soul Asylum, No Doubt, Kiss, Bush, and Radiohead. After adding bassist Ricky Wolking in 1997, the group recorded their second album for MCA. The first single from the self-titled release, "Baton Rouge", received significant mainstream rock attention, however, modern rock and Top 40 moved away from the relatively short-lived grunge sound by the late 1990s. The group also released a popular fan EP, *Scrapbook* (Rainmaker, 1999), featuring live and acoustic covers, some unreleased b-sides remaining from previous sessions. The Nixons released a final disc through Koch Records, *Latest Thing* (2000), producing a minor chart single, "First Trip", but Davis and Humphrey left the band before the promotional tour that was to follow the album's release (replaced by Ray Luzier/drums and Scott Bush/guitar). After fulfilling those dates, the Nixons ceased to be as an active band.

The Nixons, circa 1997, (l-r): Jesse Davis, Zac Maloy, Ricky Wolking, and John Humphrey.

In 2001, Davis, Brooks, and Humphrey reformed as Hover, with Garin Murdock as their lead singer. The group toured heavily, released one independent EP, and disbanded in 2002.[1] Since then, **Zac Maloy** entered into a songwriting a production role for a variety of artists and bands, first in Tulsa, and then eventually relocating to Nashville where he opened his own studio and writing retreat. John Humphrey became the drummer for the rock band Seether in 2003, and was still active in that role for their 2011 album, *Holding on to Strings Better Left to Fray*, which featured his galloping tom-tom work and powerful cymbal accents. Original drummer Tye Robison went on to operate a recording studio in Dallas. Ricky Wolking became the bassist for Edgewater, a Dallas-based rock band, and recorded a solo album titled, *Honky Mofo* (Sick Pup), and as of 2011 was working on a new project titled The Better Death. Jesse Davis also operates a recording studio in Oklahoma City, and has released an EP and full-length album with rootsy jam band called 4 Points West. Featured prominently in the Oklahoma History Center's 2008 exhibit on rock music from the state, The Nixons band members remain friends and continued adding photos, rare demos, recordings, and writing blogs on their myspace.com site, the last post being in February, 2009.

References
www.myspace.com/thenixonsofficial/blog
www.seether.com (John Humphrey)
www.myspace.com/zacmaloy and www.zacmaloymusic.com (Zac Maloy)
www.rickywolking.com and www.thebetterdeath.com (Ricky Wolking)
www.myspace.com/4pointswest (Jesse Davis)

Note
1. Matt Gleason details John Humphrey's career from the drummer's high school band days at Moore High School through joining Seether in a January 27, 2006 article in the *Tulsa World's Spot* magazine, "Gut, rattle, and roll," p. 15.

No Justice (See Red Dirt Music)

Nolen, Jimmy
(b. April 3, 1934 – d. December 18, 1983)

Although born in Oklahoma City, the father of funk guitar, Jimmy Nolen, grew up with his nine brothers and sisters on a farm close to Wealaka, Oklahoma, a community named for the site of Presbyterian Mission on a bluff above the Arkansas River southeast of Tulsa between Bixby and Leonard. It was there he began playing violin at age nine. Not improving fast enough, Nolen bought an acoustic guitar when he was fourteen and began teaching himself how to play by listening to blues on the radio, especially T-Bone Walker and **Lowell Fulson**. At eighteen, he picked up his first electric guitar while living with a sister in Wichita, Kansas, and began playing with J.D. Nicholson and His Jivin' Five with whom Jimmy first recorded in 1952.[1]

In 1955, blues singer Jimmy Wilson came upon Nolen playing at a club in Tulsa and hired him to go on the road with Wilson nationally, which Nolen did until the group broke up in Los Angeles in 1956. An imposing figure at 6'4," Nolen settled in L.A. where he joined trumpeter Monte Easton's band, recorded some long out-of-print singles with Jimmy Wilson and Ray Agee, and also worked and recorded with Chuck Higgins, a popular R&B saxophonist from southern California. Nolen's first national exposure came in 1957 when he began playing and recording with Johnny Otis, and contributed guitar to Otis's "Willie and the Hand Jive," a major hit in 1958. Nolen also made several recordings under his own name in the late 1950s and early 1960s for Federal, Elko, and Imperial Records, but none surfaced as hits. A good compilation, *Honky Tonk!*, on the UK label Ace, features 24 rare tracks from Federal and King records. All the instrumental R&B tracks were recorded between 1948 and 1964, and Nolen is included with Freddy King, Johnny "Guitar" Watson, and King Curtis.

After leaving Otis in the early 1960s, Nolen formed his own nine-piece group and backed up famous blues men who came to L.A. and needed a band, such as B.B. King. He and his band played constantly throughout the smaller clubs and ballrooms in the African-American communities of California in the early 1960s. In 1965, Nolen accepted James Brown's offer to join the Godfather of Soul on tour. One of Nolen's former sidemen, tenor saxophonist L.D. Williams, recommended Jimmy to James Brown, and Nolen made an instant and eternal impact with his ringing dominant 9th chords, now universally known as funk chords, first on Brown's hit "Papa's Got a Brand New Bag" (1965), but even more dramatically on "I Got You (I Feel Good)" (1966), and "It's a Man's, Man's, Man's World" (1966). While the same chords had long been used in jazz, Nolen's rhythm guitar on songs such as "Cold Sweat" and "I Got the Feelin'" set the standard for all future guitarists who would attempt the funk form. While known as the guitar style known as "chicken scratch" by guitarists, the form became widely accepted as the benchmark example for funk guitar, exemplified by a "chucka-chucka" rhythm, or funky "scratches" followed by chords, or a combination of both.[2]

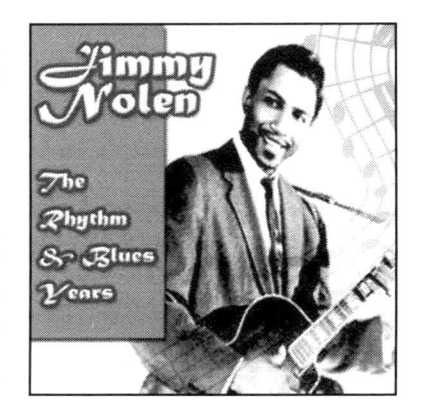

Nolen and his band mates are also roundly given credit for converting the soul music of the 1960s into funk, but Brown never gave the musicians credit on any album, and rarely in concert. Nevertheless, Nolen's guitar work appears on all of Brown's records of the period, including *Sings Raw Soul* (1967), *Live at the Apollo Vol. 2* (1968), *Say It Loud, I'm Black and I'm Proud* (1969). Nolen and the entire group walked out on Brown due to the soul master's stern leadership, which included a full-length set rehearsal before James arrived in the hall for two shows a night.[3] Led by saxophonist Maceo Parker, the musicians formed All The King's Men and played throughout California until 1972, when most of the musicians, including Nolen, returned to Brown's camp as the "J.B.'s." Along with serving as James Brown's backing band for live performances and recording sessions on *Get on the Good Foot* (1972), *Payback* (1973), and *Hell: The Payback* (1974), the J.B.'s recorded five albums under their own name from 1972 to 1975 while Nolen was in the group, to include *Damn Right I'm Somebody* (1974).

Jimmy continued playing his trademark and revolutionary style with Brown until 1983 when the big man from Oklahoma City and Wealaka had a fatal heart attack at home in Atlanta, Georgia. After Nolen's death, his recordings with Brown and as a solo instrumentalist continued resurfacing on compilations through 2003. Along with several James Brown reissues and compilations, Nolen could be found on Ace UK import compilations *Dapper Cats, Groovy Tunes, and Hot Guitars* (1992), and *Dig*

These Blues: The Legendary Dig Masters (1992).[4] Additionally, many hip-hop artists sampled Brown's music with Nolen's guitar work featured prominently, to include Eric B., Public Enemy, which featuredCredited with popularizing the "chicken scratch" guitar style through James Brown records that sold millions, Jimmy Nolen was inducted into the Oklahoma Jazz Hall of Fame in 1996 for his extremely significant contribution to American popular music. In 2010, Masters Classics records released an excellent collection of Nolen's early work, *The Rhythm and Blues Years*, containing nineteen tracks of Nolen's late 1950s and early 1960s years.

Notes
1. See Dan "Grayboy" Pollock's chronicle of Nolen's career in an online essay for, *Funky Stuff*, a website devoted to funk music, "Jimmy Nolen: Short Biography" (www.funk-stuff.com/Nolen/Index.htm) (accessed August 11, 2011).
2. For an explication of Nolen's style for more advanced guitar players, see David Rubin's *Birth of the Groove: R and B, Soul and Funk Guitar: 1945-1965,* (Hal Leonard Corporation, 2000).
3. James Brown's rehearsal requirements were detailed by the author's father, Rev. Hugh Tudor-Foley, in a 2002 e-mail in which the elder Foley recounted seeing James Brown's band rehearse after arriving to the venue by bus, and then again with Brown who arrived after flying in on a lear jet, in Beaumont, Texas, circa 1963-64.
4. Nolen's further contributions to James Brown's music and the circumstances surrounding Nolen's death are recounted in an Oklahoma Jazz Hall of Fame press release, published by the *Stillwater News Press*, May 30, 1995, A11.

Norma Jean

(b. January 30, 1938)

With a voice plaintive enough to commiserate with in heartbreak, and tough enough to kick that melancholy out the door, Norma Jean will always be remembered as one of country music's outstanding voices from her emergence out of Oklahoma City's fertile country music scene in the early 1950s through her peak years of popularity from the 1960s through the early 1970s. She has remained an active performer through the present day with a strong set of well-remembered country music classics that typify a honky-tonk girl's experience of growing up poor, enduring no-good men and hoping the new one will better, and the overall experience of being a woman in a man's world during the 1950s, '60s, and 70s. She is also remembered as "Pretty Miss Norma Jean," Porter Wagoner's singing partner on his television show from 1960 to 1967. Norma Jean Beasler was born in a little farmhouse to a Depression-era family near Wellston, Oklahoma, a town of roughly 1,000 residents northeast of Oklahoma City. Her family moved to Oklahoma City when Norma Jean was five, and she soon traded her bicycle for a guitar. Taking lessons from her aunt who was a skilled guitarist, Norma Jean debuted on KLPR radio in Oklahoma City at age twelve singing "If Teardrops Were Pennies", which resulted in her own show three times a week, and a long lasting friendship with **Wanda Jackson**, another future Oklahoma music star, who was also performing on the same station. While in high school she toured with Oklahoma Western swing bands led by Billy Gray, Merl Lindsay, and Leon McAuliffe. She also performed on the *Jude and Jody Show*, a weekly television program on WKY in Oklahoma City.

With several years of local radio and television experience and the assistance of Wanda Jackson, Norma Jean Beasler was invited in 1958 to join the cast of the *Ozark Jubilee*, an ABC television show broadcast from Springfield, Missouri. Red Foley, host of the series, requested that she shorten her name to "Norma Jean." It was also here in Springfield that she met Porter Wagoner, a regular on the *Ozark Jubilee*, and during which time she signed a contract with Columbia in 1959 for her first album. In 1960, Norma Jean left the *Ozark Jubilee* and headed to Nashville where she joined the Porter Wagoner touring group and appeared regularly as his singing partner on his syndicated television show.

With considerable exposure on television and under the tutelage of Chet Atkins, she signed with RCA Victor for which she made twenty-seven albums during her recording career with the label from 1963 to 1973. After performing "Let's Go All the Way" in 1964 on the Porter Wagoner Show, the song climbed to into the Top 15 of the *Billboard* country charts. She followed with "I'm a Walkin' Advertisement (For the Blues)" and "Put Your Arms Around Her", both of which crossed over to the Top 40, as well as striking pay dirt on the country charts. As rock music began to make a comeback in the national marketplace due to the British Invasion, she released the Harlan Howard composition, "Go Cat Go" in 1964, a Top 10 country hit, where it remained on the country charts for four months, also crossing-over to the pop charts. Based on these early recording successes, she was invited to join the Grand Ole Opry cast in 1965. In the same year, she released "I Cried All the Way to the Bank" and "I Wouldn't Buy a Used Car from Him", which became of Top 10 hit. Her most successful singles in 1966 were "The Shirt", a maudlin song about the song's singer finding an old lover's shirt that still smells like him, and provides a list of vanished memories. Along with "Pursuing Happiness", another hit for her that year about doing her best to enjoy life in the wake of loneliness, and "The Game of Triangles", a trio with Bobby Bare and Liz Anderson, which was nominated for a Grammy. Following her successful (although somewhat dark) theme of broken homes and hearts, "The Game of Triangles" explores three sides of a relationship, the husband's, the wife's, and the man's lover. The song became Norma Jean's biggest selling record and went Top 5 on the country charts.

Norma Jean, circa 1960s

During her tenure with Porter Wagoner, Norma Jean became romantically involved with him, and the ensuing romance's end notes resulted in Norma Jean's departure from the Porter Wagoner Show in 1967. The break-up did not affect Norma Jean's career, however, as she continued to perform on the Grand Ole Opry and record with RCA. In

Norma Jean, early 2000s

early 1967 she scored another Top 25 hit with the feisty kiss-off song, "Don't Let That Doorknob Hit You", and later that year, released "Heaven Help the Working Girl (In a World That's Run by Men)", a Top 20 hit that was embraced by the burgeoning feminist movement of the late 1960s. Also in 1967 she recorded *Norma Jean Sings: A Tribute to Kitty Wells*, an album dedicated to her life-long role model that rips back and forth at the heart with reminders of why Kitty Wells was the original honky-tonk angel. In 1968, she recorded "Truck Drivin' Woman", one of the first female-oriented truck driving songs. Able to singing convincingly from a point of view of one who has been there, her 1972 album, *I Guess that Comes From Being Poor*, included such downtrodden tracks as "Hundred Dollar Funeral", "There Won't Be Any Patches in Heaven", and "The Lord Must Have Loved Poor Folks (He Made So Many of Them)".

In the late 1960s she married Jody Taylor of the popular *Jude and Jody Show* on Oklahoma City television, and returned to her Oklahoma roots, while commuting to the Opry and remaining with RCA until 1973. Her last albums for RCA were *Love's A Woman's Job* (1968), *The Best of Norma Jean* (1969), *Another Man Loved Me Last Night* (1970), *It Wasn't God Who Made Honky Tonk Angels* (1971), *Norma Jean Sings: A Tribute to Hank Cochran* (1971), and *It's Time for Norma Jean* (1971). She returned to Nashville in 1984 to record *Pretty Miss Norma Jean* for Roma, a label named after her only daughter. In 2000, Collector's Choice music released *The Best of Norma Jean*, a perfect collection of her greatest hits. Since then, some of her most popular albums have been re-issued on compact disc and are available as electronic downloads.

After Norma Jean and Jody Taylor divorced in 1982, she married long-time country music front man George Riddle in 1990. She has remained active in R.O.P.E. (Reunion of Professional Entertainers) organization and, for several years performed with **Jean Shepard**, another native Oklahoman, Jan Howard, Helen Cornelius, Margo Smith, and Leona Williams in The Grand Ladies of Country Show in Branson, Missouri. Toward the end of the first decade of the 21st century, Norma began touring internationally, where she is thought of as an authentic representation of classic country music, which she is. She has performed in Germany, Norway, Denmark, Sweden, France, Holland, Austria, and various Caribbean islands. As of 2011, she continued working on her autobiography, *All the Way and Back*, certain to be an important chronicle of the country music industry from one who experienced the complete gamut of its highs and lows. Along with periodic appearances with The Grand Ladies of the Grand Ole Opry in 2011, she could also be heard every Sunday morning at 10:30 (central standard time) on Cowboy Church Internet Radio, broadcast from the God & Country Theater in Branson, Missouri.

www.prettymissnormajean.com

N.O.T.A. (None of the Above)
(formed 1979 – disbanded 1987)

None of the Above (N.O.T.A.) is one of the very few nationally recognized bands that can be classified as punk or hardcore from Oklahoma during the period in which those movements were primary parts of the American rock underground from roughly 1976 through late 1980s, the others from Oklahoma being **Debris** and **Los Reactors.** Comprised of Jeff Klein (vocals/guitar), Russell Love (guitar), Bruce Hendrickson (bass), and Bob Purdom (drums), None of the Above united in 1980 when the Tulsa punk scene found a home in the Bleu Grotto, a club that booked bands performing original material. Originally a trio, the band added guitarist Russell Love in 1982 and shortened their name to N.O.T.A. As the house band at the Crystal Pistol, N.O.T.A. opened for most national hardcore bands touring the country on the path blazed by Black Flag via a very loose network of urban all-ages clubs, college towns with college radio stations to spread the word, smaller, "dive" bars, and warehouses in rugged parts of cities. With influences ranging from both the first wave of proto-punk, garage rock, and rougher blues rock, such as Iggy and the Stooges, and the Who, as well as the mid-seventies usual suspects of the Clash, Sex Pistols, and the Ramones, N.O.T.A. opened for groups like the Dead Kennedys and Husker Du, which brought them to the attention of *Maximum RocknRoll*'s editor, Tim Yohannon. Without any Internet at the time, magazines like *Maximum RocknRoll* and *The Big Takeover* were the networking tools and tip sheets of the era. Yohannon included N.O.T.A.'s "Propaganda Control" as one of two representations of US hardcore for that year on the magazine's compilation LP, *Welcome to 1984*, which helped establish the band as a national act that achieved an international following in England, mainland Europe, and Australia. So ubiquitous was N.O.T.A. at the time, when the U.S. map is shown in the quintessential punk documentary, *American Hardcore*, that documents the progression of punk and hardcore in America from 1978 to 1986, Oklahoma is tagged with N.O.T.A.'s logo.

N.O.T.A., circa 1985

The *Welcome to 1984* vinyl is not impossible to find via e-bay, however, most copies were being auctioned by owners in the UK in 2011. Aside from some stutter step demos, most of the band's primary period material is available as either a re-issue or online. *Live at the Crystal Pistol* (re-issued by Prank Records, 2000) was meant to be a live demo of the band recorded on "punk night" January 11, 1983, and was still available in limited quantities via amazon.com as of August, 2011. As a compilation, the N.O.T.A. Collection: 1983 – 1986 contains the track included on the *Maximum RocknRoll* compilation, the "Moscow" 7" EP (Unclean, 1984), the "Toy Soldiers" 7" EP (Rabid Cat, 1984), "Empty Skulls" tape (1984), None of the Above LP outtakes (unreleased, 1985), and a 1986 demo with Dave Scum replacing Jeff Klein on vocals. As the blogger who posted the tracks says, "39 tracks in 79 minutes. All keepers. All great quality. Enjoy."[1]

As one might expect, the language in the songs would get a parental advisory sticker if they had them back then, but it was before that time. The tracks begin as most hardcore of the period does, with a slow intro, and then kicks into double time thrash with speedy snare work, lots of fast-as-you-can power chord strumming, and less aversion to the occasional searing guitar solo than many hardcore acts (often due more to skill than desire to keep the music unpretentious). For this reason, N.O.T.A. might be thought of as a "crossover thrash", relevant both in the hardcore environment, but also related to the developing guitar solo based thrash metal of Slayer and Metallica, also developing in 1983 (hear "Justice in America"). Additionally, on occasion, N.O.T.A. verges into the style of melodic hooks used by The Clash "Toy Soldier" and counterpoint between the singer and the combo, a la Joe Strummer and Mick Jones of The Clash ("Frustration"). Not only that, N.O.TA. doesn't completely forego the twang intrinsic to their hometown, ironically used in a tune called "Moscow" that is a musical country cousin to "cow-punks" of the West Coast, Rank and File, X, or the Gun Club, and Jason and the Nashville Scorchers from Tennessee, also of that period. And nobody has more right to throw in some twang than a band from Tulsa, which N.O.T.A. does without seeming gratuitous or cheesy. Of course, the lyrics and vocals depart from twangville with sneering punk vocals decrying society's ills ("Taking Away Your Rights"/"Nightstick Mentality") and contradictions ("Identity Crisis"), with humor ("Redneck Mentality"/"War on the Wankers"), and commentary on various social hypocrisies "Keeping You Out". Illuminating regressive or unfair issues in a community's social order is a primary those of most punk and hardcore. One can also hear the influences of the Ramones on tracks like "Reckless", and how they fit into the larger hardcore milieu of the Southwest with a sound imprint often analogous to their neighbors across the Red River, Texas' Dirty Rotten Imbeciles (D.R.I.). As compared to a lot of other hardcore in America at the time, N.O.T.A. exhibits more musical dexterity with well-timed "turnarounds" between chord progressions, the previously mentioned melodic elements and simpatico with thrash metal, and a confidence with allowing their influences to show, even inching toward pop with "Summer of '82". And, at other times, the group is just everything a hardcore band should be: fast, chaotic, irreverent, cynical yet witty, and indicting.

Interestingly, bassist Bruce Hendrickson's letter to the author includes some thoughtful insights into why the social commentary and ultimate validity of the hard-

Hugh W. Foley / 577

core movement faded by the late 1980s. According to Hendrickson, who published a fanzine, *Sour Grapes,* in the late 1980s, while punk and hardcore advocated, at minimum, a magnified look at discrepancies in the social order ("Angry and Free"), and at best advocated social change, the scene also encouraged nihilistic values of existential worthlessness ("Self Destruct") on the part of those in the movement, two concepts that could not cohabitate. As a result, according to Hendrickson, "the two ideologies were frequently at odds - which led to the collapse of the movement. Today, punk continues as a fairly predictable musical genre and exists as its own subculture. We were aiming for a more profound social transformation back in the day." An additional element to that concept that might also be considered is the pure catharsis that punk and hardcore offered for its creators and fans. By expressing the displeasure with society via art, one is able to at least channel the substantive frustration into a communication vehicle for like-minded people. However, as with other genre-specific musical forms such as country, folk, and hip-hop, the ideas and concepts endemic to the cultural group that produces the art are often "preaching to the choir" instead of reaching the needed ears due to the inaccessibility of the music for ears that tune it out before the lyrical message is ever perceived. Such is the challenge of creating progressive and satisfying art that also has its intended effect on those viewers or listeners who are often the object of the art's commentary or theme. Luckily, as of 2010, Hendrickson was writing a monograph on the cultural impact of 1980s punk as a social movement, sure to be an interesting read based on his already stated thesis, and the fact that he was in the middle of it all. In the 1990s, he pursued an academic career; As of 2011, he worked as a social critic and free lance writer, as well as working with another early Tulsa punk musician, and an Osage Nation tribal member, on progressive rock music recordings under the name, All of the Below.[2]

www.myspace.com/realnota

Notes

1. A full set of details about N.O.TA.'s 1980s recordings, and a free, downloadable compilation of the primary material by the band are available online at http://bloggedquartered.blogspot.com/2009/06/nota-1983-1986.html (accessed August 16, 2011). Interested listeners may pursue more details about some of the demo recordings at another blog titled The Last Days of Man on Earth at http://www.lastdaysofmanonearth.com/blog/?p=141 (accessed August 16, 2011).
2. Several historical details were gleaned from a letter to the author by N.O.T.A. bassist Bruce Hendrickson, circa 2008.

Nunn, Gary P.
(b. December 4, 1945)

Composer of one of Texas's best-known honky-tonk sing-along songs, "London Homesick Blues," better known as "Home With the Armadillo", the theme song of the long-running PBS show, *Austin City Limits,* for the past three decades, Gary P. Nunn was born in Okmulgee, a community of roughly 14,000 residents fifty miles south of Tulsa and home to the Muscogee (Creek) Nation's headquarters. A singer, songwriter, and guitarist, Nunn's musical career started in Brownfield, Texas, where he moved when he was in the sixth grade. By the seventh grade, he was playing in a garage band. Following high school graduation in Brownfield, where he was an honor student and athlete, he completed courses at Texas Tech University and South Plains College, and played in a group called The Fabulous Sparkles. In 1968 he transferred to the University of Texas to pursue a pharmacy degree, and began joining in the vibrant outlaw country scene taking shape in Austin in the personages of Michael Martin Murphey, Jerry Jeff Walker, Willie Nelson, Waylon Jennings, et al.

Austin had morphed into the center for a new movement in country music, often referred to as "outlaw country", "progressive country", or "redneck rock", wherein musicians began incorporating elements of rock into country, getting away from the highly produced Nashville Sound engineered by Chet Atkins with its string sections and big choruses. By the early 1970s, Gary began playing bass for Nelson, Murphey, and Walker, three acknowledged instigators of the genre fostered by a bunch of country music fans hanging around Austin with hair down to their backsides. By 1973, Nunn was leading The Lost Gonzo Band, the back-up group for Walker, that had to endure his high-flying (literally) Lear jet lifestyle, and joined Walker to record five albums in five years. A climactic moment in the process that was fueled by a number of stimulants and other artificial inspirations that kept the Gonzos going beyond what most people thought they could, or should, be doing, occurred in 1973 when Walker chided Nunn into singing lead vocals on the "London Homesick Blues" track for the monumentally successful album, *Viva Terlingua!* Recorded in the small town of Luckenbach, Texas, which also featured **Ray Wylie Hubbard**'s "Up Against the Wall, Redneck Mother", the Walker's album defined the outlaw country era as much as Willie Nelson's 1975 LP *Red Headed Stranger* or Waylon Jennings' 1976 album, *Wanted! The Outlaws*. Nunn played keyboards and sang back-up vocals on three additional Walker albums, including *Ridin' High* (1975), *It's A Good Night for Singin'* (1976), and *Man Must Carry On* (1977). Nunn continued finding good fortune with his songs, several of which were recorded by artists such as David Allen Coe, maybe the most "outlaw" of all the outlaw country figures (since he did time in prison), and as well as Roseanne Cash, Walker, Murphey, and Nelson.

Gary P. Nunn

The Lost Gonzo Band also recorded a self-titled album in 1975 under Nunn's leadership, followed by *Loose & On My Way* (1975), *Thrills* (1976), and *Signs of Life* (1978); all on the Capitol label. In 1980, the Lost Gonzo Band had enough of "the life" and called it quits, so Gary went out on his own, and began writing songs with his singer-songwriter wife, Karen Brooks. Beginning in 1979 and 1980, when Gary was featured on two albums of various artists recorded at the Kerrville Folk Festival in Kerrville, Texas, Nunn has released a tremendous catalog of albums, usually filled with a Texas themes, lyrically or referentially via music that wavered between Spanish, Western swing, and cowboy singer story songs. Nunn has released several well received albums solo albums, and while none necessarily scorched the national charts, Nunn's fans enjoyed the dependability of Nunn's reflective songs about Texas, love, life, and good memories, always couched in the musical textures of excellent Western musicianship. His various album titles reflect the lyrical tropes he often repeats to glorify his adopted home state: *Nobody But Me* (1980), *Home With the Armadillo* (1984), *Border States* (1987), *For Old Times Sake* (1989), *Live at Poor David's* (1992), *Totally Guacamole* (1993), *Roadtrip* (1994), *Under My Hat* (1996), *What I Like About Texas* (1997), *It's a Texas Thing* (2000), *Greatest Hits: Live from Mingus, Texas* (2001), and *Something for the Trail* (2004). So, well liked is Nunn in the Lone Star State that in 1985 he was designated by Mark White, governor of Texas, as the state's Official Ambassador to the World. In 1990, he was presented an Award of Appreciation by the San Antonio chapter of the Texas Music Association, followed by his inclusion on the list of Lone Star Greats by the Texas Department of Commerce and Tourism. In 1991, Gary was given a Citation of Recognition by the Oklahoma House of Representatives for his preservation of Southwestern music and, in 1995, was placed in the West Texas Walk of Fame in Lubbock alongside Buddy Holly, Waylon Jennings, Tanya Tucker, Joe Ely, and many other notable musicians from the area. According to his official website, Nunn performs throughout Texas and the Southwest with his band, The Sons of the Bunkhouse. He had several dates scheduled in the fall of 2011, in such venues as the Famous Broken Spoke in Austin, the Crystal Ballroom in Houston, the Miles Cotton Fest, and the Burleson County Fair. Even though he has turned being Texan in to a cottage industry, he has also returned to Oklahoma where he and Karen operate an 800-acre cattle ranch (A-O Ranch) near Hanna, or the "northern frontier", as Gary calls his refuge on the Canadian River's banks. Ok, so he did mostly grow up down there south of the Red River where dust actually reproduces on mesquite trees, but no matter how much Texas claims him, and irregardless of how many songs he sings about the big cow pastures, oil fields, pretty girls, armadillos, good country music, and longneck warehouses in Texas, that old boy is still a native Oklahoman, and he's got a big ranch and home place to prove it.

Gary P. Nunn, circa 1993

www.garypnunn.com

O

O'Dell, Kenny
(b. 1946)

A prolific songwriter of the 1970s and 1980s, notable especially for "Behind Closed Doors" and "Mama He's Crazy," Kenneth Gist, Jr. was born in Antlers, Oklahoma in 1946, but was raised in Santa Maria, California where he attended high school and participated in local talent shows. He also began writing songs as a teenager, and following high school, formed his own Mar-Kay record label in California. In 1963, he recorded a self-penned song, "Old Time Love", which enjoyed some regional popularity. While on the West Coast, he worked briefly with twang guitar master, Duane Eddy; then, formed a group called Guys and Dolls, with whom he toured the West Coast for several years. In 1967, Kenny wrote and recorded "Beautiful People", the title track of his 1968 LP for Vegas Records. The song was also later recorded by Bobby Vee, and both versions slipped into the pop charts. O'Dell released several singles between 1968 and 1973, none of which charted.

Having moved to Nashville in 1970, O'Dell managed the Bobby Goldsboro publishing company, and continued writing songs, often with Larry Henley. The Henley/O'Dell team co-wrote the #1 country hit for Tanya Tucker, "Lizzie and the Rain Man." Sandy Posey's recording of their tune, "Why Don't We Go Somewhere and Love", cracked the charts and was noticed by record producer Billy Sherrill. Sherrill began to use some of Kenny's songs on Charlie Rich's recordings, such as "I Take It on Home" and "Behind Closed Doors". With its not-so-subtle bedroom references, the latter was a smash hit on both country and pop charts and earned several 1973 accolades, to include a Grammy for Best Country Song, CMA's Song and Single of the Year, and ACM's Song and Single of the Year. With its ultimately imagery left up to listeners' imaginations, "Behind Closed Doors" also earned the BMI Three Million-Airplay Award, and ranked in the Top 50 most performed songs of all time. Kenny also played guitar on the Rich recording. Charlie Rich also has a minor connection to Oklahoma, in that he played in and around Enid, Oklahoma while stationed at Vance Air Force Base.

Kenny O'Dell

Riding the wave of success from "Behind Closed Doors", Kenny released a self-titled album on the Capricorn label in 1974, which produced a minor hit single, "You Bet Your Sweet, Sweet Love (#58 country), and one Top 20 country single, "Soulful Woman". His 1978 album, *Let's Shake Hands and Come Out Lovin'*, produced two hit singles, the album's title track (#9 country), and "As Long as I Can Wake Up in Your Arms (#12 country). His final chart entry as a solo artist was "Medicine Woman" in 1979 (#32 country), but Kenny was not through making an impact as a songwriter.

In 1984 when the mother/daughter act, The Judds, recorded "Mama He's Crazy", O'Dell received numerous awards, including BMI Country Song of the Year and Nashville Songwriters Association Song of the Year, and nominated for Song of the Year by the CMA in 1985. Kenny was also named Songwriter of the Year by Nashville Songwriters association in 1984. The song eventually won the BMI Million-Air Award.

In addition to the aforementioned songs, O'Dell penned such numbers as "I've Got Mine", "Too Much Is Not Enough", and "When It's Just You and Me". His songs have been recorded by a diverse group of artists, including Bobby "Blue" Bland, Glen Campbell, Floyd Cramer, Sammy Davis, Jr., Freddy Fender, Bobby Goldsboro, Tom Jones, Albert King, Little Milton, Loretta Lynn, Boots Randolph, Ray Stevens, **B. J. Thomas**, Bobby Vee, Bobby Womack, Percy Sledge, Billie Jo Spears, Dottie West,

Tanya Tucker, Anthony Armstrong Jones, Bellamy Brothers, Forrester Sisters, and The Rat Pack of Frank Sinatra, Dean Martin, and Sammy Davis, Jr. In 1996, he was inducted into the Nashville Songwriters Hall of Fame, and later served on the Board of Directors for the Nashville Songwriters Association in 2001-02.[1]

Note
1. Kenny O'Dell's career is covered very similarly by Colin Larkin in *The Virgin Encyclopedia of Country Music*, (London: Virgin, 1998), 312; and by Jason Ankeny in Kenny O'Dell's biography published online in the *All Music Guide* at http://www.allmusic.com/artist/kenny-odell (accessed August 22, 2011). Finally, Kenny O'Dell's biographical entry on Wikipedia says essentially the same thing as the two previous references, and includes an accurate accounting for his most significant chart hits.

O'Hara, Kelli
(b. April 16, 1976)

With a voice that can soar through a stadium, deliver subtle and delicate lines from the musical theater stage, or pound out torchy ballads, Kelli O'Hara is one of Broadway's most significant contemporary leading ladies. Born in Tulsa, but raised in Edmond, Oklahoma, Kelli has received particular notice for her sparkling performances in musicals such as *The Light in the Piazza* (2003-2005) (Tony Award nomination for Best Featured Actress in a Musical), the starring role alongside Harry Connick, Jr. in *The Pajama Game* (2006) (Drama Desk Award nomination, Outer Circle Critics Award nomination, and Tony Award nominations for Best Actress/Leading Actress in a Musical), and *South Pacific* (2010) (Drama Desk Award nomination for Outstanding Actress/ Tony Award nomination for Best Leading Actress in a Musical).[1]

O'Hara graduated with a bachelor of music degree in vocal performance and opera from Oklahoma City University where she studied with famed voice teacher, Florence Birdwell, and became a sorority sister of Kristen Chenoweth in Gamma Phi Beta. After graduation, Kelli won the State Metropolitan Opera Competition, moved to New York City and enrolled in the Lee Strasberg Institute, the noted school for training in method acting and performance. She also studies at Julliard and the Broadway Dance Center, building on the foundation in dance established at OCU. She made her Broadway debut in *Jekyll & Hyde* (2000), and subsequently appeared in Sondheim's *Follies* (2001), *Sweet Smell of Success* (2002) opposite John ithgow, and *Dracula* (2004), which began a tumult of Tony Award and Drama Desk nominations. Along with her previously mentioned successes, Kelli has worked in theaters throughout the Northeastern U.S., and Off Broadway in *Sunday at the Park with George, My Life with Albertine, Beauty,* and *Bells Are Ringing*. In 2007, she received more critical acclaim for her role as Eliza Doolittle in the New York Philharmonic production of *My Fair Lady*, and has also performed solo concerts with a number of different prestigious orchestras at some of the nation's most notable venues, to include singing with the New York Pops under Steven Reineke at Carnegie Hall; at the Kennedy Center with Marvin Hamlisch and the National Symphony Orchestra, with the New York Philharmonic under Hamlisch; the Boston Pops; Lincoln Center; Town Hall; the Kennedy Center; the Philly Pops conducted by Peter Nero; the Seattle Sympony, and several others.

In 2008, she performed at the Kennedy Center Honors as part of a tribute to Barbara Streisand, and again in 2010 for the same function in tribute to Jerry Herman (known for *Hello, Dolly!, Mame,* and *La Cage aux Folles*. In 2009, she sang a now-lionized, spine-tingling version of "God Bless America" in the famous seventh inning stretch tradition at Yankee Stadium during Game 6 of the World Series that year. With a reception unseen since Kate Smith filled New York's summer baseball sky with her operatic tones, the Yankees brought her back in 2010 to sing the National Anthem prior to Game 5 of the American League Championship Series. In 2010, Kelli also sang on PBS's *Memorial Day Concert Live from Washington DC*, and performed her solo show to rave reviews wherever it appeared. In 2008, Kelli released her first album, the jazzy and light, pop-filled, *Wonder in the World* (Ghostlight), a lush, orchestrated palate suitable for her chanteuse status, and produced by Harry Connick, Jr., who also wrote three tunes on the disc, with O'Hara contributing two of her own songs. Also in 2008, Kelli's notable performance in *South Pacific* was released by Sony Classics. In addition, Nonesuch Records released the cast soundtrack of *The Light in the Piazza*, which received a GRAMMY nomination, and Sony released the cast recording of *The Pajama Game*, also garnering a GRAMMY nomination. Additional cast soundtracks on which she has appeared include *The Sweet Smell of Success* (Sony), *My Life with Albertine* (PS Classics), *Dream True* (PS Classics), and *Jule Styne Goes Hollywood* (PS Classics). In 2011, Ghostlight Records released her album, *Always*, featuring a more subtle ensemble backing than her first solo effort, and magnifying her wide ranging vocal abilities of interpreting ballads, belting out show tunes, sing-talking through cabaret numbers, and smiling all the way through THE delightful "They Don't Let You in the Opera (If You're a Country Star)," where she gets to use her Oklahoma background to put on an accent that she had to work off back at Oklahoma City University.

Kelli O'Hara, 2008

Along with her stellar musical background, Kelli also has several film and television credits, to include *Sex & The City 2* (2010), Martin Scorcese's short, *The Key to Reserva* (2007), *The Dying Gaul* (2005), *Blue Blood* (NBC Pilot), *All Rise* (NBC Pilot), *Alexander Hamilton* (PBS), *Number3rs* (CBS), *and All My Children* (ABC). She has appeared on numerous live television shows, to include a 2011 nationwide appearance on the PBS 4th of July concert from Washington, D.C. For young and aspiring musicians, O'Hara's multiple skills re-enforce a common theme among successful musicians in the *Oklahoma Music Guide*. Those who stretch their performance and/or show business acumen are able to fulfill a variety of entertainment jobs, avoiding being cornered into only one set of artistic opportunities. With her dynamic singing range within multiple vocal performance formats, along with her acting skills, and recording career, Kelli O'Hara appears poised for a career as long as she chooses to make it. According to her website, in 2012 she resided in New York City with her husband Greg and their son Owen. Also in 2012, she appeared on Broadway with Matthew Broderick in the lighthearted musical comedy, *Nice Work if You Can Get It*, for which she received a Tony nomination for best actress in a musical.

www.kelliohara.com

Note
1. The majority of the information included here is included in Kelli O'Hara's biography on her website, however, James Watts noted O'Hara's birthplace in Tulsa and rearing in Edmond in his article "Her ship has come in: Kelli O'Hara returns to *South Pacific*." *Tulsa World*, August 15, 2010, D4.

Oklahoma City Blue Devils

The author first learned about the Oklahoma City Blue Devils from noted Robert Johnson researcher, and blues historian, Robert Palmer, in the late 1980s in New York. Upon finding out I was from Oklahoma, the first thing he said was, "Ah, the Blue Devils. They are the Robert Johnson of jazz, only tougher because they left so few recordings only two that we know of," and that's still all we know of the primary Southwestern jazz group that would both employ hot hands, and foster upcoming talent, all while sharing just about everything equally. All that is left is the oral histories of people who remember seeing them play, describing how great they were, and how they had regular band battles with the region's other dominating band, the better-known and better-recorded Bennie Moten Orchestra. The Oklahoma City Blue Devils formed around 1923-1924 in Kansas City as Billy King's Road Show, a traveling vaudeville troupe. Acknowledged band boss was trombonist Ermir "Bucket" Coleman, however, the musical leader was Walter Page, who had studied under both Major N. Clark Smith and Charles Watts, two of the best music teachers in Kansas City during the 1920s. The Billy King Road Show disbanded in 1925 in Oklahoma City, where Page kept the band intact and renamed it. Some say it was "Walter Page's Original Blue Devils" and others contend it was the "Oklahoma City Blue Devils." Page expanded the band from its original nine members to as many as thirteen to fifteen members.[1]

Oklahoma City Blue Devils, 1931

When the Blue Devils were reorganized in Oklahoma City, Page persuaded a group of Oklahoma City businessmen to back the venture. The backing consisted of a little cash, a set of uniforms, a supply of meal tickets good at a restaurant owned by one of the sponsors, and the donation of a large hotel room in the Littlepage Hotel in the

"Deep Deuce" district, or Northeast 2nd Street of Oklahoma City. The hotel served the band as a dormitory, mess hall, rehearsal hall, and recruiting office.

From 1925 to 1933, the Blue Devils epitomized the spirit of the era in many ways—dance halls packed with enthusiastic dancers, long drives between jobs on dusty Southwestern and Midwestern roads, and competing against other bands in cutting contests where musicians and bands dueled against one another, often for hours, and often in the great horn blues key of B flat. The Ritz Ballroom in Oklahoma City was home base for the Blue Devils as the group had a standing contract to play there during the winter months, while playing engagements at nearby Oklahoma towns, including El Reno, Chickasha, Shawnee, Enid, and Tulsa. During the fall and spring, the band traveled the ballroom circuit ranging from Omaha in the north to Houston in the south to El Paso in the west and Little Rock to the east. Occasional forays took them to western states, such as New Mexico and Colorado as well as to such northern states as Iowa and Minnesota.

Early members of the Blue Devils included Oran "Hot Lips" Page, Jimmy Lu Grand, Harry Youngblood, James Simpson (trumpets); Ermir Coleman, Eddie Durham, Druie Bess, and Dan Minor (trombones); Reuben Roddy, Ted Manning, Theodore Ross, and Buster Smith (reeds); Willie Lewis and Turk Thomas (piano); Reuben Lynch (guitar); Edward McNeil and Alvin Burroughs (drums); Walter Page (bass, tuba, and baritone saxophone); Ernie Williams (vocals). Four native Oklahomans, at one time or another, were members of the Blue Devils, including Abe Bolar (bass), Lemuel C. Johnson (clarinet/tenor saxophone), **Jimmy Rushing** (vocals) from Oklahoma City, and **Don Byas** (tenor/alto saxophone) from Muskogee.

During their heyday, the Blue Devils added such luminary jazz artists as Lester Young (tenor saxophone) in 1930 and again in 1932-33; and William, later known as "Count," Basie (piano) from 1928 to 1929 (for approximately eight months). Several of the Blue Devils alumni organization went on to provide the nucleus of such legendary bands as Bennie Moten and Count Basie, including "Lips" Page, Jimmy Rushing, Eddie Durham, and Walter Page. The personnel included some of the finest musicians produced in two decades of jazz in the Southwest and Midwest. The single recording session made by the Blue Devils was in Kansas City in 1929 on Vocalion 1463. The session produced two three-minute performances: *Squabblin'*, a riff tune taken at medium tempo, and *Blue Devil Blues*, with a Jimmy Rushing vocal, both of which would not sound out of place in an animated feature of the 1920s, but neither of which are ultimately representative of their nightly repertoire. Jazz historians can only surmise what the band sounded like.[1] In any case, the Oklahoma City Blue Devils represent the apex of Oklahoma's contribution to the evolving jazz form in the 1920s and early 1930s, but by providing some its most dynamic soloists, as well as some of its driving rhythmic and riffing sources for the lead men, the group is legendary in Oklahoma and Southwestern jazz scholarship.Friends of Oklahoma Music inducted the The Blue Devils band into the Oklahoma Music Hall of Fame in 2000.

Notes

1. Douglas Henry Daniels cornered the market not only in primary Blue Devils reading when Beacon Press published his thorough and engaging book, *One O'Clock Jump: The Unforgettable History of the Oklahoma City Blue Devils* (Beacon Press, 2006), the book also serves as a grand testimony to the significant African-American history of Oklahoma City, as well as the city's significant contributions to American jazz. Due to Daniels's detailed research work, interviewing many surviving Oklahomans and musicians who remembered salient details of Oklahoma City's jazz scene and its players,the text is primary reading

for those wishing to have a well-rounded understanding of the Blue Devils and their impact on jazz in Oklahoma City, and the southwestern United States.
2. For further discussions of the Oklahoma City Blue Devils history, style, ethos, and personnel changes, see Ross Russell's *Jazz Style in Kansas City and the Southwest*, (Berkeley: University of California Press, 1973), chapters 7, 8, and 9; also see Nathan W. Pearson, Jr.'s *Goin to Kansas City* (Urbana: University of Illinois Press, 1987), chapter 5; and John Wooley, *From the Blue Devils to Red Dirt: The Colors of Oklahoma Music*, (Tulsa: Hawk Publishing, 2006), chapter 1.

Oklahoma!

(Opened March 31, 1943 on Broadway in New York City)

Based on the play *Green Grow the Lilacs* by Claremore native, *Lynn Riggs*, the musical *Oklahoma!*, has become the most prominent image of Oklahomans in the national popular culture mindset, narrowly edging out the Oklahoma City bombing of the Murrah Federal Building on April 19, 1995, but clearly overwhelming oil and gas, college football, and American Indians, all of which received much lower recognition in a 2007 Zogby International Poll.[1]

Recognized as Rodgers and Hammerstein's most successful musical, *Oklahoma!* is touted for everything from selling a million copies of its title song's sheet music within a year of opening, to instigating a new form of "pop opera" that created a Broadway musical built around a story instead of a series of song and dance numbers.[2] Additionally, the musical was outrageously popular in England during the late 1940s and early 1950s as a paradigm for a hope after the country's dark experience in World War II. The show broke a 287-year-old record at London's Drury Lane Theater (three-and-a-half-years), and ultimately made millionaires out of Rodgers and Hammerstein.[3] According to a June 24, 2007 article by Rick Rogers in the *Daily Oklahoman*, the musical is staged more than 600 times per year around the world; in 2007, the centennial anniversary of Oklahoma's statehood, Rogers cited an official from the Rodgers and Hammerstein Organization that the musical was licensed for more than 900 performances across the United States and Canada (D 1-2).

To further understand the scope of the musical's popularity and omnipresence in American popular culture, one should consider the original *Oklahoma!* Soundtrack from the 1955 film (shot in Arizona, by the way). Recorded by stars of the film, including the debut of the future Mrs. Partridge, Shirley Jones, the *Oklahoma!* motion picture soundtrack was a #1 *Billboard* gold pop album in 1956 and has remained in print ever since, ultimately named multi-platinum by the RIAA in 1992. As an antidote to Oklahoma's image as a Dust Bowl state, the show's signature number was championed by future governor George Nigh as the state's official song, a task he saw accomplished as a legislator in 1953. Nigh's vision emerged in complete fruition with the 2007 Zogby International Poll results when barely 2% of respondents mentioned the bleak imagery often associated with 1930s-era Oklahoma. Furthermore, *Oklahoma!* is also held up as an important "American" populist musical that represented the strong morale and ethos of small-town America in the midst of a national crisis during World War II.

Tim Carter, author of the book length work, *Oklahoma! The Making of an American Musical*, theorizes the production hits the right spots of "nostalgia, idealism, community, spirit, and patriotism", recounts interviews in which Rodgers claimed he was making something truly "American," reaching into Aaron Copland's musical sphere. Carter further points out that the pristine Territory of the musical is related to the mythical ancient lands of Greece, full of bounty and there for the taking, by just the right sort of a happy folks riding Manifest Destiny right down the Great White Way.[4] Carter also relates further symbolic connections to the characters in the play in which Jud is a symbol for the Fascism grabbing at the world's throat at the time of World War II, and Curly is the representative solution who is willing to take action and get engaged literally in the story, as well as globally. Curly's character change is when he realizes he must also become a farmer, getting involved with the earth. A similar shift occurs within the character played by Humphrey Bogart in *Casablanca*, interestingly released in 1942, a year before *Oklahoma!* hit the Broadway stage. At the beginning of *Casablanca*, Rick is the only cause he is interested in, and sticks his neck out for nobody, with additional clear references to "isolationism" in the film's dialogue. By the end of *Casablanca*, Rick's makes the decision for all the characters in the plot, and chooses what is best for the greater good instead of his own self-serving interests. Likewise, Curly is able to give up his prized possessions to try and win his girl, which reduces him from the exalted status of a cowboy to the more proletariat role of farmer who will be in touch with the earth. And, if in order to save the world, Curly is involved in some kind of death, he will be pardoned easily through a sympathetic court of his peers, which is how the musical ends when evil Jud shows up drunk at the wedding wielding a knife, and after a scuffle with Curly, falls on the knife and dies the death of an evil aggressor of whom there were more than a few in 1943. Round up the usual suspects, indeed.

Granted, while the musical's title song has echoed the name Oklahoma throughout the world in an exuberant and optimistic tone wherein anyone's spanking new physical, mental, or metaphoric state is puffed up with a million universal possibilities, the musical's cornpone dialogue and simplistic worldview of the characters has also instilled an image in the national mindset of Oklahomans as an earnest, if not a quaintly conservative and naïve citizenry. Then CBS-TV correspondent Connie Chung said as much in 1995 after the Oklahoma City bombing, when she asked an Oklahoma City Fire Department spokesperson, "Can the Oklahoma City Fire Department handle *this*?" One could argue the constant repetition of the musical has created a sort of fossilization of what an Oklahoman is in American popular culture. Faithful or parody versions of title theme songs by disparate artists have both subverted and re-interpreted the song's original intent and lend themselves to post-modern interpretations, allowing the hearer to make up their own meaning while re-contextualizing the music and words in a contemporary era. The musical's title song has been spoofed in *South Park: Bigger, Longer, & Uncut* and on TV's the *Muppet Show* (Episode 317), and the *Rachel Maddow Show* (2008). The state song has also appeared in films such as *Twister* and *Dave*, and made television appearances on *Sesame Street*, *Why We Fight* (2001), and the final chorus, "Oklahoma, OK" is added as a tag at the end of Pete Townshend's "Jools and Jim", from his 1980 *Empty Glass* album, as a musical message to punk rockers as to what "real music is." Obviously meant as Broadway entertainment, *Oklahoma!* should not be held to any more concrete standards of realism than Rodgers and Hammerstein's *South Pacific* compares to its namesake geographical region, or an Italian opera intended to replicate an accurate depiction of society in Naples. Oklahoma and the time period depicted is merely a dramatic setting, albeit based on Riggs' play and set in Claremore. While Hammerstein references play parties, hoedowns, and square dances, Rodgers had no intent on replicating the music of the Southwest or any lame attempt on his part to write second rate "hillbilly ballads."[5]

To this writer's ears, Rodgers does make a noticeable, if predictable, musical nod to the state's American Indian past in the finale of the musical's stage production before the final chorus of "Oklahoma." Before its final crescendo, the singers break into the pseudo-chant over a contrived tom-tom rhythm, "Okla-homa, Okla-homa, Okla-homa, Okla-homa," the word itself, of course, a Choctaw saying or word, for the "land of the Red man," or "land where the Red man's languages are spoken." The musical *Oklahoma!* is certainly not totally to blame for this national perspective of Oklahomans as randy rubes and rubettes. However, the liner-notes for the 1956 Columbia Records release of the musical's "complete score" doesn't provide any other way to look at the plot's characters in their milieu: "The story, in brief, is that of the courtship of pretty Laurey by the bashful but manly rancher, Curly, and the attempts of the sinister and ugly Jud to break up the romance. Adding bright patterns to the story are Ado Annie, the girl who couldn't say no, and the various cowboys and girls, travelling salesmen, and would-be city slickers such as one might have found in Oklahoma at the turn of the century."[6]

Of course, at the turn of the twentieth century in 1900 Indian or Oklahoma Territory, one would certainly have encountered or dealt with the appearance of an American Indian or African-American somewhere in the picture, however, only the closest readings of highly coded musical or lyrical symbols imply any non-white presence. The one appearance of a non-Anglo person is the now-ironic figure of the Persian peddler, Ali Hakim, who is forced into a shotgun wedding with the girl who "cain't" say "No," Ado Annie. The scene itself is a nod to the melting pot concept popular in the American consciousness up through the middle of the twentieth century. To explore this "absence of color", director Molly Smith staged a 2010 production of *Oklahoma!* in Washington DC at the Arena Stage to mirror both DC's current population and the vastly multi-cultural 1906 Oklahoma or Indian Territory setting of the musical. Tremendously successful, Smith's production has received bookings for additional seasons. Contemporary critics such as *The Oregonian's* Marty Hughley admit

Ed Sullivan Presents Oklahoma! (1959)

the musical's vision is "Pollyannish" and "even a bit narrow-minded"; and, given the play's setting in Indian Territory, he wonders where the American Indians are. However, Hughley also dismisses those concerns by saying "this ground-breaking musical celebrates good old American rural virtues while rejoicing in the endless possibilities and national growth."[7] In other words, viewers of the musical should get over their hang ups on the lack of reality in the musical, and go deeper to the universal human truths contained within the story's contextual meanings in the scope of World War II occurring when no greater need existed for both an entertaining escape, but one that would also celebrate the bright beginnings of a great new morning when everything is going a person's way. Carter also admonishes viewers of the musical who are looking for the realism miss the point of theater in the first place, where artifice is implied the moment the curtain goes up.[8] While that is a fine and sensible disconnected viewpoint from an Oregonian (Hughley), and an accomplished scholar of the American musical theater (Carter), citizens of the actual state of Oklahoma are impacted in a different way by the musical's continued production, with no cessation in sight, ever.

In many ways, while the state has shed the dustbowl image in the national mindset, with the term "Okie" even evolving to a positive badge of one's ability to press on in the face of adversity, the replacement is Oscar Hammerstein's depiction of pre-statehood Anglos as rustics and oversimplified caricatures. Aside from that well-defined concept, Oklahoma's popular culture is rarely more nationally than an authentic source of Anglo-Americana, where country music singers and songwriters receive validity almost by birthrights. Native Oklahoman country musicians from the **Marvin Brothers** of the 1920s through **Blake Shelton** in the 2010s have mined this musical vein of the state's heritage, and others have either moved to the state (**Bob Wills, Hank Thompson, Gene Autry, etc.,**) or claimed to be from it to enhance their own authenticity (**Cowboy Copas, Eddie Cochran**). So what, *Oklahoma!* portrays a one-dimensional and oversimplified aspect of the state's history? As a cultural discussion about the state's image, one can muse on the long range needs to transition to an image somewhere between the land's first inhabitants and Oklahoma's famous astronauts, with a multi-genre soundtrack that portrays the entire story of America in music and song. The *real* Oklahoma musical has yet to be made. Nevertheless, given the omnipresent success and the continued widespread enjoyment of the musical's repeated productions, *Oklahoma!* will continue to promote the stereotype of the state's inhabitants either as simpletons, or highly-principled rural figures with an austere belief in both their destiny and a God-given right to woo. While the Oklahoma City Thunder basketball team may go some distance in establishing at least OKC as a major league city, the state's artistic, intellectual, business, and political leadership must continue to help

Oklahoma Territory dwellers, 1890.

Hugh W. Foley / 589

refine the state's image as one couched both in its unique historical development and multi-faceted contributions to American life, art, history, music, energy, commerce and science, as well as its many potentials for those same reasons.

Notes

1. The 2007 Zogby International Poll was detailed in a February 7, 2007 article, "Poll: Musical, OKC Bombing Most Associated with Oklahoma; A change in perception," by Randy Krehbiel in the Tulsa World, A-1, 4.
2. For more details on Oklahoma! as a turning point in the history of musical theatre, see Colin Larkin's essay on the subject in the Virgin Encyclopedia of Stage and Film Musicals (London: Virgin, 1999), 456.
3. Frederick Nolan explains the reception of Oklahoma! in London, and also enumerates the money generated by the musical for its creators and investors, in The Sounds of Their Music: The Story of Rodgers & Hammerstein (Milwaukee: Hal Leonard, 2002), 24.
4. For a detailed history of the musical Oklahoma!, a close accounting for the development of its music and lyrics, as well as expert chronicling of the musical's broader cultural significance, and critical acceptance in the U.S. and England, see Tim Carter's Oklahoma! The Making of an American Musical (New Haven: Yale University Press, 2007). Carter's specific summary statements on the cultural symbolism of the musical are found on pages 186-187.
5. Rodgers is very clear about his avoidance of even the slightest influence of the Southwestern United States' authentic music in his autobiography, Musical Stages: An Autobiograhy (New York: Da Capo Press), 222. He indicates his only concern was being true to his own musical identity, and since he wasn't from the area he would not be able to do justice to it beyond representing the locale through his own particular aural point of view.
6. The un-credited liner notes summarizing the musical's plot are found on Nelson Eddy in Oklahoma! ("Complete Score") (Columbia LP CL 828), notable for its inclusion of the desperate "Lonely Room" and lively "Entrance of Ensemble" which are not included on the 1955 Capitol release of the motion picture soundtrack. Ironically, the cover for Nelson Eddy in Oklahoma! is a scene from Arizona Highways Magazine.
7. Michael Hughley, "Theater review: Clackamas Rep lets the sun shine on Oklahoma!," The Oregonian, August 10, 2011 (www.oregononline.com).
8. Carter, ibid, 210-11.

Oldaker, Jamie

(born September 5, 1951)

As one of American popular music's most notable drummers for artists such as Eric Clapton, Bob Seger, Leon Russell, the GAP Band, Peter Frampton, Freddie King, Phil Collins, the Tractors, and Ronnie Dunn, just to get started, Jamie Oldaker's name is synonymous with his rock solid tempos featuring the casual confidence of an extremely gifted player. Born in Oakland, California, to parents Dee Dee and Carl Robert Oldaker, Jamie moved to Tulsa as a child where his father, a former drummer, inspired Jamie to take up the drums. Along with enjoying the steady marches of John Phillip Sousa, and Benny Goodman's drummer Gene Krupa as a child, Jamie knew his calling after seeing The Beatles on Ed Sullivan's variety show, and the young drummer's parents were always supportive and tolerant of the never- ending line of musicians jamming in the family's household. After graduating Tulsa Edison High School, Jamie left town for St. Louis to perform with Phil Driscoll at the Chase Park Plaza Hotel's famed music hot spot The Basement, leading to an appearance with Driscoll on the Ed Sullivan TV Show where The Beatles had inspired him years earlier.

Via his friendship with Tulsa musicians and friends, Teagarden and Van Winkle, who had been playing with Bob Seger, Jamie was hired to join Bob Seger's band to record the album, *Back in '72,* including the original version of Seger's classic "Turn the Page". Upon returning to Tulsa in about 1973, Oldaker played locally, often with J.J. Cale, who had been signed to Leon Russell's newly formed Shelter Records, which in turn introduced Jamie to Leon who was in town looking for musicians to record for

Shelter. Hired as a session musician at Shelter Records' home in the famed Church Studio located in Tulsa, Jamie was part of many sessions for Leon Russell and The GAP Band, along with many other album projects in between touring with Leon Russell and the Wilson Brothers. Also during this period, Jamie began working with his friend Carl Radle, one of rock's legendary bassists, and also an Oklahoma Music Hall of Fame Inductee, who had been playing with Eric Clapton on the Derek and the Domino's project which produced the hit "Layla". Trying to inspire Clapton to get back into the studio and on the road again, Carl sent Eric some of the live recordings Radle had of Jamie playing with Bob Seger and others. Over a year passed, and just two weeks before Jamie was scheduled to go on tour with Leon Russell and the GAP Band, he received a call from Carl who said,

Jamie Oldaker, 2007

"Eric wants to make a record. He said bring Jamie and the other players from Tulsa." Subsequently, Jamie recorded on Clapton's *461 Ocean Blvd.* which included the hit cover of Bob Marley's "I Shot the Sheriff", and was the first of eleven albums Oldaker recorded with Clapton, some of which include *Slowhand, There's One in Every Crowd, EC Was Here,* and *Backless*, starting a twenty-five-year-plus friendship with the British blues, rock, and pop guitarist that exists to the present day.

Recording with Clapton also began a hectic period in which Jamie bounced back and forth between Clapton and Seger's band, and in between tours found time to record two albums with Texas blues giant, Freddie King. As a result of the *Slowhand* recordings, Jamie came to the attention of Peter Frampton who hired Jamie immediately after Clapton's tour ended and went into the studio where they recorded Frampton's Gold album, *Where I Should Be*, followed by a world tour with Frampton. Along with recording some mysterious drum tracks for the Bee Gees in the late 1970s, Jamie also recorded with Phil Collins on Clapton's *Behind the Sun* album, precipitating a worldwide television audience performance with Clapton for approximately two billion people as part of the Live Aid benefit concert, followed by a world tour to support the album.

Another Oklahoma artist (and OMHOF inductee) who benefitted from Jamie's expertise and talent

Jamie Oldaker, Tulsa, early 1960s

Hugh W. Foley / 591

was Ronnie Dunn, as it was Jamie who entered Dunn into a Marlboro Country Music Contest whereby Dunn attained national recognition by winning the finals in 1988. Jamie performed with and managed Dunn during the Marlboro Country Music Tour, recording the original versions of "Boot Scootin' Boogie", "Neon Moon", "She's Not the Cheatin' Kind", and "She Used to Be Mine". Next, Oldaker joined former Kiss guitarist Ace Frehley for a world tour with metal acts Iron Maiden and Alice Cooper, then joined Frampton and Clapton for more touring and recording in the early 1990s. At Clapton's Royal Albert Hall shows that were recorded for the album and video *24 Nights*, Jamie performed with blues artist Buddy Guy, Jimmie Vaughn, Albert Collins, Johnny Johnson and Robert Cray. He followed this up with tours laying down the rhythm for Stephen Stills, Peter Frampton (again), and English rockabilly artist, Dave Edmunds. In 1994, Oldaker's founding membership in The Tractors, led by friend Steve Ripley whom he had known since the 1970s during the Shelter Records period, was rewarded with the group's debut album for Arista selling over 3.5 million albums. Along with winning CMA Video of the Year, *The Tractors* album also included the GRAMMY nominated hit "Baby Likes to Rock it (Like a Boogie Woogie Choo Choo Train)", which prominently features Oldaker's rolling drum work, as did subsequent Tractors releases, *Have Yourself a Tractors Christmas* and *Farmers in a Changing World*.

Jamie Oldaker with Eric Clapton, circa 2005.

In 2005, Jamie produced a supergroup album, *Mad Dogs & Okies*, featuring many of the friends with whom he has worked through the years: Eric Clapton, Vince Gill, Tony Joe White, Willis Alan Ramsey, Taj Mahal, Peter Frampton, Bonnie Bramlett, Ray Benson, JJ Cale, Willie Nelson, and others who are either from Oklahoma or have been involved or influenced by Oklahoma music over the years. He is also working on his autobiography, *The Best Seat in the House*, and recently was musical director for the PBS/ HDNET TV special, *The Out-*

Jamie Oldaker with Sally, 2008.

law Trail, featuring artists Raul Malo, Ray Benson, Rodney Crowell, Carlene Carter, Russel Smith, Jesse Colter, Joe Ely, Ray Wylie Hubbard and others. As of 2011, Jamie resided in San Marcos, Texas with his wife, Darlene, and dog, Sally (named after Clapton's "Lay Down Sally"), Jamie just finished producing a thirty-four track Texas- based CD, *Voices*, a benefit album to help raise awareness for returning American veterans and their families. In 2010, Oldaker was inducted into the Oklahoma Music Hall of Fame in Muskogee, Oklahoma.

Oliver Mangum

With their one album of power metal for Restless Records in 1989, Enid's Oliver Mangum entered the rock arena in the vein of Queensrÿche, Manowar or Anvil. Founded in 1983 by fleet-fingered guitarist Monte Humphrey, who started the band with Dan Kurts on bass, Curt Daugherty on drums, and Mark Mueller on vocals, many of the group's early songs were written by sound engineer Howard Worthen (who later toured with Seether). After Mueller developed issues within the band's format, he was first replaced with James Randel from the Oklahoma City band, Forté, and ultimately by Jimmy King, also an Oklahoma City singer. Oliver Mangum attacked p.a. systems and crowds with their big vocal sound, fast powerful back beat, and ferocious guitars that spin, climb, descend and grind in perfect time with the rhythm section of Curts and Daugherty, smashing out any doubt about the band's rockworthiness. With the release of their first album on Restless Records, Oliver Mangum kicked fancy pants pop metal acts off to the side of the road while jumping on board the extreme metal concert train with Pantera, Metal Church, and Celtic Frost before breaking up due largely to grunge's flannel whale beaching on the shores of American popular music. Nirvana's 1991 release, *Nevermind* (Geffen), altered the rock music landscape, whereby metal bands either evolved into nu metal styles incorporating rap, raced along with the limited thrash demographic, became retro 80s groups in smaller clubs, or just gave it up, which is apparently what Oliver Mangum decided to do about 1993 after one sonically impressive disc failed to register stateside, although the album did gain some notice overseas, notably in Germany, but subsequent demos failed to earn the group another deal.

www.myspace.com/olivermangum

Oliver Mangum, circa 1989 (l-r): Curt, Monte, James, and Dan.

Osage Nation

[In the area known as Oklahoma for many generations as hunters and traders; officially assigned to Osage Reservation, which the tribe purchased, in 1865]

The Osage people descended from the stars, according to the first panel of a mural painted on the Osage Nation Council Room wall in Pawhuska at the tribe's headquarters. The same mural depicts the Osage hunters running buffalo off cliffs in ancient times before horses were available, indicating the tribe's primary participation in the buffalo culture in which the animal was essentially a supermarket for the Native tribal person of the bison's habitat. Subsequent scenes show the Osage as a people of the mounds, which could be anywhere from 600 to 1400 A.D. Tribal oral history also reports the Osage have long-known the area that is now the Osage Nation in north central Oklahoma, the geographical boundaries of which coincide with Osage County. The tribe may have known the buffalo trails for millennia, and already had names for the places in the current Osage nation where they ultimately purchased land in 1865 after their fifty years on the first reservation in Neosho, Kansas ended badly due to the Civil War and general U.S. government mismanagement. By the time they walked across the Kansas line to their new land, the Osage population had been reduced 95%. Multiple Osage histories recount the tribe's affiliation with four other linguistically related Siouan-speaking tribes, known as the Dhegiha people, who were all at one time united and over the course of time separated into different tribes from the Mississippi River to the Great Plains. The Dhegiha include four contemporary tribes based in Oklahoma: the Ponca, Kansa (Kaw), Quapaw, and Osage; and the Omaha now known as the Omaha Tribe of Nebraska and Iowa with headquarters in Macy, Nebraska. As the Osage Nation's website indicated in 2011, not much is written about the tribe before the 1670.[1]

Surveying Osage music can be as difficult as trying to pull together a timeline of the Osage past, a project the Osage Tribal Museum has taken on and which any interested Osage historian should see, or at least visit the museum's website and . However, as for the music, oral history again says that the Osage transitioned out of their warrior culture after 1865, and with that transition went the songs and ceremonies of that ancient warrior society the Osage had maintained to that time from time immemorial. Entering the picture were missionaries such as the Quakers (Friends) and Catholics who delivered Christianity to the Osages, depicted peacefully in a scene from the Tribal Council Room's mural of Christ accepting the Osages into the water for Baptism. As early as 1867 there was an Osage Hymn Book written by Father Paul Ponziglione who was among the Osages from 1852 to 1890.[2] In 2011, Osage hymns are still sung at the Friends Indian Church in Hominy, Oklahoma. Along with putting

Osage I'n-Lon-Schka Dancers line up before going into annual ceremonies at Pawhuska, OK, June, 2012.

down the old warrior ceremonies, and with some tribal members embracing Christian hymns, a conservative traditional element among the Osage embraced the I'n-Lon-Schka Honor Ceremony, Dance, and Song Set derived from the Ponca and Kansa (Kaw) Tribes.

Oral tradition indicates the three drums were given up by the Osage's new neighbors in Indian Territory, but who were actually their old familiar relatives, the Ponca and Kansa, both of whom felt the Osage could better take care of the drums. Those Kansa and Ponca who knew the old songs and ways were rapidly fading among those dwindling tribes who also suffered after removal to hot north-central Oklahoma from their formerly cool riverside camps and lives in Kansas and Nebraska. Therein began the Osage continuing on the ancient song and dance that may have also derived from ancient Omaha songs, as much general agreement exists among contemporary singers that the Omaha are a primary source for a large percentage of original Southern Great Plains war dance songs, to include some of those of the Ponca and Kiowa. In any case, by virtue of participating in the I'n-Lon-Schka ceremonies each year, wherein some tribal language is still heard and many family songs are still sung, modern Osage people re-affirm their contemporary identity by attending the dances and singing, dancing, cooking, or just helping out. This participation in the community's annual activities is a primary part of re-affirming one's status as a tribal member outside of being an enrolled citizen with a membership card but no spiritual or tangible connection to the tribe's reality. Therefore, the songs maintained by the Osage I'n-Lon-Schka are important identity markers for modern Osage people.[3] The June ceremonies are open to the public, but videotaping, audio recording, or photographs are usually prohibited or restricted to family members or designated documentarians. As a result no commercial recordings of I'n-Lon-Schka songs are currently in print, however, some do exist within the tribes archives for their own teaching, learning, and historical purposes.

According to a .pdf document posted to Osage Nation's Museum and downloadable by the public, the I'n-Lon-Schka drum keepers are known back to the original moment when each community received its drum. The first drum keeper for Hominy was Blackdog, starting in 1880; the first drumkeeper for Gray Horse was John Black Bird, Sr., starting in 1883; and the first drumkeeper for Pawhuska was Ben Mashunkashey, beginning in 1884, and those ceremonies continue through the present-day, with 2011 ceremonies so crowded some dancers felt there was hardly any room to move. That can only mean that more and more people with Osage heritage want to participate in modern Osage ceremonies, which bodes well for their continuation and growth, as well as their evolution. In 2010, drumkeepers for the three districts included Joel Wynn for Gray Horse (since 2007), William Shunkamolah for Hominy (since 2009), and Bruce Cass of Pawhuska (since 2007).

Aside from the Christian hymns, and the music that developed with the I'n-Lon-Schka ceremonials, the music of the Native American Church is the most significant traditional musical form still maintained by Osages who became Peyotists in the 1890s after the Ghost Dance movement faded away, and the Oklahoma land runs changed Indian Territory yet again forever more. Peyote religious historian Omer Stewart explains the "Tipi Way", "The Peyote Road", or what later became known as the Native American Church, arrived in Osage Country after 1893 via a Caddo named John Wilson who brought the syncretic Native/Christian religion from southwestern Oklahoma where he had learned the rituals from the Kiowas and Comanches. Wilson re-imagined the altar and ceremony of southwestern Oklahoma based on his own visions. While traveling through Osage country to see his Delaware relatives and lead services for Quapaws living in the Cherokee Nation, Wilson stopped on occasion to lead a service for curious Osages.[4] After taking up Wilson's "Big Moon Ceremony" and converting to Peyotism, Osages built the first permanent church structures with permanent stone altars in which to hold Native American Church prayer meetings, instead of conducting ceremonies in tipis on the ground such as the southwestern and western Plains tribes.[5] In fact, Osage Native American Church meetings may still feature several Caddo songs, as well as Osage language Native American Church Songs, and songs by many other tribes who worship in that manner and sing the songs similar to how several churches in one denomination will sing similar hymns, or hymns with similar backgrounds. Additionally, since the tribal language is used in the ceremonies and songs, and the meetings occur regularly as well as when needed, the services also serve as an identity marker for attendees who identify with the "Osageness" of the services.

Osage Native American Church services displaced older naming ceremonies as in contemporary times (circa 2011) Osage names are sometimes given in the morning after the all-night prayer and song service. Many texts written about the Osage over the last 100 years have bemoaned the loss of traditional ceremonies among the Osage, but what those writers didn't know is that some of those ancient activities went underground (and were also illegal in 1889 by the way), but are still present right in both the Osage Native American Church, as well as the contemporary I'n-Lon-Schka Ceremonies which include very old songs, dance styles and patterns, face markings, haircuts, specific regalia with specific designs and colors based on one's family or clan associations, knowledge of family and clan lineage for many generations, a constant expression of Osage tribal values, and a lot of food. So while some of the I'n-Lon-schka took on an amalgamation of older warrior dances and songs that could not be kept up by their relatives, the Osage created a new meaning for the music, to replicate the social order of bringing a young Osage man among men, and a young Osage woman among women, to

Osage tribal member, Jim Gray, is both an I'n-Lon-Schka Dancer, as well as a Road Man, or church leader, in the Osage Native American Church. Mr. Gray is pictured here before NAC services in Pawhuska, Oklahoma, 2010.

learn their potential role and responsibility in traditional Osage life, something they will be expected to keep once started. That community expectation of presence is an intrinsic aspect of tribalism, and going to a ceremony or church service just because a person is of a certain lineage may or may not make sense to the outside world, but in the real world of Indian Country, just being present in the continuum of tribal identity is often enough from the tribal person's perspective.

Singers (l to r): Vann Bighorse, Scott George, Kenny Bighorse Jr., Judie Aitken, Earl Fenner, Mary Bighorse, Kickapoo Rice, 2010.

However, from the non-Indian author's point of view, the equivalent can only be expressed as being part of a caring and reciprocating community, the members of which, for the most part, appreciate and help one another during life's various crises. The Osage Native American Church and the I'n-Lon-Schka provide that comfort through annual song and dance for tribal members who wish to sustain their tribal identities.

In 1997, Indian Sounds released a collection of Osage "Ancestral Songs" for the The Osage Sweat Ceremony sung by Louie McAlpine and recorded at Gray Horse Indian Village. The disc is one of the few available commercially that preserves traditional Osage music, with McAlpine explaining each song and then singing it while accompanying himself only on a hand rattle. Interestingly, he combines one of the Osage Catholic Hymns with the sweat lodge rattle accompaniment and tempo, as well as other sweat ceremony songs. Of even more interest is a recording of the water being poured on the hot stones that creates the steam that enhances the sweating, as well as the prayers and songs that go along with the steam in the sweat lodge. Singers in the Osage Sweat Ceremony include Louie McAlpine (Osage), Herschel Kaulaity (Cheyenne-Kiowa), Casey Swank (Osage), Chris Swank (Osage), John Schonleber (Caddo). In contemporary Pan-Indian music, or that music commonly associated with the **powwow** tradition, the mostly Osage group Yellow Spotted Horse released one album, *Out of Chute (#3)*, some humorous titles in the powwow tradition: "Getting' Down in T-Town", "Bucks on the Run" (referring to the Hominy Bucks?), "Hominy Lake Moonglow" (maybe?!), and "Opus 49". Many contemporary powwow singers who have emerged from the Osage big drum traditions, to include Osage tribal member Vann Bighorse who is a constant presence in the head powwow singer's chair at Oklahoma powwows. Additionally, Vann along with other presumed related Bighorses have appeared on several Southern Thunder powwow CDs recorded for Indian House Records, such as *Intertribal Songs of Oklahoma* (IH 2081), which contains the "Osage Flag Song". Craig Satepauhoodle (Osage/**Kiowa**) is also a common sight and a sound as a head singer at powwows across Oklahoma. Raised by his Osage mother, Genevieve, and Kiowa father, Evans Ray Satepauhoodle, who were married 44 years, Craig and his brother, Silas Satepauhoodle, as well as sisters Angela (Satepauhoodle) Toineeta, and Lynette and Charisse Satepauhoodle, grew up around the ceremonial traditions of the Osage and the Kiowa, absorbing the musical elements of both, and continue on those traditions for both tribes and widely throughout the intertribal powwow world.

With regard to contemporary music, Osage tribal member Anthony Lookout was a founding member of *New Mysterians*, one the earliest popular punk rock groups in late 1970s/early 1980s Tulsa. The group was filmed on video at popular clubs, the Bleu Grotto and the Crystal Pistol, as well as recorded on the local talent TV show of the time, *Tulsa Backstage*, all of which is available on DVD, but good luck tracking one down. Lookout also appeared as a solo artist on the 1984 *Explosive* compilation with the songs "What a Zero". Anthony began a career as producer and engineer on a project with his father to record traditional Osage I'n-Lon-Schka songs for the Osage Tribal Museum, but the disc is now out of print. Lookout also pursued a career in theatre and film, most notably in appearance in the 1994 Lawrence Kasdan film, *Wyatt Earp*. As of 2011, Anthony Lookout operated his own studios in Tulsa, where he recorded a solo blues album on which he plays all drums, bass, guitar, harmonica, and sings.

Curtis Moore, circa 2007

Another Osage tribal member, Curtis Moore (b. October 28, 1959 in Stillwater, OK) has led a regionally successful blues group to opening slot for A-listers such as Leon Russell, Marshall Tucker Band, Black Oak Arkansas, Willie Nelson, David Allan Coe, as well as notability by internet playlists from as far away as Australia. 1/8 Osage and 1/32 Choctaw, Curtis' great-great grandfather was John Wash Bigheart, a noted Osage medicine man. In 2003, Moore released a CD recorded at the Cain's Ballroom in which his tough blues guitar exhibits why the Curtis Moore Band is a favorite on the no-frills rock circuit of biker gatherings, barbecues, and any event featuring the leathery crack of rowdy blues rock (www.myspace.com/curtismooreband). A November, 2004 issue of the nationally syndicated, *Biker* magazine, proclaimed Moore as "good old-style rockin' blues that we all know, love, and dance to."

The Osage do have a further reputation for keeping people dancing, and also contributing to the wider musical entertainment scene in Tulsa with the presentation of many popular music concerts at their Osage Million Dollar Elm Casino. With the obvious popularity of their ceremonial dances, the concerted attendance at Native American Church prayer meetings, and the continuation of singing Osage Christian hymns wherein the language can also be learned, Osage music traditions appear to be poised for continued healthy subsistence and development.

www.osagetribe.com

Notes

1. Along with the Osage Nation's website (www.osagetribe.com), the author consulted texts such as George Dorsey's essential 1904 work, *Traditions of the Osage*, Field Columbian Museum Publication 88; and Garrick Bailey's groundbreaking scholarship in *Traditions of the Osage: Stories Collected and Translated by Francis La Flesche* (Albuquerque, NM: UNM Press, 2010); both are essential to understanding the

Osage traditional worldview.;
2. For extensive information about the Catholic mission's work in the Osage Nation, see Sister M. Ursula's "Sources for the Study of Oklahoma Catholic Missions: A Critical Biography", *Chronicles of Oklahoma*, (Volume 16: 3), September, 1938. The bibliography notes that Ponziglione's manuscript collection of Osage Hymns with English translations is housed at Georgetown University.
3. The starting point for learning more about how Osage identity and values are transmitted during Osage Ceremonials held each June in Gray Horse, Pawhuska, and Hominy, see Alice Anne Callahan, *The Osage Ceremonial Dance: I'n-Lon-Schka* (Norman: OU Press, 1990).
4. For more information regarding the Osage-specific elements of the Native American Church, as well as an authoritative history on the church's formal origins in Oklahoma, see Omer C. Stewart's *Peyote Religion: A History*. (Norman: University of Oklahoma Press, 1987), pp. 108-112.
5. For further details of the difference between John Wilson's "Big Moon" Native American Church Ceremony and the "Half Moon" Native American Church Ceremony more common to southern Plains people such as the Comanche and Kiowa, and later the Ponca, Kansa, Otoe-Missouria, and Pawnee located in north central Oklahoma, see Thomas C. Maroukis, *The Peyote Road: Religious Freedom and the Native American Church* (Norman: OU Press, 2010), pp. 30-31.

Other Lives
(Formed, 2003 in Stillwater, OK)

The most contemplative and spacious of the modern pop rock bands out of Oklahoma, Other Lives emerged from a similarly themed group, Kunek (2003-2008), to coalesce into the organic yet precise outfit they are as Other Lives. Fronted by Jesse Tabish, whose lead vocals have the unique aural imprint of an artist that really does not sound like anyone else, with the exception of perhaps early period Syd Barrett of Pink Floyd, Tabish's lyrics ride the tension zone between hopeful and helpless, or simultaneously wonder-filled while also brimming with disappointment. The band's music is richly textured with strings, horns, keyboards, piano, acoustic and electric guitar, harmony background vocals, and an unhurried, meditative pace. Combined with Jenny Hsu's cello, Jonathon Mooney's multi-instrumental skills, a lockstep rhythm section of Josh Onstott (bass) and Colby Owens (drums), and Tabish's incantatory piano chords and

Other Lives, 2011, (l to r): Jenny Hsu, Colby Owens, Jesse Tabish, Josh Onstott, and Jonathan Mooney.

guitar arpeggios provide melodic drive and contour to Other Lives' dreamy songs.

For background on the group, bassist Josh Onstott (b. 8/16/1979, Fort Worth, TX) grew up in Cushing, started playing guitar at age seventeen, moved to Stillwater in 2000, and switched to bass about age 23 as Kunek began to form. Jonathon Mooney (b. 10/10/1984, Stillwater, OK) started playing guitar and piano at about age thirteen, and learned his primary music fundamentals from his father, also a musician. Drummer Colby Owens (b. 2/5/1983, Stillwater, OK) began playing in middle school band before his interests switched to guitars and drums outside of the school's formal band system. Cellist Jenny Hsu (b. 8/25/1983, Pullman, WA) moved to Stillwater in 1990, started playing cello at age 9 in the Stillwater Public Schools Music, continuing through her high school graduation. Jesse Tabish (b. 8/9/1983, Stillwater, OK) started playing music at age 7 when he began taking piano lessons, and started began guitar lessons with **Jeff Parker** at age 13. While in high school Tabish played guitar in a group called The Drowning Fish, with Nick Wheeler on drums and Tyson Ritter on bass and vocals, which progressed into an early version of the **All-American Rejects**. Tabish left in the Rejects in the early 2000s to forge his own musical direction, began teaching guitar at Daddy O's Music Store in Stillwater, and started forming Kunek in 2003.

After releasing Kunek's first and only album, *Flight of the Flynns*, in 2006, and numerous regional and national appearances, Eric Kiner left the group in 2008, just prior to the band going into the studio to record their follow-up album. Out of respect to Kiner, the remaining members did not want to continue with the same moniker featuring a different instrumental configuration, and changed their name during the recordings for the new album in March, 2008. With the album nearly finished, the band returned to Stillwater to take advantage of the low rent and low-key lifestyle in the college town of Stillwater, where they just kept practicing in the older part of town where the streets are still bricked instead of paved. The first formal Other Lives gig occurred at The Conservatory in Oklahoma City in October, 2008, followed by other local performances in Stillwater, as well various high profile opening slots, and major festival gigs at Sasquatch and Lollapalooza after the album came out in April, 2009. Produced by Joey Waronker (The Eels, Lisa Germano), and engineer DarrellThorp (Radiohead, Outkast, Beck), the LP's first single, "Black Tables", struck a receptive nerve among L.A. television producers, as the song appeared in shows such as *Ugly Betty, Grey's Anatomy,* and *One Tree Hill*. Overall, the album is a comforting atmospheric palate with dynamic string, horn, and keyboard arrangements that provide rich textural foundations for the songs, and fresh turnarounds between verses and choruses. If it weren't for Tabish's unforced singing style that sounds like listeners are hearing him think to himself, the music might sound a little stilted due to the heavily arranged style. However, just the right balance is achieved between Tabish's casual plaintiveness and the group's formal excellence, as the ensemble is as comfortable with a bolero as a waltz.

Other Lives finished their second full-length album in February, 2011 for TBD/Play It Again Sam Records. Released as *Tamer Animals* in May, 2011, the album achieved a minute of notoriety on *Billboard*'s Heatseeker Chart, but did not go any higher on a national scale. However, the band enjoyed healthy audiences for its shows nationwide, garnered repeated ornately worded reviews for their more-than-four-on-the-floor rock, and a British tour in the summer and fall of 2011. *Tamer Animals* further polished the ethereal aspects of Other Lives with even more multi-tracked orchestration ("Dark Horse"), meshed continuo of strings and horns ("As I Lay My Head Down"), and hushed atmospherics ("Woodwind"/"3 for 12"). The group even ranges towards the Beach Boys' *Pet Sounds* era with "Weather", and adds a little more twangy, reverb-laden guitar here and there than they had to that point on their recordings. With *Tamer Animals*, the aural focus of the group remains a lush quality of strings, horns, and keyboards, all supported with rhythmic subtlety by drummer Colby Owens and bassist Josh Onstott whose long-time work as a unit grounds the group in dependable timekeeping while being extremely adept at the multiple changes in Other Lives' songs. Achieving Brian Eno-like soundscapes with echoes of Aaron Copland's neo-Classical American symphonies, "Heading East" demonstrates the significant classical influences ruminating through the group's work, and "Dust Bowl III" could easily be the soundtrack for a Spaghetti Western set in the Glass Mountains out in Major County, Oklahoma. Listening to both the first album and *Tamer Animals* back to back, one can hear the sonic development of Other Lives in just the span of two years. Because of their elevated musical skills, Other Lives can try things beyond the reach of average rock bands based on the guitar, bass, drums format. At Other Lives' best, the music is transcendent in manners consistent with the sumptuous aspects of orchestrated rock music recordings from the Beatles' *Yellow Submarine*, *Magical Mystery Tour*, and *Sgt. Pepper* period, along with the previously mentioned references to Pink Floyd or Can. In a more contemporary sense (from the 1980s forward), the band's sound is at times analogous to British groups such as the Cocteau Twins, Chameleons UK, or Coldplay. Lyrically, Tabish connects the melancholy beauty of a sensitively examined life by a songwriter comfortable with creating art based on the interior spaces of the heart and mind that less eloquent folks have difficulty expressing. With their sophomore album as Other Lives, the group builds on what they have already accomplished sonically, adding more because they can. The result of which often sends the album's aesthetic backwards to the 1960s soundscapes of Pink Floyd, and could even logically be linked to the experimental avant-garde German rock group, Can, who merged classical sensibilities within progressive rock constructs. Occasionally, the group's musical predecessors are relatively easy to pinpoint, as opposed to the harder to define first album that established new "space" for Other Lives. Either way, the compositions, performances,

Other Lives' Jenny Hsu (cello) and Jesse Tabish (guitar/vocals), circa 2005, Stillwater, OK.

and production on *Tamer Animals* are exemplary, and practically no other American band can sound like Other Lives, which is the ultimate goal of an original pop or rock group, to be instantly identifiable in a sea of hopefuls or sound-a-likes. With regard to Oklahoma, Other Lives' relatively unique contemporary sound is likely shaped by the relative lack of pressure to develop a specific commercial sound fast in a larger urban environment where the financial pressures often force decisions unrelated to a desired artistic path.

By staying based in Stillwater, where the cost of living is somewhat cheap, and no overabundance of bands exists who are trying to sound like each other to get gigs, the group appears to have evolved in a more and natural way. As Jesse Tabish said in a 2009 *OMG* interview, "Because there is not a lot of stimulation here (in Stillwater) outside of sports and rural activities, people have the time and inclination to explore their musical worlds in more depth without the usual pressures of instant success."

In 2012, the band landed a major series of concert dates as a sympatico opening act for Radiohead, and continued touring the world on the strength of their album and reputation as a musically dynamic and lyrically challenging modern rock group. Jesse Tabish also found a little extra time to knock out a vinyl single release, "Daffodils," under the collaborative name of Winter Boys, with vocals by **Tyson Meade (Chainsaw Kittens)**, extra keyboards by Derek Brown (**Flaming Lips**, Crocodile), and percussion by local scenester, Aaron Frisby.. The recording features Tabish's now signature "space epic" compositional style layered with melodic and contoured subtleties that reward repeat listening, as is the norm with all Other Lives recordings as well. The group planned to start their next album in early 2013

www.otherlives.com

www.myspace.com/otherlives

Otoe-Missouria Tribe
(Removed to reservation near present-day, Red Rock, Oklahoma, in 1881)

While some older ceremonial dances and songs faded in the late 19th century with removal to Indian Territory, and subsequent attrition due to their socio-economic and political circumstance as Native American people bounced around by the pinball machine of federal government policies, the Otoe-Missouria Tribe of Oklahoma entered the 21st century with a very strong set of tribally specific songs for a variety of ceremonies, commemorations, and annual dances. Additionally, tribal members have not only contributed a century's worth of Native American Church songs to the collective catalogue of that music, but also have made nationally recognized recordings of Native American Church songs, and intertribal powwow songs. Various groups sponsor a number of dances at the tribal facilities near Red Rock each year, such as birthday dances, memorial dances, veterans' dances, holiday dances, gourd dances (a dance

The Otoe-Missouria Tribe's official seal depicts the seven clans of the Otoe-Missouria people.

they received permission to use from the Kiowa in the early 20th century, one of the only such grants by the Kiowa to any other tribe), and various honor dances are held by organizations within the tribe such as the Otoe War Mothers. As far as *Oklahoma Music Guide* is aware, all dances are free and open to the public, to include the annual Otoe-Missouria Encampment, occurring in mid-July each summer since the tribe arrived in the area in 1881. Throughout the year, the Encampment Committee holds various benefit dances as fundraisers for the annual gathering's expenses. In 2012, the tribe celebrated its 131st summer encampment. If attending, visitors will hear some music that continues serving the same purposes it has for millennia, to make the people dance, to remind those within earshot of tribal stories via Otoe words in the songs, or to suggest a whole clan or family's identity in a song that may have lyrics, or just a melody that everyone recognizes as this or that family's song.

Tribal history places the Otoe and Missouria people with their Siouan speaking ancestors near the Great Lakes more than five centuries ago. As many ancient people did for a variety of reasons (climate, subsistence improvements, intra-tribal politics), a group of Otoe and Missouria people split off from the main body of their tribe and began moving south, some of whom settled along the western side of Lake Michigan and became the Winnebago. Another group broke off at the confluence of the Mississippi and Rock Rivers near modern Rock Island, Illinois, and became the **Iowa** people, explaining the ancient connections between the Otoe-Missouria and the Iowa. Eventually, the Otoe settled along the Platte River in Nebraska, and the Missouria on the Grand River in what is now the state of Missouri, named, of course, after the tribe. Even though separated geographically, the tribal relatives met regularly for dances, some being held by the Buffalo Moccasin Lodge to provide for those less fortunate in the tribe, and others, such as the Peace Pipe Dance, held to formalize diplomatic relations with neighboring people or the newcomers. Being further east than the Otoe, the Missouria first encountered Europeans in the form of French traders in the 1690s, which caused problems with other tribes in the north, such as the Sac and Fox, who were already trading with the French. This began a turbulent century in which the Otoe and Missouria interacted, traded, fought, or otherwise dealt with the French, the British, the Spanish, and neighboring tribes such as the **Kansa** to the south. The 1800s also saw the tribe caught in the crossfire of many competing interests for the area by the British, then the Americans, and other tribes from the north being pushed out of their areas. After establishing a camping stronghold at St. Louis, the famous Lewis and Clark expedition visited the Otoe, after which more and more Americans followed to trade and

Otoe Encampment Benefit Dance, 2012.

settle in Otoe lands. The Otoe's first treaty with the American government was in 1817, about the same time the Otoes and Missourias reunited as one tribe due to depletion of the Otoe's numbers due to warfare with neighboring tribes to the north such as the Sac and Fox. According to tribal history, about one hundred members of the Missouria people were taken in by the Otoes, and were recognized jointly following that event by the federal government as one people, even though some tribal members still maintain individual traditions within the tribe as distinctly Otoe or Missouria, such as the Otoe War Mothers who are specific to say that they are not to be called the Otoe-Missouria War Mothers. The Otoe ceded huge tracts of land in the 1830s, but continued fighting other unsettled tribes in the 1840s, such as the Sioux to the north and the Pawnee to the south, as well as Americans who were encroaching on Otoe lands from the east. After a decade of warfare, the tribe realized it could not defend the totality of its territory, and ceded all but a tiny portion of land east of the Missouri River.

In 1855, they were moved to a reservation on the Nebraska and Kansas border before controversy arose again within the tribe regarding their potential removal to Indian Territory. By 1869, progressive tribal members ("The Quaker Band") who were in favor acculturation wanted to remain on their land in Nebraska, accept allotments, and continue moving toward an Americanized lifestyle. Traditionalists ("The Coyote Band"), such as Arkeketah, Medicine Horse, and Pipestem, advocated a move to Indian Territory where they would not have to deal with the Americans and could continue their traditional way of life. In 1880, as many as 200 members of the Coyote Band had removed themselves to an area in central Indian Territory near the Sac and Fox. The next year, after the federal government was influenced by the persuasions of the Quaker Band, the Otoe-Missouria Reservation was actually decreed to be where it is today, with the Quaker Band getting to select their land first upon arrival in 1881. Many of the Coyote Band stayed with their old relatives the Iowa, but when the Iowa reservation was allotted, almost all the Coyote Band returned to the Red Rock area.[2] Many Otoe people opposed the breaking up and allotment of tribal lands, so much so much so that tribal members would follow government surveyors after nightfall and pull up their land mark stakes. Unable to stop the inevitable, Otoe-Missouria lands were allotted to tribal members, and some of the remaining lands were opened up to settlers in the famous Oklahoma land runs; however, some lands were transferred in an extremely unscrupulous manner, process that set off a series of events and court cases that were not resolved until the 1960s, wherein they became the first tribe to garner proper settlement improper compensation for land taken from them .[3] After Oklahoma's settlement, and the subsequent abolishment of any tribal government, the Otoe-Missouria people experienced the common timeline of American Indians in the early twentieth century that included government boarding schools, reforming their tribal government in 1936 under the Oklahoma Indian Welfare Act, and slowly re-building their world to the point where in 2013 they own four casinos and operate a tribal facility with all the accoutrements of a tiny nation state to include the gamut of education, health, and social services for its people, as well as environment, legal, economic, and administrative departments.

With regard to traditional Otoe-Missouria music, a rare window into the tribal music traditions of the Otoe-Missouria people was offered to the author in exchange for duplicating a historic set of family recordings made by Otoe-Missouria tribal member Grant Cleghorn. Cleghorn produced the original transcriptions in the 1950s on a homemade record making machine. The author digitized them for archival and educational purposes only, ultimately to be housed at the Otoe-Missouria tribal library, tribal colleges, and other interested archives. As a an excellent cross-representation of Otoe-Missouria musical traditions as of the mid-twentieth century, the recordings include the following songs: "War Dance", "Horse Giveaway", "Half Breed", "Bear Dance", songs just labeled "Oto (sic) Songs", "Clan Songs" for the Elk, Owl, Otter, and Bear Clans, "Hand Game Songs", "49 Songs", "Otoe Church Songs and Hymns", "Social Dance", "Iowa Songs", several "Otoe Songs", "Round Dance", "Two Step", "Buffalo Headman Song". For a more readily example of Otoe traditional music, Indian House Records has *Ten Otoe Warrior Dance Songs* in its catalogue of American Indian Soundchiefs Series. Recorded in 1953, the album features Fred Ely, Johnny Moore, and Mrs. Johnny Moore on songs featuring only vocals and the "big drum" associated with American Indian Plains war dance music. However, the drum was of such significance to the Otoe people, the tribe's Christian Hymns were also occasionally sung using a drum. Otoe-Missouria singers and religious leaders also have contributed significantly to the Native American Church singing tradition.

Otoe specific Peyote Songs began developing after a tribal headman received the Native American Church rites and procedures in 1891from the Tonkawa who were located just northwest of the Otoe-Missouria reservation near present-day Tonkawa, Oklahoma. The Otoe developed their own "Opening Song", "Midnight Song", "Water Song", and "Morning" or "Quitting Song".[4] According to Native American Church scholar, Thomas Maroukis, the Otoe were responsible for spreading a Christian focused theology within the service to their old relatives, the Winnebago. An Otoe Peyotist, Jonathan Koshiway, also incorporated in 1914 as the First Born Church of Christ in Red Rock, Oklahoma, both to proselytize and deflect criticism from the church. However, later Otoe advocates of Peyotism thought Koshiway's charter was not specific enough and did not address the important issue of the Peyote as the sacrament and/or medicine for the church.[5] In any case, many Otoe Native American Church songs mention Jesus Christ specifically either as an intrinsic part of the belief system, or as an early attempt to insure a Christian "front" for the church, a technique not uncommon with some other early tribal adherents who fought to maintain the religion that was under scrutiny by the government, Christian missionaries, local Indian agents, and even some tribal members who did not believe the Native American Church was a legitimate denomination of Christianity. However, discussing the varying points of view of this issue is beyond the scope of the *Oklahoma Music Guide*. What's important is that the contemporary Otoe Chapter of the Native American Church is

Otoe-Missouria tribal elder, and long-time Native American Church drum carrier, Marvin Diamond, presents a lecture on instruments he makes, such as this rattle, to accompany Native American Church singing, Stillwater, OK, 2010.

Hugh W. Foley / 605

active and maintains this musical tradition that has found its way on to recordings by the Littlecook Family who are of both Otoe and Ponca descent, as are many people in the immediate vicinity between Red Rock and Ponca City where members of the two tribes have lived, socialized, gone to school, ceremonies, and church services since being moved to reservations there in the late 19th century.

The Littlecooks, to include Stephen, Oliver, Ed, and O.J., have at least five different commercial recordings of Oklahoma Native American Church Songs on the Cool Runnings record label out of Window Rock, Arizona. While the Littlecooks are members of the Ponca Chapter of the Native American Church, they sing many Otoe songs because of their family background, the proximity of the Ponca to the Otoe geographically, and the intertribal nature of the Native American Church. As an educational effort, Otoe-Missouria elder and former president of the Otoe-Missouria chapter of the Native American Church, Marvin Diamond, has also worked to produce educational videos on the musical instruments of the Native American Church which are available by searching his name on the commercial video internet service, youtube.com. Jeff McClellan and Kyle Robedeaux, both of Otoe descent, have also recorded an album of Native American Church songs with Brian Stoner for Canyon Records, *For Our Loved Ones* (2005, CR-6397), containing four Otoe Songs. Additionally, a primary Otoe Native American Church leader, Truman Daily, recorded at least one cassette of NAC songs in the Otoe language for archival and educational purposes, but which is only available as "a copy of a copy" from someone who owns a dub of it.

In the realm of intertribal powwow music, general knowledge among Oklahoma powwow singers and observers credit the Brave Scout Singers as one of the first named Oklahoma powwow groups, as well as the first big drum powwow group to sing in both the lower pitched Southern powwow singing style native to Oklahoma, as well as the more aggressive, higher pitched Northern style that did not emerge in Oklahoma until the late 1960s and early 1970s. Favored by young people and those who were perceived to be associated with the American Indian activism of the period, the style of singing was not universally liked nor welcome by more traditional Oklahoma powwow organizers, but slowly became an accepted part of most intertribal powwows, not including those hosted by a specific tribe which often focuses more on that particular tribe's music with only one center drum, such as an Otoe, Ponca, or Pawnee dance.

Formed around 1967 and amed after founder Sidney Moore's Otoe name, which translates into "Brave Scout," the first configuration of the Brave Scout Singers included Pete Moore, Sr. (Otoe/Pawnee), Anthony "Tony" Arkeketa (Ponca/Otoe), Terry Williams (Otoe/Pawnee), George Williams (Otoe/Pawnee), Noble Grant, Sr. (Otoe), and George Shields, Sr. (Pawnee/Sioux). While the northern style of singing was not prominent in the Oklahoma intertribal powwow world from the early part of the 20th century through the 1960s, Sidney Moore's travels among northern tribes familiarized him with the style of singing now commonly referred to as "northern singing." Back in Oklahoma, Moore's Pawnee relatives relayed to him the Pawnee used to sing in the higher-pitched register, as did the Pawnee's ancient relatives, the Arikira who would travel to Pawnee during mid-20th century celebrations and share those songs in that style. One recording of the Brave Scout Singers is still barely available (while supplies last) via cassette through Canyon Records. *Otoe & Pawnee Pow-Wow Songs* (CR-6172). The following singers are on the only official Brave Scout recording,: Pete Moore, Sr., Auck NewRider,

Cricket Shields, Edward Yellowfish, Conrad Gayly, Rick Tosee, Dynomite Mitholo, TeeTee Shields, Gwendy Williams,

Several Otoe singers have sung at powwows across the country, and recorded with the powwow singing group Yellow Hammer (formed circa 1990) on at least nine albums through 2011. Three discs were recorded for the prestigious Native American music label, Indian House Records. *Live at Hollywood, Florida* includes the "Otoe Flag Song" and "Victory Song"; *Red Rock, Oklahoma* contains ten intertribal songs; and *World Champions*, was recorded at the original Otoe Agency at Red Rock. Yellowhammer won the Southern Plains singing competition at the Schemitzun World Championship in Connecticut four times, and has recorded several more albums, to include *In Memory of Perry Lee Botone, Sr.* (2006), *Old School*, and *Yellowhammer* (2011).

Yellow Hammer Singers, circa 2001

Another group of intertribal powwow singers with several Otoe members, Bad Moon Rising, formed mostly for the purpose of recording one album, *Southern*, for Cool Runnings Records in 2003. One of the Otoe-Missouria's most active contemporary singers in 2012, of all forms of Otoe traditional music, is Gary "Chink" Whitecloud, Jr. who was the Head War Dance Singer at the 130th Annual Otoe-Missouria Summer Encampment at 2011, and is frequently called upon for his extensive knowledge of War Dance songs, Veterans songs, and Native American Church songs. The Otoe-Missouria sponsor dances throughout the late winter and early spring months to raise funds and awareness for their annual encampment, as well as to celebrate the accomplishments or memories of tribal members.

www.omtribe.org

Notes

1. No such printed book such as the *Peyote Hymn Book* exists, but regular attendees of Native American Church know a whole range of Peyote Songs that have been made over the last hundred years or more. The songs are often sung collectively by a variety of tribal people, no matter the host church or home language of the songs. The reference here is to suggest there is a virtual *Peyote Hymn Book* in the minds and memories of NAC members in north central Oklahoma, and Otoe singers have contributed significantly to that body of work. The archived recordings of Truman Daily are especially important in that regard.
2. For more details on Otoe-Missouria history, see R. David Edmunds, *The Otoe-Missouria People* (Phoenix, AZ: Indian Tribal Series,1976).
3. For an outrageous story regarding the corruption at every level of government and private interests regarding how Otoe lands were allotted and sold, and then how the tribe pursued a court case to seek justice and

retribution that was finally resolved in the 1960s, see Berlin Basil Chapman's *The Otoes and Missourias* (Time Journal Publishing,1965).
4. For discussion of the early rites of the Otoe Native American Church service, see Edward S. Curtis, "The Peyote Cult," *The North American Indian, Volume 19* (Cambridge, MA: Harvard University Press, 1930), pp. 199-213.
5. For more details on the spread of Peyotism among the tribes in north-central Oklahoma, as well as discussion of the Otoe impact on a Christianized version of the Native American Church, see Thomas C. Maroukis, *The Peyote Road: Religious Freedom and the Native American Church*(Norman: University of Oklahoma Press, 2010), pp. 29-30, and further discussion of the incorporation of the First Born Church of Christ in Red Rock, pp. 48, as well as opposition to it, pp. 59.
6. A phone interview with Patrick Moore, Sr. filled in details, date, and personnel of the formation and evolution of the Brave Scout Singers, July 3, 2012.

Overstreet, Tommy
(b. September 10, 1937)

With his "ladies man" good looks, and not a few songs about cheating men and or love gone wrong, Tommy Overstreet was named as the Most Promising New Male Vocalist in country music by the *Music City News* in 1971, appeared as a frequent guest on *Hee Haw* in the 1970s, and was honored in 1985 with induction into the Country Music Hall of Fame Walkway of Stars. Billed contemporarily on his website as "The King of Countrypolitan", Thomas Cary Overstreet was born in Oklahoma City, but raised in Houston, Texas.

Tommy's parents gave him a guitar when he was about thirteen that led to his first professional appearance on radio station KTHT in Houston for about four months. He then joined a local production called *Hit the Road* as a replacement for pop vocalist Tommy Sands, who was a high school chum. He graduated from Mirabeau B. Lamar High School in Houston in 1955.

Tommy's family moved to Abilene, Texas after he completed high school. While in college studying radio and television production, he was featured on local television as "Tommy Dean from Abilene," singing and playing guitar, and toured during summers with cousin Gene Austin, a singer who was well known for his hit records, "My Blue Heaven" and "Ramona". After a two-year stint in the armed forces, Overstreet moved to Los Angeles, where he worked as a songwriter for Pat Boone's Cooga Music and signed with Dunhill Records, although no records were released. His unsuccessful recording career resulted in a move back to Texas, where he appeared on the Slim Willet television show in the mid-1960s, and formed his own band to play club dates in the Houston area.

In 1967, Tommy moved to Nashville, where he used his college degree in radio and television production to gain a position as manager of Dot Records, and signed with the label as a recording artist. His first two singles, "Rocking a Memory (That Won't Go to Sleep" (1969) and "If You're Looking for a Fool" (1971) slipped into the country charts at #73 and #56, respectively. He finally scored his first major hit later in 1971 with "Gwen (Congratulations)", the title track of his first album, which charted at #5 with a song about a honky-tonk temptress, and was followed with "I Don't Know You (Anymore)", which also notched a #5 position on the country charts. As with many country artists whose initial hits establish themes to which they return again and again, Overstreet's songs tended toward the ends of relationships, a well-worn country music trope. Often his music was ornately, if not baroquely, produced in the commercial Nashville style popular in the 1960s and 1970s, with the addition of horns, background singers, and string sections to make it seem more pop. And, for Overstreet, it seemed to work out.

In 1972, Overstreet produced three more chart singles, including "A Seed Before the Rose", "Heaven Is My Woman's Love", and "Ann (Don't Go Runnin')", which reached #2 and became his overall biggest hit. The next two years, he charted with "Send Me No Roses", "I'll Never Break These Chains", "If I Miss You Again Tonight", "I'm a Believer", and "(Jeannie Marie) You Were a Lady", the latter reaching the Top 3. During the remainder of the 1970s, Tommy scored several Top 20 hits, such as "That's When My Woman Begins" (1975), "From Woman to Woman" (1975), "Here Comes that Girl Again" (1976), "Young Girl" (1976), "If Love Was a Bottle" (1977), "Don't Go City Girl on Me" (1977), which reached #5 on the charts, "This Time I'm In It for Love" (1977), "Yes Ma'am" (1978), "Better Me" (1978), and "Fadin' In, Fadin' Out" (1978).

After leaving the Dot label in 1979, Tommy moved to Tina Records, and then on to Elektra, where his most successful singles were "I'll Never Let You Down", "What More Could a Man Need", "Fadin' Renegade", "Down in the Quarter", and "Sue". Although he never achieved a #1 hit, Tommy registered twenty-seven *Billboard* entries during the 1970s. He has appeared on numerous television shows on all the major networks, to include *Merv Griffin Show*, *The Tonight Show*, *The Midnight Special*, *The Dean Martin Show*, and several others.

During the 1980s, Overstreet and his band, the Nashville Express, continued to tour nationally and internationally. He was especially popular in Germany, where his "Heaven Is My Woman's Love", sung in German, was a hit, and had completed thirty-two European tours by 2011. He was named Entertainer of the Year by the International Rodeo Association for the years 1979, 1980, and 1981 because of his extensive appearances throughout the U.S. on the rodeo circuit. In 1985, Tommy and his wife, Diane, moved to Branson, Missouri where he opened a restaurant and signed with Silver Dollar Records, a local Branson label. Continuing to perform, Overstreet has released several albums in the last decade, with 2000's *Tommy Overstreet: Country's Best, Vol. 1* including ten of his hits, such as "Gwen", "I Don't Know You (Anymore)", and "I'm A Believer". Another Greatest Hits package surfaced as an import in 2006, *Tommy Overstreet Sings His Hits* (IMC); and Tommy also produced a collection of inspirational music in 2006, *Country Gospel Favorites* (Madacy Christian), an all-star tribute to Oklahoma gospel songwriting legend, Albert E. Brumley; and in 2008 Varese Fontana released another collection of his best-known songs, *20 Classic Songs of Tommy Overstreet*. As of 2011 he continued to perform and tour, but Tommy and Diane have moved to the Pacific

Northwest, where, according to his website, they are "raising two daughters, four horses, three cats, and a black Lab."

www.tommyoverstreet.net

Bonnie Owens
(b. October 1, 1932 – d. April 24, 2006)

Recognized as the first woman singer-songwriter to emerge from the Bakersfield Sound country music movement in the 1950s, Bonnie Owens parlayed her perky personality and honky-tonk vocal style into a solid career as a country singer, but she may be best remembered as the singing wife of two major Bakersfield Sound country stars, **Buck Owens** and **Merle Haggard**. Born Bonnie Campbell near Blanchard, Oklahoma, a town of about 2,000 citizens southwest of Oklahoma City, her father worked for the WPA during the Great Depression of the 1930s, and her mother made all the children's clothes. As a child, she picked cotton on their Oklahoma sharecropper farm before the family, which eventually consisted of six daughters and two sons before the family follow a familiar Okie trail that came to a "can't go any further" halt in Arizona.

As a teenager, Bonnie developed a talent for yodeling and won contests throughout Arizona. After performing in various clubs, she met Alvis Edgar "Buck" Owens at the Mazona Roller Rink in Mesa. Bonnie immediately liked Buck because he could play the guitar. She soon joined Owens on the Buck and Britt Show on station KTYL in Mesa. Bonnie and Buck then signed up with Mac MacAtee's Skillet Lickers band and toured throughout the western U.S. In 1948, the two were married and within a year, Alan Edgar "Buddy" Owens was born, followed by a second son, Michael Lynn Owens. Buck was picking oranges in the daytime and playing music at night, while Bonnie was a stay at home mom.

By 1951, the marriage was not working, and Bonnie and the two boys left for Bakersfield, where they moved in with Buck's aunt and uncle. Buck. soon followed his family to Bakersfield and hooked on with a local band, Bill Woods and the Orange Blossom Playboys. Though legally married, Buck and Bonnie remained separated because neither could afford a divorce. In order to support the children, Bonnie took several jobs as a carhop and cocktail waitress at the Clover Club and The Blackboard, two venues that were to play an important role in her career. At the Clover Club, while serving up drinks, she sang with Fuzzy Owen and Lewis Tally. Her first single was "Dear John Letter," a duet with Fuzzy Owen (1953) on the Tally label. In 1953, when the Clover Club band landed a job as the house band for The Trading Post Show on KERO-TV, Bonnie joined Fuzzy and Lewis as a singer.

Continuing her career as a cocktail waitress at

The Blackboard, Bonnie met **Merle Haggard** one evening in 1961; however, she did not see him again until he was a guest performer on The Trading Post Show. He had just finished a 2 ½ year sentence for burglary in San Quentin. By this time, Merle's marriage to Leona Hobbs was in shambles. Merle soon called Bonnie in Alaska where she was on tour and asked her to marry him, and they were hitched on June 28, 1965 in Tijuana, Mexico. Bonnie continued recording for independent labels with singles for Mar-Vel and Tally, including "I Traded My Heart for His Gold" (1953), "Why Don't Daddy Live Here Anymore" (1963), "Don't Take Advantage of Me" (1964), and a duet with Merle Haggard, "Just Between the Two of Us" (1964), a pairing suggested by her old friend, Fuzzy Owen, who had by then become Merle's manager.

Shortly after their marriage, Bonnie and Merle signed with the Capitol label. She soon released her first two solo albums, *Bonnie Owens* and *Don't Take Advantage of Me*, in 1965. Singles from those albums produced mid-chart scores, including "Number One Heel", "Consider the Children", and "Lead Me On". In 1966, Bonnie and Merle recorded their first duet album for Capitol, *Just Between the Two of Us*, just as the two of them were becoming major country music stars and among those bringing the Bakersfield Sound to national attention. Merle and Bonnie were named Best Vocal Group by the ACM in 1965, 1966, and 1967, and Bonnie was selected as Top Female Vocalist by the ACM in 1965. The two were also nominated for the Best Vocal Duo of the Year Award by the CMA in 1970.

Solo albums for Capitol during the next five years included *All of Me Belongs to You* (1967), *Your Tender Lovin' Care* (1967), *Somewhere Between* (1968), *Lead Me On* (1969), *A Hi-Fi to Cry By* (1969), and *Mother's Favorite Hymns* (1970), as well as another duet album with Merle in 1971, *The Land of Many Churches*.

By 1974 Bonnie had stopped touring with The Merle Haggard Show after almost ten years to focus on handling Haggard's business affairs. She soon filed for legal separation from Haggard and the marriage was dissolved in 1978. Bonnie and Merle remained good friends and when Merle married Leona Williams in 1978, Bonnie was a bridesmaid.

Bonnie Owens with Merle Haggard, circa late 1960s.

She eventually resumed touring with Merle and The Strangers in the 1980s and remained a part of the group through the early 2000s as a back-up singer for Merle. When the author saw them perform in Stillwater in 2003, as Merle sang he "was proud to be an Okie from Muskogee", he would leave a space in one of the choruses where "Muskogee" would ordinarily appear and Bonnie would yell "Blanchard!" Owens died at a Bakersfield hospice after a long bout with Alzheimer's, just about a month after Buck Owens died.

Owens, Buck

(b. 1929 – d. March 25, 2006)

Not from Oklahoma, although being born just about fifteen miles south of Lake Texoma in Sherman, Texas put him in the general vicinity, Alvis Edgar "Buck" Owens, Jr. emerged into the harsh world of a Depression-era sharecropping family. Like so many others of the era, the Owens family high-tailed it west in the late 1930s to try and survive.

Multiple #1 hits from the mid-1960s through the 1970s elevated Owens to the archetype of the Bakersfield Sound (really just another way of describing transplanted Oklahoma and Texas honky-tonk hauled west by Oklahomans and Texans). He is occasionally linked to Oklahoma because he was once married to Blanchard native, Bonnie Owens, whom he divorced in 1955, and because Owens recorded a nationally syndicated country music variety show based in Oklahoma City, from 1966 through 1973. According to Owens website, he was friends with Bud and Don Mathes, owners of Mathes Brothers Furniture in Oklahoma City. The OKC furniture magnates asked Owens to host half-hour television that they would sponsor locally. Owens would record the show, and then syndicate it nationally from there. *Buck Owens' Ranch* was taped before a Spanish-flavored set at WKY-TV in Oklahoma City.

Buck Owens (far righ) on set at WKY-TV, OKC, for the Buck Owens' Ranch Show.

At its peak, *Buck Owens' Ranch* ran in 100 markets from its Oklahoma City base where four times a year Buck would come into town and record a dozen more shows in one stint, using backing tracks he had already recorded at his studio back in California. The show made Buck a national star and an experience television host.

As a result, in 1969 Owens also began co-hosting *Hee Haw* with **Roy Clark**, however, it was obvious to anyone who watched both shows Owens was often performing the same material on both programs, and the owners of *Hee Haw* made him drop *Buck Owens' Ranch*. Interestingly, while *Buck Owens' Ranch* provided Buck national notoriety and credibility as country music artist, *Hee Haw* sort of "dumbed down" his musical stature, and Owens only achieved one more hit after the show ended, a 1988 duet with 1980s retro-country specialist, Dwight Yoakam, "Streets Bakersfield" which brought Buck full circle to the style he helped popularize.

www.buckowens.com

P

Page, Patti
(b. November 8, 1927 – d. January 1, 2013)

The most consistent beautiful voice of 20th century American popular music for over thirty years, Grammy Award winner Patti Page has sold more than 100 million records. With fifteen certified gold records, Page will always be remembered for her mega-crossover hit of 1950, "Tennessee Waltz", the most successful single in country music history with ten million sold, and to a lesser extent for her novelty song recorded for a children's album, "The Doggie in the Window". She has charted 111 songs on the pop, country, and R & B charts, and her hit "Confess" is the first song in music history to feature a vocalist performing both lead and backup vocals via overdubbing in the studio. Riding the smooth crest of her lilting voice, Page notched eighty-four *Billboard* Top 40 hits from over 100 albums from 1949 to 1982. With at least 160 singles during that period, Patti is one of the few artists to have had country hits in five decades.

Born Clara Ann Fowler in Claremore, Oklahoma, a town about fifteen miles northeast of Tulsa that humorist Will Rogers also called home, her father was a section hand for the Midland Valley Railroad and her mother picked cotton to help support the eleven Fowler children, eight of whom were girls, and all of whom sang in church. Since Clara had hoped for a career as an artist, and her family needed financial help at home, she applied for a job in the art department at KTUL radio in Tulsa. She did not stay in the art department long, however, when a KTUL radio executive heard her sing "Frankie and Johnny" at a local high school function. Soon thereafter, she began singing country songs on KTUL, and playing weekend gigs with Al Clauser and his Oklahoma Cowboys. Shortly thereafter, she was selected for KTUL's program *Meet Patti Page*, sponsored by the Page Milk Company, which provided the name she kept for the rest of her career. Having heard Page sing on the radio in 1946, Jack Rael, a baritone saxophonist and road manager for the Jimmy Joy Band, hired her as a vocalist for the group. The job became a 40-plus year partnership with Rael as her manager. Soon she was appearing as Patti Page in clubs and small theaters throughout the Mid-west, and by 1947 had moved to Chicago where she had her own show on the CBS Radio Network, sang with the Benny Goodman Septet, and signed with Mercury Records, with whom she released at least fifty-nine albums from 1955 through 1971.

In June of 1948, Patti had her first hit record, "Confess", on which she and Rael collaborated on the idea of adding her own backup vocals to the track to create the impression of a vocal group. While guitarist Les Paul received a lot of credit for popularizing the process of overdubbing, now standard practice in the music industry, Patti made the first multi-track recording with "Confess", in which she harmonizes with herself.

While her home state acknowledged her success in 1983 when she was inducted into the Oklahoma Hall of Fame, Patti has made significant impact of two important music and show business cities. As a result, she has a star on the Hollywood Walk of Fame, and her name is on the Country Music Walk of Fame in Nashville. In 1988, she released an album of Lou Stein's music, and garnered strong reviews for performances in New York City. In 1992, she received the Lynn Riggs Award, named after the Claremore, OK, author whose play, *Green Grow the Lilacs*, became the inspiration for Rogers and Hammerstein's **Oklahoma!.** In 1995 Mercury released three "Best of" compilations, with re-mastered versions of her early hits, complete with stunning cover photos from the era of Patti's outrageous pop music prominence in the 1950s.

When the first class of the Oklahoma Music Hall of Fame was discussed without the eventual nomination and voting process, Patti Page was a clear and obvious choice to be one of the hall of fame's inaugural inductees in 1997, along with **Woody Guthrie**, **Merle Haggard**, and **Claude "Fiddler" Williams**. That year, she also celebrated her 50th year in show business with a well-received concert at New York's Carnegie Hall, a 1998 live album of which earned Patti her first Grammy Award in 1999 as "Best Traditional Pop Music Performance". Also in 1998, a public television documentary, *Miss Patti Page: The Singing Rage*, featured classic songs, clips from her TV shows in the 1950s, and concert performances from her long career to that point. In 1999, Verve reissued her 1956 album, *Patti Page in the Land of Hi-Fi*, which finds Patti fronting a big band style orchestra on several jazz standards. In 2001, Patti released *New Tennessee Waltz* through the Gold label, including new renditions of "Tennessee Waltz" and "The Doggie in the Window", as well as guest vocal appearances from admirers Emmy Lou Harris, **Trisha Yearwood**, Kathy Mattea, and Alison Krauss.

In 2002, *Mercury* released an 80-song retrospective of her career, and Patti began doing a two-hour weekly radio show on the Music of Your Life radio network, featuring popular music in her vein from the big band era, the 1950s, and 1960s. Also in 2002, the Oklahoma Jazz Hall of Fame honored Patti with the *Living Legend Award*, the *Tulsa World* inducted her into their Spot Awards Hall of Fame, and she released a holiday album, *Sweet Sounds of Christmas*. In 2003, Patti released her first children's album (although "That Doggie in the Window" has been a hit with children since its release). Available exclusively on her website, *Child of Mine* had its genesis when Patti and her now-deceased husband (from 1990 forward), best friend (from 1973 forward), and traveling companion, Jerome "Jerry" Filicotto, raised two of their 13 grandchildren. The album includes her famous pet store classic, as well as "Rainbow Connection", "Ants in their Pants", and "Somewhere Over the Rainbow". The title track was written by Carole King.

In 2006, Page's "Mockin' Bird Hill" appeared on the Oklahoma Centennial musical tribute to the state, *Oklahoma Rising* (EMI), and in 2007, she gave a keynote speech and sang "Child of Mine" for the first international conference for the National Committee of Grandparents for Children's Rights, with the theme of "Caring for Children – A Global Challenge".

Ready to tell her own story, in 2009 Patti released her autobiography, *This is My Song: a memoir* on Kathdan Books, the introduction for which was written by another Oklahoma vocalist know for their smooth vocal abilities, **Vince Gill**. Publicity for the book announced, "Page takes her readers on a moving and heartwarming journey from her poor upbringing to her greatest challenges and successes as a woman. Patti shares her most personal thoughts, fears, and triumphs as she goes from a small-town girl from Oklahoma to one of the biggest selling female recording artists in history." Indeed the book does those things, but will not be summarized here. All Oklahoma music fans should pick up Page's memoir not only for the historic nature of her tale in relation to Oklahoma, but for also understanding the over-arching trends and shifts in American popular culture that helped shape her career, and recurring patterns in the music industry over generations no matter the technological delivery method of music to the people.

In 2010 Patti was an inductee into the America's Old Time Gospel Hall of Fame located in LeMars, Iowa, and made a sold-out hometown appearance in Claremore at the Robson Performing Arts Center. Also that year, she sang at the Hollywood Walk of Fame 50th Anniversary Celebration, in addition to nationwide concerts at select theatres, auditoriums, and concert halls. In April, 2011, the University of Central Oklahoma staged the World Premier of *Flipside: The Patti Page Story*, in which Patti herself appeared. Of course, "Flipside" refers to her mega-smash "Tennessee Waltz" becoming a hit as the B-side, or "Flipside", of the "Boogie Woogie Santa Claus" single.

Along with the obvious success of her musical career for more than sixty years, Patti's shift from popular music to country demonstrates a repeated theme in the *Oklahoma Music Guide*: the most successful artists are those who have more than one musical specialty. As a result of genre mutability, technical knowledge, songwriting skills, or music business acumen, musical artists who develop more than one aspect of music have a better chance of success. Prior to her 2010 concert in Claremore, Patti Page told a crowd of junior high students in an afternoon assembly, "Always remember the music business is two words: *music*, that's the fun part; and *business*, that's the serious part". Before the business could honor Patti Page with a lifetime achievement award from the National Academy of Recording Arts and Sciences in February, 2013, she died on New Year's Day of that year at home in Encinitas, California.

Patti Page with OMG author Hugh Foley, Claremore, OK. 2010.

www.misspattipage.com

Parker, Andy

(b. March 17, 1913 – d. October 2, 1977)

Best known as the singing cowboy on NBC radio's *Death Valley Days* and leader of one of the early western music and vocal harmony groups (The Plainsmen), singer, songwriter, and guitarist Andy Parker was born in Mangum, Oklahoma, a Greer County town of about 3,500 residents located in the southwestern part of the state. At age 16, Andy made his radio debut on KGMP in Elk City, Oklahoma. In 1937, he relocated to San Francisco where he began to appear as the singing cowboy in *Death Valley Days* on NBC radio, a run that would last until 1941. During World War II, Andy worked in a Bay Area defense. He also sang on radio station KGO on Dude Martin's Roundup before moving to the Los Angeles area in 1944. With lyrics common to the singing cowboy era, but not too far away from his childhood experiences in Mangum, or at least the romance of it, Parker's groups featured first-rate musicians, peppy rhythms, smart harmonies, and the signature element of an accordion along with fiddles and steel guitars, a unique imprint for the Western groups

Within two years, Andy formed The Plainsmen, a trio composed of himself, Charlie Morgan (guitar), Clem Smith (bass), George Bamby (accordion), and steel guitar icon, Joaquin Murphy.

After their film debut in Cowboy Blues with Ken Curtis, by 1946 they had released some recordings on the Coast label, and began to appear regularly on the Hollywood Barn

Andy Parker (far left) with The Plainsmen.

Dance on CBS radio, as well as Sunrise Salute on local radio station KNX in Hollywood. Within another short period, the act became Andy Parker and the Plainsmen, recording more than 200 radio transcription discs for Capitol Records. Oklahoman **Noel Boggs**, another extraordinary steel guitar player, also spent time with the group. Although they appeared in several Western movies, and on several television shows, they never reached the level of fame of other Western singing groups, such as the Sons of the Pioneers. However, Andy and Charlie Morgan blipped into the American popular culture consciousness when they performed the theme song with Marilyn Monroe for the 1954 film, River of No Return.

When Morgan left in 1956, Andy dissolved the group. Parker is also noted for his songwriting, including the popular "Trail Dust," which can be found on Rounder Record's Stampede! Western Music's Late Golden Era 1945-1960. In his later years, Andy suffered from a heart condition that prevented him from working and touring. He retired in San Francisco, and died in 1977. In the 2000s, a few CDs of Andy Parker and the Plainsmen's work have been released, to include Texas Belle, a collection of Texas-themed songs, but also including "Cowboy's Meditation", "Rooty Toot Galoot", "A Calico Apron and a Gingham Gown", and "Press Along to the Big Corral". Another release, Volume 2 of the Coast Recordings included "Short Snort Polk", "I'm Gonna

Gallup into Gallup", and "I Learned to Love You Too Late". In 2010, Capitol Nashville released a Tex Ritter CD, Pecos Bill, which featured Andy Parker and the Plainsmen backing up Ritter on songs recorded in the 1950s, and released then as Songs of the Western Screen (Capitol, 1959). Also in the 2000s, Audiophonic released Call of the Rollin' Plains as part of its Western Swing Series, including forty songs and liner notes written by Andy's son, Joe.

References
Aaker, Everett. *Television Western Players of the Fifties: A Biographical Encyclopedia of All Regular Cast Members in Western Series, 1949-1959.* (McFarland, 2007).

McCloud, Barry, et Al. *Definitive Country: The Ultimate Encyclopedia of Country Music and Its Performers.*

Parker, Billy
(b. July 19, 1938)

Recognized as one of the nation's top country music disc jockeys, having won Country Music Association and Academy of Country Music honors for Disc Jockey of the Year five times in the 1970s and 1980s, and being inducted into the Country Music Disc Jockey Hall of Fame in 1992, Billy Parker was born in Okemah, Oklahoma, also the hometown of **Woody Guthrie**. Although known primarily for his deejaying work in which he has always been the quintessential communicator with a friendly style that makes listeners feel as if he knows them personally, Billy has also enjoyed success as a country music performer. He began singing and playing guitar at age eleven, and made his professional debut on the Big Red Jamboree, a local Tulsa radio program. He also spent some time later on the Ozark Jubilee. After performing in local clubs, he began his first disc jockey work in 1959 on Tulsa radio station KFMJ.

Billy Parker, Oklahoma Music Hall of Fame Induction, 2005, Muskogee, OK.

By 1963, Billy landed on radio station KFDI in Wichita, Kansas, where he was the daytime disc jockey. The same year, he recorded his first single, "The Line Between Love and Hate", followed by a second single, "I'm Drinking All the Time", released in 1966, both on the Sims label. Also in 1963, in a nationwide poll, he was voted Mr. DJ which resulted in a guest spot on Nashville's WSM, the radio home of the Grand Ole

Opry. Two years later, he joined Ernest Tubb and his Troubadours and remained with the group until 1971, when he was hired by Tulsa's **KVOO**, the Voice of Oklahoma, as a country music deejay.

Continuing his recording work as well as his on air responsibilities, Billy charted his first hit single in 1976 with "It's Bad When You're Caught (With the Goods)", a track from his Sunshine label album, *Average Man*. Several singles followed: "Thanks E.T. Thanks a Lot", a tribute to Ernest Tubb, and "Lord If I Make It to Heaven (Can I Bring My Own Angel Along)", one of his most popular recordings. During the late 1970s, his most successful singles were "You Read Between the Lines" and "Until the Next Time".

Billy's music resurfaced in the 1980s with several cuts on Soundwaves, his new recording label, including "I'll Drink to That", "I See an Angel Every Day", "If I Ever Need a Woman", "Who Said Love Was Fair?" and "Love Don't Know a Lady (From a Honky Tonk Girl)". He also appeared on an album of duets, *Something Old, Something New*, which featured "Who's Gonna Sing the Last Country Song" (with Darrell McCall) and "Too Many Irons in the Fire" (with **Cal Smith**). After moving to the Canyon Creek label in 1988, Billy charted several singles, such as "It's Time for Your Dreams to Come True", "You Are My Angel", "She's Sittin' Pretty", and "Who You're Gonna Turn To" (duet with Rosemary Sharp). In 1990, he released a gospel album, *I'll Speak Out for You, Jesus*, for which he earned the Country Personality Award from the International Gospel Music Association. Bear Family, the German company, released all his Soundwaves recordings on an album entitled *Billy Parker and Friends* in 1990.

In addition to the aforementioned honors, Billy was inducted into the Western Swing Hall of Fame in 1993, and received the Oklahoma Association of Broadcasters Lifetime Achievement Award in 1995. Billy remained with KVOO from 1971 through 2002 when the 50,000 watt AM blowtorch converted its format to newstalk, after which he did a weekly show on KVOO FM, and later on KXBL FM in Tulsa where in 2011 he continued playing classic country music, sharing his encyclopedic knowledge of country music history, and talking to folks who listen like he's known them all their lives. And, in some cases, he has. Overall, Billy had twenty-two *Billboard* chart entries, performed with Ernest Tubb, Bob Wills, and Red Foley, and appeared on the *Grand Ole Opry*, *Hee Haw*, and TNN's *Nashville Now*.

While his legacy is significant enough in country music as a performer (he was inducted into the Oklahoma Music Hall of Fame in 2005, the same year as **Toby Keith** and **Tommy Allsu**p), but Billy Parker will always be remembered as the one KVOO deejay known by truckers, housewives, farm and ranch people as a trusted radio friend. He's known by hundreds, if not thousands of musicians, as the conduit for their music to the fans they hoped to reach during his career as a country music disc-jockey. On the inside track, colleagues in radio broadcasting recognize Billy Parker as a case study in how one should operate as a radio communicator and music media professional. In 2013, he could still be heard Saturday mornings from 8 a.m. to 10 p.m. and Sunday nights from 8 p.m. to 10 p.m. on Billy Parker's Country Junction on Big Country 99.5 KXBL-FM, Tulsa.

Reference
"Billy Parker," www.bigcountry995.com (accessed September 1, 2011).

Parker, Jeffrey Gray
(b. 1956)

Multi-instrumentalist, music teacher, studio artist, and recording engineer Jeffrey Gray Parker was born in Arkansas City, Kansas in 1956, but raised in Newkirk, Oklahoma. After a few years in St. Louis, Parker moved to Norman in 1970, and lived there until 1989. Next, he headed north to Stillwater where he lived from 1989 to 1998, played guitar with all the **Red Dirt** luminaries, taught guitar lessons at Daddy-O's Music Store, set up his Cimarron Sound Lab, and recorded his first independent album, *Blood of Many Nations* (1997), the first of three albums under his studio alter ego, Coyote Zen, which are influenced not only by the red dirt sound but and his own American Indian background. *Blood of Many Nations*, *Medicine Dog* (2002), and *Coyote Zen* (Paw, 2004) also fuse multiple world music elements into a sonic imprint that diverts from the usual twang and storytelling of red dirt roads, and merges onto the tangled and tethered pathways of new age/jazz/folk and rock. As a touring and performing guitarist for more than thirty years, he has traveled extensively throughout the United States with a wide variety of bands from multiple genres. Jeff has shared the stage in an opening capacity, or performed with acts such as Jefferson Starship, Alice Cooper, Buck Owens, Rodney Crowell, Johnny Paycheck, Baillie & the Boys, Ray Wylie Hubbard, Jerry Jeff Walker, Kevin Welch, Jimmie LaFave, Brewer & Shipley, The Great Divide, Cross Canadian Ragweed, Rita Coolidge, Ricochet, and others. Parker has also had his music used in various film and television projects, as well as radio and television commercials.

Jeffrey Gray Parker

Aside from Jeffrey Parker's individual releases, his Cimarron Sound Lab in Stillwater was the site for the recording of *Red Dirt Sampler, Volume 1: A Stillwater Songwriters' Collective*. The album is a primer for red dirt music fans. Songs by all the first generation of the sound's luminaries, Tom Skinner, Brad James (lead guitarist for the Organic Boogie Band), Mike McClure, Greg Jacobs, Bob Childers are on the CD, as well as songs co-written by Parker with Skinner and Bob Kline. A **Cherokee Nation** citizen, Parker relocated his Cimarron Sound Lab to Cherokee County, near Tahlequah, in 1998. Since then, for the past several years, Jeffrey has been responding to a demand for his original music, which has been featured internationally on PBS and the Discovery Network. Additionally, his work has also been featured in exhibits such as the Smithsonian Museum of the American Indian in Washington, D.C. Jeffrey has also worked with the CMA/CMT winning Carrie Underwood, Nick Wheeler (All-American Rejects), Grammy winner Rita Coolidge, the NAMMY Award winning

Hugh W. Foley / 619

Cherokee National Youth Choir, Nammy Winner Gil Silverbird, and the world renowned Tulsa Oratorio Chorus.

With regard to his film and television credits, Parker composed and produced music for *King of the Cowboys* –A Gabriel/Rodeo Circus Films production for the Discovery Network by Academy Award-nominated director/producer Ramzy Telley. The film aired worldwide on The Learning Channel and The Travel Channel. He also composed and produced music for the documentary, *American Bullfighter*, a Miramar/Unipix documentary on bullfighters and rodeo clowns, also by Ramzy Telley, and also for the Discovery Network, which aired worldwide on The Learning Channel and The Travel Channel. Parker has also contributed to several noteworthy student projects, scoring *Melvin: A Midwestern Tale,* written and directed by Travis Graalman (now of Miramax), which won the "Outstanding Achievement in Original Score" Award at NYU's prestigious Tisch School of the Arts-First Run Festival 99. Parker also scored the film soundtrack for *Where the Dreamers Go*, an Oklahoma State University art educational documentary that aired on Oklahoma Educational Television's *Oklahoma Magazine* and was distributed to Oklahoma schools for curriculum testing and study.

Other film work includes Parker composing and producing music for the film soundtrack to *Reflections on the Little Bighorn*, a PBS nationwide documentary produced by the students and staff at the University of Nebraska-Lincoln, College of Journalism and Mass Communication. He also composed and produced music for the film soundtrack to the Oregon Public Broadcast Radio production of *Unfinished Journey: the Lewis and Clark Expedition*, which aired nationwide on public radio. Additionally, his music accompanies the Oregon Public Broadcasting television production, *The History* Detective, a program devoted to exploring the complexities and mysteries of history. Parker has also produced, engineered, and created music for high profile museum exhibits, to include the Trail of Tears Exhibit at the Cherokee Heritage Center in Tahlequah, and the Our Universes Exhibit at the Smithsonian Museum of the American Indian in Washington, D.C.

As an album producer and engineer, Jeffrey Parker has more than thirty albums to his credit in several genres, such as Native American music, country, rock, gospel, folk, and jazz. He has also been co-producer/engineer for several Cherokee Nation projects: *Cherokee Gospel Music Nation Holiday* 2000, and the 2002 Native American Music Award (Nammy) nominee *Cherokee Children's Songs"*: the 2002 Nammy-winning *Voices of The Creator's Children* featuring Rita Coolidge, and 2003's Nammy nomination, *Building One Fire*, featuring Gil Silverbird. He was also co-producer/engineer on Bliss McCain's *Grandview* which won an 2001 OMA (Ozark Music Awards) for Album Of The Year. Back in the red dirt world, he was also co-producer for Cross Canadian Ragweed's *Carney* and *Live and Loud* albums.

During the 1990's Jeffrey was an integral part of producing Oklahoma's vibrant red dirt music community, playing with, producing and/or recording a number of its notables, footnotes, and note busters, such singer/songwriters as Greg Jacobs, Tom Skinner, Bob Childers, Bill Erickson, Randy Pease, all for the singer-songwriter label, Binky-UTR-Squirrel Records of Baton Rouge, LA. He also worked with Farmboy, Dusty Children, The Farm Couple, The Great Divide, and Mike McClure. His total list of production clients in the red dirt, country, and folk rock realms is quite wide and interesting. Additional musicians who have relied on Parker's expertise for their recordings include **Byron Berline**, Jim Paul Blair, Ramona Reed, City Moon, Terry "Buffalo" Ware, **Jimmy LaFave, Jason Boland,** and the **Red Dirt Rangers.** His production of American Indian music includes previously mentioned artists such as Coolidge and Silverbird, as well as Choogie Kingfisher, JB Dreadfulwater, Ryan Wahpekeche, **John Timothy**, and The Adair Family Singers. He has also recorded the Northeastern State University Jazz Band, and several other local/regional jazz and blues artists such as Bobby Watson, Scott Wendholt, Arthur White, and Will Campbell. In 2011, Jeffrey continued working on a variety of projects to be released in 2012, played shows throughout Texas and Oklahoma, especially the new casino circuit in Oklahoma that is providing work for a number of musicians in the region. While not known to much of the public, Parker is one of Oklahoma's primary working musicians and music producers, and a further indication of a theme that has recurred throughout the *Oklahoma Music Guide*, to wit, a successful music career is built over years of dedication, and having more than one ability in the music world enhances one's chance for long-term success. As with many Oklahoma artists, Jeffrey Parker has made a career out of being able to cross musical boundaries as a musician, and also by refining several music industry skills, such as producing, engineering, and scoring music for visual media.

www.cimsound.com

Patty, Sandi
(b. July 14, 1957)

With a voice that soars to points of undeniable glory, Sandra Faye "Sandi" Patty has won thirty-nine Dove Awards, five Grammy Awards, and four *Billboard* music awards on the way to charting three platinum and five gold albums, and totaling more than eleven million units sold. Often referred to simply as "The Voice" of Contemporary Christian Music, Sandi Patty was born to Ron and Carolyn Patty in Oklahoma City, although she was raised in Anderson, Indiana and San Diego, California. Her singing debut was at the age of two when she performed "Jesus Loves Me" at the First Church of God in Anderson when she was two-years-old. Along with two younger brothers, Sandi formed the Ron Patty Family Singers who performed across the United States during school breaks over the summer and holidays.

Sandi took voice lessons at San Diego State University, and later graduated with a degree in music from Anderson College in Indiana, where she partially supported herself singing commercial jingles. During her college days, she met and married John Helvering, who helped produce her debut album, *For My Friends*.

Sandi Patty, 2011

On the album, a printer's mistake changed her name from Patty to Patti, and the name remained for some time until she changed back to her name's original spelling.

After her first independent album found its way to executives for Singspiration! Records, she was signed to that label and released her first national album in 1979, *Sandi's Song*, for which she wrote the title track. With the release of her 1981 album, *Love Overflowing,* and the resulting industry recognition in 1982 that garnered her Dove Awards for Gospel Artist of the Year and Female Vocalist of the Year from the Dove Awards, Patty's career began an ascendancy that has been heading skyward ever since. Her 1983 album, *More Than Wonderful* sold a million copies (platinum), and the follow-up album later that same year, *The Gift Goes On*, sold another 500,000 copies (gold). Her 1984 album, *Songs from the Heart*, repeated gold status, and she launched a successful U.S. tour. For the rest of the 1980s, Sandi remained contemporary Christian music's biggest star, recording five more successful albums that decade: *Hymns Just For You* (platinum), *Morning Like This* (platinum), *Make His Praise Glorious* (gold), *Sandi Patty and the Friendship Company*, and *The Finest Moments* (gold), all on the Word label.

In the 1990s, Sandi continued to produce albums at a prolific rate, including 1990's *Another Time...Another Place* (certified gold and Grammy winner), *Open for Business* and *More Than Wonderful* in 1991, *Celebrate Christmas*, a 1992 album which sold more than 1.5 million copies, *Le Voyage* in 1993, *Quiet Reflections* in 1994, *Find It on the Wings* in 1995, *O Holy Night*, *An American Songbook*, and *It's Christmas!* (1.3 million seller), all in 1996, *Artist of My Soul* and *Libertad Me Das* in 1998 (Dove Award for Best Spanish Language Album), *Together: Sandi Patty and Kathy Troccoli* in 1999, *These Days* in 2000, and *All the Best...Live* in 2001. The latter features guest appearances by various Patty family members. Worth noting is the collaboration of Sandi and Kathy Troccoli, another CCM vocalist, on the *Together* album comprised of thirteen tracks of pop tunes with emphasis on Sandi's love for George Gershwin, such as "Summertime", "The Man I Love", and "Embraceable You". Her 1998 album, *Artist of My Soul*, featured a highly charged emotional song, "Breathe on Me", reflected her personal desire to regain her audience after a well-publicized and messy end to her first marriage.

Lined up in an impressive industry trophy case, Sandi's honors include five Grammy Awards, including Best Gospel Performance-Duo or Group for the song "More Than Wonderful" with Larnelle Harris (1984), Best Gospel Performance-Duo or Group for the song "I've Just Seen Jesus" with Larnelle Harris (1986), Best Gospel Performance-Duo or Group for the song "They Say" with Deniece Williams (1987), Best Gospel Performance-Female for the album *Morning Like This* (1987), and Best Pop Gospel Album for *Another Time...Another Place* (1991). Moreover, Sandi's thirty-nine Dove Awards include eleven, consecutive Female Vocalist of the Year honors. With a career spanning thirty-one albums over thirty years of recordings, the Nashville, Tennessee-based Gospel Music Hall of Fame surprised no one by inducting her in 2007. She earned *Billboard Magazine*'s Inspirational Artist of the Year four times, and in 2008 and 2009 received nominations for Female Vocalist of the Year for her two albums of those years, *Songs for the Journey* (2008) and *Simply Sandi* (2009).

Among her other talents, Sandi has co-written several inspirational songs, including "Miracles Can Happen", "Masterpiece", "Beautiful Feet", "In the Name of the Lord", "There is a Savior", "Willing to Wait", "Who Will Call Him King of Kings", "Lift Up the Lord", "Doxology", and "All this Time (Anna's Song)", a tribute to one of her daughters. In 1997, Sandi was lead singer at the Presidential Inaugural Gala of Bill Clinton. She has performed with numerous symphony orchestras including those in Indianapolis, Dallas, Atlanta, Boston Pops, Cincinnati Pops, Houston, Louisville, Nashville, St. Louis, New York, Baltimore, and the two in her native state in Tulsa and Oklahoma City. In 2001, Sandi released *For God and Country*, a multi-artist production, commemorating the September 11 terrorist attack on the World Trade Center. She contributed three of her most celebrated renditions of "The Star Spangled Banner", "Amazing Grace", and "God Bless America". Sandi is also a published author with four books to her credit, none more gripping than her 2007 work, *Falling Forward… Into His Arms of Grace*. Regarding the book, Patty writes in her author notes that she discusses "the nitty-gritty details of recovering from a major life crisis," and "gets real about how it feels to 'fail' in some way." In 2009, Patty returned to Oklahoma where she lived in the Deer Creek area of Oklahoma County as of 2011, and where she based her operations in music recording and performing, publishing, and Christian service work. Sandi also started a record label on which she released the first solo album by Heather Payne, a founding member of **Point of Grace**. Sandi has continued performing nationally, but also has taken time out to perform a benefit concert for White Fields, a home for troubled boys in Piedmont. In the summer of 2011, she headlined Independence Day concerts presented by the Oklahoma City Philharmonic. By fall of that year, she released a cookbook, *Around the Table with Sandi Patty: Faith, Family, and Food*, and continued a steady slate of concerts across the United States through 2012 .

www.sandipatty.com

Pawnee Nation
(The Pawnee began removing to Indian Territory in 1875 from a reservation on the Platt River in Nebraska.)

With a tribal presence on the central Great Plains reaching beyond the European history marks of the 16th and 17th century to at least 700 years ago, the Pawnee people are linked linguistically and culturally to other Caddoan-speaking peoples of the Great Plains, such as the Caddo, Wichita, and Arikira. With a lifestyle subsistence based in both agriculture and bison hunting, the Pawnee lived in the river valleys of what became Kansas and Nebraska, often in permanent villages made of earthen homes. Like many Plains people, the Pawnee formed warrior societies to organize military and hunting efforts. The tribe also developed a complex understanding of the stars, mapping out many aspects of the night skies over the Great Plains and coordinating it with the Pawnee hierarchical belief system. In the early 18th century, the Pawnee numbered some 10,000 people along the Platt River in Nebraska. Due to encroachment from neighboring tribes to the west and north, as well as intrusion by non-Indian Americans from the east, the Pawnee became a "friendly tribe" to the United States government, with tribal members of all ages and genders fighting to preserve Pawnee life and livelihood. The Pawnee also had to contend with enemy tribes who were bolstered by American "placation gifts" of firearms, which often were turned on the Pawnee. Like other Plains people, the Pawnee also began raiding southern and southwestern tribes for horses, which further enhance Pawnee military abilities and stature on the Plains.

While the tribe provided the U.S. Army with valuable scouts during the Plains Indian wars, the scourges of American settlement, such as smallpox, ravaged the Pawnee people's camps and villages from the southern to north central plains. Some documentation exists the infection of the Pawnee with smallpox was intentional by non-Indian traders on the southern Plains, and spread north with traveling parties.[1] Along with being decimated by the disease for which they had no defense nor fast enough inoculation, and following further encroachment from all sides on their villages and homes in Nebraska, the Pawnee did not have much choice but to accept the sale of their reservation in 1876, and move the entire body of Pawnee to a location in what is now Pawnee County in north central Oklahoma. The move placed the tribe closer to their ancient relatives, the Wichita, with whom the tribe was once one, and rekindled a formal visitation and gift-giving exchange that exists to the present day.

Contemporarily, the primary governmental entity of the Pawnee is an elected business council, but the tribe may also still be viewed through the lens of four different bands, or tribal groups, each of which has its own chiefs, second chiefs, and other elected officers. The bands include the Chaui "Grand," the Kitkehahki "Republican," the Pitahawirata "Tappage," and the Skidi "Wolf". As with other modern American Indian tribes, the Pawnee are developing economic enterprises and providing services to their people from the tribe's headquarters in Pawnee, Oklahoma. In 2012, the tribe's enrollment is more than 3,250.[2]

Anthropologically speaking, the Pawnee have been documented about as much as anyone with multiple studies done with the tribe as the field of anthropology evolved in the early 20th century. Readers can learn as much about the Pawnee as just about any other tribe in North America. Musically speaking, the tribe's song catalogue is also as rich, well-preserved, and active as any tribe in the United States. As noted on their tribal website, the Pawnee support various honor dances, Native American Church meetings, and hand games, all of which serve as activities in which Pawnee music is performed in the context for which it was created. The Pawnee Indian Veterans also host a Memorial Day Dance, a Veterans Day Dance, and a Christmas Day Dance, as well as organizing the Pawnee Indian Veterans Homecoming and Powwow since 1946, originally held to honor and recognize returning World War II veterans, a purpose it still serves today. Additionally, several Pawnee people are active and highly noted as singers in the intertribal powwow world.

Exploring the world of Pawnee music is to gain insight into the whole perspective of how significant music has always been to American Indians. Looking at just the list of song titles collected by government ethnologists and ethnomusicologists from 1906 through 1936 illustrates the concept of Native people having a song for practically every occasion in life worthy of being marked with an inspired musical product. While various scholarly treatises have explored aspects of music along with ancient Pawnee ceremonies, as well as the embracement by the Pawnee of the Ghost Dance religion and its accompanying songs,[3] the first and still primary exploration of Pawnee musical traditions is Frances Densmore's 1929 publication for the Smithsonian Institution, *Pawnee Music*, which documents the broad palate of Pawnee music.[4] Densmore details music from the various Pawnee warrior societies ("Lance Dance" and "War

Songs"), elaborate and highly complex ceremonies "Morning Star Ceremony", along with "songs of affection," several "Chiefs' songs," and various unclassified songs such as "Everything Will Be Right," "The Message of a Star," "Song to Comfort a Child's Grief," and "Song Received from a Dead Relative." Densmore made eighty-six recordings of Pawnee singers in 1919 and 1920 in Pawnee, Oklahoma, but only seventeen of the songs have been released by the Library of Congress on *Songs of the Pawnee and Songs of the Northern Ute* (L25).

Retired Oklahoma State University professor, classical musician, and ethnomusicologist, Evan Tonsing of Glencoe, Oklahoma, has devoted tremendous efforts to documenting what recordings exist in the Library of Congress and Smithsonian Institution pertaining to Pawnee music history. He has noted that only one song, "Ghost Dance 9 possibly of Cheyenne Origin," is available from the nearly forty Pawnee songs recorded by German field recording specialist, E.M. von Hornbostel, in 1906, and later released in 1963 on a compilation, *The Demonstration Recordings of E.M. von Hornbostel* (Smithsonian/Folkways). He has

Pawnee Singers lead dancers into the arena at the annual Pawnee Veterans Homecoming.

further petitioned the Library of Congress to release the sixty-nine unissued recordings that Densmore made in Pawnee, and references in her text. Tonsing also explains that the seven recordings issued on the album *Plains: Comanche, Cheyenne, Kiowa, Caddo, Wichita, Pawnee* (L39) are likely only a portion of the Pawnee recordings made by Willard Rhodes between 1937 and 1951 when he was the director of Indian Education for the Bureau of Indian Affairs. The album includes a "Pawnee Prayer song," "Hand Game song," "Ghost Dance song," "Flag song," and "War Dance song," among others either sung by Philip Gover or Frank Murie. The final major historical recording of Pawnee music was released by Smithsonian/Folkways, *Music of the Pawnee* (FE 4334), and is available through the Smithsonian's website as a compact disc or electronic download. The collection has at least seventy Pawnee songs sung by Mark Evarts and recorded in 1936 in Madison, New Jersey. Along with many historically significant ceremonial songs, love songs, war dance songs, and animal dance songs, the collection includes a song that demonstrates how American Indian music often historicizes events with a lyric that often needs explanation, but provides a memory aid for tribal history when that song's context is fully revealed. Only titled "War Dance song," the song refers to the first council of Pawnee chiefs with the U.S. government in 1811 in St. Louis. The singer repeats in the Pawnee language, "They are all sitting around against the walls talking." Fortunately, almost every song on the album contains an explanation of the song's title, meaning, and translation.[5] The album also includes Evarts singing one of the very few Pawnee peyote songs ever released commercially, although some do exist contemporarily via the commercial video sharing website, youtube.com, sung by Aaron Adson.

Like many other Plains tribes, the Pawnee adopted the Ghost Dance behind the backs of their government agents in 1891, and like all other Plains tribes, the Pawnee ultimately put down the Ghost Dance due to governmental pressures. However, tribal members also absorbed the Native American Church, and added their own language and worldview to the pan-Indian religion that spread from the Comanche, Kiowa, and Caddo in southwestern Oklahoma to the tribes in north central Oklahoma and beyond. Interestingly, few of the authoritative texts on the Native American Church, or Peyote Religion, have much to say about the Pawnee version of the Native American Church, other than to say it came to the Pawnee from Quanah Parker, the Comanche leader often credited with spreading the way of worship to several tribes based in northern Oklahoma.[6] Prior to becoming an officially sanctioned church, however, the Pawnee ceremonial way in the Native American Church tipi was a primary location for tribally specific healing and business to take place. While contemporary Pawnee members of the Native American Church sing a wide variety of Pawnee songs in the all-night services, using the traditional instruments of a small water drum and gourd rattle, elders do and did not believe the songs should be recorded and sold commercially. As a result, very few recordings of publicly available Pawnee peyote songs exist. While that particular genre of Pawnee music may well be out of earshot for most listeners, Pawnee presence in the world of intertribal powwow music world is far from scant. In fact, some of the best recordings made of intertribal powwow music have been made by singers of Pawnee heritage, or intertribal singing groups led by Pawnees.

As noted in the *OMG II* entry for the **Otoe-Missouria Tribe**, many members of the original northern style powwow singing group from Oklahoma, the Brave Scout Singers, were both Pawnee and Otoe, not surprising since the two tribes are located near each other, and tribal members have been attending many of the same social and ceremonial functions, as well as boarding schools, for over 130 years in what is now north central Oklahoma. As mentioned earlier, the Pawnee and the Arikira are ancient relatives, connected by their mutual Caddoan linguistic background. As a result, once the Pawnee Indian Veterans started the annual Homecoming and Powwow in 1946, Arikira singers visited the Pawnee for many years and sang in a higher-pitched style than most Southern powwow singers who traditionally remain in a lower register. With this connection to the northern singing style as their original style, singers with Pawnee heritage fit right in with Brave Scout founder Sidney Moore, Sr., who initiated the northern singing style in Oklahoma after traveling among northern tribal dances, and which can be heard on the landmark Canyon Records 1980 recording, *Brave Scout Singers (Otoe-Missourian & Pawnee)*. Original members of the Brave Scout singers with Pawnee heritage include Pete Moore, Sr., George Shields, Sr., Terry Williams, and George Williams. One cannot go very far at all in 20th century Pawnee music and/or dance without running into one of many members of the Moore family who are known widely throughout the intertribal powwow world as acclaimed singers and dancers, as well as respected ceremonial and traditional leaders among the Pawnee people of the modern era, many of whom prefer to remain under the radar of American popular culture, and so are not singled out here.

Among notable Pawnee powwow singers, Vance Horsechief, Jr. (b. January 10, 1954, Pawnee) was widely recognized for his singing and song-making skills until his untimely death in automobile accident, on October 25, 2000. A full-blooded Pawnee, Horsechief performed as a singer and dancer with the internationally known singing group, Up with People, in 1973. Later, he organized the powwow singing group, Pawnee YellowHorse, composing most of the group's songs, many of which are in the Pawnee language. Pawnee YellowHorse released two albums, *Spirit of the Plains* (Without Rez Productions, 1997) and *Look to the Stars* (Echo Hawk, 2000). Additional singers on the Pawnee YellowHorse recordings include Phil Minthorn, Gary Leadingfox, Bryan Hodshire, Bunky Echo-Hawk, Walter Echo-Hawk, Jason Lightfoot, Debbie Echo-Hawk, Jennifer Folsom-Minthorn, Colleen Gorman, Kay Hodshire, Vance Horsechief III, Greg Leadingfox, C.D. Moore, Marcie Muth, and Carrie Howell.

Also recognized for several stellar powwow recordings, as well as many appearances around the United States is the Pawnee-based southern Plains singing group, Southern Thunder. Of particular note are three recordings for Tony Isaacs and the Indian House label, to include *From the Heart: Powwow Songs Recorded at Cabazon Reservation, CA* (IH 2083, 1995), *Live* (IH 2085, 1997) recorded at the Citizen Potawatomi Nation's 24th Annual Powwow at Shawnee, Oklahoma in 1997, and *Listen to the Thunder* (IH 2086, 1999) recorded at the Pawnee Nation Reserve Tribal Campground in June, 1999. All three recordings demonstrate not only the powerful presence and pace of Southern Plains powwow singing, as well as many songs composed by group members in the Pawnee language, the albums also feature the strong, practically operatic voice of lead singer Frank Adson and his many family members, helpers, and friends who create a bold and powerful sound on these collections. No better representative example exists of Southern Plains powwow singing backed up by a soaring women's chorus than these recordings. Many singers are listed on the liner notes of each compact disc, several of whom have Pawnee heritage. A representative sample of singers may be gleaned from the 1999 *Listen to the Thunder* recording, to include Aaron Adson, Frank M. Adson, Herb Adson, Gilbert Beard, Jason Lightfoot, Jordan Moore, Ron Rice, Jr., Jimmy Starr, Kyle Tipps, George Vallier, Crystal Pewo Lightfoot, Erin Plumley, Ni'vy Starr, Georgia Tiger, and Julia Tiger. While not detailed here, the GRAMMY-nominated Southern singing group, **Young Bird**, has several Pawnee connections, to include leader Curtis Hamilton-Young Bird, and additional singers with Pawnee heritage, such as Ron James, Sr., Ben Nakai, Jeff McClellan, Rusty Diamond, and Sunny Rose Yellowmule.[8]

Pawnee Yellowhorse, 2007

While many aspects of historic and

contemporary Pawnee music traditions have either been documented or shared by their composers, some Pawnee music remains only as part of the ceremonies for which it was intended, such as the Young Dog Dances, Skidi Men's Dances, or Native American Church songs, with limited exceptions of where a few recordings of those songs exist in the various archives already mentioned. Pawnee Christian hymns also are still sung contemporarily in Christian church services, but have yet to be fully documented, although a 2011 tribal survey indicated a desire for such a collection was high on the list of those who filled out the survey to provide the tribe with actionable administrative directions. Softly sung meditational songs, or hymns, have long been part of Pawnee music history as indicated from previously mentioned scholarly surveys, but the songs that are noted as "hymns" are usually related to a traditional aspect of Pawnee life such as meditations on the stars, life and death, or agriculture. Of the many good things about modern Pawnee music is that the songs often use Pawnee words, thereby vitalizing the language and passing it on to all those who learn the songs, which, by all counts, will continue being sung under the southern Plains skies for many generations to come, as those Pawnees who sacrificed so much all those years ago would have wanted it to be.

www.pawneenation.org

Notes

1. One of the most stated "facts" without documentation in American Indian history is that Native Americans, especially Plains tribes, were intentionally infected by the U.S. Army with smallpox, a version of germ warfare during the Plains Indian Wars. While a few, well-known documented examples exist of pre-colonial use of smallpox as a weapon by British slave traders against the Cherokee, the British forces against enemy American Indians (and again colonists led by George Washington), no one has ever documented the intentional transmission of smallpox to Plains Indians. However, one such mention exists in the papers of missionary Isaac McCoy, who traveled extensively in Indian Territory in the 1830s and 1840s. See McCoy's *History of the Baptist Missions* (Washington: William M. Morrison, 1840), pages 441 and 442 for more details on McCoy's understanding of how traders between Missouri and Santa Fe, New Mexico, being harassed by Pawnees and Comanches, transmitted smallpox to Pawnees via tobacco and clothing, which then spread to northern Pawnee villages after people returned from the south who had been visiting their relatives. For a fairly reliable text on Pawnee history, see Geoge E. Hyde, *The Pawnee Indians* (Norman: University of Oklahoma Press, 1951).
2. www.pawneenation.org
3. For insight into a variety of ancient Pawnee ceremonies, see Alice C. Fletcher, *Song, Pipe, and Unity in a Pawnee Calumet Ceremony: The Hako* (Lincoln: University of Nebraska Press, 1996), reprinted from the Twenty-second annual report of the Bureau of American Ethnology, Government Printing Office, 1904; Ralph Linton, *Annual Ceremony of the Pawnee Medicine Men* (Chicago: Field Museum of Natural History, 1923); Todd E. Leahy, "So That a Nation May Live: The Pawnee Ghost Dance and Cultural Renaissance." *Chronicles of Oklahoma* (November, 2007).
4. For complete details regarding Frances Densmore's work among the Pawnee, see *Pawnee Music* (Washington: Government Printing Office, 1929), published by the Smithsonian Institution's Bureau of American Ethnology, Bulletin 93.
5. No scholar has set a better example of working with, and on behalf of, a tribal entity that may or may not have the resources to spend hours-on-end searching the Library of Congress for every extant recording of existing tribal music. At the 2001 Pawnee Veterans Homecoming and Powwow, Evan Tonsing made available free copies of his research and documentation of Pawnee music that has been released commercially, and also noted that music which has yet to be released by the Library of Congress. Professor Tonsing's annotated discography and accompanying letter that came with a copy of the cassette sent to me by request guided the author in pursuit of several Pawnee recordings mentioned in this essay, and provided otherwise unknown-to-the-author perspective on Pawnee recordings in existence.
6. For more information on the history of the Native American Church's formal origins in Oklahoma, see Omer C. Stewart's *Peyote Religion: A History*. (Norman: University of Oklahoma Press, 1987), pp. 117-18.
7. For more information on the formation of the Brave Scout singers, see entry for Otoe-Missouria Tribe.
8. For more details on the Young Bird Singers, see entry for Young Bird.

Paxton, Tom

(b. October 31, 1937)

Emerging in the 1960s as one of the most talented folksingers of the protest era, singer, songwriter, guitarist Tom Paxton was born on the south side of Chicago, Illinois, but raised in Bristow, Oklahoma, where he graduated from high school. His family moved to Bristow when he was nine, but his father died soon after their arrival in Oklahoma. Thus, he was raised by a single parent and had to face the harsh realities of life at an early age. His aunt gave him a guitar at age sixteen, and when Tom entered the University of Oklahoma, he began working up his own repertoire of folk songs (more than 200 songs by the time he graduated) and later performed as a folksinger in a campus variety show. His first inspirations for folk music were **Woody Guthrie**, Cisco Houston, Pete Seeger, and the Weavers. He wrote his first song in an English literature class while avoiding the professor's lecture on Shakespeare. He earned a bachelor's degree in fine arts (drama major) in 1959, and still considers Oklahoma his home state. In 2012, one can say Tom Paxton is one of the most recognized and notable folksingers recording and performing in the contemporary era. A funny, thought-provoking folk singer and songwriter, Tom Paxton evokes the polished possibilities of American roots music, as well as the new-folk movement of early 1960s Greenwich Village, New York. Paxton also continued writing new songs about current events of recent years. His multiple GRAMMY nominations are also a testament to this status.

Following his years in Norman while at the University of Oklahoma, Paxton joined the U.S. Army and spent six months stationed at New Rochelle, New York, and later, Fort Dix, New Jersey. The location proffered the opportunity to spend his weekends in Greenwich Village, a hot spot for the beginning of the folk music revival of the 1960s with such newcomers as Bob Dylan, Joan Baez, and Phil Ochs. Learning that people's minds could be changed with a song, Paxton began trading sets and swapping songs with such noted folk artists as Dave Van Ronk and Paul Stookey of Peter, Paul, and Mary, and eventually settled in Greenwich Village after completion of his active duty. After working the coffeehouse circuit at such venues as The Bitter End and The Gaslight, he auditioned for the Chad Mitchell Trio, but was rejected as the group's director thought Tom was more adept at songwriting.

Beginning in 1962 Tom penned a long list of songs inspired by his idols Burl Ives and Woody Guthrie, some of which impressed his folk colleagues who incorporated his songs in their shows, including the Weavers, who performed Paxton's "Ramblin' Boy" in their 1963 Carnegie Hall concert and included on their subsequent album. As his writing abilities increased, Tom thought it was time to try recording an album, and in 1964, Jac Holzman of Elektra Records auditioned him in his living room. His debut album, *Ramblin' Boy*, released in 1964 served notice to the folk music community that Paxton was the real deal. The late 1960s proved to be one of Tom's most prolific songwriting and recording periods, with albums such as *Ain't That News* (1965), *Outward Bound, Morning Again* (1967), *The Things I Notice* (1968), *Tom Paxton 6* (1969), and *The Compleat Tom Paxton* (1970). Paxton magnified the inspiration of Woody Guthrie when he recorded Guthrie's "Pastures of Plenty" and "Biggest Thing Man Has Ever Done" for the 1972 *A Tribute to Woody Guthrie* collection.

In 1971, Paxton switched to the Reprise label to record four albums, *How Come the Sun* (1971), *Peace Will Come* (1972), *New Songs for Old Friends* (1973), and *Something in My Life* (1975). By the mid-1970s the folk music revival had waned, leading Tom and his family to move England where he remains highly regarded as a folk troubadour. Paxton returned to the U.S. in 1977 and settled in East Hampton on Long Island, New York. Renewed by experiences overseas and rediscovery of his own country, Tom launched a new album, *New Songs from the Briarpatch* (1977), on the Vanguard label, followed by *Heroes* in 1978, and three albums for the Flying Fish label, *Up & Up* (1979), *The Paxton Report* (1980), and *Even a Gray Day* (1983).

During the 1980s and 1990s, Tom toured throughout the U.S., performing on college campuses and in folk clubs. By 1995, he had recorded thirty-two albums, including several children's albums, such as *The Marvelous Toy and Other Gallimaufry* (1984), *Balloon-alloon-alloon* (1987), *A Child's Christmas* (1992), *Suzy is a Rocker* (1992), and *Peanut Butter Pie* (1992). In addition to his children's works, Tom completed a number of satiric topical albums in the 1980s and 1990s, including *Bulletin* (1983), *One Million Lawyers and Other Disasters* (1986), *Politics* (1988), and *Wearing the Time* (1995), the latter was nominated as Best Folk Album of the Year by the National Association of Independent Record Distributors. The 1995 album included "Getting Up Early," a Paxton original that premiered on NPR's *Prairie Home Companion*.

Paxton released a live collection in 1996, *Live for the Record*, where he continued unapologetically in the mode of folk singer discussing his own time ("Lament for a Lost Election," "Tonya Harding," and "Let's Got to Michael Jackson's House"). In 1997, Paxton released two more children's albums, *Goin' to the Zoo* and *I've Got a Yo-Yo*. Two years later, the BBC launched a highly acclaimed radio show dubbed *Paxton's Picks*, later renamed *Tom Paxton's America*, which included special guests such as Pete Seeger, Iris DeMent, and John Prine.

Paxton's songwriting credits include a host of well-known songs that he penned, including "Ramblin' Boy," in which he mentions Tulsa town; "The Last Thing on My Mind" (a major hit for Peter, Paul, and Mary as well as Dolly Parton and Porter Wagoner); "Bottle of Wine" (a Top 10 hit for The Fireballs); and "All Night Long" (a 1968 chronicle of the assassinations of Martin Luther King, Jr. and Robert Kennedy). Additional topical songs reflecting the protest movements of the 1960s and 1970s include "Bring Back the Chair" (capital punishment); "Talking Vietnam Potluck Blues," "Jimmy Newman," and "Lyndon Johnson Told the Nation" (anti-Vietnam War songs); "Talking Watergate" (Nixon tapes); "I'm Changing My Name to Chrysler (an attack on the government bailout of the auto giant); and "Litty Bitty Gun" (a mock of Nancy Reagan). Many of these Paxton classics were assembled for the retrospective *I Can't*

Help Wonder Where I'm Bound: The Elektra Years, released by Rhino in 1999. In addition to those aforementioned artists who have recorded Paxton's songs, others include Joan Baez, John Denver, Judy Collins, Arlo Guthrie, Nanci Griffith, Chet Atkins, Jose Feliciano, Neil Diamond, Placido Domingo, Willie Nelson, and Tiny Tim. The *Best of Broadside* released in 2000 by Smithsonian Folkways Recordings contained four of Tom's original songs, including "Ain't That News," "Train for Auschwitz," "Christine," and "What Did You Lean in School Today?" Tom teamed with Anne Hills for a 2001 release, *Under American Skies*, on the Appleseed label.

Paxton performed a 9/11 tragedy tribute at the Library of Congress in 2002, including his composition "The Bravest," a song written to remember the heroes of the New York City police and fire departments who died on September 11, 2001. Paxton's honors include winner of the prestigious Parents' Choice Gold Medal for his album, *Suzy is a Rocker*, and appointment as honorary chair of the World Folk Music Association. In 2003, Paxton earned a GRAMMY nomination in the category of Best Musical Album for Children for his album, *Your Shoes, My Shoes* (Red House), which included the memorable "Barney Ate My Homework," and the downright hilariously goofy "It's Time Out Time Again," "I'm a Raisin in a Bowl of Raisin Bran" and "The Pizza that Ate Chicago." Another GRAMMY nomination followed for Paxton's 2002 release, *Looking for the Moon*, as did another for his 2005 live disc, *Tom Paxton Live in the U.K.*, which emerged from his 39th tour of the U.K. where audiences are large and celebratory of Paxton's esteemed status. The disc has a very relaxed feel, and according to the liner notes has no over-dubs or editing, and is pretty much a document of how it happened. Head honcho of the famous McCabe's Guitar Shop in Santa Monica, CA, Bob Riskin, ensured the subtle deftness of Paxton's pure Americana guitar style would be recorded with a guitarist's ear on *Live at McCabe's, February 23, 1991* (Shout Factory, 2006). Paxton starts out with an "old one" ("Ramblin' Boy") to one written "two weeks ago" before the recording was made. GRAMMY nominators recognized Paxton in 2008 for his *Comedians and Angels* album, which is a collection of his favorite songs about love, although all are not necessarily prototypical love songs, as he also pays homage to various compatriots from his fifty-year career as a socio-musical observer of American ironies, joys, and despair.

Back in Oklahoma, in 2009 Paxton performed at the grand opening of Freeland Center for the Performing Arts in Bristow, his old hometown. In 2012, Tom continues writing folk songs and children's songs for his own label (Pax), as well as children's books. He also maintains an active touring schedule with performances booked through the spring of 2013.

www.tompaxton.com

Pepper, Jim
(b. June 18, 1941 – d. February, 1992)

Jim Pepper was born in Oregon to Kaw and Muscogee (Creek) parents, and turned to the state's Native American music for inspiration, which he then incorporated into widely recognized progressive jazz. He is also one of very few jazz artists in the post-big band era (after 1940), to have an original jazz based composition on the American popular music charts. His albums reflect an extreme familiarity with traditional tribal music in Oklahoma, both that of his mother's tribe, the **Muscogee (Creek) Nation**, and his father's tribe, the **Kaw Nation**. Just as much as Merle Haggard is often considered a de facto product of Oklahoma's cultural environment on the Anglo-European side, Jim Pepper should be considered an intrinsic representative of the presence and development of American Indian music from the state.

Saxophonist, singer, and composer, Jim Pepper, was born June 18, 1941 in Salem, Oregon, descended from the traditional chief line of the Pepper family on his father's Kaw side, and from the Muscogee (Creek) Nation via his mother, Floy Pepper. He grew up in Portland, Oregon. However, as a youth and young man, Pepper traveled to Oklahoma for visits to stay with his family there, where he became exposed to both the traditional ceremonial music of the **Muscogee (Creek)** commonly known as "stomp dances", as well as the songs of the Native American Church from his Kaw relatives. Ultimately, he learned a Native American Church song from his grandfather, Ralph Pepper. Described by Pepper as a Comanche chant used when water is brought into the tipi at midnight or dawn, the song that evolved into "Wichi-Tai-To" was recorded first on an album with a group called Everything is Everything, featuring Pepper on lead vocals and saxophone. Within the song's grounding are real imagery (waterbirds) and song stylings of the Native American Church (vocables, prayers, and Native language). Although the majority of non-Indians did not get the song's references, the song spent five weeks on the *Billboard* U.S. Hot 100, peaking at #69 in the spring of 1969, and was also popular in England when it was released there on Vanguard Records.

Jim Pepper appeared on as many as thirteen albums, several of which were solo albums, starting with *Pepper's Powwow* (Embryo, 1971). The album includes several songs with traditional American Indian music as their foundation, to include a different version

Jim Pepper

of "Wichi-Tai-To" than the one that became a hit, fast and slow war dances, and one track which is a Muscogee (Creek) stomp dance, indicating he also wanted to represent that side of his tribal heritage as well. To that end, in the version of "Wichi-Tai-To" on *Pepper's Powwow*, and all the subsequent live versions available for viewing through online video services, Pepper does some free form vocalizing in which he says a variety of things, presumably in a tribal language, but the one word that always emerges from his extemporaneous vocals is "Hohmbucks-che" (or in the Muscogee (Creek) spelling -"Hompvksce") which translates into "Let's eat!" Pepper also played with renowned jazz artists, often some of its most visionary and experimental figures, such as **Don Cherry** (also from Oklahoma), modern jazz guitarist, Bill Frisell, and John Scofield (perhaps, *the* jazz fusion guitarist). All three appeared on Pepper's most lionized solo album, *Comin' and Going* (Island, 1983), which is considered the manifesto of his "American Indian jazz" with nine songs that merge American Indian traditional music, and jazz, perfecting what he had started with *Pepper's Powwow*. While Pepper's music is accessible, it is still considered collectible, and, therefore, can be quite costly to obtain on compact disc, although less expensive downloads are available from standard online music services. Pepper died in Portland, Oregon, February 10, 1992 of lymphoma at only age 50, but his music and life continues to be celebrated with concerts, festivals, posthumous awards, and new recordings of his music, such as the 2008 version of "Witchi-Tai-To" recorded by Muscogee (Creek) poet and saxophonist, Joy Harjo, and included on her album, *Winding Through the Milky Way* (Fast Horse).

Even though Jim Pepper is not an Oklahoman by birth, he is descended from people who are considered first Oklahomans, those who are descendants of the tribes and nations whose tribal governments are located on mostly federal Indian Country within the boundaries of the contemporary state. By returning to the state where traditional American Indian music was being maintained, Pepper could gain greater insight to his own musical identity, and then channel through his considerable skills, the end result being the first time American Indian music was also American popular music.

Note

See *OMG II* entries for **Kaw Nation** and **Muscogee (Creek) Nation** to gain more insight into Jim Pepper's tribal music heritage.

Petree, Stephen

According to the Los Angeles-based Overcomer's Church 2012 website, where Stephen Petree was leading musical worship services twice a week, Petree "grew up listening to his father preach in a little church in his hometown of Shawnee." The press release for Petree's 2010 solo disc goes a step further out into the sticks by explaining was reared on a turkey farm outside Shawnee by his Pentecostal pastor and entrepreneur father, and vocal coach mother. Since then, he served some teen idol time, recorded several independent rock CDs, co-wrote major label modern rock songs, and has enjoyed national recognition as a modern pop rock and contemporary Christian songwriter, singer, and band leader. Along with a soaring tenor voice and uber-pop production value on his contemporary Christian music, Stephen is also known in modern rock circles as the brother of **Shiny Toy Guns** co-founder, Chad Petree, with whom Stephen wrote several songs on the GRAMMY-nominated electronica/dance album, *We Are Pilots* (Universal, 2006).

Stephen experienced the temporal side of the popular music industry before the end of his teens as a member (along with brother, Chad) of the RCA vocal pop group, pc Quest. Featured in *Teen Beat*, the group emerged in the wake of worldwide success of New Kids on the Block, but managed only two singles in 1991 that chipped into the *Billboard* Hot 100. With Jackson 5-esque vocals and somewhat dated sounding keyboards, "Can I Call You Girl" and "After the Summer's Gone" reached #58 and #41 respectively. "After the Summer's Gone" at least includes a telling guitar solo that indicated the band had a rock leaning, and foretold later more successful sounds for the Petree brothers in their future musical endeavors after pc Quest, which included the independent rock group, Paradigm, and Chad's eventual startup of Shiny Toy Guns with another Shawnee-ite, Jeremy Dawson. Stephen received co-writing credits on the three *Billboard* top 30 modern rock singles from *We Are Pilots* ("Le Disko," "You Are the One," and "Rainy Monday"). After hearing Stephen's later solo work, "You Are the One" and "Rainy Monday" both bear his obvious creative imprint, even if "Rainy Monday" leans mightily toward a tribute to the sound of New Order or Erasure's 1980s electro-dance-pop standards.

While Petree has continued to collaborate with Shiny Toy Guns, he has also become known as smooth Christian pop-rock singer and songwriter whose music fits mainstream national television programs (*Dancing with the Stars*, *America's Top Model, Guiding Light,* MTV's *The Real World*), and national commercial campaigns (Honda, Motorola). Petree has also recorded several independent contemporary Christian music albums, toured with prominent televangelist, Kenneth Copeland, and sung at the Rose Bowl in Los Angeles for the Billy Graham Crusade. Petree's 2009 solo release *Resolve to Relax*, is a good example of his punchy pop-rock songwriting and vocal style. Featuring catchy melodic hooks usually played on guitar or synthesizer, Petree's music also showcases his made-for-pop that voice that has its own sound yet inhabits the space between Queen's lead singer, Freddie Mercury, Ian McCulloch of 1980s electro-guitar group, Echo and the Bunnymen, and the majestic rock vocals of 1994-era Jeff Buckley. As with much of the most intriguing contemporary Christian music, Petree's songwriting allows for multiple interpretations of lyrics in songs such as "Good News Travels Fast," "My Spirit is Settled," "Walk the Waves," and "You're Gonna Make It."

Stephen Petree

In 2010, Stephen released the eponymous solo project *Every Weakness Makes You Beautiful* (Dream/Universal), demonstrating the breadth of his multi-genre musical skills with tight versions of modern rock, techno, and pop songs. Some of the songs are re-worked versions of songs that appeared on *Resolve to Relax*, but re-recorded with the new line up, and all guided by lyrics with dualistic sacred and secular themes. As a group in 2010, Petree was fronted by Stephen on lead vocals, rhythm guitar and keyboards, as well as Konawa native and bassist/engineer, Dave Eropkin. Lead guitarist Aaron Joseph and drummer Adam Welch, both from the Okie-transplant town of Bakersfield, California, filled out the group and the band's crystalline modern pop-rock sound with a faith-based focus.

In 2012, Stephen Petree continued creating new music, playing with his group, and leading contemporary music worship services at Overcomers Church in Los Angeles, where he lived with his wife, Sally, and two daughters.

www.myspace.com/stephenpetree/music

Pettiford, Oscar

(b. September 30, 1922 – d. September 8, 1960)

Designated by exalted Oklahoma jazz guitarist Barney Kessel as "one of the five best bassists of all time," Oscar Pettiford appeared under his own name on more than twenty albums under his own name during his brilliant career as bassist, cellist, and bandleader. All testament one needs for Pettiford's abilities can also be found on his recordings with jazz giants such as Louis Armstrong, Charlie Christian, Miles Davis, Duke Ellington, Stan Getz, Dizzy Gillespie, Lionel Hampton, Coleman Hawkins, Billie Holiday, Thelonious Monk, Charlie Parker, Sonny Rollins, and Ben Webster. Born of mixed African and American Indian heritage in Okmulgee, Oklahoma, the capital of the Muscogee (Creek) Nation where many slaves of African descent began their post-Civil War freedom, and to which many African-Americans migrated as a result of the large population of blacks in the town, Oscar came into a musical family where his mother was a pianist and music teacher. His father, Harry "Doc" Pettiford, was a practicing veterinarian as well as a guitarist, drummer, and leader of the Doc Pettiford Family Orchestra.

With Doc Pettiford's wife on piano and the six children who preceded Oscar, the group included sisters Leontine and brother Harry on the reed instruments, Marjorie on reeds and flute, Ira on trumpet, Alonzo on various brass, Rose May on guitar, and three younger sisters on vocals. The band toured the Midwest, and when Oscar was three the family moved to Minneapolis, Minnesota. While Pettiford family music history is rooted in the development of music in the early days of Oklahoma's statehood through the 1920s, they also left the state for Minneapolis in 1925 as part of larger migration of African-Americans out of Oklahoma due to increasing racial and economic strife in the state.

Once in Minnesota, Oscar studied guitar, trombone, and piano, sang in front of the orchestra at age ten, and ultimately became designated for the vacant bass chair at fourteen. When he expressed disinterest in that instrument, Harry Sr. conked his son on the head with a pair of drumsticks to convince Oscar otherwise. After Oscar, five more Pettifords followed to re-supply the band until "Doc" Pettiford's death in 1943. Influenced by Duke Ellington's bassist of the 1930s and 1940s, Jimmy Blanton, and Milt Hinton who encouraged Pettiford to not give up music for a secure day job, Oscar started playing bass with Charlie Barnet in 1943. Pettiford parlayed that visibility into an integral role in New York City's formative bebop scene with Dizzy Gillespie and Charlie Parker, a good example of which exists on *Dizzy Gillespie Volume 4: 1943 and 1944* (Masters of Jazz). The recordings mark the early stages of the bebop era with a jam between Parker, Gillespie, and Pettiford on "Sweet Georgia Brown." Oscar was "the" bassist on 52nd Street from 1943 to 1945, whose playing with Coleman Hawkins, Thelonious Monk, Roy Eldridge, Errol Garner, and Max Roach had a permanent influence on the development of bebop as a form and the bass as an instrument in jazz. Fans and critics took notice of his elevated skill and status in 1944 when he won *Esquire*'s "All Star Bassist" award, and in 1945 when he repeated the *Esquire* award and won the *Metronome* poll for best bassist.

Hugh W. Foley

Oscar's 1949 stint with Woody Herman was cut short when Pettiford broke his arm playing softball with the band team, he did have the opportunity to introduce the cello into jazz, for which he is roundly given credit. As a joke on Herman, Pettiford substituted a cello for his bass solo. Subsequently, audience members convinced Pettiford the instrument had great possibilities for jazz.

In addition to his instrumental accomplishments, Pettiford composed "Blues in the Closet," "Bohemia After Dark," "Tricrotism," "Black-Eyed Peas and Collard Greens," "Laverne Walk," and "Swingin' Til the Girls Come Home." Musicians who have recorded his compositions include Cannonball Adderly, **Chet Baker**, Herbie Mann, Charlie Mingus, and Oscar Peterson. By his career's end, his list of credits as a side man on various jazz recordings included sessions with Louis Armstrong, Art Blakey, Kenny Burrell, Charlie Parker, **Don Byas**, **Charlie Christian**, John Coltrane, Miles Davis, Billy Eckstine, Lionel Hampton, and Quincy Jones.

Pettiford's surprising death came in Copenhagen, Denmark, at the young age of thirty-eight, but not before he established the double bass as a solo instrument equal to any other horn voice in jazz. He was inducted into the Oklahoma Jazz Hall of Fame in 1995, and in 1998, Topaz records released a wonderful retrospective of Pettiford's career, *Bass Hits*, featuring recordings with Duke Ellington, Dizzy Gillespie, Coleman Hawkins, and Ben Webster, and others.

Petty, Tom
(born October 20, 1950)

Droll rocker Tom Petty is often associated with Tulsa because his first two albums, the 1976 self-titled release that contained the FM rock radio staple, "Breakdown," and 1978's *You're Gonna Get It!*, were both released by **Leon Russell** and Denny Cordell's Shelter Records. However, the Gainesville, Florida native is not from Oklahoma, and never lived in the state. In an interview with Petty published in *Billboard* on December 3, 2005, the lanky Florida singer and guitarist explained that Shelter co-owner Cordell encouraged Petty (whose band was called Mudcrutch at the time) to stop by the Church Studio in Tulsa on their way back to Florida after passing out demos in Los Angeles.

As Jennifer Chancellor noted in a *Tulsa World* article on September 19, 2010, Petty did play bass for Tulsa power pop rocker, Dwight Twilley, on a short-lived 1977 CBS children's comedy show, *Wacko!* Also as a result of being label mates with Twilley on Shelter Records, Petty played guitar on Twilley's 1977 *Twilley Don't Mind* LP, and added vocals to Twilley's 1984 Top 20 pop single, "Girls." Even though the blonde Floridian is not from Oklahoma, the hefty music business presence in Tulsa did provide Tom Petty his initial break into pop music with the release of his first major label recordings on Russell and Cordell's Shelter label.

www.tompetty.com

Pewewardy, Cornel Derek
(b. January 20, 1952)

In 2012, Cornel Pewewardy is an assistant professor and director of Indigenous Nations Studies at Portland State University in Portland, Oregon. He is also an author of many academic papers, essays, and articles, an avid intellectual opponent of American Indian mascots, and a sought after keynote speaker in American Indian education, leadership, and history circles. Additionally, Pewewardy is a widely recognized Plains Indian singer and flutist throughout world music circles. Pewewardy has recorded acclaimed albums of his own flute music, Southern Plains powwow music, multiple **Comanche** and **Kiowa** traditional songs, and contemporary hybrid recordings of traditional music and contemporary instrumentation laden with studio effects. His Kiowa hymns have been distributed internationally on compilations of musicians and singers who are the pinnacle performers of their respective international traditions.

Cornel Pewewardy

Born to a Kiowa mother, Mary Lee Pewewardy, and a Comanche father, "Doc" Pewewardy, in Lawton, Oklahoma, Cornel is an enrolled member of the Comanche Nation and grew up around the collective musical traditions of his extended family and tribes. His first musical memories as a child were hearing his grandfather sing peyote songs as the elder drove around in the family car. While Pewewardy played saxophone in junior high and high school band, Kiowa flutist Woody Bigbow **(Kiowa)** gave Cornel his first flute in 1975 at home in Anadarko, Oklahoma, and his uncle, George "Woogie" Watchetaker, a noted Comanche dancer and artist, mentored Cornel in flute composition and performance in the Plains traditions, most of which were historically linked to courting. Pewewardy credits his quick progress on the flute to his saxophone training since the fingerings for both instruments were often the same.

Additional music experiences came for Pewewardy from learning Ponca songs from Morris Lookout, and Kiowa hymns from Ralph Kotay. In 1976, Cornel received a B.S. in Education from Northeastern Oklahoma State University in Tahlequah, Oklahoma, and a Master's in Education in 1977 from the same school. That year, Pewewardy moved to New Mexico where he taught for Navajo schools in Crown Point and Cuba, New Mexico until 1984, and earned his Master of Arts in Educational Management and Development from New Mexico State. In 1986, he became director of research and development at Southwestern Indian Polytechnic in Albuquerque, received another degree from New Mexico State in Education Administration, and in 1987 released his first collection of music, *Flute and Prayer Songs* (Tribal Music International). Next, Pewewardy was off to Pennsylvannia State University where he earned his Doctor of Education in 1989, and then spent a year as a post-doctoral fellow at the university in Norman.

In 1991, Cornel moved to Saint Paul, Minnesota and became the founding principal at an American Indian magnet school. Given the amount of relocations he experienced in a relatively short amount of time, no wonder he named his 1992 release *Spirit Journey* (Sound of America Records). Anchored by ancient melodies, *Spirit Journey* explores the sonic possibilities of multi-track recording, studio effects, and contemporary instrumentation that gained Pewewardy notice in some new age music circles for the album's atmospheric and meditative qualities.

By 1994, Cornel felt the need to return to southwestern Oklahoma, and became a lecturer at the University of Science and Arts in Chickasha, a thirty-minute drive from his hometown of Lawton. That year, Cornel and the Alliance West Singers also released the first of their highly acclaimed albums, *Dancing Buffalo: Dances and Flute Songs from the Southern Plains* (Sound of the World, 1994). The album is an excellent introduction to the varied musical abilities of Pewewardy and the Alliance West Singers, as well as the music of the Southern Plains, including several songs that accompany Plains dances, *a cappella* Kiowa Hymns, and flute songs by Cornel. While the drum group's songs were recorded in New Mexico, the hymns and flute songs were recorded in McGee Chapel in Broken Bow, Oklahoma.

In 1994, Cornel moved to Lawton and taught for two years at Cameron University. In 1995, Narada Records included two songs, "Kiowa Hymn III" and "Love Song," that represent Pewewardy's more contemporary sound, a hybrid of traditional flute and contemporary instruments on *Between Father Sky and Mother Earth*. In 1996, Sound of America Records released Pewewardy and other Comanche singers on *Comanche Hymns from the Prairie*, and Cornel moved to Lawrence, Kansas where and began teaching for the University of Kansas. Also in 1996, Pewewardy's "Voices from the Sky," originally released on 1992's *Spirit Journey*, was included on *Arctic Refuge: A Gathering of Tribes*, an album dedicated to raising awareness of the wilderness and indigenous people of the Arctic.

In 1997, The Wordcraft Circle of Native Writers and Storytellers named Cornel its musician of the year. The following year Pewewardy's "Kiowa Hymn" appeared on *Invocations* (Music of the World), a compilation of international faith-based songs designed to invoke the divine, and on *Native American Music: The Rough Guide* (World Music Network). Also in 1997, the Lawrence, Kansas art commission gave Cornel their "Phoenix Award for Music," and he harmonized with Robbie Robertson on *Contact from the Underworld of Red Boy* (Capitol), an album coordinated by Oklahoma City native Jim Wilson. In 1999, Shortwave Records released *The Warrior's Edge: Songs from the Southern Plains Powwows* by Pewewardy, the Alliance West Singers, and Intertribal Veterans. The album contains intertribal war dance songs, a "Kiowa O-homah Lodge song," "Kiowa Round Dances," the "Comanche Little Ponies' Gourd Dance song," "Alvin Tsosie's Gourd Dance Song," a "Comanche Gourd Dance song," and a "Comanche Prisoner of War Song."

In 2000, the compilation *Spirit of the Native American Indians: Songs and Dances of the Kiowa, Comanche, Navajo* featured Cornel both on new compositions and traditional songs with the Alliance West Singers. Along with his recordings, Pewewardy also travels extensively and works with students on developing their traditional music skills. In a 2001 essay about American Indian music he writes, "Our music, in both its longevity and its diversity, is a testimony to our survival as a people. Our drums beat strong, our flutes still sing like birds, and our rattles sound like rain. We still sing in the ancient tongues and perform dances in the prescribed manner."

In 2002, Cornel provided some background vocals for the contemporary new age American Indian group Brulé. While many American Indian musicians are widely recorded and distributed throughout Indian Country, Cornel Pewewardy is one of the few whose music has crossed international boundaries to be considered on par with other leading figures of world music. Along with his distinguished career as a nationally recognized educator, his recordings and performances have placed him in an elite group of recognizable voices and flutists in the traditional and contemporary American Indian music world. As of 2013, he was an associate professor of Native American Studies at Portland State University in Portland, Oregon.

Phillips, John
(b. August 30, 1935 – d. March 19, 2001)

Primary songwriter, vocalist, and arranger of the 1960s pop group, The Mamas and the Papas, who are best-known for Top 10 hits such as "California Dreamin'," and "Monday, Monday," John Phillips has been periodically associated with Oklahoma; however, he was not born in, nor did he ever live in the state. The confusion generally centers around Phillips' father, who reportedly won an Okmulgee bar in a poker game on the way home from World War I. According to John Phillips' biography, *Papa John*, Phillips' mother, Edna Gertrude Gaines, was a full-blooded Cherokee born in Okmulgee, who met and married his father, Claude, a career U.S. Marine, in Oklahoma before they moved to Parris Island, South Carolina where John Phillips was born. Perhaps this fact is an explanation for why Phillips shows an alarming lack of knowledge about the town of Okmulgee, and the geography of eastern Oklahoma, as well as writing romantically and stereotypically about Cherokee and Muscogee (Creek) people when describing them, or not knowing the difference if/when his co-writer did the actual writing.[1]

Note
1. For more information on the lives of John Phillips' mother and father in Okmulgee, see Phillips' autobiography written with Jim Jerome, *Papa John: An Autobiography by John Phillips* (New York: Dell, 1987).

Pillar
(formed, 1998 in Hays, KS; relocated to Tulsa as a home base circa 2000 through the present)

Parlaying a harder edged Christian rock into crossover mainstream modern rock airplay in the mid-2000s, as well as continued success through 2010's #1 Christian Rock single, "Whatever it Takes," Pillar has sold more than a million records worldwide in proving to be one of the most prominent and consistent contemporary Christian hard rock bands since their emergence on the national scene in 2000. While many Christian teens like rocking out, they do not necessarily like the lyrical themes of secular metal, creating a large contemporary market for spiritual rock that sounds like other contemporary rock of the same era. Along with peers Creed, P.O.D., and Switchfoot, Pillar emerged in what would still be considered the post-grunge era, and mined the vein of other 1980s and '90s "Nu-metal" groups who successfully merged rock and rap with big pop hooks and tight song arrangements. While the group's sound mirrored the popular rock music on which they grew up, and which later became highly commercial, Pillar's obvious faith-based lyrics registered with millions of modern Christian rock fans. The group won three Dove Awards, headlined nine national tours where they performed for more than three million people, and earned ten #1 singles on various Christian music radio charts.

Pillar formed in Hays, Kansas when devout Christian Rob Beckley, a songwriter and vocalist with a full modern rock tonal range, began playing music with his Fort Hays State University roommate and drummer Brad Noone, in 1981. Soon, they started jamming with friends Travis Jenkins (guitar), Dustin Adams (guitar), and bassist Michael Wittig (a.k.a. Kalel). None of the original members of the group are from Oklahoma, however. Hays is a small northwestern-"ish" Kansas way-station on the cross-country corridor, US Interstate 70, just about equidistant (240 miles either way) from the Kansas State University community of Manhattan, Kansas to the east, and the Colorado/Kansas border to the west. None of the original band members are from Oklahoma, but relocated their base of operations to Tulsa on the advice of an early band manager.

Pillar, 2006

The band's hybrid musical trajectory, and varied influences from life in a Midwestern college town, may be heard on the funky title track from the band's first independently released album, *Metamorophosis* (1999). As a whole, the album shows a considerable musical presence from their secular rock forbears of the 1990s, such as Alice in Chains or Rage Against the Machine, but with the lyrical stance of an overt Christian rock band. "Metamorphosis" sounds like the Red Hot Chili Peppers showed up at your local sanctuary as the modern praise or worship band. Only the lyrics have been changed to protect the innocent.

After starting to gig and travel more on the strength of their 1999 self-released debut that capitalized on their ability to provide the sonic power of contemporary pop rock without the lyrical nihilism, the band received more encouragement via the reception of their next independent production, *Original Superman*. The 2000 album shows the group evolving firmly in the post-grunge rock and rap traditions of the 1990s, but also willing to range out into reggae's offbeat grooves. The album's title track is a ska-metal tribute to Christian rock's "original superman," and firmly established the ethos of Pillar's lyrical center without the duplicity of some Christian rock and pop bands that hope for crossover success by vague references to spiritual awakenings or confirmations, but do not mention Jesus Christ specifically.

Flicker Records took note of the buzz emerging from the Midwest's Christian rock circles about Pillar, signed them and had the group record several of the songs from *Original Superman* for what became their first official "paid-for" release, *Above* (Flicker, 2000). Boosted by the already significant regional popularity of "Original Superman," *Above* also featured "Open Your Eyes," a song that merged musical dashes of Rage Against the Machine and other post-grunge Nu-metal, along with screaming lyrical encouragement (if not evangelizing) for listeners to open up and "reach out for the Christ." The song earned the group a 2001 Dove Award for Best Hard Music Song of the Year.

(Insert Pillar image 2 Fireproof with caption including names of 2003 lineup)

Pillar relocated to Tulsa circa 2000 on the promises of a manager who wound up not fulfilling the guarantees subsequent to the band up and moving everything to northeastern Oklahoma. After firing the manager, the group liked Tulsa so much they decided to stay. In a 2012 e-mail to the author, singer Rob Beckley wrote, "We really liked Tulsa once we got down here, so we stayed. Even in the years when we were being tugged to Nashville, we fought the urges and stayed here in Tulsa." Using Tulsa as a touring base in the center of the U.S., Pillar's original members began transitioning out of the group. Adams, Jenkins, and Noone were out of the band in 1999, 2001, and 2002, respectively. Beckley and Wittig added guitarist, Noah Hanson, who beefed up the guitars in a major way on their breakthrough album in 2002 for Flicker/Universal. The band's first single chart successes were not on Christian charts, but on *Billboard*'s mainstream charts, where *Fireproof*'s title track sneaked into the Hot Mainstream Rock Tracks at #37 in August, 2003. *Fireproof* also eventually earned Pillar its third Dove Music Award for Hard Music Album of the Year in 2003. After *Fireproof,* the band hired Kansas City-native Lester Estelle II to be the drummer and provide additional vocals. The first result was "Bring Me Down," from their next Flicker release, *Where Do We Go From Here* (Flicker), which rode more of the same formula to #26 on the *Billboard* Hot Mainstream Track Chart, as well as significant airplay on Christian and secular rock stations. As for Pillar's core audience, the albums also did very well on the Contemporary Christian Charts where *Fireproof* garnered a respectable #6 slot in 2002, and *Where Do We Go From Here* (Flicker, 2004) made it to #3 in July, 2004. Next, the band toured and took almost two years to ready their next release, *The Reckoning* (Flicker, 2006), which became Pillar's biggest crossover success. Additionally, *The Reckoning* demonstrated their widespread appeal to secular hard rock fans.

While Pillar's singles did not break into the mainstream rock radio charts after *Where Do We Go From Here,* album sales were another story. As an indication of the band's wide-spread fan base, and Pillar's accomplishment of producing quality rock music with a spiritual focus, *The Reckoning* landed on several *Billboard* charts: Top Independent Albums (#3), Top Christian and Gospel Albums (#6), Top Rock Albums (#21), and the Top 200 Album Chart (#70). The group achieved similar results with 2008's *For the Love of the Game,* notching spots on eight different *Billboard* charts, to include Top Christian Albums (#3), Top Hard Rock Albums (#8), and the *Billboard* Top 200 (#71). Additionally, ESPN's *Baseball Tonight* used the album's title track in 2008 for a montage highlighting the 2007 World Series, a move which alerted other ESPN programming elements to include Pillar's music as bumpers in and out of commercials on ESPN's *Game Day* and popular *Sportscenter* highlight show. The band received the pinnacle of popular music industry notice in 2008 when *The Reckoning* received a 2008 GRAMMY nomination for Best Rock or Rap Gospel Album.

Estelle left the group in 2008 to be replaced by Taylor Carroll on drums, which also led to Phil Gilliland taking over bass duties for Kalel who wanted to spend more time at home with his family instead of being on the road all the time. With an established following that produced consistent sales and airplay, Pillar continued its success with the final album in the group's catalogue as of 2012, *Confessions.* The album's title and thematic center is based on a program of unburdening one's self by confessing among peers and members of Beckley's Tulsa church, where he has been the musical director since 2009. *Confessions* landed chart positions on a variety of *Billboard* charts: Modern Rock, Hard Rock, and Christian Albums. While the band has enjoyed nine #1 singles either on charts published by the now-defunct *Radio and Records* tip-sheet, or the Christian Radio Weekly's rock chart, *Confessions* also provided Pillar with its first #1 *Billboard* song in 2010, "Whatever It Takes," a lumbering pop rock anthem that juxtaposes melodic metal verses with crunchy guitar hooks and Beckley's signature "scream-o" vocals that hearken to the band's biggest crossover success. Interestingly, the song features more melody and less screaming, which may just be the softening that was necessary to push it to the top of the Christian Rock charts. The album was also Pillar's last as an act signed to a label, a turning point for Beckley, who had to start making more decisions based not only on his status as a lead singer of one of Christian rock's stalwart acts from 2000 through 2011, but also as a husband – married in 2001, and father to children Hudson, Emily, and Dawson, with another on the way in 2012.

Reaching out to fans of both his signature voice and Christian lyrical center, Rob Beckley announced a solo album in early 2012 with Idefi Music, an online music label, and spoke of Pillar in the "suspended" sense in a press release for his solo project. The first single for the album, "Value of My Heart," was made available though iTunes in June, 2012, and had already begun climbing reputable internet charts such as Christianrockadio.net, where it had reached the Top 25 after just a few weeks of being out. Featuring an almost plain-spoken vocal delivery introduction in which the song's speaker questions his past, what it means to him now, and how that legacy can be best managed for the good as time progresses, the song ultimately resolves that the "Son rising up" will provide guidance for the new day. The music is crunchy but not aggressive, and while Beckley's recognizable melodic voice soars in the song's choruses, absent is the angst-filled screaming that has been part of just about every one of Pillar's most popular songs. One has to think that sound will re-appear when necessary for a given song, but fatherhood, home life, and a steady local gig has a way of calming down some musicians, or driving them crazy to get back out on the road. For Beckley, the former seems to be the case.

According to a 2012 post on his social networking site, Beckley is happy with his music ministry in Tulsa, and being around for his family more than when he was on the road with Pillar. Planning to release singles as they are ready, Beckley was quoted in an Idefi Records press release about his contemporary work: "The solo record is an opportunity to just be myself and not worry about sounding like what Pillar is supposed to sound like." He continued, "I love rock. I love worship, and I love anthemic songs. This will be a straightforward rock record with the same passionate lyrics people grew used to in Pillar." Beckley also indicated through Pillar's social media sites that a new (independent) Pillar album could possibly be heard "in late 2012 or early 2013," but would only be Pillar if he's not the only one from the band on the album, which is one reason why he chose the solo route in 2012. While some metal and rock purists decry Christian rock as somehow "whitewashed," not to mention musically inferior to "real rock music," no one can argue that the original rockers of the 1940s and '50s merged country, blues, and gospel to create rockabilly, R&B, and early 1950s rock 'n' roll styles. Contemporary spiritual rockers are essentially doing the same thing without the lyrical focus on reckless behavior, hedonistic and nihilistic lifestyles, and perceived spiritual dangers of secular hard rock's often unhealthy environment and cynical lyrical ethos.

Operating from a Tulsa base since 2000, Pillar experienced the peak of Christian rock music's commercial and aesthetic success. Interestingly, the band also fits into a larger theme that emerges from most of the most successful artists profiled in the *Oklahoma Music Guide*, which is that those who are capable of success in at least two different areas of the music industry have the best chance for long-term success. Pillar was able to not only hold onto their contemporary Christian music base, but also crossed over into the mainstream rock realm, enhancing their overall career as musical artists with two target markets for their work. However, no matter what genre musicians are a part of, they ultimately have to reckon with realities of life on the road, record contracts, creating good new work, and continuing to evolve as inspired musicians who want to keep playing together. As far as bands go, Pillar has lasted longer than most, and enjoyed more success than a thousand groups with ambitions never realized.

Given his wide-ranging vocal abilities, personal convictions and ability to express them lyrically, as well as a catalogue of popular songs to draw from, Rob Beckley's music will certainly be heard in years to come, either as part of a revived Pillar for thousands of fans who would like to hear the band's songs again in concert, or on his own solo projects that continue elevating, expressing, andsharing his faith for those who enjoy his signature vocal sounds in a modern rock setting.

www.idefimusic.com, www.myspace.com/pillar, www.pillarmusic.com

Pinson, Bobby
(b. 1970)

Although country music singer and songwriter Bobby Pinson is called a "Panhandle Texan" in his own website's bio, and he is placed in Texas at the time of his 1970 birth on allmusic.com, long-time Oklahoma music chronicler, John Wooley, reported Pinson as a Tulsa native and Claremore High School graduate in a *Tulsa World* article on February 28, 2004. The son of a high school football coach and elementary school teacher, Pinson's family moved around a lot due to the elder Pinson's coaching career, during which the future songwriter for **Blake Shelton,** Marty Stuart, and LeAnn Rimes went to four different high schools, the final one being Claremore High School. After graduation, Pinson joined the United States Army.

While stationed at Fort Ord, California, he formed a country cover band near the end of his military stint. After his discharge from the service, Pinson hit the county fair and honky-tonk circuit, a period in which he met songwriters Larry Boone and Paul Nelson. Kathy Mattea, Tracy Lawrence, Marie Osmond, Ricky Van Shelton and others have recorded Boone's work, while Nelson's songs appear on recordings by the likes of Glen Campbell, Kathy Mattea, Don Williams, Joe Diffie, and Chris LeDoux. After hearing Pinson's originals on his first CD, 1994's *I Mean Business*, the experienced songwriters encouraged the former Claremore Zebra to try for a music career

Bobby Pinson, Nashville, 2012

in the country music capitol of Nashville, Tennessee. Pinson moved to Music City in 1996 where he worked a series of odd jobs (banquet server, delivery driver, and junk dealer) in order to survive. His second independent CD, *A Little Country*, emerged in 1997 with enough quality to eventually get him a deal with Sony Publishing as a staff writer in 1999.

Pinson's solo career as a Nashville country star lasted for all of about one album, 2005's *Man Like Me*, which peaked at #23 on *Billboard's* Top Country Albums. *Man Like Me* produced one Top 20 country single, "Don't Ask Me How I Know" (#16), in which Pinson tries to warn listeners about lessons he has already learned, but don't ask him how. While he did not catch on as a country singer, Pinson training as a country songwriter benefitted from his multiple experiences in a variety of small Texas towns as the new kid, playing football and being in musical theater productions in high school, and then enduring a military career before humbling himself in Nashville to make it any way possible. Plying bucolic images and common small-town Americana country tropes in his songs, Pinson's affable lyrics caught the ear of artists such as Tracy Lawrence, Marty Stuart, LeAnn Rimes, and **Blake Shelton**, all of whom recorded his songs. He also co-wrote Sugarland's #1 hit, "Want To", which topped *Billboard's* Hot Country Songs chart in 2006. Since then, he has written several songs with Toby Keith, to include the #1 *Billboard* country hit, "She Never Cried in Front of Me", as well as "She's a Hottie", "Lost You Anyway", and several others on Keith's 2008 album, *That Don't Make Me a Bad Guy*.

Also in 2008, several more Pinson co-writes with Sugarland struck the #1 single target's bull's eye ("All I Want to Do", "Already Gone", and "It Happens". The industry took notice by awarding him the BMI Songwriter of the Year Award in 2008. All totaled, Pinson has enjoyed five #1 hits and had more than sixty of his songs recorded by previously mentioned artists, as well as country music luminaries such as Brooks and Dunn ("Honky Tonk Stomp"), Rascal Flatts, and Jason Aldean. While he may not have spent a great deal of time in Oklahoma, he did graduate high school in the state, which leaves an indelible imprint on just about everyone, and is an Oklahoman by birthright (according to at least two sources). Pinson's regional sensibility has certainly resonated with other musicians from the state who appreciate the weathered but wizened songsmithing of the "Panhandle Texan". In 2013, Pinson lived in Nashville with his wife, Lucy.

www.bobbypinson.com

Place, Mary Kay
(b. August 23, 1947)

Named Top New Female Country & Western Singer by Record World in 1977, singer and actress Mary Kay Place was born in Tulsa, Oklahoma, to Brad and Gwen Place. She had two brothers, Phil and Ken. Her father was an art professor and chair of the art department at the University of Tulsa, while her mother was a public school teacher. She graduated from Tulsa's Nathan Hale High and from the University of Tulsa with a degree in radio and television production. While growing up in the state, Mary Kay enjoyed singing both pop and country songs for school and local events. In an October 20, 2002 interview with James D. Watts Jr. for the Tulsa World, Mary Kay fondly recalled her music experiences in and around Tulsa, especially singing for her grandparents at an early age.

After graduation from TU, Mary Kay headed to Hollywood to seek a career in writing and comedy performance. As a temporary receptionist at CBS, she was noticed by Tim Conway, who hired her as an assistant for the short-lived Tim Conway Comedy Hour in 1970. This led to a job as secretary to producer/creator Norman Lear on the set of Maude. Lear overheard Mary Kay and a co-worker singing one of her quirky songs, and decided to have her sing it for another one of Lear's sitcoms, All in the Family. She made her television debut as a friend of Gloria (Sally Struthers) and sang the song, "If Communism Comes Knockin' on Your Door, Don't Answer It," for Archie Bunker.

When Lear created the Mary Hartman, Mary Hartman nightly soap opera in 1976, Mary Kay was cast as the wise-cracking, twang-talking country singer Loretta Haggers, who was Mary Hartman's best friend in the series. During the two-year run of the show, Mary Kay wrote more than seventy-five songs for the character, for which she won an Emmy Award. As a result of the character's popularity and convincing country style, Columbia Records signed her to a contract and released Tonite! At the Capri Lounge Loretta Haggers (1976), an eventual GRAMMY nominee.

Mary Kay Place

Accompanied by Emmylou Harris' Hot Band, including **Byron Berline** on fiddle, with back-up vocals provided by Dolly Parton, Emmylou Harris, and Anne Murray, the album produced a Billboard #10 Hot Country single, "Baby Boy," one of Mary Kay's own songs. Additional tracks worth noting include "Vitamin L", one of Mary Kay's compositions, "All I Can Do", a Dolly Parton song, "Settin' the Woods on Fire", a Hank Williams obscurity, and two country gospel songs, "Have a Little Talk with Jesus" and "Good Old Country Baptizin'".

Mary Kay's second Columbia album, Aimin' to Please (1977), included another Top 10 hit, "Something to Brag About", a duet with Willie Nelson. Back-up musicians on this album included fellow Oklahoman **Leon Russell**, as well as James Burton, Emmylou Harris, and Albert Lee. Along with the sassy cowgirl LPcover and marketing campaign, the album featured some funny songs that are as much comedy routine as honky tonk truth: "Don't Make Love to a Country Music Singer", "You Can't Go to Heaven (If You Don't Have a Good Time", a popular version of Rodney Crowell's "Even Cowgirls Get the Blues", and Shel Silverstein's "Paintin' Her Fingernails". Place's co-writes on the album include "Marlboro Man," "Dolly's Dive", and "Cattle Kate".

After Place's experience as a country music artist that she essentially created for herself via Loretta Haggers' character, Place emphasized her acting skills with an exemplary television, movie, and theater career during through 2013. She has written scripts for such television sitcoms as the Mary Tyler Moore Show, Phyllis, The Paul Sand Show, and M*A*S*H, and made guest appearances in such television series as The West Wing and Law and Order. She has appeared in more than thirty films, including Bound for Glory (1976), The Big Chill (1983), Captain Ron (1992), Manny & Lo (1996), The

Rainmaker (1997), Pecker (1998), Being John Malkovich (1999), Girl, Interrupted (1999), Committed (2000), My First Mister (2001), Human Nature (2002), Sweet Home Alabama (2002), HBO's original series, Big Love, and as a band singer in Martin Scorsese's New York, New York (1977). She also sings and plays bass on John Stewart's 1979 album, Bombs Away Dream Babies.

In 2001, Raven Records, an Australian company, released the Ahern Sessions: 1976-1977, an album of twenty tracks from the Tonite! At the Capri Lounge and Aimin' to Please collections.

Place returned to Tulsa from her Los Angeles home to serve as keynote speaker for the 2002 Harwelden Awards ceremony, presented by the Tulsa Arts and Humanities Council to recognize supporters of the arts and humanities. And in 2009, she returned again to receive the Tulsa Award for Theatre Excellence established by the George Kaiser Foundation. In 2013, she made her home in Los Angeles where she continued working in the film and television business.

Point of Grace
(formed 1990 at Ouachita Baptist University, Arkadelphia, AR)

Featuring three graduates of Norman High School – Denise (Masters) Jones, Heather (Floyd) Payne, and Terry (Lang) Jones – Point of Grace formed when the three women were students at Ouachita Baptist University in Arkadelphia, Arkansas, along with another OBU student, Shelley (Breen) Phillips. While part of the university's choral group, The Ouachitones, the Oklahoma girls began harmonizing during a break before a performance. Those within earshot encouraged the women to form a group. After coalescing as a unit by adding Breen, the Contemporary Christian ensemble began performing at a variety functions on campus. After earning first place in a talent contest, Word Records wisened to the quartet's sacred popular music qualities.

With the release of their self-titled debut album in 1993, no one could have predicted the incredible string of twenty seven #1 radio singles and seven million albums sold from through 2012's *A Thousand Little Things*. Featuring the hallmark of Contemporary Christian Music (CCM), or music production that coordinates with a given era's successful popular sound of the moment, Point of Grace added both brilliant harmonies and soulful solo turns that kept the group's sound dynamic and evolving throughout their career.

Along with receiving thirteen Gospel Music Association Dove Awards and two GRAMMY nominations, Point of Grace received numerous Gold and Platinum sales certifications, and is one of the Top 10 best-selling artists in CCM history. As the only original member left in the group, Denise Jones continues leading Point of Grace through tours and recording. She has also written ten books and is actively involved in Mercy

Ministries of America, which helps women suffering from life-controlling issues. As of 2013, Jones lived in Franklin, Tennessee with her husband, Stu, their two sons, Spencer and Price, and their two dogs, Boomer and Sooner.

www.pointofgrace.net

Polygon, Johnny
(b. May 15, 1984)

Born in Cleveland but reared in Tulsa where his family relocated and which he claims as his hometown, Polygon performed with local Tulsa theater groups and began rapping, Johnny Polygon (John Armour) has worked with Russell Simmons, Nas, Amanda Diva, Dead Prez, and others. After an independent video for his song "Bag" perked up the ears of DJ Green Lantern's record label, Future Green Entertainment, after which Polygon's first EP, *Group Hug* appeared in 2009. His song "Price On Your Head" appeared on the video game *Grand Theft Auto IV: Liberty City Invasion..*

Released on an official Polygon mixtape, *Rebel Without Applause*, "The Riot Song" sparked repeated airplay on MTV2, bouncing it into MTV's Top 100 video chart, peaking at #8. Following the success of "The Riot Song" and another popular official mix tape to promote his next EP project, *Wolf in Cheap Clothing*, Polygon decided to go independent and headed back to Tulsa to refresh and record a first full-length album in 2013.

Johnny Polygon

Polygon's song cycles are for smart adults with an urban dance sensibility. Polygon flows full of original rhymes, but can also sing the new soul. With a confident style that could be pop (minus the curses), Polygon's raps are engaging, but he sings better than just about any rapper you can name whoa also 'sings". Check "Limosexsuperstar" on youtube.com to get the vibe as more than 200,000 other watchers have (keep hand on volume if kids are around). Aside from Nitro, Ester Dean, Meant2B, and Uncle Charlie Wilson, Oklahoma has not yet produced a break out pop hip-hop artist nationally. Is Polygon the one to make the pantheon?

www.johnnypolygononline.com

Ponca Tribe
(Arrived in Indian Territory from Nebraska in 1877)

One of several tribes removed to Indian Territory in the 19th century from their settlements on the Great Plains, and now one of thirty-eight federally recognized American Indian tribes, bands, nations or tribal towns in Oklahoma, the Ponca Tribe is one of the primary musical sources for much of what has become the Southern Plains powwow singing tradition, dispersed in the 20th century through the intertribal, pan-Indian powwow now prominent throughout North America. Their songs and style are derived from ancient times when they were one people with the Omaha, Osage, Kansa, and Quapaw, all of whom form the Dhegiha group in the Siouan linguistic family. Additionally, the Ponca's powwow tradition and song history produced the first "world champion fancy dancer," Augustus MacDonald, and the Ponca "hethoshka" war dance and tail dance ceremonies are the model for the intertribal men's powwow dance, the straight dance. The hethoshka songs and dances are also the source of the Osage Inlonshka drums and ceremonies in Hominy, Fairfax, and Pawhuska, Oklahoma. Marking their first modern powwow with the year they left Nebraska in 1876, the Ponca Tribe hosted its 136th powwow in 2012. The Ponca Powwow is both a homecoming opportunity for tribal members who live outside the area, and a chance for people who live around White Eagle, to see friends and relatives at the annual gathering. Before removal from Nebraska, Ponca dances were more ceremonial as a way to honor and commemorate tribal member's accomplishments, or as a community day of thanks and tribal celebration. Contemporarily, the powwow is based both around Ponca songs and dance traditions, but also social and contest dancing. Family songs and individual songs may also be heard throughout the weekend of the annual powwow.

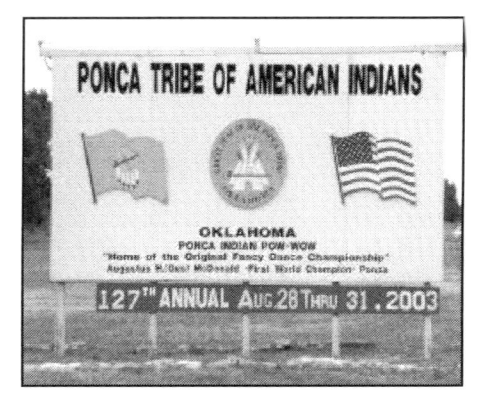

Ponca songs are often credited as deriving from the Omaha, but Ponca singers, such as Anthony "Tony"Arkeketa (b. March 7, 1943, Pawnee, Oklahoma), who grew up and still lived on his family's allotment land on the Ponca reservation when interviewed in 2002, believed the cultural wellspring was the same for all five Dhegiha tribes before they split in the 1600s. The Omaha language and Ponca languages are the same, but have different dialects. Ponca elder, historian, and one of the few remaining fluent speakers of the Ponca language, Louis Headman, explained in a 2001 interview that Dhegiha means "people on our side."

Ponca songs name places where the Dhegiha camped on migrations east to the Atlantic Coast of Virginia and the Carolinas, and then back west to the Mississippi River before dividing. The Quapaw went downstream, and the other four groups traveled to the mouth of the Osage River in Missouri where they divided again. The Osage stayed in Missouri, the Kansa (Kaw) migrated up the Missouri River into Kansas, and the Ponca separated from the Omaha and began traveling toward the Black Hills of South Dakota and southwestern Minnesota's pipestone quarries.

Historical records place the Ponca along the Niobrara River as early as 1673. The Omaha appear to have rejoined the Ponca for a time, but increasing pressure from settlers and the Sioux presaged the Ponca ceding all of their lands in a treaty with the U.S. Government in 1858. Assigned to a reservation in north central Nebraska at the confluence of the Niobrara River and Missouri Rivers, the Ponca began peaceful, agrarian progress toward self-subsistence. In 1865, the Ponca ceded one-third of their reservation to the U.S.

Fancy War Dancers Ponca Powwow, 2002.

Anthony Arkeketa, circa 2003

Government in exchange for permanent title of certain land tracts totaling about 96,000 acres. Nonetheless, the year after Nebraska's statehood, an "oversight" included the Ponca reservation on a large tract of land set aside for the Dakota Sioux in the Treaty of Fort Laramie in 1868. While the Laramie Treaty spells out very minute details such as how many yards of calico and cotton would be provided to Dakota reservation girls over the age of twelve for their clothing, the drafters "forgot" the Ponca were living on land given to the Dakota. Since the Poncas were all of a sudden on Sioux lands, the Dakota began raiding the Ponca reservation for eight years and the Government had a major "Indian problem" on their hands.

Without consulting the tribe, Congress claimed the rest of the Ponca lands in 1876 and began removing the tribe to Indian Territory, a journey of nearly 600 miles over muddy roads made worse by spring rains, and on which many people died. In the summer of 1877, 681 Ponca arrived on the wooded Quapaw Reservation in the flint hills of northeastern corner of Indian Territory. After several months, the Ponca and their agent traveled west and located the space for a reservation along the Salt Fork River in north central Oklahoma near present day Ponca City.

In 1883, a boarding school opened near the Ponca Agency, a Methodist mission began operation in 1890, and the Ponca began their uneasy journey of negotiating the two distinctly different worlds of traditional American Indian life and the American mainstream. According to Tony Arkeketa, Ponca oral tradition says, "The people were lost at that time, no longer a community, and their social structure was in disarray. Alcohol came into the tribe via traders and became prevalent to the extent that there were killings within the tribe." Arkeketa further explained, "The remaining Ponca traditional leaders saw this happening, and picked three men of the tribe to go and find a means of bringing the people back together. The men traveled to Cache, Oklahoma, where they met Quanah Parker, the Comanche who had synthesized Christianity with the Native American Church's peyote religion. From there, they created a Native American Church chapter around 1900 that was openly derided by drunken tribal members outside of the tipi. Since the men of the church only brought back four Comanche Native American Church songs, more songs had to be created."

Tony Arkeketa's grandfather, Ed Roy, was one of the three men, along with Robert Buffalohead. Roy became afireman for the church ceremonies, a role that requires tending the fire in the all-night Native American Church ceremonhy.. Roy also composed some of the songs sung contemporarily, which began a spiritual rejuvenation of the tribe, according to Arkeketa.. The same people who had been outside of the tipi making noise began to go inside out of curiosity, and a meaningful spiritual change took place in the tribe. These songs are best heard on *Ponca Peyote Songs Vol. 1, 2, & 3* (Indian House, 1972), an album recorded by Tony Isaacs in 1972 in Ponca City, Oklahoma. The songs praise the medicine (peyote) and God's word, ask Jesus for help, and celebrate the coming daylight of each service as well just being alive. Singing in the Ponca language are Sylvester Warrior, Harry Buffalohead, James Clark, and Franklin Smith. The songs are typical of other Native American Church songs with vocals, water drum, and rattle all played a fast pace, but their uniqueness lies in the Ponca language and perspective. Contemporary, the LittleCook family, led by Oliver LittleCook, has released several albums of Peyote songs under the titles *Songs of the Native American Church from Oklahoma* (Volumes I through IV), and a further series of ceremonial songs on four albums in collaboration with Perry Botone, Jr. (Otoe/Kiowa). Also, Brian Stoner (Ponca/Cherokee) has recorded Peyote songs for the Canyon label, such as *For Our Loved Ones* (Canyon CR-6397). While the Peyote songs are a fairly recent development of traditional Ponca life in the last 100 years, the original music of the "hethoshka" may be the most influential Ponca contribution to world music in general, but specifically to the North American powwow singing tradition.

Ponca Peyote Song singers in the tipi (l-r): Sylvester Warrior, Harry Buffalohead, James Clark, Franklin Smith, and Joe H. Rush.

"Hethoshka" songs are derived from Ponca history and tell stories about the tribe's experiences in battle and on the hunt. Although never used in preparation for war, nor for the period after conflict, the "hethoshka" ceremony is called a war dance because the songs refer to experiences warriors had in battle, and were a way of preserving Ponca history. The dance continues unabated today with annual gatherings at White Eagle, and one often sees the traditional "straight dancer" at intertribal powwows in regalia whose roots are settled into Ponca traditions. Additionally, through the Ponca "hethoshka," the Osage derived their "I'n-Lon-Schka" drums from the Ponca via the Otoe-Missouria and the Kansa.

According to Archie Mason, an Osage/Cherokee elder and long-time Tulsa public school and university educator, "When the Poncas first arrived on their reservation in Indian Territory, they did not arrive in time to plant crops and were starving. The Osage were already in place on their reservation across the Arkansas River and had plenty of corn and other crops. At that time, one could ford the Arkansas River in a wagon, and the Osage took a lot of corn over to the Ponca. As a return gesture, the Ponca gave the Osage people at Grayhorse a drum and the ceremonial religion of hethoshka, or war dance, and the Grass Dance, most likely from the Omaha. The Osage translated the words into "I'n-Lon-Shka," meaning "war dance."

Contemporarily, that story explains why many songs the Osage use in the Gray Horse I'n-Lon-Shka are of Ponca Origin. One also finds several Ponca people at the Grayhorse I'n-Lon-Shka, usually the first weekend of June. Subsequently, the Ponca gave the Otoe a drum and permission to perform the ceremonies, however, the Otoe could not fulfill the requirements for the drum and they passed it on to the Osage at Hominy, who still have it today. The Ponca also gave the Kansa (Kaw) a drum and permission to dance the hethoshka, but the Kansa could not fulfill the requirements for keeping the drum and passed it on to the Osage at Pawhuska, Oklahoma where it remains until the present time for the annual Pawhuska I'n-Lon-Shka ceremonies. Many of these songs can be heard on *War Dance Songs of the Ponca, Vol. 1 and 2* (Indian House 1967).

The albums are full of ancient Ponca songs recorded at Ponca City in May of 1967, and include singers Lamont Brown, Harry Buffalohead, Joe H. Rush, Russell Rush, Sylvester Warrior, Albert Waters, Louis Yellow Horse, Alice Cook, Lucy C.F. Ribs, and Stella Yellow Horse. A few of the songs were later released on *Proud Heritage: A Celebration of American Indian Music* (Indian House 1996).

One of the Ponca songs on the album recounts the bravado of a warrior during battle with these taunting lyrics: "The enemy, they are coming. There they are. They're coming to seek me out. Enemy, if you're looking for me, here I stand. Come over here!" *Volume 2* includes twenty-two "War Dance Songs" with the same singers but also includes trot songs and charging, or contest, songs.

In addition to the album of Ponca songs released by Canyon Records, *Ponca War Dances* (CR-6143), the historic American Indian Soundchiefs label, founded by Rev. Linn D. Pauahty (Kiowa), also produced albums of Ponca tribal songs and Ponca war dance songs in 1967 that are available on reissue cassette through Indian House Records. *Ponca Tribal Songs* (SC119), recorded August, 1967, contains the "Ponca Flag Song," "Veterans' Song," "Memorial Song," "Three Trot Dance Songs," "Seven War Dance Songs, and "Four Contest Songs," and includes singers Lamont Brown, Sylvester Warrior, Albert Waters, and Henry Snake. *Ponca Warriors Dance Songs and Pawnee Warriors Dance Songs* (SC118) presents ten Ponca "Warrior Dance Songs" sung by Sylvester Warrior, Albert Waters, and Francis Eagle. Finally, the Oklahoma State Arts Council's *Songs of Indian Territory* cassette includes Tony Arkeketa, Edwin Littlecook, and Maynard Hinman singing Ponca War and Scalp Dance Songs.

While the Ponca tried to get back to some semblance of normalcy in the early 20th century, the 101 Wild West Show opened in 1905 just about eight miles south of White Eagle and the Ponca Reservation. The 101 expanded its annual rodeos to include cowboy sports of roping, riding, bulldogging, all sorts of trick riding, and Ponca dancers doing war dances for Eastern tourists who came to Indian Territory in hopes of seeing some "wild Indians." Since the stately and reserved "hethoshka" dances were not quite flashy enough for tourists, the Ponca evolved regalia based on the single bustle they and the Omaha once wore, and started performing athletic dances with a lot of movement to the fast war dance songs as part of the wild West show. The long-term effect of these performances was to popularize Ponca songs outside of their original context to create some of the first "Pan-Indian" music, and to draw interest to the annual Ponca powwows where contemporary fancy dancing was in its infant stages. While the dance was new to the American public and other tribes, the fancy war dance has its roots in both Ponca musical and cultural traditions.

Although various explanations exist for the origin of the fancy dance that has become so emblematic of the contemporary powwow, to include the replication of the moves of a champion stallion, the Ponca have a song about the creation of the dance that has diffused through throughout the powwow world. According to Ponca elder Louis Headman, in the fast war dance songs, one song tells the Ponca story of the origin of the fancy war dance. Headman explains the English translation is, "When I was young, my elder brother took me to see them kill the buffalo." The story behind the words is that the elder brother, a chief's son, took the younger brother out to see the Poncas kill the buffalo. In those days the hunters would drive the buffalo off a cliff by waving buckskin in the air in hopes that the buffalo would fall to their death. Sometimes the buffalo would not die, but would just get angry. Headman says, "The Ponca hunters would wave the buckskin and do all kinds of crazy antics in front of the buffalo so the other hunters could creep around behind them and kill them. The boy saw this and when he got back to the camp he began to mimic the hunters, do somersaults, and do a fast dance with his feet." When the song maker saw this, he began to roll the drum and keep time with the boy's impression of the buffalo hunters. Contemporarily, one will see a lot of quick footwork, fast head movements, and whip sticks twirled around in time with the drum in the manner of the previously mentioned hunters' buckskin.

Given the historic musical connection between the fancy dance and the Ponca, it was not surprising for Ponca dancer Augustus MacDonald to win the first fancy dance championship in 1926 at Haskell Indian Nations Institute in Lawrence, Kansas. MacDonald's victory also secured the right for the Ponca to host the annual world fancy dance championship during the annual Ponca Powwow at White Eagle. The Ponca Powwow remained "the" proving ground for champion fancy dancers throughout the 20th century. While mega-powwows may offer more prize money, no first place trophy means more to a fancy dancer than the one they can win at Ponca. Additional information and history of the fancy war dance can be gleaned from the video *Fancy Dance* (Full Circle Productions, 1997).

Contemporary Ponca singers continue to make an impact on the intertribal powwow world. Anthony Arkeketa grew up around the Native American Church, sleeping behind his grandfather in tipi services as a small child. As he matured into a teenager and began to show musical inclinations, Arkeketa's grandparents paid for his place at the Ponca drum so he could develop into a singer in the late 1950s. Once there, he sat and sang with the famous names of Ponca singing, such as Charlie Waters, Albert Waters, Joe Rush, Russell Rush, Sylvester Warrior, Lamont Brown, and Harry Buffalohead. During that period, Arkeketa was tasked with learning the songs through the oral tradition with Harry Buffalohead. After learning the songs through the oral tradition, as opposed to the modern way of learning from an audio recording, Tony maintains many of the songs today. Arkeketa pointed out that many Ponca songs exist about the way the Ponca's dress, to include the bustle that is now worn by many contemporary traditional dancer, songs for children, songs for society, famous chiefs like Sioux leader Spotted Tail, and places the Ponca lived along the Niobrara River.

As World War I developed the Ponca sang songs about German Kaiser Wilhelm, and during World War II they created songs with Hitler in them. Older men of the tribe wrote songs for returning service people who returned from World War II, and those songs became individual songs that are only performed when the individual or the family of the individual requests them, unless they are "put back on the drum" so everyone can sing them. Every Ponca song has a story behind in it, and in many cases the origin relates directly to Ponca history. Since Tony's generation was the last to learn the Ponca language from fluent speakers, one of the few places Ponca youth can learn the language and history the tribe are through the songs. Some of the music is so old, however, no one knows what some of the words in the songs mean, and the tribe continues singing the songs with the words in them anyway. While some songs related to family groups still exist, others have been forgotten, such as the Sun Dance Songs that seem to have vanished with the participants of the last Ponca Sun Dance held in 1902, while new ones are written for new events and people.

With regard to contemporary intertribal singers, Tony Arkeketa is also generally credited with being an original member of the Brave Scout Singers who brought the higher pitched, northern style of American Indian singing to Oklahoma powwows. In the early 1960s, Tony began traveling on his vacations to the Dakotas, Wyoming, and Montana where he sang with Arikarees, Mandans, Hidatsas, Sioux, all of whom sing in the northern style. Upon returning to Oklahoma, Arkeketa was an original member of the Brave Scout Singers before forming his own group of intertribal singers to replicate the northern style. Singing in public as the Redland Singers since 1968, the group served as host drum from Washington D.C. to Los Angeles, and the North Country Fair to Corpus Christi, Texas, but have never been recorded commercially. An agreement among the group dictated they not profit personally from the music, but only provide the music for people and communities, and record only for historic preservation.

Yellowhammer, Sac and Fox Nation Powwow Near Stroud, OK, 2012.

Some Ponca singers have appeared on commercial recordings, most notably Yellowhammer who have recorded three albums for Indian House Records: *Live at Hollywood, Florida* (1995), *Red Rock, Oklahoma* (1995), and *World Champions* (2001). Although some Otoe-Missouria songs are included on the discs representing the current geographic proximity and intermarriage between the Ponca and the Otoe in north central Oklahoma, Yellowhammer is made up primarily of Ponca singers. Singers on the albums have included Perry Lee Botone, Jr., Mike Gawhega, Jim Grant, Wesley J. Hudson, James Kemble, Jim Kemble, Jr. Garland Kent, Jr., Gregory Lieb, Kinsel Lieb, John McIntosh, Patrick T. Moore, Jade Roubedeaux, Stephen Little Cook, Patrick Moore, Sr., Oliver Littlecook, Jr., Tesa Roubedeaux, and Andrea Morning Star Kemble.

In 1995, Yellowhammer won first place in the Southern Plains singing competition at the Schemitzun, Connecticut Powwow, and repeated the feat in 1997, 1998, and 2001. Many of these same singers contributed to the Fort Oakland Ramblers' initial release in 1992 on Indian House Records, *Oklahoma Intertribal and Contest Songs*, recorded at White Eagle. These last few recordings represent the intertribal, cross-cultural influences that have taken place since the 1800s in Oklahoma, where a shared sense of "Indianness" and a need for commonality in a non-Indian world developed a community of singers who learned from one another and sang together to play a primary role in creating Oklahoma's powwow music. By extension, Ponca singers have had a hand in creating a good share of the southern style intertribal powwow music now commonly heard at powwows across North America.

www.ponca.com

R

Rains, Chick
(b. May 11, 1941)

Born in Muskogee, Oklahoma, Chick Rains is a highly successful guitarist and songwriter who has written several #1 hits for artists such as Johnny Lee ("One In a Million"/1981), Janie Fricke ("Down to My Last Broken Heart"/1981), Mickey Gilley ("A Headache Tomorrow or a Heartache Tonight"/1981), Reba McEntire ("Somebody Should Leave"), Holly Dunn ("That's What Your Love Does to Me"/1988), and two #1 songs for **Wade Hayes** ("Old Enough to Know Better" and "I'm Still Dancin' With You" – both in 1995).

After graduating Muskogee public schools, Chick migrated through a number of colleges before working his way out west in the middle 1960s where here he played clubs in Los Angeles and San Francisco before signing with Capitol Records. After serving in Vietnam for the U.S. Army in 1969 and '70, Rains tried out so more college in Santa Cruz, California before moving back to L.A. where he signed with MGM Records and RCA, and shared a house with Jay Leno.. Not long thereafter, Rains had his first song recorded by an artist bigger than himself, Eddy Arnold. Subsequent to getting a song recorded by The Oak Ridge Boys in 1977, Chick moved to Nashville where he lived from 1978 to 1988 when he scored the previously listed #1 hits, plus a few more in the Top 20 for Michael Martin Murphy and Gary Morris.

Wade Hayes (l) with Chick Rains, at Chick Rains' induction into the Oklahoma Music Hall of Fame.

Flush with what one imagines must have been nice chunk of change, he moved to the spacious environs of New Mexico and played with Michael Martin Murphy's band for about three years before moving back to Nashville in 1990. Top 5 hits penned by Rains followed for Mark Collie ("Born to Love You") and Laurie White "Now I Know" before Wade Hayes took the two previously mentioned songs to the promised-land at the top of the *Billboard* Hot Country Singles chart.

Along with his own compositions, Rains has also co-written with Harlan Howard, Marty Stewart, Keith Whitley, Kix Brooks, John Rich, Michael Martin Murphy, and others. On top of the artists referenced already, Chick's songs have also been recorded by Johnny Cash, Waylon Jennings, George Jones, Roy Clark, Lone Star, and Laurie White.

In 2008, Chick was inducted into the Oklahoma Music Hall of Fame in Muskogee. To honor Rains, Wade Hayes performed the #1 songs Wade enjoyed that were written by Chick.

Red Dirt Music

With Jimmy LaFave, Tom Skinner, Bob Childers, The Great Divide, Red Dirt Rangers, Cross Canadian Ragweed, Jason Boland and the Stragglers, No Justice, John Fullbright, and a host of other rootsy singer songwriters and groups centered around north-central Oklahoma, especially Stillwater where its primary musicians met, usually as college students at Oklahoma State University, or musicians surrounding the musical opportunties in a cowboy college town. When humor is not the object of a song's lyrically focused intent, subtle and melancholy appraisals of rural and small town society's decay fill the verses of red dirt music, and, occasionally, a song about love lost or gained creeps or weeps its way into the mix. In 2003, Cross Canadian Ragweed's Cody Canada suggested the term should possibly be transmogrified to Red River music because of the propensity of the Oklahoma bands to have more success south of the Oklahoma border than in the state where they started.

The first Oklahoman to hint at the "genre" is Kiowa-Comanche-Muscogee guitarist Jesse Ed Davis, whose "Red Dirt Boogie, Brother," a funky, self-defining tune about "plain old rock and roll," appeared on his 1972 album *Ululu* (Atco). Close behind in name, if not definition, is Steve Ripley whose early 1970s band, Moses, recorded for Ripley's independent Red Dirt Records. Liner notes by Mike Dougan on the band's self-titled debut in 1974 explains Red Dirt is a record label and "also the color of the earth surrounding Enid and nearby Stillwater, Moses' home base. More important, Red Dirt is a hue of funk, a shade of sound, a basic spirit embodied in Moses' music."

While the genre's anthem is Jimmy LaFave's "Red Dirt Roads at Night," and LaFave recorded his first album in Stillwater in 1978, the first artist to emerge on a national scale from the Stillwater scene was Garth Brooks who began singing at Willie's Saloon on Washington Street in 1985. After a failed attempt that year at breaking through Nashville's long established musical hierarchy, Brooks returned to Stillwater and started a group called Santa Fe in 1986. Filling out Santa Fe were Tom Skinner, roundly considered along with Bob Childers as one of red dirt music's early shapers, as well as Tom's brothers Mike and Craig, on fiddle and guitar respectively, and other Stillwater musicians such as Matt O'Melia (drums), Dale Pierce (b. 11/29/1960, OKC - d. 2/9/2004, Stillwater, OK)/(steel guitar and dobro), and Jed Lindsey (guitar).[1] After graduating from OSU with a degree in marketing, Garth again headed for Nashville. There, he rec-connected with Bob Childers who introduced the one-time OSU javelin thrower to the manager who would elevate Brooks' career.

Referred to as the godfather of red dirt music, Bob Childers was born in West Virginia, studied music at the University of California-Berkeley, and began traveling the country in 1972 when he arrived in Stillwater and discovered Chuck Dunlap, a local Stillwater-based singer songwriter who still reins as the elder statesman of the musical crowd. Childers decided to stay in Stillwater and played locally until 1978 when he met Jimmy LaFave. With LaFave's assistance, Bob recorded his first album, *I Ain't No Jukebox* (1979). Childers' second album, 1982's *Singing Trees, Dancing Waters*, gained him enough critical attention for a White House gig in Washington, D.C., and enough confidence to move to Nashville in 1986, followed closely by Tom Skinner and Garth. (Childers' career is covered in an entry under his name in *OMG II*).

Although Tom Skinner was born in San Francisco, he and his two musically inclined brothers, Mike and Craig, grew up in the Route 66 town of Bristow about thirty miles

Santa Fe, 1987 (l-r): Tom Skinner, Jed Lindsey, Garth Brooks, Mike Skinner, Matt O'Melia is not pictured here.

southwest of Tulsa. Skinner moved to Stillwater in 1972 where a short attempt at Oklahoma State University bore few fruits other than Skinner's first guitar chords. After a stint in the Air Force where he played in his first bands, Tom returned to Oklahoma in 1978 and re-enrolled at Oklahoma State. Soon, his brothers followed and they soon began performing around town as The Skinner Brothers Band, most notably at Willie's Saloon where Garth Brooks also frequented the open microphone nights. Garth hooked up with the brothers who eventually became the nucleus of his first group, Santa Fe, where the evolving red dirt sound began to take solid commercial shape. Skinner moved to Nashville for a short time in the late 1980s, but returned to Oklahoma for his young son's sake, migrated to Louisiana for a while where he began recording for Binky Records, to include *Times Have Changed* (1996), and *Acoustic Skinner* (1998). Skinner's 2012 self-titled album produced by **Mike McClure** for 598 Recordings is a must for red dirt followers. Garth even says so. Skinner continues to be an active performer in Oklahoma as of 2013 and could be heard weekly at his Wednesday Night Science Project at the Blue Rose Cafe in Tulsa..

Tom Skinner

Along with Bob Childers' albums, Binky has also released two compact discs by Greg Jacobs, the Choctaw, Oklahoma native who found his way to Stillwater in the 1970s for college, and turned into another singer-songwriter now associated with the red dirt sound. After rambling through Kentucky and then taking a shot at the Nashville scene that did not take to his highly personal songs, Jacobs returned to Oklahoma. Working as an opening act for **Kevin Welch** and Jimmy LaFave, Jacobs recorded two independent albums, *Looking at the Moon* (1994), and *Reclining with Age* (1996) Currently a high school history teacher in Checotah, Jacobs' albums, *South of Muskogee Town* (1997) and *Look at Love* (1999), are chock full of stories about Oklahoma's hard rural history in the 20th century - "A Little Rain Will Do," and "Okie Wind," as well as seldom-told stories like that of **Muscogee (Creek)** patriot Chitto Harjo in "South of Muskogee Town," a song about the Green Corn Rebellion of 1918. His 2001 release that recycled an earlier album title, *Reclining with Age* (Binky), continued Jacobs' themes and storytelling style of his earlier releases. Greg Johnson at the Carnegie Hall of red dirt music, the Blue Door in Oklahoma City, released a live album recorded at the legendary intimate room in 2009, released as *Lucky (Live)* (Blue Door), and distills what is captivating about Jacobs' storytelling songs.

Greg Jacobs

Young bands and singer-songwriters have played local talent nights and open microphones in Stillwater for as long as college students have been drinking beer in the north central Oklahoma town, but a unique environment opened in May of 1979 when John Cooper (Red Dirt Rangers) and recreation specialist major Danny Pierce moved into a rural six-bedroom farmhouse on 149 acres for a hundred bucks a month. Only a few miles west of

Stillwater, "The Farm" quickly gained a reputation as a communal jam space, party center, and flophouse for local musicians and college students throughout the 1990s. Roughly 60 roommates moved through The Farm during its ten-year existence, and although the Red Dirt Rangers' Brad Piccolo didn't live there, he was a constant presence and credits his inspiration for seeking a music career to seeing Jimmy LaFave singing a Bob Dylan song on the front porch one night. Also present at various times were Bob Childers, Tom Skinner, Greg Jacobs, and Garth, all of whom headed out to The Farm when Stillwater's bars closed and musicians still had the desire to jam. Texas singer-songwriter Robert Earl Keen stopped by at one time or another where bonfires were set and musicians played until dawn, as did Brandon Jenkins, Mark Lyons, Curt Nielsen, and Chuck Dunlap. Dunlap recorded a 1980 album called *Daze Gone By* (Snowbound), featuring Kevin Welch on guitar, and sporting a jazzy, folk feel with pedal steel, bongos, saxophone, banjo, and plenty of harmony vocals. In 2005, Dunlap released a retrospective of his songwriting, *Journeyman* (Fringe Records).

Chuck Dunlap, 1980

In the last year or two of The Farm's existence, before a Methodist church bought the property in 1999, relative newcomers to Stillwater, Cody Canada of Cross Canadian Ragweed, Mike McClure of the Great Divide, and Jason Boland emerged on the scene. Boland had one of the Stragglers' first promo pictures taken on the porch of The Farm, and images of the now legendary homestead have been forever preserved on **Mike McClure**'s website (www.mikemcclure.com). Other bands that played in the garage, the front room, the basement, or the fields throughout the 1990s included the Cimarron Swingsters, the Red Valley Barnstormers, the Flat Mountain Boys, and the Medicine Show, whose 1994 album, *Medicine Show Live at the Tower Theater* (recorded in 1992), stirs up great jam clouds of red dirt music, as does their 1997 release, *Midnight Ramble,* recorded live in Fayetville, Arkansas. Other local Stillwater artists who have close connections to the scene include Mitch Cason, Beverly Mayes, and DaddyO's Music owner, songwriter and guitarist, Mike Shannon (b. Tulsa, 1953), and Jeffrey Gray Parker. Also, Monica Taylor and Patrick Williams, both Cherokee Nation citizens better known as The Farm Couple who currently live in Afton, have been performing together since 1996 when they debuted at the Winfield Bluegrass Festival. Monica was living at The Farm at that time, and Patrick was living near Grove, Oklahoma. Their independent CD, *Songs from the Kitchen Table*, was recorded in "one take per song" in a studio overlooking a lake in Eureka Springs, Arkansas, and features songs about ramblers, Civil War veterans, and other down-and-outers.

Monica Taylor, 2012

Other singer/songwriters generally placed in the red dirt genre include Tulsa-based Larry Spears (b. Sapulpa), whose CD, *Reflection in the Wishing Well*, featuring songs about Woody Guthrie, Jesus, and better times that have passed. Tom Skinner also adds bass and vocals to the album. The as association between red dirt musicians swirls as much as the Oklahoma wind in May. Skinner covers Larry Spears on his 2013 self-titled album mentioned earlier on 598 Recordings, and Greg Jacobs does a Spears tune on live album recorded at the Blue Door. Gene Collier (b. Drumright, r. Cushing) is another songwriter better known through other red dirt artists, having penned the perennial college bar favorite, "Oklahoma Boys," carried out to the world by Cross Canadian Ragweed. Exhibiting the

Hugh W. Foley / 657

back-and-forth-from-Oklahoma-to-Texas-nature of red dirt groups, The Burtschi Brothers' debut album, *Uncertain Texas*, was recorded in Travis Linville's Norman bedroom, and after a little success, the group recorded CD number two in Austin, Texas, followed by a live recording in Tahlequah which exhibits their extended jams where "Jimi Hendrix meets Willie Nelson in outer space." Formed in Norman in 2000, The Burtschi Brothers are allied with the red dirt groups, but also work outside of the roots music formula playing pop, alternative, jazz, or jam band pieces, extending their repertoire, as it were.. The Brothers' band includes Travis Linville (guitar), Mike Phenix (bass), Kevin Webb (guitars), and Chris Foreman (drums). Linville is also an in-demand session player and touring musician for several groups from the southwest region. Other sidemen who are well-known for fleshing out the textureof multiple red dirt groups include guitarist Terry "Buffalo" Ware (Ray Wylie Hubbard/Jimmy LaFave/John Fullbright, et al.) fiddler/guitarist Randy Crouch (a.k.a. "the Hillbilly Hendrix" for his rock fiddle work), and multi-instrumentalist Nokosee Fields (b. Stillwater) who has recorded with Travis Linville and **Other Lives**.

Another Oklahoma native musician with red dirt tendencies, Brandon Jenkins (b. June 7, 1969, Tulsa), has made his home in Austin after growing up in Tulsa. Jenkins attended Oklahoma State where he graduated with a B.A. in Sociology, tried out Nashville for a while after he had signed with a label in Alabama that tried to market him as a country act, and then returned to Tulsa before heading south across the border to Austin's intensely music friendly environment. Jenkins' 1998 CD, *Faded*, brands his style as "Western Soul, a hybrid of country, blues, and rock-n-roll," which allies it closely with basic tenets of red dirt music. By 2013, Jenkins had released nine albums of his grittier take on the soul reflected through his stories couched in a grooving blues rock. Also fitting into the more rocking side of red dirt are the Turnpike Troubadours (f. OKC, 2007), whose 2012 country rock album, *Goodbye Normal Street*, peaked at #57 on *Billboard's Top 200* album chart. No Justice rocks just hard enough to be thought of outside of red dirt music realm, but they are more or less guilty by association, if nothing else for the fact they formed in Stillwater (circa 2001). The group has really started to come into its with a corner on the tougher end of country rock; their last two albums, *2nd Avenue* (Carved, 2010) and *America's Son* (Smith Ent., 2012) have both inched into *Billboard*'s South Central heatseekers charts, along with presence in the upper reaches of the Texas Music Chart, which not every red dirt artist does.

Blessed with a honky-tonk crooner's voice, Stoney LaRue joined up with the Organic Boogie Band in 2001 to become concert favorites throughout the red dirt touring region of OK, TX, MO, KS, NM, and CO. His 2011 effort, *Velvet*, distillshis musical imprint, but his live albums capture what makes Stoney LaRue a solid preference for red dirt fans. LaRue has made Mike Hosty's "Oklahoma Breakdown" so well know that Hosty is always getting asked in Texas why he is doing Stoney LaRue's song. LaRue's recognition of the red dirt intertwinings is certainly obvious on his first album *Downtown* (2005). Larue, who is originally from Texas but has spent much of his time in Oklahoma since his teens, and began playing around 1999 in Stillwater. Downtown is has red dirt in all its windowsills, with two songs co-written by LaRue and Jason Boland, and covers of songs by Brandon Jenkins, Bob Childers, and Mike McClure.

Another historic cog in the red dirt story is multi-instrumentalist, music teacher, studio artist, and recording engineer **Jeffrey Gray Parker** who was born in Arkansas City, Kansas in 1956, but raised in Newkirk, Oklahoma. After a short stint in St. Louis, was in Norman from 1970 to 1989, and moved to Stillwater where he lived from 1989 to 1998. Aside from Jeffrey Parker's individual releases, his Cimarron Sound Lab in Stillwater was the site for the recording of *Red Dirt Sampler, Volume 1: A Stillwater Songwriters' Collective*. The album is a primer for red dirt music fans. Songs by all the first generation of the sound's luminaries, Tom Skinner, Brad James (lead guitarist for the Organic Boogie Band), Mike McClure, Greg Jacobs, Bob Childers are on the CD, as well as songs co-written by Parker with Skinner and Bob Kline. A **Cherokee Nation** citizen, Parker relocated his Cimarron Sound Lab to Cherokee County, near Tahlequah, in 1998. His career is covered in more detail under his name in *OMG II*.

The Norman-based The Damn Quails are on the precipice of being the region's next favorite band on the red dirt circuit due to their lyrical originality, musical sophistication, and unique vocal stamp. Mike McClure recognized it, producing and releasing their first album, *Down the Hatch* on his 598 Recordings. The biggest dust cloud in 2012 and 2013 got kicked up by Okemah homeboy, John Fullbright (b. April 23, 1988). Of course, in the spirit of collective musical enjoyment, Fullbright appears on The Damn Quails album, but it was Fullbright's first studio album, *From the Ground Up* (Blue Dirt Records) that was nominated for a GRAMMY as Best Americana Album. While Fullbright did not pick up the GRAMMY, he did get to perform "Gawd Above" at the 2013 GRAMMY pre-telecast which was streamed live on the GRAMMY website. He also won the 2012 ASCAP Foundation's Harold Adamson Lyric Award, and toured the UK in 2013 where his first show in London was a sell-out. Fullbright's fans dig his deft guitar skills, sensitive/inightfully humorous lyrics, and very pleasant singing voice, which is a contradistinction to a lot of the red dirt talk-singers whose stories are usually more important than how well they are sung.

John Fullbright performing in Cushing, OK, 2013.

While DaddyO's Music store, run by songwriter/guitarist, Mike Shannon, is still the folkloric center for Stillwater's musicians since the 1980s, the epicenter of red dirt may have shifted to Glencoe, Lone Chimney, and Cushing. Two of the Red Dirt Rangers live in rural areas east of Stillwater near the small town of Glencoe; same for Steve Ripley who sold the Church Studio in Tulsa and moved out to his family's land acquired in a land run to build an ultimate studio environment (where the Rangers recorded their 2013 release, *Lone Chimney*). Cushing is in the mix now because of the regular Tuesday Night Music Club for local singer/songwriters, as well as having a journalistic champion, Rick Reily, who is also a songwriter, and pens monthly columns in *The Corridor* magazine about new and established red dirt artists such as Sean Kelly, Chad Sullins, Scott Carson, and Slapout. More names in the mix of red dirt music include John Amos, K.C. Clifford, Amanda Cunningham, Travis Kidd, and Bruce Henderson.

While red dirt music may often only be a tag placed on musicians from the Stillwater area (and now much of central Oklahoma) who write their own songs and play in traditional American music veins, the category is also useful for describing music that is at times one person with a guitar and a story to tell, and at other times a gutsy jam band freak-out not afraid of a little twang; all of which draws inspiration from **Woody Guthrie**'s lyrical abilities, **Bob Wills**' wide open approach to popular music, and Will Rogers' plain-spoken humor to create a sound and story unique to north central Oklahoma, but enjoyed throughout the southwest.

Notes
1. For more insight into 1980s Stillwater, see Matt O'Melia's book about those years in Stillwater, *Garth Brooks: The Road Out of Santa Fe* (OU Press, 1997).

Red Dirt Rangers

Inspired by **Jimmy LaFave**'s song "Red Dirt Roads" and the red dirt around north central Oklahoma where the group took its primary shape in the 1980s, the Red Dirt Rangers are one of the most representative and long-lasting groups who emerged from the roots music **Red Dirt Music** scene from around Stillwater, Oklahoma from the 1980s through the 2000-teens.

Comprised initially when Stillwater native Brad Piccolo (b. April 22, 1961), Oklahoma City-born John Cooper, and Bob Wiles (b. Tulsa, OK) all became musically inspired during their college days at Oklahoma State. Piccolo had picked up a guitar when he was fifteen, strumming it alone and learning chords, but never played with anyone until meeting Cooper in college. Cooper's first musical experience was singing in church choirs, and started playing mandolin when he arrived at O.S.U. and met Piccolo who had one and showed Cooper a few chords. With Bob Wiles, they traveled to the Winfield Bluegrass Festival in Winfield, Kansas, known as "the picker's paradise," and gained both confidence and a bluegrass base that would stay with their music for the duration of their playing and recording career.

The first semblance of a gig between future members of the Red Dirt Rangers occurred in 1981 at Aunt Molly's Coffee House, an open microphone setting in the Oklahoma State student union. The group did not play formally until the mid 1980s when Cooper and Piccolo would get together because of the lack of a music scene in Oklahoma City and jam on covers, eventually adding Ben Han (b. Borneo) on lead guitar, and connecting with drummers. **Jimmy LaFave** came by their place one night and invited them to his annual Stillwater reunion show at Willie's Saloon in the late 1980s and early 1990s. As a result of the success of that performance, the Red Dirt Rangers formed and had their official paid debut in May of 1990 at a festival in Oklahoma City. Piccolo lived in Austin at the time where he played in another band and would drive up from Texas to play with the Rangers.

Red Dirt Rangers (l-r) Brad Piccolo, John Cooper, Ben Han.

Keeping their day jobs, the Rangers played around once a month experimenting with various musical configurations, one of which involved two accordionists, one on rhythm and one on lead. Gradually, the Rangers began to get better gigs and played in New York City in 1993 because of an old friend, which turned into more dates in upstate New York. Subsequently, Piccolo relocated to Oklahoma City and the band recorded their first album in 1992, a cassette-only release intended as a demo, *Cimarron Soul*, now the name of the Rangers' publishing company. The group recorded and mixed the album in one night at Stillwater's Lamb Studios and its primal rawness still makes it a fan favorite, although it is long out-of-print and circulates primarily by bootlegs. Later in 1992, The Rangers' dropped the accordion players, and added Dale Pierce, who had played in early incarnations of Garth Brooks' band, on dobro, banjo, and Melobar, drummer Scott Buxton, and Dave Clark on guitar. The band recorded their first proper album, *Red Dirt Music*, at Bill Belknap's Long Branch Studio in Tulsa, and called in red dirt luminary Tom Skinner to help with the mixing. Along with a geographic nod to the area around Stillwater in "Cimarron Valley," the man often referred to as the godfather of red dirt music, Bob Childers, wrote two songs and co-wrote another song on the album.

In 1994, the band decided to tour Oklahoma in a school bus and do thirty shows in thirty days across the state. The Rangers played from Black Mesa to Wilburton at clubs, weddings, festivals, and campfire gigs at state parks. They also met multi-instrumentalist Benny Craig in Tahlequah on the tour and he started playing fiddle and steel in the group in time for the 1994 independent recording, *Oklahoma Territory*. The album was a watershed moment for the band as they enlisted legendary producer Lloyd Maines in Lubbock, Texas, and had their first taste of national chart success in the developing Americana radio format. The band spent fourteen hours a day in the studio for a week and recorded songs with a lot of Oklahoma references such as "Cimarron Valley" and "Idabel Blues." Continuing to play regionally, the Rangers' used the disc as a springboard to Europe where they played a trucker festival in Switzerland in 1997.

On returning to the states, the Rangers recorded a one-off track for the Lazy SOB compilation, *The Songs of Route 66*. As a result of "Used to Be," a Bob Childers/Bob Wiles composition about a once active and now lonely stretch of Route 66, the band negotiated a deal with Lazy SOB to record their next album, and continued touring until 1999 when they began laying down *Rangers' Command* in Austin, Texas. Again working with Lloyd Maines, the band added **Alvin Crow** on fiddle and mandocaster for one track, Cindy Cashdollar from Asleep at the Wheel and Bob Dylan's band on dobro and steel guitar, and rough country sizzler Dale Watson on electric guitar on another. While drawing on major southwestern musical sources for inspiration and players, the lyrics drew a blueprint for red dirt music's literary perspective: original tunes with a sense of humor, two songs with Bob Childers as a co-writer, one song with Tom Skinner as a co-writer (an eerie foreshadowing of Benny Craig's premature death on "The Day the Mandolin Died"), two sets of obscure Woody Guthrie lyrics that had not been put to music before, and a wacky bluegrass cover of Prince's "1999." Partly due to the millennium change in 2000 and the inclusion of the Prince song, *Rangers' Command* made it to #21 on the Americana chart in January of 2000. That success led to constant regional touring, ceasing only in the spring of 2002 to record a new album with the Tractors' **Steve Ripley** at the legendary Church Studio in Tulsa, once owned by Leon Russell, and from 1987 to the present is owned and operated by Ripley.

Released independently by the Rangers, *Starin' Down the Sun* marked a shift in personnel for the group as they recruited a new drummer, Jim Karstein, known for his work with Gary Lewis and the Playboys, Leon Russell, Eric Clapton, J.J. Cale, Joe Cocker, Bobby "Blue" Bland, and Taj Mahal, and lesser known for his work on Cheech and Chong's "Basketball Jones." Rocky Frisco, another J.J. Cale luminary, plays on the record, as does their old friend from the Medicine Show, **Corey Mauser**. Muskogee trombonist and trumpeter Lee Norfleet adds tracks, as does Terry "Buffalo" Ware, Steve Ripley, Bob Childers, and **Byron Berline**. **Dwight Twilley** makes an appearance on vocals as well as being the topic of one song, "Dwight Twilley's Garage Sale." While Piccolo and Cooper wrote several songs on the album, as did Bob Childers and Brandon Jenkins, Bob Wiles also wrote or co-wrote a few tunes on the record as his swan song performance with the band due to carpal tunnel syndrome, as well as just a general need for a change after 13 years with the group. With a new album full of Oklahoma music luminaries, a new bassist in Jamie Kelly, and starting to work with steel/fiddle/guitarist Randy Crouch, the Red Dirt Rangers toured consistently through 2003. They added an additional element to their performance repertoire by releasing a children's album, *Blue Shoe: Music for Kids of All Ages*, which garnered them gigs at elementary schools and other children's activities across the state.

Since 2003, the group has continued on as the de facto amabassadors for red dirt music, equally adept at bluegrass, folk, country, blues, rock, or a combination of all those elements, which is in a nutshell - red dirt music.. The band survived a horrible scare in 2004 when a helicopter in which they were riding crashed into the Cimarron River, killing the pilot and another passenger. Han, Piccolo , and Cooper held on to each other on the wrecked aircraft until help arrived. After recovering, the band seemed to have a new joy about life, and pursued every opportunity that came their way. After releasing their next project, *Ranger Motel* in 2007, the band continued playing gobs of gigs, doing their *Red Dirt Radio Hour* (heard on KOSU-FM, Stillwater, Sunday nights at 9 p.m. CST/or online at KOSU.org. as of February, 2013.

In 2013, their 25th year as a band, the Rangers expected to release their new album, Lone Chimney, recorded by **Steve Ripley** at his farm-based studio near Glencoe, and not too far from Lone Chimney, OK. Along with performing their two-man play, Time Changes Everything (co-authored by Thomas Conner and John Wooley), in which Cooper and Piccolo portray a fictional meeting between Bob Wills and Woody Guthrie. At the core of Oklahoma's grass roots, red dirt, and folk scenes for years, in the spring of 2013, the Rangers were scheduled to play at the opening of the new Woody Guthrie Center in Tulsa, the facility housing the Woody Guthrie Archives. At last contact with the author, the band was also ey planning an Oklahoma World Tour that would take them back and forth across the state throughout the year.

wwww.reddirtrangers.com

Reinhart, Dick

(b. February 17, 1907 – d. December 3, 1948)

One of the finest Western swing vocalists due to his combined ability of crooning cowboy pop and singing the blues convincingly, Dick Reinhart is also recognized for his compositions "Fort Worth Jail", "Hot Rod Baby" and "A Broken Heart for a Souvenir". A former Light Crust Doughboy, Reinhart was born in Tishomingo, Oklahoma, the county seat of Johnston County, and home to about 3,000 residents. By the late 1920s, he was living in Dallas, where he learned to sing the blues from African-American musicians in Deep Ellum, the well-known blues district that produced "Blind Lemon" Jefferson.

Dick recorded with the Three Virginians on the Okeh label in 1929, when he displayed a falsetto jazz voice on such songs as "June Tenth Blues." Two years later, Dick formed the Wanderers with Roy Newman and Bert Dodson and they recorded for Bluebird. Later that year, Dick joined the Light Crust

Dick Reinhart

Doughboys, in which he played rhythm guitar and shared the vocals with Dodson until the latter departed. Two of his classic performances with the Doughboys were "Ding Dong Daddy" in 1936 and "Sittin' on Top of the World" in 1938.

Reinhart left the Doughboys in 1938 to join the Universal Cowboys for a recording session in Dallas with Vocalion. On June 23, 1939, they recorded "Aloha Means Goodbye" and "Cow Town Swing" with Dick singing. On April 21, 1940, he recorded four more songs, including "Just a Honky Tonk Girl," "It Won't Do you No Good," "Don't Ever Say Adieu," and "Little Brown Eyed Girl." Before leaving the Dallas area, Dick formed The Lone Star Boys to be found on a rare recording of "Truck Driver's Coffee Shop" on the Country Music Hall of Fame and Diesel Only Records collaboration *Truck Driver's Boogie: Big Rig Hits, 1939-1969*. In the 1940s, Reinhart moved to Oklahoma City where he teamed with **Johnny Bond** and **Jimmy Wakely** to form The Bell Boys on a daily radio show on WKY in Oklahoma City and on KVOO in Tulsa. After **Gene Autry** had toured Oklahoma and suggested he could use the trio, Dick joined Johnny Bond and Jimmy Wakely and their families for the trek to California in May of 1940. Autry hired the trio as regulars on his CBS Melody Ranch show.

After the move to California, Dick signed with Art Satherly on the Okeh label, a subsidiary of Columbia Records. In the early 1940s, he recorded several sides for Okeh, including "Don't Make Me Wait Too Long," "I Know What You're Thinkin'," "No One to Kiss Me Goodnight," "You're the Red Red Rose of My Heart," "Hey Toots," and the timeless "Wooly Booger." Bond and Wakely accompanied him on the Okeh sessions.

Reinhart's composition, "Fort Worth Jail," was recorded by such diverse artists as Lonnie Donegan, Woody Herman, Skeets McDonald, and Ernest Tubb. Dick's final recording session for (Okeh) Columbia in 1947 included "Muddy Water", and demonstrated his saturation in the blues as a primary stylistic influence. After returning to Fort Worth, he suffered a fatal heart attack at age forty-one. Reinhart appears on at least three early 20th century compilations, *Night Spot Blues* released by the U.K.'s Krazy Kat Records, and *Hot Rod Baby* (Binge), a German imprint. as well as on the 2001 Bloodshot release of *Country & Western*, a compilation of Johnny Bond's hits.

Restless Heart
Gregg, Paul (b. December 3, 1954)
Innis, Dave (b. April 9, 1959)
Jennings, Greg (b. October 2, 1954)

Formed in 1983 as the "Okie Project," Restless Heart included three native Oklahomans (Gregg born in Altus, Innis born in Bartlesville, and Jennings born in Nicoma Park) and were produced by Scott Hendricks, another Oklahoman from Clinton and an Oklahoma State University alumnus, and Tim Dubois, born in Grove, Oklahoma, and holder of a master's degree in accounting from OSU. The original Restless Heart was a quintet with John Dittrich and Larry Stewart as the non-Okies. Some called the group the latter-day Eagles with their soft country rock harmonies and adult contemporary sound.

Stewart, a Kentucky native, moved to Nashville and enrolled at Belmont College, where he met Innis at a recording studio on campus. Innis introduced Stewart to DuBois. The latter and Hendricks needed an outlet for specific compositions because some of their material was "too popular" for Nashville and "too country" for Los Angeles. Thus, the two Oklahomans invited five musicians to cut some demo tapes, and the combination worked as the group scored a streak of fifteen Top 10 country hit singles in a row with six of those topping the country charts, beginning in 1986 and ending in 1990. DuBois and Hendricks were already familiar with the musicianship of keyboard player Innis, who had written the Pointer Sisters hit "Dare Me," while guitarist Jennings had played on several Dan Seals hits.

Restless Heart, 1987 (l-r): David Innis, Greg Jennings, Larry Stewart, Paul Gregg, John Dittrich.

The group's first single, "Let the Heartache Ride," broke into the Top 40 of the country charts, and they were signed to a RCA recording contract in 1985. Their debut album in 1985, *Restless Heart*, spawned a Top 10 hit single, "I Want Everyone to Cry." However, it was their second album, *Wheels*, released in 1986, that became their most successful with three #1 hits, including "Wheels," "Why Does He Have To Be (Wrong or Right)," and "I'll Still Be Loving You," which has become a wedding classic, entered the Top 40 of the popular charts at #33, and reached #3 on the adult-contemporary charts. The ten-track album also contained four songs penned by DuBois, Jennings, Innis, and Gregg, including "The Boy's on a Roll," "Victim of the Game," "Hummingbird," and "We Owned This Town." As a result of their accomplishments, Restless Heart was nominated for the CMA Horizon Award and Vocal Group of the Year in 1987.

Although the *Big Dreams in a Small Town* (1988) and *Fast Movin' Train* (1989) albums, both RCA releases, did not fare as well as *Wheels*, their 1991 collection, *The Best of Restless Heart*, featured three more of their #1 hit singles, "Bluest Eyes in Texas," "That Rock Won't Roll," and "A Tender Lie." It was followed by the 1992 album, *Big Iron Horses*, which produced one the biggest crossover hits in 1992, "When She Cries." It became a Top 10 country hit, soared to #3 on the adult-contemporary charts, and reached #11 on *Billboard*'s Hot 100 pop singles. For these successes, it captured the ASCAP Song of the Year award in 1992.

The *Matters of the Heart* (1994) and *Tell Me What You Dream* (1995), both RCA productions, were the last of the early 1990s albums as the group began to disintegrate. Stewart had already departed the group in 1990, whereas Jennings joined **Vince Gill**'s band as guitarist and Gregg took a three-year hiatus from music, managing several family-owned businesses. The group members, however, remained in contact, and, in 1996, produced a tape for an ill fan. This resulted in a reunion album, *Greatest Hits*, released by RCA in 1998. The thirteen-track come back collection included the five #1 hits, as well as "When She Cries." Shortly thereafter, Stewart, Jennings, Gregg, and Dittrich joined Vince Gill on a national tour. During their peak years, Restless Heart had five certified gold albums, received a dozen GRAMMY, CMA, and ACM nominations, and were named ACM's Vocal Group of the Year in 1990. As a result of this #1 pop country legacy, the group has continued touring regularly, with a slate concerts book across the U.S. in 2013.

www.restless-heart.com

Ricochet

(formed Columbia, Misouri in 1984)

Known for their dynamic and twangy stage shows, multi-part *a cappella* harmonies, and renditions of "The Star-Spangled Banner" at major professional sporting events, Ricochet bounced to the top of country music in 1996 with a the #1 country hit, "Daddy's Money," and have been on the road since. While other original members hail from such diverse places as East Greenbush, New York and Lafayette, Tennessee, Ricochet's Perry Heath Wright (lead vocals/lead guitar/fiddle – b. April 22, 1967) and Greg Cook (bass/vocals – b. January 28, 1965) were both born in the east central Oklahoma town of Vian, ten miles west of Sallisaw, and have been playing together at least since 1988. In 1993, Drummer Jeff Bryant (drums/vocals) first hired Heath Wright into Bryant's group Lariat, already featuring his brother, Junior, who played anything with strings and sings. Lariat disbanded shortly thereafter, and players came and went for a year until Ricochet settled into Teddy Carr (pedal steel), Eddie Kilgallon (keyboards/horns/vocals), and Greg Cook, Wright's childhood friend, in early 1994.

The group played widely for a couple of years in the honky-tonk and dance hall country circuit that extends from coast to coast in the southern half of the United States. The band developed a fan base, practiced, and cut a demo that landed in the hands and ears of a Columbia Records-Nashville talent scout, who then signed the band to a development deal, which provides a little cash for a group under a pre-determined producer. By 1995 the group's vocal and instrumental talent became more and more obvious to record executives through live performances and subsequent crowd reactions, and the deal quickly escalated into an official contract. They recorded their first album, *Ricochet* (Columbia), and toured with **Merle Haggard**, Doug Stone, and Charlie Daniels while the label released their first single, "What Do I Know," that became a Top 5 country hit. Presto, Ricochet was rolling, and since the full album came out in early 1996, the wheels of their tour bus have not stopped rolling around the country.

Behind the #1 country single, "Daddy's Money," and Top 10 hit, "Love Is Stronger Than Pride," *Ricochet* careened through the charts as the best selling group in country music for nineteen weeks that year. The ACM awarded Ricochet Top Vocal Group and Top New Vocal Group honors for 1996, and the radio industry publication, *Radio and Records*, named Ricochet as "Group of the Year" in their 1996 readers' poll, voted on by radio programmers from around the U.S. After being named CMA's Vocal Group of the Year in 1997, their follow-up effort, *Blink of an Eye* (1997), did not keep up the first album's sales figures, but the album did garner three humble country chart singles, "Connected at the Heart," "He Left a Lot to be Desired," and the title track. Continuing to tour through 1998 and 1999, and again named the ACM's Top Vocal Group in 1998, the band had a few more modest charting singles taken from recordings that were never released as an album.

The fast ride and long haul had worn out a couple of members; drummer Jeff Bryant's carpal tunnel syndrome necessitated a replacement (Tim Chewning), and steel guitarist Shannon Farmer took over for Carr who left the road for home, family, and a successful carpet cleaning business. With Farmer's additional vocal abilities, Ricochet began finding further success with specialty *a cappella* (voice only) recordings and performances.

Hugh W. Foley

In 2000, the group's third release, *What You Leave Behind* (Columbia), is a transitional collection of unreleased songs from a few years previous, some new tunes written or co-written by the band, a first in itself for Ricochet albums, and a few songs contributed by their producers. The album's first single, "She's Gone," enjoyed subtle chart success, and the song's video received substantial airing on CMT.

The only group to ever chart the National Anthem, Ricochet has become a constant presence at major sporting events with their *a cappella* rendition of "The Star Spangled Banner," which one can hear free on their website. They have also become closely connected to the hugely popular NASCAR racing circuit. They are the first musical act to sponsor a qualifying day for a major NASCAR race, having signed on for the 2000 "Ricochet Qualifying Day" at the Winston 500, and have opened numerous races with their beautifully layered harmonies. Every year since 1995, Ricochet headlines the Annual Green Country Jam in the Vian Football Stadium to benefit St. Jude Children's Research Hospital. Well-known acts the band has met through the years appear as well, such as Steve Wariner, **Bryan White**, and Lila McCann. The band continued touring through 2002, gaining accolades for a July 30th show in which they "wowed country fans" with their sonically powerful vocal harmonies, full force country band, and confidence that only comes with being a #1 group. Continuing to tour through 2012, two Ricochet greatest hits packages were released by Mi Records, *Ricochet Reloaded-Hits/Plus* (2008) and *Ricochet 15 Years of Hits and Counting* (2012)..

Ripley, Steve
(b. January 1, 1950)

Recognized as an ace studio engineer, record producer, multi-faceted guitarist, vocalist and guitar craftsman, Steve Ripley led the Tractors, a roots-rocking country outfit whose aesthetics run from **Bob Wills** and 1950s rock and roll, to the evolving bluesy shuffle of the Tulsa sound of the 1960s and 70s, as well as **Red Dirt Music**'s equally hyphenated descriptions from the 1980s and 1990s, to multi-platinum status with the best selling album in country music for 1994. With its Top 10 country hit, "Baby Likes to Rock It," co-written by Ripley and keyboardist Walt Richmond, the debut, self-titled album sold over two million copies, earning double platinum status and a gaggle of accolades. The album earned The Tractors three ACM award nominations (Top Vocal Group, Top New Vocal Group, and Album of the Year), a TNN/*Music City News* Award nomination (Stars of Tomorrow/Vocal Duo or Group), two Grammy nominations (Best Country Performance by a Group for "Baby Likes to Rock It" and "Tryin' to Get to New Orleans"), and won the Country Music Association's Video of the Year Award for "Baby Likes to Rock It." *USA Today* raved about the album, and *Entertainment Weekly* gave it an "A."

Steve Ripley (right) with Jamie Oldaker.

Grasping The Tractors comes with understanding Steve Ripley, born in Boise, Idaho to Oklahoma native Robert, then a mid-twenties traveling cookware salesman just out of the Army, and Mary (Bonser) Ripley, whose family came from Oregon. The couple traveled throughout the north and mid-western United States, moving as many as twenty times before buying a farm next to the old Ripley homestead Steve's great grandfather acquired about ten miles southwest of Pawnee in the Cherokee Strip land run of 1893 when "excess" tribal lands were opened to white settlement. The cookware business led the family from the farm to Tulsa in 1954, then on to Oklahoma City for three years, a period in which Ripley's first musical experiences came when the family returned to the homestead on Christmas holidays and summers. At the farm his Uncle Elmer, a Bob Wills fan, had a great collection of Bob Wills, **Johnnie Lee Wills**, and Hank Williams 78 rpm singles that became Steve's earliest musical passion. Subsequent musical influences were his older cousins, then teenagers in 1955, who came back from working the west Texas oil fields talking about a guy tearing it up down there named Elvis Presley, at the time still touring the southwest and southeast United States on the strength of his Sun singles.

Ripley's parents gave him his first guitar in 1956, and Presley's domination of shifting American popular music tastes collided with the six-year-old's energy, and there was a match. In a 2002 interview, Ripley remembered being firmly convinced he was Elvis at that age, and could sing the songs banging along on an out-of-tune guitar. In the summer of 1958, the family relocated permanently to the farm near Glencoe, an agricultural and former copper mining community of about 500 people in north central Oklahoma, and within a year Steve learned his first chords on guitar. Ripley's age also put him in line to hear and be influenced by the music of the Ventures in 1962 and '63 with their guitar heavy sound fronted by native Oklahoman **Nokie Edwards**, leading Ripley and early musician buddies to play surf tunes like the Surfaris' "Wipeout," later covered by the Ventures, and about a hundred other bands. By 1965, Ripley began playing with various incarnations of rock and roll bands, and made his first recordings with The Verzatiles at age 15 in Gene Sullivan's Oklahoma City studio, then one of the few recording studios in Oklahoma, and most of the primary equipment from which Ripley now owns and has in his Church Studio in Tulsa.

Just as Ripley became confident with the 1950s rock of Elvis and Chuck Berry in various guitar-based bands, the Beatles elevated the American roots music of Chuck Berry, Motown, and rockabilly to the next level by writing their own songs and experimenting with developing studio technology. Evolving with the times musically and becoming more aware of the significant lyrical developments in rock through Bob Dylan, Ripley joined his next band, the Stillwater-based In-Keepers, who played teen dances and became regulars on Ronny Kaye's Oklahoma City television show, *The Scene*, an Oklahoma version of *American Bandstand*. Ripley remembered the band "had seven or eight guys and two go-go dancers."

After graduating high school in 1968, and since he had already been playing with the In-Keepers out of Stillwater, Steve enrolled in the state school known for "pigs and plans," Oklahoma State University, just about 10 miles as the crow flies from his home in Glencoe. While at OSU, Ripley continued playing with In-Keepers at frat parties, teen dances, and around the various bars in and around Stillwater. A nucleus of the In-Keepers evolved into the band, Moses, and that group helped put its members through college by playing a steady line of gigs in the area. Graduating in 1972 with a B.S. in Broadcasting and a double major in sociology, Ripley worked steadily with Moses and started his own label, Red Dirt Records to release an album by Moses. The record became the first release locally of any consequence in the town that would come to be known as the center of **Red**

Dirt Music, and also marks the beginning of Ripley's engineering and producing career enhanced by his radio/TV training in college.

While red dirt music is generally associated with Stillwater, *Moses Live* (Red Dirt Records, 1974) was actually recorded in Enid at the Fillin' Station. The liner notes for the album, written by Mike Dougan, imply the geographical inspiration for the music comes from "the color of the earth surrounding Enid and nearby Stillwater, Moses' home base." Recorded live to an Ampex eight-track tape machine Ripley hauled to Enid in a pickup, and mixed at Stillwater Sound, the studio started in 1973 by Ripley with a Small Business Administration loan, *Moses Live* features Ripley on guitar and vocals, Steve Irby on keyboards and vocals, Bruce Hueston on drums and vocals, and Robert Hatfield on bass and vocals. Of particular interest is the early version of Ripley's composition, "Oklahoma Blues," the only original on the album and a clear aural window through which one can hear the infant musical rumblings of Ripley's future success with The Tractors.

After a couple of years trying to run the Stillwater studio as a business and not getting ahead significantly beyond meeting his wife, Charlene, who came through the studio in 1974 as a trumpeter and keyboardist in the Perkins High School jazz band. Ripley closed the studio in 1975, continued playing in bands, and married Charlene in 1976. The young couple moved to Nashville for a couple of broke months before returning to Oklahoma City that same year where he worked for a couple of weeks at Benson Sound in Oklahoma City as a recording engineer, a job that didn't last because of Steve's "hands-on" approach to the recording process that clashed with the owner's production philosophy. Out of work, Ripley called an old friend who was working as an engineer for Leon Russell's Shelter label at the Church Studio, and talked his way into a job running monitors for Leon's live shows through the rest of 1976.

By early 1977 and the end of the tour, Russell decided to relocate his operation back west, and Ripley picked up a side gig driving Leon's motor home filled with various studio and band gear to California, and is when Ripley played some of his demos, recorded at the Church Studio, for Leon. While Russell liked the way they sounded, and subsequently hired Ripley as an engineer in his studio, a gig that did not last for similar reasons as Ripley's Benson Sound experience: mainly that Ripley wanted to be involved in the process of the music's creation, an ethos Russell perceived as "too busy," and so he let the twenty-eight-year-old engineer go. With his newly acquired free agent status, Ripley and Charlene returned to Tulsa in 1977 where Steve started working for the Oklahoma-based talent impresario, Jim Halsey, who had plans to build a studio in Tulsa and put Ripley in charge of assembling the studio space and equipment.

In April of 1978, Halsey enlisted Ripley's services as a producer and engineer for Johnnie Lee Wills' *Reunion* album for Flying Fish Records, a recording that brought back many of the elder and active Western swing players, and in the fall of the same year Ripley produced and played on a collaboration album by Roy Clark, then managed by Halsey, and Clarence Gatemouth Brown, *Makin' Music* (MCA, 1979). By 1979, Leon Russell called Ripley again, however, since Ripley basically set up the California studio, and was really the only person who knew how it was put together.

Charlene and Steve move back to California in 1979 where Ripley again assumes the engineering duties for Leon, and has the occasion to stick his head into the open Steinway while Russell is playing it, which begins an obsession by Ripley with getting the same full sound out of a guitar that he heard in Leon's piano. With all of Leon's equipment at his disposal, Ripley begins experimenting with using a guitar, fabricated by an old steel player out of Steve's favorite Fender Telecaster, to create an output from each string and then run them through six different amplifiers at the same time. "Everybody loved it and people kept coming around to play it," Steve remembers, and just as word started getting around the Los Angeles music scene about Ripley's invention, Russell decided to leave California again, and left Steve wondering what to do next. He would not wait long as fellow-Oklahoman, and all-world drummer, Jim Keltner called and invited Steve to some rehearsals for Bob Dylan who wanted to try out some new material before recording it, and urged Keltner to bring along anybody he wanted to play guitar. Keltner called Ripley, who had long admired Dylan, and whose guitar now had six outputs for six amplifiers. Not wanting to bring in six amps, which were all Leon's anyway, Ripley stopped at a music store on the way to the rehearsals and bought a small mixer to run the six outputs through, and then took a stereo output from that mixer into two amplifiers. Dylan and Steve hit it off, and after five or six weeks of rehearsals, Ripley played guitar on Dylan's "Shot of Love" in 1981, and toured Europe and the states with Dylan throughout the rest of the year.

After getting off the tour, Ripley began working with building a small mixer into the guitar, and everyone he showed it to wanted one, including Ry Cooder and Eddie Van Halen, who introduced Ripley to the Kramer Guitar Company. Ripley started working for Kramer, with his guitars favored by artists such as **J.J. Cale,** John Hiatt, and Jimmy Buffett, as well as being Eddy Van Halen's friend, guitar man, and business partner from 1982 through 1986 when Steve's mother became ill, and necessitated Ripley's return to Oklahoma with not only a little assistance from Van Halen who funded the expensive move.

After moving back to Tulsa in the fall of 1986, Ripley, along with friend and partner Glen Mitchell, bought the building at 304 S. Trenton Avenue in the fall of 1987, known more famously as Leon Russell's Church Studio, and began writing and recording songs. Ripley's first release as The Tractors was a Christmas single in 1988, and he subsequently spent several years creating the Tractors' debut album by putting together an excellent collection of musicians: Walt Richmond (b. McAlester, OK, April 18, 1947), pianist and co-producer for the album, played keyboards for years with Bonnie Raitt and Rick Danko; Ron Getman (b. Fairfax, OK, December 13, 1948) is a guitarist and steel guitarist who has toured with Janis Ian and Leonard Cohen; Casey Van Beek (b. Leiden, Holland, December 1, 1942) anchored Linda Ronstadt and the Righteous Brothers' stage bands with his steady basslines; and Jamie Oldaker (b. Oakland, CA, September 5, 1951) kept time for many years on stage and in the studio as Eric Clapton's drummer.

Taking his time to figure out how the group could embody his vision of "Hank Williams meets Chuck Berry" the Tractors' debut, self-titled album with its persistent nods to the musical heritage of country music, brought down the houses on Music Row when it came out of Oklahoma in 1994 to outsell major acts like Alan Jackson and Brooks & Dunn. With guest shots by Ry Cooder and James Burton, *The Tractors'* success opened up multiple touring opportunities and the group hit the road in 1995 to play a hundred shows to roughly half a million people in the U.S. and Europe. Riding completely unexpected mega-success, the group released a full Christmas album (with plenty to celebrate) in 1995, *Have Yourself a Tractors Christmas* (ARISTA-Nashville), featuring "Baby Likes to Rock It" as "Santa Claus is Comin' (In a Boogie Woogie Choo Choo Train)." Over the next couple of years, the group rarely played out in public, but contributed tracks to well-received tribute compilations. In 1996, the band provided "Think It Over" for *Not Fade Away: (Remembering Buddy Holly)* (MCA), and received a Grammy nomination as Best Country Duo or Group for "Tryin' to Get to New Orleans." In 1997 the group covered

"It's All Over Now," on *Stone Country* (Beyond), an album of country artists twanging up Rolling Stones songs.

Given Ripley's penchant for perfection, and following his own schedule of quality over quickness in the Church Studio, The Tractors' second album, *Farmers in a Changing World* (1998), arrived in a pop country world altered by Shania Twain and other country pop icons who enjoyed the cyclical return of Nashville pop that has taken place since Chet Atkins added brush drums and tinkling piano to Elvis Presley's music in 1956. The same retro-**Tulsa Sound** that boosted the first album into the commercial stratosphere hindered the sophomore effort's acceptance in Nashville. The album also arrived on shelves just as ARISTA's Nashville office, bolstered by The Tractors' success in 1994, and headed by Oklahoma State University alum Tim Dubois, closed its doors, effectively shutting off any promotional effort on behalf of the album. Fans loved *Farmers in a Changing World* for exactly what it was not, another hackneyed Nashville studio production geared toward the video market. Bonnie Raitt plays slide on the album, and Ripley shows off James Burton, Scotty Moore, and D.J. Fontana, all of whom made careers with Elvis Presley, among others, and many historians would say helped make the career of Elvis Presley. Hear the guts of Elvis's greatest musical periods on "The Elvis Thing." Also reaching back to Tulsa's Western swing history, Ripley enlisted **Bob Wills**' long-time fiddler, Curly Lewis, for "Way Too Late," on which the spirit of Wills' guitarist Eldon Shamblin is also invoked via recordings made by Steve before Shamblin's death. Additionally, as a result of Ripley's long career as an engineer privy to moments the public never hears, a fun element of Tractors' albums includes the various sound clips, musicians' commentary, and hidden tracks from the sessions, all of which are crystalline moments that really encapsulate the recordings, but rarely make it onto commercial country albums. Whatever qualities the album possesses for Tractors fans, it got lost in the Nashville music industry shuffle.

With no record deal, Ripley went back to the business of the studio and preparing material for the next Tractors release. In 2000, he signed with Audium records and in 2001 released *Fast Girl*. The project again brought together great players from all corners of Steve's long career of acquaintances and friendships. "Ready to Cry" was co-written by Leon Russell who played Steinway piano and Hammond organ on the track. Bluegrass mandolin virtuoso Sam Bush is on the recording, as are repeat offenders D.J. Fontana, and James Burton who has played on every Tractor release up to *Fast Girl*. Tulsa-born drummer Jimmy Karstein, who has played with Gary Lewis and the Playboys, Leon Russell, Eric Clapton, J.J. Cale, Joe Cocker, Bobby "Blue" Bland, and Taj Mahal, makes a guest percussion appearance, while Fontana's drums and Burton's guitar fuel the album's primary single, "Can't Get Nowhere," the video for which features shots around various Tulsa locations, to include the Church Studio and Cain's Ballroom, the legendary home of Bob Wills and Johnnie Lee Wills, and includes cameos from Leon's Russell's daughter, Tina Rose, **Zac Hanson**, and various other insiders and musicians who do and don't play on the song.

Fast Girl also contains a spooky reminder of September 11th, 2001. "911" was certainly never intended as such (it was meant as a tribute to New Orleans pianist Huey Piano Smith) but now has a macabre resonance. Ripley laments the digital age in "Computer Controlled," a lazy J.J. Cale-influenced tune drenched in the **Tulsa Sound**, and covers a Moon Mullican Western swing number, "Don't Ever Take My Picture Down." He also reflects on the people of his rural background in Oklahoma on "Higher Ground," with mentions of Pawnee County and Black Bear Creek.

In 2001, "Baby Likes to Rock It" resurfaced on a patriotic country compilation, *This Is Your Country: 20 Contemporary Country Classics* (Universal), a collection that places the song on par with Lee Greenwood's "God Bless the U.S.A." and tracks by Shania Twain and **Vince Gill**. Also in 2001, Steve Ripley began working on his first solo release, spent time at the helm of recording projects for contemporary Oklahoma artists such as the **Red Dirt Rangers**, and contributed two songs to the soundtrack of an independent Oklahoma film, *Round and Round*, the subject of which is the issue of cockfighting in Oklahoma, since banned in the 2002 state election by a narrow vote, but broadly ignored by several county judges. Ripley wrote and performed both the film's title track, "Round and Round," and "Oklahoma Blues," the latter of which can be traced back to Ripley's Stillwater group, Moses. Both songs appear on Steve's 2002 solo album, *Ripley*, released jointly through his own Rocking Boy Records and Audium.

While the J.J. Cale-tinged "Round and Round" was originally written with the cockfighting film in mind, Ripley was also influenced by the events of September 11, 2001 and re-reading of Revelation that harkens back to his days in the Baptist church. For "Gone Away," also from his solo album, Ripley enlisted the advice of ex-ARISTA Nashville executive Tim Dubois and *Tulsa World* music writer John Wooley for help on the song which is a rumination of many American popular culture icons that have gone by the wayside or into nostalgic status, such as Marilyn Monroe, Elvis, '57 Chevys, and *Leave It To Beaver*. Lyrically, the entire album is a meditation on aging and its inherent loss of connection to popular culture, old friends, and the death of loved ones. Through the first eight tracks on *Ripley*, the singer laments the dissolution of his personal connections to popular culture from the 1930s through the 1960s, faded childhood dreams, and absent adult lovers before finding salvation in an old 1937 Alvin Carter song, "No Depression (In Heaven)," and a Southern gospel influenced song with the Jordanaires on backing vocals, "Crossing Over," the final cut on the album where the singer's mother waits to welcome him home on the other side of the River Jordan.

The Jordanaires, who backed Elvis Presley on his most significant gospel recordings, further extend Ripley's associations with musicians who worked with Elvis. With sharp guitar solos, shuffling drum beats played mostly by Ripley, and the warm resonance of the antique tube microphones he uses in the studio for vocals, the album represents both the modernity of the Tulsa Sound and the evolution of Ripley as a solo artist who has deeply personal themes to express in his music.

Ripley released a ten-track Christmas CD under The Tractors' name, *The Big Night* (Boy Rocking/Audium, 2002), and has plans for a 2003 children's album, *Chicken Covers* (Boy Rocking/Audium), the title song for which was co-written by Tulsa-based character Gailard Sartain. Also in 2003, his solo album reached #10 on *Radio and Records* Americana Radio Chart

Ripley recorded two more records under The Tractors moniker, *The Kids Record* (Boy Rocking, 2005) and *Trade Union* (Boy Rocking, 2009), and also produced a 20-part radio series based on Oklahoma rock and roll in 2009, all of which happened about the same time Ripley sold the historic Church Studio and moved back out to the family land in Pawnee County, where he began building a new studio and became the Oklahoma version of British rockers of the 1960s who moved out to the English countryside to get away from the city.

Openly acknowledged as one of Steve's biggest influences, Bob Dylan singled out Ripley as one of the good guitarists who had played with him in a May 9, 2009 *Rolling*

Stone interview (p. 45) - - legendary status secure. Along with rescuing, repairing, and re-configuring all manner of audio equipment and stringed instruments, Ripley recorded the Red Red Dirt Rangers' 2013 release, *Lone Chimney*, and continued living the quiet life with his wife and co-farmer, Charlene out there in the country where he can think (and hear) a little more clearly.

www.thetractors.com

Rivers, Sam
(b. September 25, 1930 - d. December 26, 2011)

As one of the leading *avant-garde* jazz composers, arrangers, and instrumentalists of the 1960s, Samuel Carthorne Rivers was born in El Reno, Oklahoma, a community of approximately 15,000 population located immediately west of Oklahoma City. Sam was immersed with music at an early age as his father and mother, as well as grandparents were musicians, especially in the gospel genre. His father was a graduate of Fisk University and sang with the Fisk Jubilee Singers and the Silvertone Quartet, while his mother was a pianist who gave him lessons as early as four years old. Sam's grandfather wrote and published in 1882, *A Collection of Revival Hymns and Plantation Melodies*. He was also exposed to other styles of music including jazz (listened with his father to Count Basie and Cab Calloway) and classical, primarily Stravinsky. At age eleven, Sam began working on the trombone and tenor sax, and played soprano sax in school marching band at age twelve. Sam's family left El Reno and moved to Chicago, then on to Little Rock, where his mother taught music and sociology at Shorter College. Thus, more or less ending the free-jazz giant's connection to Oklahoma, as he never appears to have returned. Nonetheless, he was born into an formally educated musical family in the state demonstrating the high level of education of some African-Americans in the state, a legacy of the Black town movement. One aspect of Rivers' incredible career does relate to the story of other Oklahoma musicians. Several Oklahoma jazz, rock, and pop artists were successful because of their ability to cross over to other styles of music. Rivers is quoted on his website as saying, "I have the distinct honor of eing the only musician inthe history of jazz to have performed with the most important musicians in blues, swing, bebop, and the avant garde," which places him in that tradition.

Sam Rivers

www.rivbea.com.

Romanello, Tony
(b. March 8, 1977)

By starting to play guitar at age six in his native Tulsa and forming his first band at age fourteen (YSY), it should be no major surprise Tony Romanello surfaced in 2003 as the latest Oklahoma pop/rock musician to receive national critical recognition, and appears poised to transform his multi-layered, lush arrangements, sensitive lyrics, and pleading vocal style into wider success beyond the national college radio charts.

Tony Romanello (center) with the Black Jackets, 2013

After taking guitar lessons from Dick Gordon, Sr. from ages six to twelve, and graduating Tulsa Bishop Kelley High School in 1995, Tony attended the University of Oklahoma where he formed the independent rock group, Murmur, and recorded a six-song CD with Matt Vandever (bass) and high school buddy, Ben Marshall (drums). After adding Eric Knox on keyboards, Murmur played regionally with some limited success before disbanding in 1999. After the group dissolved, Romanello went into the studio with Trent Bell, long known for his guitar work in the Chainsaw Kittens and a multitude of production and engineering credits (Chainsaw Kittens, Starlight Mints, Pistol Arrows, **Flaming Lips**). Having all the songwriting credits on Murmur's songs, Romanello added several and converted the lot into his first solo project, *The Mumble Odd* (Engine Shed, 2000), an album that makes many promises of bigger things to come

Full of Romanello's talented guitar work that ranges from simple power chords, flashy leads, and lyrical melody lines ("Fingertips," "Run Away," "Sky"), *The Mumble Odd* also exhibits his more contemplative acoustic guitar ("How to Drop Things," "Can You Feel This"). Vocally, Romanello is often compared to the tragically-fated Jeff Buckley, largely because of a singing style that often soars over the music without dominating it obtrusively ("Everything"), or Brian Wilson of the Beach Boys due to the upper register singing backed by layers of harmonics ("Lo-Fi Dreams in Stereo"). Inner-self lyrics are often written in the first person, making the singer the spokesperson for an introspective life channeled through a sparkling melancholy ("A Red Shade of Somber," "Under the Blue." Pianist Eric Knox also adds some beautiful keyboard work to the album that elevates it beyond the basic drums, bass, guitar rock format. Additionally in 2000, Romanello released an independent collection of out-takes, demos, sketches, and finished works, *Lo-Fi Dreams in Stereo*, an album whose title takes its name from the final track on *The Mumble Odd*, and is available only through his website.

After graduating OU in 2000, Tony returned to Tulsa and formed The Tony Romanello Band (TRB). Assembled with the intention of being able to play *The Mumble Odd* live, the group consisted of Josiah Borgos (drums), Andy Callis (guitar), Brad Hall (bass), and Blaine Nelson (Rhodes piano). TRB played regionally most of the way through 2001 before returning to Tulsa and recording the EP, *Shades of Grey* (Engine Shed, 2001). A three-part suite of his now trademark crushing guitars, stratospheric vocals and ability to assemble musicians who provide just the right musical atmosphere and cohesion, *Shades of Gray* earned the *Tulsa World's* Best Rock Act of 2001 at the annual Spotnik Awards, just one of several he has earned from his hometown's paper (Artist of the Year 2002, Best Local Album 2002, Best Rock Act 2001 and 2002, Rising Star 2000).

Following *Shades of Gray*, Romanello returned to Bell Labs to again record with Trent Bell where they worked together to assemble a massive studio album that is diverse as it is glistening. At times recalling The Beatles' *Magical Mystery Tour* and *Yellow Submarine* period ("An Insomniac's Diary," "Finally Found") and continuing to channel the ghost of Buckley ("The Amazing Disappearing Man," "The Artist"), *Counting Stars* (Engine Shed, 2003) features a multitude of overdubs, samples, experimental instrumentation (string quartet, horns, tablas), and effects-laden vocals that place it in line with Oklahoma's other pop mad scientists, **The Flaming Lips** (Lips' drummer Steven Drozd plays all drums and percussion on the album) and Starlight Mints. Lyrically, the album continues Romanello's thematic fascination with lonely and misguided characters trying to find the big answers ("Finally Found," "Algiers," "Tell Me Please"). Hook after memorable hook ("Novocain," "De Leon") makes one wonder how long it will be before some major label discovers this talented songwriter and musician who is making epic pop songs for the post-rock & rap world.

Critical raves for *Counting Stars* have come from as far away as France and England, but Romanello's appeal to the American college radio market has cemented his status as an up-and-coming artist in the U.S. While the album did not break the *College Media Journal*'s top fifty, it did receive airplay on at least fifty college stations nationwide from California to New York, by all counts a national success for an independently released album in Tulsa by an artist who is really just starting what could be a career of significant distinction. In July, 2003, Romanello released a four song EP, *Where Are You Tonight*, produced by Brad Mitcho (Glass House, Molly's Yes). The EP includes a song recorded live at Rogers State University's college radio station, KRSC-FM. Not long after, Tony relocated to Texas where he worked on solo material which led to his 8th album, *Lo-Fi Dreams in Stereo: Vol 2.* In 2009, Romanello returned to Tulsa and formed the Black Jackets, releasing a five-song EP, *Pleased to Meet Me* in 2012. The group includes Romanello (vocals/guitar), Andy Callis (guitars/backing vocals), Mike Taylor (guitars/backing vocals), Matt Vandaveer (bass), Mike Friedemann (drums), and special guest Philip Zoellner on keys.

www.tonyromanello.com

Rooney, Joe Don
(b. September 13, 1975)

As a member of the contemporary country trio, Rascal Flatts, winner of the CMA Horizon Award in 2002, talented instrumentalist (plays guitar and mandolin), vocalist, and songwriter Joe Don Rooney was born to Windel and Jo Rooney in Baxter Springs, Kansas, but raised in Picher, Oklahoma, a community of roughly 2,000 residents located in extreme northeastern Oklahoma that is a former lead-and-zinc mining town and still a source of environmental controversy as the U.S.'s oldest Superfund site. Joe Don graduated from Picher-Cardin High School and attended Northeastern Oklahoma A & M junior college in Miami, for two years.

Joe Don's primary musical influences were his siblings (Robin, Kelly, and Mike), all interested in myriad forms of music. Several Oklahomans were influential in Rooney's early musical training, including **Steve Gaines**, **Merle Haggard**, and **Vince Gill**, who Joe Don lists as his favorite singer. His first musical performance was with his mother, father, and sister Kelly, when they sang for church. "Freight Train," composed by the legendary Elizabeth "Libba" Cotton, was the first song Joe Don learned as a child. As a teenager, Joe Don was an electrical apprentice to his father and worked various janitorial jobs.

Country music became an important professional element in Joe Don's early career

Joe Don Rooney

when he began working at age nineteen at the Grand Lake Opry in Grove, Oklahoma, located approximately thirty miles south of his hometown. The Grand Lake Opry, modeled after the Grand Ole Opry, sponsored monthly shows featuring country music artists from Nashville and Bakersfield, such as Porter Wagoner, **Billy Parker**, **Wanda Jackson**, Connie Smith, and **Merle Haggard**.

Rooney met the other two members of Rascal Flatts (Jay DeMarcus and Gary LeVox, second cousins and close friends from Columbus, Ohio) when he and Jay were working in Chely Wright's band in 2001. At the same time, the two cousins were playing gigs in Nashville. Lacking a full time guitarist, they invited Joe Don to sit in with them at a weekend show at Printers Alley in Nashville, and the trio was complete. According to Joe Don, his high voice blended well with the other two members and the Rascal Flatts chemistry was born, although the group was originally called Okla-hio, combining the states of origin of the band members. As Joe Don recalled after hearing themselves on stage, "It really, really was magical. We honestly didn't have to work hard at it. It was so natural and so much fun."

The threesome recorded some demo tapes that were sent to producer Dan Huff, who liked the group's strong vocal harmonies and outstanding musicianship. Although not involved in the project, Huff recommended the group to Lyric Street Records Senior Vice-President of A&R, Doug Howard. Within four days, Howard had signed the trio to a contract.

Their self-titled album went platinum in 2002, and resulted in four consecutive Top 10 hits, including the first single, "Prayin' for Daylight," followed by "This Everyday Love," "While You Loved Me," and "I'm Movin' On." Rascal Flatts was invited to perform at Nashville's Wild Horse Saloon as part of Country's Class of 2000 during the Country Radio Seminar in March of 2000. Because of their ties with the Disney Corporation, the group recorded a new Sting song ("Walk the Llama Llama") for the movie soundtrack, *The Emperor's New Groove*, released in 2000. They were invited in 2001 to the 74th annual Macy's Thanksgiving Day Parade in New York City, where they rode the Santaland Express float, performing their "Prayin' for Daylight" single.

Rascal Flatts received their first major award in 2000, given by the ACM for Top New Vocal Duo or Group. The video of "I'm Movin' On," the single from their eponymous album that soared to the top of the country charts in 2002, was nominated for the CMT Flameworthy Video Awards in the category of Best Video From an Artist's Debut Album. At the 2002 CMA awards press conference in Nashville, where Rascal Flatts helped with the announcements, the trio was nominated for two honors: Vocal Group of the Year and the Horizon Award. They won the latter at the televised CMA awards show in October of 2002. The group released their next single, "These Days," from their second album, the platinum-plus *Melt*, that hit the record stores in the fall of 2002. "These Days" debuted at #2 on Yahoo's LAUNCH, the highest spot a country group had achieved on the Yahoo chart, and also charted #4 on *Radio & Records*, #1 on *Billboard*, and #4 on Blue Chip Radio Report, in the fall of 2002. In October of 2002, ABC Radio's *Country Coast to*

Coast, broadcast on more than 150 stations to some 1.5 million listeners, nominated Rascal Flatts as Best Vocal Group/Duo for 2002 for their Best Country Around-Fan's Choice Awards. Competing with **Brooks and Dunn**, Dixie Chicks, Trick Pony, and Montgomery Gentry, the latter was declared the winner.

Joe Don's songwriting credits include "1/2 That Makes Me Whole," "How Do You Feel," and "Right Now," recorded by Chad Brock, and co-writer on "Like I Am" and "Shine On," both on the *Melt* CD. The latter song is Rooney's tribute to students and faculty at Picher-Cardin High School. Rooney believes the group is successful because of the eclectic mix of their musical roots, including bluegrass, gospel, and rhythm-and-blues. Moreover, the trio reports that Lyric Street Records, a division of the Disney Corporation, has allowed the band to take country music in a a new direction focusing on highly polished pop music production without all the usual country music trappings. The concept has obviously worked with seven albums being released on the label were certified platinum (one million units sold). After Lyric Street closed up shop in 2012, the band switched to Big Machine Records. The group has one multiple CMA, ACM, CMT, AMA, People's Choice and *Billboard* awards, with a GRAMMY for Best Country Song/Songwriter Award in 2006 for "Bless the Broken Road". Rascal Flatts became members of the Grand Ole Opry in 2011 and received a star onthe Hollywood Walk of Fame in 2012. According to the group's website, they would be touring the world and the U.S. for most of 2013.

www.rascalflatts.com

Royal, Marshal Walton
(b. May 12, 1912 - d. May 9, 1995)

As lead alto sax player and music director of the Count Basic Orchestra for almost twenty years (1951-1970), instrumentalist, bandleader, and arranger Marshal Royal was born in Sapulpa, Oklahoma, immediately west of Tulsa. Marshal was raised around music as his father was a bandleader, music teacher, and played all the reeds, strings, and some of the valve instruments, while his mother was a pianist.

The family moved to Los Angeles in 1916. Prompted by his father at age four, Marshal studied violin under a graduate of the Paris Conservatory, and while in high school, he was first chair (concert master) in his high school orchestra. His father had organized a family orchestra, known as The Three Royals, and Marshal made his professional debut with the group at age twelve in Los Angeles. Often compared to Benny Carter, Royal's rich alto sax solos with a string of excellent big bands made him popular both nationally and internationally. He died in Los Angeles on May 9, 1995.

Marshal Royal

Marshal Royal: Jazz Survivor, an autobiography written with Claire P. Gordon, was released in 2001 by Continuum Press.

Rubin, Mark
(b. August 8, 1966)

Having anchored country/punk/rock Bad Livers from 1991 to 2000 on string bass, tuba, and band management, as of 2003 Stillwater native Mark Rubin continues rumble-thumping, popping and oomping through an ever-growing musical career of live performances and recordings both in the U.S. and internationally. Born in Stillwater to musically inclined parents who met in the University of Arizona marching band, Mark's father was national secretary of the Kappa Kappa Psi Marching Band Fraternity, announcer for the Oklahoma State University Cowboy marching band, and member of several community orchestras. After a childhood in Stillwater where he would sit in awe of the Oklahoma State tuba players while his father prepared to announce the band's halftime show, Rubin spent his teen years in Norman where his father became director of the University of Oklahoma's Hillel House.

Mark Rubin

After an aborted attempt on violin as child, he started playing tuba in the Norman High School symphony in 1982 and 1983, just as the national hardcore and alternative rock scene developed around the U.S. Oklahoma City became a primary stopover between larger gigs for Black Flag and other groups who followed their pioneering path that eventually became the alternative music trail for bands from the West Coast, Minneapolis, Austin, Athens, Georgia, and, ultimately, Seattle. After switching to electric bass after high school, and seeing reggae artists like Eek-a-Mouse, Rubin played in the Legendary Streetpeople, a reggae group in which he debuted at the Norman High School cafeteria in 1984. After a couple of years of traveling back and forth to Dallas, making connections, and managing bands from his Norman apartment, Mark moved to Dallas in 1986 where he had his first stage experience, singing "Suspicious Minds" on stage with **The Flaming Lips**. He played bass with a punk rock group, The Bedrockers, and became inspired to take up string bass by Smiling Jack Barton, the Reverend Horton Heat's bassist. Barton guided Rubin in picking up a string bass in a 1988 classified ad for $100, and soon thereafter, Mark joined Killbilly, a Dallas-based roots band with a punk rock attitude. That same aesthetic connected Mark to Killbilly's newly arriving banjo player and musician extraordinaire, Danny Barnes. After a year-and-a-half, the two musicians left Killbilly in simpatico and moved to Austin, played as a trio for a year with fiddler Ralph White, and began to form Bad Livers in 1989.

After starting with their first single, a cover of Iggy Pop's "Lust for Life" recorded in the Butthole Surfers' Paul Leary's living room, the Bad Livers partnership produced six albums appreciated both by fans and music critics, but not always by bluegrass or country traditionalists because of the band's eclectic take on Americana. With a raging hybrid of rock, country, and blues played on traditional instruments one usually hears in bluegrass or other American folk styles, Bad Livers released *Delusion of Banjer* (1992), *Horses in the Mines* (1994), a collection of old-time gospel songs, *Dust on the Bible* (1994), and three releases on the Sugar Hill roots-oriented label, *Hogs on the Highway* (1997), *Industry and Thrift* (1998), and *Blood and Mood* (2000). While Rubin humbly admits he has only been the bass and tuba player for Bad Livers and did not write any of the songs, 1998's *Industry and Thrift* bears his most indelible print. From the opening notes of the tuba on "Lumpy, Beanpole, & Dirt," to his rapid-fire bass on "Brand New Hat" or "Cannonball Rag," to his traditional arrangement of "A Yid ist Geboren inz Oklahoma," a nod to his Jewish heritage (he has the ten commandments tattooed on his arm in Hebrew) and love of klezmer music, Rubin's mark is obvious on the album, and clearly demonstrates his influence on the Bad Livers' songwriting. The album not only features their popular

"I'm Going Back to Mom and Dad," but a hidden jam track with Mark pulling and popping hard on the string bass while Barnes rolls the banjo.

In 1998, Barnes moved to Washington state and the group really ceased to be a touring group, although more albums could be released from live recordings and yet-to-be-heard studio material. Since then, Rubin has supervised and composed for a film soundtrack, *The Newton Boys* (1998), hosted a music television show, *Breakin' In*, on local access TV in Austin, and a radio show on KUT, the University of Texas' college station. He has also worked consistently with Texas western swing traditionalist, Don Walser, both supporting Walser on bass, and releasing some of Walser's live radio recordings from the early 1960s on a "house label" Rubin has established, LumpyDisc. His interests have also diversified deeper into ethnic music beyond the traditional American styles that first inspired him, to include Tex-Mex, Tex-Polish, and Persian music. In 1999, Mark traveled to France with his Yiddish ensemble, Rubinchik's Orchestra, which mutated into a bluegrass band, a Tex-Mex conjunto, or a Hungarian folk band, depending on the occasion. In 2001, he played tuba on *Brotherhood of Brass*, a release by Frank London's Klezmer Brass Allstars, and contributed bass and tuba to *buttermilk & rifles*, a solo effort by Kevin Russell, well known for leading the Austin favorite roots radicals, the Gourds. He also recorded an album of old-time string band music with the Bing Bang Boys in Port Townsend, Washington, and released in 2002. Also in 2K2, Rubin's Yiddish band accompanied Neil Blumofe on a few of the tracks on *Hazzan Neil Blumofe*, and released an album of all-acoustic old time music with Texas-Polish dance band fiddler, Brian Marshall, called *Texas Kapela*. In 2013, he continues as a member of The Other Europeans, a 14-piece collective of Jewish and Rroma musicians.

Rubin continues his eclectic career of musician, producer, writer, and teacher, His website is a thorough and constantly updated resource to keep track of this outrageously diverse creative person and musician.

www.markrubin.com

Rushing, Jimmy
(b. August 26, 1903 - d. June 8, 1972)

Achieving his greatest fame as the vocalist for the Count Basie band from 1935 to 1950 and solo recording in the 1960s, James Andrew Rushing was born in Oklahoma City. His father, Andrew Rushing, who played the trumpet, ran Rushing's Café on Northeast Second Street in Oklahoma City, an African-American business district that was to become known as "Deep Deuce." His mother, Cora Freeman, played piano and sang in choirs, and at one time was a professional religious singer. His brother was a singer. Thus, Jimmy was around music throughout his early home life, and eventually played piano at his father's café, however, the first instrument he learned was the violin. While at Douglass High School in Oklahoma City, he studied music theory under the tutelage of Zelia Page Breaux, a well-known music teacher who also influenced several other jazz greats to come out of Oklahoma City, including **Buddy Anderson** and Lem Johnson. As a teenager, Jimmy sang at any venue available, including school pageants, glee clubs, church choirs, and opera houses in the Oklahoma City area. His piano and vocal talents were influenced by his Uncle Wesley Manning, who played and sang in a local sporting house. A barrelhouse pianist in Oklahoma City by the name of Gerry Stoner was also an influence on Jimmy's piano talents. During the summers of his high school years, he hoboed from Chicago to Dallas, playing music. As he matured, Jimmy was known as "Mr. Five By Five" because of his physical stature.

After high school Rushing attended Wilberforce University in Wilberforce, Ohio, where he was the "official" pianist at the university dances. After two years of college, he moved to Los Angeles, where he worked several non-music jobs, but occasionally played with Jelly Roll Morton and Paul Howard at private parties and nightclubs, such as the Quality Night Club and the Jump Steady Club.

Around 1926, Jimmy returned to Oklahoma City because he became unhappy with life in Los Angeles. He worked in his father's café for more than a year, but an opportunity arose where Jimmy would reenter music. The Billy King Road Show disbanded in 1925 in Oklahoma City, where Walter Page kept the band intact and renamed it—some sources say it "Walter Page's Original Blue Devils," while others contend it was the "**Oklahoma City Blue Devils**." Page expanded the band from its original nine members to as many as thirteen to fifteen members, and one of those was Jimmy. In addition to Jimmy, three other native Oklahomans were at one time or another member of the Blue Devils, including Abe Bolar, Lemuel C. Johnson, and **Don Byas**. Rushing also played with several artists who would become legendary, including Lester Young and William "Count" Basie.

When the Blue Devils were reorganized in Oklahoma City, Page persuaded a group of Oklahoma City businessmen to back the venture. The backing consisted of a little cash, a set of uniforms, a supply of meal tickets good at any restaurant owned by one of the sponsors, and the donation of a large hotel room (Littlepage Hotel in the "Deep Deuce District" district) that served as a dormitory, mess hall, rehearsal hall, and recruiting office. The Blue Devils used the Ritz Ballroom in downtown Oklahoma City as their home base while they performed on the Territorial Band circuit from Omaha, Nebraska, to Little Rock, Arkansas. The Blue Devils traveled to Kansas City for a "battle of the bands" competition and recorded their only music on the Vocalion label in 1929, featuring Jimmy on the vocal number, "Blue Devil Blues."

While in Kansas City, Jimmy, as well as Basie and Page, was invited to join the Bennie Moten Orchestra, one of the top bands in the Kansas City jazz scene. The Moten Orchestra had drawn national attention and was on tour around the country. Jimmy was also the vocalist on all the Moten recordings for Victor through 1935, when Moten died. Basie reorganized the Moten ensemble into the Count Basie Orchestra, and Jimmy became the lead vocalist until 1950.

The Basie Orchestra's 1936 recording of "Boogie Woogie" featured Jimmy and marked his presence on the national scene. Rushing appears on all the Basie recordings during this period and can be found on several reissues on Decca, Columbia, and RCA. While with Basie, Jimmy also performed in a number of films, including *Crazy Horse*, *Take Me Back Baby*, *Air Mail Special*, and *Top Man*, as well as the "From Spirituals to Swing" concerts at Carnegie Hall in 1938.

In 1950 Basie dissolved his orchestra due to hard times for big bands, and Rushing briefly retired to South Carolina. But it was not long until Jimmy was again on the music scene with his own combo, as well as doing solo work. Basie and Rushing were reunited in 1954 when they appeared on the *Tonight Show*, hosted by Steve Allen. Jimmy's recording output increased in the 1950s, especially a series of albums with Vanguard, such as *Jimmy*

Rushing Sings the Blues and *Listen to the Blues*, both released in 1955.

Jimmy then signed with Columbia Records and released several notable albums, *The Jazz Odyssey of James Rushing, Esq.* (1955), *Cat Meets Chick* (1956), *Little Jimmy Rushing and the Big Brass* (1958), *Rushing Lullabies* (1959), and *Jimmy Rushing and the Smith Girls* (1960). For this work, Jimmy won the *Down Beat* Critics Poll for Best Male Singer in 1957, 1958, 1959, and 1960; British magazine *Melody Maker* Critics Poll as Best Male Singer for the same years; and the German magazine *Jazz Podium* Critics Award in 1958. The same year, Jimmy and Benny Goodman performed together at the World's Fair in Brussels, which resulted in collaboration on "Brussels Blues." Jimmy also appeared in a CBS film, *The Sound of Jazz*, and reunited with Count Basie at the Newport Jazz Festival; both occurring in 1957.

The 1960s also proved to be a productive period for Jimmy. He toured the world with several jazz greats, including Dave Brubeck, Thelonious Monk, Eddie Condon, Harry James Orchestra, and Joe Newman; won *Jazz & Pop* Critics Award in 1967, completed a singing and acting role in *The Learning Tree* film in 1969, and was guest on the *Mike Douglas Show* on television.

Rushing became ill in 1971, but the awards kept rolling in with *Down Beat* Critics Poll Record of the Year in 1972 for *The You and Me That Used to Be*; *Down Beat* Critics Poll for Best Male Singer in 1972; and the Kansas City Jazz Hall of Fame Award in 1971. Jimmy was considered a first-class jazz singer, but his numbers were always tinged with the blues. In his later years, he favored certain songs, such as "Going to Chicago," "Everyday I Have the Blues," "Exactly Like You," "I Surrender Dear," and "When I Grow Too Old to Dream." On June 8, 1972 "Mr. Five By Five"died with leukemia at the Flower and Fifth Avenue Hospital in New York City. He is buried at the Maple Grove Cemetery, Kew Gardens, in Queens.

Rushlow, Tim

Born in Midwest City at Tinker Air Force base where his father, Tom, was stationed in the Air Force, Tim Rushlow went on to be the lead singer of the country rock group Little Texas, one of the most popular country acts of the 1990s to the tune of more than six million albums sold. After being discharged from the military, Tom Rushlow moved the family to Arlington, Texas, where he formed the band Moby Dick and the Whalers with three of his brothers-in-law via his wife, and Tim's mom, Patricia. The group toured regionally and released some of their own records, but more importantly they provided the environment in which Tim could learn to play music. Picking up drums, bass, piano, and guitar from his father and uncles, Tim sang along with his parents' record collection, inspired especially by the country group, Alabama. As a teenager, Tim sang in school choirs, formed garage bands around 1984 with vocalist/guitarist Dwayne O'Brien that landed gigs in the north Texas and southern Oklahoma area, and performed in the live music shows at Six Flags Over Texas that led to a job in 1986 imitating country music legends at Opryland in Nashville.

Tim Rushlow

When Rushlow left Arlington for Nashville, O'Brien attended East Central Oklahoma State University in Ada where he earned a chemistry degree, and then followed Rushlow to Nashville where they formed Little Texas with Rushlow's high school buddies, lead guitarist Porter Howell and bassist Duane Propes who were attending Nashville's Belmont University. Starting to tour in the country by booking themselves and being their own roadies, the band met keyboardist Brady Seals and drummer Del Gray in Massachussetts, who joined the band shortly thereafter. By 1988 the group had been signed to Warner Brothers and named themselves Little Texas, after Little Texas Boulevard where they practiced in Nashville. Buying a 1972 Chevy van for $300 and building a trailer themselves, the group played clubs around the country, appeared on *Star Search* (they didn't win), and by 1990 had developed enough material to record their first album, *First Time for Everything* (Warner Brothers, 1992). The band's debut single, "Some Guys Have All the Love," became a top ten country hit and launched the band on a six-year ride of top ten hits, million-selling albums, and sold out concerts.

Merging glam rock looks (and some music not that far from the genre), earthy lyrics about Daddy, high school football games, hayfields, and plenty of references to Texas, the group continued its meteoric rise in 1994 with *Big Time* (Warner Brothers, 1993). The platinum-selling album provided two, top five country hits, "What Might Have Been" and the line-dancing favorite, "God Blessed Texas," as well as the #1 country hit, "My Love." Little Texas followed up *Big Time* with *Kick a Little* (Warner Brothers, 1993). The album's title track went top ten, as did "Amy's Back in Austin," and the group had another platinum album in its catalogue. In 1995, the band released a greatest hits package with two new songs, to include the foreshadowing "Life Goes On." Once 1997's self-titled album did not produce any hits, the group of old friends who were doing just fine financially, decided to call it quits in 1998.

With a little time and a comfy cash cushion to think about what to do next, Rushlow took time out from the music business, cut his hair, and began writing songs, the fruit of which was his 2001 self-titled solo album on Atlantic Records. A conservative effort with all of the safe studio trappings of Nashville's corporate country establishment, the album can only be looked at as Rushlow stretching out to find out who he was outside of Little Texas. While some of the songs are about inspirational people who make sacrificial choices in life ("In the Meantime"), and love their partners through something so difficult as Alzheimer's disease ("She Misses Him"), which did make the country top ten, the album was so far away from the rowdy rural insights of Little Texas that only the most ardent fans picked it up. The singer-songwriter apparently got the message. By spring of 2002, he had formed a group, Rushlow, with Billy Welch (keyboards, vocals), Kurt Allison (lead guitar), Tully Kennedy (bass guitar, vocals), Rich Redmond (drums), and Tishomingo native (and Rushlow's cousin) Doni Harris on acoustic guitar and vocals.

Furthering Rushlow's connection to Oklahoma, Doni Harris grew up on Lake Texoma near the Texas border. "Everybody in our family plays or sings," Harris says on the band's website, "and Tim and I grew up singing on the Oklahoma Opry and places like that." Harris played in a local band, Atlantis, and was the president of the Tishomingo High School Marching Band. After a period of commuting from Oklahoma to Nashville to sing demos for songwriters, he settled in Nashville permanently and landed a publishing deal. Before long, he hooked up with his cousin Tim who was putting together Rushlow. In March, 2003, the group signed to Lyric Street Records, the label that has released debut albums by SheDaisy and Rascal Flatts. The band's first single, "I Can't Be Your Friend," reached #15 *Billboard* Hot Country Singles chart, but even with a rush released of the band's album, no momentum could be sustained due to Lyric Street re-organizing their company. After touring the world in 2007 and '08 as the duo Rushlow Harris signed by Toby Keith's Show Dog Universal label, Tim worked on a Christian pop album which did not have the hoped-for success, and began doing his "One Man, One Guitar, One Night" solo acoustic show which was booked across the South in early 2013.

www.timrushlow.com

Russell, Leon
(b. April 2, 1941)

As one of pop and rock's most significant artists from the early 1960s through the mid-1970s, Leon Russell's career as a multi-instrumentalist, record producer, arranger, studio owner and stylistic iconoclast is legendary in music circles. His gold albums, pop hits, and continued success as a touring performer as of 2003 are testament to his popularity among legions of worldwide music fans. Born Claude Russell Bridges in the southwestern Oklahoma town of Lawton, home to the massive Fort Sill army base, he studied classical piano from age three to thirteen. Having moved to Tulsa when he was fourteen, he attended Tulsa's Will Rogers High School, played briefly with Ronnie Hawkins and the Hawks, and eventually formed a group called the Starlighters with local musicians Leo Feathers (guitar), Chuck Blackwell (drums), Jack Dunham (vocals), Lucky Clark (bass), and Johnny Williams (saxophone). The group played locally until Jerry Lee Lewis signed the musicians as his touring band in the late 1950s. They toured the Midwest for two years with the fifties rock and roll icon known for "Great Balls of Fire" and "Whole Lotta Shakin' Goin' On." The Lewis influence on Russell is obvious on Leon's first two singles, "Swanee River" and "All Right," recorded in Tulsa and released on the Chess label in 1959.

In January of 1962, Russell and drummer Chuck Blackwell headed to California where they met up with **David Gates** and formed a group that played country and rock in supper clubs, and began getting session work around Los Angeles. That led to a friendship with Rick Nelson's guitarist, James Burton, who taught Leon how to play guitar. Russell became a member of an elite group of session musicians known as the "Wrecking Crew," and he built and an impressive resumé during the 1960s with his presence on hit recordings such as Herb Albert's "A Taste of Honey," the Righteous Brothers "You've Lost That Loving Feeling" (also featuring Muskogee guitarist **Barney Kessel**), and the Byrds' cover of Dylan's "Mr. Tambourine Man." He also appeared on a dizzying array of sessions with the likes of Glen Campbell, Dorsey Burnette, Frank Sinatra, Bob Dylan, Ike and Tina Turner, Aretha Franklin, The Rolling Stones, Barbara Streisand, The Ventures, Bobby Darin, Wayne Newton, Sam Cooke, Nitty Gritty Dirt Band, Johnny Mathis, and The Byrds. As an arranger, he supervised the musical production Gary Lewis and the Playboys' #1 hit of 1965, "This Diamond Ring." His piano playing is prominent on Jan and Dean's "Surf City," Bobby Doris Pickett's "Monster Mash," the Carpenters' "Superstar," The Byrds'

Leon Russell

"Mr. Tambourine Man," Herb Alpert's "A Taste of Honey," The Beach Boys' "California Girls" and *Pet Sounds* album, and virtually all of Phil Spector's hit recordings, to include the Crystals' "He's a Rebel," one of the quintessential girl group recordings.

From 1965 to 1967, Russell built his own studio in California where he began experimenting with recording techniques, producing the critically lauded but commercially unsuccessful *Asylum Choir* in 1968. He also recorded and toured with Delaney and Bonnie that year, and enjoyed his first major success as a songwriter with Joe Cocker who had a hit with Russell's "Delta Lady" in 1969, a song originally written for Rita Coolidge. As a result of serving as Joe Cocker's musical director and arranger for *Joe Cocker!* (1969), and the live album that resulted from Cocker's famous Mad Dogs and Englishmen tour in 1970, the 43 member band for which Leon assembled and led, Russell became an important figure in the royal British music scene of Eric Clapton, with whom he wrote "Blues Power," Steve Winwood, the Rolling Stones, and soon-to-be ex-Beatles George Harrison and Ringo Starr.

Russell formed Shelter Records in 1969 and recorded *Asylum Choir II* with Marc Benno, unreleased until 1972 and producing no hits, but clearly indicating Russell's musical directions with its honky-tonk piano-driven blues-rock. *Asylum Choir II* also features usually unexamined strong political statements on some of the most resonant anti-war songs of the Vietnam era, such as "Down on the Base" and "Ballad for a Soldier," which may account for the hesitancy on the part of the label that would not release it. Shelter also provided the forum for such notable artists as Tom Petty, Freddie King, **J.J. Cale**, Phoebe Snow, **The GAP Band**, and **Dwight Twilley**. In 1970, Leon's first album surfaced under his own name and produced one hit single, "Roll Away the Stone," a gospel anti-war anthem, "Give Peace a Chance," and his own version of Cocker's hit, "Delta Lady," as well as now-standard Russell concert pieces, "Shoot Out at the Plantation," and "A Song for You." In 1971, Russell released the Top 20 album, *Leon Russell and the Shelter People*, which featured, among others, George Harrison as a "performer," **Jesse Ed Davis**, and a backup group called the Tulsa Tops on songs such as "Home Sweet Oklahoma," "The Ballad of Mad Dogs and Englishmen," and "Stranger in a Strange Land." Also in 1971, as a result of George Harrison guesting on Russell's first solo album, Leon played for Harrison's Concert for Bangladesh, at New York's Madison Square Garden, and is featured prominently on the resulting album.

In 1972, Russell bought the tapes for *Asylum Choir II* and released it to some success as it reached the top 100 album charts, largely as a result of his significant rock star status at the time. He also released the gold-selling *Carney* in 1972, his best-selling album ever, which produced the Top 20 pop hit "Tightrope," and the song "This Masquerade," later a Grammy winning song for Russell in 1977 via George Benson who had a Top 10 hit with it on the #1 album *Breezin'* (1976) when it became the first song in music history to land at the top spot on the pop, jazz, and R & B charts.

Needing a rest from the constant pressures of touring, recording, writing, and performing, Russell returned to Oklahoma in 1972 when he bought 7 ½ acres on Grand Lake in northeastern Oklahoma and began building a massive spread to include a 3,500-square foot house, studio, swimming pool, and guest apartments that became known as "the hippie place" by locals. In 1973, at the peak of his popularity as a rock artist, Russell surfaced for the first time with his alter ego, Hank Wilson, the country performer Leon uses as a vehicle for traditional country and gospel songs that are an obvious cornerstone of his music. Recorded in Owen Bradley's famous barn studio in Mt. Juliet, Tennessee, which burned not long afterwards, *Hank Wilson's Back* features country standards such as "Rollin' in My Sweet Baby's Arms," "I'm So Lonesome I Could Cry," **Hank Thompson**'s "Six Pack to Go," and "Truck Drivin' Man." Also in 1973, when *Billboard Magazine* reported Leon was the top concert attraction in the world, Russell's *Leon Live*, a triple album recorded in front of 70,000 people at Long Beach Arena and released in late 1972, went gold. Late in 1972, Russell released a Christmas single, "Slipping into Christmas," that rose to #4 on the pop charts.

Given this tremendous success, Russell also began acquiring several properties around Tulsa, to include the First Church of God at Third and Trenton. Russell converted the building into the now famous Church Studio, currently owned and operated by **Steve Ripley** of the Tractors. The Church Studio provided a nexus through which some of rock's biggest performers of the 1970s channeled their recording sessions away from the microscopic pressures of New York or L.A. While musicians such as Bob Dylan and **J.J. Cale** recorded there in the 1970s, Tulsa power popster **Dwight Twilley** recorded his 1975 Top 20 hit, "I'm On Fire," in the studio, and the GAP Band experienced some of their early tastes of recording on Russell's 1974 album, *All That Jazz*, recorded in part at the studio. *All That Jazz* featured Russell's version of Tim Hardin's "If I Were A Carpenter," a humble pop hit at #74, and the album peaked at #34 on the album charts. Leon's 1975 release, the gold-selling *Will O' The Wisp*, provided Russell's last Top 20 hit, "Lady Blue," in the fall of 1974, and "Bluebird" which was a Top 40 hit for Helen Reddy in 1975.

Also in 1975, Leon formed Sheltervision, a video branch of Shelter that began documenting various elements of the music industry milieu swirling about Russell who was the ever-calm eye of the hurricane. While a film has yet to be released, Russell said in a 2001 interview that live performances will surface on DVD. Russell ended his ties with Shelter in 1976 and started a new label, Paradise Records, a formative training ground for members of Concrete Blonde and Steve Ripley. Subsequently, Shelter released the *Best of Leon Russell*, which went gold. Also that year, Russell married Mary McCreary, a vocalist with the Sly and the Family Stone spin-off group, Little Sister. The two recorded *Wedding Album* (Paradise, 1976), which produced Russell's last chart single, "Rainbow in Your Eyes."

Make Love to the Music went practically unnoticed in 1977, and in 1979, his solo album, *Americana*, sold modestly; however, Leon also released a duet album with Willie Nelson in 1979, *One for the Road*, which earned gold status, and peaked at #25 on the pop album chart. *One for the Road* was the CMA's Album of the Year, and the version of "Heartbreak Hotel" included on the album topped the country charts. Leon's association with Willie included doing some overdubs on some of Willie's early 1960s recordings, and later hosting the first of Nelson's 4th of July Picnics, which began a significant mixing of the country and rock audiences around Austin in the 1970s.

In the early 1980s, Russell relocated permanently to Nashville, and toured with the New Grass Revival, a bluegrass band with whom he recorded rock standards on *The Live Album* in 1981. Also during the 1980s, Leon toured with Edgar Winter around the world to include concerts in Russia, Brazil, Mexico, Canada, and throughout the United States. In 1984, Leon released *Hank Wilson Volume II*, another collection of country standards, and in 1989 his initial solo release from 1970 was reissued with additional tracks. In 1992, Bruce Hornsby urged Leon back into the studio for a largely unsuccessful commercial release, *Anything Can Happen*, and in 1995 Leon released a set of traditional Christmas songs, *Hymns of Christmas*, on his own label, Leon Russell Records. In 1996, The Right Stuff label re-released *Leon Live*, a two-CD set that includes all the material from the original three-record set, and also released *Retrospective* (1997), a compilation of Russell's major hits from the Shelter period of 1970 to 1975. In 1998, Ark 21 Records released the third installment of Leon's Hank Wilson series, *Legend in My Time, Hank Wilson Volume III*. Along with covers of **Merle Haggard**'s "Okie from Muskogee," and Willie Nelson's "Crazy," the album features excellent musicians such as Marty Stuart on mandolin, Willie Nelson's harmonica player, Micky Raphael, and background vocals by the Oak Ridge Boys on "Daddy Sang Bass" and Willie Nelson on two songs. An extra bonus is an audio interview with Russell that is included prior to the first track on the album.

Russell released a new collection of his own material in 1999 with *Face in the Crowd*, and a collection of Russell's blues-flavored material, *Blues: Same Old Song*. In 2000, Atlantic Records released a live set recorded at Gilley's, and in 2001 Leon started releasing a series of albums on his Leon Russell Records label, to include a tribute to himself on *Signature Songs*, his greatest hits reinterpreted acoustically just on piano and vocals. Also in 2001, Leon re-released an album of blues songs in which he plays the guitar exclusively, *Guitar Blues*, previously available only in Japan, and in 2002 released a compilation of standards such as "My Funny Valentine," "'Round Midnight," and "As Time Goes By," with Leon accompanied by the Nashville Symphony Orchestra.

Leon lives in Nashville, but has had a whirlwind of a life for the past few years. After toiling about the country in his bus doing shows in every kind of venue imagineable through the 1990s and early 2000s, he teamed up with Elton John in 2010 for *The Union*, a collaboratve album garnering Leon his first appearance on the charts since 1981, as well as a GRAMMY nomination for best pop collaboration.Also in 2011, Russell was inducted into the Songwriters Hall of Fame in New York City (the same year as Garth Brooks), and Omnivore Records released *Live in Japan*, which had only been available in Japan up until this point. Along with the 1973 recording of the Japanese concert, several bonus tracks from a 1971 concert in Houston are also featured on the disc. In 2013, the Oklahoma Museum of Popular Culture received a donation of more than 4,500 pieces of Leon Russell memorabilia with the stipulation the materials to into the new museu proposed by the Oklahoma History Center for Tulsa's Brady District. If it happens, a whole lot of Leon Russell will be going back to Tulsa, one more time. Leon was booked for several gigs across the U.S. in the first half of 2013.

www.leonrussellrecords.com

Russell, Tom

(b. February 8, 1955)

With nineteen albums of original songs and a host of compositions recorded by the likes of Johnny Cash, Nanci Griffith, Doug Sahm, Ian Tyson, Suzy Boggess, and Iris DeMent, Tom Russell was born in Oklahoma City. As a child Tom's family moved to southern California, where he grew up listening to artists such as **Merle Haggard**, Buck Owens, and **Spade Cooley**. In the 1960s, he was influenced by such folk artists as Bob Dylan and Ian & Sylvia, and began to haunt the folk clubs in Los Angeles. Russell has been described as the "songwriter's

Tom Russell

songwriter" and "one of the finest folk artists Americans never heard of." Excellent as he is, Russell left the state at a very early age, and the influence of the state on his work must be seen as marginal, outside of whatever music his parents played around the house, many of which seem to be of a common Oklahoma aesthetic focusing on hard core country such as that listed as some of his influences in various interviews. Again, Oklahoma has a heavy environmental music presence on those who stayed in the state through some of its tougher mid-twentieth century years, and then took those sounds with them, or embraced familiar sounds when they got wherever they were going.

www.tomrussell.com

S

Schon, Neal
(b. 2/27/1954)

Neal Schon, the lead guitarist and primary songwriter for the pop rock group, Journey, was born at Tinker Air Force Base in Midwest City, OK. After moving to San Francisco at a very early age, he began playing various instruments at age five because both of his parents were musicians.

www.schonmusic.com

Neal Schon

Seaton, Lynn
(b. July 18, 1957)

One of the most in-demand jazz bass players during the last twenty years, Lynn Seaton was born in Tulsa. He started at the age of seven on the guitar, but soon switched to the bass at nine. While studying music at the University of Oklahoma, he performed at various clubs within the state. By 1980, Lynn had relocated to Cincinnati, Ohio, where he joined pianist Steve Schmidt's Trio and John Von Ohlen's big band at the Blue Wisp jazz club. About a year later, he was awarded a NEA Jazz Studies Fellowship to study under Rufus Reid in New York City. In 1984, he joined Woody Herman's Young Thundering Heard, and in July of the following year, he began a two-year stint with the Count Basie Orchestra. Following his time with the Basie ensemble, he worked with Tony Bennett, George Shearing, and Monty Alexander.

In 1993 Seaton turned to freelancing and during the next five years performed in forty-nine of the fifty states as well as more than thirty-five countries abroad, appearing at such prestigious jazz festivals as Concord, Newport, North Sea, and Bern. His freelance work included performances with such notable jazz artists as Clark Terry, Buck Clayton, Herb Ellis, Thad Jones, Mel Lewis, Marian McPartland, and Teddy Wilson. In addition, he appeared on more than 100 albums as side bassist for such artists as Diane Schuur, Kenny Drew, Jr., Nancy Wilson, Joe Williams, Bucky Pizzarelli, Milt Hinton, Hoagy Carmichael,

Ernestine Anderson, and Al Cohn. Seaton's only recorded album during this period was *Bassman's Basement*, a 1991 release on the Timeless label, on which he is accompanied by pianist Lee Musiker and drummer Tim Horner. Three of Lynn's compositions are included on the ten tracks, including "Major's Grand Slam," "Marianna's Waltz," and "Naptown Zebras."

By the late 1990s Seaton had become a respected jazz educator, instructing students at Cincinnati's College Conservatory of Music, Long Island University, State University of New York at New Paulz, William Patterson College, and North Texas University in Denton, where he joined the faculty in 1998.

In 2000 the OmniTone label released *Solo Flights*, a 12-track collection with seven of the selections written by Seaton. Seaton's solos run the gamut of musical genres, including "Ode to Jimi," a tribute to the late rock icon Jimi Hendrix, "Liltin' with Milton," dedicated to the late jazz bassist Milt Hinton, two of his compositions. Additional forays into other genres include "Moten Swing" (Big Band jazz), "How High the Moon" (bebop), and "Barcelona" (flamenco). He also appears on the Woody Herman *50th Anniversary Tour* album (Concord 1986) and *Live at the 1990 Concord Jazz Festival* with Frank Wess (Concord 1990).

As of 2013, Seaton resides in Denton, where he is lecturer in the Jazz Studies Division of the College of Music at the University of North Texas. He teaches applied jazz bass lessons, jazz fundamentals and styles, jazz improvisation, and a rhythm section master class. Finally, he continues to perform by leading his own jazz trio with gigs in the Dallas-Fort Worth metroplex.

Sessions, Ronnie

(b. December 7, 1948)

A childhood prodigy known for recording ten Top 10 hits, singer, guitarist, and songwriter, Ronnie Sessions was born in Henryetta, Oklahoma, a community of roughly 6,000 residents located east of Oklahoma City on Interstate 40. Ronnie's family moved to Bakersfield, California, when he was about nine years old, and he began to take guitar lessons from Andy Moseley, another native Oklahoman and inventor of the Moserite guitar.

In 1957, Ronnie signed his first recording contract with the Pike label. The next year, he was invited to sing on stage during a Grand Ole Opry troupe tour at the Bakersfield Civic Center. So impressed with Ronnie's performance, the troupe invited him to continue on the tour. Sessions signed with **Gene Autry's** Republic label, and broke into the Top 10 in 1968 with **Hoyt Axton's** "Never Been to Spain," which was followed with "I Never Go Around Mirrors," a #6 hit. He also recorded on Republic a revival of the pop song, "Tossin' and Turnin'," as well as several regional hits, such as "The Life of Riley" and "More Than Satisfied." In 1969, Ronnie moved to MCA Records, and scored with "Wiggle Wiggle," which reached #4 in 1969. He recorded two albums with MCA, *Ronnie Sessions* (1969) and *Ronnie Sessions Live* (1970), but was eventually dropped by the label in 1980.

Ronnie Sessions

After moving to Nashville, Sessions wrote several songs, most notably "When I Play the Fiddle," which Kenny Rogers recorded on his 1977 album, *Lucille*. His last charted single, "I Bought the Shoes That Just Walked Out on Me," was in 1986. He retired from the music business in 1987.

Settle, Mike

(b. March 20, 1941)

Composer or co-composer of more than 130 songs, co-founder of The First Edition with Kenny Rogers, and musical director of the New Christy Minstrels, singer, songwriter, instrumentalist (guitar and harmonica), and producer Mike Settle was born in Tulsa, but, in the ninth grade, moved to Muskogee, a city of roughly 38,000 residents located southeast of Tulsa. While in Tulsa, he was a member of the Tulsa Boy Singers (fifth through seventh grade) in which he received much of his early musical training. According to Mike, he considers Muskogee his "hometown" because of the friends and relatives who still live there, as well as the many pleasant memories he recalls from his early years spent in the community.

Mike Settle

Upon completion of high school, Mike majored in music at Oklahoma City University. After performing at coffeehouses in Oklahoma, Mike replaced John Montgomery in the Cumberland Three in 1960, including a Carnegie Hall concert with Shelley Berman. The group, which patterned themselves as another Kingston Trio, disbanded in 1961 when John Stewart left to replace Dave Guard in the Kingston Trio. He had also performed at New York City's Bitter End as a solo artist. Settle performed at the 1963 Newport Folk Festival in one of the festival workshops, made several appearances on the ABC television series *Hootenanny*, and toured the coffee house circuit as a soloist before leaving New York City for California as a replacement for one of the last original members in The New Christy Minstrels.

Settle spent 1966-67 with The New Christy Minstrels, serving as musical director while with the group. He left the Minstrels, along with Kenny Rogers, to form The First Edition with Thelma Comacho, Terry Williams, and drummer Mickey Jones. On the group's *The First Edition '69* album for the Reprise label, Mike is credited with writing or co-writing five of the ten tracks, including his signature song, "But You Know I Love You," which became a major hit for Bill Anderson in the 1970s, a #1 hit for Dolly Parton in the 1980s, and logged more than two million performances with BMI. Mike also served as music director for Glenn Yarbrough as well as The New Seekers. In 1971 Mike released his only solo album, *Mike Settle*, on the Uni label. It included "But You Know I Love You," "Saturday's Only," "The Nights of Your Life," and "Nobody Knows."

Settle's songs have been recorded by myriad artists. In addition to those previously mentioned, they include "But You Know I Love You" (**Henson Cargill**, Buck Owens, Kenny Rogers, and Alison Krauss), "Sing Hallelujah" (Judy Collins, Joe & Eddie, and Stephane Grappelli), "Settle Down [Goin' Down That Highway]" (The Springfields, Peter, Paul, & Mary, and Bobby Darin), "I'd Build a Bridge" (Glen Campbell, Charlie Rich, Wayne Newton, and Johnny Rodriguez), "Lady Lonely" (Wayne Newton), "Morning Star"

(Glenn Yarbrough), "Bound for Zion" (Lonnie Donegan), "Nights of Your Life" (Bobby Goldsboro), "Saturday's Only" (Bobby Goldsboro), "Goo Ga Gee" (Kingston Trio), and "Little Boy" (The Highwaymen, Kingston Trio, and Andy Williams). Other artists to record Mike's songs include Harry Belafonte and The Limelighters. Additional songwriting credits to Mike include "Sometimes Love is Better When It's Gone," and three songs for the film *Vanishing Point*, including "Nobody Knows," "Where Do We Go From Here," and "The Girl Done Got It Together." In addition to writing songs, Mike has appeared as a back-up vocalist and instrumentalist for such artists and groups as Kim Carnes, John Stewart, Glenn Yarbrough, and the Kingston Trio.

As of 2003, Settle remains active in the songwriting business and works as a freelance journalist, while residing in the Nashville area.

Shelton, Blake

(b. June 18, 1976)

With his single, "Austin" reaching #1 on the country charts for five consecutive weeks in 2002, (which tied a *Billboard* record for an artist's debut album), Blake Tollison Shelton through the first batch of kerosene on the fire that was about to become his colossal country music career. Born to Dick and Dorothy Shelton in Ada, Oklahoma, a college town (East Central University) of approximately 15,000 population southeast of Oklahoma City.

Blake started singing in his bedroom at an early, and his mother was so excited, she entered him in a beauty pageant talent show with fifty little girls when he was eight, singing "Old Time Rock-n-Roll." According to Blake, he was so embarrassed that he vowed never to sing again. Blake kept his interest in country music primarily because his Uncle Dearl taught him the basic chords of C, F, and G on the guitar. By the time he reached his teens, Blake was singing at local honky tonks in and around Ada, including the Country Music Palace and Legends, and became a regular on a local country music show. He also wrote his first song, "Once in a Long, Long While"m when he was fifteen. Blake began receiving statewide attention when he captured the Denbo Diamond Award for young Oklahoma entertainers. Based on this award and his local singing reputation, Blake was invited to perform at a tribute show in Ada for Mae Boren Axton, the noted Nashville songwriter (co-wrote "Heartbreak Hotel" recorded by Elvis Presley). Ms. Axton was impressed and encouraged him to come to Nashville, where she long established a reputation for assisting young musicians.

Two weeks after graduating from Ada High School in 1994, Blake at age seventeen moved to Nashville where he reunited with Ms. Axton, who provided him with his first paying job in Music City—painting her house, taking care of her yard, and various other odd jobs.. While working for Ms. Axton, Blake met **Hoyt Axton**, Mae's son and influential singer-songwriter who was temporarily living in his tour bus parked in Mae's

Blake Shelton (center) with Trace Adkins (left) and producer Scott Hendricks (right).

driveway. Hoyt gave Blake several tips about the music industry and presented him with a long Bowie knife on his eighteenth birthday. Hoyt also introduced Blake to the song "Ol' Red," which was included on Shelton's debut album *Austin*, and has become a 2002 Top 20 hit single.

For the next few years, Blake performed at several Nashville venues, such as Douglas Corner and the Bluebird Café, while working for Sony Tree publishing house making tape copies of writers' songs. Unfortunately, Blake spent too much time visiting with the writers and was terminated. During this period, he had several songs published with Naomi Martin Music, Warner/Chappell Music, and Jerry Crutchfield Music. In 1997 Bobby Braddock, veteran songwriter-producer, member of the Nashville Songwriters Hall of Fame, and co-composer of such songs as "D-I-V-O-R-C-E," " Time Marches On", and "He Stopped Loving Her Today", was given a tip on Blake. Braddock secured a contract for Blake with Tree Productions for which they recorded "Ol' Red," the song Hoyt had given him. *Austin* (Warner Bros) was released in 2001, and included several of Blake's songs, such as "That's What I Call Home," "Every Time I Look at You," "Problems at Home," and "All Over Me," co-written with Earl Thomas Conley, one of Blake's mentors and idols. "All Over Me" cracked the Top 20 on country charts in 2002,

Shelton was named *Radio & Records'* Breakthrough Artist of the Year in 2001, received the coveted Critics Pick Award from *Music Row Magazine*, and was nominated for Favorite New Artist in Country Music for *Billboard*, American Music, Country Weekly Fan Favorite, and ACM awards in 2001-02. His single, "Ol' Red," nudged into the Top 10 of the *Billboard* Hot Country Singles chart in the summer of 2002, and the video of the same title was given considerable broadcast time on CMT.

Blake Shelton Day was proclaimed on March 15, 2002 in Blake's hometown of Ada, and he will make a stop with his band, Road Kill, on his 2002 tour at Legends, a country music bar in Ada, where he performed as a teenager. His latest single, "Baby," was the Blue Chip Radio Report Song of the Week for October 28, 2002, debuted on the country charts at #33, and cracked the Top 25 in November of 2002. As Blake recently stated: "It's weird to think people are calling for me now. That's new to me. I've always dealt with begging somebody for a job."In 2003, Blake released his sophomore CD, *The Dreamer* (Warner Brothers). The album sold 77,000 copies the first week it was on the shelves, debuting at #2 on *Billboard*'s country album charts, and within three weeks "Baby" became his second #1 country hit where it stayed at the top of the *Billboard* country charts for three weeks, and also reached #1 at *Radio and Records*. By spring, 2003, Blake was nominated by the ACM as the Top New Male Vocalist, sang on Tracy Byrd's wildly popular "The Truth About Men," had a #1 video hit at GAC with his second single from *The Dreamer*, "Heavy Liftin'," and joined **Toby Keith** on the massively successful Shock'n Y'all tour through the fall of tha year and the show was *on*.

Since then, Shelton has winked, smirked, and channelled a husky baritone voice bad-country-boy-good-looks through numerous double entendres and love gone wrong songs.. Since 2001, Shelton has charted twenty-two singles, include twelve #1 hits. His first three albums were also certified gold (500,000 units sold). As if he weren't having enough professional success, in 2011 he became a coach on the NBC reality talent show, *The Voice*, which elevated his notoriety in the non-country music market, leading to even more popularity. Also in 2011, he married country singer **Miranda Lambert**, and the two mega-stars liveon a ranch near Tishomingo, Oklahoma in rural south-central Oklahoma.

www.blakeshelton.com

Shepard, Jean

(b. November 21, 1933)

Paul's Valley native Jean Shepard is noted for several firsts in the field of country music. She was one of the first women to break the country music barrier in the 1950s. Upon the recommendation of **Hank Thompson**, Shepard signed with Capitol Records in 1952. One year later, she scored with a #1 country hit, a Korean War song entitled "A Dear John Letter" with narration from Ferlin Husky, who was appointed as her guardian for tours outside the state as Jean was not yet twenty-one. It topped the country charts for twenty-three weeks and crossed over to the Top 5 pop charts, selling some ten million records in 1953. This success made her California's first major female recording artist since Patsy Montana. Moreover, she was one of the first women to join the Grand Ole Opry in 1955, and is the first woman to hold membership in the "mode lode of country music" for more than forty-seven years. In addition, Jean was the first country music female vocalist to overdub her voice on records. Furthermore, she was the first female in country music to sell a million records. Finally, she was the first woman in country music to record a concept album. Jean's 1956 *Songs of a Love Affair* featured twelve songs, all written by her, from a single woman's point of view on one side, while the other side portrayed the wife's perspective.

Jean Shepard

Born to parents, Hoit and Alla Mae Shepard, who raised eleven children in rural Oklahoma, Ollie Imogene Shepard was an avid listener to the Grand Ole Opry and **Bob Wills'** radio broadcasts over KVOO in Tulsa. She learned to sing by listening to Jimmie Rodgers records on a wind-up Victrola. After living in Hugo, Jean and her family relocated to Visalia, California, near Bakersfield, at the conclusion of World War II. At the age of fourteen, she and several friends formed The Melody Ranch Girls, an all-female western swing band, named after Noble's Melody Ranch, owned by Noble Fosberg, who managed and booked the band. Jean sang and played upright bass, an instrument that overwhelmed her five feet, one inch height. She recalled her mother and father hocking every stick of furniture in their home to pay for the bass which cost $350, a sum that would have bought a whole house full of furniture at the time. In 1948, the group recorded Hank Thompson's song "Help."

Jean was becoming a well known music personality in the San Joaquin Valley, while working three nights a week at Pismo Beach, performing on local radio station KNGS, and appearing on Jelly Sanders' radio show on Porterville's KTNV. Through these appearances, she came to the attention of Thompson, who was personally responsible for her first recording contract with Capitol. Her first solo recording was "Crying Steel Guitar Waltz/ Twice the Lovin'" in 1953 with Speedy West on steel. The aforementioned "A Dear John Letter" was followed with "Forgive Me John," which charted at #4 on the country lists as well as on the Top 25 pop charts. Her early Capitol recordings were backed by Bill Woods'

Hugh W. Foley

band out of Bakersfield, which included guitarist Buck Owens. She later formed her own band called The Second Fiddles, after her 1964 hit "Second Fiddle (to an Old Guitar)." With the Capitol and United Artists labels, she produced several Top Five country hits such as "A Satisfied Mind," "Beautiful Lies," "Second Fiddle to a Steel Guitar," "Take Possession," and "Slippin' Away." The latter won her a Grammy Award nomination in 1973 for Best Country Female Vocalist of the Year.

The same year Jean joined the Grand Ole Opry (1955), she helped launch the *Ozark Jubilee* telecast on ABC television as part of Red Foley's cast, where she remained until 1957. She was named Top Female Singer by *Cash Box* magazine in 1959 following such hits as "I Want to Got Where No One Knows Me" and "Have Heart, Will Love." In 1963, her husband Hawkshaw Hawkins was killed in a plane crash near Camden, Tennessee, which also killed Patsy Cline and Cowboy Copas.

Jean's string of medium-sized hits in the 1960s on Capitol included "Many Happy Hangovers to You," "If Teardrops Were Silver," "I'll Take the Dog," "Mr. Do-It-Yourself," "Heart, We did All We Could," "Your Forevers (Don't Last Very Long)," and "Seven Lonely Days." The late Jim Reeves was quoted as saying, "All the girl singers should sound like Jean Shepard. She always hits her notes, holds them and wraps them around an audience like nobody else can."

In 1973, Jean moved to the United Artists and remained with that label until 1977. Her biggest hits with UA included "At the Time," "I'll Do Anything It Takes (To Stay With You)," "Poor Sweet Baby," and "The Tips of My Fingers." Her last hit single was in 1978, "The Real Thing," which peaked at #85. Thereafter, she made fewer and fewer recordings, mostly on small, independent labels. Her greatest successes in the 1970s were with Bill Anderson's songs, such as "Slippin' Away," "The Tips of My Fingers," and "Mercy," all of which were released in an album of Anderson penned songs, *Poor Sweet Baby*. In 1975, Jean recorded a tribute to her late husband Hawkshaw Hawkins, "Two Little Boys," written by their sons, Don Robbins (named after Don Gibson and Marty Robbins) and Harold Franklin Hawkins II after his father.

During the 1980s and 1990s Jean continued to tour, especially the U.K., where she was well received. It was at the Wembley Country Festival in the U.K. in 1977 that she stated to the audience, "John Denver, Glen Campbell, and Mac Davis are not country," reaffirming her viewpoint on the retention of pure country sounds. She helped form the Association of Country Entertainers to "keep it country," after her objections to Olivia Newton-John's award from the Country Music Association. In 1996, two of the best collections of Jean's recordings were released, including the Country Music Foundation's *Honky Tonk Heroine: Classic Capitol Recordings, 1952-1964*, a 24-track compilation of Jean's #1 hits plus such songs as "Twice the Lovin' (In Half the Time)," "Under Your Spell Again," and "The Root of All Evil (Is A Man)," and the Bear Family five-disc box set, *The Melody Ranch Girl*, which included all 151 tracks recorded on Capitol from 1952 to 1964. This Oklahoma "honky tonk heroine" charted forty-five hits from 1953 to 1978.

Since 1968 Jean has been married to bluegrass guitarist Benny Birchfield, who was Roy Orbison's road manager at the time of Orbison's death. Her latest releases are *Jean Shepard, Precious Memories*, a gospel album, and *The Tennessee Waltz*. Shepard's role in the development of the country music on the West Coast is highlighted with one of her selections ("Dear John Letter") on the 1996 *Heroes of Country Music, Vol. 4: Legends of the West Coast* (Rhino).

As of this 2013, she continues to perform on the Grand Ole Opry (now for more than 50 years) as well as in Branson, Missouri, in "Grand Ladies of Country Music," a show launched in 2000 that includes Jan Howard, Helen Cornelius, Margo Smith, Leona Williams, and **Norma Jean**, another Oklahoman. She also appeared at Dollywood in 2002 in a show called "Grand Ladies of the Grand Ole Opry," which included Jeanie Seely and Jan Howard. Finally, Jean was the Golden Voice Awards winner for 2002 in the Female Golden Voice category, and was a participant in the fourth annual show held in Nashville to "honor the men and women who have given country music her voice." In 2010, Shepard was inducted into the Oklahoma Music Hall of Fame. and in 2011 she was inducted into the Country Music Hall of Fame.

www.jeanshepardcountry.com

Simmons, John Jacob

(b. June 14, 1918 – d. September 19, 1979)

One of the most highly regarded and in-demand jazz bassists in the 1940s and 1950s, John Jacob Simmons was born in Haskell, Oklahoma, a community of about 2,000 residents located southeast of Tulsa. John's family relocated to Tulsa, where he attended school until 1936, first playing the trumpet, but forced to switch to the bass after a football injury affected his mouth. While in high school, John's family moved to California, and he played his first gigs in the Los Angeles and San Diego areas.

During the 1940s and 1950s, Simmons played with James P. Johnson, Hot Lips Page, Sid Catlett, Ben Webster, Dexter Gordon, Sidney DeParis, Bill DeArango, Al Casey, Charles Thompson, Milt Jordan, Cozy Cole, Benny Carter, Billie Holliday, and the Rolf Ericson-Duke Jordan band in Scandinavia. He performed with both Dixieland and Big Bands, as well as Bebop combos during this period, including sessions with fellow Oklahoman **Don Byas** on 52nd Street in New York City, and other beboppers such as Coleman Hawkins and Thelonious Monk. He also toured and recorded with Harry "Sweets" Edison, Tadd Dameron, Art Tatum, John Coltrane, Andre Previn, Buddy Rich, and Phineas Newborn, as well as recording with the famed vocalists Billie Holliday, Ella Fitzgerald, and Lena Horne. Plagued by illness in the 1960s and 1970s, Simmons died in Los Angeles, California, on September 19, 1979.

Smotherman Michael

(b. Erick, OK)

A keyboardist/songwriter born on "a little hard scrabble ranch out side of Erick, OK". who went to California after high school with a band, and then moved to Nashville in 1994, Michael Smotherman has written songs that have been recorded byWaylon Jennings, RayCharles, Cher, Bonnie Raitt, Willie Nelson, Brooks and Dunn, Kenny Rogers, B.J. Thomas, Glen Campbell, Kenny Rogers, Luther Vandross, Tom Jones, Greg Allman, The Poiner Sisters, Kenny Chesney, Hank Williams, Jr., and "a bunch of others [he] can't remember." He's played keyboars and many sessions and toured with Rogers Miller, Mick Fleetwood, Glen Campbell, and Captain Beefheart. "I am a fortunate man," Mr. Smotherman wrote in facebook message to the author on 7/26/2010.

Smith, Cal

(b. July 4, 1932)

With three #1 country hits to his credit, including "The Lord Knows I'm Drinking," "Country Bumpkin," and "It's Time to Pay the Fiddler," Calvin Grant Shofner was born in Gans, Oklahoma, a small hamlet of around 200 people located in eastern Oklahoma near the Arkansas border. Cal and his family moved to California when he was a youngster, and they settled in the Oakland area.. Smith was active in country music from 1960, when he began playing guitar for Ernest Tubb , through 1986 when he released he final album, *Stories of Life*, before retiring with his wife, Darlene, to Branson, Missouri. Smith was inducted into the Oklahoma Music Hall of Fame in Muskogee in 2007.

Cal Smith

Spencer, Tim

(b. July 13, 1908 – April 26, 1974)

One of the original members of the Sons of the Pioneers formed in 1934 and an inductee into the Nashville Songwriters Hall of Fame in 1971, Vernon Tim Spencer was born in Webb City, Missouri, but was raised in Picher, Oklahoma, a former lead and zinc mining community of approximately 1,700 residents in extreme northeastern Oklahoma, where he attended grade school. As a teenager, he left home because of an argument with his father over the purchase of a music instrument without parental permission, and began working in the lead and zinc mines of the Tri-State Mining District until a mine accident hospitalized him with a cracked vertebra. Unable to return to the mines, he began singing in local venues, and eventually relocated to his brother Glenn's home in Los Angeles in 1931. During the day Tim worked at a Safeway warehouse, and played and sang music at night, hooking up with short-lived bands, such as the Rocky Mountaineers, International Cowboys, and O-Bar-O Cowboys.

In 1933, Spencer, Leonard Slye (Roy Rogers), and Bob Nolan formed the Pioneer Trio, later to become known as the Sons of the Pioneers, and the trio soon added brothers Hugh (fiddle) and Karl (guitar) Farr. The group was featured on radio station KFWB in Hollywood, where their show captured an immediate audience, and gained enough popularity for invitations to appear with Oklahoman Will Rogers and at the Texas Centennial. The Pioneers featured unique western themes, developed a smooth harmony style later emulated by almost every western singing group in the U.S., and may have been the first western ensemble to feature group yodeling. In 1935, the Pioneers became only the third West Coast unit signed by Decca Records, following Bing Crosby and Stuart Hamblen. Filmmakers soon noticed the group, and they were cast in a 1935 Liberty Studio film, *The Old Homestead*, followed by an appearance in **Gene Autry**'s first feature film, the 1936 *Tumbling Tumbleweeds*. They were then hired by Columbia Studios to provide music for a series of westerns starring Charles Starrett. It should be noted that another Oklahoman, **Shug Fisher**, born in Tabler near Chickasha, was member of The Pioneers (1943-46 and 1949-51) as comedian and bass player.

Spencer, who had not written any songs prior to the group's formulation, soon began to compose, including his first song in 1934, "Will You Love Me (When My Hair Turns to

Silver)," later recorded by the Pioneers. Many of the their most successful songs, including "The Everlasting Hills of Oklahoma," "Room Full of Roses," "Cigarettes, Whiskey and Wild, Wild Women," "Over the Santa Fe Trail," and "The Timber Trail," were written by Spencer, while he also co-wrote "Yippi-Yi, Yippi-Yo" and "Roses" with his brother Glenn, "Blue Prairie" with Bob Nolan, and "Ride'em Cowboy" with Roy Rogers. Additional songs credited to Spencer include "Careless Kisses," "Cowboy's Sunday Prayer," "Bunkhouse Bugle Boy," "Go West, Young Man," and "I'm Happy in My Levi Britches." His most successful song was "Room Full of Roses," which soared to the top of the *Billboard* pop charts in 1949, went to #1 on the country charts in 1974 with Mickey Gilley's version, and received a one million performance award from BMI.

Spencer retired from the The Pioneers in 1949 because of vocal problems, finding his own replacement, Ken Curtis, or Festus of *Gunsmoke* fame. He continued to serve as the group's manager until 1955, and added his nephew, Sunny Spencer. After leaving the Pioneers, he headed the religious record division of RCA Victor, and eventually started his own gospel publishing company, Manna Music, where he wrote "We've Got a Great Big Wonderful God," "Open Your Heart," and "Cowboy Campmeetin'." He later handed down the company to his son, Hal, and died in 1974 in Apple Valley, California.

Spencer was recipient of many honors because of his affiliation with The Sons of the Pioneers, such as Walk of Stars on Hollywood Boulevard (1974), Country Music Hall of Fame (1978), and Western Music Hall of Fame (1989). As an individual, he was inducted into the Nashville Songwriters Hall of Fame (1971), Gospel Music Hall of Fame, Cowboy Hall of Fame (Oklahoma City), and Western Music Hall of Fame, all in 1985, primarily because of his songwriting career.

Stafford, Terry

(b. November 22, 1941 – d. March 17, 1996)

Best known for his Top 10 1964 hit single, "Suspicion" and composer of such country hits as Buck Owens' "Big in Vegas" and George Strait's "Amarillo by Morning," Terry LaVerne Stafford was born in Hollis, a town of about 2,500 residents located in extreme southwestern Oklahoma, but later moved to Amarillo, Texas, where he excelled in athletics, listened to Elvis Presley and Buddy Holly as a teenager, and graduated from Palo Duro High School in 1960. During his senior year, Terry told his classmates that he planned to leave for California to make hit records. With his parents' consent, he moved to Hollywood, and worked for two years as a nightclub entertainer. In one of these performances, he was spotted by John Fisher and Les Worden, who had just launched Crusader Records, and was looking for talent.

Terry's first single, "Suspicion", was released in February of 1964, and soared to #3 in 1964 on the U.S. charts with the Beatles holding down the other four positions of the Top 5. His voice resembled Elvis Presley, who had earlier recorded "Suspicion" on his 1962 album, *Pot Luck*. Following this first success, his second single, "I'll Touch a Star," reached #23 on the charts. Subsequently, none of his singles made the Top 40.

Realizing that he might be destined for the "one hit wonder" status, Stafford turned to professional songwriting in the late 1960s, and composed for the next twenty years. One of his greatest achievements in songwriting was his "Amarillo by Morning," which Terry recorded as a "B" side for Atlantic Records, while the "A" side was a country cover, "Has Anyone Seen My Sweet Gypsy Rose." Atlantic eventually promoted the "B" side because it reached #31 on the country charts in 1973, and received the attention of country artists such as Chris LeDoux, Moe Bandy, and George Strait. LeDoux was the first to include it in his *Life As A Rodeo Man* album (1975), and again in his *American Cowboy* collection (1994). Strait's single shot to the top of the country charts in 1982, and the song was also included on *Strait From the Heart* (1982), *Greatest Hits* (1986), and *Strait Out of the Box* (1995). Finally, Bandy included it in his 1987 *Act Naturally* album.

Stafford returned from Nashville to Amarillo in 1995, and died from liver complications on March 17, 1996. He is buried in Llano Cemetery in Amarillo.

Kay Starr

(b. July 21, 1922)

One of the most celebrated pop singers of the 1950s, recognized for charting numerous hit singles, including "Bonaparte's Retreat," "Side By Side," "Wheel of Fortune," and "Rock and Roll Waltz," Kathryn LaVerne Starks was born in Dougherty, Oklahoma, a hamlet of about 100 residents south of Oklahoma City. Her father Harry was a full-blooded Iroquois and mother Annie was of mixed American Indian and Irish descent. And contrary to some reports, Kay was not born on a reservation. When Kay was three the family moved to Dallas where her father found work installing sprinkler systems (Automatic Sprinkler Company) in buildings. When the Great Depression hit, Kay's mother raised chickens in a hen house behind their home, and it was here that Kay first began singing concerts each day after school to the chickens at age nine.

Although her parents considered the hen house concerts amusing, Kay's Aunt Nora recognized her singing potential and suggested to her parents that she enter a talent contest sponsored by radio station WRR in Dallas. Performing at the Dallas Melba Theatre, she won the contest singing "Now's the Time to Fall in Love." Because of the overwhelming response to her singing, Kay was given her own fifteen-minute radio program broadcast three times per week. Singing primarily pop and country music, she earned three dollars for each appearance, but her family soon moved to Memphis. Here Kay soon landed her own show, *Starr Time* on WREC radio, and was also featured on WMPS radio's popular *Saturday Night Jamboree* program. Dubbed "The Kid" by station management, she was given the opportunity to sing requests whenever someone would call. Around this time, she changed her name to Kay Starr because of continual misspellings received in fan mail.

Starr's first major break was when noted big band leader and jazz violinist Joe Venuti came to Memphis in 1937. Venuti's contract with the Peabody Hotel in Memphis specified that he have a girl singer with his band—a void that he had not been able to fill. Venuti's road manager heard Kay on radio and was so impressed that he an
. Her first Top 10 hit came in 1949 with "So Tired," followed by "Hoop-Dee-Doo," which charted at #2 in 1950. Interestingly, on a hometown visit to Dougherty, Kay heard a fiddle tune being played on a jukebox in the local honky tonk. It was Pee Wee King's "Bonaparte's Retreat." She called Roy Acuff's publishing house in Nashville and received permission from Acuff to record it with lyrics provided by Acuff. It was released by Capitol in 1950 and became Kay's first major hit as it sold almost a million copies. After several successful duets ("I'll Never Be Free" and "You're My Sugar") with country singer, Ten-

nessee Ernie Ford, Kay was called into the Capitol studio on January 17, 1952. Management wanted her to record a rush release of a new song, "Wheel of Fortune," which was also recorded by two competing labels. It is the song that has become historically associated with Starr, and resulted in her first gold record. It remained on the charts at #1 for ten weeks and eventually became the number two selling single in 1952. From 1948 to 1954, Kay charted twenty-seven hits with Capitol, but the studio failed to renew her contract in 1955, and she accepted an offer from RCA.

In 1956, Starr hit both American and British charts with her million selling gold record, "Rock and Roll Waltz." It stayed on the charts at #1 for six weeks, and eventually became the number two selling single in 1956 in the U.S., and the number one single of the year in the U.K. It was the first #1 single by a female singer in the rock era, the first to have "rock and roll" in the title, and the first #1 single for RCA Records.Kay remained with RCA until 1959 when she returned to Capitol, and recorded several new albums, including *Movin'* (1959) which included "Lazy River," *Losers, Weepers* (1960), *I Cry By Night* (1962), and *Just Plain Country* (1962), which included Patsy Cline's "Crazy" and Buck Owens' "Foolin' Around."

By the mid-1960s, rock and roll had changed American music tastes that led to Kay's second departure from Capitol. She continued to perform at major concert venues in the U.S. and England, including the Riveria, Sands, and Fremont Hotels in Las Vegas, and Harrah's in Reno. Recording with several independent jazz and country labels, she teamed with Count Basie in 1968 for an album of classic jazz, *Back to the Roots* (1975). In the 1980s, she teamed with Helen O'Connell and Margaret Whiting for a 3 Girls 3 revue and later with Kaye Ballard as 4 Girls 4. In 1993, she joined Pat Boone on The April Love tour of the U.K.

Starr is also remembered as one of the first recording artists to "overdub" her own voice in her recording of "Side by Side." Along with Jo Stafford, Rosemary Clooney, and **Patti Page**, Kay Starr was one of the most influential women in American music during the early 1950s. In 2001, Kay was featured on Tony Bennett's new album for Capitol to commemorate his 75th birthday, *Playin' With My Friends: Tony Bennett Sings the Blues*, in which she duetted with Tony on "Blue and Sentimental." Starr was inducted into the Oklahoma Jazz Hall of Fame in 2000, and into the Oklahoma Music Hall of Fame in 2002.

T

Talley, James

(b. November 9, 1943)

Considered by some critics as the modern-day **Woody Guthrie** and recognized by former President Jimmy Carter's wife, Rosalyn, as her favorite singer, James Talley was born in a Tulsa hospital, but never lived there. His parents were living in Pryor and went to Tulsa to have James delivered. Both parents were from Oklahoma with his father's family from Welch in the northeastern part, while his mother's parents (Ogden and Mary) were farmers near Mehan, where they resided in a pyramidal house with a well for water and no indoor plumbing. It was here that James spent much of childhood learning about Oklahoma, such as his great grandfather participating in two land rushes into Oklahoma (1889

James Tallley

and 1893). While working near Pryor, Oklahoma, his parents met while making munitions and gunpowder at the Oklahoma Ordinance. One of the venues where his parents courted was Cain's Ballroom in Tulsa, dancing to the sounds of **Bob Wills and the Texas Playboys**. James' mother, who was raised on a small farm near Glencoe, received a degree in elementary education from Oklahoma A & M (Oklahoma State University) in Stillwater in the 1930s. When James was age three, the family eventually migrated to Washington state where his father worked at the Hanford Works in Richland, and his mother taught school for five years. Wages for teachers and construction workers in the booming town of Richland were good, and when the Talleys left for Albuquerque, New Mexico, they had accumulated $8,000 in their coffers. But his father paid a dear price for the wages at Hanford for a large tumor in one of his lungs was detected shortly after they moved to New Mexico. Half of one of his lungs was removed, but the doctors never fully diagnosed the problem and its causes. During the next few years, his father suffered three heart attacks and died in 1969 at age fifty-seven. James always believed that the plutonium use by his father at Hanford caused his father's death, and wrote a song about the plant entitled "Richland, Washington," included in his 2002 CD, *Touchstones*. James recalls fond memories of his father, such as playing the guitar, singing Jimmie Rodgers songs, and listening to the music of Bob Wills, especially Tommy Duncan, crooner for the Texas Playboys, who his father met in Washington. James paid tribute to the western swing genre on his first album with a song, "W. Lee O'Daniel and the Light Crust Doughboys." One of the stories James relates about his father is when he faced poverty: "It ain't no disgrace to be poor, it's just unhandy as hell."

After graduation from high school in Albuquerque, Talley attended Oklahoma State University the fall semester of 1961. He was a singer with the Student Entertainers, under the leadership of Ashley Alexander, participated in Air Force ROTC, and, according to James, almost memorized Dante's *Inferno* in a humanities course. While visiting James in Stillwater, his father suffered a massive heart attack and was hospitalized in Stillwater until James was able to transport him to Albuquerque. Lacking funds, he enrolled at the University of New Mexico, where he received a degree in fine arts, and then completed two years of graduate study at U.C.L.A. and Univeristy of New Mexico in American Studies, but failed to finish his Ph.D. While in graduate school at U.C.L.A. in 1966, he read Woody Guthrie's book, *Born to Win*, which he says changed his life. He soon discovered his favorite songs were also by Guthrie, and claims to have learned almost all of them before he left campus. In his autobiography, he says Guthrie became his idol probably because of his "Okie" roots. After employment for a year as a caseworker for the New Mexico Department of Public Welfare, he moved to Nashville in 1968, and while continuing as a caseworker, he met his wife, Jan.

In the mid-1970s, Talley recorded four critically acclaimed albums for Capitol Records, *Got No Bread, No Milk, No Money, But We Sure Got Lots of Love* ((1975), which was originally released on Talley's own Torreon label, but then picked up by Capitol;

Tryin' Like the Devil (1976), which included the brutally honest track, "Give My Love to Marie," with lyrics describing a coal miner with black lung disease; *Blackjack Choir* (1977), on which B.B. King appeared on James' tribute to King in the track entitled "Bluesman"); and *Ain't It Somethin'* (1978). By 1978, James was dropped from the Capitol label because the recordings received little radio airplay, and James was forced to lay off his band, which included such notable instrumentalists as Josh Graves, Johnny Gimble, and Charlie McCoy. One bright spot for James is when President Jimmy Carter and wife, Rosalynn, informed the media that he was one of their favorite artists and invited him to sing at the 1977 Inauguration Ball, and later performed twice at the Carter White House. Thus, James was forced to enter the real estate business in Nashville in 1983 to support his family because his Capitol albums soon fell out of print.

In 1985, Talley signed with the German label, Bear Family Records, after Richard Weize, head of the label, asked him to perform at the company's tenth anniversary party. Weize reissued the magnificent Capitol albums, as well as releasing several new ones, including *American Originals* (1985), *Lovesongs and the Blues* (1989), and *James Talley: Live* (1994), recorded at The Lone Star Café in New York and The Great Southeast Music Hall in Atlanta. Talley launched an ambitious project in 1992 with the publication and accompanying CD entitled *The Road to Torreon: Love Songs and Other Writings by James Talley*. The contents of the book featured Talley's prose and incredible photographs of New Mexican villages by Cavalliere Ketchum. The book was published by the University of New Mexico Press and the CD was released by Bear Family Records, a German company.

In 1994, Talley went to Santa Fe, where he recorded a tribute album, *Woody Guthrie and Songs of My Oklahoma Home*, one of the best collections to date of Guthrie's classic material from the 1930s and 1940s, including "Dust Bowl Blues," "Do Re Mi," and "Pretty Boy Floyd." After unsuccessful negotiations with Capitol, James released the album on his own Cimarron label, followed by *Nashville City Blues* (2000) and *Touchstones* (2002). The latter contains an eclectic variety of songs in the sixteen tracks, including such cuts as "W. Lee O'Daniel and the Light Crust Doughboys" with some Oklahoma images of Tulsa and Cain's Ballroom. After hearing the Woody tribute album, Nora Guthrie (Woody's daughter) was quoted: "You sound eerily like my father." In 2009, Talley released *Journey - The Second Voyage* on Cimarron Records.

www.jamestalley.com

Thomas, B. J.
(b. August 7, 1942)

A career that has spanned four different genres of American music (pop, country, rock, and gospel) and best known for his "Rain Drops Keep Fallin' on My Head," Billy Joe Thomas was born in Hugo, a southeastern Oklahoma town boasting roughly 5,000 citizens and county seat of Choctaw County. He was raised in Rosenberg, Texas, near Houston, and grew up singing in church. His early influences were both country and rhythm and blues artists, including Hank Williams, Sr., Ernest Tubb, and Jackie Wilson. The first record he purchased was "Miss Ann" by Little Richard. He chose the initials B.J., when he was ten, because there were five Billy's on his Little League baseball team. At fourteen, B.J. joined his church choir and also sang in his high school choral group. While still in high school, he joined The Triumphs, a Houston-based group, who recorded a local hit entitled "Lazy

Man." Collaborating with songwriter Mark Charron, a member of The Triumphs, B.J. co-wrote "Billy and Sue," which also failed to gain any attention.

On July 4, 1965, The Triumphs performed at a state park in Houston, where they were noticed by Charles Booth, owner of Pacemaker Records. He signed the group to his label and released their first album, which included as one of the tracks the Hank Williams, Sr. song, "I'm So Lonesome I Could Cry," which B.J. recorded for his father, who had suggested this might be a hit. Backed by his old group The Triumphs, B.J. recorded the number at the Houston studio of Huey P. Meaux. A Houston disc jockey named Bob White thought it was a potential hit and gave it airplay. Pacemaker Records released it as a single and New York-based Scepter Records picked it up for national distribution, and it peaked at #8 on the Hot 100 in 1966.

B.J. Thomas

Based on the success of using Hank Williams material, B.J. recorded "I Can't Help It (If I'm Still in Love With You)," which failed to achieve the same popularity as his first recording, as well as a re-release of "Billy and Sue."

Thomas did not enter the Top 10 list until 1968 when he recorded "Hooked on a Feeling," which charted at #5 and became a million seller. It was Dionne Warwick, recording colleague at Scepter, who suggested to Burt Bacharach and Hal David that B.J. be given the opportunity to sing "Raindrops Keep Fallin' on My Head," for the motion picture *Butch Cassidy and the Sundance Kid* in 1969. Apparently, Bacharach and David had approached both Bob Dylan and Ray Stevens, but both had conflicts, and B.J. became their next choice. The night before he was to record "Raindrops" B.J. was ordered by his doctor not to use his voice for two weeks because he was suffering from a severe case of laryngitis. B.J. pleaded with the doctor and was given some medication to lubricate his throat. The next day, B.J. did five takes of the song before Bacharach was satisfied. An executive from 20th Century Fox present at the recording session congratulated B.J. on sounding so much like Paul Newman, and inquired how the thought of using such a raspy voice. A few weeks later with his voice healed, B.J. recorded the single version of "Raindrops", and at this session Bacharach added the "da-da-da-da-da" tag. It won an Academy Award, was B.J.'s biggest hit, and was Bacharach and David's first million seller. B.J. sang it on the 1970 Academy Awards telecast before a national audience.

By the late 1960s, Thomas had captured four gold records, including "The Eyes of a New York Woman," "Hooked on a Feeling," "It's Only Love," and "Raindrops." In addition, he had a series of soft rock hits, such as "Everybody's Out of Town," "I Just Can't Help Believing," "No Love at All," "Rock and Roll Shoes" (a duet with Ray Charles), and "Rock and Roll Lullaby." The latter featured guitarist Duane Eddy and the Beach Boys. In 1968, he married Gloria and they raised three daughters—Paige, Erin, and Nora.

Following Scepter Records' demise, B.J. signed with Paramount with little success, and he moved in 1975 to ABC Records to pursue a more country-oriented style. "(Hey Won't You Play) Another Somebody Done Somebody Wrong Song," his first single at

700 / Oklahoma Music Guide II

ABC, reached #1 in both the pop and country charts, and became his second biggest seller. It also won the 1975 Grammy for Best Country Song and was nominated for the CMA Single of the Year in 1975. It still retains the record for having the longest title for a #1 hit. In his autobiography, B.J. admits he barely remembers the recording session for his second #1 hit. At the time, he was spending up to $3,000 per week to feed a drug habit that included Valium, cocaine, and amphetamines.

Plagued by a series of personal problems, including bankruptcy and drug addiction, B.J. emerged as a born-again Christian in 1976, and recorded on the Christian label, Myrrh, including the platinum *Home Where I Belong* album, as well as penning his autobiography, *Home Where I Belong*. He and his wife, Gloria, also wrote another book, *In Tune*. He received two Dove awards and five Grammys for his gospel recordings, one each year from 1977 to 1981, including the albums *Happy Man* in 1978, *You Gave Me Love (When Nobody Gave Me a Prayer)* in 1979, and *Amazing Grace* in 1981.

Thomas returned to the country field in the 1980s and peaked with such hits as "Whatever Happened to Old Fashioned Love" and "New Looks From an Old Lover," both of which hit No. 1 on the country charts. These were followed by two Top 10 hits, "The Whole World's in Love When You're Lonely" and "Two Car Garage." On his thirty-ninth birthday in 1981, B.J. became a member of the Grand Ole Opry, its sixtieth member.

In 1985, Thomas released *Throwin' Rocks at the Moon*, which contained "As Long as We've Got Each Other," the theme song for the highly successful ABC-TV sitcom *Growing Pains*. His final album for Columbia was *Night Life*, a collection of country standards produced in Nashville. As of 2002, a live album is in the works as well as a dance mix of some of his classic pop hits.

B.J. and Gloria, his wife of thirty-four years, reside in Arlington, Texas, and he continues to maintain an active tour schedule (approximately 100 dates per year) performing at various venues, including Tulsa's Brady Theater, the Toledo Symphony, and the Hiawassee, Georgia Mountain Fair, and performs on the Grand Ole Opry about four times a year. During his career, Thomas has sold more than fifty million records, and earned two platinum and eleven gold records.

www.bjthomas.com

Thompson, Hank
(b. September 3, 1925 - November 6, 2007)

A musical career spanning more than seven decades and producing some 60 million records, Country Music Hall of Famer Henry William Thompson was born in Waco, Texas, the only child of Ilda and Jule Thompson. Although a native Texan, Thompson is associated with Oklahoma in many ways, including host of a variety show on WKY-TV in Oklahoma City during the mid-1950s; sponsor of and teacher at the Hank Thompson School of Country Music in Claremore in 1973, the first such entity in the U.S.; owner of a radio station in Sand Springs, where he made his home for several years; his recordings of such songs as "Oklahoma Hills" and "Oklahoma Home Brew," his 1969 album, *Hank Thompson Salutes Oklahoma*, and serving as mentor for such Oklahoma country music stars as **Wanda Jackson** and **Norma Jean**.

Growing up in Waco, Hank was influenced by a variety of country music ranging from **Gene Autry** to Jimmie Rodgers. His first choice was the harmonica, an instrument he used to win several local amateur contests. But Gene Autry strummed the guitar and

Hank Thompson

young Hank at age ten was given a $4 model for Christmas by his parents. He devoted hour upon hour to learning chord patterns and guitar runs, as well as ventriloquist skills, and it resulted in a job performing on a Saturday morning program in the early 1940s at a local theater broadcast over radio station WACO. A local flour company liked what they heard, and provided sponsorship for six months for a show dubbed "Hank the Hired Hand," while Hank completed high school.

Following graduation in 1943, Hank enlisted in the U.S. Navy and, while stationed in San Diego, he convinced his superiors to allow him to play in local clubs. While at sea, Hank also entertained on board and broadcast over a small network of stations established by the Navy in the South Pacific. During his tour of duty, he completed several college credits though Southern Methodist University and the University of Texas-Austin. It is also reported that he attended Princeton University after his discharge from the Navy. Studying primarily electrical engineering at these three universities, Hank is one of the most educated of the country music artists, although he never completed a degree.

Returning to Waco, Hank started a noon show on KWTX, and the response was so positive that he formed his own band, the Brazos Valley Boys (named after the river running through Waco), and began to play dances throughout Texas. Hank had tried his hand at writing songs in the Navy, and continued this endeavor after his discharge. He recorded two of his songs, "Whoa Sailor" and "Swing Wide Your Gate of Love," both on the local Globe label, and with the help of Hal Horton, a disc jockey on KRLD, a 50,000 watt station in Dallas, "Whoa Sailor" became a regional hit. After recording four more cuts with the Blue Bonnet label (most notable was "A Lonely Heart Knows"), another independent company in Texas, Hank was given a break by Capitol recording artist, Tex Ritter, who assisted him in obtaining a contract with this major label in 1948, an association that lasted until 1966. During the next two years, Hank justified Ritter's faith in him by releasing four hits, "Humpty Dumpty Heart," "Today," a redo of "Whoa Sailor," and a new composition, "Green Light."

In 1951, Hank began a thirteen-year partnership with the Hollywood record producer, Ken Nelson, who produced his first number one hit and signature song, "Wild Side of Life," in one take. The single remained at the top of the country charts for fifteen weeks in 1952, and Hank earned a gold record, as well as prompting an answer song from Miss Kitty Wells, "It Wasn't God Who Made Honky Tonk Angels." In 1953-54, Hank charted seven Top 10 singles, including "Wake Up Irene," and answer song to "Goodnight, Irene," "No Help Wanted," "Breakin' the Blues," "Honky Tonk Girl," "New Green Light," "We've Gone Too Far," and "You Can't Have My Love," the last five songs written or co-written by him. Hank was also instrumental in helping a future country star on "You Can't Have My Love." Her name was Wanda Jackson.

During the late 1950s and on into the 1960s, Hank and the band averaged about 240 personal appearances annually, taking them to all fifty states, Canada, Far East, and Europe.

Moreover, he continued to record at a furious pace with such hits as "Don't Take It Out on Me," "Wildwood Flower," a Carter Family song that Hank learned as a youngster, "I'm Not Mad, Just Hurt," "I've Run Out of Tomorrows," "A Six Pack to Go," "Squaws Along the Yukon," "Oklahoma Hills," "Waitin' in the Lobby of Your Heart," "Rub-A-Dub-Dub," "Rockin' in the Congo," "The Blackboard of My Heart," and "Breakin' in Another Heart," the latter co-written with his wife Dorothy.

Hank left Capitol in 1964, but signed with Warner Brothers in 1966. By the time Hank had left Capitol, he had generated record sales of more than 30 million and had produced roughly 100 singles on the hit charts. His tenure with Warner Brothers lasted only two years, but he did produce the *Where is the Circus* album. He then moved in 1968 to ABC/Dot Records, an association that lasted a decade. While at the new label, Hank celebrated his twenty-fifth year as a recording artist in 1971, and the company issued a two-record set in his honor, *Hank Thompson's 25th Anniversary* album. Additional hits during his period with ABC included "On Tap, in the Can, or in the Bottle," "Smokey the Bar," "Next Time I Fall in Love (I Won't)," "Kindly Keep It Country," "The Older the Violin, the Sweeter the Music," "Who Left the Door to Heaven Open," "The Mark of a Heel," "Mama Don't 'Low," and "I Hear the South Calling Me."

Over the years, Hank and the Brazos Valley Boys were featured on several television shows, including *The Tonight Show* (Johnny Carson), *Jimmy Dean Show*, and *Swingin' Country*, as well as singing the theme song for the movie *Smoky*, starring Fess Parker and **Hoyt Axton**. He was elected to the Country Music Hall of Fame in 1989, and the Country Music Foundation released a package of hits titled *Hank Thompson Country Music Hall of Fame Series*.

Hank Thompson was a pioneer in country music during the twentieth century, including the first color broadcast of a variety show on television (WKY-TV in Oklahoma City), first act to use a sound and lighting system developed through Hank's engineering skills, first music act to receive corporate tour sponsorship, first "live" country music album recorded at the Golden Nugget in Las Vegas, first act to use drums on the Grand Ole Opry, first country music artist to play Las Vegas, and the Brazos Valley Boys, Hank's group, were voted the number one country band for fifteen consecutive years by *Billboard* magazine.

From Carnegie Hall to Las Vegas to the Hollywood Palladium, Hank's contributions to country music are immeasurable. In 1997, the *Hank Thompson and Friends* album was released on Curb. The thirteen tracks include such notables as Marty Stuart, **Brooks and Dunn**, George Jones, Kitty Wells, and **Vince Gill**. The latter is featured in a duet with Hank on "Six Pack to Go." Thompson's 2000 album on the Hightone label was produced by the veteran Lloyd Maines. *Seven Decades* includes songs ranging from the traditional "Wreck of the Old 97" to Jimmie Rodgers' "In the Jailhouse Now" to the Kingston Trio's "Scotch and Soda." Only one other artist, Frank Sinatra, has achieved the honor of recording for seven decades, a remarkable feat. His latest release in 2001 is *Humpty Dumpty Heart* on the Country Stars label. Hank was inducted into the Nashville Songwriters Hall of Fame in 1997, and the Oklahoma Music Hall of Fame in 2002. His last public performance was October 8, 2007 in Waco, Texas. Diagnosed with lung cancer, Thompson died at aged 82.

Tillman, Floyd
(b. December 8, 1914)

Member of the Country Music Hall of Fame (1984) and Nashville Songwriters Hall of Fame (1970), as well as one of the first to champion the use of the electric guitar in country music (first known country singer to accompany himself with an electric guitar) and the first to define the honky tonk subgenre of country music, Floyd Tillman was born near Ryan, Oklahoma, a community of about 1,000 residents located just north of the Red River boundary between Oklahoma and Texas. Floyd was the youngest of eleven children born into a sharecropper family that moved to Post, Texas, a cotton mill town, when he was only a few months old. He attended grade school in Post from 1923 to 1929, and worked as a messenger boy for Western Union when he was in his early teens.

Floyd started his musical career on the mandolin and banjo, but later changed to the guitar (it is reported he played his first job after two weeks of practice) in order to backup local fiddle players, and in 1931, he and his brothers formed a string band trio. At age nineteen Floyd started writing songs and joined Adolph and Emil Hofner's western swing house band at the Gus' Palm Garden in San Antonio, where he played lead electric guitar and sang with the group, although he admitted that he could not sing and wanted to become a songwriter. He also performed on radio station KABC in San Antonio.

During the mid-1930s, Tillman played banjo, mandolin, and guitar with Mack Clark's dance band in Houston, and then left to join the Blue Ridge Playboys led by Leon "Pappy" Selph, during which time they recorded with Vocalion Records. He departed from the Clark ensemble because members of the band claimed that Floyd's song, "It Makes No Difference Now," was too hillbilly. As personnel changed often during the Depression, Floyd also worked with such western swing and honky tonk notables as Cliff Bruner, Moon Mullican, and **Bob Dunn**.

In 1938, Cliff Bruner and the Texas Wanderers recorded Floyd's first songwriting hit, "It Makes No Difference Now," which has become a country classic and covered by such diverse artists as Eddy Arnold, Bing Crosby, The Supremes, **Gene Autry**, Ray Charles, Willie Nelson and Hank Snow, **Hank Thompson**, Burl Ives, and Jimmie Davis. The latter bought the song from Floyd in 1938 for $300, and both are listed as co-writers. "It Makes No Difference Now," along with "San Antonio Rose," was the first crossover hit when Bing Crosby in 1940 sang both songs on the same record. In 1939, Floyd made his first recording with his own song, "I'll Keep on Loving You" on the Victor label.

During World War II, Tillman served as a radio operator in Army Air Corps, and was stationed near Houston, where he continued his songwriting and recording. His first No. 1 hit as a recording artist came in 1944 with "They Took the Stars Out of Heaven" on the Decca label. It was followed by a string of Top 10 hits for Floyd, including "G.I. Blues," "Drivin' Nails in My Coffin," "Each Night at Nine," "I Love You So Much It Hurts," "I Gotta Have My Baby Back," "Slippin' Around," and "I'll Never Slip Around Again."

From 1945 to 1950, Floyd and his band, Floyd Tillman and All the Gang, performed on radio station KTRH in Houston. In 1945, he signed with Columbia Records where his first major hit was "Drivin' Nails in My Coffin." In 1948, he hit the Top 5 country charts with "I Love You So Much It Hurts Me," which was covered by such pop and country artists as Vic Damone, Red Foley, Ernest Tubb, Ray Charles, Ray Price, Mickey Gilley, Andy Williams, Marie Osmond, Eddy Arnold, and **Jimmy Wakely**.

In 1949, Tillman wrote and released the song that would define his career, "Slippin' Around," regarded by music historians as the first song to deal with cheating and infidelity. It, too, was covered by a wide array of artists, such as Margaret Whiting and Jimmy Wakely, which made it into a #1 pop hit and a million seller for them in 1949, and Ernest Tubb, who took it to #1 on the country charts and #17 on the pop charts also in 1949. Additional artists to cover the song included Texas Jim Robertson (1950), Marion Worth and George Morgan (1964), Roy Drusky and Priscilla Mitchell (1965), and Mack Abernathy (1988). "Slippin" Around" was also selected by the Smithsonian Institution as one of the tracks of an eight record set titled *The Smithsonian Collection of Classic Country Music* released in 1981.

In the early 1950s, Tillman dissolved his band and discussed retirement. The last song he recorded with his band, "I Don't Care Anymore," perhaps summarized his feelings. Floyd's last charted solo success was in 1960 with "It Just Tears Me Up," however, he made further recordings on minor labels, including an album of his songs with various friends such as **Merle Haggard** and Willie Nelson, both of whom were influenced by his style. Nelson was on hand to celebrate Floyd's 85th birthday bash in Llano, Texas in 1999.

Several other songs written by Tillman not previously mentioned include "I Am Music," recorded by Skeets McDonald, "This Cold War With You," "Some Other World," "Daisy Mae," recorded by Ernest Tubb, "Please Don't Pass Me By," and "I'll Never Slip Around Again," released by Margaret Whiting and Jimmy Wakely. His 1944 hit, "Each Night at Nine," captured the feelings of lonely servicemen so well that both Axis Sally and Tokyo Rose played it heavily to encourage desertion among American troops during World War II.

In addition to the aforementioned honors and accolades, "I Love You So Much It Hurts" earned Tillman a BMI One-Million Performance Award. When he was inducted into the Nashville Songwriters Hall of Fame, Floyd said: "You don't know when it's time to write a song. You just feel the song. It comes through you. . . . Sometimes you get an idea from what somebody said . . . But you don't write it unless you feel like it . . .They're personal songs, but they weren't written during the time they were personal. In other words when you have these problems you don't . . . the last thing you think of is writing a song about a problem. But later on you laugh at it, and then you write a song about it."

One of the best recent CD releases of Tillman's songs is *Country Music Hall of Fame 1984* (King Records-2000) that includes "I Love You So Much, It Hurts," "Drivin' Nails in My Coffin," and "This Cold War With You."

As of 2003, Tillman in his 88th year resides in Marble Falls, Texas.

Tisdale, Wayman
(b. 6/9/1964 - d. 5/15/2009)

Although Wayman Tisdale will always be remembered as a basketball legend in the state of Oklahoma, his notable music career is active and fruitful with five nationally released jazz albums that explore his preferred funky, smooth jazz style, and a collection of gospel songs to his credit. Born June 9, 1964 in Ft. Worth, Texas but reared in Tulsa,

Wayman Tisdale

Wayman used the bass as a lead instrument in the model of his greatest influences, Stanley Clark and Marcus Miller, and his vocals are representative of his upbringing in the gospel choir and its association with American soul music.

Tisdale's father, Reverend Louis Tisdale, bought Wayman a toy guitar and the ten-year-old eventually broke all but the fattest strings, so he began playing bass lines on what was left. He also began playing basketball that year, eventually reaching 6'9". A foot taller than his teen contemporaries, he became the first Oklahoma high school player ever to have his number retired.

Known for his massive dunks and his left-handed jumper at the University of Oklahoma, Wayman is roundly considered the greatest player in school history. He is the only three-time, first-team, consensus All-American in college basketball history, and completed his career #3 on the all-time NCAA scoring list. Leaving OU as a junior, he was second overall pick in the 1985 NBA draft, after Patrick Ewing. He was also a member, along with Michael Jordan, of the 1984 Olympic gold-medal team coached by Bob Knight. Tisdale averaged fifteen points-per-game over twelve years in the NBA, four years each with Indiana, Sacramento, and Phoenix, and appeared in twenty-two career playoff games before retiring in 1998.

Throughout his basketball career, Wayman kept playing bass not only out of enjoyment, but to keep his spirits up through the long non-stop NBA road trips and changes in urban locations with trades to new teams. By the time he signed with the Phoenix Suns in 1994, he had also signed with Mo Jazz, an offshoot of Motown Records, and released his first CD, *Power Forward* in 1995, a top ten album on *Billboard*'s Contemporary Jazz Chart, then 1996's *In the Zone*, another Top 10 jazz album. When Mo Jazz folded in 1997, Atlantic Records signed Tisdale, spurring the 1998 release of *Decisions*, recorded in Tisdale's home studio, and featuring some of the biggest names in contemporary jazz, such as Gerald Albright and Marcus Miller. In 2001, Wayman released *Face to Face*, a highly successful contemporary jazz album that hit #1 on *Billboard's* jazz chart. As a result, The Smooth Jazz Awards named him the 2002 Bassist of the Year, and the Oklahoma Jazz Hall of Fame also presented Wayman with its Legacy Tribute Award that year. After his diagnosis and treatment for cancer in March, 2007, Tisdale recorded *Rebound*, and was planning both a tour and more recordings when he fell ill, and died, May 15, 2009 in Tulsa. Tisdale and his wife, Regina, were married from 1981 through his passing and had four children together. As many as 4,000 mourners paid their respects to the Tisdale family at Wayman's funeral held in Tulsa's BOK Center.

Asked for a comment on his career in 2003, Tisdale said, "I am very conscious not to take credit for what I do. It is all rooted in family and grounded firmly in God. I had great parents that helped show me the way and I knew everything would turn out all right. From being the #1 basketball player in the nation in high school to a gold medal in the Olympics, and success in both my professional careers, God is smiling on me."

Toppah, Cheevers

Raised by parents Jeannie and D.K. Toppah in Weatherford, Oklahoma, Grammy-nominee Cheevers Toppah is of Navajo descent on his mother's side and Kiowa heritage on his father's side. As a result, he is connected to a long family line of traditional American Indian singers, and has released nine albums of Native American music between 2007 and 2011. Along with lifelong experience around the big powwow drum, he began singing in choirs during elementary school. After formal choral training at Weatherford High School with his choir teacher, John Gerber, Toppah traveled and performed with the Oklahoma All-State chorus. This experience inspired Cheevers to combine his choral training with his extensive knowledge of powwow singing.

Cheevers Toppah

Teaming with Alex E. Smith (Pawnee/Sauk & Fox), the first results of their harmonized Southern Plains vocals appeared on the 2007 Canyon Records CD, Intonation, nominated for a Grammy Award for Best Native American Album. By adding Ojibwe singer Nitanis "Kit" Landry, they expanded their sound by adding Landry's higher pitched Northern-style vocals on Harmony Nights (Canyon, 2007), and recorded a third CD as a trio, Rain in July (Canyon, 2009).

When Cheevers was 14, he began learning Kiowa traditional Christian hymns from his grandfather, noted Kiowa hymn singer, Ralph Kotay, and later from his aunt Ida Kaubin and grandmother, Dorita Horse. To re-vitalize and preserve the a cappella hymns, Toppah recorded Renewed Spirit: Harmonized Church Hymns of the Kiowa (Canyon, 2011), nominated for a 2011 Native American Music Award ("Nammy"). Cheevers has also recorded two albums of Peyote Songs with celebrated Diné Native American Church singer, Kevin Yazzie. Both 2010 Canyon releases, First Light and Awakening of Life, feature the ethereal harmonies of Yazzie and Toppah, and the up tempo rhythms of a water drum and gourd rattle used in the all-night Native American Church services. Cheevers has also composed and recorded powwow songs for three Canyon Records albums by the widely traveled repeat champion singing group, Thunder Hill, to include Clash of the Titans (2006), For the Love (2008), and Relentless (2010).

Most recently, he has been recording with the Southern-style powwow group, Wild Band of Comanches. For his extensive output of recording over the last four years, along with a widely recognized voice with talents in all areas of traditional and contemporary American Indian music, the Oklahoma Music Hall of Fame awarded Cheevers the 2011 Rising Star Award.

The Tractors (see Steve Ripley)

Tulsa Sound

By all counts the Tulsa Sound is a musical mélange of country, blues, rock, and occasionally jazz, that has its sources in the multi-faceted "Okie jazz" of **Bob Wills**, the rich R&B/jazz history of Tulsa, and the teenage musicians of the 1950s, such as **Leon Russell**, **David Gates**, **J.J. Cale**, and **Jack Dunham**, who embraced the burgeoning rock and roll movement while infusing a heady dose of R&B into the twangy blues of Elvis Presley.

Left to Right: Leo Feathers (guitar), Chuck Blackwell (drums), Ron Ryle (bass), Johnny Williams (saxophone), Russell Bridges (Leon Russell) (piano), Jack Dunham (vocals), and Junior Markhan (vocals) perform at the Tropicana Club, 1959.

What later becomes known as the Tulsa Sound of the 1970s might best be described as 50s rockers slowing down, maturing, settling down with families and changing priorities, which is reflected in the more relaxed style of music manifested most directly by J.J. Cale and Leon Russell's easy paced recordings of the early 1970s. Eric Clapton's 1974 tribute to Cale, *Slowhand* (MCA), with a rhythm section of Oklahomans Jamie Oldaker and Carl Radle, and then Dire Straits *Sultans of Swing* (Sire, 1978) is just mainstream popular music catching up with Tulsa's hip hybrid of blues, country, and rock. An updated version of the sound ran through American pop culture again in 1985 when Dire Straits' "Money for Nothing," with Mark Knopfler's thinly veiled imitation of J.J. Cale's vocal style, led to high rotations on the nascent video music channel, MTV. In the 1990s, **Steve Ripley**'s Tractors mined the same vein for their multi-platinum success, and by 2003, periodic reunions of Tulsa Sound musicians drew appreciative crowds while some of its primary musicians continued active careers in the recording studios and on concert stages around the world.

Aside from the previously mentioned R&B, Western swing, and rockabilly influences, the groundwork for what became known as the Tulsa Sound was laid in the middle 1950s as young Tulsa musicians began to form R&B leaning rock and roll bands while 50s rock and roll had a stranglehold on popular music and culture. Musicians from this era include drummers Chuck Blackwell, David Teegarden, Buddy Jones, and Jimmy Karstein, singer/songwriters J.J. Cale (then Johnny Cale) and David Gates, guitarists Tommy Crook and Leo Feathers, pianist/singer/songwriter Leon Russell (then Russell Bridges), guitarist/pianist Tom Tripplehorn, and singer/songwriter Jack Dunham, all of whom have made significant contributions to American popular and country music. Additional musicians who played important roles in Tulsa's 1950s music scene were vocalists Gene Crose, Bobby Taylor, Jack Thurman, Bill Davis, Clyde Stacy, and Billy Mecon; bassists Ron Lyle, Bill Raffensperger, Gerald Goodwin, Larry McNulty, Jimmy Strader, Tommy Lee "Lucky" Clark, and Ralph Brumett; saxophonists Johnny Williams, Bill Boatman, and Sammy Dodge,;drummers Chuck Farmer, Don Kimmel, Gerald Goodwin, Jim Turley, and C.B. Glasby; pianists Jimmy Manry, Paul Pugh, Jim Blazer, Eddie Spraker, Rocky Frisco, and Doug Cunningham; as well as guitarists Lee Weir and Tommy Rush. Although younger than the first wave of Tulsa rock musicians, Jamie Oldaker (b. September 5, 1951) has also made numerous significant recordings that are part of the Tulsa Sound's legacy, most notably with the Bob Seger Band in 1973, on Leon Russell's 1974 album, *Stop All That Jazz*, and with Eric Clapton from 1974 to 1979, and again in 1984. Oldaker also played with Freddie King, Peter Frampton, and ex-Kiss guitarist Ace Frehley, before joining Steve Ripley and The Tractors for the group's 1994 self-titled album that sold more than two million copies.

While Jack Dunham was the first of the 1950s generation of Tulsa musicians to migrate to the Los Angeles area to take advantage of recording and performance opportunities there, several followed close behind. Along with Gates, Russell, and Cale, drummer David Teegarden recorded with Skip "Van Winkle" Knape on "God, Love, and Rock & Roll," a Top 40 hit in 1970, and kept time for Bob Seger's recordings and road shows from 1972-1991. Born in Tulsa, guitarist/pianist Tommy Tripplehorn (b. Feb. 2, 1944) toured and recorded with Gary Lewis and the Playboys in the 1960s, and continued as a session musician for several years before returning to Tulsa where he also played on the Tractors' 1994 smash album. Drummer Jim Karstein, born in 1942 in Tulsa, played on several sessions with Eric Clapton, toured with Gary Lewis and the Playboys, and appeared on J.J. Cale's albums from 1972 to 1992. Karstein has also worked with **Steve Ripley**, and James Burton, and was a member of Eric Clapton's Rainbow Concert Band. Chuck Blackwell, also born in Tulsa, is a drummer and songwriter who recorded with Joe Cocker, **Jesse Ed Davis**, and Freddie King, and whose songs were recorded by Taj Majal, Freddie King, and Ian Moore.

Born in Oklahoma City in 1942, but reared in Tulsa where he played in bands with the other Tulsa Sound titans, Carl Radle was one of the most sought after rock and blues bassists of the 1970s. He played on Delaney & Bonnie's 1969-70 tour, then joined Leon Russell and Joe Cocker for the famous Mad Dogs and Englishmen tour of 1970. After that circus of a road band, Radle formed Derek and the Dominos with Eric Clapton, Bobby Whitlock, and Jim Gordon, all of whom played in Delaney and Bonnie's group. With Derek and the Dominos, Carl plays bass and percussion on the famous album *Layla and Other Assorted Love Songs* (Atco, 1970), the title track of which has long been a classic rock radio standard. In 1971, Radle joined Leon Russell, Ringo Starr, Billy Preston, Bob Dylan, **Jesse Ed Davis**, and several others, in George Harrison's Concert for Bangladesh, a benefit concert to aid victims of a massive flood in India. While playing in Eric Clapton's band throughout the 1970s, during which time the Tulsa Sound became internationally known, Carl Radle also

David Teegarden

performed with a host of major artists, to include recording with some of the giants of the 1970s rock era: John Lee Hooker, Dave Mason, Buddy Guy, Rita Coolidge, Art Garfunkel, Doctor John, Duane Allman, and J.J. Cale. Radle died in 1980.

One musician who has foregone touring the country to remain in Tulsa, where "in-the-know" music enthusiasts recognize him as one of the premier guitarists in the United States, if not the world, is Tommy Crook. While not widely recognized as part of the Tulsa Sound per se, Crook often relies on its multiple elements for his musical inspiration, and played in bands with some of its primary movers and shakers in the early 1960s. With his unique fingerpicking style, and placement of bass strings on the bottom two positions on his guitar, Crook's sound is as unique as it is inspirational. His career is detailed under his name in *OMG II*.

Clyde Stacy, 1957

Another Tulsa Sound group that had more of cult following in Europe than anywhere else was Rockin' Jimmy and the Brothers of the Night. Led by guitarist and vocalist Jim Byfield, (b. February 7, 1949 in Tulsa) who really came of age a little later than the first generation of Tulsa Sound players, his music is very similar to both J.J. Cale's career-long style, and Eric Clapton's 1970s derivative of it. In fact, Clapton covered Byfield's "Little Rachel" on *There's One in Every Crowd* (Polydor, 1975). Before leading the Brothers of the Night, Byfield fronted Guava (1977), and then Jim Byfield and His Band (1978). In 1980, Byfield recorded for Pilgrim Records, established by former Joe Cocker roadie Peter Nichols, an engineer for Leon Russell's Shelter Records who became enthusiastic about recording local Tulsa bands. Pilgrim released at least two Tulsa band compilations, *Tulsa Sampler* (1977) and *The Green Album* (1978), as well as Rockin' Jimmy and the Brothers of the Night, *By the Light of the Moon* (1980).

Recorded at George Bingham's Ranch Studio in Glenpool, *By the Light of the Moon* relies on the laid-back, R&B influenced rock with a shuffle that has become the trademark of the Tulsa Sound. Byfield's musicians on the album include many familiar names: bassist Gary Gilmore (J.J. Cale, Taj Majal); keyboardist Walt Richmond (Bonnie Raitt, Rick Danko, The Tractors, et al.); drummer Chuck DeWalt; and guitarist Steve Hickerson. Backup vocalist Debbie Campbell (from Fort Worth, Texas) had fronted the Los Angeles-based group Buckwheat and toured with Bonnie Raitt before moving to Tulsa in the mid-1970s where she worked as a back up singer and opening solo act for multiple artists. Backup vocalist Jim Sweeney had already had his own solo album on Pilgrim in 1979, *Didn't I Blow Your Mind*, supported by the Brothers of the Night, as they did for Campbell's 1982

Carl Radle

album, *Two Hearts* (Churchill). The Brothers released a self-titled album in 1983 on Intercord with Gary Cundiff replacing Gilmore on bass, but the record saw little success outside of local music fans and those who kept track of Tulsa's music scene. Bringing the story full circle, Byfield also played guitar on The Tractors' 1994 self-titled hit album which brought the lazy Tulsa shuffle right back to the forefront of the music business, although this time in the country arena.

Rockin' Jimmy and the Brothers of the Night

Don White, born in Tulsa in 1940, is another singer and songwriter whose career has been intertwined with the Tulsa Sound. A singer, songwriter, and guitarist, J.J. Cale played guitar in White's first group and developed a deeper appreciation for country music via White. Artists who have recorded Don White's songs include Roseanne Cash, The Oak Ridge Boys, Suzy Boggus, and Razzy Bailey. His rootsy guitar work has been featured in recording sessions by J.J. Cale, Waylon Jennings, Marty Stuart, The Tractors, Katie Moffitt, and Johnny Rodriguez. While he also verges into straight-ahead country, Don White's 1999 independent CD, *Okie Fiesta*, is an ample illustration of both his guitar skills and songwriting style, both indicative at times of the common touchstones of the Tulsa Sound: relaxed and raspy vocal delivery reminiscent of Cale and Leon Russell, a shuffling rhythm section, and rootsy, blues-leaning guitar solos. Additionally, Tulsa Sound vets and old friends Tommy Tripplehorn and Casey Van Beek make appearances on the album, and White covers two songs by J.J. Cale ("Riverboat Song," "Magnolia") as well as one by Tom Waits ("Blind Love").

While the definitive Tulsa Sound history has yet to be written, many of the people who were there when it started are largely still around Tulsa. Several can be found on Sundays at the Beams of Light Family Tabernacle, pastored by former Tweed front man and guitarist, Jimmy Ray, who has recorded an inspirational CD with the many talented members of the tabernacle congregation. Given the contribution of Tulsa musicians to American pop, rock, and country music from 1960 to the present, a complete account can't be far off. For the time being, researchers can learn a lot from just going to the *Tulsa World's* online archives and putting any one of the names from this essay in the search engine.

Twilley, Dwight
(b. June 6, 1951)

Equally influenced by Sun rockabilly and Beatlesque songwriting and harmonies, Dwight Twilley and his partner, Tulsa native Phil Seymour (b. May 15, 1952 – d. August 17, 1993), created a tight and punchy pop sound in the mid-1970s that peaked early on a national scale with their Top 20 hit, "I'm on Fire." Since then, Dwight Twilley's recordings with Seymour have become landmarks of the evolving "power pop" sound that predated both punk in the U.K., and new wave in the United States. The two met at a Tulsa theater where they had both taken their brothers to see the Beatles' *A Hard Day's Night* during a matinee special's "take a friend free" promotion. Inspired by the film, the two teenagers, already accomplished instrumentalists, began writing and recording songs together, taking on the name Oister for their group, and occasionally playing with guitarist Bill Pitcock IV.

After practicing in their home-based studio, "The Shop," and making several recordings, they released two low-budget albums, *Oister Presents Swirling Clouds*, and *Oisters Greatest Hits*. Figuring New York and L.A. were too far to drive, Seymour and Twilley made a trip to Nashville, but never made it after they stopped at the legendary Sun Studios in Memphis, well-known for its recording of early blues artists like Howlin' Wolf and B.B. King, but also for being the epicenter of the rockabilly movement with Elvis Presley as its kingpin. At Sun, they met one of the label's early rockabilly artists, Ray Harris, who later invited the boys down to his Tupelo, Mississippi studios to record, and encouraged them to toughen up their sound. With some demos in hand, the Dwight Twilley Band traveled to Los Angeles and wrangled a deal with Shelter Records, co-owned by **Leon Russell**. Their first single, "I'm On Fire," mined from the same glam boogie as T. Rex's #1 hit, "Bang a Gong (Get It On), created an instant national stir by reaching #16 on the national pop charts in 1975, with practically no promotion from Shelter's haphazard industry management technique. Via the song's success, the band landed an *American Bandstand* appearance, and previewed the song they intended as the follow-up single, "Shark," recorded at Leon's home studio in Tulsa and on which Russell played bass, piano, and percussion. The label thought the group would be perceived as a novelty act trying to capitalize on the shark craze spreading through American pop culture at the time on the fins of the film 1975 film *Jaws*, and refused to release the single, which was ultimately dropped from *Sincerely*.

When *Sincerely* (Shelter) finally did hit the shelves in 1976, the band's notoriety had all but faded and the record went virtually unnoticed by anyone but critics noting the change in American pop from rebel Southern rock to a smarter, more polished sound that mirrored the punk pop emanating from England at the time via Elvis Costello and American cult figures Big Star, led by Alex Chilton. After *Sincerely* stalled at #138 on *Billboard*'s pop album charts, the band's second album, virtually all of which had been recorded during the *Sincerely* sessions, languished on the tape shelf while they negotiated a deal with ARISTA to release a new album, *Twilley Don't Mind*, on which their old Shelter label mate, Tom Petty, added backing vocals. In spite of the album's pop potential, the record only reached #70 on the pop album chart, and Seymour left the group, pursuing a solo career that produced on Top 30 hit, "Precious to Me," from his self-titled debut in 1980. After recording backing vocals for Tom Petty's first hits, "American Girl" and "Breakdown," Phil Seymour also worked with Del Shannon, Moon Mullican, and Oklahoma's other power poppers, 20/20, before joining the L.A.-based Textones. Diagnosed with Lymphoma in the middle 1980s, Seymour died in 1993 in Tarazana, California.

Soldiering on as a solo performer, Twilley had another largely unnoticed album for ARISTA, *Twilley* (1979), and an equally received album on EMI, *Scuba Divers* (1982), both of which charted at #113 and #109 respectively on the pop album charts. At least the single from *Scuba Divers*, "Somebody to Love," reached #16 on *Billboard*'s mainstream rock chart. Finally, in 1984, Twilley achieved some more commercial success with "Girls" (#16, 1984) from *Jungle*, which reached #39 on the pop album charts. His final album of the 1980s, *Wild Dogs*, created no buzz for CBS.

Twilley blipped again on the pop culture radar screen in 1992, when his "Why You Wanna Break My Heart" was included on the *Wayne's World* soundtrack.

When an earthquake destroyed his California home in 1995, Twilley returned to Tulsa and recorded his first new album since 1986, *Tulsa*, ultimately released on the Copper label in 1999, entirely in his mid-town Tulsa converted garage studio. The album ran away with a couple of Tulsa's local Spot Music Awards, sponsored by the *Tulsa World*, including Artist of the Year and National Album of the Year. In 1997, Twilley showed sixty pieces of his graphic art collection in a Tulsa exhibit titled *Out in the Rain*, and began releasing vinyl singles through Pop the Balloon Records in Europe in 1998. As a result of resurgent interest in Twilley's career, Not Lame Records released a compilation of rarities and outtakes from Twilley's thirty-year career, *Between the Cracks* (1998). In 1999, one of the largest European independent labels, Castle, picked up *Tulsa* for distribution there, as well as *Between the Cracks*.

In 2001, sessions from new material recorded in the early 1990s but never released, found new life as *Luck* on Twilley's own label, Big Oak. His tenth full-length release met with critical and commercial raves in Europe, and behind the new/old album, he headlined the Serie-B pop festival in Spain, playing alongside younger alterna-rockers Mudhoney, Bevis Frond, Cotton Mather, and Death Cab for Cutie. Also in 2001, Dwight Twilley made the magical list of potential rock and roll hall of fame inductees with other newly eligible artists, Bruce Springsteen, the Sex Pistols, and Blondie, and in 2002 hit the road nationally for the first time since the late 1980s with a group consisting of original Twilley guitarist Bill Pitcock IV, early drummer Jerry Naifeh, and bassist Dave White who played with Dwight for several years. His fall, 2003, tour through the Midwestern U.S. exchanged White for 20/20's Ron Flynt on bass and backing vocals. Twilley also told *Oklahoma Music* magazine that Capitol-EMI plans to release *Scuba Divers* and *Jungle* on CD for the first time, with bonus tracks. In 2011, he released *Soundtrack,* his autobiography set to music, and got some extra keyboard work on the album from Taylor **Hanson**.

www.dwighttwilley.com

Twine, Linda
(b. 1947)

Born in Muskogee, Broadway conductor, composer, arranger, and conductor Linda Twine is a graduate of OCU and the Manhattan School of Music. She was one of the very few female conductors working in New York's musical theater in the late 20th and early 21st centuries. She has been musical director for several big shows, *Ain't Misbehavin'*, *Big River*, *The Wiz*, et al. Twine has also composed original theatrical and choral works. Twine is also from a very prominent family of African-Americans from Muskogee, with her grandfather being W. H. Twine, known during the pre-statehood Indian Territory days as the "Black Tiger" due to the ferociousness with which he sought to proectthe rights of African-Americans.

U

Underwood, Carrie
(b. March 10, 1983)

Carrie Underwood, 2009

After winning the American Idol talent contest in 2005, Carrie Underwood has ridden her powerful, expressive, and emotive voice to multi-platinum sales status via her four hit albums: *Some Hearts* (2005), *Carnival Ride* (2007), *Play On* (2009), and *Blown Away* (2012).

Along the way, Underwood has set several recording industry records for sales, chart positions, and total number one singles on the country music charts (twelve total between 1991 and 2012, breaking Reba McEntire's record of eleven). She has won more than 100 major industry awards given by orgnaizations such as the Academy of Country Music, the American Music Association, BMI, ASCAP, Country Music Association, *Billboard*, CMT, and six GRAMMY Awards. Her 2005 album, *Some Hearts,* was named by *Billboard* as the country album of the decade.

Born to parents Stephen and Carole Underwood in Muskogee, Oklahoma, she grew up in a rural farm environemnt outside of Checotah, OK. After graduating Checotah High School, she attendend Northeastern Oklahoma State University in Tahlequah, where she majored in communications with a journalism emphasis. During the summers in Tahlequah, Carrie performed in NSU's Downtown Country show. Little did showgoers know they were watching the future queen of country music.

By 2013, Underwoodshe had amassed more than 15 million albums sold worldwide, 16 #1 singles (seven co-written by Carrie), and was the top selling country female touring artist of 2008, 2010, and was on a world and North American tour through 2013.

www.carriedunderwoodofficial.com

Carrie Underwood poses with a young fan from the stage of the Muskogee Civic Center after receiving the Rising Star Award from the Oklahoma Music Hall of Fame a short time after winning American Idol in 2005.

V

Vasquez, Andrew
(b. November 30, 1957)

An enrolled member of the Apache Tribe of Oklahoma, Andrew Vasquez is one of the nation's leading American Indian flutists whose recordings have enjoyed international success for their blend of sound effects, modern and traditional instruments, occasional philosophical musings from Vasquez, and the soothing, echo-laden Plains Indian flute. Andrew was born in Anadarko, the southwestern Oklahoma town so heavily associated with American Indians, it bills itself as the capital of Indian Country.

Along with Vasquez's own Na-I-Sha people (sometimes known as Kiowa-Apache in the history books), whose musical traditions are thousands of years old, as well as those of the neighboring **Kiowa**, Comanche, and Wichita tribes, traditional and Pan-Indian music surrounded Vasquez in his youth. Participating in the powwow dance culture of that area led to his membership in the New York-based *American Indian Dance Theater* from 1986 through 1991. While on tour, Andrew traded for his first flute, and began to develop his own style on the instrument preserved in the 20th century by Belo Cozad, **"Doc" Tate Nevaquaya**, Tom Ware, and **Cornel Pewewardy**, all American Indians from Oklahoma.

Andrew Vasquez

Andrew's Na-I-Sha name is "Ditkal Te-Bikas," which means "cedar stalk" in the Apache language and is rooted in the part of the cedar tree from which flutes are made. He has three recordings to date for the North Dakota based Makoche label. His first CD, *Vasquez* (1996), features less percussion and modern instruments than his subsequent albums, *Wind River* (1997) and *V3: An American Indian* (1999). Named 1998's Best Contemporary Native American Album at the New Age Voice Awards *Wind River*'s cover design by his wife, Myra Vasquez, also received the Best Album Cover Award. *Wind River* also garnered Vasquez several notable nominations in 1998 from organizations such as the Association of Independent Music, and the Native American Music Awards (Songwriter of the Year/Flutist of the Year). In 1999, he was nominated as Flutist of the Year and Best Male Artist while his album of that year, *V3: An American Indian*, received a nomination in the Best New Age Recording Category. *V3* features Vasquez's strongest use to date of contemporary instrumentation in his music, mixing in acoustic and electric guitars, more keyboards, and his trademark flute work.

In 2000, Andrew received the Best Male Artist Award from the Native American Music Awards for *V3*. Vasquez has also released an album of Kiowa-Apache music on the Spalax label. As a northern style traditional dancer, Andrew creates his own regalia and beadwork, and has performed professionally around the world and won many powwow dance titles around the United States. He currently resides in Bismarck, North Dakota with his wife, Myra, where he continues composing music, enjoying family life, and preparing his next artistic ventures as one of the country's leading contemporary American Indian musicians. According the Makoche Records website, Andrew says about his music: "Everything I play comes from my heart and stands for what I believe in. I compose my songs for special reasons."

www.makoche.com

Hugh W. Foley

W

Wakely, Jimmy
(b. February 16, 1914 – d. September 23, 1982)

One of the most revered singing cowboys whose recordings appealed to both country and pop music audiences, and a 1971 inductee into the Nashville Songwriters Hall of Fame, James Clarence Wakely was born in Mineola, Arkansas, but when he was a small child, the Wakely family relocated to Battiest, Oklahoma, a tiny hamlet in McCurtain County in the southeastern part of the state. The family moved several times around the state as struggling sharecroppers, and Jimmy wound up graduating from Cowden High School, located in Washita County southwest of Oklahoma City. He was musically inclined at an early age, learning both the piano and guitar, as well as singing in both country and pop styles. According to his son, Johnny, Jimmy played the piano in church and later directed the church choir. After winning a local radio talent contest, he decided to become a musician.

In 1937, Jimmy married Inez Miser, and they moved to Oklahoma City, where he worked part time in a service station, played piano with Merle Salathiel (better known as Merl Lindsay) and his Barnyard Boys, and traveled the summer with Little Doc Roberts' Medicine Show. He auditioned for local radio shows, where he met **Johnny Bond**, who was to become a life long friend. The two formed a trio patterning their sound after the popular singing cowboy group, the Sons of the Pioneers. The third member of the trio alternated between Scotty Harrell and former Lightcrust Doughboy, **Dick Reinhart**, a native Oklahoman born in Tishomingo. At the outset, the trio called themselves The Singing Cowboy Trio, but later changed their name to The Bell Boys because of sponsorship by Bell Clothiers on radio station WKY in Oklahoma City, where they played on a daily show. In addition, the trio cut transcription discs and also played live on radio station KVOO in Tulsa. On the daily radio broadcasts, the trio used Johnny Bond's "Cimarron (Roll On)," which he had composed in 1938, as their theme song

According to Wakely's son, Johnny, Jimmy was hitchhiking one night in the rain and a bolt of lightning lighted up a sign reading "**Gene Autry** Now Appearing" at a local fair. Jimmy caught a ride to the fair and met Autry, who discovered that Jimmy was living in Oklahoma. Autry told Jimmy to write him and they began corresponding after Autry's return to California. During this correspondence, Autry encouraged Jimmy to move to Hollywood and, if he became a member of the musician's union, he would try to find a spot on his *Melody Ranch* radio show.

A second source indicates that Gene Autry was on tour promoting his movie *Rancho Grande* in Oklahoma and Kansas in the late 1930s, and the trio traveled to Okemah, Oklahoma, and Lawrence, Kansas, to meet Autry and audition for him. After hearing the trio, Autry was impressed by their repertoire, which included some of his songs. Autry suggested that he could use the trio on his *Melody Ranch* show should they ever decide to move to California.

Whatever the case, Jimmy and Inez and their two daughters, Deanna and Carol, Johnny and Dorothy Bond, and Dick Reinhart packed their belongings in Jimmy's Dodge automobile and left for California on May, 31, 1940, leaving Scotty behind as he wanted to remain in Oklahoma. Autry hired them as the Jimmy Wakely Trio for his CBS *Melody Ranch* radio show. For the next two years, Jimmy worked for Autry, often known as

"The Melody Kid." After leaving Autry, Jimmy formed his own band, which off and on included such legendary country artists as Merle Travis, Cliffie Stone, and **Spade Cooley**. He signed a recording contract with Decca in 1942, and over the next five years, released some thirty-four sides, including "I Wonder Where You Are Tonight," "Cimarron (Roll On)," Bond's composition, "There's A Star Spangled Banner Waving Somewhere," a cover of Elton Britt's song, and "I'm Sending You Red Roses," his first record on the country charts, peaking at #3 in 1944.

Wakely's first acting appearance was in 1939 in a B movie western, *Saga of Death Valley*, starring Roy Rogers. He went on to appear in support roles during the next six years, usually with the Jimmy Wakely Trio or Jimmy Wakely's Rough Riders, in western movies starring such legendaries as Johnny Mack Brown, Charles Starrett, and Slim Summerville. He finally starred in his first movie in 1945, *Song of the Range*, which resulted in a series of twenty-eight leading roles for Monogram over the next five years to his last, *Lawless Code*, in 1949. In a poll conducted in 1948, he was voted the #4 cowboy star after Rogers, Autry, and Starrett, and only Autry, Rogers, and Tex Ritter starred in more musical westerns.

In 1948 Wakely decided to devote his career to music, including penning his own song, "Song of the Sierras," and switched to the Capitol label, and returned to the Top 10 with "Signed, Sealed, and Delivered." It was followed by two of the most successful records of the post-World War II decade, "One Has My Name (The Other Has My Heart)," which held the top spot on the country charts for eleven weeks and crossed over to the Top 10 pop charts, and **Floyd Tillman**'s song, "I Love You So Much It Hurts," which held the #1 position on the country charts for five weeks and crossed over to the Top 25 of the pop charts. His final hit for 1948 was "Mine All Mine," which cracked the Top 10 of the country charts.

Jimmy Wakely

Wakely's recording success continued in early 1949 with "Forever More" (Top 10), "Till the End of the World" (Top 10), "I Wish I Had Nickel" (Top 5), and "Someday You'll Call My Name" (Top 10). Later the same year, he teamed with Margaret Whiting, celebrated pop singer, to record a cover of another Tillman song, "Slippin' Around," which reached #1 on both country (seventeen weeks) and pop charts and became a million seller for the duet. "Wedding Bells," the flip side, also went Top 10 on the country charts and crossed over to the Top 30 of the pop charts. To round out the year, Jimmy and Whiting released another Tillman song, "I'll Never Slip Around Again," which charted at No. 3 on the country list and crossed over to the Top 10 of the pop charts.

Referred to as the "Bing Crosby of Country Music," Jimmy became so popular that in a nationwide poll in 1948, he was voted America's third most popular singer behind Perry Como and Frankie Laine, edging Bing Crosby into fourth place. His solo successes in 1950 included "Peter Cottontail" and "Mona Lisa." The flourishing partnership with

Whiting also continued the same year with the double-sided Top 3 release, "Broken Down Merry-Go-Round"/"The Gods Were Angry With Me," another Top 3 single, "Let's Go to Church (Next Sunday Morning)," and a Top 10 release, "Bushel and a Peck."

Wakely returned the charts in 1951 with his solo hits, "My Heart Cries for You" (Top 10) and "Beautiful Brown Eyes" (Top 5). His final hits with Whiting included "When You and I Were Young Maggie Blues" (Top 10) and "I Don't Want to Be Free" (Top 5). Overall, Jimmy and Whiting had nine total hits during their career as one of the most popular partnerships in American musical history. Jimmy never made the country charts again. During the late 1940s and 1950s, he toured extensively in the U.S., the Pacific, the Far East, including Alaska and Korea, where he often appeared with the Bob Hope Show. In 1952 Jimmy starred in his own CBS radio network show, *The Jimmy Wakely Show*, which remained on the air until 1958. In 1953 he signed with Coral Records and in 1955 joined Decca, Coral's parent label. Although Jimmy was never able to attain the singles success of the later 1940s, he released several albums on Decca worth noting, including *Santa Fe Trail*, a 1956 production of excellent cowboy songs. With the exception of two albums for Dot in 1966, he remained on the Decca label through 1970.

In the early 1950s, Wakely built a recording studio in his home, where his son Johnny assisted him, and they eventually formed their own record label, Shasta. Jimmy released in 1959, *Merry Christmas*, a seasonal album, and *Country Million Sellers*, both on his label. In addition to his own albums, Shasta released material by other singing cowboy stars, including Rex Allen, Johnny Bond, Tex Ritter, and Eddie Dean. In 1961, Jimmy co-hosted the ABC television network series *Five Star Jubilee* with another singing cowboy star, Tex Ritter. During the remainder of the 1960s and 1970s, he formed a family act with his children, Johnny and Linda, and they played the nightclub circuit including Reno, Tahoe, Las Vegas, and Elko. He was elected to the Nashville Songwriters Hall of Fame in 1971.

Due to age and emphysema, Jimmy died on September 23, 1982 at his home in Mission Hills, California, with Inez and four children (Johnny, Carol, Linda, and Deanna) at his bedside.

Wakely's songs were recorded by numerous artists, including Gene Autry ("I'll Never Let You Go", co-written with Autry), Spade Cooley ("The Solid South"), Woody Herman ("Too Late"), Louvin Brothers ("Too Late"), Elvis Presley ("It Wouldn't Be the Same Without You"), **Jean Shepard** ("You Can't Break the Chains of Love"), T. Texas Tyler ("Follow Thru"), Slim Whitman ("I'm Casting My Lasso Towards the Sky"), and Leona Williams and **Merle Haggard** ("You Can't Break the Chains of Love"). In 2000, *The Very Best of Jimmy Wakely* was released on Varese Sarabande, the U.K. label, and included such hits as "Beautiful Brown Eyes," "Slippin' Around," "I Love You So Much It Hurts," "One Has My Name (The Other Has My Heart)," and "I'll Never Let You Go, Little Darlin'." *Heroes of Country Music, Vol. 4: Legends of the West Coast* (Rhino-1996) celebrates Wakely's contribution to that region's importance in country music with his "One Has My Name (The Other Has My Heart)." One of the most recent releases of Wakely material is *Jimmy Wakely: The Singing Cowboy* (Varese Sarabande-2002) which contains such songs as "I'm An Old Cowhand," "Tumbling Tumbleweeds," and "The Last Roundup".

Walker, Wayne

(b. December 13, 1925 – d. January 2, 1979)

Recipient of more than twenty BMI Awards for songwriting and an inductee into the Nashville Songwriters Hall of Fame in 1975, Wayne Paul Walker was born in Quapaw, Oklahoma, a community of roughly 1,000 people located in the northeastern part of the state, but was raised in Kilgore, Texas, and attended Kilgore High School from 1940 to 1942, apparently never graduating. He worked at various jobs throughout his early career, including car and vacuum cleaner salesman and roofing houses. Walker's greatest achievements were in the field of songwriting, especially after he signed in 1954 with Cedarwood Publishing Company, organized by Webb Pierce and Jim Denny. Cedarwood became one of the most important publishers in Nashville with its roster including such legendary songwriters as John D. Loudermilk, Danny Dill, Mel Tillis, Marijohn Wilkin, and Pierce.

The list of songs written or co-written by Wayne and recorded by various artists representing genres from country to rock is impressive. It includes "Burning Memories" (Ray Price, Waylon Jennings, Kitty Wells, Jerry Lee Lewis and Mel Tillis), "It's My Way" (Tammy Wynette, Webb Pierce, and Don Gibson), "Pride" (Janie Fricke, Ray Price, and Dean Martin), "Cut Across Shorty" (Carl Smith, Nat Stuckey, Eddie Cochran, and Rod Stewart), "Walk on Boy" (Dion and the Belmonts and Doc Watson), "Leavin' On Your Mind" (Patsy Cline and LeAnn Rimes), "Thoughts of a Fool" (Ernest Tubb and George Strait), "All the Time" (Kitty Wells, Jack Greene, and Anne Murray), which was nominated for Song of the Year by the CMA in 1967, "Little Boy Sad" (Johnny Burnette, Bill Phillips, and James Darren), "Pathway of Teardrops" (Ricky Skaggs and K.T. Oslin), "Holiday for Love" (Webb Pierce), "She's Gone, Gone, Gone" (Lefty Frizzell), "Cajun Queen" (Jimmy Dean), "Why, Why" (Carl Smith), "How Do You Talk to a Baby?" (Webb Pierce), "Fallen Angel" (Webb Pierce), "Sweet Lips" (Webb Pierce), "Hello Out There" (**Carl Belew**), "Unloved, Unwanted" (Kitty Wells), "A Little Heartache" (Eddy Arnold), "I Thank My Lucky Stars" (Eddy Arnold), "Memory No. 1" (Webb Pierce), "Since She Turned Seventeen" (Billy "Crash" Craddock), "Ancient History" (Johnny Cash), "Rock the Bop" (Brenda Lee), "Dream Baby (How Long Must I Dream)" (Jerry Lee Lewis), "I Chased You 'Til I You Caught Me" (Ernest Tubb), "Lonely Island" (Marvin Rainwater), "I'll Be Satisfied With Love" (Faron Young), "(I Wished for an Angel) The Devil Sent Me" (Johnny Horton), "When I Look in the Mirror" (Kalin Twins), "(Is My) Ring on Your Finger" (Hawkshaw Hawkins), "Money Tree" (**Merle Haggard**), "In the Misty Moonlight" (Bobby Bare), "You Don't Know Me" (Elvis Presley), "Honey 'Cause I Love You" (Carl Perkins), "Set Up Two Glasses, Joe" (Ernest Tubb), "Papers and Pens" (Ernest Tubb), "Answer the Phone" (Ernest Tubb), "Forgive Me" (Ernest Tubb), "Fool, Fool, Fool" (Webb Pierce), "Livin' Alone" (Hank Locklin), and "Foreign Love Affair" (Hank Locklin).

When inducted into the Nashville Songwriters Hall of Fame, Wayne said, "If I write enough songs, some of them will get recorded, and some of these will sell records. You know the law of averages is bound to work out. I figure a good songwriter can write a song anytime he has to. It may not be a good song, but it will be a song. Of course, there are times when I'm in different moods and can write better than at other times, but that is true of any business. This is the business I'm in, and I enjoy it." Walker died at his home in Nashville on January 2, 1979.

www.nashvillesongwritersfoundation.com/fame/walkerw

Wallace, Billy
(b. March 26, 1917 – d. June 3, 1978)

Composer of the #1 hit in 1952 for Webb Pierce, "Back Street Affair," as well as several other country hits in the 1950s, Cright "Billy" Wallace was born in Oklahoma City, but raised in Alabama. He is reported to have learned guitar from the Delmore Brothers, but cited Ernest Tubb and Roy Acuff as the major influences on his singing style. As a vocalist, he never charted any hits, but recorded for several labels, such as Decca (1952), for which he recorded "Back Street Affair," Blue Hen (1955), Mercury (1956), Deb (1957), Del-Ray (1962), and Acadia, a Canadian label for which he recorded an album in 1963.

Ellen Wallace and Billy Wallace perform on stage, 1939.

Wallace's first radio job was in Decatur, Alabama, and he later worked on WSB in Atlanta and WLAC in Nashville. He joined the cast of the *Louisiana Hayride* in 1951. Webb Pierce heard Billy's recording of "Back Street Affair" and took it to #1 in 1952. It was a song based on Billy's lifestyle experiences, and was later covered by such stars as Loretta Lynn, Billy Walker, and John Prine. Pierce also scored with Billy's "Don't Throw Your Life Away," later covered by the Johnson Mountain Boys, a bluegrass group.

Kitty Wells was the country artist who later recorded most of Billy's songs, including "Whose Shoulder Will You Cry On," which was later covered by two bluegrass groups, Del McCoury and the Dixie Pals and IIIrd Tyme Out, "Cheatin's a Sin," "I'm Paying for That Back Street Affair," and "Honky Tonk Waltz."

Additional songs that Wallace wrote include "We're Steppin' Out Tonight," recorded by David Ball and Bobby Hicks; "I've Just Got to See You Once More," cut by Little Jimmy Dickins, and "Slaves of a Hopeless Love Affair," waxed by Red Foley.

Several of Billy's songs have been compiled into a compact disc by Cattle Records, a German company. The album is entitled *Billy Wallace Sings His Hits*, and includes "Ghost of a Honky Tonk Slave," "Honky Tonk Row," "I'm Going Out of Your Arms," "If All Other Girls Were Like You," "Judge of Hearts," "The Sycamore Tree," "Your Kisses and Lies," and "My Heart Needs an Overhaul Job."

Wallace died in 1978 at his home in Huntsville, Alabama.

Webb, Jimmy
(b. August 15, 1946)

One of the most prolific songwriters of the twentieth century having composed such hits as "By the Time I Get to Phoenix," "Wichita Lineman," "Up, Up and Away," and "MacArthur Park," and the only artist to ever receive Grammy awards for music, lyrics, and orchestration, songwriter, producer, arranger, singer, and keyboard artist James Layne Webb was born in Elk City, Oklahoma, a community of roughly 10,000 inhabitants west of Oklahoma City. Jimmy learned to play piano at age six, and wrote his first song, "Someone Else," when he was about twelve. Jimmy's father was a Baptist minister in

Elk City, where he made his first public appearance, playing organ in his father's church, while rearranging, improvising, and re-harmonizing church hymns. Jimmy also led his own rock and roll band, and began writing songs, primarily religious in nature, although one was a musical.

In 1964 Jimmy and his family moved to California, and he enrolled at San Bernardino Valley College as a music major, but dropped out shortly thereafter when his mother died. While in college, he arranged a single for The Contessas, a girl group, as well as writing another musical, *Dancing Girl*, for his girlfriend. The college drama department rejected it, although it included a song, "Didn't We." In 1965, he headed for Hollywood where he was employed with Jobete Music, the publishing division of Tamla-Motown Records. While here, he wrote "This Time Last Summer" for Brenda Holloway and "My Christmas Tree" for the Supremes, as well as publishing his "Honey Come Back" composition. These reached singer Johnny Rivers, and in 1966, Jimmy signed a contract with Johnny Rivers Music Company and Rivers' new Soul City Records. Rivers recorded the original version of Jimmy's "By the Time I Get to Phoenix" in 1966. It was here that Jimmy met The Fifth Dimension, who recorded his "Up, Up and Away" in 1967. An immediate hit, the song sold one million copies, was eventually used by TWA for a series of commercials, and played in the locker room of the Apollo XI astronauts as they journeyed to the moon. His strong relationship with The Fifth Dimension continued with two albums, *Up, Up and Away* (contributed five of the fourteen tracks) and *The Magic Garden* (wrote all but one of the twelve tracks, including "Carpet Man"), both released in 1967. Jimmy also wrote a majority of the songs for Rivers' 1967 album, *Rewind*. His connection to The Fifth Dimension waned, however, Glen Campbell released "By the Time I Get to Phoenix" in 1967. Jimmy's "Up, Up and Away" and "By the Time I Get to Phoenix" had garnered eight Grammy Awards by 1968. Jimmy formed his own company that provided jingles for such companies as Chevrolet, Doritos, and Hamm's beer, and was a millionaire by age twenty-one.

In 1968, *Jim Webb Sings Jim Webb* was released on the Epic label, an album that Jimmy reportedly disliked, contained none of his hit songs, and released without his consent. An earlier venture into singing resulted in a 1967 single, "Love Years Coming," with an obscure group called the Strawberry Children. Also in 1968, the Brooklyn Bridge scored a hit with Jimmy's "The Worst That Could Happen." Jimmy continued writing songs, one of which was "MacArthur Park," a melodramatic composition some seven minutes in length backed by a rock combo, full orchestra, and choir. First offered to The Association, which rejected it, Jimmy persuaded his friend, Richard Harris, the brilliant Irish actor, to record it. The orchestral part was recorded in Los Angeles, while Harris' voice was added in a Dublin studio. Released in 1968 by Dunhill Records, it reached #2 on the pop charts, and was later covered by Waylon Jennings (won a Grammy in 1969 with it), Donna Summer, and the Four Tops. The accompanying Richard Harris album, *A Tramp Shining*, was written entirely by Jimmy, and reached #4 in the summer of 1968. It also included one of Jimmy's finest compositions

Jimmy Webb

that he had written in college, "Didn't We," later recorded by Frank Sinatra and Barbara Streisand. Jimmy also scored another entire album for Harris, *The Yard Went On Forever*, also released by Dunhill in 1968, but it never sold well, although critics had called it more impressive than the first. A banner year continued for Jimmy as Glen Campbell released "Wichita Lineman," which went to #1 on the country charts, followed by another Campbell hit, "Galveston," in 1969.

In 1969, Webb scored the music for the films, *How Sweet It Is* and *Tell Them Willie Boy Is Here*, began work on a semi-autobiographical Broadway musical, *His Own Dark City*, and was composer-arranger for Thelma Houston's debut album, *Sunshower*.

In 1970, Jimmy decided to launch a solo concert tour kicked off in Los Angeles, as well to record a series of solo albums. His concert tour was largely unsuccessful because of his inexperience as a performer, but his albums were well received, although sales were not.

Jimmy's official debut album, *Words and Music*, included a tribute to P.F. Sloan, a neglected songwriter. It was followed in 1971 with *And So On*, which featured jazz musician Larry Coryell, in 1972 with *Letters*, highlighted by Jimmy's own version of "Galveston" and a cameo appearance by Joni Mitchell, in 1974 with *Land's End*, featuring Art Garfunkel on "Crying in My Sleep" and another cameo appearance from Joni Mitchell, and 1977 with *El Mirage*, produced, conducted, and arranged by George Martin of Beatles fame, and a track entitled "The Highwayman," a title popularized by the noted country group consisting of Johnny Cash, Willie Nelson, Kris Kristofferson, and Waylon Jennings.

The decade of the 1970s also saw Jimmy producing such albums as *The Supremes Produced and Arranged by Jimmy Webb* (1973), Glen Campbell's *Reunion* (1974), The Fifth Dimension's *Earthbound* (1975), Cher's *Stars* (1975), and Art Garfunkel's *Watermark* (1978).

In 1981, Webb moved to New York in hopes of breaking through on Broadway, a dream he never realized. During the 1980s, he scored the animated feature film, *The Last Unicorn*, as well as other film soundtracks such as *Doc*, *Voices*, and *Hanoi Hilton*. He also wrote music for television, including *Amazing Stories*, *Tales From the Crypt*, and *Faerie Tale Theater*. He released only one solo album during the decade, *Angel Heart* (1982), one of his weakest compilations.

In the 1990s, Webb released his highly acclaimed *Suspending Disbelief*, produced by Linda Ronstadt, one of his biggest fans, in 1993, and included his own version of David Crosby's "Too Young to Die." It was followed in 1996 by *Ten Easy Pieces*, a remake of several of his most classic songs accompanying himself on the piano. Two 1993 tribute concerts to Jimmy were held in New York, featuring Glen Campbell, David Crosby, Art Garfunkel, Brooklyn Bridge, Michael Feinstein, and Nanci Griffith. In 1998, Jimmy published his first book, *Tunesmith: Inside the Art of Songwriting*, acclaimed as the "finest book about songwriting of our time," by *Musician* magazine. In the late 1990s, Australia's Raven Records issued two albums, *Richard Harris: The Webb Sessions, 1968-69* and *Reunited*, a collection of Glen Campbell's recordings of Jimmy's songs. A multi-artist tribute to Webb, *Someone Left the Cake Out in the Rain*, was released by Debutante Records in 1999. It featured tracks by Glen Campbell, Linda Ronstadt, Four Tops, Judy Collins, and the Johnny Mann Singers.

Recent activities include his tribute to **Garth Brooks** at the ASCAP Golden Note Awards ceremony in Washington, DC, where he sang "By the Time I Get to Phoenix" and "MacArthur Park," featured vocalist on *An All-Star Tribute to Brian Wilson* DVD release on which he sings "In My Room" with Carly Simon and David Crosby and "Surf's Up" with Crosby and **Vince Gill**, performances at Mountain Stage in Charleston, West Virginia along with **Hank Card** and the Austin Lounge Lizards, a concert with Vince Gill in Oklahoma City, an overseas tour in Australia, and performance at the dedication of the new Capitol dome in Oklahoma City on November 16, 2002, during which he sang and played the piano for two of his memorable songs, "By the Time I Get to Phoenix" and "Wichita Lineman."

Awards and honors bestowed upon Jimmy are impressive, including ACM/Song of the Year for "Wichita Lineman" (1968), induction into the National Academy of Popular Music-Songwriter's Hall of Fame (1986), Nashville Songwriter's Hall of Fame (1990), National Academy of Songwriters-Lifetime Achievement Award (1993), Oklahoma Hall of Fame (1999), two of his songs included in the BMI list of Top 100 Songs of the Century ("By the Time I Get to Phoenix" and "Up, Up and Away"), election to Board of Directors of ASCAP, and recipient of the Johnny Mercer Award in 2003 at the Songwriters Hall of Fame. Also in 2003, Webb released a Jimmy Webb boxed set only available through his website. In 2007, Webb teamed with **Vince Gill** to write "Oklahoma Rising" to recognize the state's centennial. In May, 2012, Jimmy traveled to England where he received the Ivor Novello Special International Award, recognizing non-U.K. writers who make extraordinary contributions to the global musical landscape. Jimmy Webb is the only performer to every receive GRAMMY awards for music, lyrics,and orchestration.

www.jimmywebb.com

Welch, Kevin
(b. August 17, 1955)

One of the most prominent Americana/alternative country music songwriters and performers to hail from Oklahoma, Kevin Welch was born in Long Beach, California, but raised in Midwest City, Oklahoma, a suburb of Oklahoma City and home of Tinker Air Force Base. He moved throughout the U.S. during his early childhood as the family followed his father's job, but at age seven, finally settled in Oklahoma. Because of his extensive travels as a child, he claims to have learned to read by viewing billboards and highway signs. Following graduation from Midwest City High School, Kevin attended the University of Central Oklahoma for one semester as a music major. During his time in Oklahoma, he met John Hadley, a songwriter for Tree International, who was an art instructor at the University of Oklahoma in Norman. Hadley criticized Kevin's guitar playing, which made Welch work harder in developing his picking talents. Early examples of his playing can be heard on Stillwater musician Chuck Dunlap's 1980 album, *Daze Gone By* (Snowbound).

Kevin Welch

After leaving UCO, Kevin traveled the nightclub and honky tonk circuit for five years in a van and a truck dubbed "Phyllis." During this time he first played with a band called New Rodeo and then joined a band named Blue Rose Café, named after a popular restaurant in Tulsa.

After life on the road, he married Jennifer Patten and they moved in 1978 to Nashville, where he spent ten years as a staff writer for Sony Tree, and began raising a family of three children, Dustin, Savannah, and Ada. During that decade, he wrote or co-wrote songs for **Roger Miller** ("Everyone Gets Crazy Now and Then"), Ricky Skaggs ("Let It Be You"), Gary Morris ("Plain Brown Wrapper" and "Velvet Chains"), Carlene Carter ("Time's Up"), Moe Bandy ("Too Old to Die Young"), Trisha Yearwood ("That's What I Like About You"), **Garth Brooks** ("Pushing Up Daisies"), Jimmie Dale Gilmore ("Headed for a Fall"), Marie Osmond ("Steppin' Stone"), Randy Travis ("Heart of Hearts"), Del McCoury ("True Love Never Dies"), Charley Pride ("I Came Straight To You"), **Reba McEntire** ("Whoever's Watchin'" and "What Do You Know About a Heartache"), and Fairfield Four ("Life Down Here on Earth"). Other recording artists who used Welch's songs included Pam Tillis, Conway Twitty, The Highwaymen, T. Graham Brown, The Judds, Waylon Jennings, Patty Loveless, Don Williams, The Kendalls, and Sweethearts of the Rodeo. He is in great demand as a session musician and vocalist having performed with Carlene Carter, **Gail Davies**, **Ray Wylie Hubbard**, and **Kelly Willis** during the 1990s.

After playing the club circuit in Nashville with bands like The Roosters, which included Mike Henderson and Harry Stinson, Kevin formed his own band, The Overtones, in about 1988. Several of his colleagues at Tree, including Kieran Kane and Paul Worley, suggested Kevin pursue a recording contract with Warner Brothers/Reprise. His self-titled debut album was released in 1990. It yielded three minor country hits, "Stay November" "Till I See You Again," and "True Love Never Dies," as well as "The Mother Road," Kevin's tribute to Route 66. His second album, *Western Beat*, was released in 1992, also by Reprise. It was critically acclaimed, but produced no hits because mainstream country radio did not buy into Kevin's acoustic sound and Jack Kerouac-type lyrics. Kevin and Warner Brothers mutually agreed to release him.

In 1995, Kevin and cohorts Kieran Kane, Harry Stinson, Mike Henderson, and Tammy Rogers decided to form their own independent recording label they named Dead Reckoning Records. They released more than twenty records over the next seven years, as well as touring as a group called A Night of Reckoning throughout Europe, Canada, and the U.S. Kevin's first album on Dead Reckoning, Life Down Here on Earth, was released in 1995 to rave reviews by those who said he defined the new "Americana" sound. His second Dead Reckoning album, Beneath My Wheels, also was well received. In 2000, Kevin and Kieran developed a two-person show (two guitars and two voices), and recorded a live album in Melbourne, Australia, titled 11/12/13: Live in Melbourne. During the last two years, Kevin recorded Millionaire, an album featuring several of his friends from Denmark. It reached the Top 15 of the Americana charts in the summer of 2002. That same year, Welch launched an extensive overseas tour with performances in Sweden, Denmark, Australia, and Canada. In 2004, Kane Welch Kaplin made a three-man acoustic record, then made two more albums, Lost John Dean, and a self-titled album, both of which did well onthe Americana charts. The trio was nominated for Duo/Group of the year in 2007 and 2008, but lost out to Robert Plant and Alison Krauss. Welch now lives in log cabin outside of Austin and touring behind his most recent release, A Patch of Blue Sky.

www.kevinwelch.com

White, Bryan
(b. February 17, 1974)

Having country music hits is hard enough, but how about two #1 singles right out of the box? That was the story's opening for Bryan Shelton White, a singer, songwriter, guitarist, and drummer, born in Lawton, Oklahoma, but raised in Oklahoma City, where he graduated from Putnam City West High School. Bryan was the oldest child (younger brother Daniel) of two professional musicians (Bud and Anita), while his great-grandmother was a popular square dance caller in Oklahoma. His grandfather, Wilford White, was an auctioneer, and gave Bryan some early advice: "You've got to have rhythm, a lot of endurance and a strong throat."

At an early age, Bryan began banging on pots and pans, and his parents bought him his first drum set when he was five. His mother directed him toward country music at about age ten, when she took him to a show she opened for Loretta Lynn. After his parents divorced, Bryan was shuttled between homes, but both encouraged him to pursue music and allowed him to play drums with their respective music groups. While during a sound check, his mother heard him sing "Stand By Me," and she suggested he also try vocals with the drums. While in high school at Putnam West, he switched from drums to guitar, formed a trio, and began writing songs. He decided after high school, he would try his luck in Nashville. According to Bryan, "mowing lawns and fishing were the only two options I had besides music."

Thus, in 1992, after high school graduation, White headed to Nashville. For the first year, his parents had to wire money each month for him to survive. But he soon connected with Billy Joe Walker, Jr., a friend of the family who was a session musician in Music City. Over the next two years, Walker helped Bryan refine his act and assisted him in landing a position as a demo singer, as well as a staff songwriter's job and artist management deal with Glen Campbell Music and GC Management. This relationship eventually resulted in Bryan meeting Kyle Lehning, who had worked with Randy Travis and Dan Seals. Lehning was president of Asylum Records, which signed Bryan to a contract in 1993, with Walker producing his first two singles, "Eugene You Genius" and "Look at Me Now," both of which made Top 40.

Bryan's management team outlined a performance schedule that included opening for such stars as Pam Tillis, Tracy Lawrence, and Diamond Rio. He did not have a backup band, it was just he and his acoustic guitar. He performed some 200 concerts across the U.S. and Canada. Later, he hired members of Pearl River for his band.

His debut album, *Bryan White*, crafted by Lehning and Walker, was released in 1994, and two #1 hit singles ensued, "Someone Else's Star" and "Rebecca Lynn." The eponymous album eventually went platinum, and CMT's poll named him Rising Video Star of the Year. Bryan continued to co-write songs for other artists, including the Top 5 "I Don't Believe in Goodbye" for Sawyer Brown and "Imagine That" for Diamond Rio.

In early 1996 White completed his second album for Asylum, *Between Now and Forever*, which included four songs he had co-written, "Blindhearted," "So Much for Pretending," "On Any Given Night," and the title track. From this album, "I'm Not Supposed to

Love You Anymore" and "So Much for Pretending" became his third and fourth #1 hits. Honors for White include the ACM's Top New Male Vocalist for 1995, followed by the CMA's Horizon Award and Best New Touring Artist for 1996, the *TNN/Music City News* Male Star of Tomorrow Award in 1996, "Up and Coming Artist" for the 1998 Viewpoint Award, and nominations for Male Vocalist of the Year by the CMA in 1996 and 1997.

Following the Oklahoma City bombing in April of 1995, Bryan returned home for a benefit concert to raise scholarship money for children injured or orphaned in the blast, and helped raise funds for the Oklahoma City Bombing Memorial. In 2001, Bryan and Patty Loveless were among several stars to perform for the grand opening of the newly-renovated Oklahoma City Civic Center. He has also participated in benefit concerts for Cerebral Palsy, Cystic Fibrosis Foundation, Native American Clothing Drive, "Country Cares", Boys and Girls Clubs of America, Buddies of Nashville, and St. Jude Children's Research Hospital.

White's recorded output for 1996 included his version of "When You Wish Upon a Star," from the animated Disney film *Pinocchio*, for the *Disney Country* album. In 1997, Bryan released his third album, *The Right Place*, which included "Love Is the Right Place," "Leave My Heart Out of This," "Bad Day to Let You Go," and "One Small Miracle," the latter penned by his good friend, Steve Wariner. He opened for **Vince Gill** on a highly successful tour the same year. Two years later, Bryan recorded the *How Lucky I Am* album, and released his first seasonal album, *Dreaming of Christmas*. Bryan is also in great demand as a backup vocalist and instrumentalist as he has sung vocals on albums for LeAnn Rimes, Lila McCann, Shania Twain, and was a guest drummer on Steve Wariner's *No More Mr. Nice Guy* album.

In 2000, Elektra Records put together four of Bryan's #1 hits and several other Top 20 hits for his *Greatest Hits* album. Also in 2000, he married actress Erika Page, who stars on the television soap opera *One Life to Live*, and with whom he has two sons.

In 2002, Bryan appeared with Traveling Light: Songs From the 23rd Psalm, released in 2002 by the Creative Trust Workshop label, and featuring Bryan and several other CCM, pop, and country artists, such as Amy Grant. In 2012, Bryan released Dust Bowl Dreams, with eight of the ten songs on the disc written by White. According to a statement from his website, White says, "I want to keep making positive music that not only inspires me, but everyone else out there to have hope in what they want to strive for. I want it to be a real light to them and a good influence, to encourage them all I can."

www.bryanwhite.com

Wichita and Affiliated Tribes

Based in Anadarko, Oklahoma with a tribal enrollment of about 2,500 in 2010, Wichita memories exist to the beginning of time in southwestern Oklahoma. Modern historians indicate the tribe's ancestors have been in the Anadarko area for at least 3,000 years, making the Wichita and Affiliated Tribes one of the very first contemporary tribes in the state once known as Indian Territory.

After decades of hardship in the 19th century, the Wichita were settled on their reservation in southwestern Oklahoma. Once there, some Wichita people became members of churches established by Muscogee (Creek) missionaries, notably Rock Spring Baptist Church, still active today north of Anadarko where hymns are sung in the Wichita language. Many people also joined the Native American church, which combines traditional and Christian beliefs and has its own unique set of songs. Other tribal members took up the Ghost Dance religion in the 1890s, the songs of which are still sung today at Wichita gatherings.

Historically, the Wichita had many songs for many purposes, such as healing songs, prayer songs, lullabies, war dance songs, morning star songs, and ceremonial rain dance songs. Field recordings of Wichita music were first made in 1902 making the tribe's singers some of the first recording artists in pre-statehood history. Ethnomusicologists visited the tribe again in the 1930s and 1950s, with some of those recordings being released on vinyl by the Smithsonian Institution. Contemporarily, the Wichita celebrate their music each year in August at the Annual Wichita Tribal Dance where one hears ancient songs in a modern context, songs that celebrate their country, veterans, their young people and elders, and the tribe's long association with the Pawnee, as well songs related to the long tradition of Wichita tradition of ceremonial dance. Contemporarily, the tribe has several cultural programs to preserve and revitalize its language and songs, as well as a committee that plans the yearly Wichita Dance to celebrate its elders, its veterans, and its children in song and fellowship. In 2008, the tribe was inducted into the Oklahoma Music Hall of Fame for their legacy and contemporary maintenance of ancient musical tradition in the face overwhelming odds.

Wichita singer, Jimmy Reeder accepts the induction award for his tribe from the Oklahoma Music Hall of Fame in Muskogee, 2008.

Wiley and Gene
Wiley Walker (b. November 17, 1911 – d. May 17, 1966)
Gene Sullivan (b. November 16, 1914 – d. October 24, 1984)

One of the most successful duets in the 1930s and 1940s and co-writers of two country music classics, "Live and Let Live" and "When My Blue Moon Turns to Gold Again," Winston Lee Moore (Wiley's birth name) was born in Laurel Hill, Florida, while Gene Sullivan was born in Carbon Hill, Alabama. Although born outside of Oklahoma and spent several years of their career in Louisiana and Texas, Wiley and Gene spent some of their most productive years in Oklahoma from 1941 on when they joined radio station KWXX. Wiley and Gene teamed as a duet in 1939 in Dallas.

After their move to Oklahoma, Wiley and Gene wrote and recorded "Live and Let Live" and "When My Blue Moon Turns to Gold Again" in 1941. Neither song was successful as a record at the outset, but was frequently requested on their radio program. In 1943, Zeke Manners recorded "When My Blue Moon Turns to Gold Again" and it became a hit. Wiley and Gene's record was reissued on a more successful basis. Others who recorded the song were Elvis Presley, who had the biggest hit with it in 1956, Slim Whitman, Cindy Walker, Eddy Arnold, Cliffie Stone, Jim and Jesse, Jerry Lee Lewis, Bashful Brother Oswald, Red Allen and Frank Wakefield, Clarence "Gatemouth" Brown, Bill Monroe, **Leon Russell** and the Newgrass Revival, Tex Ritter, Foy Willing and the Riders of the Purple Sage, and **Merle Haggard**.

Jimmie Davis, Carl Smith, Johnny and Jack, Joe Val and the New England Bluegrass Boys, and Hank Williams, Sr. recorded "Live and Let Live," while another one of their songs, "I Want to Live and Love," became Rose Maddox' theme song. Additional songs they co-wrote were "I Might Have Known," "Kansas City Blues," "Teardrop Waltz," and "Make Room in Your Heart For a Friend." Because of their achievements in songwriting, Wiley and Gene were inducted into the Nashville Songwriters Hall of Fame in 1971.

In the late 1940s, Wiley and Gene entered the new medium of television. For years, they hosted the *Oklahoma Jamboree* on KOCO-TV in Oklahoma City that featured local bands, such as the Bluestem Boys, a bluegrass group that included Bill Caswell, **Byron Berline**, Frank Deramus, and Gary Price. Television gave them an opportunity to expand their talents for comedy and dancing as Wiley was a buck dancer and fiddler and Gene liked to recite humorous poetry, such as "Sleeping at the Foot of the Bed,' which became a popular recording for Little Jimmy Dickens, and "Wash Your Feet Before You Go to Bed."

(l-r) Wiley and Gene

In 1946, Wiley and Gene recorded for Columbia, "Make Room in Your Heart For a Friend," which reached #3 on the country charts, and was selected for the *Anthology of Country Music, Volume 2: Early Country Harmony 1940's*. By the early 1950s, Wiley and Gene began to fade from prominence on the music scene, but Gene had one more recording that achieved notoriety, "Please Pass the Biscuits," a 1957 novelty song with recitation that cracked the Top 10. He had originally cut a demo of it for Little Jimmy Dickens, however, Columbia Records like Gene's version best.

Wiley and Gene continued to make occasional public appearances in the early 1960s, until Wiley's death in 1966. Gene ran a music store in Oklahoma City during the 1970s and died in 1984. In 1988, Old Homestead Records released a 24-track album entitled *Radio Favorites*, including all the Wiley and Gene favorites plus several not previously mentioned songs, such as "After I'm Gone," "Don't That Moon Look Lonesome," and "Take Away Those Blues From My Heart."

Wiley, Lee
(b. October 9, 1915 - d. December 11, 1975)

One of the first jazz singers to organize a set of songs around a common composer or theme known later as the songbook or concept album, as well as one of the first women jazz composers, vocalist and songwriter, Lee Wiley was born in Fort Gibson, Oklahoma, a community of approximately 3,000 residents northeast of Muskogee. She had three siblings, including two brothers (Ted and Floyd) and one sister (Pearl). One of her ancestors, Worcester Willey was a missionary to the Cherokee Indians, and helped found Dwight Mission near Fort Gibson. Believed to have been of Cherokee heritage, she began her jazz career as a run away from home teenager in Tulsa, where she studied music (heavily influenced by the "race" records of Mildred Bailey and Ethel Waters) and sang on local radio. Sometime during her teenage years, Lee's singing career was briefly interrupted when she was temporarily blinded due to a fall while horseback riding.

When Lee was about fifteen, she migrated to New York City and sang on the Paramount Show. By seventeen, she joined the Leo Reisman Orchestra at the Central Park Casino, and remained with Reisman until 1933, during which she made one of her first recordings, "Time on My Hands." Wiley's career peaked in the mid-1930s when she launched a successful radio series on CBS titled *Saturday Night Swing*. From 1936-38, she was the star vocalist. Sometime during her early jazz career, Lee dropped the second "l" in Willey because she thought her original last name sounded unprofessional for a jazz singer.

Lee also began recording her own sides for the Kapp label, backed by the Casa Loma Orchestra and the Dorsey Brothers. Married to swing pianist Jess Stacy from 1943 to 1948, Wiley was vocalist for Stacy's big band jazz ensemble. In addition to Stacy, she was vocalist for several other big bands, including Eddie Condon and Paul Whiteman. Lee also worked with several small combos, including those led by Bud Freeman, Max Kaminsky, Fats Waller, and Bobby Hackett.

During the 1940s, Lee appeared at several New York City jazz clubs, such as Kelly's, Hickory House, Famous Door, and the Stable, and performed a Town Hall concert organized by Condon. In 1947, Lee recorded a duet with Bing Crosby, "It Still Suits Me," reportedly completed in one take. According to Harold Arlen, her manager, "Lee was a divine-looking girl. She was beautiful in a very unsophisticated way and yet she was a very sophisticated singer."

Lee was an exceptional interpreter of such songs as "I've Got a Crush on You," "How Long Has This Been Going On?" "Baby's Awake Now," and "You Took Advantage of Me," primarily with Waller, Freeman, and Condon. Collaborating with composer and arranger Victor Young, she is noted for co-composing as lyricist such hits as "Got the South in My Soul," "Eerie Moan," and "Anytime, Anyday, Anywhere," the latter becoming an R & B hit in the 1950s for Joe Morris and Laurie Tate. With more than fifty recordings to her credit, Wiley was the first jazz vocalist to record albums devoted to one composer's works, including Irving Berlin, Cole Porter, Vincent Youmans, Rodgers & Hart, Harold Arlen, and George Gershwin. Cited in more than forty jazz publications, Wiley was featured in a 1963 television drama based on her life *Something About Lee Wiley*, starring Piper Laurie.

Lee signed with Columbia Records in 1950, recording *Night in Manhattan* with Joe Bushkin and Bobby Hackett and *Lee Wiley Sings Irving Berlin* (1951), her first concept album. She made her television debut in 1951 on the *Once Upon a Tune* show, and later appeared on the *Tonight* show hosted by Steve Allen.

In 1952, Wiley performed a live concert at Carnegie Hall that was recorded on the Audophile label. After recording her Rodgers & Hart album with Storyville in 1954, she moved to RCA Victor where she recorded *West of the Moon* (1956) and *A Touch of the Blues* (1957). The most notable of the two, *West of the Moon*, featured Lee's versions of "Can't Get Out of This Mood," "East of the Sun," and "Who Can I Turn to Now," backed by such fine instrumentalists as trumpeter Billy Butterfield and trombonist Urbie Green.

Lee retired in 1958 after becoming disenchanted with the music business. Her final studio recording in

Lee Wiley

1971 was *Back Home Again*, but by this time Lee's voice was no longer in its prime and she continued to bemoan the fact she was not a commercial success. She was persuaded by Condon and George Wein, festival organizer, to make a farewell performance at the first Newport in New York Jazz Festival in 1972, and died in New York three years later at the age of sixty-seven from colon cancer.

Several of Lee's recordings have been released in CD format, including *Back Home Again* (1995) and *Lee Wiley at Carnegie Hall-1972* (1996), both on Audiophile, *Hot House Rose* (1996) on Pearl, *Rarities: Thinking of You* (1997) on Jazz Classics, *Lee Wiley: Complete Fifties Studio Masters* (2-CD set) and *Lee Wiley: Manhattan Moods* (2-CD set), both from the Jazz Factory label, *Legendary Lee Wiley* (1999) on Baldwin Street Music, and *Lee Wiley: Manhattan Nights-The Complete Golden Years Studio Sessions* (4-CD set with 92 tracks) available from Collectors Choice distributors.

Wiley was inducted into the Oklahoma Jazz Hall of Fame in 2000 and Oklahoma Music Hall of Fame in 2003. She is survived by a brother in California and a niece in Fort Gibson, and she is buried in Fort Gibson where the family home remains standing. A Lee Wiley documentary by a Japanese filmmaker, part of which was shot in Muskogee and Fort Gibson, was also scheduled for release in 2003.

Williams, Claude "Fiddler"

(b. February 22, 1908 - 4/27/2004)

Known as one of "the" primary jazz fiddlers in a career that spans nearly the entire history of jazz, Claude "Fiddler" Williams suffered early professional setbacks, such as being replaced by John Hammond in the Count Basie Orchestra on the eve of that band's national success in 1937, but has outlived all of his detractors to enjoy status as one of the premier jazz violinists of the twentieth — and now – twenty-first century. He continues performing and recording actively as of 2003, and well-deserved attention, slowly forthcoming during most of the twentieth century, has mounted impressively in the last few years for this important musician who is the primary living proponent of the jazz string band tradition. Born in Muskogee, the same jazz hotbed that produced Jay McShann, Don Byas, and Barney Kessel, Williams grew up in a house surrounded by music. He learned piano by ear through playing with his older brother, and at ten, he began playing mandolin and bass with his brother-in-law's string band in the hotels and barber shops in Muskogee and surrounding towns. The group played ragtime standards, blues, and occasional Western songs like "Wagoner" and "Red Wing." Of course, these ingredients form a large part of jazz's nucleus.

Williams switched to violin upon hearing a Joe Venuti concert in Muskogee, and Venuti is often cited as making a giant impression on Williams. An interesting aspect about the concert that is usually left untold in Williams' multitude of interviews about his life is that because he was African-American, he and his family were not allowed into the park where Venuti played. Williams heard the music over and above the bushes, without amplification, which convinced him he wanted to play the ubiquitous instrument of the 19th century American west.

After apprenticing with his brother-in-law's string band, and other traveling groups who would come through town and pick him up for area engagements, Williams played with the Pettiford Family Band, although the great bassist Oscar Pettiford was only an infant at the time, and went on the road with a traveling variety show called Kid Thomas and

Claude "Fiddler" Williams

His Jazz Babies. By the time he was nineteen, in 1927, Williams joined Torrence (sometimes spelled Terrence) "T" Holder's territory band in Muskogee, which became the Clouds of Joy under the leadership of Andy Kirk when "T" Holder ran into money troubles. The Clouds of Joy were one of the leading territory bands of the area, playing in Kansas City in 1929 and recording for the Brunswick label, on which Williams appears on fiddle. After recording, the group began touring the East Coast. Although he played banjo and violin in the Clouds of Joy all the way to New York's Roseland Ballroom and Harlem's Savoy Theater, Kirk wanted Williams to focus more on guitar, which Williams did not want to do. So, when Williams hurt his leg during a string of one-night stands, Kirk left Williams behind, calling Williams' wife to let her know where to send for him. Those years are preserved on two albums, *The Territories, Vol. 1* (Arcadia) and *Loose Ankles* (Brunswick).

Back in Kansas City, Williams worked with Alphonso Trent in 1932 and moved to Chicago where he played fiddle with bassist Eddie Cole, whose brother, Nat, was featured on piano. Williams left the group when jobs started to slow down with the Cole brothers. After leaving the Coles, Williams went back to Chicago where Count Basie sent for him to join that orchestra in 1936. Williams only played on one recording session for Basie in 1937, before John Hammond replaced him with Freddie Green, who would stay with Basie for fifty years. Although different accounts exist as to why Williams was replaced, the end result was the same and Claude moved on. Williams does speak for himself musically on MCA's three-CD late-'30s Basie collection, *The Original MCA Recordings*, as well as *The Count at the Chatterbox: 1937* (Jazz Archives), and *Count Basie: The Complete Decca Recordings 1937-1939* (GRP).

After being released from the Basie orchestra, Williams returned to Kansas City where he started a string band that was a fairly successful live draw, but did not record, so he moved to Flint, Michigan where he stayed until being called up for service during World War II. Afterwards, Williams worked as a guitarist in a WPA band in Michigan, and with The Four Shades of Rhythm in Chicago. In 1951 and 1952, he was a member of the Los Angeles-based R & B band led by Oklahoman Roy Milton, then moved back to Kansas City where he had his own combos, one of which featured saxophonist Eddie "Cleanhead" Vinson. From the mid 1950s through the 1960s, Claude toiled in relative obscurity, leading groups in Denver and Las Vegas before returning to Kansas City in 1969. Williams returned to the spotlight when he started playing with Jay McShann in the early 1970s, and was featured prominently on McShann's *The Man from Muskogee* (1972).

While Williams seems to have fought an uphill battle throughout the early and mid-twentieth century to keep his fiddle in the jazz mix, his playing became appreciated more and more throughout the 1970s and 1980s because of his obvious connection to the string band tradition and territory bands, which made him a historic, if not romantic, figure.

During that period, he performed at numerous major festivals in the United States and overseas, and began recording again. Steeplechase Records released *Call for the Fiddler* (1976), Classic Jazz released *Fiddler's Dream* (1977), and in 1980, Big Bear Records released *Claude Willliams' Kansas City Giants*. Showing his stylistic range and further demonstrating the multi-musical influences of his Oklahoma background, in 1982 Williams was featured with the Johnnie Lee Wills Western swing band at the Smithsonian Folklife Festival in Washington, D.C. Subsequently, Claude played in the Broadway production of *Black and Blue*, along with continuing a constant schedule of touring, performing and recording. He surfaced again on two highly acclaimed discs recorded in New York, *Live at J's Volume 1* and *Volume 2* (Arhoolie, 1989), the same year he was inducted into the Oklahoma Jazz Hall of Fame.

Since 1990, Williams has received more critical attention than he has in his entire life. Williams has been featured on the network television program *CBS News Sunday Morning*, played Carnegie Hall twice, and opened Lincoln Center's *Kansas City Swing and Shout* event with his trio. Williams performed for President Clinton's first inaugural, and toured Australia. The two previously mentioned CDs, *Claude Williams, Live at J's, Volumes 1 & 2*, landed on the Best of 1994 jazz critics' polls in the *Village Voice* and *Pulse!* In 1994 and 1995, his live recordings aired on NPR's *Jazz Set* and he toured twenty-three cities headlining a *Masters of the Folk Violin* tour. In 1994, he earned the first and only Charlie Christian Jazz Award from Black Liberated Arts Incorporated in Oklahoma City. Also in 1994, he recorded a highly lauded session released as *Swingtime in New York* on Progressive Records in 1995.

Williams' successes and accolades continued in 1997. He celebrated his 89th birthday in Washington D. C. educating and entertaining students at the Smithsonian by day, and playing with a trio at night to great reviews in the *Washington Post*. Along with his successes around the U. S. and abroad, his home town honored Claude Williams in 1997 by making him one of the first inductees into the newly formed Oklahoma Music Hall of Fame in Muskogee, Oklahoma. Williams was inducted with three other giants of American music, whose roots are in Oklahoma: Woody Guthrie, Patti Page, and Merle Haggard. In 1998, Williams performed at the White House, the recording of which was subsequently featured in a PBS special. In 1999, Williams was the first installment in *Down Beat's* First Person Project, which plans to round up jazz's elder statesmen for a history of the music in their own words. Although only two pages with two photographs, the article signaled the permanent return and historical significance for the man who was written out of jazz history in 1937 when he was given his notice to leave the Count Basie Orchestra. By the end of 1999, the then-91-year-old, toured consistently, stopping at Oklahoma State University on September 16 for a day in classes with students and a concert that night at the Seretean Center.

Critically lauded by *The New York Times* and the *Los Angeles Times*, Claude Williams has come to be one of a handful of contemporary jazz violin masters. Oscar-nominee Mark O'Connor has said there is no doubt Williams is one of the great, original musicians of the twentieth century. For the yearning, sweet sound of Claude Williams' fiddle, listen to his composition "Fiddler's Dream" on *Claude Williams Live at J's Part 2*. The first notes he strikes are long, mournful blue notes. Then, Williams proceeds to establish the head riff, or the guiding theme of the tune, before cascading through improvisations on the blues, which ultimately adds up to jazz. Claude exemplifies many elements of the 19th and 20th century African-American musical tradition with his playing — the haunting and sad melodies of the blues, as well as the spritely nature of the early 20th century string bands that mirrored the evolution of dixieland, and, finally, the harmonic improvisations on a blues theme which is at the foundation of jazz. The violin is not often thought of as a contemporary jazz instrument outside of the legendary Stephane Grappelli or Joe Venuti, however, Claude Williams may be solely responsible for raising the consciousness of it at the end of the twentieth century, and establishing it as a fixture in the twenty-first. His resurrection of the early string band style, of which he has been a player since he was 10-years-old in Muskogee, is testament both to his tremendous abilities and the hotbed of jazz from which he came in Muskogee, Oklahoma.

The Willis Brothers

Willis, James Ylisis "Guy" (b. July 5, 1915 – d. April 13, 1981)
Willis, Charles Ray "Skeeter" (b. December 20, 1917 – d. March 5, 1976)
Willis, John Victor "Vic" (b. May 31, 1922 – d. January 15, 1995)

Known variously as the Oklahoma Wranglers and the Willis Brothers, these multi-instrumentalists were long-time country music stars in the middle of the 20th century, famous for a blend of Western swing, old-time country, cowboy songs, and several tunes about the open road as a truck driver. Their truck driving songs are still a common sight in truck stop budget display cassette and CD cases throughout the United States. The Willis family moved from Alex, Arkansas, where Guy was born, to Coalton, Oklahoma, where Skeeter was born, and finally landed for good in Schulter, Oklahoma, a small town just south of Okmulgee, where "Vic" was born. Trained informally on front porch family singings, all three brothers sang and played various instruments. Their first gig as the Oklahoma Wranglers occurred at KGEF radio in Shawnee, Oklahoma in 1932, and they continued appearing on various radio programs throughout Oklahoma, to include KTUL, Tulsa in 1933 and 1934, and in Gallup, New Mexico in 1935.

In 1940, the brothers moved to Kansas City where they appeared KITE radio, and then on the KMBC weekly radio program, *Brush Street Follies*, before calling it quits due to World War II. They reunited in 1946, moved to Nashville and joined the Grand Ole Opry. Signed to Sterling Records, they recorded four songs one December morning as the Oklahoma Wranglers, and took a lunch break. On returning, they were assigned a backing job for a young hillbilly singer named Hank Williams, and the group became the Country Boys for a session when they recorded eight original songs with Williams, including several sacred, gospel flavored songs, "Calling You," "Wealth Won't Save Your Soul," and "When God Comes and Gathers His Jewels." Additionally, the brothers and Williams recorded four secular songs, the immortal "Honky Tonkin'", and a couple of darker tunes, "I Don't Care (If Tomorrow Never Comes)" and "My Love For You (Has Turned to Hate)." Had the Willis Brothers not done anything else they would still be forever ensconced in the history of American country music via Hank Williams' initial recording session.

The brothers left the Grand Ole Opry in 1949, and toured with Eddy Arnold as his band from 1949 to 1953, appearing in two films with Arnold, *Feuding Rhythm* (1949) and *Hoe Down* (1950). It was Arnold who suggested they change their name to avoid being typecast as only a Western group. Already having recorded in 1948 for MCA and Sterling, the Willis Brothers recorded for RCA in 1950, and Coral in 1954, before moving to Starday where they had major chart successes.

After becoming members of the *Ozark Jubilee* in Springfield, Missouri in 1953,

The Willis Brothers

the brothers toured the U.S. extensively and were in high demand as session players. In 1956, they joined the *Midwestern Hayride* television program, and over the next several years enjoyed television stints in Chattanooga, Tennessee and Birmingham, Alabama before rejoining the Grand Ole Opry in 1960 where they remained as regulars until Guy's death in 1981. While Guy wrote most of the songs, such as "I Miss My Old Oklahoma," "My Pillow Talk," and "Drive My Blues Away," the group did not enjoy commercial success until their 1964 Top Ten hit, "Give Me 40 Acres (To Turn This Rig Around)," landed them on the country charts. That began a long series of recordings in which they chronicled the ups and downs of being a truck driver, to include "The Only Shoulder (A Trucker Can Cry On)," "Diesel Drivin' Donut Dunkin' Dan," "Diesel Smoke on Danger Road," and "Soft Shoulders and Dangerous Curves."

The Willis Brothers charted again with a novelty tune in 1965, "A Six Foot Two-by-Four," and revisited the country charts only two more times with "Bob" and "Somebody Knows My Dog," both in 1967. Highlight albums include *Code of the West* (Starday, 1963), *Road Stops – Juke Box Hits* (Starday, 1965), *The Willis Brothers Goin' to Town* (Starday, 1967), and *The Best of the Willis Brothers* (Starday, 1975). Not only were the Willis Brothers known for their instrumental prowess, they could all sing well, which endeared them to fans through the U.S., as well as Europe and Central America where they performed on USO tours. Skeeter died in 1976 from Lymphoma, and Guy and Vic continued as a duo. Guy died in 1981, and Vic became Secretary/Treasurer of the American Federation of Musicians, AFM Local 257, in Nashville. He was killed when his car went out of control late at night on a Mississippi highway in 1995. The group's recordings with Hank Williams resurfaced in 1998 on *The Complete Hank Williams* boxed set, and in 1999, First Generation Records released a self-titled album by the Vic Willis Trio, although it offered none of the originality, humor, nor traditional country music quality of the early material.

Willis, Kelly
(b. October 1, 1968)

Pretty much a military kid who moved around a lot, alt country singer/songwriter Kelly Willis was born in Lawton, Oklahoma, the third largest city in the state and home of Fort Sill military base where her father, a career Army officer, was stationed. As the youngest of three children, she was raised primarily in Virginia and North Carolina, especially in the Washington, D.C. area, but some of her family was from Sentinel, a very small town in southwestern Oklahoma, and she spent many holidays and summer breaks there. According to a *Washington Post* online chat in which she participated in 2003, she considers herself an Okie. While Kelly was a child, her mother was involved in musicals and that influence may have affected her interest in singing. Her singing idols as a child were the likes of **Wanda Jackson** and Patsy Cline. As a teenager Kelly entered a pay recording booth and sang "Teddy Bear," one of Elvis Presley's hits. Using this demo tape at age sixteen, she convinced her boyfriend (and future husband) percussionist Max Polermo to join his rockabilly band.

Kelly's powerhouse vocals attracted a large following in the D.C. area, and Polermo's band renamed itself to Kelly and the Fireballs in 1987. Following Kelly's graduation from high school, the band headed to Austin, Texas, where they dissolved shortly thereafter. Kelly and Palermo launched a new group, Radio Ranch, consisting of Kelly on vocals and rhythm guitar, Polermo on drums, Michael Hardwick on steel guitar, Michael Foreman on bass, and David Murray on lead guitar. The band received great reviews at the 1989 Austin South By Southwest Music Festival. While playing the Austin live music circuit, Kelly was noticed at the Continental Club by singer Nanci Griffith, one of the mainstays of the Austin music scene. Griffith contacted MCA producer Tony Brown, who had signed Griffith, Lyle Lovett, and Steve Earle. Shortly thereafter, a record deal was consummated that resulted in Kelly's debut album, *Well Traveled Love*, released in 1990. The album received critical acclaim, but fared poorly on radio airplay.

In 1991 Kelly recorded her second album, *Bang Bang*, the title track taken from an obscure song from rockabilly artist Janis Martin. Her sophomore album was also not well received by the buying public, but, by this time, she was the opening act for Dwight Yoakum and honing her considerate abilities. A third effort for MCA, a 1993 self-titled production that included the majority of tracks penned by Kelly and performed without a band. One of the highlights of the release was a duet with another Oklahoman, **Kevin Welch**, on "That'll Be Me." The album also failed to generate any improvement in sales over the previous recordings. Thus, MCA dropped Kelly from their roster shortly after its release.

During the early 1990s, Willis contributed songs to the soundtracks of the films *Thelma & Louise* ("I Don't Want to Love You But I Do") and *Boys*, appeared as Clarissa Flan, a folksinger, in Tim Robbins' satirical film *Bob Roberts*, and was featured on television's *P.S. I Love You* program with Dwight Yoakum. Following a couple of inactive years in recording, Kelly resurfaced in 1995 duetting with Son Volt's Jay Farrar on the *Red Hot & Bothered* compilation. A year later, she released *Fading Fast*, a four song EP, on A&M Records. She married fellow Austin singer/songwriter

Kelly Willis performs with her husband, Bruce Robison, 2013.

Bruce Robison in 1996, following a divorce from her first husband. Her EP release was followed by *Wrapped*, a 1997 production on the independent label Lucky Dog, and the same year, she joined Sarah McLachlan, Jewel, and other female singers in the Lilith Fair concert tour.

In 1998 Kelly switched labels and recorded for Rykodisc, *What I Deserve*, a 1999 thirteen track album featuring several of her own songs with a portion of the album's sales going to the National Coalition Against Domestic Violence. The album continued to elevate her status as a premier songwriter. She has also now written or co-written (several with Robison) such songs as "Baby Take a Piece of My Heart," a crowd favorite at such Austin venues as the Cactus Club, "Shadows of Love," "World Without You," "Not Long for This World," "Happy With That," "Take Me Down," "What I Desire," "Talk Like That," and "Fading Fast." She took some time off after the 1998 album because of the birth of Kelly and Bruce's first child in 2001, a son they named Deral Otis.

Kelly is featured on the tribute album to Johnny Cash, *Dressed in Black*, released in 2002 on the Dualtone label, and in the summer of 2002 released her latest recording, *Easy*, a ten track album which she co-produced on the Ryko label. Seven of the ten tracks were written or co-written by Kelly, including "Not What I Had in Mind," "If I Left You," "Easy (As Falling Apart)," and "Reason to Believe." The latter cut is dedicated to Deral Otis, her two-year-old son, and spawned a conversational CD titled *Reason to Believe* in 2002. Backgrounds vocals on the *Easy* CD are provided by **Vince Gill**, Alison Krauss, Dan Tyminski, and Robison (her husband). The *Easy* album reached #1 on the Americana Roots chart in the summer of 2002. Kelly's "If I Left You" video reached #2 on the CMT Most Wanted Live's Great Eight in the fall of 2002. In 2003, the Dwight Yoakam box set, *Reprise Please Baby: The Warner Bros. Years*, contained two previously unreleased duets with Kelly, and she performed a few shows in Texas in the summer of 2003. After taking some time off to devote her attention to being a new mother, she and her husband, singer/songwriter Bruce Robison, released an album of love songs (mostly covers), *Cheater's Game*, inspired by their sixteen years of marriage, and performed a few shows together to suport the album, and, well, get out of the house.

www.kellywillis.com

Wills Brothers
Bob Wills (b. March 6, 1905 - d. May 13, 1975)
Johnnie Lee Wills (b. September 2, 1912 – d. October 25, 1984)
Luke Wills (b. September 20, 1920 – d. October 21, 2000)
Billy Jack Wills (b. February 26, 1926 – d. March 6, 1991)

Emerging from the East Texas fiddle and string bands of the 1920s, but gaining their fame in Oklahoma through daily broadcasts on KVOO-Tulsa from 1934 to 1958, Bob Wills and his Texas Playboys, as well the bands of his brothers, Johnnie Lee, and to a lesser extent Billy Jack and Luke, popularized the hybrid country music offshoot, Western swing, in the 1930s and 1940s. Johnnie Lee began leading the radio program in 1942 when Bob left Tulsa for opportunities in film, and it was Johnnie Lee who led the primary Tulsa band on-air until 1958 and until 1964 from his Tulsa base. As a result of the KVOO broadcasts and countless shows within a day's or weekend's drive of Tulsa, along with subsequent recordings that became very popular, the Wills brothers became synonymous with the music that was a direct product of the multi-ethnic population of the southwestern United States, particularly Oklahoma and Texas.

An improvisationally based form, Western swing is the country musician's way of playing jazz. The music turns where it needs to go to fit the audience, shape-shifting square dances into blues, old time fiddle reels into jazz, and mariachi, polkas, and waltzes into danceable pop. With a beat and a riffing horn section influenced by the big band movement of the 1930s, a western sound via steel guitar, and the country comfort of old time fiddles, the Wills bands featured dexterous virtuosos improvising on electric guitar and smooth vocalists to rival any crooner of the swing era. As Western swing guitarist Don Tolle explained in a 2002 interview, the essence of Western swing is related to jazz, and to play it a musician wants to "get as far out as you can, improvising as far away from the melody as possible while staying within the chord structure of the song."

Luke, Johnnie Lee, Bob, and Billy Jack

Add Bob, a cigar-smoking, charismatic leader, bantering with the band as they played, and urging them on with his "Ah-ha's," and the Wills' brand of cowboy jazz bounded into the grateful ears of Oklahomans being smacked daily by the Depression era.

While Milton Brown, **Spade Cooley**, and Hoyle Nix had bands that may have been equal to the Wills groups in musical caliber, Bob's added gimmicks and reputation as a great bandleader catapulted him and the music to immense popularity. Granted, Western swing surfaced first in Fort Worth, Texas, but the style leapt to the national stage from Tulsa via the clear channel mega-wattage of KVOO. Along with providing the Wills with both a significant live and radio audience, Oklahoma also contributed to Bob and Johnnie Lee's excellent crew of musicians with notables such as Eldon Shamblin (b. April 24, 1916, Weatherford, OK – d. August 5, 1998), Tommy Perkins (r. Oklahoma City – d. June 7, 2003, Oklahoma), Julian "Curly" Lewis (b. Stigler, 1924), Glen "Blub" Rhees (b. Oilton, July 28, 1924 – d. March 28, 1996), "Famous" Amos Headrick (b. Van Buren, AR), Clarence Cagle (b. April 19, 1920, Oklahoma City), Noel Boggs (b. November 14, 1917, Oklahoma City – d. August 31, 1974, California), Tommy Elliot (Ponca City), Jack Rider (Stillwell), **Benny Garcia** (b. March 20, 1926, Oklahoma City), Millard Kelso (b. Cleveland, OK), Keith Coleman (b. Chickasha?), Gene Crownover (b. Cromwell), Don Tolle (b. April 24, 1924, Rushville, IL, reared near Shidler, OK – d. December 5, 2002, Cushing, OK), Robert "Zeb" McNally (Tulsa), Art Haines (Oklahoma City), Gene and Lester "Junior" Bernard (Leonard), William "Smoky" Dacus (Quinton), James Guy "Cotton" Thompson (b. Tulsa – d. June 8, 1953, Muskogee), Buster Magnus (Tulsa), Gene Crownover (Muskogee), Charles and Ted Adams (Tulsa), Bob and Glen Morris (Tulsa), Tommy Dee (b. April 6, 1928, Wetumka, OK), Jay and Ray DeGeer (Oilton), Ramona Reed (b. November 16, 1930, Talihina), and **Tommy Allsup** (b. November 24, 1931, Owasso).

The often-told Wills story begins with Bob (born James Robert), the eldest of ten children descended from fiddle players on both sides of John Wills' and Emma (Foley)

Wills' families. As a child in the east Texas cotton fields near Kosse, about 40 miles southeast of Waco, the inherent musical multiplicity of that area filled Bob's ears: the old time fiddle tunes, reels, and square dances of his family, the field hollers, work songs, and country blues of the African-American cotton pickers, the omnipresent black and white church music traditions, as well as the various styles of dance music styles brought in by Mexican, Czechs, and Germans immigrants. In 1913, the family moved to a farm between Turkey and Memphis in the Texas panhandle, about seventy five miles from the Oklahoma border, where Bob started on mandolin, but switched over to fiddle by necessity and ease since the strings on both instruments are the same, G-D-A-E. He launched his professional career playing square dances and fiddle contests at age ten, first urged into soloing due to his father's lack of sobriety at a performance. After graduating an Amarillo barber school in 1927, Bob cut hair in Turkey, Texas, until he moved to Fort Worth in 1929 where he joined a medicine show, played on KTAT radio, played house parties, and added Milton and Durwood Brown to his group on fiddle and guitar respectively.

After winning a fiddle contest on KFJZ, Fort Worth in 1930, the Wills fiddle group landed a gig on the hugely popular cross-town station, WBAP, that boosted attendance at dances and elevated their star to the top of the Fort Worth music scene, bubbling with the nascent Western swing style. When the group's popularity as a dance band grew, so did the need for extended versions of familiar tunes. This led Bob to encourage his musicians to take improvisational solos on choruses that swung out and linked the music to the primary creative elements of jazz. The group's heightened notoriety led to another radio program for sponsor Burrus Mill and Elevator Company of Fort Worth. Burris's Light Crust Flour inspired the Light Crust Doughboys, the band's working name during the period. After only a few weeks on the air, Burris Mills' General Manager W. Lee "Pappy" O'Daniel moved the show to noon on WBAP, officially launching the Western swing rocket into the peak listening period of lunch time. Within six months, the program was simulcast in San Antonio and Houston, and eventually aired via the Southwest Quality Network over several more stations in Texas and Oklahoma. The radio programs served not only as entertainment, but also as music lessons for many young people who had acquired an instrument through their family or some other means, and had little else but the radio as a source of information and entertainment during the poverty-stricken 1930s.

The group cut their first two first two records in a Dallas hotel for Victor Records in 1932, "Suebonnet Sue" and "Nancy Jane." While the records were not hits in any sense of the word, Burrus Mills and Pappy O'Daniel envisioned big financial returns from the group and built a studio at the mill where the band was supposed to practice eight hours a day. O'Daniel also required the group to stop playing dances, which caused Milton and Durwood Brown to leave the group and form the most popular Western swing group in Texas, Milton Brown and his Musical Brownies, featuring **Bob Dunn** on steel guitar, and Milton's smooth vocals that served as a benchmark for future crooners of the style. While Wills stayed with the Light Crust Doughboys until 1933, having added his brother Johnnie Lee on tenor banjo in 1931, his "artistic differences" with Pappy O'Daniel (and occasional alcoholic lapses in judgement) forced a separation between the two headstrong entities, and Bob moved to Waco, taking several of the Doughboys with him.

Once in Waco, Wills formed Bob Wills and the Playboys and began broadcasting over radio station WACO. Not long after, Bob met future manager O.W. Mayo, who began booking gigs for the group around Waco. Having peaked in Waco, the two drove to Oklahoma City in 1934 to explore the possibilities of getting hired on KOMA, a station familiar with Wills since the Light Crust Doughboy days. Unfortunately, the station was also familiar with O'Daniel and knew the future Texas governor and U.S. Senator would not stand for Wills to be on the same station as O'Daniel's "new" Doughboys. Wills and Mayo then headed for WKY who booked the band and then pulled the rug out due to financial intimidation from O'Daniel. Subsequently, the WKY program director made a call to KTUL in Tulsa where he secured the group an offer to play on the relatively new station with only a small power output.

On the trip to Tulsa, Mayo convinced Bob to stop at the 25,000-watt radio station, KVOO, "the voice of Oklahoma," and the group was hired for a midnight spot February of 1934. During that first broadcast, the band (now called Bob Wills and the Texas Playboys) promised a promotional photo to the listener who sent in a letter from the most distant place, and a woman from Oakland, California won the contest. Convinced of the group's audience appeal, KVOO began broadcasting the Playboys straight from the stage of the Cain's Ballroom on February 9, 1934. Within weeks, the group began receiving piles of mail and multiple offers to play throughout Oklahoma where the Depression hung heavy over many rural communities. While the Wills band offered a moment of sunshine during an otherwise bleak existence for many rural Oklahomans caught up in the Depression, several towns, such as Oilton, Bristow, Cushing, Drumright, and Seminole, were still in the midst of heavy oil production that provided dance gigs where flush oil field workers were ready to dance away the weekends.

Of course, O'Daniel tried to hijack the Playboys again in Tulsa, but KVOO held out and before long the Wills band had a prime lunchtime slot of 12:30 to 1 p.m. that provided the foundation for their ascent to fame which lasted until 1958 between the bands of Bob and Johnnie Lee, all broadcast from the stage of the Cain's Ballroom, a building

Bob Wills Ranch House, 1951 (l-r) Bobby Koefer (steel), Kenny ? (trombone) Wayne Nichols (trumpet), Bill Briggs (sax), Ramona Reed (vocals), Luke Wills (standing), Billy Houck (drums), Bob Jack Lloyd (bass), Snuffy Smith (standing), Skeeter Elkin (piano), Eldon Shamblin (guitar), announcer on stool is either Dan Valentine or Lynn Bigler.

Hugh W. Foley

that began its life in 1924 as a garage for city founder Tate Brady, evolved into the Louvre Ballroom in the late 1920s, and became Cain's Dance Academy in 1930 when Madison W. "Daddy" Cain purchased it and featured the swinging country jazz string ensembles from Texas that became the foundation sounds of Western swing. With KVOO's raised power to 50,000 watts and status as one of America's "clear channel" radio stations, preventing any other station from the AM dial position of 1170, Bob Wills and the Texas Playboys became known throughout much of the United States, Canada, and Mexico as well as any big band leaders of the 1930s.

After shifting personnel through 1935, Wills added Texas-born steel guitarist Leon McAuliffe, who was heavily influenced by **Bob Dunn**, to the group. Wills also brought in more Texans, pianist Al Stricklin, and Everett Stover who began fleshing out choruses with his trumpet. Oklahoma's first contribution came to the band in the form of saxophonist Robert "Zeb" McNally, the son of the apartment manager where the Wills band lived in Tulsa, followed by trombonist Art Haines who filled out a horn section that led to Nashville's derisive term for Wills' music, "Okie Jazz." Another Oklahoman in Wills' pioneering band was drummer William Eschol "Smokey" Dacus (b. Quinton) who had played music on scholarship at the University of Tulsa and was working in a Tulsa hotel orchestra when Bob found him in 1935 and added him to the Playboys. Dacus is thought of as one of the very first drummers of country music. Until Bob added the drum kit to his group in 1935, the instrument was not accepted in the country music genre due to its association with African-American music, specifically jazz. Dacus played drums in the Dixieland style that put a swing in the music that made it premier for dancing and allied it with the big band movement of the 1930s. Set for the moment, the group's popularity landed them a recording contract with Art Satherley and Brunswick Records in Dallas.

At those first Brunswick sessions in September of 1935, Wills recorded several songs with Oklahoma titles and themes in the style that has come to be known as Western swing: "Good Old Oklahoma," "Tulsa Waltz," "Oklahoma Rag," and "Osage Stomp." Other favorites from the session included "Sittin' on Top of the World" and "Get With It," along with a cover of Big Bill Broonzy's "I Can't Be Satisfied." Interestingly, the jazz element in the music, with Dacus on drums, Zeb McNally on sax, and Haines on fiddle and trombone, is provided by Oklahomans, which further exemplifies the strength of Oklahoma's jazz and blues scene from the turn of the 20th century through World War II. The 1935 Wills recordings sold well and Satherly booked the group again, although trombonist Haines left to form the Ragtime Rascals in Shawnee, Oklahoma.

In 1936, Wills recorded several more jazz and blues-tinged numbers in Chicago, none more significant than "Steel Guitar Rag," "Trouble in Mind," and "Bring It On Down To My House," all of which became long-time Wills standards. The group's 1936 recordings on Brunswick's Vocalion label outsold other major artists that year such as Louis Armstrong, **Gene Autry**, Fletcher Henderson, and Bix Beiderbicke. The 1937 recordings in Dallas produced "Tulsa Stomp," and several blues-jazz numbers, including "Oozlin' Daddy Blues," "Old Jelly Roll Blues," "The New St. Louis Blues," as well as a cover of Jimmie Rodgers' "Blue Yodel #1," further exhibiting the group's diverse abilities and foundation in all American roots music forms. By 1937, Eldon Shamblin, born in Weatherford, Oklahoma, joined the group and began providing a completely unique sound on guitar by duplicating bass lines on the bass strings of the guitar while playing chords of tunes on the tenor strings. Shamblin went on to make the guitar a frontline solo instrument in the group and represented the guitar sound evolving nationally in jazz via Oklahoma City's

Charlie Christian in Benny Goodman's band. One of Wills' best biographers, Charles R. Townsend, in his excellent account of Wills' career, *San Antonio Rose: The Life and Music of Bob Wills*, speculates Christian heard Shamblin in Wills' band over KVOO in 1938 and began emulating some of Shamblin's work. Whatever similarities and cross-fertilization occurred between Shamblin and Christian, the two musicians who matured in Oklahoma were intrinsic to the developing significance of the electric guitar as a frontline instrument in American popular music. Shamblin's significant duet recordings with steel guitarist Leon McAuliffe on "Bob Wills Special" and "Twin Guitar Special" are Western swing standards and benchmarks of the genre. By century's end *Rolling Stone* magazine called Eldon the world's greatest rhythm guitarist, and *Musician* magazine declared him one of the twenty prime movers in guitar history.

In the spring of 1938, the Wills band recorded again in Dallas for Columbia, who had purchased Brunswick, and Wills continued producing music linked more closely to jazz and blues than country, such as "Alexander's Ragtime Band," "Mississippi Delta Blues," "Gambling Polka Dot Blues," by Jimmie Rodgers, and "Empty Bed Blues." However, the group also shifted more toward Tin Pan Alley type numbers such as "Oh You Beautiful Doll" and "I'll See You in My Dreams," and George and Ira Gershwin's, "Oh, Lady Be Good." In November of 1938, Wills recorded a number of fiddle tunes for Art Satherly and Columbia, to include "San Antonio Rose," "Dreamy Eyes Waltz," "Prosperity Special," and "Drunkard's Blues," as well as "Twinkle, Twinkle Little Star," "Silver Bells," and "Little Girl Go Ask Your Mother." With his rapidly growing popularity and considerable record sales, Bob purchased a large house and piece of land in north Tulsa where his parents moved, and where the group often rehearsed and had dances after home-cooked meals.

The Playboys' career continued skyrocketing in late '30s as they became one of the best-known and best selling bands in the United States, popular as a dance band for thousands of people each week, perennial jukebox favorites, and omnipresent via KVOO radio. Clarence Cagle's wife, Kathrean, remembered in a 2002 interview, "During that time you could walk down the street and never miss a beat of their music because all the windows were open and all the radios were playing the band." By most counts, the band's peak was from 1938 to 1941 until World War II broke up the group. By 1940, however, the group's eighteen members made it one of the biggest orchestras in the country, and the band could alternate between a horn-led swing band and a fiddle-led country group, often combining the two. In the April, 1940 sessions in Saginaw, Texas, the group had three fiddlers, a steel guitarist, a rhythm and lead guitarist (hinting at the oncoming rock movement), a drummer, five saxophonists, two trumpet players, bass, banjo, piano, and a vocalist, with some men having the ability to play two instruments. The group made their definitive recordings in 1940, to include "Corrine Corrina," "Bob Wills Special," "Big Beaver," and a new version of Bob's composition, "San Antonio Rose," which in many ways defines the concept of Western-swing. With a swing beat, a Spanish melody played by horns, Tommy Duncan's crooned vocal, Bob's trademark commentary, and its danceability, the record sold over 500,000 copies in 1940 for Columbia whose only other gold record of the year was Frank Sinatra's "All or Nothing at All." The known Oklahomans who contributed to the recording include Eldon Shamblin (guitar), Smokey Dacus (drums), and Zeb McNally (saxophone). Bing Crosby eventually sold more than 1.5 million copies of his version of "New San Antonio Rose," and the song elevated Bob Wills to genuine pop star status.

With the success of Bob's big band and "New San Antonio Rose," Hollywood came calling to capitalize on Bob's status as a potential musical cowboy star. Bob's first role, along with established singing cowboy Tex Ritter, came in *Take Me Back to Oklahoma* (1940). In 1941, Wills recorded his last sessions with the original Playboys group in Dallas, the products of which included one of his best known songs, "Take Me Back to Tulsa" and the previously mentioned Shamblin/McAuliffe duet, "Twin Guitar Special." After performing in another film, *Go West Young Lady* (1941), and recording tracks such as "Cherokee Maiden" and "Bob Wills Stomp" while in California with the smaller group he had taken out west to be in the film, Bob and his movie band returned from California to Tulsa where the glory days of Bob Wills and the Texas Playboys ended when the Japanese attacked Pearl Harbor, Hawaii on December 7. Vocalist Tommy Duncan Left, as did pianist Al Stricklin. By 1942, all that remained of the original group was Bob, Leon McAuliffe and Eldon Shamblin.

Bob assembled a new group complete with horns, fiddles, steel and electric guitar that recorded in Hollywood in the summer of 1942. Later in the year he performed as part of the broadcasts Johnnie Lee kept going on KVOO, but World War II eventually took most of the band, including Bob who landed in the Army by the end of that year, a few days after Christmas. The life of musician had not prepared the thirty-seven-year-old for the rigors of the Army, and by the summer of 1943 he was discharged. Bob made it back to Tulsa where he put a band together by borrowing some of Johnnie Lee's musicians. By this time, Johnnie Lee had solidly established himself at Cain's and on KVOO after having started his own band when Bob continued going west to make movies, record, and play to the large number of displaced Oklahomans who had sought out California as a respite from the dust bowl in the 1930s. Among the films Bob appeared in, often with various incarnations of his band, include *The Lone Prarie* (1942), *Silver City Raiders* (1943), *Saddles and Sagebrush* (1943), *Riders of the Northwest Mounted* (1943), *The Vigilantes Ride* (1944), *Wyoming Hurricane* (1944), *Bob Wills and His Texas Playboys* (1944), *The Last Horseman* (1944), *Rhythm Roundup* (1945), *Blazing the Western Trail* (1945), *Frontier Frolic* (1946), and *Lawless Empire* (1946).

The musical hits also continued for Bob throughout the 1940s in California, to include the following #1 songs: "Smoke on the Water" (1945), "Stars and Stripes in Iwo Jima" (1945), "Silver Dew on the Bluegrass Tonight" (1945), "White Cross on Okinawa" (1945), "New Spanish Two Step" (1946), and "Sugar Moon" (1947). Along with recording roughly 200 songs for the Tiffany Music Company from mid-1945 through 1947, usually referred to as The Tiffany Transcriptions, the band also recorded several other Western swing standards and favorites during the period: "Roly Poly," "Bob Wills Boogie," "Brain Cloudy Blues," "Might as Well Forget It," "Texas Playboy Rag," "Bob Wills Boogie," and "Bubbles in My Beer." With Bob's movie career in full swing and his brothers leading bands in Sacramento and Tulsa, opportunities were ripe for many musicians who could play the Wills standards, swing out, and take off on their instruments. The process of drafting musicians back and forth between Wills bands was not unlike baseball teams who trade players or bring them up through a farm system. A long line of Oklahoma musicians made their way through the Wills bands of the 1940s, '50s, and '60s with Bob or Johnnie Lee, or eventually in bands led by the other Wills brothers, Billy Jack and Luke. Additionally, the groups provided a professional training ground for musicians who would go on to form their own groups like Leon Rausch, Leon McAuliffe, and Tommy Duncan.

From the time Johnnie Lee started his band in 1940, the younger Wills held sway over the Western swing music scene throughout Oklahoma, Kansas, Missouri, and Arkansas by continuing the broadcasts over KVOO until 1958 when the cosmopolitan Nashville Sound and rock and roll had all but subsumed Western swing as an important musical in popular consciousness. While Johnnie Lee's band did not reach the heights of Bob's triumphs, Johnnie Lee and his boys did have some national success with hits such as "Milk Cow Blues" (1941), "Rag Mop" (1949), and "Peter Cottontail" (1950). Oklahoma musicians who made significant contributions to Johnnie Lee's recordings of the 1940s and early 1950s include pianist Clarence Cagle, who played with **Charlie Christian** in the 1930s, Junior Barnard, whose "country boogie" guitar work is a harbinger of the rockabilly movement of the 1950s, fiddler and vocalist Cotton Thompson, and later, Don Tolle, recommended to Johnnie Lee by Merl Lindsay in whose Oklahoma Night Riders Don had been playing. While most of the major players in the Wills bands have had their stories documented, Don Tolle's career has been relegated to footnotes and asides, until now.

Like most of the musicians who played with Bob and Johnnie Lee, Don Tolle was classically trained (on violin) but heard the Playboys on the radio as a child and wanted nothing more than to be a jazz player in the Wills style. While Tolle was born in Rushville, Illinois to tenant farmers, at age one he moved with his family to a rural home between Denoya and Shidler in Osage County where his father worked in the oil fields. Surrounded by musical instruments in the home, he began playing fiddle at the age of five when his father arranged for lessons from a Jewish music teacher, Julian Choates. Tolle had already begun playing mandolin, and switched to violin for the lessons wherein he became formally trained to read, much like many of the other Western swing players who could read and play from charts the same as most big band musicians. His earliest public musical experiences occurred when he accompanied his father, also an accomplished fiddle player, at various dances and other social events. He attended high school in Wolf, Oklahoma and began his professional career in 1939 playing with bands around Seminole, Oklahoma. After a stint in the service, and performing on radio in Portland, Oregon in 1945, Don played fiddle and guitar in Fresno, California Western swing bands sponsored by Bob Wills in 1946, and moved back to Oklahoma City where he began playing guitar exclusively with Merl Lindsay and his Oklahoma Night Riders in 1947.

After recording one single with Lindsay, "Grade A Pasteurized Baby," Tolle moved to Nashville to play guitar for Paul Howard and His Arkansas Cotton Pickers with whom he toured the southeastern United States until 1951 when he received a call from Johnnie Lee Wills who needed a "take off man," the term for a hot soloist in Western swing. Don returned to Tulsa and joined Johnnie Lee as lead guitarist in August of 1951, just in time for the group's RCA Victor recording sessions, made in the KVOO studios, that produced three singles, "The Thingamijig," "There Are Just Two I's in Dixie," and a cover of Tennessee Ernie Ford's "Blackberry Boogie," all re-released in 1983 through Bear Family Records as part of their *Rompin' Stompin' Singin' Swingin'* series of American roots music artists. Tolle's leads on these recordings are clear indications of the guitar's evolution in American popular music by way of Junior Bernard's style, which permeated Western swing, and surfaced in many ways through the guitar work of Scotty Moore on the Elvis Presley

Sun Sessions (Presley's own awareness of the Wills music sprouts on the 1966 home recording by Elvis of "San Antonio Rose," and later on the recording of "Faded Love" by Elvis in 1970, which appeared on the 1971 gold-selling RCA album, *Elvis Country*). As a guitarist and fiddler, Don Tolle played regularly with Johnnie Lee on KVOO radio, Tulsa television station KVOO (where Don eventually hosted his own Sunday night show), and throughout the region's dance halls with Johnnie Lee and His Boys. When Johnnie Lee needed a break from the rigors of the road life, namely the constant partying, Tolle took to the highways with his own Western All Stars.

After leaving Johnnie Lee and His Boys in 1961, Tolle moved to Big Springs, Texas, and spent four years playing guitar with Hoyle Nix and His West Texas Cowboys from 1962 to 1966, and in 1966 opened the Don Tolle School of Music in Big Springs which he operated until 1988. Don also continued fronting his own Western All-Stars, a rotating lineup he began using in 1957 and continued booking through 1969.

Another one of the Oklahoma native musicians who had an important part of the Wills legacy is Glenn "Blub" Rhees who became a Texas Playboy for Bob in 1957 and played saxophone on all of the Liberty Recordings through 1962 when he returned to Johnnie Lee's band. Glenn began playing sax in the seventh grade in Jennings, Oklahoma, moved on to Oilton High School where he played in the high school band, and finally wound up at Tulsa Webster High School where he performed with **Patti Page** before graduating. Subsequently, he worked in the oil business for a few years in Texas, New Mexico, Wyoming, and Louisiana before returning to Tulsa where he played with Art Davis and the Rhythm Riders from 1946 to 1948 throughout the Oklahoma, Texas, and Arkansas region. While with Art Davis, Lucky Moeller heard Glenn and offered him a job with the Western Okies. When Lucky was hired to be Bob Wills manager, Rhees moved to New Mexico where he found steady work in clubs.

In 1950, Glenn moved back to Oklahoma City where he joined Luke Wills' group, the Rhythm Busters, at the Trianon Ballroom. A year later, he moved to Lawton where he joined the Southernaires where he packed up Nashville stars such as Lefty Frizzel, Hank Williams, Webb Pierce, and others. By 1955, Rhees was back in Tulsa and working for Johnnie Lee, and when Bob was looking for a sax man in 1957, Johnnie Lee suggested "Blub," a nickname given to him because of his expansive waistline. After the Liberty recordings with Bob, Glenn returned to Tulsa where he recorded again with Johnnie Lee where he was featured on two successful singles, "Blub Twist" and "Slush," in 1962. Johnnie Lee kept the band active until 1964, the year of the Beatles' arrival in America, when Wills dissolved the group and opened a western wear store on Memorial Drive in Tulsa.

Johnnie Lee did regroup the surviving and available musicians from the Wills' salad days for two albums. 1978's *Reunion* album, produced by **Steve Ripley** for Flying Fish Records, featured many of the old time Western swing musicians including Tolle, Johnny Gimble, Gene Crownover, Eldon Shamblin, Glen Rhees, Curly Lewis, and Clarence Cagle. Don Tolle plays all the lead guitar parts on *Reunion*, while Shamblin was satisfied to hold down the rhythm on the album. The musicians got together for one more recording session in 1980 for *Dance All Night* (Delta), which followed much the same format of elder Playboys playing Western swing favorites.

While the height of Johnnie Lee's national popularity passed by 1950, Bob Wills made one of his most memorable hits that year, the eternal Western swing favorite, "Faded Love," an old fiddle tune Bob learned from his father that featured lyrics written by brother Billy Jack. The song became #1 country hit on *Billboard's* country and western chart in the fall of 1950 and is Oklahoma's official state country and western song. One of the players on the session, drummer Tommy Perkins, was only fifteen-years-old at the time.

Tommy Perkins was born in Oklahoma City in 1934. At age three, he performed with his parents' group, The Arkansawyers, and by age fourteen played six nights a week with a three-piece band in Clinton. At fifteen, Perkins joined the Bob Wills band for California tour that started in Oklahoma. Perkins was still in school at the time, and had to get special permission from the Oklahoma Lt. Governor, James E. Berry, to leave school for a month to six weeks to do the California tour. While in California, Perkins was the drummer on the recording of Wills' "Fade Love," a #1 hit in 1950, and now the state country song of Oklahoma.

Returning from California, Perkins went to work with Richard Rozelle's band, when Rozelle had country hits with "Old, Man" and "Mom and Dad's Waltz." He worked with Rozelle for a year, and then played with Little Jimmy Dickens and Hank Thompson. Back in California by 1952, Perkins played with Billy Jack Wills', Bob's youngest brother who was leading a band at Wills Point, also known as the West Coast base for Western swing. Perkins played on Billy Jack's two rockabilly, or country boogie albums, recorded in total from 1952 to 1954. Perkins then returned to Oklahoma where he worked for Leona Culp in Tulsa at the Cimarron Ballroom, off and on for about four years. It was during that stint when Tommy met Western Swing vocalist Leon Rausch, an association that continued into the 1990s when Perkins joined the touring and recording Playboys II group, primarily made up of living Playboys getting together in the 1990s on old favorites from the Western swing's peak period of the late 1930s through the early 1950s.

In 1992, he also recorded an album with jazz guitar giant Herb Ellis, known as *Texas Swings*, and recorded an album called *Life's Like Poetry* with traditional country singer and songwriter Lefty Frizzell.

Modern Drummer magazine featured Perkins in its July, 2000 issue, and he was also a member of the Western Swing Hall of Fame. Demonstrating his diverse ability and longevity, during his sixty-plus career, he also played with the Ink Spots and Arlo Guthrie. Tommy Perkins always kept a basic, steady tempo without all the "butterflying around," as Bob Wills called overactive drummers who like to roll around the tom-toms a lot, instead of just keeping good dance time. Perkins died tragically in an automobile accident in June 7, 2003, returning from the Legends of Western Swing Festival in Wichita Falls, Texas.

Even though financial and health problems plagued Bob Wills throughout the 1950s, he still maintained a steady recording and performance schedule that benefited from his tremendous fame through 1957, although his music did not enjoy the success of his peak period of the 1930s and early 1940s. Bob returned to Tulsa in 1957 to join forces with Johnnie Lee for two years before heading back out west to Las Vegas where he performed regularly through 1962. From 1960 to 1961, he reunited with his old singer, Tommy Duncan, for three albums on Liberty Records containing new recordings of some of their hits and several other selections that exhibited Bob's wide ranging musical tastes of blues, jazz, fiddle tunes, swing and pop. Bob had the first of his heart attacks in 1962, and after recovering in Tulsa, started touring and recording again before settling in Fort Worth, Texas in 1963.

All but worn out, Wills had another heart attack in 1964, ending his days as a bandleader. He sold the management of the band to Missouri-born singer and guitarist Leon Rausch for $10,000, and the Texas Playboys soldiered on under Rausch's direction, sometimes with Bob and sometimes not. While he continued fronting other leaders' bands, he kept recording through 1969, but the music had little impact on the national scene, treasured as the recordings are by Wills enthusiasts. He traveled Texas and Oklahoma by car in the middle 1960s, carrying with him only a vocalist or guitarist, and would play with various local pickup musicians at one-night stands throughout Texas and Oklahoma.

Inducted into the Country Music Hall of Fame in 1968, the plaque commemorating his contributions reads, "Bob Wills – established himself as King of Western Swing – a living legend whose road map has chartered new pathways into the world of American stage, radio, TV, records, and movies." In May of 1969, Bob had a stroke that incapacitated him.

Not willing to let his idol go quietly into the forgetful night of popular culture's memory, **Merle Haggard** supervised a *Tribute to the Best Damn Fiddle Player in the World (Or My Salute to Bob Wills)* from his home studio in 1971 which reunited many of Wills' original Playboys. In 1973, a final session was organized in Dallas where Bob just added voice tracks on recordings released as *For the Last Time* (United Artists). On the second day of the sessions, when Merle Haggard was to play fiddle, Wills had a massive stroke that left him comatose until he died in 1975, after which he was buried in Tulsa's

1978 Reunion of Western swing greats, seated (left to right): Johnny Gimble Claude Clemmons (drums), Gene Crownover, Don Tolle, and Eldon Shamblin; standing (left to right) Roy Ferguson, Curly Lewis, Joe Holley, Ted Adams, Glenn "Blub" Rhees, Johnnie Lee Wills, Wayne Johnson, Clarence Cagle, ohn Thomas Wills, Alex Brasheare, and O.W. Mayo.

Memorial Park Cemetery in section 15, lot 560, space 2, next to which his wife Betty was buried in 1993.

In 1997, Bob Wills won a posthumous Grammy Hall of Fame Award, and in 1999, the Rock and Roll Hall of Fame inducted Bob Wills and His Texas Playboys as an early influence on rock. The Wills legacy's latest accolade came in 2001 when Friends of Oklahoma Music inducted Bob, Johnnie Lee, Luke, and Billy Jack, along with special recognition for all those Oklahomans who recorded with any of the brothers, into the Oklahoma Music Hall of Fame.

While Bob Wills' music will be forever associated with the zenith of Western swing's popularity, the music of his brothers, Johnnie Lee and Billy Jack, is now also receiving acclaim through reissues available on Rounder, Rhino, and Bear Family Records. One particularly insightful compilation, *Heroes of Country Music, Volume One: Legends of Western Swing* (Rhino, 1996), has Bob's "Faded Love," Johnnie Lee's "Milk Cow Blues," and Billy Jack's "Troubles (Those Lonesome Kind)," as well as songs by **Hank Thompson**, **Spade Cooley**, and Milton Brown and His Brownies featuring the extremely significant steel player **Bob Dunn** on "Taking Off." As Johnnie Lee is being given more credit as an important Western swing band leader, younger brother Billy Jack is now often cited as leading a significant group that was a pre-cursor to rock and roll by leaning more toward the R&B and jump blues of the 1940s than the Western swing of his brothers. Billy Jack started playing bass with Johnnie Lee's group before relocating to California with Bob and ultimately leading his own band when Bob left California for Oklahoma City. The two representative recordings from Billy Jack's career as a bandleader based in Sacramento, California, include *Crazy Man Crazy* (Western, 1952 – reissued in 1999 on Joaquin Records) and *Billy Jack Wills and his Western Swing Band* (Western, 1952). Harder to find, but worth the search, are Billy Jack's *There's Good Rockin' Tonight* (Bear Family) and *Sacramento 1952-54* (Bear Family). Luke Wills' sole and out-of-print album *High Voltage Gal* features "(Gotta Get To) Oklahoma City," "Cain's Stomp," and "Oklahoma Blues."

While Charles R. Townsend's previously mentioned biography of Bob Wills is the most comprehensive source for information regarding Wills' professional career, discography, and recording sessions, the 1998 biography by Bob's daughter, Rosetta, *The King of Western Swing: Bob Wills Remembered*, is an excellent insider's view into the legendary band leader's life. A more obscure book certainly worth seeking out is John E. Perkins, Jr.'s *Leon Rausch – The Voice of the* Playboys (Swing, 1996), which provides a wealth of anecdotal information about various Wills bands, sidemen, and performances, as well as a thorough document of the life of vocalist and guitarist Leon Rausch, who fronted the Texas Playboys with Bob starting in 1958, but whose musical connections in Tulsa go back to 1955 when he was performing with Don Tolle's Western All Stars, and who lived in Tulsa until 1965. The Hal Leonard music company has also made an important contribution to the preservation of Bob Wills' music with *Bob Wills: King of Western Swing*, a compilation of piano/vocal/guitar sheet music scores.

Demonstrating the continuing impact of Bob Wills on contemporary musicians, a group of alternative-country-tinged musicians, to include Jimmie Dale Gilmore, Robbie Fulks, Jon Langford, Neko Case, Alejandro Escovedo, and The Meat Purveyors, more known for underground success on the college radio level or in the alt- country Americana radio format, appear on *The Pine Valley Cosmonauts Salute the Majesty of Bob Wills* (Bloodshot 1998). The collection features Wills standards redone with both the reverence and rowdiness one might expect from the artists on the album. In 1999, the group that is most representative contemporarily of the Western swing tradition, Asleep at the Wheel, released their own tribute to Wills on *Ride with Bob* (Dreamworks), covering the Playboys' best-known songs and featuring Oklahomans such as **Tommy Allsup, Vince Gill** and **Reba McEntire**. Through 2003, former Playboys continued reunion gigs at celebrations such as the annual Bob Wills Day on the Oklahoma capitol's house floor, the annual Bob Wills celebration in Turkey, Texas, and at regular gatherings for fans in Medicine Park and Pawhuska, Oklahoma. Since 1975, the Cain's Ballroom, forever known as the House That Bob Built, features any remaining active musicians of the Wills bands, or younger guys who know the changes, Fans were still lucky in 2013 getting to see Leon Rausch lead the Texas Playobys, and **Tommy Allsup** lead the Round Up Boys at the annual event.

While many recordings exist for the various incarnations of the Playboys, first-time listeners should begin with a standard compilation of Bob Wills' best-known songs, such as *The Essential Bob Wills: 1935-1947* (Columbia Classics, 1992), Rhino's excellent compilation, *Bob Wills & His Texas Playboys: Anthology 1935-1973*, or Bear Family Records eleven-CD boxed set, *San Antonio Rose*, that includes a DVD of *Take Me Back to Oklahoma* and a 168-page book full of photos and copies of movie posters. In 2006, SONY released a definitive re-mastered collection to celebrate the 100th birth of Bob Wills. The four-CD set contains 105 songs, starting with his first recordings in 1932 and ending with his final session in 1972.

Wilson, Charlie (see The GAP Band)

Wilson, Joe Lee
(b. December 22, 1935)

One of the most popular jazz vocal stylists of the 1970s, Joe Lee (Joseph) Wilson was born on a farm near Bristow, Oklahoma, a community of roughly 4,000 population located southwest of Tulsa. Of African-American and American Indian ancestry (maternal grandmother was Creek), Joe Lee, or J. L., spent his early childhood singing while doing farm chores, as well as vocalizing in school and church functions. It is also reported that he took piano lessons for about two years from ages seven to nine.

Although documentation is scarce regarding Joe Lee's schooling in Oklahoma, he apparently relocated to California around 1955. He was a voice major at the Los Angeles Conservatory from 1956 to 1957, and then studied jazz at Los Angeles City College, majoring in music from 1957 to 1958. He began his professional career in Santa Monica, California, in 1958, and then toured the West Coast and spent a year in Mexico.

In 1962 Joe Lee moved to New York City, where he worked with Sonny Rollins, Freddie Hubbard, Lee Morgan, Miles Davis, Roy Haynes, Jackie McLean, Frank Foster, **Sunny Murray**, Pharaoh Sanders, and Archie Shepp, with whom he is lead vocalist on Shepp's notable albums in the early 1970s, *Cry of My People*, *Attica Blues*, and *Things Have Got to Change*. The latter was reissued in 2002 on the Universal International label.

Joe Lee Wilson

During the 1960s and 1970s, Wilson made New York City his base of operations. Dubbed "The Big Voice," he appeared at the Newport in New York and Live Lofts Jazz Festivals during this time, opened and operated the Lady's Fort Jazz Club, hosted his own jazz radio show, performed on a U.S. State Department tour with his own group, Joy of Jazz, and was one of the innovators of the Loft Movement which gave struggling young jazz musicians performance opportunities. During this time, Joe Lee recorded three solo albums with guitar, including *Livin' High off Nickels and Dimes*, *Secrets from the Sun*, and *Without A Song*, all on independent labels. One of his greatest achievements during this period was winning the *Down Beat* Critics Poll in 1973 in the category of Talent Deserving Wider Recognition-Male Vocalist.

In 1978 Wilson performed at Ronnie Scott's Club in London, and was guest vocalist with Humphrey Lyttelton's Big Band while in the U.K. He thus discovered and liked the European jazz scene, and eventually moved to Europe, living in the U.K. and France from the late 1970s on. The *London Evening Standard* newspaper once described Joe Lee as "the male equivalent of Ella Fitzgerald, Sarah Vaughan, and Carmen McRae."

As of 2002, Wilson is still performing a combination of jazz, blues, and gospel music at age sixty-seven with appearances on three continents and release of two recent albums, *Feelin' Good* (Candid Records) and *What Would It Be Without You* (Knitting Factory Records). He toured the U.K. and Ireland twice in 2001 with his Joy of Jazz group, led a six-week series of gospel workshops at King's School Canterbury, and sang for sold out crowds at the Faith and Light Festival at Lourdes.

Wooley, Sheb
(b. April 10, 1921)

One of the most versatile performers in country music as a songwriter, recording artist, actor, and comedian, Sheb Wooley was born to William Curtis and Ora Wooley on a farm near Erick, Oklahoma, a community of about 1,000 residents just off Interstate 40 near the Texas border. Sheb learned to ride a horse by age four and later competed in rodeos while in high school. Local sources say his father traded a shotgun for Sheb's first guitar, and while in high school, Sheb formed a country music band (The Plainview Melody Boys), playing at neighborhood dances and on local radio in Elk City.

Sheb Wooley

Sheb liked music, but realized it would not provide much of a living, therefore, he worked as a welder in the Oklahoma oil fields after graduating from high school. As with many other Oklahomans, Sheb pulled up stakes in the 1930s and headed to California, where he found work in a plant moving orange crates. In the meantime, Sheb had married Melba Laurie Miller, a cousin of Roger Miller, whom he had met at Erick, where the Miller family lived. At the outset of World War II, Sheb was declared unfit for military service (4-F) due to injuries suffered during his rodeo days, but he did work in defense plants during the war.

Following the war, Wooley headed to Nashville, where he cut his first records for the Bullet label in the studios of WSM, the radio home of the Grand Ole Opry. He also appeared on radio station WLAC as a singer/guitarist, but neither the record deal or radio work proved fruitful, and Sheb relocated to Fort Worth after about a year in Music City.

From 1946 to 1949, Sheb fronted his own show on radio station WBAP in Fort Worth, sponsored by Calumet Baking Powder, and formed his own band, The Calumet Indians. While in the area, he recorded several cuts for the Bluebonnet label in Dallas. Several of these vintage recordings have been reissued by Bear Family as *Country Boogies Wild Wooley*. He then left Texas and returned to California, thinking that movies might fit into his future plans. About the same time, Sheb signed on as a songwriter with Hill & Range publishing company, which resulted in 1950, a recording contract with a new company MGM Records, remaining with the label for more than twenty years. In hopes of some movie work, Sheb took acting lessons at the Jack Koslyn School of Acting in Los Angeles, which led to his first screen role in 1949 as a heavy in the Errol Flynn film *Rocky Mountain*. Three years later, he was cast as Ben Miller, the whiskey-drinking killer in the Gary Cooper film *High Noon*, in which he gained considerable notice.

In the 1950s, Wooley appeared in several other films, including *Little Big Horn* (1951), *Distant Drums* (1951), *Man Without a Star* (1955), *Giant* (1956), and *Rio Bravo* (1959), but his most memorable work was in television, where he was cast as Pete Nolan in the *Rawhide* series from 1959 to 1967. He also appeared in several other television shows, such as *Lassie*, *Cheyenne*, *Range Rider*, and *The Lone Ranger*, as well as writing several scripts for *Rawhide*. During his career in Hollywood from 1950 to 1979, Sheb appeared in more than seventy films.

During his acting career, Sheb continued to write songs and make records. His songs were recorded by such artists as Hank Snow, who had a big hit in 1953 with "When Mexican Joe Met Jole Blon," Theresa Brewer's million seller "Too Young to Tango" in 1954, and Rusty Draper scored a Top 20 hit in 1955 with "Are You Satisfied?" But it was the novelty hit "The Purple People Eater," released in 1958, which turned Sheb into an international star. MGM Records was at first reluctant to release the single, but it became a million seller (in 2002 it had sold more than 100 million copies worldwide), remained atop the U.S. pop charts for six weeks, and became a Top 20 hit in the U.K. His next major hit was in 1962, another novelty number titled "That's My Pa," which reached #1 on the country charts. It is reported that Sheb was in line to record "Don't Go Near the Indians," but because of film obligations, Rex Allen's version was released before he could record it. He jokingly told MGM he would write a sequel that resulted in another comic parody, "Don't Go Near the Eskimos," featuring a new drunken persona to present it—Ben Colder.

As Ben Colder, Sheb recorded several more humorous parodies of popular hits, such as "Almost Persuaded No. 2," "Harper Valley PTA (Later That Same Day)," "Hello Wall No. 2," and "Fifteen Beers (Years) Ago." Under his own name, he recorded a few minor hits, including "Blue Guitar" and "Tie a Tiger Down." He received a *Cash Box* magazine special award in 1964 for his contributions to country and popular music. In 1967, 1968, 1969, and 1979, Ben Colder was nominated as Comedian of the Year by the CMA, and captured top honors in 1968. In 2002 Bear Family released *Eskimos, Mean Old Queen & Itty Bitty Steers*, a twenty-six track compilation under the Ben Colder name, and includes all the well-known parodies of popular hits, such as "Ballad of a Mean Old Queen" ("Ballad of a Teenage Queen"), "Detroit City #2," and "Make the World Go Away #2."

In 1969 when the popular television show *Hee Haw* went on the air, Sheb was hired to perform as Ben Colder, served as the resident songwriter, and wrote the show's theme music. He appeared in thirteen segments of the show.

Album credits for Sheb include his self-titled debut (1956), *Songs from the Days of*

Rawhide (1960), *That's My Ma and That's My Pa* (1962), *Tales of How the West Was Won* (1963), *It's a Big Land* (1965), *Warm and Wooley* (1969), and *The Purple People Eater*, released in 1997 by Bear Family, the German label.

Wooley's songs have been recorded by a variety of artists, including Johnny Bond, Ray Stevens, Frenchie Burke, Flying Burrito Brothers, Johnny Cash, Bob Wills, Connie Francis, and even Judy Garland.

As of 2003, Wooley continued to write songs with his entertainment company, Dotson-Wooley, based in Hendersonville, Tennessee, where he makes his home.

www.ben-colder.com

Young Bird
(formed in Pawnee, OK in 1997)

While other Oklahoma intertribal singing groups may have been in existence longer, such as Southern Thunder, Gray Horse, Cozad, Yellow Hammer, Red Land, and Fort Oakland Ramblers, the Young Bird drum, led by Curtis Hamilton-Young Bird (Cheyenne/Sauk & Fox) has risen to national status as one of the most significant southern style powwow drum groups in the United States. On the strength of their powerful group sound, Young Bird has toured nationally and internationally, released eight albums through Canyon Records, one of which was Grammy nominee in 2001, and has won a host of singing competitions throughout North America.

Curtis Hamilton-Young Bird

Born June 25, 1976 in the north central Oklahoma town of Pawnee, where the Pawnee Nation maintains its headquarters, Curtis Hamilton-Young Bird's first musical experiences were through his attendance of Native American Church peyote meetings with his father, Don Hamilton (Cheyenne/Apache (Na-I-Sha)/Tonkawa), and his mother, June Hamilton-Young Bird (Pawnee/Sauk & Fox/Otoe). Curtis started dancing early in powwows, first as a tiny tot straight dancer, then a junior fancy dancer, and finally as a teen-aged traditional dancer. Growing up around his grandfathers, uncles, and father who sang around the big center drum in the powwow circle, Curtis sat with them for the first time when he was eight years old. When he was twelve and thirteen, Curtis traveled and sang with a northern style group, Blue Hawk, before joining the Rose Hill Singers, led by Lloyd Gwen, in 1989. After singing with Rose Hill for several years at powwows, and a trip to the 1996 summer Olympics in Atlanta where his family's group performed with 112 dancers and singers for four weeks in a fixed venue, Curtis started the Young Bird singers in 1997 with his father, brothers, friends, and other family members.

The group recorded their debut album, *Déjà vu: Pow-Wow Songs from Oklahoma*, in 1998 for Canyon Records, one of the premier outlets for American Indian music since 1951. The album was recorded in the 1st National Bank of Pawnee for its acoustics, and included titles that show the group's affinity for rap and R&B, as in "Getting' Jiggy," "Wu Tan," and "R&B Connection." Not to say the songs mirror those musical genres in any way, other than attitude, but the group has been noted as a favorite by artists such as Busta

Rhymes and 'N Sync. In 1998, Young Bird won the United Tribes Singing Contest, and in 1999 released their second album, *Rendezvous*, also recorded in the Pawnee 1st National Bank. Also in 1999, the group toured Italy for a week with six performances at different venues throughout the country.

Word Up (Canyon, 2000) is the group's first live recording, made in Tempe, Arizona at Arizona State University's Powwow, and includes a "Cheyenne Flag and Victory Song," as well as a song dedicated to the northern district of the Sac and Fox Nation, "Skushy Strut," and a tune called "Flipmode," which is the pseudonym the group has used when they get together with singers from other groups at powwows. Also released in 2000, *Down for Life* was recorded live at the annual Shakopee Mdewankanton Sioux Community Pow-Wow, and is one of the first non-compilation albums to feature a Northern plains and a Southern plains style powwow group on the same album. Paired with The Boyz, a championship northern-style drum group from St. Paul, Minnesota, among Young Bird's contributions are "Bling, Bling," "Road Warrior," and "Killing Time."

In 2000, the group was the youngest ever to win the overall world singing competition at Schemitzun Powwow in Connecticut, and their 2001 *Change of Life* album for Canyon Records was nominated for a Grammy as the Best Native American Album of 2001. As a result, the group traveled to Los Angeles where they performed at a pre-Grammy Awards reception in early 2002. Young Bird followed *Change of Life* in 2001 with *Double Platinum* (Canyon) featuring them and another northern style group, *River Cree*, on alternate tracks recorded live at the annual Ermine Skin Band Pow-Wow in Alberta, Canada. In 2002, Young Bird released another live album, *Only the Strong Survive* (Canyon), recorded in Iowa City, Iowa at the University of Iowa's 13th annual powwow. The album featured more of their trademark big drum and strong, soaring vocal stylings for which they have become known through Indian Country.

While the group has had a number of singers from many different tribes in the group since 1997, all of which are listed on their various albums, the lineup for *Only the Strong Survive* included Curtis as lead singer, and additional singers Ron (Ski) James, Sr. (Arapaho/Colville/Pawnee/Otoe), G.C. Tsouhlarakis (Muscogee/Navajo), Hah-Tee Delgado (Comanche), Ben Nakai (Navajo/Pawnee), Danita Cornelison (Sauk & Fox), Jeff McClellan (Sauk & Fox), Sunny Rose Yellowmule (Pawnee/Crow), Anthony Monoessy (Comanche/Kiowa), Sam Cook (Muscogee/Kiowa), Rusty Diamond (Pawnee/Otoe), and Curtis's father, Don Hamilton-Young Bird.

In October, 2002, the group received the Oklahoma Music Hall

YoungBird Singers, Sarcee Champs, 2011

of Fame's first Rising Star Award for the outstanding achievements the group has made thus far. By late fall of 2002, the group shifted between three vehicles they owned to crisscross the United States and Canada to perform at the biggest powwows in North America. In 2003, Young Bird's music appeared in *The World of American Indian Dance*, an NBC television special focusing on contemporary powwow dances.

Also released in 2003, *Southern and Northern Pow-Wow Songs* (Canyon) featured both Young Bird and a northern-style group, Midnite Express, alternating tracks throughout the disc. The group released a new album, *Beautiful Life, in 2009.*

YoungBird Singers have continued winning singing competitions throughout the U.S. and Canada: Apache Gold Singing Champs, San Carols, AZ (2003-05), , Ft. Hall Idaho Champions (2006), and 1st Place Drum, San Manuel Powwow (2012).

Discussing the group's passion for their music, Curtis Hamilton-Youngbird says, "Once you start singing around the drum, you want to do it more and more, to celebrate the spirit of the creator, and the songs he gives us."

www.myspace.com/youngbird97

One More for the Road

The Woody Guthrie Center in Tulsa is the newest music-focused museum in Oklahoma. The center is a state of the art facility that not only houses Guthrie's papers, but also guides visitors through his life and career in music through interactive displays, historic artifacts, and music listening stations.

2013 People's List of Oklahoma Music & *OMG II* Cross Index

"The People's List" of Oklahoma music is comprised of musicians, musical groups, music professionals, music traditions, music journalists, musical educators, national musical figures with mythical or reputed ties to Oklahoma, and/or significant and/or obscure local music entities of Oklahoma suggested by many sources, spoken or written, to the author, or picked up by the author by continuously reading the usual and unusual suspects. Space, deadlines, or available information may have impacted fuller documentation in this printing of individuals or group's deserving more coverage. Future editions of OMG may include fuller entries of those listed here and/or those musicians just beginning their journey, still practicing, or now out paying their show business dues by playing free, cheap, or anywhere that asks.

Corrections, additions, or suggestions for the list are encouraged and may be submitted by writing and e-mail to the author@oklahomamusicguide.com.

People's List and Cross Index Format and Abbreviation Key:
Individual or Group
Oklahoma Connection & Musical Notability
b=born, r=resided, d=died, f=formed

alt = Alternative
AI = American Indian
BG = Bluegrass
CCM = Contemporary Christian Music
CW = Country & Western
et al. = and others
HS = High School
I.T. = Indian Territory
OCU = Oklahoma City University
OKC = Oklahoma City
OSU = Oklahoma State University
OU = University of Oklahoma
R&B = Rhythm and Blues
R&R = Rock and Roll, baby
TU = Tulsa University
vox = vocals
*=unknown at press time

Bold text indicates the name of the artist, group, or tribe is included in the biographical entry listed in boldface text.

A

Abeyta, David
Absentee Shawnee Tribe/based in Shawnee, moved to I.T. in 1868/powwows
Absher, Brad/r. Tulsa/blues/rock guitarist and singer
Acoustic Ross/f. Tulsa/singer, songwriter, guitarist
Act Casual/f. Oklahoma City, 1991/blues band
  Ellis, Dorothy "Miss Blues"
    b. Texas, r. Oklahoma City/singer
  Ford, Kenneth/b. Tom/vocalist, songwriter, bassist
Adams, Frank/r. Tulsa/jazz saxophonist
Adams, Joe/r. Tulsa/opera singer
Adams, Jody/r. Oklahoma/bluegrass fiddler, mandolinist, songwriter
Adams, Ron/r. Tulsa/jazz bassist
Admirals/f. Stillwater/industrial-folk-space-rock band, debut EP by **Trent Bell**, released February, 2013 (Idol Records)
  Bair, Andrew (keyboards/piano/guitar)
  Brewer, Cory (drums)
  Murphy, Brett (bass)
  Tucker, Colton (guitar/vocals)
Admiral Twin
  Agent, Dan/r. Tahlequah co-managed Randy Crouch and the Flying Horse Opera
A Girl Thang/f. Oklahoma City/rock group
Agony Scene
  Aguilar, Albert/r., OKC, Putnam City North H.S. grad/ singer, songwriter, guitarist,
  Ahhaitty, Bill/r. Oklahoma/powwow head singer, round dance singer, recorded for Canyon Records
Ahhaitty, Walter
AJ and Why Not/f. Oklahoma/blues group
Akin, Anna Jean "Smoki"/b. 6/2/1924, Clovis, NM - d. 5/6/2013/pianist who played with Count Basie Lefty Frizzell, Sammi Smith, and her own Smoki Durham Band
Aldrich, "Walkin' Talkin'" Charlie/b. Ogawana, 1913/classical guitarist, country singer, songwriter
Aldridge, Harold/reared in Taft, r.Tahlequah blues guitarist, vocalist, performer, educator
Alexander, Adrian/b. 1968, McAlester – d. Krebs, 2012 drummer (Down for Five/Sybil's Machine)
Alexander, Dave/r. Broken Arrow Western swing bandleader
Alexandria, Jonettia/r. Broken Arrow composer, music educator, children's music
All-American Rejects
ALLBLAK/f. Tulsa/rap, hip-hop
Allen, Bill/b. OK, 1925, r. Wewoka/Western swing rhythm guitarist, fiddler
Allen, Steve/r. Tulsa/guitarist & vocalist with pop rock group 20/20
Al-Jibouri, Sean/r. Tulsa/blues rock guitarist
Alred, Casi/b. OK, 1988/country singer
Allsup, Tommy
Altamont Speedway/f. Norman
Alter Ego/f. Oklahoma City, 1995/blues rock group
Alvaro's Brazilian Jazz/r. Edmond, 2002 Latin jazz group
AM
Amazing Rhythm Chickens/f. Norman, 1973 classic rock and roll group
Ambassador Bill/f. Oklahoma City, 1995 punk rock group
Ambient Music Cartel/f. Oklahoma City, 1998 rock group
American Boyfriends/f. Oklahoma City, 1992 pop rock group
  Goad, Matt/r. Oklahoma City/guitarist, vocalist
  Harmon, Eric/r. Oklahoma City/drummer
  Johnson, Matt/r. Oklahoma City/bassist
  York, Richard/r. Oklahoma City/guitarist
American Girlz/f. Broken Arrow/retro pop music
American Horse/f. Tulsa/rock group
AMF/f. Tulsa/punk metal rock group

Anderson, Buddy
Anderson, Jonathan/b. 1990 – d. 2001, r. Enid rapper and leader of Midwest Hustlaz
Anderson, Keith
Andrews, Jack /b. Oklahoma City, 1930 country music talent scout
Anderson, Kenny/Oklahoma Opry guitarist
Andress, Tuck
And There Stands Empires/f. Tulsa/ loud rock group
Animation/f. Oklahoma City/rock group
Anita's Anger/f. Weatherford neo-punk pop rock group
Another Roadside Attraction/f. Stillwater/acoustic folk
Anquoe, Jack, Sr. (Kiowa)/b. Mountain View 1933 head singer with Grayhorse,
Anquoe, Jack, Jr.(Kiowa/Cherokee)/b. Claremore singer with Grayhorse, Redlands
Anquoe, Jim (Kiowa)/b. Mountain View Kiowa and intertribal powwow singer
Anquoe, Kelly (Kiowa/Cherokee)/r. Tahlequah . intertribal powwow singer
Anquoe, Mary Ann (Kiowa)/b. Mountain View singer (War Mothers' songs)
Anquoe, Quentin/r. Oklahoma/ intertribal powwow head singer
Anquoe, Rick/r. Oklahoma intertribal powwow head singer
Anquoe, Ron/r. Oklahoma intertribal powwow head singer
Antenna Lodge/f. Tulsa/hardcore punk rock group
  Forbis, Jeremy/drummer
  Kendrick, Kelly/singer, guitarist
  Sutliff, Danel/bassist
Anthony, David/r. Oklahoma City/guitarist & songwriter for George Strait
Anti-Mortem/f. 2008, Chickasha/heavy metal rock group signed to Nuclear Blast Records in 2013 began recording first album in March
  Dickerson, Levi/drummer
  Henderson, Corey/bassist
  Romo, Larado/lead vocalist
  Romo, Nevada/guitarist
  Smith, Zain/guitarist
Apache Tribe of Oklahoma
Apparitions in Blue/r. Norman/techno dance music
Aqueduct
Aranda/f. Oklahoma City/rock group
The Arbuckles/f. Shawnee/bluegrass group
  Talley, Tony/r. Shawnee/dobro player, lead vocalist
  Thomas, Don/b. Cushing/banjo, lead/tenor vocalist
  Thomas, Russell/r. Shawnee/bassist, lead & baritone vocalist
  Thomas, Steve/b. Cushing/guitarist,lead/tenor vocalist
Archer, Charlie/r. Stratford/guitarist for Conway Twitty, 1970s-1993
Arkeketa, John (Otoe/Cherokee)/r. Tahlequah intertribal powwow head singer
The Arnolds/f. Tulsa/Southern gospel group
ARRAKIS/f. Oklahoma City/rock group
Atkinson, Taylor/b. Midwest City, r. Edmond red dirt and country-rock singer/bandleader
Austin, Larry
Austin, William, W/b. Lawton, 1920/musicologist
Autry, Gene
Awake/f. Oklahoma City, 1998/CCM group
Axolotls/f. Seminole 1999/rock group
Axton, Hoyt
Axton, Mae Boren
Aycock, Jesse/r. Tulsa/singer, songwriter guitarist of many textures and dynamics
Aycock, Scott and Empty Pockets/f. Tulsa, 1999 Americana music group
  Aycock, Scott/singer, songwriter, guitarist, and KWGS Folk Salad radio program host
  Grant, Russell/drummer

754 / Oklahoma Music Guide II

Leonard, Tom/bassist
Murphy, J. Pat/guitarist
Parker, Charlie/saxophone
Schad, Carolyn/harmony vocals

B

Baby M/f. Tulsa/modern rock group
Bageyes/f. Tulsa/loud rock group
Baggot, Edward/r. Oklahoma/traditional fiddler
Bagsby, David/r. Tulsa/keyboardist, electronic music
Bagsby, Steve/r. Tulsa/banjo player
Bryce Bailey/AI singer, recording engineer, producer
  Oklahoma Red: Live at Red Earth Vol. 1 (Arbor)
Bailey, Fred/b. northwest Oklahoma/singer songwriter
Baker, Adam/b. Oklahoma City, 1964
  graphic artist for album covers
Baker, Andrea/b. Muskogee/jazz singer
Baker, Bobby/r. Clarerore/Western swing steel guitarist
  fiddler with Cowjazz
Baker, Chet
Baker, Danny/b. Tulsa, 1964/blues-rock band leader
Baker, Jimmie/b. Tulsa/big band leader in Stillwater
Baker, Mark
Bakerville/r. Tulsa/country group
Balageur, Jean-Michel/r. Tulsa/guitarist
Ballard, John R.(Ottawa/Cherokee)/r. Oklahoma
  song leader, Stomp Dance Blues (Indian House, 1999)
Ballard, Joyce (Shawnee/Peoria)/r. Oklahoma
  shell shaker on Stomp Dance Blues (Indian House, 1999)
Ballard, Louis
Balletto, Luigi/r. Tulsa/lounge singer, entertainer
Ballista/f. Oklahoma City/rock group
  Almanza, Cesar/b. Harlingen, TX, 1975/
    guitarist/back-up vocalist
  DuVall, Rick/b. Muskogee, 1974/bassist, lead vocalist
  Martinek, Billy/b. Oklahoma City, 1973/drummer
Ballistic/f. Tulsa/rock group
Banana Seat/f. Tulsa/rock group
Banish Misfortune/f. Oklahoma City/Celtic music group
  Morrow, Dana/pianist
  Reid, Phil/fiddler
  Vaniandingham, Steve/banjo, mandolinist
Banks, Damen/b. Tulsa/rapper
Banks, Hobart/r. Muskogee/jazz pianist, 1930s
Barbata, Johnny
Barber, Glenn
Barker, Brandy Michelle/r. Moore/country singer
Barker,Rolland/r.Cushing
  intertribalpowwow headsinger
Barnes, Ben/r. Oklahoma/stomp dance leader
  Stomp Dance Blues (Indian House, 1999)
Barnett, Bobby
Barnett, Jeremy/Kelleyville Ceremonial Grounds
  stomp dance leader
Barton, George/r. Tahlequah/singer, songwriter
  guitarist for Barton and Sweeney
Bass, Sam D./b. Oklahoma/played cello with
  Tommy Duncan, Tex Ritter, and Moon Mullican
The Bastions/f. Oklahoma/Southern gospel group
Batcheller, Joe/r. Oklahoma/singer, songwriter
Baylor, Helen/r. Tulsa/contemporary gospel
Bayton, Dennis/r. Catoosa/f. Big Band Sound, 1991
Beams of Light Family Church/Tulsa/CCM
Bearpaw. Josh/Kelleyville Ceremonial Grounds
  stomp dance leader
Beck, Chelsea/b. Laverne, 1993/country
  singer, yodeler, www.chelseabeck.com
Beckham, Bob
Bee, Molly
Beef & Lemons/f. Tulsa/indy rock group
Beefeater Project/f. OKC/psychedelic rock band
Been, Michael (see entry for The Call)
Belanger, Paul/r. Gene Autry/cowboy singer,yodeler
Belew, Carl
Belken, Jim/b. Dallas, TX, 1931, r. Oklahoma
  Western swing fiddler
Belknap, Bill/r. Oklahoma/pop rock group 20/20
Bell, Aaron
Bell, Ann/r. Oklahoma/rock vocals

Bell, Larry/r. Tulsa/keyboardist, played with
  Jerry Lee Lewis, recorded with Paul Anka
Bell, Trent
Bellvue/f. Norman, 1995/rock group
Benjaman, Paul/f. Tulsa/blues rock
  Paul Benjaman Band
Ben.Ben/f. Tulsa/jazz fusion group
Bennett, Mike/r. Tulsa/trumpeter
  Johnnie Lee Wills, Ray Charles,
  Cab Calloway, Flash Terry
Bennett, Wayne/b. Sulphur/blues guitarist
Bentley, Rick/r. Oklahoma/banjo player
Bentonelli, Giuseppe Joseph Benton/b. Sayre, 1898
  opera singer
Berline, Byron
Berline, Lue/r. Oklahoma/old time fiddler
  (Byron Berline's father)
Bernard, Gene/b. Leonard/Western swing
Bernard, Lester "Junior"/b. Leonard/
  Western swing guitarist
Bernston, David/r. Tulsa/blues harmonica
Berryman, Ric/r. Broken Arrow/rock
  multi-instrumentalist and vocalist
Bibb, Teri/b. Altus/Broadway musical performer
Big Big Brains/f. Broken Arrow/classic rock
Big Daddy & the Blueskickers/f. Beggs/blues
  Big Daddy/guitarist, vocalist
  Gallie, John/pianist, organist
  McCallister, Donn/drummer, percussionist
  McDuffie, Doug/bassist, vocalist
Bigelow, Tracy/r. Tiawah/rhythm guitarist,
  lead guitarist for retro-jazz group Early Swing Now
BigHorse, Vann/r. Pawhuska
  intertribal powwow head singer
Bihari, Jules, Joe, Saul and Lester/r. Oklahoma
  Modern Records founders
Bill & Bink/country music duo
  recorded for Hobart-based Hu-Se-Co label in the 1950s
Billy & Baby Gap/r. Tulsa/R & B vocal duo
  (Billy Young and Anthony Walker)
Billy, Bryon Mahli/Choctaw chanter, circa 2013
Billy Joe Winghead/f. Oklahoma/psychobilly,
  country, punk rock group
Binge/Purge Society/f. Oklahoma/heavy metal group
Bingham. Ray/r. Tulsa/music promoter, booking agent
Bio Mass/f. Norman/rock group
Bird, Margery/r. Tulsa/music philanthropist
Birdwell, Florence/OCU music faculty. 2003/voice
Bishop, Elvin
Bishops Alley/f. Oklahoma City, 2000/rock
Blair, Jim/r. Muskogee/multi-instrumentalist
  country, bluegrass (Neverly Brothers)
Blackbear Creek/f. Pawnee/intertribal powwow group
Blackbird/f. Shawnee and Norman, 1990
  intertribal northern style powwow group
  (Arbor Records)
  Primeaux, Graham/r. Shawnee/head singer
Blackhawk Blues Band/f. Oklahoma City, 1990/ blues
  Garcia, Al/r. Oklahoma City/drummer
  Gray, Cecil/r. Oklahoma City/guitar/vocalist
  Jones, Batiste/r. Oklahoma City/guitarist,
    harmonica, vocalist
  Scott, Melvin/r. Oklahoma City/bass/vocalist
Blackstone, Tsianina Redfeather
  b. Dec. 13, 1883, I.T. – d. January, 1985
  concert/opera performer through the 1930s
Black Out/f. Locust Grove/skater pop group
Blackstone, Tsianina/b. I. T., 1882/opera
Blackwell, Chuck
Blair, Greg/b. Claremore/CCM singer
Blair, Jim
  b. Odessa, TX, r. Clayton & Muskogee
  multi-instrumentalist, vocalist w/
  Neverly Brothers, City Moon, Delicious Militia
  Hank Williams, Sr. tribute performer
Blake, Al/r. Oklahoma City/blues guitarist
Blak Kat Bone/f. Hartshorne/blues rock group
Blalock, Jay (Shawnee/Ojibwe)/r. Oklahoma
  intertribal powwow head singer
Blane, Ralph

Blazer, Jim/r. Tulsa/pianist
The Blue Cats/f. Oklahoma City/blues/R & B
The Blue Collars/f. Tulsa/pop rock group
  Abbot, Nick/trombonist
  Dalby, Mike/baritone saxophonist
  Halka, Charles/keyboardist
  Halka, Dan/bassist
  Hull, Jojo/drummer
  Plumlee, James/drummer
  Swain, Todd/tenor saxophonist
  VanValkenburgh, Parker/vocalist, guitarist, sax

Blue Combo/f. Tulsa/blues group
  Armstrong, Robby/b. Tulsa/drums, vocalist
  Davis, Shannon/b. Tulsa/vocalist
  Elmore, Steve/b. Tulsa/keyboardist
  Miller, Rusty/b. Chattanooga, TN/guitar, vocalist
  Waggoner, "Tex"/b. Wichita Falls, TX/bass
Blued/f. Tulsa/heavy metal group
Blue Diamond/f. Muskogee/classic rock group
Blue, Leon/r. Oklahoma/keyboardist for B.B. King
The Blue Flame/f. Oklahoma City/blues group
Blues Nation/f. Anadarko, 1980s/American Indian
  blues band
  Klinekole, Sonny/b. Lawton/bass
  Mauchahty-Ware, Tom/b. Lawton/guitar, vocals,
    Kiowa/Comanche flutist
  Miller, Dusty/b. Lawton/guitar
  Sullivan, Obie/b. Okmulgee/keyboards
  Tsotigh, Terry/b. Carnegie/drums/harmonica
BMP (ill Murray's Prostate)/f. Pryor, 1998/rock
Boggs, Noel
Bogle, Bob
Bointy, Joe/r. Oklahoma/powwow singer
  (Kiowa/Comanche)
Boland, Jason and the Stragglers
Bolar, Abe/b. Oklahoma City, 1909/jazz bassist for
  Oklahoma City Blue Devils
Bolding, Katie/b. Edmond, 1979/opera singer,
  NY Metropolitan Opera chorus, Dallas Opera
  (Countess Ceprana in Verdi's Rigoletto, 2013)
Bolen, Chuck/r. Oklahoma/pop, rock vocalist,
  recorded for Sheridan Records in Tulsa
Bond, Johnny
Bond, Ridge/b. Tulsa/performed as "Curly"
  in1950s Broadway productions of Oklahoma!
Bonham, Virgil/b. Talihina/bluegrass
  Bill Grant's Kiamichi Mountain Boys
  Bonham Review (bluegrass)
Bonham, Glen
Booker, Scott
Boondogs/f. Tulsa/rootsy, Americana group
Bop Cats/f. Tulsa/rock and roll revival group
Bordeaux, Tonya/r. Tulsa/CCM, world music
  guitarist, singer, songwriter
Bostic, Earl
The Bourgeois/f. Tulsa, 2012/modern rock
Boydst un, S.F. "Max"/b. Tulsa, r. Muskogee/
  bluegrass/country/blues guitarist, singer
Browa, Frank/Duck Creek Ceremonial Grounds
  stomp dance leader
Boyd, Clarence/b. Vinita, r. Kellyville/
  co-wrote "Release Me"
Bowlsey/f. OKC, 2013/alternative foik/pop
Boykin, Orval/r. Oklahoma City/country bassist
Brackeen, Charles
Brady, Felicia/r. Oklahoma/folk & pop singer
  songwriter
Brant, Nathan/r. Tulsa/pop rock singer,
  songwriter
Brave (Sierra Brown)/OKC Classen HS, 2013/
  alternadramapop
Bravo Brass Quintet/f. OKC/chamber music
Bray, Frank/r. Broken Arrow/jazz vocalist
Brazille, Emmitt/r. Oklahoma City/jazz pianist
  multi-genre and multi-instrumental
Bread, Phillip "Yogie"/r. Oklahoma
  American Indian flutist, Kiowa
Breaux, Zelia Page/b. MO, r. Langston, OKC/
  legendary music educator

Hugh W. Foley / 755

Breeden, Harold/b. Guthrie, 1921
  jazz reeds and educator
Brewer, Mike
Brice, Bill/b. Knoxville, TN, r. Oklahoma circa
  1980s to his death in 2012/church organist
Brice, Carol/b. Sedalia, NC, 4/16/1918 - d.
  Norman, OK, 2/15/1985/opera singer, OU faculty
Brick Face Lovely/f. Tulsa/rock group
Bridges, Henry (Hank)/b. OKC, circa 1908/jazz
  saxophone
British Invasion/f. OKC/1960s pop tribute band
Broncho/f. Norman and Tulsa, 2010
  Okie garage pop, www.bronchoband.com
  Ford, Johnathon/bass, vocals
  King, Ben/guitar, vocals
  Lindsey, Ryan/guitar, vocals
  Price, Nathan/drums
Brooks, Colleen/b. in Kansas City, MO, r. Yukon
  country singer on Capitol Records,
  Garth Brooks's mother
Brooks, Garth
Brooks, Joan/r. Edmond/classical music
Brooks, William/b. Ardmore, 1959/singer,
  songwriter
Brother Bear/f. Stillwater, 2008/space pop
Broughton, J.C./r. Sapulpa/old time fiddler
Brown, Buddy/r. Oklahoma/blues guitarist
  led Buddy Brown and the Hound Dogs
Brown, Darrell/r. Oklahoma/gospel producer
Brown, Felix, Jr/Duck Creek Ceremonial Grounds
  stomp dance leader
Brown, Joseph/b. Wagoner/JOB Records founder
Brown, Kyle/b. Stilwell, 1981, r. Tahlequah/singer,
  songwriter associated w/Red Dirt music
Brown, Nathan/b. Longview, TX, 1965, reared
  in Oklahoma/country songwriter
Brown, Tanya Rae/r. Mounds/country singer
  (a.k.a. Mrs. Junior Brown)
Brown, W. Lawson/r. Bethany/gospel singer
Bruce, Buddy
Brumley, Albert, Sr.
Bruner, Mark/reared in Frederick, r. Tulsa/guitarist
Bryant, Anita
Bryan, Mark/r. Stillwater/pianist
Bryant, Freddie/r. Norman/guitarist
Buchanan, Roy/r. Tulsa in 1955/blues guitarist
Buckner, Acee/song leader
  Tallahassee Wvkokye Ceremonial Grounds
Buffalomeat, Lavern/r. Oklahoma
  intertribal powwow head singer
Bunds, Monica/Tulsa University student, 2003/
  sings on TU jazz CD, Sophisticated Ladies
Burford, Annette/b. Oklahoma City/opera singer
Burkhart, Sara Maybelle/b. Tulsa, 1910/
  classical composer
Burleigh, Glenn Edward/b. Guthrie/gospel
  composer, conductor
Burns, William O./b. Calvin, 1921/
  Texas State Champion old time fiddler
Burris, Eddie/r. Tulsa/co-wrote "Okie from
  Muskogee", drummer for Merle Haggard
Burtschi Brothers/f. Norman/Okie rock, dirt jazz,
  Americana, Red Dirt, roots music group
  Foreman, Chris/drums
  Linville, Travis/guitar
  Phenix, Mike/bass
  Webb, Kevin/guitars
Busey, Gary
Butcher, Marlin/b. Oklahoma City, 1951/
  rock and country bassist
Butler, John (**Kaw/Otoe**)/r. Oologah/
  intertribal powwow head singer
Butler, Wesley/stomp dance leader
  Peach Ceremonial Grounds/
Butler, Zachary/r. Oklahoma/song leader
  Stomp Dance Blues (Indian House, 1999)
Byars, Mike/r. Norman/drums (see **Hosty Duo**)
Byas, Don

Byfield, Jim/b. Tulsa, 1949/vocalist, guitarist,
  (see **Tulsa Sound**)
Byington, Presley/r. Idabel/**Choctaw** flutist
Bynum, David/r. Tulsa
  opened Vinyl Countdown record store, 2012

C

Cable, Kelly/r. Oklahoma/
  intertribal powwow head singer
Caddo Nation of Oklahoma
Cagle, Chris/b. 1969, TX/country singer
  ("Chicks Dig It", "Got My Country On"),
  moved to Marietta, Oklahoma in 2008
Cagle, Clarence/b. Oklahoma City, 1920/
  Western swing pianist for **Bob Wills**
Cain, Cindy/b. April 5, 1959, N.M., r. Pryor/jazz
  and blues singer
Cain's Ballroom, Tulsa concert hall, 1920s –
  present, National Register of Historic Places
Caldwell, Chuck
Cale, J.J.
Caliman, Hadley/b. Idabel, 1932/
  jazz saxophonist
The Call
Call of the West/r. Strang/cowboy singers
Campbell, Debbie/b. Ft. Worth, r. Tulsa/
  rock, pop, jazz vocalist
Campbell, Royce/r. Oklahoma/
  finger picking guitarist
Canada, Cody/b. Pampa, TX, 1976/r. Yukon
  and Stillwater/ (See **Cross Canadian
  Ragweed** and **Red Dirt Music** entries)
The Candles/f. Norman, 2003/pop rock group,
  formerly The Pistol Arrows (1999-2003)
  Flato, Chance/b. July 21, 1975, Houston, TX/
    bassist (w/ The Green Owls 1996-97)
  Sarmiento, Adam/b. 4/4/1976, Rochester, NY
    drummer, songwriter (The New Tribe 1993-96)
  Sarmiento, Eric/b. 3/20/1974, Rochester, NY
    singer, guitarist, songwriter (The New Tribe 1993-96)
  Williams, Brent/b. 5/25/1976, Riverdale, GA/
    violinist, also plays with OKC Philharmonic
Candy, Stewart/r. Hammond/
  Cheyenne church song singer
The Canis/f. Tulsa/rap group
  recorded for Made Records
Canning, Jessi/r. Tulsa/sparkle pop
  based in Washington D. C. circa 2002
The Cannons
Cantrell, Jerry
Cantwell, Wayne/r. Del City/old time musician
  fiddle/dulcimer/mandolin/banjo/guitar
Card, Hank
Cargill, Henson
Cardin, Fred/b. Quapaw Reservation, I.T., 1895
  classical composer
Cardinal, Arnold "Curly"/b. 1921, Old Forge, PA –
  d. 2007, OKC/mandolin, banjo, guitar, bass –
  jazz/country, Nashville session musician
Carlton, Larry
Carman/b. Trenton, NJ, r. Tulsa/gospel singer
Carnival Groove/f. Okahoma City/rock group
Caroline's Spine
Carroll, Claudia/OCU music faculty, 2003/pianist
Carothers, Dale/r. Cushing/old time fiddler
Carrington, Rodney/b. Texas, r. Tulsa
  country singer
Carson, Jeff
Carson, Ken/b. Coalgate-Centrahoma vicinity/
  singer with Sons of the Pioneers
Carter, Dave/b. Oxnard, CA, r. Oklahoma/
  folk singer
Carter, Rose (Chuck Wagon Gang)
Carter, Roy (Chuck Wagon Gang)
Cassity, Marca/r. Oklahoma City/
  acoustic guitarist, singer, songwriter
Castle, Jeremy/b. Oklahoma City, 1974,
  r. Blanchard/country singer

Caswell, Bill/r. Oklahoma City/Bartlesville/
  country, bluegrass guitarist
Cate, Merry Kay/r. Tulsa/CCM singer
Catfish String Band/performed KFRU -1920s,
  later on KVOO/old time country group
Cats of the Thin Earth/f. Norman, OK/rock group
Cawley, Jack/r. Stillwater/
  led Oklahoma Ridge Runners
Cedar Ridge/f. Shawnee/bluegrass group
Certified Fools/f. Stillwater, 1993/blues, funk rock group
  Andrew, Brett/reared in Perkins, r. Stillwater/vocalist
  Hardy, Brad/b. Stillwater/bassist
  Headrick, Adam/b. Stillwater/guitarist
  Labow, Benji/b. Toronto, r. Stillwater/drummer
    who recorded on CD
  Presley, Jason/b. Stillwater/guitarist
  Suratt, Toby/b. Fremont, CA, r. Stillwater/
    live drummer
  Turner, Travis/r. Stillwater/drummer
Chainsaw Kittens
  glam pop rock group
  Bell, Trent/guitarist after Mark Metzger
  Bones Edward, Eric/drummer (1996)
  Harmon, Eric/drummer (1993)
  Johnson, Matt/bass guitarist (1993-1996)
  Leader, Ted/drummer (1990)
  McElhaney, Kevin/bassist (1990)
  Meade, Tyson/guitarist, vocalist, songwriter
  Metzger, Mark/lead guitarist (1990)
Chalapa, Sean/song leader
  Gar Creek Ceremonial Grounds
Chalepah, Alonzo (Apache Tribe of OK)/
  r. Anadarko/intertribal powwow head singer
Chamberlain, Sheree/b. 1996, r. OKC, 2012/
  OSU grad/winsome folk-singer, songwriter
Chanate, Jake (Kiowa)/r. Tahlequah/
  intertribal powwow head singer
Chance, Greyson
Chapman, Gary/b. Waurika, 1957/
  gospel singer
Charles, Bobby/r. Oklahoma City/soul singer
Charles, Hank/r. Broken Arrow/keyboards&guitar
  owns and operates Valcour Sound studio,
  guitarist/keyboardist for Wanda Jackson
Charles, Jeremy/r. Tulsa/music photographer,
  www.jeremycharles.com
Charm Pops/f. Oklahoma City, 1997/pop rock
Chenoweth, Kristin
Chenoweth, Vida/r. Enid/classical marimbist
Cher/b. CA, 1946/Cher's mother, Jackie Jean
  Crouch, told Jay Leno on the Tonight Show
  that Crouch left OKC for California with her
  father in 1936 when she was ten years old.
Cherokee
Cherry Blossom Clinic/f. Altus/rock group
Cherry, Don
Cherry Playground/f. OKC/modern rock band
Cheyenne/f. Norman, 2004, moved to Brooklyn, NY
  droll and contemplative Okie pop
  Fisher, Heath/drums
  Harper, Josh/guitar
  Jennings, Beau/vocals, guitar, piano
  Walker, Elliot/bass
Cheyenne-Arapaho Tribes
Chickasaw Nation
Childer, Lemuel Jennings/b. Tulsa
  composed "Pictures from Hiawatha"
Childers, Bob
Childers, Lemuel/b. Tulsa or Pawhuska/classical composer
Choctaw Nation
Chosen/f. Hugo/Southern Gospel group
  Compton, Carol/r. Broken Bow/lead vocalist, harmonies
  Grissam, Gary "Butter/r. Duncan/drummer
  Harvey, Del/r. Duncan/lead vocalist, harmonies
  Leach, B.J./b. Bartlesville/bassist
  Tims, Jerry/r. Hugo/keyboardist, vocalist
  Tims, Stacy/r. Broken Bow/harmony vocalist
Chozen/f. Tulsa/rock group
Chozen Figgaz/r. Tulsa/rap group

Christie, Chooch/Chewey Ceremonial Grounds stomp dance leader
Christian, Charlie
Chuck and Sandy/f. Tulsa/jazz duo
Chunk/f. Oklahoma City, 1995/rock group
Chute 5/f. Oklahoma City/country group
Cinematic Blue/f. Tulsa, 2001/pop rock trio
 Bartee, Brandon/bassist
 Finton, Zane/drums
 Moore, Chris/vocals, guitar
Cinocca, Joe/r. Tulsa/owner, Yawn Records
Cissel, Charles/b. Tulsa, 1948/R & B singer
Citizen Potawatomi Nation/based in Shawnee annual powwow
City Moon/f. 1988, OKC/honky-tonk, country
 Blair, Jim P./b. Odessa, TX, r. Muskogee multi-instrumentalist, vocalist
 Blair, John/b. Odessa, TX, r. Oklahoma City/fiddler
 Bonham, Virgil/b. Talihina/vocalist, guitarist, band leader
 Parret, Clifford/b. Nowata/bassist, banjo
 Wyatt, Cory/b. Norman/drummer
Claroscuro/f. OKC/Latino rock, world music
Clark, Annie/b. Tulsa, reared in Dallas/ethereal singer, poetic songwriter performs as St. Vincent
 2012 album w/David Byrne, *Love This Giant*
Clark, Bobby/b. OKC/bluegrass, Grand Ole Opry
Clark, Earl/b. Tulsa/jazz saxophonist
Clark, Jim/r. Owasso/steel guitar maker, steel guitarist
Clark, John/Drumright H.S. Grad, 1978/country singer, songwriter, also w/Hank Thompson
Clark, Lucky/r. Tulsa/Tulsa Sound vocalist and bandleader from 1958 to 1960
Clark, Millard/r. Moore/intertribal powwow singer operates Indian Sounds Records
Clark, Roy
Clark, Sanford
Clauser, Al
Clear Creek Band/f. Guymon/traditional country
Cletro, Eddie/b. Trenton, NJ, 10/28/1918 rockabilly singer, bandleader claimed OK for press purposes
Cleveland, Ingram/b. Vinita, 1908/OKclassical composer
Click, Joey/b. Altus/bassist for Trace Adkins
Clifford, K.C./b. Oklahoma City/folk singer songwriter
Clour, Deral/country boogie singer recorded for Hobart-based Hu-Se-Co label in the 1950s
Clupper, Dave/r. Jenks/spiritual alternative folk
C-Note/r. Tulsa/hip hop artist
Cobb, Bob/r. Wagoner/Western swing bassist
Coburn, Sarah
Cochran, Eddie/b. Albert Lea, MN, various family members from OKC rockabilly singer ("Summer Time Blues")
Codynah, Van/r. Oklahoma/Gourd Dance singer intertribal powwow head singer
Coe, David/r. Oklahoma/traditional fiddler
Coe, Richard/r. Oklahoma/mountain dulcimer
Coffey, Kellie
Cogan, Mary and The Sundowners/r. Tulsa/ singer, songwriter
 Bruner, Mark/guitarist
 Cogan, Mary/singer
 DeWalt, Chuck/drummer
 Eicher, Shelby/fiddler-mandolinist
 Morgan, Ron/bassist
 Sutton, Spencer/keyboardist
Cole, Darrel and the New Country Revolution f.Tulsa/country group
Coleman, Keith/b. Chickasha/fiddler w/Bob Wills
Collins, Henry/r. Oklahoma/powwow head singer
Collins Larry (The Collins Kids)
Collins, Lorrie (The Collins Kids)
Collins, Tommy

Collum, Bob/b. Tulsa/folk rock singer songwriter
Color Me Badd
Colourmusic
Colton, Graham
Colvard, Molly/b. 1989, r. Owasso/blues singer, guitarist
Comanche Nation
Come Together/f. Oklahoma City/Beatles tribute band
Common Tyme/f. Blanchard/bluegrass group
Commonwealthy/f. Tulsa, Bixby/rock group
Composition B/f. Pryor, 2001/rock group
Compston, Don/r. Tulsa/steel guitarist, Oklahoma Steel Guitar Association president
Conaway, Shane/b. Tahlequah, r. Muskogee, Edmond, Yukon guitarist with Ty England
Conklin, Roscoe/r. Oklahoma/intertribal powwow head singer
Conlon, Paula/OU professor of music, 1996-pres. American Indian music specialist, "Doc" Tate Nevaquaya biographer
Connor Raus/f. Tulsa/rock group
Conoscenti, Don/r. Oklahoma City, from Atlanta folk singer
Convertino, John
Cook, David
Cooley, Spade
Cooper, Jerry/b. Texas, r. OKC, 1970s-1990s country, gospel singer/songwriter
Cooper, Kieth/r. Tulsa, 1979-2004/tenor saxophonist with Bopcats, Debbie Campbell, KMOD's live band, et al., moved to FL, 2004
Copas, Cowboy/b. Ohio/country, singer claimed Muskogee for press purposes died in plane crash with Patsy Cline
Copenhaver, Dave/staff engineer of Studio Seven in OKC/producer, Lunacy Records
Council Oak Trio/r. Tulsa/chamber music group
Cox, Richard/r. Tulsa/cool jazz saxophonist
Coy, Vernon/b. Muskogee/country guitarist 1950s and 1960s
Cozad, Daniel (Kiowa)/r. Oklahoma/ intertribal powwow head singer
Cozad, Kenneth (Kiowa)/r. Carnegie/intertribal powwow head singer
Cozad, Larry (Kiowa)/r. Hominy/Gourd Dance & intertribal head powwow singer
Cozad, Leonard, Sr. (Kiowa)/b. Hog Creek Cozad Family Singers
Cozad, Leonard, Jr. (Kiowa)/r. Oklahoma City/ intertribal powwow head singer
Cozad, Lewis (Kiowa)/r. Oklahoma/Gourd Dance singer, intertribal powwow head singer
Cozad, Vernon (Kiowa)/r. Norman/intertribal powwow head singer
Cozad, Rusty (Kiowa)/r. Oklahoma/intertribal powwow head singer
CPH (Corporate Puppet Halitosis)/f. Tulsa/ Christian rock, pop group
Cradle/f. Mustang, 1998/rock group
Craig, Forrest, H./b. MO, r. OK four time grand champion fiddler
Crain, Samantha
Crank, M.A. "Mac"/b. Arkansas City, KS, 1948 r. Stillwater/started Stillwater Blues Festival
Criss, Marie/r. Oklahoma/ intertribal powwow singer
Critchlow, Slim/r. Oklahoma as a child/ cowboy singer
Crittenden, Melodie/b. Moore, 1969/ country singer
Croney, Merle/r. Oklahoma/band leader, multi-instrumentalist/Merle Croney Family bluegrass group:
 Croney, Danny/fiddle, guitar, mandolin player
 Croney, Frank/banjo, bass, guitar player
 Croney, Karen/bass, mandolin, fiddle, guitar player
 Croney, Mark/mandolin, guitar, fiddle player
Crook, Tommy
Crooked X
Crosby, Bill/r. Tulsa/jazz bassist

Crose, Gene/r. Tulsa/1950s rock and roll singer, guitarist, band leader, Tulsa Sound
Cross Canadian Ragweed
Crosset, Steve/b. Oklahoma City/guitarist for Glen Campbell
Crouch, Randy/b. April 1, 1952, r. Tahlequah/ fiddler, singer, guitarist, songwriter extraordinaire often intertwined with **Red Dirt Music**
Crowder, Ione Sassano/b. 6/21/1908, Tulsa - d. 5/25/2005 co-founder of Tulsa Opera, opera singer, voice teacher
Crownover, Gene/b. Cromwell, steel guitarist for Bob Wills
Crow, Alvin
Crow, Kyle/based, OKC, 2013/modern rock singer, songwriter
Crumbley, Elmer/b. Kingisher, 1908/ jazz of the territory band era
Crush Molly Sunshine/r. Moore, 1996/rock
Cruz, Edgar, Manuel, and Mark/r. OKC/ multi-genre guitarists (pop/classical/Spanish)
Cryout Reggae Band/f. Tulsa/ "reggae with a funky twist"
 Criner, Jerry/vocals, guitar
 Ewing, Beau/drums
 Heidon, Eric/bass
Cubie, Greta/b. near Stroud, 1933, OU grad multi-instrumentalist
Cummings, Boss/stomp dance leader Rocky Ford Ceremonial Grounds
Cummins, Jon/r. Tulsa/jazz bassist
Cunningham, Agnes "Sis"
Cunningham, Amanda/b. Elgin, 1978, r. OKC Red Dirt singer, songwriter
Curtis Lowe Band/f. Tulsa/rock group
Curtis Moore Band/f. Tulsa/blues-rock group
Cynderplay/f. Blackwell/CCM - rock

D

Daddy D/r. Oklahoma City/rapper
Daisy Strange/f. Tulsa/pop rock group
Dalton, Karen/b. Enid, 1937/folk singer songwriter referenced by Bob Dylan in his 2004 biography, Chronicles: Volume I
Dalton, Larry/b. Big Stone Gap, VA, 1946 – d. Tulsa, 2009/classical/sacred pianist arranger (Paula Abdul, Al Green, et al.)
Damascus Road/f. Sapulpa/Christian rock
Damn Quails/f. 2009/poetic country rock
Daniels, Jack/b. Choctaw, 1949/ guitars, vocals Highway 101
Dansby, Brad/r. Valliant/contemporary Christian
Dark, Danny (Danny Croskery)/b. Tulsa/1950s jazz and pop trumpeter, bandleader, voiceover talent
The Darlings/f. Tulsa/independent, Emo rock
David R/r. Oklahoma/singer-songwriter
Davies, Gail
Davis, Bill/r. Tulsa/blues harmonica, vocalist
Davis, Dale/born Dale Siegenthaler in Morris, 1928/1950s rock and roll singer, guitarist, Stardale Recordes
Davis, Harvey "Preacher"/r. Cushing/fiddler, vocalist
Davis, Jesse Ed
Davis, LaVonne "Sister Boogie" Faris/r. Noble/ pianist, played and sang w/Bob Wills in 1960s
Davis, Kevin/b. Walters/country singer
Davis, Michael Rees/b. Tulsa/opera tenor
Davis, Ray/r. Lawton and Ada/blues singer
Dawes, Kevin (Ottawa)/r. Baxter Springs, KS/ intertribal powwow head singer
Day by Day/f. Tulsa/hard rock group
Day One/f. Oklahoma City, 2009/alt. hip hop
 Coldstone, Lucious/flow
 Dexter, Jim/guitar, vocals
 Fox, Thomas/guitar
Dayton, Ronny/b. Tulsa/Ronny and the Daytonas

DDS/f. Tulsa/hard rock group
Dean, Ester
Debris
Deck Sachse/f. Tulsa/independent rock group
Deer, Richard (Iowa/Sac & Fox/Cheyenne)/
   r. Tulsa/intertribal powwow head singer
Deerinwater, Joe (Cherokee/Muscogee)/
   r. Tahlequah/intertribal powwow head singer
Deerpeople/f. Stillwater, 2009/
   galloping space rock, recorded two EPs
   with Trent Bell at Bell Labs in Norman
   Barnes, Brennan
   Bayhylle, Jordan
   Larrea, Alex
   Looney, Kendall
   Moore, Derek
   Shen, Julian
Defining Times/f. OKC, 2011/ambient rock
DeGeer, Jay/r. Oilton/multi-instrumentalist
DeGeer, Rae/r. Oilton/saxophonist
   w/Charlie Barnett and Johnnie Lee Wills
Delavan, Mark/b. Tulsa (ORU Graduate)/
   opera singer
Delaware, Marcella/r. Oklahoma/
   intertribal powwow singer
Delaware Nation (Western)/based near
   Anadarko, moved to I.T. in 1859/powwow
Delaware Tribe of Indians (Eastern)/based in
   Bartlesville, moved to I.T. in 1867/powwow
The Delicious Militia/1997-2005/country rock,
   Red Dirt music
   Greteman, Blaine/b. Oklahoma City, 1975/
      singer, songwriter, guitarist
   Martin, Doug/b. Clinton, IN, r. Stillwater and
      Claremore/singer, songwriter, guitarist
   McBride-Smith/r. Stillwater/guitar, vox, songs
   McCubbin, Derek/b. Stillwater, 1978/drummer
   Phillips, Brandon/r. Stillwater/keyboardist
   Phillips, Mark/r. Stillwater/bassist
   Wolfe, Aleks/r. Stillwater/bassist
   Foley, Hugh/r. Stillwater/trombone
Delladova, John/r. Tulsa/jazz drummer
Delta Rhythm Boys
The Del Toros/f. Tulsa, 2010/modern rock, pop
DeNada/f. Tulsa/reggae, jazz, R & B, soul
   Edwards, Matthew/drummer, percussionist
   Fite, Travis/vocalist, guitarist
   Hebert, Al Ray/bassist
Denim/recorded in Broken Bow/country group
Denison, Cal/b. Fairfax, 1956/gospel acoustic
   guitarist
Denizens/f. Oologah, 2002/rock group
Dennie, "Al" George/b. Arcadia, 1903/
   jazz bandleader
Dennis, James, T/OU graduate, 1951
   invented phonograph and CD changers
Dennis, Jody/r. Oklahoma/banjo player
Dennis, Levi/b. Sapulpa/country fiddler
Denver, John
Depth and Current/f. Norman, 2009
   gothic electro pop
   Hariss, Chris
   Lemke, Derek
   McKenzie, Tommy
DeRamus, Judy/r. Broken Bow/gospel singer
Derrick, Harvey/b. Pawhuska, r. Edmond/
   country, Gospel, and cowboy singer,
   songwriter, guitarist
Desi and Cody/f. Tulsa/sweet folk pop
   Clinton, Cody/guitars
   Roses, Desirae/from Portland, OR/vocals
DeVaney, Yvonne
Dewitt, Scotty/r. Yukon/steel guitar
Diamond, Marvin/b. near Red Rock, r. Pawnee
   Otoe-Missouria Native American Church
   drum carrier, singer, instrument maker
Dick, Luke/b. Cogar, OK/graduate of OCU and
   OSU with philosophy degrees/singer,
   songwriter, multi-media artist, lukedick.org
Diffie, Joe

Dillard, Ernestine
Dinning Sisters
Dinning, Mark
Dixon, Gabe/b. Guymon/singer w/Copperhead
Dizmal Failure/f. Hartshorne, 1999/rock group
DJ Dvyne/r. Emond/dance music dj, mixologist
DOG & LOC/r. Oklahoma City, 2002/rap
   (The Okla-Homiez)
Donnelly, Ted
Dosher, Kennon/r. Tipton/country singer,
   songwriter
Double Excel/r. Tulsa/R & B vocal group,
   recorded for Made records
Double Not Spyz/f. Oklahoma/disbanded folk
   music group now the Hapless Romantics
Dowd, Johnny/b. Fort Worth, TX, r. Pauls Valley/
   singer, songwriter
Down for Five/f. Tulsa/heavy metal rock group,
Downing, Big Al
Downing, Don/b. Lenapah, 1940/dance band
   singer/pianist, and brother of Big Al Downing
Dozier, Billy/r. Oklahoma/Western swing guitarist
Drake, Charly/singer, recorded for Hobart-based
   Hu-Se-Co label in the 1950s/country boogie singer
Dramacyde/f. Tulsa/shock rock group
Dreadfulwater, J.B./b. Oklahoma/Cherokee
   gospel singer, bandleader
Drew, Ray/r. Oklahoma City/blues singer
Driscoll, Phil/b. Seattle, r. Tulsa, 1961/gospel
   singer, trumpeter
Drive by Romeo/f. Tulsa/techno group
Driven/f. Tulsa/rock group
   Autry, Brandon/guitarist
   Campbell, Gary/drummer
   Montgomery, Matt/lead singer
   Nipps, Colt/bassist
Dru, Daniel/b. near Thomas, 1924/
   Cheyenne drum maker
The Drum Busters/f. Tahlequah/
   intertribal powwow singing group
DuBois, Tim
Due North/f. Oklahoma City/
   contemporary Christian duo
Duhon, Olivia/2003 TU music student/
   sings on TU jazz CD, Sophisticated Ladies
Duke, Johnny and Shootout/f. Tulsa/country
Dulcinea/f. Tulsa/acoustic duo
   Fort, Andrea/double bassist, harpist,
      percussionist
   Loman, Kasey/guitarist, vocalist
Duncan, Jake/r. Jenks/old time fiddler
   won 1st place in 2006 at Walnut Valley
   Old Time Fiddle Championship
Dunham, Jack
Dunlap, Chuck/r. Stillwater/Red Dirt Music
Dunn, Bob
Dunn, Donald/b. Sallisaw/blues guitarist
Dunn, Ronnie
Dupoint, Phil "The Fish"/r. Carnegie/
   intertribal powwow head singer, Kiowa
Durrill, John
Duvall, Brad/b. Tulsa/touring lead guitarist for
   Gus Hardin and Pake McEntire
D.W. Sides/f. Atoka/Christian rock band
Dysart, Eric/r. Disney/fiddle, piano, mandolin,
   guitar, two-time Oklahoma State Jr. Fiddle
   Champion, Branson, MO performer

E

Eagle, Wilke D., Sr. (Ponca)/r. Marland/
   intertribal powwow head singer
Earlene, Gayla/r. Tulsa/country-gospel singer
East, Lyndel/b. Oklahoma City/country singer
Eastern Shawnee Tribe/based in Seneca, MO,
   just across state line, since 1832/powwow
Eaton, Bobby/b. Tulsa/bassist for Natalie Cole
Eaves, Jimmy/b. Eaves City/rockabilly singer
Echols, Justin/b. 1980, r. Oklahoma City/jazz
   singer, pianist, OKC police officer

Edgar, Jim/r. Perry/1950s and 60s rock and roll
   vocalist, bandleader
Edwards, Jim/b. Tulsa, r. Okmulgee, 2011/
   traditional country singer who has performed
   at many local music events in Oklahoma
Edwards, Nokie
Edwards, Stoney
Egerton, Stephen
Eicher, Shelby
Eighth Day/f Oklahoma City/CCM - rock
Eisenhauer, Kathy Jean/b. Chelsea, 1979/
   country singer
Elam, Katrina
Elcombe, Arthur/r. Snow/luthier, guitarist,
   worked with the Tractors, and Janis Ian
Electric Rag Band/f. 1994, Tulsa/blues band
Element/f. Oklahoma City, 1998/loud rock
Elija's Ride/f. Tulsa/Christian hard rock group
   Brown, Matt/vocalist
   Ballinger, Aaron/drummer
   Cross, Shannon/bassist
   Williamson, Kenny/guitarist
Elling, Hank/b. Lawton, 1948/cowboy singer
Ellis, E.P. "Vep"/r. Tulsa/gospel singer
Ellis Family/f. Tulsa/Southern gospel group
Ellis, Jimmy/reared in Oklahoma/blues singer
Ellison, Scott
El Paso Hot Button/emerged, 2003, OKC/
   one-man industrial/experimental rocknoise
   (see Mickey Reece)
Enevoldsen, Adam/b. Charlottesville, VA/vocals,
   guitars w/Plastic Jack, bassist for Fried Okra Jones
Enevoldsen, Kyle/b. Ponca City/percussionist,
   drummer with Fried Okra Jones and Plastic Jack
The Engine Hearts/f. Tulsa/rock group
   Disney, Andy/drummer
   Foster, Jo/bassist
   Scott, Justin/guitarist, vocalist
   Simmons, Alex/guitarist, vocalist
England, Tyler
Enlow/f. Tulsa/Christian hardcore rock group
Enrico, Eugene/OU music faculty, 2013/
   musicologist
Enriquez, Mikaila
Entry 5/f. Oklahoma City/acoustic
   singer/ songwriter duo
Erotic Suicide/f. Oklahoma City/hard rock band
Ester Drang
Estes, Billy/r. Tulsa/drummer, father of Toni Estes
Estes, Toni
Eternal Decision/f. Oklahoma City, 1997/punk rock
Evangelicals
Evans, Falkner/b. Tulsa/jazz pianist
   based in New York City as of 2007
Even the Dogs/f. 2006, Tulsa/metalcore rock
Euchee Tribe/based in Sapulpa, moved to I.T., 1829/
   Green Corn ceremonials, stomp dance
   Euchee Christian hymns
Exit 125/f. Oklahoma City/rock group
Eye/f. Norman/rock group
Ezell, Ellis/b. Tahlequah, 1913, r. Muskogee/
   jazz saxophonist, bandleader, (see **Barney Kessel**)

F

Factor 9/f. Norman/rock group
Failsafe/f. Tulsa/hard rock group
Falcon Five-0/rock group
   Falcon, J./vocalist, guitarist
   King, Wally/guitarist
   Simon, "Sugar Stick"/drummer
Falderal String Band/f. Oklahoma City/folk group
Falkner, Jay, & the South 40 Band/f. Panama/
   classic rock, country and western group
Fallen Hero/f. Sapulpa/Christian pop group
Fanny Grace/r. Oklahoma City/gypsy soul
Fanzine/f. Tulsa/rock group
Far from Sanity/f. Tulsa/Christian hard rock
   Edens, Christian/b. St. Louis, r. Tulsa/drummer
   Goodnight, Mark/b. Kansas, r. Tulsa area/vocalist, samples

Laywell, Eddie/b. Maryland, r. Tulsa/bassist, vocalist
Melton, Jimmy/b. Tulsa/guitarist
Sanchez, Willie/b. Fredericksburg, TX, r. Tulsa/guitarist, vocalist
The Farm Couple/f. outside Stillwater, 1996/folk singers, Red Dirt Music
Taylor, Monica/r. Stillwater/singer, songwriter, guitarist
Williams, Patrick/r. Grove/singer, songwriter, guitarist
Farmer, Kelly/b. Tulsa, 1977/opera singer (Tulsa Opera)
Farrell, Gail/b. Salinas, CA (10/6/1947), r. Durant, vocalist with The Lawrence Welk Show
Farrier, Marshall/r. Tulsa/leads pop rock group
Feathers, Leo/b. Stilwell/country, rock guitarist for Jerry Lee Lewis, Tulsa Sound
Fenton, Paul "Happy"
  b. Rantoul, IL, 1900, d. Wagoner, 1975 organist, accordionist, bandleader
Ferguson, Charles, E./r. Newkirk, circa 1902/sheet music publisher, composer
Ferguson, Roy/r. Tulsa/country, Western swing singer, guitarist (Roy and Candy's Music, Tulsa)
Ferris, James/r. Oklahoma City/rock singer, songwriter
Fields, Ernie
Fields, Nokosee/reared in Stillwater/classical vocalist and violinist, bluegrass/old time fiddler, recorded with Other Lives, Deerpeople
Finley, Gail/b. 9/30/1970, OK/country singer on Grand Old Opry in 1995
Fireside Bluegrass/f. Oklahoma City/bluegrass
Fisher, Jerry/b. Oklahoma, 1943/lead singer with Blood, Sweat, and Tears
Fischer, Blake/r. OKC/pop singer, songwriter
Fisher, Shug
Fisher, Starr/r. Oklahoma/pop, jazz singer & Miss Black Oklahoma
Fisher, Steve/b. Tulsa, 1954/folk singer
Five Americans
Flaming Lips
Flash Terry
Flatland Travelers/f. Sapulpa, 2009 multi-genre college town party/jam band
  Bell, Chris/guitar, lead vocals
  Cahwee, Dylan/drums, backing vocals
  Linden, Ryan/bass, backing vocals
  Naifeh, Sam/guitar, backing vocals
Flowers, Danny/b. North Carolina/wrote "Tulsa Time," made famous by Don Williams and Eric Clapton
Flowers, Darren/r. Oklahoma City/singer-songwriter, guitarist, keyboardist
Floy, John/r. Oklahoma City/pop rock guitarist
Floyd, Heather/r. Oklahoma/CCM, singer
Flying Clouds/f. Cushing/gospel group led by Alceed Thomas, circa 1950s
Flying L Ranch Quartet/r. Oklahoma/barbershop singing group
Flynn, Mike/r. Tulsa/folk music historian
Foley, Nokose "Blue Fire"/b. Claremore, 1994/traditional blues guitar/vocals & intertribal powwow singer wtih Young Buffalo Horse
Force 4D/f. Oklahoma/metal group
Ford Brothers Band/f. Oklahoma City/R&R
Ford, Brownie/b. Oklahoma/singing cowboy
Ford, Marty/b. 8/26/1972, Tulsa/country guitarist
Forgiven/f. Ponca City/Southern gospel quartet
  Brooke, Mark/b. Ponca City/tenor vocals
  Green, Mark/b. Ponca City/lead vocals
  Johnson, Stan/b. Enid/bass vocals
For Love Not Lisa
Formerly/f. Gore and Tulsa/rock group
Forsyth, Kris/r. Oklahoma/country singer
Fortner, Rick/r. Tulsa/jazz pianist, music director of All Souls Unitarian Church

Fort Oakland Ramblers/f. Tonkawa/Southern style powwow group, recorded *When He Paints His Face* (Canyon, 1997)
  Begs-His-Own, Joe/singer
  Flores, J.R./singer
  Patterson, Don/b. near Tonkawa/lead singer
  Patterson, Henry/singer
  Robedeaux, Alde/singer
  Robedeaux, Kyle/singer
  Roy, Chief/singer
  Street, Anthony/singer
Fort Sill-Chiricahua-Warm Springs Apache/based in Apache, arrived in I.T., 1894 Known for Mountain Spirit or Fire Dance Songs, and Apache hymns
Fortune Tellers/f. OKC, circa 1981/rock group recorded for French label, New Rose Records
  Kolliopoulos, Basile/bassist
  Kolliopoulos, Miho/lead guitarist
  Newberry, Mike/drums
Foster, Billy Joe/r. Duncan/bluegrass fiddler, guitarist, toured with Bill Monroe, Ricky Skaggs, and The Whites, early booster of Joe Diffie
Foust, Steve/r. near Ripley/CCM singer, songwriter
Francis, Riley/r. Tulsa/1950s R&R singer, Tulsa Sound
Franklin, Sam/b. Clearview, 1932/R & B saxophonist
Frazier-Adams, Carleen/r. Tulsa/recorded an album of Scottish fiddle tunes
Frazier, Dallas
Freakshow/f. Tulsa/psycho rock
Frejo, Brian/r. Oklahoma City/hip hop producer
Fried Okra Jones/f. Stillwater, 1999/blues rock
  Enevoldsen, Adam/bassist
  Enevoldsen, Kyle/drummer
  Isom, "Texas" Ray/b. Ennis, TX/lead guitarist
  Watermelon Slim/b. Boston, MA/vocalist, harp player, slide guitarist
Frierson, Jewel/b. Hominy, 1946 Tulsa Booker T. Washington grad/blues, jazz, R&B singer in Chicago
Friesen, Gordon/b. Weatherford/folk singer, composer, husband of Agnes Cunningham
Frisco, Rocky (also see **Tulsa Sound**)
From Tomorrow/f. Tulsa/goth rock group
Frost, Cody/r. Afton/flat pick guitarist
Fullbright, John/b. Okemah/singer, songwriter (See **Red Dirt Music**)
Full Flava Kings/f. Tulsa/R&B, rock group
  Fary, Stanley/drummer
  Fite, Travis/guitarist
  Marrow, Rick/keyboardist
  Redd, Charlie/lead singer, bassist, also tours as background singer for Jimmie Vaughan
Full Swing/f. Tulsa/R & B group, recorded for Made Records
Fulson, Lowell
Funkhouser, Joe/b. Hobart/singer, songwriter of songs about rural Oklahoma
Furr, Ronnie/r. Oklahoma/country singer, songwriter, guitarist
Fuzz/f. Tulsa/rock group

G

Gaea Spore/f. Norman
Gagle, Dickie/r. Bartlesville/drummer for Mel McDaniel and Randy Crouch
Gaines, Steve and Cassie
Ganem, I.J.Jr. Sand Springs/singer, producer in Branson, MO
Ganem, Morgan/r. Sand Springs/rock guitarist, songwriter
Gant, Dave/b. Ada/Garth Brooks's bandleader, keyboardist, fiddler
GAP Band
Garcia, Benny, Jr.
Garcia, Edwin, Jr. "Canito"/r. Tulsa/electric, acoustic, upright double bass in jazz, Latin, and pop styles
Garcia, Lynda/b. Washington, D.C., r. Muskogee organist at Tuskegee Institute
Garcia, Opalee Randolph/b. Enid, July 7, 1907/Latin musician
The Gardes/f. Ponca City, 1993/funky folk rock
  Grover, Lance/guitars
  Horton, Brett/b. Delaware, r. Ponca City/singer, songwriter, guitarist
  Lenhart, Ricky/drummer
Gardner, Chuck/r. Tulsa/jazz pianist
Gardner, Sandy/reared in Tulsa/bassist, jazz vocalist
Gardner, Max P./b. Oklahoma City, 1932/country music publisher, broadcaster
Gardner, Sandy/b. Tulsa/jazz singer
Gaston, Lyle
Gates, David
Gawhega, Michael/r. Oklahoma/intertribal powwow head singer
Gaylord, Dave/r. Vinita/traditional fiddler
Gaylord, Monte/b. Oologah/traditional fiddler
Gears of Redemption/f. OKC/CCM - rock
Geary, Barbara/r. Tulsa/classical pianist
George, Demetra/grad. Putnam City H.S. 1970, OCU, 1974/Broadway and opera singer
George, Scott (Osage)/r. Oklahoma City/intertribal powwow head singer
Getman, Ron/b. Fairfax, 1948/multi-instrumentalist (strings) with Leonard Cohen, Steve Ripley, Tractors
Geyer, Joyce/b. Okmulgee/opera singer
Ghosts/f. 2002, Tulsa/psychedelic pop/rock
Gibbs, Vince/r. Tulsa/Prince impersonator appears in Missy Elliot's "Work It" video
Gibson, John, A. (Shawnee)/r. Claremore/songleader,Stomp Dance Blues (Indian House, 1999)
Gibson, Johnna/r. (Shawnee/Sac & Fox/Seneca-Cayuga) Claremore/shell shaker on Stomp Dance Blues (Indian House, 1999)
Gibson, Mark/r. Tulsa, 2013/singer, songwriter blue-eyed soul, groove rock
Gibson, Terri (Sac & Fox/Seneca-Cayuga)/r. Claremore/shell shaker on Stomp Dance Blues (Indian House, 1999)
Gibson, Tony/r. Claremore/stomp dance leader on Stomp Dance Blues (Indian House, 1999)
Gill, Vince
Gillette, Betty Barber/r. Tulsa/radio singer on KTUL and KVOO-AM, Tulsa in the 1940s
Gillian, Steve/r. Oklahoma/traditional fiddler
Gilliam, Les
Gilliland, Danny/b. Bartlesville, 1958/champion banjo player
Gilliland, Henry, C./ b. MO, r. Altus, OK/made some of the first fiddle recordings
Gilmore, Gary
Gilyard, James/b. Stillwater, 1945/jazz bassist
Gimble, Dick/b. Oklahoma/country bassist
Glare/f. Tulsa, disbanded 2002/rock group
Glasgow, Robert/b. Shawnee, 1925/classical organist
Glaude, Joe/b. Virginia, 1966, r. Tulsa/new age guitarist
Glazer, Jon/r. Tulsa/jazz and country keyboardist, performed with The Judds
Glenn, Eddie/r. Tahlequah/"hick hop" singer, songwriter
Glytch/f. Oklahoma City, 1997/rock group
Godsey, Glen/r. Tulsa/old time country singer
God's Unwanted Children/f. Tulsa/heavy metal rock group
Goff, Carl, Jr./b. Lexington/country songwriter
Go For Baroque/f. OKC/Baroque music group
Goff, Carl Reber "Chuck"/b. 1964, r. Noble d. 2/27/2013/bassist, songwriter, bandleader for Toby Keith for 25 years

Hugh W. Foley / 759

Gogo Plumbay/f. Tulsa/www.gogoplumbay.com psychedelic-blues-jazz-trance group,
Go With Girls/f. Tahlequah/independent rock
Goldston, Darin/b. Ada, 1967/blues guitarist with Memphis P. Tails
Good, Al
Goodfox, Arlen (Pawnee)/r. Shawnee/ intertribal powwow head singer
Gordon, Dick, Jr./r. Tulsa/guitar teacher
(Tony Romanello)
Gossell, Karen/2003 TU music student/singer Sophisticated Ladies TU CD, saxophonist
Gouge, Felix/song leader New Tulsa Ceremonial Grounds
Gouge, Thompson/stomp dance leader/ Hullabee Ceremonial Grounds/song leader
Grace, Fanny/r. Oklahoma City/country singer
Graham, Bret/r. Stroud/country singer
Graham, Jeff/b. Joplin, MO, r. Tulsa/singer, songwriter, guitarist
Graham, Phillip/b. Ada/concert pianist
Grant, Bill
Grant, Earl/b. Oklahoma City, 1933/pianist
Grant, Russell/r. Tulsa/jazz drummer
Grantham, Donald/b. Duncan, 1947/classical composer
Grantham, George
Gravity Propulsion System/f. Norman/rock
Gray, Otto
Gray, Sonny/r. Tulsa/jazz pianist, band leader, Rubiot Club owner, TU music faculty
Greenberg, Clay/b. Texas, reared in Oklahoma/folk singer, songwriter
Gray, Wardell
Great Divide
The Green Police/f. Claremore and Verdigris, 2001/ punk rock
Greenawalt, Ross/r. Tulsa circa 2002/anti-folk singer, songwriter
Greenview Circle/f. Sand Springs/pop, rock
Deleon, Carlos/bassist
Deleon, Tony/drummer
Storm, Dustin/vocalist, guitarist
Weaver, Cartwright/guitarist
Grey/r. Enid/rock and pop singer
Griffin, "Big" Mike/b. Lawton/blues guitarist singer
Griffiths, Barrick
Griffith, Lance/r. Oklahoma City/country singer, also with the Long Riders
Grogran, Phil/b. Oklahoma City/classical composer
Groner, Duke/b. 3/25/1906, Ardmore/jazz bassist, vocalist, bandleader
Groove Pilots/f. Tulsa/rock group
Growing Mylow/f. Norman/pop rock group
Guardant/f. Tulsa, 2011/electronic pop
Guthrie, Gwen/b. 7/9/1950, Okemah – d. 2/3/1999, Orange, NJ/backup singer for Aretha Franklin, Stevie Wonder, Madonna, et al. (raised in Newark, NJ)
Guthrie, Jack
Guthrie, Woody
Gut Wrench/f. Broken Arrow/heavy metal rock
Guyer, Joyce/b. Okmulgee/opera soprano
Gyles, Jimmy/r. Tahlequah/flatpick guitarist, man0dolinist

H

Habit/f. Ardmore, 2001/rock group
Hadley, John/r. Norman/country songwriter (Dixie Chicks)
Hager, Ty/r. Tulsa/country singer-songwriter
Haggard, Jerry/r. Stillwater/Red Dirt Sound, singer-songwriter
Haggard, Merle
Haley, Fred/d. 1/14/2002, OKC/organist
Half These Girls/f. Norman/rock group

Hall, Charley/r. Oklahoma City/CCM singer, guitarist
Halley, David
Halsey, Jim
Ham, Steve/r. Tulsa/trombonist with Johnnie Lee Wills, Ray Charles, Cab Calloway, Flash Terry
Hamilton, John (Kiowa)/r. Anadarko/ intertribal powwow head singer
Hammons, Thomas/b. Shawnee/opera baritone
Hampton, John/b. Coalgate/old time fiddler
Hampton, Rhonda/b. Altus/country singer
Haney, Woodrow, Sr./b. Red Mound/American Indian flutist
Hanna, Jack/r. Tulsa/jazz bassist
Hanson
Hanson, Andrea/r. Tahlequah & OKC/ Miss Oklahoma
Hanson, Eric/b. Shawnee/drummer w/ Jimmy LaFave and Mike McClure
Hanson, Halie/b. OKC/CCM, singer/songwriter
Hapless Romantics/f. Tulsa/folk music group leaning toward Red Dirt Music
Cooper, David/drummer, vocalist
Frisco, Rocky/keyboardist, Tulsa Sound
Gasaway, Wes/fiddler, mandolinist, vocalist
Skinner, Tom/bassist, vocalist
Spears, Larry/guitarist, singer, songwriter
Williams, Gene/electric guitarist
Harbingers/f. Tulsa/gospel group
Hardin, Bud/r. Calumet/country singer
Hardin, Glen/b. in Hollis, OK, (4/18/1939)/ pianist for Buddy Holly, Elvis Presley, Frank Sinatra, and others.
Hardin, Gus
Hardin, Steve
Hardy, Brad/b. Stillwater/funk, blues, jazz bassist
Harjo, Joy/b. Tulsa, 1951/Muscogee shell shaker, saxophonist, spoken-word artist, poet, singer
Harjo, Scotty/song leader Tallahassee Wvkokye Ceremonial Grounds
Harlow, Dan/r. Oklahoma/BG mandolin player
Harold, Robert/b. Tulsa, 1951/rock guitarist
Harper, Monty/b. Stillwater/children's music songwriter, singer, guitarist
Harper, Thomas/b. Oklahoma/opera tenor with Seattle Opera
Harrington-Hernandez Heather Marie r. Muskogee/classical organist
Harris, Berry/b. Chockie, 1929/blues guitarist, singer
Harris, Kent/b. Oklahoma City/leader of Boogaloo & His Gallant Crew (R & B/soul)
Harris, Rodger/b. Duncan, 1945/ old-time country and folk music
Harris, Roy
Harris, Sam
Harrison, Pete/b. Sallisaw/Western swing guitarist
Harry, Simon/Duck Creek Ceremonial Grounds/ stomp dance leader
Harry, Virgle/Duck Creek Ceremonial Grounds/ stomp dance leader
Harter, Ali
Harvest Pickers/f. Spavinaw/bluegrass group
Harvey and the Wallbangers/f. Oklahoma City/ classic rock and roll group
Hate Furnace/f. Pryor/heavy metal rock group
Hauck, Ross/b. Bartlesville/opera tenor with Wolf Trapp Opera Co.
Hay, Kata/b. Skiatook, 1987/ Yodeling Champion (2001), country singer, youtube favorite (1.8 million views), tours w/ Grassabilities
Hayes, Amber/b. Weleetka/country singer/ songwriter
Hayes, Don/b. Early Mart, CA, 1948/1970s and early 1980s country singer, father of Wade Hayes

Hayes, Chandler/b. Tulsa/singer, songwriter
Hayes, Wade
Hazlewood, Lee
Headrick, Amos/b. Van Buren, AR, r. Oklahoma/ fiddler for Bob Wills
Headroom/f. Oklahoma City/rock group
Heap-a-bird, Alfrich/b. Thomas/ Cheyenne singer
Heartland Express/f. Oklahoma/bluegrass
Hedges, Michael
Heimdale, Gregg/r. Tulsa/jazz bassist
Heitzke, Brett/r. Oklahoma City/folksinger
Helms, Mark/r. Hochatown/songwriter
Hembree, Gene/r. Tulsa/polka multi-instrumentalist
Henderson, Mary Kay/b. Muskogee/gospel singer, Cherokee Youth Choir director
Henderson, Bruce/b. Stillwater/country-rock singer, songwriter
Henderson, Mike/b. Independence, MO, 1951, r. OKC/country singer, songwriter with Kevin Welch
Hendricks, Scott
Hendricks, Ray/b. Jim Caldwell, r. Stillwater/ Louisiana Hayride performer
Hendrickson, Britni/b. Tulsa, 1987/country singer, songwriter
Henley, Jimmy/b. Sayre/banjo, w/ Roy Clark
Henry, John/r. Tulsa/blues disc jockey (KMOD-FM, Tulsa), emcee for 50s rock revival group, Bop Cats
Henry, Shane/r. Oklahoma/blues guitarist, singer
Herbst, Jim/b. Oklahoma City, 1950/country singer
Herndon, Susan/b. St. Louis, reared in Tulsa/ folk, blues, country, rock singer, songwriter, appreciated worldwide
Herron, John
Herrin Burt & The Stringers/f. Edmond/blues
Hetradox/f. Tulsa/rock group
Hicks, Benson/song leader Tallahassee Wvkokye Ceremonial Grounds
Hi-Def Howlers/f. Oklahoma City/pop, rock
High Eagle, J.C./b. Oklahoma/ Cherokee-Osage flutist
Highfill, George/b. Ft. Smith, AR, r. Stigler, OK/ country singer, songwriter, harmonica player
High Ground/f. Oklahoma City/bluegrass group
Higley, Brewster/r. Shawnee, d. 1911/wrote "Home on the Range"
Hill, Buffalo/song leader Peach Ceremonial Grounds
Hill, Charlie/r. Tulsa, circa 2012/guitarist, instrumental recording artist, charliehillguitar.com
Hill, Jack/song leader Peach Ceremonial Grounds
Hill-Chief, Roman/song leader Peach Ceremonial Grounds
Hill, Sonny/r. Tulsa, 1950s/blues harmonica
Hill, Steve/b. Tulsa keyboardist and bassist for Bloodrock
Hills of Home/f. Oklahoma/bluegrass group
Hinder
Hinex, Suzi/r. Cushing/CCM singer, songwriter, released CD, Welcome Here, in 2005
Hinton, Sam
HNNC/f. Oklahoma City/rap group
Hobbs, Becky
Hockensmith, Hadley
Hoffman, Billy/r. Poteau/country singer, songwriter
Hoffman Brothers/f. Muskogee/rock group
Hoffman, Kirby/b. Tulsa, 1954/CCM musician, educator
Hoke, Jim/b. Oklahoma City/ woodwinds for Kenny Loggins
Holder, Brandon/r. Tulsa/drummer w/Leon Russell

Holder, Terrence "T"/b. Texas, r. Muskogee/ territory jazz band leader
Holladay, Marvin "Doc"/studied at Phillips University, Enid/baritone saxophonist
Hollis/f. Tulsa/independent rock group
Holly, Doyle
Holmberg, Frederick
first director of Oklahoma City Symphony
Holt, Culley/b. McAlester, 1925/ singer with the Jordonaires
The Homesteaders/gospel group/
  Brandt, James/r. Okemah/singer
  Chesser, Lisa/r. Konawa/singer
  Richardson, Wayne/r. Henryetta/singer
  Williamson, Donnie/r. Weleetka/singer
Honeywagon/f. Edmond/rock group
Hooten, David/r. Oklahoma City/trumpeter, CCM artist, recognized for rendition of "Amazing Grace"
Hopkins, Bubba/b. Spavinaw/traditional fiddler
Hopkins, David "Hoppy"/r. Tulsa/guitarist with the Swamptones, also played w/ Larry Bell, Jim Dowing, and Bill Davis
Horse Thief/f. OKC, 2012/psychedelic rock
  Neal, Cameron/lead vocals
  Coleman, Alex/guitar
  Fowler, Cody/bass
  Roubert, Alberto/drums
  Zeller, Zach/keyboards
Hosty Duo
  Hosty, Mike
  Byars, Mike
HotrodboB/f. Claremore, 2002/rockabilly, punk,
  Layton, Bo/drummer
  Layton, Clay/guitarist, vocalist
  Pitts, Jay/bassist, vocalist
House, Don/r. Thomas/guitarist for Bob Wills, leader of Thomas Country Opry Band, a.k.a. The House Band
Howard, Eddie/Oklahoma Opry house band drummer
Howlin' 88/f. Norman/blues band
Hubbard, Ray Wylie
Huckaby, Ed/NEOSU-Broken Arrow music professor/trumpeter, contemporary classical composer
Hudson, Richard/b. Seminole, reared Konawa/ gospel finger style guitarist
Hudson Roar/f, Oklahoma, circa 2012 melancholy dream pop played by 1 girl w/ 1 machine
Huff, Cowboy Charlie
Huffer, Jerry/r. Muskogee/music educator
Hughes, Frank Clayton/b. Ada, 1915 classical composer
Hughes, Billy
Hughes, Jack/r. Stratford, OK/ country bassist, songwriter
Hunt, William/b. SE Oklahoma/ folk music preserver and performer
Hurricane, Jane/f. Oklahoma City/pop rock
Hurricane Mason/f. Tulsa/blues-rock group
  Flint, Kevin/bassist
  Mason, Matt/guitarist, vocalist
  Montgomery, Shawn/drummer
Hurte, Leroy/b. Muskogee/1940s R & B record company entrepreneur, notably with Bronze Records in Los Angeles
Hutchison, "Uncle" Dick/b. Disney/old time country fiddler

I

Idabel/f. OKC/atmospheric folk, Americana
  Coppinger, Andy
  Khodabakhsh, Michael
  Godsey, Taylor
The Ills/f. Norman/progressive jazz group
  Ahmadi, Kasra George/saxophonist
  Jones, Ryan/keyboardist
  Littell, Boyd/drummer
  Nelson, Blaine/guitarist

Infamus/f. Tulsa/rock group
Ingersoll, Clint/r. Pryor/Locust Grove/singer, songwriter (songs recorded by Chris Ledoux & John Michael Montgomery)
Insect Lounge/f. Norman/rock group
Insult to Injury/f. Oklahoma/hardcore punk rock
Iowa Tribe of Oklahoma
Ira/f. Tulsa/pop rock group
Isco-say/r. Muskogee, Tulsa/rapper
Ivy Mike/f. Norman/rock group
Ivy, Thomas/r. Altus/bluegrass banjoist

J

Jabee/r. OKC, 2013/hip hop, underground soul
Jack, Karen & Lucy/f. Skiatook/Americana, roots
Jackson, Wanda
Jacob Fred Jazz Odyssey
Jacobs, Greg/b. Choctaw/singer, songwriter, **Red Dirt Music**
Jacobson, Garrett "Big G"/b. OKC,1983/blues guitarist and singer
Jae, Jana
Jahruba/r. Norman/African percussionist
Jakober, Andrew/b. Tulsa, 1986/indie folk/pop singer, songwriter (A. Jakober)
Jambalaya Jass Band/f. Sapulpa/ traditional Dixieland jazz group
  Bennett, Mike/trumpeter
  Chitton, Mike/banjoist
  Crosby, Bill/bassist
  Ham, Steve/trombonist
  Yohe, Tony/drummer
James, Brett
James, George/b. Beggs, 1906/jazz woodwinds, bandleader
James, Jana/r. Enid/CCM and Celtic singer
James, Jenny/r. Oklahoma/ intertribal powwow singer
James, Patricia/r. Oklahoma/ intertribal powwow singer
The James Ray/f. Stillwater, 1995/rock group
  Anderson, Steve/bassist
  Bello, John/guitarist
  Lichtenberger, James/guitarist
  Unruh, Tod/drummer
  Young, Bill/vocalist
James, Tom/b. Oklahoma/country singer, songwriter for Flatt and Scruggs, Rex Allen, started Klix Records in 1957
Jantzen, Riley/r. Enid/acoustic indie folk singer/ songwriter
Jarvis/r. Tulsa, OK/R&B singer, recorded "Pretty Girls" for Ludacris' DTP Records,
  collaborated with Lil Scrappy and Waka Flocka
Jazzcow/f. Tulsa, 2001/jazz jam band
  Andrews, Airrion/bassist
  Combs, Chris/guitarist
  Loomis, Mike/drummer
  Staub, Michael/saxophonist
Jefferson, Harold/b. 1948, Pontiac, MI, moved to OKC, 1957/guitarist for Etta James, Wilson Pickett, Joe Tex, Sam and Dave, et al.
Jeffrey, Robert/b. Tulsa, 1915/blues pianist, guitarist, vocalist
Jenkins, Brandon/b. Tulsa, 1969/singer, songwriter, Red Dirt Music, OSU graduate
Jennings, Beau/reared, OK, resided Brooklyn, NY country, roots rock, guitarist, singer/songwriter leads Beau Jennings and the Tigers
Jennings, Christina/r. Oklahoma/classical flutist/ Julliard graduate
Jernigan, Dennis
Jesse D/f. Tulsa/classic rock, hard rock, pop
  De La O, Jesse/vocalist, guitarist, bassist, keyboardist
Jewett, Bryan/r. Tulsa/techno folk musician
Jify Trip/f. Tulsa, 1995/rock group
Jimijank/f. Norman/rock group

J-Mal/r. Oklahoma City/hip hop producer, Loud Noyz Productions, 2007
Joe and Ellen Felzke/f. Tulsa/brother and sister jazz, folk duo
Johnny Reliable/f. Tulsa/1950s-style, contemporary rock group
Johns, Val/b. Shattuck/pianist
Johns, William
Johnson, Cecil and Herman
Johnson, Christopher/b. Tulsa/classical pipe organist for New York City's Riverside Church as of 2003
Johnson, Greg/b. Oklahoma/owner of the Blue Door, a long-time (and the best) intimate singer/songwriter venue in OKC
Johnson, Jeff/r. Oklahoma City/jazz bassist
Johnson, Larry/b. Oklahoma City/R & B vocalist, guitarist
Johnson, Lemuel/b. Oklahoma City, 1909/jazz woodwinds, bandleader, vocals, Blue Devils
Johnson, Lewis/enrolled member of the Seminole Nation of OK/American Indian flutist
Johnson, Michael/r. Jones/acoustic guitar
Johnson, Seminem/song leader Nuyaka Ceremonial Grounds
Johnston, Janet/b. Muskogee, 4/28/1937 children's Christian music writer
Jones, Anthony Armstrong/b. Ada, 1949, d. 1996/ Top 40 covers singer
Jones, Charles and the Starduster s f. Oklahoma, 1950s/rock and roll recorded for Sully Records
Jones, Claude/b. Boley, 1901/jazz trombonist
Jones, Denise/b. Norman/gospel singer with (see **Point of Grace**)
Jones, Dustin/Oklahoma Opry house band guitarist, sound engineer
Jones, Norah
Jones, Shawn/b. Lawton, OCU graduate/ singer, songwriter
Jones, Stacey/b.Tulsa/singer for rock group American Hi-Fi
Joose/f. Oklahoma/urban-dance group
Joplin, Scott/ragtime pianist, composer performed his opera A Guest of Honor in Oklahoma City in 1903
Josephson, Kim/b. Ohio, r. Tulsa/opera singer
Jude and Jody/f. OKC, 1950s and 1960s/ country duo, Jude Northcutt and Jody Taylor
Just for U/f. Tulsa/CCM

K

Karma Syndicate/f. Tulsa/jazz with spoken word
Karstein, Jimmy/b. Tulsa, 1943
Katz, Robert, S./r. Tulsa/educator classical double bassist
Kaw (Kanza) Nation of Oklahoma/ based in Kaw City since 1902/powwow/ straight dance songs
Kay, Billy/r. Oklahoma/flatpick guitar player
Kayka Momma/r. Tulsa/rapper
Kearney, Jason/r. Tulsa/folk music singer, guitarist
Keeton, Scott/r. Del City/blues guitarist, singer
Keith, Jeff/b. Texarkana, r. Idabel/rock singer
Keith, Krystal/r. Norman/country singer,songwriter
Keith, Toby
Kelley, Pat/r. Tulsa/jazz guitarist, Tulsa Will Rogers H.S. and Tulsa University graduate
Kelly, Jamie/b. Ada/bassist, guitarist, vocalist for Linville Band
Kelly, Lori Lee/b. Clinton/singer, Miss Oklahoma
Kelly, Mark/b. 6/28/1956, Enid/bassist for Christian rock group Petra from 1981 through 1987;recorded seven albums before retiring
Kelly, Sean/b. Tulsa, 1960/Americana singer, songwriter, drummer with Slapout owner/operator of 1600-AM, KUSH Radio

Kelly, Walter/b. Stillwater/guitarist, educator Berklee School of Music and UCO graduate
Keltner, Jim/b. Claremore, 1942/drummer
Kemble, John (**Ponca**)/r. OKC intertribal powwow head singer
Kemble, Kirby/r. Oklahoma/ intertribal powwow head singer
Kemp, Julia/r. Oklahoma/opera soprano
Kemp, Wayne
Kenner, Clarence/b. Oklahoma/jazz trumpeter
Kentucky Blue/f. Tulsa/bluegrass group
Kern, Michael/r. Lawton/guitarist
Kersting, Kathleen/b. Enid/opera singer
Kessel, Barney
Ketchum, Benny/r. Tulsa/country bandleader, singer
Kettle of Fish/f. Tulsa, 1999/pop rock group
The Kevorkians/f. Tulsa/rock group
KGB/f. Oklahoma City/rock group
Kickapoo Tribe of Oklahoma/based in McLoud area since 1839/traditional music, socialpowwows
Kidd, Travis/"hometown" Tulsa/Americana, alt-country, blues, singer, songwriter, guitarist, occasionally connected to **Red Dirt** music
Kihega, Michael/r. Oklahoma intertribal powwow head singer
Kilgore, Ben/r. Tulsa/acoustic guitarist, singer, songwriter
Kilgore, Merle
Kilpatrick, Jack F./b. Stilwell/classical composer
Kimera/f. Tulsa/rock group
King, Aaron Harvey/b. Paris, TX, 1954/OKC blues guitarist has woked with KoKo Taylor, Z.Z. Hill, Little Johnny Taylor, et al.
King, Bug/r. Oklahoma City, OC Douglas graduate/R & B vocalist
King James Verzion/f. Stillwater/rock group
King, Kathy Weinstock/r. Tulsa/educator, classical cellist
Kings of Leon
Kinky Slinky/f. Oklahoma City/dread rock
Kiowa Tribe of Oklahoma
Kirk, Jean/r. Cushing/Gospel songwriter
Kirkpatrick, Albert J./b. Oklahoma City/classical composer
Kiser, Bob/r. Tulsa/guitarist for John T. Wills
Kishketon, Rowe (Kickapoo/Sac & Fox)/ r. Shawnee/intertribal powwow head singer
Kizer, Glen/r. Okemah/Broadway musicals
Kleefeld, Daniel/r. Tulsa/CCM, jazz, classical multi-instrumentalist
Klipspringer/f. Norman, 1994/"one guy hits things, one guy keys things, two guys strum things, everyone yells", off their rocker group
Klondike 5 String Band/f. Tulsa/bluegrass and traditional American roots music
Francen, Eric/b. Louisville, KY, r. Tulsa/banjo
Gifford, Josh/harmonica, washboard
El Gaucho Loco/bass fiddle
Skelton, Carmen/b. Houston, r. Tulsa/fiddle
Skelton, Matt/b. Tulsa/rhythm guitar, vocals
Knape, Skip/r. Turley/organist for Bob Seger
Knie, Roberta/r. Cordell/opera singer
Knight, Justin/b. Tulsa/New Age, contemporary Christian pianist, composer, recording artist
Knifechief, John (Pawnee)/r. Pawnee/intertribal powwow head singer
Knifechief, Steve (Pawnee)/r. Pawnee/intertribal powwow head singer
Knifechief, Tom (Pawnee)/r. Pawnee/ intertribal powwow head singer
Koenig, Willie/r. Oklahoma City/Latin percussionist
Koomsa, Bill, Jr. (Kiowa)/ intertribal powwow head singer
Kotay, Ralph/r. Oklahoma/ intertribal powwow head singer
Kottke, Leo/b. Athens, GA, r. Muskogee/ multi-genre guitarist
Kubiak, Benny/r. Oklahoma/old time fiddler

Kubik, Gail
Kuehn, Bill/r. Oklahoma/percussionist
Kuney, Amy/b. Tulsa/singer-songwriter based in Los Angeles, released first CD in 2006

L

Labow, Jenny/b. Canada, Stillwater HS grad, 1991/ pop, rock singer, songwriter, and guitarist
LaCroix, Ryan/b. OKC, 1979, r. Yukon/ Oklahoma music journalist/writer, operator of www.oklahomarock.com
Lacy, Robin H./b. McAlester/country singer, songwriter, drummer for Johnny Paycheck and Merle Haggard
Lacy, Rudy/b. McAlester, r. Stillwater/CCM country singer, songwriter
LaFave, Jimmy
Lafort 3/f. Bartlesville/heavy metal group
Lakes, Gary/b. Woodward, 1914/opera tenor
Lambert, Miranda
Lamond, Don
Lancaster, Sound/f. Oklahoma City/modern rock group
  Alsip, Marshall/drummer
  Gulley, Chad/guitarist, keyboardist, vocalist
  Mills, Jennifer/cellist, keyboardist, vocalist
  Rosenhamer, Steve/bassist
  Stanley, Adam/guitarist, keyboardist, vocalist
Lang, Kelly/b. Oklahoma City, 1967/country singer
Lang, Terry/r. Oklahoma/gospel singer with **Point of Grace**
LaRue, Stoney/(see **Red Dirt Music**)
Larkin/f. Tulsa/Irish music group
  Lawrence, David/whistle
  Malone, Chad/lead singer
  Modglin, Aaron/guitarist
  Naifeh, Karen/violinist
  Tuttle, Kelly/bassist
  Walker, Johnnie/drummer
LaRue, Stoney and the Organic Boogie Band/f. Stillwater/(see **Red Dirt Music**)
Lasso/f. Norman/rock group
Last Exit/f. Tulsa/rock group
Laurence, Dave/r. Oklahoma City/folk singer and songwriter
Lay, Rodney
Leadingfox, Randal/r. Oklahoma/ intertribal powwow head singer
Ledford, Brian/"son of Oklahoma concrete finishers and oilmen", r. Seattle, WA, 2011/ Alt-country-Americana singer/songwriter
Lee, Brian/r. Tulsa/pianist
Leeper, Jane and Jean/known as "Oklahoma Sweethearts"/recorded for Capitol records
Leftwich, Brad/b. Stillwater/old time and bluegrass fiddler, Oklahoma Opry manager
Lehman, Lavern/b. Tahlequah, 1944/bass guitarist with Pat Benatar, Joe Cocker, Eric Burdon, Mitch Mitchell
Lehman, Tom/r. Tahlequah/ jazz educator (NEOSU), trombonist
The Leveling/f. Tulsa/modern rock group
Leverette, Ken/r. Tulsa/jazz drummer
Levine, Joel/r. Oklahoma City for 27 years/ director, OKC Philharmonic
Levy, Marcy/r. Oklahoma/vocalist for Bob Seger and Eric Clapton
Lewis, Curly/b. Stigler/fiddler for Johnnie Lee Wills and Hank Thompson
Lewis, Ed
Lewis, Sheila/b. Broken Bow/gospel singer
Lewis, William/b. Tulsa, 1935/opera tenor
Liddell/f. Tulsa/soft rock group
The Lids/f. Norman/rock group
Lieb, Kensil or Kinsel/r. Ponca City/ intertribal powwow head singer
Liggins, Jimmy and Joe
Lightfoot, Jason/r. Oklahoma/ intertribal powwow headsinger

Lincoln, Robert/b. Lawton/ intertribal group Young Buffalo Horse
Lindsay, Merl/b. Oklahoma City/country and rockabilly singer, bandleader, recorded for Hu-Se-Co
Lindsey Ryan
Linville, Travis/b. Chickasha/lead singer for Travis Linville and the Burtschi Brothers multi-instrumentalist (see **Red Dirt Music**)
Litefoot/r. Tulsa, attended Tulsa University/ actor, rapper on Red Vinyl Records
Lithium/f. Owasso/rock group
Littleaxe, Dennis (Shawnee)/r. Oklahoma/ intertribal powwow singer
Littleaxe, Troy, Sr. (Shawnee)/r. Bartlesville/ intertribal powwow head singer, stomp dance leader
Littlebear, Newman/Kelleyville Ceremonial Grounds/stomp dance leader
Littlecreek, Wiley (Shawnee)/r. Oklahoma/ intertribal powwow head singer
Littlecook, Oliver (Ponca)/b. Ponca City/ intertribal powwow singer, Native American Church singer
Little League Hero/f. Oklahoma, 1999/pop rock group
Little Man, Creg/r. Thomas/ intertribal powwow head singer
Little Texas
Little Thunder/r. Tahlequah/ intertribal powwow singing group
Lloyd, Larry/r. Collinsville/steel guitarist played on Grand Ole Opry and with Roy Clark
Lobb, Betty Lou/b. Bennington/Big D Jamboree vocalist
Local Hero/f. Tulsa/reggae group
  Bee/drummer
  Cheryl/saxophonist
  Campbell, Kelly/guitarist
  James, Doc/bassist
  Perry, Deborah/keyboardist
  Santanna/percussionist
  U.E./saxophonist
Logan, Charles/r. Oklahoma/ intertribal powwow head singer
Logan, Gene/r. Oklahoma/ intertribal powwow head singer
Logan, Stacey/OCU grad/Broadway performer and singer
Logsdon, Guy
Loman, Michael (Choctaw)/r. Tulsa/ American Indian flutist
Lon, Dave/r. Oklahoma/singer, songwriter, Red Dirt Music
Long, Fiddlin' Sam/r. Oklahoma/old time fiddler
Longhorn, Colleen (Shawnee/Sac & Fox/ Seneca-Cayuga)/r. Oklahoma/shell shaker on Stomp Dance Blues (Indian House, 1999)
Loose Shoes/r. Oklahoma City/roots music group
Los Reactors
Love, Clarence
Love, Rusti/r. Glenpool/jazz and country rock singer
Loving, Thesa/reared in Tulsa, resided in Tahlequah/cabaret, jazz singer in New York City, former Tulsa Union drama teacher
Low Water Crossing/f. Bowlegs/bluegrass
Lower 40/f. Oklahoma, 2011/pop country
Loyal Opposition/f. Stillwater, 1985/pop rock
Luber, Willie/r. Okarche and Oklahoma City, 1970s/country steel player
Luchsinger, Susie (see Susie McEntire)
Luker, Jack/r. Oklahoma City/old time fiddler and fiddle judge
Lunceford, Jimmy
Lunsford, Mike/b. Guymon, 1950/country singer and songwriter
Lure/f. Oklahoma City, 1999/rock group
Lushanya, Tessie Mobley/b. near Ardmore/ Chickasaw opera singer known as "Songbird of the Chickasaws" in the 1930s and 1940s

Lyons, Malyne "Poochie Love"/b. Stillwater/ Kansas City blues diva, backup singer for Heatwave, featured in Jet magazine
Lyons, Robert/r. Lawton/steel beach picnic entertainer (guitars and vocals) aboard USS Kitty Hawk, 2003

M

Mabrey, "Shy" Willie/b. Webbers Falls, 1942/ blues singer
Mack, Joe/reared in Lawton, r. Tahlequah, 2012/ folksinger, bouncy guitar player, music writer for Currentland magazine.
Madden, Doyle/recorded for Hobart-based Hu-Se-Co label in the 1950s/country singer
Mad Verb/f. Tulsa, 1999, disbanded melodic hard rock
Mae, Audra/b. 2/20/1984, OKC; graduated Putnam City High School/folk singer, songwriter, wrote "Why I Was Born to Die" for Susan Boyle
Maggi, Tanya/r. Tulsa/educator, classical viola
Magruder Everett, Kyle/b. St. Joseph, MO, r. Oklahoma City/country singer, songwriter, recorded with Jason Boland
Maguire, Beth/b. Texas, reared in Tulsa/country singer
Majnun/f. Tulsa/rock group
Malave, Alvaro "Ted"/b. Stillwater, 1960/ classical and Spanish guitar
Maloy, Paul/b. Allen/songwriter, co-wrote "Someone Walkin' Around Upstairs," recorded by George Strait
Maloy, Zac (also see The Nixons)
Manifest Destiny/f. Stillwater, 1989/heavy metal
Allensworth, Trey/b. Stillwater/drummer, vocalist
Big John/b. Enid/bassist and vocalist
Filonow, John/b. Lansing, MI. r. Stillwater/ lead guitarist
Hock, Matt/b. Temple, TX, r. Stillwater/lead vocalist
Moffat, Jake/b. Stillwater/rhythm guitarist and vocalist
Mannafest/f. Tulsa/Christian rock group
Manning, Kim
Marble Phrog/f. Tulsa, circa 1968/psychedelic and garage rock group
Marcotte, Joseph B./b. near Purcell, 1913/ cowboy singer and instrumentalist on KFXR, Oklahoma City, in 1933
Mariachi Orgullo/f. Norman/mariachi music
Mariachi Tulsa/f. Tulsa/mariachi music
Markham, Jimmy "Jr."
Markley, Bob/b. Oklahoma/vocalist and songwriter for The West Coast Pop Art Experimental Band
Marquis, Aldee/b. Tulsa/classical violinist
Marsh, Sharon/b. Broken Bow/gospel singer
Marshallcity/f. Tulsa, 2000 – disbanded 2003/ rock group
Cayton, Jeff/b. California/drummer
Cook, Colby/b. Joplin, MO, 1973, r. Broken Arrow, 1975\ bassist
Parsons, Jody/b. Mustang, 1976/vocalist, guitarist, mandolinist
Zoellner, Philip/b. Tulsa/vocalist, guitarist (moved to New York City in 2003)
Martin, Dusty/b. Sallisaw, 1938/country singer for Texas Rose Records
Martini Kings/f. Norman/rock and swing combo
Martin, Moon
Martin, Rudi/r. Enid/Western swing clarinetist
Martinez, Thomas and Wild Frontier/f. Tulsa/ country group
Marvin, Frankie and Johnny
Marvin, Rex/b. California, 1947, reared in OK UCO vocal student/country singer
Mashunkashey, Russell/r. Oklahoma intertribal powwow head singer
Mason/f. Tulsa, 1970s/hard rock group
Mason, Ashley/2003 TU music student/ sings on TU jazz CD, Sophisticated Ladies

The Masopust Polka Band/f. Oklahoma just like the name says, a polka group
Mass Reality/f. Tulsa, 1992/CCM
Masters, Denise/b. Norman/CCM, gospel singer Point of Grace
Masters, Sammy/b. Sasakawa, 1930 rockabilly guitarist and singer
Mathews, Berta Leah/b. August 10, 1925, McAlester/ jazz singer soloist at Café Society, New York, 1950, toured with Woody Herman (1954-55)
Mathews, Tony
Mathis, Reed
Mattingly, Paul/b. Sand Springs, 1921/steel guitarist
Matlock, Jarrid/r. Oklahoma City, b. 1974/country singer
Matlock, W.N./r. Cleveland/gospel singer
Mauser, Corey/b. Phoenix, AZ, 1968, moved to Tulsa, 1971/pianist and organist
Maxwell, Bill/b. OKC/drummer, composer
Mayday Malone/f. Oklahoma City/punk rock
Mayo, O.W./b. Texas, r. Oklahoma/Bob Wills' manager
Mayola/f. Stillwater, circa 2006/experimental rock, released independent EP, Everybody, and full-length CD, Money/War.
McAlister, Barbara
McAuliffe, Leon
McCann, Terry/r. Oklahoma City/blues flutist
McBee, Cecil
McBride, Laura Lee
McClarty, Matthew/r. Ada/gospel group leader
McClellan, Billy E., Sr./b. Arkansas City, KS, 1954, r. Agra/Native American Church singer
McClure, Mike
McClurg, Mark/b. Claremore/fiddler for Alan Jackson, formed duet with Wade Hayes, McHayes, 2002
McCollum, Jeffrey/r. Oklahoma/ baritone with Indianapolis Opera
McCombs, Cody/r. Tulsa/blues singer, guitarist
McDaniel, Mel
McReynolds, Samuel/b. Oklahoma City/ composer, cellist w/ Oklahoma City Symphony
McDonald, "Rusty"/b. Myrl Edwards, Norge/ Western swing, rockabilly, country boogie singer
McDonald, Tomy/r. Tulsa/rock guitarist
McEntire, Pake
McEntire, Reba
McEntire, Susie
McFarland, T.J./r. Tulsa/cosmic country singer, songwriter
McGhee, Howard
McGhee, Paul/b. Tulsa/drummer w/ Texas Playboys
McGinty, Billy/b. MO, parents made land run of 1889/cowboy band leader, (see **Otto Gray**)
McGraw, Clarence/r. Oklahoma/old time fiddler
Mcgrew, Shane/b. Enid/singer, songwriter, fiddler, rhythm guitaris, solo and w/ Fishin' Naked, Hippie the Cowboy)
McCrey, Gary/b. Shawnee/country singer, songwriter
McGuire, Barry
McIntosh, John/r. Oklahoma intertribal powwow head singer
McKinney, Elizabeth/r. Oklahoma/ soprano with Santa Fe Chorale
McKinnon, Russ
McLinn, Steve/r. Oklahoma City/electro-acoustic world fusion multi-instrumentalist
McNulty, Larry/r. Tulsa/bassist
McPherson, J.D.
McQuarters, R.W./b. Tulsa/rapper and founder of Franchise Records, pro football player
McReynolds, Samuel/b. Oklahoma City/classical composer and cellist
McShann, Jay
Meade, Tyson Todd
Meadows, Jason/b. June 9, 1971, r. Calera/ country singer finalist on Nashville Star, 2005 released 100% Cowboy (Baccerstick, 2007)

Meandering Orange/f. Tahlequah/ Okie-delic groove rock
Meant2B/f. 2001, Edmond, UCO/R&B/hip-hop vocal group
Meazell, Tiger/r. Oklahoma City/jazz alto saxophonist, Selmer artist/clinician
Mecom, Billy/r. Tulsa/1950s country singer with Billy Mecom and the Country Cousins
Medicine Show (See Red Dirt Music)
Mediocre Music Makers/f. Erick, 1999/country, bluegrass duo
Russell, Annabelle/guitar, vocals
Russell, Harley/guitar, vocals
MEDU-NETR/comprised of 3 Tulsa rap groups/ Somatic Souls, HORSEMAN, Black Cosmic Posse
Meehan, Dennis, a.k.a. Clovis Roblaine/b. Oklahoma/bassist with Ray Wylie Hubbard,
Melatonin/f. Tulsa/loud rock group
Mendia, Francis/r. Oaks/ intertribal powwow head singer
Men of Made/f. Bixby/R & B and hip hop artists
Mercury 1/f. Weatherford/rock group
Mericle, Don/r. Wagoner/music educator
Meridian/f. Tulsa/pop rock group
Brown, Gary/drummer
Gaylor, Dennis/acoustic guitarist, vocalist, keyboardist
Hoy, Bill/vocalist, percussionist
Jarret, Tim/electric guitar
Mayeux, Ed/bassist
Merrick, Joe/b. Oklahoma City/country songwriteriner
Merritt, Chris
Meyer, Carolyn/b. Nowata, 1952, r. Stillwater children's music composer, singer (Giant Blueberry Music)
Meyer, Edgar
Mezclave Latin Jazz Ensemble/f. Tulsa/
Michaels, Gus/r. Stillwater/singer, songwriter
Miami Nation/based in Miami moved to I.T. in 1873/stomp dances, powwow
Microlight/f. Oklahoma City, 1996/rock group
Midwest Kings/f. Tulsa/rock group released first CD in 2003
Briggs, Justin/bassist
Skibb, Andy/vocalist
Tiemann, Neal/guitarist, lyricist
Mikaila
Milke/f. Tulsa/singer, songwriter
Miller, George/b. Tulsa, 1964/African percussionist
Miller, Jody
Miller, Roger
Miller, Lula Mae/b. Rentiesville/gospel singer
Milner, Chuck/b. Cheyenne/country songwriter
Millsap, Parker/r. OK/growling (but melodic) folk singer in duo with Michael Rose
Milton, Roy
The Mimsies/f. Norman/glam rock band
Minner, DC & Selby
Minutes Too Far/f. Oklahoma City/rock group
Missing Link Band/f. Claremore/blues band
Mistress X/f. Tulsa/rock band
Mitchell, Glen/recorded in Tulsa/organist with Steve Ripley and The Tractors
Mitchell, Leona
Mizelle, Dary John/b. Stillwater, 1940/classical composer
Mobley, Tessie/b. Ardmore, 1906 - d.1964, Ft. Worth, TX/operatic soprano who performed in Chicago and Italy, a.k.a. "Songbird of the Chickasaws"
Mockingbird Lane/f. Shawnee/rock group
Blizzard/drummer, background vocalist
Christophe/lead vocalist, guitarist
Elecktra/bassist, background vocalist
Model 2551/f. Oklahoma City/rock group

Hugh W. Foley / 763

Modern Rock Diaries/emerged OKC, 2008
Indy rock, classically trained
Allen, Angela/multi-instrumentalist, vocals
Allen, John/multi-instrumentalist, vocals
Cowan, Brantley/guitar, vocals
Trench, Clinton/bass, vocals
recorded EP at Blackwatch Studios w/ Jarod Evans
Modoc Tribe/based in Miami,
moved to I.T. in 1873
stomp dance, powwow
Moeller, Lucky
Moffat, Jake/r. Stillwater/singer, songwriter
Moguin, Sharon/r. Tulsa/jazz, blues, standards vocalist
Molly's Yes/f. Tulsa, 1998/rock group on Republic/Universal Records
Goggin, Ed/r. Tulsa/vocalist, keyboardist
Mitcho, Brad/bassist, vocalist, programming
Ross, Mac/guitarist, vocalist
Taylor, Scott/drummer
Mondaine, Jermaine/b. Muskogee, 1973/jazz, Gospel, R&B saxophonist
Monossey, Elrod/r. Oklahoma/intertribal powwow head singer
Monossey, Spencer Ray/r. Oklahoma/intertribal powwow head singer
Montgomery, Melissa/r. Choctaw/country singer
Montgomery, Merle/b. Davidson, 1904/classical composer
Montgomery, Randy/b. 1951, OKC/folk-singer, songwriter
Mont Lyons/f. OKC/progressive indy rock
Crews, Brandon/ vocals, guitar
Freudenberger, Kurt/drums
Oliver, Bryan/vocals, keyboards
Trevor Smith/bass
Moody, Harley/b. Altus, resided Olustee/country, bluegrass, Gospel singer/songwriter, and Steel Beach Picnic performer
Mooney, Ralph
Moore, Curtis/blues guitarist/(**See Osage Nation**)
Moore, David, A./r. Tulsa/educator, music composition
Moore, Gary Lee/b. Oklahoma, 1950, r. Seattle/Pacific Northwest old time fiddler
Moore, Marilyn
Moore, Melvin/b. Oklahoma City, 1917/jazz singer
Moore, Pat/b. Tulsa, 1948/gospel singer, pianist
Moran, David/r. Oklahoma/hammer dulcimer
Moran, Pat/b. Enid, 1934/jazz pianist, bandleader
Moreland, James "Ace"/b. Miami, d. Feb. 8, 2003
Cherokee blues guitarist for King Snake Records
Moreland, John/b. Kentucky, reared in Tulsa/roots-rock/Red Dirt/country singer/songwriter
Morgan, Kylie/b. July 3, 1995, OKC, graduated Newcastle High School/CMA "Who New to Watch", country singer, songwriter
Morris, Bobby/b. Tulsa/rhythm guitar w/ The Champs
Morris, Steve/song leader
NewTulsa Ceremonial Grounds
Morris, Theodora/University of Central Oklahoma music faculty, 2003/violinist
Morrow, Rick/r. Tulsa/keyboardist
Morton, Ann/b. Muldrow, 1942/rock singer
Moseley, Andy/b. Durant, 1933/co-founder of Mosrite guitars used by Nokie Edwards and The Ventures, The Ramones, et al.
Moseley, Semie/b. Durant, 1935/co-founder of Mosrite guitars used by Nokie Edwards and The Ventures
Mosely, Keith/b. Edmond
bassist for String Cheese Incident
Moses, Ted/r. Tulsa/jazz pianist
Mourning September
Mourning Star/f. Shawnee
intertribal powwow singing group
Mourning Three/f. Tulsa/rock group

Moye, Felicia/r. Norman/classical violinist, concertmaster for OKC Philharmonic, 2003
Mucker, Baby Ray/b. Slick, OK, reared in Stockton, CA/keyboardist for Bobby Blue Bland, B.B. King, The Whispers, et al.
Muddy Chucks/f. Verdigris/Christian punk rock
Munde, Alan/b. Norman, 1946/country music historian, banjoist, played with Byron Berline
Munds, Ken/r. Okmulgee/gospel singer with Brush Arbor
Mundy, Emily Miller (Smith)/r. Tulsa/vocalist (Tulsa Sound)
Mundy, Jim/b. Muldrow, 1934/country singer
Mundy, Marilyn/b. Bokoshe/country singer
Murray, Sonny
Muscogee (Creek) Nation
Musick, Scott (The Call)
Myers, Helen/b. Oklahoma City/ethnomusicologist
Myrick, Chris (Cherokee)/r. Oklahoma City country singer 1960, 1970s
recorded for Caprice Records

N

Naifeh, Jerry/b. Tulsa/drummer
for Twilley and Phil Seymour
Nail, Austin/r. Oklahoma City/blues guitarist, leads Austin Nail band
Nance, Colin/r. OKC/electronica
Nance, Kregg/r. Ardmore/country singer
Natural Grass/f. Oklahoma/bluegrass group
Baker, Pat/bassist, lead vocalist
Campbell, Pat/guitarist, vocalist
Campbell, Royce/lead guitarist, vocalist
Farrar, Ronnie/banjoist, vocalist
Nuneley, Dick/mandolinist, vocalist
Nauni, Marla
Navel Orange/f. Norman/rock group
Navrath, Joe/b. Ada, r. Stroud/country rock singer, songwriter
Naylor Family/f. Guthrie, 1998/bluegrass group
N-Dex/f. Oklahoma City/rapper
Black Face Entertainment

Negative Nancy/f. Tulsa/rock group
Brown, J. "Brushdog/b. Tulsa, 1972/drummer, also w/Jump Suit Love, File 13, & Tricinella
Cates, Travis/b. Muskogee, 1975, graduated Oktaha High School/bassist, also w/Hurricane Mason
Endacott, Steve/b. 1969, attended OSU/singer
Morris, Steve "Doc"/b. Anaheim, CA, 1968, graduated Pryor High School/lead guitarist
Nelson, Jerry/r. Claremore/blues guitarist, vocalist
Nelson, Willie/r. Perkins
intertribal powwow head singer
Nevaquaya, "Doc" Tate
Nevaquaya, Sonny/b. Apache, OK/Al flutist, son of **"Doc" Tate Nevaquaya**
Newman, Tessa Rae/reared in "central Oklahoma" on a horse farm/country-rock singer, songwriter
New Plainsmen Quartet/f. Chickasha gospel group
New Science/f. Tulsa, 2002/rock group
Gilardi, Jason/drummer
Hosterman, Ben/guitarist
Jameson, Mike/guitarist, vocalist
Jones, Scott/bassist
Nichols, Grady
Nitro
The Nixons
Noe, Candy/r. Tulsa/multi-genre vocalist for Johnnie Lee Wills, et al.
(Roy and Candy's Music, Tulsa)
Noeebo/f. Broken Arrow/electronic dance duo
Hopiard, Chris/keyboards, synthesizers
Smith, Dough/keyboardist, synthesizers

No Justice/f. Stillwater/blues rock group (see **Red Dirt Music**)
Grauberger, Tim/drummer
Payne, Jerry/bassist
Payne, Tony/guitarist
Rice, Steve/vocalist
Nolen, Jimmy
Norfleet, Lee/r. Muskogee/trombonist
Norful, Smoke/b. Muskogee/gospel singer (EMI)
Norma Jean Beasler
Northcutt, Jude/r. Slaughterville/country singer with Jude and Jody, OKC, 1950s-1960s
Norton, Spencer Hilton/b. Anadarko, 1909 classical composer
No Small Change/f. Choctaw and Alva Christian rock group
N.O.T.A.
Nude Furniture/f. Tulsa, OK/pop group
Null, Annette/b. Quinton, 1929/country singer
Nunn, Gary P.
Nymphomercial/f. Bartlesville/modern rock

O

O'Bannon, Evan/r. Oklahoma mountain dulcimer
Obrien, Amy/b. Oklahoma City/opera singer
O'Brien, Dwayne/b. Ada, 1963 guitarist and vocalist for Little Texas
O'Dell, Kenny
Ogden, Dave/b. Stillwater/bassist w/Fried Okra Jones
O'Hara, Kelli
O'Kelly's Celtic Band/r. Jones/Celtic music
Oklahoma!/Broadway musical, 1943
Oklahoma Bass Maniax/f. Tecumseh and Shawnee rap duo
Oklahoma City Blue Devils
OK Sweetheart/f. Tulsa, 2008/progressive pop, won 2008 John Lennon songwriting contest for pop music, www.oksweetheart.com
Oldaker, Jamie
Old School/f. Tulsa/rock group
Olive, Marcus/r. Olive Springs/holler guitarist, folk-singing interpreter and reporter of human introspectivity and celestial design
Oliver Mangum
Olsen, Jennie/r. Oklahoma soprano with Santa Fe Chorale
O'Mealey, Julie/r. Oklahoma alto with Santa Fe Chorale
One Accord/f. Stillwater/CCM
One Eyed Buffalo/f. Lawton/rock group
1 G.O.P./f. Tulsa/CCM
Higher Dimensions Family Church
Orange, Richard/r. Tulsa/multi-genre musician
Orloski, Stephanie/2003 TU music student sings on TU jazz CD, Sophisticated Ladies
Orphium/f. Tulsa, 1998/rock group
Osage Nation
Osage Sweat/recorded at Grayhorse, Osage Nation, 1997/sweat lodge singers
Kaulaity, Herschel (Cheyenne-Kiowa)/singer
McAlpine Louis (Osage)/singer
Schonleber, John (Caddo)/singer
Swank, Casey (Osage)/singer
Swank, Chris (Osage)/singer
Oscillators/f. Tulsa, 1995/blues group
O'Shea, B.J./r. Oklahoma/blues guitarist, singer
Osterhaus, Carveth/d. 5/15/2013, OKC/
music faculty at OCU (1973-89) and UCO (1990-2003)/ opera and music theater director
Osternaus, Megan/b. OKC, 1976/Broadway performer, singer, dancer, actor in Mama Mia!, Mary Poppins, Martin Guerre
Other Lives
The Other Side/f. Oklahoma/rock group
Otoe-Missouria Tribe
Ottawa Tribe/based in Miami, moved to I.T. in 1867/powwow, Native American Church

Ott, Doy/b. McAlester or Ada/singer with Statesmen Quartet
Oulds, Jerry/r. Bartlesville/R & B, pop singer, songwriter, multi-instrumentalist
Outcast Bluegrass/f. Oklahoma/bluegrass
The Outlaws/f. Hominy/country group
Overland Bluegrass Express/f. Cushing/BG
  Blackburn, Fred/guitar, vocals
  Blackburn, Marcella/bass, songwriter
  Hargrove, Jim/guitar, fiddle, vocals
  Hargrove, Wanda/vocals
  Watson, Buddy/banjo, vocals
Overstreet, Tommy
Owens, Bonnie
Owens, Buck
The Oxfords/f. Tulsa, 1960s/garage rock band included on 1960s garage rock compilation, Teenage Shutdown (Vol. 10)
Oyebi, Pat (Kiowa)/r. Stilwell/ intertribal powwow head singer
OZMA/f. Tulsa/rock group

P

Padgett, Bill/r. Tulsa/drummer with Brian Parton, Brandon McGovern
Page, Patti
Page, Walter/b. Gallatin, MS, r. Oklahoma City/ leader of **Oklahoma City Blue Devils**
Pagna, Sammy/r. Tulsa/pianist
Pahsetopah, Michael, P. (Osage/Euchee)/ r. Oklahoma/intertribal powwow head singer
Pakanli, Princess/b. Ardmore/opera singer
Palmer, Mallory/r. Oklahoma/country singer
Paper Scissors/f. Yukon/pop rock
Parker, Andy
Parker, Billy
Parker, Chris/r. Tulsa/singer, songwriter
Parker, Jeffrey Gray
Parton, Brian and the Nashville Rebels/ f. Tulsa, 1993/rockabilly
Parton, Thurman (Caddo)/r. Binger/Caddo Turkey Dance head singer
Patterson, Donald (Tonkawa)/b. near Tonkawa/ head singer w/Fort Oakland Ramblers
Patterson, Henry (Tonkawa)/r. Tonkawa/ intertribal powwow head singer
Patty, Sandi
Paul's Electric Lemonade/r. Tulsa/pop group
Pawnee Nation
Pawnee YellowHorse/f. Pawnee, 1996/ Pawnee drum group
  Echo-Hawk, Bunky/singer
  Echo-Hawk, Debbie/back-up singer
  Echo-Hawk, Walter/singer
  Folsom-Minthorn Jennifer/back-up singer.
  Gorman, Colleen/back-up singer
  Horsechief, Vance, Jr./lead singer, composer
  Horsechief, Vance III/singer
  Hodshire, Bryan/singer
  Hodshire, Kay/back-up singer
  Howell, Carrie/back-up singer
  Leadingfox, Gary/singer
  Leadingfox, Greg/singer
  Lightfoot, Jason/singer
  Minthorn, Phil/singer
  Moore, C.D./singer
  Muth, Marcie/back-up singer
Paxton, Tom
Pearson, Carlton/r. Tulsa/gospel singer (Warner Alliance Records)
Peck, Hayley/r. Oklahoma/country rock singer
Peevey, Gayla/b. Ponca City, 1943/recorded 1953 novelty hit, "I Want a Hippopotamus for Christmas", and later recorded as Jamie Horton
Pegues, Holly Michelle/b. Tulsa/opera soprano
Pendarvis, Paul/b. Oklahoma/violinist, bandleader
Pendleton, Ema Jane/b. 1993, Tulsa/old time fiddle award winner at Walnut Valley Old Time Fiddle Championships, 2011

Peoria Tribe/based in Miami, moved to I.T. in 1867/powwow
Pepper, Jim/b. June 18, 1941 in Oregon to Oklahoma parents of Muscogee (Creek) and **Kansa (Kaw)** descent – d. Feb. 1992/ jazz saxophonist
Peterson, Quinn/r. Stillwater/country singer, songwriter
Peter's Volcano/f. Newscastle/rock group
Petree, Stephen
Pettiford, Oscar
Petty, Brian/b. Clay Center, KS, r. Stillwater/ singer with Dale Warland Singers
Petty Tom
Pewewardy, Cornel
Phat Phly/f. Pryor/rock and roll cover band circa 2002
Phelps, Shelly/b. Pauls Valley, 1964/singer songwriter
Phillips, Eva/r. Tulsa, from 1982/country/gospel songwriter
Phillips, John (of The Mamas and The Papas)
Phillips, Marvin/b. Guthrie, 1931/singer with Jesse Belvin as Jesse & Marvin
Pickens, Kel/b. Tulsa, 1949, r. Stillwater/ children's music producer (Giant Blueberry Music), lyricist
Pierce, Mike/b. Muskogee, 1960, r. Braggs/ band road manager, concert merchandising
Pillar
Pilot, Jim (a.k.a. Pylant)/r. Oklahoma/country singer
Pinkie & the Snakeshakers/f. Oklahoma City, 1998/blues
Pinson, Bobby
Pipestem, Rock/r. Oklahoma intertribal powwow head singer
Pishney-Floyd, Annette/b. Enid, 1942 classical music performer
Pishney-Floyd, Monte/b. Oklahoma City, 1941/ classical composer
Pitcock, Bill IV/b. Tulsa/producer, singer, songwriter, bassist for Dwight Twilley
Pitts, Alan/b. Bristow/country singer
Pittsenbarger, Kent/b. Oklahoma City, 1954/ drummer w/Memphis P. Tails
Pittsley, Dustin/b. Tulsa, 1983, r. Chandler/ blues guitarist/vocalist
Place, Mary Kay
Plastic Jack/R & B, rock group
  Enevoldsen, Adam/vocals, guitars
  Enevoldsen, Kyle/drummer
  Isom, Ray/guitars, vocals
  Ogden, Dave/bassist
Platt, Carol/r. Oklahoma/soprano
Playya 1000 & The Deeksta/f. Tulsa, 2007/ hip-hop duo
Plumb, Dilla Jean/r. Oklahoma City/singer with Woody Herman in late 1930s and early 1940s
The Plumbers/f. Tulsa, late 1990s/rock group
  Mitcho, Brad/guitarist
  Quinn, John/bassist
  Taylor, Scott/drummer
Podank String Band/f. Oklahoma/alternabilly released first, independent CD in 2003
Poe, Bobby & the Poe Cats/f. Vinita/rockabilly group included Big Al Downing, backed Wanda Jackson
Point of Grace
Poison Okies/f. Oklahoma City, 1994/rockabilly
Polygon, Johnny
Ponca Tribe
Poor Boys/f. jabeMeeker/southern style intertribal powwow singing group (Arbor Records)
  Anquoe, Quinton/singer
  Deer, Michael/singer
  Gawhega, Mike/singer
  Kihega, Mike/singer
  Littlecrow, Amos/singer
  Locust, Knokkovtee/singer
  Logan, Charles/singer

Tehaund, Rueben/singer
White, Geoff/b. Tahlequah, r. Claremore
Potter, Kim & Southern Reign/f. Kiefer, 1998/ country group
  Green, Clyde/r. Cushing/lead guitar
  Green, Rick/r. Kiefer/keyboards/vocals
  Harris, Jim/r. Tulsa/bassist, mandolinist
  Murphy, Dean/r. Bristow/drummer
  Pierce, Dale/r. Stillwater/dobro, banjo, steel, guitar player, Red Dirt Music
  Potter, Doug/r. Kiefer/harmony vocals
  Potter, Kim/r. Kiefer/lead singer
Potts, Wes/r. Woodward/country singer, songwriter, guitarist with Merl Lindsay, Bobby Barnett
Powell, Doug/b. Stillwater/singer, songwriter
Powell, Susan/b. Elk City/1981 Miss America, classical & opera singer
Powerglide/f. Tulsa, 1999/1960s and 70s rock cover band
  Blue, David/r. Bartlesville/drummer
  Lyon, Wes/Tulsa Will Rogers H.S. grad/ guitarist
  Ryan, David/Tulsa Will Rogers H.S. keyboardist, guitarist
  Shoun, Paul/Tulsa Will Rogers H.S.l lead singer
  Sullivan, Don/Tulsa Will Rogers H.S./bassist, also played with Roy Clark
Prairie Land String Band/f. Oklahoma City/folk
The Prairie Twins/b. Oklahoma/cowgirl singers
Prana/f. Tulsa, 2003/loud rock
Prentiss, Spencer/b. 1905, Washington, D.C. r. Bartlesville/cellist, founding member of Bartlesville Symphony Orchestra
Preslar, Casey/r. Tulsa/singer, Miss Oklahoma 2002
The Rickey Preston Band/f. Tulsa/R & B, blues, soul group
Pretty Black Chains/f. OKC, circa 2010/independent rock group www.prettyblackchains.com
Price, Gary/b. Johnston County/banjo mandolin player, luthier
Price, John Elwood/b. Tulsa, 1935 classical musician
Prill, Julie Baker/r. Terlton/country singer
Prix Teen/f. Stillwater, 2011/electronic pop
Proctor, David/Mekko, Tallahassee Wvkokye Ceremonial Grounds/song leader
Proctor, Michael/Tallahassee Wvkokye Ceremonial Grounds/stomp dance leader
Proctor, Sam/Heles Haya, Tallahassee Wvkokye Ceremonial Grounds/stomp dance leader
Pryor, Steve/b. Tulsa/Cherokee blues guitarist, singer, songwriter, see **Cherokee** entry
Pro Musica Tulsae/f. Tulsa/medieval and Renaissance era music
Pruitt, Bill/r. Oklahoma/champion yodeler
Pugh, Paul/r. Tulsa/pianist

Q

Quapaw Tribe/based in Quapaw/moved to I.T. from AR in 1833/oldest listed powwow in Ok, annually on July 4
Quarterless/f. Tulsa/classic and modern rock
  Harrington, Mel/bassist
  Kay, Matt/vocalist
  Kruse, Ben/lead guitarist
  McCracken, Kelly/percussionist
  Sears, Jeremy/rhythm guitarist
Quetone, Brian/r. Oklahoma/intertribal powwow head singer
Quetone, John (Sac & Fox/Kiowa/Otoe)/r. Oklahoma/intertribal powwow head singer
Quinn, Kenny/r. Tulsa/jazz, blues pianist
Quinton, Wade/b. Fairfax, VA, r. Tulsa/country singer

R

R, David/b. Oklahoma/folk singer/songwriter
Rabbit, Jimmy/b. Holdenville/country singer
Radford, Ronald/b. California, moved to Tulsa at four/flamenco guitarist
Radial Angel/f. Norman/contemporary Christian group signed by Warner Brothers' Squint Records 2003
  Jones, Eddie/bassist
  Dolezel, Jeremy/guitarist
  Perkins, Tommy/r. Noble/drummer
  Taber, Jared/lead singer
Radial Spangle/f. Oklahoma City, 1991/ indy rock group evolved into Charm Pops
Radle, Carl/b. Oklahoma City, 1942/bassist for Eric Clapton and Leon Russell, **Tulsa Sound**
Rae, Lana/b. Oklahoma/country singer
Raffensperger, Bill/b. Tulsa, 1941/bassist associated with the **Tulsa Sound**
Rains, Chick
Rains, Peggy/b. Adair County, Chalk Bluff Community/country singer
Rains, Ron/Texas native, OCU grad, music, 1974/Broadway performer, actor, singer
Rains, Shan/r. Stillwater/country singer
Rainwater, Marvin/b. Wichita, KS, 1925, reared in Oklahoma/country, rockabilly singer
Rambler/f. Oklahoma/21st century honky tonk
  Brown, Dave/bassist, vocalist
  Brown, Tim/lead singer, rhythm guitarist
  Chavez, Troy/guitarist, vocalist
  Emmons, Matt/drummer
RamDogg & Anloc/f. Oklahoma City/hip hop
Ramirez, Debra/b. Buffalo, r. Guymon/ contemporary Christian singer
Randall, Lawrence/r. Owasso/gospel singer with The Ambassadors
Raphael/b. Tulsa, 1948/pianist
Ratley, Rob/r. Muskogee/blues drummer with DC Minner and Shy Willie
Raus, Connor/r. Tulsa/jazz keyboardist
Rausch, Leon/r. Tulsa/Western swing singer
Red Dirt Rangers
Reid, Ryan/b. Stillwater, reared in Cushing/blues-rock singer/songwriter
Reinhart, Dick/b. Tishomingo/Western singer
Reverb Brothers/f. OKC, 1990/roots rockers
The Rhoades Sisters/r. Tulsa/Gospl duo numerous Christian TV & radio appearances
Richards, Jamie/b. Shawnee/country singer
Richardson, Jeff/r. Tulsa/rapper, a.k.a. Yung Hog
Rich, Charlie/r. Enid/country singer "The Gambler", "Lucille", et al./stationed at Vance Air Force Base where he organized a jazz band
Richie and the Resonators/f. Tulsa/blues rock group with a country alter-ego, Audio Rodeo
  Buchman, Randy/drummer
  Duncan, Billy/organist
  Gray, Mitch/bassist
  Starks, Mike/harmonica player
  Starks, Richard/guitarist, vocalist
Richmond, Walter/b. McAlester, OK April 18, 1947/keyboardist with Bonnie Raitt, Tractors, **Tulsa Sound**
Richter, Brad/b. Enid/classical guitarist
Ricochet
Riddlin' Kids/f. Tulsa/punk rock group
Riggs, Debbie/b. Ada, r. Stillwater/gospel singer
Riggs, Lynn/b. Claremore/wrote play Green Grow the Lilacs, the basis for the musical Oklahoma!
Ripley, Steve
Rippinger, Rockwell Ryan/b. Orlando, FL, reared in Tulsa/CCM singer, songwriter
Ripple Green/f. 2006, OKC/epic space funk
Ritter, Steve/r. Blackgum, graduated Vian HS, NSU/country singer, songwriter
Rivers, Jimmy (See **Cherokee**)
Rivers, Sam
Roark-Strummer, Linda/b. Tulsa/opera singer,

Robbins, Everett "Happy"/r. Oklahoma jazz pianist of the 1920s
Rockumentalists/f. Norman/rock group
Rogers, Doug/r. Tulsa/drummer for The Brazos Valley Boys
Rogers, Harlan/r. Oklahoma/keyboardist and pianist with Ricky Skaggs
Rodgers, Jesse/b. Claremore, 1913 rockabilly singer
Rohrer, Leah/r. Oklahoma, OCU graduate/ Broadway performer/singer
Rollerson, Leon/r. Tulsa/bassist, organized group that became the GAP Band, played with Al Green, et al.
Romaine, Karl/r. Walters/guitarist
Romanello, Tony
Rooney, Joe Don
Rosales, Antonio/b. Oklahoma City/country singer, Oklahoma Country Music Assn. president
Rose Hill/southern style powwow group/ recorded for Indian House Records, 1995
  Barker, Roland/singer
  Frejo, Brian/singer
  Gwen, Lloyd/singer, leader
  Hamilton, Curtis/singer (Young Bird)
  Hamilton, Donnie/singer (Young Bird)
  Hamilton, Juaquin/singer (Young Bird)
  Harris, R.G., Jr./singer
  Victors, Greg/singer
  Victors, Shude/singer
  Walker, Henry, Jr./singer
  Whitecloud, Hootie/singer
  Whitecloud, J.R./singer
  Whitecloud, Michael/singer
Rose Stone Trio/r. Tulsa/flute, harp, harpsichord chamber group
Ross, Billy/b. Cushing/country songwriter
Ross, Jason/r. Stilwell intertribal powwow head singer
Ross, J.R. (Cherokee/Kiowa)/r. Sapulpa/ intertribal powwow head singer
Roubedoux, Jade/r. Oklahoma/ intertribal powwow head singer
Roubedoux, Kyle (Ponca/Otoe)/r. Enid/ intertribal powwow head singer
Roulain, Cole/r. Stillwater/singer, songwriter, guitarist
The Rounders/f. early 2000s, Putnam City/ progressive blues/recorded for Blind Pig (04) and Rykodisc (2007)
Round-Up Boys/f. Tulsa/traditional country
The Roustabouts/f. Enid, 1997/punk rock
  Felton, Daniel/b. Enid, r. Waukomis/bassist, guitarist, vocalist
  Smith, Jesse/b. Enid, r. Hennessey/drummer
  Waggoner, Nick/b. Enid, r. Hennessey/ guitarist, vocalist
Rowe, Ray D./r. Tulsa/early vocalist with the GAP Band, fronts Down Home Blues Band
Rowland, William/b. MO, r. Broken Arrow ragtime pianist
Royal Crush/f. Tulsa, 1997/modern pop rock
Royal, Marshall
Roy, George/r. Salina intertribal powwow head singer
Rubin, Mark
Rucker, Laura/b. Oklahoma/jazz, blues singer
Rucker, Lee/UCO music faculty/ jazz trumpeter /p/ with Woody Herman Orchestra)
R.U.I./f. Tulsa/rap group
Rush, Tommy/r. Tulsa/1950s rock and roll singer, Tulsa Sound
Rushing, Jimmy
Rushlow, Tim
Rushlow, Tom/r. Midwest City/guitarist, father of Tim Rushlow, lead singer for Little Texas
Russell, Leon
Russell, Pee Wee/b. St. Louis, MO, r. Muskogee/Dixieland clarinetist

Russell, Shawna/b. 1979, reared in Okemah/ country singer, songwriter, on Way Out West Records, www.shawnarussell.com
Russell, Tom
Ryan, Donald/r. Tulsa/jazz pianist
Ryan, Frank/r. Tulsa/educator, classical conductor

S

Sac & Fox Nation/based south of Stroud since 1869/Native American Church songs/ powwow songs/hymns
SafetySuit/f. 2004 by ORU students, relocated to Nashville in 2004/pop rock group with 2012 Top 10 Billboard single, "These Times"
Saied, Jimmy/r. Tulsa/conductor
Salama, Kareem/b. Ponca City, 1978/country singer with Egyptian immigrant parents toured Middle East for U.S. State Dept., 2011
Sallee, Josh/b. 1988, r. OKC/hip hop emcee
Salmon, Scottie/r. Red Oak/choreographer w/ Radio City Rockettes, Miss American Pageant, and Barbara Mandrell
Sam and the Stylees/f. Tulsa/reggae group
  Frye, Nigel/bassist
  Glendening, Thomas/drummer, guitarist, vocalist
  Jones, Sam/guitarist
  Lokey, Maria/percussionist, vocalist
  Meddler, Brian/vocalist
  Reynolds, Lance/guitarist
  Santana/percussionist
Same Day Service/f. Oklahoma/riot girl punk rock
Samsarah/f. Tulsa/rock group
Sampson, Carter/reared OKC, r. Fayetville, AR, 2012 folk singer/songwriter, plays with The County Seat
Sampson, Phil/b. Chickasha/country singer, songwriter
Samsara/f. Tulsa/independent rock group
Sanders, Nathan/b. Oklahoma City/mandolinist, bassist, guitarist
Sanders, Sarah Nicole/b. Muskogee, 1985/ gospel singer
San Dimas/f. Tulsa/rock group
Sandkuhl, Ron/r. Broken Arrow/inventor of the G-Stand a guitar stand attached to a guitar's neck plate
Sandman Band/f. Norman/rock group
Sankey, O.T./r. Oklahoma intertribal powwow head singer
Sarcone (Martin), John/b. Stillwater, 1981/ singer, songwriter
Sarmiento, Adam/r. OKC/composer, drums, bass, vocals, programming/(see The Candles)
Satepauhoodle, Craig (Kiowa/Osage) b. Hominy/intertribal powwow head singer
Satepauhoodle, Evans Ray (Kiowa) b.Carnegie/intertribal powwow head singer
Satepauhoodle, Silas (Kiowa/Osage) b. Pawhuska/intertribal powwow head singer
Savage, William/OU history professor wrote Singing Cowboys and All That Jazz (1983)
Scaggs, Boz/b. Ohio, 1944, r. OK as a child pop rock singer, songwriter
Schmidt, Scott/r. Bartlesville national mandolin champion
Schneider, Moe/b. Bessie, 1919/ Dixieland trombonist
Schnorrenberg, Nathan/r. Owasso, Norman/ singer, songwriter
Schon, Neal
Scott-Garrison Duo/performing together in Tulsa since 1980s/award-winning chamber music ensemble
Scotty (b. Concho) and Tommie/traditional country, bluegrass, and gospel duo
Scowden, Grant/b. Little Rock, 1994, reared in Poteau/multi-instrumentalist, singer, songwriter
Scroggins, Enois/b. Muskogee/gospel singer
Scroggins, Janice/b. Idabel/blues piano

Seaton, Lynn
Sebran, Harry/b. 1921, Romania – d. Tulsa, 2008 Jewish cantor
Seglem, Sara/b. Midwest City/opera soprano
Selby, Mark/b. Oklahoma/guitarist, singer, songwriter (Dixie Chicks, Trisha Yearwood)
Seldom Seen/f. Weleetka/country, bluegrass
  Burden, Phillip/fiddler, rhythm guitarist, vocalist
  Burden, Steve/banjoist, guitarist, fiddler, vocalist
Sellers, Rick/r. Drumright/music promoter
Seminole Nation/based in Wewoka, began moving to I.T. reluctantly, in 1835/stomp dance/flute/Christian hymns
Seneca-Cayuga/based in Miami, in I.T. by 1832/cycle of Longhouse Green Corn Ceremonial songs
Sessions, Ronnie
Settle, Mike
Sever/f. Oklahoma City/heavy metal group
Sewell, Ace/b. Blanchard/old time fiddler
Sewell, Wally/r. Tulsa/1950s rock and roll singer
Seymour, Phil/b. Tulsa, 1952/Dwight Twilley Band
Shade of the Son/f. Cyril/Christian rock group
Shade Seven/f. Oklahoma City/rock group
Shadid, Margie/r. Oklahoma City/jazz singer
Shadowlake 8/f. Stillwater, circa 1957 and '58/ rock and roll band
The Shadows Five/f. Oklahoma/1960s R&R recorded for Sully Records
Shaffer, Larry/r. Tulsa/concert promoter
Shamblin, Eldon/b. Weatherford, 1916/ guitarist for Bob Wills
Shamrock/f. Tulsa/rock group
Shanghai Automatic/f. Tulsa/rock group
Shannon, Mark/b. Tahlequah, r. Tulsa/country l lead guitarist
Shannon, Mike/b. Tulsa, 1953, raised around McAlester, r. Stillwater/songwriter, guitarist (**Red Dirt Music**), Daddy O's Music store
Shannon, Tom/r. Tulsa/jazz saxophonist
Shatswell, Danny/b. Oklahoma, 1953/country singer, songwriter
Shaw, Charlie/b. Texas, r. Oklahoma City, 1960s/country guitarist, vocalist, bandleader
Shaw, Danial Alexander (DA)/b. Hartford, AR, resided. Poteau, OK/hymn writer ("Just Beyond the Rolling River" – 1925)
Shaw, Lee/b. Oklahoma/jazz pianist
Shawnee, Mike (Shawnee/Quapaw/Delaware/ Muscogee)/r. Owasso/intertribal powwow head singer
Shawnee Tribe/based in Miami area since 1871/White Oak Ceremonial Grounds/stomp dance/powwow
Sheehan, Megan/r. Broken Arrow/country singer
Sheffield-Charles, Ellen/r. OKC/ jazz and ballet pianist
Sheffield, Leslie/r. Oklahoma City/ jazz band leader
Sheff, Spade/b. Tahlequah/country singer, songwriter
Shelton, Blake
Shepard, Jean
Sherley, Glen/b. Oklahoma, 1936/country singer, songwriter
Shiny Toy Guns/f. Los Angeles, 2002 founding members, Chad Petree and Jeremy Dawson/industrial pop rock group
Shofner, Laura/r. Cushing, OCU Music grad/ opera singer
Short, Steve/r. Oklahoma City/drummer for Reba McEntire and Byron Berline, Gospel groups, recording engineer, producer
Shortt Dogg/r. Oklahoma City/blues, R & B group
Shryok, Gordon/r. Tulsa/owned Shriok Studios in Tulsa (1960s-1980s)/recording engineer
Sidewinder/r. Tulsa, 2003/rock, Top 40, country
  Davis, Tresa/singer
  Dunlap, Bruce/bassist, vocalist

Harlan, Joel/lead guitarist
Huffman/drummer
Lowther, Chris/rhythm guitarist, vocalist
Significant Other/f. Tulsa/rock group
Siksigma/f. Tulsa/heavy metal rock group
Siller, Nathan/r. OKC, moved to NYC in 2008/ classical singer, guitarist, released 2013 "rock-tronic" CD w/ group-name Portraiture
Silver Creek Bluegrass/f. Oklahoma/bluegrass
  Bryant, Glenn/banjo player
  Keith, James/fiddler
  Lins, Sue/mandolinist
  Miller, Ken/guitarist
  Rohr, Florence/bassist
Simmons, John
Simon, Billy/b. Cleveland/gospel songwriter, vocalist with 4 Runner Quartet
Simpleton/f. Stillwater, 2001/pop rock
  Beier, Matt/drummer
  Hall, James/bassist
  Jones, Chris/guitarist, vocalist
  Simpson, John/r. Oklahoma/polka band leader
Singer, Harold "Hal"/b. Tulsa, 1918/jazz clarinetist and tenor saxophonist
Singer, Margaret Ann/r. Oklahoma/classical pianist for the Oklahoma City Symphony
Siren/f. Tahlequah/rock group
Siva/f. OKC, 2007/heavy metal
Six Foot Landing/f. Tulsa/pop rock group
6point/f. Norman/rock group
Six Foot Six/f. Tulsa/metal group
Skarekrow/f. Tulsa/progressive rock, metal
Skating Polly/f. 2009, Edmond/punk-rock-pop duo 2013 album produced by Exene Cervenka
  Bighorse, Peyton
  Mayo, Kelli
Skinner, Craig/r. Oklahoma/guitarist, Red Dirt Music
Skinner, Mike/r. Oklahoma/fiddler, Red Dirt Music
Skinner, Tom/b. Bristow, 1954/singer, songwriter, Red Dirt Music
Skruface/f. Tulsa/independent rock group
  Aaron, Chris/vocalist
  Deason, Mike/drummer, vocalist
  McCullough, Sean/bassist
  Owens, Glen/guitarist
Slapout/f. Stillwater, 2002/folk-rock duo
  Mccubbin, Derek/guitar, vocals, songwriter
  Foley, Hugh/trombone, gtr, vocals, songwriter
Sloan, J. David/b. Kingfisher, 7/9/1942/country singer, songwriter, toured with Red Sovine
Slow Children at Play/f. Norman/rock group
Slow Head Soul/f. Tulsa/improvisational jams
  Al-Hammami, Zee/drummer, percussionist, vocalist
  Harry, Lelan/bassist, vocalist
  Turner, Isaac/guitarist, vocalist
  Turner, Joshua/guitarist, vocalist
Slowvein/f. Yukon, 1997/rock group
  Berry, Danny/guitarist
  Kruel, Tommy/bassist
  Lea, Susan/backup vocalist
  Leiter, Gary/guitarist
  Ramsey, Mark/drummer
  Turner, Elizabeth/vocalist
Smalley, John Jacob/r. Edmond/ American Idol performer, 2003
Smarty Pants/f. Oklahoma City, 1997/pop rock
Smilin' Vic & and the Soul Monkeys/ f. 1995,OKC/blues group
  Feuerborn, Larry/b. Norman/bassist
  Gutierrez, Victor/b. Tulsa/vocalist
  Taylor, Mitch/b. Tulsa/guitarist
  Warren, Cleve/b. Oklahoma City/drummer
Smith, Alex E./r. Pawnee/Southern plains powwow singer/nominated for GRAMMY in 2006 with Cheevers Toppah
Smith, Big Walter/b. Tulsa, 1930/blues singer spent most of his career in Minnesota
Smith Cal
Smith, Chester/b. Wade, 1930/rockabilly singer

Smith, "Sweet" Emily/b. Sullivan, IN, 1944, moved to Tulsa, 1959/Tulsa nightclub owner, Tulsa Sound insider, inspired Leon Russell's song, "Sweet Emily"
Smith, Fred/b. Tulsa/jazz keyboardist
Smith, Howard/bGe. Ardmore, 1910/jazz pianist, arranger, composer
Smith, J.T./b. Texas, recorded in OK, 1930s/ blues artist
Smith, Jami/r. Edmond/CCM singer, songwriter
Smith, Jo Ann/r. Oklahoma/autoharp champion
Smith, Katie Thomas/r. Coweta/bluegrass guitarist with Umy and the Goodtimers
Smith, Sam/stomp dance leader Tallahassee Wvkokye Ceremonial Grounds
Smith, Sammi/b. CA, 1943, r.l/d. OK/country singer "Help Me Make It Through the Night"
Smith, Steve/r. Oklahoma mountain dulcimer champion
Smith, Steve/r. Tulsa/singer, songwriter
Smith, "Big" Walter/b. Tulsa, 1930 - d. Minnesota, 2012/blues singer
Smittle, Betsy/b. Oklahoma/country bassist, vocalist, and **Garth Brooks**' sister
Smoke/f. Tulsa/spoken word, multi-ethnic music
  Glass, Mingo/r. Tulsa/percussionist, flute
  Harris, Nancy/b. Tulsa/poet, spoken word artist
  Henry, Tom/b. near Spring Creek, Cherokee County/guitarist, percussionist
The Smok'n Coyotes/classic country, rock
  Ecker, Ken/r. on a lake near Edmond/ keyboardist
  Embrey, Bo/r. Mustang/drummer
  Embrey, Mike/r. Mustang/lead guitarist
  Hudson, Larry/r. Norman/bassist
  Keesee, Steve/r. Shawnee/lead vocalist, rhythm guitarist
Smotherman, Michael
SnapDragon/f. Tulsa/pop rock group
  Boren, Russell/bassist
  Capps, Matt/drummer
  Gibbons, Kelly/guitarist, keyboardist
  Horn, Robert/guitarist
  Jude, Christine/vocalist
  Sabelo, Tony/percussionist, keyboardist
Sneed, Sherman Brooks/b. OKC, 1921/backup singer for Harry Belafonte (1957-72), manager/producer for Lena Horne (1972-97)
The SNOTROKITZ/f. Norman/rock group
Snow, Bill/r. Tulsa/singer, songwriter
SOAHC/f. Tulsa/Christian rock group
Sol Mist/f. Oklahoma/CCM
Sol Raven/f. Tulsa/heavy metal group
Soul Avengers/f. Tulsa/blues rock group
  Bruce, Mike "Monk"/guitarist, vocalist
  Dragoo, Mike/drummer, vocalist
  Munson, Steve/bassist
Sounds Good/f. Tulsa/jazz group
  Bruce, Buddy/guitarist
  Cope, Rick/drummer
  Cummins, Jon/bassist
  Williamson, Gayle/pianist
  Wright, Shelly/vocalist
Sounds of the Southwest/official OK state Western swing band via Oklahoma legislature in 1997
  Keith, Becky/r. Oklahoma/lead vocalist, guitarist
  Keith, Matt/r. Oklahoma/vocalist, fiddler
  McLin, Wil/r. Oklahoma/vocalist, guitarist
  Sharp, Richard/r. Oklahoma/vocalist and bassist (also plays with Byron Berline)
Southern Boys/r. Oklahoma/southern style powwow group (Arbor Records)
  Cable, Darrell/singer
  Cable, Kelly/singer
  Chasenah, Finton/singer
  Hindsley, Corey/singer
  Mashunkashey, Russell/singer
  Monossey, Althea/back-up singer

Monossey, Anthony/singer
Monossey, Dobbin/back-up singer
Monossey, Carl/singer
Monossey, Larry/singer
Monossey, Ronald/singer
Monossey, Sukie/back-up singer
Redbone, Edgar/singer
Starr, Marlena/back-up singer
Starr, Ni'vy/backup singer
Southern Steel/f. Collinsville/country metal
  Casger, Bryan/r. Collinsville/drummer
  Johnson, Richard/r. Collinsville/guitarist
  Overholt, Ryan/r. Collinsville/lead singer
  Rowe, Corbin/r. Collinsville/guitarist
  Thurman, Zak/r. Collinsville/bassist
Southern Thunder/f. Pawnee, 1991/southern style powwow group (Indian House)
  Adson, Aaron/singer
  Adson, Frank M.(Pawnee/Navajo)/head singer
  Adson, Herb/singer
  Adson, Robert/singer
  Beard, Gilbert/singer
  Lightfoot, Crystal Pewo/ back-up singer
  Lightfoot, Jason/singer
  Moore, Jordan/singer
  Plumley, Erin/back-up singer
  Rice, Ron, Jr./singer
  Starr, Jimmy/singer
  Starr, Ni'vy/back-up singer
  Tiger, Georgia/back-up singer
  Tiger, Julia/back-up singer
  Tipps, Kyle/singer
  Valliere, George, Jr./singer
South 40 Band/f. southeastern Oklahoma/country rock group
Sovo, Gene/r. Oklahoma intertribal powwow head singer
Spears, Billy/b. Hartshorne, OK circa 1919 - d. Lawrence, KS, 2013/country fiddler
Spears, Larry/b. Sapulpa/Red Dirt Music
Spears, Sheena/r. Oklahoma/country singer
Special Disaster Team/f. Norman/ska, punk rock
Special Purpose/f. Tulsa/rock group
Spencer, Tim
SphereGazer/f. Norman/rock group
Spiral/f. Tulsa/independent rock group
Spivery, John/r. Oklahoma/keyboardist, recorded for Made Records
Spookie Jar/f. Oklahoma City/hard rock group
Spotted Horse, Brent/r. Edmond intertribal powwow head singer
Spradlin, Kelly/r. Tulsa/blues vocalist, guitarist
Spraker, Eddie/r. Tulsa/1950s R&R singer, Tulsa Sound
Springstreet/f. Tulsa/bluegrass group
Squareforce/f. Tulsa/blues rock group
Squirrel, James (Shawnee)/r. Oklahoma/stomp dance leader on Stomp Dance Blues (Indian House, 1999)
Stacy, Clyde/b. Checotah/Briartown vicinity, 8/11/1936/rockabilly singer, guitarist
Stafford, Terry
The Standels/f. Muskogee, 1960s/garage rock band included on 1960s garage rock compilation, Teenage Shutdown (Vol. 12)
Standing on Zero/f. Tulsa/rock group
Stanley, Tommy/b. 1985, TX, r. Cushing/2008 finalist on Nashville Star, the NBC-TV reality talent show
Stardeath and White Dwarfs/f. Norman/2004
Starlight Mints/f. Norman, circa 1999 supercool-progressive-pop-rock-group
  Love-Nunez, Marian/bassist
  Nunez, Andy/drummer
  Vest, Allan/singer, guitarist
Starling, Kristy/r. Putnam City/CCM singer
Starr, Arigon/Kickapoo Tribe of OK tribal member with Muscogee (Creek) heritage/Native-themed country-rock singer, songwriter, performer

Starr, Jimmy/r. Stroud intertribal powwow head singer
Starr, Kay
Starr, Moses/r. Hydro intertribal powwow head singer
Stars Go Dim/f. Tulsa, 2007/CCM pop/rock #1 hits in Singapore/multi-business commercial placement of their songs
The Stellas/f. Emond/rock group on Edmond-based Sonic Blitz Records, produced by Trent Bell
  Duncan, Raechel/r. Choctaw/music educator by day/guitarist, vocalist by night
  London, John/drummer, programmer
Stella Luna/f. Norman/experimental music
  Fitzpatrick, Darin/drummer
  Hanson, Susan/guitarist, vocalist
  Roberts, Rhonda/bassist
  Smith, Devon/guitarist, vocalist
Sterling, Jennifer/keyboardist, sampler
Sterling, Tom/r. Tulsa/jazz saxophonist
Steven Speaks/f. Tulsa/independent pop rock
Steveson, Kristin/b. Broken Arrow/opera singer
Steward, Jackie/r. Oklahoma City/1960s and '70s country singer, pianist, night club owner
Stewart, Kathryn/b. Bartlesville/opera singer
Still Breathing/f.Oklahoma/Christian metal on Solid State Records, disbanded 2002
Stidham, Jack/r. Chickasha/old time Western swing fiddler
Stokes, Adam/r. Stillwater (Stillwater H.S. grad) folk singer, songwriter
Stonehorse/f. Claremore, 1980/country, Western swing group
  Caple, Roger/bassist, vocalist
  O'Brien, Rich/guitarist
  Passmore, Darlene/drummer
  Self, Mike/guitarist and vocalist
  Stockton, Wade/fiddler, tenor banjo player
  Talbert, Brenda/pianist
  Talbert, Dale/steel guitarist
  Talbert, Donnie/b. Claremore/fiddler, vocalist, bandleader, also plays with Alan Jackson
Stone Soup/f. Oklahoma/rock group
Stovall, Vern/b. Altus, 1928/country singer
Strader, Jimmy/b. Tulsa/blues singer, bassist
Straight Shooter/f. Lexington/rock group
Streamline/f. Tulsa/rock group
Stricklin, Al/b. Texas, r. Tulsa/pianist w/ Bob Wills
The Stringents/f. Oklahoma City, 2006/string quartet versions of classic rock and pop
The Struggle/f. Norman/rock group
Stubbs, Deni/Oklahoma Opry house band bassist
Stubbs, Dick/b. Seminole/guitarist and steel guitarist for Johnny Horton, Gene Autry, and Hank Thompson
Studi, Wes/b. No Fire Hollow, 1946/Cherokee actor, Firecat of Discord bassist
Stump, Adley/b. Tulsa, OSU graduate, r. Nashville/performed on The Voice, 2012, released independent CD, Like a Lady (2011)
Subject to Blackout/f. Tulsa/modern rock group
Sub Rosa/f. OKC and Norman/rock group
Subseven/f. Oklahoma City/CCM - rock
The Suburbillies/f. OKC/alt countryl
Sugar Free Allstars/f. Norman/pop rock group
Sullins, Chad/b. Hobart, reared in Altus, based in Stillwater, 2012/singer, songwriter leads Red Dirt group, Last Call Coalition,
Sullivan Family/formed Boggy Depot, 2002/gospel group
  Sullivan, Elizabeth/family matriarch who taught her children music
  Sullivan, Heather/singer, songwriter whose voice and songs have appeared on The Sopranos, General Hospital, Guiding Light, et al.
  Sullivan, Kathleen/opera soprano, cabaret and Broadway singer
  Sullivan, Pat/physician and singer

  for community events in Vian, OK
  Sullivan, Stacy/film, TV, & stage performer, won 2002 Manhattan Assn. of Cabarets and Clubs Award for Female New York Debut
  Sullivan, Tim/singer, songwriter, co-wrote theme song for Boston Red Sox in 2003
Sullivan, Morey/r. Bartlesville (1975 – 1985)/vocalist, Brazos Valley Boys' leader
Sun Cured Red/f. Stillwater, 1998/improvisational rock group
  Bourland, Chris/saxophonist, flutist, keyboardist, electronics
  Cathey, Josh/bassist
  Loyd, Daniel/vocalist, guitarist
  Seary, Darin/drummer
  Stapp, Jimmy/guitarist, vocalist
SuperChild/f. Miami/rock group
Sutherlin, Aly/reared in Lawton/award-winning country and CCM guitarist, songwriter
Sutter, Lynn/r. Oklahoma/gospel singer
Sutton, Spencer Dale/b. 10/10/1953, OK played with Gus Hardin, Ronnie Dunn Steve Ripley, Hank Thompson, et al.
Sweatt, Al/recorded on the Tulsa-based KEEN label in the 1950s/rockabilly singer
Sweeney, Arthur/r. Tulsa/recording studio engineer, gospel record label operator
Sweney, Jim/r. Tulsa/R & B vocalist
Sweeney, Mark/r. Tahlequah/singer, songwriter, guitarist Barton and Sweeney
Swingin' Utters/f. San Francisco, circa 1990/punk rock/hard core group, front man Johnny Bonnel's mother born in Oklahoma
Sybil's Machine/f. Tulsa/rock group
Syringe/f. Norman/rock group
System X/f. Oklahoma/metal group

T

Taddy Porter/f. Stillwater/rock
  Brewer, Andy/vocals
  Jones, Doug/drums
  Jones, Kevin/bass
  Selby, Joe/lead guitar, backing vocals
Tallows.f. OKC, 2012/ethereal electro-pop
Tae Meyulks/f. Tulsa/fusion jazz
Tahchawwickah, Victor (Comanche)/r. OK intertribal powwow head singer
Tahhawah, Jerome (Comanche)/r. OK intertribal powwow head singer
Talley, James
Tallows/f. Oklahoma City, circa 2012 experimental pop
Taming Enos/f. Tulsa/rock group
Tanner, David Case/b. Tulsa, 1951/blues rock pianist
Tate, Bob, Jr./b. Oklahoma/jazz, R & B saxophonist
Tate, Mary Ann/b. Tulsa/blues singer
Tate, Jerod Impichchaachaaha'/b. Norman/Chickasaw classical composer
Taylor, Bobby/r. Tulsa/1950s rock and roll singer, Tulsa Sound
Taylor, Jody/r. Lexington/country guitarist in 1950s and '60s Oklahoma City-based duo, Jude and Jody
Taylor, Jovonia/2003 TU music student sings on TU jazz CD, Sophisticated Ladies
Taylor, Lester/r. Oklahoma City/jazz and R & B percussionist, singer
Taylor, Little Eddy/b. Oklahoma City/blues guitarist, soul singer
Taylor, Scott/r. Bartlesville
Taylor, Ted/b. Okmulgee, 1934/soul and blues singer
Teagarden, Charlie/b. Texas, r. Oklahoma City/jazz trumpeter
Teegarden, David/b. Tulsa/drummer writer, producer, See **Tulsa Sound**

Teagarden, Jack/b. Texas, r. Oklahoma City, played in Central High School Band/jazz trombonist
Tedder, Ryan/reared in Tulsa/producer musician/songwriter for Beyonce, B.o.B., Jennifer Lopez, Maroon 5, Kelly Clarkson, Wiz Khalifa, Hillar Duff, Adele, et. al., also front man for OneRepublic
Teegarden, David/b. Tulsa/producer, singer, songwriter, singer, drummer, **Tulsa Sound**
Te-Ata/b. December 3, 1895, Emet/Chickasaw singer and storyteller
Terrell, Stephen W./b. Oklahoma City/alternative country artist and journalist
Tex Montana's Fireball 4/f. Tulsa/rock group
Thacker, Ron/b. Duncan/lead guitarist for rock group Aggro
13 Stars/f. Oklahoma City/rock group
36 Inches/f. Oklahoma City/rock group
Thai Music/f. Tulsa/Thai Music at Lanna Thai Restaurant in Tulsa
Thirteen Stars/f. 1998, OKC/power pop/rock
Thomas, B.J.
Thomas, Chance/reared, OKC/composer for computer games/The Hobbit, et al.
Thomas, Guthrie/b. Lawton/folksinger
Thomas, Jesse "Babyface"/r. Oklahoma City/blues singer
Thomas, Joe/b. Muskogee, 1908/jazz tenor saxophonist
Thomas, Paul Wesley/b. Oklahoma City/symphony composer
Thomas, Tony/r. Hugo/old time fiddler
Thomas, Walter "Foots"/b. Muskogee, 1907/jazz flutist, saxophonist, bandleader, arranger
Thompson, Charlie/r. Oklahoma City, 1960s, d. 1991/bass vocalist for Elvis Presley, Sawyer Brown, et al.
Thompson, Chester, D./b. Oklahoma City/pianist and keyboardist with Tower of Power and Santana
Thompson, Hank
Thompson, Lee "Trippy"/b. Enid, 1962/rock singer for Dragmules (Atlantic Records)
Thompson, Patti/r. Tulsa, 1965/lead singer for ORU World Action Signers
Thompson, Paulina/b. Saratov, Russia, r. OKC/singer, songwriter
Thompson Square/country duo
Thompson, Kiefer/b. Miami/guitar, vocals
Thompson, Shawna/vocals
Thompson, Tony/b. Waco, TX, reared in OKC lead singer of Hi-Five, 1990s R & B group
Three Strange Days/f. Tulsa/rock group
351 Windsor/f. Tulsa/jazz jam band
Jones, Jeffrey/drummer
Karleskint, Paul/guitarist
Mayo, Matt/bassist
The Throwbacks/f. Tulsa/Christian rock group
Thompson, Verlin/b. 1/5/1954, Ardmore/songwriter for Loretta Lynn Music, CBS Songs, Capitol Records, co-producer for Guy Clark
Thunderhorse/f. 2000, Stillwater/northern style intertribal powwow group (Arbor Records) evolved into Young Buffalo Horse
Allen, Andy/lead singer
American Horse, Coleman (Northern Cheyenne/Lakota)/singer
Bear, Jeremy/lead singer
Coser, Pete, Jr. (Muscogee/Choctaw)/singer
Frank, Seymour (Euchee)/singer
Gabbard, Wayne/singer
Larson, Ahsinees/lead singer
Lincoln, Kyle (Shoshone/Choctaw)/singer
Lincoln, Robert (Choctaw/Ojibwa)/ b. Lawton/lead singer

Longhorn, Wayne (Navajo/Absentee Shawnee)/singer
McDaniel, Symphony/back-up singer
Moyer, Dana (Ojibwa)/back-up singer
Scott, Gregg (Choctaw)/singer
Shipman, Paul (Delaware/Cherokee)/ b. Pittsburgh, KS/singer
Ware, Bambi (Kiowa)/back-up singer
Washee, Timmy (Cheyenne-Arapaho)/singer
Thurman, Katrina/b. Moore/opera soprano
Thurman, Marty (Comanche/Sac & Fox)/intertribal powwow head singer
Tickle Monsters/f. Tulsa/rock group
Tiddark, Nipper/r. Oklahoma/intertribal powwow head singer
Tidwell, Natalie/b. Oklahoma City country singer
Tiger, B.J./r. Weleetka/Muscogee stomp dance leader (Indian House Records)
Tiger-J/b. Tulsa/rapper
Tiger, Chebon/r. Oklahoma/Muscogee blues singer/guitarist
Tiger, Junior/Nuyaka Ceremonial Grounds/stomp dance leader
Tillison, Roger/b. Oklahoma/rock guitarist for **J.J. Cale**, Gary Lewis, **Jesse Ed Davis**
Tillman, Floyd
Tindle, Mark/b. Ft. Monmouth, NJ, r. Tulsa guitar, banjo, mountain dulcimer player
Tipton, Billy/b. OKC, 1914/ d. Jan. 21, 1989, Spokane, WA/jazz pianist, saxophonist, also a woman who portrayed herself as a man to work as a musician
Tisdale, Wayman
Tisha/b. Tisha Campbell in OKC, 1970 R & B, hip hop singer
Tomlin, Truman, "Pinky"/r. Oklahoma pop composer
Tonkawa Tribe/based in Tonkawa, moved to I.T., 1855/Scalp Dance powwow
Tonsing, Evan/r. Glencoe/cellist, music professor at OSU, ethnomusicologist
Too Fair for Julie/f. Owasso/raw emo group
Tooisgah, Velma/r. Oklahoma intertribal powwow singer
Toppah, Cheevers
Toppah, Ernest "Iron" (Kiowa)/intertribal powwow head singer, Kiowa songs
Toppah, Sidney (Kiowa)/r. Wichita, KS/intertribal powwow head singer
Totty, Dennis/r. Tulsa/guitarist, singer, songwriter for Totty, CCM rock
Totty, Byron/r. Tulsa/bassist for Totty, CCM rock
Tovar, Jacob/r. Perry, Tulsa/country singer, guitarist
Tower, Wade/r. Stillwater/pop crooner
Townsend, Glenn R./b. Sulphur, 1948/blues vocalist and guitarist
The Tractors (see **Steve Ripley**)
Trader Price/f. Foss, OK/country group
Traindodge/f. Norman/rock group
Travis, Merle/b. Kentucky - d. Park Hill, Ok country guitarist
Trent Malloy/f. Oklahoma City, 2002/indy rock
Bell, Mitch/electric guitarist
Coe, James/bassist, vocalist
Dani, David/guitarist, vocalist
Ragland, Dustin/drummer
Tres Hombres/f. Stillwater, 2011/fusion of jazz, rock, and additional disparate influences of being from Stillwater
Tribe of Souls/f. Tulsa/reggae, funk, rock, ska
Butler, Charles/drummer
Rigney, Mike/bassist, keyboardist
Simmons, Brian/vocalist, guitarist
Tricinella/f. Tulsa/rock group
Tri-Lads/f. Tulsa 1957-1960/classic R&R, doo-wop style group

Fournier, Chuck/lead singer
Miller, Bill/bass singer, 1957-1960
Ragan, Bill/guitarist, harmony singer
Webb, James/bass singer, 1957, became Hollywood sound engineer
Trilogy/f. Catoosa, 2002/rock group
Barnes, Jason/r. Catoosa/lead guitarist
Poplin, Brandon/r. Coweta/bassist
Wise, Josh/r. Tulsa/drummer
Trinikas/f. OKC Douglas High School, 1970/R&B group who recorded "Black is Beautiful", released on Pearce Records in 1972
Trio Tulsa/r. Tulsa/chamber music
TripC/Owasso High School graduate, 2002/hip-hop artist with a punk rock ethos
Triplett, Gene/b. 1949, LaJolla, CA, reared in OKC/Daily Oklahoman music writer, editor, 1981-present, OMHOF Inductee, 2011
Tripplehorn, Tommy/b. Tulsa, 1944 drummer with Gary Lewis and the Playboys, Bill Davis, Tulsa Sound
Troutman, Tory/b. Yukon/music reviewer
Trudell, John/r. Tulsa/American Indian poet who recorded with Jesse Ed Davis
The Truthettes/based in Oklahoma City gospel group
2treal/f. Oklahoma/hip-hop, rap
Tsoodle, Gene/b. 1940, r. OKC/contemporary American Indian music singer/songwriter
Tucker Road/f. Stillwater/pop, rock, country
Cook, Terry/vocals, lead guitarist, rhythm guitarist
Grauberger, Tim/drummer
Reynolds, Mike/pianist, organist
Rogers, Jason/vocals, rhythm guitarist, mandolin and harmonica player
Talasaz, Afshean/bass guitar
Turnpike Troubadours/f. 2007, Oklahoma City/country rock, 2012 album, Goodbye Normal Street, peaked at #57 on Billboard's Top 200 album chart. (See Red Dirt Music)
Edwards, RC/bass, vocals
Engleman, Ryan/lead guitar
Felker, Evan/vocals, guitar
Nix, Kyle/fiddle, backing vocals
Pearson, Gabe/drums, backing vocals
Tulsa Sound
Tulsa Wildcards/f. Tulsa, 1999/pop/rock cover group driven to save the paddlefish, be the Western Hills house band, and force smiles statewide
Freeland, David/saxophone
Lienhart, Edward/lead vocalist, guitarist, keyboardist
Norfleet, Lee/bassist, vocalist
Winkle, John/drummer, vocalist
Tweedie, David/b. Stillwater/fiddler with Molasses Creek
Twelve Pearls/f. Stillwater, 1997/rock group
Crabtree, Matt/drummer
Doolen, Jordan/vocalist, guitarist
Jackson, Brad/guitarist
Nowlin, Kit/bassist
20 Minutes to Vegas/f. Oklahoma City/punk rock
20/20/f. Tulsa, 1970s/pop rock group
Allen, Steve/r. Tulsa/guitarist, vocalist
Flynt, Ron/r. Tulsa/bassist, vocalist
27 Ends/f. Stillwater/"American music" group, a.k.a. a country band
Good, Brad/r. Apache/singer, songwriter, bass guitarist
Lafave, Jesse/r. Cashion/guitarist
McGrew, Shane/r. Enid/fiddler
Woodson, Travis/r. Dewey/drummer
Yarbrough, Josh/r. Purcell, Prosper, Texas/guitarist
Twilley, Dwight
Twine, Linda/b. Muskogee, 1947/Broadway conductor, arranger, Tony Award winner

Twitty, Conway/r. Oklahoma City, 1960s-1975/ country, rock and roll singer
Tyler, Jared/r. Tulsa/singer, songwriter, guitarist, recorded with Malcolm Holcombe, Nora Jones, Jamie Kindleyside
Tyler, Stephen of Aerosmith/**not from OK** the parents of Teresa Barrick, the singer's wife, are from Tulsa

U

Ugly Tree/circa 2001-2003, Stillwater/punk rock group with members from Shawnee and Stillwater
Ultrafix/f. Tulsa/2002 Jim Beam/Rolling Stone Rock Band Search "Band of the Year"
 Charron, Beau/guitar
 DeVore, Angie/singer
 Fawcett, Mike/bassist
 Green, TJ/drummer
Ultraviolet Seraphic/f. Oklahoma City
Uncle Joey and the Mudpuppies/f. Edmond
Uncle Rumple/f. Tulsa/rock group
Underwood, Carrie
Unexpected Bliss/f. OKC, Bethany/rock group
Ungerman, Rebecca/r. Tulsa/blues singer with Blue Combo, Jon Glazer, and her own combo
United Keetoowah Band of Cherokees/based in Tahlequah, in I.T. since 1828/ceremonials, powwow
The Unreliables/f. Sapulpa/pop rock group
Upchurch, Greg/b. Kingston/drummer for hard rock group, Puddle of Mudd
Upside/f. Tulsa/rock group
The Uptown Horns/f. Tulsa/blues group, formerly Flash Terry's horn section

V

Vagabundus/f. Tulsa/modern rock group
Valliere, George, Jr. (Quapaw/Shawnee) r.Claremore/intertribal powwow head singer
Van Beek, Casey/b. Leiden, Holland/bassist w/ Linda Ronstadt, Steve Ripley, The Tractors
Van, Buddy/b. Indianola/lead guitarist for Henson Cargill, Little Jimmy Dickens, Wanda Jackson, et. al.
Vance, Karen/r. Tulsa/blues vocalist
Van Dyke, Pam/r. Tulsa/jazz vocalist
Vasquez, Andrew
Vaughn, Countess/b. Idabel, 1978/singer, actress on television program 227
The Velveteen Habit/f. Tulsa/rock group
Velvet Leaf/originally from New Orleans, r. Tulsa circa 2002/modern rock group
Verde/f. Tulsa/modern rock group
Vineyard, Randy/r. Tulsa/Barbara Streisand and Cher tribute performer
von Thurn, Reta Ruth/b. Tulsa, 1917/classical composer

W

Wackerly, Gary/r. Oklahoma/old time fiddler
Waffle/f. Oklahoma City, 1995/rock group
 Hart, Brian/guitarist
 Ray, Curtis/guitarist, bassist
 Ray, Travis/drummer
 Wilkinson, Mark/vocalist
Wagner, Carson/r. Tulsa/pianist (classical/ragtime/standards/Christian)
Wagner, Sarah & the Popadelphics/f. Tulsa old wave pop
Wahkinney, Rusty/r. Oklahoma intertribal powwow head singer
Wahpepah, Nick/r. Oklahoma/ intertribal powwow head singer
Wainright, Maci/b. 1/8/1998, Edmond/pop, rock singer, songwriter, guitarist, released independent CD, Good Day in 2005

Wakeland/f. Stillwater, 1990/pop rock group (Giant Records)
 Heinrichs, Brad/guitarist
 Litsch, Shane/drummer
 Nunez, Andy/bassist
 Sullivan, Chris/vocalist
Wakely, Jimmy
Walcher, Daniel/b. 1985, TX, reared Edmond indy folk-rock singer/songwriter
Walker, Aaron "T-Bone"/b. Linden, TX, 1910, r. OKC, 1930/blues vocalist, guitarist
Walker, Forrest "Kisko"/r. Shawnee intertribal powwow head singer
Walker, Harvey/b. Talihina, 1937/banjo player for the Wagonmasters
Walker, Henry, Jr./r. Oklahoma intertribal powwow head singer
Walker, Tom/Oklahoma State University music faculty, 2003/trombonist, recorded for Salvationist Records
Walker, Wayne
Wallace, Billy
Wallace, Matt/b. Tulsa, 1960/record producer (Sheryl Crow)
Walters, JD/r. Tulsa/steel-guitarist (Brazos Valley Boys)
Wand, Hart/r. Oklahoma City wrote one of the first published blues in music history, "Dallas Blues," in 1912
Wanzer, Lloyd/b. Enid/national fiddle champion
Ware, Bill/r. Bartlesville/drummer for BeauSoleil
Ware, Bill/r. Oklahoma intertribal powwow singer
Ware, Pearl/r. Oklahoma intertribal powwow singer
Ware, Terry "Buffalo"/b. Shattuck, 1950 solo guitarist, songwriter & guitarist for Ray Wylie Hubbard (also see Red Dirt Music)
Ware, Tom (Kiowa/Comanche)/b. Lawton/ intertribal powwow singer, Blues Nation, flutist, "49" singer
Ware, John/b. Tulsa, 1944/rock drummer with The West Coast Pop Art Experimental Band
Warford, Tony/r. Collinsville/CCM guitarist
Warren, Bobby/b. Norman/guitarist and founder of Shorebird Inpel Records
Warrenpeace/f. Oklahoma City/rock group
 Brann, Steve/guitarist
 King, J.J./vocalist
 McCord, Robbie/drummer
 Scott, Craig/bass
Washington, Wiley/song leader Duck Creek Ceremonial Grounds
Watermelon Slim (a.k.a. Bill Homans)/blues attended OSU/led Fried Okra Jones
Way Out West/f. Okemah/traditional country
Wayne, Curtis/r. Lawton, Nashvillecountry songwriter, songs recorded by George Strait
Weatherford, Lily Fern/b. 11/25/1928, Bethany/ Gospel singer in the Southern Gospel Music Hall of Fame, moved to CA as a child, moved back to OK in 1970S, returned to CA, resided Broken Arrow as of 2013
Weaver, Smiley/b. Ada/vocalist with Bob Wills steel guitarist for Les Gilliam
Webb, Amy/b. Oklahoma/folk singer, songwriter
Webb, Jimmy
Webb, Toby Lee/r. Tulsa/country singer
Webster, Joe/r. Bartlesville/singer
Weems, Ted/died in Tulsa, May 6, 1963/ big band leader
Welborn, Larry/r. Mead, OK/rockabilly jingled keys on "That'll Be The Day"/B. Holly
Welch, Herbie/b. Muskogee/R & B guitarist, singer
Welch, Kevin
Wensell, Craig/b. Stillwater/classical double bassist
Wesley, George, Jr./b. Oklahoma City/gospel singer
Western Justice/f. Tulsa/country group
 Arnold, Jim/r. Tulsa/drummer

Bennett, Bruce/r. Rogers, AR/bassist
 Duvall, Brad/r. Tulsa/acoustic guitarist
 Lane, Michael/r. Tulsa/singer, guitarist
West, Speedy/b. Springfield, MO, 1924, r. Tulsa, 1960/steel guitarist recorded with Loretta Lynn, Tenn. Ernie Ford
West, Speedy, Jr/ b. Hollywood, CA, 1953 d. 5/4/2011, OKC/country and rock guitarist
We The Ghost/f. Tulsa, 2012/hybridindy pop
Wheeler, Ron/r. Tulsa/educator, classical conductor
Wheeler, Ron/b. Alva/folk singer, songwriter
Whisperloud/f. Oklahoma, recording since 1999/CCM
 Blumer, Keri/singer
 Carris, Alana/singer
 Gaskill, Tessa/singer
Whister, Norman/b. 10/9/1933, Elk City, KS, r. Bartlesville/fiddler for Roger Miller and Merle Haggard
White, Bill/b. Muldrow, 1934/country singer
White, Bryan
White, Buck/b. Oklahoma/singer and mandolinist in country group The Whites
WhiteCloud, Gary "Chink" (Otoe/Muscogee) r. Tulsa, OK/intertribal powwow singer
White, Craig/Rose State College professor, 2003 started a music recording option as part of liberal studies program
White, Dionne/Miss Okmulgee, 2003 pop and jazz singer
White, Don/b. Tulsa, 1940/country, rock singer, guitarist for J.J. Cale, et al. songwriter, Tulsa Sound
White, Geoff/r. Tahlequah intertribal powwow head singer
Whitehorse, Mac/r. Oklahoma/ intertribal powwow singer
Whitekiller, Johnny/r. Hulbert, Tahlequah area country and rock singer, guitarist, bandleader since early 1970s
Whittle, Elmer/b. Tahlequah, 1927 Western swing guitarist
Wichita & Affiliated Tribes
Wiggins, Wally/r. Tulsa/Tulsa Sound vocalist and bandleader from 1957 to 1960
Wig Head/f. Owasso/trippy rock band
Wilcox, Harlow/b. Norman/country guitarist known for "Groovy Grubworm"
Wild Band of Comanches/f. Fletcher, OK/ Southern-style intertribal powwow singing group from the Comanche Nation in OK
 Adson, Aaron/singer
 Brown, Spud/singer
 Cable, Kelly/singer
 Cozad, Howard/singer
 Cozad, Kenneth/singer
 Delgado, Hah-Tee/singer
 Delgado, Starr/singer
 Dobbin/singer
 Lightfoot, Crystal/singer
 Lightfoot, Jason/singer
 Monoessy, Anthony/singer
 Monoessy, Larry/singer
 Monoessy, Ronald/singer
 Monoessy, Thea/singer
 Motah, Joe/singer
 Ross, JR/singer
 Tahchawwickah, Chad/singer
 Thompson, Tish/singer
 Toppah, Cheevers/singer
Wilder, Christian Logan/b. Lawton/opera singer
Wilder, Walt/b. Taloga, r. Edmond/country singer, songwriter, publisher
Wiley and Gene
Wiley, Lee
Wiley, Stephen/r. Muskogee/Christian hip hop
Wilkerson, Zac/b. Buffalo/singer, songwriter
Williams, Claude "Fiddler"

Williams, Dennis/r. Oklahoma City/gospel singer w/ The Mighty Wonders
Williams, Gary/b. Pryor, 1971/blues guitarist
Williams, John/b. Tulsa, OK, 1940/50s rock and contemporary jazz saxophonist, played with Leon Russell
Williams, Lew/b. 1/12/1934, Chillicothe, TX Rockabilly singer on KTAT, Frederick, OK "Cab Calloway of rockabilly"
Williams, Mason/b. Abilene, TX, r. OKC//classical guitarist, known for "Classical Gas", also part of early 1960s OKC folk scene
Williamson, Gayle/b. Tulsa/jazz pianist with Sounds Good
Williamson, Josh (Sac & Fox/Choctaw)/intertribal powwow head singer
Willis, Aunt Minerva and Uncle Wallace/r. Choctaw Nation/first documented singing of "Swing Low, Sweet Chariot"
Willis, Bill/r. Tulsa/jazz and blues organist
Willis Brothers (Guy, Skeeter, and Vic)
Willis, Kelly
Wills Brothers (Bob, Johnnie Lee, Luke, and Billy Jack)
Wills, Roger/b. Kiowa/bassist, Alan Jackson's bandleader
Willyecho/formed Tulsa, 2011/harmony-laden soul, pop duo
  Rappe, Micheal/guitar, vocals
  Williams, Kyle/guitar, vocals
Wilson, Charlie (see **The GAP Band**)
Wilson, J. Paul/enrolled Sac & Fox intertribal powwow head singer
Wilson, Jim/b. Oklahoma City/Choctaw world music producer and musician
Wilson, Jimmie/r. Oklahoma/bandleader, Catfish String Band
Wilson, Joe Lee
Wilson, Kenny/b. El Reno/country singer, songwriter
Wilson, Mark/r. Oklahoma/opera baritone
Wilson, Reuben/b. Mounds, 1935/soul and jazz organist
Windsor 351/f. Tulsa/modern rock group
Wingers, Warren/r. Owasso/singer, songwriter
Winslett, Jerry, Jr./b. Del City/country music singer, songwriter
Winter Boys, f. in a Stillwater kitchen, 2012
  Brown, Derek/additional keyboards
  Frisby, Aaron/percussion
  Meade, Tyson/vocals
  Tabish, Jesse/guitar/keyboard (Other Lives)
Winters, Zach/r. Norman/singer, songwriter
Wiseman, Craig/b. Lexington/songwriter (Tim McGraw's "Cowboy and Me")
Wooley, John/b. MN, r. Chelsea, OK/music journalist, writer with more 25 books, many covering Oklahoma music, OMHOF inductee, co-wrote "Gone Away" with Steve Ripley
Wooley, Sheb
Wooten, Bob/r. Sand Springs Johnny Cash's guitarist from 1968
Wooten, Steve/b. Tulsa, 1957/independent country vocalist, guitarist
Wooten, Ruby (Rowan)/b. Fort Gibson/pop, country guitarist, vocalist who performed with Porter Wagoner
Word, Lucky/b. Wright City/bassist, guitarist, played with Merl Lindsay
Word of Mouth/f. Oklahoma/rock group
Wright, Claude, H./b. 1893, Lebanon, KS, moved to Collinsville, I.T. in 1899 music educator, bandleader
Wright, Dempsey/b. Calumet, 1929/jazz guitarist
Wrightsman, Stan/b. Gotebo or OKC, 1910 Dixieland pianist
The WuWus/f. OKC, 2012/electronic pop
The Wurly Birds/f. 2010, OKC/R&B, soul, rock
Wyandotte Nation/based in Wyandotte since 1893/powwow

Y

Yarbrough, Tom/r. Oklahoma/country songwriter
Yard, Jocelyn/b. Oklahoma City, 1984 finger style guitarist
Yeagley, David, A./b. Oklahoma City classical pianist
Yearwood, Trisha/r. Owasso, 2005-present/country music singer who married **Garth Brooks** and relocated to the state.
Yellow Hammer/f. Ponca City and Red Rock, 1995/southern style powwow group (See Otoe-Missoria and Ponca entries)
  Botone, Perry Lee, Jr./singer
  Gawhega, Michael, N./singer
  Grant, James, Sr./singer
  Hudson, Wesley/singer
  Kemble, James, Jr./singer
  Kemble, James, Sr. b. Wichita, KS, r. Ponca City/singer
  Kent, Garland, Jr./singer
  Lieb, Kinsel, V./singer
  Little Cook, Oliver, Jr./singer
  Little Cook, Stephen T./singer
  McIntosh, John, Sr./singer
  Moore, Patrick, L., Sr./singer
  Morning Star Kemble, Andrea/back-up singer
  Roubedoux, Jade/back-up singer
  Roubedoux, Tesa Dee/back-up singer
Yellow Spotted Horse/f. 1992/southern style powwow group
  Bighorse, Kenny Bob/lead singer
  Bills, K.C./singer
  Blackstar, Linda/singer
  Goodeagle, Guideon/singer
  Goodeagle, Laura/singer
  Goodeagle, Tesa/singer
  Hutchins, Roman/singer
  Kimble, Andrea/singer
  Kemble, James, Jr./singer
  Lazelle, Linda/singer
  Littlecook, Littlebear/singer
  Littlecook, O.J./singer
  Littlecook, Oliver (Ponca)/b. Ponca City lead singer
  Mashunkashey, Russell/singer
Yohe, Tony/r. Tulsa/jazz, blues drummer
Yoon, Hooby/b. Tulsa, 1975/award-winning competitive classical pianist
York, Paris/b. Indianola, 1934/jazz educator, co-owner with son (Larry) and grandson (Adam) of Music Store, Tulsa, OK
York, Walter Wynn/b. Claremore, 1914/classical composer
The Young Aristocracy/f. Tulsa, 1960s garage rock band included on 1960s garage rock compilation, Teenage Shutdown (Vol. 9)
Youngbear, J.R./r. Oklahoma intertribal powwow head singer
Young Bird
Young Buffalo Horse/f. Shawnee, early 2000s/northern style powwow singing group on P-Dub Records (2013)
  Robert Lincoln/head singer
  Coleman American Horse/singer
  Bryce Bailey/singer
  Robby Boston/singer
  Pete RG Coser/singer
  Nokose Foley/singer
  Chiefy Greenwood/singer
  Colt Lincoln/singer
  Shema Lincoln/singer
  Shannon Ross/singer
  Coltin Shawnee/singer
  Mikael Toledo/singer
Young Hustlas Coalition/f. Tulsa/rap group
  A-Game/rapper
  Anjorin, Femi/rapper
  Brown, Reginald (Dibiasi)/rapper
  CO2/rapper
  Droop Locc/rapper
  Profit/rapper
Young, Ruth Alexander/b. Ardmore opera singer

Z

Zaremba, Kathryn/b. Broken Arrow/Broadway musical performer, (played Annie on Broadway)
Zeabra/f. Shawnee, 1967 as Sage, renamed Zeabra in Stillwater, 1970s/pop rock group (Circus Records)
  Baird, Rusty/r. Shawnee/2nd bassist
  Brown, Donald/r. Shawnee/2nd drummer
  Fuller, Mick/r. Shawnee/original drummer
  Hawkins, Jeff/r. Shawnee/guitarist, vocalist
  Hembree, Mark/r. Shawnee/guitarist, vocalist
  Kelly, Chris/r. Shawnee/keyboards
  McGehee, Tommy/r. Shawnee/original bassist
Zen Hipster/f. Tulsa/alternative rock group
Zero for Conduct/f. Tulsa/space rock group
Ziff/f. Tulsa/rock group
Zion Rex/f. Norman/rock group
Zoellner, Philip/r. Tulsa/roots-rock singer, songwriter, guitarist, formerly led alt-country outfit, Marshall City
Zotigh, Dennis (Kiowa)/r. Norman, AI music history intertribal powwow head singer,

Image Credits for Oklahoma Music Guide II

The author of the *Oklahoma Music Guide II* wishes to thank all of the people, companies, media outlets, and private archivists who have contributed historic images to help illustrate this book. If any information included in these credits is incorrect, or if an image's copyright has been improperly transferred to its current ownership, please contact the authors for a timely resolution and/or correction for subsequent editions of the guide. Send comments, concerns, questions, or additional images to hughwfoley@gmail.com.

Introductory Essay Images: Muskogee Musicians, date unkown (likely 1910s or 1920s), courtesy Leo Cundiff; Carrie Underwood in Checotah, 2005, courtesy Cathy Coomer; Jimmy Webb courtesy of Greg Johnson at the Blue Door in OKC; additional images from the Hugh Foley collection; **Abeyta, David** image courtesy of Yep Roc Records; **Admiral Twin** photo by C Taylor Crothers/courtesy Admiral Twin; **Ahaitty, Walter** images courtesy Walter Ahhaitty and The Sound of Indian America Records; **All-American Rejects** image courtesy Honda Corporation, Chris Gaylor and Tyson Ritter images by Hugh Foley; **Tommy Allsup** images courtesy of Hugh Foley; **AM** image courtesy of www.amsounds.com; **Keith Anderson** images courtesy www.keithanderson.com and ARISTA Nashville; **Tuck Andress** images courtesy www.tuckandpatti.com; **Apache Tribe of Oklahoma** images courtesy *Music of the Plains Apache* (AHM 4252); **Aqueduct's** David Terry image courtesy of Alicia J. Rose; **Larry Austin** image courtesy Larry Austin; **Gene Autry** photo from Foley collection; **Hoyt Axton** photos from Foley collection and courtesy Jeremiah Records (JH 5000) from the cover of *Rusty Old Halo* (1979); **Mae Boren Axton** image courtesy Cantrell Publishing, Ada, OK; **Chet Baker** album cover images courtesy of Universal Music and Video Distribution for *Verve Jazz Masters 32* (1994), Entertainers Records (CD 284), Enja Records with cover photo from *My Favourite Songs: The Last Great Concert* (R179600) by Calle Hesslefors, and picture of Chet Baker in front of mirror courtesy Kestone Pressedienst, GMBH; **Baker, Mark** image courtesy Florida Institute of Technology Office of University Communications; **Louis Ballard** 2004 image courtesy Louis Ballard from Hugh Foley collection, photo at piano by Abe Eilot courtesy of Louis Ballard; **Johny Barbata** image courtesy www.johnybarbata. com; **Glenn Barber** image courtest EDsel Records, *The Crazy Cajun Recordings of Glenn Barber* (NESTCD927); **Bobby Barnett** courtesy Bear Family Records; **Carl Belew** photo from Foley collection; **Aaron Bell** image by Bob Ghiraldini from *John Coltrane & Duke Ellington* (1962) liner notes (Impulse, MCA-39103); **Trent Bell** image courtesy Trent Bell at myspace.com/trentbell; **Wayne Bennett** courtesy www.mikereillyband.com; **Byron Berline** photos courtesy of Byron Berline and Hugh Foley collection; **Elvin Bishop** album covers courtesy of Alligator Records; 2010 promo image by Jen Taylor and courtesy Delta Groove Music; **Chuck Blackwell** 2006 images by Foley at Oklahoma Music Hall of Fame Induction for Carl Radle, 2006; 1969 image from inside cover of Taj Mahal's *Giant Step* (Columbia GP 18); **Bob Bogle** playing bass courtesy of Mel Taylor via album cover for *The Ventures: Live in Japan '65* (EMI, 1995) courtesy EMI/Liberty/Dolton Records, Bogle in sunglasses from back cover of *Rock and Roll Forever* (SPC-3589) courtesy of Pickwick International Records; **Jason Boland and the Stragglers** photos courtesy Brandy Reed of RPR Marketing and Public Relations, Nashville; **Johnny Bond** album cover courtesy of Bloodshot Revival and Soundies www.bloodshotrecords.com , design by M Greiner; **Glen Bonham** image courtesy Glen Bonham; **Earl Bostic** image courtesy Foley collection; **Mike Brewer** photo by Jeff Nicholson/courtesy Brewer and Shipley; **Garth Brooks** young image with guitar courtesy Chrome Dreams, UK from the 1999 narrative history CD, *Maximum Garth Brooks*; studio publicity photo by Beverly Parker courtesy Capitol Records, action shot from Foley collection; image of Garth Brooks going away party at Willie's courtesy Bill Bloodworth; **Junior Brown** cover image by George Brainard from *Down Home Chrome* (Telarc CD 83612) courtesy Telarc Records; **Albert Brumley, Sr.** photo courtesy Hartford Music Company and Albert E. Brumley and Sons; **Anita Bryant** album cover photo for *Abide With Me* (WST-8532) by Russ Busby courtesy of WORD Records; second image from album cover for *The World of Lonely People* (Columbia CL 22220; **Don Byas** cassette cover of *All the Things You Are* (2673734) courtesy Jazz Life Records, Holland; second image courtesy CD cover of *Midnight at Minton's* (Highnote 7044) courtesy of Highnote Records, New York City; cover image of *Savoy Jam Party* courtesy Universal Music Development Group; **Caddo Nation** seal courtesy of the Caddo Nation; image of Caddo singers courtesy of Thurmon Parton; **J.J. Cale** album cover of *Millennium Collection – 20th Century Masters* (2002) courtesy Universal Music Development Group; photo sitting with guitar uncredited press photo courtesy The Rosebud Agency; photo of J.J. Cale with Hugh Foley by Christine Lakeland with Hugh's camera in NYC; Elder photo of J.J. Cale by Anton Cobijn courtesy Anton Corbijn and The Rosebud Agency; **The Call** image courtesy MCA Records; **Jerry Cantrell** image courtesy Bill Ebbesen; **Hank Card** image courtesy www.austinloungelizards.com; **Henson Cargill** image courtesy Mega Records for the back cover of *On the Road* (Buckboard, BBS-1012); **Larry Carlton** cover image from *The Best of Larry Carlton* (GRP, 2005)) courtesy Universal Music Development Group; **Jeff Carson** fan club image from Hugh Foley collection; **Rose and Roy Carter** courtesy the Chuck Wagon Gang courtesy GOGR at www.grandolegospelreunion.com; **Chainsaw Kittens** press kit image from Foley collection by Craig S. Smith; image of Tyson Meade courtesy Aaron Frisby; **Greyson Chance** image courtesy Universal Music Development Group; **Kristin Chenoweth** headshot photo courtesy PMK HBH Management; additional images courtesy Sony Music and www.kristin-chenoweth.com; **Cherokee** images of stomp dance, flute workshop, flutes, and Cherokee National Youth Choir by Hugh Foley; image of fiddlers Sam O'Fields and John Church courtesy Cara Cowan; J.B. Dreadfulwater image courtesy of J.B. Dreadfulwater from the album *Guide Me Jehovah* (JB 447), Ace Moreland album cover *Give It to Get It* (IHR 9438) photo by Peter J. Everett courtesy icehouse and King Snake Records; image of Elvis Presley from an 8X10 publicity shot of unknown origin with no photo or copyright credits and is part of the author's collection; **Cheyenne-Arapaho** images by Hugh Foley; **Charlie Christian** image courtesy of Leo Valdes, and Universal Music and Video Distribution for album cover of *Radio Land 1939-1941* (2001); **Eddie Cletro** image courtesy Diane Cletro Johnson; **Sarah Coburn** image courtesy Barrett Vantage Artists by Stacy Boge; **Kellie Coffey** photo courtesy of Roseann and Robert Coffey; **Color Me Badd** album cover photos for *Now and Forever* (Giant, 1996) by Jon Ragel, courtesy of Giant and Warner Brothers Records; **Graham Colton** publicity image courtesy Graham Colton; live image placed in public domain on www.wikipedia.org; **John Convertino** image by Hugh Foley taken at WNYU-FM studios, NYC, 1988; **David Cook** publicity cover of *Star* magazine, www.starmagazine.com; **Spade Cooley** album cover courtesy of Bloodshot Revival and Soundies www.bloodshotrecords.com , design by M Greiner; **Cowboy Copas** image from Starday LP, *Inspirational Songs* (SLP 133); **Samantha Crain** photo appeared in Ramseur Records *Songs of the Night* (RR2727) liner notes courtesy Ramseur Records and Samantha Lamb, photographer; **Tommy Crook** photo by Hugh Foley; **Crooked X** image courtesy www.myspace.com/crookedx and www.rockbandent.com; **Cross Canadian Ragweed** 1999 image by Matthew Gambrell from Foley collection; live shots by Foley at the Tumbleweed in Stillwater; later studio shots courtesy Brandy Reed of RPR Marketing and Public Relations, Nashville and Universal Music Development Group; **Alvin Crow** image courtesy of Alvin Crow and www.mypace.com/alvincrow; 1978 image from now defunct and undated *Country Music* Magazine article; **Edgar Cruz** image courtesy Edgar Cruz and www.edgarcruz.com; **Agnes "Sis" Cunningham** image with Almanac Singers courtesy of Bess L. Hawes, and Prism Records from the *Songs of Protest* CD (Prism, B00005Q4AQ); **Gail Davies** courtesy of Gail Davies; **Jesse Ed Davis** with "Ed's in town button" image courtesy Epic Records bonus record AS7 1067, 1973; 1966 photo on stage while backing up Conway Twitty in Oklahoma City, courtesy Gene Jones; playing guitar image by Jim Marshall from 1973 CBS (Epic) LP AL 31233; **Debris** image from archives of Karl Ikola, Chuck Ivey, and Johnny Gregg, appeared in Debris, *Static Disposal* (Anopheles Records 004); Debris at Opolis in Norman courtesy www.myspace.com/debris1975; **John Denver** image from *Rocky Mountain High: Live in Japan* (Eagle Rock/Fontana, 2009) courtesy of Universal Music Group Development; **Yvonne DeVaney** image courtesy of Yvonne DeVaney; **Joe Diffie** 2010 image courtesy Universal Music and Development Group by Scott Simontacchi; early 1990s photo courtesy of Joe Diffie Fan Club; album cover artwork for Joe Diffie, *The Ultimate Collection* (2009) courtesy Rounder Records; **Ernestine Dillard** image courtesy www.ernestinedillard.com; **Dinning Sisters** images courtesy Dolores Dinning Edgin at www.doloresdinningedgin.com and Foley collection; **Mark Dinning** image from MGM single "A Star is Born (A Love Has Died)" (K12688); **Big Al Downing** publicity photo courtesy Martha Moore, So Much Moore Media and Marketing; 1960s image and later image in overalls courtesy Wanda Jackson; **Tim Dubois** photo courtesy Vanderbilt University Media Department; **Jack Dunham** photo courtesy of Jack Dunham; **Ronnie Dunn** photos from Foley collection; Red Dirt Tour poster from direct marketing postcard; image of Brooks and Dunn with Reba courtesy Arista Nashville and MCA Nashville; **Nokie Edwards**

photo courtesy Judy and Nokie Edwards; **Stoney Edwards** press photos courtesy Foley collection; Stoney sitting in chair on cover of *Mississippi You're On My Mind* (Capitol ST-11401) art direction by Roy Kohara; Stoney at bar from cover of *No Way to Drown a Memory* (Music America) courtesy Curtis Wayne; **Stephen Egerton** image courtesy Stephen Egerton; **Shelby Eicher** image courtesy Shelby Eicher; **Katrina Elam** images courtesy Universal South Records and Katrina Elam; **Scott Ellison** image courgesy Scott Ellison; **Tyler England** album cover for *Two Ways to Fall* (RCA 66930-2) courtesy of RCA Records; **Ester Dean** image courtesy *BMI Music World*; **Ester Drang** image courtesy www.esterdrang.com; **Toni Estes image** courtesy Toni Estes; **Evangelicals** image by Matthew Isaac courtest www.myspace.com/evangelicals; **Ernie Fields Orchestra** image courtesty Delmark Records from cover of *Big Band Jazz Tulsa to Harlem* (Delmark DL-439) via the Frank Driggs Collection; **Shug Fisher** youthful image courtesy Collection of Karl E. Farr, which his son donated to the Southern Folklife Collection at the Library of the University of North Carolina at Chapel Hill. The image is also courtesy of the Elizabeth Drake McDonald Collection (Inventory #20355), Manuscripts Department, University of North Carolina at Chapel Hil; later image of Fisher in character from Foley collection; **Five Americans** Spanish 7" image courtesy of www.thefiveamericans.com; **Flaming Lips** group photo courtesy Warner Brothers Records; Wayne Coyne, 2006, courtesy Kris Krug; image of Steven Drozd courtesy of Ella Mullins; images of Lollapalooza performance courtesy Alex Gaylon; image of OKC Zoo Amphitheater performance courtesy of Morgan Tepsic; image of Michael Ivins, 2006, courtesy Liz Berry; live shot of Wayne Coyne hitting gong courtesy Hellfire Management; **Flash Terry** photo by Mac; **For Love Not Lisa** image courtesy www.forlovenotlisa.com; **Rocky Frisco** 1950s images courtesy Rocky Frisco; Rocky Frisco on stage with Eric Clapton and J.J. Cale Image courtesy of Rosebud Agency photographer Johnny A; Rocky Frisco backstage at 2008 Oklahoma Music Hall of Fame Show, 2008 by Hugh Foley; **Lowell Fulson** publicity photo by E.K. Waller courtesy of Bullseye and Rounder Records; **Steve and Cassie Gaines** as part of Lynyrd Skynyrd group photo originally sent out by Famous Toby Mami's Public Relations, now in Foley collection; un-credited 8X10 publicity photo of Steve Gaines in Foley collection; **GAP Band** album cover of *Millennium Collection – 20th Century Masters* (2000) and GAP Band III courtesy Universal Music Group Development; GAP Band receiving BMI Award courtesy BMI Music World; **Benny Garcia, Jr.** photo by Hugh Foley; photo with Don Tolle by Berniece Cook; **David Gates** courtesy of Selwyn Miller Management; **Vince Gill** publicity photo courtesy MCA Nashville/Universal Music Group Development by Andrew Eccles, 2002; group picture with Barney Kessel and Byron Berline by Hugh Foley; image of Gill at the Crossroads Guitar Festival by Truejustice; **Gary Gilmore** image by Hugh Foley; **Al Good** images courtesy Al Good; **Bill Grant** and Delia Bell image #1 by Howard Clay; Bill Grant and Delia Image #2 courtesy Kiamichi Records; Bill Grant image by Anne Howze courtesy www.myspace.com/billgrantmusic; **George Grantham** with Poco from uncredited Epic Records publicity still; **Otto Gray** and Billy McGinty photos courtesy of Carla and Dale Chlouber at the Washington Irving Trail Museum and Foley collection; **Wardell Gray** image 1 from Foley collection, image 2 from Wardell Gray, *Memorial Recordings, Volume I and II* (Fantasy) courtesy Universal Music Group Development; **Great Divide** group photo by Jim Herrington courtesy of The Great Divide; **Barrick Griffiths** images courtesy of Barrick Griffiths; **Woody Guthrie** images with guitar courtesy Woody Guthrie Archives; Image of Woody Guthrie's home as it appeared in Okemah in the 1970s by George Carney; Ribbon of Highway/Endless Skyway courtesy Shout Factory Records; **Merle Haggard** image circa 1960s by George Herman of Capitol Photo Studio and from Merle Haggard, *Strangers* (Capitol T2373) courtesy Capitol Records; image with Merle playing fiddle by Jimmy Latham of Odessa, Texas, appeared in liner notes of *Bob Wills and His Texas Playboys for the Last Time* (United Artists, 1973); un-credited Haggard press photo circa 2000 from Foley collection; "Okie from Muskogee" promotional bookmark courtesy City of Muskogee Chamber of Commerce; **David Halley** CD image courtesy of www.artistdirect.com; **Jim Halsey** image with Oak Ridge Boys courtesy Jim Halsey; "Starmaker" image courtesy Jim Halsey and Oklahoma Historical Society from invitation to the opening to the 2010 Jim Halsey "Starmaker" exhibit at the Oklahoma History Center in Oklahoma City; image with Johnnie Lee Wills band by David Montgomery courtesy the Jim Halsey company, appeared on back cover Wills' *Reunion* (Flying Fish FF069, 1978); Jim Halsey with Dr. Bob Blackburn by Hugh Foley; **Hanson** image courtesy www.hanson.net; Best of Hanson CD cover courtesy Universal Music Group Development; Hanson 2001 press image courtesy Universal Music Group Development, by Dewey Nicks; **Roy Harris** image from Dan Stehman, *Roy Harris: A Bio-Bibliography* (New York: Greenwood, 1992) courtesy Johana Harris Heggie and Greenwood Press, 88 Post Road West, Westport, CT, 06881; **Sam Harris** image by Hugh Foley, 2010; **Ali Harter** image performing live at the Conservatory, OKC, courtesy Doug Schwarz; profile image courtesy Little Mafia Records; **Wade Hayes, 2011 image by Deana Tackett** courtesy wadehayes.com; OMHOF, 2008 performance image by Hugh Foley; **Lee Hazlewood** on back cover of Nancy Sinatra's *Country My Way* LP (WB/Reprise RS 6251) with photo credit to Ron Joy; **Michael Hedges** publicity photo by Ebet Roberts courtesy Windham Hill Records and in Foley collection; **Scott Hendrickns** image courtesy www.scotthendricksinfo.com; **Sam Hinton** image courtesy of www.sandiegohistory.org; **Becky Hobbs** photo by Dean Dixon courtesy Beckaroo Productions; **Hadley Hockensmith** image courtesy of Hadley Hockensmith via his facebook page; **Doyle Holly** album cover image photo from *Just Another Cowboy Song* (BR-15011) by Ken Kim courtesy Barnaby Records; **Mike Hosty** images by Hugh Foley; **Ray Wylie Hubbard** photo by Todd Woolfson courtesy Ray Wylie Hubbard; **Charlie Huff** images from a 1950s Charlie Huff independently published songbook in Foley collection; **Iowa Tribe of Oklahoma** seal courtesy Iowa Tribe of Oklahoma Powwow Program; Billy McClellan Sr. fancy dance image courtesy Indian Health Care Resource Center of Tulsa; Jeff McClellan image courtesy Canyon Records by Stephen Butler from *For Our Loved Ones* (CR-6397); Iowa Powwow image by Foley; **Wanda Jackson** Wanda Jackson 1950s and 1990s publicity images courtesy Wendell Goodman and Wanda Jackson Entertainment; Let's Have a Party Album cover art Universal Music Group Development for her 2011 CD, *Let's Have a Party: Best of Wanda Jackson* (Fontana, 2011); album cover photo from *Rock 'n' Roll Away Your Blues* (VR-025) courtesy Varrick and Rounder Records; image of Wanda singing in 2009 by Hugh Foley; **Jacob Fred Jazz Odyssey** 2011 group image courtesy www.jfjo.com; image of Brian Haas playing keyboards by Hugh Foley; **Jana Jae** image by Chuck Monson courtesy prunepicker.blogspot.com; **Brett James** image by JenST213 at photobucket.com; **William Johns** image courtesy William Johns; **Cecil Johnson** image by Jack Reynolds from the album Cecil Johnson, *Country Style Fiddling* ; **Herman Johnson** image from the album Herman Johnson , *National Champion*; **Claude Jones** image by William P. Gottlieb, courtesy Ira and Leonore S. Gershwin Fund Collection, Music Division, Library of Congress; **Stacy Jones** image by Colin Lane courtesy Universal Music Development Group; **Kaw Nation** seal courtesy of the Kaw Nation; **Toby Keith** 2010 publicity image courtesy Show Dog Universal; 1993 Mercury Records publicity image by Mark Tucker; 1996 image courtesy Universal Music Group Development; 2003 publicity image by Richard McLaren courtesy Universal Music Group Development and Dreamworks-Nashville Records; 2009 USO Afghanistan USO tour image courtesy U.S. Department of Defense Public Information Office by Sgt. Joshua LaPere; **Barney Kessel** photo by William Gullette courtesy Barney and Phyllis Kessel; **Merle Kilgore** photo by Gordy Collins courtesy Merle Kilgore; **Kings of Leon** photos courtesy Rockvizion Concert Photos, Australia; **Kiowa** images by Hugh Foley courtesy Kiowa Gourd Clan, the Cozad Family, and Evans Ray Satepauhoodle; **Leo Kottke** image by Anthony Pepitone courtesy Wikimedia Commons; **Gail Kubik** image courtesy www.dvdtoile.com of Paris, France; **Jimmy LaFave** publicity photo by Jim Herrington courtesy Bohemia Beat and Rounder Records; live concert images of Jimmy LaFave from the 2010 Woody Guthrie Folk Festival in Okemah, OK, courtesy of Candy Harsany; **Miranda Lambert** image 1 by Randee St. Nicholas courtesy Sony Nashville; images 2 and 3 courtesy www.graphicshunt.com; **Don Lamond** image from Slingerland Drums ad from Foley collection; **Rodney Lay and the Blazers** image courtesy Rodney Lay; Rodney Lay circa 2000s image courtesy www.myspace.com/kellyskountryjunctionshow; **Merl Lindsay and his Night Riders** group image from cover of *Boppin' Hillbilly Vol. 7* (Collector, WLP 2807); **Little Texas** image of Dwayne O'Brien byJeremy Cowart courtesy www.littletexasonline.com; **Guy Logsdon** image courtesy Guy Logsdon from www.guylogsdon.com; **Los Reactors** image courtesy www.myspace.com/losreactors; **Clarence Love** image courtesy of Clarence Love; **Jimmie Lunceford** image by William P. Gottlieb, courtesy Ira and Leonore S. Gershwin Fund Collection, Music Division, Library of Congress; **Zac Maloy** image courtesy http://www.myspace.com/zacmaloy; **Kim Manning** image by Hugh Foley; **Junior Markham** image by Hugh Foley; **Moon Martin** image courtesy Moon Martin and www.moonmartin.com; **Tony Matthews** by Hugh Foley; **Barbara McAlister** image by Kelly Studios, Muskogee, OK; **Leon McAuliffe** image 1 from Leon McAuliffe, *The Dancin'est Band Around* (Capitol T2016), image 2 courtesy *Country Music*

People, Vol. 3, No. 5, May 1972 issue (Kent, England), image 3 from Rogers State College yearbook, 1987, courtesy Rogers State University, Claremore, OK; **Cecil McBee** image courtesy Zagreb Jazz Festival, 2011: **Mike McClure** image by Hugh Foley; **Mel McDaniel** image from Foley collection; **Reba McEntire** profile publicity photo by McGuire courtesy MCA-Nashville; contemporary image from Foley collection; *For My Broken Heart* cover courtesy Universal Music Group Development; 2008 performance image courtesy vwbeetleboy via wikimediacommons; **Susie McEntire** image courtesy www.susiemcentire.com; **Howard McGhee** image by Tom Marcello, Webster, NY; **Barry McGuire** image by Nambassa Trust and Peter Terry courtesy www.nambassa.com; **J.D. McPherson** image courtesy of Hi-Style Records; **Jay McShann** 1940s and 1980s photos courtesy Jay McShann; 1995 image by Phil Wight taken in Edinburgh, Scotland, 1995; performance photo in Tulsa by Hugh Foley; **Tyson Meade** image Chainsaw Kittens publicity photo courtesy Mammoth Records by Bill Phelps; **Chris Merritt** publicity headshot image by Jack Reznicki; **Mikaila** images courtesy Universal Music Group Development; **JodyMiller** images courtesy Jody Miller at Jody Miller Music. **Roger Miller** album cover for *All Time Greatest Hits* (Mercury Nashville, 2003) courtesy Universal Music and Video Distribution, photo by Pikow from album cover of *The Return of Roger Miller* (Smash, MGS 27061) courtesy Smash Records; photo of bilboard by Hugh Foley; **DC Minner** photos courtesy of DC and Selby Minner, photo from Oklahoma Jazz Hall of Fame Induction by Hugh Foley; **Leona Mitchell** courtesy of Leona Mitchell; **Lucky Moeller** images courtesy Dixie (Moeller) Andrews; **Ralph Mooney** early 2000s publicity image courtesy Ralph Mooney; **Marilyn Moore** album cover courtesy Toshibi/EMI Japan; **Mosrite Records** and **Semie Moseley** image courtesy Mosrite Records; **Semie Moseley** image with Nokie Edwards courtesy Kiyoshi Mochizuki, Yokohama, Japan; **Andy Moseley** 2010 image courtesy Andy Moseley; **Sunny Murray** image courtesy ESP Records ; **Muscogee (Creek)** images by Hugh Foley courtesy of Tallahassee (Wvkokye) Ceremonial Grounds and Hvtce Cvpv Baptist Church; American Indian Hymn Singers courtesy Canyon Records (CR-611-C); Joy Harjo photo by Hulleah Tsinhnahjinnie courtesy Joy Harjo, photo of Julian B! courtesy Julian B!; artistic rendering of John "Yafke" Timothy by Johnny Tiger, Jr."; image of Jamie Coon courtesy www.jamiecoon.com; image of Pete Coser and Tony Arkeketa by Hugh Foley; image of Young Buffalo Horse courtesy of Michael Roberts; **Scott Musick** image courtesy Lanna Thai Tulsa at www.lannathaitulsa.com; **Marla Nauni** image courtesy Marla Nauni; **Doc Tate Nevaquaya** image courtesy Riversong Soundworks, Ashville, NC; **Grady Nichols** image courtesy www.gradynichols.com; **Nitro** image courtesy Derrick Brooks via www.myspace.com/nitro405; **Norma Jean** album cover image from *Norma Jean Sings a Tribute to Kitty Wells* (LSP-3664) courtesy RCA Records; **N.O.T.A.** images courtesy Bruce Hendrickson and www.myspace.com/realnota; **Gary P. Nunn** photo 1 by Rick Henson courtesy Ruth Nunn; image 2 courtesy Guacamole Records; **Kenny O'Dell** image courtesy Nashville Songwriters Association; **Kelli O'Hara** image by Rubenstein courtesy of Wikimedia Commons; *Oklahoma!* images from *Oklahoma!* (Coronet, CXS 46); Territory Dwellers courtesy Oklahoma Historical Society; *Ed Sullivan Presents the Songs of Oklahoma* (Little and Ives, ES6); **Osage** image of Vann Bighorse and singers courtesy of Wierd Wayne; Andrew Gray images courtesy Andrew Gray; image of Craig Satepauhoodle by Foley; Curtis Moore image courtesy of Curtis Moore; **Other Lives** press image courtesy of Other Lives; live images by Hugh; **Otoe-Missouria** seal courtesy Otoe-Missouria Tribe; image of Marvin Diamond by Hugh Foley; images of Brave Scout Singers and Yellow Hammer Singers courtesy of Canyon Records; **Tommy Overstreet** publicity photo 1 from Foley collection; 2006 image courtesy Tommy Overstreet; **Bonnie Owens** album cover image from Merle Haggard and Bonnie Owens, *That Makes Two of Us* (JS-6106), courtesy Pickwick and Capitol Records; the image with Merle Haggard by George Herman of Capitol Photo Studio and from Merle Haggard, *Strangers* (Capitol T2373) courtesy Capitol Records; **Buck Owens' Ranch** image courtesy Doyle Holly at myspace.com/doyleholly; **Patti Page** 1950s and 1990s publicity photos courtesy of Hot Schatz Public Relations; 1963 image by Bud Fraker; Album covers courtesy of Universal Music and Video Distribution; 2010 images in Claremore by Hugh Foley or whoever was asked to use Hugh's camera; **Billy Parker** photos by Hugh; **Jeff Parker** image courtesy Jeff Parker and TRAphotography; **Sandi Patti** publicity photo from Foley collection; **Pawnee** untitled painting by Nathan McCray at nmedesigns@yahoo.com or www.facebook.com/nmedesigns; **Tom Paxton** album cover photo by Irene Young from *And Loving You* (FF414) courtesy Flying Fish and Rounder Records; **Jim Pepper** image by Ron Schwerin from *Comin' and Goin'* (Antilles 7 90680-1); **Stephen Petree** image courtesy Jeff of www.cornerstonefestival.com; **Oscar Pettiford** album cover image from *The New Oscar Pettiford Sextet* (OJC-112) courtesy Fantasy Records; **Tom Petty** image courtesy wikimediacommons; **Cornel Pewewardy** publicity photo courtesy Cornel Pewewardy; **Pillar** 2006 *Reckoning* cover image by Tec Petaja courtesy Flicker Records; **Bobby Pinson** publicity image courtesy bobbypinson.com, image of Bobby Pinson playing guitar courtesy *BMI MUSICWORLD*, Fall 2012; **Mary Kay Place** image courtesy Krisicher via Wikimedia Commons, *Aimin' to Please* 1977 advertisement courtesy Columbia Records; **Point of Grace** album cover image from *Point of Grace, 24* (Word/Curb/WB WD2-886573) courtesy Word Records; **Johnny Polygon** image by Karine Simon courtesy Wikimedia Commons; **Ponca** seal by Mac, photo of elder singers by Tony Isaacs and cover of *Ponca Peyote Songs Vol. 1* courtesy of Tony Isaacs and Indian House Records, images of Tony Arkeketa, Eddie Arkeketa leading the Redland Singers, and Yellowhammer by Hugh Foley; **Red Dirt Music** photo of Garth Brooks and Santa Fe courtesy *Stillwater News Press*, image of Bob Childers courtesy www.bobchilders.com , Greg Jacobs image by Hugh Foley, Stoney Larue photo by Todd V. Wolfson courtesy Brandy Reed of RPR Marketing and Public Relations, Nashville; **Red Dirt Rangers** photos courtesy John Cooper; **Restless Heart** images of Dave Innis and Greg Jennings courtesy www.restless-heart.com; **Jimmie Revard** cover photo from Jimmie Revard and his Oklahoma Playboys, *Oh! Swing It* (Rambler 108) courtesy Mutual Music Corporation, San Francisco; **Ricochet** sign coming in to Vian, Oklahoma by Hugh Foley; **Steve Ripley** photo by Walt Richmond courtesy Charlene and Steve Ripley; **Tony Romanello** publicity photo courtesy of Tony Romanello; **Joe Don Rooney** with Rascal Flatts from album cover of *Live* (Hollywood, 2003) courtesy Universal Music and Press Distribution; **Mark Rubin** by Todd Woolfson; **Jimmy Rushing** album cover of *Everyday I Have the Blues/Livin' the Blues* (Verve, 1999) courtesy Universal Music and Press Distribution; **Leon Russell** courtesy Ark 21 Records; **Tom Russell** photo by David Burckhalter courtesy of Hightone Records; **Mike Settle** photo courtesy Mike Settle; **Blake Shelton** photo by Kristin G. Barlowe courtesy Warner Brothers Records; **Kay Starr** photo from sheet music for "Half a Photograph" courtesy Vesta Music Corporation; **James Talley** photo courtesy James Talley; **B.J. Thomas** photo courtesy B.J. Thomas; **Hank Thompson** photo by Lori Eanes courtesy of Hank Thompson Enterprises; **Wayman Tisdale** publicity photo courtesy Warner Brothers Records; **Tulsa Sound** 1959 group photo courtesy of Jack Dunham who also assembled the photos for this entry with the assistance of Janine Stovall, Clyde Stacy photo courtesy of Clyde Stacy, Bobby Taylor photo courtesy of Bobby Taylor, Gene Crose photo courtesy of Gene Crose, Tommy Rush photo courtesy of Tommy Rush, Junior Markham photo courtesy of Junior Markham, Tommy Crook photo courtesy of Tommy Crook, photo of Rockin' Jimmy and the Brothers of the Night from the album cover of 1980's *By the Light of the Moon* (0060-326) courtesy of Pilgrim and Metronome GMBH Records; **Dwight Twilley** 7" cover of "Girls" single courtesy EMI-Capitol Records; **Andrew Vasquez** publicity photo copyright 1996 and courtesy Makoché Recording Company; **Billy Wallace** performance still from Foley collection, possibly taken by Jerome Robinson from Bronx, New York; **Lily Fern Weatherford** photo with the Weatherfords courtesy Bob Duke Talent; **Jimmy Webb** courtesy Jimmy Webb Music; **Kevin Welch** image by Rodney Bursiel; **Bryan White** publicity photo courtesy Warner Brothers Records Publicity; **Claude "Fiddler" Williams** publicity photo by Russ Dantzler courtesy of Hot Jazz Management and Production; **Wiley and Gene** publicity photo courtesy of Jack Dunham; **Willis Brothers** publicity photo from Foley Collection; **Kelly Willis** iamge courtesy Kelly Willis via facebook; **Wills Brothers** group photo courtesy Friends of Oklahoma Music, Inc., Bob Wills headshot from Foley collection; Bob Wills group 1940s group photo courtesy Jack Dunham; Cain's Ballroom image by Hugh Foley; Bob Wills 1960s group photo courtesy Berniece Cook and Don Tolle, Johnnie Lee Wills *Reunion* album photo courtesy of Berniece Cook and Don Tolle, Tommy Perkins photo by Hugh Foley; Pine Valley Cosmonauts cover art by Jon Langford courtesy of Bloodshot Records,www.bloodshotrecords.com; **Sheb Wooley** album cover photo from *The Very Best of Sheb Wooley* (E-4275) courtesy Metro-Goldwyn-Mayer, Inc.; **Young Bird** group photo courtesy Canyon Records, photo of Curtis Hamilton-Youngbird by Hugh Foley.ley. *Wooley* (E-4275) courtesy Metro-Goldwyn-Mayer, Inc.; **Young Bird** group photo courtesy Canyon Records, photo of Curtis Hamilton-Youngbird by Hugh Foley.

About the Author

A professor of fine arts at Rogers State University in Claremore, where he has taught since 1996, Dr. Hugh W. Foley, Jr. has contributed scholarly articles, book chapters, and encyclopedia entries on American Indian music, rock, jazz, blues, and country music to *Oklahoma Humanities* (2013), *The Encyclopedia of Oklahoma History and Culture* (2010), *Another Hot Oklahoma Night: A Rock and Roll Story* (2009), *The Encyclopedia of New York State* (2007), *The Sound of People and Places* (2003), *The New York Encyclopedia of the Humanities* (2002), *The Guide to United States Popular Culture* (2001), and *Living Blues* (1998). Additionally, he has written several essays on American Indian historical subjects for the *Encyclopedia of Politics of the American West* (2012), *Oklahoma @ the Movies* (2012), *Encyclopedia of American Indian Literature, Native Peoples of the World* (2011), *Encyclopedia of American Indian History* (2009), and *Encyclopedia of Native American Treaties* (2004). He is also the author of the *Oklahoma Route 66 Music Guide* (2004), and wrote "The Music of Route 66" for the *Encyclopedia of U.S. Cultural Geography* (2013).

Hugh Foley

Actively involved in radio since 1977, Foley has worked as a disc-jockey, program director, producer, and announcer at commercial, military, public, and college radio stations in Oklahoma, Atlanta, New York, Connecticut, Berkeley, CA, Germany, and Japan.

Along with creating the college radio music format in 2000 for Rogers State University's radio station, KRSC-FM, he is also the music director for KUSH-AM in Cushing, Oklahoma, where he programs Americana music, and has hosted a weekly American Indian music, news, and public affairs program, *Native Air*, since 1998.

Also at Rogers State University, he teaches courses in music appreciation, cinema, and Native American Studies on KRSC-TV, the university's television station, amassing more than 1,000 hours of live television on-air broadcasting since 1998. As a result, he has shot, edited, and produced a number of video lessons, features, and longer-form documentaries on cinema, Oklahoma music and American Indian life-ways. Along with being aired on television for his classes, the productions have been shown at conferences, personal lecture appearances, film festivals, and on public television stations across the United States. Interested viewers may see some of these videos under the producer names "ekvcate" and "docfo" on www.youtube.com.

Private Foley, GI DJ American Forces Network Europe (Germany), 1980

Dr. Foley is a founding member of the Oklahoma Music Hall of Fame in Muskogee (the beginnings of which were in 1995), was its first vice-president, and has chaired the Oklahoma Music Hall of Fame induction selection committee since 2003. He also serves as a governor's appointee to the OMHOF board of directors until 2016, and was also president of the Oklahoma Folklife Council from 2005 to 2010. In 2013, he fulfilled the role of conulsting state scholar for *New Harmonies*, a Smithsonian Institution traveling exhibit about American roots music, touring six communites across the state of Oklahoma via the Oklahoma Humanities Council (Idabel, Spiro, Frederick, Hobart, El Reno, and Alva).

A Stillwater, Oklahoma resident, Foley is also a volunteer bugler for Bugles Across America, a nationwide non-profit organization that provides live renditions of "Taps" for Veterans memorial services.

His favorite musical experience by far is listening to his son, "Blue Fire" Foley, playing roots and blues music, or singing American Indian songs of many different types.

Nokose "Blue Fire" Foley
Claremore, OK 2012

Hugh Foley's maternal grandfather, Paul "Happy" Fenton (1900-1975) was the first entertainer ever heard over Tulsa radio station, KTUL, and was also a regular performer on KVOO, Tulsa; WKY, Oklahoma City; and KDFM, Beaumont, TX, before becoming the recreational director and dining room organist for Western Hills lodge at Sequoyah State Park in 1957 through his retirement in 1974. He also sang with the earliest incarnation of the Tulsa Barbershop Harmony Society (now Tulsa Founders Chorus) and is listed on the original invitation to join the first group by founder O.C. Cash in 1938. Among other gigs, he led a German polka group in which Lawrence Welk once played, counted Liberace as an associate, played "floating lady music" for magicians conventions, was a professional photographer, and built a sound effects machine out of old junk parts (pictured in center), as well as the synthesizer pictured here on top of his organ.

Paul "Happy" Fenton, circa 1960s
Western Hills Lodge, Sequoyah State Park, OK

776 / Oklahoma Music Guide II

Outro Vamp: Some Lessons Learned from Compiling *OMG II*

This history of Oklahoma music is fascinating and intrinsic to understanding the history of American traditional and popular music. The continued emergence of significant Oklahoma musical figures to the present day is equally inspirational both an entertainment and socio-cultural artistic manifestation. To understand this history, one must recognized the music of the American Indian, both traditional and Christian, as well as the spirituals, hymns, and blues of the slaves of African descent who came into Indian Territory with Five Tribes of the Southeastern US, and then in the subsequent migrations of African-American in the late 19th and early 20th century black town movement of Oklahoma. Alongside those musical stories are the foundations of country music emerging from Anglo, Scot, Welsh, Irish, and German immigrants to the state. All are all extremely important to establishing the first important musical milieu of the socio-cultural zone that becomes Oklahoma.

For country music specifically, the first defining moment is the migration of people from the American South, Upland South, and Ohio Valley into Indian Territory, then Oklahoma Territory, and, finally, Oklahoma. One must also take into account that some Scottish and English musical traditions migrated with people who had married into the Five Tribes and were removed to Indian Territory in the 1830s, indicated by the Anglo-influenced mountain fiddle style that came with the Cherokees on their removals of the 1830s. After the Civil War, however, the subsequent Anglo-Scot-Irish-German immigrants brought all of their traditional music to pre and post-statehood Oklahoma. These songs are the foundation for the "Old Time" country music that evolves into the gospel, folk music and bluegrass of the eastern half of rural Oklahoma. Without that environment of house parties, "play parties", square dances, barn dances, etc., not to mention the cultural mix of a place like Okemah, OK, Woody Guthrie most likely does not surface in the same way that he did. Talking about Guthrie jumps the gun of talking about Oklahoma's major establishment of the singing cowboy in American popular culture during the 1920s and '30s. Because of the fame of singing cowboys like Otto Gray (the first Western band on national radio) from Ripley, OK, and, of course, Gene Autry, the state was an important area for the development of Western music, both the singing cowboy and Western swing of Bob Wills and his Texas Playboys, based in Tulsa. The singing cowboy identity of the state was so prominent that musicians who were not from the state claimed to be so for purposes of appearing more authentic as Western or cowboy music performers (Eddie Cletro, Cowboy Copas, and Al Clauser). While Oklahoma was well-known for its status as a cowboy state, it was less known (and still is to a large extent) as a producer of significant jazz musicians. If one adds developing jazz traditions into the mix of Western music from the period of statehood through the 1930s, an understanding can start to take shape of the of the musical hybrids that are part of Oklahoma's musical story through the modern era (Western swing through Red Dirt music). Without those jazz scenes, Charlie Christian does not take the electric guitar and turn it into a lead solo instrument, which was also being featured by Bob Wills at the same time. Some musicians have suggested Charlie Christian heard the electric guitar over KVOO radio when already had it in his band of the 1930s; others say Wills' guitarists heard Charlie Christian and added it to their own repertoire. Either way, the cross-cultural influences of the state are a continued part of its musical history. Clearly, the musicians of 1950s Tulsa are influenced by the rock and roll surfacing on the national stage by 1954. However, Tulsa musicians were also influenced by blues and Western swing. What is often called the "Tulsa Sound" sits in a comfortable pocket between blues, rock, and country with what is often a defining "shuffle" beat. That whole topic leads listeners through a whole list of Tulsa musicians now familiar to millions (J.J. Cale, Leon Russell, David Gates, the GAP Band, etc.).

Without digressing too much, a couple of years ago the author was asked for a list of the most influential Oklahoma musical entities. This is a tricky question because it depends on whether one mean historically significant, innovative and inspirational, or just popular/commercially successful? To start, I would leave off a few titans who either were born in the state and left at an early age (Nokie Edward and Oscar Pettiford), those who were tremendously popular in an established genre (Reba McEntire, Carrie Underwood), and may even define their era (Patti Page), but are not necessarily what you might call influential as artists, meaning they don't necessarily transcend their influences or start a new musical movement. Good for discussion, and only my opinion, I would say some of the most the following list is a good place to begin talking about significant Oklahoma artists, leaving out the story of "Swing Low Sweet Chariot" for the time being.

Most Influential Artists of Oklahoma Music History (For starters)

1. The Plains Indian music of the Ponca and Kiowa has influenced Pan-Indian powwow music across the United States.
2. Oklahoma City Blue Devils -primary, hot swinging territory band of the 1920s that leads to the Count Basie Orchestra
3. Otto Gray and His Oklahoma Cowboys - precursor of singing cowboys, Western swing, and Red Dirt music
4. Gene Autry - popularized the singing cowboy of radio, film, and stage
5. Charlie Christian - electric guitarist, jazz innovator
6. Woody Guthrie - *the* Anglo folk musician
7. Barney Kessel - jazz guitarist
8. Chet Baker -jazz trumpeter
9. Howard McGhee - jazz trumpeter
10. Lowell Fulson – forged "uptown blues", which combined horn sections with electric blues, inspiring B.B. King
11. Wanda Jackson - 1950s rockabilly queen who was the first woman to have significant success in rock music
12. Leon Russell - rock musician, producer, singer, songwriter
13. Lee Hazlewood (pop/rock producer/songwriter, i.e. "These Boots are Made for Walking")
14. Roger Miller - major crossover artist
15. Jimmy Nolen - James Brown's guitarist and father of the funk guitar in popular music

16. J.J. Cale - major influence on Eric Clapton and Lynyrd Skynyrd, defines so-called "Tulsa Sound"
17. Hoyt Axton - (major hits and furthering the Oklahoma songwriting trope of humorous wisdom born of disaster
18. GAP Band and Charlie Wilson - primary R&B success story from Oklahoma
19. Debris - acknowledged as important punk rock figures whose first album pre-dates The Ramones first album
20. Michael Hedges - primary new age artist - totally unique and complicated guitar style
21. Vince Gill – helped re-introduce a more traditional country sound into Nashville in the 1980s (a.k.a. "neo-traditional country")
22. Flaming Lips – Oklahoma's biggest rock artists of the last from the 1980s through the current era
23. Garth Brooks – Along with delivering the right songs for his audience, Brooks' long-lasting influence may be more in "saving country music" by his marketing savvy that made country music popular with non-country music audience, major stage shows that used techniques from the rock environment to create a more exciting experience for concert goers, and then just picking the right songs for his audience; either way, he is still the biggest selling solo music artist in history.
24. Jacob Fred Jazz Odyssey - most progressive jazz group in America today... has evolved over the years, so one never knows exactly what will happen, but the genius or pianist Brian Haas is not to be denied.
25. Oklahoma City University's School of Music - produced an incredible number of classical, opera and Broadway performers.

    Having said all that, one can say for sure that Oklahoma music is most often a hybrid form, merging more than one musical and/or ethnic influence, directly related to the sociological formation of the state's population. As a result, its musicians are often comfortable with more than form, and often can crossover supposed stylistic boundary lines, or adapt to shifts in a musical genre, such as big band jazz musicians who transitioned into be-bop players, or any Tulsa Sound musician who merged rock, blues, and country, or any Western swing musician who played multiple styles, or any Red Dirt musician who may perform at any number of different venues on one weekend in which bluegrass, folk, country rock, blues, or country is a primary focus, and then the next weekend be working with the same group at festival with a different musical focus. Without any real foundation for it, I'll say that up until about the 1970s or so, an Oklahoma musician grew up singing or playing in church, learning more about the formal aspects of music in the school band, and then took off on their own rebellious journey inspired by the popular music of their time, with which they were prepared to play and evolve. Two other primary lessons also emerged through repeated appearance in the various musicians discussed in the text:

    Sometimes talented and innovative people are not successful financially, and sometimes moderately talented or average artists become very successful financially.

    The most successful musicians from Oklahoma were ones that could either play more than style of music, so they would always have work, or excelled in another aspect of the music business, such as publishing, production, promotion, or management.

A Note on Popular Music/Show Business Scholarship

Plagiarism is rampant within pop music scholarship. At times, it is difficult to see who is copying who and what the original source is of a "fact." Occasionally, artists' websites will copy other websites, and then the books and newspapers print what is on the sites, and then that information disappears from the online source, is inaccurate compared to other sources, and finally you have four to five different sources that either say slight variations of the same thing (changing verbs and adjectives), but may have some primary fact up for conjecture. The author has tried to be careful in corroborating facts with more than one source and to cite original, trustworthy material, and yet not clutter the text with notes and references to commonly accepted facts. Along with basic sources for checking material included in the guide (artist website, online databases such as allmusic.com, billboard.com, or Wikipedia when sources are used), the author also turns to years of collected print files of press releases, obscure clippings, album liner notes, correspondence and personal interviews with artists, as well as various older print popular music reference works collected, often outdated, or just plain wrong. Occasionally, something as simple as an e-bay search will turn up very valuable research materials as liner notes are routinely included as product descriptions of items for sale; additionally images of albums or singles often indicate label changes, studios, and songwriting credits not found anywhere else. This is one of the scholarly issues in the new era of popular culture documentation: sometimes it's happening faster than people can actually keep up with it, so we are turning to the great amorphous scholar of Wikipedia, with its constant updates, evolving reference base, and varying degrees of critically interpretive acumen. While not always a dependable source, popular culture scholarship often takes extreme tangential forms with the smallest key being learned to understand the big picture. That fact may not necessarily come from an established reference source, but might come from an obscure sources such as liner notes, myspace.com, Wikipedia.com, a youtube video, a fan website, an official website, a publicist's bio, or the artist themselves in an interview or blog. Only after becoming aware of all the particulars regarding an artist can one start to assemble a true summary statement about them in the context necessary to understand them properly as part of a genre or historical period. Of course, that is the challenge of any historical writer, to not only chronicle facts, but to try and interpret what they mean in a bigger picture.

Listening to Popular Music Critically

Finally, one must listen to as much of the music by an artist while writing about them. While the *OMG* archives are fairly extensive with regard to Oklahoma artists, it does not contain everything released by every musician in this book. However, the difference contemporarily in listening to music for critical and historical writing is that you have almost anything you want to hear by significant artists online, either as a full track on the artist's website or as a sample of the track intended for purchase as a download, which one can then buy, if necessary, on the spot. Additionally, because of video archive sites like youtube.com, we can also see film and/or video of most popular American artists since the 1930s. Therefore, not only do we now have an artist's own perspective of themselves via their own website at our fingertips, we also have instant access to an accurate discography of their recorded output with audio samples via the website allmusicguide.com. With regard to critical comments on music, making pointed or negative statements toward someone's art with a snarky attitude is a lot easier when you have never had any personal contact with that person, their people, or anyone you might know who values their music, which is why sometimes writing about music can be a challenge critically, especially if you have some personal contact with that person or their milieu. Instead of just hearing the music and seeing the artist perform from a distance, when we meet a musician, get a sense of them as a human, sometimes we get sucked in by the splendor of being associated with the artist, and are not critical enough. The author has been fortunate enough to see, interview, and meet several significant Oklahoma musicians, which definitely colors a critical interpretation of them. When about an artist, we think about our job as pop music scholars, writers, and journalists: Are we to be critical in a mean way with no concern for feelings by stating the obvious without concern for any multiple human factors (such as where, when, and why a given piece of music is produced), or to try and explain why an artist's music is or is not accepted at a particular time. The latter is more challenging, to interpret, explain, and critique an artist's music in the context of the era in which it was created and released into the world. Along with analyzing the music itself (melody, rhythm, lyrics, texture, or timbre), as well as the musicians' conscious or subconscious influences and the general music scene that helped shape it, pop music scholars should try to discuss the socio-political environment into which a music it was born that made it resonate enough with a group of people to make it popular.

Oklahoma music knowledge and primary musical resources have been developed via the Oklahoma History Center's rock music research that formed the basis for the *Another Hot Oklahoma Night* exhibit on rock history in 2009, as well as informing the exhibit's accompanying book, *Another Hot Oklahoma Night: A Rock and Roll Story*. Information from the extensive interviews with Oklahoma musicians conducted by the Larry O'Dell and Jeff Moore has had additional influence by informing new writing about Oklahoma music, and will further form the foundation for the rock and popular music aspects of the planned Oklahoma Museum of Popular Culture ("OK Pop") for Tulsa in the next decade, money for which is already being volunteered by the Kaiser Foundation. Another huge development in Oklahoma music research occurred in 2013 with the announcement of the Woody Guthrie Center in Tulsa, which will house the Woody Guthrie Archives for further research and study.

Last Call

The author makes no claim of knowing everything there is to know about Oklahoma music. There is just too much to know, and way more than can be published. Many people know more than the author about individual artists, groups, and musical traditions. *OMG* only hopes to coalesce as much information as possible about musical entities from Oklahoma, explain or debunk their connections to the state, and contextualize their place in the wider context of their respective musical genre.

Through the course of this text, the author has also included occasional personal anecdotes about his experience with the music or musicians discussed in a given section of the book. This technique comes from a modern trend in popular music writing to inject oneself into a story to give the reader a sense of the writer's investment in the subject. Not meant to be a boast of "I met so and so," or "back when I saw so and so", these personal observations are ossified in the writer's mind as primary thoughts about those musicians, and stand as examples of what make those musical figures unique or important to the writer.

More than anything, this text is meant to be a celebration of the music of Oklahoma, and one of the primary aspects of Oklahoma culture that makes the state a unique place. Hopefully, future volumes will address some of the disparities of this volume, in which some major figures of Oklahoma music have been given so much space they squeezed out some new or lesser known but still significant Oklahoma artists. The author also hopes will encourage those who are working selflessly to promote and preserve the Oklahoma music story. With whatever flaws it contains, the *Oklahoma Music Guide* seeks to inspire more people to keep sharing the huge impact Oklahoma musicians have had on the world of music. Also, the author hopes the book will inspire current and future musicians to keep on practicing, so they too might succeed in ways that so many from the state already have. Keep on going!

                          Hugh Foley
                          Stillwater, OK
                          March 12, 2013

Chalkline 259 of Hochatown, Oklahoma, whose dual-lead vocals, excellent vocal harmonies, original songs, and fine musicianship indicate they could be a group many more people will know about beyond 2013 when this image was taken after a performance in Idabel, Oklahoma.

Made in the USA
Charleston, SC
05 October 2013